The Norton Anthology
of American Literature

SIXTH EDITION

VOLUME E

American Literature since 1945

The Norton Anthology
of American Literature

SIXTH EDITION

Nina Baym, *General Editor*

SWANLUND CHAIR AND CENTER FOR
ADVANCED STUDY PROFESSOR OF ENGLISH
JUBILEE PROFESSOR OF LIBERAL ARTS AND SCIENCES
UNIVERSITY OF ILLINOIS AT URBANA-CHAMPAIGN

VOLUME E

American Literature since 1945

W · W · NORTON & COMPANY · *New York* · *London*

Editor: Julia Reidhead
Developmental Editor: Marian Johnson
Manuscript Editors: Candace Levy, Anne Hellman, Carol Flechner
Assistant Editor: Brian Baker
Production Manager: Diane O'Connor
Permissions Manager: Nancy Rodwan
Permissions Clearing: Margaret Gorenstein
Text Design: Antonina Krass
Art Research: Neil Ryder Hoos

The text of this book is composed in Fairfield Medium
with the display set in Bernhard Modern.
Composition by Binghamton Valley Composition.
Manufacturing by R. R. Donnelley & Sons.

ISBN 0-393-97901-6 (pbk.)

bW. W. Norton & Company, Inc., 500 Fifth Avenue, New York, NY 10110
www.wwnorton.com

W. W. Norton & Company Ltd., Castle House, 75/76 Wells Street, London W1T 3QT

Contents

American Poetry since 1945

Preface to the Sixth Edition

In this first edition of *The Norton Anthology of American Literature* to appear in the twenty-first century, we respond to numerous requests for a more flexible, more portable format by introducing five individual volumes in two slipcased packages corresponding to the former Volumes 1 and 2. This new format accommodates the many instructors who use the anthology in a two-semester survey, but also opens up possibilities for mixing and matching the five volumes for a variety of courses organized by period or topic.

As with earlier editions, the editors have worked closely with teachers who assign the book and, through these teachers, with the students who use it. From the anthology's inception, three goals have been paramount: first, to present a variety of works rich and substantial enough to enable teachers to build their own courses according to their own ideals (thus, teachers are offered more authors and more selections than they will probably choose to teach); second, to make the anthology self-sufficient by featuring many works in their entirety and longer selections so that individual authors can be covered in depth; and third, to balance traditional interests with developing critical concerns. This commitment to balance has been evident from the first edition of 1979, where, in response to teachers who found that the traditional canon was insufficiently representative of American literary history, we included Anne Bradstreet, Mary Rowlandson, Sarah Kemble Knight, Phillis Wheatley, Margaret Fuller, Harriet Beecher Stowe, Frederick Douglass, Sarah Orne Jewett, Kate Chopin, Mary E. Wilkins Freeman, Booker T. Washington, Charles Chesnutt, Edith Wharton, W. E. B. Du Bois, and many others. Yet we did not shortchange writers like Franklin, Emerson, Thoreau, Hawthorne, Poe, Melville, Hemingway, Fitzgerald, or Faulkner, whom teachers then and now would not think of doing without.

That the "untraditional" authors listed above have now become part of the American literary canon shows that canons are not fixed, but emerge and change. At the same time, teachers over the last thirty years have seen a striking expansion in the extent and diversity of the authors they are expected and want to teach. In endeavoring to ensure that our inclusions—extensive as they are—do not outrun what might conceivably be of use in the classroom, we have always revised our selections in response to detailed suggestions from many teachers. For this Sixth Edition, we have drawn on the careful commentary of 111 reviewers. We are delighted with the new materials we bring to this Sixth Edition, which take several forms:

Volume A
Under the new rubric *Literature to 1700*, for the opening section, we incorporate Native American and explorer materials with settler literature up

through the Salem witchcraft episode. This configuration corresponds to the new emphasis in early American literary studies on the Atlantic Rim, on the multiethnicity of the early colonies, and on the position of Puritan New England as a key but not the only determinant in early American writing. The multilingual, multiethnic colonies are stressed in the expanded period introduction and in the travel writings and biographical narratives of newly included authors Garcilaso de la Vega, Jacob Steendam, Adriaen Van der Donck, and Francis Pastorious. The much-assigned cluster of Native American trickster tales has been expanded with a tale from the Sioux tradition. Also included are additional writings by Samuel de Champlain and Samuel Sewall and Cotton Mather's sensationalist accounts of criminal trials from *Pillars of Salt.*

American Literature 1700–1820 In this section, newly edited by Philip F. Gura, University of North Carolina at Chapel Hill, we distinguish the eighteenth century as a period of consolidation and development in an emergent American literature. Newly included to better convey the range of genres and writers that found readers in early America are voices, free and slave, from the Atlantic Rim: the plantation owner James Grainger and the slaves Briton Hammon and the anonymous author of "The Speech of Moses Bon Sàam." Also new are the poet Annis Boudinot Stockton, the novelist Charles Brockden Brown, and the playwright Royall Tyler, represented by his comedy *The Contrast.*

Volume B

American Literature 1820–1865 broadens our geographical scope by introducing two new California writers, Louise Amelia Smith Clappe and Bayard Taylor. Clappe's "Dame Shirley" letters, among the earliest classics for students of western American literature, constitute a vivid report from the gold mines. Taylor, the era's best-known and most prolific travel writer, depicts in our selection the early days of San Francisco. The esteemed poet Emma Lazarus is newly included with poems, most famously "The New Colossus," that gave a highly cultured voice to Jewish American identity. New selections by Poe, Stowe, and Douglass—three chapters of whose later autobiography, *My Bondage and My Freedom*, have been added—deepen the representation of these central figures.

Volume C

As a convenience to some instructors, Volume C: *American Literature 1865–1914* opens with the selections by Walt Whitman and Emily Dickinson that are included in Volume B. Sarah Morgan Bryan Piatt, increasingly recognized as a major woman poet in the era, is newly represented, as are fiction writers Constance Fenimore Woolson, Abraham Cahan, and Sui Sin Far. These three writers extend this period's regional and ethnic representation, while demonstrating anew the capacious possibilities of American realism.

Volume D

American Literature between the Wars, 1914–1945, now includes two important longer works of fiction by American women—Nella Larsen's *Quicksand*, a tragedy of African American identity, and Katherine Anne Porter's beautifully written novella of romance in a time of war, *Pale Horse, Pale Rider,* both presented here in their entirety—as well as chapters from John Steinbeck's *The Grapes of Wrath*. Short fiction, too, is strengthened with two stories by Willa Cather, "The Sculptor's Funeral" and "Neighbour Rosicky"; the addition of a second story by F. Scott Fitzgerald, the 1922 *Metropolitan Magazine* version of "Winter Dreams"; and two new fiction writers, the Native American writer D'arcy McNickle and the Filipino American Carlos Bulosan. *Trifles*, Susan Glaspell's teachable short play, is newly included.

Volume E

American Prose since 1945 strengthens the anthology's offerings by Latino and Latina writers with the addition of Rudolfo A. Anaya's short story "The Christmas Play," selections from Gloria Anzaldúa's influential work of theory, *Borderlands/La Frontera*, and short fiction by Judith Ortiz Cofer. Strengthening the anthology's rich offerings in modern American drama is Pulitzer Prize-winner Suzan-Lori Parks's *The America Play*. Ralph Ellison's searing story "Cadillac Flambé," excised from the posthumously published *Juneteenth*, Donald Barthelme's "The Balloon," and a dazzling, poignant set piece from Richard Powers's *Galatea 2.2* enrich the representation of recent fiction.

American Poetry since 1945 newly anthologizes work by five important poets: United States Poet Laureate Billy Collins, Stanley Kunitz, Charles Wright, Charles Simic, and Jorie Graham. Frank O'Hara's poems have been reselected, and recent work by Robert Creeley, Galway Kinnell, W. S. Merwin, and Rita Dove is newly anthologized.

The student Web site to accompany the anthology (www.wwnorton.com/naal), by Bruce Michelson, offers timelines, outlines of the period introductions, over 400 annotated links, author resource pages for 160 writers in the anthology, searchable "Explorations" that provide questions and research projects, and, a new feature, self-grading quizzes. *Teaching with* The Norton Anthology of American Literature: *A Guide for Instructors*, by Bruce Michelson and Marjorie Pryse, is a lively, practical resource for questions to motivate close reading and discussion, as well as concise teaching notes for individual periods, authors, and works; model exam questions and essay topics; and reading lists for a wide variety of courses using the anthology.

As in past editions, editorial features—period introductions, headnotes, and annotation—are designed to be concise yet full and to give students the information needed without imposing an interpretation. In the Sixth Edition, much of this editorial material has been revised in response to new scholarship. Several period introductions have been entirely or substantially rewritten, and a number of headnotes have been tightened or rewritten to be more useful to students. The Selected Bibliographies have been thoroughly updated. The Sixth Edition retains two editorial features that help students place their reading in historical and cultural context—a Texts/Contexts timeline following each period introduction and a map on the front endpaper of each volume—and adds to these a third feature to help students consider the relationships among writers within a given period: a chronological chart, located on the back endpaper, showing the lifespans of many of the writers anthologized.

Our policy has been to reprint each text in the form that accords, as far as it is possible to determine, to the intention of its author. There is one exception: we have modernized most spellings and (very sparingly) the punctuation in the sections *Literature to 1700* and *American Literature 1700–1820* on the principle that archaic spellings and typography pose unnecessary problems for beginning students. We have used square brackets to indicate titles supplied by the editors for the convenience of students. Whenever a portion of a text has been omitted, we have indicated that omission with three asterisks.

The editors of this anthology were selected on the basis of their expertness in their individual area. We note with pleasure the addition to the editorial team of Philip F. Gura, William S. Newman Distinguished Professor of American Literature and Culture and Adjunct Professor of Religious Studies at the University of North Carolina at Chapel Hill. He succeeds Francis Murphy as period editor of *American Literature 1700–1820*. Each editor was given ultimate responsibility for his or her period, but all collaborated in the final enterprise. Arnold Krupat edited Native American Literatures in Volumes A and B and the oratory, songs, and chants, Eastman, Oskison, and Black Elk selections in Volumes C and D. Ronald Gottesman prepared the texts and introductions for Abraham Lincoln and Frederick Douglass; and Nina Baym prepared the texts and introductions for Harriet Beecher Stowe and Harriet Jacobs.

We take this opportunity to thank the hundreds of teachers throughout the country who have answered our questions. Those teachers who prepared detailed critiques, or who offered special help in preparing texts, are listed under Acknowledgments, on a separate page. The editors would like to express appreciation for their assistance to Kenneth L. Baughman, Brad Campbell, Samuel L. Gladden, Vince Gotera, Tim Gustafson, Katrina Huffman, Julie Huffman-Klinkowitz, Julie Husband, Judith Kicinski, Daniel Lane, Maurice Lee, David Wei Li, Brenda Lin, Allison McCabe, Anne Myles, James O'Loughlin, Steven Olsen-Smith, Julian Rice, Todd Richardson, Heddy Richter, Monica Rodriguez, Jacob Schoenly, Beth Shube, Alan Shucard, Jesse Swan, John Swope, Karen Tracey, Catherine Waitinas, Jennie Wang, Rachel Watson, and Thomas Wolfe. We also thank the many people at Norton who contributed to the Sixth Edition: Julia Reidhead, who supervised the Sixth Edition; Marian Johnson, development editor; Candace Levy, Anne Hellman, and Carol Flechner, manuscript editors; Brian Baker, who prepared timelines and maps; Eileen Connell, Web site editor; Diane O'Connor, production manager; Toni Krass, designer; Neil Ryder Hoos, art researcher; Nancy Rodwan, permissions manager; and Margaret Gorenstein, who cleared permissions. We also wish to acknowledge our debt to the late George P. Brockway, former president and chairman at Norton, who invented this anthology, and to M. H. Abrams, Norton's advisor on English texts. All have helped us to create an anthology that, more than ever, is testimony to the continuing richness of American literary traditions.

NINA BAYM

Acknowledgments

Michel Aaij (University of Alabama), Alan Ainsworth (Houston Community College), David Allen (University College of the Fraser Valley), Robert Allen Alexander Jr. (Nicholls State University), Scott Andrews (California State University, Northridge), Scott Ash (Nassau Community College), Diana Badur (Black Hawk College), Donald Bahr (Arizona State University), Ellen Barker (Georgia Perimeter College), Don Barkin (Yale University), Jonathan N. Barron (University of Southern Mississippi), Craig Bartholomus (Penn Valley College), Laura Behling (Gustavus Adolphus College), Alfred Bendixen (California State University), Denny Berthiaume (Foothill College), Philip Biedler (University of Alabama), Stanley S. Blair (Monmouth University), Nancy J. Brown (Lourdes College), William F. Browne (Brooklyn College), Lisa D. Chavez (Albion College), Colin Clarke (George Washington University), Sheila Coghill (Minnesota State University, Moorhead), Marc Conner (Washington and Lee University), Nancy Cook (University of Rhode Island), John Cosenza (St. John's University), Elana Crane (Miami University), Robert Croft (Gainesville College), Dianne M. Daily (Northern Virginia Community College), Robin G. Daniel (Broward Community College), Michel de Benedictis (Miami-Dade Community College), William J. De-Saegher (Point Loma Nazarene University), L. C. DiCicco (University of London), Brian Diemert (Brescia College), Mary Lynn Dodson (Amarillo College), Sam Dodson (Tarleton State University), Paul Downes (University of Toronto), Gregory Eiselein (Kansas State University), Julie Ellison (University of Michigan), Sharon Felton (Belmont University), Paul Ferlazzo (Northern Arizona University), Marie Foley (Santa Barbara City College), Dean Flower (Smith College), Brian Folker (Central Connecticut State University), Lee Foreman (Edison College), Robert Forman, Andrew Furman (Florida Atlantic University), Ronald Gervais (San Diego State University), Leonard S. Goldberg (Gettysburg College), Henry Golemba (Wayne State University), Lisa Gordis (Barnard College), Richard Grande (Pennsylvania State University), Timothy Gray (College of Staten Island, CUNY), James Green (Arizona State University), Loren C. Gruber (Missouri Valley College), Peter L. Hays (University of California, Davis), Roy Hill (Westark College), Carl S. Horner (Flagler College), Ronald Hurlburt (St. Johns River Community College), Mark Johnson (Missouri State University), AnaLouise Keating (Aquinas College), J. Gerald Kennedy (Louisiana State University), Elizabeth Rodriguez Kessler (California State University at Northridge), David Ketterer (Concordia University), Elizabeth Lamont (Lincoln Memorial University), Philip J. Landon (University of Maryland, Baltimore County), Genevieve Later (University College of the Cariboo), Bruce Levy (Southern Methodist University), Margrit D. Loomis (University of Louisiana at Monroe), Ginny Brown Machann (Blinn College), Veronica Makowsky (University of Connecticut), Saundra Rose Maley (George Washington University), Joseph Malof (University of Texas, Austin), Jean Carwile Masteller (Whitman College), Richard N. Masteller (Whitman College), Philip Mayfield (Fullerton College), David McDowell (Anne Arundel Community College), Ken McLean (Bishop's University), Philip Milner (St. Francis Xavier University, Antigonish, Nova Scotia), Madonne Minter (Texas Tech University), Margaret P. Murray (Western Connecticut State University), Jacqueline O'Connor (University of St. Thomas), James Obertino (Central Missouri State University), Jean Pfaelzer (University of Delaware), Bruce H. Price (McLean Hospital), Larus Reed (Virginia State University), Charles James Reuse (Minnesota State University Moorhead), Eliza Richards (Boston University), Susan Rieke (Saint Mary College), Becky Roberts, Jane Rose (Purdue University), Sherry L. Rosenthal (Community College of South Nevada), Richard E. Rosol (Central Connecticut State University), Michael Runyan (Saddleback College), David Rota (University of Missouri, St. Louis), Jack Ryan (Gettysburg College), Mary Segall (Quinnipiac College), Robert Seltzer (Nova University), Dorothy U. Seyler (Northern Virginia Community College, Annandale), David Shawn (Endicott College), David Shields (The Citadel), Conrad Sienkiewicz, Father Joseph Stefanelli, S.J., Jeffrey Steele (University of Wisconsin, Madison), Gary Storhoff (University of Connecticut, Stamford), Kathleen Thornton (University of Albany), Trysh Travis (Southern Methodist University), John Trimble (University of Texas, Austin), Michael Trussler (University of Regina), Mary Katherine Wainwright (Manatee Community College), Michael Warner (Rutgers University), John Wenke (Salisbury State University), Jill Knight Weinberger (Central Connecticut State University), Susan P. Willens (George Washington University), Ann Winters (Westark College), James N. Wise (University of Missouri, Rolla), Lisa Wittmeyer (Park University), Margaret J. Yonce (Augusta State University).

The Norton Anthology
of American Literature

SIXTH EDITION

VOLUME E

American Literature since 1945

American Prose since 1945

THE UNITED STATES AND WORLD POWER

Distribution of power is a purpose of war, and the consequences of a world war are necessarily global. Having agreed to a policy of unconditional surrender, the allied countries of Britain, the Soviet Union, and the United States positioned themselves to achieve nothing short of total victory over their enemies in World War II: Germany and Japan. Yet each country's contribution to victory made for startling contrasts in the following half century. Britain, beleaguered since the war's start in September 1939, fought against odds that depleted its resources and severely disrupted its traditional class structure. The Soviet Union, an amalgamation of nations under the central power of Russia, suffered the war's worst casualties when attacked by Germany in June 1941 and afterward during the hideous contest of attrition along the war's bitter eastern front well into 1945. Although newly established as a world power after the end of hostilities, the U.S.S.R. remained at an economic disadvantage and dissolved in 1991 after five decades of Cold War against its ideological adversaries in the West. It was the United States, entering the war after Japan's attack on Pearl Harbor on December 7, 1941, that emerged as a world power in excellent economic shape. This new power, experienced both at home and abroad, became a major force in reshaping American culture for the balance of the twentieth century.

The great social effort involved in fighting World War II reorganized America's economy and altered its people's lifestyles. Postwar existence revealed different kinds of men and women, with new aspirations among both majority and minority populations. New possibilities for action empowered individuals and groups in the pursuit of personal freedom and individual self-expression. During World War II American industry had expanded dramatically for military purposes; plants that had manufactured Chevrolets, Plymouths, Studebakers, Packards, and Fords now made B-24 Liberators and Grumman Avengers. With three million men in uniform, the vastly expanded workforce comprised increasing numbers of women. After hostilities were concluded many of these women were reluctant to return to homemaking; after a decade or so of domesticity, women emerged as a political force on behalf of rights and opportunities in the workplace. This pattern extended to other groups as well. African Americans, whether they enlisted or were drafted, served in fighting units throughout the war and were unwilling to return to second-class status afterward; nor could a majority culture aware of their contribution continue to enforce segregation and other forms of prejudice so easily as before the war.

Economic power at the world level continued to influence American culture through the first two postwar decades. The first two—and only two—atomic bombs were exploded in Japan in August 1945; their effect was so horrific that a strategy of geographical "containment" emerged as a military policy. When Communist North Korea invaded South Korea in 1950, therefore, the United States rejected responding with atomic weapons in favor of a United Nations–sponsored "police action" that fought with conventional weapons only and declined to pursue enemy forces beyond specific boundaries. But if hot war was out, cold war was in, specifically the type of contest in which military strength was built up for deterrence rather than combat. Here economic conduct would be a major factor in the American decision to contain the Soviet Union's attempt to expand its influence. In the years following World War II the U.S.S.R. had assumed a stance considered adversarial to Western interests. Ideologically, the opposition was between Western capitalism and Soviet state socialism; militarily, the contest exhibited itself in the West's rebuilding of Germany and the formation of the North Atlantic Treaty Organization (NATO) versus the Soviet Union's influence over Eastern Europe's nations by means of the Warsaw Pact. Geopolitically, the U.S.S.R. sponsored the formation of socialist governments in what became known as its satellite nations of Poland, Hungary, and Czechoslovakia, separated by what British Prime Minister Winston Churchill characterized as an Iron Curtain inhibiting contact with the democracies of Western Europe. In Africa, where new nations gained independence from colonial rule, West and East competed for influence. Overall, the West perceived a threat in the U.S.S.R.'s 1948 attainment of nuclear weaponry and its maintenance of massive troop strength beyond its borders. When Communist revolutionaries took control of mainland China in 1949, the Cold War moved beyond European boundaries to encompass the entire globe. Until the collapse of the Soviet Union, economic warfare motivated American activity as decisively as had the waging of World War II.

Throughout the 1950s and into the early 1960s, social critics perceived a stable conformity to American life, a dedication to an increasingly materialistic standard of living, whose ethical merit was ensured by a continuity with the prewar world—a continuity that proved to be delusory. In this initial postwar period white males benefited especially from the economy and saw the nature of their lives change. The G.I. Bill provided veterans with a college education; after World War II America would eventually have as much as 50 percent of its population college educated, a percentage unthinkable in prewar years and unmatched by any other nation. With world markets open to American goods, the expanded economy offered sophisticated technical and professional jobs for these college graduates; within a generation the alphabet soup of great corporations—IT&T, GE, RCA, IBM, and so forth—came to dominate employment patterns at home and around the globe. Higher incomes and demographic expansion created vast new suburbs beyond the limits of older cities, and the population of the United States began a westward shift. New roads accommodated this increasingly mobile society, including the interstate highway system begun in 1955. By 1960 the average American family was moving to a new place of residence at the rate of once every five years, as new opportunities beckoned and lifestyles expanded beyond the more traditional stability of "home." An age of plenty created a new managerial class, but also ensured an ample piece of the pie for workers protected by well-organized, secure unions.

Named for the man who served as president from 1953 to 1961, the early postwar period came to be known as the "Eisenhower Era." Dwight D. Eisenhower had commanded the Allied forces during their push to total victory in World War II. Comparatively apolitical, he was asked to run as a Democratic presidential candidate in 1948 before accepting the Republican nomination in 1952. His impact on American culture of the 1950s suggested the presence of a benign father figure who had fought to make the world secure and who now could preside over its enjoyment of achieved ideals. At home, he provided federal funds to build freeways that swept suburban workers home from their city jobs. Militarily, he was commander-in-chief of a globally powerful but never-used force, the Strategic Air Command, a fleet of bombers up to half of which were in the air at all times, poised to deliver a nuclear strike measured in how many times over it could annihilate an enemy. Yet education was a weapon, too, and when the Soviet Union's 1957 launch of the *Sputnik* satellite suggested the West was lagging behind, a new technology race began that reendowed American schools and colleges with rich resources and a crucial sense of commitment. Also during this era the movement for African American civil rights, directed to overturning legislated segregation in the South rather than reforming de facto abuses throughout the country, proceeded through local court action and only occasionally with federal involvement. The push was on to return women to a domesticity made pleasurable by new labor-saving machinery and consumer goods.

But ways of life consonant with an isolated, stable economy could not survive in the new atmosphere of American power and wealth. The passage from the 1950s to the 1960s marks the great watershed of the postwar half century. Conflicts between conformity and individuality, tradition and innovation, stability and disruption were announced and anticipated even before they effectively influenced history and culture. The earliest harbinger was the 1960 election of John F. Kennedy as president. Former senator from Massachusetts, heir to a large (but comparatively recently made) family fortune, Kennedy was a generation younger and immensely more glamorous than Eisenhower. To a mainstream society that might have become complacent with the material success of Eisenhower's years and had neglected the less fortunate, Kennedy offered an energetic program of involvement. Formally titled "The New Frontier," it reached from the participation of individual Americans in the Peace Corps (working to aid underdeveloped countries around the world) to the grand effort at conquering space. In the midst of his brief presidency, in October 1962, the Soviet Union installed ballistic missiles in Cuba; when Kennedy protested this act and began a naval blockade of the island nation, the possibility of nuclear warfare came closer than ever before, until the U.S.S.R. relented and withdrew its weapons. Domestic tensions also rose when Robert Kennedy, the president's brother and U.S. attorney general, took a newly activist approach toward desegregation, sending federal troops into the South to enforce the law. But there was a cultural grace to the Kennedy era as well, with the president's wife, Jacqueline, making involvement in the arts not just fashionable but also a matter of government policy.

The Sixties, as they are known, really began with the assassination of John F. Kennedy on November 22, 1963. The tumultuous dozen years of American history that followed embraced a more combative period in civil rights, climaxing with the most sustained and effective attempts to remedy the evils of racial discrimination since the years of Reconstruction after the Civil War. For the first time since the Suffrage movement following World War I, women organized to pursue their legal, ethical, and cultural interests, now defined as feminism. Active dissension within the culture emerged in response to military involvement in Vietnam, where in 1961 President Kennedy had sent small numbers of advisers to help the Republic of South Vietnam resist pressures from Communist North Vietnam. Presidents Lyndon Johnson and Richard Nixon expanded and continued the U.S. presence; and an increasingly strident opposition—fueled by protests on American college campuses and among the country's liberal intellectuals—turned into a much larger cultural revolution. Between 1967 and 1970 the nation experienced many outbreaks of violence, including political assassinations (of presidential candidate Robert Kennedy and civil rights leader Dr. Martin Luther King Jr. in 1968), urban riots, and massive campus disruptions.

Torn apart by opposition to President Johnson and the climate of violence surrounding its national convention in Chicago in August 1968, the Democratic Party lost to Republican candidate Richard Nixon, who was himself burdened with the Vietnam War and escalating dissent (leading to student deaths at Kent State and Jackson State universities in May 1970). By the time the Vietnam War ended in 1975 with the collapse of Saigon to North Vietnamese and Viet Cong forces, the United States had also been buffeted by large-scale domestic troubles in the form of the Watergate scandal: a revelation of President Nixon's abuses of governmental privileges that led to his resignation in August 1974. These events mark the end of one of the more discomfortingly disruptive eras in American history.

By the end of the 1970s some characteristics of the previous decade's countercultural revolt had been accepted in the mainstream, including informalities of dress, relaxation of sexual codes of behavior, and an increased respect for individual rights. The 1980s experienced a call for traditional values, which were interpreted not as a return to community and self-sacrifice but the pursuit of wealth. During the presidency of Ronald Reagan incomes rose while taxes fell; the Sixties' distrust of government mutated into a defense of personal acquisition. Following the debacle in Vietnam, where more than fifty thousand Americans died in a losing war, the military restricted itself in the 1980s and early 1990s to quick, sharply specified interventions (in Grenada, Panama, and most dramatically in Iraq) relying less on vague deterrence than on precise applications of technological expertise. Economically, America boomed, but in new ways: manufacturing dominance was replaced by service efficiency, massive workforces were downsized into more profitable units, while investment and entrepreneurship replaced older modes of development.

As the twentieth century approached its turn, global power experienced its greatest readjustment since World War II. American economic might had depleted the Soviet Union's ability to compete, and as that state's ethnic republics achieved independence and the old Warsaw Pact alliance of Eastern European nations collapsed, the European Union—once restricted to Western democracies—assumed even greater importance. With the attack on New York's World Trade Center and the Pentagon by terrorists on September 11, 2001, the third millennium threatened to echo the first with a renewed emphasis on religion setting political agendas and working to see those agendas fulfilled.

LITERARY DEVELOPMENTS

In such a turbulent half century, literature also encompasses a great deal of change. Not surprisingly, during this period many important writers reexamined both what fiction and drama are meant to accomplish and how to accomplish it.

Just as people in the first two decades following World War II addressed themselves to taking material advantage of the extensive gains won by global victory, so too did writers seek to capitalize on the successes of a previous literary generation. Cultural homogeneity was an ideal during the 1950s, patriotically so in terms of building up the foundations of American society to resist and contain Communism, materialistically so when it came to enjoying the benefits of mass marketing in a consumer-driven world. Following this trend, writers assumed that a short story, a novel, or a play could represent the experiences of an entire people, that a common national essence lay beneath distinctions of gender, race, ethnicity, religion, or region. Literature between 1945 and the Sixties let readers believe that there could be such a thing as the representative American short story, nuanced for upper-middle-class patrons in the pages of *The New Yorker* magazine while slanted to more homely interests in *Collier's* and *The Saturday Evening Post*.

It was typical for a story in these journals to be set within the same context as the medium's advertising: Cadillacs, suburban station wagons, and the occasional European-delivered Mercedes-Benz in *The New Yorker*, Fords and Chevrolets in *Collier's* and the *Post*. An ad for an all-electric kitchen might well appear on the page opposite a short story starting off with its characters sharing breakfast in an all-electric kitchen, or at least wishing they could have one. American life, of course, was far from being so uniform. But there was great success in selling the idea of cultural conformity to a people supposedly united by the war effort, by their patiently saving during the years of wartime shortages, and by the threat of Communism. These same impulses to homogenization could be transferred from the pages of weekly magazines to the medium that would replace them, television; here situation comedies and the occasional serious drama would murmur reassurances that all the best features of American life could be held in common.

Novels of the immediate postwar period followed this trend in more depth, in larger scale, and with more self-conscious justification. Ernest Hemingway, a master of the short story himself, had fostered the notion of novel writing as "going the distance," slugging it out all the way, as it were, in a fifteen-round championship prizefight. Publicized by others as one of the dominant literary figures of his day, Hemingway promoted his own example to influence a new generation of novelists who believed they had to act like him to be taken seriously. Hence the desire to write what was called "the great American novel," a major work that would characterize the larger aspects of experience. Ambitions were not simply to write a war novel, for example, but *the* war novel; not just a work about corporate big business, but something that generalized the subject for all times. Regionalism could remain an interest, but only if it provided deeper meaning; here the example of William Faulkner encouraged the belief among younger writers that dealing with the American South meant grappling with monumental issues of guilt and the inexorable power of history. Major dramatists behaved the same way; if their immediate predecessors had drawn on classically tragic allusions in deepening their themes, postwar playwrights embraced otherwise mundane characters as universal types; the death of a salesman, for example, would be examined in the same spotlight once reserved for great people, for here indeed was a figure who stood for the postwar human being.

Like the notion of cultural conformity itself, this understanding of literature came under serious challenge during the 1960s. Critical movements of the time articulated a new literary unease, and writers began responding to critical movements with new literary strategies. The first such challenge was the "death of the novel" controversy, sparked by some writers' sense that social reality had become too unstable to serve as a reliable anchor for their narratives and fueled by certain critics' conviction that fiction had exhausted its formal possibilities. The short story and the novel, it was argued, demanded a set of fairly limited conventions; these conventions, such as characterization and development by means of dialogue, imagery, and symbolism, however, relied on a securely describable world to make sense. Just as these conventions were becoming stale by overuse, so the subjects to which they were applied increasingly exceeded any orderly account. Even as American life in the 1950s espoused conformity, technological advances in the exchange of information had made the particulars of such life ever more hard to manage. As boundaries of time and space were eclipsed by television, air travel, and an accompanying global awareness, the once essential unities of representation (time, space, and action) no longer provided ground on which to build a work of literary art. As more became known about the world itself, the writer's ability to make sense of the whole was challenged. A culture that looked for totalized expressions from its writers now seemed to demand the impossible.

A parallel development in literary theory posed another great threat to conventional literature. Known as "Deconstruction" and brought to American shores from France by means of a series of university conferences and academic publications beginning in 1966, this style of criticism questioned the underlying assumptions behind any statement, exposing how what was accepted as absolute truth usually depended on rhetoric rather than fact, exposing indeed how "fact" itself was constructed by intellectual operations. This style of criticism became attractive to literary scholars who had been framing social and political questions in much the same terms—believing, for example, that the Vietnam War had been presented to the American people through slogans rather than realities. Many fiction writers and dramatists, who had sought stable employment in universities and colleges, took part vigorously in these discussions. The Death of the Novel debates and Deconstruction converged to destabilize literary genres that were once thought to be a most reliable window on the world.

Two literary developments emerged in response. For writers who valued reportage and had developed literary techniques that kept pace with the explosive growth of the information age, the traditional conventions of fiction were not dead: it was rather that the novel and the short story were no longer their proper home. Hence the invention of the nonfiction novel and its attendant school of New Journalism, which held that characterization, imagery, symbol, and the like were no longer the exclusive province of fiction but appropriate tools for an improved journalism. One of Deconstruction's claims was that there is no absolute objectivity; every author, journalist or not, writes from a point of view whose perspective carries with it any number of colorings and biases. Why not capitalize on that perspective—be honest about it, and report not so much the event as the writer's place in it? Given all that literary art can tell about the human imagination, techniques that could be called fraudulent in a fiction writer's hands might be praiseworthy as a journalist's most candid honesty. In the process, the subject matter— itself an ungraspable object, under the new terms of literary theory—would be enriched with the more knowable sense of the writer's presence. Thus book-length studies of newsworthy events began to be crafted in the manner of novels, while feature journalism read more like a short story, using as it did the writing techniques more traditionally associated with fictive artists.

The second development involved not transposing the conventions of fiction to another medium but discarding them as completely as possible. The beginnings of this movement involved rejecting the principal convention of traditional fiction, the suspension of disbelief that enabled an invented story to be presented as factual. By emphasizing their own presence as creators of the tale and making their main subject the procedures by which their narratives were brought into being, writers of Metafiction (as the form was called) sidestepped objections from both the Deconstructionists and the Death of the Novel critics. There were no false illusions in Metafiction; what you saw was what you got, a literary work representing nothing other than itself. The value of such work lay in the author, not the tale: how interesting the writer could make the process, how much evidence of imagination and intelligence and creative personality showed through. A good analogy for Metafiction was the practice of Abstract Expressionist painters from a generation before, who had made the canvas not a surface on which to represent but an arena in which to act, the action of their paint taking precedence over anything else being depicted. From the specific technique of Metafiction, innovative writers of this period expanded their repertoire to include more broadly expressive narratives involving not just writing but existence itself. Fiction is not about experience, these authors claimed; it is experience itself. The difficult aim here was to capture the essence of experience without the mediating conventions of representative illusion.

Fiction in the 1960s, much like the decade itself, was often extreme in its methods and disruptive in its effects. Yet much like the social and political legacy of the decade, the legacies of Sixties writing influenced later literary developments. Even in the heyday of Deconstruction and the Death of the Novel, realistic fiction continued to be written, in a style enriched by having its previously unquestioned practices so rigorously cross-examined. A new group of realistic writers called Minimalists made these challenges central to their work, crafting a manner of description that with great intensity limited itself to what could be most reliably accepted. What the Minimalists described was not endorsed by the authors as true; rather they were signs of what their characters accepted as truth, not objects from nature but conventions accepted by societies to go about the business of living. In a typically Minimalist story, although nothing sad is mentioned and no character grieves, someone does indeed make a sign that she is saying something meant to be sad, and another character emits a perfect sign of being deeply unhappy in response. Objects that abound in such works are drawn from the consumer's world not for what they are but for what they signify, be it good taste or poor, wealth or deprivation. All told, it is a capable way of writing realism in a world where philosophical definitions discourage such a term.

Social revolutions of the 1960s left a legacy even richer than those of critical and philosophical change. Civil rights activism helped create the Black Arts Movement, which in turn replaced the tokenistic notion of accepting only one African American writer at a time with a much broader awareness of imaginative expression by a wide range of literary talent. A parallel movement saw southern writers seeking other styles of response than mourning the loss of the Civil War or feeling guilty about slavery; another saw Jewish American writers moving beyond thematics of assimilation and identity to embrace subjects and techniques reaching from the personal to the metafictive. Feminist and nonfeminist women writers found that subgenres such as fantasy and science fiction could be useful in overthrowing long-held stereotypes of gender; present-day life could be described with a new frankness and expanded awareness appropriate to women's wider and more egalitarian role in society. Native American writers received new attention from mainstream culture, first initiated by attention to the land's ecology and a recognition that the "Wild West" view of American history involved strategic stereotyping of Indian peoples. Welcome now were artistic expressions of the cultural complexity of the American population from Chinese Americans, Japanese Americans, Mexican Americans, and other groups previously excluded from the literary canon.

The most dramatic development, one that indicated the much broadening range of achievement among writers of many different backgrounds and persuasions, was the success of African American women during the 1970s and 1980s in finding a literary voice and making it heard as an important articulation of experience. Here was a reminder of how so much of what passes for reality is nothing but artifice, fabrication, and convention—for here was a large group of people who had been written out of history and denied a speaking part in national dialogue. With identity repressed and so much of a usable past effaced, these writers nevertheless were able to find a means of expression that helped redefine readers' understanding of the world.

WRITERS AND THEIR WORK

A hallmark of the postwar period is its shift from unity as an ideal to diversity, and during these times American writing has been characterized by a great variety of styles all employed at the same time. Yet as these writers engage in a dialogue with each other's themes and approaches, certain patterns emerge—sometimes merely responsive, other times developmental, and occasionally revolutionary. If there is anything in common to the period, it is an appreciation of and sometimes outright delight in language as a tool of literary expression. Finding a voice is any person's first task in seeking to be heard; and because words are the basic component of literature, the writer's use of them will be the first evidence of his or her artistic talent. In American writing since 1945, the invitation to compare and contrast is richly rewarding.

Consider the approaches taken to a common figure, the salesperson, by Arthur Miller and David Mamet. The older playwright poses his character struggling to articulate his identity as an antihero, fighting to keep his head above water in a world so powerful as to overwhelm him. Four decades later, David Mamet's sales staff is awash in a tide of language, their slick talking managing to submerge all traces of reality in a realty world built on illusive premises; as long as a character can talk, he survives. A similar contrast distinguishes older and newer writers of the American South. Tennessee Williams, like Arthur Miller, presents characters desperately seeking to articulate their problems, problems that story writers Eudora Welty and Flannery O'Connor choose to portray as either picturesque or grotesque. A generation later Barry Hannah, whose narrator from Mississippi is faced with articulating something much tougher, the nature of the war he's fighting in Vietnam, finds a comforting solution in the power of his speech, an ability to couch this horrific experience in language whose ongoing power manages to construct a narrative of his own making that carries him safely home (where grotesqueries reminiscent of O'Connor's await his equally smooth treatment). Ultimately, language can become the event itself, as in Suzan-Lori Parks's ritualization of the assassination of President Abraham Lincoln in *The American Play*, a work whose power indicates how this event continues to influence the lives of African Americans a century and a half later.

In a world that would define away human dignity, writers strive to find a place for it, no matter how hard they have to search. Such a quest characterizes Saul Bellow's "Looking for Mr. Green" but also motivates Grace Paley's search for more effective ways to do so in "A Conversation with My Father." In this latter piece the narrator's parent asks for a narrative reminiscent of the same Russian masters who influenced Saul Bellow's development as a deeply philosophical fiction writer; but Paley's narrator, who is a writer much like herself, resists the world's tragic sense of closure as if telling stories were itself a way to change reality. Writers dealing with specific problems, such as Ralph Ellison, James Baldwin, and Bernard Malamud, find ritualization a helpful way of understanding the natures of the African American and Jewish American experience; and in a more general sense, their contemporary Kurt Vonnegut works to expose rituals for the devices that they are. His examination of the potency of the phrase "fates worse than death" (in an essay that uses, in the manner of the New Journalism, many devices characteristic of fiction) shows how language once again shapes perceptions of reality and encourages certain ways of conduct, a reminder that Vonnegut himself did not become popular until the 1960s, when such understandings were a more prominent cultural feature.

New voices and new styles of expression also distinguish the half century following World War II. Beginning in the 1950s, James Baldwin found imaginative forms for issues politicized in the civil rights struggle; half a generation later, Amiri Baraka (then known as LeRoi Jones) spoke more stridently for African American male identity, giving center stage to a character whose pronouncements are received as so threatening that his encompassing society cannot accept him. Women with a feminist perspective, such as Ursula K. Le Guin, turn to a previously male domain, science fiction, to create utopias where everything is quite literally renamed (a reminder that the name precedes how a thing is perceived). At the same time, African American women strive for a voice of their own, neglected as it has been by historical forces since America's birth. It is noteworthy that Paule Marshall, Toni Morrison, and Alice Walker must first of all have their characters sit down and talk with each other before such redefinitions can emerge. Sometimes it's for agreement, other times for dialogue and debate; but in all cases, as in Le Guin's "She Unnames Them," the ability to speak must itself be developed before conditions can be changed. This speech testifies to the period's developing awareness that describing the terms of existence centrally influences the nature of existence itself.

Tradition itself becomes something pliable in these writers' hands. Whether Philip Roth challenging the dimensions of Jewish American societal practice in "Defender of the Faith," N. Scott Momaday revitalizing tribal understandings in *The Way to Rainy Mountain*, Maxine Hong Kingston incorporating the dreams of her Chinese American protagonist in *Tripmaster Monkey* into the larger sweep of both American popular culture and canonical literature, or Ishmael Reed critiquing the subculture of African Americans in *The Last Days of Louisiana Red*, individual cultures are now seen as participants in a richly interchanging multiculture that redefines an America less a melting pot than a collage of immense variety, each part drawing certain strengths from others. In this context the nature of reality changes, whether defined scientifically by Thomas Pynchon, socio-culturally by Rudolfo Anaya, or in terms of dominating emotions by Stephen Dixon. People can well be what they make of themselves, as Gerald Vizenor shows in his update of the trickster figure (from Native American legend) in "Almost Browne." Freed from the stricter constraints of literary realism, a writer like Donald Barthelme can examine the imaginative importance of human relations from a multiplicity of perspectives, including not just reminiscence but that of the full inventory of popular representational forms. Thanks to computer technology, novelists may now include artificial intelligence among their cast of characters, as Richard Powers demonstrates in *Galatea 2.2*.

Challenged by new understandings of how reality is constructed, literary realism is transformed. John Cheever's "The Swimmer" takes recourse to the magical to express what in an earlier time might have been a sociologically and psychologically inclined story. John Updike uses the occasion of a family's dissolution to explore lyrical dimensions of the experience as well as its dynamics of severed relations. In "Medley" Toni Cade Bambara constructs a society in terms of its musical language rather than simply its behavioral styles, while Raymond Carver's "Cathedral" quite minimally feels out the shape of things as if its auditor were blind, as the story's character in question is. Carver's method assumes nothing, patiently constructing its world from scratch. But postwar writing also provides opportunities for great expansion, as Annie Dillard undertakes in "Holy the Firm," where the occasion of a little girl suffering severe burns is examined from perspectives encompassing the philosophical and spiritual as well as more immediate concerns.

The postwar world offers multiform varieties of existence, and if there is a progress to writing it is in authors' success at finding ways to treat unique experiences in ways accessible to and enjoyable by a general readership. Ann Beattie's world, one that in the hands of a realistic, socially inclined writer might once have been assumed to conform with a national ideal, is in fact made of its characters' own constructions—constructs that present a compelling picture by virtue of their play of signs rather than correspondences to similar objects in the reader's world. The worlds of Diane Glancy, Leslie Silko, and Louise Erdrich, while typically described as Native American, are more than sociological representations of a particular group; instead each writer uses idiosyncratic techniques to describe an experience that exists primarily in the writing, in the nature of the event's perception, as opposed to any reductive explanation of events themselves. Gloria Anzaldúa and Sandra Cisneros display a similar range of techniques in building their Mexican American worlds, worlds that are distinguished by their unique style of language—again, examples of how different names for things yield an experience of different things, all as shaped by the writer's descriptive power. In a similar manner, fables from Puerto Rico influence the American lives lived by protagonists in the fiction of Judith Ortiz Cofer, lending her work a multicultural potency that exceeds any simple recounting of existence.

It has been said that our contemporary culture provides the greatest variety of literary expression available at any one time. From a war effort that demanded unity of purpose and a cold war period that for a time encouraged conformity to a homogenetic ideal, American writing has emerged at the end of this century to include a sophisticated mastery of technique in service of a task broadened by an understanding of literature's role in characterizing reality. With inclusiveness the new rule and imaginative potential as a fresh ideal, writing has survived threats of its death to flourish more fully than ever.

AMERICAN PROSE SINCE 1945

TEXTS	CONTEXTS
1941 Eudora Welty, "Petrified Man"	
	1945 U.S. drops atomic bombs on Hiroshima and Nagasaki; Japan surrenders, ending World War II • Cold War begins
1947 Tennesse Williams, *A Streetcar Named Desire*	1947 Jackie Robinson becomes the first black Major League ballplayer
1949 Arthur Miller, *Death of a Salesman*	
	1950 Senator Joseph McCarthy begins attacks on communism
	1950–53 Korean War
1951 Saul Bellow, "Looking for Mr. Green"	
1952 Ralph Ellison, *Invisible Man*	
	1953 House Concurrent Resolution 108 dictates government's intention to "terminate" its treaty relations with the Native American tribes
	1954 *Brown v. Board of Education* declares segregated schools unconstitutional
1955 Flannery O'Connor, "Good Country People"	
	1956 Martin Luther King Jr. leads bus boycott in Montgomery, Alabama
1958 Bernard Malamud, "The Magic Barrel"	
1959 Philip Roth, "Defender of the Faith"	
1960 Thomas Pynchon, "Entropy"	1960 Woolworth lunch counter sit-in in Greensboro, N.C., marks beginning of civil rights movement
	1963 King delivers "I Have a Dream" speech • black church in Birmingham, Alabama, bombed, killing four girls • President John F. Kennedy assassinated
1964 John Cheever, "The Swimmer" • Amiri Baraka (LeRoi Jones), *Dutchman*	
1965 James Baldwin, "Going to Meet the Man"	1965 Riots break out in Watts section of Los Angeles • Malcolm X assassinated
	1965–73 Vietnam War
	1966 National Organization for Women (NOW) founded
1968 Donald Barthelme, "The Balloon" • Norman Mailer, *The Armies of the Night*	1968 King assassinated • Senator Robert F. Kennedy assassinated
1969 N. Scott Momaday, *The Way to Rainy Mountain*	1969 U.S. astronauts land on the moon • Stonewall riots in New York City initiate gay liberation movement • Woodstock Festival held near Bethel, New York

Boldface titles indicate works in the anthology.

TEXTS	CONTEXTS
1970 Ishmael Reed, "Neo-HooDoo Manifesto"	1970 National Guard kills four students during antiwar demonstration at Kent State University, Ohio
	1972 Watergate scandal • military draft ends
1973 Alice Walker, "Everyday Use"	1973 *Roe. v. Wade* legalizes abortion • American Indian Movement members occupy Wounded Knee
1974 Grace Paley, "A Conversation with My Father"	1974 President Richard Nixon resigns in wake of Watergate, avoiding impeachment
1975 Barry Hannah, "Midnight and I'm Not Famous Yet" • John Updike, "Separating"	
	1976 U.S. bicentennial
1977 Annie Dillard, "Holy the Firm"	
1978 Ann Beattie, "Weekend"	
1980 Toni Cade Bambara, "Medley"	
1981 Leslie Marmon Silko, "Lullaby"	
1982 Rudolfo Anaya, "The Christmas Play" • Raymond Carver, "Cathedral" • David Mamet, *Glengarry Glen Ross* • Kurt Vonnegut, "Fates Worse Than Death"	1982 Equal Rights Amendment defeated • antinuclear movement protests manufacture of nuclear weapons • AIDS officially identified in the United States
1983 Paule Marshall, "Reena" • Toni Morrison, "Recitatif"	
1984 Stephen Dixon, "Time to Go"	
1985 Ursula K. Le Guin, "She Unnames Them" • Don DeLillo, *White Noise*	
1986 Louise Erdrich, "Fleur"	
1987 Gloria Anzaldúa, *Borderlands / La Frontera*	
1989 Maxine Hong Kingston, *Tripmaster Monkey*	1989 Soviet Union collapses; Cold War ends • oil tanker *Exxon Valdez* runs aground in Alaska
	1990 Congress passes Native American Graves Protection and Repatriation Act
1991 Sandra Cisneros, *Woman Hollering Creek* • Gerald Vizenor, "Almost Browne"	1991 United States enters Persian Gulf War • World Wide Web introduced
1993 Diane Glancy, "Polar Breath"	
1995 Suzan-Lori Parks, *The America Play* • Richard Powers, *Galatea 2.2.*	1995 Federal building in Oklahoma City bombed in a terrorist attack
	1997 *Pathfinder* robot explores Mars
1999 Ralph Ellison, *Juneteenth*	
	2001 Execution of Timothy McVeigh, convicted in 1995 Oklahoma City bombing • September 11 terrorist attacks on Pentagon and World Trade Center

EUDORA WELTY
1909–2001

In her essay titled "Place in Fiction," Eudora Welty spoke of her work as filled with the spirit of place: "Location is the ground conductor of all the currents of emotion and belief and moral conviction that charge out from the story in its course." Both her outwardly uneventful life and her writing are most intimately connected to the topography and atmosphere, the season and the soil of the native Mississippi that was her lifelong home.

Born in Jackson in 1909, to parents who came from the North, and raised in comfortable circumstances (her father headed an insurance company), she attended Mississippi State College for Women, then graduated from the University of Wisconsin in 1929. After a course in advertising at the Columbia University School of Business, she returned to Mississippi, first working as a radio writer and newspaper society editor, then for the Works Progress Administration, taking photographs of and interviewing local residents. Those travels would be reflected in her fiction and also in a book of her photographs, *One Time and Place*, published in 1971.

She began writing fiction after her return to Mississippi in 1931 and five years later published her first story, "Death of a Traveling Salesman," in a small magazine. Over the next two years, six of her stories were published in the *Southern Review*, a serious literary magazine one of whose editors was the poet and novelist Robert Penn Warren. She also received strong support from Katherine Anne Porter, who contributed an introduction to Welty's first book of stories, *A Curtain of Green* (1941). That introduction hailed the arrival of another gifted southern fiction writer, and in fact the volume contained some of the best stories she was ever to write, such as "Petrified Man" (printed here). Her profusion of metaphor and the difficult surface of her narrative—often oblique and indirect in its effect—were in part a mark of her admiration for modern writers like Virginia Woolf and (as with any young southern writer) William Faulkner. Although Welty's stories were as shapely as that of her mentor, Porter, they were more richly idiomatic and comic in their inclination. A second collection, *The Wide Net*, appeared two years later; and her first novel, *The Robber Bridegroom*, was published in 1942.

In that year and the next she was awarded the O. Henry Memorial Prize for the best piece of short fiction, and from then on she received a steady stream of awards and prizes, including the Pulitzer Prize for her novel *The Optimist's Daughter* (1972). Her most ambitious and longest piece of fiction is *Losing Battles* (1970), in which she aimed to compose a narrative made up almost wholly out of her characters' voices in mainly humorous interplay. Like Robert Frost, Welty loves gossip in all its actuality and intimacy, and if that love failed in the novels to produce compelling, extended sequences, it did result in many lively and entertaining pages. Perhaps her finest single book after *A Curtain of Green* was *The Golden Apples* (1949), a sequence of tales about a fabulous, invented, small Mississippi community named Morgana. Her characters appear and reappear in these related stories and come together most memorably in the brilliant "June Recital," perhaps her masterpiece.

As an entertainer, her wonderfully sharp sense of humor is strongly evident. Although the characters and themes that fill the pages of her fiction consist, in part, of involuted southern families, physically handicapped, mentally retarded, or generally unstable kinfolk—and although this fiction is shot through with undercurrents of death, violence, and degradation—everything Welty touches is transformed by the incorrigibly humorous twist of her narrative idiom. No matter how desperate a situation may be, she makes us listen to the way a character talks about it; it is style rather than information we find ourselves paying attention to. And although her attitude toward human folly is satiric, it is satire devoid of the wish to undermine and mock her characters. Instead, they are given irresistible life and a memorable expressiveness in the vivid realizations of her prose. Her narrative unfolds on the principle of varied repetitions or reiterations that have (she has claimed) the function of a deliberate double exposure in photography. She once remarked in an essay that "fine story writers seem to be in a sense obstructionists." By making us pay attention to who is speaking and what the implications are of that speech, by asking us to imagine the way in which a silent character is responding to that speech, and by making us read behind the deceptively simple response she gives to that character, we are made active readers, playfully engaged in the complicated scene of a typical Welty story. "Why I Live at the P.O.," "Keela, the Outcast Indian Maiden," the unforgettable "Powerhouse" with its Fats Waller-like hero, "Petrified Man," "June Recital," and many others are solid proof of both the strength and the joy of her art. And although she has been called a "regional" writer, she herself has noted the condescending nature of that term, which she says is an "outsider's term; it has no meaning for the insider who is doing the writing, because as far as he knows he is simply writing about life" (*On Writing*). So it is with Eudora Welty's fiction.

The text is that published in *A Curtain of Green* (1941).

Petrified Man

"Reach in my purse and git me a cigarette without no powder in it if you kin, Mrs. Fletcher, honey," said Leota to her ten o'clock shampoo-and-set customer. "I don't like no perfumed cigarettes."

Mrs. Fletcher gladly reached over to the lavender shelf under the lavender-framed mirror, shook a hair net loose from the clasp of the patent-leather bag, and slapped her hand down quickly on a powder puff which burst out when the purse was opened.

"Why, look at the peanuts, Leota!" said Mrs. Fletcher in her marvelling voice.

"Honey, them goobers has been in my purse a week if they's been in it a day. Mrs. Pike bought them peanuts."

"Who's Mrs. Pike?" asked Mrs. Fletcher, settling back. Hidden in this den of curling fluid and henna[1] packs, separated by a lavender swing-door from the other customers, who were being gratified in other booths, she could give her curiosity its freedom. She looked expectantly at the black part in Leota's yellow curls as she bent to light the cigarette.

"Mrs. Pike is this lady from New Orleans," said Leota, puffing, and pressing into Mrs. Fletcher's scalp with strong red-nailed fingers. "A friend, not a customer. You see, like maybe I told you last time, me and Fred and Sal and Joe all had us a fuss, so Sal and Joe up and moved out, so we didn't do a thing but rent out their room. So we rented it to Mrs. Pike. And Mr. Pike." She flicked an ash into the basket of dirty towels. "Mrs. Pike is a very decided blonde. *She* bought me the peanuts."

"She must be cute," said Mrs. Fletcher.

"Honey, 'cute' ain't the word for what she is. I'm tellin' you, Mrs. Pike is attractive. She has her a good time. She's got a sharp eye out, Mrs. Pike has."

---

1. Reddish brown dye for tinting hair.

She dashed the comb through the air, and paused dramatically as a cloud of Mrs. Fletcher's hennaed hair floated out of the lavender teeth like a small storm-cloud.

"Hair fallin'."

"Aw, Leota."

"Uh-huh, commencin' to fall out," said Leota, combing again, and letting fall another cloud.

"Is it any dandruff in it?" Mrs. Fletcher was frowning, her hair-line eyebrows diving down toward her nose, and her wrinkled, beady-lashed eyelids batting with concentration.

"Nope." She combed again. "Just fallin' out."

"Bet it was that last perm'nent you gave me that did it," Mrs. Fletcher said cruelly. "Remember you cooked me fourteen minutes."

"You had fourteen minutes comin' to you," said Leota with finality.

"Bound to be somethin'," persisted Mrs. Fletcher. "Dandruff, dandruff. I couldn't of caught a thing like that from Mr. Fletcher, could I?"

"Well," Leota answered at last, "you know what I heard in here yestiddy, one of Thelma's ladies was settin' over yonder in Thelma's booth gittin' a machineless, and I don't mean to insist or insinuate or anything, Mrs. Fletcher, but Thelma's lady just happ'med to throw out—I forgotten what she was talkin' about at the time—that you was p-r-e-g., and lots of times that'll make your hair do awful funny, fall out and God knows what all. It just ain't our fault, is the way I look at it."

There was a pause. The women stared at each other in the mirror.

"Who was it?" demanded Mrs. Fletcher.

"Honey, I really couldn't say," said Leota. "Not that you look it."

"Where's Thelma? I'll get it out of her," said Mrs. Fletcher.

"Now, honey, I wouldn't go and git mad over a little thing like that," Leota said, combing hastily, as though to hold Mrs. Fletcher down by the hair. "I'm sure it was somebody didn't mean no harm in the world. How far gone are you?"

"Just wait," said Mrs. Fletcher, and shrieked for Thelma, who came in and took a drag from Leota's cigarette.

"Thelma, honey, throw your mind back to yestiddy if you kin," said Leota, drenching Mrs. Fletcher's hair with a thick fluid and catching the overflow in a cold wet towel at her neck.

"Well, I got my lady half wound for a spiral," said Thelma doubtfully.

"This won't take but a minute," said Leota. "Who is it you got in there, old Horse Face? Just cast your mind back and try to remember who your lady was yestiddy who happ'm to mention that my customer was pregnant, that's all. She's dead to know."

Thelma drooped her blood-red lips and looked over Mrs. Fletcher's head into the mirror. "Why, honey, I ain't got the faintest," she breathed. "I really don't recollect the faintest. But I'm sure she meant no harm. I declare, I forgot my hair finally got combed and thought it was a stranger behind me."

"Was it that Mrs. Hutchinson?" Mrs. Fletcher was tensely polite.

"Mrs. Hutchinson? Oh, Mrs. Hutchinson." Thelma batted her eyes. "Naw, precious, she come on Thursday and didn't ev'm mention your name. I doubt if she ev'm knows you're on the way."

"Thelma!" cried Leota staunchly.

"All I know is, whoever it is 'll be sorry some day. Why, I just barely knew it myself!" cried Mrs. Fletcher. "Just let her wait!"

"Why? What're you gonna do to her?"

It was a child's voice, and the women looked down. A little boy was making tents with aluminum wave pinchers[2] on the floor under the sink.

"Billy Boy, hon, mustn't bother nice ladies," Leota smiled. She slapped him brightly and behind her back waved Thelma out of the booth. "Ain't Billy Boy a sight? Only three years old and already just nuts about the beauty-parlor business."

"I never saw him here before," said Mrs. Fletcher, still unmollified.

"He ain't been here before, that's how come," said Leota. "He belongs to Mrs. Pike. She got her a job but it was Fay's Millinery. He oughtn't to try on those ladies' hats, they come down over his eyes like I don't know what. They just git to look ridiculous, that's what, an' of course he's gonna put 'em on: hats. They tole Mrs. Pike they didn't appreciate him hangin' around there. Here, he couldn't hurt a thing."

"Well! I don't like children that much," said Mrs. Fletcher.

"Well!" said Leota moodily.

"Well! I'm almost tempted not to have this one," said Mrs. Fletcher. "That Mrs. Hutchinson! Just looks straight through you when she sees you on the street and then spits at you behind your back."

"Mr. Fletcher would beat you on the head if you didn't have it now," said Leota reasonably. "After going this far."

Mrs. Fletcher sat up straight. "Mr. Fletcher can't do a thing with me."

"He can't!" Leota winked at herself in the mirror.

"No, siree, he can't. If he so much as raises his voice against me, he knows good and well I'll have one of my sick headaches, and then I'm just not fit to live with. And if I really look that pregnant already—"

"Well, now, honey, I just want you to know—I habm't told any of my ladies and I ain't goin' to tell 'em—even that you're losin' your hair. You just get you one of those Stork-a-Lure dresses and stop worryin'. What people don't know don't hurt nobody, as Mrs. Pike says."

"Did you tell Mrs. Pike?" asked Mrs. Fletcher sulkily.

"Well, Mrs. Fletcher, look, you ain't ever goin' to lay eyes on Mrs. Pike or her lay eyes on you, so what diffunce does it make in the long run?"

"I knew it!" Mrs. Fletcher deliberately nodded her head so as to destroy a ringlet Leota was working on behind her ear. "Mrs. Pike!"

Leota sighed. "I reckon I might as well tell you. It wasn't any more Thelma's lady tole me you was pregnant than a bat."

"Not Mrs. Hutchinson?"

"Naw, Lord! It was Mrs. Pike."

"Mrs. Pike!" Mrs. Fletcher could only sputter and let curling fluid roll into her ear. "How could Mrs. Pike possibly know I was pregnant or otherwise, when she doesn't even know me? The nerve of some people!"

"Well, here's how it was. Remember Sunday?"

"Yes," said Mrs. Fletcher.

2. Clips used to form and hold (or set) hair curl or wave.

"Sunday, Mrs. Pike an' me was all by ourself. Mr. Pike and Fred had gone over to Eagle Lake, sayin' they was goin' to catch 'em some fish, but they didn't a course. So we was gettin' in Mrs. Pike's car, it's a 1939 Dodge—"

"1939, eh," said Mrs. Fletcher.

"—An' we was gettin' us a Jax beer apiece—that's the beer that Mrs. Pike says is made right in N.O., so she won't drink no other kind. So I seen you drive up to the drugstore an' run in for just a secont, leavin' I reckon Mr. Fletcher in the car, an' come runnin' out with looked like a perscription. So I says to Mrs. Pike, just to be makin' talk, 'Right yonder's Mrs. Fletcher, and I reckon that's Mr. Fletcher—she's one of my regular customers,' I says."

"I had on a figured print," said Mrs. Fletcher tentatively.

"You sure did," agreed Leota. "So Mrs. Pike, she give you a good look— she's very observant, a good judge of character, cute as a minute, you know— and she says, 'I bet you another Jax that lady's three months on the way.' "

"What gall!" said Mrs. Fletcher. "Mrs. Pike!"

"Mrs. Pike ain't goin' to bite you," said Leota. "Mrs. Pike is a lovely girl, you'd be crazy about her, Mrs. Fletcher. But she can't sit still a minute. We went to the travellin' freak show yestiddy after work. I got through early— nine o'clock. In the vacant store next door. What, you ain't been?"

"No, I despise freaks," declared Mrs. Fletcher.

"Aw. Well, honey, talkin' about bein' pregnant an' all, you ought to see those twins in a bottle, you really owe it to yourself."

"What twins?" asked Mrs. Fletcher out of the side of her mouth.

"Well, honey, they got these two twins in a bottle, see? Born joined plumb together—dead a course." Leota dropped her voice into a soft lyrical hum. "They was about this long—pardon—must of been full time, all right, wouldn't you say?—an' they had these two heads an' two faces an' four arms an' four legs, all kind of joined *here*. See, this face looked this-a-way, and the other face looked that-a-way, over their shoulder, see. Kinda pathetic."

"Glah!" said Mrs. Fletcher disapprovingly.

"Well, ugly? Honey, I mean to tell you—their parents was first cousins and all like that. Billy Boy, git me a fresh towel from off Teeny's stack—this 'n's wringin' wet—an' quit ticklin' my ankles with that curler. I declare! He don't miss nothin'."

"Me and Mr. Fletcher aren't one speck of kin, or he could never of had me," said Mrs. Fletcher placidly.

"Of course not!" protested Leota. "Neither is me an' Fred, not that we know of. Well, honey, what Mrs. Pike liked was the pygmies. They've got these pygmies down there, too, an' Mrs. Pike was just wild about 'em. You know, the teeniniest men in the universe? Well, honey, they can just rest back on their little bohunkus an' roll around an' you can't hardly tell if they're sittin' or standin'. That'll give you some idea. They're about forty-two years old. Just suppose it was your husband!"

"Well, Mr. Fletcher is five foot nine and one half," said Mrs. Fletcher quickly.

"Fred's five foot ten," said Leota, "but I tell him he's still a shrimp, account of I'm so tall." She made a deep wave over Mrs. Fletcher's other temple with the comb. "Well, these pygmies are a kind of a dark brown, Mrs. Fletcher. Not bad lookin' for what they are, you know."

"I wouldn't care for them," said Mrs. Fletcher. "What does that Mrs. Pike see in them?"

"Aw, I don't know," said Leota. "She's just cute, that's all. But they got this man, this petrified man, that ever'thing ever since he was nine years old, when it goes through his digestion, see, somehow Mrs. Pike says it goes to his joints and has been turning to stone."

"How awful!" said Mrs. Fletcher.

"He's forty-two too. That looks like a bad age."

"Who said so, that Mrs. Pike? I bet she's forty-two," said Mrs. Fletcher.

"Naw," said Leota, "Mrs. Pike's thirty-three, born in January, an Aquarian. He could move his head—like this. A course his head and mind ain't a joint, so to speak, and I guess his stomach ain't, either—not yet, anyways. But see—his food, he eats it, and it goes down, see, and then he digests it"— Leota rose on her toes for an instant—"and it goes out to his joints and before you can say 'Jack Robinson,' it's stone—pure stone. He's turning to stone. How'd you liked to be married to a guy like that? All he can do, he can move his head just a quarter of an inch. A course he *looks* just *terrible*."

"I should think he would," said Mrs. Fletcher frostily. "Mr. Fletcher takes bending exercises every night of the world. I make him."

"All Fred does is lay around the house like a rug. I wouldn't be surprised if he woke up some day and couldn't move. The petrified man just sat there moving his quarter of an inch though," said Leota reminiscently.

"Did Mrs. Pike like the petrified man?" asked Mrs. Fletcher.

"Not as much as she did the others," said Leota deprecatingly. "And then she likes a man to be a good dresser, and all that."

"Is Mr. Pike a good dresser?" asked Mrs. Fletcher sceptically.

"Oh, well, yeah," said Leota, "but he's twelve or fourteen years older'n her. She ast Lady Evangeline about him."

"Who's Lady Evangeline?" asked Mrs. Fletcher.

"Well, it's this mind reader they got in the freak show," said Leota. "Was real good. Lady Evangeline is her name, and if I had another dollar I wouldn't do a thing but have my other palm read. She had what Mrs. Pike said was the 'sixth mind' but she had the worst manicure I ever saw on a living person."

"What did she tell Mrs. Pike?" asked Mrs. Fletcher.

"She told her Mr. Pike was as true to her as he could be and besides, would come into some money."

"Humph!" said Mrs. Fletcher. "What does he do?"

"I can't tell," said Leota, "because he don't work. Lady Evangeline didn't tell me enough about my nature or anything. And I would like to go back and find out some more about this boy. Used to go with this boy until he got married to this girl. Oh, shoot, that was about three and a half years ago, when you was still goin' to the Robert E. Lee Beauty Shop in Jackson. He married her for her money. Another fortune-teller tole me that at the time. So I'm not in love with him any more, anyway, besides being married to Fred, but Mrs. Pike thought, just for the hell of it, see, to ask Lady Evangeline was he happy."

"Does Mrs. Pike know everything about you already?" asked Mrs. Fletcher unbelievingly. "Mercy!"

"Oh, yeah, I tole her ever'thing about ever'thing, from now on back to I don't know when—to when I first started goin' out," said Leota. "So I ast Lady Evangeline for one of my questions, was he happily married, and she says, just like she was glad I ask her, 'Honey,' she says, 'naw, he idn't. You write down this day, March 8, 1941,' she says, 'and mock it down: three years from today him and her won't be occupyin' the same bed.' There it is, up on the wall with them other dates—see, Mrs. Fletcher? And she says, 'Child, you ought to be glad you didn't git him, because he's so mercenary.' So I'm glad I married Fred. He sure ain't mercenary, money don't mean a thing to him. But I sure would like to go back and have my other palm read."

"Did Mrs. Pike believe in what the fortune-teller said?" asked Mrs. Fletcher in a superior tone of voice.

"Lord, yes, she's from New Orleans. Ever'body in New Orleans believes ever'thing spooky. One of 'em in New Orleans before it was raided says to Mrs. Pike one summer she was goin' to go from State to State and meet some grey-headed men, and, sure enough, she says she went on a beautician convention up to Chicago. . . ."

"Oh!" said Mrs. Fletcher. "Oh, is Mrs. Pike a beautician too?"

"Sure she is," protested Leota. "She's a beautician. I'm goin' to git her in here if I can. Before she married. But it don't leave you. She says sure enough, there was three men who was a very large part of making her trip what it was, and they all three had grey in their hair and they went in six States. Got Christmas cards from 'em. Billy Boy, go see if Thelma's got any dry cotton. Look how Mrs. Fletcher's a-drippin'."

"Where did Mrs. Pike meet Mr. Pike?" asked Mrs. Fletcher primly.

"On another train," said Leota.

"I met Mr. Fletcher, or rather he met me, in a rental library," said Mrs. Fletcher with dignity, as she watched the net come down over her head.

"Honey, me an' Fred, we met in a rumble seat[3] eight months ago and we was practically on what you might call the way to the altar inside of half an hour," said Leota in a guttural voice, and bit a bobby pin open. "Course it don't last. Mrs. Pike says nothin' like that ever lasts."

"Mr. Fletcher and myself are as much in love as the day we married," said Mrs. Fletcher belligerently as Leota stuffed cotton into her ears.

"Mrs. Pike says it don't last," repeated Leota in a louder voice. "Now go git under the dryer. You can turn yourself on, can't you? I'll be back to comb you out. Durin' lunch I promised to give Mrs. Pike a facial. You know—free. Her bein' in the business, so to speak."

"I bet she needs one," said Mrs. Fletcher, letting the swing-door fly back against Leota. "Oh, pardon me."

A week later, on time for her appointment, Mrs. Fletcher sank heavily into Leota's chair after first removing a drug-store rental book, called *Life Is Like That,* from the seat. She stared in a discouraged way into the mirror.

"You can tell it when I'm sitting down, all right," she said.

Leota seemed preoccupied and stood shaking out a lavender cloth. She began to pin it around Mrs. Fletcher's neck in silence.

"I said you sure can tell it when I'm sitting straight on and coming at you this way," Mrs. Fletcher said.

---

3. Folding seat at the rear of an automobile.

"Why, honey, naw you can't," said Leota gloomily. "Why, I'd never know. If somebody was to come up to me on the street and say, 'Mrs. Fletcher is pregnant!' I'd say, 'Heck, she don't look it to me.' "

"If a certain party hadn't found it out and spread it around, it wouldn't be too late even now," said Mrs. Fletcher frostily, but Leota was almost choking her with the cloth, pinning it so tight, and she couldn't speak clearly. She paddled her hands in the air until Leota wearily loosened her.

"Listen, honey, you're just a virgin compared to Mrs. Montjoy," Leota was going on, still absent-minded. She bent Mrs. Fletcher back in the chair and, sighing, tossed liquid from a teacup on to her head and dug both hands into her scalp. "You know Mrs. Montjoy—her husband's that premature-grey-headed fella?"

"She's in the Trojan Garden Club, is all I know," said Mrs. Fletcher.

"Well, honey," said Leota, but in a weary voice, "she come in here not the week before and not the day before she had her baby—she come in here the very selfsame day, I mean to tell you. Child, we was all plumb scared to death. There she was! Come for her shampoo an' set. Why, Mrs. Fletcher, in an hour an' twenty minutes she was layin' up there in the Babtist Hospital with a seb'm-pound son. It was that close a shave. I declare, if I hadn't been so tired I would of drank up a bottle of gin that night."

"What gall," said Mrs. Fletcher. "I never knew her at all well."

"See, her husband was waitin' outside in the car, and her bags was all packed an' in the back seat, an' she was all ready, 'cept she wanted her shampoo an' set. An' havin' one pain right after another. Her husband kep' comin' in here, scared-like, but couldn't do nothin' with her a course. She yelled bloody murder, too, but she always yelled her head off when I give her a perm'nent."

"She must of been crazy," said Mrs. Fletcher. "How did she look?"

"Shoot!" said Leota.

"Well, I can guess," asid Mrs. Fletcher. "Awful."

"Just wanted to look pretty while she was havin' her baby, is all," said Leota airily. "Course, we was glad to give the lady what she was after—that's our motto—but I bet a hour later she wasn't payin' no mind to them little end curls. I bet she wasn't thinkin' about she ought to have on a net. It wouldn't of done her no good if she had."

"No, I don't suppose it would," said Mrs. Fletcher.

"Yeah man! She was a-yellin'. Just like when I give her perm'nent."

"Her husband ought to make her behave. Don't it seem that way to you?" asked Mrs. Fletcher. "He ought to put his foot down."

"Ha," said Leota. "A lot he could do. Maybe some women is soft."

"Oh, you mistake me, I don't mean for her to get soft—far from it! Women have to stand up for themselves, or there's just no telling. But now you take me—I ask Mr. Fletcher's advice now and then, and he appreciates it, especially on something important, like is it time for a permanent—not that I've told him about the baby. He says, 'Why, dear, go ahead!' Just ask their *advice*."

"Huh! If I ever ast Fred's advice we'd be floatin' down the Yazoo River on a houseboat or somethin' by this time," said Leota. "I'm sick of Fred. I told him to go over to Vicksburg."

"Is he going?" demanded Mrs. Fletcher.

"Sure. See, the fortune-teller—I went back and had my other palm read, since we've got to rent the room agin—said my lover was goin' to work in Vicksburg, so I don't know who she could mean, unless she meant Fred. And Fred ain't workin' here—that much is so."

"Is he going to work in Vicksburg?" asked Mrs. Fletcher. "And—"

"Sure. Lady Evangeline said so. Said the future is going to be brighter than the present. He don't want to go, but I ain't gonna put up with nothin' like that. Lays around the house an' bulls—did bull—with that good-for-nothin' Mr. Pike. He says if he goes who'll cook, but I says I never get to eat anyway— not meals. Billy Boy, take Mrs. Grover that *Screen Secrets* and leg it."

Mrs. Fletcher heard stamping feet go out the door.

"Is that that Mrs. Pike's little boy here again?" she asked, sitting up gingerly.

"Yeah, that's still him." Leota stuck out her tongue.

Mrs. Fletcher could hardly believe her eyes. "Well! How's Mrs. Pike, your attractive new friend with the sharp eyes who spreads it around town that perfect strangers are pregnant?" she asked in a sweetened tone.

"Oh, Mizziz Pike." Leota combed Mrs. Fletcher's hair with heavy strokes.

"You act like you're tired," said Mrs. Fletcher.

"Tired? Feel like it's four o'clock in the afternoon already," said Leota. "I ain't told you the awful luck we had, me and Fred? It's the worst thing you ever heard of. Maybe *you* think Mrs. Pike's got sharp eyes. Shoot, there's a limit! Well, you know, we rented out our room to this Mr. and Mrs. Pike from New Orleans when Sal an' Joe Fentress got mad at us 'cause they drank up some home-brew we had in the closet—Sal an' Joe did. So, a week ago Sat'day Mr. and Mrs. Pike moved in. Well, I kinda fixed up the room, you know—put a sofa pillow on the couch and picked some ragged robbins and put in a vase, but they never did say they appreciated it. Anyway, then I put some old magazines on the table."

"I think that was lovely," said Mrs. Fletcher.

"Wait. So, come night 'fore last, Fred and this Mr. Pike, who Fred just took up with, was back from they said they was fishin', bein' as neither one of 'em has got a job to his name, and we was all settin' around their room. So Mrs. Pike was settin' there, readin' a old *Startling G-Man Tales* that was mine, mind you, I'd bought it myself, and all of a sudden she jumps!—into the air—you'd 'a' thought she'd set on a spider—an' says, 'Canfield'—ain't that silly, that's Mr. Pike—'Canfield, my God A'mighty,' she says, 'honey,' she says, 'we're rich, and you won't have to work.' Not that he turned one hand anyway. Well, me and Fred rushes over to her, and Mr. Pike, too, and there she sets, pointin' her finger at a photo in my copy of *Startling G-Man*. 'See that man?' yells Mrs. Pike. 'Remember him, Canfield?' 'Never forget a face,' says Mr. Pike. 'It's Mr. Petrie, that we stayed with him in the apartment next to ours in Toulouse Street in N.O. for six weeks. Mr. Petrie.' 'Well,' says Mrs. Pike, like she can't hold out one secont longer, 'Mr. Petrie is wanted for five hundred dollars cash, for rapin' four women in California, and I know where he is.'"

"Mercy!" said Mrs. Fletcher. "Where was he?"

At some time Leota had washed her hair and now she yanked her up by the back locks and sat her up.

"Know where he was?"

"I certainly don't," Mrs. Fletcher said. Her scalp hurt all over.

Leota flung a towel around the top of her customer's head. "Nowhere else but in that freak show! I saw him just as plain as Mrs. Pike. *He* was the petrified man!"

"Who would ever have thought that!" cried Mrs. Fletcher sympathetically.

"So Mr. Pike says, 'Well whatta you know about that', an' he looks real hard at the photo and whistles. And she starts dancin' and singin' about their good luck. She meant our bad luck! I made a point of tellin' that fortune-teller the next time I saw her. I said, 'Listen, that magazine was layin' around the house for a month, and there was the freak show runnin' night an' day, not two steps away from my own beauty parlor, with Mr. Petrie just settin' there waitin'. An' it had to be Mr. and Mrs. Pike, almost perfect strangers.' "

"What gall," said Mrs. Fletcher. She was only sitting there, wrapped in a turban, but she did not mind.

"Fortune-tellers don't care. And Mrs. Pike, she goes around actin' like she thinks she was Mrs. God," said Leota. "So they're goin' to leave tomorrow, Mr. and Mrs. Pike. And in the meantime I got to keep that mean, bad little ole kid here, gettin' under my feet ever' minute of the day an' talkin' back too."

"Have they gotten the five hundred dollars' reward already?" asked Mrs. Fletcher.

"Well," said Leota, "at first Mr. Pike didn't want to do anything about it. Can you feature that? Said he kinda liked that ole bird and said he was real nice to 'em, lent 'em money or somethin'. But Mrs. Pike simply tole him he could just go to hell, and I can see her point. She says, 'You ain't worked a lick in six months, and here I make five hundred dollars in two seconts, and what thanks do I get for it? You go to hell, Canfield,' she says. So," Leota went on in a despondent voice, "they called up the cops and they caught the ole bird, all right, right there in the freak show where I saw him with my own eyes, thinkin' he was petrified. He's the one. Did it under his real name—Mr. Petrie. Four women in California, all in the month of August. So Mrs. Pike gits five hundred dollars. And my magazine, and right next door to my beauty parlor. I cried all night, but Fred said it wasn't a bit of use and to go to sleep, because the whole thing was just a sort of coincidence—you know: can't do nothin' about it. He says it put him clean out of the notion of goin' to Vicksburg for a few days till we rent out the room agin—no tellin' who we'll git this time."

"But can you imagine anybody knowing this old man, that's raped four women?" persisted Mrs. Fletcher, and she shuddered audibly. "Did Mrs. Pike *speak* to him when she met him in the freak show?"

Leota had begun to comb Mrs. Fletcher's hair. "I says to her, I says, 'I didn't notice you fallin' on his neck when he was the petrified man—don't tell me you didn't recognize your fine friend?' And she says, 'I didn't recognize him with that white powder all over his face. He just looked familiar,' Mrs. Pike says, 'and lots of people look familiar.' But she says that ole petrified man did put her in mind of somebody. She wondered who it was! Kep' her awake, which man she'd ever knew it reminded her of. So when she seen the photo, it all come to her. Like a flash. Mr. Petrie. The way he'd turn his head and look at her when she took him in his breakfast."

"Took him in his breakfast!" shrieked Mrs. Fletcher. "Listen—don't tell me. I'd 'a' felt something."

"Four women. I guess those women didn't have the faintest notion at the time they'd be worth a hundred an' twenty-five bucks apiece some day to Mrs. Pike. We ast her how old the fella was then, an's she says he musta had one foot in the grave, at least. Can you beat it?"

"Not really petrified at all, of course," said Mrs. Fletcher meditatively. She drew herself up. "I'd 'a' felt something," she said proudly.

"Shoot! I did feel somethin'," said Leota. "I tole Fred when I got home I felt so funny. I said, 'Fred, that ole petrified man sure did leave me with a funny feelin'.' He says, 'Funny-haha or funny-peculiar?' and I says, 'Funny-peculiar.'" She pointed her comb into the air emphatically.

"I'll bet you did," said Mrs. Fletcher.

They both heard a crackling noise.

Leota screamed, "Billy Boy! What you doin' in my purse?"

"Aw, I'm just eatin' these ole stale peanuts up," said Billy Boy.

"You come here to me!" screamed Leota, recklessly flinging down the comb, which scattered a whole ashtray full of bobby pins and knocked down a row of Coca-Cola bottles. "This is the last straw!"

"I caught him! I caught him!" giggled Mrs. Fletcher. "I'll hold him on my lap. You bad, bad boy, you! I guess I better learn how to spank little old bad boys," she said.

Leota's eleven o'clock customer pushed open the swing-door upon Leota's paddling him heartily with the brush, while he gave angry but belittling screams which penetrated beyond the booth and filled the whole curious beauty parlor. From everywhere ladies began to gather round to watch the paddling. Billy Boy kicked both Leota and Mrs. Fletcher as hard as he could, Mrs. Fletcher with her new fixed smile.

Billy Boy stomped through the group of wild-haired ladies and went out the door, but flung back the words, "If you're so smart, why ain't you rich?"

1941

TENNESSEE WILLIAMS
1911–1983

Speaking of Blanche DuBois, the heroine of *A Streetcar Named Desire*, Tennessee Williams once said, "She was a demonic creature; the size of her feeling was too great for her to contain." In Williams's plays—he wrote and rewrote more than twenty full-length dramas as well as films and shorter works—his characters are driven by the size of their feelings, much as Williams himself felt driven to write about them.

He was born Thomas Lanier Williams in Columbus, Mississippi, on March 26, 1911. His mother, "Miss Edwina," the daughter of an Episcopalian minister, was repressed and genteel, very much the southern belle in her youth. His father, Cornelius, was a traveling salesman, often away from his family and often violent and drunk when at home. As a child, Williams was sickly and overly protected by his mother; he was closely attached to his sister, Rose, repelled by the roughhouse world of boys, and alienated from his father. The family's move from Mississippi to St. Louis, where Cornelius became a sales manager of the shoe company he had traveled for, was a shock to Mrs. Williams and her young children, used to living in small southern towns where a minister's daughter was an important person. Yet Mrs. Williams was a woman who could take care of herself, a "survivor."

Williams went to the University of Missouri, but left after two years; his father then found him a job in the shoe-factory warehouse. He worked there for nearly three years, writing feverishly at night. His closest friend at the time was a burly co-worker, easygoing and attractive to women, named Stanley Kowalski. Williams found the life so difficult, however, that he succumbed to a nervous breakdown. After recovering at the home of his beloved grandparents, he went on to further studies, finally graduating at the age of twenty-seven. Earlier, Rose had been suffering increasing mental imbalance; the final trauma was apparently brought on by one of Cornelius's alcoholic rages, in which he beat Edwina and, trying to calm Rose, made a gesture that she took to be a sexual one. Shortly thereafter, Edwina signed the papers allowing Rose to be "tragically becalmed" by a prefrontal lobotomy. She spent most of her life in sanatoriums, except when Williams brought her out for visits.

The next year Williams left for New Orleans, the first of many temporary homes; it would provide the setting for *A Streetcar Named Desire*. In New Orleans, he changed his name to "Tennessee," later giving—as often when discussing his life—various romantic reasons for doing so. There also he actively entered the homosexual world.

Williams had had plays produced at local theaters and in 1939 he won a prize for a collection of one-act plays, *American Blues*. The next year, *Battle of Angels* failed (it would later be rewritten as *Orpheus Descending*, 1957). His first success was *The Glass Menagerie* (1945). Williams called it a "memory play," seen through the recollections of the writer, Tom, who talks to the audience about himself and about the scenes depicting his mother, Amanda, poverty-stricken but genteelly living on memories of her southern youth and her "gentlemen callers"; his crippled sister, Laura, who finds refuge in her "menagerie" of little glass animals; and the traumatic effect of a modern "gentleman caller" on them. While there are similarities between Edwina, Rose, and Tennessee, on the one hand, and Amanda, Laura, and Tom on the other, there are also differences: the play is not literally autobiographical.

The financial success of *Menagerie* was at first exhilarating, then debilitating. Williams fled to Mexico, to work full time on an earlier play, *The Poker Night*. It had begun as *The Moth*; its first image, as Williams's biographer, Donald Spoto, tells us, was "simply that of a woman, sitting with folded hands near a window, while moonlight streamed in and she awaited in vain the arrival of her boy friend": named Blanche, she was at first intended as a young Amanda. During rehearsals of *Menagerie*, Williams had asked members of the stage crew to teach him to play poker, and he began to visualize the play as a series of confrontations between working-class poker players and two refined southern women.

As the focus of his attention changed from Stanley to Blanche, *The Poker Night* gradually turned into *A Streetcar Named Desire*. When it opened in 1947, it was an even greater success than *Glass Menagerie*, and it won the Pulitzer Prize. Williams was able to travel and to buy a home in Key West, Florida, where he did much of his ensuing work. At about this time his "transitory heart" found "a home at last" in a young man named Frank Merlo.

For more than a decade thereafter, a new Williams play appeared almost every two years. Among the most successful were *The Rose Tattoo* (1950), in which the tempestuous heroine Serafina, worshiping the memory of her dead husband, finds love again; the Pulitzer Prize–winning *Cat on a Hot Tin Roof* (1955), which portrays the conflict of the dying Big Daddy and his impotent son, Brick, watched and controlled by Brick's wife, "Maggie the Cat"; and *The Night of the Iguana* (1961), which brings a varied group of tormented people together at a rundown hotel on the Mexican coast. His plays were produced widely abroad and also became equally successful films. Yet some of the ones now regarded as the best of this period were commercial failures: *Summer and Smoke* (1948), for example, and the surrealistic and visionary *Camino Real* (1953).

For years, Williams had depended on a wide variety of drugs, especially to help him sleep and to keep him awake in the early mornings when he invariably worked. In the 1960s, these began to take a real toll. Other factors contributed to the decline of his later years: the death of Frank Merlo, the emergence of younger playwrights of whom he felt blindly jealous, and the violent nature of the 1960s themselves, which seemed both to mirror his own inner chaos and to leave him behind.

Yet, despite Broadway failures, critical disparagements, and a breakdown for which he was hospitalized, he kept valiantly working. His biographer notes that in his late work, Rose was "the source and inspiration of everything he wrote, either directly—with a surrogate character representing her—or indirectly, in the situation of romanticized mental illness or unvarnished verisimilitude." This observation is certainly true of his last Broadway play, the failed *Clothes for a Summer Hotel* (1980), ostensibly about the ghosts of Scott and Zelda Fitzgerald, and of the play he obsessively wrote and rewrote, *The Two Character Play*, which chronicles the descent into madness and death of a brother and sister who are also lovers.

Despite Williams's self-destructiveness, both in his writing and in his social life, the work of his great years was now being seriously studied and often revived by regional and community theaters. Critics began to see that he was one of America's best and most dedicated playwrights. And he kept on working. He was collaborating on a film of two stories about Rose when he died on February 23, 1983, apparently having choked to death on the lid of a pill bottle.

Williams, who was always reluctant to talk about his work (likening it to a "bird that will be startled away, as by a hawk's shadow"), did not see himself in a tradition in American dramaturgy. He acknowledged the influence of Anton Chekhov, the nineteenth-century Russian writer of dramas with lonely, searching characters; of D. H. Lawrence, the British novelist who emphasized the theme of a sexual life force; and above all of the American Hart Crane, homosexual *poète maudit*, who, he said, "touched fire that burned [himself] alive," adding that "perhaps it is only through self-immolation of such a nature that we living beings can offer to you the entire truth of ourselves." Such a statement indicates the deeply confessional quality of Williams's writing, even in plays not directly autobiographical.

Although he never acknowledged any debt to Eugene O'Neill, Williams shared with that playwright an impatience over realistic theater conventions. *The Glass Menagerie*, for example, uses screened projections, lighting effects, and music to emphasize that it takes place in Tom's memory. *A Streetcar Named Desire* moves in and out of the house on Elysian Fields, while music and lighting reinforce all the major themes. Williams also relies on the effects of language, especially of a vivid and colloquial southern speech that may be compared with that of William Faulkner, Eudora Welty, or Flannery O'Connor. Rhythms of language become almost a musical indication of character, distinguishing Blanche from other characters. Reading or seeing his plays, we become aware of how symbolic repetitions—in Blanche's and Stanley's turns of phrase, the naked light bulb and the paper lantern, the Mexican woman selling flowers for the dead, the "Varsouviana" waltz and the reverberating voices—produce a heightening of reality: what Williams called "poetic realism."

More than a half century later, does the destruction of Blanche, the "lady," still have the power to move us? Elia Kazan, in his director's notes, thought of her as "an outdated creature, approaching extinction . . . like a dinosaur." But Blythe Danner, who played Blanche in a 1988 revival, acutely observes that Williams "was attached to the things that were going to destroy him" and that Blanche, similarly, is both attracted to and repelled by Stanley: "It's Tennessee fighting, fighting, fighting what he doesn't want to get into, what is very prevalent in his mind. That incredible contradiction in so many people is what he captures better than any other playwright."

From our present perspective, moreover, we are less concerned over contemporary criticisms of Williams's plays for their violence and their obsession with sexuality, which in some of the later work was regarded by some critics as an almost morbid preoccupation with "perversion"—murder, rape, drugs, incest, nymphomania. We now know that the shriller voices making such accusations were attacking Williams for his homosexuality, which, we must remember, could not be publicly spoken of in this country until comparatively recently. These topics, however, also figure as instances of his deeper subject, the themes of desire and loneliness. As he said in an interview, "Desire is rooted in a longing for companionship, a release from the loneliness that haunts every individual." Loneliness and desire propel his characters into extreme behavior, no doubt, but such behavior literally dramatizes the plight that Williams saw as universal.

The text is taken from *The Theatre of Tennessee Williams*, volume 1 (1971).

A Streetcar Named Desire

And so it was I entered the broken world
To trace the visionary company of love, its voice
An instant in the wind (I know not whither hurled)
But not for long to hold each desperate choice.
        —"The Broken Tower" by Hart Crane[1]

THE CHARACTERS

BLANCHE	PABLO
STELLA	A NEGRO WOMAN
STANLEY	A DOCTOR
MITCH	A NURSE
EUNICE	A YOUNG COLLECTOR
STEVE	A MEXICAN WOMAN

Scene One

The exterior of a two-story corner building on a street in New Orleans which is named Elysian Fields and runs between the L & N tracks and the river.[2] The section is poor but, unlike corresponding sections in other American cities, it has a raffish charm. The houses are mostly white frame, weathered grey, with rickety outside stairs and galleries and quaintly ornamented gables. This building contains two flats, upstairs and down. Faded white stairs ascend to the entrances of both.

It is first dark of an evening early in May. The sky that shows around the dim white building is a peculiarly tender blue, almost a turquoise, which invests the scene with a kind of lyricism and gracefully attenuates the atmosphere of decay. You can almost feel the warm breath of the brown river beyond the river warehouses with their faint redolences of bananas and coffee. A corresponding air is evoked by the music of Negro entertainers at a barroom around the corner. In this part of New Orleans you are practically always just around the corner, or a few doors down the street, from a tinny piano being played with the infatuated fluency of brown fingers. This "Blue Piano" expresses the spirit of the life which goes on here.

---

1. American poet (1899–1932).
2. Elysian Fields is in fact a New Orleans street at the northern tip of the French Quarter, between the Louisville & Nashville railroad tracks and the Mississippi River. In Greek mythology, the Elysian Fields are the abode of the blessed in the afterlife.

Two women, one white and one colored, are taking the air on the steps of the building. The white woman is EUNICE, *who occupies the upstairs flat; the colored woman a neighbor, for New Orleans is a cosmopolitan city where there is a relatively warm and easy intermingling of races in the old part of town.*

Above the music of the "Blue Piano" the voices of people on the street can be heard overlapping.

> [*Two men come around the corner,* STANLEY KOWALSKI *and* MITCH. *They are about twenty-eight or thirty years old, roughly dressed in blue denim work clothes.* STANLEY *carries his bowling jacket and a red-stained package from a butcher's. They stop at the foot of the steps.*]

STANLEY [*bellowing*]   Hey there! Stella, baby!

> [STELLA *comes out on the first floor landing, a gentle young woman, about twenty-five, and of a background obviously quite different from her husband's.*]

STELLA [*mildly*]   Don't holler at me like that. Hi, Mitch.

STANLEY   Catch!

STELLA   What?

STANLEY   Meat!

> [*He heaves the package at her. She cries out in protest but manages to catch it: then she laughs breathlessly. Her husband and his companion have already started back around the corner.*]

STELLA [*calling after him*]   Stanley! Where are you going?

STANLEY   Bowling!

STELLA   Can I come watch?

STANLEY   Come on. [*He goes out.*]

STELLA   Be over soon. [*to the white woman*] Hello, Eunice. How are you?

EUNICE   I'm all right. Tell Steve to get him a poor boy's sandwich 'cause nothing's left here.

> [*They all laugh; the colored woman does not stop.* STELLA *goes out.*]

COLORED WOMAN   What was that package he th'ew at 'er? [*She rises from steps, laughing louder.*]

EUNICE   You hush, now!

NEGRO WOMAN   Catch *what!*

> [*She continues to laugh.* BLANCHE *comes around the corner, carrying a valise. She looks at a slip of paper, then at the building, then again at the slip and again at the building. Her expression is one of shocked disbelief. Her appearance is incongruous to this setting. She is daintily dressed in a white suit with a fluffy bodice, necklace and earrings of pearl, white gloves and hat, looking as if she were arriving at a summer tea or cocktail party in the garden district. She is about five years older than* STELLA. *Her delicate beauty must avoid a strong light. There is something about her uncertain manner, as well as her white clothes, that suggests a moth.*]

EUNICE [*finally*]   What's the matter, honey? Are you lost?

BLANCHE [*with faintly hysterical humor*]   They told me to take a street-car named Desire, and then transfer to one called Cemeteries[3] and ride six blocks and get off at—Elysian Fields!

---

3. The end of a streetcar line that stopped at a cemetery. Desire is a street in New Orleans.

EUNICE   That's where you are now.

BLANCHE   At Elysian Fields?

EUNICE   This here is Elysian Fields.

BLANCHE   They mustn't have—understood—what number I wanted . . .

EUNICE   What number you lookin' for?

[BLANCHE *wearily refers to the slip of paper.*]

BLANCHE   Six thirty-two.

EUNICE   You don't have to look no further.

BLANCHE   [*uncomprehendingly*]   I'm looking for my sister, Stella DuBois,
I mean—Mrs. Stanley Kowalski.

EUNICE   That's the party.—You just did miss her, though.

BLANCHE   This—can this be—her home?

EUNICE   She's got the downstairs here and I got the up.

BLANCHE   Oh. She's—out?

EUNICE   You noticed that bowling alley around the corner?

BLANCHE   I'm—not sure I did.

EUNICE   Well, that's where she's at, watchin' her husband bowl. [*There is
a pause.*] You want to leave your suitcase here an' go find her?

BLANCHE   No.

NEGRO WOMAN   I'll go tell her you come.

BLANCHE   Thanks.

NEGRO WOMAN   You welcome. [*She goes out.*]

EUNICE   She wasn't expecting you?

BLANCHE   No. No, not tonight.

EUNICE   Well, why don't you just go in and make yourself at home till they
get back.

BLANCHE   How could I—do that?

EUNICE   We own this place so I can let you in.

[*She gets up and opens the downstairs door. A light goes on behind the
blind, turning it light blue.* BLANCHE *slowly follows her into the downstairs flat. The surrounding areas dim out as the interior is lighted. Two
rooms can be seen, not too clearly defined. The one first entered is primarily a kitchen but contains a folding bed to be used by* BLANCHE. *The
room beyond this is a bedroom. Off this room is a narrow door to a
bathroom.*]

EUNICE [*defensively, noticing* BLANCHE's *look*]   It's sort of messed up right
now but when it's clean it's real sweet.

BLANCHE   Is it?

EUNICE   Uh-huh, I think so. So you're Stella's sister?

BLANCHE   Yes. [*wanting to get rid of her*] Thanks for letting me in.

EUNICE   *Por nada,*[4] as the Mexicans say, *por nada!* Stella spoke of you.

BLANCHE   Yes?

EUNICE   I think she said you taught school.

BLANCHE   Yes.

EUNICE   And you're from Mississippi, huh?

BLANCHE   Yes.

EUNICE   She showed me a picture of your home-place, the plantation.

BLANCHE   Belle Reve?[5]

---

4. It's nothing (Spanish).   5. Beautiful Dream (French).

EUNICE A great big place with white columns.

BLANCHE Yes . . .

EUNICE A place like that must be awful hard to keep up.

BLANCHE If you will excuse me, I'm just about to drop.

EUNICE Sure, honey. Why don't you set down?

BLANCHE What I meant was I'd like to be left alone.

EUNICE [offended] Aw. I'll make myself scarce, in that case.

BLANCHE I didn't meant to be rude, but—

EUNICE I'll drop by the bowling alley an' hustle her up. [She goes out the door.]

> [BLANCHE sits in a chair very stiffly with her shoulders slightly hunched and her legs pressed close together and her hands tightly clutching her purse as if she were quite cold. After a while the blind look goes out of her eyes and she begins to look slowly around. A cat screeches. She catches her breath with a startled gesture. Suddenly she notices something in a half opened closet. She springs up and crosses to it, and removes a whiskey bottle. She pours a half tumbler of whiskey and tosses it down. She carefully replaces the bottle and washes out the tumbler at the sink. Then she resumes her seat in front of the table.]

BLANCHE [faintly to herself] I've got to keep hold of myself! [STELLA comes quickly around the corner of the building and runs to the door of the downstairs flat.]

STELLA [calling out joyfully] Blanche!

> [For a moment they stare at each other. Then BLANCHE springs up and runs to her with a wild cry.]

BLANCHE Stella, oh, Stella, Stella! Stella for Star!

> [She begins to speak with feverish vivacity as if she feared for either of them to stop and think. They catch each other in a spasmodic embrace.]

BLANCHE Now, then, let me look at you. But don't you look at me, Stella, no, no, no, not till later, not till I've bathed and rested! And turn that over-light off! Turn that off! I won't be looked at in this merciles glare! [STELLA laughs and complies.] Come back here now! Oh, my baby! Stella! Stella for Star! [She embraces her again.] I thought you would never come back to this horrible place! What am I saying? I didn't mean to say that. I meant to be nice about it and say—Oh, what a convenient location and such—Ha-a-ha! Precious lamb! You haven't said a word to me.

STELLA You haven't given me a chance to, honey! [She laughs, but her glance at BLANCHE is a little anxious.]

BLANCHE Well, now you talk. Open your pretty mouth and talk while I look around for some liquor! I know you must have some liquor on the place! Where could it be, I wonder? Oh, I spy, I spy!

> [She rushes to the closet and removes the bottle; she is shaking all over and panting for breath as she tries to laugh. The bottle nearly slips from her grasp.]

STELLA [noticing] Blanche, you sit down and let me pour the drinks. I don't know what we've got to mix with. Maybe a coke's in the icebox. Look'n see, honey, while I'm—

BLANCHE No coke, honey, not with my nerves tonight! Where—where—where is—?

STELLA Stanley? Bowling! He loves it. They're having a—found some soda!—tournament . . .

BLANCHE   Just water, baby, to chase it! Now don't get worried, your sister hasn't turned into a drunkard, she's just all shaken up and hot and tired and dirty! You sit down, now, and explain this place to me! What are you doing in a place like this?

STELLA   Now, Blanche—

BLANCHE   Oh, I'm not going to be hypocritical, I'm going to be honestly critical about it! Never, never, never in my worst dreams could I picture—Only Poe! Only Mr. Edgar Allan Poe!—could do it justice! Out there I suppose is the ghoul-haunted woodland of Weir![6] [*She laughs.*]

STELLA   No, honey, those are the L & N tracks.

BLANCHE   No, now seriously, putting joking aside. Why didn't you tell me, why didn't you write me, honey, why didn't you let me know?

STELLA   [*carefully, pouring herself a drink*]   Tell you what, Blanche?

BLANCHE   Why, that you had to live in these conditions!

STELLA   Aren't you being a little intense about it? It's not that bad at all! New Orleans isn't like other cities.

BLANCHE   This has got nothing to do with New Orleans. You might as well say—forgive me, blessed baby! [*She suddenly stops short.*] The subject is closed!

STELLA   [*a little drily*]   Thanks.

[*During the pause,* BLANCHE *stares at her. She smiles at* BLANCHE.]

BLANCHE   [*looking down at her glass, which shakes in her hand*]   You're all I've got in the world, and you're not glad to see me!

STELLA   [*sincerely*]   Why, Blanche, you know that's not true.

BLANCHE   No?—I'd forgotten how quiet you were.

STELLA   You never did give me a chance to say much, Blanche. So I just got in the habit of being quiet around you.

BLANCHE   [*vaguely*]   A good habit to get into . . . [*then, abruptly*] You haven't asked me how I happened to get away from the school before the spring term ended.

STELLA   Well, I thought you'd volunteer that information—if you wanted to tell me.

BLANCHE   You thought I'd been fired?

STELLA   No, I—thought you might have—resigned . . .

BLANCHE   I was so exhausted by all I'd been through my—nerves broke. [*nervously tamping cigarette*] I was on the verge of—lunacy, almost! So Mr. Graves—Mr. Graves is the high school superintendent—he suggested I take a leave of absence. I couldn't put all of those details into the wire . . . [*She drinks quickly.*] Oh, this buzzes right through me and feels so *good!*

STELLA   Won't you have another?

BLANCHE   No, one's my limit.

STELLA   Sure?

BLANCHE   You haven't said a word about my appearance.

STELLA   You look just fine.

BLANCHE   God love you for a liar! Daylight never exposed so total a ruin! But you—you've put on some weight, yes, you're just as plump as a little partridge! And it's so becoming to you!

STELLA   Now, Blanche—

6. From the refrain of Poe's gothic ballad "Ulalume" (1847).

BLANCHE   Yes, it is, it is or I wouldn't say it! You just have to watch around the hips a little. Stand up.

STELLA   Not now.

BLANCHE   You hear me? I said stand up! [STELLA *complies reluctantly.*] You messy child, you, you've spilt something on that pretty white lace collar! About your hair—you ought to have it cut in a feather bob with your dainty features. Stella, you have a maid, don't you?

STELLA   No. With only two rooms it's—

BLANCHE   What? *Two* rooms, did you say?

STELLA   This one and—[*She is embarrassed.*]

BLANCHE   The other one? [*She laughs sharply. There is an embarrassed silence.*]

BLANCHE   I am going to take just one little tiny nip more, sort of to put the stopper on, so to speak. . . . Then put the bottle away so I won't be tempted. [*She rises.*] I want you to look at *my* figure! [*She turns around.*] You know I haven't put on one ounce in ten years, Stella? I weigh what I weighed the summer you left Belle Reve. The summer Dad died and you left us . . .

STELLA   [*a little wearily*]   It's just incredible, Blanche, how well you're looking.

BLANCHE   [*They both laugh uncomfortably.*]   But, Stella, there's only two rooms, I don't see where you're going to put me!

STELLA   We're going to put you in here.

BLANCHE   What kind of bed's this—one of those collapsible things?
        [*She sits on it.*]

STELLA   Does it feel all right?

BLANCHE [*dubiously*]   Wonderful, honey. I don't like a bed that gives much. But there's no door between the two rooms, and Stanley—will it be decent?

STELLA   Stanley is Polish, you know.

BLANCHE   Oh, yes. They're something like Irish, aren't they?

STELLA   Well—

BLANCHE   Only not so—highbrow? [*They both laugh again in the same way.*] I brought some nice clothes to meet all your lovely friends in.

STELLA   I'm afraid you won't think they are lovely.

BLANCHE   What are they like?

STELLA   They're Stanley's friends.

BLANCHE   Polacks?

STELLA   They're a mixed lot, Blanche.

BLANCHE   Heterogeneous—types?

STELLA   Oh, yes. Yes, types is right!

BLANCHE   Well—anyhow—I brought nice clothes and I'll wear them. I guess you're hoping I'll say I'll put up at a hotel, but I'm not going to put up at a hotel. I want to be *near* you, got to be *with* somebody, I *can't* be *alone!* Because—as you must have noticed—I'm—*not* very *well*. . . . [*Her voice drops and her look is frightened.*]

STELLA   You seem a little bit nervous or overwrought or something.

BLANCHE   Will Stanley like me, or will I be just a visiting in-law, Stella? I couldn't stand that.

STELLA   You'll get along fine together, if you'll just try not to—well—compare him with men that we went out with at home.

BLANCHE Is he so—different?

STELLA Yes. A different species.

BLANCHE In what way; what's he like?

STELLA Oh, you can't describe someone you're in love with! Here's a picture of him! [*She hands a photograph to* BLANCHE.]

BLANCHE An officer?

STELLA A Master Sergeant in the Engineers' Corps. Those are decorations!

BLANCHE He had those on when you met him?

STELLA I assure you I wasn't just blinded by all the brass.

BLANCHE That's not what I—

STELLA But of course there were things to adjust myself to later on.

BLANCHE Such as his civilian background! [STELLA *laughs uncertainly.*] How did he take it when you said I was coming?

STELLA Oh, Stanley doesn't know yet.

BLANCHE [*frightened*] You—haven't told him?

STELLA He's on the road a good deal.

BLANCHE Oh. Travels?

STELLA Yes.

BLANCHE Good. I mean—isn't it?

STELLA [*half to herself*] I can hardly stand it when he is away for a night . . .

BLANCHE Why, Stella!

STELLA When he's away for a week I nearly go wild!

BLANCHE Gracious!

STELLA And when he comes back I cry on his lap like a baby . . . [*She smiles to herself.*]

BLANCHE I guess that is what is meant by being in love . . . [STELLA *looks up with a radiant smile.*] Stella—

STELLA What?

BLANCHE [*in an uneasy rush*] I haven't asked you the things you probably thought I was going to ask. And so I'll expect you to be understanding about what *I* have to tell *you.*

STELLA What, Blanche? [*Her face turns anxious.*]

BLANCHE Well, Stella—you're going to reproach me, I know that you're bound to reproach me—but before you do—take into consideration—you left! I stayed and struggled! You came to New Orleans and looked out for yourself! *I* stayed at *Belle Reve* and tried to hold it together! I'm not meaning this in any reproachful way, but *all* the burden descended on *my* shoulders.

STELLA The best I could do was make my own living, Blanche.

[BLANCHE *begins to shake again with intensity.*]

BLANCHE I know, I know. But you are the one that abandoned Belle Reve, not I! I stayed and fought for it, bled for it, almost died for it!

STELLA Stop this hysterical outburst and tell me what's happened? What do you mean fought and bled? What kind of—

BLANCHE I knew you would, Stella. I knew you would take this attitude about it!

STELLA About—what?—please!

BLANCHE [*slowly*] The loss—the loss . . .

STELLA Belle Reve? Lost, is it? No!

BLANCHE Yes, Stella.

[*They stare at each other across the yellow-checked linoleum of the table.* BLANCHE *slowly nods her head and* STELLA *looks slowly down at her hands folded on the table. The music of the "Blue Piano" grows louder.* BLANCHE *touches her handkerchief to her forehead.*]

STELLA   But how did it go? What happened?

BLANCHE [*springing up*]   You're a fine one to ask me how it went!

STELLA   Blanche!

BLANCHE   You're a fine one to sit there *accusing me* of it!

STELLA   *Blanche!*

BLANCHE   I, I, *I* took the blows in my face and my body! All of those deaths! The long parade to the graveyard! Father, mother! Margaret, that dreadful way! So big with it, it couldn't be put in a coffin! But had to be burned like rubbish! You just came home in time for the funerals, Stella. And funerals are pretty compared to deaths. Funerals are quiet, but deaths— not always. Sometimes their breathing is hoarse, and sometimes it rattles, and sometimes they even cry out to you, "Don't let me go!" Even the old, sometimes, say, "Don't let me go." As if you were able to stop them! But funerals are quiet, with pretty flowers. And, oh, what gorgeous boxes they pack them away in! Unless you were there at the bed when they cried out, "Hold me!" you'd never suspect there was the struggle for breath and bleeding. You didn't dream, but I saw! *Saw! Saw!* And now you sit there telling me with your eyes that I let the place go! How in hell do you think all that sickness and dying was paid for? Death is expensive, Miss Stella! And old Cousin Jessie's right after Margaret's, hers! Why, the Grim Reaper had put up his tent on our doorstep! . . . Stella. Belle Reve was his headquarters! Honey—that's how it slipped through my fingers! Which of them left us a fortune? Which of them left a cent of insurance even? Only poor Jessie—one hundred to pay for her coffin. That was all, Stella! And I with my pitiful salary at the school. Yes, accuse me! Sit there and stare at me, thinking I let the place go! *I* let the place go? Where were *you!* In bed with your—Polack!

STELLA [*springing*]   Blanche! You be still! That's enough! [*She starts out.*]

BLANCHE   Where are you going?

STELLA   I'm going into the bathroom to wash my face.

BLANCHE   Oh, Stella, Stella, you're crying!

STELLA   Does that surprise you?

BLANCHE   Forgive me—I didn't mean to—

[*The sound of men's voices is heard.* STELLA *goes into the bathroom, closing the door behind her. When the men appear, and* BLANCHE *realizes it must be* STANLEY *returning, she moves uncertainly from the bathroom door to the dressing table, looking apprehensively toward the front door.* STANLEY *enters, followed by* STEVE *and* MITCH. STANLEY *pauses near his door,* STEVE *by the foot of the spiral stair, and* MITCH *is slightly above and to the right of them, about to go out. As the men enter, we hear some of the following dialogue.*]

STANLEY   Is that how he got it?

STEVE   Sure that's how he got it. He hit the old weather-bird for 300 bucks on a six-number-ticket.

MITCH   Don't tell him those things; he'll believe it.

[*Mitch starts out.*]

STANLEY [*restraining Mitch*]   Hey, Mitch—come back here.

[BLANCHE, *at the sound of voices, retires in the bedroom. She picks up* STANLEY's *photo from dressing table, looks at it, puts it down. When* STANLEY *enters the apartment, she darts and hides behind the screen at the head of bed.*]

STEVE [*to* STANLEY *and* MITCH]   Hey, are we playin' poker tomorrow?

STANLEY   Sure—at Mitch's.

MITCH [*hearing this, returns quickly to the stair rail*]   No—not at my place. My mother's still stick!

STANLEY   Okay, at my place . . . [MITCH *starts out again.*] But you bring the beer!

[MITCH *pretends not to hear—calls out "Good night, all," and goes out, singing.* EUNICE's *voice is heard, above.*]

Break it up down there! I made the spaghetti dish and ate it myself.

STEVE [*going upstairs*]   I told you and phoned you we was playing. [*to the men*] Jax⁷ beer!

EUNICE   You never phoned me once.

STEVE   I told you at breakfast—and phoned you at lunch . . .

EUNICE   Well, never mind about that. You just get yourself home here once in a while.

STEVE   You want it in the papers?

[*More laughter and shouts of parting come from the men.* STANLEY *throws the screen door of the kitchen open and comes in. He is of medium height, about five feet eight or nine, and strongly, compactly built. Animal joy in his being is implicit in all his movements and attitudes. Since earliest manhood the center of his life has been pleasure with women, the giving and taking of it, not with weak indulgence, dependently, but with the power and pride of a richly feathered male bird among hens. Branching out from this complete and satisfying center are all the auxiliary channels of his life, such as his heartiness with men, his appreciation of rough humor, his love of good drink and food and games, his car, his radio, everything that is his, that bears his emblem of the gaudy seed-bearer. He sizes women up at a glance, with sexual classifications, crude images flashing into his mind and determining the way he smiles at them.*]

BLANCHE [*drawing involuntarily back from his stare*]   You must be Stanley. I'm Blanche.

STANLEY   Stella's sister?

BLANCHE   Yes.

STANLEY   H'lo. Where's the little woman?

BLANCHE   In the bathroom.

STANLEY   Oh. Didn't know you were coming in town.

BLANCHE   I—uh—

STANLEY   Where you from, Blanche?

BLANCHE   Why, I—live in Laurel.

[*He has crossed to the closet and removed the whiskey bottle.*]

STANLEY   In Laurel, huh? Oh, yeah. Yeah, in Laurel, that's right. Not in my territory. Liquor goes fast in hot weather. [*He holds the bottle to the light to observe its depletion.*] Have a shot?

BLANCHE   No, I—rarely touch it.

7. A local brand of beer.

STANLEY Some people rarely touch it, but it touches them often.

BLANCHE [*faintly*] Ha-ha.

STANLEY My clothes're stickin' to me. Do you mind if I make myself com-
.fortable? [*He starts to remove his shirt.*]

BLANCHE Please, please do.

STANLEY Be comfortable is my motto.

BLANCHE It's mine, too. It's hard to stay looking fresh. I haven't washed
or even powdered my face and—here you are!

STANLEY You know you can catch cold sitting around in damp things,
especially when you been exercising hard like bowling is. You're a
teacher, aren't you?

BLANCHE Yes.

STANLEY What do you teach, Blanche?

BLANCHE English.

STANLEY I never was a very good English student. How long you here for,
Blanche?

BLANCHE I—don't know yet.

STANLEY You going to shack up here?

BLANCHE I thought I would if it's not inconvenient for you all.

STANLEY Good.

BLANCHE Traveling wears me out.

STANLEY Well, take it easy.

[*A cat screeches near the window.* BLANCHE *springs up.*]

BLANCHE What's that?

STANLEY Cats . . . Hey, Stella!

STELLA [*faintly, from the bathroom*] Yes, Stanley.

STANLEY Haven't fallen in, have you? [*He grins at* BLANCHE. *She tries
unsuccessfully to smile back. There is a silence.*] I'm afraid I'll strike you
as being the unrefined type. Stella's spoke of you a good deal. You were
married once, weren't you?

[*The music of the polka rises up, faint in the distance.*]

BLANCHE Yes. When I was quite young.

STANLEY What happened?

BLANCHE The boy—the boy died. [*She sinks back down.*] I'm afraid I'm—
going to be sick! [*Her head falls on her arms.*]

Scene Two

It is six o'clock the following evening. BLANCHE *is bathing.* STELLA *is completing
her toilette.* BLANCHE's *dress, a flowered print, is laid out on* STELLA's *bed.*

STANLEY *enters the kitchen from outside, leaving the door open on the perpetual "Blue Piano" around the corner.*

STANLEY What's all this monkey doings?

STELLA Oh, Stan! [*She jumps up and kisses him, which he accepts with
lordly composure.*] I'm taking Blanche to Galatoire's for supper and then
to a show, because it's your poker night.

STANLEY How about my supper, huh? I'm not going to no Galatoire's for
supper!

STELLA I put you a cold plate on ice.

STANLEY Well, isn't that just dandy!

STELLA I'm going to try to keep Blanche out till the party breaks up because I don't know how she would take it. So we'll go to one of the little places in the Quarter afterward and you'd better give me some money.

STANLEY Where is she?

STELLA She's soaking in a hot tub to quiet her nerves. She's terribly upset.

STANLEY Over what?

STELLA She's been through such an ordeal.

STANLEY Yeah?

STELLA Stan, we've—lost Belle Reve!

STANLEY The place in the country?

STELLA Yes.

STANLEY How?

STELLA [vaguely] Oh, it had to be—sacrificed or something. [There is a pause while STANLEY considers. STELLA is changing into her dress.] When she comes in be sure to say something nice about her appearance. And, oh! Don't mention the baby. I haven't said anything yet, I'm waiting until she gets in a quieter condition.

STANLEY [ominously] So?

STELLA And try to understand her and be nice to her, Stan.

BLANCHE [singing in the bathroom] "From the land of the sky blue water, They brought a captive maid!"

STELLA She wasn't expecting to find us in such a small place. You see I'd tried to gloss things over a little in my letters.

STANLEY So?

STELLA And admire her dress and tell her she's looking wonderful. That's important with Blanche. Her little weakness!

STANLEY Yeah. I get the idea. Now let's skip back a little to where you said the country place was disposed of.

STELLA Oh!—yes . . .

STANLEY How about that? Let's have a few more details on that subjeck.

STELLA It's best not to talk much about it until she's calmed down.

STANLEY So that's the deal, huh? Sister Blanche cannot be annoyed with business details right now!

STELLA You saw how she was last night.

STANLEY Uh-hum, I saw how she was. Now let's have a gander at the bill of sale.

STELLA I haven't seen any.

STANLEY She didn't show you no papers, no deed of sale or nothing like that, huh?

STELLA It seems like it wasn't sold.

STANLEY Well, what in hell was it then, give away? To charity?

STELLA Shhh! She'll hear you.

STANLEY I don't care if she hears me. Let's see the papers!

STELLA There weren't any papers, she didn't show any papers, I don't care about papers.

STANLEY Have you ever heard of the Napoleonic code?[8]

---

8. This codification of French law (1802), made by Napoleon as emperor, is the basis for Louisiana's civil law.

STELLA No, Stanley, I haven't heard of the Napoleonic code and if I have, I don't see what it—

STANLEY Let me enlighten you on a point or two, baby.

STELLA Yes?

STANLEY In the state of Louisiana we have the Napoleonic code according to which what belongs to the wife belongs to the husband and vice versa. For instance if I had a piece of property, or you had a piece of property—

STELLA My head is swimming!

STANLEY All right. I'll wait till she gets through soaking in a hot tub and then I'll inquire if *she* is acquainted with the Napoleonic code. It looks to me like you have been swindled, baby, and when you're swindled under the Napoleonic code I'm swindled *too*. And I don't like to be *swindled*.

STELLA There's plenty of time to ask her questions later but if you do now she'll go to pieces again. I don't understand what happened to Belle Reve but you don't know how ridiculous you are being when you suggest that my sister or I or anyone of our family could have perpetrated a swindle on anyone else.

STANLEY Then where's the money if the place was sold?

STELLA Not sold—*lost, lost!*

[*He stalks into bedroom, and she follows him.*]

Stanley!

[*He pulls open the wardrobe trunk standing in middle of room and jerks out an armful of dresses.*]

STANLEY Open your eyes to this stuff! You think she got them out of a teacher's pay?

STELLA Hush!

STANLEY Look at these feathers and furs that she come here to preen herself in! What's this here? A solid-gold dress, I believe! And this one! What is these here? Fox-pieces! [*He blows on them.*] Genuine fox fur-pieces, a half a mile long! Where are your fox-pieces, Stella? Bushy snow-white ones, no less! Where are your white fox-pieces?

STELLA Those are inexpensive summer furs that Blanche has had a long time.

STANLEY I got an acquaintance who deals in this sort of merchandise. I'll have him in here to appraise it. I'm willing to bet you there's thousands of dollars invested in this stuff here!

STELLA Don't be such an idiot, Stanley!

[*He hurls the furs to the day bed. Then he jerks open a small drawer in the trunk and pulls up a fistful of costume jewelry.*]

STANLEY And what have we here? The treasure chest of a pirate!

STELLA Oh, Stanley!

STANLEY Pearls! Ropes of them! What is this sister of yours, a deep-sea diver? Bracelets of solid gold, too! Where are your pearls and gold bracelets?

STELLA Shhh! Be still, Stanley!

STANLEY And diamonds! A crown for an empress!

STELLA A rhinestone tiara she wore to a costume ball.

STANLEY What's rhinestone?

STELLA Next door to glass.

STANLEY Are you kidding? I have an acquaintance that works in a jewelry store. I'll have him in here to make an appraisal of this. Here's your plantation, or what was left of it, here!

STELLA   You have no idea how stupid and horrid you're being! Now close that trunk before she comes out of the bathroom!

[*He kicks the trunk partly closed and sits on the kitchen table.*]

STANLEY   The Kowalskis and the DuBoises have different notions.

STELLA [*angrily*]   Indeed they have, thank heavens!—*I'm* going outside.
[*She snatches up her white hat and gloves and crosses to the outside door.*] You come out with me while Blanche is getting dressed.

STANLEY   Since when do you give me orders?

STELLA   Are you going to stay here and insult her?

STANLEY   You're damn tootin' I'm going to stay here.

[STELLA *goes out to the porch.* BLANCHE *comes out of the bathroom in a red satin robe.*]

BLANCHE [*airily*]   Hello, Stanley! Here I am, all freshly bathed and scented, and feeling like a brand new human being!

[*He lights a cigarette.*]

STANLEY   That's good.

BLANCHE [*drawing the curtains at the windows*]   Excuse me while I slip on my pretty new dress!

STANLEY   Go right ahead, Blanche.

[*She closes the drapes between the rooms.*]

BLANCHE   I understand there's to be a little card party to which we ladies are cordially *not* invited!

STANLEY [*ominously*]   Yeah?

[BLANCHE *throws off her robe and slips into a flowered print dress.*]

BLANCHE   Where's Stella?

STANLEY   Out on the porch.

BLANCHE   I'm going to ask a favor of you in a moment.

STANLEY   What could that be, I wonder?

BLANCHE   Some buttons in back! You may enter!

[*He crosses through drapes with a smoldering look.*]
How do I look?

STANLEY   You look all right.

BLANCHE   Many thanks! Now the buttons!

STANLEY   I can't do nothing with them.

BLANCHE   You men with your big clumsy fingers. May I have a drag on your cig?

STANLEY   Have one for yourself.

BLANCHE   Why, thanks!. . . . It looks like my trunk has exploded.

STANLEY   Me an' Stella were helping you unpack.

BLANCHE   Well, you certainly did a fast and thorough job of it!

STANLEY   It looks like you raided some stylish shops in Paris.

BLANCHE   Ha-ha! Yes—clothes are my passion!

STANLEY   What does it cost for a string of fur-pieces like that?

BLANCHE   Why, those were a tribute from an admirer of mine!

STANLEY   He must have had a lot of—admiration!

BLANCHE   Oh, in my youth I excited some admiration. But look at me now!
[*She smiles at him radiantly.*] Would you think it possible that I was once considered to be—attractive?

STANLEY   Your looks are okay.

BLANCHE   I was fishing for a compliment, Stanley.

STANLEY   I don't go in for that stuff.

BLANCHE   What—stuff?

STANLEY   Compliments to women about their looks. I never met a woman
that didn't know if she was good-looking or not without being told, and
some of them give themselves credit for more than they've got. I once
went out with a doll who said to me, "I am the glamorous type, I am the
glamorous type!" I said, "So what?"

BLANCHE   And what did she say then?

STANLEY   She didn't say nothing. That shut her up like a clam.

BLANCHE   Did it end the romance?

STANLEY   It ended the conversation—that was all. Some men are took in
by this Hollywood glamor stuff and some men are not.

BLANCHE   I'm sure you belong in the second category.

STANLEY   That's right.

BLANCHE   I cannot imagine any witch of a woman casting a spell over you.

STANLEY   That's—right.

BLANCHE   You're simple, straightforward and honest, a little bit on the
primitive side I should think. To interest you a woman would have to—
[*She pauses with an indefinite gesture.*]

STANLEY [*slowly*]   Lay . . . her cards on the table.

BLANCHE [*smiling*]   Well, I never cared for wishy-washy people. That was
why, when you walked in here last night, I said to myself—"My sister
has married a man!"—Of course that was all that I could tell about you.

STANLEY [*booming*]   Now let's cut the re-bop![9]

BLANCHE [*pressing hands to her ears*]   Ouuuuu!

STELLA [*calling from the steps*]   Stanley! You come out here and let Blanche
finish dressing!

BLANCHE   I'm through dressing, honey.

STELLA   Well, you come out, then.

STANLEY   Your sister and I are having a little talk.

BLANCHE [*lightly*]   Honey, do me a favor. Run to the drugstore and get me
a lemon Coke with plenty of chipped ice in it!—Will you do that for me,
sweetie?

STELLA [*uncertainly*]   Yes. [*She goes around the corner of the building.*]

BLANCHE   The poor little thing was out there listening to us, and I have
an idea she doesn't understand you as well as I do. . . . All right; now,
Mr. Kowalski, let us proceed without any more double-talk. I'm ready to
answer all questions. I've nothing to hide. What is it?

STANLEY   There is such a thing in this state of Louisiana as the Napoleonic
code, according to which whatever belongs to my wife is also mine—and
vice versa.

BLANCHE   My, but you have an impressive judicial air!
[*She sprays herself with her atomizer; then playfully sprays him with it.
He seizes the atomizer and slams it down on the dresser. She throws back
her head and laughs.*]

STANLEY   If I didn't know that you was my wife's sister I'd get ideas about
you!

BLANCHE   Such as what!

STANLEY   Don't play so dumb. You know what!

---

9. Nonsense syllables (from "bop," a form of jazz).

BLANCHE [*she puts the atomizer on the table*]   All right. Cards on the table. That suits me. [*She turns to* STANLEY.] I know I fib a good deal. After all, a woman's charm is fifty per cent illusion, but when a thing is important I tell the truth, and this is the truth: I haven't cheated my sister or you or anyone else as long as I have lived.

STANLEY   Where's the papers? In the trunk?

BLANCHE   Everything that I own is in that trunk.

[STANLEY *crosses to the trunk, shoves it roughly open and begins to open compartments.*]

BLANCHE   What in the name of heaven are you thinking of! What's in the back of that little boy's mind of yours? That I am absconding with something, attempting some kind of treachery on my sister?—Let me do that! It will be faster and simpler . . . [*She crosses to the trunk and takes out a box.*] I keep my papers mostly in this tin box. [*She opens it.*]

STANLEY   What's them underneath? [*He indicates another sheaf of paper.*]

BLANCHE   These are love-letters, yellowing with antiquity, all from one boy. [*He snatches them up. She speaks fiercely.*] Give those back to me!

STANLEY   I'll have a look at them first!

BLANCHE   The touch of your hands insults them!

STANLEY   Don't pull that stuff!

[*He rips off the ribbon and starts to examine them.* BLANCHE *snatches them from him, and they cascade to the floor.*]

BLANCHE   Now that you've touched them I'll burn them!

STANLEY [*staring, baffled*]   What in hell are they?

BLANCHE [*on the floor gathering them up*]   Poems a dead boy wrote. I hurt him the way that you would like to hurt me, but you can't! I'm not young and vulnerable any more. But my young husband was and I—never mind about that! Just give them back to me!

STANLEY   What do you mean by saying you'll have to burn them?

BLANCHE   I'm sorry, I must have lost my head for a moment. Everyone has something he won't let others touch because of their—intimate nature . . .

[*She now seems faint with exhaustion and she sits down with the strong box and puts on a pair of glasses and goes methodically through a large stack of papers.*]

Ambler & Ambler. Hmmmmm. . . . Crabtree. . . . More Ambler & Ambler.

STANLEY   What is Ambler & Ambler?

BLANCHE   A firm that made loans on the place.

STANLEY   Then it *was* lost on a mortgage?

BLANCHE [*touching her forehead*]   That must've been what happened.

STANLEY   I don't want no ifs, ands or buts! What's all the rest of them papers?

[*She hands him the entire box. He carries it to the table and starts to examine the paper.*]

BLANCHE [*picking up a large envelope containing more papers*]   There are thousands of papers, stretching back over hundreds of years, affecting Belle Reve as, piece by piece, our improvident grandfathers and father and uncles and brothers exchanged the land for their epic fornications— to put it plainly! [*She removes her glasses with an exhausted laugh.*] The four-letter word deprived us of our plantation, till finally all that was left—and Stella can verify that!—was the house itself and about twenty acres of ground, including a graveyard, to which now all but Stella and I have retreated. [*She pours the contents of the envelope on the table.*] Here all of them are, all papers! I hereby endow you with them! Take them, peruse them—commit them to memory, even! I think it's wonderfully fitting that Belle Reve should finally be this bunch of old papers in your big, capable hands! . . . I wonder if Stella's come back with my lemon Coke . . . [*She leans back and closes her eyes.*]

STANLEY   I have a lawyer acquaintance who will study these out.

BLANCHE   Present them to him with a box of aspirin tablets.

STANLEY [*becoming somewhat sheepish*]   You see, under the Napoleonic code—a man has to take an interest in his wife's affairs—especially now that she's going to have a baby.

[BLANCHE *opens her eyes. The "Blue Piano" sounds louder.*]

BLANCHE   Stella? Stella going to have a baby? [*dreamily*] I didn't know she was going to have a baby!

[*She gets up and crosses to the outside door.* STELLA *appears around the corner with a carton from the drugstore.* STANLEY *goes into the bedroom with the envelope and the box. The inner rooms fade to darkness and the outside wall of the house is visible.* BLANCHE *meets* STELLA *at the foot of the steps to the sidewalk.*]

BLANCHE   Stella, Stella for star! How lovely to have a baby! It's all right. Everything's all right.

STELLA   I'm sorry he did that to you.

BLANCHE   Oh, I guess he's just not the type that goes for jasmine perfume, but maybe he's what we need to mix with our blood now that we've lost Belle Reve. We thrashed it out. I feel a bit shaky, but I think I handled it nicely, I laughed and treated it all as a joke. [STEVE *and* PABLO *appear, carrying a case of beer.*] I called him a little boy and laughed and flirted. Yes, I was flirting with your husband! [*as the men approach*] The guests are gathering for the poker party. [*The two men pass between them, and enter the house.*] Which way do we go now, Stella—this way?

STELLA   No, this way. [*She leads* BLANCHE *away.*]

BLANCHE [*laughing*]   The blind are leading the blind!

[*A tamale* VENDOR *is heard calling.*]

VENDOR'S VOICE   Red-hot!

Scene Three

THE POKER NIGHT[1]

*There is a picture of Van Gogh's[2] of a billiard-parlor at night. The kitchen now suggests that sort of lurid nocturnal brilliance, the raw colors of childhood's spectrum. Over the yellow linoleum of the kitchen table hangs an electric bulb with a vivid green glass shade. The poker players—*STANLEY, STEVE, MITCH *and* PABLO—*wear colored shirts, solid blues, a purple, a red-and-white check, a light green, and they are men at the peak of their physical manhood, as coarse*

1. Williams's first title for *A Streetcar Named Desire.*

2. *The Night Café,* by Vincent Van Gogh (1853–1890), Dutch postimpressionist painter.

and direct and powerful as the primary colors. There are vivid slices of watermelon on the table, whiskey bottles and glasses. The bedroom is relatively dim
with only the light that spills between the portieres and through the wide window on the street.

For a moment, there is absorbed silence as a hand is dealt.

STEVE   Anything wild this deal?
PABLO   One-eyed jacks are wild.
STEVE   Give me two cards.
PABLO   You, Mitch?
MITCH   I'm out.
PABLO   One.
MITCH   Anyone want a shot?
STANLEY   Yeah. Me.
PABLO   Why don't somebody go to the Chinaman's and bring back a load
   of chop suey?
STANLEY   When I'm losing you want to eat! Ante up! Openers? Openers!
   Get y'r ass off the table, Mitch. Nothing belongs on a poker table but
   cards, chips and whiskey.
      [He lurches up and tosses some watermelon rinds to the floor.]
MITCH   Kind of on your high horse, ain't you?
STANLEY   How many?
STEVE   Give me three.
STANLEY   One.
MITCH   I'm out again. I oughta go home pretty soon.
STANLEY   Shut up.
MITCH   I gotta sick mother. She don't go to sleep until I come in at night.
STANLEY   Then why don't you stay home with her?
MITCH   She says to go out, so I go, but I don't enjoy it. All the while I keep
   wondering how she is.
STANLEY   Aw, for the sake of Jesus, go home, then!
PABLO   What've you got?
STEVE   Spade flush.
MITCH   You all are married. But I'll be alone when she goes.—I'm going
   to the bathroom.
STANLEY   Hurry back and we'll fix you a sugar-tit.
MITCH   Aw, go rut. [He crosses through the bedroom into the bathroom.]
STEVE   [dealing a hand]   Seven card stud.³ [telling his joke as he deals] This
   ole farmer is out in back of his house sittin' down th'owing corn to the
   chickens when all at once he hears a loud cackle and this young hen
   comes lickety split around the side of the house with the rooster right
   behind her and gaining on her fast.
STANLEY   [impatient with the story]   Deal!
STEVE   But when the rooster catches sight of the farmer th'owing the corn
   he puts on the brakes and lets the hen get away and starts pecking corn.
   And the old farmer says, "Lord God, I hopes I never gits that hongry!"
      [STEVE and PABLO laugh. The sisters appear around the corner of the
      building.]

<hr />

3. An adventurous and risky variant of poker.

STELLA   The game is still going on.

BLANCHE   How do I look?

STELLA   Lovely, Blanche.

BLANCHE   I feel so hot and frazzled. Wait till I powder before you open the door. Do I look done in?

STELLA   Why no. You are as fresh as a daisy.

BLANCHE   One that's been picked a few days.

[STELLA *opens the door and they enter.*]

STELLA   Well, well, well. I see you boys are still at it?

STANLEY   Where you been?

STELLA   Blanche and I took in a show. Blanche, this is Mr. Gonzales and Mr. Hubbell.

BLANCHE   Please don't get up.

STANLEY   Nobody's going to get up, so don't be worried.

STELLA   How much longer is this game going to continue?

STANLEY   Till we get ready to quit.

BLANCHE   Poker is so fascinating. Could I kibitz?

STANLEY   You could not. Why don't you women go up and sit with Eunice?

STELLA   Because it is nearly two-thirty. [BLANCHE *crosses into the bedroom and partially closes the portieres.*] Couldn't you call it quits after one more hand?

[*A chair scrapes.* STANLEY *gives a loud whack of his hand on her thigh.*]

STELLA [*sharply*]   That's not fun, Stanley.

[*The men laugh.* STELLA *goes into the bedroom.*]

STELLA   It makes me so mad when he does that in front of people.

BLANCHE   I think I will bathe.

STELLA   Again?

BLANCHE   My nerves are in knots. Is the bathroom occupied?

STELLA   I don't know.

[BLANCHE *knocks.* MITCH *opens the door and comes out, still wiping his hands on a towel.*]

BLANCHE   Oh!—good evening.

MITCH   Hello. [*He stares at her.*]

STELLA   Blanche, this is Harold Mitchell. My sister, Blanche DuBois.

MITCH [*with awkward courtesy*]   How do you do, Miss DuBois.

STELLA   How is your mother now, Mitch?

MITCH   About the same, thanks. She appreciated your sending over that custard.—Excuse me, please.

[*He crosses slowly back into the kitchen, glancing back at* BLANCHE *and coughing a little shyly. He realizes he still has the towel in his hands and with an embarrassed laugh hands it to* STELLA. BLANCHE *looks after him with a certain interest.*]

BLANCHE   That one seems—superior to the others.

STELLA   Yes, he is.

BLANCHE   I thought he had a sort of sensitive look.

STELLA   His mother is sick.

BLANCHE   Is he married?

STELLA   No.

BLANCHE   Is he a wolf?

STELLA   Why, Blanche! [BLANCHE *laughs.*] I don't think he would be.

BLANCHE   What does—what does he do? [*She is unbuttoning her blouse.*]

STELLA   He's on the precision bench in the spare parts department. At the plant Stanley travels for.

BLANCHE   Is that something much?

STELLA   No. Stanley's the only one of his crowd that's likely to get anywhere.

BLANCHE   What makes you think Stanley will?

STELLA   Look at him.

BLANCHE   I've looked at him.

STELLA   Then you should know.

BLANCHE   I'm sorry, but I haven't noticed the stamp of genius even on Stanley's forehead.

[*She takes off the blouse and stands in her pink silk brassiere and white skirt in the light through the portieres. The game has continued in undertones.*]

STELLA   It isn't on his forehead and it isn't genius.

BLANCHE   Oh. Well, what is it, and where? I would like to know.

STELLA   It's a drive that he has. You're standing in the light, Blanche!

BLANCHE   Oh, am I!

[*She moves out of the yellow streak of light.* STELLA *has removed her dress and put on a light blue satin kimona.*]

STELLA   [*with girlish laughter*]   You ought to see their wives.

BLANCHE   [*laughingly*]   I can imagine. Big, beefy things, I suppose.

STELLA   You know that one upstairs? [*more laughter*] One time [*laughing*] the plaster—[*laughing*] cracked—

STANLEY   You hens cut out that conversation in there!

STELLA   You can't hear us.

STANLEY   Well, you can hear me and I said to hush up!

STELLA   This is my house and I'll talk as much as I want to!

BLANCHE   Stella, don't start a row.

STELLA   He's half drunk!—I'll be out in a minute.

[*She goes into the bathroom.* BLANCHE *rises and crosses leisurely to a small white radio and turns it on.*]

STANLEY   Awright, Mitch, you in?

MITCH   What? Oh!—No, I'm out!

[BLANCHE *moves back into the streak of light. She raises her arms and stretches, as she moves indolently back to the chair. Rhumba music comes over the radio.* MITCH *rises at the table.*]

STANLEY   Who turned that on in there?

BLANCHE   I did. Do you mind?

STANLEY   Turn it off!

STEVE   Aw, let the girls have their music.

PABLO   Sure, that's good, leave it on!

STEVE   Sounds like Xavier Cugat![4]

[STANLEY *jumps up and, crossing to the radio, turns it off. He stops short at the sight of* BLANCHE *in the chair. She returns his look without flinching. Then he sits again at the poker table. Two of the men have started arguing hotly.*]

---

4. Cuban bandleader, well known for composing and playing rhumbas.

STEVE   I didn't hear you name it.

PABLO   Didn't I name it, Mitch?

MITCH   I wasn't listenin'.

PABLO   What were you doing, then?

STANLEY   He was looking through them drapes. [*He jumps up and jerks roughly at curtains to close them.*] Now deal the hand over again and let's play cards or quit. Some people get ants when they win.

[MITCH *rises as* STANLEY *returns to his seat.*]

STANLEY [*yelling*]   Sit down!

MITCH   I'm going to the "head." Deal me out.

PABLO   Sure he's got ants now. Seven five-dollar bills in his pants pocket folded up tight as spitballs.

STEVE   Tomorrow you'll see him at the cashier's window getting them changed into quarters.

STANLEY   And when he goes home he'll deposit them one by one in a piggy bank his mother give him for Christmas. [*dealing*] This game is Spit in the Ocean.[5]

[MITCH *laughs uncomfortably and continues through the portieres. He stops just inside.*]

BLANCHE [*softly*]   Hello! The Little Boys' Room is busy right now.

MITCH   We've—been drinking beer.

BLANCHE   I hate beer.

MITCH   It's—a hot weather drink.

BLANCHE   Oh, I don't think so; it always makes me warmer. Have you got any cigs? [*She has slipped on the dark red satin wrapper.*]

MITCH   Sure.

BLANCHE   What kind are they?

MITCH   Luckies.

BLANCHE   Oh, good. What a pretty case. Silver?

MITCH   Yes. Yes; read the inscription.

BLANCHE   Oh, is there an inscription? I can't make it out. [*He strikes a match and moves closer.*] Oh! [*reading with feigned difficulty*] "And if God choose,/I shall but love thee better—after—death!" Why, that's from my favorite sonnet by Mrs. Browning![6]

MITCH   You know it?

BLANCHE   Certainly I do!

MITCH   There's a story connected with that inscription.

BLANCHE   It sounds like a romance.

MITCH   A pretty sad one.

BLANCHE   Oh?

MITCH   The girl's dead now.

BLANCHE [*in a tone of deep sympathy*]   Oh!

MITCH   She knew she was dying when she give me this. A very strange girl, very sweet—very!

BLANCHE   She must have been fond of you. Sick people have such deep, sincere attachments.

MITCH   That's right, they certainly do.

BLANCHE   Sorrow makes for sincerity, I think.

---

5. Another variant of poker.
6. Elizabeth Barrett Browning, 19th-century British poet, was most famous for her sequence of love
poems *Sonnets from the Portuguese*.

MITCH   It sure brings it out in people.

BLANCHE   The little there is belongs to people who have experienced some sorrow.

MITCH   I believe you are right about that.

BLANCHE   I'm positive that I am. Show me a person who hasn't known any sorrow and I'll show you a shuperficial—Listen to me! My tongue is a little—thick! You boys are responsible for it. The show let out at eleven and we couldn't come home on account of the poker game so we had to go somewhere and drink. I'm not accustomed to having more than one drink. Two is the limit—and *three!* [*She laughs.*] Tonight I had three.

STANLEY   Mitch!

MITCH   Deal me out. I'm talking to Miss—

BLANCHE   DuBois.

MITCH   Miss DuBois?

BLANCHE   It's a French name. It means woods and Blanche means white, so the two together mean white woods. Like an orchard in spring! You can remember it by that.

MITCH   You're French?

BLANCHE   We are French by extraction. Our first American ancestors were French Huguenots.

MITCH   You are Stella's sister, are you not?

BLANCHE   Yes, Stella is my precious little sister. I call her little in spite of the fact she's somewhat older than I. Just slightly. Less than a year. Will you do something for me?

MITCH   Sure. What?

BLANCHE   I bought this adorable little colored paper lantern at a Chinese shop on Bourbon. Put it over the light bulb! Will you, please?

MITCH   Be glad to.

BLANCHE   I can't stand a naked light bulb, any more than I can a rude remark or a vulgar action.

MITCH [*adjusting the lantern*]   I guess we strike you as being a pretty rough bunch.

BLANCHE   I'm very adaptable—to circumstances.

MITCH   Well, that's a good thing to be. You are visiting Stanley and Stella?

BLANCHE   Stella hasn't been so well lately, and I came down to help her for a while. She's very run down.

MITCH   You're not—?

BLANCHE   Married? No, no. I'm an old maid schoolteacher!

MITCH   You may teach school but you're certainly not an old maid.

BLANCHE   Thank you, sir! I appreciate your gallantry!

MITCH   So you are in the teaching profession?

BLANCHE   Yes. Ah, yes . . .

MITCH   Grade school or high school or—

STANLEY [*bellowing*]   Mitch!

MITCH   Coming!

BLANCHE   Gracious, what lung-power! . . . I teach high school. In Laurel.

MITCH   What do you teach? What subject?

BLANCHE   Guess!

MITCH   I bet you teach art or music? [BLANCHE *laughs delicately.*] Of course I could be wrong. You might teach arithmetic.

BLANCHE   Never arithmetic, sir; never arithmetic! [*with a laugh*] I don't even know my multiplication tables! No, I have the misfortune of being an English instructor. I attempt to instill a bunch of bobby-soxers and drugstore Romeos with reverence for Hawthorne and Whitman and Poe!

MITCH   I guess that some of them are more interested in other things.

BLANCHE   How very right you are! Their literary heritage is not what most of them treasure above all else! But they're sweet things! And in the spring, it's touching to notice them making their first discovery of love! As if nobody had ever known it before!

[*The bathroom door opens and* STELLA *comes out.* BLANCHE *continues talking to* MITCH.]

Oh! Have you finished? Wait—I'll turn on the radio.

[*She turns the knobs on the radio and it begins to play "Wien, Wien, nur du allein."*[7] BLANCHE *waltzes to the music with romantic gestures.* MITCH *is delighted and moves in awkward imitation like a dancing bear.* STANLEY *stalks fiercely through the portieres into the bedroom. He crosses to the small white radio and snatches it off the table. With a shouted oath, he tosses the instrument out the window.*]

STELLA   Drunk—drunk—animal thing, you! [*She rushes through to the poker table.*] All of you—please go home! If any of you have one spark of decency in you—

BLANCHE [*wildly*]   Stella, watch out, he's—

[STANLEY *charges after* STELLA.]

MEN [*feebly*]   Take it easy, Stanley. Easy, fellow.—Let's all—

STELLA   You lay your hands on me and I'll—

[*She backs out of sight. He advances and disappears. There is the sound of a blow.* STELLA *cries out.* BLANCHE *screams and runs into the kitchen. The men rush forward and there is grappling and cursing. Something is overturned with a crash.*]

BLANCHE [*shrilly*]   My sister is going to have a baby!

MITCH   This is terrible.

BLANCHE   Lunacy, absolute lunacy!

MITCH   Get him in here, men.

[STANLEY *is forced, pinioned by the two men, into the bedroom. He nearly throws them off. Then all at once he subsides and is limp in their grasp. They speak quietly and lovingly to him and he leans his face on one of their shoulders.*]

STELLA [*in a high, unnatural voice, out of sight*]   I want to go away, I want to go away!

MITCH   Poker shouldn't be played in a house with women.

[BLANCHE *rushes into the bedroom.*]

BLANCHE   I want my sister's clothes! We'll go to that woman's upstairs!

MITCH   Where is the clothes?

BLANCHE [*opening the closet*]   I've got them! [*She rushes through to* STELLA.] Stella, Stella, precious! Dear, dear little sister, don't be afraid!

[*With her arm around* STELLA, BLANCHE *guides her to the outside door and upstairs.*]

STANLEY [*dully*]   What's the matter; what's happened?

MITCH   You just blew your top, Stan.

---

7. Vienna, Vienna, you are my only (German); a waltz from an operetta by Franz Lehar.

PABLO   He's okay, now.

STEVE   Sure, my boy's okay!

MITCH   Put him on the bed and get a wet towel.

PABLO   I think coffee would do him a world of good, now.

STANLEY [*thickly*]   I want water.

MITCH   Put him under the shower!

[*The men talk quietly as they lead him to the bathroom.*]

STANLEY   Let the rut go of me, you sons of bitches!

[*Sounds of blows are heard. The water goes on full tilt.*]

STEVE   Let's get quick out of here!

[*They rush to the poker table and sweep up their winnings on their way out.*]

MITCH [*sadly but firmly*]   Poker should not be played in a house with women.

[*The door closes on them and the place is still. The Negro entertainers in the bar around the corner play "Paper Doll"[8] slow and blue. After a moment STANLEY comes out of the bathroom dripping water and still in his clinging wet polka dot drawers.*]

STANLEY   Stella! [*There is a pause.*] My baby doll's left me!

[*He breaks into sobs. Then he goes to the phone and dials, still shuddering with sobs.*]

Eunice? I want my baby! [*He waits a moment; then he hangs up and dials again.*] Eunice! I'll keep on ringin' until I talk with my baby!

[*An indistinguishable shrill voice is heard. He hurls phone to floor. Dissonant brass and piano sounds as the rooms dim out to darkness and the outer walls appear in the night light. The "Blue Piano" plays for a brief interval. Finally, STANLEY stumbles half-dressed out to the porch and down the wooden steps to the pavement before the building. There he throws back his head like a baying hound and bellows his wife's name: "Stella! Stella, sweetheart! Stella!"*]

STANLEY   Stell-lahhhhh!

EUNICE [*calling down from the door of her upper apartment*]   Quit that howling out there an' go back to bed!

STANLEY   I want my baby down here. Stella, Stella!

EUNICE   She ain't comin' down so you quit! Or you'll git th' law on you!

STANLEY   Stella!

EUNICE   You can't beat on a woman an' then call 'er back! She won't come! And her goin' t' have a baby! . . . You stinker! You whelp of a Polack, you! I hope they do haul you in and turn the fire hose on you, same as the last time!

STANLEY [*humbly*]   Eunice, I want my girl to come down with me!

EUNICE   Hah! [*She slams her door.*]

STANLEY [*with heaven-splitting violence*]   *STELL-LAHHHHH!*

[*The low-tone clarinet moans. The door upstairs opens again. STELLA slips down the rickety stairs in her robe. Her eyes are glistening with tears and her hair loose about her throat and shoulders. They stare at each other. Then they come together with low, animal moans. He falls to his knees on the steps and presses his face to her belly, curving a little with*]

---

8. Popular song of the early 1940s by Johnny Black.

maternity. Her eyes go blind with tenderness as she catches his head and raises him level with her. He snatches the screen door open and lifts her off her feet and bears her into the dark flat. BLANCHE comes out the upper landing in her robe and slips fearfully down the steps.]

BLANCHE   Where is my little sister? Stella? Stella?

[She stops before the dark entrance of her sister's flat. Then catches her breath as if struck. She rushes down to the walk before the house. She looks right and left as if for a sanctuary. The music fades away. MITCH appears from around the corner.]

MITCH   Miss DuBois?

BLANCHE   Oh!

MITCH   All quiet on the Potomac now?

BLANCHE   She ran downstairs and went back in there with him.

MITCH   Sure she did.

BLANCHE   I'm terrified!

MITCH   Ho-ho! There's nothing to be scared of. They're crazy about each other.

BLANCHE   I'm not used to such—

MITCH   Naw, it's a shame this had to happen when you just got here. But don't take it serious.

BLANCHE   Violence! Is so—

MITCH   Set down on the steps and have a cigarette with me.

BLANCHE   I'm not properly dressed.

MITCH   That don't make no difference in the Quarter.

BLANCHE   Such a pretty silver case.

MITCH   I showed you the inscription, didn't I?

BLANCHE   Yes. [During the pause, she looks up at the sky.] There's so much—so much confusion in the world . . . [He coughs diffidently.] Thank you for being so kind! I need kindness now.

Scene Four

It is early the following morning. There is a confusion of street cries like a choral chant.

STELLA is lying down in the bedroom. Her face is serene in the early morning sunlight. One hand rests on her belly, rounding slightly with new maternity. From the other dangles a book of colored comics. Her eyes and lips have that almost narcotized tranquility that is in the faces of Eastern idols.

The table is sloppy with remains of breakfast and the debris of the preceding night, and STANLEY's gaudy pyjamas lie across the threshold of the bathroom. The outside door is slightly ajar on a sky of summer brilliance.

BLANCHE appears at this door. She has spent a sleepless night and her appearance entirely contrasts with STELLA's. She presses her knuckles nervously to her lips as she looks through the door, before entering.

BLANCHE   Stella?

STELLA [stirring lazily]   Hmmh?

[BLANCHE utters a moaning cry and runs into the bedroom, throwing herself down beside STELLA in a rush of hysterical tenderness.]

BLANCHE   Baby, my baby sister!

STELLA [*drawing away from her*]   Blanche, what is the matter with you?
   [BLANCHE *straightens up slowly and stands beside the bed looking down
   at her sister with knuckles pressed to her lips.*]
BLANCHE   He's left?
STELLA   Stan? Yes.
BLANCHE   Will he be back?
STELLA   He's gone to get the car greased. Why?
BLANCHE   Why! I've been half crazy, Stella! When I found out you'd been
   insane enough to come back in here after what happened—I started to
   rush in after you!
STELLA   I'm glad you didn't.
BLANCHE   What were you thinking of? [STELLA *makes an indefinite gesture.*]
   Answer me! What? What?
STELLA   Please, Blanche! Sit down and stop yelling.
BLANCHE   All right, Stella. I will repeat the question quietly now. How
   could you come back in this place last night? Why, you must have slept
   with him!
   [STELLA *gets up in a calm and leisurely way.*]
STELLA   Blanche, I'd forgotten how excitable you are. You're making much
   too much fuss about this.
BLANCHE   Am I?
STELLA   Yes, you are, Blanche. I know how it must have seemed to you
   and I'm awful sorry it had to happen, but it wasn't anything as serious
   as you seem to take it. In the first place, when men are drinking and
   playing poker anything can happen. It's always a powder-keg. He didn't
   know what he was doing. . . . He was as good as a lamb when I came
   back and he's really very, very ashamed of himself.
BLANCHE   And that—that makes it all right?
STELLA   No, it isn't all right for anybody to make such a terrible row, but—
   people do sometimes. Stanley's always smashed things. Why, on our wedding night—soon as we came in here—he snatched off one of my slippers
   and rushed about the place smashing light bulbs with it.
BLANCHE   He did—*what?*
STELLA   He smashed all the light bulbs with the heel of my slipper! [*She
   laughs.*]
BLANCHE   And you—you *let* him? Didn't *run*, didn't *scream?*
STELLA   I was—sort of—thrilled by it. [*She waits for a moment.*] Eunice
   and you had breakfast?
BLANCHE   Do you suppose I wanted any breakfast?
STELLA   There's some coffee left on the stove.
BLANCHE   You're so—matter of fact about it, Stella.
STELLA   What other can I be? He's taken the radio to get it fixed. It didn't
   land on the pavement so only one tube was smashed.
BLANCHE   And you are standing there smiling!
STELLA   What do you want me to do?
BLANCHE   Pull yourself together and face the facts.
STELLA   What are they, in your opinion?
BLANCHE   In my opinion? You're married to a madman!
STELLA   No!
BLANCHE   Yes, you are, your fix is worse than mine is! Only you're not

being sensible about it. I'm going to *do* something. Get hold of myself and make myself a new life!

STELLA   Yes?

BLANCHE   But you've given in. And that isn't right, you're not old! You can get out.

STELLA [*slowly and emphatically*]   I'm not in anything I want to get out of.

BLANCHE [*incredulously*]   What—Stella?

STELLA   I said I am not in anything that I have a desire to get out of. Look at the mess in this room! And those empty bottles! They went through two cases last night! He promised this morning that he was going to quit having these poker parties, but you know how long such a promise is going to keep. Oh, well, it's his pleasure, like mine is movies and bridge. People have got to tolerate each other's habits, I guess.

BLANCHE   I don't understand you. [STELLA *turns toward her.*] I don't understand your indifference. Is this a Chinese philosophy you've—cultivated?

STELLA   Is what—what?

BLANCHE   This—shuffling about and mumbling—'One tube smashed—beer bottles—mess in the kitchen!'—as if nothing out of the ordinary has happened! [STELLA *laughs uncertainly and picking up the broom, twirls it in her hands.*]

BLANCHE   Are you deliberately shaking that thing in my face?

STELLA   No.

BLANCHE   Stop it. Let go of that broom. I won't have you cleaning up for him!

STELLA   Then who's going to do it? Are you?

BLANCHE   I? I!

STELLA   No, I didn't think so.

BLANCHE   Oh, let me think, if only my mind would function! We've got to get hold of some money, that's the way out!

STELLA   I guess that money is always nice to get hold of.

BLANCHE   Listen to me. I have an idea of some kind. [*Shakily she twists a cigarette into her holder.*] Do you remember Shep Huntleigh? [STELLA *shakes her head.*] Of course you remember Shep Huntleigh. I went out with him at college and wore his pin for a while. Well—

STELLA   Well?

BLANCHE   I ran into him last winter. You know I went to Miami during the Christmas holidays?

STELLA   No.

BLANCHE   Well, I did. I took the trip as an investment, thinking I'd meet someone with a million dollars.

STELLA   Did you?

BLANCHE   Yes. I ran into Shep Huntleigh—I ran into him on Biscayne Boulevard, on Christmas Eve, about dusk . . . getting into his car—Cadillac convertible; must have been a block long!

STELLA   I should think it would have been—inconvenient in traffic!

BLANCHE   You've heard of oil wells?

STELLA   Yes—remotely.

BLANCHE   He has them, all over Texas. Texas is literally spouting gold in his pockets.

STELLA   My, my.

BLANCHE   Y'know how indifferent I am to money. I think of money in terms
of what it does for you. But he could do it, he could certainly do it!

STELLA   Do what, Blanche?

BLANCHE   Why—set us up in a—shop!

STELLA   What kind of a shop?

BLANCHE   Oh, a—shop of some kind! He could do it with half what his
wife throws away at the races.

STELLA   He's married?

BLANCHE   Honey, would I be here if the man weren't married? [STELLA
laughs a little. BLANCHE *suddenly springs up and crosses to phone. She
speaks shrilly.*] How do I get Western Union?—Operator! Western
Union!

STELLA   That's a dial phone, honey.

BLANCHE   I can't dial, I'm too—

STELLA   Just dial O.

BLANCHE   O?

STELLA   Yes, "O" for Operator! [BLANCHE *considers a moment; then she puts
the phone down.*]

BLANCHE   Give me a pencil. Where is a slip of paper? I've got to write it
down first—the message, I mean . . . [*She goes to the dressing table, and
grabs up a sheet of Kleenex and an eyebrow pencil for writing equipment.*]
Let me see now . . . [*She bites the pencil.*] 'Darling Shep. Sister and I in
desperate situation.'

STELLA   I beg your pardon!

BLANCHE   'Sister and I in desperate situation. Will explain details later.
Would you be interested in—?' [*She bites the pencil again.*] 'Would you
be—interested—in . . . ' [*She smashes the pencil on the table and springs
up.*] You never get anywhere with direct appeals!

STELLA [*with a laugh*]   Don't be so ridiculous, darling!

BLANCHE   But I'll think of something, I've *got* to think of—*some*thing!
Don't laugh at me, Stella! Please, please don't—I—I want you to look at
the contents of my purse! Here's what's in it! [*She snatches her purse
open.*] Sixty-five measly cents in coin of the realm!

STELLA [*crossing to bureau*]   Stanley doesn't give me a regular allowance,
he likes to pay bills himself, but—this morning he gave me ten dollars
to smooth things over. You take five of it, Blanche, and I'll keep the rest.

BLANCHE   Oh, no. No, Stella.

STELLA [*insisting*]   I know how it helps your morale just having a little
pocket-money on you.

BLANCHE   No, thank you—I'll take to the streets!

STELLA   Talk sense! How did you happen to get so low on funds?

BLANCHE   Money just goes—it goes places. [*She rubs her forehead.*] Sometime today I've got to get hold of a Bromo![9]

STELLA   I'll fix you one now.

BLANCHE   Not yet—I've got to keep thinking!

STELLA   I wish you'd just let things go, at least for a—while . . .

9. Short for Bromo-seltzer, a headache remedy.

BLANCHE   Stella, I can't live with him! You can, he's your husband. But how could I stay here with him, after last night, with just those curtains between us?

STELLA   Blanche, you saw him at his worst last night.

BLANCHE   On the contrary, I saw him at his best! What such a man has to offer is animal force and he gave a wonderful exhibition of that! But the only way to live with such a man is to—go to bed with him! And that's your job—not mine!

STELLA   After you've rested a little, you'll see it's going to work out. You don't have to worry about anything while you're here. I mean—expenses . . .

BLANCHE   I have to plan for us both, to get us both—out!

STELLA   You take it for granted that I am in something that I want to get out of.

BLANCHE   I take it for granted that you still have sufficient memory of Belle Reve to find this place and these poker players impossible to live with.

STELLA   Well, you're taking entirely too much for granted.

BLANCHE   I can't believe you're in earnest.

STELLA   No?

BLANCHE   I understand how it happened—a little. You saw him in uniform, an officer, not here but—

STELLA   I'm not sure it would have made any difference where I saw him.

BLANCHE   Now don't say it was one of those mysterious electric things between people! If you do I'll laugh in your face.

STELLA   I am not going to say anything more at all about it!

BLANCHE   All right, then, don't!

STELLA   But there are things that happen between a man and a woman in the dark—that sort of make everything else seem—unimportant. [*Pause.*]

BLANCHE   What you are talking about is brutal desire—just—Desire!—the name of that rattle-trap streetcar that bangs through the Quarter, up one old narrow street and down another . . .

STELLA   Haven't you ever ridden on that streetcar?

BLANCHE   It brought me here.—Where I'm not wanted and where I'm ashamed to be . . .

STELLA   Then don't you think your superior attitude is a bit out of place?

BLANCHE   I am not being or feeling at all superior, Stella. Believe me I'm not! It's just this. This is how I look at it. A man like that is someone to go out with—once—twice—three times when the devil is in you. But live with? Have a child by?

STELLA   I have told you I love him.

BLANCHE   Then I *tremble* for you! I just—*tremble* for you. . . .

STELLA   I can't help your trembling if you insist on trembling!

   [*There is a pause.*]

BLANCHE   May I—speak—*plainly*?

STELLA   Yes, do. Go ahead. As plainly as you want to.

   [*Outside, a train approaches. They are silent till the noise subsides. They are both in the bedroom. Under cover of the train's noise* STANLEY *enters from outside. He stands unseen by the women, holding some packages in his arms, and overhears their following conversation. He wears an undershirt and grease-stained seersucker pants.*]

BLANCHE Well—if you'll forgive me—he's *common!*

STELLA Why, yes, I suppose he is.

BLANCHE Suppose! You can't have forgotten that much of our bringing up, Stella, that you just *suppose* that any part of a gentleman's in his nature! *Not one particle, no!* Oh, if he was just—*ordinary!* Just *plain*— but good and wholesome, but—*no*. There's something downright—*bestial*—about him! You're hating me saying this, aren't you?

STELLA [*coldly*] Go on and say it all, Blanche.

BLANCHE He acts like an animal, has an animal's habits! Eats like one, moves like one, talks like one! There's even something—sub-human— something not quite to the stage of humanity yet! Yes, something—ape- like about him, like one of those pictures I've seen in—anthropological studies! Thousands and thousands of years have passed him right by, and there he is—Stanley Kowalski—survivor of the Stone Age! Bearing the raw meat home from the kill in the jungle! And you—*you* here—*waiting* for him! Maybe he'll strike you or maybe grunt and kiss you! That is, if kisses have been discovered yet! Night falls and the other apes gather! There in the front of the cave, all grunting like him, and swilling and gnawing and hulking! His poker night! you call it—this party of apes! Somebody growls—some creature snatches at something—the fight is on! *God!* Maybe we are a long way from being made in God's image, but Stella—my sister—there has been *some* progress since then! Such things as art—as poetry and music—such kinds of new light have come into the world since then! In some kinds of people some tenderer feelings have had some little beginning! That we have got to make *grow!* And *cling* to, and hold as our flag! In this dark march toward whatever it is we're approaching. . . . *Don't—don't hang back with the brutes!*

[*Another train passes outside.* STANLEY *hesitates, licking his lips. Then suddenly he turns stealthily about and withdraws through front door. The women are still unaware of his presence. When the train has passed he calls through the closed front door.*]

STANLEY Hey! Hey, Stella!

STELLA [*who has listened gravely to* BLANCHE] Stanley!

BLANCHE Stell, I—

[*But* STELLA *has gone to the front door.* STANLEY *enters casually with his packages.*]

STANLEY Hiyuh, Stella. Blanche back?

STELLA Yes, she's back.

STANLEY Hiyuh, Blanche. [*He grins at her.*]

STELLA You must've got under the car.

STANLEY Them darn mechanics at Fritz's don't know their ass fr'm—Hey!

[STELLA *has embraced him with both arms, fiercely, and full in the view of* BLANCHE. *He laughs and clasps her head to him. Over her head he grins through the curtains at* BLANCHE. *As the lights fade away, with a lingering brightness on their embrace, the music of the "Blue Piano" and trumpet and drums is heard.*]

Scene Five

BLANCHE *is seated in the bedroom fanning herself with a palm leaf as she reads over a just-completed letter. Suddenly she bursts into a peal of laughter.* STELLA *is dressing in the bedroom.*

STELLA   What are you laughing at, honey?

BLANCHE   Myself, myself, for being such a liar! I'm writing a letter to Shep. [*She picks up the letter.*] "Darling Shep. I am spending the summer on the wing, making flying visits here and there. And who knows, perhaps I shall take a sudden notion to *swoop* down on *Dallas!* How would you feel about that? Ha-ha! [*She laughs nervously and brightly, touching her throat as if actually talking to* SHEP.] Forewarned is forearmed, as they say!"—How does that sound?

STELLA   Uh-huh . . .

BLANCHE [*going on nervously*]   "Most of my sister's friends go north in the summer but some have homes on the Gulf and there has been a continued round of entertainments, teas, cocktails, and luncheons—"
[*A disturbance is heard upstairs at the Hubbells' apartment.*]

STELLA   Eunice seems to be having some trouble with Steve.
[EUNICE'*s voice shouts in terrible wrath.*]

EUNICE   I heard about you and that blonde!

STEVE   That's a damn lie!

EUNICE   You ain't pulling the wool over my eyes! I wouldn't mind if you'd stay down at the Four Deuces, but you always going up.

STEVE   Who ever seen me up?

EUNICE   I seen you chasing her 'round the balcony—I'm gonna call the vice squad!

STEVE   Don't you throw that at me!

EUNICE [*shrieking*]   You hit me! I'm gonna call the police!
[*A clatter of aluminum striking a wall is heard, followed by a man's angry roar, shouts and overturned furniture. There is a crash; then a relative hush.*]

BLANCHE [*brightly*]   Did he *kill* her?
[EUNICE *appears on the steps in daemonic disorder.*]

STELLA   No! She's coming downstairs.

EUNICE   Call the police, I'm going to call the police! [*She rushes around the corner.*]
[*They laugh lightly.* STANLEY *comes around the corner in his green and scarlet silk bowling shirt. He trots up the steps and bangs into the kitchen.* BLANCHE *registers his entrance with nervous gestures.*]

STANLEY   What's a matter with Eun-uss?

STELLA   She and Steve had a row. Has she got the police?

STANLEY   Naw. She's gettin' a drink.

STELLA   That's much more practical!
[STEVE *comes down nursing a bruise on his forehead and looks in the door.*]

STEVE   She here?

STANLEY   Naw, naw. At the Four Deuces.

STEVE   That rutting hunk! [*He looks around the corner a bit timidly, then turns with affected boldness and runs after her.*]

BLANCHE   I must jot that down in my notebook. Ha-ha! I'm compiling a notebook of quaint little words and phrases I've picked up here.

STANLEY   You won't pick up nothing here you ain't heard before.

BLANCHE   Can I count on that?

STANLEY   You can count on it up to five hundred.

BLANCHE   That's a mighty high number. [*He jerks open the bureau drawer, slams it shut and throws shoes in a corner. At each noise* BLANCHE *winces slightly. Finally she speaks.*] What sign were you born under?

STANLEY [*while he is dressing*]   Sign?

BLANCHE   Astrological sign. I bet you were born under Aries. Aries people are forceful and dynamic. They dote on noise! They love to bang things around! You must have had lots of banging around in the army and now that you're out, you make up for it by treating inanimate objects with such a fury!

[STELLA *has been going in and out of closet during this scene. Now she pops her head out of the closet.*]

STELLA   Stanley was born just five minutes after Christmas.

BLANCHE   Capricorn—the Goat!

STANLEY   What sign were *you* born under?

BLANCHE   Oh, my birthday's next month, the fifteenth of September; that's under Virgo.

STANLEY   What's Virgo?

BLANCHE   Virgo is the Virgin.

STANLEY [*contemptuously*]   Hah! [*He advances a little as he knots his tie.*] Say, do you happen to know somebody named Shaw?

[*Her face expresses a faint shock. She reaches for the cologne bottle and dampens her handkerchief as she answers carefully.*]

BLANCHE   Why, everybody knows somebody named Shaw!

STANLEY   Well, this somebody named Shaw is under the impression he met you in Laurel, but I figure he must have got you mixed up with some other party because this other party is someone he met at a hotel called the Flamingo.

[BLANCHE *laughs breathlessly as she touches the cologne-dampened handkerchief to her temples.*]

BLANCHE   I'm afraid he does have me mixed up with this "other party." The Hotel Flamingo is not the sort of establishment I would dare to be seen in!

STANLEY   You know of it?

BLANCHE   Yes, I've seen it and smelled it.

STANLEY   You must've got pretty close if you could smell it.

BLANCHE   The odor of cheap perfume is penetrating.

STANLEY   That stuff you use is expensive?

BLANCHE   Twenty-five dollars an ounce! I'm nearly out. That's just a hint if you want to remember my birthday! [*She speaks lightly but her voice has a note of fear.*]

STANLEY   Shaw must've got you mixed up. He goes in and out of Laurel all the time so he can check on it and clear up any mistake.

[*He turns away and crosses to the portieres.* BLANCHE *closes her eyes as if faint. Her hand trembles as she lifts the handkerchief again to her forehead.* STEVE *and* EUNICE *come around corner.* STEVE's *arm is around* EUNICE's *shoulder and she is sobbing luxuriously and he is cooing love-*

words. There is a murmur of thunder as they go slowly upstairs in a tight embrace.]

STANLEY [*to* STELLA] I'll wait for you at the Four Deuces!

STELLA Hey! Don't I rate one kiss?

STANLEY Not in front of your sister.

[*He goes out.* BLANCHE *rises from her chair. She seems faint; looks about her with an expression of almost panic.*]

BLANCHE Stella! What have you heard about me?

STELLA Huh?

BLANCHE What have people been telling you about me?

STELLA Telling?

BLANCHE You haven't heard any—unkind—gossip about me?

STELLA Why, no, Blanche, of course not!

BLANCHE Honey, there was—a good deal of talk in Laurel.

STELLA About *you*, Blanche?

BLANCHE I wasn't so good the last two years or so, after Belle Reve had started to slip through my fingers.

STELLA All of us do things we—

BLANCHE I never was hard or self-sufficient enough. When people are soft—soft people have got to shimmer and glow—they've got to put on soft colors, the colors of butterfly wings, and put a—paper lantern over the light. . . . It isn't enough to be soft. You've got to be soft *and attractive*. And I—I'm fading now! I don't know how much longer I can turn the trick.

[*The afternoon has faded to dusk.* STELLA *goes into the bedroom and turns on the light under the paper lantern. She holds a bottled soft drink in her hand.*]

BLANCHE Have you been listening to me?

STELLA I don't listen to you when you are being morbid! [*She advances with the bottled Coke.*]

BLANCHE [*with abrupt change to gaiety*] Is that Coke for me?

STELLA Not for anyone else!

BLANCHE Why, you precious thing, you! Is it just Coke?

STELLA [*turning*] You mean you want a shot in it!

BLANCHE Well, honey, a shot never does a Coke any harm! Let me! You mustn't wait on me!

STELLA I like to wait on you, Blanche. It makes it seem more like home. [*She goes into the kitchen, finds a glass and pours a shot of whiskey into it.*]

BLANCHE I have to admit I love to be waited on . . .

[*She rushes into the bedroom.* STELLA *goes to her with the glass.* BLANCHE *suddenly clutches* STELLA's *free hand with a moaning sound and presses the hand to her lips.* STELLA *is embarrassed by her show of emotion.* BLANCHE *speaks in a choked voice.*]

You're—you're—so *good* to me! And I—

STELLA Blanche.

BLANCHE I know, I won't! You hate me to talk sentimental! But honey, *believe* I feel things more than I *tell* you! I *won't* stay long! I won't, I *promise* I—

STELLA Blanche!

BLANCHE [*hysterically*]   I won't, I promise, *I'll* go! Go *soon!* I will *really!* I *won't* hang around until he—throws me out . . .

STELLA   Now will you stop talking foolish?

BLANCHE   Yes, honey. Watch how you pour—that fizzy stuff foams over!
[BLANCHE *laughs shrilly and grabs the glass, but her hand shakes so it almost slips from her grasp.* STELLA *pours the Coke into the glass. It foams over and spills.* BLANCHE *gives a piercing cry.*]

STELLA [*shocked by the cry*]   Heavens!

BLANCHE   Right on my pretty white skirt!

STELLA   Oh . . . Use my hanky. Blot gently.

BLANCHE [*slowly recovering*]   I know—gently—gently . . .

STELLA   Did it stain?

BLANCHE   Not a bit. Ha-ha! Isn't that lucky? [*She sits down shakily, taking a grateful drink. She holds the glass in both hands and continues to laugh a little.*]

STELLA   Why did you scream like that?

BLANCHE   I don't know why I screamed! [*continuing nervously*] Mitch— Mitch is coming at seven. I guess I am just feeling nervous about our relations. [*She begins to talk rapidly and breathlessly.*] He hasn't gotten a thing but a good-night kiss, that's all I have given him, Stella. I want his respect. And men don't want anything they get too easy. But on the other hand men lose interest quickly. Especially when the girl is over—thirty. They think a girl over thirty ought to—the vulgar term is—"put out." . . . And I—I'm not "putting out." Of course he—he doesn't know—I mean I haven't informed him—of my real age!

STELLA   Why are you sensitive about your age?

BLANCHE   Because of hard knocks my vanity's been given. What I mean is—he thinks I'm sort of—prim and proper, you know! [*She laughs out sharply.*] I want to *deceive* him enough to make him—want me . . .

STELLA   Blanche, do you want *him?*

BLANCHE   I want to *rest!* I want to breathe quietly again! Yes—I *want* Mitch . . . *very badly!* Just think! If it happens! I can leave here and not be anyone's problem . . .
[STANLEY *comes around the corner with a drink under his belt.*]

STANLEY [*bawling*]   Hey, Steve! Hey, Eunice! Hey, Stella!
[*There are joyous calls from above. Trumpet and drums are heard from around the corner.*]

STELLA [*kissing* BLANCHE *impulsively*]   It *will* happen!

BLANCHE [*doubtfully*]   It will?

STELLA   It *will!* [*She goes across into the kitchen, looking back at* BLANCHE.] It will, honey, *it will*. . . . But don't take another drink! [*Her voice catches as she goes out the door to meet her husband.*]
[BLANCHE *sinks faintly back in her chair with her drink.* EUNICE *shrieks with laughter and runs down the steps.* STEVE *bounds after her with goat-like screeches and chases her around corner.* STANLEY *and* STELLA *twine arms as they follow, laughing. Dusk settles deeper. The music from the Four Deuces is slow and blue.*]

BLANCHE   Ah, me, ah, me, ah, me . . .
[*Her eyes fall shut and the palm leaf fan drops from her fingers. She slaps her hand on the chair arm a couple of times. There is a little glimmer*]

of lightning about the building. A YOUNG MAN *comes along the street and rings the bell.*]

BLANCHE   Come in.

[*The* YOUNG MAN *appears through the portieres. She regards him with interest.*]

BLANCHE   Well, well! What can I do for *you*?

YOUNG MAN   I'm collecting for *The Evening Star.*

BLANCHE   I didn't know that stars took up collections.

YOUNG MAN   It's the paper.

BLANCHE   I know, I was joking—feebly! Will you—have a drink?

YOUNG MAN   No, ma'am. No, thank you. I can't drink on the job.

BLANCHE   Oh, well, now, let's see. . . . No, I don't have a dime! I'm not the lady of the house. I'm her sister from Mississippi. I'm one of those poor relations you've heard about.

YOUNG MAN   That's all right. I'll drop by later. [*He starts to go out. She approaches a little.*]

BLANCHE   Hey! [*He turns back shyly. She puts a cigarette in a long holder.*] Could you give me a light? [*She crosses toward him. They meet at the door between the two rooms.*]

YOUNG MAN   Sure. [*He takes out a lighter.*] This doesn't always work.

BLANCHE   It's temperamental? [*It flares.*] Ah!—thank you. [*He starts away again.*] Hey! [*He turns again, still more uncertainly. She goes close to him.*] Uh—what time is it?

YOUNG MAN   Fifteen of seven, ma'am.

BLANCHE   So late? Don't you just love these long rainy afternoons in New Orleans when an hour isn't just an hour—but a little piece of eternity dropped into your hands—and who knows what to do with it? [*She touches his shoulders.*] You—uh—didn't get wet in the rain?

YOUNG MAN   No, ma'am. I stepped inside.

BLANCHE   In a drugstore? And had a soda?

YOUNG MAN   Uh-huh.

BLANCHE   Chocolate?

YOUNG MAN   No, ma'am. Cherry.

BLANCHE [*laughing*]   Cherry!

YOUNG MAN   A cherry soda.

BLANCHE   You make my mouth water. [*She touches his cheek lightly, and smiles. Then she goes to the trunk.*]

YOUNG MAN   Well, I'd better be going—

BLANCHE [*stopping him*]   Young man!

[*He turns. She takes a large, gossamer scarf from the trunk and drapes it about her shoulders. In the ensuing pause, the "Blue Piano" is heard. It continues through the rest of this scene and the opening of the next. The young man clears his throat and looks yearningly at the door.*]

Young man! Young, young, young man! Has anyone ever told you that you look like a young Prince out of the Arabian Nights?

[*The* YOUNG MAN *laughs uncomfortably and stands like a bashful kid.* BLANCHE *speaks softly to him.*]

Well, you do, honey lamb! Come here. I want to kiss you, just once, softly and sweetly on your mouth!

[*Without waiting for him to accept, she crosses quickly to him and presses her lips to his.*]

Now run along, now, quickly! It would be nice to keep you, but I've got to be good—and keep my hands off children.

[*He stares at her a moment. She opens the door for him and blows a kiss at him as he goes down the steps with a dazed look. She stands there a little dreamily after he has disappeared. Then* MITCH *appears around the corner with a bunch of roses.*]

BLANCHE [*gaily*] Look who's coming! My Rosenkavalier! Bow to me first . . . now present them! Ahhhh—Merciiii![1]

[*She looks at him over them, coquettishly pressing them to her lips. He beams at her self-consciously.*]

Scene Six

It is about two A.M *on the same evening. The outer wall of the building is visible.* BLANCHE *and* MITCH *come in. The utter exhaustion which only a neurasthenic personality can know is evident in* BLANCHE'S *voice and manner.* MITCH *is stolid but depressed. They have probably been out to the amusement park on Lake Pontchartrain, for* MITCH *is bearing, upside down, a plaster statuette of Mae West, the sort of prize won at shooting galleries and carnival games of chance.*

BLANCHE [*stopping lifelessly at the steps*] Well—[MITCH *laughs uneasily.*] Well . . .

MITCH I guess it must be pretty late—and you're tired.

BLANCHE Even the hot tamale man has deserted the street, and he hangs on till the end. [MITCH *laughs uneasily again.*] How will you get home?

MITCH I'll walk over to Bourbon and catch an owl-car.

BLANCHE [*laughing grimly*] Is that streetcar named Desire still grinding along the tracks at this hour?

MITCH [*heavily*] I'm afraid you haven't gotten much fun out of this evening, Blanche.

BLANCHE I spoiled it for *you.*

MITCH No, you didn't, but I felt all the time that I wasn't giving you much—entertainment.

BLANCHE I simply couldn't rise to the occasion. That was all. I don't think I've ever tried so hard to be gay and made such a dismal mess of it. I get ten points for trying!—I *did* try.

MITCH Why did you try if you didn't feel like it, Blanche?

BLANCHE I was just obeying the law of nature.

MITCH Which law is that?

BLANCHE The one that says the lady must entertain the gentleman—or no dice! See if you can locate my door key in this purse. When I'm so tired my fingers are all thumbs!

MITCH [*rooting in her purse*] This it?

BLANCHE No, honey, that's the key to my trunk which I must soon be packing.

MITCH You mean you are leaving here soon?

BLANCHE I've outstayed my welcome.

1. "Merci": thank you (French). "My Rosenkavalier": Knight of the Rose (German); title of a romantic opera (1911) by Richard Strauss.

MITCH   This it?

[*The music fades away.*]

BLANCHE   Eureka! Honey, you open the door while I take a last look at the sky. [*She leans on the porch rail. He opens the door and stands awkwardly behind her.*] I'm looking for the Pleiades, the Seven Sisters, but these girls are not out tonight. Oh, yes they are, there they are! God bless them! All in a bunch going home from their little bridge party. . . . Y' get the door open? Good boy! I guess you—want to go now . . .

[*He shuffles and coughs a little.*]

MITCH   Can I—uh—kiss you—good night?

BLANCHE   Why do you always ask me if you may?

MITCH   I don't know whether you want me to or not.

BLANCHE   Why should you be so doubtful?

MITCH   That night when we parked by the lake and I kissed you, you—

BLANCHE   Honey, it wasn't the kiss I objected to. I liked the kiss very much. It was the other little—familiarity—that I—felt obliged to—discourage. . . . I didn't resent it! Not a bit in the world! In fact, I was somewhat flattered that you—desired me! But, honey, you know as well as I do that a single girl, a girl alone in the world, has got to keep a firm hold on her emotions or she'll be lost!

MITCH   [*solemnly*]   Lost?

BLANCHE   I guess you are used to girls that like to be lost. The kind that get lost immediately, on the first date!

MITCH   I like you to be exactly the way that you are, because in all my— experience—I have never known anyone like you.

[BLANCHE *looks at him gravely; then she bursts into laughter and then claps a hand to her mouth.*]

MITCH   Are you laughing at me?

BLANCHE   No, honey. The lord and lady of the house have not yet returned, so come in. We'll have a nightcap. Let's leave the lights off. Shall we?

MITCH   You just—do what you want to.

[BLANCHE *precedes him into the kitchen. The outer wall of the building disappears and the interiors of the two rooms can be dimly seen.*]

BLANCHE   [*remaining in the first room*]   The other room's more comfortable—go on in. This crashing around in the dark is my search for some liquor.

MITCH   You want a drink?

BLANCHE   I want *you* to have a drink! You have been so anxious and solemn all evening, and so have I; we have both been anxious and solemn and now for these few last remaining moments of our lives together—I want to create—*joie de vivre!* I'm lighting a candle.

MITCH   That's good.

BLANCHE   We are going to be very Bohemian. We are going to pretend that we are sitting in a little artists' cafe on the Left Bank in Paris! [*She lights a candle stub and puts it in a bottle.*] *Je suis la Dame aux Camellias! Vous êtes—Armand!*[2] Understand French?

MITCH   [*heavily*]   Naw. Naw, I—

2. I am the Lady of the Camellias! You are— Armand! (French). Both are characters in the popular romantic play *La Dame aux Camélias* (1852) by the French author Alexandre Dumas *fils;* she is a courtesan who gives up her true love, Armand.

BLANCHE   *Voulez-vous couchez avec moi ce soir? Vous ne comprenez pas? Ah, quelle dommage!*[3]—I mean it's a damned good thing. . . . I've found some liquor! Just enough for two shots without any dividends, honey . . .

MITCH [*heavily*]   That's—good.

[*She enters the bedroom with the drinks and the candle.*]

BLANCHE   Sit down! Why don't you take off your coat and loosen your collar?

MITCH   I better leave it on.

BLANCHE   No. I want you to be comfortable.

MITCH   I am ashamed of the way I perspire. My shirt is sticking to me.

BLANCHE   Perspiration is healthy. If people didn't perspire they would die in five minutes. [*She takes his coat from him.*] This is a nice coat. What kind of material is it?

MITCH   They call that stuff alpaca.

BLANCHE   Oh. Alpaca.

MITCH   It's very light-weight alpaca.

BLANCHE   Oh. Light-weight alpaca.

MITCH   I don't like to wear a wash-coat even in summer because I sweat through it.

BLANCHE   Oh.

MITCH   And it don't look neat on me. A man with a heavy build has got to be careful of what he puts on him so he don't look too clumsy.

BLANCHE   You are not too heavy.

MITCH   You don't think I am?

BLANCHE   You are not the delicate type. You have a massive bone-structure and a very imposing physique.

MITCH   Thank you. Last Christmas I was given a membership to the New Orleans Athletic Club.

BLANCHE   Oh, good.

MITCH   It was the finest present I ever was given. I work out there with the weights and I swim and I keep myself fit. When I started there, I was getting soft in the belly but now my belly is hard. It is so hard now that a man can punch me in the belly and it don't hurt me. Punch me! Go on! See? [*She pokes lightly at him.*]

BLANCHE   Gracious. [*Her hand touches her chest.*]

MITCH   Guess how much I weigh, Blanche?

BLANCHE   Oh, I'd say in the vicinity of—one hundred and eighty?

MITCH   Guess again.

BLANCHE   Not that much?

MITCH   No. More.

BLANCHE   Well, you're a tall man and you can carry a good deal of weight without looking awkward.

MITCH   I weigh two hundred and seven pounds and I'm six feet one and one half inches tall in my bare feet—without shoes on. And that is what I weigh stripped.

BLANCHE   Oh, my goodness, me! It's awe-inspiring.

MITCH [*embarrassed*]   My weight is not a very interesting subject to talk about. [*He hesitates for a moment.*] What's yours?

---

3. Would you like to sleep with me this evening? You don't understand? Ah, what a pity! (French).

BLANCHE   My weight?

MITCH   Yes.

BLANCHE   Guess!

MITCH   Let me lift you.

BLANCHE   Samson![4] Go on, lift me. [*He comes behind her and puts his hands on her waist and raises her lightly off the ground.*] Well?

MITCH   You are light as a feather.

BLANCHE   Ha-ha! [*He lowers her but keeps his hands on her waist.* BLANCHE *speaks with an affectation of demureness.*] You may release me now.

MITCH   Huh?

BLANCHE [*gaily*]   I said unhand me, sir. [*He fumblingly embraces her. Her voice sounds gently reproving.*] Now, Mitch. Just because Stanley and Stella aren't at home is no reason why you shouldn't behave like a gentleman.

MITCH   Just give me a slap whenever I step out of bounds.

BLANCHE   That won't be necessary. You're a natural gentleman, one of the very few that are left in the world. I don't want you to think that I am severe and old maid school-teacherish or anything like that. It's just—well—

MITCH   Huh?

BLANCHE   I guess it is just that I have—old-fashioned ideals! [*She rolls her eyes, knowing he cannot see her face.* MITCH *goes to the front door. There is a considerable silence between them.* BLANCHE *sighs and* MITCH *coughs self-consciously.*]

MITCH [*finally*]   Where's Stanley and Stella tonight?

BLANCHE   They have gone out. With Mr. and Mrs. Hubbell upstairs.

MITCH   Where did they go?

BLANCHE   I think they were planning to go to a midnight prevue at Loew's State.

MITCH   We should all go out together some night.

BLANCHE   No. That wouldn't be a good plan.

MITCH   Why not?

BLANCHE   You are an old friend of Stanley's?

MITCH   We was together in the Two-forty-first.[5]

BLANCHE   I guess he talks to you frankly?

MITCH   Sure.

BLANCHE   Has he talked to you about me?

BLANCHE   Oh—not very much.

BLANCHE   The way you say that, I suspect that he has.

MITCH   No, he hasn't said much.

BLANCHE   But what he *has* said. What would you say his attitude toward me was?

MITCH   Why do you want to ask that?

BLANCHE   Well—

MITCH   Don't you get along with him?

BLANCHE   What do you think?

MITCH   I don't think he understands you.

BLANCHE   That is putting it mildly. If it weren't for Stella about to have a baby, I wouldn't be able to endure things here.

---

4. Legendary strong man, in the Old Testament.   5. Battalion of engineers, in World War II.

MITCH   He isn't—nice to you?

BLANCHE   He is insufferably rude. Goes out of his way to offend me.

MITCH   In what way, Blanche?

BLANCHE   Why, in every conceivable way.

MITCH   I'm surprised to hear that.

BLANCHE   Are you?

MITCH   Well, I—don't see how anybody could be rude to you.

BLANCHE   It's really a pretty frightful situation. You see, there's no privacy here. There's just these portieres between the two rooms at night. He stalks through the rooms in his underwear at night. And I have to ask him to close the bathroom door. That sort of commonness isn't necessary. You probably wonder why I don't move out. Well, I'll tell you frankly. A teacher's salary is barely sufficient for her living expenses. I didn't save a penny last year and so I had to come here for the summer. That's why I have to put up with my sister's husband. And he has to put up with me, apparently so much against his wishes. . . . Surely he must have told you how much he hates me!

MITCH   I don't think he hates you.

BLANCHE   He hates me. Or why would he insult me? The first time I laid eyes on him I thought to myself, that man is my executioner! That man will destroy me, unless——

MITCH   Blanche—

BLANCHE   Yes, honey?

MITCH   Can I ask you a question?

BLANCHE   Yes. What?

MITCH   How old are you?
    [*She makes a nervous gesture.*]

BLANCHE   Why do you want to know?

MITCH   I talked to my mother about you and she said, "How old is Blanche?" And I wasn't able to tell her. [*There is another pause.*]

BLANCHE   You talked to your mother about me?

MITCH   Yes.

BLANCHE   Why?

MITCH   I told my mother how nice you were, and I liked you.

BLANCHE   Were you sincere about that?

MITCH   You know I was.

BLANCHE   Why did your mother want to know my age?

MITCH   Mother is sick.

BLANCHE   I'm sorry to hear it. Badly?

MITCH   She won't live long. Maybe just a few months.

BLANCHE   Oh.

MITCH   She worries because I'm not settled.

BLANCHE   Oh.

MITCH   She wants me to be settled down before she—[*His voice is hoarse and he clears his throat twice, shuffling nervously around with his hands in and out of his pockets.*]

BLANCHE   You love her very much, don't you?

MITCH   Yes.

BLANCHE   I think you have a great capacity for devotion. You will be lonely when she passes on, won't you? [MITCH *clears his throat and nods.*] I understand what that is.

MITCH   To be lonely?

BLANCHE   I loved someone, too, and the person I loved I lost.

MITCH   Dead? [*She crosses to the window and sits on the sill, looking out. She pours herself another drink.*] A man?

BLANCHE   He was a boy, just a boy, when I was a very young girl. When I was sixteen, I made the discovery—love. All at once and much, much too completely. It was like you suddenly turned a blinding light on something that had always been half in shadow, that's how it struck the world for me. But I was unlucky. Deluded. There was something different about the boy, a nervousness, a softness and tenderness which wasn't like a man's, although he wasn't the least bit effeminate looking—still— that thing was there. . . . He came to me for help. I didn't know that. I didn't find out anything till after our marriage when we'd run away and come back and all I knew was I'd failed him in some mysterious way and wasn't able to give the help he needed but couldn't speak of! He was in the quicksands and clutching at me—but I wasn't holding him out, I was slipping in with him! I didn't know that. I didn't know anything except I loved him unendurably but without being able to help him or help myself. Then I found out. In the worst of all possible ways. By coming suddenly into a room that I thought was empty—which wasn't empty, but had two people in it . . . the boy I had married and an older man who had been his friend for years . . .

[*A locomotive is heard approaching outside. She claps her hands to her ears and crouches over. The headlight of the locomotive glares into the room as it thunders past. As the noise recedes she straightens slowly and continues speaking.*]

Afterward we pretended that nothing had been discovered. Yes, the three of us drove out to Moon Lake Casino, very drunk and laughing all the way.

[*Polka music sounds, in a minor key faint with distance.*]

We danced the Varsouviana![6] Suddenly in the middle of the dance the boy I had married broke away from me and ran out of the casino. A few moments later—a shot!

[*The polka stops abruptly.* BLANCHE *rises stiffly. Then, the polka resumes in a major key.*]

I ran out—all did!—all ran and gathered about the terrible thing at the edge of the lake! I couldn't get near for the crowding. Then somebody caught my arm. "Don't go any closer! Come back! You don't want to see!" See? See what! Then I heard voices say—Allan! Allan! The Grey boy! He'd stuck the revolver into his mouth, and fired—so that the back of his head had been—blown away!

[*She sways and covers her face.*]

It was because—on the dance floor—unable to stop myself—I'd suddenly said—"I saw! I know! You disgust me . . ." And then the searchlight which had been turned on the world was turned off again and never for one moment since has there been any light that's stronger than this— kitchen—candle . . .

[MITCH *gets up awkwardly and moves toward her a little. The polka music increases.* MITCH *stands beside her.*]

---

6. Fast Polish dance, similar to the polka.

MITCH [*drawing her slowly into his arms*] You need somebody. And I need somebody, too. Could it be—you and me, Blanche?

> [*She stares at him vacantly for a moment. Then with a soft cry huddles in his embrace. She makes a sobbing effort to speak but the words won't come. He kisses her forehead and her eyes and finally her lips. The Polka tune fades out. Her breath is drawn and released in long, grateful sobs.*]

BLANCHE Sometimes—there's God—so quickly!

Scene Seven

It is late afternoon in mid-September.

The portieres are open and a table is set for a birthday supper, with cake and flowers.

STELLA *is completing the decorations as* STANLEY *comes in.*

STANLEY What's all this stuff for?

STELLA Honey, it's Blanche's birthday.

STANLEY She here?

STELLA In the bathroom.

STANLEY [*mimicking*] "Washing out some things"?

STELLA I reckon so.

STANLEY How long she been in there?

STELLA All afternoon.

STANLEY [*mimicking*] "Soaking in a hot tub"?

STELLA Yes.

STANLEY Temperature 100 on the nose, and she soaks herself in a hot tub.

STELLA She says it cools her off for the evening.

STANLEY And you run out an' get her cokes, I suppose? And serve 'em to Her Majesty in the tub? [STELLA *shrugs.*] Set down here a minute.

STELLA Stanley, I've got things to do.

STANLEY Set down! I've got th' dope on your big sister, Stella.

STELLA Stanley, stop picking on Blanche.

STANLEY That girl calls *me* common!

STELLA Lately you been doing all you can think of to rub her the wrong way, Stanley, and Blanche is sensitive and you've got to realize that Blanche and I grew up under very different circumstances than you did.

STANLEY So I been told. And told and told and told! You know she's been feeding us a pack of lies here?

STELLA No, I don't, and—

STANLEY Well, she has, however. But now the cat's out of the bag! I found out some things!

STELLA What—things?

STANLEY Things I already suspected. But now I got proof from the most reliable sources—which I have checked on!

> [BLANCHE *is singing in the bathroom a saccharine popular ballad which is used contrapuntally with* STANLEY's *speech.*]

STELLA [*to* STANLEY] Lower your voice!

STANLEY Some canary bird, huh!

STELLA Now please tell me quietly what you think you've found out about my sister.

STANLEY Lie Number One: All this squeamishness she puts on! You should just know the line she's been feeding to Mitch. He thought she had never been more than kissed by a fellow! But Sister Blanche is no lily! Ha-ha! Some lily she is!

STELLA What have you heard and who from?

STANLEY Our supply-man down at the plant has been going through Laurel for years and he knows all about her and everybody else in the town of Laurel knows all about her. She is as famous in Laurel as if she was the President of the United States, only she is not respected by any party! This supply-man stops at a hotel called the Flamingo.

BLANCHE [singing blithely] "Say, it's only a paper moon, Sailing over a cardboard sea—But it wouldn't be make-believe If you believed in me!"[7]

STELLA What about the—Flamingo?

STANLEY She stayed there, too.

STELLA My sister lived at Belle Reve.

STANLEY This is after the home-place had slipped through her lily-white fingers! She moved to the Flamingo! A second-class hotel which has the advantage of not interfering in the private social life of the personalities there! The Flamingo is used to all kinds of goings-on. But even the management of the Flamingo was impressed by Dame Blanche! In fact they was so impressed by Dame Blanche that they requested her to turn in her room key—for permanently! This happened a couple of weeks before she showed here.

BLANCHE [singing] "It's a Barnum and Bailey world, Just as phony as it can be—But it wouldn't be make-believe If you believed in me!"

STELLA What—contemptible—lies!

STANLEY Sure, I can see how you would be upset by this. She pulled the wool over your eyes as much as Mitch's!

STELLA It's pure invention! There's not a word of truth in it and if if I were a man and this creature had dared to invent such things in my presence—

BLANCHE [singing] "Without your love, It's a honky-tonk parade! Without your love, It's a melody played In a penny arcade . . ."

STANLEY Honey, I told you I thoroughly checked on these stories! Now wait till I finished. The trouble with Dame Blanche was that she couldn't put on her act any more in Laurel! They got wised up after two or three dates with her and then they quit, and she goes on to another, the same old line, same old act, same old hooey! But the town was too small for this to go on forever! And as time went by she became a town character. Regarded as not just different but downright loco—nuts. [STELLA draws back.] And for the last year or two she has been washed up like poison. That's why she's here this summer, visiting royalty, putting on all this act—because she's practically told by the mayor to get out of town! Yes, did you know there was an army camp near Laurel and your sister's was one of the places called "Out-of-Bounds"?

BLANCHE "It's only a paper moon, Just as phony as it can be—But it wouldn't be make-believe If you believed in me!"

STANLEY Well, so much for her being such a refined and particular type of girl. Which brings us to Lie Number Two.

STELLA I don't want to hear any more!

7. From "It's Only a Paper Moon" (1933), a popular song by Harold Arlen.

STANLEY   She's not going back to teach school! In fact I am willing to bet you that she never had no idea of returning to Laurel! She didn't resign temporarily from the high school because of her nerves! No, siree, Bob! She didn't. They kicked her out of that high school before the spring term ended—and I hate to tell you the reason that step was taken! A seventeen-year-old boy—she'd gotten mixed up with!

BLANCHE   "It's a Barnum and Bailey world, Just as phony as it can be—"
[*In the bathroom the water goes on loud; little breathless cries and peals of laughter are heard as if a child were frolicking in the tub.*]

STELLA   This is making me—sick!

STANLEY   The boy's dad learned about it and got in touch with the high school superintendent. Boy, oh, boy, I'd like to have been in that office when Dame Blanche was called on the carpet! I'd like to have seen her trying to squirm out of that one! But they had her on the hook good and proper that time and she knew that the jig was all up! They told her she better move on to some fresh territory. Yep, it was practickly a town ordinance passed against her!
[*The bathroom door is opened and* BLANCHE *thrusts her head out, holding a towel about her hair.*]

BLANCHE   Stella!

STELLA   [*faintly*]   Yes, Blanche?

BLANCHE   Give me another bath-towel to dry my hair with. I've just washed it.

STELLA   Yes, Blanche. [*She crosses in a dazed way from the kitchen to the bathroom door with a towel.*]

BLANCHE   What's the matter, honey?

STELLA   Matter? Why?

BLANCHE   You have such a strange expression on your face!

STELLA   Oh—[*she tries to laugh*] I guess I'm a little tired!

BLANCHE   Why don't you bathe, too, soon as I get out?

STANLEY   [*calling from the kitchen*]   How soon is that going to be?

BLANCHE   Not so terribly long! Possess your soul in patience!

STANLEY   It's not my soul, it's my kidneys I'm worried about!
[BLANCHE *slams the door.* STANLEY *laughs harshly.* STELLA *comes slowly back into the kitchen.*]

STANLEY   Well, what do you think of it?

STELLA   I don't believe all of those stories and I think your supply-man was mean and rotten to tell them. It's possible that some of the things he said are partly true. There are things about my sister I don't approve of— things that caused sorrow at home. She was always—flighty!

STANLEY   Flighty!

STELLA   But when she was young, very young, she married a boy who wrote poetry. . . . He was extremely good-looking. I think Blanche didn't just love him but worshipped the ground he walked on! Adored him and thought him almost too fine to be human! But then she found out—

STANLEY   What?

STELLA   This beautiful and talented young man was a degenerate. Didn't your supply-man give you that information?

STANLEY   All we discussed was recent history. That must have been a pretty long time ago.

STELLA   Yes, it was—a pretty long time ago . . .

[STANLEY *comes up and takes her by the shoulders rather gently. She gently withdraws from him. Automatically she starts sticking little pink candles in the birthday cake.*]

STANLEY   How many candles you putting in that cake?

STELLA   I'll stop at twenty-five.

STANLEY   Is company expected?

STELLA   We asked Mitch to come over for cake and ice-cream.

[STANLEY *looks a little uncomfortable. He lights a cigarette from the one he has just finished.*]

STANLEY   I wouldn't be expecting Mitch over tonight.

[STELLA *pauses in her occupation with candles and looks slowly around at* STANLEY.]

STELLA   Why?

STANLEY   Mitch is a buddy of mine. We were in the same outfit together—Two-forty-first Engineers. We work in the same plant and now on the same bowling team. You think I could face him if—

STELLA   Stanley Kowalski, did you—did you repeat what that—?

STANLEY   You're goddam right I told him! I'd have that on my conscience the rest of my life if I knew all that stuff and let my best friend get caught!

STELLA   Is Mitch through with her?

STANLEY   Wouldn't you be if—?

STELLA   I said, *Is Mitch through with her?*

[BLANCHE's *voice is lifted again, serenely as a bell. She sings* "But it wouldn't be make-believe If you believed in me."]

STANLEY   No, I don't think he's necessarily through with her—just wised up!

STELLA   Stanley, she thought Mitch was—going to—going to marry her. I was hoping so, too.

STANLEY   Well, he's not going to marry her. Maybe he *was,* but he's not going to jump in a tank with a school of sharks—now! [*He rises.*] Blanche! Oh, Blanche! Can I please get in my bathroom? [*There is a pause.*]

BLANCHE   Yes, indeed, sir! Can you wait one second while I dry?

STANLEY   Having waited one hour I guess one second ought to pass in a hurry.

STELLA   And she hasn't got her job? Well, what will she do!

STANLEY   She's not stayin' here after Tuesday. You know that, don't you? Just to make sure I bought her ticket myself. A bus ticket.

STELLA   In the first place, Blanche wouldn't go on a bus.

STANLEY   She'll go on a bus and like it.

STELLA   No, she won't, no, she won't, Stanley!

STANLEY   *She'll go!* Period. P.S. She'll go *Tuesday!*

STELLA [*slowly*]   What'll—she—do? What on earth will she—*do!*

STANLEY   Her future is mapped out for her.

STELLA   What do you mean?

[BLANCHE *sings.*]

STANLEY   Hey, canary bird! Toots! Get OUT of the BATHROOM!

[*The bathroom door flies open and* BLANCHE *emerges with a gay peal of laughter, but as* STANLEY *crosses past her, a frightened look appears in her face, almost a look of panic. He doesn't look at her but slams the bathroom door shut as he goes in.*

BLANCHE [*snatching up a hairbrush*] Oh, I feel so good after my long, hot bath, I feel so good and cool and—rested!

STELLA [*sadly and doubtfully from the kitchen*] Do you, Blanche?

BLANCHE [*snatching up a hairbrush*] Yes, I do, so refreshed! [*She tinkles her highball glass.*] A hot bath and a long, cold drink always give me a brand new outlook on life! [*She looks through the portieres at* STELLA, *standing between them, and slowly stops brushing.*] Something has happened!—What is it?

STELLA [*turning away quickly*] Why, nothing has happened, Blanche.

BLANCHE You're lying! Something has!

[*She stares fearfully at* STELLA, *who pretends to be busy at the table. The distant piano goes into a hectic breakdown.*]

Scene Eight

Three quarters of an hour later.

The view through the big windows is fading gradually into a still-golden dusk. A torch of sunlight blazes on the side of a big water-tank or oil-drum across the empty lot toward the business district which is now pierced by pinpoints of lighted windows or windows reflecting the sunset.

The three people are completing a dismal birthday supper. STANLEY *looks sullen.* STELLA *is embarrassed and sad.*

BLANCHE *has a tight, artificial smile on her drawn face. There is a fourth place at the table which is left vacant.*

BLANCHE [*suddenly*] Stanley, tell us a joke, tell us a funny story to make us all laugh. I don't know what's the matter, we're all so solemn. Is it because I've been stood up by my beau?

[STELLA *laughs feebly.*]

It's the first time in my entire experience with men, and I've had a good deal of all sorts, that I've actually been stood up by anybody! Ha-ha! I don't know how to take it. . . . Tell us a funny little story, Stanley! Something to help us out.

STANLEY I didn't think you liked my stories, Blanche.

BLANCHE I like them when they're amusing but not indecent.

STANLEY I don't know any refined enough for your taste.

BLANCHE Then let me tell one.

STELLA Yes, you tell one, Blanche. You used to know lots of good stories.
[*The music fades.*]

BLANCHE Let me see, now. . . . I must run through my repertoire! Oh, yes—I love parrot stories! Do you all like parrot stories? Well, this one's about the old maid and the parrot. This old maid, she had a parrot that cursed a blue streak and knew more vulgar expressions than Mr. Kowalski!

STANLEY Huh.

BLANCHE And the only way to hush the parrot up was to put the cover back on its cage so it would think it was night and go back to sleep. Well, one morning the old maid had just uncovered the parrot for the day— when who should she see coming up the front walk but the preacher! Well, she rushed back to the parrot and slipped the cover back on the cage and then she let in the preacher. And the parrot was perfectly still, just as quiet as a mouse, but just as she was asking the preacher how much sugar he wanted in his coffee—the parrot broke the silence with a loud—[*She whistles.*]—and said—"God *damn,* but that was a short day!"

[*She throws back her head and laughs.* STELLA *also makes an ineffectual effort to seem amused.* STANLEY *pays no attention to the story but reaches way over the table to spear his fork into the remaining chop which he eats with his fingers.*]

BLANCHE   Apparently Mr. Kowalski was not amused.

STELLA   Mr. Kowalski is too busy making a pig of himself to think of anything else!

STANLEY   That's right, baby.

STELLA   Your face and your fingers are disgustingly greasy. Go and wash up and then help me clear the table.

[*He hurls a plate to the floor.*]

STANLEY   That's how I'll clear the table! [*He seizes her arm.*] Don't ever talk that way to me! "Pig—Polack—disgusting—vulgar—greasy!"—them kind of words have been on your tongue and your sister's too much around here! What do you two think you are? A pair of queens? Remember what Huey Long[8] said—"Every Man is a King!" And I am the king around here, so don't forget it! [*He hurls a cup and saucer to the floor.*] My place is cleared! You want me to clear your places?

[STELLA *begins to cry weakly.* STANLEY *stalks out on the porch and lights a cigarette. The Negro entertainers around the corner are heard.*]

BLANCHE   What happened while I was bathing? What did he tell you, Stella?

STELLA   Nothing, nothing, nothing!

BLANCHE   I think he told you something about Mitch and me! You know why Mitch didn't come but you won't tell me! [STELLA *shakes her head helplessly.*] I'm going to call him!

STELLA   I wouldn't call him, Blanche.

BLANCHE   I am, I'm going to call him on the phone.

STELLA [*miserably*]   I wish you wouldn't.

BLANCHE   I intend to be given some explanation from someone!

[*She rushes to the phone in the bedroom.* STELLA *goes out on the porch and stares reproachfully at her husband. He grunts and turns away from her.*]

STELLA   I hope you're pleased with your doings. I never had so much trouble swallowing food in my life, looking at that girl's face and the empty chair! [*She cries quietly.*]

BLANCHE [*at the phone*]   Hello. Mr. Mitchell, please. . . . Oh. . . . I would like to leave a number if I may. Magnolia 9047. And say it's important to call. . . . Yes, very important. . . . Thank you.

[*She remains by the phone with a lost, frightened look.* STANLEY *turns slowly back toward his wife and takes her clumsily in his arms.*]

STANLEY   Stell, it's gonna be all right after she goes and after you've had the baby. It's gonna be all right again between you and me the way that it was. You remember the way that it was? Them nights we had together? God, honey, it's gonna be sweet when we can make noise in the night

---

8. Demagogic Louisiana political leader, governor, and senator (1893–1935).

the way that we used to and get the colored lights going with nobody's sister behind the curtains to hear us!

[*Their upstairs neighbors are heard in bellowing laughter at something.* STANLEY *chuckles.*]

Steve an' Eunice . . .

STELLA Come on back in. [*She returns to the kitchen and starts lighting the candles on the white cake.*] Blanche?

BLANCHE Yes. [*She returns from the bedroom to the table in the kitchen.*] Oh, those pretty, pretty little candles! Oh, don't burn them, Stella.

STELLA I certainly will.

[STANLEY *comes back in.*]

BLANCHE You ought to save them for baby's birthdays. Oh, I hope candles are going to glow in his life and I hope that his eyes are going to be like candles, like two blue candles lighted in a white cake!

STANLEY [*sitting down*] What poetry!

BLANCHE [*she pauses reflectively for a moment*] I shouldn't have called him.

STELLA There's lots of things could have happened.

BLANCHE There's no excuse for it, Stella. I don't have to put up with insults. I won't be taken for granted.

STANLEY Goddamn, it's hot in here with the steam from the bathroom.

BLANCHE I've said I was sorry three times. [*The piano fades out.*] I take hot baths for my nerves. Hydrotherapy, they call it. You healthy Polack, without a nerve in your body, of course you don't know what anxiety feels like!

STANLEY I am not a Polack. People from Poland are Poles, not Polacks. But what I am is a one-hundred-per-cent American, born and raised in the greatest country on earth and proud as hell of it, so don't ever call me a Polack.

[*The phone rings.* BLANCHE *rises expectantly.*]

BLANCHE Oh, that's for me, I'm sure.

STANLEY I'm not sure. Keep your seat. [*He crosses leisurely to phone.*] H'lo. Aw, yeh, hello, Mac.

[*He leans against wall, staring insultingly in at* BLANCHE. *She sinks back in her chair with a frightened look.* STELLA *leans over and touches her shoulder.*]

BLANCHE Oh, keep your hands off me, Stella. What is the matter with you? Why do you look at me with that pitying look?

STANLEY [*bawling*] QUIET IN THERE!—We've got a noisy woman on the place.—Go on, Mac. At Riley's? No, I don't wanta bowl at Riley's. I had a little trouble with Riley last week. I'm the team captain, ain't I? All right, then, we're not gonna bowl at Riley's, we're gonna bowl at the West Side or the Gala! All right, Mac. See you!

[*He hangs up and returns to the table.* BLANCHE *fiercely controls herself, drinking quickly from her tumbler of water. He doesn't look at her but reaches in a pocket. Then he speaks slowly and with false amiability.*]

Sister Blanche, I've got a little birthday remembrance for you.

BLANCHE Oh, have you, Stanley? I wasn't expecting any, I—I don't know why Stella wants to observe my birthday! I'd much rather forget it—when you—reach twenty-seven! Well—age is a subject that you'd prefer to—ignore!

STANLEY Twenty-seven?

BLANCHE [*quickly*]   What is it? Is it for *me*?
   [*He is holding a little envelope toward her.*]
STANLEY   Yes, I hope you like it!
BLANCHE   Why, why—Why, it's a—
STANLEY   Ticket! Back to Laurel! On the Greyhound! Tuesday!
   [*The Varsouviana music steals in softly and continues playing.* STELLA
   rises abruptly and turns her back. BLANCHE *tries to smile. Then she tries
   to laugh. Then she gives both up and springs from the table and runs
   into the next room. She clutches her throat and then runs into the bath-
   room. Coughing, gagging sounds are heard.*]
   Well!
STELLA   You didn't need to do that.
STANLEY   Don't forget all that I took off her.
STELLA   You needn't have been so cruel to someone alone as she is.
STANLEY   Delicate piece she is.
STELLA   She is. She was. You didn't know Blanche as a girl. Nobody,
   nobody, was tender and trusting as she was. But people like you abused
   her, and forced her to change.
   [*He crosses into the bedroom, ripping off his shirt, and changes into a
   brilliant silk bowling shirt. She follows him.*]
   Do you think you're going bowling now?
STANLEY   Sure.
STELLA   You're not going bowling. [*She catches hold of his shirt.*] Why did
   you do this to her?
STANLEY   I done nothing to no one. Let go of my shirt. You've torn it.
STELLA   I want to know why. Tell me why.
STANLEY   When we first met, me and you, you thought I was common.
   How right you was, baby. I was common as dirt. You showed me the
   snapshot of the place with the columns. I pulled you down off them
   columns and how you loved it, having them colored lights going! And
   wasn't we happy together, wasn't it all okay till she showed here?
   [STELLA *makes a slight movement. Her look goes suddenly inward as if
   some interior voice had called her name. She begins a slow, shuffling
   progress from the bedroom to the kitchen, leaning and resting on the
   back of the chair and then on the edge of a table with a blind look and
   listening expression.* STANLEY, *finishing with his shirt, is unaware of her
   reaction.*]
   And wasn't we happy together? Wasn't it all okay? Till she showed here.
   Hoity-Toity, describing me as an ape. [*He suddenly notices the change in*
   STELLA.] Hey, what is it, Stel? [*He crosses to her.*]
STELLA [*quietly*]   Take me to the hospital.
   [*He is with her now, supporting her with his arm, murmuring indistin-
   guishably as they go outside.*]

Scene Nine

A while later that evening. BLANCHE *is seated in a tense hunched position in
a bedroom chair that she has recovered with diagonal green and white stripes.
She has on her scarlet satin robe. On the table beside chair is a bottle of liquor
and a glass. The rapid, feverish polka tune, the "Varsouviana," is heard. The*

music is in her mind; she is drinking to escape it and the sense of disaster closing in on her, and she seems to whisper the words of the song. An electric fan is turning back and forth across her.

MITCH comes around the corner in work clothes: blue denim shirt and pants. He is unshaven. He climbs the steps to the door and rings. BLANCHE is startled.

BLANCHE   Who is it, please?
MITCH [*hoarsely*]   Me. Mitch.
   [*The polka tune stops.*]
BLANCHE   Mitch!—Just a minute.
   [*She rushes about frantically, hiding the bottle in a closet, crouching at the mirror and dabbing her face with cologne and powder. She is so excited that her breath is audible as she dashes about. At last she rushes to the door in the kitchen and lets him in.*]
Mitch!—Y'know, I really shouldn't let you in after the treatment I have received from you this evening! So utterly uncavalier! But hello, beautiful!
   [*She offers him her lips. He ignores it and pushes past her into the flat. She looks fearfully after him as he stalks into the bedroom.*]
My, my, what a cold shoulder! And such uncouth apparel! Why, you haven't even shaved! The unforgivable insult to a lady! But I forgive you. I forgive you because it's such a relief to see you. You've stopped that polka tune that I had caught in my head. Have you ever had anything caught in your head? No, of course you haven't, you dumb angel-puss, you'd never get anything awful caught in your head!
   [*He stares at her while she follows him while she talks. It is obvious that he has had a few drinks on the way over.*]
MITCH   Do we have to have that fan on?
BLANCHE   No!
MITCH   I don't like fans.
BLANCHE   Then let's turn it off, honey. I'm not partial to them!
   [*She presses the switch and the fan nods slowly off. She clears her throat uneasily as MITCH plumps himself down on the bed in the bedroom and lights a cigarette.*]
I don't know what there is to drink. I—haven't investigated.
MITCH   I don't want Stan's liquor.
BLANCHE   It isn't Stan's. Everything here isn't Stan's. Some things on the premises are actually mine! How is your mother? Isn't your mother well?
MITCH   Why?
BLANCHE   Something's the matter tonight, but never mind. I won't cross-examine the witness. I'll just—[*She touches her forehead vaguely. The polka tune starts up again.*]—pretend I don't notice anything different about you! That—music again . . .
MITCH   What music?
BLANCHE   The "Varsourviana"! The polka tune they were playing when Allan—Wait!
   [*A distant revolver shot is heard. BLANCHE seems relieved.*]
There now, the shot! It always stops after that.
   [*The polka music dies out again.*]
Yes, now it's stopped.

MITCH Are you boxed out of your mind?

BLANCHE I'll go and see what I can find in the way of—[*She crosses into the closet, pretending to search for the bottle.*] Oh, by the way, excuse me for not being dressed. But I'd practically given you up! Had you forgotten your invitation to supper?

MITCH I wasn't going to see you any more.

BLANCHE Wait a minute. I can't hear what you're saying and you talk so little that when you do say something, I don't want to miss a single syllable of it. . . . What am I looking around here for? Oh, yes—liquor! We've had so much excitement around here this evening that I *am* boxed out of my mind! [*She pretends suddenly to find the bottle. He draws his foot up on the bed and stares at her contemptuously.*] Here's something. Southern Comfort! What is that, I wonder?

MITCH If you don't know, it must belong to Stan.

BLANCHE Take your foot off the bed. It has a light cover on it. Of course you boys don't notice things like that. I've done so much with this place since I've been here.

MITCH I bet you have.

BLANCHE You saw it before I came. Well, look at it now! This room is almost—dainty! I want to keep it that way. I wonder if this stuff ought to be mixed with something? Ummm, it's sweet, so sweet! It's terribly, terribly sweet! Why, it's a *liqueur*, I believe! Yes, that's what it *is*, a liqueur! [MITCH *grunts.*] I'm afraid you won't like it, but try it, and maybe you will.

MITCH I told you already I don't want none of his liquor and I mean it. You ought to lay off his liquor. He says you been lapping it up all summer like a wild cat!

BLANCHE What a fantastic statement! Fantastic of him to say it, fantastic of you to repeat it! I won't descend to the level of such cheap accusations to answer them, even!

MITCH Huh.

BLANCHE What's in your mind? I see something in your eyes!

MITCH [*getting up*] It's dark in here.

BLANCHE I like it dark. The dark is comforting to me.

MITCH I don't think I ever seen you in the light. [BLANCHE *laughs breathlessly.*] That's a fact!

BLANCHE Is it?

MITCH I've never seen you in the afternoon.

BLANCHE Whose fault is that?

MITCH You never want to go out in the afternoon.

BLANCHE Why, Mitch, you're at the plant in the afternoon!

MITCH Not Sunday afternoon. I've asked you to go out with me sometimes on Sundays but you always make an excuse. You never want to go out till after six and then it's always some place that's not lighted much.

BLANCHE There is some obscure meaning in this but I fail to catch it.

MITCH What it means is I've never had a real good look at you, Blanche. Let's turn the light on here.

BLANCHE [*fearfully*] Light? Which light? What for?

MITCH This one with the paper thing on it. [*He tears the paper lantern off the light bulb. She utters a frightened gasp.*]

BLANCHE   What did you do that for?

MITCH   So I can take a look at you good and plain!

BLANCHE   Of course you don't really mean to be insulting!

MITCH   No, just realistic.

BLANCHE   I don't want realism. I want magic! [MITCH *laughs.*] Yes, yes, magic! I try to give that to people. I misrepresent things to them. I don't tell truth, I tell what *ought* to be truth. And if that is sinful, then let me be damned for it!—*Don't turn the light on!*

> [MITCH *crosses to the switch. He turns the light on and stares at her. She cries out and covers her face. He turns the lights off again.*]

MITCH   [*slowly and bitterly*]   I don't mind you being older than what I thought. But all the rest of it—Christ! That pitch about your ideals being so old-fashioned and all the malarkey that you've dished out all summer. Oh, I knew you weren't sixteen any more. But I was a fool enough to believe you was straight.

BLANCHE   Who told you I wasn't—"straight"? My loving brother-in-law. And you believed him.

MITCH   I called him a liar at first. And then I checked on the story. First I asked our supply-man who travels through Laurel. And then I talked directly over long-distance to this merchant.

BLANCHE   Who is this merchant?

MITCH   Kiefaber.

BLANCHE   The merchant Kiefaber of Laurel! I know the man. He whistled at me. I put him in his place. So now for revenge he makes up stories about me.

MITCH   Three people, Kiefaber, Stanley and Shaw, swore to them!

BLANCHE   Rub-a-dub-dub, three men in a tub! And such a filthy tub!

MITCH   Didn't you stay at a hotel called The Flamingo?

BLANCHE   Flamingo? No! Tarantula was the name of it! I stayed at a hotel called The Tarantula Arms!

MITCH   [*stupidly*]   Tarantula?

BLANCHE   Yes, a big spider! That's where I brought my victims. [*She pours herself another drink.*] Yes, I had many intimacies with strangers. After the death of Allan—intimacies with strangers was all I seemed able to fill my empty heart with. . . . I think it was panic, just panic, that drove me from one to another, hunting for some protection—here and there, in the most—unlikely places—even, at last, in a seventeen-year-old boy but—somebody wrote the superintendent about it—"This woman is morally unfit for her position!"

> [*She throws back her head with convulsive, sobbing laughter. Then she repeats the statement, gasps, and drinks.*]

True? Yes, I suppose—unfit somehow—anyway. . . . So I came here. There was nowhere else I could go. I was played out. You know what played out is? My youth was suddenly gone up the water-spout, and—I met you. You said you needed somebody. Well, I needed somebody, too. I thanked God for you, because you seemed to be gentle—a cleft in the rock of the world that I could hide in! But I guess I was asking, hoping—too much! Kiefaber, Stanley and Shaw have tied an old tin can to the tail of the kite.

> [*There is a pause.* MITCH *stares at her dumbly.*]

MITCH   You lied to me, Blanche.

BLANCHE   Don't say I lied to you.

MITCH   Lies, lies, inside and out, all lies.

BLANCHE   Never inside, I didn't lie in my heart . . .

[A VENDOR comes around the corner. She is a blind MEXICAN WOMAN *in a dark shawl, carrying bunches of those gaudy tin flowers that lower-class Mexicans display at funerals and other festive occasions. She is calling barely audibly. Her figure is only faintly visible outside the building.*]

MEXICAN WOMAN   Flores. Flores, Flores para los muertos.[9] Flores. Flores.

BLANCHE   What? Oh! Somebody outside . . . [*She goes to the door, opens it and stares at the* MEXICAN WOMAN.]

MEXICAN WOMAN [*she is at the door and offers* BLANCHE *some of her flowers*]   Flores? Flores para los muertos?

BLANCHE [*frightened*]   No, no! Not now! Not now!

[*She darts back into the apartment, slamming the door.*]

MEXICAN WOMAN [*she turns away and starts to move down the street*]   Flores para los muertos.

[*The polka tune fades in.*]

BLANCHE [*as if to herself*]   Crumble and fade and—regrets—recriminations . . . "If you'd done this, it wouldn't've cost me that!"

MEXICAN WOMAN   Corones[1] para los muertos. Corones . . .

BLANCHE   Legacies! Huh. . . . And other things such as bloodstained pillow-slips—"Her linen needs changing"—"Yes, Mother. But couldn't we get a colored girl to do it?" No, we couldn't of course. Everything gone but the—

MEXICAN WOMAN   Flores.

BLANCHE   Death—I used to sit here and she used to sit over there and death was as close as you are. . . . We didn't dare even admit we had ever heard of it!

MEXICAN WOMAN   Flores para los muertos, flores—flores . . .

BLANCHE   The opposite is desire. So do you wonder? How could you possibly wonder! Not far from Belle Reve, before we had lost Belle Reve, was a camp where they trained young soldiers. On Sunday nights they would go in town to get drunk—

MEXICAN WOMAN [*softly*]   Corones . . .

BLANCHE   —and on the way back they would stagger onto my lawn and call—"Blanche! Blanche!"—the deaf old lady remaining suspected nothing. But sometimes I slipped outside to answer their calls. . . . Later the paddy-wagon would gather them up like daisies . . . the long way home . . .

[*The* MEXICAN WOMAN *turns slowly and drifts back off with her soft mournful cries.* BLANCHE *goes to the dresser and leans forward on it. After a moment,* MITCH *rises and follows her purposefully. The polka music fades away. He places his hands on her waist and tries to turn her about.*]

BLANCHE   What do you want?

MITCH [*fumbling to embrace her*]   What I been missing all summer.

---

9. Flowers for the dead (Spanish).   1. Wreaths (Spanish).

BLANCHE Then marry me, Mitch!

MITCH I don't think I want to marry you any more.

BLANCHE No?

MITCH [*dropping his hands from her waist*] You're not clean enough to bring in the house with my mother.

BLANCHE Go away, then. [*He stares at her.*] Get out of here quick before I start screaming fire! [*Her throat is tightening with hysteria.*] Get out of here quick before I start screaming fire.

[*He still remains staring. She suddenly rushes to the big window with its pale blue square of the soft summer light and cries wildly.*]

Fire! Fire! Fire!

[*With a startled gasp,* MITCH *turns and goes out the outer door, clatters awkwardly down the steps and around the corner of the building.* BLANCHE *staggers back from the window and falls to her knees. The distant piano is slow and blue.*]

Scene Ten

It is a few hours later that night.

BLANCHE *has been drinking fairly steadily since* MITCH *left. She has dragged her wardrobe trunk into the center of the bedroom. It hangs open with flowery dresses thrown across it. As the drinking and packing went on, a mood of hysterical exhilaration came into her and she has decked herself out in a some-what soiled and crumpled white satin evening gown and a pair of scuffed silver slippers with brilliants set in their heels.*

Now she is placing the rhinestone tiara on her head before the mirror of the dressing-table and murmuring excitedly as if to a group of spectral admirers.

BLANCHE How about taking a swim, a moonlight swim at the old rock-quarry? If anyone's sober enough to drive a car! Ha-ha! Best way in the world to stop your head buzzing! Only you've got to be careful to dive where the deep pool is—if you hit a rock you don't come up till tomorrow . . .

[*Tremblingly she lifts the hand mirror for a closer inspection. She catches her breath and slams the mirror face down with such violence that the glass cracks. She moans a little and attempts to rise.* STANLEY *appears around the corner of the building. He still has on the vivid green silk bowling shirt. As he rounds the corner the honky-tonk music is heard. It continues softly throughout the scene. He enters the kitchen, slamming the door. As he peers in at* BLANCHE *he gives a low whistle. He has had a few drinks on the way and has brought some quart beer bottles home with him.*]

BLANCHE How is my sister?

STANLEY She is doing okay.

BLANCHE And how is the baby?

STANLEY [*grinning amiably*] The baby won't come before morning so they told me to go home and get a little shut-eye.

BLANCHE Does that mean we are to be alone in here?

STANLEY Yep. Just me and you, Blanche. Unless you got somebody hid under the bed. What've you got on those fine feathers for?

BLANCHE   Oh, that's right. You left before my wire came.
STANLEY   You got a wire?
BLANCHE   I received a telegram from an old admirer of mine.
STANLEY   Anything good?
BLANCHE   I think so. An invitation.
STANLEY   What to? A fireman's ball?
BLANCHE   [throwing back her head]   A cruise of the Caribbean on a yacht!
STANLEY   Well, well. What do you know?
BLANCHE   I have never been so surprised in my life.
STANLEY   I guess not.
BLANCHE   It came like a bolt from the blue!
STANLEY   Who did you say it was from?
BLANCHE   An old beau of mine.
STANLEY   The one that give you the white fox-pieces?
BLANCHE   Mr. Shep Huntleigh. I wore his ATO pin my last year at college.
   I hadn't seen him again until last Christmas. I ran in to him on Biscayne
   Boulevard. Then—just now—this wire—inviting me on a cruise of the
   Caribbean! The problem is clothes. I tore into my trunk to see what I
   have that's suitable for the tropics!
STANLEY   And come up with that—gorgeous—diamond—tiara?
BLANCHE   This old relic? Ha-ha! It's only rhinestones.
STANLEY   Gosh. I thought it was Tiffany diamonds. [He unbuttons his
   shirt.]
BLANCHE   Well, anyhow, I shall be entertained in style.
STANLEY   Uh-huh. It goes to show, you never know what is coming.
BLANCHE   Just when I thought my luck had begun to fail me—
STANLEY   Into the picture pops this Miami millionaire.
BLANCHE   This man is not from Miami. This man is from Dallas.
STANLEY   This man is from Dallas?
BLANCHE   Yes, this man is from Dallas where gold spouts out of the
   ground!
STANLEY   Well, just so he's from somewhere! [He starts removing his shirt.]
BLANCHE   Close the curtains before you undress any further.
STANLEY [amiably]   This is all I'm going to undress right now. [He rips the
   sack off a quart beer bottle] Seen a bottle-opener?
      [She moves slowly toward the dresser, where she stands with her hands
      knotted together.]
   I used to have a cousin who could open a beer bottle with his teeth.
   [pounding the bottle cap on the corner of table] That was his only accomplishment, all he could do—he was just a human bottle-opener. And then
   one time, at a wedding party, he broke his front teeth off! After that he
   was so ashamed of himself he used t' sneak out of the house when company came . . .
      [The bottle cap pops off and a geyser of foam shoots up. Stanley laughs
      happily, holding up the bottle over his head.]
   Ha-ha! Rain from heaven! [He extends the bottle toward her] Shall we
   bury the hatchet and make it a loving-cup? Huh?
BLANCHE   No, thank you.
STANLEY   Well, it's a red-letter night for us both. You having an oil millionaire and me having a baby.

[*He goes to the bureau in the bedroom and crouches to remove something from the bottom drawer.*]

BLANCHE [*drawing back*]   What are you doing in here?

STANLEY   Here's something I always break out on special occasions like this. The silk pyjamas I wore on my wedding night!

BLANCHE   Oh.

STANLEY   When the telephone rings and they say, "You've got a son!" I'll tear this off and wave it like a flag! [*He shakes out a brilliant pyjama coat.*] I guess we are both entitled to put on the dog. [*He goes back to the kitchen with the coat over his arm.*]

BLANCHE   When I think of how divine it is going to be to have such a thing as privacy once more—I could weep with joy!

STANLEY   This millionaire from Dallas is not going to interfere with your privacy any?

BLANCHE   It won't be the sort of thing you have in mind. This man is a gentleman and he respects me. [*improvising feverishly*] What he wants is my companionship. Having great wealth sometimes makes people lonely! A cultivated woman, a woman of intelligence and breeding, can enrich a man's life—immeasurably! I have those things to offer, and this doesn't take them away. Physical beauty is passing. A transitory possession. But beauty of the mind and richness of the spirit and tenderness of the heart—and I have all of those things—aren't taken away, but grow! Increase with the years! How strange that I should be called a destitute woman! When I have all of these treasures locked in my heart. [*A choked sob comes from her.*] I think of myself as a very, very rich woman! But I have been foolish—casting my pearls before swine!

STANLEY   Swine, huh?

BLANCHE   Yes, swine! Swine! And I'm thinking not only of you but of your friend, Mr. Mitchell. He came to see me tonight. He dared to come here in his work clothes! And to repeat slander to me, vicious stories that he had gotten from you! I gave him his walking papers . . .

STANLEY   You did, huh?

BLANCHE   But then he came back. He returned with a box of roses to beg my forgiveness! He implored my forgiveness. But some things are not forgivable. Deliberate cruelty is not forgivable. It is the one unforgivable thing in my opinion and it is the one thing of which I have never, never been guilty. And so I told him, I said to him, "Thank you," but it was foolish of me to think that we could ever adapt ourselves to each other. Our ways of life are too different. Our attitudes and our backgrounds are incompatible. We have to be realistic about such things. So farewell, my friend! And let there be no hard feelings . . .

STANLEY   Was this before or after the telegram came from the Texas oil millionaire?

BLANCHE   What telegram? No! No, after! As a matter of fact, the wire came just as—

STANLEY   As a matter of fact there wasn't no wire at all!

BLANCHE   Oh, oh!

STANLEY   There isn't no millionaire! And Mitch didn't come back with roses 'cause I know where he is—

BLANCHE   Oh!

STANLEY   There isn't a goddam thing but imagination!

BLANCHE   Oh!

STANLEY   And lies and conceit and tricks!

BLANCHE   Oh!

STANLEY   And look at yourself! Take a look at yourself in that worn-out
Mardi Gras outfit, rented for fifty cents from some rag-picker! And with
the crazy crown on! What queen do you think you are?

BLANCHE   Oh—God . . .

STANLEY   I've been on to you from the start! Not once did you pull any
wool over this boy's eyes! You come in here and sprinkle the place with
powder and spray perfume and cover the light-bulb with a paper lantern,
and lo and behold the place has turned into Egypt and you are the Queen
of the Nile! Sitting on your throne and swilling down my liquor! I say—
Ha!—Ha! Do you hear me? Ha—ha—ha! [*He walks into the bedroom.*]

BLANCHE   Don't come in here!

[*Lurid reflections appear on the walls around* BLANCHE. *The shadows are
of a grotesque and menacing form. She catches her breath, crosses to the
phone and jiggles the hook.* STANLEY *goes into the bathroom and closes
the door.*]

Operator, operator! Give me long-distance, please. . . . I want to get in
touch with Mr. Shep Huntleigh of Dallas. He's so well known he doesn't
require any address. Just ask anybody who—Wait!!—No, I couldn't find
it right now. . . . Please understand, I—No! No, wait! . . . One moment!
Someone is—Nothing! Hold on, please!

[*She sets the phone down and crosses warily into the kitchen. The night
is filled with inhuman voices like cries in a jungle. The shadows and
lurid reflections move sinuously as flames along the wall spaces. Through
the back wall of the rooms, which have become transparent, can be seen
the sidewalk. A prostitute has rolled a drunkard. He pursues her along
the walk, overtakes her and there is a struggle. A policeman's whistle
breaks it up. The figures disappear. Some moments later the Negro
Woman appears around the corner with a sequined bag which the prostitute had dropped on the walk. She is rooting excitedly through it.*
BLANCHE *presses her knuckles to her lips and returns slowly to the phone.
She speaks in a hoarse whisper.*]

BLANCHE   Operator! Operator! Never mind long-distance. Get Western
Union. There isn't time to be—Western—Western Union!

[*She waits anxiously.*]

Western Union? Yes! I—want to—Take down this message! "In desperate, desperate circumstances! Help me! Caught in a trap. Caught in—"
Oh!

[*The bathroom door is thrown open and* STANLEY *comes out in the brilliant silk pyjamas. He grins at her as he knots the tasseled sash about his
waist. She gasps and backs away from the phone. He stares at her for a
count of ten. Then a clicking becomes audible from the telephone, steady
and rasping.*]

STANLEY   You left th' phone off th' hook.

[*He crosses to it deliberately and sets it back on the hook. After he has
replaced it, he stares at her again, his mouth slowly curving into a grin,
as he weaves between* BLANCHE *and the outer door. The barely audible
"Blue Piano" begins to drum up louder. The sound of it turns into the*

roar of an approaching locomotive. BLANCHE crouches, pressing her fists to her ears until it has gone by.]

BLANCHE [finally straightening]   Let me—let me get by you!

STANLEY   Get by me? Sure. Go ahead. [He moves back a pace in the doorway.]

BLANCHE   You—you stand over there! [She indicates a further position.]

STANLEY [grinning]   You got plenty of room to walk by me now.

BLANCHE   Not with you there! But I've got to get out somehow!

STANLEY   You think I'll interfere with you? Ha-ha!

[The "Blue Piano" goes softly. She turns confusedly and makes a faint gesture. The inhuman jungle voices rise up. He takes a step toward her, biting his tongue which protrudes between his lips.]

STANLEY [softly]   Come to think of it—maybe you wouldn't be bad to—interfere with . . .

[BLANCHE moves backward through the door into the bedroom.]

BLANCHE   Stay back! Don't you come toward me another step or I'll—

STANLEY   What?

BLANCHE   Some awful thing will happen! It will!

STANLEY   What are you putting on now?

[They are now both inside the bedroom.]

BLANCHE   I warn you, don't, I'm in danger!

[He takes another step. She smashes a bottle on the table and faces him, clutching the broken top.]

STANLEY   What did you do that for?

BLANCHE   So I could twist the broken end in your face!

STANLEY   I bet you would do that!

BLANCHE   I would! I will if you—

STANLEY   Oh! So you want some roughhouse! All right, let's have some roughhouse!

[He springs toward her, overturning the table. She cries out and strikes at him with the bottle top but he catches her wrist.]

Tiger—tiger! Drop the bottle-top! Drop it! We've had this date with each other from the beginning!

[She moans. The bottle-top falls. She sinks to her knees: He picks up her inert figure and carries her to the bed. The hot trumpet and drums from the Four Deuces sound loudly.]

Scene Eleven

It is some weeks later. STELLA is packing BLANCHE's things. Sounds of water can be heard running in the bathroom.

The portieres are partly open on the poker players—STANLEY, STEVE, MITCH and PABLO—who sit around the table in the kitchen. The atmosphere of the kitchen is now the same raw, lurid one of the disastrous poker night.

The building is framed by the sky of turquoise. STELLA has been crying as she arranges the flowery dresses in the open trunk.

EUNICE comes down the steps from her flat above and enters the kitchen. There is an outburst from the poker table.

STANLEY   Drew to an inside straight and made it, by God.

PABLO   Maldita sea tu suerto!

STANLEY   Put it in English, greaseball.

PABLO   I am cursing your rutting luck.

STANLEY [*prodigiously elated*]   You know what luck is? Luck is believing you're lucky. Take at Salerno.² I believed I was lucky. I figured that 4 out of 5 would not come through but I would . . . and I did. I put that down as a rule. To hold front position in this rat-race you've got to believe you are lucky.

MITCH   You . . . you . . . you . . . Brag . . . brag . . . bull . . . bull.

[STELLA *goes into the bedroom and starts folding a dress.*]

STANLEY   What's the matter with him?

EUNICE [*walking past the table*]   I always did say that men are callous things with no feelings, but this does beat anything. Making pigs of yourselves. [*She comes through the portieres into the bedroom.*]

STANLEY   What's the matter with her?

STELLA   How is my baby?

EUNICE   Sleeping like a little angel. Brought you some grapes. [*She puts them on a stool and lowers her voice.*] Blanche?

STELLA   Bathing.

EUNICE   How is she?

STELLA   She wouldn't eat anything but asked for a drink.

EUNICE   What did you tell her?

STELLA   I—just told her that—we'd made arrangements for her to rest in the country. She's got it mixed in her mind with Shep Huntleigh.

[BLANCHE *opens the bathroom door slightly.*]

BLANCHE   Stella.

STELLA   Yes, Blanche.

BLANCHE   If anyone calls while I'm bathing take the number and tell them I'll call right back.

STELLA   Yes.

BLANCHE   That cool yellow silk—the bouclé. See if it's crushed. If it's not too crushed I'll wear it and on the lapel that silver and turquoise pin in the shape of a seahorse. You will find them in the heart-shaped box I keep my accessories in. And Stella . . . Try and locate a bunch of artificial violets in that box, too, to pin with the seahorse on the lapel of the jacket.

[*She closes the door.* STELLA *turns to* EUNICE.]

STELLA   I don't know if I did the right thing.

EUNICE   What else could you do?

STELLA   I couldn't believe her story and go on living with Stanley.

EUNICE   Don't ever believe it. Life has got to go on. No matter what happens, you've got to keep on going.

[*The bathroom door opens a little.*]

BLANCHE [*looking out*]   Is the coast clear?

STELLA   Yes, Blanche. [*to* EUNICE] Tell her how well she's looking.

BLANCHE   Please close the curtains before I come out.

STELLA   They're closed.

STANLEY   —How many for you?

PABLO   Two.

STEVE   Three.

---

2. Important beachhead in the Allied invasion of Italy in World War II.

[BLANCHE *appears in the amber light of the door. She has a tragic radiance in her red satin robe following the sculptural lines of her body. The "Varsouviana" rises audibly as* BLANCHE *enters the bedroom.*]

BLANCHE [*with faintly hysterical vivacity*] I have just washed my hair.

STELLA Did you?

BLANCHE I'm not sure I got the soap out.

EUNICE Such fine hair!

BLANCHE [*accepting the compliment*] It's a problem. Didn't I get a call?

STELLA Who from, Blanche?

BLANCHE Shep Huntleigh . . .

STELLA Why, not yet, honey!

BLANCHE How strange! I—

[*At the sound of* BLANCHE's *voice* MITCH's *arm supporting his cards has sagged and his gaze is dissolved into space.* STANLEY *slaps him on the shoulder.*]

STANLEY Hey, Mitch, come to!

[*The sound of this new voice shocks* BLANCHE. *She makes a shocked gesture, forming his name with her lips.* STELLA *nods and looks quickly away.* BLANCHE *stands quite still for some moments—the silver-backed mirror in her hand and a look of sorrowful perplexity as though all human experience shows on her face.* BLANCHE *finally speaks but with sudden hysteria.*]

BLANCHE What's going on here?

[*She turns from* STELLA *to* EUNICE *and back to* STELLA. *Her rising voice penetrates the concentration of the game.* MITCH *ducks his head lower but* STANLEY *shoves back his chair as if about to rise.* STEVE *places a restraining hand on his arm.*]

BLANCHE [*continuing*] What's happened here? I want an explanation of what's happened here.

STELLA [*agonizingly*] Hush! Hush!

EUNICE Hush! Hush! Honey.

STELLA Please, Blanche.

BLANCHE Why are you looking at me like that? Is something wrong with me?

EUNICE You look wonderful, Blanche. Don't she look wonderful?

STELLA Yes.

EUNICE I understand you are going on a trip.

STELLA Yes, Blanche *is*. She's going on a vacation.

EUNICE I'm green with envy.

BLANCHE Help me, help me get dressed!

STELLA [*handing her dress*] Is this what you—

BLANCHE Yes, it will do! I'm anxious to get out of here—this place is a trap!

EUNICE What a pretty blue jacket.

STELLA It's lilac colored.

BLANCHE You're both mistaken. It's Della Robbia blue.[3] The blue of the robe in the old Madonna pictures. Are these grapes washed?

[*She fingers the bunch of grapes which* EUNICE *had brought in.*]

---

3. A shade of light blue seen in terra cottas made by the Della Robbia family in the Italian Renaissance.

EUNICE   Huh?

BLANCHE   Washed, I said. Are they washed?

EUNICE   They're from the French Market.

BLANCHE   That doesn't mean they've been washed. [*The cathedral bells chime.*] Those cathedral bells—they're the only clean thing in the Quarter. Well, I'm going now. I'm ready to go.

EUNICE [*whispering*]   She's going to walk out before they get here.

STELLA   Wait, Blanche.

BLANCHE   I don't want to pass in front of those men.

EUNICE   Then wait'll the game breaks up.

STELLA   Sit down and . . .

[BLANCHE *turns weakly, hesitantly about. She lets them push her into a chair.*]

BLANCHE   I can smell the sea air. The rest of my time I'm going to spend on the sea. And when I die, I'm going to die on the sea. You know what I shall die of [*She plucks a grape.*] I shall die of eating an unwashed grape one day out on the ocean. I will die—with my hand in the hand of some nice-looking ship's doctor, a very young one with a small blond mustache and a big silver watch. "Poor lady," they'll say, "the quinine did her no good. That unwashed grape has transported her soul to heaven." [*The cathedral chimes are heard.*] And I'll be buried at sea sewn up in a clean white sack and dropped overboard—at noon—in the blaze of summer—and into an ocean as blue as [*chimes again*] my first lover's eyes!

[A DOCTOR *and a* MATRON *have appeared around the corner of the building and climbed the steps to the porch. The gravity of their profession is exaggerated—the unmistakable aura of the state institution with its cynical detachment. The* DOCTOR *rings the doorbell. The murmur of the game is interrupted.*]

EUNICE [*whispering to* STELLA]   That must be them.

[STELLA *presses her fists to her lips.*]

BLANCHE [*rising slowly*]   What is it?

EUNICE [*affectedly casual*]   Excuse me while I see who's at the door.

STELLA   Yes.

[EUNICE *goes into the kitchen.*]

BLANCHE [*tensely*]   I wonder if it's for me.

[A *whispered colloquy takes place at the door.*]

EUNICE [*returning, brightly*]   Someone is calling for Blanche.

BLANCHE   It *is* for me, then! [*She looks fearfully from one to the other and then to the portieres. The "Varsouviana" faintly plays.*] Is it the gentleman I was expecting from Dallas?

EUNICE   I think it is, Blanche.

BLANCHE   I'm not quite ready.

STELLA   Ask him to wait outside.

BLANCHE   I . . .

[EUNICE *goes back to the portieres. Drums sound very softly.*]

STELLA   Everything packed?

BLANCHE   My silver toilet articles are still out.

STELLA   Ah!

EUNICE [*returning*]   They're waiting in front of the house.

BLANCHE   They! Who's "they"?

EUNICE   There's a lady with him.

BLANCHE   I cannot imagine who this "lady" could be! How is she dressed?

EUNICE   Just—just a sort of a—plain-tailored outfit.

BLANCHE   Possibly she's—[*Her voice dies out nervously.*]

STELLA   Shall we go, Blanche?

BLANCHE   Must we go through that room?

STELLA   I will go with you.

BLANCHE   How do I look?

STELLA   Lovely.

EUNICE [*echoing*]   Lovely.

> [BLANCHE *moves fearfully to the portieres.* EUNICE *draws them open for her.* BLANCHE *goes into the kitchen.*]

BLANCHE [*to the men*]   Please don't get up. I'm only passing through.

> [*She crosses quickly to outside door.* STELLA *and* EUNICE *follow. The poker players stand awkwardly at the table—all except* MITCH *who remains seated, looking down at the table.* BLANCHE *steps out on a small porch at the side of the door. She stops short and catches her breath.*]

DOCTOR   How do you do?

BLANCHE   You are not the gentleman I was expecting. [*She suddenly gasps and starts back up the steps. She stops by* STELLA, *who stands just outside the door, and speaks in a frightening whisper.*] That man isn't Shep Huntleigh.

> [*The "Varsouviana" is playing distantly.* STELLA *stares back at* BLANCHE. EUNICE *is holding* STELLA'*s arm. There is a moment of silence—no sound but that of* STANLEY *steadily shuffling the cards.* BLANCHE *catches her breath again and slips back into the flat. She enters the flat with a peculiar smile, her eyes wide and brilliant. As soon as her sister goes past her,* STELLA *closes her eyes and clenches her hands.* EUNICE *throws her arms comfortingly about her. Then she starts up to her flat.* BLANCHE *stops just inside the door.* MITCH *keeps staring down at his hands on the table, but the other men look at her curiously. At last she starts around the table toward the bedroom. As she does,* STANLEY *suddenly pushes back his chair and rises as if to block her way. The* MATRON *follows her into the flat.*]

STANLEY   Did you forget something?

BLANCHE [*shrilly*]   Yes! Yes, I forgot something!

> [*She rushes past him into the bedroom. Lurid reflections appear on the walls in odd, sinuous shapes. The "Varsouviana" is filtered into a weird distortion, accompanied by the cries and noises of the jungle.* BLANCHE *seizes the back of a chair as if to defend herself.*]

STANLEY [*sotto voce*][4]   Doc, you better go in.

DOCTOR [*sotto voce, motioning to the* MATRON]   Nurse, bring her out.

> [*The* MATRON *advances on one side,* STANLEY *on the other. Divested of all the softer properties of womanhood, the* MATRON *is a peculiarly sinister figure in her severe dress. Her voice is bold and toneless as a firebell.*]

MATRON   Hello, Blanche.

> [*The greeting is echoed and re-echoed by other mysterious voices behind the walls, as if reverberated through a canyon of rock.*]

STANLEY   She says that she forgot something.

---

4. In an undertone.

[*The echo sounds in threatening whispers.*]

MATRON   That's all right.

STANLEY   What did you forget, Blanche?

BLANCHE   I—I—

MATRON   It don't matter. We can pick it up later.

STANLEY   Sure. We can send it along with the trunk.

BLANCHE   [*retreating in panic*]   I don't know you—I don't know you. I want to be—left alone—please!

MATRON   Now, Blanche!

ECHOES   [*rising and falling*]   Now, Blanche—now, Blanche—now, Blanche!

STANLEY   You left nothing here but spilt talcum and old empty perfume bottles—unless it's the paper lantern you want to take with you. You want the lantern?

> [*He crosses to dressing table and seizes the paper lantern, tearing it off the light bulb, and extends it toward her. She cries out as if the lantern was herself. The* MATRON *steps boldly toward her. She screams and tries to break past the* MATRON. *All the men spring to their feet.* STELLA *runs out to the porch, with* EUNICE *following to comfort her, simultaneously with the confused voices of the men in the kitchen.* STELLA *rushes into* EUNICE's *embrace on the porch.*]

STELLA   Oh, my God, Eunice help me! Don't let them do that to her, don't let them hurt her! Oh, God, oh, please God, don't hurt her! What are they doing to her? What are they doing? [*She tries to break from* EUNICE's *arms.*]

EUNICE   No, honey, no, no, honey. Stay here. Don't go back in there. Stay with me and don't look.

STELLA   What have I done to my sister? Oh, God, what have I done to my sister?

EUNICE   You done the right thing, the only thing you could do. She couldn't stay here; there wasn't no other place for her to go.

> [*While* STELLA *and* EUNICE *are speaking on the porch the voices of the men in the kitchen overlap them.* MITCH *has started toward the bedroom.* STANLEY *crosses to block him.* STANLEY *pushes him aside.* MITCH *lunges and strikes at* STANLEY. STANLEY *pushes* MITCH *back.* MITCH *collapses at the table, sobbing. During the preceding scenes, the* MATRON *catches hold of* BLANCHE's *arm and prevents her flight.* BLANCHE *turns wildly and scratches at the* MATRON. *The heavy woman pinions her arms.* BLANCHE *cries out hoarsely and slips to her knees.*]

MATRON   These fingernails have to be trimmed. [*The* DOCTOR *comes into the room and she looks at him.*] Jacket, Doctor?

DOCTOR   Not unless necessary.

> [*He takes off his hat and now he becomes personalized. The unhuman quality goes. His voice is gentle and reassuring as he crosses to* BLANCHE *and crouches in front of her. As he speaks her name, her terror subsides a little. The lurid reflections fade from the walls, the inhuman cries and noises die out and her own hoarse crying is calmed.*]

DOCTOR   Miss DuBois.

> [*She turns her face to him and stares at him with desperate pleading. He smiles; then he speaks to the* MATRON.]

It won't be necessary.

BLANCHE [*faintly*]   Ask her to let go of me.

DOCTOR [*to the* MATRON]   Let go.

> [*The* MATRON *releases her.* BLANCHE *extends her hands toward the* DOCTOR. *He draws her up gently and supports her with his arm and leads her through the portieres.*]

BLANCHE [*holding tight to his arm*]   Whoever you are—I have always depended on the kindness of strangers.

> [*The poker players stand back as* BLANCHE *and the* DOCTOR *cross the kitchen to the front door. She allows him to lead her as if she were blind. As they go out on the porch,* STELLA *cries out her sister's name from where she is crouched a few steps up on the stairs.*]

STELLA   Blanche! Blanche, Blanche!

> [BLANCHE *walks on without turning, followed by the* DOCTOR *and the* MATRON. *They go around the corner of the building.* EUNICE *descends to* STELLA *and places the child in her arms. It is wrapped in a pale blue blanket.* STELLA *accepts the child, sobbingly.* EUNICE *continues downstairs and enters the kitchen where the men, except for* STANLEY, *are returning silently to their places about the table.* STANLEY *has gone out on the porch and stands at the foot of the steps looking at* STELLA.]

STANLEY [*a bit uncertainly*]   Stella?

> [*She sobs with inhuman abandon. There is something luxurious in her complete surrender to crying now that her sister is gone.*]

STANLEY [*voluptuously, soothingly*]   Now, honey. Now, love. Now, now, love. [*He kneels beside her and his fingers find the opening of her blouse.*] Now, now, love, Now, love. . . .

> [*The luxurious sobbing, the sensual murmur fade away under the swelling music of the "Blue Piano" and the muted trumpet.*]

STEVE   This game is seven-card stud.

CURTAIN

1947

JOHN CHEEVER
1912–1982

"It seems to me that man's inclination toward light, toward brightness, is very nearly botanical—and I mean spiritual light. One not only needs it, one struggles for it." These sentences from an interview with John Cheever, conducted by the novelist John Hersey, at first glance look strange coming from a "*New Yorker* writer" of entertaining stories in which harried, comfortably off, white middle-class suburbanites conduct their lives. "Our Chekhov of the exurbs," he was dubbed by the reviewer John Leonard, with reference to the mythical community of Shady Hill (which Cheever created along the lines of existing ones in Fairfield or Westchester county). Yet Chekhov's own characters, living as they do in darkness, are aspirers toward "spiritual light," with a similarly "botanical" inclination. Trapped in their beautifully appointed houses and neighborhoods but carried along by the cool, effortless prose of their creator, Cheever's characters are viewed with a sympathetic irony, well-seasoned by sadness.

Cheever's early years were not notable for their idyllic quality, and he reveals little nostalgia for a lost childhood. Born in Quincy, Massachusetts, he grew up in what he describes as shabby gentility, with his father departing the family when his son was fifteen. (Cheever had an older brother, Fred, with whom he formed a strong and troubled relationship.) Two years later his father lost his money in the crash of 1929, and by that time Cheever had been expelled from Thayer Academy, in Braintree. The expulsion marked the end of his formal education and the beginning of his career as a writer; for, remarkably, he wrote a short story about the experience, titled it "Expelled," and sent it to the *New Republic*, where Malcolm Cowley (who would become a lifelong friend) published it.

During the 1930s Cheever lived in New York City, in impoverished circumstances, taking odd jobs to support himself and winning a fellowship to the writer's colony at Yaddo, in Saratoga Springs. His New York life would provide the material for many of his early stories, whose protagonists are rather frequently in desperate economic situations. With the coming of World War II, Cheever joined the armed forces and served in the Pacific theater but saw no combat. In 1941 he married Mary Winternitz, a marriage that was to produce three children and last through four decades. About the marriage Cheever said, "That two people—both of us temperamental, quarrelsome and intensely ambitious—could have gotten along for such a vast period of time is for me a very good example of the boundlessness of human nature." Meanwhile, with the help of Malcolm Cowley, he began to publish in *The New Yorker* and in 1943, while in service, his first book of stories (*The Way Some People Live*) was published to favorable reviews. Over the decades to follow, the stories continued to appear, largely in *The New Yorker*, where he became—along with J. D. Salinger and John Updike—a recurrent phenomenon. Five further volumes of short fiction were published, and in 1978 *The Stories of John Cheever* gathered together those he wished to be remembered for.

But although he is praised for his skill as a realist depictor of suburban manners and morals, Cheever's art cannot be adequately understood in such terms. As Stephen C. Moore has usefully pointed out, "His best stories move from a base in a mimetic presentation of surface reality—the *scenery* of apparently successful American middle class life—to fables of heroism." Cheever's embattled heroes express themselves in taking up challenges that are essentially fabulous, and foolhardy: swimming home across the backyard pools of Westchester ("The Swimmer," printed here); performing feats of physical daredeviltry in suburban living rooms ("O Youth and Beauty"); or dealing with the myriad demands and temptations that beset the hero who, having escaped death in an airplane, returns home to more severe trials ("The Country Husband"). Whatever the specific narrative, we are always aware of the storyteller's art, shaping ordinary life into the odder, more willful figures of fantasy and romance.

Although Cheever will be remembered primarily as a writer of short stories, his output includes a respectable number of novels. In 1957 he won a National Book Award for his first one, *The Wapshot Chronicle* (it was followed by *The Wapshot Scandal*, in 1964), notable for its New England seacoast and domestic flavor, if less so for a continuously engaging narrative line. Perhaps his most gripping novel is *Bullet Park* (1969), which, like the best of the stories, is both realistic and fabulous. The suburban milieu, seen from the 5:42 train from New York, has never been done more accurately, even lovingly, by Cheever. And as is to be expected, his protagonist's carefully built, pious suburban existence turns out to be a mess. Although the novel provoked interesting disagreement about its merits (some critics felt the narrative manipulations both ruthless and sentimental), there was no disagreement about the vivid quality of its represented life, on the commuter train or at the cocktail party. In the years just previous to his death, and after a bout with alcohol and drug addiction, Cheever published his two final novels, *Falconer* (1978) and *Oh What a Paradise It Seems* (1980), the former of which was much praised for its harrowing rendering of prison life. (Farragut, the novel's hero, is sent to Falconer Prison for killing his brother; Cheever lived in Ossining, New York, home of Sing Sing Prison, during his later years.)

From the beginning to the end of his career, he was and remained a thoroughly professional writer, wary of pronouncing on the world at large (there is a noticeable absence of politics and ideology in his work) or on the meaning and significance of his own art. As one sees from his published *Journals* (1991), he agonized over the disruptive facts of his alcoholism and his homosexuality. But he also managed to remain a private man, seemingly untouched by experiments—or fads—in the writing of fiction. Whether or not, as T. S. Eliot said about Henry James, he had a mind so fine that no idea could violate it, Cheever remained firmly resistant to ideas of all sorts. This insular tendency is probably a reason why his work makes less than a "major" claim on us, but it is also the condition for his devoted and scrupulous attention to the particularities of middle-class life at the far edge of its promised dream.

The text is from *The Brigadier and the Golf Widow* (1964).

The Swimmer

It was one of those midsummer Sundays when everyone sits around saying: "I *drank* too much last night." You might have heard it whispered by the parishioners leaving church, heard it from the lips of the priest himself, struggling with his cassock in the *vestiarium*,[1] heard it from the golf links and the tennis courts, heard it from the wildlife preserve where the leader of the Audubon group was suffering from a terrible hangover. "I *drank* too much," said Donald Westerhazy. "We all *drank* too much," said Lucinda Merrill. "It must have been the wine," said Helen Westerhazy. "I *drank* too much of that claret."

This was at the edge of the Westerhazys' pool. The pool, fed by an artesian well with a high iron content, was a pale shade of green. It was a fine day. In the west there was a massive stand of cumulus cloud so like a city seen from a distance—from the bow of an approaching ship—that it might have had a name. Lisbon. Hackensack.[2] The sun was hot. Neddy Merrill sat by the green water, one hand in it, one around a glass of gin. He was a slender man—he seemed to have the especial slenderness of youth—and while he was far from young he had slid down his banister that morning and given the bronze backside of Aphrodite[3] on the hall table a smack, as he jogged toward the smell of coffee in his dining room. He might have been compared to a summer's day, particularly the last hours of one, and while he lacked a tennis racket or a sail bag the impression was definitely one of youth, sport, and clement weather. He had been swimming and now he was breathing deeply, stertorously as if he could gulp into his lungs the components of that moment, the heat of the sun, the intenseness of his pleasure. It all seemed to flow into his chest. His own house stood in Bullet Park,[4] eight miles to

1. Cloakroom for religious vestments adjacent to a church's sanctuary.
2. A town in New Jersey. Lisbon is the capital of Portugal.
3. Greek goddess of love and beauty.
4. Fictive suburb used as a location for many of Cheever's stories and novels.

the south, where his four beautiful daughters would have had their lunch and might be playing tennis. Then it occurred to him that by taking a dogleg to the southwest he could reach his home by water.

His life was not confining and the delight he took in this observation could not be explained by its suggestion of escape. He seemed to see, with a cartographer's eye, that string of swimming pools, that quasi-subterranean stream that curved across the county. He had made a discovery, a contribution to modern geography; he would name the stream Lucinda after his wife. He was not a practical joker nor was he a fool but he was determinedly original and had a vague and modest idea of himself as a legendary figure. The day was beautiful and it seemed to him that a long swim might enlarge and celebrate its beauty.

He took off a sweater that was hung over his shoulders and dove in. He had an inexplicable contempt for men who did not hurl themselves into pools. He swam a choppy crawl, breathing either with every stroke or every fourth stroke and counting somewhere well in the back of his mind the one-two one-two of a flutter kick. It was not a serviceable stroke for long distances but the domestication of swimming had saddled the sport with some customs and in his part of the world a crawl was customary. To be embraced and sustained by the light green water was less a pleasure, it seemed, than the resumption of a natural condition, and he would have liked to swim without trunks, but this was not possible, considering his project. He hoisted himself up on the far curb—he never used the ladder—and started across the lawn. When Lucinda asked where he was going he said he was going to swim home.

The only maps and charts he had to go by were remembered or imaginary but these were clear enough. First there were the Grahams, the Hammers, the Lears, the Howlands, and the Crosscups. He would cross Ditmar Street to the Bunkers and come, after a short portage, to the Levys, the Welchers, and the public pool in Lancaster. Then there were the Hallorans, the Sachses, the Biswangers, Shirley Adams, the Gilmartins, and the Clydes. The day was lovely, and that he lived in a world so generously supplied with water seemed like a clemency, a beneficence. His heart was high and he ran across the grass. Making his way home by an uncommon route gave him the feeling that he was a pilgrim, an explorer, a man with a destiny, and he knew that he would find friends all along the way; friends would line the banks of the Lucinda River.

He went through a hedge that separated the Westerhazys' land from the Grahams', walked under some flowering apple trees, passed the shed that housed their pump and filter, and came out at the Grahams' pool. "Why, Neddy," Mrs. Graham said, "what a marvelous surprise. I've been trying to get you on the phone all morning. Here, let me get you a drink." He saw then, like any explorer, that the hospitable customs and traditions of the natives would have to be handled with diplomacy if he was ever going to reach his destination. He did not want to mystify or seem rude to the Grahams nor did he have the time to linger there. He swam the length of their pool and joined them in the sun and was rescued, a few minutes later, by the arrival of two carloads of friends from Connecticut. During the uproarious reunions he was able to slip away. He went down by the front of the Grahams' house, stepped over a thorny hedge, and crossed a vacant lot to the Hammers'. Mrs. Hammer, looking up from her roses, saw him swim by although she wasn't quite sure who it was. The Lears heard him splashing past the open windows of their living room. The Howlands and the Crosscups were away. After leaving the Howlands' he crossed Ditmar Street and started for the Bunkers', where he could hear, even at that distance, the noise of a party.

The water refracted the sound of voices and laughter and seemed to suspend it in midair. The Bunkers' pool was on a rise and he climbed some stairs to a terrace where twenty-five or thirty men and women were drinking. The only person in the water was Rusty Towers, who floated there on a rubber raft. Oh how bonny and lush were the banks of the Lucinda River! Prosperous men and women gathered by the sapphire-colored waters while caterer's men in white coats passed them cold gin. Overhead a red de Haviland trainer was circling around and around and around in the sky with something like the glee of a child in a swing. Ned felt a passing affection for the scene, a tenderness for the gathering, as if it was something he might touch. In the distance he heard thunder. As soon as Enid Bunker saw him she began to scream: "Oh look who's here! What a marvelous surprise! When Lucinda said that you couldn't come I thought I'd *die*." She made her way to him through the crowd, and when they had finished kissing she led him to the bar, a progress that was slowed by the fact that he stopped to kiss eight or ten other women and shake the hands of as many men. A smiling bartender he had seen at a hundred parties gave him a gin and tonic and he stood by the bar for a moment, anxious not to get stuck in any conversation that would delay his voyage. When he seemed about to be surrounded he dove in and swam close to the side to avoid colliding with Rusty's raft. At the far end of the pool he bypassed the Tomlinsons with a broad smile and jogged up the garden path. The gravel cut his feet but this was the only unpleasantness. The party was confined to the pool, and as he went toward the house he heard the brilliant, watery sound of voices fade, heard the noise of a radio from the Bunkers' kitchen, where someone was listening to a ballgame. Sunday afternoon. He made his way through the parked cars and down the grassy border of their driveway to Alewives' Lane. He did not want to be seen on the road in his bathing trunks but there was no traffic and he made the short distance to the Levys' driveway, marked with a private property sign and a green tube for the *New York Times*. All the doors and windows of the big house were open but there were no signs of life; not even a dog barked. He went around the side of the house to the pool and saw that the Levys had only recently left. Glasses and bottles and dishes of nuts were on a table at the deep end, where there was a bathhouse or gazebo, hung with Japanese lanterns. After swimming the pool he got himself a glass and poured a drink. It was his fourth or fifth drink and he had swum nearly half the length of the Lucinda River. He felt tired, clean, and pleased at that moment to be alone; pleased with everything.

It would storm. The stand of cumulus cloud—that city—had risen and darkened, and while he sat there he heard the percussiveness of thunder again. The de Haviland trainer was still circling overhead and it seemed to Ned that he could almost hear the pilot laugh with pleasure in the afternoon; but when there was another peal of thunder he took off for home. A train whistle blew and he wondered what time it had gotten to be. Four? Five? He thought of the provincial station at that hour, where a waiter, his tuxedo concealed by a raincoat, a dwarf with some flowers wrapped in newspaper, and a woman who had been crying would be waiting for the local. It was suddenly growing dark; it was that moment when the pin-headed birds seem to organize their song into some acute and knowledgeable recognition of the storm's approach. Then there was a fine noise of rushing water from the crown of an oak at his back, as if a spigot there had been turned. Then the noise of fountains came from the crowns of all the tall trees. Why did he love storms, what was the meaning of his excitement when the door sprang open and the rain wind fled rudely up the stairs, why had the simple task of shutting the windows of an old house seemed fitting and urgent, why did the first watery notes of a storm wind have for him the unmistakable sound of good news, cheer, glad tidings? Then there was an explosion, a smell of cordite, and rain lashed the Japanese lanterns that Mrs. Levy had bought in Kyoto the year before last, or was it the year before that?

He stayed in the Levys' gazebo until the storm had passed. The rain had cooled the air and he shivered. The force of the wind had stripped a maple of its red and yellow leaves and scattered them over the grass and the water. Since it was midsummer the tree must be blighted, and yet he felt a peculiar sadness at this sign of autumn. He braced his shoulders, emptied his glass, and started for the Welchers' pool. This meant crossing the Lindleys' riding ring and he was surprised to find it overgrown with grass and all the jumps dismantled. He wondered if the Lindleys had sold their horses or gone away for the summer and put them out to board. He seemed to remember having heard something about the Lindleys and their horses but the memory was unclear. On he went, barefoot through the wet grass, to the Welchers', where he found their pool was dry.

This breach in his chain of water disappointed him absurdly, and he felt like some explorer who seeks a torrential headwater and finds a dead stream. He was disappointed and mystified. It was common enough to go away for the summer but no one ever drained his pool. The Welchers had definitely gone away. The pool furniture was folded, stacked, and covered with a tarpaulin. The bathhouse was locked. All the windows of the house were shut, and when he went around to the driveway in front he saw a for-sale sign nailed to a tree. When had he last heard from the Welchers—when, that is, had he and Lucinda last regretted an invitation to dine with them. It seemed only a week or so ago. Was his memory failing or had he so disciplined it in the repression of unpleasant facts that he had damaged his sense of the truth? Then in the distance he heard the sound of a tennis game. This cheered him, cleared away all his apprehensions and let him regard the overcast sky and the cold air with indifference. This was the day that Neddy Merrill swam across the county. That was the day! He started off then for his most difficult portage.

Had you gone for a Sunday afternoon ride that day you might have seen him, close to naked, standing on the shoulders of route 424, waiting for a chance to cross. You might have wondered if he was the victim of foul play, had his car broken down, or was he merely a fool. Standing barefoot in the deposits of the highway—beer cans, rags, and blowout patches—exposed to all kinds of ridicule, he seemed pitiful. He had known when he started that this was a part of his journey—it had been on his maps—but confronted with the lines of traffic, worming through the summery light, he found himself unprepared. He was laughed at, jeered at, a beer can was thrown at him, and he had no dignity or humor to bring to the situation. He could have gone back, back to the Westerhazys', where Lucinda would still be sitting in the sun. He had signed nothing, vowed nothing, pledged nothing not even to himself. Why, believing as he did, that all human obduracy was susceptible to common sense, was he unable to turn back? Why was he determined to complete his journey even if it meant putting his life in danger? At what point had this prank, this joke, this piece of horseplay become serious? He could not go back, he could not even recall with any clearness the green water at the Westerhazys', the sense of inhaling the day's components, the friendly and relaxed voices saying that they had *drunk* too much. In the space of an hour, more or less, he had covered a distance that made his return impossible.

An old man, tooling down the highway at fifteen miles an hour, let him get to the middle of the road, where there was a grass divider. Here he was exposed to the ridicule of the northbound traffic, but after ten or fifteen minutes he was able to cross. From here he had only a short walk to the Recreation Center at the edge of the Village of Lancaster, where there were some handball courts and a public pool.

The effect of the water on voices, the illusion of brilliance and suspense, was the same here as it had been at the Bunkers' but the sounds here were louder, harsher, and more shrill, and as soon as he entered the crowded enclosure he was confronted with regimentation. "ALL SWIMMERS MUST TAKE A SHOWER BEFORE USING THE POOL. ALL SWIMMERS MUST USE THE FOOTBATH. ALL SWIMMERS MUST WEAR THEIR IDENTIFICATION DISKS." He took a shower, washed his feet in a cloudy and bitter solution and made his way to the edge of the water. It stank of chlorine and looked to him like a sink. A pair of lifeguards in a pair of towers blew police whistles at what seemed to be regular intervals and abused the swimmers through a public address system. Neddy remembered the sapphire water at the Bunkers' with longing and thought that he might contaminate himself—damage his own prosperousness and charm—by swimming in this murk, but he reminded himself that he was an explorer, a pilgrim, and that this was merely a stagnant bend in the Lucinda River. He dove, scowling with distaste, into the chlorine and had to swim with his head above water to avoid collisions, but even so he was bumped into, splashed and jostled. When he got to the shallow end both lifeguards were shouting at him: "Hey, you, you without the identification disk, get outa the water." He did, but they had no way of pursuing him and he went through the reek of suntan oil and chlorine out through the hurricane fence and passed the handball courts. By crossing the road he entered the wooded part of the Halloran estate. The woods were not cleared and the footing was treacherous and difficult until he reached the lawn and the clipped beech hedge that encircled their pool.

The Hallorans were friends, an elderly couple of enormous wealth who seemed to bask in the suspicion that they might be Communists. They were zealous reformers but they were not Communists, and yet when they were accused, as they sometimes were, of subversion, it seemed to gratify and excite them. Their beech hedge was yellow and he guessed this had been blighted like the Levys' maple. He called hullo, hullo, to warn the Hallorans of his approach, to palliate his invasion of their privacy. The Hallorans, for reasons that had never been explained to him, did not wear bathing suits. No explanations were in order, really. Their nakedness was a detail in their uncompromising zeal for reform and he stepped politely out of his trunks before he went through the opening in the hedge.

Mrs. Halloran, a stout woman with white hair and a serene face, was reading the *Times*. Mr. Halloran was taking beech leaves out of the water with a scoop. They seemed not surprised or displeased to see him. Their pool was perhaps the oldest in the county, a fieldstone rectangle, fed by a brook. It had no filter or pump and its waters were the opaque gold of the stream.

"I'm swimming across the county," Ned said.

"Why, I didn't know one could," exclaimed Mrs. Halloran.

"Well, I've made it from the Westerhazys'," Ned said. "That must be about four miles."

He left his trunks at the deep end, walked to the shallow end, and swam this stretch. As he was pulling himself out of the water he heard Mrs. Halloran say: "We've been *terribly* sorry to hear about all your misfortunes, Neddy."

"My misfortunes?" Ned asked. "I don't know what you mean."

"Why, we heard that you'd sold the house and that your poor children . . ."

"I don't recall having sold the house," Ned said, "and the girls are at home."

"Yes," Mrs. Halloran sighed. "Yes . . ." Her voice filled the air with an unseasonable melancholy and Ned spoke briskly. "Thank you for the swim."

"Well, have a nice trip," said Mrs. Halloran.

Beyond the hedge he pulled on his trunks and fastened them. They were loose and he wondered if, during the space of an afternoon, he could have lost some weight. He was cold and he was tired and the naked Hallorans and their dark water had depressed him. The swim was too much for his strength but how could he have guessed this, sliding down the banister that morning and sitting in the Westerhazys' sun? His arms were lame. His legs felt rubbery and ached at the joints. The worst of it was the cold in his bones and the feeling that he might never be warm again. Leaves were falling down around him and he smelled woodsmoke on the wind. Who would be burning wood at this time of year?

He needed a drink. Whiskey would warm him, pick him up, carry him through the last of his journey, refresh his feeling that it was original and valorous to swim across the county. Channel swimmers took brandy. He needed a stimulant. He crossed the lawn in front of the Hallorans' house and went down a little path to where they had built a house for their only daughter Helen and her husband Eric Sachs. The Sachses' pool was small and he found Helen and her husband there.

"Oh, *Neddy*," Helen said. "Did you lunch at Mother's?"

"Not *really*," Ned said. "I *did* stop to see your parents." This seemed to be explanation enough. "I'm terribly sorry to break in on you like this but I've taken a chill and I wonder if you'd give me a drink."

"Why, I'd *love* to," Helen said, "but there hasn't been anything in this house to drink since Eric's operation. That was three years ago."

Was he losing his memory, had his gift for concealing painful facts let him forget that he had sold his house, that his children were in trouble, and that his friend had been ill? His eyes slipped from Eric's face to his abdomen, where he saw three pale, sutured scars, two of them at least a foot long. Gone was his navel, and what, Neddy thought, would the roving hand, bed-checking one's gifts at 3 A.M. make of a belly with no navel, no link to birth, this breach in the succession?

"I'm sure you can get a drink at the Biswangers'," Helen said. "They're having an enormous do. You can hear it from here. Listen!"

She raised her head and from across the road, the lawns, the gardens, the woods, the fields, he heard again the brilliant noise of voices over water. "Well, I'll get wet," he said, still feeling that he had no freedom of choice about his means of travel. He dove into the Sachses' cold water and, gasping, close to drowning, made his way from one end of the pool to the other. "Lucinda and I want *terribly* to see you," he said over his shoulder, his face set toward the Biswangers'. "We're sorry it's been so long and we'll call you *very* soon."

He crossed some fields to the Biswangers' and the sounds of revelry there. They would be honored to give him a drink, they would be happy to give him a drink, they would in fact be lucky to give him a drink. The Biswangers invited him and Lucinda for dinner four times a year, six weeks in advance. They were always rebuffed and yet they continued to send out their invitations, unwilling to comprehend the rigid and undemocratic realities of their society. They were the sort of people who discussed the price of things at cocktails, exchanged market tips during dinner, and after dinner told dirty stories to mixed company. They did not belong to Neddy's set—they were not even on Lucinda's Christmas card list. He went toward their pool with feelings of indifference, charity, and some unease, since it seemed to be getting dark and these were the longest days of the year. The party when he joined it was noisy and large. Grace Biswanger was the kind of hostess who asked the optometrist, the veterinarian, the real-estate dealer and the dentist. No one was swimming and the twilight, reflected on the water of the pool, had a wintry gleam. There was a bar and he started for this. When Grace Biswanger saw him she came toward him, not affectionately as he had every right to expect, but bellicosely.

"Why, this party has everything," she said loudly, "including a gate crasher."

She could not deal him a social blow—there was no question about this and he did not flinch. "As a gate crasher," he asked politely, "do I rate a drink?"

"Suit yourself," she said. "You don't seem to pay much attention to invitations."

She turned her back on him and joined some guests, and he went to the bar and ordered a whiskey. The bartender served him but he served him rudely. His was a world in which the caterer's men kept the social score, and to be rebuffed by a part-time barkeep meant that he had suffered some loss of social esteem. Or perhaps the man was new and uninformed. Then he heard Grace at his back say: "They went for broke overnight—nothing but income—and he showed up drunk one Sunday and asked us to loan him five thousand dollars. . . ." She was always talking about money. It was worse than eating your peas off a knife. He dove into the pool, swam its length and went away.

The next pool on his list, the last but two, belonged to his old mistress,

Shirley Adams. If he had suffered any injuries at the Biswangers' they would be cured here. Love—sexual roughhouse in fact—was the supreme elixir, the painkiller, the brightly colored pill that would put the spring back into his step, the joy of life in his heart. They had had an affair last week, last month, last year. He couldn't remember. It was he who had broken it off, his was the upper hand, and he stepped through the gate of the wall that surrounded her pool with nothing so considered as self-confidence. It seemed in a way to be his pool as the lover, particularly the illicit lover, enjoys the possessions of his mistress with an authority unknown to holy matrimony. She was there, her hair the color of brass, but her figure, at the edge of the lighted, cerulean water, excited in him no profound memories. It had been, he thought, a lighthearted affair, although she had wept when he broke it off. She seemed confused to see him and he wondered if she was still wounded. Would she, God forbid, weep again?

"What do you want?" she asked.

"I'm swimming across the county."

"Good Christ. Will you ever grow up?"

"What's the matter?"

"If you've come here for money," she said, "I won't give you another cent."

"You could give me a drink."

"I could but I won't. I'm not alone."

"Well, I'm on my way."

He dove in and swam the pool, but when he tried to haul himself up onto the curb he found that the strength in his arms and his shoulders had gone, and he paddled to the ladder and climbed out. Looking over his shoulder he saw, in the lighted bathhouse, a young man. Going out onto the dark lawn he smelled chrysanthemums or marigolds—some stubborn autumnal fragrance—on the night air, strong as gas. Looking overhead he saw that the stars had come out, but why should he seem to see Andromeda, Cepheus, and Cassiopeia? What had become of the constellations of midsummer? He began to cry.

It was probably the first time in his adult life that he had ever cried, certainly the first time in his life that he had ever felt so miserable, cold, tired, and bewildered. He could not understand the rudeness of the caterer's barkeep or the rudeness of a mistress who had come to him on her knees and showered his trousers with tears. He had swum too long, he had been immersed too long, and his nose and his throat were sore from the water. What he needed then was a drink, some company, and some clean dry clothes, and while he could have cut directly across the road to his home he went on to the Gilmartins' pool. Here, for the first time in his life, he did not dive but went down the steps into the icy water and swam a hobbled side stroke that he might have learned as a youth. He staggered with fatigue on his way to the Clydes' and paddled the length of their pool, stopping again and again with his hand on the curb to rest. He climbed up the ladder and wondered if he had the strength to get home. He had done what he wanted, he had swum the county, but he was so stupefied with exhaustion that his triumph seemed vague. Stooped, holding onto the gateposts for support, he turned up the driveway of his house.

The place was dark. Was it so late that they had all gone to bed? Had

Lucinda stayed at the Westerhazys' for supper? Had the girls joined her there or gone someplace else? Hadn't they agreed, as they usually did on Sunday, to regret all their invitations and stay at home? He tried the garage doors to see what cars were in but the doors were locked and rust came off the handles onto his hands. Going toward the house, he saw that the force of the thunderstorm had knocked one of the rain gutters loose. It hung down over the front door like an umbrella rib, but it could be fixed in the morning. The house was locked, and he thought that the stupid cook or the stupid maid must have locked the place up until he remembered that it had been some time since they had employed a maid or a cook. He shouted, pounded on the door, tried to force it with his shoulder, and then, looking in at the windows, saw that the place was empty.

1964

BERNARD MALAMUD
1914–1986

Bernard Malamud began late as a writer, publishing his first novel at age thirty-eight and reaching a wider audience only about a decade later. In addition, he had the unusual distinction of having written a second novel (*The Assistant*, 1957) that most readers rightly consider to be his best. Malamud knew well the urban life he wrote about in that book. He was born in Brooklyn, graduated from Erasmus Hall High School and the City College of New York, then took a master's degree at Columbia. During the 1940s he taught evening classes at Erasmus Hall and Harlem Evening High School, while writing short stories that by 1950 had begun to appear in such magazines as *Partisan Review* and *Commentary*. Along with Saul Bellow, he was an important member of the group of Jewish novelists who flourished in the 1950s and beyond, but unlike Bellow, his stories were usually notable for the way they captured the speech and manners of working-class, recently immigrated Jews.

That urban Jewish milieu was absent from his first novel, *The Natural* (1952), which tells of an injured Major League pitcher reborn into a splendid outfielder. (Malamud may have been influenced by John R. Tunis's popular boy's book, *The Kid from Tompkinsville*, 1939.) The book contains much allegorical play with the Grail legend and other myths, but it held at arm's length Malamud's deeper concerns, which came to full expression only in *The Assistant*, with its vivid rendering of a grocer's day-to-day existence. Rejecting the frenetic verbal energy of his first novel, Malamud wrote *The Assistant* in a low-key, rather toneless style, just right for catching the drab solemnities of his characters' lives. As with Bellow's *The Victim*, published a few years previously, the novel is about human responsibility and the possibilities for conversion, seen through the conflict between Jew and gentile. The conflict is given life through faithfully rendered speech and through the patient yet always surprising turns of event with which the story unfolds. If the allegorical twist at its end is too ingenious for belief, still *The Assistant* remains an unforgettable, if depressing, book.

In subsequent novels he extended and relaxed his style. The comic *A New Life* (1962) is about a hapless college professor at a West Coast university (Malamud taught at Oregon State for a time). *The Fixer* (1966) is a parable-history of the ritual murder of a Christian child, while *The Tenants* (1971) attempted, in eventually violent, sensationalistic terms, to portray one minority's experience confronting another's—Jew against African American. Later, in *Dubin's Lives* (1979), he produced a readable if slightly conventional tale of a writer of biographies who is suddenly overtaken by life, in the form of a desirable young woman (the novel is set in Vermont, where Malamud lived for years, teaching at Bennington College from 1961 until he retired). In *God's Grace* (1982), he returned to the mode of parable or fable, writing a novel whose setting is a post-thermonuclear one.

In comparison with *The Assistant* and his shorter fiction, Malamud's later novels seem sometimes abstract and often insistently willed. In the short fiction, by contrast, we are given memorable portraits of embattled Jews in grotesque circumstances. At times they are close to becoming heroes of folklore; at other times they threaten to collapse into human caricatures. In a story such as "The Lady in the Lake," the pathetic-comic hero becomes both. At his best, as in that story or ones such as "The Magic Barrel" (printed here), "Idiots First," and "The Last Mohican," there is an intensity and a purity in the way Malamud imagines his lonely questers for perfection who become entangled in the imperfections of a social world. And on such occasions of tragicomic humiliation, this writer succeeded in sounding the deeper note that was his particular trademark.

The text is that of *The Magic Barrel* (1958), a collection of short stories.

The Magic Barrel

Not long ago there lived in uptown New York, in a small, almost meager room, though crowded with books, Leo Finkle, a rabbinical student at the Yeshiva University.[1] Finkle, after six years of study, was to be ordained in June and had been advised by an acquaintance that he might find it easier to win himself a congregation if he were married. Since he had no present prospects of marriage, after two tormented days of turning it over in his mind, he called in Pinye Salzman, a marriage broker whose two-line advertisement he had read in the *Forward*.[2]

The matchmaker appeared one night out of the dark fourth-floor hallway of the graystone rooming house where Finkle lived, grasping a black, strapped portfolio that had been worn thin with use. Salzman, who had been long in the business, was of slight but dignified build, wearing an old hat, and an overcoat too short and tight for him. He smelled frankly of fish, which he loved to eat, and although he was missing a few teeth, his presence was not displeasing, because of an amiable manner curiously contrasted with mournful eyes. His voice, his lips, his wisp of beard, his bony fingers were animated, but give him a moment of repose and his mild blue eyes revealed a depth of sadness, a characteristic that put Leo a little at ease although the situation, for him, was inherently tense.

He at once informed Salzman why he had asked him to come, explaining that his home was in Cleveland, and that but for his parents, who had married comparatively late in life, he was alone in the world. He had for six years devoted himself almost entirely to his studies, as a result of which, under-

---

1. In New York City, it offers courses in theological as well as secular disciplines. Generically, *yeshiva* is a term for a Jewish seminary.

2. *The Jewish Daily Forward,* a Yiddish-language daily newspaper published in New York City.

standably, he had found himself without time for a social life and the company of young women. Therefore he thought it the better part of trial and error—of embarrassing fumbling—to call in an experienced person to advise him on these matters. He remarked in passing that the function of the marriage broker was ancient and honorable, highly approved in the Jewish community, because it made practical the necessary without hindering joy. Moreover, his own parents had been brought together by a matchmaker. They had made, if not a financially profitable marriage—since neither had possessed any worldly goods to speak of—at least a successful one in the sense of their everlasting devotion to each other. Salzman listened in embarrassed surprise, sensing a sort of apology. Later, however, he experienced a glow of pride in his work, an emotion that had left him years ago, and he heartily approved of Finkle.

The two went to their business. Leo had led Salzman to the only clear place in the room, a table near a window that overlooked the lamp-lit city. He seated himself at the matchmaker's side but facing him, attempting by an act of will to suppress the unpleasant tickle in his throat. Salzman eagerly unstrapped his portfolio and removed a loose rubber band from a thin packet of much-handled cards. As he flipped through them, a gesture and sound that physically hurt Leo, the student pretended not to see and gazed steadfastly out the window. Although it was still February, winter was on its last legs, signs of which he had for the first time in years begun to notice. He now observed the round white moon, moving high in the sky through a cloud menagerie, and watched with half-open mouth as it penetrated a huge hen, and dropped out of her like an egg laying itself. Salzman, though pretending through eyeglasses he had just slipped on, to be engaged in scanning the writing on the cards, stole occasional glances at the young man's distinguished face, noting with pleasure the long, severe scholar's nose, brown eyes heavy with learning, sensitive yet ascetic lips, and a certain, almost hollow quality of the dark cheeks. He gazed around at shelves upon shelves of books and let out a soft, contented sigh.

When Leo's eyes fell upon the cards, he counted six spread out in Salzman's hand.

"So few?" he asked in disappointment.

"You wouldn't believe me how much cards I got in my office," Salzman replied. "The drawers are already filled to the top, so I keep them now in a barrel, but is every girl good for a new rabbi?"

Leo blushed at this, regretting all he had revealed of himself in a curriculum vitae he had sent to Salzman. He had thought it best to acquaint him with his strict standards and specifications, but in having done so, he felt he had told the marriage broker more than was absolutely necessary.

He hesitantly inquired, "Do you keep photographs of your clients on file?"

"First comes family, amount of dowry, also what kind promises," Salzman replied, unbuttoning his tight coat and settling himself in the chair. "After come pictures, rabbi."

"Call me Mr. Finkle. I'm not yet a rabbi."

Salzman said he would, but instead called him doctor, which he changed to rabbi when Leo was not listening too attentively.

Salzman adjusted his horn-rimmed spectacles, gently cleared his throat and read in an eager voice the contents of the top card:

"Sophie P. Twenty four years. Widow one year. No children. Educated high school and two years college. Father promises eight thousand dollars. Has wonderful wholesale business. Also real estate. On the mother's side comes teachers, also one actor. Well known on Second Avenue."

Leo gazed up in surprise. "Did you say a widow?"

"A widow don't mean spoiled, rabbi. She lived with her husband maybe four months. He was a sick boy she made a mistake to marry him."

"Marrying a widow has never entered my mind."

"This is because you have no experience. A widow, especially if she is young and healthy like this girl, is a wonderful person to marry. She will be thankful to you the rest of her life. Believe me, if I was looking now for a bride, I would marry a widow."

Leo reflected, then shook his head.

Salzman hunched his shoulders in an almost imperceptible gesture of disappointment. He placed the card down on the wooden table and began to read another:

"Lily H. High school teacher. Regular. Not a substitute. Has savings and new Dodge car. Lived in Paris one year. Father is successful dentist thirty-five years. Interested in professional man. Well Americanized family. Wonderful opportunity."

"I knew her personally," said Salzman. "I wish you could see this girl. She is a doll. Also very intelligent. All day you could talk to her about books and theater and what not. She also knows current events."

"I don't believe you mentioned her age?"

"Her age?" Salzman said, raising his brows. "Her age is thirty-two years."

Leo said after a while, "I'm afraid that seems a little too old."

Salzman let out a laugh. "So how old are you, rabbi?"

"Twenty-seven."

"So what is the difference, tell me, between twenty-seven and thirty-two? My own wife is seven years older than me. So what did I suffer?—Nothing. If Rothschild's[3] daughter wants to marry you, would you say on account her age, no?"

"Yes," Leo said dryly.

Salzman shook off the no in the yes. "Five years don't mean a thing. I give you my word that when you will live with her for one week you will forget her age. What does it mean five years—that she lived more and knows more than somebody who is younger? On this girl, God bless her, years are not wasted. Each one that it comes makes better the bargain."

"What subjects does she teach in high school?"

"Languages. If you heard the way she speaks French, you will think it is music. I am in the business twenty-five years, and I recommend her with my whole heart. Believe me, I know what I'm talking, rabbi."

"What's on the next card?" Leo said abruptly.

Salzman reluctantly turned up the third card:

"Ruth K. Nineteen years. Honor student. Father offers thirteen thousand cash to the right bridegroom. He is a medical doctor. Stomach specialist with marvelous practice. Brother in law owns own garment business. Particular people."

---

3. Once prominent, enormously wealthy family of Jewish international bankers and business leaders.

Salzman looked as if he had read his trump card.

"Did you say nineteen?" Leo asked with interest.

"On the dot."

"Is she attractive?" He blushed. "Pretty?"

Salzman kissed his finger tips. "A little doll. On this I give you my word. Let me call the father tonight and you will see what means pretty."

But Leo was troubled. "You're sure she's that young?"

"This I am positive. The father will show you the birth certificate."

"Are you positive there isn't something wrong with her?" Leo insisted.

"Who says there is wrong?"

"I don't understand why an American girl her age should go to a marriage broker."

A smile spread over Salzman's face.

"So for the same reason you went, she comes."

Leo flushed. "I am pressed for time."

Salzman, realizing he had been tactless, quickly explained. "The father came, not her. He wants she should have the best, so he looks around himself. When we will locate the right boy he will introduce him and encourage. This makes a better marriage than if a young girl without experience takes for herself. I don't have to tell you this."

"But don't you think this young girl believes in love?" Leo spoke uneasily.

Salzman was about to guffaw but caught himself and said soberly, "Love comes with the right person, not before."

Leo parted dry lips but did not speak. Noticing that Salzman had snatched a glance at the next card, he cleverly asked, "How is her health?"

"Perfect," Salzman said, breathing with difficulty. "Of course, she is a little lame on her right foot from an auto accident that it happened to her when she was twelve years, but nobody notices on account she is so brilliant and also beautiful."

Leo got up heavily and went to the window. He felt curiously bitter and upbraided himself for having called in the marriage broker. Finally, he shook his head.

"Why not?" Salzman persisted, the pitch of his voice rising.

"Because I detest stomach specialists."

"So what do you care what is his business? After you marry her do you need him? Who says he must come every Friday night in your house?"

Ashamed of the way the talk was going, Leo dismissed Salzman, who went home with heavy, melancholy eyes.

Though he had felt only relief at the marriage broker's departure, Leo was in low spirits the next day. He explained it as arising from Salzman's failure to produce a suitable bride for him. He did not care for his type of clientele. But when Leo found himself hesitating whether to seek out another matchmaker, one more polished than Pinye, he wondered if it could be—his protestations to the contrary, and although he honored his father and mother—that he did not, in essence, care for the match-making institution? This thought he quickly put out of mind yet found himself still upset. All day he ran around in the woods—missed an important appointment, forgot to give out his laundry, walked out of a Broadway cafeteria without paying and had to run back with the ticket in his hand; had even not recognized his landlady in the street when she passed with a friend and courteously called out, "A good evening to you, Doctor Finkle." By nightfall, however, he had regained sufficient calm to sink his nose into a book and there found peace from his thoughts.

Almost at once there came a knock on the door. Before Leo could say enter, Salzman, commercial cupid, was standing in the room. His face was gray and meager, his expression hungry, and he looked as if he would expire on his feet. Yet the marriage broker managed, by some trick of the muscles, to display a broad smile.

"So good evening. I am invited?"

Leo nodded, disturbed to see him again, yet unwilling to ask the man to leave.

Beaming still, Salzman laid his portfolio on the table. "Rabbi, I got for you tonight good news."

"I've asked you not to call me rabbi. I'm still a student."

"Your worries are finished. I have for you a first-class bride."

"Leave me in peace concerning this subject," Leo pretended lack of interest.

"The world will dance at your wedding."

"Please, Mr. Salzman, no more."

"But first must come back my strength," Salzman said weakly. He fumbled with the portfolio straps and took out of the leather case an oily paper bag, from which he extracted a hard, seeded roll and a small, smoked white fish. With a quick motion of his hand he stripped the fish out of its skin and began ravenously to chew. "All day in a rush," he muttered.

Leo watched him eat.

"A sliced tomato you have maybe?" Salzman hesitantly inquired.

"No."

The marriage broker shut his eyes and ate. When he had finished he carefully cleaned up the crumbs and rolled up the remains of the fish, in the paper bag. His spectacled eyes roamed the room until he discovered, amid some piles of books, a one-burner gas stove. Lifting his hat he humbly asked, "A glass tea you got, rabbi?"

Conscience-stricken, Leo rose and brewed the tea. He served it with a chunk of lemon and two cubes of lump sugar, delighting Salzman.

After he had drunk his tea, Salzman's strength and good spirits were restored.

"So tell me, rabbi," he said amiably, "you considered some more the three clients I mentioned yesterday?"

"There was no need to consider."

"Why not?"

"None of them suits me."

"What then suits you?"

Leo let it pass because he could give only a confused answer.

Without waiting for a reply, Salzman asked, "You remember this girl I talked to you—the high school teacher?"

"Age thirty-two?"

But, surprisingly, Salzman's face lit in a smile. "Age twenty-nine."

Leo shot him a look. "Reduced from thirty-two?"

"A mistake," Salzman avowed. "I talked today with the dentist. He took me to his safety deposit box and showed me the birth certificate. She was twenty-nine years last August. They made her a party in the mountains where she went for her vacation. When her father spoke to me the first time I forgot to write the age and I told you thirty-two, but now I remember this was a different client, a widow."

"The same one you told me about? I thought she was twenty-four?"

"A different. Am I responsible that the world is filled with widows?"

"No, but I'm not interested in them, nor for that matter, in school teachers."

Salzman pulled his clasped hands to his breast. Looking at the ceiling he devoutly exclaimed, "Yiddishe kinder,[4] what can I say to somebody that he is not interested in high school teachers? So what then you are interested?"

Leo flushed but controlled himself.

"In what else will you be interested," Salzman went on, "if you not interested in this fine girl that she speaks four languages and has personally in the bank ten thousand dollars? Also her father guarantees further twelve thousand. Also she has a new car, wonderful clothes, talks on all subjects, and she will give you a first-class home and children. How near do we come in our life to paradise?"

"If she's so wonderful, why wasn't she married ten years ago?"

"Why?" said Salzman with a heavy laugh. "—Why? Because she is *partikiler*.[5] This is why. She wants the *best*."

Leo was silent, amused at how he had entangled himself. But Salzman had aroused his interest in Lily H., and he began seriously to consider calling on her. When the marriage broker observed how intently Leo's mind was at work on the facts he had supplied, he felt certain they would soon come to an agreement.

Late Saturday afternoon, conscious of Salzman, Leo Finkle walked with Lily Hirschorn along Riverside Drive. He walked briskly and erectly, wearing with distinction the black fedora he had that morning taken with trepidation out of the dusty hat box on his closet shelf, and the heavy black Saturday coat he had thoroughly whisked clean. Leo also owned a walking stick, a present from a distant relative, but quickly put temptation aside and did not use it. Lily, petite and not unpretty, had on something signifying the approach of spring. She was au courant,[6] animatedly, with all sorts of subjects, and he weighed her words and found her surprisingly sound—score another for Salzman, whom he uneasily sensed to be somewhere around, hiding perhaps high in a tree along the street, flashing the lady signals with a pocket mirror; or perhaps a cloven-hoofed Pan,[7] piping nuptial ditties as he danced his invisible way before them, strewing wild buds on the walk and purple grapes in their path, symbolizing fruit of a union, though there was of course still none.

Lily startled Leo by remarking, "I was thinking of Mr. Salzman, a curious figure, wouldn't you say?"

Not certain what to answer, he nodded.

She bravely went on, blushing, "I for one am grateful for his introducing us. Aren't you?"

He courteously replied, "I am."

---

4. Jewish children (Yiddish); the sense is, what do these children know of the world as their parents knew it.
5. Yiddish corruption of "particular."

6. In keeping with the times (French).
7. Greek rural deity, part man and part goat, who presided over shepherds and flocks.

"I mean," she said with a little laugh—and it was all in good taste, or at least gave the effect of being not in bad—"do you mind that we came together so?"

He was not displeased with her honesty, recognizing that she meant to set the relationship aright, and understanding that it took a certain amount of experience in life, and courage, to want to do it quite that way. One had to have some sort of past to make that kind of beginning.

He said that he did not mind. Salzman's function was traditional and honorable—valuable for what it might achieve, which, he pointed out, was frequently nothing.

Lily agreed with a sigh. They walked on for a while and she said after a long silence, again with a nervous laugh, "Would you mind if I asked you something a little bit personal? Frankly, I find the subject fascinating." Although Leo shrugged, she went on half embarrassedly, "How was it that you came to your calling? I mean was it a sudden passionate inspiration?"

Leo, after a time, slowly replied, "I was always interested in the Law."

"You saw revealed in it the presence of the Highest?"

He nodded and changed the subject. "I understand that you spent a little time in Paris, Miss Hirschorn?"

"Oh, did Mr. Salzman tell you, Rabbi Finkle?" Leo winced but she went on, "It was ages ago and almost forgotten. I remember I had to return for my sister's wedding."

And Lily would not be put off. "When," she asked in a trembly voice, "did you become enamored of God?"

He stared at her. Then it came to him that she was talking not about Leo Finkle, but of a total stranger, some mystical figure, perhaps even passionate prophet that Salzman had dreamed up for her—no relation to the living or dead. Leo trembled with rage and weakness. The trickster had obviously sold her a bill of goods, just as he had him, who'd expected to become acquainted with a young lady of twenty-nine, only to behold, the moment he laid eyes upon her strained and anxious face, a woman past thirty-five and aging rapidly. Only his self control had kept him this long in her presence.

"I am not," he said gravely, "a talented religious person," and in seeking words to go on, found himself possessed by shame and fear. "I think," he said in a strained manner, "that I came to God not because I loved Him, but because I did not."

This confession he spoke harshly because its unexpectedness shook him.

Lily wilted. Leo saw a profusion of loaves of bread go flying like ducks high over his head, not unlike the winged loaves by which he had counted himself to sleep last night. Mercifully, then, it snowed, which he would not put past Salzman's machinations.

He was infuriated with the marriage broker and swore he would throw him out of the room the minute he reappeared. But Salzman did not come that night, and when Leo's anger had subsided, an unaccountable despair grew in its place. At first he thought this was caused by his disappointment in Lily, but before long it became evident that he had involved himself with Salzman without a true knowledge of his own intent. He gradually realized—with an emptiness that seized him with six hands—that he had called in the broker to find him a bride because he was incapable of doing it himself. This terrifying insight he had derived as a result of his meeting and conversation with Lily Hirschorn. Her probing questions had somehow irritated him into revealing—to himself more than her—the true nature of his relationship to God, and from that it had come upon him, with shocking force, that apart from his parents, he had never loved anyone. Or perhaps it went the other way, that he did not love God so well as he might, because he had not loved man. It seemed to Leo that his whole life stood starkly revealed and he saw himself for the first time as he truly was—unloved and loveless. This bitter but somehow not fully unexpected revelation brought him to a point of panic, controlled only by extraordinary effort. He covered his face with his hands and cried.

The week that followed was the worst of his life. He did not eat and lost weight. His beard darkened and grew ragged. He stopped attending seminars and almost never opened a book. He seriously considering leaving the Yeshiva, although he was deeply troubled at the thought of the loss of all his years of study—saw them like pages torn from a book, strewn over the city—and at the devastating effect of this decision upon his parents. But he had lived without knowledge of himself, and never in the Five Books and all the Commentaries—mea culpa[8]—had the truth been revealed to him. He did not know where to turn, and in all this desolating loneliness there was no *to whom,* although he often thought of Lily but not once could bring himself to go downstairs and make the call. He became touchy and irritable, especially with his landlady, who asked him all manner of personal questions; on the other hand, sensing his own disagreeableness, he waylaid her on the stairs and apologized abjectly, until mortified, she ran from him. Out of this, however, he drew the consolation that he was a Jew and that a Jew suffered. But gradually, as the long and terrible week drew to a close, he regained his composure and some idea of purpose in life: to go on as planned. Although he was imperfect, the ideal was not. As for his quest of a bride, the thought of continuing afflicted him with anxiety and heartburn, yet perhaps with this new knowledge of himself he would be more successful than in the past. Perhaps love would now come to him and a bride to that love. And for this sanctified seeking who needed a Salzman?

The marriage broker, a skeleton with haunted eyes, returned that very night. He looked, withal, the picture of frustrated expectancy—as if he had steadfastly waited the week at Miss Lily Hirschorn's side for a telephone call that never came.

Casually coughing, Salzman came immediately to the point: "So how did you like her?"

Leo's anger rose and he could not refrain from chiding the matchmaker: "Why did you lie to me, Salzman?"

Salzman's pale face went dead white, the world had snowed on him.

"Did you not state that she was twenty-nine?" Leo insisted.

"I gave you my word—"

"She was thirty-five, if a day. *At least* thirty-five."

"Of this don't be too sure. Her father told me—"

8. I have sinned (Latin). "Five Books and all the Commentaries": the Pentateuch (Five Books of Moses) consists of Genesis, Exodus, Leviticus, Numbers, and Deuteronomy—that part of Old Testament scripture referred to as the Torah, or "Law," and on which explanatory commentaries have been written.

"Never mind. The worst of it was that you lied to her."

"How did I lie to her, tell me?"

"You told her things about me that weren't true. You made me out to be more, consequently less than I am. She had in mind a totally different person, a sort of semimystical Wonder Rabbi."

"All I said, you was a religious man."

"I can imagine."

Salzman sighed. "This is my weakness that I have," he confessed. "My wife says to me I shouldn't be a salesman, but when I have two fine people that they would be wonderful to be married, I am so happy that I talk too much." He smiled wanly. "This is why Salzman is a poor man."

Leo's anger left him. "Well, Salzman, I'm afraid that's all."

The marriage broker fastened hungry eyes on him.

"You don't want any more a bride?"

"I do," said Leo, "but I have decided to seek her in a different way. I am no longer interested in an arranged marriage. To be frank, I now admit the necessity of premarital love. That is, I want to be in love with the one I marry."

"Love?" said Salzman, astounded. After a moment he remarked, "For us, our love is our life, not for the ladies. In the ghetto they—"

"I know, I know," said Leo. "I've thought of it often. Love, I have said to myself, should be a by-product of living and worship rather than its own end. Yet for myself I find it necessary to establish the level of my need and fulfill it."

Salzman shrugged but answered, "Listen, rabbi, if you want love, this I can find for you also. I have such beautiful clients that you will love them the minute your eyes will see them."

Leo smiled unhappily. "I'm afraid you don't understand."

But Salzman hastily unstrapped his portfolio and withdrew a manila packet from it.

"Pictures," he said, quickly laying the envelope on the table.

Leo called after him to take the pictures away, but as if on the wings of the wind, Salzman had disappeared.

March came. Leo had returned to his regular routine. Although he felt not quite himself yet—lacked energy—he was making plans for a more active social life. Of course it would cost something, but he was an expert in cutting corners; and when there were no corners left he would make circles rounder. All the while Salzman's pictures had lain on the table, gathering dust. Occasionally as Leo sat studying, or enjoying a cup of tea, his eyes fell on the manila envelope, but he never opened it.

The days went by and no social life to speak of developed with a member of the opposite sex—it was difficult, given the circumstances of his situation. One morning Leo toiled up the stairs to his room and stared out the window at the city. Although the day was bright his view of it was dark. For some time he watched people in the street below hurrying along and then turned with a heavy heart to his little room. On the table was the packet. With a sudden relentless gesture he tore it open. For a half-hour he stood by the table in a state of excitement, examining the photographs of the ladies Salzman had included. Finally, with a deep sigh he put them down. There were six, of varying degrees of attractiveness, but look at them long enough and they all became Lily Hirschorn: all past their prime, all starved behind bright smiles, not a true personality in the lot. Life, despite their frantic yoohooings, had passed them by; they were pictures in a brief case that stank of fish. After a while, however, as Leo attempted to return the photographs into the envelope, he found in it another, a snapshot of the type taken by a machine for a quarter. He gazed at it a moment and let out a cry.

Her face deeply moved him. Why, he could at first not say. It gave him the impression of youth—spring flowers, yet age—a sense of having been used to the bone, wasted; this came from the eyes, which were hauntingly familiar, yet absolutely strange. He had a vivid impression that he had met her before, but try as he might he could not place her although he could almost recall her name, as if he had read it in her own handwriting. No, this couldn't be; he would have remembered her. It was not, he affirmed, that she had an extraordinary beauty—no, though her face was attractive enough; it was that *something* about her moved him. Feature for feature, even some of the ladies of the photographs could do better; but she leaped forth to his heart—had *lived*, or wanted to—more than just wanted, perhaps regretted how she had lived—had somehow deeply suffered: it could be seen in the depths of those reluctant eyes, and from the way the light enclosed and shone from her, and within her, opening realms of possibility: this was her own. Her he desired. His head ached and eyes narrowed with the intensity of his gazing, then as if an obscure fog had blown up in the mind, he experienced fear of her and was aware that he had received an impression, somehow, of evil. He shuddered, saying softly, it is thus with us all. Leo brewed some tea in a small pot and sat sipping it without sugar, to calm himself. But before he had finished drinking, again with excitement he examined the face and found it good: good for Leo Finkle. Only such a one could understand him and help him seek whatever he was seeking. She might, perhaps, love him. How she had happened to be among the discards in Salzman's barrel he could never guess, but he knew he must urgently go find her.

Leo rushed downstairs, grabbed up the Bronx telephone book, and searched for Salzman's home address. He was not listed, nor was his office. Neither was he in the Manhattan book. But Leo remembered having written down the address on a slip of paper after he had read Salzman's advertisement in the "personals" column of the *Forward*. He ran up to his room and tore through his papers, without luck. It was exasperating. Just when he needed the matchmaker he was nowhere to be found. Fortunately Leo remembered to look in his wallet. There on a card he found his name written and a Bronx address. No phone number was listed, the reason—Leo now recalled—he had originally communicated with Salzman by letter. He got on his coat, put a hat on over his skull cap and hurried to the subway station. All the way to the far end of the Bronx he sat on the edge of his seat. He was more than once tempted to take out the picture and see if the girl's face was as he remembered it, but he refrained, allowing the snapshot to remain in his inside coat pocket, content to have her so close. When the train pulled into the station he was waiting at the door and bolted out. He quickly located the street Salzman had advertised.

The building he sought was less than a block from the subway, but it was not an office building, nor even a loft, nor a store in which one could rent office space. It was a very old tenement house. Leo found Salzman's name in pencil on a soiled tag under the bell and climbed three dark flights to his apartment. When he knocked, the door was opened by a thin, asthmatic, gray-haired woman, in felt slippers.

"Yes?" she said, expecting nothing. She listened without listening. He could have sworn he had seen her, too, before but knew it was an illusion.

"Salzman—does he live here? Pinye Salzman," he said, "the matchmaker?"

She stared at him a long minute. "Of course."

He felt embarrassed. "Is he in?"

"No." Her mouth, though left open, offered nothing more.

"The matter is urgent. Can you tell me where his office is?"

"In the air." She pointed upward.

"You mean he has no office?" Leo asked.

"In his socks."

He peered into the apartment. It was sunless and dingy, one large room divided by a half-open curtain, beyond which he could see a sagging metal bed. The near side of a room was crowded with rickety chairs, old bureaus, a three-legged table, racks of cooking utensils, and all the apparatus of a kitchen. But there was no sign of Salzman or his magic barrel, probably also a figment of the imagination. An odor of frying fish made Leo weak to the knees.

"Where is he?" he insisted. "I've got to see your husband."

At length she answered, "So who knows where he is? Every time he thinks a new thought he runs to a different place. Go home, he will find you."

"Tell him Leo Finkle."

She gave no sign she had heard.

He walked downstairs, depressed.

But Salzman, breathless, stood waiting at his door.

Leo was astounded and overjoyed. "How did you get here before me?"

"I rushed."

"Come inside."

They entered. Leo fixed tea, and a sardine sandwich for Salzman. As they were drinking he reached behind him for the packet of pictures and handed them to the marriage broker.

Salzman put down his glass and said expectantly, "You found somebody you like?"

"Not among these."

The marriage broker turned away.

"Here is the one I want." Leo held forth the snapshot.

Salzman slipped on his glasses and took the picture into his trembling hand. He turned ghastly and let out a groan.

"What's the matter?" cried Leo.

"Excuse me. Was an accident this picture. She isn't for you."

Salzman frantically shoved the manila packet into his portfolio. He thrust the snapshot into his pocket and fled down the stairs.

Leo, after momentary paralysis, gave chase and cornered the marriage broker in the vestibule. The landlady made hysterical outcries but neither of them listened.

"Give me back the picture, Salzman."

"No." The pain in his eyes was terrible.

"Tell me who she is then."

"This I can't tell you. Excuse me."

He made to depart, but Leo, forgetting himself, seized the matchmaker by his tight coat and shook him frenziedly.

"Please," sighed Salzman. "*Please.*"

Leo ashamedly let him go. "Tell me who she is," he begged. "It's very important for me to know."

"She is not for you. She is a wild one—wild, without shame. This is not a bride for a rabbi."

"What do you mean wild?"

"Like an animal. Like a dog. For her to be poor was a sin. This is why to me she is dead now."

"In God's name, what do you mean?"

"Her I can't introduce to you," Salzman said.

"Why are you so excited?"

"Why, he asks," Salzman said, bursting into tears. "This is my baby, my Stella, she should burn in hell."

Leo hurried up to bed and hid under the covers. Under the covers he thought his life through. Although he soon fell asleep he could not sleep her out of his mind. He woke, beating his breast. Though he prayed to be rid of her, his prayers went unanswered. Through days of torment he endlessly struggled not to love her; fearing success, he escaped it. He then concluded to convert her to goodness, himself to God. The idea alternately nauseated and exalted him.

He perhaps did not know that he had come to a final decision until he encountered Salzman in a Broadway cafeteria. He was sitting alone at a rear table, sucking the bony remains of a fish. The marriage broker appeared haggard, and transparent to the point of vanishing.

Salzman looked up at first without recognizing him. Leo had grown a pointed beard and his eyes were weighted with wisdom.

"Salzman," he said, "love has at last come to my heart."

"Who can love from a picture?" mocked the marriage broker.

"It is not impossible."

"If you can love her, then you can love anybody. Let me show you some new clients that they just sent me their photographs. One is a little doll."

"Just her I want," Leo murmured.

"Don't be a fool, doctor. Don't bother with her."

"Put me in touch with her, Salzman," Leo said humbly. "Perhaps I can be of service."

Salzman had stopped eating and Leo understood with emotion that it was now arranged.

Leaving the cafeteria, he was, however, afflicted by a tormenting suspicion that Salzman had planned it all to happen this way.

Leo was informed by letter that she would meet him on a certain corner, and she was there one spring night, waiting under a street lamp. He appeared, carrying a small bouquet of violets and rosebuds. Stella stood by the lamp post, smoking. She wore white with red shoes, which fitted his expectations, although in a troubled moment he had imagined the dress red, and only the shoes white. She waited uneasily and shyly. From afar he saw that her eyes—clearly her father's—were filled with desperate innocence. He pictured, in her, his own redemption. Violins and lit candles revolved in the sky. Leo ran forward with flowers outthrust.

Around the corner, Salzman, leaning against a wall, chanted prayers for the dead.

1958

RALPH ELLISON
1914–1994

"If the Negro, or any other writer, is going to do what's expected of him, he's lost the battle before he takes the field." This remark of Ralph Ellison's, taken from his *Paris Review* interview of 1953, serves in more than one sense as an appropriate motto for his own career. He did not do what his critics, literary or political, suggested that he ought to but insisted on being a writer rather than a spokesman for a cause or a representative figure. His importance to American letters is partly due to this independence. It is also true, that he did the unexpected in not following his fine first novel with the others that were predicted. While maintaining a strong presence on the literary scene by writing essays on a wide variety of social and cultural issues, Ellison published only excerpts from his work in progress: a massive novel that may well have run to three volumes, a single book of which was assembled after his death and published as *Juneteenth* (1999).

Ellison was born in Oklahoma; grew up in Oklahoma City; won a state scholarship; and attended the Tuskegee Institute, where he was a music major, his instrument, the trumpet. His musical life was wide enough to embrace both "serious music" and the world of Southwest–Kansas City jazz just reaching its heyday when Ellison was a young man. He became friends with Jimmy Rushing, the blues singer, and was acquainted with other members of what would be the great Count Basie band of the 1930s; this "deep, rowdy stream of jazz" figured for him as an image of the power and control that constituted art. Although he was a serious student of music and composition, his literary inclinations eventually dominated his musical ones; but testimony to his abiding knowledge and love of music may be found in some of the essays from *Shadow and Act* (1964), a collection of his prose.

Ellison left Tuskegee and went north to New York City. There, in 1936, he met Richard Wright, who encouraged him as a writer, and Ellison began to publish reviews and short stories. *Invisible Man*, begun in 1945, was published seven years later and won the National Book Award. Ellison subsequently received a number of awards and lectureships, taught at the Salzburg Seminar, at Bard College, and at the University of Chicago, and in 1970 was named Albert Schweitzer Professor of the Humanities at New York University, where he taught until his retirement. Yet he admitted to being troubled by the terms in which *Invisible Man*'s success—and perhaps his own career as well—were defined. In the *Paris Review* interview he deprecatingly referred to his novel as largely a failure, wished that rather than a "statement" about the American Negro it could be read "simply as a novel," and hoped that in twenty years it would be so read, casually adding, "if it's around that long."

Invisible Man may have outlived Ellison's expectations, but not without suffering attacks from critics. The most powerful of these, Irving Howe, took the author to task for not following the lead of Richard Wright and devoting his fiction to the Negro cause. Howe believed that African Americans should write social protest novels about the tragedy of black ghetto life. *Invisible Man* had used its protagonist's "invisibility" to entertain a much broader range of possibilities; and though by no means socially irresponsible, the novel is dedicated to the richness of life and art that becomes possible when the imagination is liberated from close realism.

"Cadillac Flambé," printed here, is one of the several excerpts from his work in progress that appeared during Ralph Ellison's lifetime. Scholars have yet to determine how it may have fit into Ellison's plans for the larger work that occupied him from 1952 until his death. But his literary executor, John F. Callahan, included just a paragraph from it in the posthumous novel titled *Juneteenth*, while suggesting that the piece deserved consideration as a free-standing short story. *Juneteenth* itself, based on Ellison's plan for Book II of his projected three-volume work, features the voices of two major characters: the African American minister, Alonzo "Daddy" Hickman, and Bliss, the presumably white orphan child he raises and who after running away becomes the notorious race-baiting Senator Adam Sunraider. "Cadillac Flambé" introduces an ancillary character who in the process of reacting against the senator's racism becomes a major interest by himself. Jazzman LeeWillie Minifees is a good example of how Ellison could create a character from the properties of a voice alone; his impassioned complaint about how Senator Sunraider debases African American culture is such a noteworthy performance that including it in *Juneteenth* might have distracted readers from the important verbal portraits of Hickman and Bliss.

Cadillac Flambé[1]

It had been a fine spring day made even pleasanter by the lingering of the cherry blossoms and I had gone out before dawn with some married friends and their children on a bird-watching expedition. Afterwards we had sharpened our appetites for brunch with rounds of bloody marys and bullshots. And after the beef bouillon ran out, our host, an ingenious man, had improvised a drink from chicken broth and vodka which he proclaimed the "chicken-shot." This was all very pleasant and after a few drinks my spirits were soaring. I was pleased with my friends, the brunch was excellent and varied—chili con carne, cornbread, and oysters Rockefeller, etc.—and I was pleased with my tally of birds. I had seen a bluebird, five rose-breasted grosbeaks, three painted buntings, seven goldfinches, and a rousing consort of mockingbirds. In fact, I had hated to leave.

Thus it was well into the afternoon when I found myself walking past the Senator's estate. I still had my binoculars around my neck, and my tape recorder—which I had along to record bird songs—was slung over my shoulder. As I approached, the boulevard below the Senator's estate was heavy with cars, with promenading lovers, dogs on leash, old men on canes, and laughing children, all enjoying the fine weather. I had paused to notice how the Senator's lawn rises from the street level with a gradual and imperceptible elevation that makes the mansion, set far at the top, seem to float like a dream castle; an illusion intensified by the chicken-shots, but which the art editor of my paper informs me is the result of a trick copied from the landscape architects who designed the gardens of the Bellevedere Palace in Vienna.[2] But be that as it may, I was about to pass on when a young couple blocked my path, and when I saw the young fellow point up the hill and say

---

1. The text is that of "Cadillac Flambé" as first published in the *American Review* in 1973.

2. Designed in the rococo manner by Johann Lucas von Hildebrandt between 1714 and 1722.

to his young blonde of a girl, "I bet you don't know who that is up there," I brought my binoculars into play, and there, on the right-hand terrace of the mansion, I saw the Senator.

Dressed in a chef's cap, apron, and huge asbestos gloves, he was armed with a long-tined fork which he flourished broadly as he entertained the notables for whom he was preparing a barbecue. These gentlemen and ladies were lounging in their chairs or standing about in groups sipping the tall iced drinks which two white-jacketed Filipino boys were serving. The Senator was dividing his attention between the spareribs cooking in a large chrome grill-cart and displaying his great talent for mimicking his colleagues with such huge success that no one at the party was aware of what was swiftly approaching. And, in fact, neither was I.

I was about to pass on when a gleaming white Cadillac convertible, which had been moving slowly in the heavy traffic from the east, rolled abreast of me and suddenly blocked the path by climbing the curb and then continuing across the walk and onto the Senator's lawn. The top was back and the driver, smiling as though in a parade, was a well-dressed Negro man of about thirty-five, who sported the gleaming hair affected by their jazz musicians and prize-fighters, and who sat behind the wheel with that engrossed, yet relaxed, almost ceremonial attention to form that was once to be observed only among the finest horsemen. So closely did the car brush past that I could have reached out with no effort and touched the rich ivory leather upholstery. A bull fiddle[3] rested in the back of the car. I watched the man drive smoothly up the lawn until he was some seventy-five yards below the mansion, where he braked the machine and stepped out to stand waving toward the terrace, a gallant salutation grandly given.

At first, in my innocence, I placed the man as a musician, for there was, after all, the bull fiddle; then in swift succession I thought him a chauffeur for one of the guests, a driver for a news or fashion magazine or an advertising agency or television network. For I quickly realized that a musician wouldn't have been asked to perform at the spot where the car was stopped, and that since he was alone, it was unlikely that anyone, not even the Senator, would have hired a musician to play serenades on a bull fiddle. So next I decided that the man had either been sent with equipment to be used in covering the festivities taking place on the terrace, or that he had driven the car over to be photographed against the luxurious background. The waving I interpreted as the expression of simple-minded high spirits aroused by the driver's pleasure in piloting such a luxurious automobile, the simple exuberance of a Negro allowed a role in what he considered an important public spectacle. At any rate, by now a small crowd had gathered and had begun to watch bemusedly.

Since it was widely known that the Senator is a master of the new political technology, who ignores no medium and wastes no opportunity for keeping his image ever in the public's eye, I wasn't disturbed when I saw the driver walk to the trunk and begin to remove several red objects of a certain size and place them on the grass. I wasn't using my binoculars now and thought these were small equipment cases. Unfortunately, I was mistaken.

For now, having finished unpacking, the driver stepped back behind the

3. Slang for bass viol.

wheel, and suddenly I could see the top rising from its place of concealment to soar into place like the wing of some great, slow, graceful bird. Stepping out again, he picked up one of the cases—now suddenly transformed into the type of can which during the war was sometimes used to transport high-octane gasoline in Liberty ships[4] (a highly, dangerous cargo for those round bottoms and the men who shipped in them)—and, leaning carefully forward, began emptying its contents upon the shining chariot.

And thus, I thought, *is gilded an eight-valved, three-hundred-and-fifty-horsepowered air-conditioned lily!*

For so accustomed have we Americans become to the tricks, the shenanigans, and frauds of advertising, so adjusted to the contrived fantasies of commerce—indeed, to pseudo-events of all kinds—that I thought that the car was being drenched with a special liquid which would make it more alluring for a series of commercial photographs.

Indeed, I looked up the crowded boulevard behind me, listening for the horn of a second car or station wagon which would bring the familiar load of pretty models, harassed editors, nervous wardrobe mistresses, and elegant fashion photographers who would convert the car, the clothes, and the Senator's elegant home, into a photographic rite of spring.

And with the driver there to remind me, I even expected a few ragged colored street urchins to be brought along to form a poignant but realistic contrast to the luxurious costumes and high-fashion surroundings: an echo of the somber iconography in which the crucified Christ is flanked by a repentant and an unrepentant thief, or that in which the three Wise Eastern Kings bear their rich gifts before the humble stable of Bethlehem.

But now reality was moving too fast for the completion of this foray into the metamorphosis of religious symbolism. Using my binoculars for a closer view, I could see the driver take a small spherical object from the trunk of the car and a fuzzy tennis ball popped into focus against the dark smoothness of his fingers. This was joined by a long wooden object which he held like a conductor's baton and began forcing against the ball until it was pierced. This provided the ball with a slender handle which he tested delicately for balance, drenched with liquid, and placed carefully behind the left fin of the car.

Reaching into the back seat now, he came up with a bass fiddle bow upon which he accidently spilled the liquid, and I could see drops of fluid roping from the horsehairs and falling with an iridescent spray into the sunlight. Facing us now, he proceeded to tighten the horsehairs, working methodically, very slowly, with his head gleaming in the sunlight and beads of sweat standing over his brow.

As I watched, I became aware of the swift gathering of a crowd around me, people asking puzzled questions, and a certain tension, as during the start of a concert, was building. And I had just thought, *And now he'll bring out the fiddle,* when he opened the door and hauled it out, carrying it, with the dripping bow swinging from his right hand, up the hill some thirty feet above the car, and placed it lovingly on the grass. A gentle wind started to blow now, and I swept my glasses past his gleaming head to the mansion, and as I screwed the focus to infinity, I could see several figures spring

4. World War II American troop transports.

suddenly from the shadows on the shaded terrace of the mansion's far wing. They were looking on like the spectators of a minor disturbance at a dull baseball game. Then a large woman grasped that something was out of order and I could see her mouth come open and her eyes blaze as she called out soundlessly, "Hey, you down there!" Then the driver's head cut into my field of vision and I took down the glasses and watched him moving, broad-shouldered and jaunty, up the hill to where he'd left the fiddle. For a moment he stood with his head back, his white jacket taut across his shoulders, looking toward the terrace. He waved then, and shouted words that escaped me. Then, facing the machine, he took something from his pocket and I saw him touch the flame of a cigarette lighter to the tennis ball and begin blowing gently upon it; then, waving it about like a child twirling a Fourth of July sparkler, he watched it sputter into a small blue ball of flame.

I tried, indeed I anticipated what was coming next, but I simply could not accept it! The Negro was twirling the ball on that long, black-tipped wooden needle—the kind used for knitting heavy sweaters—holding it between his thumb and fingers in the manner of a fire-eater at a circus, and I couldn't have been more surprised if he had thrown back his head and plunged the flame down his throat than by what came next. Through the glasses now I could see sweat beading out beneath his scalp line and on the flesh above the stiff hairs of his moustache as he grinned broadly and took up the fiddle bow, and before I could move he had shot his improvised, flame-tipped arrow onto the cloth top of the convertible.

"Why that black son of the devil!" someone shouted, and I had the impression of a wall of heat springing up from the grass before me. Then the flames erupted with a stunning blue roar that sent the spectators scattering. People were shouting now, and through the blue flames before me I could see the Senator and his guests, running from the terrace to halt at the top of the lawn, looking down, while behind me there were screams, the grinding of brakes, the thunder of footfalls as the promenaders broke in a great spontaneous wave up the grassy slope, then sensing the danger of exploding gasoline, receded hurriedly to a safer distance below, their screams and curses ringing above the roar of the flames.

How, oh, how, I wished for a cinema camera to synchronize with my tape recorder!—which automatically I now brought into play as heavy fumes of alcohol and gasoline, those defining spirits of our age, filled the air. There before me unfolding in *tableau vivant*[5] was surely the most unexpected picture in the year: in the foreground at the bottom of the slope, a rough semicircle of outraged faces; in the mid-foreground, up the gentle rise of the lawn, the white convertible shooting into the springtime air a radiance of intense blue flame, a flame like that of a welder's torch or perhaps of a huge fowl being flambéed in choice cognac; then on the rise above, distorted by heat and flame, the dark-skinned, white-suited driver, standing with his gleaming face expressive of high excitement as he watched the effect of his deed. Then, rising high in the background atop the grassy hill, the white-capped Senator surrounded by his notable guests—all caught in postures eloquent of surprise, shock, or indignation.

The air was filled with an overpowering smell of wood alcohol, which, as

5. Living picture (French); a 19th-century practice of arranging people in static poses.

the leaping red and blue flames took firm hold, mingled with the odor of burning paint and leather. I became aware of the fact that the screaming had suddenly faded now, and I could hear the swoosh-pop-crackle-and-hiss of the fire. And with the gaily dressed crowd become silent, it was as though I were alone, isolated, observing a conflagration produced by a stroke of lightning flashed out of a clear blue springtime sky. We watched with that sense of awe similar to that with which medieval crowds must have observed the burning of a great cathedral. We were stunned by the sacrificial act and, indeed, it was as though we had become the unwilling participants in a primitive ceremony requiring the sacrifice of a beautiful object in appeasement of some terrifying and long-dormant spirit, which the black man in the white suit was summoning from a long, black sleep. And as we watched, our faces strained as though in anticipation of the spirit's materialization from the fiery metamorphosis of the white machine, a spirit that I was afraid, whatever the form in which it appeared, would be powerfully good or powerfully evil, and absolutely out of place here and now in Washington. It was, as I say, uncanny. The whole afternoon seemed to float, and when I looked again to the top of the hill the people there appeared to move in slow motion through watery waves of heat. Then I saw the Senator, with chef cap awry, raising his asbestos gloves above his head and beginning to shout. And it was then that the driver, the firebrand, went into action.

Till now, looking like the chief celebrant of an outlandish rite, he had held firmly to his middle-ground; too dangerously near the flaming convertible for anyone not protected by asbestos suiting to risk laying hands upon him, yet far enough away to highlight his human vulnerability to fire. But now as I watched him move to the left of the flames to a point allowing him an uncluttered view of the crowd, his white suit reflecting the flames, he was briefly obscured by a sudden swirl of smoke, and it was during this brief interval that I heard the voice.

Strong and hoarse and typically Negro in quality, it seemed to issue with eerie clarity from the fire itself. Then I was struggling within myself for the reporter's dedicated objectivity and holding my microphone forward as he raised both arms above his head, his long, limber fingers wide-spread as he waved toward us.

"Ladies and gentlemen," he said, "please don't be disturbed! I don't mean you any harm, and if you'll just cool it a minute I'll tell you what this is all about . . ."

He paused and the Senator's voice could be heard angrily in the background.

"Never mind that joker up there on top of the hill," the driver said. "You can listen to him when I get through. He's had too much free speech anyway. Now it's *my* turn."

And at this a man at the other end of the crowd shouted angrily and tried to break up the hill. He was grabbed by two men and an hysterical, dark-haired woman wearing a well-filled chemise-style dress, who slipped to the ground holding a leg, shouting, "No, Fleetwood. No! That crazy nigger will kill you!"

The arsonist watched with blank-faced calm as the man was dragged protesting back into the crowd. Then a shift in the breeze whipped smoke down upon us and gave rise to a flurry of coughing.

"Now believe me," the arsonist continued, "I know that it's very, very hard for you folks to look at what I'm doing and not be disturbed, because for you it's a crime and a sin."

He laughed, swinging his fiddle bow in a shining arc as the crowd watched him fixedly.

"That's because you know that most folks can't afford to own one of these Caddies. Not even good, hard-working folks, no matter what the pictures in the papers and magazines say. So deep down it makes you feel some larceny. You feel that it's unfair that everybody who's willing to work hard can't have one for himself. That's right! And you feel that in order to get one it's OK for a man to lie and cheat and steal—yeah, even swindle his own mother *if* she's got the cash. That's the difference between what you *say* you believe and the way you *act* if you get the chance. Oh yes, because words is words, but life is hard and earnest and these here Caddies is way, way out of this world!"

Pausing, he loosened the knot in his blue and white tie so that it hung down the front of his jacket in a large loop, then wiped his brow with a blue silk handkerchief.

"I don't mean to insult you," he said, bending toward us now, the fiddle bow resting across his knee, "I'm just reminding you of the facts. Because I can see in your eyes that it's going to cost me more to get *rid* of this Caddy the way I have to do it than it cost me to get it. I don't rightly know what the price will be, but I know that when you people get scaird and shook up, you get violent. —No, wait a minute . . ." He shook his head. "That's not how I meant to say it. I'm sorry. I apologize.

"Listen, here it is: This *morning,*" he shouted now, stabbing his bow toward the mansion with angry emphasis. "This morning that fellow Senator *Sunraider* up there, *he* started it when he shot off his mouth over the *radio.* That's what this is all about! I realized that things had gotten out of control. I realized all of a sudden that the man was *messing* . . . with . . . my *Cadillac,* and ladies and gentlemen, that's serious as all *hell* . . .

"Listen to me, y'all: A little while ago I was romping past *Richmond,* feeling fine. I had played myself three hundred and seventy-five dollars and thirty-three cents worth of gigs down in Chattanooga, and I was headed home to *Harlem* as straight as I could go. I wasn't bothering any*body.* I didn't even mean to stop by here, because this town has a way of making a man feel like he's living in a fool's *paradise.* When I'm *here* I never stop thinking about the difference between what it is and what it's *supposed* to be. In fact, I have the feeling that somebody put the *Indian* sign[6] on this town a long, long time ago, and I don't want to be around when it takes effect. So, like I say, I wasn't even thinking about this town. I was rolling past Richmond and those whitewalls were slapping those concrete slabs and I was rolling and the wind was feeling fine on my face—and that's when I made my sad mistake. Ladies and gentlemen, I turned on the radio. I had nothing against anybody. I was just hoping to hear some Dinah, or Duke, or Hawk [7] so that I could study their phrasing and improve my style and enjoy myself. —But what do I get? I'll tell you what I got—"

6. A curse (slang).
7. Coleman Hawkins (1904–1969), American jazz musician. Dinah Washington (1924–1963), born Ruth Lee Jones, American jazz singer. Edward Kennedy "Duke" Ellington (1899–1976), American jazz composer and orchestra leader.

He dropped his shoulders with a sudden violent twist as his index finger jabbed toward the terrace behind him, bellowing, "I GOT THAT NO GOOD, NOWHERE SENATOR SUNRAIDER! THAT'S WHAT I GOT! AND WHAT WAS HE DOING? HE WAS TRYING TO GET THE UNITED STATES GOVERNMENT TO MESS WITH MY CADILLAC! AND WHAT'S MORE, HE WAS CALLING MY CADDY A 'COON CAGE.'

"Ladies and gentlemen, I couldn't believe my *ears*. I don't know that Senator, and I know he doesn't know me from old *Bodiddly*.[8] But just the same, there he is, talking straight to me and there was no use of my trying to dodge. Because I do live in Harlem and I lo-mo-sho do drive a Cadillac. So I had to sit there and take it like a little man. There he was, a United States SENATOR, coming through my own radio telling me what I ought to be driving, and recommending to the United States Senate and the whole country that the name of my car be changed simply because *I*, me, LeeWillie Minifees, was driving it!

"It made me feel faint. It upset my mind like a midnight telegram!

"I said to myself, 'LeeWillie, what on earth is this man *talking* about? Here you been thinking you had it *made*. You been thinking you were as free as a bird—even though a black bird. That good-rolling Jersey Turnpike is up ahead to get you home. —And now here comes this Senator putting you in a cage! What in the world is going on?'

"I got so nervous that all at once my foot weighed ninety-nine pounds, and before I knew it I was doing *seventy-five*. I was breaking the law! I guess I was really trying to get away from that voice and what the man had said. But I was rolling and I was listening. I couldn't *help* myself. What I was hearing was going against my whole heart and soul, but I was listening *anyway*. And what I heard was beginning to make me see things in a new light. Yes, and that new light was making my eyeballs ache. And all the time Senator Sunraider up in the Senate was calling my car a 'coon cage.'

"So I looked around and I saw all that fine ivory leather there. I looked at the steel and at the chrome. I looked through the windshield and saw the road unfolding and the houses and the trees was flashing by. I looked up at the top and I touched the button and let it go back to see if that awful feeling would leave me. But it wouldn't leave. The *air* was hitting my face and the *sun* was on my head and I was feeling that good old familiar feeling of *flying*— but ladies and gentlemen, it was no longer the same! Oh, no—because I could still hear that Senator playing the *dozens*[9] with my Cadillac!

"And just then, ladies and gentlemen, I found myself rolling toward an old man who reminded me of my granddaddy by the way he was walking beside the highway behind a plow hitched to an old, white-muzzled Missouri mule. And when that old man looked up and saw me he waved. And I looked back through the mirror as I shot past him and I could see him open his mouth and say something like, 'Go on, fool!' Then him and that mule was gone even from the mirror and I was rolling on.

"And then, ladies and gentlemen, in a twinkling of an eye it struck me. A voice said to me, 'LeeWillie, that old man is right: you are a fool. And that doggone Senator Sunraider is right, LeeWillie, you are a fool in a coon cage!'

---

8. Bo Diddley (b. 1928), American rock and roll musician.

9. African American folk practice of trading insults in an antiphonal, escalating manner.

"I tell you, ladies and gentlemen, that old man and his mule both were talking to me. I said, 'What do you mean about his being right?' And they said, 'LeeWillie, look who he *is*,' and I said, 'I *know* who he is,' and they said, 'Well, LeeWillie, if a man like that, in the position he's in, can think the way he doin, then LeeWillie, you have GOT to be wrong!'

"So I said, 'Thinking like that is why you've still got that mule in your lap,' man. 'I worked hard to get the money to buy this Caddy,' and he said, '*Money?* LeeWillie, can't you see that it ain't no longer a matter of money? Can't you see it's done gone way past the question of money? Now it's a question of whether you can afford it in terms *other than money.*'

"And I said, 'Man, what are you talking about, "terms other than money,"' and he said, 'LeeWillie, even this damn mule knows that if a man like that feels the way he's talking and can say it right out over the radio and the T.V., and from the place where he's saying it—there's got to be something drastically wrong with you for even wanting one. Son, the man's done made it mean something different. All you wanted was to have a pretty automobile, but fool, he done changed the Rules on you!'

"So against myself, ladies and gentlemen, I was forced to *agree* with the old man and the mule. That Senator up there wasn't simply degrading my Caddy. That wasn't the *point.* It's that he would low-rate a thing so truly fine as a *Cadillac* just in order to degrade *me* and my *people.* He was accusing *me* of lowering the value of the auto, when all I ever wanted was the very best!

"Oh, it hurt me to the quick, and right then and there I had me a rolling revelation. The *scales* dropped from my eyes. I had been BLIND, but the Senator up there on that hill was making me SEE. He was making me see some things I didn't *want* to see! I'd thought I was dressed real FINE, but I was as naked as a jaybird sitting on a limb in the drifting snow. I THOUGHT I was rolling past *Richmond,* but I was really trapped in a COON CAGE, running on one of those little TREADMILLS like a SQUIRREL or a HAMSTER. So now my EYEBALLS were aching. My head was in such a whirl that I shot the car up to ninety, and all I could see up ahead was the road getting NARROW. It was getting as narrow as the eye of a NEEDLE, and that needle looked like the Washington MONUMENT lying down. Yes, and I was trying to thread that Caddy straight through that eye and I didn't care if I made it or not. But while I managed to get that Caddy through I just couldn't thread that COON CAGE because it was like a two-ton knot tied in a piece of fine silk thread. The sweat was pouring off me now, ladies and gentlemen, and my brain was on fire, so I pulled off the highway and asked myself some questions, and I got myself some answers. It went this way:

" 'LeeWillie, who put you in this cage?'

" 'You put your own self in there,' a voice inside me said.

" 'But I paid for it, it's mine. I own it . . . ' I said.

" 'Oh, no, LeeWillie,' the voice said, 'what you mean is that it owns *you,* that's why you're *in* the cage. *Admit* it, daddy; you have been NAMED. Senator Sunraider has put the badmouth, the NASTY mouth on you and now your Cadillac ain't no Caddy anymore! Let's face it, LeeWillie, from now on everytime you sit behind this wheel you're going to feel those RINGS shooting round and round your TAIL and one of those little black COON'S masks is going to settle down over your FACE, and folks standing on the streets and hanging out the windows will sing out, "HEY! THERE GOES MISTER COON AND HIS COON CAGE!" That's right, LeeWillie! And all those little husky-voiced colored CHILDREN playing in the gutters will point at you and say, "THERE GOES MISTAH GOON AND HIS GOON GAGE"—and that will be right in Harlem!'

"And that did it, ladies and gentlemen; that was the capper, and THAT'S why I'm here!

"Right then and there, beside the *highway*, I made my decision. I rolled that Caddy, I made a U-turn and I stopped only long enough to get me some of that good white wood *alcohol* and good *white* gasoline, and then I headed straight here. So while some of you are upset, you can see that you don't have to be afraid because LeeWillie means nobody any harm.

"I am here, ladies and gentlemen, to make the Senator a present. Yes, sir and yes, mam, and it's Sunday and I'm told that *confession* is good for the *soul*. —So Mister Senator," he said, turning toward the terrace above, "this is my public testimony to my coming over to your way of thinking. This is my surrender of the Coon Cage Eight! You have unconverted me from the convertible. In fact, I'm giving it to you, Senator Sunraider, and it is truly mine to give. I hope all my people will do likewise. Because after your speech they ought to run whenever they even *look* at one of these. They ought to make for the bomb shelters whenever one comes close to the curb. So I, me, LeeWillie Minifees, am setting an example and here it is. You can HAVE it, Mister Senator. I don't WANT it. Thank you KINDLY and MUCH obliged . . ."

He paused, looking toward the terrace, and at this point I saw a great burst of flame which sent the crowd scurrying backward down the hill, and the white-suited firebrand went into an ecstatic chant, waving his violin bow, shaking his gleaming head and stamping his foot:

"Listen to me, Senator: I don't want no JET! (stamp!) But thank you kindly.

"I don't want no FORD! (stamp!)

"Neither do I want a RAMBLER! (stamp!)

"I don't want no NINETY-EIGHT! (stamp!)

"Ditto the THUNDERBIRD! (stamp-stamp!)[1]

"Yes, and keep those CHEVYS and CHRYSLERS away from me—do you (stamp!) *hear* me, Senator?

"YOU HAVE TAKEN THE BEST," he boomed, "SO, DAMMIT, TAKE ALL THE REST! Take ALL the rest!

"In fact, now I don't want anything you think is too good for me and my people. Because, just as that old man and the mule said, if a man in your position is against our having them, then there must be something WRONG in our *wanting* them. So to keep you happy, I, me, LeeWillie Minifees, am prepared to WALK. I'm ordering me some club-footed, pigeon-toed SPACE SHOES. I'd rather crawl or FLY. I'd rather save my money and wait until the A-RABS make a car. The Zulus even. Even the ESKIMOS! Oh, I'll walk and wait. I'll grab me a GREYHOUND or a FREIGHT! So you can have my coon cage, fare thee well!

"Take the TAIL FINS and the WHITEWALLS. Help yourself to the poor

---

1. Popular automobile makes and models, including the Nash Rambler, Oldsmobile 98, and Ford Thunderbird.

raped RADIO. ENJOY the automatic dimmer and the power brakes. ROLL, Mister Senator, with that fluid DRIVE. Breathe that air-conditioned AIR. There's never been a Caddy like this one and I want you to HAVE IT. Take my scientific dreamboat and enjoy that good ole GRACIOUS LIVING! The key's in the ignition and the REGISTRATION'S in the GLOVE compartment! And thank you KINDLY for freeing me from the Coon Cage. Because before I'd be in a CAGE, I'll be buried in my GRAVE—Oh! Oh!"

He broke off, listening; and I became aware of the shrilling of approaching sirens. Then he was addressing the crowd again.

"I knew," he called down with a grin, "that THOSE would be coming soon. Because they ALWAYS come when you don't NEED them. Therefore, I only hope that the Senator will beat it on down here and accept his gift before they arrive. And in the meantime, I want ALL you ladies and gentlemen to join LeeWillie in singing 'God Bless America' so that all this won't be in vain.

"I want you to understand that that was a damned GOOD Caddy and I loved her DEARLY. That's why you don't have to worry about me. I'm doing fine. Everything is copacetic.[2] Because, remember, nothing makes a man feel better than giving AWAY something, than SACRIFICING something, that he dearly LOVES!"

And then, most outrageous of all, he threw back his head and actually sang a few bars before the noise of the short-circuited horn set the flaming car to wailing like some great prehistoric animal heard in the throes of its dying.

Behind him now, high on the terrace, the Senator and his guests were shouting, but on the arsonist sang, and the effect on the crowd was maddening. Perhaps because from the pleasurable anticipation of watching the beginning of a clever advertising stunt, they had been thrown into a panic by the deliberate burning, the bizarre immolation of the automobile. And now with a dawning of awareness they perceived that they had been forced to witness (and who could turn away?) a crude and most portentous political gesture.

So suddenly they broke past me, dashing up the hill in moblike fury, and it was most fortunate for Minifees that his duet with the expiring Cadillac was interrupted by members of the police and fire departments, who, arriving at this moment, threw a flying wedge between the flaming machine and the mob. Through the noisy action I could see him there, looming prominently in his white suit, a mocking smile flickering on his sweaty face, as the action whirled toward where he imperturbably stood his ground, still singing against the doleful wailing of the car.

He was still singing, his wrists coolly extended now in anticipation of handcuffs—when struck by a veritable football squad of asbestos-garbed policemen and swept, tumbling, in a wild tangle of arms and legs, down the slope to where I stood. It was then I noted that he wore expensive black alligator shoes.

And now, while the crowd roared its approval, I watched as LeeWillie Minifees was pinned down, lashed into a straitjacket and led toward a police car. Up the hill two policemen were running laboredly toward where the Senator stood, silently observing. About me there was much shouting and

2. Excellent (slang).

shoving as some of the crowd attempted to follow the trussed-up and still grinning arsonist but were beaten back by the police.

It was unbelievably wild. Some continued to shout threats in their outrage and frustration, while others, both men and women, filled the air with a strangely brokenhearted and forlorn sound of weeping, and the officers found it difficult to disperse them. In fact, they continued to mill angrily about even as firemen in asbestos suits broke through, dragging hoses from a roaring pumper truck and sprayed the flaming car with a foamy chemical, which left it looking like the offspring of some strange animal brought so traumatically and precipitantly to life that it wailed and sputtered in protest, both against the circumstance of its debut into the world and the foaming presence of its still-clinging afterbirth . . .

And what had triggered it? How had the Senator sparked this weird conflagration? Why, with a joke! The day before, while demanding larger appropriations for certain scientific research projects that would be of great benefit to our electronics and communications industries, and of great importance to the nation as a whole, the Senator had aroused the opposition of a liberal Senator from New York who had complained, in passing, of what he termed the extreme vapidness of our recent automobile designs, their lack of adequate safety devices, and of the slackness of our quality-control standards and procedures. Well, it was in defending the automobile industry that the Senator passed the remark that triggered LeeWillie Minifees's bizarre reply.

In his rebuttal—the committee session was televised and aired over radio networks—the Senator insisted that not only were our cars the best in the world, the most beautiful and efficiently designed, but that, in fact, his opponent's remarks were a gratuitous slander. Because, he asserted, the only ground which he could see for complaint lay in the circumstance that a certain make of luxury automobile had become so outrageously popular in the nation's Harlems—the archetype of which is included in his opponent's district—that he found it embarrassing to own one. And then with a face most serious in its composure he went on to state:

"We have reached a sad state of affairs, gentlemen, wherein this fine product of American skill and initiative has become so common in Harlem that much of its initial value has been sorely compromised. Indeed, I am led to suggest, and quite seriously, that legislation be drawn up to rename it the 'Coon Cage Eight.' And not at all because of its eight, super-efficient cylinders, nor because of the lean, springing strength and beauty of its general outlines. Not at all, but because it has now become such a common sight to see eight or more of our darker brethren crowded together enjoying its power, its beauty, its neo-pagan comfort, while weaving recklessly through the streets of our great cities and along our super-highways. In fact, gentlemen, I was run off the road, forced into a ditch by such a power-drunk group just the other day. It is enough to make a citizen feel alienated from his own times, from the abiding values and recent developments within his own beloved nation.

"And yet, we continue to hear complaints to the effect that these constituents of our worthy colleague are ill-housed, ill-clothed, ill-equipped and under-*treated!* But, gentlemen, I say to you in all sincerity: Look into the streets! Look at the statistics for automobile sales! And I don't mean the economy cars, but our most expensive luxury machines. Look and see who is purchasing them! Give your attention to who it is that is creating the scarcity and removing these superb machines from the reach of those for whom they were intended! With so many of these good things, what, pray, do those people desire—is it a jet plane on every Harlem rooftop?"

Now for Senator Sunraider this had been mild and far short of his usual maliciousness. And while it aroused some slight amusement and brought replies of false indignation from some of his opponents, it was edited out, as is frequently the case, when the speech appeared in the Congressional Record and in the press. But who could have predicted that Senator Sunraider would have brought on LeeWillie Minifees's wild gesture? Perhaps he had been putting on an act, creating a happening, as they say, though I doubted it. There was something more personal behind it. Without question, the Senator's remarks were in extremely bad taste, but to cap the joke by burning an expensive car seemed so extreme a reply as to be almost metaphysical.

And yet, I reminded myself, it might simply be a case of overreacting expressed in true Negro abandon, an extreme gesture springing from the frustration of having no adequate means of replying, or making himself heard above the majestic roar of a Senator. There was, of course, the recent incident involving a black man suffering from an impacted wisdom tooth who had been so maddened by the blaring of a moisture-shorted automobile horn which had blasted his sleep about three o'clock of an icy morning, that he ran out into the street clothed only in an old-fashioned nightshirt and blasted the hood of the offending automobile with both barrels of a twelve-gauge over-and-under shotgun.

But while toothaches often lead to such extreme acts—and once in a while to suicide—LeeWillie Minifees had apparently been in no pain—or at least not in *physical* pain. And on the surface at least his speech had been projected clearly enough (allowing for the necessity to shout) and he had been smiling when they led him away. What would be his fate? I wondered; and where had they taken him? I would have to find him and question him, for his action had begun to sound in my mind with disturbing overtones which had hardly been meaningful. Rather they had been like the brief interruption one sometimes hears while listening to an F.M. broadcast of the musical *Oklahoma!*,[3] say, with original cast, when the signal fades and a program of quite different mood from a different wavelength breaks through. It had happened but then a blast of laughter had restored us automatically to our chosen frequency.

1973

---

3. Broadway musical by Richard Rodgers and Oscar Hammerstein II first staged in 1943 and popular as a film and soundtrack recording throughout the 1950s and 1960s.

From Invisible Man[1]

Prologue

I am an invisible man. No, I am not a spook like those who haunted Edgar Allan Poe; nor am I one of your Hollywood-movie ectoplasms. I am a man of substance, of flesh and bone, fiber and liquids—and I might even be said to possess a mind. I am invisible, understand, simply because people refuse to see me. Like the bodiless heads you see sometimes in circus sideshows, it is as though I have been surrounded by mirrors of hard, distorting glass. When they approach me they see only my surroundings, themselves, or figments of their imagination—indeed, everything and anything except me.

Nor is my invisibility exactly a matter of a bio-chemical accident to my epidermis. That invisibility to which I refer occurs because of a peculiar disposition in the eyes of those with whom I come in contact. A matter of the construction of their *inner* eyes, those eyes with which they look through their physical eyes upon reality. I am not complaining, nor am I protesting either. It is sometimes advantageous to be unseen, although it is most often rather wearing on the nerves. Then too, you're constantly being bumped against by those of poor vision. Or again, you often doubt if you really exist. You wonder whether you aren't simply a phantom in other people's minds. Say, a figure in a nightmare which the sleeper tries with all his strength to destroy. It's when you feel like this that, out of resentment, you begin to bump people back. And, let me confess, you feel that way most of the time. You ache with the need to convince yourself that you do exist in the real world, that you're a part of all the sound and anguish, and you strike out with your fists, you curse and you swear to make them recognize you. And, alas, it's seldom successful.

One night I accidentally bumped into a man, and perhaps because of the near darkness he saw me and called me an insulting name. I sprang at him, seized his coat lapels and demanded that he apologize. He was a tall blond man, and as my face came close to his he looked insolently out of his blue eyes and cursed me, his breath hot in my face as he struggled. I pulled his chin down sharp upon the crown of my head, butting him as I had seen the West Indians do, and felt his flesh tear and the blood gush out, and I yelled, "Apologize! Apologize!" But he continued to curse and struggle, and I butted him again and again until he went down heavily, on his knees, profusely bleeding. I kicked him repeatedly, in a frenzy because he still uttered insults though his lips were frothy with blood. Oh yes, I kicked him! And in my outrage I got out my knife and prepared to slit his throat, right there beneath the lamplight in the deserted street, holding him in the collar with one hand, and opening the knife with my teeth—when it occurred to me that the man had not *seen* me, actually; that he, as far as he knew, was in the midst of a walking nightmare! And I stopped the blade, slicing the air as I pushed him away, letting him fall back to the street. I stared at him hard as the lights of a car stabbed through the darkness. He lay there, moaning on the asphalt; a man almost killed by a phantom. It unnerved me. I was both disgusted and

1. The text is from *Invisible Man* (1952). Ras the Destroyer, Rinehart, and Brother Jack, mentioned in the prologue, are characters who will appear later.

ashamed. I was like a drunken man myself, wavering about on weakened legs. Then I was amused: Something in this man's thick head had sprung out and beaten him within an inch of his life. I began to laugh at this crazy discovery. Would he have awakened at the point of death? Would Death himself have freed him for wakeful living? But I didn't linger. I ran away into the dark, laughing so hard I feared I might rupture myself. The next day I saw his picture in the *Daily News*, beneath a caption stating that he had been "mugged." Poor fool, poor blind fool, I thought with sincere compassion, mugged by an invisible man!

Most of the time (although I do not choose as I once did to deny the violence of my days by ignoring it) I am not so overtly violent. I remember that I am invisible and walk softly so as not to awaken the sleeping ones. Sometimes it is best not to awaken them; there are few things in the world as dangerous as sleepwalkers. I learned in time though that it is possible to carry on a fight against them without their realizing it. For instance, I have been carrying on a fight with Monopolated Light & Power for some time now. I use their service and pay them nothing at all, and they don't know it. Oh, they suspect that power is being drained off, but they don't know where. All they know is that according to the master meter back there in their power station a hell of a lot of free current is disappearing somewhere into the jungle of Harlem. The joke, of course, is that I don't live in Harlem but in a border area. Several years ago (before I discovered the advantages of being invisible) I went through the routine process of buying service and paying their outrageous rates. But no more. I gave up all that, along with my apartment, and my old way of life: That way based upon the fallacious assumption that I, like other men, was visible. Now, aware of my invisibility, I live rent-free in a building rented strictly to whites, in a section of the basement that was shut off and forgotten during the nineteenth century, which I discovered when I was trying to escape in the night from Ras the Destroyer. But that's getting too far ahead of the story, almost to the end, although the end is in the beginning and lies far ahead.

The point now is that I found a home—or a hole in the ground, as you will. Now don't jump to the conclusion that because I call my home a "hole" it is damp and cold like a grave; there are cold holes and warm holes. Mine is a warm hole. And remember, a bear retires to his hole for the winter and lives until spring; then he comes strolling out like the Easter chick breaking from its shell. I say all this to assure you that it is incorrect to assume that, because I'm invisible and live in a hole, I am dead. I am neither dead nor in a state of suspended animation. Call me Jack-the-Bear,[2] for I am in a state of hibernation.

My hole is warm and full of light. Yes, *full* of light. I doubt if there is a brighter spot in all New York than this hole of mine, and I do not exclude Broadway. Or the Empire State Building on a photographer's dream night. But that is taking advantage of you. Those two spots are among the darkest of our whole civilization—pardon me, our whole *culture* (an important distinction, I've heard)—which might sound like a hoax, or a contradiction, but that (by contradiction, I mean) is how the world moves: Not like an arrow, but a boomerang. (Beware of those who speak of the *spiral* of history; they

2. Also the title of a jazz recording by Duke Ellington and his orchestra (1940).

are preparing a boomerang. Keep a steel helmet handy.) I know; I have been boomeranged across my head so much that I now can see the darkness of lightness. And I love light. Perhaps you'll think it strange that an invisible man should need light, desire light, love light. But maybe it is exactly because I *am* invisible. Light confirms my reality, gives birth to my form. A beautiful girl once told me of a recurring nightmare in which she lay in the center of a large dark room and felt her face expand until it filled the whole room, becoming a formless mass while her eyes ran in bilious jelly up the chimney. And so it is with me. Without light I am not only invisible, but formless as well; and to be unaware of one's form is to live a death. I myself, after existing some twenty years, did not become alive until I discovered my invisibility.

That is why I fight my battle with Monopolated Light & Power. The deeper reason, I mean: It allows me to feel my vital aliveness. I also fight them for taking so much of my money before I learned to protect myself. In my hole in the basement there are exactly 1,369 lights. I've wired the entire ceiling, every inch of it. And not with fluorescent bulbs, but with the older, more-expensive-to-operate kind, the filament type. An act of sabotage, you know. I've already begun to wire the wall. A junk man I know, a man of vision, has supplied me with wire and sockets. Nothing, storm or flood, must get in the way of our need for light and ever more and brighter light. The truth is the light and light is the truth. When I finish all four walls, then I'll start on the floor. Just how that will go, I don't know. Yet when you have lived invisible as long as I have you develop a certain ingenuity. I'll solve the problem. And maybe I'll invent a gadget to place my coffee pot on the fire while I lie in bed, and even invent a gadget to warm my bed—like the fellow I saw in one of the picture magazines who made himself a gadget to warm his shoes! Though invisible, I am in the great American tradition of tinkers. That makes me kin to Ford, Edison and Franklin. Call me, since I have a theory and a concept, a "thinker-tinker." Yes, I'll warm my shoes; they need it, they're usually full of holes. I'll do that and more.

Now I have one radio-phonograph; I plan to have five. There is a certain acoustical deadness in my hole, and when I have music I want to *feel* its vibration, not only with my ear but with my whole body. I'd like to hear five recordings of Louis Armstrong playing and singing "What Did I Do to Be So Black and Blue"—all at the same time. Sometimes now I listen to Louis while I have my favorite dessert of vanilla ice cream and sloe gin. I pour the red liquid over the white mound, watching it glisten and the vapor rising as Louis bends that military instrument into a beam of lyrical sound. Perhaps I like Louis Armstrong because he's made poetry out of being invisible. I think it must be because he's unaware that he *is* invisible. And my own grasp of invisibility aids me to understand his music. Once when I asked for a cigarette, some jokers gave me a reefer, which I lighted when I got home and sat listening to my phonograph. It was a strange evening. Invisibility, let me explain, gives one a slightly different sense of time, you're never quite on the beat. Sometimes you're ahead and sometimes behind. Instead of the swift and imperceptible flowing of time, you are aware of its nodes, those points where time stands still or from which it leaps ahead. And you slip into the breaks and look around. That's what you hear vaguely in Louis' music.

Once I saw a prizefighter boxing a yokel. The fighter was swift and amazingly scientific. His body was one violent flow of rapid rhythmic action. He hit the yokel a hundred times when the yokel held up his arms in stunned surprise. But suddenly the yokel, rolling about in the gale of boxing gloves, struck one blow and knocked science, speed and footwork as cold as a well-digger's posterior. The smart money hit the canvas. The long shot got the nod. The yokel had simply stepped inside of his opponent's sense of time. So under the spell of the reefer I discovered a new analytical way of listening to music. The unheard sounds came through, and each melodic line existed of itself, stood out clearly from all the rest, said its piece, and waited patiently for the other voices to speak. That night I found myself hearing not only in time, but in space as well. I not only entered the music but descended, like Dante, into its depths. *And beneath the swiftness of the hot tempo there was a slower tempo and a cave and I entered it and looked around and heard an old woman singing a spiritual as full of Weltschmerz as flamenco, and beneath that lay a still lower level on which I saw a beautiful girl the color of ivory pleading in a voice like my mother's as she stood before a group of slaveowners who bid for her naked body, and below that I found a lower level and a more rapid tempo and I heard someone shout:*

"*Brothers and sisters, my text this morning is the 'Blackness of Blackness.'*"

And a congregation of voices answered: "That blackness is most black, brother, most black . . ."

"*In the beginning . . .*"

"*At the very start," they cried.*

". . . *there was blackness . . .*"

"*Preach it . . .*"

". . . *and the sun . . .*"

"*The sun, Lawd . . .*"

". . . *was blood red . . .*"

"*Red . . .*"

"*Now black is . . ." the preacher shouted.*

"*Bloody . . .*"

"*I said black is . . .*"

"*Preach it, brother . . .*"

". . . *an' black ain't . . .*"

"*Red, Lawd, red: He said it's red!*"

"*Amen, brother . . .*"

"*Black will git you . . .*"

"*Yes, it will . . .*"

". . . *an' black won't . . .*"

"*Naw, it won't!*"

"*It do . . .*"

"*It do, Lawd . . .*"

". . . *an' it don't.*"

"*Halleluiah . . .*"

". . . *It'll put you, glory, glory, Oh my Lawd, in the* WHALE'S BELLY."

"*Preach it, dear brother . . .*"

". . . *an' make you tempt . . .*"

"*Good God a-mighty!*"

"*Old Aunt Nelly!*"

"*Black will make you . . .*"

"*Black . . .*"

". . . or black will un-make you."

"Ain't it the truth, Lawd?"

And at that point a voice of trombone timbre screamed at me, "Git out of here, you fool! Is you ready to commit treason?"

And I tore myself away, hearing the old singer of spirituals moaning, "Go curse your God, boy, and die."

I stopped and questioned her, asked her what was wrong.

"I dearly loved my master, son," she said.

"You should have hated him," I said.

"He gave me several sons," she said, "and because I loved my sons I learned to love their father though I hated him too."

"I too have become acquainted with ambivalence," I said. "That's why I'm here."

"What's that?"

"Nothing, a word that doesn't explain it. Why do you moan?"

"I moan this way 'cause he's dead," she said.

"Then tell me, who is that laughing upstairs?"

"Them's my sons. They glad."

"Yes, I can understand that too," I said.

"I laughs too, but I moans too. He promised to set us free but he never could bring hisself to do it. Still I loved him . . ."

"Loved him? You mean . . . ?"

"Oh, yes, but I loved something else even more."

"What more?"

"Freedom."

"Freedom," I said. "Maybe freedom lies in hating."

"Naw, son, it's in loving. I loved him and give him the poison and he withered away like a frost-bit apple. Them boys woulda tore him to pieces with they homemade knives."

"A mistake was made somewhere," I said, "I'm confused." And I wished to say other things, but the laughter upstairs became too loud and moan-like for me and I tried to break out of it, but I couldn't. Just as I was leaving I felt an urgent desire to ask her what freedom was and went back. She sat with her head in her hands, moaning softly; her leather-brown face was filled with sadness.

"Old woman, what is this freedom you love so well?" I asked around a corner of my mind.

She looked surprised, then thoughtful, then baffled. "I done forgot, son. It's all mixed up. First I think it's one thing, then I think it's another. It gits my head to spinning. I guess now it ain't nothing but knowing how to say what I got up in my head. But it's a hard job, son. Too much is done happen to me in too short a time. Hit's like I have a fever. Ever' time I starts to walk my head gits to swirling and I falls down. Or if it ain't that, it's the boys; they gits to laughing and wants to kill up the white folks. They's bitter, that's what they is . . ."

"But what about freedom?"

"Leave me 'lone, boy; my head aches!"

I left her, feeling dizzy myself. I didn't get far.

Suddenly one of the sons, a big fellow six feet tall, appeared out of nowhere and struck me with his fist.

"What's the matter, man?" I cried.

"You made Ma cry!"

"But how?" I said, dodging a blow.

"Askin' her them questions, that's how. Git outa here and stay, and next time you got questions like that, ask yourself!"

He held me in a grip like cold stone, his fingers fastening upon my windpipe until I thought I would suffocate before he finally allowed me to go. I stumbled about dazed, the music beating hysterically in my ears. It was dark. My head cleared and I wandered down a dark narrow passage, thinking I heard his footsteps hurrying behind me. I was sore, and into my being had come a profound craving for tranquillity, for peace and quiet, a state I felt I could never achieve. For one thing, the trumpet was blaring and the rhythm was too hectic. A tom-tom beating like heart-thuds began drowning out the trumpet, filling my ears. I longed for water and I heard it rushing through the cold mains my fingers touched as I felt my way, but I couldn't stop to search because of the footsteps behind me.

"Hey, Ras," I called. "Is it you, Destroyer? Rinehart?"

No answer, only the rhythmic footsteps behind me. Once I tried crossing the road, but a speeding machine struck me, scraping the skin from my leg as it roared past.

Then somehow I came out of it, ascending hastily from this underworld of sound to hear Louis Armstrong innocently asking,

> What did I do
> To be so black
> And blue?

At first I was afraid; this familiar music had demanded action, the kind of which I was incapable, and yet had I lingered there beneath the surface I might have attempted to act. Nevertheless, I know now that few really listen to this music. I sat on the chair's edge in a soaking sweat, as though each of my 1,369 bulbs had everyone become a klieg light[3] in an individual setting for a third degree with Ras and Rinehart in charge. It was exhausting—as though I had held my breath continuously for an hour under the terrifying serenity that comes from days of intense hunger. And yet, it was a strangely satisfying experience for an invisible man to hear the silence of sound. I had discovered unrecognized compulsions of my being—even though I could not answer "yes" to their promptings. I haven't smoked a reefer since, however; not because they're illegal, but because to see around corners is enough (that is not unusual when you are invisible). But to hear around them is too much; it inhibits action. And despite Brother Jack and all that sad, lost period of the Brotherhood, I believe in nothing if not in action.

Please, a definition: A hibernation is a covert preparation for a more overt action.

Besides, the drug destroys one's sense of time completely. If that happened, I might forget to dodge some bright morning and some cluck would run me down with an orange and yellow street car, or a bilious bus! Or I might forget to leave my hole when the moment for action presents itself.

Meanwhile I enjoy my life with the compliments of Monopolated Light &

---

3. Arc light used in making motion pictures.

Power. Since you never recognize me even when in closest contact with me, and since, no doubt, you'll hardly believe that I exist, it won't matter if you know that I tapped a power line leading into the building and ran it into my hole in the ground. Before that I lived in the darkness into which I was chased, but now I see. I've illuminated the blackness of my invisibility—and vice versa. And so I play the invisible music of my isolation. The last statement doesn't seem just right, does it? But it is; you hear this music simply because music is heard and seldom seen, except by musicians. Could this compulsion to put invisibility down in black and white be thus an urge to make music of invisibility? But I am an orator, a rabble rouser—Am? I *was*, and perhaps shall be again. Who knows? All sickness is not unto death, neither is invisibility.

I can hear you say, "What a horrible, irresponsible bastard!" And you're right. I leap to agree with you. I am one of the most irresponsible beings that ever lived. Irresponsibility is part of my invisibility; any way you face it, it is a denial. But to whom can I be responsible, and why should I be, when you refuse to see me? And wait until I reveal how truly irresponsible I am. Responsibility rests upon recognition, and recognition is a form of agreement. Take the man whom I almost killed: Who was responsible for that near murder—I? I don't think so, and I refuse it. I won't buy it. You can't give it to me. *He* bumped *me, he* insulted *me.* Shouldn't he, for his own personal safety, have recognized my hysteria, my "danger potential"? He, let us say, was lost in a dream world. But didn't *he* control that dream world— which, alas, is only too real!—and didn't *he* rule me out of it? And if he had yelled for a policeman, wouldn't *I* have been taken for the offending one? Yes, yes, yes! Let me agree with you, I was the irresponsible one; for I should have used my knife to protect the higher interests of society. Some day that kind of foolishness will cause us tragic trouble. All dreamers and sleepwalkers must pay the price, and even the invisible victim is responsible for the fate of all. But I shirked that responsibility; I became too snarled in the incompatible notions that buzzed within my brain. I was a coward . . .

But what did *I* do to be so blue? Bear with me.

Chapter I

[BATTLE ROYAL]

It goes a long way back, some twenty years. All my life I had been looking for something, and everywhere I turned someone tried to tell me what it was. I accepted their answers too, though they were often in contradiction and even self-contradictory. I was naïve. I was looking for myself and asking everyone except myself questions which I, and only I, could answer. It took me a long time and much painful boomeranging of my expectations to achieve a realization everyone else appears to have been born with: That I am nobody but myself. But first I had to discover that I am an invisible man!

And yet I am no freak of nature, nor of history. I was in the cards, other things having been equal (or unequal) eighty-five years ago. I am not ashamed of my grandparents for having been slaves. I am only ashamed of myself for having at one time been ashamed. About eighty-five years ago they were told that they were free, united with others of our country in everything pertaining to the common good, and, in everything social, separate like the fingers of the hand. And they believed it. They exulted in it. They stayed in their place, worked hard, and brought up my father to do the same. But my grandfather is the one. He was an odd old guy, my grandfather, and I am told I take after him. It was he who caused the trouble. On his deathbed he called my father to him and said, "Son, after I'm gone I want you to keep up the good fight. I never told you, but our life is a war and I have been a traitor all my born days, a spy in the enemy's country ever since I give up my gun back in the Reconstruction. Live with your head in the lion's mouth. I want you to overcome 'em with yeses, undermine 'em with grins, agree 'em to death and destruction, let 'em swoller you till they vomit or bust wide open." They thought the old man had gone out of his mind. He had been the meekest of men. The younger children were rushed from the room, the shades drawn and the flame of the lamp turned so low that it sputtered on the wick like the old man's breathing. "Learn it to the younguns," he whispered fiercely; then he died.

But my folks were more alarmed over his last words than over his dying. It was as though he had not died at all, his words caused so much anxiety. I was warned emphatically to forget what he had said and, indeed, this is the first time it has been mentioned outside the family circle. It had a tremendous effect upon me, however. I could never be sure of what he meant. Grandfather had been a quiet old man who never made any trouble, yet on his deathbed he had called himself a traitor and a spy, and he had spoken of his meekness as a dangerous activity. It became a constant puzzle which lay unanswered in the back of my mind. And whenever things went well for me I remembered my grandfather and felt guilty and uncomfortable. It was as though I was carrying out his advice in spite of myself. And to make it worse, everyone loved me for it. I was praised by the most lily-white men of the town. I was considered an example of desirable conduct—just as my grandfather had been. And what puzzled me was that the old man had defined it as *treachery*. When I was praised for my conduct I felt a guilt that in some way I was doing something that was really against the wishes of the white folks, that if they had understood they would have desired me to act just the opposite, that I should have been sulky and mean, and that that really would have been what they wanted, even though they were fooled and thought they wanted me to act as I did. It made me afraid that some day they would look upon me as a traitor and I would be lost. Still I was more afraid to act any other way because they didn't like that at all. The old man's words were like a curse. On my graduation day I delivered an oration in which I showed that humility was the secret, indeed, the very essence of progress. (Not that I believed this—how could I, remembering my grandfather?—I only believed that it worked.) It was a great success. Everyone praised me and I was invited to give the speech at a gathering of the town's leading white citizens. It was a triumph for our whole community.

It was in the main ballroom of the leading hotel. When I got there I discovered that it was on the occasion of a smoker, and I was told that since I was to be there anyway I might as well take part in the battle royal to be fought by some of my schoolmates as part of the entertainment. The battle royal came first.

All of the town's big shots were there in their tuxedoes, wolfing down the buffet foods, drinking beer and whiskey and smoking black cigars. It was a large room with a high ceiling. Chairs were arranged in neat rows around three sides of a portable boxing ring. The fourth side was clear, revealing a gleaming space of polished floor. I had some misgivings over the battle royal, by the way. Not from a distaste for fighting, but because I didn't care too much for the other fellows who were to take part. They were tough guys who seemed to have no grandfather's curse worrying their minds. No one could mistake their toughness. And besides, I suspected that fighting a battle royal might detract from the dignity of my speech. In those pre-invisible days I visualized myself as a potential Booker T. Washington. But the other fellows didn't care too much for me either, and there were nine of them. I felt superior to them in my way, and I didn't like the manner in which we were all crowded together into the servants' elevator. Nor did they like my being there. In fact, as the warmly lighted floors flashed past the elevator we had words over the fact that I, by taking part in the fight, had knocked one of their friends out of a night's work.

We were led out of the elevator through a rococo hall into an anteroom and told to get into our fighting togs. Each of us was issued a pair of boxing gloves and ushered out into the big mirrored hall, which we entered looking cautiously about us and whispering, lest we might accidentally be heard above the noise of the room. It was foggy with cigar smoke. And already the whiskey was taking effect. I was shocked to see some of the most important men of the town quite tipsy. They were all there—bankers, lawyers, judges, doctors, fire chiefs, teachers, merchants. Even one of the more fashionable pastors. Something we could not see was going on up front. A clarinet was vibrating sensuously and the men were standing up and moving eagerly forward. We were a small tight group, clustered together, our bare upper bodies touching and shining with anticipatory sweat; while up front the big shots were becoming increasingly excited over something we still could not see. Suddenly I heard the school superintendent, who had told me to come, yell, "Bring up the shines, gentlemen! Bring up the little shines!"

We were rushed up to the front of the ballroom, where it smelled even more strongly of tobacco and whiskey. Then we were pushed into place. I almost wet my pants. A sea of faces, some hostile, some amused, ringed around us, and in the center, facing us, stood a magnificent blonde—stark naked. There was dead silence. I felt a blast of cold air chill me. I tried to back away, but they were behind me and around me. Some of the boys stood with lowered heads, trembling. I felt a wave of irrational guilt and fear. My teeth chattered, my skin turned to goose flesh, my knees knocked. Yet I was strongly attracted and looked in spite of myself. Had the price of looking been blindness, I would have looked. The hair was yellow like that of a circus kewpie doll, the face heavily powdered and rouged, as though to form an abstract mask, the eyes hollow and smeared a cool blue, the color of a baboon's butt. I felt a desire to spit upon her as my eyes brushed slowly over her body. Her breasts were firm and round as the domes of East Indian temples, and I stood so close as to see the fine skin texture and beads of pearly perspiration glistening like dew around the pink and erected buds of her nipples. I wanted at one and the same time to run from the room, to sink through the floor, or go to her and cover her from my eyes and the eyes of the others with my body; to feel the soft thighs, to caress her and destroy her, to love her and murder her, to hide from her, and yet to stroke where below the small American flag tattooed upon her belly her thighs formed a capital V. I had a notion that of all in the room she saw only me with her impersonal eyes.

And then she began to dance, a slow sensuous movement; the smoke of a hundred cigars clinging to her like the thinnest of veils. She seemed like a fair bird-girl girdled in veils calling to me from the angry surface of some gray and threatening sea. I was transported. Then I became aware of the clarinet playing and the big shots yelling at us. Some threatened us if we looked and others if we did not. On my right I saw one boy faint. And now a man grabbed a silver pitcher from a table and stepped close as he dashed ice water upon him and stood him up and forced two of us to support him as his head hung and moans issued from his thick bluish lips. Another boy began to plead to go home. He was the largest of the group, wearing dark red fighting trunks much too small to conceal the erection which projected from him as though in answer to the insinuating low-registered moaning of the clarinet. He tried to hide himself with his boxing gloves.

And all the while the blonde continued dancing, smiling faintly at the big shots who watched her with fascination, and faintly smiling at our fear. I noticed a certain merchant who followed her hungrily, his lips loose and drooling. He was a large man who wore diamond studs in a shirtfront which swelled with the ample paunch underneath, and each time the blonde swayed her undulating hips he ran his hand through the thin hair of his bald head and, with his arms upheld, his posture clumsy like that of an intoxicated panda, wound his belly in a slow and obscene grind. This creature was completely hypnotized. The music had quickened. As the dancer flung herself about with a detached expression on her face, the men began reaching out to touch her. I could see their beefy fingers sink into the soft flesh. Some of the others tried to stop them and she began to move around the floor in graceful circles, as they gave chase, slipping and sliding over the polished floor. It was mad. Chairs went crashing, drinks were spilt, as they ran laughing and howling after her. They caught her just as she reached a door, raised her from the floor, and tossed her as college boys are tossed at a hazing, and above her red, fixed-smiling lips I saw the terror and disgust in her eyes, almost like my own terror and that which I saw in some of the other boys. As I watched, they tossed her twice and her soft breasts seem to flatten against the air and her legs flung wildly as she spun. Some of the more sober ones helped her to escape. And I started off the floor, heading for the anteroom with the rest of the boys.

Some were still crying and in hysteria. But as we tried to leave we were stopped and ordered to get into the ring. There was nothing to do but what we were told. All ten of us climbed under the ropes and allowed ourselves to be blindfolded with broad bands of white cloth. One of the men seemed to feel a bit sympathetic and tried to cheer us up as we stood with our backs against the ropes. Some of us tried to grin. "See that boy over there?" one of the men said. "I want you to run across at the bell and give it to him right in the belly. If you don't get him, I'm going to get you. I don't like his looks." Each of us was told the same. The blindfolds were put on. Yet even then I had been going over my speech. In my mind each word was as bright as flame. I felt the cloth pressed into place, and frowned so that it would be loosened when I relaxed.

But now I felt a sudden fit of blind terror. I was unused to darkness. It was as though I had suddenly found myself in a dark room filled with poisonous cottonmouths. I could hear the bleary voices yelling insistently for the battle royal to begin.

"Get going in there!"

"Let me at that big nigger!"

I strained to pick up the school superintendent's voice, as though to squeeze some security out of that slightly more familiar sound.

"Let me at those black sonsabitches!" someone yelled.

"No, Jackson, no!" another voice yelled. "Here, somebody, help me hold Jack."

"I want to get at that ginger-colored nigger. Tear him limb from limb," the first voice yelled.

I stood against the ropes trembling. For in those days I was what they called ginger-colored, and he sounded as though he might crunch me between his teeth like a crisp ginger cookie.

Quite a struggle was going on. Chairs were being kicked about and I could hear voices grunting as with a terrific effort. I wanted to see, to see more desperately than ever before. But the blindfold was tight as a thick skin-puckering scab and when I raised my gloved hands to push the layers of white aside a voice yelled, "Oh, no you don't, black bastard! Leave that alone!"

"Ring the bell before Jackson kills him a coon!" someone boomed in the sudden silence. And I heard the bell clang and the sound of the feet scuffling forward.

A glove smacked against my head. I pivoted, striking out stiffly as someone went past, and felt the jar ripple along the length of my arm to my shoulder. Then it seemed as though all nine of the boys had turned upon me at once. Blows pounded me from all sides while I struck out as best I could. So many blows landed upon me that I wondered if I were not the only blindfolded fighter in the ring, or if the man called Jackson hadn't succeeded in getting me after all.

Blindfolded, I could no longer control my motions. I had no dignity. I stumbled about like a baby or a drunken man. The smoke had become thicker and with each new blow it seemed to sear and further restrict my lungs. My saliva became like hot bitter glue. A glove connected with my head, filling my mouth with warm blood. It was everywhere. I could not tell if the moisture I felt upon my body was sweat or blood. A blow landed hard against the nape of my neck. I felt myself going over, my head hitting the floor. Streaks of blue light filled the black world behind the blindfold. I lay prone, pretending that I was knocked out, but felt myself seized by hands and yanked to my feet. "Get going, black boy! Mix it up!" My arms were like lead, my head smarting from blows. I managed to feel my way to the ropes and held on, trying to catch my breath. A glove landed in my mid-section and I went over again, feeling as though the smoke had become a knife jabbed into my guts. Pushed this way and that by the legs milling around me, I finally pulled erect and discovered that I could see the black, sweat-washed forms weaving in the smoky-blue atmosphere like drunken dancers weaving to the rapid drum-like thuds of blows.

Everyone fought hysterically. It was complete anarchy. Everybody fought everybody else. No group fought together for long. Two, three, four, fought one, then turned to fight each other, were themselves attacked. Blows landed below the belt and in the kidney, with the gloves open as well as closed, and with my eye partly opened now there was not so much terror. I moved carefully, avoiding blows, although not too many to attract attention, fighting from group to group. The boys groped about like blind, cautious crabs crouching to protect their mid-sections, their heads pulled in short against their shoulders, their arms stretched nervously before them, with their fists testing the smoke-filled air like the knobbed feelers of hypersensitive snails. In one corner I glimpsed a boy violently punching the air and heard him scream in pain as he smashed his hand against a ring post. For a second I saw him bent over holding his hand, then going down as a blow caught his unprotected head. I played one group against the other, slipping in and throwing a punch then stepping out of range while pushing the others into the melee to take the blows blindly aimed at me. The smoke was agonizing and there were no rounds, no bells at three minute intervals to relieve our exhaustion. The room spun around me, a swirl of lights, smoke, sweating bodies surrounded by tense white faces. I bled from both nose and mouth, the blood spattering upon my chest.

The men kept yelling, "Slug him, black boy! Knock his guts out!"

"Uppercut him! Kill him! Kill that big boy!"

Taking a fake fall, I saw a boy going down heavily beside me as though we were felled by a single blow, saw a sneaker-clad foot shoot into his groin as the two who had knocked him down stumbled upon him. I rolled out of range, feeling a twinge of nausea.

The harder we fought the more threatening the men became. And yet, I had begun to worry about my speech again. How would it go? Would they recognize my ability? What would they give me?

I was fighting automatically when suddenly I noticed that one after another of the boys was leaving the ring. I was surprised, filled with panic, as though I had been left alone with an unknown danger. Then I understood. The boys had arranged it among themselves. It was the custom for the two men left in the ring to slug it out for the winner's prize. I discovered this too late. When the bell sounded two men in tuxedoes leaped into the ring and removed the blindfold. I found myself facing Tatlock, the biggest of the gang. I felt sick at my stomach. Hardly had the bell stopped ringing in my ears than it clanged again and I saw him moving swiftly toward me. Thinking of nothing else to do I hit him smash on the nose. He kept coming, bringing the rank sharp violence of stale sweat. His face was a black blank of a face, only his eyes alive—with hate of me and aglow with a feverish terror from what had happened to us all. I became anxious. I wanted to deliver my speech and he came at me as though he meant to beat it out of me. I smashed him again and again, taking his blows as they came. Then on a sudden impulse I struck him lightly and as we clinched, I whispered, "Fake like I knocked you out, you can have the prize."

"I'll break your behind," he whispered hoarsely.

"For *them*?"

"For *me*, sonofabitch!"

They were yelling for us to break it up and Tatlock spun me half around with a blow, and as a joggled camera sweeps in a reeling scene, I saw the howling red faces crouching tense beneath the cloud of blue-gray smoke.

For a moment the world wavered, unraveled, flowed, then my head cleared and Tatlock bounced before me. That fluttering shadow before my eyes was his jabbing left hand. Then falling forward, my head against his damp shoulder, I whispered,

"I'll make it five dollars more."

"Go to hell!"

But his muscles relaxed a trifle beneath my pressure and I breathed, "Seven?"

"Give it to your ma," he said, ripping me beneath the heart.

And while I still held him I butted him and moved away. I felt myself bombarded with punches. I fought back with hopeless desperation. I wanted to deliver my speech more than anything else in the world, because I felt that only these men could judge truly my ability, and now this stupid clown was ruining my chances. I began fighting carefully now, moving in to punch him and out again with my greater speed. A lucky blow to his chin and I had him going too—until I heard a loud voice yell, "I got my money on the big boy."

Hearing this, I almost dropped my guard. I was confused: Should I try to win against the voice out there? Would not this go against my speech, and was not this a moment for humility, for nonresistance? A blow to my head as I danced about sent my right eye popping like a jack-in-the-box and settled my dilemma. The room went red as I fell. It was a dream fall, my body languid and fastidious as to where to land, until the floor became impatient and smashed up to meet me. A moment later I came to. An hypnotic voice said FIVE emphatically. And I lay there, hazily watching a dark red spot of my own blood shaping itself into a butterfly, glistening and soaking into the soiled gray world of the canvas.

When the voice drawled TEN I was lifted up and dragged to a chair. I sat dazed. My eye pained and swelled with each throb of my pounding heart and I wondered if now I would be allowed to speak. I was wringing wet, my mouth still bleeding. We were grouped along the wall now. The other boys ignored me as they congratulated Tatlock and speculated as to how much they would be paid. One boy whimpered over his smashed hand. Looking up front, I saw attendants in white jackets rolling the portable ring away and placing a small square rug in the vacant space surrounded by chairs. Perhaps, I thought, I will stand on the rug to deliver my speech.

Then the M.C. called to us, "Come on up here boys and get your money."

We ran forward to where the men laughed and talked in their chairs, waiting. Everyone seemed friendly now.

"There it is on the rug," the man said. I saw the rug covered with coins of all dimensions and a few crumpled bills. But what excited me, scattered here and there, were the gold pieces.

"Boys, it's all yours," the man said. "You get all you grab."

"That's right, Sambo," a blond man said, winking at me confidentially.

I trembled with excitement, forgetting my pain. I would get the gold and the bills, I thought. I would use both hands. I would throw my body against the boys nearest me to block them from the gold.

"Get down around the rug now," the man commanded, "and don't anyone touch it until I give the signal."

"This ought to be good," I heard.

As told, we got around the square rug on our knees. Slowly the man raised his freckled hand as we followed it upward with our eyes.

I heard, "These niggers look like they're about to pray!"

Then, "Ready," the man said. "Go!"

I lunged for a yellow coin lying on the blue design of the carpet, touching it and sending a surprised shriek to join those rising around me. I tried frantically to remove my hand but could not let go. A hot, violent force tore through my body, shaking me like a wet rat. The rug was electrified. The hair bristled up on my head as I shook myself free. My muscles jumped, my nerves jangled, writhed. But I saw that this was not stopping the other boys. Laughing in fear and embarrassment, some were holding back and scooping up the coins knocked off by the painful contortions of the others. The men roared above us as we struggled.

"Pick it up, goddamnit, pick it up!" someone called like a bass-voiced parrot. "Go on, get it!"

I crawled rapidly around the floor, picking up the coins, trying to avoid the coppers and to get greenbacks and the gold. Ignoring the shock by laughing, as I brushed the coins off quickly, I discovered that I could contain the electricity—a contradiction, but it works. Then the men began to push us onto the rug. Laughing embarrassedly, we struggled out of their hands and kept after the coins. We were all wet and slippery and hard to hold. Suddenly I saw a boy lifted into the air, glistening with sweat like a circus seal, and dropped, his wet back landing flush upon the charged rug, heard him yell and saw him literally dance upon his back, his elbows beating a frenzied tattoo upon the floor, his muscles twitching like the flesh of a horse stung by many flies. When he finally rolled off, his face was gray and no one stopped him when he ran from the floor amid booming laughter.

"Get the money," the M.C. called. "That's good hard American cash!"

And we snatched and grabbed, snatched and grabbed. I was careful not to come too close to the rug now, and when I felt the hot whiskey breath descend upon me like a cloud of foul air I reached out and grabbed the leg of a chair. It was occupied and I held on desperately.

"Leggo, nigger! Leggo!"

The huge face wavered down to mine as he tried to push me free. But my body was slippery and he was too drunk. It was Mr. Colcord, who owned a chain of movie houses and "entertainment palaces." Each time he grabbed me I slipped out of his hands. It became a real struggle. I feared the rug more than I did the drunk, so I held on, surprising myself for a moment by trying to topple *him* upon the rug. It was such an enormous idea that I found myself actually carrying it out. I tried not to be obvious, yet when I grabbed his leg, trying to tumble him out of the chair, he raised up roaring with laughter, and, looking at me with soberness dead in the eye, kicked me viciously in the chest. The chair leg flew out of my hand and I felt myself going and rolled. It was as though I had rolled through a bed of hot coals. It seemed a whole century would pass before I would roll free, a century in which I was seared through the deepest levels of my body to the fearful breath within me and the breath seared and heated to the point of explosion. It'll all be over in a flash, I thought as I rolled clear. It'll all be over in a flash.

But not yet, the men on the other side were waiting, red faces swollen as though from apoplexy as they bent forward in their chairs. Seeing their fingers coming toward me I rolled away as a fumbled football rolls off the receiver's fingertips, back into the coals. That time I luckily sent the rug sliding out of place and heard the coins ringing against the floor and the boys scuffling to pick them up and the M.C. calling, "All right, boys, that's all. Go get dressed and get your money."

I was limp as a dish rag. My back felt as though it had been beaten with wires.

When we had dressed the M.C. came in and gave us each five dollars, except Tatlock, who got ten for being last in the ring. Then he told us to leave. I was not to get a chance to deliver my speech, I thought. I was going out into the dim alley in despair when I was stopped and told to go back. I returned to the ballroom, where the men were pushing back their chairs and gathering in groups to talk.

The M.C. knocked on a table for quiet. "Gentlemen," he said, "we almost forgot an important part of the program. A most serious part, gentlemen. This boy was brought here to deliver a speech which he made at his graduation yesterday . . ."

"Bravo!"

"I'm told that he is the smartest boy we've got out there in Greenwood. I'm told that he knows more big words than a pocket-sized dictionary."

Much applause and laughter.

"So now, gentlemen, I want you to give him your attention."

There was still laughter as I faced them, my mouth dry, my eye throbbing. I began slowly, but evidently my throat was tense, because they began shouting, "Louder! Louder!"

"We of the younger generation extol the wisdom of that great leader and educator," I shouted, "who first spoke these flaming words of wisdom: 'A ship lost at sea for many days suddenly sighted a friendly vessel. From the mast of the unfortunate vessel was seen a signal: "Water, water; we die of thirst!" The answer from the friendly vessel came back: "Cast down your bucket where you are." The captain of the distressed vessel, at last heeding the injunction, cast down his bucket, and it came up full of fresh sparkling water from the mouth of the Amazon River.' And like him I say, and in his words, 'To those of my race who depend upon bettering their condition in a foreign land, or who underestimate the importance of cultivating friendly relations with the Southern white man, who is his next-door neighbor, I would say: "Cast down your bucket where you are"—cast it down in making friends in every manly way of the people of all races by whom we are surrounded . . . ' "

I spoke automatically and with such fervor that I did not realize that the men were still talking and laughing until my dry mouth, filling up with blood from the cut, almost strangled me. I coughed, wanting to stop and go to one of the tall brass, sand-filled spittoons to relieve myself, but a few of the men, especially the superintendent, were listening and I was afraid. So I gulped it down, blood, saliva and all, and continued. (What powers of endurance I had during those days! What enthusiasm! What a belief in the rightness of things!) I spoke even louder in spite of the pain. But still they talked and still they laughed, as though deaf with cotton in dirty ears. So I spoke with greater emotional emphasis. I closed my ears and swallowed blood until I was nauseated. The speech seemed a hundred times as long as before, but I could not leave out a single word. All had to be said, each memorized nuance considered, rendered. Nor was that all. Whenever I uttered a word of three or more syllables a group of voices would yell for me to repeat it. I used the phrase "social responsibility," and they yelled:

"What's that word you say, boy?"

"Social responsibility," I said.

"What?"

"Social . . ."

"Louder."

". . . responsibility."

"More!"

"Respon—"

"Repeat!"

"—sibility."

The room filled with the uproar of laughter until, no doubt, distracted by having to gulp down my blood, I made a mistake and yelled a phrase I had often seen denounced in newspaper editorials, heard debated in private.

"Social . . ."

"What?" they yelled.

". . . equality—"

The laughter hung smokelike in the sudden stillness. I opened my eyes, puzzled. Sounds of displeasure filled the room. The M.C. rushed forward. They shouted hostile phrases at me. But I did not understand.

A small dry mustached man in the front row blared out, "Say that slowly, son!"

"What, sir?"

"What you just said!"

"Social responsibility, sir," I said.

"You weren't being smart, were you, boy?" he said, not unkindly.

"No, sir!"

"You sure that about 'equality' was a mistake?"

"Oh, yes, sir," I said. "I was swallowing blood."

"Well, you had better speak more slowly so we can understand. We mean to do right by you, but you've got to know your place at all times. All right, now, go on with your speech."

I was afraid. I wanted to leave but I wanted also to speak and I was afraid they'd snatch me down.

"Thank you, sir," I said, beginning where I had left off, and having them ignore me as before.

Yet when I finished there was a thunderous applause. I was surprised to see the superintendent come forth with a package wrapped in white tissue paper, and, gesturing for quiet, address the men.

"Gentlemen, you see that I did not overpraise the boy. He makes a good speech and some day he'll lead his people in the proper paths. And I don't have to tell you that that is important in these days and times. This is a good, smart boy, and so to encourage him in the right direction, in the name of the Board of Education I wish to present him a prize in the form of this . . ."

He paused, removing the tissue paper and revealing a gleaming calfskin brief case.

". . . in the form of this first-class article from Shad Whitmore's shop."

"Boy," he said, addressing me, "take this prize and keep it well. Consider it a badge of office. Prize it. Keep developing as you are and some day it will be filled with important papers that will help shape the destiny of your people."

I was so moved that I could hardly express my thanks. A rope of bloody saliva forming a shape like an undiscovered continent drooled upon the leather and I wiped it quickly away. I felt an importance that I had never dreamed.

"Open it and see what's inside," I was told.

My fingers a-tremble, I complied, smelling the fresh leather and finding an official-looking document inside. It was a scholarship to the state college for Negroes. My eyes filled with tears and I ran awkwardly off the floor.

I was overjoyed; I did not even mind when I discovered that the gold pieces I had scrambled for were brass pocket tokens advertising a certain make of automobile.

When I reached home everyone was excited. Next day the neighbors came to congratulate me. I even felt safe from grandfather, whose deathbed curse usually spoiled my triumphs. I stood beneath his photograph with my brief case in hand and smiled triumphantly into his stolid black peasant's face. It was a face that fascinated me. The eyes seemed to follow everywhere I went.

That night I dreamed I was at a circus with him and that he refused to laugh at the clowns no matter what they did. Then later he told me to open my brief case and read what was inside and I did, finding an official envelope stamped with the state seal; and inside the envelope I found another and another, endlessly, and I thought I would fall of weariness. "Them's years," he said. "Now open that one." And I did and in it I found an engraved document containing a short message in letters of gold. "Read it," my grandfather said. "Out loud!"

"To Whom It May Concern," I intoned. "Keep This Nigger-Boy Running."

I awoke with the old man's laughter ringing in my ears.

(It was a dream I was to remember and dream again for many years after. But at that time I had no insight into its meaning. First I had to attend college.)

1952

SAUL BELLOW
b. 1915

When Saul Bellow was awarded the Nobel Prize for literature in 1976 his citation read: "For the human understanding and subtle analysis of contemporary culture that are combined in his work." Except for the poet Robert Lowell, no American writer of the post–World War II period has a better claim to these virtues than Bellow, who has devoted himself almost exclusively and passionately to the novel and its attempt to imagine life in the United States, particularly in the great cities of Chicago and New York.

He was born in Lachine, Quebec, grew up in the Jewish ghetto of Montreal, and moved to Chicago when he was nine. He attended the University of Chicago, then transferred to Northwestern, where he took a degree in anthropology and sociology, the effects of which study are everywhere evident in the novels he was to write. He taught English for a time, served in the merchant marine during World War II, then after the war spent some fifteen years away from Chicago, teaching at New York University and Princeton and living in Paris. In 1962 he returned to Chicago and since then has been a lecturer at the University of Chicago. He has married five times.

Bellow's first novel, *Dangling Man,* was not published until he was nearly thirty and is a short series of elegantly morose meditations, told through the journal of a young man waiting to be inducted into the army and with the "freedom" of having nothing to do but wait. Eventually he is drafted: "Long live regimentation," he sardonically exults. His second novel, *The Victim* (1947), continues the investigation of ways people strive to be relieved of self-determination. This book concerns a week in the life of Asa Leventhal, alone in New York City while his wife visits a relative, who is suddenly confronted by a figure from the past (Kirby Allbee, a Gentile) who succeeds in implicating Leventhal with the past and its present manifestations. *The Victim* is Bellow's most somberly naturalistic depiction of a man brought up against forces larger than himself, yet from the opening sentence ("On some nights New York is as hot as Bangkok") a poetic dimension makes itself felt and helps create the sense of mystery and disturbance felt by both the main character and the reader.

Dangling Man and *The Victim* are highly wrought, mainly humorless books; in two long novels published in the 1950s Bellow opened up into new ranges of aspiration and situational zaniness, which brought him respectful admiration from many critics. *The Adventures of Augie March* (1953) and *Henderson the Rain King* (1959) are each narrated by an "I" who, like his predecessor Huck Finn, is good at lighting out for the territory ahead of whoever means to tie him down. The hero's adventures, whether occurring in Chicago, Mexico, or Africa, are exuberantly delivered in an always stimulating and sometimes overactive prose. *Augie* is filled with sights and sounds, colors and surfaces; its tone is self-involved, affectionate, and affirmative in its ring; *Henderson,* Bellow's most extravagant narrative, has the even more fabulous air of a quest-romance in which the hero returns home from Africa at peace with the world he had been warring against.

The ironic motto for Bellow's novels of the 1950s may well be "Seize the Day," as in the title of perhaps his finest piece of fiction. This short novel is both painful and exhilarating because it so fully exposes its hero (Tommy Wilhelm, an aging out-of-work ex-actor) to the insults of other people who don't understand him, to a city (New York's Upper West Side) impervious to his needs, and to a narrative prose that mixes ridicule and affection so thoroughly as to make them scarcely distinguishable. *Seize the Day* combines, within Tommy's monologues, a wildness and pathos of bitter comedy that was a powerful new element in Bellow's work.

In "Where Do We Go from Here?: The Future of Fiction," an essay published in 1965, Bellow pointed out that nineteenth-century American literature—Emerson, Thoreau, Whitman, Melville—was highly didactic in its efforts to "instruct a young and raw nation." Bellow sees himself in this instructive tradition and in the international company of "didactic" novelists like Dostoyevsky, D. H. Lawrence, and Joseph Conrad; he believes also that "the imagination is looking for new ways to express virtue . . . we have barely begun to comprehend what a human being is." These concerns animate the novels Bellow has written in the years since *Henderson.* In *Herzog* (1964) the hero is another down-and-outer, a professor-intellectual, a student of Romanticism and of the glorification of Self, which Herzog believes both modern life and modernist literature have been working to undercut. At the same time he is a comic and pathetic victim of marital disorder; like all Bellow's heroes, Herzog has a terrible time with women, yet cannot live without them. In *Mr. Sammler's Planet* (1970), written out of the disorders of the late 1960s, the atmosphere is grimmer.

Sammler, an aging Jew living (again) on New York's West Side, analyzes and judges but cannot understand the young or blacks, or the mass of people gathered at Broadway and Ninety-sixth Street. He sees about him everywhere "poverty of soul" but admits that he too has "a touch of the same disease—the disease of the single self explaining what was what and who was who."

These novels, as well as *Humboldt's Gift* (1975), have been accused of parading too single-handedly attitudes toward which their author is sympathetic, whereas *The Dean's December* (1982) was criticized by John Updike, in a review, for being too much "*about* Saul Bellow," even though indirectly. Subsequently, a collection of shorter fiction, *Him with His Foot in His Mouth* (1984); the novels, *More Die of Heartbreak* (1987) and *Ravelstein* (2000); three novellas, *The Bellarosa Connection* (1989), *A Theft* (1989), and *The Actual* (1997); and three stories collected as *Something to Remember Me By* (1991) exhibit various talky, informal protagonists and narrators with a lot on their minds. Matters of form and plot in these works seem less important than the ideas and active energy struck off by human beings in turmoil— usually comic turmoil. What Bellow finds moving in Theodore Dreiser's work, "his balkiness and sullenness, and then his allegiance to life," is still found in his own: complaint and weariness, fault-finding, accusation of self and others—these gestures directed at "life" also make up the stuff of life and the "allegiance" out of which Bellow's heroes are made. We read him for this range of interest; for flexibility and diversity of style and idiom; and for the eloquences of nostalgia, invective, and lamentation that make up his intensely imagined world. These are the qualities evident in one of his most important short stories, "Looking for Mr. Green," in which the protagonist rejects both cynicism and snobbery in favor of establishing an individual's worth; only if Mr. Green exists as a person worthy of respect can Bellow's character feel the same way about himself.

The text is that of *Mosby's Memoirs and Other Stories* (1968).

Looking for Mr. Green

Whatsoever thy hand findeth to do, do it with thy might. . . . [1]

Hard work? No, it wasn't really so hard. He wasn't used to walking and stair-climbing, but the physical difficulty of his new job was not what George Grebe felt most. He was delivering relief checks in the Negro district, and although he was a native Chicagoan this was not a part of the city he knew much about—it needed a depression to introduce him to it. No, it wasn't literally hard work, not as reckoned in foot-pounds, but yet he was beginning to feel the strain of it, to grow aware of its peculiar difficulty. He could find the streets and numbers, but the clients were not where they were supposed to be, and he felt like a hunter inexperienced in the camouflage of his game. It was an unfavorable day, too—fall, and cold, dark weather, windy. But, anyway, instead of shells in his deep trenchcoat pocket he had the cardboard of checks, punctured for the spindles of the file, the holes reminding him of the holes in player-piano paper. And he didn't look much like a hunter, either; his was a city figure entirely, belted up in this Irish conspirator's coat.[2] He was slender without being tall, stiff in the back, his legs looking shabby in a pair of old tweed pants gone through and fringy at the cuffs. With this

---

1. From Ecclesiastes 9.10; the verse continues, "for there is no work, nor device, nor knowledge, nor wisdom, in the grave, whither thou goest."

2. Like those worn by members of the anti-British underground in Ireland.

stiffness, he kept his head forward, so that his face was red from the sharpness of the weather; and it was an indoors sort of face with gray eyes that persisted in some kind of thought and yet seemed to avoid definiteness of conclusion. He wore sideburns that surprised you somewhat by the tough curl of the blond hair and the effect of assertion in their length. He was not so mild as he looked, nor so youthful; and nevertheless there was no effort on his part to seem what he was not. He was an educated man; he was a bachelor; he was in some ways simple; without lushing, he liked a drink; his luck had not been good. Nothing was deliberately hidden.

He felt that his luck was better than usual today. When he had reported for work that morning he had expected to be shut up in the relief office at a clerk's job, for he had been hired downtown as a clerk, and he was glad to have, instead, the freedom of the streets and welcomed, at least at first, the vigor of the cold and even the blowing of the hard wind. But on the other hand he was not getting on with the distribution of the checks. It was true that it was a city job; nobody expected you to push too hard at a city job. His supervisor, that young Mr. Raynor, had practically told him that. Still, he wanted to do well at it. For one thing, when he knew how quickly he could deliver a batch of checks, he would know also how much time he could expect to clip for himself. And then, too, the clients would be waiting for their money. That was not the most important consideration, though it certainly mattered to him. No, but he wanted to do well, simply for doing-well's sake, to acquit himself decently of a job because he so rarely had a job to do that required just this sort of energy. Of this peculiar energy he now had a superabundance; once it had started to flow, it flowed all too heavily. And, for the time being anyway, he was balked. He could not find Mr. Green.

So he stood in his big-skirted trenchcoat with a large envelope in his hand and papers showing from his pocket, wondering why people should be so hard to locate who were too feeble or sick to come to the station to collect their own checks. But Raynor had told him that tracking them down was not easy at first and had offered him some advice on how to proceed. "If you can see the postman, he's your first man to ask, and your best bet. If you can't connect with him, try the stores and tradespeople around. Then the janitor and the neighbors. But you'll find the closer you come to your man the less people will tell you. They don't want to tell you anything."

"Because I'm a stranger."

"Because you're white. We ought to have a Negro doing this, but we don't at the moment, and of course you've got to eat, too, and this is public employment. Jobs have to be made. Oh, that holds for me too. Mind you, I'm not letting myself out. I've got three years of seniority on you, that's all. And a law degree. Otherwise, you might be back of the desk and I might be going out into the field this cold day. The same dough pays us both and for the same, exact, identical reason. What's my law degree got to do with it? But you have to pass out these checks, Mr. Grebe, and it'll help if you're stubborn, so I hope you are."

"Yes, I'm fairly stubborn."

Raynor sketched hard with an eraser in the old dirt of his desk, left-handed, and said, "Sure, what else can you answer to such a question. Anyhow, the trouble you're going to have is that they don't like to give information about anybody. They think you're a plain-clothes dick or an installment collector, or summons-server or something like that. Till you've been seen around the neighborhood for a few months and people know you're only from the relief."

It was dark, ground-freezing, pre-Thanksgiving weather; the wind played hob with the smoke, rushing it down, and Grebe missed his gloves, which he had left in Raynor's office. And no one would admit knowing Green. It was past three o'clock and the postman had made his last delivery. The nearest grocer, himself a Negro, had never heard the name Tulliver Green, or said he hadn't. Grebe was inclined to think that it was true, that he had in the end convinced the man that he wanted only to deliver a check. But he wasn't sure. He needed experience in interpreting looks and signs and, even more, the will not to be put off or denied and even the force to bully if need be. If the grocer did know, he had got rid of him easily. But since most of his trade was with relievers, why should he prevent the delivery of a check? Maybe Green, or Mrs. Green, if there was a Mrs. Green, patronized another grocer. And was there a Mrs. Green? It was one of Grebe's great handicaps that he hadn't looked at any of the case records. Raynor should have let him read files for a few hours. But he apparently saw no need for that, probably considering the job unimportant. Why prepare systematically to deliver a few checks?

But now it was time to look for the janitor. Grebe took in the building in the wind and gloom of the late November day—trampled, frost-hardened lots on one side; on the other, an automobile junk yard and then the infinite work of Elevated frames, weak-looking, gaping with rubbish fires; two sets of leaning brick porches three stories high and a flight of cement stairs to the cellar. Descending, he entered the underground passage, where he tried the doors until one opened and he found himself in the furnace room. There someone rose toward him and approached, scraping on the coal grit and bending under the canvas-jacketed pipes.

"Are you the janitor?"

"What do you want?"

"I'm looking for a man who's supposed to be living here. Green."

"What Green?"

"Oh, you maybe have more than one Green?" said Grebe with new, pleasant hope. "This is Tulliver Green."

"I don't think I c'n help you, mister. I don't know any."

"A crippled man."

The janitor stood bent before him. Could it be that he was crippled? Oh, God! what if he was. Grebe's gray eyes sought with excited difficulty to see. But no, he was only very short and stooped. A head awakened from meditation, a strong-haired beard, low, wide shoulders. A staleness of sweat and coal rose from his black shirt and the burlap sack he wore as an apron.

"Crippled how?"

Grebe thought and then answered with the light voice of unmixed candor, "I don't know. I've never seen him." This was damaging, but his only other choice was to make a lying guess, and he was not up to it. "I'm delivering checks for the relief to shut-in cases. If he weren't crippled he'd come to collect himself. That's why I said crippled. Bedridden, chair-ridden—is there anybody like that?"

This sort of frankness was one of Grebe's oldest talents, going back to childhood. But it gained him nothing here.

"No suh. I've got four buildin's same as this that I take care of. I don' know all the tenants, leave alone the tenants' tenants. The rooms turn over so fast, people movin' in and out every day. I can't tell you."

The janitor opened his grimy lips but Grebe did not hear him in the piping of the valves and the consuming pull of air to flame in the body of the furnace. He knew, however, what he had said.

"Well, all the same, thanks. Sorry I bothered you. I'll prowl around upstairs again and see if I can turn up someone who knows him."

Once more in the cold air and early darkness he made the short circle from the cellarway to the entrance crowded between the brickwork pillars and began to climb to the third floor. Pieces of plaster ground under his feet; strips of brass tape from which the carpeting had been torn away marked old boundaries at the sides. In the passage, the cold reached him worse than in the street; it touched him to the bone. The hall toilets ran like springs. He thought grimly as he heard the wind burning around the building with a sound like that of the furnace, that this was a great piece of constructed shelter. Then he struck a match in the gloom and searched for names and numbers among the writings and scribbles on the walls. He saw WHOODY-DOODY GO TO JESUS, and zigzags, caricatures, sexual scrawls, and curses. So the sealed rooms of pyramids were also decorated, and the caves of human dawn.

The information on his card was, TULLIVER GREEN—APT 3D. There were no names, however, and no numbers. His shoulders drawn up, tears of cold in his eyes, breathing vapor, he went the length of the corridor and told himself that if he had been lucky enough to have the temperament for it he would bang on one of the doors and bawl out "Tulliver Green!" until he got results. But it wasn't in him to make an uproar and he continued to burn matches, passing the light over the walls. At the rear, in a corner off the hall, he discovered a door he had not seen before and he thought it best to investigate. It sounded empty when he knocked, but a young Negress answered, hardly more than a girl. She opened only a bit, to guard the warmth of the room.

"Yes suh?"

"I'm from the district relief station on Prairie Avenue. I'm looking for a man named Tulliver Green to give him his check. Do you know him?"

No, she didn't; but he thought she had not understood anything of what he had said. She had a dream-bound, dream-blind face, very soft and black, shut off. She wore a man's jacket and pulled the ends together at her throat. Her hair was parted in three directions, at the sides and transversely, standing up at the front in a dull puff.

"Is there somebody around here who might know?"

"I jus' taken this room las' week."

He observed that she shivered, but even her shiver was somnambulistic and there was no sharp consciousness of cold in the big smooth eyes of her handsome face.

"All right, miss, thank you. Thanks," he said, and went to try another place.

Here he was admitted. He was grateful, for the room was warm. It was full of people, and they were silent as he entered—ten people, or a dozen, perhaps more, sitting on benches like a parliament. There was no light, properly speaking, but a tempered darkness that the window gave, and everyone seemed to him enormous, the men padded out in heavy work clothes and winter coats, and the women huge, too, in their sweaters, hats, and old furs. And, besides, bed and bedding, a black cooking range, a piano piled towering to the ceiling with papers, a dining-room table of the old style of prosperous Chicago. Among these people Grebe, with his cold-heightened fresh color and his smaller stature, entered like a schoolboy. Even though he was met with smiles and good will, he knew, before a single word was spoken, that all the currents ran against him and that he would make no headway. Nevertheless he began. "Does anybody here know how I can deliver a check to Mr. Tulliver Green?"

"Green?" It was the man that had let him in who answered. He was in short sleeves, in a checkered shirt, and had a queer, high head, profusely overgrown and long as a shako;[3] the veins entered it strongly, from his forehead. "I never heard mention of him. Is this where he live?"

"This is the address they gave me at the station. He's a sick man, and he'll need his check. Can't anybody tell me where to find him?"

He stood his ground and waited for a reply, his crimson wool scarf wound about his neck and drooping outside his trenchcoat, pockets weighted with the block of checks and official forms. They must have realized that he was not a college boy employed afternoons by a bill collector, trying foxily to pass for a relief clerk, recognized that he was an older man who knew himself what need was, who had had more than an average seasoning in hardship. It was evident enough if you looked at the marks under his eyes and at the sides of his mouth.

"Anybody know this sick man?"

"No suh." On all sides he saw heads shaken and smiles of denial. No one knew. And maybe it was true, he considered, standing silent in the earthen, musky human gloom of the place as the rumble continued. But he could never really be sure.

"What's the matter with this man?" said shako-head.

"I've never seen him. All I can tell you is that he can't come in person for his money. It's my first day in this district."

"Maybe they given you the wrong number?"

"I don't believe so. But where else can I ask about him?" He felt that this persistence amused them deeply, and in a way he shared their amusement that he should stand up so tenaciously to them. Though smaller, though slight, he was his own man, he retracted nothing about himself, and he looked back at them, gray-eyed, with amusement and also with a sort of courage. On the bench some man spoke in his throat, the words impossible to catch, and a woman answered with a wild, shrieking laugh, which was quickly cut off.

"Well, so nobody will tell me?"

"Ain't nobody who knows."

"At least, if he lives here, he pays rent to someone. Who manages the building?"

"Greatham Company. That's on Thirty-ninth Street."

Grebe wrote it in his pad. But, in the street again, a sheet of wind-driven paper clinging to his leg while he deliberated what direction to take next, it seemed a feeble lead to follow. Probably this Green didn't rent a flat, but a room. Sometimes there were as many as twenty people in an apartment; the real-estate agent would know only the lessee. And not even the agent could tell you who the renters were. In some places the beds were even used in shifts, watchmen or jitney drivers or short-order cooks in night joints turning out after a day's sleep and surrendering their beds to a sister, a nephew, or perhaps a stranger, just off the bus. There were large numbers of newcomers in this terrific, blight-bitten portion of the city between Cottage Grove and

3. Stiff military headdress with a high crown and a plume.

Ashland, wandering from house to house and room to room. When you saw them, how could you know them? They didn't carry bundles on their backs or look picturesque. You only saw a man, a Negro, walking in the street or riding in the car, like everyone else, with his thumb closed on a transfer. And therefore how were you supposed to tell? Grebe thought the Greatham agent would only laugh at his question.

But how much it would have simplified the job to be able to say that Green was old, or blind, or consumptive. An hour in the files, taking a few notes, and he needn't have been at such a disadvantage. When Raynor gave him the block of checks he asked, "How much should I know about these people?" Then Raynor had looked as though he were preparing to accuse him of trying to make the job more important than it was. He smiled, because by then they were on fine terms, but nevertheless he had been getting ready to say something like that when the confusion began in the station over Staika and her children.

Grebe had waited a long time for this job. It came to him through the pull of an old schoolmate in the Corporation Counsel's office, never a close friend, but suddenly sympathetic and interested—pleased to show, moreover, how well he had done, how strongly he was coming on even in these miserable times. Well, he was coming through strongly, along with the Democratic administration itself. Grebe had gone to see him in City Hall, and they had had a counter lunch or beers at least once a month for a year, and finally it had been possible to swing the job. He didn't mind being assigned the lowest clerical grade, nor even being a messenger, though Raynor thought he did.

This Raynor was an original sort of guy and Grebe had taken to him immediately. As was proper on the first day, Grebe had come early, but he waited long, for Raynor was late. At last he darted into his cubicle of an office as though he had just jumped from one of those hurtling huge red Indian Avenue cars. His thin, rough face was wind-stung and he was grinning and saying something breathlessly to himself. In his hat, a small fedora, and his coat, the velvet collar a neat fit about his neck, and his silk muffler that set off the nervous twist of his chin, he swayed and turned himself in his swivel chair, feet leaving the ground; so that he pranced a little as he sat. Meanwhile he took Grebe's measure out of his eyes, eyes of an unusual vertical length and slightly sardonic. So the two men sat for a while, saying nothing, while the supervisor raised his hat from his miscombed hair and put it in his lap. His cold-darkened hands were not clean. A steel beam passed through the little makeshift room, from which machine belts once had hung. The building was an old factory.

"I'm younger than you; I hope you won't find it hard taking orders from me," said Raynor. "But I don't make them up, either. You're how old, about?"

"Thirty-five."

"And you thought you'd be inside doing paper work. But it so happens I have to send you out."

"I don't mind."

"And it's mostly a Negro load we have in this district."

"So I thought it would be."

"Fine. You'll get along. *C'est un bon boulot.*[4] Do you know French?"

"Some."

---

4. It's a good job (French slang).

"I thought you'd be a university man."

"Have you been in France?" said Grebe.

"No, that's the French of the Berlitz School. I've been at it for more than a year, just as I'm sure people have been, all over the world, office boys in China and braves in Tanganyika. In fact, I damn well know it. Such is the attractive power of civilization. It's overrated, but what do you want? *Que voulez-vous?*[5] I get *Le Rire* and all the spicy papers, just like in Tanganyika. It must be mystifying, out there. But my reason is that I'm aiming at the diplomatic service. I have a cousin who's a courier, and the way he describes it is awfully attractive. He rides in the *wagon-lits*[6] and reads books. While we—What did you do before?"

"I sold."

"Where?"

"Canned meat at Stop and Shop. In the basement."

"And before that?"

"Window shades, at Goldblatt's."

"Steady work?"

"No, Thursdays and Saturdays. I also sold shoes."

"You've been a shoe-dog too. Well. And prior to that? Here it is in your folder." He opened the record. "Saint Olaf's College, instructor in classical languages. Fellow, University of Chicago, 1926–27. I've had Latin, too. Let's trade quotations—*'Dum spiro spero.'* "

" *'Da dextram misero.'* "

" *'Alea jacta est.'* "

" *'Excelsior.'* "[7]

Raynor shouted with laughter, and other workers came to look at him over the partition. Grebe also laughed, feeling pleased and easy. The luxury of fun on a nervous morning.

When they were done and no one was watching or listening, Raynor said rather seriously, "What made you study Latin in the first place? Was it for the priesthood?"

"No."

"Just for the hell of it? For the culture? Oh, the things people think they can pull!" He made his cry hilarious and tragic. "I ran my pants off so I could study for the bar, and I've passed the bar, so I get twelve dollars a week more than you as a bonus for having seen life straight and whole. I'll tell you, as a man of culture, that even though nothing looks to be real, and everything stands for something else, and that thing for another thing, and that thing for a still further one—there ain't any comparison between twenty-five and thirty-seven dollars a week, regardless of the last reality. Don't you think that was clear to your Greeks? They were a thoughtful people, but they didn't part with their slaves."

This was a great deal more than Grebe had looked for in his first interview with his supervisor. He was too shy to show all the astonishment he felt. He laughed a little, aroused, and brushed at the sunbeam that covered his head with its dust. "Do you think my mistake was so terrible?"

"Damn right it was terrible, and you know it now that you've had the whip of hard times laid on your back. You should have been preparing yourself for trouble. Your people must have been well off to send you to the university.

---

5. What do you want? (French).
6. European railroad sleeping-cars.
7. The Latin phrases are translated, in order, as

follows: "Where there's life there's hope" (literally, "while I breathe I hope"); "Give the right hand to the wretched"; "The die is cast"; "Higher!"

Stop me, if I'm stepping on your toes. Did your mother pamper you? Did your father give in to you? Were you brought up tenderly, with permission to go and find out what were the last things that everything else stands for while everybody else labored in the fallen world of appearances?"

"Well, no, it wasn't exactly like that." Grebe smiled. *The fallen world of appearances!* no less. But now it was his turn to deliver a surprise. "We weren't rich. My father was the last genuine English butler in Chicago—"

"Are you kidding?"

"Why should I be?"

"In a livery?"

"In livery. Up on the Gold Coast."

"And he wanted you to be educated like a gentleman?"

"He did not. He sent me to the Armor Institute to study chemical engineering. But when he died I changed schools."

He stopped himself, and considered how quickly Raynor had reached him. In no time he had your valise on the table and all your stuff unpacked. And afterward, in the streets, he was still reviewing how far he might have gone, and how much he might have been led to tell if they had not been interrupted by Mrs. Stakia's great noise.

But just then a young woman, one of Raynor's workers, ran into the cubicle exclaiming, "Haven't you heard all the fuss?"

"We haven't heard anything."

"It's Staika, giving out with all her might. The reporters are coming. She said she phoned the papers, and you know she did."

"But what is she up to?" said Raynor.

"She brought her wash and she's ironing it here, with our current, because the relief won't pay her electric bill. She has her ironing board set up by the admitting desk, and her kids are with her, all six. They never are in school more than once a week. She's always dragging them around with her because of her reputation."

"I don't want to miss any of this," said Raynor, jumping up. Grebe, as he followed with the secretary, said, "Who is this Staika?"

"They call her the 'Blood Mother of Federal Street.' She's a professional donor at the hospitals. I think they pay ten dollars a pint. Of course it's no joke, but she makes a very big thing out of it and she and the kids are in the papers all the time."

A small crowd, staff and clients divided by a plywood barrier, stood in the narrow space of the entrance, and Staika was shouting in a gruff, mannish voice, plunging the iron on the board and slamming it on the metal rest.

"My father and mother came in a steerage, and I was born in our house, Robey by Huron. I'm no dirty immigrant. I'm a U.S. citizen. My husband is a gassed veteran from France with lungs weaker'n paper, that hardly can he go to the toilet by himself. These six children of mine, I have to buy the shoes for their feet with my own blood. Even a lousy little white Communion necktie, that's a couple drops of blood; a little piece of mosquito veil for my Vadja so she won't be ashamed in church for the other girls, they take my blood for it by Goldblatt. That's how I keep goin'. A fine thing if I had to depend on the relief. And there's plenty of people on the rolls—fakes! There's nothin' *they* can't get, that can go and wrap bacon at Swift and Armour any time. They're lookin' for them by the Yards. They never have to be out of work. Only they rather lay in their lousy beds and eat the public's money."

She was not afraid, in a predominantly Negro station, to shout this way about Negroes.

Grebe and Raynor worked themselves forward to get a closer view of the woman. She was flaming with anger and with pleasure at herself, broad and huge, a golden-headed woman who wore a cotton cap laced with pink ribbon. She was barelegged and had on black gym shoes, her Hoover apron[8] was open and her great breasts, not much restrained by a man's undershirt, hampered her arms as she worked at the kid's dress on the iron board. And the children, silent and white, with a kind of locked obstinacy, in sheepskins and lumberjackets, stood behind her. She had captured the station, and the pleasure this gave her was enormous. Yet her grievances were true grievances. She was telling the truth. But she behaved like a liar. The look of her small eyes was hidden, and while she raged she also seemed to be spinning and planning.

"They send me out college case workers in silk pants to talk me out of what I got comin'. Are they better'n me? Who told them? Fire them. Let 'em go and get married, and then you won't have to cut electric from people's budget."

The chief supervisor, Mr. Ewing, couldn't silence her and he stood with folded arms at the head of his staff, bald, bald-headed, saying to his subordinates like the ex-school principal he was, "Pretty soon she'll be tired and go."

"No she won't," said Raynor to Grebe. "She'll get what she wants. She knows more about the relief even then Ewing. She's been on the rolls for years, and she always gets what she wants because she puts on a noisy show. Ewing knows it. He'll give in soon. He's only saving face. If he gets bad publicity, the Commissioner'll have him on the carpet, downtown. She's got him submerged; she'll submerge everybody in time, and that includes nations and governments."

Grebe replied with his characteristic smile, disagreeing completely. Who would take Staika's orders, and what changes could her yelling ever bring about?

No, what Grebe saw in her, the power that made people listen, was that her cry expressed the war of flesh and blood, perhaps turned a little crazy and certainly ugly, on this place and this condition. And at first, when he went out, the spirit of Staika somehow presided over the whole district for him, and it took color from her; he saw her color, in the spotty curb fires, and the fires under the El, the straight alley of flamy gloom. Later, too, when he went into a tavern for a shot of rye, the sweat of beer, association with West Side Polish streets, made him think of her again.

He wiped the corners of his mouth with his muffler, his handkerchief being inconvenient to reach for, and went out again to get on with the delivery of his checks. The air bit cold and hard and a few flakes of snow formed near him. A train struck by and left a quiver in the frames and a bristling icy hiss over the rails.

Crossing the street, he descended a flight of broad steps into a basement grocery, setting off a little bell. It was a dark, long store and it caught you with its stinks of smoked meat, soap, dried peaches, and fish. There was a fire wrinkling and flapping in the little stove, and the proprietor was waiting,

8. Woman's coverall, popular during World War I.

an Italian with a long, hollow face and stubborn bristles. He kept his hands warm under his apron.

No, he didn't know Green. You knew people but not names. The same man might not have the same name twice. The police didn't know, either, and mostly didn't care. When somebody was shot or knifed they took the body away and didn't look for the murderer. In the first place, nobody would tell them anything. So they made up a name for the coroner and called it quits. And in the second place, they didn't give a goddamn anyhow. But they couldn't get to the bottom of a thing even if they wanted to. Nobody would get to know even a tenth of what went on among these people. They stabbed and stole, they did every crime and abomination you ever heard of, men and men, women and women, parents and children, worse than the animals. They carried on their own way, and the horrors passed off like a smoke. There was never anything like it in the history of the whole world.

It was a long speech, deepening with every word in its fantasy and passion and becoming increasingly senseless and terrible: a swarm amassed by suggestion and invention, a huge, hugging, despairing knot, a human wheel of heads, legs, bellies, arms, rolling through his shop.

Grebe felt that he must interrupt him. He said sharply, "What are you talking about! All I asked was whether you knew this man."

"That isn't even the half of it. I been here six years. You probably don't want to believe this. But suppose it's true?"

"All the same," said Grebe, "there must be a way to find a person."

The Italian's close-spaced eyes had been queerly concentrated, as were his muscles, while he leaned across the counter trying to convince Grebe. Now he gave up the effort and sat down on his stool. "Oh—I suppose. Once in a while. But I been telling you, even the cops don't get anywhere."

"They're always after somebody. It's not the same thing."

"Well, keep trying if you want. I can't help you."

But he didn't keep trying. He had no more time to spend on Green. He slipped Green's check to the back of the block. The next name on the list was FIELD, WINSTON.

He found the back-yard bungalow without the least trouble; it shared a lot with another house, a few feet of yard between. Grebe knew these two-shack arrangements. They had been built in vast numbers in the days before the swamps were filled and the streets raised, and they were all the same— a board-walk along the fence, well under street level, three or four ball-headed posts for clotheslines, greening wood, dead shingles, and a long, long flight of stairs to the rear door.

A twelve-year-old boy let him into the kitchen, and there the old man was, sitting by the table in a wheel chair.

"Oh, it's d' Government man," he said to the boy when Grebe drew out his checks. "Go bring me my box of papers." He cleared a space on the table.

"Oh, you don't have to go to all that trouble," said Grebe. But Field laid out his papers: Social Security card, relief certification, letters from the state hospital in Manteno, and a naval discharge dated San Diego, 1920.

"That's plenty," Grebe said. "Just sign."

"You got to know who I am," the old man said. "You're from the Government. It's not your check, it's a Government check and you got no business to hand it over till everything is proved."

He loved the ceremony of it, and Grebe made no more objections. Field emptied his box and finished out the circle of cards and letters.

"There's everything I done and been. Just the death certificate and they can close book on me." He said this with a certain happy pride and magnificence. Still he did not sign; he merely held the little pen upright on the golden-green corduroy of his thigh. Grebe did not hurry him. He felt the old man's hunger for conversation.

"I got to get better coal," he said. "I send my little gran'son to the yard with my order and they fill his wagon with screening. The stove ain't made for it. It fall through the grate. The order says Franklin County egg-size coal."

"I'll report it and see what can be done."

"Nothing can be done, I expect. You know and I know. There ain't no little ways to make things better, and the only big thing is money. That's the only sunbeams, money. Nothing is black where it shines, and the only place you see black is where it ain't shining. What we colored have to have is our own rich. There ain't no other way."

Grebe sat, his reddened forehead bridged levelly by his close-cut hair and his cheeks lowered in the wings of his collar—the caked fire shone hard within the isinglass-and-iron frames but the room was not comfortable—sat and listened while the old man unfolded his scheme. This was to create one Negro millionaire a month by subscription. One clever, good-hearted young fellow elected every month would sign a contract to use the money to start a business employing Negroes. This would be advertised by chain letters and word of mouth, and every Negro wage earner would contribute a dollar a month. Within five years there would be sixty millionaires.

"That'll fetch respect," he said with a throat-stopped sound that came out like a foreign syllable. "You got to take and organize all the money that gets thrown away on the policy wheel and horse race. As long as they can take it away from you, they got no respect for you. Money, that's d' sun of human kind!" Field was a Negro of mixed blood, perhaps Cherokee, or Natchez; his skin was reddish. And he sounded, speaking about a golden sun in this dark room, and looked, shaggy and slab-headed, with the mingled blood of his face and broad lips, the little pen still upright in his hand, like one of the underground kings of mythology, old judge Minos himself.

And now he accepted the check and signed. Not to soil the slip, he held it down with his knuckles. The table budged and creaked, the center of the gloomy, heathen midden of the kitchen covered with bread, meat, and cans, and the scramble of papers.

"Don't you think my scheme'd work?"

"It's worth thinking about. Something ought to be done, I agree."

"It'll work if people will do it. That's all. That's the only thing, any time. When they understand it in the same way, all of them."

"That's true," said Grebe, rising. His glance met the old man's.

"I know you got to go," he said. "Well, God bless you, boy, you ain't been sly with me. I can tell in a minute."

He went back through the buried yard. Someone nursed a candle in a shed, where a man unloaded kindling wood from a sprawl-wheeled baby buggy and two voices carried on a high conversation. As he came up the sheltered passage he heard the hard boost of the wind in the branches and against the house fronts, and then, reaching the sidewalk, he saw the needle-eye red of cable towers in the open icy height hundreds of feet above the river and the factories—those keen points. From here, his view was obstructed all the way to the South Branch and its timber banks, and the cranes beside the water. Rebuilt after the Great Fire,[9] this part of the city was, not fifty years later, in ruins again, factories boarded up, buildings deserted or fallen, gaps of prairie between. But it wasn't desolation that this made you feel, but rather a faltering of organization that set free a huge energy, an escaped, unattached, unregulated power from the giant raw place. Not only must people feel it but, it seemed to Grebe, they were compelled to match it. In their very bodies. He no less than others, he realized. Say that his parents had been servants in their time, whereas he was not supposed to be one. He thought that they had never done any service like this, which no one visible asked for, and probably flesh and blood could not even perform. Nor could anyone show why it should be performed; or see where the performance would lead. That did not mean that he wanted to be released from it, he realized with a grimly pensive face. On the contrary. He had something to do. To be compelled to feel this energy and yet have no task to do—that was horrible; that was suffering; he knew what that was. It was now quitting time. Six o'clock. He could go home if he liked, to his room, that is, to wash in hot water, to pour a drink, lie down on his quilt, read the paper, eat some liver paste on crackers before going out to dinner. But to think of this actually made him feel a little sick as though he had swallowed hard air. He had six checks left, and he was determined to deliver at least one of these: Mr. Green's check.

So he started again. He had four or five dark blocks to go, past open lots, condemned houses, old foundations, closed schools, black churches, mounds, and he reflected that there must be many people alive who had once seen the neighborhood rebuilt and new. Now there was a second layer of ruins; centuries of history accomplished through human massing. Numbers had given the place forced growth; enormous numbers had also broken it down. Objects once so new, so concrete that it could have occurred to anyone they stood for other things, had crumbled. Therefore, reflected Grebe, the secret of them was out. It was that they stood for themselves by agreement, and were natural and not unnatural by agreement, and when the things themselves collapsed the agreement became visible. What was it, otherwise, that kept cities from looking peculiar? Rome, that was almost permanent, did not give rise to thoughts like these. And was it abidingly real? But in Chicago, where the cycles were so fast and the familiar died out, and again rose changed, and died again in thirty years, you saw the common agreement or covenant, and you were forced to think about appearances and realities. (He remembered Raynor and he smiled. Raynor was a clever boy.) Once you had grasped this, a great many things became intelligible. For instance, why Mr. Field should conceive such a scheme. Of course, if people were to agree to create a millionaire, a real millionaire would come into existence. And if you wanted to know how Mr. Field was inspired to think of this, why, he had within sight of his kitchen window the chart, the very bones of a successful scheme—the El with its blue and green confetti of signals. People consented to pay dimes and ride the crash-box cars, and so it was a success. Yet how absurd it looked; how little reality there was to start with. And yet Yerkes,[1] the great financier who built it, had known that he could get people to agree to do it. Viewed as itself, what a scheme of a scheme if seemed, how close to an appearance. Then why wonder at Mr. Field's idea?

9. The Chicago Fire of 1871.
1. Charles Tyson Yerkes (1837–1905), American financier.

He had grasped the principle. And then Grebe remembered, too, that Mr. Yerkes had established the Yerkes Observatory and endowed it with millions. Now how did the notion come to him in his New York museum of a palace or his Aegean-bound yacht to give money to astronomers? Was he awed by the success of his bizarre enterprise and therefore ready to spend money to find out where in the universe being and seeming were identical? Yes, he wanted to know what abides; and whether flesh is Bible grass; and he offered money to be burned in the fire of suns. Okay, then, Grebe thought further, these things exist because people consent to exist with them—we have got so far—and also there is a reality which doesn't depend on consent but within which consent is a game. But what about need, the need that keeps so many vast thousands in position? You tell me that, you *private* little gentleman and *decent* soul—he used these words against himself scornfully. Why is the consent given to misery? And why so painfully ugly? Because there is *something* that is dismal and permanently ugly? Here he sighed and gave it up, and thought it was enough for the present moment that he had a real check in his pocket for a Mr. Green who must be real beyond question. If only his neighbors didn't think they had to conceal him.

This time he stopped at the second floor. He struck a match and found a door. Presently a man answered his knock and Grebe had the check ready and showed it even before he began. "Does Tulliver Green live here? I'm from the relief."

The man narrowed the opening and spoke to someone at his back.

"Does he live here?"

"Uh-uh. No."

"Or anywhere in this building? He's a sick man and he can't come for his dough." He exhibited the check in the light, which was smoky—the air smelled of charred lard—and the man held off the brim of his cap to study it.

"Uh-uh. Never seen the name."

"There's nobody around here that uses crutches?"

He seemed to think, but it was Grebe's impression that he was simply waiting for a decent interval to pass.

"No, suh. Nobody I ever see."

"I've been looking for this man all afternoon"—Grebe spoke out with sudden force—"and I'm going to have to carry this check back to the station. It seems strange not to be able to find a person to *give* him something when you're looking for him for a good reason. I suppose if I had bad news for him I'd find him quick enough."

There was a responsive motion in the other man's face. "That's right, I reckon."

"It almost doesn't do any good to have a name if you can't be found by it. It doesn't stand for anything. He might as well not have any," he went on, smiling. It was as much of a concession as he could make to his desire to laugh.

"Well, now, there's a little old knot-back man I see once in a while. He might be the one you lookin' for. Downstairs."

"Where? Right side or left? Which door?"

"I don't know which. Thin-face little knot-back with a stick."

But no one answered at any of the doors on the first floor. He went to the end of the corridor, searching by matchlight, and found only a stairless exit to the yard, a drop of about six feet. But there was a bungalow near the alley, an old house like Mr. Field's. To jump was unsafe. He ran from the front door, through the underground passage and into the yard. The place was occupied. There was a light through the curtains, upstairs. The name on the ticket under the broken, scoop-shaped mailbox was Green! He exultantly rang the bell and pressed against the locked door. Then the lock clicked faintly and a long staircase opened before him. Someone was slowly coming down—a woman. He had the impression in the weak light that she was shaping her hair as she came, making herself presentable, for he saw her arms raised. But it was for support that they were raised; she was feeling her way downward, down the wall, stumbling. Next he wondered about the pressure of her feet on the treads; she did not seem to be wearing shoes. And it was a freezing stairway. His ring had got her out of bed, perhaps, and she had forgotten to put them on. And then he saw that she was not only shoeless but naked; she was entirely naked, climbing down while she talked to herself, a heavy woman, naked and drunk. She blundered into him. The contact of her breasts, though they touched only his coat, made him go back against the door with a blind shock. See what he had tracked down, in his hunting game!

The woman was saying to herself, furious with insult. "So I cain't——k, huh? I'll show that son-of-a-bitch kin I, cain't I."

What should he do now? Grebe asked himself. Why, he should go. He should turn away and go. He couldn't talk to this woman. He couldn't keep her standing naked in the cold. But when he tried he found himself unable to turn away.

He said, "Is this where Mr. Green lives?"

But she was still talking to herself and did not hear him.

"Is this Mr. Green's house?"

At last she turned her furious drunken glance on him. "What do you want?"

Again her eyes wandered from him; there was a dot of blood in their enraged brilliance. He wondered why she didn't feel the cold.

"I'm from the relief."

"Awright, what?"

"I've got a check for Tulliver Green."

This time she heard him and put out her hand.

"No, no, for *Mr.* Green. He's got to sign," he said. How was he going to get Green's signature tonight!

"I'll take it. He cain't."

He desperately shook his head, thinking of Mr. Field's precautions about identification. "I can't let you have it. It's for him. Are you Mrs. Green?"

"Maybe I is, and maybe I ain't. Who want to know?"

"Is he upstairs?"

"Awright. Take it up yourself, you goddamn fool."

Sure, he was a goddamn fool. Of course he could not go up because Green would probably be drunk and naked, too. And perhaps he would appear on the landing soon. He looked eagerly upward. Under the light was a high narrow brown wall. Empty! It remained empty!

"Hell with you, then!" he heard her cry. To deliver a check for coal and clothes, he was keeping her in the cold. She did not feel it, but his face was burning with frost and self-ridicule. He backed away from her.

"I'll come tomorrow, tell him."

"Ah, hell with you. Don' never come. What you doin' here in the nighttime? Don' come back." She yelled so that he saw the breadth of her tongue. She stood astride in the long cold box of the hall and held on to the banister and the wall. The bungalow itself was shaped something like a box, a clumsy, high box pointing into the freezing air with its sharp, wintry lights.

"If you are Mrs. Green, I'll give you the check," he said, changing his mind.

"Give here, then." She took it, took the pen offered with it in her left hand, and tried to sign the receipt on the wall. He looked around, almost as though to see whether his madness was being observed, and came near believing that someone was standing on a mountain of used tires in the auto-junking shop next door.

"But are you Mrs. Green?" he now thought to ask. But she was already climbing the stairs with the check, and it was too late, if he had made an error, if he was now in trouble, to undo the thing. But he wasn't going to worry about it. Though she might not be Mrs. Green, he was convinced that Mr. Green was upstairs. Whoever she was, the woman stood for Green, whom he was not to see this time. Well, you silly bastard, he said to himself, so you think you found him. So what? Maybe you really did find him—what of it? But it was important that there was a real Mr. Green whom they could not keep him from reaching because he seemed to come as an emissary from hostile appearances. And though the self-ridicule was slow to diminish, and his face still blazed with it, he had, nevertheless, a feeling of elation, too. "For after all," he said, "he *could* be found!"

1951, 1968

ARTHUR MILLER
1915–2005

For much modern American drama the family is the central subject, as the anthology selections show. In *Long Day's Journey into Night*, O'Neill studied his own family through the Tyrones; in Tennessee Williams's *A Streetcar Named Desire* the Kowalskis are one family, which Blanche invades, while Blanche and Stella, as sisters, are another. Most of Arthur Miller's plays, as well, concentrate on the family and envision an ideal world as, perhaps, an enlarged family. Often the protagonist's sense of family draws him into conflict with—and eventual doom in—the outside world. Yet, Miller recognized that an ideal is sometimes a rationalization. Joe Keller insists in *All My Sons* (1947) that he shipped damaged airplane parts during the war to support his family, but a desire for commercial success was part of his motive. Eddie Carbone in *A View from the Bridge* (1955) accepts death because of his sense of responsibility to his niece, but married man though he is, he may also be in love with that same niece. In *Death of a Salesman* (1949), Willy Loman's delusions and self-deceptions derive from, and return to, his image of himself as family provider, an image he cannot live up to; driven by his desire to be "well liked," a successful social personality, he fails to connect with either of his sons and neglects his wife. Thus Miller's treatment of the family leads to a treatment both of personal ideals and of the society within which families have to operate.

Miller was born on October 17, 1915, into a German-Jewish family in Manhattan; his father was a well-to-do but almost illiterate clothing manufacturer, his mother an avid reader. When his father's business collapsed after the stock market crash in 1929, the family moved to Brooklyn, where Miller graduated from high school. His subsequent two years of work in an automobile-parts warehouse to earn money for college tuition are warmly recalled in his play *A Memory of Two Mondays* (1955). At the University of Michigan he enrolled as a journalism student. These were the years of the Spanish Civil War, the rise of fascism, and the attraction of Marxism as a way out of the Depression, and here Miller formed his political views. He also began to write plays, which won prizes at the university and in New York. He then went to work for the Federal Theater Project, wrote radio plays, toured army camps gathering material for a film, and married Mary Slattery, the first of his three wives.

In 1947, his first Broadway success, *All My Sons*, was produced (*The Man Who Had All the Luck* had failed in 1944). This strongly realistic portrayal of a family divided because of the father's insistence on business as usual during World War II drew the attention of audience and theater critics. *Death of a Salesman*, his masterpiece, was produced two years later; it won the Pulitzer Prize. An adaptation (in 1951) of Ibsen's *An Enemy of the People* followed. It was suggested to him by the actors Fredric March and Florence Eldridge, but Miller himself was clearly drawn by Ibsen's hero, Dr. Stockmann, who leads a fight against pollution with strong but confused idealism.

In the 1950s the hysterical search for supposed communist infiltration of American life reached its height, as Senator Joseph McCarthy summoned suspect after suspect to hearings in Washington. Miller later said that at this time he was reading a book about the Salem witch trials and saw that "the main point of the hearings, precisely as in seventeenth-century Salem, was that the accused make public confession, damn his confederates as well as his Devil master, and guarantee his sterling new allegiance by breaking disgusting old vows—whereupon he was let loose to rejoin the society of extremely decent people." Out of this came *The Crucible* (1953), in which the hero, John Proctor, allows himself to be executed rather than sign away his name and his children's respect. Later, the hysteria touched Miller personally: he was denied a passport and in 1957 was convicted of contempt of Congress for refusing to name suspected communists (this conviction was unanimously overturned by the Supreme Court the following year).

Miller had long been looking for a way to dramatize what he had earlier learned about mob control of the Brooklyn waterfront and finally did so in the one-act play *A View from the Bridge*, produced with *A Memory of Two Mondays* in 1955; later he would rework *View* into a full-length play. Meanwhile, he had met the glamorous movie actress Marilyn Monroe; they married in 1956, after he divorced his first wife. He wrote the screenplay *The Misfits* for Monroe, but in their private life, their complex natures were ill-sorted. The marriage ended in divorce in 1961, and a year later he married the photographer Ingeborg Morath, with whom he collaborated on several books of photographs and essays.

In 1964 two plays opened: *After the Fall*—in which the protagonist is a thinly disguised Miller investigating his family, his responsibilities, and his wives—and *Incident at Vichy*—about Jews and Nazis in Vichy, France. While these were by no means as successful as *Salesman*, they returned him seriously to the stage. Among later plays are *The Price* (1968), *The Creation of the World and Other Business* (1972), *The Archbishop's Ceiling* (1977), and two one-act plays under the title *Danger: Memory!* (1986). These last fared poorly in New York, but found successful productions elsewhere in the world. Miller in his later years was something of an activist. In the late 1960s he was asked to become president of PEN (Poets, Essayists, Novelists), the international writers' group. By opening this organization to writers in what were Iron Curtain countries and speaking out for those repressed by totalitarian regimes, he became a respected champion of human rights.

Like his contemporary Tennessee Williams, Miller rejected the influence of "mawkish twenties slang" and "deadly repetitiveness." Again like Williams, Miller was impatient with prosy dialogue and well-made structures. As he explained, the success of *A Streetcar Named Desire* in 1947 helped him to write *Death of a Salesman*:

With *Streetcar,* Tennessee had printed a license to speak at full throat, and it helped strengthen me as I turned to Willy Loman, a salesman always full of words, and better yet, a man who could never cease trying, like Adam, to name himself and the world's wonders. I had known all along that this play could not be encompassed by conventional realism, and for one integral reason: in Willy the past was as alive as what was happening at the moment, sometimes even crashing in to completely overwhelm his mind. I wanted precisely the same fluidity of form.

In *Salesman,* the action moves effortlessly from the present—the last twenty-four hours of Willy's life—into moments in his memory symbolized in the stage setting by the idyllic leaves around his house that, in these past moments, block out the threatening apartment houses. The successful realization of this fluidity on the stage was greatly aided by Miller's director, Elia Kazan, and his stage designer, Jo Mielziner, both of whom had worked with Williams two years earlier on *Streetcar.* A striking difference between Williams and Miller, however, is the latter's overt moralizing, which adds a didactic element to his plays not to be found in those of Williams.

Because of Miller's political involvements, such plays as *All My Sons* and *Death of a Salesman* were seen—especially during the Cold War years—as political tracts. At the other extreme, a later play, *The Ride Down Mount Morgan* (1992), impressed theatergoers as a moral commentary on cultural values in decline, a theme more common at the political spectrum's opposite end. It is good to remember that for both earlier and later plays Miller's protagonists have death on their minds, a concern greater than any political affiliation.

The text is that of *Arthur Miller's Collected Plays* (1957).

Death of a Salesman

Certain Private Conversations in Two Acts and a Requiem

THE CHARACTERS

WILLY LOMAN	THE WOMAN	JENNY
LINDA	CHARLEY	STANLEY
BIFF	UNCLE BEN	MISS FORSYTHE
HAPPY	HOWARD WAGNER	LETTA
BERNARD		

The action takes place in WILLY LOMAN's *house and yard and in various places he visits in the New York and Boston of today.*

Act One

A melody is heard, playing upon a flute. It is small and fine, telling of grass and trees and the horizon. The curtain rises.

Before us is the Salesman's house. We are aware of towering, angular shapes behind it, surrounding it on all sides. Only the blue light of the sky falls upon the house and forestage; the surrounding area shows an angry flow of orange. As more light appears, we see a solid vault of apartment houses around the small, fragile-seeming home. An air of the dream clings to the place, a dream rising out of reality. The kitchen at center seems actual enough, for there is a kitchen table with three chairs, and a refrigerator. But no other fixtures are seen. At the back of the kitchen there is a draped entrance, which leads to the living-room. To the right of the kitchen, on a level raised two feet, is a bedroom furnished only with a brass bedstead and a straight chair. On a shelf over the bed a silver athletic trophy stands. A window opens onto the apartment house at the side.

Behind the kitchen, on a level raised six and a half feet, is the boys' bedroom, at present barely visible. Two beds are dimly seen, and at the back of the room a dormer window. (This bedroom is above the unseen living-room.) At the left a stairway curves up to it from the kitchen.

The entire setting is wholly or, in some places, partially transparent. The roof-line of the house is one-dimensional; under and over it we see the apartment buildings. Before the house lies an apron, curving beyond the forestage into the orchestra. This forward area serves as the back yard as well as the locale of all WILLY'*s imaginings and of his city scenes. Whenever the action is in the present the actors observe the imaginary wall-lines, entering the house only through its door at the left. But in the scenes of the past these boundaries are broken, and characters enter or leave a room by stepping "through" a wall onto the forestage.*

From the right, WILLY LOMAN, *the Salesman, enters, carrying two large sample cases. The flute plays on. He hears but is not aware of it. He is past sixty years of age, dressed quietly. Even as he crosses the stage to the doorway of the house, his exhaustion is apparent. He unlocks the door, comes into the kitchen, and thankfully lets his burden down, feeling the soreness of his palms. A word-sigh escapes his lips—it might be "Oh, boy, oh, boy." He closes the door, then carries his cases out into the living-room, through the draped kitchen doorway.*

LINDA, *his wife, has stirred in her bed at the right. She gets out and puts on a robe, listening. Most often jovial, she has developed an iron repression of her exceptions to* WILLY'*s behavior—she more than loves him, she admires him, as though his mercurial nature, his temper, his massive dreams and little cruelties, served her only as sharp reminders of the turbulent longings within him, longings which she shares but lacks the temperament to utter and follow to their end.*

LINDA [*hearing* WILLY *outside the bedroom, calls with some trepidation*] Willy!

WILLY It's all right. I came back.

LINDA Why? What happened? [*slight pause*] Did something happen, Willy?

WILLY No, nothing happened.

LINDA You didn't smash the car, did you?

WILLY [*with casual irritation*] I said nothing happened. Didn't you hear me?

LINDA Don't you feel well?

WILLY I'm tired to the death. [*The flute has faded away. He sits on the bed beside her, a little numb.*] I couldn't make it. I just couldn't make it, Linda.

LINDA [*very carefully, delicately*] Where were you all day? You look terrible.

WILLY I got as far as a little above Yonkers. I stopped for a cup of coffee. Maybe it was the coffee.

LINDA What?

WILLY [*after a pause*] I suddenly couldn't drive any more. The car kept going off onto the shoulder, y'know?

LINDA [*helpfully*] Oh. Maybe it was the steering again. I don't think Angelo knows the Studebaker.

WILLY No, it's me, it's me. Suddenly I realize I'm goin' sixty miles an hour and I don't remember the last five minutes. I'm—I can't seem to—keep my mind to it.

LINDA Maybe it's your glasses. You never went for your new glasses.

WILLY No, I see everything. I came back ten miles an hour. It took me nearly four hours from Yonkers.

LINDA [*resigned*] Well, you'll just have to take a rest, Willy, you can't continue this way.

WILLY I just got back from Florida.

LINDA But you didn't rest your mind. Your mind is overactive, and the mind is what counts, dear.

WILLY I'll start out in the morning. Maybe I'll feel better in the morning. [*She is taking off his shoes.*] These goddam arch supports are killing me.

LINDA Take an aspirin. Should I get you an aspirin? It'll soothe you.

WILLY [*with wonder*] I was driving along, you understand? And I was fine. I was even observing the scenery. You can imagine, me looking at scenery, on the road every week of my life. But it's so beautiful up there, Linda, the trees are so thick, and the sun is warm. I opened the windshield and just let the warm air bathe over me. And then all of a sudden I'm goin' off the road! I'm tellin' ya, I absolutely forgot I was driving. If I'd've gone the other way over the white line I might've killed somebody. So I went on again—and five minutes later I'm dreamin' again, and I nearly—[*He presses two fingers against his eyes.*] I have such thoughts, I have such strange thoughts.

LINDA Willy, dear. Talk to them again. There's no reason why you can't work in New York.

WILLY They don't need me in New York. I'm the New England man. I'm vital in New England.

LINDA But you're sixty years old. They can't expect you to keep traveling every week.

WILLY I'll have to send a wire to Portland. I'm supposed to see Brown and Morrison tomorrow morning at ten o'clock to show the line. Goddammit, I could sell them! [*He starts putting on his jacket.*]

LINDA [*taking the jacket from him*] Why don't you go down to the place tomorrow and tell Howard you've simply got to work in New York? You're too accommodating, dear.

WILLY If old man Wagner was alive I'd a been in charge of New York now! That man was a prince, he was a masterful man. But that boy of his, that Howard, he don't appreciate. When I went north the first time, the Wagner Company didn't know where New England was!

LINDA Why don't you tell those things to Howard, dear?

WILLY [*encouraged*] I will, I definitely will. Is there any cheese?

LINDA I'll make you a sandwich.

WILLY No, go to sleep. I'll take some milk. I'll be up right away. The boys in?

LINDA They're sleeping. Happy took Biff on a date tonight.

WILLY [*interested*] That so?

LINDA It was so nice to see them shaving together, one behind the other, in the bathroom. And going out together. You notice? The whole house smells of shaving lotion.

WILLY   Figure it out. Work a lifetime to pay off a house. You finally own it, and there's nobody to live in it.

LINDA   Well, dear, life is a casting off. It's always that way.

WILLY   No, no, some people—some people accomplish something. Did Biff say anything after I went this morning?

LINDA   You shouldn't have criticized him, Willy, especially after he just got off the train. You mustn't lose your temper with him.

WILLY   When the hell did I lose my temper? I simply asked him if he was making any money. Is that a criticism?

LINDA   But, dear, how could he make any money?

WILLY   [worried and angered]   There's such an undercurrent in him. He became a moody man. Did he apologize when I left this morning?

LINDA   He was crestfallen, Willy. You know how he admires you. I think if he finds himself, then you'll both be happier and not fight any more.

WILLY   How can he find himself on a farm? Is that a life? A farmhand? In the beginning, when he was young, I thought, well, a young man, it's good for him to tramp around, take a lot of different jobs. But it's more than ten years now and he has yet to make thirty-five dollars a week?

LINDA   He's finding himself, Willy.

WILLY   Not finding yourself at the age of thirty-four is a disgrace!

LINDA   Shh!

WILLY   The trouble is he's lazy, goddammit!

LINDA   Willy, please!

WILLY   Biff is a lazy bum!

LINDA   They're sleeping. Get something to eat. Go on down.

WILLY   Why did he come home? I would like to know what brought him home.

LINDA   I don't know. I think he's still lost, Willy. I think he's very lost.

WILLY   Biff Loman is lost. In the greatest country in the world a young man with such—personal attractiveness, gets lost. And such a hard worker. There's one thing about Biff—he's not lazy.

LINDA   Never.

WILLY   [with pity and resolve]   I'll see him in the morning; I'll have a nice talk with him. I'll get him a job selling. He could be big in no time. My God! Remember how they used to follow him around in high school? When he smiled at one of them their faces lit up. When he walked down the street . . . [He loses himself in reminiscences.]

LINDA   [trying to bring him out of it]   Willy, dear, I got a new kind of American-type cheese today. It's whipped.

WILLY   Why do you get American when I like Swiss?

LINDA   I just thought you'd like a change—

WILLY   I don't want a change! I want Swiss cheese. Why am I always being contradicted?

LINDA   [with a covering laugh]   I thought it would be a surprise.

WILLY   Why don't you open a window in here, for God's sake?

LINDA   [with infinite patience]   They're all open, dear.

WILLY   The way they boxed us in here. Bricks and windows, windows and bricks.

LINDA   We should've bought the land next door.

WILLY   The street is lined with cars. There's not a breath of fresh air in the neighborhood. The grass don't grow any more, you can't raise a carrot in the back yard. They should've had a law against apartment houses. Remember those two beautiful elm trees out there? When I and Biff hung the swing between them?

LINDA   Yeah, like being a million miles from the city.

WILLY   They should've arrested the builder for cutting those down. They massacred the neighborhood. [*lost*] More and more I think of those days, Linda. This time of year it was lilac and wisteria. And then the peonies would come out, and the daffodils. What fragrance in this room!

LINDA   Well, after all, people had to move somewhere.

WILLY   No, there's more people now.

LINDA   I don't think there's more people. I think—

WILLY   There's more people! That's what ruining this country! Population is getting out of control. The competition is maddening! Smell the stink from that apartment house! And another one on the other side . . . How can they whip cheese?

[*On* WILLY's *last line,* BIFF *and* HAPPY *raise themselves up in their beds, listening.*]

LINDA   Go down, try it. And be quiet.

WILLY   [*turning to* LINDA, *guiltily*]   You're not worried about me, are you, sweetheart?

BIFF   What's the matter?

HAPPY   Listen!

LINDA   You've got too much on the ball to worry about.

WILLY   You're my foundation and my support, Linda.

LINDA   Just try to relax, dear. You make mountains out of molehills.

WILLY   I won't fight with him any more. If he wants to go back to Texas, let him go.

LINDA   He'll find his way.

WILLY   Sure. Certain men just don't get started till later in life. Like Thomas Edison, I think. Or B. F. Goodrich. One of them was deaf. [*He starts for the bedroom doorway.*] I'll put my money on Biff.

LINDA   And Willy—if it's warm Sunday we'll drive in the country. And we'll open the windshield, and take lunch.

WILLY   No, the windshields don't open on the new cars.

LINDA   But you opened it today.

WILLY   Me? I didn't. [*He stops.*] Now isn't that peculiar! Isn't that a remarkable—[*He breaks off in amazement and fright as the flute is heard distantly.*]

LINDA   What, darling?

WILLY   That is the most remarkable thing.

LINDA   What, dear?

WILLY   I was thinking of the Chevvy. [*slight pause*] Nineteen twenty-eight . . . when I had that red Chevvy—[*breaks off*] That funny? I coulda sworn I was driving that Chevvy today.

LINDA   Well, that's nothing. Something must've reminded you.

WILLY   Remarkable. Ts. Remember those days? The way Biff used to simonize that car? The dealer refused to believe there was eighty thousand miles on it. [*He shakes his head.*] Heh! [*to* LINDA] Close your eyes, I'll be right up. [*He walks out of the bedroom.*]

HAPPY [*to* BIFF]   Jesus, maybe he smashed up the car again!

LINDA [*calling after* WILLY]   Be careful on the stairs, dear! The cheese is on the middle shelf! [*She turns, goes over to the bed, takes his jacket, and goes out of the bedroom.*]

> [*Light has risen on the boys' room. Unseen,* WILLY *is heard talking to himself, "Eighty thousand miles," and a little laugh.* BIFF *gets out of bed, comes downstage a bit, and stands attentively.* BIFF *is two years older than his brother* HAPPY, *well built, but in these days bears a worn air and seems less self-assured. He has succeeded less, and his dreams are stronger and less acceptable than* HAPPY'S. HAPPY *is tall, powerfully made. Sexuality is like a visible color on him, or a scent that many women have discovered. He, like his brother, is lost, but in a different way, for he has never allowed himself to turn his face toward defeat and is thus more confused and hard-skinned, although seemingly more content.*]

HAPPY [*getting out of bed*]   He's going to get his license taken away if he keeps that up. I'm getting nervous about him, y'know, Biff?

BIFF   His eyes are going.

HAPPY   No, I've driven with him. He sees all right. He just doesn't keep his mind on it. I drove into the city with him last week. He stops at a green light and then it turns red and he goes. [*He laughs.*]

BIFF   Maybe he's color-blind.

HAPPY   Pop? Why he's got the finest eye for color in the business. You know that.

BIFF [*sitting down on his bed*]   I'm going to sleep.

HAPPY   You're not still sour on Dad, are you Biff?

BIFF   He's all right, I guess.

WILLY [*underneath them, in the living-room*]   Yes, sir, eighty thousand miles—eighty-two thousand!

BIFF   You smoking?

HAPPY [*holding out a pack of cigarettes*]   Want one?

BIFF [*taking a cigarette*]   I can never sleep when I smell it.

WILLY   What a simonizing job, heh!

HAPPY [*with deep sentiment*]   Funny, Biff, y'know? Us sleeping in here again? The old beds. [*He pats his bed affectionately.*] All the talk that went across those two beds, huh? Our whole lives.

BIFF   Yeah. Lotta dreams and plans.

HAPPY [*with a deep and masculine laugh*]   About five hundred women would like to know what was said in this room.

> [*They share a soft laugh.*]

BIFF   Remember that big Betsy something—what the hell was her name— over on Bushwick Avenue?

HAPPY [*combing his hair*]   With the collie dog!

BIFF   That's the one. I got you in there, remember?

HAPPY   Yeah, that was my first time—I think. Boy, there was a pig! [*They laugh, almost crudely.*] You taught me everything I know about women. Don't forget that.

BIFF   I bet you forgot how bashful you used to be. Especially with girls.

HAPPY   Oh, I still am, Biff.

BIFF Oh, go on.

HAPPY I just control it, that's all. I think I got less bashful and you got more so. What happened, Biff? Where's the old humor, the old confidence? [*He shakes* BIFF'*s knee.* BIFF *gets up and moves restlessly about the room.*] What's the matter?

BIFF Why does Dad mock me all the time?

HAPPY He's not mocking you, he—

BIFF Everything I say there's a twist of mockery on his face. I can't get near him.

HAPPY He just wants you to make good, that's all. I wanted to talk to you about Dad for a long time, Biff. Something's—happening to him. He—talks to himself.

BIFF I noticed that this morning. But he always mumbled.

HAPPY But not so noticeable. It got so embarrassing I sent him to Florida. And you know something? Most of the time he's talking to you.

BIFF What's he say about me?

HAPPY I can't make it out.

BIFF What's he say about me?

HAPPY I think the fact that you're not settled, that you're still kind of up in the air . . .

BIFF There's one or two other things depressing him, Happy.

HAPPY What do you mean?

BIFF Never mind. Just don't lay it all to me.

HAPPY But I think if you just got started—I mean—is there any future for you out there?

BIFF I tell ya, Hap, I don't know what the future is. I don't know—what I'm supposed to want.

HAPPY What do you mean?

BIFF Well, I spent six or seven years after high school trying to work myself up. Shipping clerk, salesman, business of one kind or another. And it's a measly manner of existence. To get on that subway on the hot mornings in summer. To devote your whole life to keeping stock, or making phone calls, or selling or buying. To suffer fifty weeks of the year for the sake of a two-week vacation, when all you really desire is to be outdoors, with your shirt off. And always to have to get ahead of the next fella. And still—that's how you build a future.

HAPPY Well, you really enjoy it on a farm? Are you content out there?

BIFF [*with rising agitation*] Hap, I've had twenty or thirty different kinds of jobs since I left home before the war, and it always turns out the same. I just realized it lately. In Nebraska when I herded cattle, and the Dakotas, and Arizona, and now in Texas. It's why I came home now, I guess, because I realized it. This farm I work on, it's spring there now, see? And they've got about fifteen new colts. There's nothing more inspiring or—beautiful than the sight of a mare and a new colt. And it's cool there now, see? Texas is cool now, and it's spring. And whenever spring comes to where I am, I suddenly get the feeling, my God, I'm not gettin' anywhere! What the hell am I doing, playing around with horses, twenty-eight dollars a week! I'm thirty-four years old. I oughta be makin' my future. That's when I come running home. And now, I get here, and I don't know what to do with myself. [*after a pause*] I've always made a point of not wasting my life, and everytime I come back here I know that all I've done is to waste my life.

HAPPY   You're a poet, you know that, Biff? You're a—you're an idealist!

BIFF   No, I'm mixed up very bad. Maybe I oughta get married. Maybe I oughta get stuck into something. Maybe that's my trouble. I'm like a boy. I'm not married. I'm not in business, I just—I'm like a boy. Are you content, Hap? You're a success, aren't you? Are you content?

HAPPY   Hell, no!

BIFF   Why? You're making money, aren't you?

HAPPY [*moving about with energy, expressiveness*]   All I can do now is wait for the merchandise manager to die. And suppose I get to be merchandise manager? He's a good friend of mine, and he just built a terrific estate on Long Island. And he lived there about two months and sold it, and now he's building another one. He can't enjoy it once it's finished. And I know that's just what I would do. I don't know what the hell I'm workin' for. Sometimes I sit in my apartment—all alone. And I think of the rent I'm paying. And it's crazy. But then, it's what I always wanted. My own apartment, a car, and plenty of women. And still, goddammit, I'm lonely.

BIFF [*with enthusiasm*]   Listen why don't you come out West with me?

HAPPY   You and I, heh?

BIFF   Sure, maybe we could buy a ranch. Raise cattle, use our muscles. Men built like we are should be working out in the open.

HAPPY [*avidly*]   The Loman Brothers, heh?

BIFF [*with vast affection*]   Sure, we'd be known all over the counties!

HAPPY [*enthralled*]   That's what I dream about, Biff. Sometimes I want to just rip my clothes off in the middle of the store and outbox that goddam merchandise manager. I mean I can outbox, outrun, and outlift anybody in that store, and I have to take orders from those common, petty sons-of-bitches till I can't stand it any more.

BIFF   I'm tellin' you, kid, if you were with me I'd be happy out there.

HAPPY [*enthused*]   See, Biff, everybody around me is so false that I'm constantly lowering my ideals . . .

BIFF   Baby, together we'd stand up for one another, we'd have someone to trust.

HAPPY   If I were around you—

BIFF   Hap, the trouble is we weren't brought up to grub for money. I don't know how to do it.

HAPPY   Neither can I!

BIFF   Then let's go!

HAPPY   The only thing is—what can you make out there?

BIFF   But look at your friend. Builds an estate and then hasn't the peace of mind to live in it.

HAPPY   Yeah, but when he walks into the store the waves part in front of him. That's fifty-two thousand dollars a year coming through the revolving door, and I got more in my pinky finger than he's got in his head.

BIFF   Yeah, but you just said—

HAPPY   I gotta show some of those pompous, self-important executives over there that Hap Loman can make the grade. I want to walk into the store the way he walks in. Then I'll go with you, Biff. We'll be together yet, I swear. But take those two we had tonight. Now weren't they gorgeous creatures?

BIFF   Yeah, yeah, most gorgeous I've had in years.

HAPPY   I get that any time I want, Biff. Whenever I feel disgusted. The only trouble is, it gets like bowling or something. I just keep knockin' them over and it doesn't mean anything. You still run around a lot?

BIFF   Naa. I'd like to find a girl—steady, somebody with substance.

HAPPY   That's what I long for.

BIFF   Go on! You'd never come home.

HAPPY   I would! Somebody with character, with resistance! Like Mom, y'know? You're gonna call me a bastard when I tell you this. That girl Charlotte I was with tonight is engaged to be married in five weeks. [*He tries on his new hat.*]

BIFF   No kiddin'!

HAPPY   Sure, the guy's in line for the vice-presidency of the store. I don't know what gets into me, maybe I just have an overdeveloped sense of competition or something, but I went and ruined her, and furthermore I can't get rid of her. And he's the third executive I've done that to. Isn't that a crummy characteristic? And to top it all, I go to their weddings! [*indignantly, but laughing*] Like I'm not supposed to take bribes. Manufacturers offer me a hundred-dollar bill now and then to throw an order their way. You know how honest I am, but it's like this girl, see. I hate myself for it. Because I don't want the girl, and, still, I take it and—I love it!

BIFF   Let's go to sleep.

HAPPY   I guess we didn't settle anything, heh?

BIFF   I just got one idea that I think I'm going to try.

HAPPY   What's that?

BIFF   Remember Bill Oliver?

HAPPY   Sure, Oliver is very big now. You want to work for him again?

BIFF   No, but when I quit he said something to me. He put his arm on my shoulder, and he said, "Biff, if you ever need anything, come to me."

HAPPY   I remember that. That sounds good.

BIFF   I think I'll go to see him. If I could get ten thousand or even seven or eight thousand dollars I could buy a beautiful ranch.

HAPPY   I bet he'd back you. 'Cause he thought highly of you, Biff. I mean, they all do. You're well liked, Biff. That's why I say to come back here, and we both have the apartment. And I'm tellin' you, Biff, any babe you want . . .

BIFF   No, with a ranch I could do the work I like and still be something. I just wonder though. I wonder if Oliver still thinks I stole that carton of basketballs.

HAPPY   Oh, he probably forgot that long ago. It's almost ten years. You're too sensitive. Anyway, he didn't really fire you.

BIFF   Well, I think he was going to. I think that's why I quit. I was never sure whether he knew or not. I know he thought the world of me, though. I was the only one he'd let lock up the place.

WILLY [*below*]   You gonna wash the engine, Biff?

HAPPY   Shh!

         oBIFF *looks at* HAPPY, *who is gazing down, listening.* WILLY *is mumbling in the parlor.*]

HAPPY   You hear that?

[*They listen.* WILLY *laughs warmly.*]

BIFF [*growing angry*]   Doesn't he know Mom can hear that?

WILLY   Don't get your sweater dirty, Biff!

[*A look of pain crosses* BIFF'S *face.*]

HAPPY   Isn't that terrible? Don't leave again, will you? You'll find a job here. You gotta stick around. I don't know what to do about him, it's getting embarrassing.

WILLY   What a simonizing job!

BIFF   Mom's hearing that!

WILLY   No kiddin', Biff, you got a date? Wonderful!

HAPPY   Go on to sleep. But talk to him in the morning, will you?

BIFF [*reluctantly getting into bed*]   With her in the house. Brother!

HAPPY [*getting into bed*]   I wish you'd have a good talk with him.

[*The light on their room begins to fade.*]

BIFF [*to himself in bed*]   That selfish, stupid . . .

HAPPY   Sh . . . Sleep, Biff.

[*Their light is out. Well before they have finished speaking,* WILLY's *form is dimly seen below in the darkened kitchen. He opens the refrigerator, searches in there, and takes out a bottle of milk. The apartment houses are fading out, and the entire house and surroundings become covered with leaves. Music insinuates itself as the leaves appear.*]

WILLY   Just wanna be careful with those girls, Biff, that's all. Don't make any promises. No promises of any kind. Because a girl, y'know, they always believe what you tell 'em, and you're very young, Biff, you're too young to be talking seriously to girls.

[*Light rises on the kitchen.* WILLY, *talking, shuts the refrigerator door and comes downstage to the kitchen table. He pours milk into a glass. He is totally immersed in himself, smiling faintly.*]

WILLY   Too young entirely, Biff. You want to watch your schooling first. Then when you're all set, there'll be plenty of girls for a boy like you. [*He smiles broadly at a kitchen chair.*] That so? The girls pay for you? [*He laughs.*] Boy, you must really be makin' a hit.

[WILLY *is gradually addressing—physically—a point offstage, speaking through the wall of the kitchen, and his voice has been rising in volume to that of a normal conversation.*]

WILLY   I been wondering why you polish the car so careful. Ha! Don't leave the hubcaps, boys. Get the chamois to the hubcaps. Happy, use newspaper on the windows, it's the easiest thing. Show him how to do it, Biff! You see, Happy? Pad it up, use it like a pad. That's it, that's it, good work. You're doin' all right, Hap. [*He pauses, then nods in approbation for a few seconds, then looks upward.*] Biff, first thing we gotta do when we get time is clip that big branch over the house. Afraid it's gonna fall in a storm and hit the roof. Tell you what. We get a rope and sling her around, and then we climb up there with a couple of saws and take her down. Soon as you finish the car, boys, I wanna see ya. I got a surprise for you, boys.

BIFF [*offstage*]   Whatta ya got, Dad?

WILLY   No, you finish first. Never leave a job till you're finished—remember that. [*looking toward the "big trees"*] Biff, up in Albany I saw a beautiful hammock. I think I'll buy it next trip, and we'll hang it right between those two elms. Wouldn't that be something? Just swingin' there under those branches. Boy, that would be . . .

[YOUNG BIFF and YOUNG HAPPY *appear from the direction* WILLY *was addressing.* HAPPY *carries rags and a pail of water.* BIFF, *wearing a sweater with a block "S," carries a football.*]

BIFF [*pointing in the direction of the car offstage*]   How's that, Pop, professional?

WILLY   Terrific. Terrific job, boys. Good work, Biff.

HAPPY   Where's the surprise, Pop?

WILLY   In the back seat of the car.

HAPPY   Boy! [*He runs off.*]

BIFF   What is it, Dad? Tell me, what'd you buy?

WILLY [*laughing, cuffs him*]   Never mind, something I want you to have.

BIFF [*turns and starts off*]   What is it, Hap?

HAPPY [*offstage*]   It's a punching bag!

BIFF   Oh, Pop!

WILLY   It's got Gene Tunney's[1] signature on it!

[HAPPY *runs onstage with a punching bag.*]

BIFF   Gee, how'd you know we wanted a punching bag?

WILLY   Well, it's the finest thing for the timing.

HAPPY [*lies down on his back and pedals with his feet*]   I'm losing weight, you notice, Pop?

WILLY [*to* HAPPY]   Jumping rope is good too.

BIFF   Did you see the new football I got?

WILLY [*examining the ball*]   Where'd you get a new ball?

BIFF   The coach told me to practice my passing.

WILLY   That so? And he gave you the ball, heh?

BIFF   Well, I borrowed it from the locker room. [*He laughs confidentially.*]

WILLY [*laughing with him at the left*]   I want you to return that.

HAPPY   I told you he wouldn't like it!

BIFF [*angrily*]   Well, I'm bringing it back!

WILLY [*stopping the incipient argument, to* HAPPY]   Sure, he's gotta practice with a regulation ball, doesn't he? [*to* BIFF] Coach'll probably congratulate you on your initiative!

BIFF   Oh, he keeps congratulating my initiative all the time, Pop.

WILLY   That's because he likes you. If somebody else took that ball there'd be an uproar. So what's the report, boys, what's the report?

BIFF   Where'd you go this time, Dad? Gee we were lonesome for you.

WILLY [*pleased, puts an arm around each boy and they come down to the apron*]   Lonesome, heh?

BIFF   Missed you every minute.

WILLY   Don't say? Tell you a secret, boys. Don't breathe it to a soul. Someday I'll have my own business, and I'll never have to leave home any more.

HAPPY   Like Uncle Charley, heh?

WILLY   Bigger than Uncle Charley! Because Charley is not—liked. He's liked, but he's not—well liked.

BIFF   Where'd you go this time, Dad?

---

1. World heavyweight boxing champion from 1926 to 1928.

WILLY   Well, I got on the road, and I went north to Providence. Met the Mayor.

BIFF   The Mayor of Providence!

WILLY   He was sitting in the hotel lobby.

BIFF   What'd he say?

WILLY   He said, "Morning!" And I said, "You got a fine city here, Mayor." And then he had coffee with me. And then I went to Waterbury. Waterbury is a fine city. Big clock city, the famous Waterbury clock. Sold a nice bill there. And then Boston—Boston is the cradle of the Revolution. A fine city. And a couple of other towns in Mass., and on to Portland and Bangor and straight home!

BIFF   Gee, I'd love to go with you sometime, Dad.

WILLY   Soon as summer comes.

HAPPY   Promise?

WILLY   You and Hap and I, and I'll show you all the towns. America is full of beautiful towns and fine, upstanding people. And they know me, boys, they know me up and down New England. The finest people. And when I bring you fellas up, there'll be open sesame for all of us, 'cause one thing, boys: I have friends. I can park my car in any street in New England, and the cops protect it like their own. This summer, heh?

BIFF and HAPPY [together]   Yeah! You bet!

WILLY   We'll take our bathing suits.

HAPPY   We'll carry your bags, Pop!

WILLY   Oh, won't that be something! Me comin' into the Boston stores with you boys carryin' my bags. What a sensation!

   [BIFF is prancing around, practicing passing the ball.]

WILLY   You nervous, Biff, about the game?

BIFF   Not if you're gonna be there.

WILLY   What do they say about you in school, now that they made you captain?

HAPPY   There's a crowd of girls behind him everytime the classes change.

BIFF [taking WILLY's hand]   This Saturday, Pop, this Saturday—just for you, I'm going to break through for a touchdown.

HAPPY   You're supposed to pass.

BIFF   I'm takin' one play for Pop. You watch me, Pop, and when I take off my helmet, that means I'm breakin' out. Then you watch me crash through that line!

WILLY [kisses BIFF]   Oh, wait'll I tell this in Boston!

   [BERNARD enters in knickers. He is younger than BIFF, earnest and loyal, a worried boy.]

BERNARD   Biff, where are you? You're supposed to study with me today.

WILLY   Hey, looka Bernard. What're you lookin' so anemic about, Bernard?

BERNARD   He's gotta study, Uncle Willy. He's got Regents[2] next week.

HAPPY [tauntingly, spinning BERNARD around]   Let's box, Bernard!

BERNARD   Biff! [He gets away from HAPPY.] Listen, Biff, I heard Mr. Birnbaum say that if you don't start studyin' math he's gonna flunk you, and you won't graduate. I heard him!

WILLY   You better study with him, Biff. Go ahead now.

---

2. Compulsory statewide high school examinations in New York.

BERNARD   I heard him!

BIFF   Oh, Pop, you didn't see my sneakers! [*He holds up a foot for* WILLY *to look at.*]

WILLY   Hey, that's a beautiful job of printing!

BERNARD [*wiping his glasses*]   Just because he printed University of Virginia on his sneakers doesn't mean they've got to graduate him, Uncle Willy!

WILLY [*angrily*]   What're you talking about? With scholarships to three universities they're gonna flunk him?

BERNARD   But I heard Mr. Birnbaum say—

WILLY   Don't be a pest, Bernard! [*to his boys*] What an anemic!

BERNARD   Okay, I'm waiting for you in my house, Biff.
   [BERNARD *goes off. The Lomans laugh.*]

WILLY   Bernard is not well liked, is he?

BIFF   He's liked, but he's not well liked.

HAPPY   That's right, Pop.

WILLY   That's just what I mean. Bernard can get the best marks in school, y'understand, but when he gets out in the business world, y'understand, you are going to be five times ahead of him. That's why I thank Almighty God you're both built like Adonises.[3] Because the man who makes an appearance in the business world, the man who creates personal interest, is the man who gets ahead. Be liked and you will never want. You take me, for instance. I never have to wait in line to see a buyer. "Willy Loman is here!" That's all they have to know, and I go right through.

BIFF   Did you knock them dead, Pop?

WILLY   Knocked 'em cold in Providence, slaughtered 'em in Boston.

HAPPY [*on his back, pedaling again*]   I'm losing weight, you notice, Pop?
   [LINDA *enters, as of old, a ribbon in her hair, carrying a basket of washing.*]

LINDA [*with youthful energy*]   Hello, dear!

WILLY   Sweetheart!

LINDA   How'd the Chevvy run?

WILLY   Chevrolet, Linda, is the greatest car ever built. [*to the boys*] Since when do you let your mother carry wash up the stairs?

BIFF   Grab hold there, boy!

HAPPY   Where to, Mom?

LINDA   Hang them up on the line. And you better go down to your friends, Biff. The cellar is full of boys. They don't know what to do with themselves.

BIFF   Ah, when Pop comes home they can wait!

WILLY [*laughs appreciatively*]   You better go down and tell them what to do, Biff.

BIFF   I think I'll have them sweep out the furnace room.

WILLY   Good work, Biff.

BIFF [*goes through wall-line of kitchen to doorway at back and calls down*]   Fellas! Everybody sweep out the furnace room! I'll be right down!

VOICES   All right! Okay, Biff.

BIFF   George and Sam and Frank, come out back! We're hangin' up the wash! Come on, Hap, on the double!
   [*He and* HAPPY *carry out the basket.*]

---

3. In Greek mythology, Adonis was a beautiful youth favored by Aphrodite, goddess of love.

LINDA   The way they obey him!

WILLY   Well, that training, the training. I'm tellin' you, I was sellin' thousands and thousands, but I had to come home.

LINDA   Oh, the whole block'll be at that game. Did you sell anything?

WILLY   I did five hundred gross in Providence and seven hundred gross in Boston.

LINDA   No! Wait a minute, I've got a pencil. [*She pulls pencil and paper out of her apron pocket.*] That makes your commission . . . Two hundred—my God! Two hundred and twelve dollars!

WILLY   Well, I didn't figure it yet, but . . .

LINDA   How much did you do?

WILLY   Well, I—I did—about a hundred and eighty gross in Providence. Well, no—it came to—roughly two hundred gross on the whole trip.

LINDA   [*without hesitation*]   Two hundred gross. That's . . . [*She figures.*]

WILLY   The trouble was that three of the stores were half closed for inventory in Boston. Otherwise I woulda broke records.

LINDA   Well, it makes seventy dollars and some pennies. That's very good.

WILLY   What do we owe?

LINDA   Well, on the first there's sixteen dollars on the refrigerator—

WILLY   Why sixteen?

LINDA   Well, the fan belt broke, so it was a dollar eighty.

WILLY   But it's brand new.

LINDA   Well, the man said that's the way it is. Till they work themselves in, y'know
[*They move through the wall-line into the kitchen.*]

WILLY   I hope we didn't get stuck on that machine.

LINDA   They got the biggest ads of any of them!

WILLY   I know, it's a fine machine. What else?

LINDA   Well, there's nine-sixty for the washing machine. And for the vacuum cleaner there's three and a half due on the fifteenth. Then the roof, you got twenty-one dollars remaining.

WILLY   It don't leak, does it?

LINDA   No, they did a wonderful job. Then you owe Frank for the carburetor.

WILLY   I'm not going to pay that man! That goddam Chevrolet, they ought to prohibit the manufacture of that car!

LINDA   Well, you owe him three and a half. And odds and ends, comes to around a hundred and twenty dollars by the fifteenth.

WILLY   A hundred and twenty dollars! My God, if business don't pick up I don't know what I'm gonna do!

LINDA   Well, next week you'll do better.

WILLY   Oh, I'll knock 'em dead next week. I'll go to Hartford. I'm very well liked in Hartford. You know, the trouble is, Linda, people don't seem to take to me.
[*They move onto the forestage.*]

LINDA   Oh, don't be foolish.

WILLY   I know it when I walk in. They seem to laugh at me.

LINDA   Why? Why would they laugh at you? Don't talk that way, Willy.
[WILLY *moves to the edge of the stage.* LINDA *goes into the kitchen and starts to darn stockings.*]

WILLY   I don't know the reason for it, but they just pass me by. I'm not
noticed.

LINDA   But you're doing wonderful, dear. You're making seventy to a hundred dollars a week.

WILLY   But I gotta be at it ten, twelve hours a day. Other men—I don't
know—they do it easier. I don't know why—I can't stop myself—I talk
too much. A man oughta come in with a few words. One thing about
Charley. He's a man of few words, and they respect him.

LINDA   You don't talk too much, you're just lively.

WILLY [smiling]   Well, I figure, what the hell, life is short, a couple of jokes.
[to himself] I joke too much! [The smiles goes.]

LINDA   Why? You're—

WILLY   I'm fat. I'm very—foolish to look at, Linda. I didn't tell you, but
Christmas time I happened to be calling on F. H. Stewarts, and a salesman I know, as I was going in to see the buyer I heard him say something
about—walrus. And I—I cracked him right across the face. I won't take
that. I simply will not take that. But they do laugh at me. I know that.

LINDA   Darling . . .

WILLY   I gotta overcome it. I know I gotta overcome it. I'm not dressing to
advantage, maybe.

LINDA   Willy, darling, you're the handsomest man in the world—

WILLY   Oh, no, Linda.

LINDA   To me you are. [slight pause] The handsomest.
[From the darkness is heard the laughter of a woman. WILLY doesn't turn
to it, but it continues through LINDA's lines.]

LINDA   And the boys, Willy. Few men are idolized by their children the
way you are.
[Music is heard as behind a scrim,[4] to the left of the house, THE WOMAN,
dimly seen, is dressing.]

WILLY [with great feeling]   You're the best there is, Linda, you're a pal, you
know that? On the road—on the road I want to grab you sometimes and
just kiss the life outa you.
[The laughter is loud now, and he moves into a brightening area at the
left, where THE WOMAN has come from behind the scrim and is standing,
putting on her hat, looking into a "mirror" and laughing.]

WILLY   'Cause I get so lonely—especially when business is bad and there's
nobody to talk to. I get the feeling that I'll never sell anything again, that
I won't make a living for you, or a business, a business for the boys. [He
talks through THE WOMAN's subsiding laughter; THE WOMAN primps at the
"mirror."] There's so much I want to make for—

THE WOMAN   Me? You didn't make me, Willy. I picked you.

WILLY [pleased]   You picked me?

THE WOMAN [who is quite proper-looking, WILLY's age]   I did. I've been sitting at that desk watching all the salesmen go by, day in, day out. But
you've got such a sense of humor, and we do have such a good time
together, don't we?

WILLY   Sure, sure. [He takes her in his arms.] Why do you have to go now?

THE WOMAN   It's two o'clock . . .

---

4. In a stage set, a painted gauze curtain that becomes transparent when lighted from the back.

WILLY   No, come on in! [*He pulls her.*]

THE WOMAN   . . . my sisters'll be scandalized. When'll you be back?

WILLY   Oh, two weeks about. Will you come up again?

THE WOMAN   Sure thing. You do make me laugh. It's good for me. [*She squeezes his arm, kisses him.*] And I think you're a wonderful man.

WILLY   You picked me, heh?

THE WOMAN   Sure. Because you're so sweet. And such a kidder.

WILLY   Well, I'll see you next time I'm in Boston.

THE WOMAN   I'll put you right through to the buyers.

WILLY [*slapping her bottom*]   Right. Well, bottoms up!

THE WOMAN [*slaps him gently and laughs*]   You just kill me, Willy. [*He suddenly grabs her and kisses her roughly.*] You kill me. And thanks for the stockings. I love a lot of stockings. Well, good night.

WILLY   Good night. And keep your pores open!

THE WOMAN   Oh, Willy!

> [THE WOMAN *bursts out laughing, and* LINDA's *laughter blends in.* THE WOMAN *disappears into the dark. Now the area at the kitchen table brightens.* LINDA *is sitting where she was at the kitchen table, but now is mending a pair of her silk stockings.*]

LINDA   You are, Willy. The handsomest man. You've got no reason to feel that—

WILLY [*coming out of* THE WOMAN's *dimming area and going over to* LINDA]   I'll make it all up to you, Linda. I'll—

LINDA   There's nothing to make up, dear. You're doing fine, better than—

WILLY [*noticing her mending*]   What's that?

LINDA   Just mending my stockings. They're so expensive—

WILLY [*angrily, taking them from her*]   I won't have you mending stockings in this house! Now throw them out!

> [LINDA *puts the stockings in her pocket.*]

BERNARD [*entering on the run*]   Where is he? If he doesn't study!

WILLY [*moving to the forestage, with great agitation*]   You'll give him the answers!

BERNARD   I do, but I can't on a Regents! That's a state exam! They're liable to arrest me!

WILLY   Where is he? I'll whip him, I'll whip him!

LINDA   And he'd better give back that football, Willy, it's not nice.

WILLY   Biff! Where is he? Why is he taking everything?

LINDA   He's too rough with the girls, Willy. All the mothers are afraid of him!

WILLY   I'll whip him!

BERNARD   He's driving the car without a license!

> [THE WOMAN's *laugh is heard.*]

WILLY   Shut up!

LINDA   All the mothers—

WILLY   Shut up!

BERNARD [*backing quietly away and out*]   Mr. Birnbaum says he's stuck up.

WILLY   Get outa here!

BERNARD   If he doesn't buckle down he'll flunk math! [*He goes off.*]

LINDA   He's right, Willy, you've gotta—

WILLY [*exploding at her*]   There's nothing the matter with him! You want him to be a worm like Bernard? He's got spirit, personality . . .

[*As he speaks,* LINDA, *almost in tears, exist into the living-room.* WILLY *is alone in the kitchen, wilting and staring. The leaves are gone. It is night again, and the apartment houses look down from behind.*]

WILLY   Loaded with it. Loaded! What is he stealing? He's giving it back, isn't he? Why is he stealing? What did I tell him? I never in my life told him anything but decent things.

[HAPPY *in pajamas has come down the stairs;* WILLY *suddenly becomes aware of* HAPPY's *presence.*]

HAPPY   Let's go now, come on.

WILLY   [*sitting down at the kitchen table*]   Huh! Why did she have to wax the floors herself? Everytime she waxes the floors she keels over. She knows that!

HAPPY   Shh! Take it easy. What brought you back tonight?

WILLY   I got an awful scare. Nearly hit a kid in Yonkers. God! Why didn't I go to Alaska with my brother Ben that time! Ben! That man was a genius, that man was success incarnate! What a mistake! He begged me to go.

HAPPY   Well, there's no use in—

WILLY   You guys! There was a man started with the clothes on his back and ended up with diamond mines!

HAPPY   Boy, someday I'd like to know how he did it.

WILLY   What's the mystery? The man knew what he wanted and went out and got it! Walked into a jungle, and comes out, the age of twenty-one, and he's rich! The world is an oyster, but you don't crack it open on a mattress!

HAPPY   Pop, I told you I'm gonna retire you for life.

WILLY   You'll retire me for life on seventy goddam dollars a week? And your women and your car and your apartment, and you'll retire me for life! Christ's sake, I couldn't get past Yonkers today! Where are you guys, where are you? The woods are burning! I can't drive a car!

[CHARLEY *has appeared in the doorway. He is a large man, slow of speech, laconic, immovable. In all he says, despite what he says, there is pity, and, now, trepidation. He has a robe over pajamas, slippers on his feet. He enters the kitchen.*]

CHARLEY   Everything all right?

HAPPY   Yeah, Charley, everything's . . .

WILLY   What's the matter?

CHARLEY   I heard some noise. I thought something happened. Can't we do something about the walls? You sneeze in here, and in my house hats blow off.

HAPPY   Let's go to bed, Dad. Come on.

[CHARLEY *signals to* HAPPY *to go.*]

WILLY   You go ahead, I'm not tired at the moment.

HAPPY   [*to* WILLY]   Take it easy, huh? [*He exits.*]

WILLY   What're you doin' up?

CHARLEY   [*sitting down at the kitchen table opposite* WILLY]   Couldn't sleep good. I had a heartburn.

WILLY   Well, you don't know how to eat.

CHARLEY   I eat with my mouth.

WILLY   No, you're ignorant. You gotta know about vitamins and things like that.

CHARLEY   Come on, let's shoot. Tire you out a little.

WILLY [*hesitantly*]   All right. You got cards?

CHARLEY [*taking a deck from his pocket*]   Yeah, I got them. Someplace. What is it with those vitamins?

WILLY [*dealing*]   They build up your bones. Chemistry.

CHARLEY   Yeah, but there's no bones in a heartburn.

WILLY   What are you talkin' about? Do you know the first thing about it?

CHARLEY   Don't get insulted.

WILLY   Don't talk about something you don't know anything about.
   [*They are playing. Pause.*]

CHARLEY   What're you doin' home?

WILLY   A little trouble with the car.

CHARLEY   Oh. [*pause*] I'd like to take a trip to California.

WILLY   Don't say.

CHARLEY   You want a job?

WILLY   I got a job, I told you that. [*after a slight pause*] What the hell are you offering me a job for?

CHARLEY   Don't get insulted.

WILLY   Don't insult me.

CHARLEY   I don't see no sense in it. You don't have to go on this way.

WILLY   I got a good job. [*slight pause*] What do you keep comin' in here for?

CHARLEY   You want me to go?

WILLY [*after a pause, withering*]   I can't understand it. He's going back to Texas again. What the hell is that?

CHARLEY   Let him go.

WILLY   I got nothin' to give him, Charley, I'm clean, I'm clean.

CHARLEY   He won't starve. None a them starve. Forget about him.

WILLY   Then what have I got to remember?

CHARLEY   You take it too hard. To hell with it. When a deposit bottle is broken you don't get your nickel back.

WILLY   That's easy enough for you to say.

CHARLEY   That ain't easy for me to say.

WILLY   Did you see the ceiling I put up in the living-room?

CHARLEY   Yeah, that's a piece of work. To put up a ceiling is a mystery to me. How do you do it?

WILLY   What's the difference?

CHARLEY   Well, talk about it.

WILLY   You gonna put up a ceiling?

CHARLEY   How could I put up a ceiling?

WILLY   Then what the hell are you bothering me for?

CHARLEY   You're insulted again.

WILLY   A man who can't handle tools is not a man. You're disgusting.

CHARLEY   Don't call me disgusting, Willy.
   [UNCLE BEN, *carrying a valise and an umbrella, enters the forestage from around the right corner of the house. He is a stolid man, in his sixties, with a mustache and an authoritative air. He is utterly certain of his destiny, and there is an aura of far places about him. He enters exactly as* WILLY *speaks.*]

WILLY   I'm getting awfully tired, Ben.

[BEN's *music is heard.* BEN *looks around at everything.*]

CHARLEY Good, keep playing; you'll sleep better. Did you call me Ben?

[BEN *looks at his watch.*]

WILLY That's funny. For a second there you reminded me of my brother Ben.

BEN I only have a few minutes. [*He strolls, inspecting the place.* WILLY *and* CHARLEY *continue playing.*]

CHARLEY You never heard from him again, heh? Since that time?

WILLY Didn't Linda tell you? Couple of weeks ago we got a letter from his wife in Africa. He died.

CHARLEY That so.

BEN [*chuckling*] So this is Brooklyn, eh?

CHARLEY Maybe you're in for some of his money.

WILLY Naa, he had seven sons. There's just one opportunity I had with that man . . .

BEN I must make a train, William. There are several properties I'm looking at in Alaska.

WILLY Sure, sure! If I'd gone with him to Alaska that time, everything would've been totally different.

CHARLEY Go on, you'd froze to death up there.

WILLY What're you talking about?

BEN Opportunity is tremendous in Alaska, William. Surprised you're not up there.

WILLY Sure, tremendous.

CHARLEY Heh?

WILLY There was the only man I ever met who knew the answers.

CHARLEY Who?

BEN How are you all?

WILLY [*taking a pot, smiling*] Fine, fine.

CHARLEY Pretty sharp tonight.

BEN Is Mother living with you?

WILLY No, she died a long time ago.

CHARLEY Who?

BEN That's too bad. Fine specimen of a lady, Mother.

WILLY [*to* CHARLEY] Heh?

BEN I'd hoped to see the old girl.

CHARLEY Who died?

BEN Heard anything from Father, have you?

WILLY [*unnerved*] What do you mean, who died?

CHARLEY [*taking a pot*] What're you talkin' about?

BEN [*looking at his watch*] William, it's half-past eight!

WILLY [*as though to dispel his confusion he angrily stops* CHARLEY's *hand*] That's my build!

CHARLEY I put the ace—

WILLY If you don't know how to play the game I'm not gonna throw my money away on you!

CHARLEY [*rising*] It was my ace, for God's sake!

WILLY I'm through, I'm through!

BEN When did Mother die?

WILLY Long ago. Since the beginning you never knew how to play cards.

CHARLEY [*picks up the cards and goes to the door*]   All right! Next time I'll bring a deck with five aces.

WILLY   I don't play that kind of game!

CHARLEY [*turning to him*]   You ought to be ashamed of yourself!

WILLY   Yeah?

CHARLEY   Yeah! [*He goes out.*]

WILLY [*slamming the door after him*]   Ignoramus!

BEN [*as* WILLY *comes toward him through the wall-line of the kitchen*]   So you're William.

WILLY [*shaking* BEN'*s hand*]   Ben! I've been waiting for you so long! What's the answer? How did you do it?

BEN   Oh, there's a story in that.

[LINDA *enters the forestage, as of old, carrying the wash basket.*]

LINDA   Is this Ben?

BEN [*gallantly*]   How do you do, my dear.

LINDA   Where've you been all these years? Willy's always wondered why you—

WILLY [*pulling* BEN *away from her impatiently*]   Where is Dad? Didn't you follow him? How did you get started?

BEN   Well, I don't know how much you remember.

WILLY   Well, I was just a baby, of course, only three or four years old—

BEN   Three years and eleven months.

WILLY   What a memory, Ben!

BEN   I have many enterprises, William, and I have never kept books.

WILLY   I remember I was sitting under the wagon in—was it Nebraska?

BEN   It was South Dakota, and I gave you a bunch of wild flowers.

WILLY   I remember you walking away down some open road.

BEN [*laughing*]   I was going to find Father in Alaska.

WILLY   Where is he?

BEN   At that age I had a very faulty view of geography, William. I discovered after a few days that I was heading due south, so instead of Alaska, I ended up in Africa.

LINDA   Africa!

WILLY   The Gold Coast!

BEN   Principally diamond mines.

LINDA   Diamond mines!

BEN   Yes, my dear. But I've only a few minutes—

WILLY   No! Boys! Boys! [YOUNG BIFF *and* HAPPY *appear.*] Listen to this. This is your Uncle Ben, a great man! Tell my boys, Ben!

BEN   Why, boys, when I was seventeen I walked into the jungle, and when I was twenty-one I walked out. [*He laughs.*] And by God I was rich.

WILLY [*to the boys*]   You see what I been talking about? The greatest things can happen!

BEN [*glancing at his watch*]   I have an appointment in Ketchikan Tuesday week.

WILLY   No, Ben! Please tell about Dad. I want my boys to hear. I want them to know the kind of stock they spring from. All I remember is a man with a big beard, and I was in Mamma's lap, sitting around a fire, and some kind of high music.

BEN   His flute. He played the flute.

WILLY   Sure, the flute, that's right!

    [*New music is heard, a high, rollicking tune.*]

BEN   Father was a very great and a very wild-hearted man. We would start in Boston, and he'd toss the whole family into the wagon, and then he'd drive the team right across the country; through Ohio, and Indiana, Michigan, Illinois, and all the Western states. And we'd stop in the towns and sell the flutes that he'd made on the way. Great inventor, Father. With one gadget he made more in a week than a man like you could make in a lifetime.

WILLY   That's just the way I'm bringing them up, Ben—rugged, well liked, all-around.

BEN   Yeah? [*to* BIFF] Hit that, boy—hard as you can. [*He pounds his stomach.*]

BIFF   Oh, no, sir!

BEN   [*taking boxing stance*]   Come on, get to me! [*He laughs.*]

WILLY   Go to it, Biff! Go ahead, show him!

BIFF   Okay! [*He cocks his fist and starts in.*]

LINDA   [*to* WILLY]   Why must he fight, dear?

BEN   [*sparring with* BIFF]   Good boy! Good boy!

WILLY   How's that, Ben, heh?

HAPPY   Give him the left, Biff!

LINDA   Why are you fighting?

BEN   Good boy! [*Suddenly comes in, trips* BIFF, *and stands over him, the point of his umbrella poised over* BIFF's *eye.*]

LINDA   Look out, Biff!

BIFF   Gee!

BEN   [*patting* BIFF's *knee*]   Never fight fair with a stranger, boy. You'll never get out of the jungle that way. [*taking* LINDA's *hand and bowing*] It was an honor and a pleasure to meet you, Linda.

LINDA   [*withdrawing her hand coldly, frightened*]   Have a nice—trip.

BEN   [*to* WILLY]   And good luck with your—what do you do?

WILLY   Selling.

BEN   Yes. Well . . . [*He raises his hand in farewell to all.*]

WILLY   No, Ben, I don't want you to think . . . [*He takes* BEN's *arm to show him.*] It's Brooklyn, I know, but we hunt too.

BEN   Really, now.

WILLY   Oh, sure, there's snakes and rabbits and—that's why I moved out here. Why, Biff can fell any one of these trees in no time! Boys! Go right over to where they're building the apartment house and get some sand. We're gonna rebuild the entire front stoop right now! Watch this, Ben!

BIFF   Yes, sir! On the double, Hap!

HAPPY   [*as he and* BIFF *run off*]   I lost weight, Pop, you notice?

    [CHARLEY *enters in knickers, even before the boys are gone.*]

CHARLEY   Listen, if they steal any more from that building the watchman'll put the cops on them!

LINDA   [*to* WILLY]   Don't let Biff . . .

    [BEN *laughs lustily.*]

WILLY   You shoulda seen the lumber they brought home last week. At least a dozen six-by-tens worth all kinds a money.

CHARLEY   Listen, if that watchman—

WILLY   I gave them hell, understand. But I got a couple of fearless characters there.

CHARLEY   Willy, the jails are full of fearless characters.

BEN [*clapping* WILLY *on the back, with a laugh at* CHARLEY]   And the stock exchange, friend!

WILLY [*joining in* BEN'S *laughter*]   Where are the rest of your pants?

CHARLEY   My wife bought them.

WILLY   Now all you need is a golf club and you can go upstairs and go to sleep. [*to* BEN] Great athlete! Between him and his son Bernard they can't hammer a nail!

BERNARD [*rushing in*]   The watchman's chasing Biff!

WILLY [*angrily*]   Shut up! He's not stealing anything!

LINDA [*alarmed, hurrying off left*]   Where is he? Biff, dear! [*She exits.*]

WILLY [*moving toward the left, away from* BEN]   There's nothing wrong. What's the matter with you?

BEN   Nervy boy. Good!

WILLY [*laughing*]   Oh, nerves of iron, that Biff!

CHARLEY   Don't know what it is. My New England man comes back and he's bleedin', they murdered him up there.

WILLY   It's contacts, Charley, I got important contacts!

CHARLEY [*sarcastically*]   Glad to hear it, Willy. Come in later, we'll shoot a little casino. I'll take some of your Portland money. [*He laughs at* WILLY *and exits.*]

WILLY [*turning to* BEN]   Business is bad, it's murderous. But not for me, of course.

BEN   I'll stop by on my way back to Africa.

WILLY [*longingly*]   Can't you stay a few days? You're just what I need, Ben, because I—I have a fine position here, but I—well, Dad left when I was such a baby and I never had a chance to talk to him and I still feel— kind of temporary about myself.

BEN   I'll be late for my train.

  [*They are at opposite ends of the stage.*]

WILLY   Ben, my boys—can't we talk? They'd go into the jaws of hell for me, see, but I—

BEN   William, you're being first-rate with your boys. Outstanding, manly chaps!

WILLY [*hanging on to his words*]   Oh, Ben, that's good to hear! Because sometimes I'm afraid that I'm not teaching them the right kind of—Ben, how should I teach them?

BEN [*giving great weight to each word, and with a certain vicious audacity*]   William, when I walked into the jungle, I was seventeen. When I walked out I was twenty-one. And, by God, I was rich! [*He goes off into darkness around the right corner of the house.*]

WILLY   . . . was rich! That's just the spirit I want to imbue them with! To walk into a jungle! I was right! I was right! I was right!

  [BEN *is gone, but* WILLY *is still speaking to him as* LINDA, *in nightgown and robe, enters the kitchen, glances around for* WILLY, *then goes to the door of the house, looks out and sees him. Comes down to his left. He looks at her.*]

LINDA   Willy, dear? Willy?

WILLY   I was right!

LINDA   Did you have some cheese? [*He can't answer.*] It's very late, darling. Come to bed, heh?

WILLY [*looking straight up*]   Gotta break your neck to see a star in this yard.

LINDA   You coming in?

WILLY   Whatever happened to that diamond watch fob? Remember? When Ben came from Africa that time? Didn't he give me a watch fob with a diamond in it?

LINDA   You pawned it, dear. Twelve, thirteen years ago. For Biff's radio correspondence course.

WILLY   Gee, that was a beautiful thing. I'll take a walk.

LINDA   But you're in your slippers.

WILLY [*starting to go around the house at the left*]   I was right! I was! [*half to* LINDA, *as he goes, shaking his head*] What a man! There was a man worth talking to. I was right!

LINDA [*calling after* WILLY]   But in your slippers, Willy!

[WILLY *is almost gone when* BIFF, *in his pajamas, comes down the stairs and enters the kitchen.*]

BIFF   What is he doing out there?

LINDA   Sh!

BIFF   God Almighty, Mom, how long has he been doing this?

LINDA   Don't, he'll hear you.

BIFF   What the hell is the matter with him?

LINDA   It'll pass by morning.

BIFF   Shouldn't we do anything?

LINDA   Oh, my dear, you should do a lot of things, but there's nothing to do, so go to sleep.

[HAPPY *comes down the stair and sits on the steps.*]

HAPPY   I never heard him so loud, Mom.

LINDA   Well, come around more often; you'll hear him. [*She sits down at the table and mends the lining of* WILLY's *jacket.*]

BIFF   Why didn't you ever write me about this, Mom?

LINDA   How would I write to you? For over three months you had no address.

BIFF   I was on the move. But you know I thought of you all the time. You know that, don't you, pal?

LINDA   I know, dear, I know. But he likes to have a letter. Just to know that there's still a possibility for better things.

BIFF   He's not like this all the time, is he?

LINDA   It's when you come home he's always the worst.

BIFF   When I come home?

LINDA   When you write you're coming, he's all smiles, and talks about the future, and—he's just wonderful. And then the closer you seem to come, the more shaky he gets, and then, by the time you get here, he's arguing, and he seems angry at you. I think it's just that maybe he can't bring himself to—to open up to you. Why are you so hateful to each other? Why is that?

BIFF [*evasively*]   I'm not hateful, Mom.

LINDA   But you no sooner come in the door than you're fighting!

BIFF   I don't know why. I mean to change. I'm tryin', Mom, you understand?

LINDA   Are you home to stay now?

BIFF   I don't know. I want to look around, see what's doin'.

LINDA   Biff, you can't look around all your life, can you?

BIFF   I just can't take hold, Mom. I can't take hold of some kind of a life.

LINDA   Biff, a man is not a bird, to come and go with the springtime.

BIFF   Your hair . . . [He touches her hair.] Your hair got so gray.

LINDA   Oh, it's been gray since you were in high school. I just stopped
dyeing it, that's all.

BIFF   Dye it again, will ya? I don't want my pal looking old. [He smiles.]

LINDA   You're such a boy! You think you can go away for a year and . . .
You've got to get it into your head now that one day you'll knock on this
door and there'll be strange people here—

BIFF   What are you talking about? You're not even sixty, Mom.

LINDA   But what about your father?

BIFF [lamely]   Well, I meant him too.

HAPPY   He admires Pop.

LINDA   Biff, dear, if you don't have any feeling for him, then you can't have
any feeling for me.

BIFF   Sure I can, Mom.

LINDA   No. You can't just come to see me, because I love him. [with a
threat, but only a threat, of tears] He's the dearest man in the world to
me, and I won't have anyone making him feel unwanted and low and
blue. You've got to make up your mind now, darling, there's no leeway
any more. Either he's your father and you pay him that respect, or else
you're not to come here. I know he's not easy to get along with—nobody
knows that better than me—but . . .

WILLY [from the left, with a laugh]   Hey, hey, Biffo!

BIFF [starting to go out after WILLY]   What the hell is the matter with him?
    [HAPPY stops him.]

LINDA   Don't—don't go near him!

BIFF   Stop making excuses for him! He always, always wiped the floor with
you. Never had an ounce of respect for you.

HAPPY   He's always had respect for—

BIFF   What the hell do you know about it?

HAPPY [surlily]   Just don't call him crazy!

BIFF   He's got no character—Charley wouldn't do this. Not in his own
house—spewing out that vomit from his mind.

HAPPY   Charley never had to cope with what he's got to.

BIFF   People are worse off than Willy Loman. Believe me, I've seen them!

LINDA   Then make Charley your father, Biff. You can't do that, can you?
I don't say he's a great man. Willy Loman never made a lot of money.
His name was never in the paper. He's not the finest character that ever
lived. But he's a human being, and a terrible thing is happening to him.
So attention must be paid. He's not to be allowed to fall into his grave
like an old dog. Attention, attention must be finally paid to such a person.
You called him crazy—

BIFF   I didn't mean—

LINDA   No, a lot of people think he's lost his—balance. But you don't have
to be very smart to know what his trouble is. The man is exhausted.

HAPPY   Sure!

LINDA   A small man can be just as exhausted as a great man. He works for a company thirty-six years this March, opens up unheard-of territories to their trademark, and now in his old age they take his salary away.

HAPPY   [*indignantly*]   I didn't know that, Mom.

LINDA   You never asked, my dear! Now that you get your spending money someplace else you don't trouble your mind with him.

HAPPY   But I gave you money last—

LINDA   Christmas time, fifty dollars! To fix the hot water it cost ninety-seven fifty! For five weeks he's been on straight commission, like a beginner, an unknown!

BIFF   Those ungrateful bastards!

LINDA   Are they any worse than his sons? When he brought them business, when he was young, they were glad to see him. But now his old friends, the old buyers that loved him so and always found some order to hand him in a pinch—they're all dead, retired. He used to be able to make six, seven calls a day in Boston. Now he takes his valises out of the car and puts them back and takes them out again and he's exhausted. Instead of walking he talks now. He drives seven hundred miles, and when he gets there no one knows him any more, no one welcomes him. And what goes through a man's mind, driving seven hundred miles home without having earned a cent? Why shouldn't he talk to himself? Why? When he has to go to Charley and borrow fifty dollars a week and pretend to me that it's his pay? How long can that go on? How long? You see what I'm sitting here and waiting for? And you tell me he has no character? The man who never worked a day but for your benefit? When does he get the medal for that? Is this his reward—to turn around at the age of sixty-three and find his sons, who he loved better than his life, one a philandering bum—

HAPPY   Mom!

LINDA   That's all you are, my baby! [*to* BIFF] And you! What happened to the love you had for him? You were such pals! How you used to talk to him on the phone every night! How lonely he was till he could come home to you!

BIFF   All right, Mom. I'll live here in my room, and I'll get a job. I'll keep away from him, that's all.

LINDA   No, Biff. You can't stay here and fight all the time.

BIFF   He threw me out of this house, remember that.

LINDA   Why did he do that? I never knew why.

BIFF   Because I know he's a fake and he doesn't like anybody around who knows!

LINDA   Why a fake? In what way? What do you mean?

BIFF   Just don't lay it all at my feet. It's between me and him—that's all I have to say. I'll chip in from now on. He'll settle for half my pay check. He'll be all right. I'm going to bed. [*He starts for the stairs.*]

LINDA   He won't be all right.

BIFF   [*turning on the stairs, furiously*]   I hate this city and I'll stay here. Now what do you want?

LINDA   He's dying, Biff.

[HAPPY *turns quickly to her, shocked.*]

BIFF   [*after a pause*]   Why is he dying?

LINDA   He's been trying to kill himself.

BIFF [*with great horror*]   How?

LINDA   I live from day to day.

BIFF   What're you talking about?

LINDA   Remember I wrote you that he smashed up the car again? In February?

BIFF   Well?

LINDA   The insurance inspector came. He said that they have evidence. That all these accidents in the last year—weren't—weren't—accidents.

HAPPY   How can they tell that? That's a lie.

LINDA   It seems there's a woman . . . [*she takes a breath as*]

⌠BIFF [*sharply but contained*]   What woman?

⌡LINDA [*simultaneously*]   . . . and this woman . . .

LINDA   What?

BIFF   Nothing. Go ahead.

LINDA   What did you say?

BIFF   Nothing. I just said what woman?

HAPPY   What about her?

LINDA   Well, it seems she was walking down the road and saw his car. She says that he wasn't driving fast at all, and that he didn't skid. She says he came to that little bridge, and then deliberately smashed into the railing, and it was only the shallowness of the water that saved him.

BIFF   Oh, no, he probably just fell asleep again.

LINDA   I don't think he fell asleep.

BIFF   Why not?

LINDA   Last month . . . [*with great difficulty*] Oh, boys, it's so hard to say a thing like this! He's just a big stupid man to you, but I tell you there's more good in him than in many other people. [*She chokes, wipes her eyes.*] I was looking for a fuse. The lights blew out, and I went down the cellar. And behind the fuse box—it happened to fall out—was a length of rubber pipe—just short.

HAPPY   No kidding?

LINDA   There's a little attachment on the end of it. I knew right away. And sure enough, on the bottom of the water heater there's a new little nipple on the gas pipe.

HAPPY [*angrily*]   That—jerk.

BIFF   Did you have it taken off?

LINDA   I'm—I'm ashamed to. How can I mention it to him? Every day I go down and take away that little rubber pipe. But, when he comes home, I put it back where it was. How can I insult him that way? I don't know what to do. I live from day to day, boys. I tell you, I know every thought in his mind. It sounds so old-fashioned and silly, but I tell you he put his whole life into you and you've turned your backs on him. [*She is bent over in the chair, weeping, her face in her hands.*] Biff, I swear to God! Biff, his life is in your hands!

HAPPY [*to* BIFF]   How do you like that damned fool!

BIFF [*kissing her*]   All right, pal, all right. It's all settled now. I've been remiss. I know that, Mom. But now I'll stay, and I swear to you, I'll apply myself. [*kneeling in front of her, in a fever of self-reproach*] It's just—you see, Mom, I don't fit in business. Not that I won't try. I'll try, and I'll make good.

HAPPY   Sure you will. The trouble with you in business was you never tried to please people.

BIFF   I know, I—

HAPPY   Like when you worked for Harrison's. Bob Harrison said you were tops, and then you go and do some damn fool thing like whistling whole songs in the elevator like a comedian.

BIFF [*against* HAPPY]   So what? I like to whistle sometimes.

HAPPY   You don't raise a guy to a responsible job who whistles in the elevator!

LINDA   Well, don't argue about it now.

HAPPY   Like when you'd go off and swim in the middle of the day instead of taking the line around.

BIFF [*his resentment rising*]   Well, don't you run off? You take off sometimes, don't you? On a nice summer day?

HAPPY   Yeah, but I cover myself!

LINDA   Boys!

HAPPY   If I'm going to take a fade the boss can call any number where I'm supposed to be and they'll swear to him that I just left. I'll tell you something that I hate to say, Biff, but in the business world some of them think you're crazy.

BIFF [*angered*]   Screw the business world!

HAPPY   All right, screw it! Great, but cover yourself!

LINDA   Hap, Hap!

BIFF   I don't care what they think! They've laughed at Dad for years, and you know why? Because we don't belong in this nuthouse of a city! We should be mixing cement on some open plain, or—or carpenters. A carpenter is allowed to whistle!

[WILLY *walks in from the entrance of the house, at left.*]

WILLY   Even your grandfather was better than a carpenter. [*Pause. They watch him.*] You never grew up. Bernard does not whistle in the elevator, I assure you.

BIFF [*as though to laugh* WILLY *out of it*]   Yeah, but you do, Pop.

WILLY   I never in my life whistled in an elevator! And who in the business world thinks I'm crazy?

BIFF   I didn't mean it like that, Pop. Now don't make a whole thing out of it, will ya?

WILLY   Go back to the West! Be a carpenter, a cowboy, enjoy yourself!

LINDA   Willy, he was just saying—

WILLY   I heard what he said!

HAPPY [*trying to quiet* WILLY]   Hey, Pop, come on now . . .

WILLY [*continuing over* HAPPY's *line*]   They laugh at me, heh? Go to Filene's, go to the Hub, go to Slattery's, Boston. Call out the name Willy Loman and see what happens! Big Shot!

BIFF   All right, Pop.

WILLY   Big!

BIFF   All right!

WILLY   Why do you always insult me?

BIFF   I didn't say a word. [*to* LINDA] Did I say a word?

LINDA   He didn't say anything, Willy.

WILLY [*going to the doorway of the living-room*]   All right, good night, good night.

LINDA Willy, dear, he just decided . . .

WILLY [*to* BIFF] If you get tired hanging around tomorrow, paint the ceiling I put up in the living-room.

BIFF I'm leaving early tomorrow.

HAPPY He's going to see Bill Oliver, Pop.

WILLY [*interestedly*] Oliver? For what?

BIFF [*with reserve, but trying, trying*] He always said he'd stake me. I'd like to go into business, so maybe I can take him up on it.

LINDA Isn't that wonderful?

WILLY Don't interrupt. What's wonderful about it? There's fifty men in the City of New York who'd stake him. [*to* BIFF] Sporting goods?

BIFF I guess so. I know something about it and—

WILLY He knows something about it! You know sporting goods better than Spalding, for God's sake! How much is he giving you?

BIFF I don't know, I didn't even see him yet, but—

WILLY Then what're you talkin' about?

BIFF [*getting angry*] Well, all I said was I'm gonna see him, that's all!

WILLY [*turning away*] Ah, you're counting your chickens again.

BIFF [*starting left for the stairs*] Oh, Jesus, I'm going to sleep!

WILLY [*calling after him*] Don't curse in this house!

BIFF [*turning*] Since when did you get so clean?

HAPPY [*trying to stop them*] Wait a . . .

WILLY Don't use that language to me! I won't have it!

HAPPY [*grabbing* BIFF, *shouts*] Wait a minute! I got an idea. I got a feasible idea. Come here, Biff, let's talk this over now, let's talk some sense here. When I was down in Florida last time, I thought of a great idea to sell sporting goods. It just came back to me. You and I, Biff—we have a line, the Loman Line. We train a couple of weeks, and put on a couple of exhibitions, see?

WILLY That's an idea!

HAPPY Wait! We form two basketball teams, see? Two water-polo teams. We play each other. It's a million dollars' worth of publicity. Two brothers, see? The Loman Brothers. Displays in the Royal Palms—all the hotels. And banners over the ring and the basketball court: "Loman Brothers." Baby, we could sell sporting goods!

WILLY That is a one-million-dollar idea!

LINDA Marvelous!

BIFF I'm in great shape as far as that's concerned.

HAPPY And the beauty of it is, Biff, it wouldn't be like a business. We'd be out playin' ball again . . .

BIFF [*enthused*] Yeah, that's . . .

WILLY Million-dollar . . .

HAPPY And you wouldn't get fed up with it, Biff. It'd be the family again. There'd be the old honor, and comradeship, and if you wanted to go off for a swim or somethin'—well, you'd do it! Without some smart cooky gettin' up ahead of you!

WILLY Lick the world! You guys together could absolutely lick the civilized world.

BIFF I'll see Oliver tomorrow. Hap, if we could work that out . . .

LINDA Maybe things are beginning to—

WILLY [*wildly enthused, to* LINDA]   Stop interrupting! [*to* BIFF] But don't wear sport jacket and slacks when you see Oliver.

BIFF   No, I'll—

WILLY   A business suit, and talk as little as possible, and don't crack any jokes.

BIFF   He did like me. Always liked me.

LINDA   He loved you!

WILLY [*to* LINDA]   Will you stop! [*to* BIFF] Walk in very serious. You are not applying for a boy's job. Money is to pass. Be quiet, fine, and serious. Everybody likes a kidder, but nobody lends him money.

HAPPY   I'll try to get some myself, Biff. I'm sure I can.

WILLY   I see great things for you kids, I think your troubles are over. But remember, start big and you'll end big. Ask for fifteen. How much you gonna ask for?

BIFF   Gee, I don't know—

WILLY   And don't say "Gee." "Gee" is a boy's word. A man walking in for fifteen thousand dollars does not say "Gee!"

BIFF   Ten, I think, would be top though.

WILLY   Don't be so modest. You always started too low. Walk in with a big laugh. Don't look worried. Start off with a couple of your good stories to lighten things up. It's not what you say, it's how you say it—because personality always wins the day.

LINDA   Oliver always thought the highest of him—

WILLY   Will you let me talk?

BIFF   Don't yell at her, Pop, will ya?

WILLY [*angrily*]   I was talking, wasn't I?

BIFF   I don't like you yelling at her all the time, and I'm tellin' you, that's all.

WILLY   What're you, takin' over this house?

LINDA   Willy—

WILLY [*turning on her*]   Don't take his side all the time, goddammit!

BIFF [*furiously*]   Stop yelling at her!

WILLY [*suddenly pulling on his cheek, beaten down, guilt ridden*]   Give my best to Bill Oliver—he may remember me. [*He exits through the living-room doorway.*]

LINDA [*her voice subdued*]   What'd you have to start that for? [BIFF *turns away.*] You see how sweet he was as soon as you talked hopefully? [*She goes over to* BIFF.] Come up and say good night to him. Don't let him go to bed that way.

HAPPY   Come on, Biff, let's buck him up.

LINDA   Please, dear. Just say good night. It takes so little to make him happy. Come. [*She goes through the living-room doorway, calling upstairs from within the living-room*] Your pajamas are hanging in the bathroom, Willy!

HAPPY [*looking toward where* LINDA *went out*]   What a woman! They broke the mold when they made her. You know that, Biff?

BIFF   He's off salary. My God, working on commission!

HAPPY   Well, let's face it: he's no hot-shot selling man. Except that sometimes, you have to admit, he's a sweet personality.

BIFF [*deciding*]   Lend me ten bucks, will ya? I want to buy some new ties.

HAPPY I'll take you to a place I know. Beautiful stuff. Wear one of my striped shirts tomorrow.

BIFF She got gray. Mom got awful old. Gee, I'm gonna go in to Oliver tomorrow and knock him for a—

HAPPY Come on up. Tell that to Dad. Let's give him a whirl. Come on.

BIFF [steamed up] You know, with ten thousand bucks, boy!

HAPPY [as they go into the living-room] That's the talk, Biff, that's the first time I've heard the old confidence out of you! [from within the living-room, fading off] You're gonna live with me, kid, and any babe you want just say the word . . . [The last lines are hardly heard. They are mounting the stairs to their parents' bedroom.]

LINDA [entering her bedroom and addressing WILLY, who is in the bathroom. She is straightening the bed for him] Can you do anything about the shower? It drips.

WILLY [from the bathroom] All of a sudden everything falls to pieces! Goddam plumbing, oughta be sued, those people. I hardly finished putting it in and the thing . . . [His words rumble off.]

LINDA I'm just wondering if Oliver will remember him. You think he might?

WILLY [coming out of the bathroom in his pajamas] Remember him? What's the matter with you, you crazy? If he'd've stayed with Oliver he'd be on top by now! Wait'll Oliver gets a look at him. You don't know the average caliber any more. The average young man today—[he is getting into bed]—is got a caliber of zero. Greatest thing in the world for him was to bum around.

[BIFF and HAPPY enter the bedroom. Slight pause.]

WILLY [stops short, looking at BIFF] Glad to hear it, boy.

HAPPY He wanted to say good night to you, sport.

WILLY [to BIFF] Yeah. Knock him dead, boy. What'd you want to tell me?

BIFF Just take it easy, Pop. Good night. [He turns to go.]

WILLY [unable to resist] And if anything falls off the desk while you're talking to him—like a package or something—don't you pick it up. They have office boys for that.

LINDA I'll make a big breakfast—

WILLY Will you let me finish? [to BIFF] Tell him you were in the business in the West. Not farm work.

BIFF All right, Dad.

LINDA I think everything—

WILLY [going right through her speech] And don't undersell yourself. No less than fifteen thousand dollars.

BIFF [unable to bear him] Okay. Good night, Mom. [He starts moving.]

WILLY Because you got a greatness in you, Biff, remember that. You got all kinds a greatness . . . [He lies back, exhausted. BIFF walks out.]

LINDA [calling after BIFF] Sleep well, darling!

HAPPY I'm gonna get married, Mom. I wanted to tell you.

LINDA Go to sleep, dear.

HAPPY [going] I just wanted to tell you.

WILLY Keep up the good work. [HAPPY exits.] God . . . remember that Ebbets Field[5] game? The championship of the city?

5. Brooklyn sports stadium.

LINDA Just rest. Should I sing to you?

WILLY Yeah. Sing to me. [LINDA *hums a soft lullaby.*] When that team came out—he was the tallest, remember?

LINDA Oh, yes. And in gold.

> [BIFF *enters the darkened kitchen, takes a cigarette, and leaves the house. He comes downstage into a golden pool of light. He smokes, staring at the night.*]

WILLY Like a young god. Hercules—something like that. And the sun, the sun all around him. Remember how he waved to me? Right up from the field, with the representatives of three colleges standing by? And the buyers I brought, and the cheers when he came out—Loman, Loman, Loman! God Almighty, he'll be great yet. A star like that, magnificent, can never really fade away!

> [*The light on* WILLY *is fading. The gas heater begins to glow through the kitchen wall, near the stairs, a blue flame beneath red coils.*]

LINDA [*timidly*] Willy dear, what has he got against you?

WILLY I'm so tired. Don't talk any more.

> [BIFF *slowly returns to the kitchen. He stops, stares toward the heater.*]

LINDA Will you ask Howard to let you work in New York?

WILLY First thing in the morning. Everything'll be all right.

> [BIFF *reaches behind the heater and draws out a length of rubber tubing. He is horrified and turns his head toward* WILLY's *room, still dimly lit, from which the strains of* LINDA's *desperate but monotonous humming rise.*]

WILLY [*staring through the window into the moonlight*] Gee, look at the moon moving between the buildings!

> [BIFF *wraps the tubing around his hand and quickly goes up the stairs.*]

CURTAIN

Act Two

Music is heard, gay and bright. The curtain rises as the music fades away. WILLY, *in shirt sleeves, is sitting at the kitchen table, sipping coffee, his hat in his lap.* LINDA *is filling his cup when she can.*

WILLY Wonderful coffee. Meal in itself.

LINDA Can I make you some eggs?

WILLY No. Take a breath.

LINDA You look so rested, dear.

WILLY I slept like a dead one. First time in months. Imagine, sleeping till ten on a Tuesday morning. Boys left nice and early, heh?

LINDA They were out of here by eight o'clock.

WILLY Good work!

LINDA It was so thrilling to see them leaving together. I can't get over the shaving lotion in this house!

WILLY [*smiling*] Mmm—

LINDA Biff was very changed this morning. His whole attitude seemed to be hopeful. He couldn't wait to get downtown to see Oliver.

WILLY He's heading for a change. There's no question, there simply are certain men that take longer to get—solidified. How did he dress?

LINDA His blue suit. He's so handsome in that suit. He could be a—anything in that suit!

[WILLY *gets up from the table.* LINDA *holds his jacket for him.*]

WILLY There's no question, no question at all. Gee, on the way home tonight I'd like to buy some seeds.

LINDA [*laughing*] That'd be wonderful. But not enough sun gets back there. Nothing'll grow any more.

WILLY You wait, kid, before it's all over we're gonna get a little place out in the country, and I'll raise some vegetables, a couple of chickens . . .

LINDA You'll do it yet, dear.

[WILLY *walks out of his jacket.* LINDA *follows him.*]

WILLY And they'll get married, and come for a weekend. I'd build a little guest house. 'Cause I got so many fine tools, all I'd need would be a little lumber and some peace of mind.

LINDA [*joyfully*] I sewed the lining . . .

WILLY I could build two guest houses, so they'd both come. Did he decide how much he's going to ask Oliver for?

LINDA [*getting him into the jacket*] He didn't mention it, but I imagine ten or fifteen thousand. You going to talk to Howard today?

WILLY Yeah. I'll put it to him straight and simple. He'll just have to take me off the road.

LINDA And Willy, don't forget to ask for a little advance, because we've got the insurance premium. It's the grace period now.

WILLY That's a hundred . . . ?

LINDA A hundred and eight, sixty-eight. Because we're a little short again.

WILLY Why are we short?

LINDA Well, you had the motor job on the car . . .

WILLY That goddam Studebaker!

LINDA And you got one more payment on the refrigerator . . .

WILLY But it just broke again!

LINDA Well, it's old, dear.

WILLY I told you we should've bought a well-advertised machine. Charley bought a General Electric and it's twenty years old and it's still good, that son-of-a-bitch.

LINDA But, Willy—

WILLY Whoever heard of a Hastings refrigerator? Once in my life I would like to own something outright before it's broken! I'm always in a race with the junkyard! I just finished paying for the car and it's on its last legs. The refrigerator consumes belts like a goddam maniac. They time those things. They time them so when you finally paid for them, they're used up.

LINDA [*buttoning up his jacket as he unbuttons it*] All told, about two hundred dollars would carry us, dear. But that includes the last payment on the mortgage. After this payment, Willy, the house belongs to us.

WILLY It's twenty-five years!

LINDA Biff was nine years old when we bought it.

WILLY Well, that's a great thing. To weather a twenty-five year mortgage is—

LINDA It's an accomplishment.

WILLY All the cement, the lumber, the reconstruction I put in this house! There ain't a crack to be found in it any more.

LINDA   Well, it served its purpose.

WILLY   What purpose? Some stranger'll come along, move in, and that's that. If only Biff would take this house, and raise a family . . . [*He starts to go.*] Good-by, I'm late.

LINDA [*suddenly remembering*]   Oh, I forgot! You're supposed to meet them for dinner.

WILLY   Me?

LINDA   At Frank's Chop House on Forty-eighth near Sixth Avenue.

WILLY   Is that so! How about you?

LINDA   No, just the three of you. They're gonna blow you to a big meal!

WILLY   Don't say! Who thought of that?

LINDA   Biff came to me this morning, Willy, and he said, "Tell Dad, we want to blow him to a big meal." Be there six o'clock. You and your two boys are going to have dinner.

WILLY   Gee whiz! That's really somethin'. I'm gonna knock Howard for a loop, kid. I'll get an advance, and I'll come home with a New York job. Goddammit, now I'm gonna do it!

LINDA   Oh, that's the spirit, Willy!

WILLY   I will never get behind a wheel the rest of my life!

LINDA   It's changing, Willy, I can feel it changing!

WILLY   Beyond a question. G'by, I'm late. [*He starts to go again.*]

LINDA [*calling after him as she runs to the kitchen table for a handkerchief*]   You got your glasses?

WILLY [*feels for them, then comes back in*]   Yeah, yeah, got my glasses.

LINDA [*giving him the handkerchief*]   And a handkerchief.

WILLY   Yeah, handkerchief.

LINDA   And your saccharine?

WILLY   Yeah, my saccharine.

LINDA   Be careful on the subway stairs.

[*She kisses him, and a silk stocking is seen hanging from her hand.* WILLY *notices it.*]

WILLY   Will you stop mending stockings? At least while I'm in the house. It gets me nervous. I can't tell you. Please.

[LINDA *hides the stocking in her hand as she follows* WILLY *across the forestage in front of the house.*]

LINDA   Remember, Frank's Chop House.

WILLY [*passing the apron*]   Maybe beets would grow out there.

LINDA [*laughing*]   But you tried so many times.

WILLY   Yeah. Well, don't work hard today. [*He disappears around the right corner of the house.*]

LINDA   Be careful!

[*As* WILLY *vanishes,* LINDA *waves to him. Suddenly the phone rings. She runs across the stage and into the kitchen and lifts it.*]

LINDA   Hello? Oh, Biff! I'm so glad you called, I just . . . Yes, sure, I just told him. Yes, he'll be there for dinner at six o'clock, I didn't forget. Listen, I was just dying to tell you. You know that little rubber pipe I told you about? That he connected to the gas heater? I finally decided to go down the cellar this morning and take it away and destroy it. But it's gone! Imagine? He took it away himself, it isn't there! [*She listens.*] When? Oh, then you took it. Oh—nothing, it's just that I'd hoped he'd taken it away himself. Oh, I'm not worried, darling, because this morning he left in such high spirits, it was like the old days! I'm not afraid any more. Did Mr. Oliver see you? . . . Well, you wait there then. And make a nice impression on him, darling. Just don't perspire too much before you see him. And have a nice time with Dad. He may have big news too! . . . That's right, a New York job. And be sweet to him tonight, dear. Be loving to him. Because he's only a little boat looking for a harbor. [*She is trembling with sorrow and joy.*] Oh, that's wonderful, Biff, you'll save his life. Thanks, darling. Just put your arm around him when he comes into the restaurant. Give him a smile. That's the boy . . . Good-by, dear. . . . You got your comb? . . . That's fine. Good-by, Biff dear.

> [*In the middle of her speech,* HOWARD WAGNER, *thirty-six, wheels in a small typewriter table on which is a wire-recording machine and proceeds to plug it in. This is on the left forestage. Light slowly fades on* LINDA *as it rises on* HOWARD. HOWARD *is intent on threading the machine and only glances over his shoulder as* WILLY *appears.*]

WILLY Pst! Pst!

HOWARD Hello, Willy, come in.

WILLY Like to have a little talk with you, Howard.

HOWARD Sorry to keep you waiting. I'll be with you in a minute.

WILLY What's that, Howard?

HOWARD Didn't you ever see one of these? Wire recorder.

WILLY Oh. Can we talk a minute?

HOWARD Records things. Just got delivery yesterday. Been driving me crazy, the most terrific machine I ever saw in my life. I was up all night with it.

WILLY What do you do with it?

HOWARD I bought it for dictation, but you can do anything with it. Listen to this. I had it home last night. Listen to what I picked up. The first one is my daughter. Get this. [*He flicks the switch and "Roll out the Barrel" is heard being whistled.*] Listen to that kid whistle.

WILLY That is lifelike, isn't it?

HOWARD Seven years old. Get that tone.

WILLY Ts, ts. Like to ask a little favor if you . . .

> [*The whistling breaks off, and the voice of* HOWARD's *daughter is heard.*]

HIS DAUGHTER "Now you, Daddy."

HOWARD She's crazy for me! [*Again the same song is whistled.*] That's me! Ha! [*He winks.*]

WILLY You're very good!

> [*The whistling breaks off again. The machine runs silent for a moment.*]

HOWARD Sh! Get this now, this is my son.

HIS SON "The capital of Alabama is Montgomery; the capital of Arizona is Phoenix; the capital of Arkansas is Little Rock; the capital of California is Sacramento . . ." [*and on, and on*]

HOWARD [*holding up five fingers*] Five years old, Willy!

WILLY He'll make an announcer some day!

HIS SON [*continuing*] "The capital . . ."

HOWARD Get that—alphabetical order! [*The machine breaks off suddenly.*] Wait a minute. The maid kicked the plug out.

WILLY It certainly is a—

HOWARD Sh, for God's sake!

HIS SON   "It's nine o'clock, Bulova watch time. So I have to go to sleep."
WILLY   That really is—
HOWARD   Wait a minute! The next is my wife.
       [*They wait.*]
HOWARD'S VOICE   "Go on, say something." [*pause*] "Well, you gonna talk?"
HIS WIFE   "I can't think of anything."
HOWARD'S VOICE   "Well, talk—it's turning."
HIS WIFE [*shyly, beaten*]   "Hello." [*silence*] "Oh, Howard, I can't talk into
   this . . ."
HOWARD [*snapping the machine off*]   That was my wife.
WILLY   That is a wonderful machine. Can we—
HOWARD   I tell you, Willy, I'm gonna take my camera, and my bandsaw,
   and all my hobbies, and out they go. This is the most fascinating relax-
   ation I ever found.
WILLY   I think I'll get one myself.
HOWARD   Sure, they're only a hundred and a half. You can't do without it.
   Supposing you wanna hear Jack Benny,[6] see? But you can't be at home
   at that hour. So you tell the maid to turn the radio on when Jack Benny
   comes on, and this automatically goes on with the radio . . .
WILLY   And when you come home you . . .
HOWARD   You can come home twelve o'clock, one o'clock, any time you
   like, and you get yourself a Coke and sit yourself down, throw the switch,
   and there's Jack Benny's program in the middle of the night!
WILLY   I'm definitely going to get one. Because lots of time I'm on the
   road, and I think to myself, what I must be missing on the radio!
HOWARD   Don't you have a radio in the car?
WILLY   Well, yeah, but who ever thinks of turning it on?
HOWARD   Say, aren't you supposed to be in Boston?
WILLY   That's what I want to talk to you about, Howard. You got a minute?
   [*He draws a chair in from the wing.*]
HOWARD   What happened? What're you doing here?
WILLY   Well . . .
HOWARD   You didn't crack up again, did you?
WILLY   Oh, no. No . . .
HOWARD   Geez, you had me worried there for a minute. What's the trou-
   ble?
WILLY   Well, tell you the truth, Howard. I've come to the decision that I'd
   rather not travel any more.
HOWARD   Not travel! Well, what'll you do?
WILLY   Remember, Christmas time, when you had the party here? You said
   you'd try to think of some spot for me here in town.
HOWARD   With us?
WILLY   Well, sure.
HOWARD   Oh, yeah, yeah. I remember. Well, I couldn't think of anything
   for you, Willy.
WILLY   I tell ya, Howard. The kids are all grown up, y'know. I don't need
   much any more. If I could take home—well, sixty-five dollars a week, I
   could swing it.

---

6. Vastly popular radio comedian of the 1930s and 1940s.

HOWARD   Yeah, but Willy, see I—

WILLY   I tell ya why, Howard. Speaking frankly and between the two of us, y'know—I'm just a little tired.

HOWARD   Oh, I could understand that, Willy. But you're a road man, Willy, and we do a road business. We've only got a half-dozen salesmen on the floor here.

WILLY   God knows, Howard, I never asked a favor of any man. But I was with the firm when your father used to carry you in here in his arms.

HOWARD   I know that, Willy, but—

WILLY   Your father came to me the day you were born and asked me what I thought of the name of Howard, may he rest in peace.

HOWARD   I appreciate that, Willy, but there just is no spot here for you. If I had a spot I'd slam you right in, but I just don't have a single solitary spot.

[*He looks for his lighter.* WILLY *has picked it up and gives it to him. Pause.*]

WILLY [*with increasing anger*]   Howard, all I need to set my table is fifty dollars a week.

HOWARD   But where am I going to put you, kid?

WILLY   Look, it isn't a question of whether I can sell merchandise, is it?

HOWARD   No, but it's a business, kid, and everybody's gotta pull his own weight.

WILLY [*desperately*]   Just let me tell you a story, Howard—

HOWARD   'Cause you gotta admit, business is business.

WILLY [*angrily*]   Business is definitely business, but just listen for a minute. You don't understand this. When I was a boy—eighteen, nineteen—I was already on the road. And there was a question in my mind as to whether selling had a future for me. Because in those days I had a yearning to go to Alaska. See, there were three gold strikes in one month in Alaska, and I felt like going out. Just for the ride, you might say.

HOWARD [*barely interested*]   Don't say.

WILLY   Oh, yeah, my father lived many years in Alaska. He was an adventurous man. We've got quite a little streak of self-reliance in our family. I thought I'd go out with my older brother and try to locate him, and maybe settle in the North with the old man. And I was almost decided to go, when I met a salesman in the Parker House. His name was Dave Singleman. And he was eighty-four years old, and he'd drummed merchandise in thirty-one states. And old Dave, he'd go up to his room, y'understand, put on his green velvet slippers—I'll never forget—and pick up his phone and call the buyers, and without ever leaving his room, at the age of eighty-four, he made a living. And when I saw that, I realized that selling was the greatest career a man could want. 'Cause what could be more satisfying than to be able to go, at the age of eighty-four, into twenty or thirty different cities, and pick up a phone, and be remembered and loved and helped by so many different people? Do you know? when he died—and by the way he died the death of a salesman, in his green velvet slippers in the smoker of the New York, New Haven and Hartford, going into Boston—when he died, hundreds of salesmen and buyers were at his funeral. Things were sad on a lotta trains for months after that. [*He stands up.* HOWARD *has not looked at him.*] In those days there was personality in it, Howard. There was respect, and comradeship, and grat-

itude in it. Today, it's all cut and dried, and there's no chance for bringing
friendship to bear—or personality. You see what I mean? They don't
know me any more.

HOWARD [*moving away, toward the right*]   That's just the thing, Willy.

WILLY   If I had forty dollars a week—that's all I'd need. Forty dollars, Howard.

HOWARD   Kid, I can't take blood from a stone, I—

WILLY [*desperation is on him now*]   Howard, the year Al Smith[7] was nom-
inated, your father came to me and—

HOWARD [*starting to go off*]   I've got to see some people, kid.

WILLY [*stopping him*]   I'm talking about your father! There were promises
made across this desk! You mustn't tell me you've got people to see—I
put thirty-four years into this firm, Howard, and now I can't pay my
insurance! You can't eat the orange and throw the peel away—a man is
not a piece of fruit! [*after a pause*] Now pay attention. Your father—in
1928 I had a big year. I averaged a hundred and seventy dollars a week
in commissions.

HOWARD [*impatiently*]   Now, Willy, you never averaged—

WILLY [*banging his hand on the desk*]   I averaged a hundred and seventy
dollars a week in the year of 1928! And your father came to me—or
rather, I was in the office here—it was right over this desk—and he put
his hand on my shoulder—

HOWARD [*getting up*]   You'll have to excuse me, Willy, I gotta see some
people. Pull yourself together. [*going out*] I'll be back in a little while.

[*On* HOWARD's *exit, the light on his chair grows very bright and strange.*]

WILLY   Pull myself together! What the hell did I say to him? My God, I
was yelling at him! How could I! [WILLY *breaks off, staring at the light,
which occupies the chair, animating it. He approaches this chair, standing
across the desk from it.*] Frank, Frank, don't you remember what you told
me that time? How you put your hand on my shoulder, and Frank . . .
[*He leans on the desk and as he speaks the dead man's name he accidentally
switches on the recorder, and instantly*]

HOWARD'S SON   ". . . of New York is Albany. The capital of Ohio is Cincin-
nati, the capital of Rhode Island is . . ." [*The recitation continues.*]

WILLY [*leaping away with fright, shouting*]   Ha! Howard! Howard! Howard!

HOWARD [*rushing in*]   What happened?

WILLY [*pointing at the machine, which continues nasally, childishly, with the
capital cities*]   Shut it off! Shut it off!

HOWARD [*pulling the plug out*]   Look, Willy . . .

WILLY [*pressing his hands to his eyes*]   I gotta get myself some coffee. I'll
get some coffee . . .

[WILLY *starts to walk out.* HOWARD *stops him.*]

HOWARD [*rolling up the cord*]   Willy, look . . .

WILLY   I'll go to Boston.

HOWARD   Willy, you can't go to Boston for us.

WILLY   Why can't I go?

HOWARD   I don't want you to represent us. I've been meaning to tell you
for a long time now.

WILLY   Howard, are you firing me?

---

7. Democratic candidate for president in 1928.

HOWARD I think you need a good long rest, Willy.

WILLY Howard—

HOWARD And when you feel better, come back, and we'll see if we can work something out.

WILLY But I gotta earn money, Howard. I'm in no position to—

HOWARD Where are your sons? Why don't your sons give you a hand?

WILLY They're working on a very big deal.

HOWARD This is no time for false pride, Willy. You go to your sons and you tell them that you're tired. You've got two great boys, haven't you?

WILLY Oh, no question, no question, but in the meantime . . .

HOWARD Then that's that, heh?

WILLY All right, I'll go to Boston tomorrow.

HOWARD No, no.

WILLY I can't throw myself on my sons. I'm not a cripple!

HOWARD Look, kid, I'm busy, I'm busy this morning.

WILLY [grasping HOWARD's arm] Howard, you've got to let me go to Boston!

HOWARD [hard, keeping himself under control] I've got a line of people to see this morning. Sit down, take five minutes, and pull yourself together, and then go home, will ya? I need the office, Willy. [He starts to go, turns, remembering the recorder, starts to push off the table holding the recorder.] Oh, yeah. Whenever you can this week, stop by and drop off the samples. You'll feel better, Willy, and then come back and we'll talk. Pull yourself together, kid, there's people outside.

> [HOWARD exits, pushing the table off left. WILLY stares into space, exhausted. Now the music is heard—BEN's music—first distantly, then closer, closer. As WILLY speaks, BEN enters from the right. He carries valise and umbrella.]

WILLY Oh, Ben, how did you do it? What is the answer? Did you wind up the Alaska deal already?

BEN Doesn't take much time if you know what you're doing. Just a short business trip. Boarding ship in an hour. Wanted to say good-by.

WILLY Ben, I've got to talk to you.

BEN [glancing at his watch] Haven't the time, William.

WILLY [crossing the apron to BEN] Ben, nothing's working out. I don't know what to do.

BEN Now, look here, William. I've bought timberland in Alaska and I need a man to look after things for me.

WILLY God, timberland! Me and my boys in those grand outdoors!

BEN You've a new continent at your doorstep, William. Get out of these cities, they're full of talk and time payments and courts of law. Screw on your fists and you can fight for a fortune up there.

WILLY Yes, yes! Linda, Linda!

> [LINDA enters as of old, with the wash.]

LINDA Oh, you're back?

BEN I haven't much time.

WILLY No, wait! Linda, he's got a proposition for me in Alaska.

LINDA But you've got—[to BEN] He's got a beautiful job here.

WILLY But in Alaska, kid, I could—

LINDA You're doing well enough, Willy!

BEN [to LINDA] Enough for what, my dear?

LINDA [*frightened of* BEN *and angry at him*]   Don't say those things to him! Enough to be happy right here, right now. [*to* WILLY, *while* BEN *laughs*] Why must everybody conquer the world? You're well liked, and the boys love you, and someday—[*to* BEN]—why, old man Wagner told him just the other day that if he keeps it up he'll be a member of the firm, didn't he, Willy?

WILLY   Sure, sure. I am building something with this firm, Ben, and if a man is building something he must be on the right track, mustn't he?

BEN   What are you building? Lay your hand on it. Where is it?

WILLY [*hesitantly*]   That's true, Linda, there's nothing.

LINDA   Why? [*to* BEN] There's a man eighty-four years old—

WILLY   That's right, Ben, that's right. When I look at that man I say, what is there to worry about?

BEN   Bah!

WILLY   It's true, Ben. All he has to do is go into any city, pick up the phone, and he's making his living and you know why?

BEN [*picking up his valise*]   I've got to go.

WILLY [*holding* BEN *back*]   Look at this boy!

   [BIFF, *in his high school sweater, enters carrying suitcase.* HAPPY *carries* BIFF's *shoulder guards, gold helmet, and football pants.*]

WILLY   Without a penny to his name, three great universities are begging for him, and from there the sky's the limit, because it's not what you do, Ben. It's who you know and the smile on your face! It's contacts, Ben, contacts! The whole wealth of Alaska passes over the lunch table at the Commodore Hotel, and that's the wonder, the wonder of this country, that a man can end with diamonds here on the basis of being liked! [*He turns to* BIFF.] And that's why when you get out on that field today it's important. Because thousands of people will be rooting for you and loving you. [*to* BEN, *who has again begun to leave*] And Ben! when he walks into a business office his name will sound out like a bell and all the doors will open to him! I've seen it, Ben, I've seen it a thousand times! You can't feel it with your hand like timber, but it's there!

BEN   Good-by, William.

WILLY   Ben, am I right? Don't you think I'm right? I value your advice.

BEN   There's a new continent at your doorstep, William. You could walk out rich. Rich! [*He is gone.*]

WILLY   We'll do it here, Ben! You hear me? We're gonna do it here!

   [*Young* BERNARD *rushes in. The gay music of the Boys is heard.*]

BERNARD   Oh, gee, I was afraid you left already!

WILLY   Why? What time is it?

BERNARD   It's half-past one!

WILLY   Well, come on, everybody! Ebbets Field next stop! Where's the pennants? [*He rushes through the wall-line of the kitchen and out into the living room.*]

LINDA [*to* BIFF]   Did you pack fresh underwear?

BIFF [*who has been limbering up*]   I want to go!

BERNARD   Biff, I'm carrying your helmet, ain't I?

HAPPY   No, I'm carrying the helmet.

BERNARD   Oh, Biff, you promised me.

HAPPY   I'm carrying the helmet.

BERNARD How am I going to get in the locker room?

LINDA Let him carry the shoulder guards. [*She puts her coat and hat on in the kitchen.*]

BERNARD Can I, Biff? 'Cause I told everybody I'm going to be in the locker room.

HAPPY In Ebbets Field it's the clubhouse.

BERNARD I meant the clubhouse. Biff!

HAPPY Biff!

BIFF [*grandly, after a slight pause*] Let him carry the shoulder guards.

HAPPY [*as he gives* BERNARD *the shoulder guards*] Stay close to us now.
[WILLY *rushes in with the pennants.*]

WILLY [*handing them out*] Everybody wave when Biff comes out on the field. [HAPPY *and* BERNARD *run off.*] You set now, boy?
[*The music has died away.*]

BIFF Ready to go, Pop. Every muscle is ready.

WILLY [*at the edge of the apron*] You realize what this means?

BIFF That's right, Pop.

WILLY [*feeling* BIFF's *muscles*] You're comin' home this afternoon captain of the All-Scholastic Championship Team of the City of New York.

BIFF I got it, Pop. And remember, pal, when I take off my helmet, that touchdown is for you.

WILLY Let's go! [*He is starting out, with his arm around* BIFF, *when* CHARLEY *enters, as of old, in knickers.*] I got no room for you, Charley.

CHARLEY Room? For what?

WILLY In the car.

CHARLEY You goin' for a ride? I wanted to shoot some casino.

WILLY [*furiously*] Casino! [*incredulously*] Don't you realize what today is?

LINDA Oh, he knows, Willy. He's just kidding you.

WILLY That's nothing to kid about!

CHARLEY No, Linda, what's goin' on?

LINDA He's playing in Ebbets Field.

CHARLEY Baseball in this weather?

WILLY Don't talk to him. Come on, come on! [*He is pushing them out.*]

CHARLEY Wait a minute, didn't you hear the news?

WILLY What?

CHARLEY Don't you listen to the radio? Ebbets Field just blew up.

WILLY You go to hell! [CHARLEY *laughs. Pushing them out*] Come on, come on! We're late.

CHARLEY [*as they go*] Knock a homer, Biff, knock a homer!

WILLY [*the last to leave, turning to* CHARLEY] I don't think that was funny, Charley. This is the greatest day of my life.

CHARLEY Willy, when are you going to grow up?

WILLY Yeah, heh? When this game is over, Charley, you'll be laughing out of the other side of your face. They'll be calling him another Red Grange.[8] Twenty-five thousand a year.

CHARLEY [*kidding*] Is that so?

WILLY Yeah, that's so.

---

8. Harold Edward Grange, All-American halfback at the University of Illinois from 1923 to 1925, who played professionally for the Chicago Bears.

CHARLEY Well, then, I'm sorry, Willy. But tell me something.

WILLY What?

CHARLEY Who is Red Grange?

WILLY Put up your hands. Goddam you, put up your hands!

[CHARLEY, *chuckling, shakes his head and walks away, around the left corner of the stage.* WILLY *follows him. The music rises to a mocking frenzy.*]

WILLY Who the hell do you think you are, better than everybody else? You don't know everything, you big, ignorant, stupid . . . Put up your hands!

[*Light rises, on the right side of the forestage, on a small table in the reception room of* CHARLEY'S *office. Traffic sounds are heard.* BERNARD, *now mature, sits whistling to himself. A pair of tennis rackets and an overnight bag are on the floor beside him.*]

WILLY [*offstage*] What are you walking away for? Don't walk away! If you're going to say something say it to my face! I know you laugh at me behind my back. You'll laugh out of the other side of your goddam face after this game. Touchdown! Touchdown! Eighty thousand people! Touchdown! Right between the goal posts.

[BERNARD *is a quiet, earnest, but self-assured young man.* WILLY's *voice is coming from right upstage now.* BERNARD *lowers his feet off the table and listens.* JENNY, *his father's secretary, enters.*]

JENNY [*distressed*] Say, Bernard, will you go out in the hall?

BERNARD What is that noise? Who is it?

JENNY Mr. Loman. He just got off the elevator.

BERNARD [*getting up*] Who's he arguing with?

JENNY Nobody. There's nobody with him. I can't deal with him any more, and your father gets all upset everytime he comes. I've got a lot of typing to do, and your father's waiting to sign it. Will you see him?

WILLY [*entering*] Touchdown! Touch—[*He sees* JENNY.] Jenny, Jenny, good to see you. How're ya? Workin'? Or still honest?

JENNY Fine. How've you been feeling?

WILLY Not much any more, Jenny. Ha, ha! [*He is surprised to see the rackets.*]

BERNARD Hello, Uncle Willy.

WILLY [*almost shocked*] Bernard! Well, look who's here! [*He comes quickly, guiltily to* BERNARD *and warmly shakes his hand.*]

BERNARD How are you? Good to see you.

WILLY What are you doing here?

BERNARD Oh, just stopped by to see Pop. Get off my feet till my train leaves. I'm going to Washington in a few minutes.

WILLY Is he in?

BERNARD Yes, he's in his office with the accountant. Sit down.

WILLY [*sitting down*] What're you going to do in Washington?

BERNARD Oh, just a case I've got there, Willy.

WILLY That so? [*indicating the rackets*] You going to play tennis there?

BERNARD I'm staying with a friend who's got a court.

WILLY Don't say. His own tennis court. Must be fine people, I bet.

BERNARD They are, very nice. Dad tells me Biff's in town.

WILLY [*with a big smile*] Yeah, Biff's in. Working on a very big deal, Bernard.

BERNARD   What's Biff doing?

WILLY   Well, he's been doing very big things in the West. But he decided to establish himself here. Very big. We're having dinner. Did I hear your wife had a boy?

BERNARD   That's right. Our second.

WILLY   Two boys! What do you know!

BERNARD   What kind of a deal has Biff got?

WILLY   Well, Bill Oliver—very big sporting-goods man—he wants Biff very badly. Called him in from the West. Long distance, carte blanche, special deliveries. Your friends have their own private tennis court?

BERNARD   You still with the old firm, Willy?

WILLY [after a pause]   I'm—I'm overjoyed to see how you made the grade, Bernard, overjoyed. It's an encouraging thing to see a young man really— really—Looks very good for Biff—very—[He breaks off, then] Bernard— [He is so full of emotion, he breaks off again.]

BERNARD   What is it, Willy?

WILLY [small and alone]   What—what's the secret?

BERNARD   What secret?

WILLY   How—how did you? Why didn't he ever catch on?

BERNARD   I wouldn't know that, Willy.

WILLY [confidentially, desperately]   You were his friend, his boyhood friend. There's something I don't understand about it. His life ended after that Ebbets Field game. From the age of seventeen nothing good ever happened to him.

BERNARD   He never trained himself for anything.

WILLY   But he did, he did. After high school he took so many correspondence courses. Radio mechanics; television; God knows what, and never made the slightest mark.

BERNARD [taking off his glasses]   Willy, do you want to talk candidly?

WILLY [rising, faces BERNARD]   I regard you as a very brilliant man, Bernard. I value your advice.

BERNARD   Oh, the hell with the advice, Willy. I couldn't advise you. There's just one thing I've always wanted to ask you. When he was supposed to graduate, and the math teacher flunked him—

WILLY   Oh, that son-of-a-bitch ruined his life.

BERNARD   Yeah, but, Willy, all he had to do was go to summer school and make up that subject.

WILLY   That's right, that's right.

BERNARD   Did you tell him not to go to summer school?

WILLY   Me? I begged him to go. I ordered him to go!

BERNARD   Then why wouldn't he go?

WILLY   Why? Why! Bernard, that question has been trailing me like a ghost for the last fifteen years. He flunked the subject, and laid down and died like a hammer hit him!

BERNARD   Take it easy, kid.

WILLY   Let me talk to you—I got nobody to talk to. Bernard, Bernard, was it my fault? Y'see? It keeps going around in my mind, maybe I did something to him. I got nothing to give him.

BERNARD   Don't take it so hard.

WILLY   Why did he lay down? What is the story there? You were his friend!

BERNARD Willy, I remember, it was June, and our grades came out. And he'd flunked math.

WILLY That son-of-a-bitch!

BERNARD No, it wasn't right then. Biff just got very angry, I remember, and he was ready to enroll in summer school.

WILLY [*surprised*] He was?

BERNARD He wasn't beaten by it at all. But then, Willy, he disappeared from the block for almost a month. And I got the idea that he'd gone up to New England to see you. Did he have a talk with you then?

[WILLY *stares in silence.*]

BERNARD Willy?

WILLY [*with a strong edge of resentment in his voice*] Yeah, he came to Boston. What about it?

BERNARD Well, just that when he came back—I'll never forget this, it always mystifies me. Because I'd thought so well of Biff, even though he'd always taken advantage of me. I loved him, Willy, y'know? And he came back after that month and took his sneakers—remember those sneakers with "University of Virginia" printed on them? He was so proud of those, wore them every day. And he took them down in the cellar, and burned them up in the furnace. We had a fist fight. It lasted at least half an hour. Just the two of us, punching each other down the cellar, and crying right through it. I've often thought of how strange it was that I knew he'd given up his life. What happened in Boston, Willy?

[WILLY *looks at him as at an intruder.*]

BERNARD I just bring it up because you asked me.

WILLY [*angrily*] Nothing. What do you mean, "What happened?" What's that got to do with anything?

BERNARD Well, don't get sore.

WILLY What are you trying to do, blame it on me? If a boy lays down is that my fault?

BERNARD Now, Willy, don't get—

WILLY Well, don't—don't talk to me that way! What does that mean, "What happened?"

[CHARLEY *enters. He is in his vest, and he carries a bottle of bourbon.*]

CHARLEY Hey, you're going to miss that train. [*He waves the bottle.*]

BERNARD Yeah, I'm going. [*He takes the bottle.*] Thanks, Pop. [*He picks up his rackets and bag.*] Good-by, Willy, and don't worry about it. You know, "If at first you don't succeed . . ."

WILLY Yes, I believe in that.

BERNARD But sometimes, Willy, it's better for a man just to walk away.

WILLY Walk away?

BERNARD That's right.

WILLY But if you can't walk away?

BERNARD [*after a slight pause*] I guess that's when it's tough. [*extending his hand*] Good-by, Willy.

WILLY [*shaking BERNARD's hand*] Good-by, boy.

CHARLEY [*an arm on BERNARD's shoulder*] How do you like this kid? Gonna argue a case in front of the Supreme Court.

BERNARD [*protesting*] Pop!

WILLY [*genuinely shocked, pained, and happy*] No! The Supreme Court!

BERNARD   I gotta run. 'By, Dad!

CHARLEY   Knock 'em dead, Bernard!

[BERNARD *goes off.*]

WILLY [*as* CHARLEY *takes out his wallet*]   The Supreme Court! And he didn't even mention it!

CHARLEY [*counting out money on the desk*]   He don't have to—he's gonna do it.

WILLY   And you never told him what to do, did you? You never took any interest in him.

CHARLEY   My salvation is that I never took any interest in anything. There's some money—fifty dollars. I got an accountant inside.

WILLY   Charley, look . . . [*with difficulty*] I got my insurance to pay. If you can manage it—I need a hundred and ten dollars.

[CHARLEY *doesn't reply for a moment; merely stops moving.*]

WILLY   I'd draw it from my bank but Linda would know, and I . . .

CHARLEY   Sit down, Willy.

WILLY [*moving toward the chair*]   I'm keeping an account of everything, remember. I'll pay every penny back. [*He sits.*]

CHARLEY   Now listen to me, Willy.

WILLY   I want you to know I appreciate . . .

CHARLEY [*sitting down on the table*]   Willy, what're you doin'? What the hell is goin' on in your head?

WILLY   Why? I'm simply . . .

CHARLEY   I offered you a job. You can make fifty dollars a week. And I won't send you on the road.

WILLY   I've got a job.

CHARLEY   Without pay? What kind of job is a job without pay? [*He rises.*] Now, look kid, enough is enough. I'm no genius but I know when I'm being insulted.

WILLY   Insulted!

CHARLEY   Why don't you want to work for me?

WILLY   What's the matter with you? I've got a job.

CHARLEY   Then what're you walkin' in here every week for?

WILLY [*getting up*]   Well, if you don't want me to walk in here—

CHARLEY   I am offering you a job!

WILLY   I don't want your goddam job!

CHARLEY   When the hell are you going to grow up?

WILLY [*furiously*]   You big ignoramus, if you say that to me again I'll rap you one! I don't care how big you are! [*He's ready to fight. Pause.*]

CHARLEY [*kindly, going to him*]   How much do you need, Willy?

WILLY   Charley, I'm strapped, I'm strapped. I don't know what to do. I was just fired.

CHARLEY   Howard fired you?

WILLY   That snotnose. Imagine that? I named him. I named him Howard.

CHARLEY   Willy, when're you gonna realize that them things don't mean anything? You named him Howard, but you can't sell that. The only thing you got in this world is what you can sell. And the funny thing is that you're a salesman, and you don't know that.

WILLY   I've always tried to think otherwise, I guess. I always felt that if a man was impressive, and well liked, that nothing—

CHARLEY Why must everybody like you? Who liked J. P. Morgan?[9] Was he impressive? In a Turkish bath he'd look like a butcher. But with his pockets on he was very well liked. Now listen, Willy, I know you don't like me, and nobody can say I'm in love with you, but I'll give you a job because—just for the hell of it, put it that way. Now what do you say?

WILLY I—I just can't work for you, Charley.

CHARLEY What're you, jealous of me?

WILLY I can't work for you, that's all, don't ask me why.

CHARLEY [angered, takes out more bills] You been jealous of me all your life, you damned fool! Here, pay your insurance. [He puts the money in WILLY's hand.]

WILLY I'm keeping strict accounts.

CHARLEY I've got some work to do. Take care of yourself. And pay your insurance.

WILLY [moving to the right] Funny, y'know? After all the highways, and the trains, and the appointments, and the years, you end up worth more dead than alive.

CHARLEY Willy, nobody's worth nothin' dead. [after a slight pause] Did you hear what I said?

[WILLY stands still, dreaming.]

CHARLEY Willy!

WILLY Apologize to Bernard for me when you see him. I didn't mean to argue with him. He's a fine boy. They're all fine boys, and they'll end up big—all of them. Someday they'll all play tennis together. Wish me luck, Charley. He saw Bill Oliver today.

CHARLEY Good luck.

WILLY [on the verge of tears] Charley, you're the only friend I got. Isn't that a remarkable thing? [He goes out.]

CHARLEY Jesus!

[CHARLEY stares after him a moment and follows. All light blacks out. Suddenly raucous music is heard, and a red glow rises behind the screen at right. STANLEY, a young waiter, appears, carrying a table, followed by HAPPY, who is carrying two chairs.]

STANLEY [putting the table down] That's all right, Mr. Loman, I can handle it myself. [He turns and takes the chairs from HAPPY and places them at the table.]

HAPPY [glancing around] Oh, this is better.

STANLEY Sure, in the front there you're in the middle of all kinds a noise. Whenever you got a party. Mr. Loman, you just tell me and I'll put you back here. Y'know, there's a lotta people they don't like it private, because when they go out they like to see a lotta action around them because they're sick and tired to stay in the house by theirself. But I know you, you ain't from Hackensack. You know what I mean?

HAPPY [sitting down] So how's it coming, Stanley?

STANLEY Ah, it's a dog life. I only wish during the war they'd a took me in the Army. I coulda been dead by now.

HAPPY My brother's back, Stanley.

STANLEY Oh, he come back, heh? From the Far West.

---

9. John Pierpont Morgan (1887–1943), a famous banker and financier.

HAPPY Yeah, big cattle man, my brother, so treat him right. And my father's coming too.

STANLEY Oh, your father too!

HAPPY You got a couple of nice lobsters?

STANLEY Hundred per cent, big.

HAPPY I want them with the claws.

STANLEY Don't worry, I don't give you no mice. [HAPPY *laughs.*] How about some wine? It'll put a head on the meal.

HAPPY No. You remember, Stanley, that recipe I brought you from overseas? With the champagne in it?

STANLEY Oh, yeah, sure. I still got it tacked up yet in the kitchen. But that'll have to cost a buck apiece anyways.

HAPPY That's all right.

STANLEY What'd you, hit a number or somethin'?

HAPPY No, it's a little celebration. My brother is—I think he pulled off a big deal today. I think we're going into business together.

STANLEY Great! That's the best for you. Because a family business, you know what I mean?—that's the best.

HAPPY That's what I think.

STANLEY 'Cause what's the difference? Somebody steals? It's in the family. Know what I mean? [*sotto voce*][1] Like this bartender here. The boss is goin' crazy what kinda leak he's got in the cash register. You put it in but it don't come out.

HAPPY [*raising his head*] Sh!

STANLEY What?

HAPPY You notice I wasn't lookin' right or left, was I?

STANLEY No.

HAPPY And my eyes are closed.

STANLEY So what's the—?

HAPPY Strudel's comin'.

STANLEY [*catching on, looks around*] Ah, no, there's no—
     [*He breaks off as a furred, lavishly dressed girl enters and sits at the next table. Both follow her with their eyes.*]

STANLEY Geez, how'd ya know?

HAPPY I got radar or something. [*staring directly at her profile*] Oooooooo . . . Stanley.

STANLEY I think that's for you, Mr. Loman.

HAPPY Look at that mouth. Oh, God. And the binoculars.

STANLEY Geez, you got a life, Mr. Loman.

HAPPY Wait on her.

STANLEY [*going to the girl's table*] Would you like a menu, ma'am?

GIRL I'm expecting someone, but I'd like a—

HAPPY Why don't you bring her—excuse me, miss, do you mind? I sell champagne, and I'd like you to try my brand. Bring her a champagne, Stanley.

GIRL That's awfully nice of you.

HAPPY Don't mention it. It's all company money. [*He laughs.*]

GIRL That's a charming product to be selling, isn't it?

---

1. In an undertone.

HAPPY   Oh, gets to be like everything else. Selling is selling, y'know.

GIRL   I suppose.

HAPPY   You don't happen to sell, do you?

GIRL   No, I don't sell.

HAPPY   Would you object to a compliment from a stranger? You ought to be on a magazine cover.

GIRL   [*looking at him a little archly*]   I have been.

  [STANLEY *comes in with a glass of champagne.*]

HAPPY   What'd I say before, Stanley? You see? She's a cover girl.

STANLEY   Oh, I could see, I could see.

HAPPY   [*to the* GIRL]   What magazine?

GIRL   Oh, a lot of them. [*She takes the drink.*] Thank you.

HAPPY   You know what they say in France, don't you? "Champagne is the drink of the complexion"—Hya, Biff!

  [BIFF *has entered and sits with* HAPPY.]

BIFF   Hello, kid. Sorry I'm late.

HAPPY   I just got here. Uh, Miss—?

GIRL   Forsythe.

HAPPY   Miss Forsythe, this is my brother.

BIFF   Is Dad here?

HAPPY   His name is Biff. You might've heard of him. Great football player.

GIRL   Really? What team?

HAPPY   Are you familiar with football?

GIRL   No, I'm afraid I'm not.

HAPPY   Biff is quarterback with the New York Giants.

GIRL   Well, that's nice, isn't it? [*She drinks.*]

HAPPY   Good health.

GIRL   I'm happy to meet you.

HAPPY   That's my name. Hap. It's really Harold, but at West Point they called me Happy.

GIRL   [*now really impressed*]   Oh, I see. How do you do? [*She turns her profile.*]

BIFF   Isn't Dad coming?

HAPPY   You want her?

BIFF   Oh, I could never make that.

HAPPY   I remember the time that idea would never come into your head. Where's the old confidence, Biff?

BIFF   I just saw Oliver—

HAPPY   Wait a minute. I've got to see that old confidence again. Do you want her? She's on call.

BIFF   Oh, no. [*He turns to look at the* GIRL.]

HAPPY   I'm telling you. Watch this. [*turning to the* GIRL] Honey? [*She turns to him.*] Are you busy?

GIRL   Well, I am . . . but I could make a phone call.

HAPPY   Do that, will you, honey? And see if you can get a friend. We'll be here for a while. Biff is one of the greatest football players in the country.

GIRL   [*standing up*]   Well, I'm certainly happy to meet you.

HAPPY   Come back soon.

GIRL   I'll try.

HAPPY   Don't try, honey, try hard.

[*The* GIRL *exits.* STANLEY *follows, shaking his head in bewildered admiration.*]

HAPPY   Isn't that a shame now? A beautiful girl like that? That's why I can't get married. There's not a good woman in a thousand. New York is loaded with them, kid!

BIFF   Hap, look—

HAPPY   I told you she was on call!

BIFF [*strangely unnerved*]   Cut it out, will ya? I want to say something to you.

HAPPY   Did you see Oliver?

BIFF   I saw him all right. Now look, I want to tell Dad a couple of things and I want you to help me.

HAPPY   What? Is he going to back you?

BIFF   Are you crazy? You're out of your goddam head, you know that?

HAPPY   Why? What happened?

BIFF [*breathlessly*]   I did a terrible thing today, Hap. It's been the strangest day I ever went through. I'm all numb, I swear.

HAPPY   You mean he wouldn't see you?

BIFF   Well, I waited six hours for him, see? All day. Kept sending my name in. Even tried to date his secretary so she'd get me to him, but no soap.

HAPPY   Because you're not showin' the old confidence, Biff. He remembered you, didn't he?

BIFF [*stopping* HAPPY *with a gesture*]   Finally, about five o'clock, he comes out. Didn't remember who I was or anything. I felt like such an idiot, Hap.

HAPPY   Did you tell him my Florida idea?

BIFF   He walked away. I saw him for one minute. I got so mad I could've torn the walls down! How the hell did I ever get the idea I was a salesman there? I even believed myself that I'd been a salesman for him! And then he gave me one look and—I realized what a ridiculous lie my whole life has been! We've been talking in a dream for fifteen years. I was a shipping clerk.

HAPPY   What'd you do?

BIFF [*with great tension and wonder*]   Well, he left, see. And the secretary went out. I was all alone in the waiting-room. I don't know what came over me, Hap. The next thing I know I'm in his office—paneled walls, everything. I can't explain it. I—Hap, I took his fountain pen.

HAPPY   Geez, did he catch you?

BIFF   I ran out. I ran down all eleven flights. I ran and ran and ran.

HAPPY   That was an awful dumb—what'd you do that for?

BIFF [*agonized*]   I don't know, I just—wanted to take something, I don't know. You gotta help me, Hap, I'm gonna tell Pop.

HAPPY   You crazy? What for?

BIFF   Hap, he's got to understand that I'm not the man somebody lends that kind of money to. He thinks I've been spiting him all these years and it's eating him up.

HAPPY   That's just it. You tell him something nice.

BIFF   I can't.

HAPPY   Say you got a lunch date with Oliver tomorrow.

BIFF   So what do I do tomorrow?

HAPPY   You leave the house tomorrow and come back at night and say Oliver is thinking it over. And he thinks it over for a couple of weeks, and gradually it fades away and nobody's the worse.

BIFF   But it'll go on forever!

HAPPY   Dad is never so happy as when he's looking forward to something!

[WILLY *enters.*]

HAPPY   Hello, scout!

WILLY   Gee, I haven't been here in years!

[STANLEY *has followed* WILLY *in and sets a chair for him.* STANLEY *starts off but* HAPPY *stops him.*]

HAPPY   Stanley!

[STANLEY *stands by, waiting for an order.*]

BIFF   [*going to* WILLY *with guilt, as to an invalid*]   Sit down, Pop. You want a drink?

WILLY   Sure, I don't mind.

BIFF   Let's get a load on.

WILLY   You look worried.

BIFF   N-no. [*to* STANLEY] Scotch all around. Make it doubles.

STANLEY   Doubles, right. [*He goes.*]

WILLY   You had a couple already, didn't you?

BIFF   Just a couple, yeah.

WILLY   Well, what happened, boy? [*nodding affirmatively, with a smile*] Everything go all right?

BIFF   [*takes a breath, then reaches out and grasps* WILLY's *hand*]   Pal . . . [*He is smiling bravely, and* WILLY *is smiling too.*] I had an experience today.

HAPPY   Terrific, Pop.

WILLY   That so? What happened?

BIFF   [*high, slightly alcoholic, above the earth*]   I'm going to tell you everything from first to last. It's been a strange day. [*Silence. He looks around, composes himself as best he can, but his breath keeps breaking the rhythm of his voice.*] I had to wait quite a while for him, and—

WILLY   Oliver?

BIFF   Yeah, Oliver. All day, as a matter of cold fact. And a lot of— instances—facts, Pop, facts about my life came back to me. Who was it, Pop? Who ever said I was a salesman with Oliver?

WILLY   Well, you were.

BIFF   No, Dad, I was shipping clerk.

WILLY   But you were practically—

BIFF   [*with determination*]   Dad, I don't know who said it first, but I was never a salesman for Bill Oliver.

WILLY   What're you talking about?

BIFF   Let's hold on to the facts tonight, Pop. We're not going to get any-where bullin' around. I was a shipping clerk.

WILLY   [*angrily*]   All right, now listen to me—

BIFF   Why don't you let me finish?

WILLY   I'm not interested in stories about the past or any crap of that kind because the woods are burning, boys, you understand? There's a big blaze going on all around. I was fired today.

BIFF   [*shocked*]   How could you be?

WILLY   I was fired, and I'm looking for a little good news to tell your mother, because the woman has waited and the woman has suffered. The gist of it is that I haven't got a story left in my head, Biff. So don't give me a lecture about facts and aspects. I am not interested. Now what've you got to say to me?

[STANLEY *enters with three drinks. They wait until he leaves.*]

WILLY   Did you see Oliver?

BIFF   Jesus, Dad!

WILLY   You mean you didn't go up there?

HAPPY   Sure he went up there.

BIFF   I did. I—saw him. How could they fire you?

WILLY [*on the edge of his chair*]   What kind of a welcome did he give you?

BIFF   He won't even let you work on commission?

WILLY   I'm out! [*driving*] So tell me, he gave you a warm welcome?

HAPPY   Sure, Pop, sure!

BIFF [*driven*]   Well, it was kind of—

WILLY   I was wondering if he'd remember you. [*to* HAPPY] Imagine, man doesn't see him for ten, twelve years and gives him that kind of a welcome!

HAPPY   Damn right!

BIFF [*trying to return to the offensive*]   Pop, look—

WILLY   You know why he remembered you, don't you? Because you impressed him in those days.

BIFF   Let's talk quietly and get this down to the facts, huh?

WILLY [*as though* BIFF *had been interrupting*]   Well, what happened? It's great news, Biff. Did he take you into his office or'd you talk in the waiting-room?

BIFF   Well, he came in, see, and—

WILLY [*with a big smile*]   What'd he say? Betcha he threw his arm around you.

BIFF   Well, he kinda—

WILLY   He's a fine man. [*to* HAPPY] Very hard man to see, y'know.

HAPPY [*agreeing*]   Oh, I know.

WILLY [*to* BIFF]   Is that where you had the drinks?

BIFF   Yeah, he gave me a couple of—no, no!

HAPPY [*cutting in*]   He told him my Florida idea.

WILLY   Don't interrupt. [*to* BIFF] How'd he react to the Florida idea?

BIFF   Dad, will you give me a minute to explain?

WILLY   I've been waiting for you to explain since I sat down here! What happened? He took you into his office and what?

BIFF   Well—I talked. And—he listened, see.

WILLY   Famous for the way he listens, y'know. What was his answer?

BIFF   His answer was—[*He breaks off, suddenly angry.*] Dad, you're not letting me tell you what I want to tell you!

WILLY [*accusing, angered*]   You didn't see him, did you?

BIFF   I did see him!

WILLY   What'd you insult him or something? You insulted him, didn't you?

BIFF   Listen, will you let me out of it, will you just let me out of it!

HAPPY   What the hell!

WILLY   Tell me what happened!

BIFF [*to* HAPPY]   I can't talk to him!

[*A single trumpet note jars the ear. The light of green leaves stains the house, which holds the air of night and a dream.* YOUNG BERNARD *enters and knocks on the door of the house.*]

YOUNG BERNARD [*frantically*] Mrs. Loman, Mrs. Loman!

HAPPY Tell him what happened!

BIFF [*to* HAPPY] Shut up and leave me alone!

WILLY No, no. You had to go and flunk math!

BIFF What math? What're you talking about?

YOUNG BERNARD Mrs. Loman, Mrs. Loman!
[LINDA *appears in the house, as of old.*]

WILLY [*wildly*] Math, math, math!

BIFF Take it easy, Pop!

YOUNG BERNARD Mrs. Loman!

WILLY [*furiously*] If you hadn't flunked you'd've been set by now!

BIFF Now, look, I'm gonna tell you what happened, and you're going to listen to me.

YOUNG BERNARD Mrs. Loman!

BIFF I waited six hours—

HAPPY What the hell are you saying?

BIFF I kept sending in my name but he wouldn't see me. So finally he . . .
[*He continues unheard as light fades low on the restaurant.*]

YOUNG BERNARD Biff flunked math!

LINDA No!

YOUNG BERNARD Birnbaum flunked him! They won't graduate him!

LINDA But they have to. He's gotta go to the university. Where is he? Biff! Biff!

YOUNG BERNARD No, he left. He went to Grand Central.

LINDA Grand—You mean he went to Boston!

YOUNG BERNARD Is Uncle Willy in Boston?

LINDA Oh, maybe Willy can talk to the teacher. Oh, the poor, poor boy!
[*Light on house area snaps out.*]

BIFF [*at the table, now audible, holding up a gold fountain pen*] . . . so I'm washed up with Oliver, you understand? Are you listening to me?

WILLY [*at a loss*] Yeah, sure. If you hadn't flunked—

BIFF Flunked what? What're you talking about?

WILLY Don't blame everything on me! I didn't flunk math—you did! What pen?

HAPPY That was awful dumb, Biff, a pen like that is worth—

WILLY [*seeing the pen for the first time*] You took Oliver's pen?

BIFF [*weakening*] Dad, I just explained it to you.

WILLY You stole Bill Oliver's fountain pen!

BIFF I didn't exactly steal it! That's just what I've been explaining to you!

HAPPY He had it in his hand and just then Oliver walked in, so he got nervous and stuck it in his pocket!

WILLY My God, Biff!

BIFF I never intended to do it, Dad!

OPERATOR'S VOICE Standish Arms, good evening!

WILLY [*shouting*] I'm not in my room!

BIFF [*frightened*] Dad, what's the matter? [*He and* HAPPY *stand up.*]

OPERATOR Ringing Mr. Loman for you!

WILLY   I'm not there, stop it!

BIFF [*horrified, gets down on one knee before* WILLY]   Dad, I'll make good,
I'll make good. [WILLY *tries to get to his feet.* BIFF *holds him down.*] Sit
down now.

WILLY   No, you're no good, you're no good for anything.

BIFF   I am, Dad, I'll find something else, you understand? Now don't worry
about anything. [*He holds up* WILLY's *face.*] Talk to me, Dad.

OPERATOR   Mr. Loman does not answer. Shall I page him?

WILLY [*attempting to stand, as though to rush and silence the* OPERA-
TOR]   No, no, no!

HAPPY   He'll strike something, Pop.

WILLY   No, no . . .

BIFF [*desperately, standing over* WILLY]   Pop, listen! Listen to me! I'm telling
you something good. Oliver talked to his partner about the Florida idea.
You listening? He—he talked to his partner, and he came to me . . . I'm
going to be all right, you hear? Dad, listen to me, he said it was just a
question of the amount!

WILLY   Then you . . . got it?

HAPPY   He's gonna be terrific, Pop!

WILLY [*trying to stand*]   Then you got it, haven't you? You got it! You got
it!

BIFF [*agonized, holds* WILLY *down*]   No, no. Look, Pop. I'm supposed to
have lunch with them tomorrow. I'm just telling you this so you'll know
that I can still make an impression, Pop. And I'll make good somewhere,
but I can't go tomorrow, see?

WILLY   Why not? You simply—

BIFF   But the pen, Pop!

WILLY   You give it to him and tell him it was an oversight!

HAPPY   Sure, have lunch tomorrow!

BIFF   I can't say that—

WILLY   You were doing a crossword puzzle and accidentally used his pen!

BIFF   Listen, kid, I took those balls years ago, now I walk in with his fountain pen? That clinches it, don't you see? I can't face him like that! I'll
try elsewhere.

PAGE'S VOICE   Paging Mr. Loman!

WILLY   Don't you want to be anything?

BIFF   Pop, how can I go back?

WILLY   You don't want to be anything, is that what's behind it?

BIFF [*now angry at* WILLY *for not crediting his sympathy*]   Don't take it that
way! You think it was easy walking into that office after what I'd done to
him? A team of horses couldn't have dragged me back to Bill Oliver!

WILLY   Then why'd you go?

BIFF   Why did I go? Why did I go! Look at you! Look at what's become of
you!

[*Off left,* THE WOMAN *laughs.*]

WILLY   Biff, you're going to go to that lunch tomorrow, or—

BIFF   I can't go. I've got no appointment!

HAPPY   Biff for . . . !

WILLY   Are you spiting me?

BIFF   Don't take it that way! Goddammit!

WILLY [*strikes* BIFF *and falters away from the table*]   You rotten little louse! Are you spiting me?

THE WOMAN   Someone's at the door, Willy!

BIFF   I'm no good, can't you see what I am?

HAPPY [*separating them*]   Hey, you're in a restaurant! Now cut it out, both of you? [*The girls enter.*] Hello, girls, sit down.

[THE WOMAN *laughs, off left.*]

MISS FORSYTHE   I guess we might as well. This is Letta.

THE WOMAN   Willy, are you going to wake up?

BIFF [*ignoring* WILLY]   How're ya, miss, sit down. What do you drink?

MISS FORSYTHE   Letta might not be able to stay long.

LETTA   I gotta get up early tomorrow. I got jury duty. I'm so excited! Were you fellows ever on a jury?

BIFF   No, but I been in front of them! [*The girls laugh.*] This is my father.

LETTA   Isn't he cute? Sit down with us, Pop.

HAPPY   Sit him down, Biff!

BIFF [*going to him*]   Come on, slugger, drink us under the table. To hell with it! Come on, sit down, pal.

[*On* BIFF'*s last insistence,* WILLY *is about to sit.*]

THE WOMAN [*now urgently*]   Willy, are you going to answer the door!

[THE WOMAN'*s call pulls* WILLY *back. He starts right, befuddled.*]

BIFF   Hey, where are you going?

WILLY   Open the door.

BIFF   The door?

WILLY   The washroom . . . the door . . . where's the door?

BIFF [*leading* WILLY *to the left*]   Just go straight down.

[WILLY *moves left.*]

THE WOMAN   Willy, Willy, are you going to get up, get up, get up, get up?

[WILLY *exits left.*]

LETTA   I think it's sweet you bring your daddy along.

MISS FORSYTHE   Oh, he isn't really your father!

BIFF [*at left, turning to her resentfully*]   Miss Forsythe, you've just seen a prince walk by. A fine, troubled prince. A hard-working, unappreciated prince. A pal, you understand? A good companion. Always for his boys.

LETTA   That's so sweet.

HAPPY   Well, girls, what's the program? We're wasting time. Come on, Biff. Gather round. Where would you like to go?

BIFF   Why don't you do something for him?

HAPPY   Me!

BIFF   Don't you give a damn for him, Hap?

HAPPY   What're you talking about? I'm the one who—

BIFF   I sense it, you don't give a good goddam about him. [*He takes the rolled-up hose from his pocket and puts it on the table in front of* HAPPY.] Look what I found in the cellar, for Christ's sake. How can you bear to let it go on?

HAPPY   Me? Who goes away? Who runs off and—

BIFF   Yeah, but he doesn't mean anything to you. You could help him—I can't! Don't you understand what I'm talking about? He's going to kill himself, don't you know that?

HAPPY   Don't I know it! Me!

BIFF Hap, help him! Jesus . . . help him . . . Help me, help me, I can't bear to look at his face! [*Ready to weep, he hurries out, up right.*]

HAPPY [*starting after him*] Where are you going?

MISS FORSYTHE What's he so mad about?

HAPPY Come on, girls, we'll catch up with him.

MISS FORSYTHE [*as* HAPPY *pushes her out*] Say, I don't like that temper of his!

HAPPY He's just a little overstrung, he'll be all right!

WILLY [*off left, as* THE WOMAN *laughs*] Don't answer! Don't answer!

LETTA Don't you want to tell your father—

HAPPY No, that's not my father. He's just a guy. Come on, we'll catch Biff, and, honey, we're going to paint this town! Stanley, where's the check! Hey, Stanley!

[*They exit.* STANLEY *looks toward left.*]

STANLEY [*calling to* HAPPY *indignantly*] Mr. Loman! Mr. Loman!

[STANLEY *picks up a chair and follows them off. Knocking is heard off left.* THE WOMAN *enters, laughing.* WILLY *follows her. She is in a black slip; he is buttoning his shirt. Raw, sensuous music accompanies their speech.*]

WILLY Will you stop laughing? Will you stop?

THE WOMAN Aren't you going to answer the door? He'll wake the whole hotel.

WILLY I'm not expecting anybody.

THE WOMAN Whyn't you have another drink, honey, and stop being so damn self-centered?

WILLY I'm so lonely.

THE WOMAN You know you ruined me, Willy? From now on, whenever you come to the office, I'll see that you go right through to the buyers. No waiting at my desk any more, Willy. You ruined me.

WILLY That's nice of you to say that.

THE WOMAN Gee, you are self-centered! Why so sad? You are the saddest, self-centeredest soul I ever did see-saw. [*She laughs. He kisses her.*] Come on inside, drummer boy. It's silly to be dressing in the middle of the night. [*As knocking is heard*] Aren't you going to answer the door?

WILLY They're knocking on the wrong door.

THE WOMAN But I felt the knocking. And he heard us talking in here. Maybe the hotel's on fire!

WILLY [*his terror rising*] It's a mistake.

THE WOMAN Then tell them to go away!

WILLY There's nobody there.

THE WOMAN It's getting on my nerves, Willy. There's somebody standing out there and it's getting on my nerves!

WILLY [*pushing her away from him*] All right, stay in the bathroom here, and don't come out. I think there's a law in Massachusetts about it, so don't come out. It may be that new room clerk. He looked very mean. So don't come out. It's a mistake, there's no fire.

[*The knocking is heard again. He takes a few steps away from her, and she vanishes into the wing. The light follows him, and now he is facing* YOUNG BIFF, *who carries a suitcase.* BIFF *steps toward him. The music is gone.*]

BIFF   Why didn't you answer?

WILLY   Biff! What are you doing in Boston?

BIFF   Why didn't you answer? I've been knocking for five minutes, I called you on the phone—

WILLY   I just heard you. I was in the bathroom and had the door shut. Did anything happen home?

BIFF   Dad—I let you down.

WILLY   What do you mean?

BIFF   Dad . . .

WILLY   Biffo, what's this about? [*putting his arm around* BIFF] Come on, let's go downstairs and get you a malted.

BIFF   Dad, I flunked math.

WILLY   Not for the term?

BIFF   The term. I haven't got enough credits to graduate.

WILLY   You mean to say Bernard wouldn't give you the answers?

BIFF   He did, he tried, but I only got a sixty-one.

WILLY   And they wouldn't give you four points?

BIFF   Birnbaum refused absolutely. I begged him, Pop, but he won't give me those points. You gotta talk to him before they close the school. Because if he saw the kind of man you are, and you just talked to him in your way, I'm sure he'd come through for me. The class came right before practice, see, and I didn't go enough. Would you talk to him? He'd like you, Pop. You know the way you could talk.

WILLY   You're on. We'll drive right back.

BIFF   Oh, Dad, good work! I'm sure he'll change for you!

WILLY   Go downstairs and tell the clerk I'm checkin' out. Go right down.

BIFF   Yes, sir! See, the reason he hates me, Pop—one day he was late for class so I got up at the blackboard and imitated him. I crossed my eyes and talked with a lithp.

WILLY [*laughing*]   You did? The kids like it?

BIFF   They nearly died laughing!

WILLY   Yeah? What'd you do?

BIFF   The thquare root of thixthy twee is . . . [WILLY *bursts out laughing;* BIFF *joins him.*] And in the middle of it he walked in!

[WILLY *laughs and* THE WOMAN *joins in offstage.*]

WILLY [*without hesitation*]   Hurry downstairs and—

BIFF   Somebody in there?

WILLY   No, that was next door.

[THE WOMAN *laughs offstage.*]

BIFF   Somebody got in your bathroom!

WILLY   No, it's the next room, there's a party—

THE WOMAN [*enters laughing. She lisps this*]   Can I come in? There's something in the bathtub, Willy, and it's moving!

[WILLY *looks at* BIFF, *who is staring open-mouthed and horrified at* THE WOMAN.]

WILLY   Ah—you better go back to your room. They must be finished painting by now. They're painting her room so I let her take a shower here. Go back, go back . . . [*He pushes her.*]

THE WOMAN [*resisting*]   But I've got to get dressed, Willy, I can't—

WILLY   Get out of here! Go back, go back . . . [*suddenly striving for the ordinary*] This is Miss Francis, Biff, she's a buyer. They're painting her room. Go back, Miss Francis, go back . . .

THE WOMAN   But my clothes, I can't go out naked in the hall!

WILLY [*pushing her offstage*]   Get outa here! Go back, go back!

> [BIFF *slowly sits down on his suitcase as the argument continues offstage.*]

THE WOMAN   Where's my stockings? You promised me stockings, Willy!

WILLY   I have no stockings here!

THE WOMAN   You had two boxes of size nine sheers for me, and I want them!

WILLY   Here, for God's sake, will you get outa here!

THE WOMAN [*enters holding a box of stockings*]   I just hope there's nobody in the hall. That's all I hope. [*to* BIFF] Are you football or baseball?

BIFF   Football.

THE WOMAN [*angry, humiliated*]   That's me too. G'night. [*She snatches her clothes from* WILLY, *and walks out.*]

WILLY [*after a pause*]   Well, better get going. I want to get to the school first thing in the morning. Get my suits out of the closet. I'll get my valise. [BIFF *doesn't move.*] What's the matter? [BIFF *remains motionless, tears falling.*] She's a buyer. Buys for J. H. Simmons. She lives down the hall—they're painting. You don't imagine—[*He breaks off. After a pause*] Now listen, pal, she's just a buyer. She sees merchandise in her room and they have to keep it looking just so . . . [*Pause. Assuming command*] All right, get my suits. [BIFF *doesn't move.*] Now stop crying and do as I say. I gave you an order. Biff, I gave you an order! Is that what you do when I give you an order? How dare you cry! [*putting his arm around* BIFF] Now look, Biff, when you grow up you'll understand about these things. You mustn't—you mustn't overemphasize a thing like this. I'll see Birnbaum first thing in the morning.

BIFF   Never mind.

WILLY [*getting down beside* BIFF]   Never mind! He's going to give you those points. I'll see to it.

BIFF   He wouldn't listen to you.

WILLY   He certainly will listen to me. You need those points for the U. of Virginia.

BIFF   I'm not going there.

WILLY   Heh? If I can't get him to change that mark you'll make it up in summer school. You've got all summer to—

BIFF [*his weeping breaking from him*]   Dad . . .

WILLY [*infected by it*]   Oh, my boy . . .

BIFF   Dad . . .

WILLY   She's nothing to me, Biff. I was lonely, I was terribly lonely.

BIFF   You—you gave her Mama's stockings! [*His tears break through and he rises to go.*]

WILLY [*grabbing for* BIFF]   I gave you an order!

BIFF   Don't touch me, you—liar!

WILLY   Apologize for that!

BIFF   You fake! You phony little fake! You fake! [*Overcome, he turns quickly and weeping fully goes out with his suitcase.* WILLY *is left on the floor on his knees.*]

WILLY   I gave you an order! Biff, come back here or I'll beat you! Come
  back here! I'll whip you!
  [STANLEY *comes quickly in from the right and stands in front of* WILLY.]
WILLY [*shouts at* STANLEY]   I gave you an order . . .
STANLEY   Hey, let's pick it up, pick it up, Mr. Loman. [*He helps* WILLY *to
  his feet.*] Your boys left with the chippies. They said they'll see you home.
  [*A second waiter watches some distance away.*]
WILLY   But we were supposed to have dinner together.
  [*Music is heard,* WILLY's *theme.*]
STANLEY   Can you make it?
WILLY   I'll—sure, I can make it. [*suddenly concerned about his clothes*] Do
  I—I look all right?
STANLEY   Sure, you look all right. [*He flicks a speck off* WILLY's *lapel.*]
WILLY   Here—here's a dollar.
STANLEY   Oh, your son paid me. It's all right.
WILLY [*putting it in* STANLEY's *hand*]   No, take it. You're a good boy.
STANLEY   Oh, no, you don't have to . . .
WILLY   Here—here's some more, I don't need it any more. [*after a slight
  pause*]   Tell me—is there a seed store in the neighborhood?
STANLEY   Seeds? You mean like to plant?
  [*As* WILLY *turns,* STANLEY *slips the money back into his jacket pocket.*]
WILLY   Yes. Carrots, peas . . .
STANLEY   Well, there's hardware stores on Sixth Avenue, but it may be too
  late now.
WILLY [*anxiously*]   Oh, I'd better hurry. I've got to get some seeds. [*He
  starts off to the right.*] I've got to get some seeds, right away. Nothing's
  planted. I don't have a thing in the ground.
  [WILLY *hurries out as the light goes down.* STANLEY *moves over to the right
  after him, watches him off. The other waiter has been staring at* WILLY.]
STANLEY [*to the waiter*]   Well, whatta you looking at?
  [*The waiter picks up the chairs and moves off right.* STANLEY *takes the
  table and follows him. The light fades on this area. There is a long pause,
  the sound of the flute coming over. The light gradually rises on the
  kitchen, which is empty.* HAPPY *appears at the door of the house, followed
  by* BIFF. HAPPY *is carrying a large bunch of long-stemmed roses. He enters
  the kitchen, looks around for* LINDA. *Not seeing her, he turns to* BIFF,
  who is just outside the house door, and makes a gesture with his hands,
  indicating "Not here, I guess." He looks into the living-room and freezes.
  Inside,* LINDA, *unseen, is seated,* WILLY's *coat on her lap. She rises ominously and quietly and moves toward* HAPPY, *who backs up into the
  kitchen, afraid.*]
HAPPY   Hey, what're you doing up? [LINDA *says nothing but moves toward
  him implacably.*] Where's Pop? [*He keeps backing to the right, and now*
  LINDA *is in full view in the doorway to the living room.*] Is he sleeping?
LINDA   Where were you?
HAPPY [*trying to laugh it off*]   We met two girls, Mom, very fine types. Here,
  we brought you some flowers. [*offering them to her*] Put them in your
  room, Ma.
  [*She knocks them to the floor at* BIFF's *feet. He has now come inside and
  closed the door behind him. She stares at* BIFF, *silent.*]

HAPPY   Now what'd you do that for? Mom, I want you to have some flowers—

LINDA [cutting HAPPY off, violently to BIFF]   Don't you care whether he lives or dies?

HAPPY [going to the stairs]   Come upstairs, Biff.

BIFF [with a flare of disgust, to HAPPY]   Go away from me! [to LINDA] What do you mean, lives or dies? Nobody's dying around here, pal.

LINDA   Get out of my sight! Get out of here!

BIFF   I wanna see the boss.

LINDA   You're not going near him!

BIFF   Where is he? [He moves into the living-room and LINDA follows.]

LINDA [shouting after BIFF]   You invite him for dinner. He looks forward to it all day—[BIFF appears in his parents' bedroom, looks around and exits]—and then you desert him there. There's no stranger you'd do that to!

HAPPY   Why? He had a swell time with us. Listen, when I—[LINDA comes back into the kitchen]—desert him I hope I don't outlive the day!

LINDA   Get out of here!

HAPPY   Now look, Mom . . .

LINDA   Did you have to go to women tonight? You and your lousy rotten whores!

[BIFF re-enters the kitchen.]

HAPPY   Mom, all we did was follow Biff around trying to cheer him up! [to BIFF] Boy, what a night you gave me!

LINDA   Get out of here, both of you, and don't come back! I don't want you tormenting him any more. Go on now, get your things together! [to BIFF] You can sleep in his apartment. [She starts to pick up the flowers and stops herself.] Pick up this stuff, I'm not your maid any more. Pick it up, you bum, you!

[HAPPY turns his back to her in refusal. BIFF slowly moves over and gets down on his knees, picking up the flowers.]

LINDA   You're a pair of animals! Not one, not another living soul would have had the cruelty to walk out on that man in a restaurant!

BIFF [not looking at her]   Is that what he said?

LINDA   He didn't have to say anything. He was so humiliated he nearly limped when he came in.

HAPPY   But, Mom, he had a great time with us—

BIFF [cutting him off violently]   Shut up!

[Without another word, HAPPY goes upstairs.]

LINDA   You! You didn't even go in to see if he was all right!

BIFF [still on the floor in front of LINDA, the flowers in his hand; with self-loathing]   No. Didn't. Didn't do a damned thing. How do you like that, heh? Left him babbling in a toilet.

LINDA   You louse. You . . .

BIFF   Now you hit it on the nose! [He gets up, throws the flowers in the waste-basket.] The scum of the earth, and you're looking at him!

LINDA   Get out of here!

BIFF   I gotta talk to the boss, Mom. Where is he?

LINDA   You're not going near him. Get out of this house!

BIFF [with absolute assurance, determination]   No. We're gonna have an abrupt conversation, him and me.

LINDA You're not talking to him!
> [*Hammering is heard from outside the house, off right.* BIFF *turns toward the noise.*]

LINDA [*suddenly pleading*] Will you please leave him alone?

BIFF What's he doing out there?

LINDA He's planting the garden!

BIFF [*quietly*] Now? Oh, my God!
> [BIFF *moves outside,* LINDA *following. The light dies down on them and comes up on the center of the apron as* WILLY *walks into it. He is carrying a flashlight, a hoe, and a handful of seed packets. He raps the top of the hoe sharply to fix it firmly, and then moves to the left, measuring off the distance with his foot. He holds the flashlight to look at the seed packets, reading off the instructions. He is in the blue of night.*]

WILLY Carrots . . . quarter-inch apart. Rows . . . one-foot rows. [*He measures it off.*] One foot. [*He puts down a package and measures off.*] Beets. [*He puts down another package and measures again.*] Lettuce. [*He reads the package, puts it down.*] One foot—[*He breaks off as* BEN *appears at the right and moves slowly down to him.*] What a proposition, ts, ts. Terrific, terrific. 'Cause she's suffered, Ben, the woman has suffered. You understand me? A man can't go out the way he came in, Ben, a man has got to add up to something. You can't, you can't—[BEN *moves toward him as though to interrupt.*] You gotta consider, now. Don't answer so quick. Remember, it's a guaranteed twenty-thousand-dollar proposition. Now look, Ben, I want you to go through the ins and outs of this thing with me. I've got nobody to talk to, Ben, and the woman has suffered, you hear me?

BEN [*standing still, considering*] What's the proposition?

WILLY It's twenty thousand dollars on the barrelhead. Guaranteed, gilt-edged, you understand?

BEN You don't want to make a fool of yourself. They might not honor the policy.

WILLY How can they dare refuse? Didn't I work like a coolie to meet every premium on the nose? And now they don't pay off! Impossible!

BEN It's called a cowardly thing, William.

WILLY Why? Does it take more guts to stand here the rest of my life ringing up a zero?

BEN [*yielding*] That's a point, William. [*He moves, thinking, turns.*] And twenty thousand—that *is* something one can feel with the hand, it is there.

WILLY [*now assured, with rising power*] Oh, Ben, that's the whole beauty of it! I see it like a diamond, shining in the dark, hard and rough, that I can pick up and touch in my hand. Not like—like an appointment! This would not be another damned-fool appointment, Ben, and it changes all the aspects. Because he thinks I'm nothing, see, and so he spites me. But the funeral—[*straightening up*] Ben, that funeral will be massive! They'll come from Maine, Massachusetts, Vermont, New Hampshire! All the old-timers with the strange license plates—that boy will be thunder-struck, Ben, because he never realized—I am known! Rhode Island, New York, New Jersey—I am known, Ben, and he'll see it with his eyes once and for all. He'll see what I am, Ben! He's in for a shock, that boy!

BEN [*coming down to the edge of the garden*] He'll call you a coward.

WILLY [*suddenly fearful*]   No, that would be terrible.

BEN   Yes. And a damned fool.

WILLY   No, no, he mustn't, I won't have that! [*He is broken and desperate.*]

BEN   He'll hate you, William.

>   [*The gay music of the Boys is heard.*]

WILLY   Oh, Ben, how do we get back to all the great times? Used to be so full of light, and comradeship, the sleigh-riding in winter, and the ruddiness on his cheeks. And always some kind of good news coming up, always something nice coming up ahead. And never even let me carry the valises in the house, and simonizing, simonizing that little red car! Why, why can't I give him something and not have him hate me?

BEN   Let me think about it. [*He glances at his watch.*] I still have a little time. Remarkable proposition, but you've got to be sure you're not making a fool of yourself.

>   [BEN *drifts off upstage and goes out of sight.* BIFF *comes down from the left.*]

WILLY [*suddenly conscious of* BIFF, *turns and looks up at him, then begins picking up the packages of seeds in confusion*]   Where the hell is that seed? [*indignantly*] You can't see nothing out here! They boxed in the whole goddam neighborhood!

BIFF   There are people all around here. Don't you realize that?

WILLY   I'm busy. Don't bother me.

BIFF [*taking the hoe from* WILLY]   I'm saying good-by to you, Pop. [WILLY *looks at him, silent, unable to move.*] I'm not coming back any more.

WILLY   You're not going to see Oliver tomorrow?

BIFF   I've got no appointment, Dad.

WILLY   He put his arm around you, and you've got no appointment?

BIFF   Pop, get this now, will you? Everytime I've left it's been a fight that sent me out of here. Today I realized something about myself and I tried to explain it to you and I—I think I'm just not smart enough to make any sense out of it for you. To hell with whose fault it is or anything like that. [*He takes* WILLY's *arm.*] Let's just wrap it up, heh? Come on in, we'll tell Mom. [*He gently tries to pull* WILLY *to left.*]

WILLY [*frozen, immobile, with guilt in his voice*]   No, I don't want to see her.

BIFF   Come on! [*He pulls again, and* WILLY *tries to pull away.*]

WILLY [*highly nervous*]   No, no, I don't want to see her.

BIFF [*tries to look into* WILLY's *face, as if to find the answer there*]   Why don't you want to see her?

WILLY [*more harshly now*]   Don't bother me, will you?

BIFF   What do you mean, you don't want to see her? You don't want them calling you yellow, do you? This isn't your fault; it's me, I'm a bum. Now come inside! [WILLY *strains to get away.*] Did you hear what I said to you?

>   [WILLY *pulls away and quickly goes by himself into the house.* BIFF *follows.*]

LINDA [*to* WILLY]   Did you plant, dear?

BIFF [*at the door, to* LINDA]   All right, we had it out. I'm going and I'm not writing any more.

LINDA [*going to* WILLY *in the kitchen*]   I think that's the best way, dear. 'Cause there's no use drawing it out, you'll just never get along.

[WILLY *doesn't respond.*]

BIFF People ask where I am and what I'm doing, you don't know, and you don't care. That way it'll be off your mind and you can start brightening up again. All right? That clears it, doesn't it? [WILLY *is silent, and* BIFF *goes to him.*] You gonna wish me luck, scout? [*He extends his hand.*] What do you say?

LINDA Shake his hand, Willy.

WILLY [*turning to her, seething with hurt*] There's no necessity to mention the pen at all, y'know.

BIFF [*gently*] I've got no appointment, Dad.

WILLY [*erupting fiercely*] He put his arm around . . . ?

BIFF Dad, you're never going to see what I am, so what's the use of arguing? If I strike oil I'll send you a check. Meantime forget I'm alive.

WILLY [*to* LINDA] Spite, see?

BIFF Shake hands, Dad.

WILLY Not my hand.

BIFF I was hoping not to go this way.

WILLY Well, this is the way you're going. Good-by.

[BIFF *looks at him a moment, then turns sharply and goes to the stairs.*]

WILLY [*stops him with*] May you rot in hell if you leave this house!

BIFF [*turning*] Exactly what is it that you want from me?

WILLY I want you to know, on the train, in the mountains, in the valleys, wherever you go, that you cut down your life for spite!

BIFF No, no.

WILLY Spite, spite, is the word of your undoing! And when you're down and out, remember what did it. When you're rotting somewhere beside the railroad tracks, remember, and don't you dare blame it on me!

BIFF I'm not blaming it on you!

WILLY I won't take the rap for this, you hear?

[HAPPY *comes down the stairs and stands on the bottom step, watching.*]

BIFF That's just what I'm telling you!

WILLY [*sinking into a chair at the table, with full accusation*] You're trying to put a knife in me—don't think I don't know what you're doing!

BIFF All right, phony! Then let's lay it on the line. [*He whips the rubber tube out of his pocket and puts it on the table.*]

HAPPY You crazy—

LINDA Biff! [*She moves to grab the hose, but* BIFF *holds it down with his hand.*]

BIFF Leave it there! Don't move it!

WILLY [*not looking at it*] What is that?

BIFF You know goddam well what that is.

WILLY [*caged, wanting to escape*] I never saw that.

BIFF You saw it. The mice didn't bring it into the cellar! What is this supposed to do, make a hero out of you? This supposed to make me sorry for you?

WILLY Never heard of it.

BIFF There'll be no pity for you, you hear it? No pity!

WILLY [*to* LINDA] You hear the spite!

BIFF No, you're going to hear the truth—what you are and what I am!

LINDA Stop it!

WILLY   Spite!

HAPPY [*coming down toward* BIFF]   You cut it now!

BIFF [*to* HAPPY]   The man don't know who we are! The man is gonna know!
[*to* WILLY] We never told the truth for ten minutes in this house!

HAPPY   We always told the truth!

BIFF [*turning on him*]   You big blow, are you the assistant buyer? You're
one of the two assistants to the assistant, aren't you?

HAPPY   Well, I'm practically—

BIFF   You're practically full of it! We all are! And I'm through with it. [*to*
WILLY] Now hear this, Willy, this is me.

WILLY   I know you!

BIFF   You know why I had no address for three months? I stole a suit in
Kansas City and I was in jail. [*to* LINDA, *who is sobbing*] Stop crying. I'm
through with it.

[LINDA *turns away from them, her hands covering her face.*]

WILLY   I suppose that's my fault!

BIFF   I stole myself out of every good job since high school!

WILLY   And whose fault is that?

BIFF   And I never got anywhere because you blew me so full of hot air I
could never stand taking orders from anybody! That's whose fault it is!

WILLY   I hear that!

LINDA   Don't, Biff!

BIFF   It's goddam time you heard that! I had to be boss big shot in two
weeks, and I'm through with it!

WILLY   Then hang yourself! For spite, hang yourself!

BIFF   No! Nobody's hanging himself, Willy! I ran down eleven flights with
a pen in my hand today. And suddenly I stopped, you hear me? And in
the middle of that office building, do you hear this? I stopped in the
middle of that building and I saw—the sky. I saw the things that I love
in this world. The work and the food and time to sit and smoke. And I
looked at the pen and said to myself, what the hell am I grabbing this
for? Why am I trying to become what I don't want to be? What am I
doing in an office, making a contemptuous, begging fool of myself, when
all I want is out there, waiting for me the minute I say I know who I am!
Why can't I say that, Willy? [*He tries to make* WILLY *face him, but* WILLY
pulls away and moves to the left.]

WILLY [*with hatred, threateningly*]   The door of your life is wide open!

BIFF   Pop! I'm a dime a dozen, and so are you!

WILLY [*turning on him now in an uncontrolled outburst*]   I am not a dime
a dozen! I am Willy Loman, and you are Biff Loman!

[BIFF *starts for* WILLY, *but is blocked by* HAPPY. *In his fury,* BIFF *seems on
the verge of attacking his father.*]

BIFF   I am not a leader of men, Willy, and neither are you. You were never
anything but a hard-working drummer who landed in the ash can like all
the rest of them! I'm one dollar an hour, Willy! I tried seven states and
couldn't raise it. A buck an hour! Do you gather my meaning? I'm not
bringing home any prizes any more, and you're going to stop waiting for
me to bring them home!

WILLY [*directly to* BIFF]   You vengeful, spiteful mut!

[BIFF *breaks from* HAPPY. WILLY, *in fright, starts up the stairs.* BIFF *grabs
him.*]

BIFF [*at the peak of his fury*]   Pop, I'm nothing! I'm nothing, Pop. Can't you understand that? There's no spite in it any more. I'm just what I am, that's all.

[BIFF's *fury has spent itself, and he breaks down, sobbing, holding on to* WILLY, *who dumbly fumbles for* BIFF's *face.*]

WILLY [*astonished*]   What're you doing? What're you doing? [*to* LINDA] Why is he crying?

BIFF [*crying, broken*]   Will you let me go, for Christ's sake? Will you take that phony dream and burn it before something happens? [*Struggling to contain himself, he pulls away and moves to the stairs.*] I'll go in the morning. Put him—put him to bed. [*Exhausted,* BIFF *moves up the stairs to his room.*]

WILLY [*after a long pause, astonished, elevated*]   Isn't that—isn't that remarkable? Biff—he likes me!

LINDA   He loves you, Willy!

HAPPY [*deeply moved*]   Always did, Pop.

WILLY   Oh, Biff! [*staring wildly*]   He cried! Cried to me. [*He is choking with his love, and now cries out his promise.*] That boy—that boy is going to be magnificent!

[BEN *appears in the light just outside the kitchen.*]

BEN   Yes, outstanding, with twenty thousand behind him.

LINDA [*sensing the racing of his mind, fearfully, carefully*]   Now come to bed, Willy. It's all settled now.

WILLY [*finding it difficult not to rush out of the house*]   Yes, we'll sleep. Come on. Go to sleep, Hap.

BEN   And it does take a great kind of a man to crack the jungle.

[*In accents of dread,* BEN's *idyllic music starts up.*]

HAPPY [*his arm around* LINDA]   I'm getting married, Pop, don't forget it. I'm changing everything. I'm gonna run that department before the year is up. You'll see, Mom. [*He kisses her.*]

BEN   The jungle is dark but full of diamonds, Willy.

[WILLY *turns, moves, listening to* BEN.]

LINDA   Be good. You're both good boys, just act that way, that's all.

HAPPY   'Night, Pop. [*He goes upstairs.*]

LINDA [*to* WILLY]   Come, dear.

BEN [*with greater force*]   One must go in to fetch a diamond out.

WILLY [*to* LINDA, *as he moves slowly along the edge of the kitchen, toward the door*]   I just want to get settled down, Linda. Let me sit alone for a little.

LINDA [*almost uttering her fear*]   I want you upstairs.

WILLY [*taking her in his arms*]   In a few minutes, Linda. I couldn't sleep right now. Go on, you look awful tired. [*He kisses her.*]

BEN   Not like an appointment at all. A diamond is rough and hard to the touch.

WILLY   Go on now. I'll be right up.

LINDA   I think this is the only way, Willy.

WILLY   Sure, it's the best thing.

BEN   Best thing!

WILLY   The only way. Everything is gonna be—go on, kid, get to bed. You look so tired.

LINDA   Come right up.

WILLY   Two minutes.

[LINDA *goes into the living-room, then reappears in her bedroom.* WILLY *moves just outside the kitchen door.*]

WILLY Loves me. [*wonderingly*] Always loved me. Isn't that a remarkable thing? Ben, he'll worship me for it!

BEN [*with promise*] It's dark there, but full of diamonds.

WILLY Can you imagine that magnificence with twenty thousand dollars in his pocket?

LINDA [*calling from her room*] Willy! Come up!

WILLY [*calling into the kitchen*] Yes! Yes. Coming! It's very smart, you realize that, don't you, sweetheart? Even Ben sees it. I gotta go, baby. 'By! 'By! [*going over to* BEN, *almost dancing*] Imagine? When the mail comes he'll be ahead of Bernard again!

BEN A perfect proposition all around.

WILLY Did you see how he cried to me? Oh, if I could kiss him, Ben!

BEN Time, William, time!

WILLY Oh, Ben, I always knew one way or another we were gonna make it, Biff and I!

BEN [*looking at his watch*] The boat. We'll be late. [*He moves slowly off into the darkness.*]

WILLY [*elegiacally, turning to the house*] Now when you kick off, boy, I want a seventy-yard boot, and get right down the field under the ball, and when you hit, hit low and hit hard, because it's important, boy. [*He swings around and faces the audience.*] There's all kinds of important people in the stands, and the first thing you know . . . [*suddenly realizing he is alone*] Ben! Ben, where do I . . . ? [*He makes a sudden movement of search.*] Ben, how do I . . . ?

LINDA [*calling*] Willy, you coming up?

WILLY [*uttering a gasp of fear, whirling about as if to quiet her*] Sh! [*He turns around as if to find his way; sounds, faces, voices, seem to be swarming in upon him and he flicks at them, crying,*] Sh! Sh! [*Suddenly music, faint and high, stops him. It rises in intensity, almost to an unbearable scream. He goes up and down on his toes, and rushes off around the house.*] Shhh!

LINDA Willy?

[*There is no answer.* LINDA *waits.* BIFF *gets up off his bed. He is still in his clothes.* HAPPY *sits up.* BIFF *stands listening.*]

LINDA [*with real fear*] Willy, answer me! Willy!

[*There is the sound of a car starting and moving away at full speed.*]

LINDA No!

BIFF [*rushing down the stairs*] Pop!

[*As the car speeds off, the music crashes down in a frenzy of sound, which becomes the soft pulsation of a single cello string.* BIFF *slowly returns to his bedroom. He and* HAPPY *gravely don their jackets.* LINDA *slowly walks out of her room. The music has developed into a dead march. The leaves of day are appearing over everything.* CHARLEY *and* BERNARD *somberly dressed, appear and knock on the kitchen door.* BIFF *and* HAPPY *slowly descend the stairs to the kitchen as* CHARLEY *and* BERNARD *enter. All stop a moment when* LINDA, *in clothes of mourning, bearing a little bunch of roses, comes through the draped doorway into the kitchen. She goes to* CHARLEY *and takes his arm. Now all move toward the audience, through the wall-line of the kitchen. At the limit of the apron,* LINDA *lays down the flowers, kneels, and sits back on her heels. All stare down at the grave.*]

Requiem

CHARLEY   It's getting dark, Linda.
[LINDA *doesn't react. She stares at the grave.*]
BIFF   How about it, Mom? Better get some rest, heh? They'll be closing the gate soon.
[LINDA *makes no move. Pause.*]
HAPPY [*deeply angered*]   He had no right to do that. There was no necessity for it. We would've helped him.
CHARLEY [*grunting*]   Hmmm.
BIFF   Come along, Mom.
LINDA   Why didn't anybody come?
CHARLEY   It was a very nice funeral.
LINDA   But where are all the people he knew? Maybe they blame him.
CHARLEY   Naa. It's a rough world, Linda. They wouldn't blame him.
LINDA   I can't understand it. At this time especially. First time in thirty-five years we were just about free and clear. He only needed a little salary. He was even finished with the dentist.
CHARLEY   No man only needs a little salary.
LINDA   I can't understand it.
BIFF   There were a lot of nice days. When he'd come home from a trip; or on Sundays, making the stoop; finishing the cellar; putting on the new porch; when he built the extra bathroom; and put up the garage. You know something, Charley, there's more of him in that front stoop than in all the sales he ever made.
CHARLEY   Yeah. He was a happy man with a batch of cement.
LINDA   He was so wonderful with his hands.
BIFF   He had the wrong dreams. All, all, wrong.
HAPPY [*almost ready to fight* BIFF]   Don't say that!
BIFF   He never knew who he was.
CHARLEY [*stopping* HAPPY's *movement and reply. To* BIFF]   Nobody dast blame this man. You don't understand: Willy was a salesman. And for a salesman, there is no rock bottom to the life. He don't put a bolt to a nut, he don't tell you the law or give you medicine. He's a man way out there in the blue, riding on a smile and a shoeshine. And when they start not smiling back—that's an earthquake. And then you get yourself a couple of spots on your hat, and you're finished. Nobody dast blame this man. A salesman is got to dream, boy. It comes with the territory.
BIFF   Charley, the man didn't know who he was.
HAPPY [*infuriated*]   Don't say that!
BIFF   Why don't you come with me, Happy?
HAPPY   I'm not licked that easily. I'm staying right in this city, and I'm gonna beat this racket! [*He looks at* BIFF, *his chin set.*] The Loman Brothers!
BIFF   I know who I am, kid.
HAPPY   All right, boy. I'm gonna show you and everybody else that Willy Loman did not die in vain. He had a good dream. It's the only dream you

can have—to come out number-one man. He fought it out here, and this is where I'm gonna win it for him.

BIFF [*with a hopeless glance at* HAPPY, *bends toward his mother*] Let's go, Mom.

LINDA I'll be with you in a minute. Go on, Charley. [*He hesitates.*] I want to, just for a minute. I never had a chance to say good-by.

[CHARLEY *moves away, followed by* HAPPY. BIFF *remains a slight distance up and left of* LINDA. *She sits there, summoning herself. The flute begins, not far away, playing behind her speech.*]

LINDA Forgive me, dear. I can't cry. I don't know what it is, but I can't cry. I don't understand it. Why did you ever do that? Help me, Willy, I can't cry. It seems to me that you're just on another trip. I keep expecting you. Willy, dear, I can't cry. Why did you do it? I search and search and I search, and I can't understand it, Willy. I made the last payment on the house today. Today, dear. And there'll be nobody home. [*A sob rises in her throat.*] We're free and clear. [*Sobbing more fully, released*] We're free. [BIFF *comes slowly toward her.*] We're free . . . We're free . . .

[BIFF *lifts her to her feet and moves out up right with her in his arms.* LINDA *sobs quietly.* BERNARD *and* CHARLEY *come together and follow them, followed by* HAPPY. *Only the music of the flute is left on the darkening stage as over the house the hard towers of the apartment buildings rise into sharp focus, and*]

CURTAIN

1949

GRACE PALEY
b. 1922

"A Conversation with My Father" is not Grace Paley's only story about a daughter's visit with an elderly, terminally ill father. Like other repeated situations in her work, such visits are part of the way this daughter, a short story writer much like Paley herself, uses dialogues with a traditionalist parent to explore innovative issues in her literary art. Unlike some of her contemporaries, whose concern with the making of fiction overshadows the situations such stories would otherwise convey, Paley always directs her imaginative explanations to realistic events, events in which larger social and moral issues reinforce the artistic points she wishes to make. Her ability to adapt nontraditional techniques into realistic short stories makes her accessible to a readership otherwise unfriendly to the aesthetic solipsism of self-exploratory fiction (or "metafiction" as it has come to be called).

That Paley's protagonist talks with her father rather than simply writing about him indicates an important characteristic: in such narratives the author does not wish to present a lecture (though figures in her stories sometimes give them) but rather to achieve an understanding through dialogue. This debative quality is evident in the stories in her first collection, *The Little Disturbances of Man* (1959), some of which draw on situations first encountered when adapting to marriage and family life in the difficult circumstances of an army camp. By the time of *Enormous Changes at the Last Minute* (1974) Paley develops her most noteworthy theme, that of women (often single mothers) building satisfactory relationships with the world around them by talking with each other (and sometimes to themselves). The title story from this second collection also shows Paley expanding her language to include an almost poetic phraseology whose facility with metaphors and similes makes much of her narrative action happen directly on the page. Here the same father is recalled as a child first seeing the American flag, then as a young immigrant taking advantage of what that symbol represents: "Under its protection and working like a horse, he'd read Dickens, gone to medical school, and shot like a surface-to-air missile right into the middle class." By choosing a comparison to current military technology that erupts from the sentence's quainter, almost century-old references, Paley invites her reader to be startled by the same realization that has motivated her to write.

Grace Paley was born in New York City, the child of Russian Jewish immigrants from Ukraine. She attended Hunter College, but graduated from the Merchants and Bankers Business and Secretarial School. Married during college, she had two children and then was later divorced, not remarrying until 1972. During the 1950s she became an activist for social issues, first working to close Washington Square (in her Greenwich Village neighborhood) to traffic, later protesting the Vietnam War; in 1978 she was arrested on the White House lawn in a demonstration against nuclear weapons. The success of *Enormous Changes at the Last Minute* drew her to the attention of other writers, and throughout the 1970s and 1980s she was a regular participant on literary panels with innovative fictionalists such as Donald Barthelme and William H. Gass. Her third collection, *Later the Same Day*, continues her method of using metafictive techniques for writing otherwise realistic short stories. In the front matter of *Enormous Changes at the Last Minute*, where a disclaimer about correspondences between fact and fiction would customarily appear, she posts this warning: "Everyone in this book is imagined into life except the father. No matter what story he has to live in, he's my father, I. Goodside, M.D., artist, and storyteller."

In addition to her fiction, Paley has also authored poetry and direct social commentary. Especially noteworthy is her essay from the September 1975 issue of *Ms.* magazine, "Other People's Children," objecting to the massive and hurried evacuation of South Vietnamese children during the Vietnam War's last days on the grounds that mothers' rights and interests were grossly violated.

The text is from *Enormous Changes at the Last Minute* (1974).

A Conversation with My Father

My father is eighty-six years old and in bed. His heart, that bloody motor, is equally old and will not do certain jobs any more. It still floods his head with brainy light. But it won't let his legs carry the weight of his body around the house. Despite my metaphors, his muscle failure is not due to his old heart, he says, but to a potassium shortage. Sitting on one pillow, leaning on three, he offers last-minute advice and makes a request.

"I would like you to write a simple story just once more," he says, "the kind de Maupassant wrote, or Chekhov,[1] the kind you used to write. Just recognizable people and then write down what happened to them next."

I say, "Yes, why not? That's possible." I want to please him, though I don't

---

1. Anton Chekhov (1860–1904), Russian dramatist and story writer, whose characters often discuss moral nuances at length. Guy de Maupassant (1850–1893), French author of well-made sentimental stories and novels.

remember writing that way. I *would* like to try to tell such a story, if he means the kind that begins: "There was a woman . . ." followed by plot, the absolute line between two points which I've always despised. Not for literary reasons, but because it takes all hope away. Everyone, real or invented, deserves the open destiny of life.

Finally I thought of a story that had been happening for a couple of years right across the street. I wrote it down, then read it aloud. "Pa," I said, "how about this? Do you mean something like this?"

> Once in my time there was a woman and she had a son. They lived nicely, in a small apartment in Manhattan. This boy at about fifteen became a junkie, which is not unusual in our neighborhood. In order to maintain her close friendship with him, she became a junkie too. She said it was part of the youth culture, with which she felt very much at home. After a while, for a number of reasons, the boy gave it all up and left the city and his mother in disgust. Hopeless and alone, she grieved. We all visit her.

"O.K., Pa, that's it," I said, "an unadorned and miserable tale."

"But that's not what I mean," my father said. "You misunderstood me on purpose. You know there's a lot more to it. You know that. You left everything out. Turgenev[2] wouldn't do that. Chekhov wouldn't do that. There are in fact Russian writers you never heard of, you don't have an inkling of, as good as anyone, who can write a plain ordinary story, who would not leave out what you have left out. I object not to facts but to people sitting in trees talking senselessly, voices from who knows where . . ."

"Forget that one, Pa, what have I left out now? In this one?"

"Her looks, for instance."

"Oh. Quite handsome, I think. Yes."

"Her hair?"

"Dark, with heavy braids, as though she were a girl or a foreigner."

"What were her parents like, her stock? That she became such a person. It's interesting, you know."

"From out of town. Professional people. The first to be divorced in their county. How's that? Enough?" I asked.

"With you, it's all a joke," he said. "What about the boy's father? Why didn't you mention him? Who was he? Or was the boy born out of wedlock?"

"Yes," I said. "He was born out of wedlock."

"For Godsakes, doesn't anyone in your stories get married? Doesn't anyone have the time to run down to City Hall before they jump into bed?"

"No," I said. "In real life, yes. But in my stories, no."

"Why do you answer me like that?"

"Oh, Pa, this is a simple story about a smart woman who came to N.Y.C.[3] full of interest love trust excitement very up to date, and about her son, what a hard time she had in this world. Married or not, it's of small consequence."

"It is of great consequence," he said.

"O.K.," I said.

"O.K. O.K. yourself," he said, "but listen. I believe you that she's good-looking, but I don't think she was so smart."

---

2. Ivan Turgenev (1818–1883), Russian novelist, noted for his tragic vision.   3. I.e., New York City.

"That's true," I said. "Actually that's the trouble with stories. People start out fantastic. You think they are extraordinary, but it turns out as the work goes along, they're just average with a good education. Sometimes the other way around, the person's a kind of dumb innocent, but he outwits you and you can't even think of an ending good enough."

"What do you do then?" he asked. He had been a doctor for a couple of decades and then an artist for a couple of decades and he's still interested in details, craft, technique.

"Well, you just have to let the story lie around till some agreement can be reached between you and the stubborn hero."

"Aren't you talking silly, now?" he asked. "Start again," he said. "It so happens I'm not going out this evening. Tell the story again. See what you can do this time."

"O.K.," I said. "But it's not a five-minute job." Second attempt:

> Once, across the street from us, there was a fine handsome woman, our neighbor. She had a son whom she loved because she'd known him since birth (in helpless chubby infancy, and in the wrestling, hugging ages, seven to ten, as well as earlier and later). This boy, when he fell into the fist of adolescence, became a junkie. He was not a hopeless one. He was in fact hopeful, an ideologue and successful converter. With his busy brilliance, he wrote persuasive articles for his high-school newspaper. Seeking a wider audience, using important connections, he drummed into Lower Manhattan newsstand distribution a periodical called *Oh! Golden Horse!*
>
> In order to keep him from feeling guilty (because guilt is the stony heart of nine tenths of all clinically diagnosed cancers in America today, she said), and because she had always believed in giving bad habits room at home where one could keep an eye on them, she too became a junkie. Her kitchen was famous for a while—a center for intellectual addicts who knew what they were doing. A few felt artistic like Coleridge and others were scientific and revolutionary like Leary.[4] Although she was often high herself, certain good mothering reflexes remained, and she saw to it that there was lots of orange juice around and honey and milk and vitamin pills. However, she never cooked anything but chili, and that no more than once a week. She explained, when we talked to her, seriously, with neighborly concern, that it was her part in the youth culture and she would rather be with the young, it was an honor, than with her own generation.
>
> One week, while nodding through an Antonioni[5] film, this boy was severely jabbed by the elbow of a stern and proselytizing girl, sitting beside him. She offered immediate apricots and nuts for his sugar level, spoke to him sharply, and took him home.
>
> She had heard of him and his work and she herself published, edited, and wrote a competitive journal called *Man Does Live By Bread Alone*. In the organic heat of her continuous presence he could not help but become interested once more in his muscles, his arteries, and nerve

4. Timothy Leary (1920–1996), psychologist who in the 1960s encouraged experimentation with hallucinogenic drugs. Samuel Taylor Coleridge (1772–1834), English poet whose *Kubla Khan* was written under the influence of opium.
5. Michelangelo Antonioni (b. 1912), Italian filmmaker known for his intellectual style.

connections. In fact he began to love them, treasure them, praise them with funny little songs in *Man Does Live* . . .

> *the fingers of my flesh transcend*
> *my transcendental soul*
> *the tightness in my shoulders end*
> *my teeth have made me whole*

To the mouth of his head (that glory of will and determination) he brought hard apples, nuts, wheat germ, and soybean oil. He said to his old friends, from now on, I guess I'll keep my wits about me. I'm going on the natch. He said he was about to begin a spiritual deep-breathing journey. How about you too, Mom? he asked kindly.

His conversion was so radiant, splendid, that neighborhood kids his age began to say that he had never been a real addict at all, only a journalist along for the smell of the story. The mother tried several times to give up what had become without her son and his friends a lonely habit. This effort only brought it to supportable levels. The boy and his girl took their electronic mimeograph and moved to the bushy edge of another borough. They were very strict. They said they would not see her again until she had been off drugs for sixty days.

At home alone in the evening, weeping, the mother read and reread the seven issues of *Oh! Golden Horse!* They seemed to her as truthful as ever. We often crossed the street to visit and console. But if we mentioned any of our children who were at college or in the hospital or dropouts at home, she would cry out, My baby! My baby! and burst into terrible, face-scarring, time-consuming tears. The End.

First my father was silent, then he said, "Number One: You have a nice sense of humor. Number Two: I see you can't tell a plain story. So don't waste time." Then he said sadly, "Number Three: I suppose that means she was alone, she was left like that, his mother. Alone. Probably sick?"

I said, "Yes."

"Poor woman. Poor girl, to be born in a time of fools to live among fools. The end. The end. You were right to put that down. The end."

I didn't want to argue, but I had to say, "Well, it is not necessarily the end, Pa."

"Yes," he said, "what a tragedy. The end of a person."

"No, Pa," I begged him. "It doesn't have to be. She's only about forty. She could be a hundred different things in this world as time goes on. A teacher or a social worker. An ex-junkie! Sometimes it's better than having a master's in education."

"Jokes," he said. "As a writer that's your main trouble. You don't want to recognize it. Tragedy! Plain tragedy! Historical tragedy! No hope. The end."

"Oh, Pa," I said. "She could change."

"In your own life, too, you have to look it in the face."

He took a couple of nitroglycerin. "Turn to five," he said, pointing to the dial on the oxygen tank. He inserted the tubes into his nostrils and breathed deep. He closed his eyes and said, "No."

I had promised the family to always let him have the last word when arguing, but in this case I had a different responsibility. That woman lives across the street. She's my knowledge and my invention. I'm sorry for her. I'm not going to leave her there in that house crying. (Actually neither would Life, which unlike me has no pity.)

Therefore: She did change. Of course her son never came home again. But right now, she's the receptionist in a storefront community clinic in the East Village.[6] Most of the customers are young people, some old friends. The head doctor has said to her, "If we only had three people in this clinic with your experiences . . ."

"The doctor said that?" My father took the oxygen tubes out of his nostrils and said, "Jokes. Jokes again."

"No, Pa, it could really happen that way, it's a funny world nowadays."

"No, he said. "Truth first. She will slide back. A person must have character. She does not."

"No, Pa," I said. "That's it. She's got a job. Forget it. She's in that storefront working."

"How long will it be?" he asked. "Tragedy! You too. When will you look it in the face?"

1974

---

6. Immigrant neighborhood in lower Manhattan that in the 1960s became home to anti-establishment youth counterculture.

KURT VONNEGUT
b. 1922

As a counterculture hero of the turbulent 1960s and a best-selling author among readers of popular fiction in the three decades afterwards, Kurt Vonnegut is at once more traditional and more complicated than his enthusiasts might believe. To a generation of young people who felt their country had forsaken them, he offered examples of common decency and cultural idealism as basic as a grade-school civics lesson. For a broader readership who felt conventional fiction was inadequate to express the way their lives had been disrupted by the era's radical social changes, he wrote novels structured in more pertinently contemporary terms, bereft of such unifying devices as conclusive characterization and chronologically organized plots. His most famous novel, *Slaughterhouse-Five* (1969), takes as its organizing incident the Allied fire-bombing of the German city of Dresden late in World War II, as witnessed by the American prisoner of war Billy Pilgrim. Yet despite its origins in World War II, the manner of its telling is much more akin to the writing of Americans of the time who were trying to understand the Vietnam War. Both *Slaughterhouse-Five* and the war in Southeast Asia abjured the certainties of an identifiable beginning, middle, and end; both presented a mesmerizing sense of confused, apparently directionless present, with no sense of totalization or conclusiveness. Together, this World War II novel and the later war within which it was written speak for the unsettling nature of the American 1960s. Yet, this unconventional structure is paired with the language of American vernacular (much in the manner of Vonnegut's hero, Mark Twain). Where more elevated speech would obscure his point, this author speaks plainly and simply, drawing his words, phrases, and inflections from the American middle class and its common experiences of life.

Vonnegut was born in Indianapolis, Indiana, to a family prominent in both business and the arts. During the Great Depression of the 1930s, the sensitive, well-read teenager saw his mother's inherited wealth dissipated, his father's profession as an architect crumble for lack of work, and his extended family begin scattering around the country in search of new careers. Service as a World War II infantryman taught not only how politics reshapes the world but how science (Vonnegut had been studying biochemistry in college before enlistment) could be used to create effects not always beneficial to humankind but as destructive as the Dresden firestorm. Working as a publicist for the General Electric Corporation after the war, the author learned firsthand about the strategies for managing the lifestyles of millions. In short, before writing his first story in 1950 Kurt Vonnegut had shared many formative experiences of his generation. Reworking those experiences would yield fictions and public statements that helped his fellow Americans adjust to a reinvented postwar world.

Vonnegut's advice, like Mark Twain's, would be unapologetically lowbrow. Part of each writer's appeal is that he pokes holes in the pseudo-sophistications of supposedly more serious approaches, and in "Fates Worse Than Death" (printed here) Vonnegut begins by emphasizing that the self-consciously highbrow New Yorker magazine has never published his work. Indeed, his short stories of the 1950s were written for the immensely more general readership of Collier's and The Saturday Evening Post. These narratives (collected in 1968 as Welcome to the Monkey House) deflate the pretensions of wealth, expertise, and influence with demonstrations of middle-class values and common sense. At the same time, Vonnegut was writing novels in formats borrowed from popular subgenres: science fiction dystopia for Player Piano (1952), space opera in The Sirens of Titan (1959), the spy thriller as model for Mother Night (1961), scientific apocalypse and intrigue for Cat's Cradle (1963), and a prince-and-the-pauper critique of riches in God Bless You, Mr. Rosewater (1965). Each work challenges the technical and thematic conventions of the novel, yet each time within the familiarity of a commonly available form.

In the middle 1960s, with his family magazine markets having gone out of business, Vonnegut began writing essays for popular magazines such as Esquire, McCall's, and the Ladies Home Journal. Reviewing The Random House Dictionary for the New York Times Book Review (October 30, 1966), he contrasted the assignment's linguistic complexity with his own shuffling, hands-in-pockets approach. As lexographers debated theories like prescriptive versus descriptive standards of language, for example, Vonnegut could just shrug and say that the former, "as nearly as I could tell, was like an honest cop, while descriptive was like a boozed-up war buddy from Mobile, Ala." In other essays the author would use similar self-effacing humor to undermine positions that used intellectual pretensions to support their points. To the over-enthusiasts for science fiction who try to include writers like Leo Tolstoy and Franz Kafka in their brotherhood, he objects that "it is as though I were to claim everybody of note belonged fundamentally to Delta Upsilon, my own lodge, incidentally, whether he knew it or not. Kafka would have made a desperately unhappy D. U." Thus a false analogy is transformed into a logical fallacy: that of the excluded middle, saying Kakfa is to science fiction not as science fiction is to Delta Upsilon, but as Kafka is to D. U. The argument is thus won by playing with the unquestioned standards of logic, overturning intellectual pretensions by the silliness of their own deductions.

With the success of Slaughterhouse-Five and the widespread appreciation of his essays and personal appearances, Kurt Vonnegut became much more a public spokesman. From his new home in New York City (where he moved in 1970 following nearly two decades of writing in obscurity on Cape Cod, Massachusetts) the author has written later novels such as Galápagos (1985), Hocus Pocus (1990), and Timequake (1997), works treating such large issues as the evolution and possible devolution of humankind and America's economic and social role at the end of the twentieth century. Vonnegut's challenges to the conventions of traditional fiction make him as innovative as any of the literary disruptionists of the postmodern era, yet he trusts in the honesty of plain and accurate statement. Hence his advice in "How to Write with Style," from his 1981 collection, *Palm Sunday:* "I myself find that I trust my writing most, and others seem to trust it most, when I sound like a person from Indianapolis, which I am."

The text is that of *Fates Worse Than Death* (1991).

Fates Worse Than Death

Lecture at St. John the Divine, NYC[1]
23 May 1982

Good morning,

This is a pretty small church, but I guess I have to start somewhere.

Actually, this is not my main line of work. Preaching in Cathedrals is just a hobby. I make up stories for a living. I get my ideas from dreams.

The wildest dream I have had so far is about *The New Yorker* magazine. In this dream, the magazine has published a three-part essay by Jonathan Schell,[2] which proves that life on Earth is about to end. I am supposed to go to the largest Gothic cathedral in the world, where all the people are waiting, and say something wonderful—right before a hydrogen bomb is dropped on the Empire State Building.

People as far away as Bridgeport will die instantly.

Here is how I interpret the dream: I consider myself an important writer, and I think *The New Yorker* should be ashamed that it has never published me.

•   •   •

I will speak today about the worst imaginable consequences of doing without hydrogen bombs. This should be a relief. I am sure you are sick and tired of hearing how all living things sizzle and pop inside a radioactive fireball. We have known that for more than a third of this century—ever since we dropped an atom bomb on the yellow people of Hiroshima. *They* certainly sizzled and popped.

After all is said and done, what was that sizzling and popping, despite the brilliant technology which caused it, but our old friend death? Let us not forget that Saint Joan of Arc[3] was made to sizzle and pop in old times with nothing more than firewood. She wound up dead. The people of Hiroshima wound up dead. Dead is dead.

Scientists, for all their creativity, will never discover a method for making people deader than dead. So if some of you are worried about being hydro-gen-bombed, you are merely fearing death. There is nothing new in that. If there weren't any hydrogen bombs, death would still be after you. And what is death but an absence of life? That's all it is. That is all it ever can be.

Death is nothing. What is all this fuss about?

•   •   •

1. One of the world's largest cathedrals, located at Amsterdam Avenue and 112th Street in New York City.
2. American journalist and essayist (b. 1943),

noted for the thoroughness of his research and commitment to larger implications.
3. French military leader and saint burned at the stake for witchcraft (1412–1431).

Let us "up the ante," as gamblers say. Let us talk about fates worse than death. When the Reverend Jim Jones saw that his followers in Guyana were facing fates worse than death, he gave them Kool-Aid laced with cyanide.[4] If our government sees that we are facing fates worse than death, it will shower our enemies with hydrogen bombs, and then we will be showered in turn. There will be plenty of Kool-Aid for everyone, in a manner of speaking, when the right time comes.

What will the right time look like?

I will not waste your time with trivial fates, which are only marginally worse than death. Suppose we were conquered by an enemy, for example, who didn't understand our wonderful economic system, and so Braniff Airlines and International Harvester and so on all went bust, and millions of Americans who wanted to work couldn't find any jobs anywhere. Or suppose we were conquered by an enemy who was too cheap to take good care of children and old people. Or suppose we were conquered by an enemy who wouldn't spend money on anything but weapons for World War Three. These are all tribulations we could live with, if we had to—although God forbid.

But suppose we foolishly got rid of our nuclear weapons, our Kool-Aid, and an enemy came over here and crucified us. Crucifixion was the most painful thing which the ancient Romans ever found to do to anyone. They knew as much about pain as we do about genocide. They sometimes crucified hundreds of people at one time. That is what they did to all the survivors of the army of Spartacus, which was composed mostly of escaped slaves. They crucified them all. There were several miles of crosses.

If we were up on crosses, with nails through our feet and hands, wouldn't we wish that we still had hydrogen bombs, so that life could be ended everywhere? Absolutely.

We know of one person who was crucified in olden times, who was supposedly as capable as we or the Russians are of ending life everywhere. But he chose to endure agony instead. All he said was, "Forgive them, Father—they know not what they do."

He let life go on, as awful as it was for him, because here we are, aren't we?

But he was a special case. It is unfair to use Jesus Christ as an exemplar of how much pain and humiliation we ordinary human beings should put up with before calling for the end of everything.

*   *   *

I don't believe that we *are* about to be crucified. No potential enemy we now face has anywhere near enough carpenters. Not even the Pentagon at budget time has mentioned crucifixion. I am sorry to have to put that idea into their heads. I will have only myself to blame if, a year from now, the Joint Chiefs of Staff testify under oath that we are on the brink of being crucified.

But what if they said, instead, that we would be enslaved if we did not appropriate enough money for weaponry? That could be true. Despite our world-wide reputation for sloppy workmanship, wouldn't some enemy get a kick out of forcing us into involuntary servitude, buying and selling us like so many household appliances or farm machines or inflatable erotic toys?

4. Mass suicide of an apocalyptic cult on November 18, 1978.

And slavery would surely be a fate worse than death. We can agree on that, I'm sure. We should send a message to the Pentagon: "If Americans are about to become enslaved, it is Kool-Aid Time."

They will know what we mean.

. . .

Of course, at Kool-Aid time all higher forms of life on Earth, not just us and our enemies, will be killed. Even those beautiful and fearless and utterly stupid sea birds, the blue-footed boobies of the Galapagos Islands,[5] will die, because we object to slavery.

I have seen those birds, by the way—up close. I could have unscrewed their heads, if I wanted to. I made a trip to the Galapagos Islands two months ago—in the company of, among other people, Paul Moore, the bishop of this very cathedral. That is the sort of company I keep these days—everything from bishops to blue-footed boobies. I have never seen a human slave, though. But my four great-grandfathers saw slaves. When they came to this country in search of justice and opportunity, there were millions of Americans who were slaves.

. . .

The equation which links a strong defence posture to not being enslaved is laid down in that stirring fight song, much heard lately, "Rule Britannia." I will sing the equation:

"Rule, Britannia, Britannia rule the waves—"

That, of course, is a poetic demand for a navy second to none. The next line explains why it is essential to have a navy that good:

"Britons never, never, never shall be slaves."

It may surprise some of you to learn what an old equation that is. The Scottish poet who wrote it, James Thomson, died in 1748—one quarter of a century before there was such a country as the United States of America. Thomson promised Britons that they would never be slaves at a time when the enslavement of persons with inferior weaponry was a respectable industry. Plenty of people were going to be slaves, and it would serve them right, too—but Britons would not be among them.

So that isn't really a very nice song. It is about not being humiliated which is all right. But it is also about humiliating others, which is not a moral thing to do. The humiliation of others should never be a national goal.

There is one poet who should have been ashamed of himself.

. . .

If the Soviet Union came over here and enslaved us, it wouldn't be the first time Americans were slaves. If we conquered the Russians and enslaved them, it wouldn't be the first time Russians were slaves.

And the last time Americans were slaves, and the last time Russians were slaves, they displayed astonishing spiritual strengths and resourcefulness. They were good at loving one another. They trusted God. They discovered in the simplest, most natural satisfactions, reasons to be glad to be alive.

5. Group of islands, belonging to Ecuador, in the Pacific Ocean, visited by the English naturalist Charles Darwin (1809–1882) in 1832 before he began research on natural selection as a principal force in the origin of species.

They were able to believe that better days were coming in the sweet by-and-by. And here is a fascinating statistic: they committed suicide less often than their masters did.

So Americans and Russians can both stand slavery, if they have to—and still want life to go on and on.

Could it be that slavery *isn't* a fate worse than death. After all, people are tough, you know? Maybe we shouldn't send that message to the Pentagon—about slavery and Kool-Aid time.

•   •   •

But suppose enemies came ashore in great numbers, because we lacked the means to stop them, and they pushed us out of our homes and off our ancestral lands, and into swamps and deserts. Suppose that they even tried to destroy our religion, telling us that our Great God Jehovah, or whatever we wanted to call Him, was as ridiculous as a piece of junk jewelry.

Again: this is a wringer millions of Americans have already been through—or are still going through. It is another catastrophe which Americans can endure, if they have to—and still, miraculously, maintain some measure of dignity, or self-respect.

As bad as life is for our Indians, they still like it better than death.

•   •   •

So I haven't had much luck, have I, in identifying fates worse than death. Crucifixion is the only clear winner so far, and we aren't about to be crucified. We aren't about to be enslaved, either—to be treated as white Americans used to treat black Americans. And no potential enemy that I have heard of wants to come over here to treat all of us the way we still treat American Indians.

What other fates worse than death could I name? Life without petroleum?

•   •   •

In melodramas of a century ago, a female's loss of virginity outside of holy wedlock was sometimes spoken as a fate worse than death. I hope that isn't what the Pentagon or the Kremlin has in mind—but you never know.

I would rather die for virginity than for petroleum, I think. It's more literary, somehow.

•   •   •

I may be blinding myself to the racist aspects of hydrogen bombs, whose only function is to end everything. Perhaps there are tribulations which *white* people should not be asked to tolerate. But the Russian slaves were white. The supposedly unenslavable Britons were enslaved by the Romans. Even proud Britons, if they were enslaved now, would have to say, "Here we go again." Armenians and Jews have certainly been treated hideously in modern as well as ancient times—and they have still wanted life to go on and on and on. About a third of our own white people were robbed and ruined and scorned after our Civil War. They still wanted life to go on and on and on.

•   •   •

Have there ever been large numbers of human beings of any sort who have not, despite everything, done everything they could to keep life going on and on and on?

Soldiers.

'Death before Dishonor' was the motto of several military formations during the Civil War—on both sides. It may be the motto of the Eighty-second Airborne Division[6] right now. A motto like that made a certain amount of sense, I suppose, when military death was what happened to the soldier on the right or the left of you—or in front of you—or in back of you. But military death now can easily mean the death of everything, including, as I have already said, the blue-footed boobies of the Galapagos Islands.

The webbed feet of those birds really are the brightest blue, by the way. When two blue-footed boobies begin a courtship, they show each other what beautiful, bright blue feet they have.

•   •   •

If you go to the Galapagos Islands, and see all the strange creatures, you are bound to think what Charles Darwin thought when he went there: How much time Nature has in which to accomplish simply anything. If we desolate this planet, Nature can get life going again. All it takes is a few million years or so, the wink of an eye to Nature.

Only humankind is running out of time.

My guess is that we will not disarm, even though we should, and that we really will blow up everything by and by. History shows that human beings are vicious enough to commit every imaginable atrocity, including the construction of factories whose only purpose was to kill people and burn them up.

It may be that we were put here on Earth to blow the place to smithereens. We may be Nature's way of creating new galaxies. We may be programmed to improve and improve our weapons, and to believe that death is better than dishonor.

And then, one day, as disarmament rallies are being held all over the planet, *ka-blooey!* A new Milky Way is born.

•   •   •

Perhaps we should be adoring instead of loathing our hydrogen bombs. They could be the eggs for new galaxies.

•   •   •

What can save us? Divine intervention, certainly—and this is the place to ask for it. We might pray to be rescued from our inventiveness, just as the dinosaurs may have prayed to be rescued from their size.

But the inventiveness which we so regret now may also be giving us, along with the rockets and warheads, the means to achieve what has hitherto been an impossibility, the unity of mankind. I am talking mainly about television sets.

Even in my own lifetime, it used to be necessary for a young soldier to get into fighting before he became disillusioned about war. His parents back

6. A highly effective paratroop assault unit of the U.S. Army, noted for its brilliant combat record.

home were equally ignorant, and believed him to be slaying monsters. But now, thanks to modern communications, the people of every industrialized nation are nauseated by war by the time they are ten years old. America's first generation of television viewers has gone to war and come home again—and we have never seen veterans like them before.

What makes the Vietnam veterans so somehow spooky? We could almost describe them as being 'unwholesomely mature'. They have *never* had illusions about war. They are the first soldiers in history who knew even in childhood, from having heard and seen so many pictures of actual and restaged battles, that war is meaningless butchery of ordinary people like themselves.

It used to be that veterans could shock their parents when they came home, as Ernest Hemingway[7] did, by announcing that everything about war was repulsive and stupid and dehumanizing. But the parents of our Vietnam veterans were disillusioned about war, too, many of them having seen it first hand, before their children ever went overseas. Thanks to modern communications, Americans of all ages were dead sick of war even before we went into Vietnam.

Thanks to modern communications, the poor, unlucky young people from the Soviet Union, now killing and dying in Afghanistan, were dead sick of war before they ever got there.

Thanks to modern communications, the same must be true of the poor, unlucky young people from Argentina and Great Britain, now killing and dying in the Falkland Islands.[8] *The New York Post* calls them 'Argies' and 'Brits'. Thanks to modern communications, we know that they are a good deal more marvelous and complicated than that, and that what is happening to them down there, on the rim of the Antarctic, is a lot more horrible and shameful than a soccer match.

*   *   *

When I was a boy it was unusual for an American, or a person of any nationality, for that matter, to know much about foreigners. Those who did were specialists—diplomats, explorers, journalists, anthropologists. And they usually knew a lot about just a few groups of foreigners, Eskimos, maybe, or Arabs, or what have you. To them, as to the schoolchildren of Indianapolis, large areas of the globe were *terra incognita*.

Now look what has happened. Thanks to modern communications, we have seen sights and heard sounds from virtually every square mile of the land mass on this planet. Millions of us have actually visited more exotic places than had many explorers during my childhood. Many of you have been to Timbuktu. Many of you have been to Katmandu. My dentist just got home from Fiji. He told me all about Fiji. If he had taken his fingers out of my mouth, I would have told him about the Galapagos Islands.

So we now know for *certain* that there are no potential human enemies anywhere who are anything but human beings almost exactly like ourselves. They need food. How amazing. They love their children. How amazing. They obey their leaders. How amazing. They think like their neighbors. How amazing.

---

7. American fiction writer (1899–1961).
8. At the time of this speech (1982), the former Soviet Union was attempting military suppression of the revolt in Afghanistan, and Great Britain was at war with Argentina over possession of the Falkland Islands in the south Atlantic.

Thanks to modern communications, we now have something we never had before: reason to mourn deeply the death or wounding of any human being on any side in any war.

.　　　.　　　.

It was because of rotten communications, of malicious, racist ignorance that we were able to celebrate the killing of almost all the inhabitants in Hiroshima, Japan, thirty-seven years ago. We thought they were vermin. They thought we were vermin. They would have clapped their little yellow hands with glee, and grinned with their crooked buck teeth, if they could have incinerated everybody in Kansas City, say.

Thanks to how much the people of the world now know about all the other people of the world, the fun of killing enemies has lost its zing. It has so lost its zing that no sane citizen of the Soviet Union, if we were to go to war with that society, would feel anything but horror if his country were to kill practically everybody in New York and Chicago and San Francisco. Killing enemies has so lost its zing, that no sane citizen of the United States would feel anything but horror if our country were to kill practically everybody in Moscow and Leningrad and Kiev.

Or in Nagasaki,[9] Japan, for that matter.

We have often heard it said that people would have to change, or we would go on having world wars. I bring you good news this morning: people have changed.

We aren't so ignorant and bloodthirsty any more.

.　　　.　　　.

I told you a crazy dream I had—about *The New Yorker* magazine and this cathedral. I will tell you a sane dream now.

I dreamed last night of our descendants a thousand years from now, which is to say all of humanity. If you are at all into reproduction, as was the Emperor Charlemagne,[1] you can pick up an awful lot of relatives in a thousand years. Every person in this cathedral who has a drop of white blood is a descendant of Charlemagne.

A thousand years from now, if there are still human beings on Earth, every one of those human beings will be descended from us—and from everyone who has chosen to reproduce.

In my dream, our descendants are numerous. Some of them are rich, some are poor, some are likable, some are insufferable.

I ask them how humanity, against all odds, managed to keep going for another millennium. They tell me that they and their ancestors did it by preferring life over death for themselves and others at every opportunity, even at the expense of being dishonored. They endured all sorts of insults and humiliations and disappointments without committing either suicide or murder. They are also the people who do the insulting and humiliating and disappointing.

I endear myself to them by suggesting a motto they might like to put on their belt buckles or tee-shirts or whatever. They aren't all hippies, by the way. They aren't all Americans, either. They aren't even all white people.

9. City destroyed by the second atomic bomb on August 9, 1945.

1. King of the Franks and Holy Roman Emperor (742–814).

I give them a quotation from that great 19th century moralist and robber baron, Jim Fisk, who may have contributed money to this cathedral.

Jim Fisk uttered his famous words after a particularly disgraceful episode having to do with the Erie Railroad. Fisk himself had no choice but to find himself contemptible. He thought this over, and then shrugged and said what we all must learn to say, if we want to go on living much longer:

"Nothing is lost save honor."

I thank you for your attention.

1982   1991

JAMES BALDWIN
1924–1987

James Baldwin was born in Harlem, the first of nine children. From his novel *Go Tell It on the Mountain* (1953) and his story "The Rockpile," we learn how extremely painful was the relationship between his father (actually his stepfather) and his eldest son. David Baldwin, son of a slave, was a lay preacher rigidly committed to a vengeful God who would eventually judge white people as they deserved; in the meantime, much of the vengeance was taken out on James. His father's "unlimited capacity for introspection and rancor," as the son later put it, must have had a profound effect on the sermonizing style Baldwin was to develop. Just as important was his conversion and resulting service as a preacher in his father's church, as we can see from both the rhythm and the message of his prose—which is very much a *spoken* prose.

Baldwin did well in school and, having received a hardship deferment from military service (his father was dying), began to attach himself to Greenwich Village, where he concentrated on the business of becoming a writer. In 1944 he met Richard Wright, at that time "the greatest black writer in the world for me," in whose early books Baldwin "found expressed, for the first time in my life, the sorrow, the rage, and the murderous bitterness which was eating up my life and the lives of those about me." Wright helped him win a Eugene Saxton fellowship, and in 1948, when Baldwin went to live in Paris, he was following in Wright's footsteps (Wright had become an expatriate to the same city a year earlier). It is perhaps for this reason that in his early essays written for *Partisan Review* and published in 1955 as *Notes of a Native Son* (with the title's explicit reference to Wright's novel) Baldwin dissociated himself from the image of American life found in Wright's "protest work" and, as Ralph Ellison was also doing, went about protesting in his own way.

As far as his novels are concerned, Baldwin's way involved a preoccupation with the intertwining of sexual with racial concerns, particularly in America. His interest in what it means to be black and homosexual in relation to white society is most fully and interestingly expressed in his long and somewhat ragged third novel, *Another Country* (1962). (He had previously written *Go Tell It on the Mountain*, and a second novel, *Giovanni's Room*, 1955, about a white expatriate in Paris and his male lover.) *Another Country* contains scenes full of lively detail and intelligent reflection, although it lacks—as do all his novels—a compelling design that draws the book together. In his novels Baldwin made slight use of the talents for irony and sly teasing he is master of in his essays; nor, unlike Ellison or Mailer, did he show much interest in stylistic experimentation. In his short stories collected in *Going to Meet the Man*

(1965), the racial terrorism of America as he perceived it made its own grotesque stylistic statement. The writer's challenge was to maintain steady control in the face of such atrocities that might otherwise disrupt the narrative's ability to contain such events.

His later novels, *Tell Me How Long the Train's Been Gone* (1968) and *Just above My Head* (1979), were overlong and tended toward the shapeless. Like Mailer, Baldwin risked advertising himself too strenuously and sometimes fell into stridency and sentimentality. Like Ellison, he experienced many pressures to be something more than just a writer, but he nevertheless produced a respectable series of novels and stories, even if no single fiction of his is comparable in breadth and daring to *Invisible Man*. There has surely been no black writer better able to imagine white experience, to speak in various tones of different kinds and behaviors of people or places other than his own. In its sensitivity to shades of discrimination and moral shape, and in its commitment—despite everything—to America, his voice was comparable in importance to that of any person of letters from recent decades, and tributes paid to him at his death were agreed on that fact.

The text is the title story from *Going to Meet the Man* (1965).

Going to Meet the Man

"What's the matter?" she asked.

"I don't know," he said, trying to laugh, "I guess I'm tired."

"You've been working too hard," she said. "I keep telling you."

"Well, goddammit, woman," he said, "it's not my fault!" He tried again; he wretchedly failed again. Then he just lay there, silent, angry, and helpless. Excitement filled him like a toothache, but it refused to enter his flesh. He stroked her breast. This was his wife. He could not ask her to do just a little thing for him, just to help him out, just for a little while, the way he could ask a nigger girl to do it. He lay there, and he sighed. The image of a black girl caused a distant excitement in him, like a far-away light; but, again, the excitement was more like pain; instead of forcing him to act, it made action impossible.

"Go to sleep," she said, gently, "you got a hard day tomorrow."

"Yeah," he said, and rolled over on his side, facing her, one hand still on one breast. "Goddamn the niggers. The black stinking coons. You'd think they'd learn. Wouldn't you think they'd learn? I mean, *wouldn't* you?"

"They going to be out there tomorrow," she said, and took his hand away, "get some sleep."

He lay there, one hand between his legs, staring at the frail sanctuary of his wife. A faint light came from the shutters; the moon was full. Two dogs, far away, were barking at each other, back and forth, insistently, as though they were agreeing to make an appointment. He heard a car coming north on the road and he half sat up, his hand reaching for his holster, which was on a chair near the bed, on top of his pants. The lights hit the shutters and seemed to travel across the room and then went out. The sound of the car slipped away, he heard it hit gravel, then heard it no more. Some liver-lipped students, probably, heading back to that college—but coming from where? His watch said it was two in the morning. They could be coming from anywhere, from out of state most likely, and they would be at the court-house tomorrow. The niggers were getting ready. Well, they would be ready, too.

He moaned. He wanted to let whatever was in him out; but it wouldn't come out. Goddamn! he said aloud, and turned again, on his side, away from Grace, staring at the shutters. He was a big, healthy man and he had never had any trouble sleeping. And he wasn't old enough yet to have any trouble getting it up—he was only forty-two. And he was a good man, a God-fearing man, he had tried to do his duty all his life, and he had been a deputy sheriff for several years. Nothing had ever bothered him before, certainly not getting it up. Sometimes, sure, like any other man, he knew that he wanted a little more spice than Grace could give him and he would drive over yonder and pick up a black piece or arrest her, it came to the same thing, but he couldn't do that now, no more. There was no telling what might happen once your ass was in the air. And they were low enough to kill a man then, too, every one of them, or the girl herself might do it, right while she was making believe you made her feel so good. The niggers. What had the good Lord Almighty had in mind when he made the niggers? Well. They were pretty good at that, all right. Damn. Damn. Goddamn.

This wasn't helping him to sleep. He turned again, toward Grace again, and moved close to her warm body. He felt something he had never felt before. He felt that he would like to hold her, hold her, hold her, and be buried in her like a child and never have to get up in the morning again and go downtown to face those faces, good Christ, they were ugly! and never have to enter that jail house again and smell that smell and hear that singing; never again feel that filthy, kinky, greasy hair under his hand, never again watch those black breasts leap against the leaping cattle prod, never hear those moans again or watch that blood run down or the fat lips split or the sealed eyes struggle open. They were animals, they were no better than animals, what could be done with people like that? Here they had been in a civilized country for years and they still lived like animals. Their houses were dark, with oil cloth or cardboard in the windows, the smell was enough to make you puke your guts out, and there they sat, a whole tribe, pumping out kids, it looked like, every damn five minutes, and laughing and talking and playing music like they didn't have a care in the world, and he reckoned they didn't, neither, and coming to the door, into the sunlight, just standing there, just looking foolish, not thinking of anything but just getting back to what they were doing, saying, Yes suh, Mr. Jesse. I surely will, Mr. Jesse. Fine weather, Mr. Jesse. Why, I thank you, Mr. Jesse. He had worked for a mail-order house for a while and it had been his job to collect the payments for the stuff they bought. They were too dumb to know that they were being cheated blind, but that was no skin off his ass—he was just supposed to do his job. They would be late—they didn't have the sense to put money aside; but it was easy to scare them, and he never really had any trouble. Hell, they all liked him, the kids used to smile when he came to the door. He gave them candy, sometimes, or chewing gum, and rubbed their rough bullet heads—maybe the candy should have been poisoned. Those kids were grown now. He had had trouble with one of them today.

"There was this nigger today," he said; and stopped; his voice sounded peculiar. He touched Grace. "You awake?" he asked. She mumbled something, impatiently, she was probably telling him to go to sleep. It was all right. He knew that he was not alone.

"What a funny time," he said, "to be thinking about a thing like that—you listening?" She mumbled something again. He rolled over on his back. "This nigger's one of the ringleaders. We had trouble with him before. We must have had him out there at the work farm three or four times. Well, Big Jim C. and some of the boys really had to whip that nigger's ass today." He looked over at Grace; he could not tell whether she was listening or not; and he was afraid to ask again. "They had this line you know, to register"—he laughed, but she did not—"and they wouldn't stay where Big Jim C. wanted them, no, they had to start blocking traffic all around the court house so couldn't nothing or nobody get through, and Big Jim C. told them to disperse and they wouldn't move, they just kept up that singing, and Big Jim C. figured that the others would move if this nigger would move, him being the ringleader, but he wouldn't move and he wouldn't let the others move, so they had to beat him and a couple of the others and they threw them in the wagon—but *I* didn't see this nigger till I got to the jail. They were still singing and I was supposed to make them stop. Well, I couldn't make them stop for me but I knew he could make them stop. He was lying on the ground jerking and moaning, they had threw him in a cell by himself, and blood was coming out his ears from where Big Jim C. and his boys had whipped him. Wouldn't you think they'd learn? I put the prod to him and he jerked some more and he kind of screamed—but he didn't have much voice left. "You make them stop that singing," I said to him, "you hear me? You make them stop that singing." He acted like he didn't hear me and I put it to him again, under his arms, and he just rolled around on the floor and blood started coming from his mouth. He'd pissed his pants already." He paused. His mouth felt dry and his throat was as rough as sandpaper; as he talked, he began to hurt all over with that peculiar excitement which refused to be released. "You all are going to stop your singing, I said to him, and you are going to stop coming down to the court house and disrupting traffic and molesting the people and keeping us from our duties and keeping doctors from getting to sick white women and getting all them Northerners in this town to give our town a bad name—!" As he said this, he kept prodding the boy, sweat pouring from beneath the helmet he had not yet taken off. The boy rolled around in his own dirt and water and blood and tried to scream again as the prod hit his testicles, but the scream did not come out, only a kind of rattle and a moan. He stopped. He was not supposed to kill the nigger. The cell was filled with a terrible odor. The boy was still. "You hear me?" he called. "You had enough?" The singing went on. "You had enough?" His foot leapt out, he had not known it was going to, and caught the boy flush on the jaw. *Jesus,* he thought, *this ain't no nigger, this is a goddamn bull,* and he screamed again, "You had enough? You going to make them stop that singing now?"

But the boy was out. And now he was shaking worse than the boy had been shaking. He was glad no one could see him. At the same time, he felt very close to a very peculiar, particular joy; something deep in him and deep in his memory was stirred, but whatever was in his memory eluded him. He took off his helmet. He walked to the cell door.

"White man," said the boy, from the floor, behind him.

He stopped. For some reason, he grabbed his privates.

"You remember Old Julia?"

The boy said, from the floor, with his mouth full of blood, and one eye, barely open, glaring like the eye of a cat in the dark, "My grandmother's name was Mrs. Julia Blossom. *Mrs.* Julia Blossom. You going to call our women by their right names yet.—And those kids ain't going to stop singing. We going to keep on singing until every one of you miserable white mothers go stark raving out of your minds." Then he closed the one eye; he spat blood; his head fell back against the floor.

He looked down at the boy, whom he had been seeing, off and on, for more than a year, and suddenly remembered him: Old Julia had been one of his mail-order customers, a nice old woman. He had not seen her for years, he supposed that she must be dead.

He had walked into the yard, the boy had been sitting in a swing. He had smiled at the boy, and asked, "Old Julia home?"

The boy looked at him for a long time before he answered. "Don't no Old Julia live here."

"This is her house. I know her. She's lived her for years."

The boy shook his head. "You might know a Old Julia someplace else, white man. But don't nobody by that name live here."

He watched the boy; the boy watched him. The boy certainly wasn't more than ten. *White man.* He didn't have time to be fooling around with some crazy kid. He yelled, "Hey! Old Julia!"

But only silence answered him. The expression on the boy's face did not change. The sun beat down on them both, still and silent; he had the feeling that he had been caught up in a nightmare, a nightmare dreamed by a child; perhaps one of the nightmares he himself had dreamed as a child. It had that feeling—everything familiar, without undergoing any other change, had been subtly and hideously displaced: the trees, the sun, the patches of grass in the yard, the leaning porch and the weary porch steps and the card-board in the windows and the black hole of the door which looked like the entrance to a cave, and the eyes of the pickaninny, all, all, were charged with malevolence. *White man.* He looked at the boy. "She's gone out?"

The boy said nothing.

"Well," he said, "tell her I passed by and I'll pass by next week." He started to go; he stopped. "You want some chewing gum?"

The boy got down from the swing and started for the house. He said, "I don't want nothing you got, white man." He walked into the house and closed the door behind him.

Now the boy looked as though he were dead. Jesse wanted to go over to him and pick him up and pistol whip him until the boy's head burst open like a melon. He began to tremble with what he believed was rage, sweat, both cold and hot, raced down his body, the singing filled him as though it were a weird, uncontrollable, monstrous howling rumbling up from the depths of his own belly, he felt an icy fear rise in him and raise him up, and he shouted, he howled, "You lucky we *pump* some white blood into you every once in a while—your women! Here's what I got for all the black bitches in the world—!" Then he was, abruptly, almost too weak to stand; to his bewilderment, his horror, beneath his own fingers, he felt himself violently stiffen—with no warning at all; he dropped his hands and he stared at the boy and he left the cell.

"All that singing they do," he said. "All that singing." He could not remember the first time he had heard it; he had been hearing it all his life. It was the sound with which he was most familiar—though it was also the sound of which he had been least conscious—and it had always contained an obscure comfort. They were singing to God. They were singing for mercy and they hoped to go to heaven, and he had even sometimes felt, when looking into the eyes of some of the old women, a few of the very old men, that they were singing for mercy for his soul, too. Of course he had never thought of their heaven or of what God was, or could be, for them; God was the same for everyone, he supposed, and heaven was where good people went—he supposed. He had never thought much about what it meant to be a good person. He tried to be a good person and treat everybody right: it wasn't his fault if the niggers had taken it into their heads to fight against God and go against the rules laid down in the Bible for everyone to read! Any preacher would tell you that. He was only doing his duty: protecting white people from the niggers and the niggers from themselves. And there were still lots of good niggers around—he had to remember that; they weren't all like that boy this afternoon; and the good niggers must be mighty sad to see what was happening to their people. They would thank him when this was over. In that way they had, the best of them, not quite looking him in the eye, in a low voice, with a little smile: We surely thanks you, Mr. Jesse. From the bottom of our hearts, we thanks you. He smiled. They hadn't all gone crazy. This trouble would pass.—He knew that the young people had changed some of the words to the songs. He had scarcely listened to the words before and he did not listen to them now; but he knew that the words were different; he could hear that much. He did not know if the faces were different, he had never, before this trouble began, watched them as they sang, but he certainly did not like what he saw now. They hated him, and this hatred was blacker than their hearts, blacker than their skins, redder than their blood, and harder, by far, than his club. Each day, each night, he felt worn out, aching, with their smell in his nostrils and filling his lungs, as though he were drowning—drowning in niggers; and it was all to be done again when he awoke. It would never end. It would never end. Perhaps this was what the singing had meant all along. They had not been singing black folks into heaven, they had been singing white folks into hell.

Everyone felt this black suspicion in many ways, but no one knew how to express it. Men much older than he, who had been responsible for law and order much longer than he, were now much quieter than they had been, and the tone of their jokes, in a way that he could not quite put his finger on, had changed. These men were his models, they had been friends to his father, and they had taught him what it meant to be a man. He looked to them for courage now. It wasn't that he didn't know that what he was doing was right—he knew that, nobody had to tell him that; it was only that he missed the ease of former years. But they didn't have much time to hang out with each other these days. They tended to stay close to their families every free minute because nobody knew what might happen next. Explosions rocked the night of their tranquil town. Each time each man wondered silently if perhaps this time the dynamite had not fallen into the wrong hands. They thought that they knew where all the guns were; but they could not possibly know every move that was made in that secret place where the darkies lived. From time to time it was suggested that they form a posse and search the home of every nigger, but they hadn't done it yet. For one thing, this might have brought the bastards from the North down on their backs;

for another, although the niggers were scattered throughout the town—down in the hollow near the railroad tracks, way west near the mills, up on the hill, the well-off ones, and some out near the college—nothing seemed to happen in one part of town without the niggers immediately knowing it in the other. This meant that they could not take them by surprise. They rarely mentioned it, but they *knew* that some of the niggers had guns. It stood to reason, as they said, since, after all, some of them had been in the Army. There were niggers in the Army right now and God knows they wouldn't have had any trouble stealing this half-assed government blind—the whole world was doing it, look at the European countries and all those countries in Africa. They made jokes about it—bitter jokes; and they cursed the government in Washington, which had betrayed them; but they had not yet formed a posse. Now, if their town had been laid out like some towns in the North, where all the niggers lived together in one locality, they could have gone down and set fire to the houses and brought about peace that way. If the niggers had all lived in one place, they could have kept the fire in one place. But the way this town was laid out, the fire could hardly be controlled. It would spread all over town—and the niggers would probably be helping it to spread. Still, from time to time, they spoke of doing it, anyway; so that now there was a real fear among them that somebody might go crazy and light the match.

They rarely mentioned anything not directly related to the war that they were fighting, but this had failed to establish between them the unspoken communication of soldiers during a war. Each man, in the thrilling silence which sped outward from their exchanges, their laughter, and their anecdotes, seemed wrestling, in various degrees of darkness, with a secret which he could not articulate to himself, and which, however directly it related to the war, related yet more surely to his privacy and his past. They could no longer be sure, after all, that they had all done the same things. They had never dreamed that their privacy could contain any element of terror, could threaten, that is, to reveal itself, to the scrutiny of a judgment day, while remaining unreadable and inaccessible to themselves; nor had they dreamed that the past, while certainly refusing to be forgotten, could yet so stubbornly refuse to be remembered. They felt themselves mysteriously set at naught, as no longer entering into the real concerns of other people—while here they were, out-numbered, fighting to save the civilized world. They had thought that people would care—people didn't care; not enough, anyway, to help them. It would have been a help, really, or at least a relief, even to have been forced to surrender. Thus they had lost, probably forever, their old and easy connection with each other. They were forced to depend on each other more and, at the same time, to trust each other less. Who could tell when one of them might not betray them all, for money, or for the ease of confession? But no one dared imagine what there might be to confess. They were soldiers fighting a war, but their relationship to each other was that of accomplices in a crime. They all had to keep their mouths shut.

I stepped in the river at Jordan.

Out of the darkness of the room, out of nowhere, the line came flying up at him, with the melody and the beat. He turned wordlessly toward his sleeping wife. *I stepped in the river at Jordan.* Where had he heard that song?

"Grace," he whispered. "You awake?"

She did not answer. If she was awake, she wanted him to sleep. Her breathing was slow and easy, her body slowly rose and fell.

I stepped in the river at Jordan.
The water came to my knees.

He began to sweat. He felt an overwhelming fear, which yet contained a curious and dreadful pleasure.

I stepped in the river at Jordan.
The water came to my waist.

It had been night, as it was now, he was in the car between his mother and his father, sleepy, his head in his mother's lap, sleepy, and yet full of excitement. The singing came from far away, across the dark fields. There were no lights anywhere. They had said good-bye to all the others and turned off on this dark dirt road. They were almost home.

I stepped in the river at Jordan,
The water came over my head,
I looked way over to the other side,
He was making up my dying bed!

"I guess they singing for him," his father said, seeming very weary and subdued now. "Even when they're sad, they sound like they just about to go and tear off a piece." He yawned and leaned across the boy and slapped his wife lightly on the shoulder, allowing his hand to rest there for a moment. "Don't they?"

"Don't talk that way," she said.

"Well, that's what we going to do," he said, "you can make up your mind to that." He started whistling. "You see? When I begin to feel it, I gets kind of musical, too."

Oh, Lord! Come on and ease my troubling mind!

He had a black friend, his age, eight, who lived nearby. His name was Otis. They wrestled together in the dirt. Now the thought of Otis made him sick. He began to shiver. His mother put her arm around him.

"He's tired," she said.

"We'll be home soon," said his father. He began to whistle again.

"We didn't see Otis this morning," Jesse said. He did not know why he said this. His voice, in the darkness of the car, sounded small and accusing.

"You haven't seen Otis for a couple of mornings," his mother said.

That was true. But he was only concerned about *this* morning.

"No," said his father, "I reckon Otis's folks was afraid to let him show himself this morning."

"But Otis didn't do nothing!" Now his voice sounded questioning.

"Otis *can't* do nothing," said his father, "he's too little." The car lights picked up their wooden house, which now solemnly approached them, the lights falling around it like yellow dust. Their dog, chained to a tree, began to bark.

"We just want to make sure Otis *don't* do nothing," said his father, and stopped the car. He looked down at Jesse. "And you tell him what your Daddy said, you hear?"

"Yes sir," he said.

His father switched off the lights. The dog moaned and pranced, but they ignored him and went inside. He could not sleep. He lay awake, hearing the night sounds, the dog yawning and moaning outside, the sawing of the crickets, the cry of the owl, dogs barking far away, then no sounds at all, just the heavy, endless buzzing of the night. The darkness pressed on his eyelids like a scratchy blanket. He turned, he turned again. He wanted to call his mother, but he knew his father would not like this. He was terribly afraid. Then he heard his father's voice in the other room, low, with a joke in it; but this did not help him, it frightened him more, he knew what was going to happen. He put his head under the blanket, then pushed his head out again, for fear, staring at the dark window. He heard his mother's moan, his father's sigh; he gritted his teeth. Then their bed began to rock. His father's breathing seemed to fill the world.

That morning, before the sun had gathered all its strength, men and women, some flushed and some pale with excitement, came with news. Jesse's father seemed to know what the news was before the first jalopy stopped in the yard, and he ran out, crying, "They got him, then? They got him?"

The first jalopy held eight people, three men and two women and three children. The children were sitting on the laps of the grown-ups. Jesse knew two of them, the two boys; they shyly and uncomfortably greeted each other. He did not know the girl.

"Yes, they got him," said one of the women, the older one, who wore a wide hat and a fancy, faded blue dress. "They found him early this morning."

"How far had he got?" Jesse's father asked.

"He hadn't got no further than Harkness," one of the men said. "Look like he got lost up there in all them trees—or maybe he just got so scared he couldn't move." They all laughed.

"Yes, and you know it's near a graveyard, too," said the younger woman, and they laughed again.

"Is that where they got him now?" asked Jesse's father.

By this time there were three cars piled behind the first one, with everyone looking excited and shining, and Jesse noticed that they were carrying food. It was like a Fourth of July picnic.

"Yeah, that's where he is," said one of the men, "declare, Jesse, you going to keep us here all day long, answering your damn fool questions. Come on, we ain't got no time to waste."

"Don't bother putting up no food," cried a woman from one of the other cars, "we got enough. Just come on."

"Why, thank you," said Jesse's father, "we be right along, then."

"I better get a sweater for the boy," said his mother, "in case it turns cold."

Jesse watched his mother's thin legs cross the yard. He knew that she also wanted to comb her hair a little and maybe put on a better dress, the dress she wore to church. His father guessed this, too, for he yelled behind her, "Now don't you go trying to turn yourself into no movie star. You just come on." But he laughed as he said this, and winked at the men; his wife was younger and prettier than most of the other women. He clapped Jesse on the head and started pulling him toward the car. "You all go on," he said, "I'll be right behind you. Jesse, you go tie up that there dog while I get this car started."

The cars sputtered and coughed and shook; the caravan began to move; bright dust filled the air. As soon as he was tied up, the dog began to bark. Jesse's mother came out of the house, carrying a jacket for his father and a sweater for Jesse. She had put a ribbon in her hair and had an old shawl around her shoulders.

"Put these in the car, son," she said, and handed everything to him. She bent down and stroked the dog, looked to see if there was water in his bowl, then went back up the three porch steps and closed the door.

"Come on," said his father, "ain't nothing in there for nobody to steal." He was sitting in the car, which trembled and belched. The last car of the caravan had disappeared but the sound of singing floated behind them.

Jesse got into the car, sitting close to his father, loving the smell of the car, and the trembling, and the bright day, and the sense of going on a great and unexpected journey. His mother got in and closed the door and the car began to move. Not until then did he ask, "Where are we going? Are we going on a picnic?"

He had a feeling that he knew where they were going, but he was not sure.

"That's right," his father said, "we're going on a picnic. You won't ever forget *this* picnic—!"

"Are we," he asked, after a moment, "going to see the bad nigger—the one that knocked down old Miss Standish?"

"Well, I reckon," said his mother, "that we *might* see him."

He started to ask, *Will a lot of niggers be there? Will Otis be there?*—but he did not ask his question, to which, in a strange and uncomfortable way, he already knew the answer. Their friends, in the other cars, stretched up the road as far as he could see; other cars had joined them; there were cars behind them. They were singing. The sun seemed suddenly very hot, and he was at once very happy and a little afraid. He did not quite understand what was happening, and he did not know what to ask—he had no one to ask. He had grown accustomed, for the solution of such mysteries, to go to Otis. He felt that Otis knew everything. But he could not ask Otis about this. Anyway, he had not seen Otis for two days; he had not seen a black face anywhere for more than two days; and he now realized, as they began chugging up the long hill which eventually led to Harkness, that there were no black faces on the road this morning, no black people anywhere. From the houses in which they lived, all along the road, no smoke curled, no life stirred—maybe one or two chickens were to be seen, that was all. There was no one at the windows, no one in the yard, no one sitting on the porches, and the doors were closed. He had come this road many a time and seen women washing in the yard (there were no clothes on the clotheslines), men working in the fields, children playing in the dust; black men passed them on the road other mornings, other days, on foot, or in wagons, sometimes in cars, tipping their hats, smiling, joking, their teeth a solid white against their skin, their eyes as warm as the sun, the blackness of their skin like dull fire against the white of the blue or the grey of their torn clothes. They passed the nigger church— dead-white, desolate, locked up; and the graveyard, where no one knelt or walked, and he saw no flowers. He wanted to ask, *Where are they? Where are they all?* But he did not dare. As the hill grew steeper, the sun grew colder. He looked at his mother and his father. They looked straight ahead, seeming to be listening to the singing which echoed and echoed in this graveyard silence. They were strangers to him now. They were looking at something he could not see. His father's lips had a strange, cruel curve, he wet his lips from time to time, and swallowed. He was terribly aware of his father's tongue, it was as though he had never seen it before. And his father's body suddenly seemed immense, bigger than a mountain. His eyes, which were grey-green, looked yellow in the sunlight; or at least there was a light in them which he had never seen before. His mother patted her hair and adjusted the ribbon, leaning forward to look into the car mirror. "You look all right," said his father, and laughed. "When that nigger looks at you, he's going to swear he throwed his life away for nothing. Wouldn't be surprised if he don't come back to haunt you." And he laughed again.

The singing now slowly began to cease; and he realized that they were nearing their destination. They had reached a straight, narrow, pebbly road, with trees on either side. The sunlight filtered down on them from a great height, as though they were under-water; and the branches of the trees scraped against the cars with a tearing sound. To the right of them, and beneath them, invisible now, lay the town; and to the left, miles of trees which led to the high mountain range which his ancestors had crossed in order to settle in this valley. Now, all was silent, except for the bumping of the tires against the rocky road, the sputtering of motors, and the sound of a crying child. And they seemed to move more slowly. They were beginning to climb again. He watched the cars ahead as they toiled patiently upward, disappearing into the sunlight of the clearing. Presently, he felt their vehicle also rise, heard his father's changed breathing, the sunlight hit his face, the trees moved away from them, and they were there. As their car crossed the clearing, he looked around. There seemed to be millions, there were certainly hundreds of people in the clearing, staring toward something he could not see. There was a fire. He could not see the flames, but he smelled the smoke. Then they were on the other side of the clearing, among the trees again. His father drove off the road and parked the car behind a great many other cars. He looked down at Jesse.

"You all right?" he asked.

"Yes sir," he said.

"Well, come on, then," his father said. He reached over and opened the door on his mother's side. His mother stepped out first. They followed her into the clearing. At first he was aware only of confusion, of his mother and father greeting and being greeted, himself being handled, hugged, and patted, and told how much he had grown. The wind blew the smoke from the fire across the clearing into his eyes and nose. He could not see over the backs of the people in front of him. The sounds of laughing and cursing and wrath—and something else—rolled in waves from the front of the mob to the back. Those in front expressed their delight at what they saw, and this delight rolled backward, wave upon wave, across the clearing, more acrid than the smoke. His father reached down suddenly and sat Jesse on his shoulders.

Now he saw the fire—of twigs and boxes, piled high; flames made pale orange and yellow and thin as a veil under the steadier light of the sun; grey-blue smoke rolled upward and poured over their heads. Beyond the shifting curtain of fire and smoke, he made out first only a length of gleaming chain, attached to a great limb of the tree; then he saw that this chain bound two black hands together at the wrist, dirty yellow palm facing dirty yellow palm. The smoke poured up; the hands dropped out of sight; a cry went up from the crowd. Then the hands slowly came into view again, pulled upward by the chain. This time he saw the kinky, sweating, bloody head—he had never before seen a head with so much hair on it, hair so black and so tangled that it seemed like another jungle. The head was hanging. He saw the forehead, flat and high, with a kind of arrow of hair in the center, like he had, like his father had; they called it a widow's peak; and the mangled eye brows, the wide nose, the closed eyes, and the glinting eye lashes and the hanging lips, all streaming with blood and sweat. His hands were straight above his head. All his weight pulled downward from his hands; and he was a big man, a bigger man than his father, and black as an African jungle cat, and naked. Jesse pulled upward; his father's hands held him firmly by the ankles. He wanted to say something, he did not know what, but nothing he said could have been heard, for now the crowd roared again as a man stepped forward and put more wood on the fire. The flames leapt up. He thought he heard the hanging man scream, but he was not sure. Sweat was pouring from the hair in his armpits, poured down his sides, over his chest, into his navel and his groin. He was lowered again; he was raised again. Now Jesse knew that he heard him scream. The head went back, the mouth wide open, blood bubbling from the mouth; the veins of the neck jumped out; Jesse clung to his father's neck in terror as the cry rolled over the crowd. The cry of all the people rose to answer the dying man's cry. He wanted death to come quickly. They wanted to make death wait: and it was they who held death, now, on a leash which they lengthened little by little. *What did he do?* Jesse wondered. *What did the man do? What did he do?*—but he could not ask his father. He was seated on his father's shoulders, but his father was far away. There were two older men, friends of his father's, raising and lowering the chain; everyone, indiscriminately, seemed to be responsible for the fire. There was no hair left on the nigger's privates, and the eyes, now, were wide open, as white as the eyes of a clown or a doll. The smoke now carried a terrible odor across the clearing, the odor of something burning which was both sweet and rotten.

He turned his head a little and saw the field of faces. He watched his mother's face. Her eyes were very bright, her mouth was open: she was more beautiful than he had ever seen her, and more strange. He began to feel a joy he had never felt before. He watched the hanging, gleaming body, the most beautiful and terrible object he had ever seen till then. One of his father's friends reached up and in his hands he held a knife: and Jesse wished that he had been that man. It was a long, bright knife and the sun seemed to catch it, to play with it, to caress it—it was brighter than the fire. And a wave of laughter swept the crowd. Jesse felt his father's hands on his ankles slip and tighten. The man with the knife walked toward the crowd, smiling slightly; as though this were a signal, silence fell; he heard his mother cough. Then the man with the knife walked up to the hanging body. He turned and smiled again. Now there was a silence all over the field. The hanging head looked up. It seemed fully conscious now, as though the fire had burned out terror and pain. The man with the knife took the nigger's privates in his hand, one hand, still smiling, as though he were weighing them. In the cradle of the one white hand, the nigger's privates seemed as remote as meat being weighed in the scales; but seemed heavier, too, much heavier, and Jesse felt his scrotum tighten; and huge, huge, much bigger than his father's, flaccid, hairless, the largest thing he had ever seen till then, and the blackest. The white hand stretched them, cradled them, caressed them. Then the dying man's eyes looked straight into Jesse's eyes—it could not have been as long as a second, but it seemed longer than a year. Then Jesse screamed, and the crowd screamed as the knife flashed, first up, then down, cutting the dreadful thing away, and the blood came roaring down. Then the crowd rushed forward, tearing at the body with their hands, with knives, with rocks, with stones, howling and cursing. Jesse's head, of its own weight, fell downward toward his father's head. Someone stepped forward and drenched the body with kerosene. Where the man had been, a great sheet of flame appeared. Jesse's father lowered him to the ground.

"Well, I told you," said his father, "you wasn't never going to forget *this* picnic." His father's face was full of sweat, his eyes were very peaceful. At that moment Jesse loved his father more than he had ever loved him. He felt that his father had carried him through a mighty test, had revealed to him a great secret which would be the key to his life forever.

"I reckon," he said. "I reckon."

Jesse's father took him by the hand and, with his mother a little behind them, talking and laughing with the other women, they walked through the crowd, across the clearing. The black body was on the ground, the chain which had held it was being rolled up by one of his father's friends. Whatever the fire had left undone, the hands and the knives and the stones of the people had accomplished. The head was caved in, one eye was torn out, one ear was hanging. But one had to look carefully to realize this, for it was, now, merely, a black charred object on the black, charred ground. He lay spread-eagled with what had been a wound between what had been his legs.

"They going to leave him here, then?" Jesse whispered.

"Yeah," said his father, "they'll come and get him by and by. I reckon we better get over there and get some of that food before it's all gone."

"I reckon," he muttered now to himself, "I reckon." Grace stirred and touched him on the thigh: the moonlight covered her like glory. Something bubbled up in him, his nature again returned to him. He thought of the boy in the cell; he thought of the man in the fire; he thought of the knife and grabbed himself and stroked himself and a terrible sound, something between a high laugh and a howl, came out of him and dragged his sleeping wife up on one elbow. She stared at him in a moonlight which had now grown cold as ice. He thought of the morning and grabbed her, laughing and crying, crying and laughing, and he whispered, as he stroked her, as he took her, "Come on, sugar, I'm going to do you like a nigger, just like a nigger, come on, sugar, and love me just like you'd love a nigger." He thought of the morning as he labored and she moaned, thought of morning as he labored harder than he ever had before, and before his labors had ended, he heard the first cock crow and the dogs begin to bark, and the sound of tires on the gravel road.

1965

FLANNERY O'CONNOR
1925–1964

Flannery O'Connor, one of the twentieth century's finest writers of short stories, was born in Savannah; lived with her mother in Milledgeville, Georgia, for much of her life; and died before her fortieth birthday—victim like her father of disseminated lupus, an incurable disease. She was stricken with the disease in 1950 while at work on her first novel, but injections of a cortisone derivative managed to arrest it, though the cortisone weakened her bones to the extent that from 1955 on she could get around only on crutches. She was able to write, travel, and lecture until 1964 when the lupus reactivated itself and killed her. A Roman Catholic throughout her life, she is quoted as having remarked, apropos of a trip to Lourdes, "I had the best-looking crutches in Europe." This remark suggests the kind of hair-raising jokes that centrally inform her writing as well as a refusal to indulge in self-pity over her fate.

She published two novels, *Wise Blood* (1952) and *The Violent Bear It Away* (1960), both weighty with symbolic and religious concerns and ingeniously contrived in the black-humored manner of Nathanael West, her American predecessor in this mode. But her really memorable creations of characters and actions take place in the stories, which are extremely funny, sometimes unbearably so, and finally we may wonder just what it is we are laughing at. Upon consideration the jokes are seen to be dreadful ones, as with Manley Pointer's treatment of Joy Hopewell's artificial leg in "Good Country People" or Mr. Shiftlet's of his bride in "The Life You Save May Be Your Own."

Another American "regionalist," the poet Robert Frost, whose own work contains its share of dreadful jokes, once confessed to being more interested in people's speech than in the people themselves. A typical Flannery O'Connor story consists at its most vital level in people talking, clucking their endless reiterations of clichés about life, death, and the universe. These clichés are captured with beautiful accuracy by an artist who had spent her life listening to them, lovingly and maliciously keeping track until she could put them to use. Early in her life she hoped to be a cartoonist, and there is cartoonlike mastery in her vivid renderings of character through speech and other gesture. Critics have called her a maker of grotesques, a label that like other ones—regionalist, southern lady, or Roman Catholic novelist—might have annoyed if it didn't obviously amuse her too. She once remarked tartly that "anything that comes out of the South is going to be called grotesque by the Northern reader, unless it is grotesque, in which case it is going to be called realistic."

Of course, this capacity for mockery, along with a facility in portraying perverse behavior, may work against other demands we make of the fiction writer, and it is true that O'Connor seldom suggests that her characters have inner lives that are imaginable, let alone worth respect. Instead, the emphasis is on the sharp eye and the ability to tell a tale and keep it moving inevitably toward completion. These completions are usually violent, occurring when the character—in many cases a woman—must confront an experience that she cannot handle by the old trustworthy language and habit-hardened responses. O'Connor's art lies partly in making it impossible for us merely to scorn the banalities of expression and behavior by which these people get through their lives. However dark the comedy, it keeps in touch with the things of this world, even when some force from another world threatens to annihilate the embattled protagonist. And although the stories are filled with religious allusions and parodies, they do not try to inculcate a doctrine. One of her best ones is titled "Revelation," but a reader often finishes a story with no simple, unambiguous sense of what has been revealed. Instead, we must trust the internal fun and richness of each tale to reveal what it has to reveal. We can agree also, in sadness, with the critic Irving

Howe's conclusion to his review of her posthumous collection of stories that it is intolerable for such a writer to have died at the age of thirty-nine.

The texts are from *A Good Man Is Hard to Find* (1955).

The Life You Save May Be Your Own

The old woman and her daughter were sitting on their porch when Mr. Shiftlet came up their road for the first time. The old woman slid to the edge of her chair and leaned forward, shading her eyes from the piercing sunset with her hand. The daughter could not see far in front of her and continued to play with her fingers. Although the old woman lived in this desolate spot with only her daughter and she had never seen Mr. Shiftlet before, she could tell, even from a distance, that he was a tramp and no one to be afraid of. His left coat sleeve was folded up to show there was only half an arm in it and his gaunt figure listed slightly to the side as if the breeze were pushing him. He had on a black town suit and a brown felt hat that was turned up in the front and down in the back and he carried a tin tool box by a handle. He came on, at an amble, up her road, his face turned toward the sun which appeared to be balancing itself on the peak of a small mountain.

The old woman didn't change her position until he was almost into her yard; then she rose with one hand fisted on her hip. The daughter, a large girl in a short blue organdy dress, saw him all at once and jumped up and began to stamp and point and make excited speechless sounds.

Mr. Shiftlet stopped just inside the yard and set his box on the ground and tipped his hat at her as if she were not in the least afflicted; then he turned toward the old woman and swung the hat all the way off. He had long black slick hair that hung flat from a part in the middle to beyond the tips of his ears on either side. His face descended in forehead for more than half its length and ended suddenly with his features just balanced over a jutting steel-trap jaw. He seemed to be a young man but he had a look of composed dissatisfaction as if he understood life thoroughly.

"Good evening," the old woman said. She was about the size of a cedar fence post and she had a man's gray hat pulled down low over her head.

The tramp stood looking at her and didn't answer. He turned his back and faced the sunset. He swung both his whole and his short arm up slowly so that they indicated an expanse of sky and his figure formed a crooked cross. The old woman watched him with her arms folded across her chest as if she were the owner of the sun, and the daughter watched, her head thrust forward and her fat helpless hands hanging at the wrists. She had long pink-gold hair and eyes as blue as a peacock's neck.

He held the pose for almost fifty seconds and then he picked up his box and came on to the porch and dropped down on the bottom step. "Lady," he said in a firm nasal voice, "I'd give a fortune to live where I could see me a sun do that every evening."

"Does it every evening," the old woman said and sat back down. The daughter sat down too and watched him with a cautious sly look as if he were a bird that had come up very close. He leaned to one side, rooting in his pants pocket, and in a second he brought out a package of chewing gum and offered her a piece. She took it and unpeeled it and began to chew without taking her eyes off him. He offered the old woman a piece but she only raised her upper lip to indicate she had no teeth.

Mr. Shiftlet's pale sharp glance had already passed over everything in the yard—the pump near the corner of the house and the big fig tree that three or four chickens were preparing to roost in—and had moved to a shed where he saw the square rusted back of an automobile. "You ladies drive?" he asked.

"That car ain't run in fifteen year," the old woman said. "The day my husband died, it quit running."

"Nothing is like it used to be, lady," he said. "The world is almost rotten."

"That's right," the old woman said. "You from around here?"

"Name Tom T. Shiftlet," he murmured, looking at the tires.

"I'm pleased to meet you," the old woman said. "Name Lucynell Crater and daughter Lucynell Crater. What you doing around here, Mr. Shiftlet?"

He judged the car to be about a 1928 or '29 Ford. "Lady," he said, and turned and gave her his full attention, "lemme tell you something. There's one of these doctors in Atlanta that's taken a knife and cut the human heart—the human heart," he repeated, leaning forward, "out of a man's chest and held it in his hand," and he held his hand out, palm up, as if it were slightly weighted with the human heart, "and studied it like it was a day-old chicken, and lady," he said, allowing a long significant pause in which his head slid forward and his clay-colored eyes brightened, "he don't know no more about it than you or me."

"That's right," the old woman said.

"Why, if he was to take that knife and cut into every corner of it, he still wouldn't know no more than you or me. What you want to bet?"

"Nothing," the old woman said wisely. "Where you come from, Mr. Shiftlet?"

He didn't answer. He reached into his pocket and brought out a sack of tobacco and a package of cigarette papers and rolled himself a cigarette, expertly with one hand, and attached it in a hanging position to his upper lip. Then he took a box of wooden matches from his pocket and struck one on his shoe. He held the burning match as if he were studying the mystery of flame while it traveled dangerously toward his skin. The daughter began to make loud noises and to point to his hand and shake her finger at him, but when the flame was just before touching him, he leaned down with his hand cupped over it as if he were going to set fire to his nose and lit the cigarette.

He flipped away the dead match and blew a stream of gray into the evening. A sly look came over his face. "Lady," he said, "nowadays, people'll do anything anyways. I can tell you my name is Tom T. Shiftlet and I come from Tarwater, Tennessee, but you never have seen me before: how you know I ain't lying? How you know my name ain't Aaron Sparks, lady, and I come from Singleberry, Georgia, or how you know it's not George Speeds and I come from Lucy, Alabama, or how you know I ain't Thompson Bright from Toolafalls, Mississippi?"

"I don't know nothing about you," the old woman muttered, irked.

"Lady," he said, "people don't care how they lie. Maybe the best I can tell you is, I'm a man; but listen lady," he said and paused and made his tone more ominous still, "what is a man?"

The old woman began to gum a seed. "What you carry in that tin box, Mr. Shiftlet?" she asked.

"Tools," he said, put back. "I'm a carpenter."

"Well, if you come out here to work, I'll be able to feed you and give you a place to sleep but I can't pay. I'll tell you that before you begin," she said.

There was no answer at once and no particular expression on his face. He leaned back against the two-by-four that helped support the porch roof. "Lady," he said slowly, "there's some men that some things mean more to them than money." The old woman rocked without comment and the daughter watched the trigger that moved up and down in his neck. He told the old woman then that all most people were interested in was money, but he asked what a man was made for. He asked her if a man was made for money, or what. He asked her what she thought she was made for but she didn't answer, she only sat rocking and wondered if a one-armed man could put a new roof on her garden house. He asked a lot of questions that she didn't answer. He told her that he was twenty-eight years old and had lived a varied life. He had been a gospel singer, a foreman on the railroad, an assistant in an undertaking parlor, and he come over the radio for three months with Uncle Roy and his Red Creek Wranglers. He said he had fought and bled in the Arm Service of his country and visited every foreign land and that everywhere he had seen people that didn't care if they did a thing one way or another. He said he hadn't been raised thataway.

A fat yellow moon appeared in the branches of the fig tree as if it were going to roost there with the chickens. He said that a man had to escape to the country to see the world whole and that he wished he lived in a desolate place like this where he could see the sun go down every evening like God made it to do.

"Are you married or are you single?" the old woman asked.

There was a long silence. "Lady," he asked finally, "where would you find you an innocent woman today? I wouldn't have any of this trash I could just pick up."

The daughter was leaning very far down, hanging her head almost between her knees watching him through a triangular door she had made in her overturned hair; and she suddenly fell in a heap on the floor and began to whimper. Mr. Shiftlet straightened her out and helped her get back in the chair.

"Is she your baby girl?" he asked.

"My only," the old woman said "and she's the sweetest girl in the world. I would give her up for nothing on earth. She's smart too. She can sweep the floor, cook, wash, feed the chickens, and hoe. I wouldn't give her up for a casket of jewels."

"No," he said kindly, "don't ever let any man take her away from you."

"Any man come after her," the old woman said, " 'll have to stay around the place."

Mr. Shiftlet's eye in the darkness was focused on a part of the automobile bumper that glittered in the distance. "Lady," he said, jerking his short arm up as if he could point with it to her house and yard and pump, "there ain't a broken thing on this plantation that I couldn't fix for you, one-arm jackleg or not. I'm a man," he said with a sullen dignity, "even if I ain't a whole one. I got," he said, tapping his knuckles on the floor to emphasize the immensity of what he was going to say, "a moral intelligence!" and his face pierced out of the darkness into a shaft of doorlight and he stared at her as if he were astonished himself at this impossible truth.

The old woman was not impressed with the phrase. "I told you you could hang around and work for food," she said, "if you don't mind sleeping in that car yonder."

"Why listen, lady," he said with a grin of delight, "the monks of old slept in their coffins!"

"They wasn't as advanced as we are," the old woman said.

The next morning he began on the roof of the garden house while Lucynell, the daughter, sat on a rock and watched him work. He had not been around a week before the change he had made in the place was apparent. He had patched the front and back steps, built a new hog pen, restored a fence, and taught Lucynell, who was completely deaf and had never said a word in her life, to say the word "bird." The big rosy-faced girl followed him everywhere, saying "Burrttddt ddbirrrttdt," and clapping her hands. The old woman watched from a distance, secretly pleased. She was ravenous for a son-in-law.

Mr. Shiftlet slept on the hard narrow back seat of the car with his feet out the side window. He had his razor and a can of water on a crate that served him as a bedside table and he put up a piece of mirror against the back glass and kept his coat neatly on a hanger that he hung over one of the windows.

In the evenings he sat on the steps and talked while the old woman and Lucynell rocked violently in their chairs on either side of him. The old woman's three mountains were black against the dark blue sky and were visited off and on by various planets and by the moon after it had left the chickens. Mr. Shiftlet pointed out that the reason he had improved this plantation was because he had taken a personal interest in it. He said he was even going to make the automobile run.

He had raised the hood and studied the mechanism and he said he could tell that the car had been built in the days when cars were really built. You take now, he said, one man puts in one bolt and another man puts in another bolt and another man puts in another bolt so that it's a man for a bolt. That's why you have to pay so much for a car: you're paying all those men. Now if you didn't have to pay but one man, you could get you a cheaper car and one that had had a personal interest taken in it, and it would be a better car. The old woman agreed with him that this was so.

Mr. Shiftlet said that the trouble with the world was that nobody cared, or stopped and took any trouble. He said he never would have been able to teach Lucynell to say a word if he hadn't cared and stopped long enough.

"Teach her to say something else," the old woman said.

"What you want her to say next?" Mr. Shiftlet asked.

The old woman's smile was broad and toothless and suggestive. "Teach her to say 'sugarpie,' " she said.

Mr. Shiftlet already knew what was on her mind.

The next day he began to tinker with the automobile and that evening he told her that if she would buy a fan belt, he would be able to make the car run.

The old woman said she would give him the money. "You see that girl yonder?" she asked, pointing to Lucynell who was sitting on the floor a foot away, watching him, her eyes blue even in the dark. "If it was ever a man wanted to take her away, I would say, 'No man on earth is going to take that sweet girl of mine away from me!' but if he was to say, 'Lady, I don't want to take her away, I want her right here,' I would say, 'Mister, I don't blame you none. I wouldn't pass up a chance to live in a permanent place and get the sweetest girl in the world myself. You ain't no fool,' I would say."

"How old is she?" Mr. Shiftlet asked casually.

"Fifteen, sixteen," the old woman said. The girl was nearly thirty but because of her innocence it was impossible to guess.

"It would be a good idea to paint it too," Mr. Shiftlet remarked. "You don't want it to rust out."

"We'll see about that later," the old woman said.

The next day he walked into town and returned with the parts he needed and a can of gasoline. Late in the afternoon, terrible noises issued from the shed and the old woman rushed out of the house, thinking Lucynell was somewhere having a fit. Lucynell was sitting on a chicken crate, stamping her feet and screaming, "Burrddttt! bddurrddtttt!" but her fuss was drowned out by the car. With a volley of blasts it emerged from the shed, moving in a fierce and stately way. Mr. Shiftlet was in the driver's seat, sitting very erect. He had an expression of serious modesty on his face as if he had just raised the dead.

That night, rocking on the porch, the old woman began her business, at once. "You want you an innocent woman, don't you" she asked sympathetically. "You don't want none of this trash."

"No'm, I don't," Mr. Shiftlet said.

"One that can't talk," she continued, "can't sass you back or use foul language. That's the kind for you to have. Right there," and she pointed to Lucynell sitting cross-legged in her chair, holding both feet in her hands.

"That's right," he admitted. "She wouldn't give me any trouble."

"Saturday," the old woman said, "you and her and me can drive into town and get married."

Mr. Shiftlet eased his position on the steps.

"I can't get married right now," he said. "Everything you want to do takes money and I ain't got any."

"What you need with money?" she asked.

"It takes money," he said. "Some people'll do anything anyhow these days, but the way I think, I wouldn't marry no woman that I couldn't take on a trip like she was somebody. I mean take her to a hotel and treat her. I wouldn't marry the Duchesser Windsor," he said firmly, "unless I could take her to a hotel and giver something good to eat.

"I was raised thataway and there ain't a thing I can do about it. My old mother taught me how to do."

"Lucynell don't even know what a hotel is," the old woman muttered. "Listen here, Mr. Shiftlet," she said, sliding forward in her chair, "you'd be getting a permanent house and a deep well and the most innocent girl in the world. You don't need no money. Lemme tell you something: there ain't any place in the world for a poor disabled friendless drifting man."

The ugly words settled in Mr. Shiftlet's head like a group of buzzards in the top of a tree. He didn't answer at once. He rolled himself a cigarette and lit it and then he said in an even voice, "Lady, a man is divided into two parts, body and spirit."

The old woman clamped her gums together.

"A body and a spirit," he repeated. "The body, lady, is like a house: it don't go anywhere; but the spirit, lady, is like a automobile: always on the move, always . . ."

"Listen, Mr. Shiftlet," she said, "my well never goes dry and my house is always warm in the winter and there's no mortgage on a thing about this place. You can go to the courthouse and see for yourself. And yonder under that shed is a fine automobile." She laid the bait carefully. "You can have it painted by Saturday. I'll pay for the paint."

In the darkness, Mr. Shiftlet's smile stretched like a weary snake waking up by a fire. After a second he recalled himself and said, "I'm only saying a man's spirit means more to him than anything else. I would have to take my wife off for the weekend without no regards at all for cost. I got to follow where my spirit says to go."

"I'll give you fifteen dollars for a weekend trip," the old woman said in a crabbed voice. "That's the best I can do."

"That wouldn't hardly pay for more than the gas and the hotel," he said. "It wouldn't feed her."

"Seventeen-fifty," the old woman said. "That's all I got so it isn't any use you trying to milk me. You can take a lunch."

Mr. Shiftlet was deeply hurt by the word "milk." He didn't doubt that she had more money sewed up in her mattress but he had already told her he was not interested in her money. "I'll make that do," he said and rose and walked off without treating with her further.

On Saturday the three of them drove into town in the car that the paint had barely dried on and Mr. Shiftlet and Lucynell were married in the Ordinary's office while the old woman witnessed. As they came out of the court-house, Mr. Shiftlet began twisting his neck in his collar. He looked morose and bitter as if he had been insulted while someone held him. "That didn't satisfy me none," he said. "That was just something a woman in an office did, nothing but paper work and blood tests. What do they know about my blood? If they was to take my heart and cut it out," he said, "they wouldn't know a thing about me. It didn't satisfy me at all."

"It satisfied the law," the old woman said sharply.

"The law," Mr. Shiftlet said and spit. "It's the law that don't satisfy me."

He had painted the car dark green with a yellow band around it just under the windows. The three of them climbed in the front seat and the old woman said, "Don't Lucynell look pretty? Looks like a baby doll." Lucynell was dressed up in a white dress that her mother had uprooted from a trunk and there was a Panama hat on her head with a bunch of red wooden cherries on the brim. Every now and then her placid expression was changed by a sly isolated little thought like a shoot of green in the desert. "You got a prize!" the old woman said.

Mr. Shiftlet didn't even look at her.

They drove back to the house to let the old woman off and pick up the lunch. When they were ready to leave, she stood staring in the window of the car, with her fingers clenched around the glass. Tears began to seep sideways out of her eyes and ran along the dirty creases in her face. "I ain't ever been parted with her for two days before," she said.

Mr. Shiftlet started the motor.

"And I wouldn't let no man have her but you because I seen you would do right. Good-bye, Sugarbaby," she said, clutching at the sleeve of the white dress. Lucynell looked straight at her and didn't seem to see her there at all. Mr. Shiftlet eased the car forward so that she had to move her hands.

The early afternoon was clear and open and surrounded by pale blue sky. Although the car would go only thirty miles an hour, Mr. Shiftlet imagined a terrific climb and dip and swerve that went entirely to his head so that he forgot his morning bitterness. He had always wanted an automobile but he had never been able to afford one before. He drove very fast because he wanted to make Mobile by nightfall.

Occasionally he stopped his thoughts long enough to look at Lucynell in the seat beside him. She had eaten the lunch as soon as they were out of the yard and now she was pulling the cherries off the hat one by one and throwing them out the window. He became depressed in spite of the car. He had driven about a hundred miles when he decided that she must be hungry again and at the next small town they came to, he stopped in front of an aluminum-painted eating place called The Hot Spot and took her in and ordered her a plate of ham and grits. The ride had made her sleepy and as soon as she got up on the stool, she rested her head on the counter and shut her eyes. There was no one in The Hot Spot but Mr. Shiftlet and the boy behind the counter, a pale youth with a greasy rag hung over his shoulder. Before he could dish up the food, she was snoring gently.

"Give it to her when she wakes up," Mr. Shiftlet said. "I'll pay for it now."

The boy bent over her and stared at the long pink-gold hair and the half-shut sleeping eyes. Then he looked up and stared at Mr. Shiftlet. "She looks like an angel of Gawd," he murmured.

"Hitchhiker," Mr. Shiftlet explained. "I can't wait. I got to make Tuscaloosa."

The boy bent over again and very carefully touched his finger to a strand of the golden hair and Mr. Shiftlet left.

He was more depressed than ever as he drove on by himself. The late afternoon had grown hot and sultry and the country had flattened out. Deep in the sky a storm was preparing very slowly and without thunder as if it meant to drain every drop of air from the earth before it broke. There were times when Mr. Shiftlet preferred not to be alone. He felt too that a man with a car had a responsibility to others and he kept his eye out for a hitchhiker. Occasionally he saw a sign that warned: "Drive carefully. The life you save may be your own."

The narrow road dropped off on either side into dry fields and here and there a shack or a filling station stood in a clearing. The sun began to set directly in front of the automobile. It was a reddening ball that through his windshield was slightly flat on the bottom and top. He saw a boy in overalls and a gray hat standing on the edge of the road and he slowed the car down and stopped in front of him. The boy didn't have his hand raised to thumb the ride, he was only standing there, but he had a small cardboard suitcase and his hat was set on his head in a way to indicate that he had left somewhere for good. "Son," Mr. Shiftlet said, "I see you want a ride."

The boy didn't say he did or he didn't but he opened the door of the car and got in, and Mr. Shiftlet started driving again. The child held the suitcase on his lap and folded his arms on top of it. He turned his head and looked out the window away from Mr. Shiftlet. Mr. Shiftlet felt oppressed. "Son," he said after a minute, "I got the best old mother in the world so I reckon you only got the second best."

The boy gave him a quick dark glance and then turned his face back out the window.

"It's nothing so sweet," Mr. Shiftlet continued, "as a boy's mother. She taught him his first prayers at her knee, she give him love when no other would, she told him what was right and what wasn't, and she seen that he done the right thing. Son," he said, "I never rued a day in my life like the one I rued when I left that old mother of mine."

The boy shifted in his seat but he didn't look at Mr. Shiftlet. He unfolded his arms and put one hand on the door handle.

"My mother was a angel of Gawd," Mr. Shiftlet said in a very strained voice. "He took her from heaven and giver to me and I left her." His eyes were instantly clouded over with a mist of tears. The car was barely moving.

The boy turned angrily in the seat. "You go to the devil!" he cried. "My old woman is a flea bag and yours is a stinking pole cat!" and with that he flung the door open and jumped out with his suitcase into the ditch.

Mr. Shiftlet was so shocked that for about a hundred feet he drove along slowly with the door still open. A cloud, the exact color of the boy's hat and shaped like a turnip, had descended over the sun, and another, worse looking, crouched behind the car. Mr. Shiftlet felt that the rottenness of the world was about to engulf him. He raised his arm and let it fall again to his breast. "Oh Lord!" he prayed. "Break forth and wash the slime from this earth!"

The turnip continued slowly to descend. After a few minutes there was a guffawing peal of thunder from behind and fantastic raindrops, like tin-can tops, crashed over the rear of Mr. Shiftlet's car. Very quickly he stepped on the gas and with his stump sticking out the window he raced the galloping shower into Mobile.

1955

Good Country People

Besides the neutral expression that she wore when she was alone, Mrs. Freeman had two others, forward and reverse, that she used for all her human dealings. Her forward expression was steady and driving like the advance of a heavy truck. Her eyes never swerved to left or right but turned as the story turned as if they followed a yellow line down the center of it. She seldom used the other expression because it was not often necessary for her to retract a statement, but when she did, her face came to a complete stop, there was an almost imperceptible movement of her black eyes, during which they seemed to be receding, and then the observer would see that Mrs. Freeman, though she might stand there as real as several grain sacks thrown on top of each other, was no longer there in spirit. As for getting anything across to her when this was the case, Mrs. Hopewell had given it up. She might talk her head off. Mrs. Freeman could never be brought to admit herself wrong on any point. She would stand there and if she could be brought to say anything, it was something like, "Well, I wouldn't of said it was and I wouldn't of said it wasn't," or letting her gaze range over the top kitchen shelf where there was an assortment of dusty bottles, she might remark, "I see you ain't ate many of them figs you put up last summer."

They carried on their important business in the kitchen at breakfast. Every morning Mrs. Hopewell got up at seven o'clock and lit her gas heater and Joy's. Joy was her daughter, a large blonde girl who had an artificial leg. Mrs. Hopewell thought of her as a child though she was thirty-two years old and highly educated. Joy would get up while her mother was eating and lumber into the bathroom and slam the door, and before long, Mrs. Freeman would arrive at the back door. Joy would hear her mother call, "Come on in," and then they would talk for a while in low voices that were indistinguishable in the bathroom. By the time Joy came in, they had usually finished the weather report and were on one or the other of Mrs. Freeman's daughters, Glynese or Carramae. Joy called them Glycerin and Caramel. Glynese, a redhead, was eighteen and had many admirers; Carramae, a blonde, was only fifteen but already married and pregnant. She could not keep anything on her stomach. Every morning Mrs. Freeman told Mrs. Hopewell how many times she had vomited since the last report.

Mrs. Hopewell liked to tell people that Glynese and Carramae were two of the finest girls she knew and that Mrs. Freeman was a *lady* and that she was never ashamed to take her anywhere or introduce her to anybody they might meet. Then she would tell how she had happened to hire the Freemans in the first place and how they were a godsend to her and how she had had them four years. The reason for her keeping them so long was that they were not trash. They were good country people. She had telephoned the man whose name they had given as a reference and he had told her that Mr. Freeman was a good farmer but that his wife was the nosiest woman ever to walk the earth. "She's got to be into everything," the man said. "If she don't get there before the dust settles, you can bet she's dead, that's all. She'll want to know all your business. I can stand him real good," he had said, "but me nor my wife neither could have stood that woman one more minute on this place." That had put Mrs. Hopewell off for a few days.

She had hired them in the end because there were no other applicants but she had made up her mind beforehand exactly how she would handle the woman. Since she was the type who had to be into everything, then, Mrs. Hopewell had decided, she would not only let her be into everything, she would *see to it* that she was into everything—she would give her the responsibility of everything, she would put her in charge. Mrs. Hopewell had no bad qualities of her own but she was able to use other people's in such a constructive way that she never felt the lack. She had hired the Freemans and she had kept them four years.

Nothing is perfect. This was one of Mrs. Hopewell's favorite sayings. Another was: that is life! And still another, the most important, was: well, other people have their opinions too. She would make these statements, usually at the table, in a tone of gentle insistence as if no one held them but her, and the large hulking Joy, whose constant outrage had obliterated every expression from her face, would stare just a little to the side of her, her eyes icy blue, with the look of someone who has achieved blindness by an act of will and means to keep it.

When Mrs. Hopewell said to Mrs. Freeman that life was like that, Mrs. Freeman would say, "I always said so myself." Nothing had been arrived at by anyone that had not first been arrived at by her. She was quicker than Mr. Freeman. When Mrs. Hopewell said to her after they had been on the place a while, "You know, you're the wheel behind the wheel," and winked, Mrs. Freeman had said, "I know it. I've always been quick. It's some that are quicker than others."

"Everybody is different," Mrs. Hopewell said.

"Yes, most people is," Mrs. Freeman said.

"It takes all kinds to make the world."

"I always said it did myself."

The girl was used to this kind of dialogue for breakfast and more of it for dinner; sometimes they had it for supper too. When they had no guest they ate in the kitchen because that was easier. Mrs. Freeman always managed to arrive at some point during the meal and to watch them finish it. She would stand in the doorway if it were summer but in the winter she would stand with one elbow on top of the refrigerator and look down on them, or she would stand by the gas heater, lifting the back of her skirt slightly. Occasionally she would stand against the wall and roll her head from side to side. At no time was she in any hurry to leave. All this was very trying on Mrs. Hopewell but she was a woman of great patience. She realized that nothing is perfect and that in the Freemans she had good country people and that if, in this day and age, you get good country people, you had better hang onto them.

She had had plenty of experience with trash. Before the Freemans she had averaged one tenant family a year. The wives of these farmers were not the kind you would want to be around you for very long. Mrs. Hopewell, who had divorced her husband long ago, needed someone to walk over the fields with her; and when Joy had to be impressed for these services, her remarks were usually so ugly and her face so glum that Mrs. Hopewell would say, "If you can't come pleasantly, I don't want you at all," to which the girl, standing square and rigid-shouldered with her neck thrust slightly forward, would reply, "If you want me, here I am—LIKE I AM."

Mrs. Hopewell excused this attitude because of the leg (which had been shot off in a hunting accident when Joy was ten). It was hard for Mrs. Hopewell to realize that her child was thirty-two now and that for more than twenty years she had had only one leg. She thought of her still as a child because it tore her heart to think instead of the poor stout girl in her thirties who had never danced a step or had any *normal* good times. Her name was really Joy but as soon as she was twenty-one and away from home, she had had it legally changed. Mrs. Hopewell was certain that she had thought and thought until she had hit upon the ugliest name in any language. Then she had gone and had the beautiful name, Joy, changed without telling her mother until after she had done it. Her legal name was Hulga.

When Mrs. Hopewell thought the name, Hulga, she thought of the broad blank hull of a battleship. She would not use it. She continued to call her Joy to which the girl responded but in a purely mechanical way.

Hulga had learned to tolerate Mrs. Freeman who saved her from taking walks with her mother. Even Glynese and Carramae were useful when they occupied attention that might otherwise have been directed at her. At first she had thought she could not stand Mrs. Freeman for she had found that it was not possible to be rude to her. Mrs. Freeman would take on strange resentments and for days together she would be sullen but the source of her displeasure was always obscure; a direct attack, a positive leer, blatant ugliness to her face—these never touched her. And without warning one day, she began calling her Hulga.

She did not call her that in front of Mrs. Hopewell who would have been incensed but when she and the girl happened to be out of the house together, she would say something and add the name Hulga to the end of it, and the big spectacled Joy-Hulga would scowl and redden as if her privacy had been intruded upon. She considered the name her personal affair. She had arrived at it first purely on the basis of its ugly sound and then the full genius of its fitness had struck her. She had a vision of the name working like the ugly sweating Vulcan who stayed in the furnace and to whom, presumably, the goddess had to come when called.[1] She saw it as the name of her highest creative act. One of her major triumphs was that her mother had not been able to turn her dust into Joy, but the greater one was that she had been able to turn it herself into Hulga. However, Mrs. Freeman's relish for using the name only irritated her. It was as if Mrs. Freeman's beady steel-pointed eyes had penetrated far enough behind her face to reach some secret fact. Something about her seemed to fascinate Mrs. Freeman and then one day Hulga realized that it was the artificial leg. Mrs. Freeman had a special fondness for the details of secret infections, hidden deformities, assaults upon children. Of diseases, she preferred the lingering or incurable. Hulga had heard Mrs. Hopewell give her the details of the hunting accident, how the leg had been literally blasted off, how she had never lost consciousness. Mrs. Freeman could listen to it any time as if it had happened an hour ago.

When Hulga stumped into the kitchen in the morning (she could walk without making the awful noise but she made it—Mrs. Hopewell was certain—because it was ugly-sounding), she glanced at them and did not speak. Mrs. Hopewell would be in her red kimono with her hair tied around her head in rags. She would be sitting at the table, finishing her breakfast and Mrs. Freeman would be hanging by her elbow outward from the refrigerator, looking down at the table. Hulga always put her eggs on the stove to boil and then stood over them with her arms folded, and Mrs. Hopewell would look at her—a kind of indirect gaze divided between her and Mrs. Freeman—and would think that if she would only keep herself up a little, she wouldn't be so bad looking. There was nothing wrong with her face that a pleasant expres-

---

1. Vulcan was the Greek god of fire whom Venus, goddess of love, "presumably" obeyed as her consort.

sion wouldn't help. Mrs. Hopewell said that people who looked on the bright side of things would be beautiful even if they were not.

Whenever she looked at Joy this way, she could not help but feel that it would have been better if the child had not taken the Ph.D. It had certainly not brought her out any and now that she had it, there was no more excuse for her to go to school again. Mrs. Hopewell thought it was nice for girls to go to school to have a good time but Joy had "gone through." Anyhow, she would not have been strong enough to go again. The doctors had told Mrs. Hopewell that with the best of care, Joy might see forty-five. She had a weak heart. Joy had made it plain that if it had not been for this condition, she would be far from these red hills and good country people. She would be in a university lecturing to people who knew what she was talking about. And Mrs. Hopewell could very well picture her there, looking like a scarecrow and lecturing to more of the same. Here she went about all day in a six-year-old skirt and a yellow sweat shirt with a faded cowboy on a horse embossed on it. She thought this was funny; Mrs. Hopewell thought it was idiotic and showed simply that she was still a child. She was brilliant but she didn't have a grain of sense. It seemed to Mrs. Hopewell that every year she grew less like other people and more like herself—bloated, rude, and squint-eyed. And she said such strange things! To her own mother she had said—without warning, without excuse, standing up in the middle of a meal with her face purple and her mouth half full—"Woman! do you ever look inside? Do you ever look inside and see what you are *not*? God!" she had cried sinking down again and staring at her plate, "Malebranche[2] was right: we are not our own light. We are not our own light!" Mrs. Hopewell had no idea to this day what brought that on. She had only made the remark, hoping Joy would take it in, that a smile never hurt anyone.

The girl had taken the Ph.D. in philosophy and this left Mrs. Hopewell at a complete loss. You could say, "My daughter is a nurse," or "My daughter is a school teacher," or even, "My daughter is a chemical engineer." You could not say, "My daughter is a philosopher." That was something that had ended with the Greeks and Romans. All day Joy sat on her neck in a deep chair, reading. Sometimes she went for walks but she didn't like dogs or cats or birds or flowers or nature or nice young men. She looked at nice young men as if she could smell their stupidity.

One day Mrs. Hopewell had picked up one of the books the girl had just put down and opening it at random, she read, "Science, on the other hand, has to assert its soberness and seriousness afresh and declare that it is concerned solely with what-is. Nothing—how can it be for science anything but a horror and a phantasm? If science is right, then one thing stands firm: science wishes to know nothing of nothing. Such is after all the strictly scientific approach to Nothing. We know it by wishing to know nothing of Nothing." These words had been underlined with a blue pencil and they worked on Mrs. Hopewell like some evil incantation in gibberish. She shut the book quickly and went out of the room as if she were having a chill.

This morning when the girl came in, Mrs. Freeman was on Carramae. "She thrown up four times after supper," she said, "and was up twict in the

2. Nicolas Malebranche (1638–1715), French philosopher.

night after three o'clock. Yesterday she didn't do nothing but ramble in the bureau drawer. All she did. Stand up there and see what she could run up on."

"She's got to eat," Mrs. Hopewell muttered, sipping her coffee, while she watched Joy's back at the stove. She was wondering what the child had said to the Bible salesman. She could not imagine what kind of a conversation she could possibly have had with him.

He was a tall gaunt hatless youth who had called yesterday to sell them a Bible. He had appeared at the door, carrying a large black suitcase that weighted him so heavily on one side that he had to brace himself against the door facing. He seemed on the point of collapse but he said in a cheerful voice, "Good morning, Mrs. Cedars!" and set the suitcase down on the mat. He was not a bad-looking young man though he had on a bright blue suit and yellow socks that were not pulled up far enough. He had prominent face bones and a streak of sticky-looking brown hair falling across his forehead.

"I'm Mrs. Hopewell," she said.

"Oh!" he said, pretending to look puzzled but with his eyes sparkling, "I saw it said 'The Cedars' on the mailbox so I thought you was Mrs. Cedars!" and he burst out in a pleasant laugh. He picked up the satchel and under cover of a pant, he fell forward into her hall. It was rather as if the suitcase had moved first, jerking him after it. "Mrs. Hopewell!" he said and grabbed her hand. "I hope you are well!" and he laughed again and then all at once his face sobered completely. He paused and gave her a straight earnest look and said, "Lady, I've come to speak of serious things."

"Well, come in," she muttered, none too pleased because her dinner was almost ready. He came into the parlor and sat down on the edge of a straight chair and put the suitcase between his feet and glanced around the room as if he were sizing her up by it. Her silver gleamed on the two sideboards; she decided he had never been in a room as elegant as this.

"Mrs. Hopewell," he began, using her name in a way that sounded almost intimate, "I know you believe in Chrustian service."

"Well yes," she murmured.

"I know," he said and paused, looking very wise with his head cocked on one side, "that you're a good woman. Friends have told me."

Mrs. Hopewell never liked to be taken for a fool. "What are you selling?" she asked.

"Bibles," the young man said and his eye raced around the room before he added, "I see you have no family Bible in your parlor, I see that is the one lack you got!"

Mrs. Hopewell could not say, "My daughter is an atheist and won't let me keep the Bible in the parlor." She said, stiffening slightly, "I keep my Bible by my bedside." This was not the truth. It was in the attic somewhere.

"Lady," he said, "the word of God ought to be in the parlor."

"Well, I think that's a matter of taste," she began. "I think . . ."

"Lady," he said, "for a Chrustian, the word of God ought to be in every room in the house besides in his heart. I know you're a Chrustian because I can see it in every line of your face."

She stood up and said, "Well, young man, I don't want to buy a Bible and I smell my dinner burning."

He didn't get up. He began to twist his hands and looking down at them, he said softly, "Well lady, I'll tell you the truth—not many people want to buy one nowadays and besides, I know I'm real simple. I don't know how to say a thing but to say it. I'm just a country boy." He glanced up into her unfriendly face. "People like you don't like to fool with country people like me!"

"Why!" she cried, "good country people are the salt of the earth! Besides, we all have different ways of doing, it takes all kinds to make the world go 'round. That's life!"

"You said a mouthful," he said.

"Why, I think there aren't enough good country people in the world!" she said, stirred. "I think that's what's wrong with it!"

His face had brightened. "I didn't inraduce myself," he said. "I'm Manley Pointer from out in the country around Willohobie, not even from a place, just from near a place."

"You wait a minute," she said. "I have to see about my dinner." She went out to the kitchen and found Joy standing near the door where she had been listening.

"Get rid of the salt of the earth," she said, "and let's eat."

Mrs. Hopewell gave her a pained look and turned the heat down under the vegetables. "I can't be rude to anybody," she murmured and went back into the parlor.

He had opened the suitcase and was sitting with a Bible on each knee.

"You might as well put those up," she told him. "I don't want one."

"I appreciate your honesty," he said. "You don't see any more real honest people unless you go way out in the country."

"I know," she said, "real genuine folks!" Through the crack in the door she heard a groan.

"I guess a lot of boys come telling you they're working their way through college," he said, "but I'm not going to tell you that. Somehow," he said, "I don't want to go to college. I want to devote my life to Chrustian service. See," he said, lowering his voice, "I got this heart condition. I may not live long. When you know it's something wrong with you and you may not live long, well then, lady . . ." He paused, with his mouth open, and stared at her.

He and Joy had the same condition! She knew that her eyes were filling with tears but she collected herself quickly and murmured, "Won't you stay for dinner? We'd love to have you!" and was sorry the instant she heard herself say it.

"Yes mam," he said in an abashed voice, "I would sher love to do that!"

Joy had given him one look on being introduced to him and then throughout the meal had not glanced at him again. He had addressed several remarks to her, which she had pretended not to hear. Mrs. Hopewell could not understand deliberate rudeness, although she lived with it, and she felt she had always to overflow with hospitality to make up for Joy's lack of courtesy. She urged him to talk about himself and he did. He said he was the seventh child of twelve and that his father had been crushed under a tree when he himself was eight years old. He had been crushed very badly, in fact, almost cut in two and was practically not recognizable. His mother had got along the best she could by hard working and she had always seen that her children went to Sunday School and that they read the Bible every evening. He was now nineteen years old and he had been selling Bibles for four months. In that time he had sold seventy-seven Bibles and had the promise of two more sales. He wanted to become a missionary because he thought that was the way you could do most for people. "He who losest his life shall find it," he said simply and he was so sincere, so genuine and earnest that Mrs. Hopewell would not for the world have smiled. He prevented his peas from sliding onto the table by blocking them with a piece of bread which he later cleaned his plate with. She could see Joy observing sidewise how he handled his knife and fork and she saw too that every few minutes, the boy would dart a keen appraising glance at the girl as if he were trying to attract her attention.

After dinner Joy cleared the dishes off the table and disappeared and Mrs. Hopewell was left to talk with him. He told her again about his childhood and his father's accident and about various things that had happened to him. Every five minutes or so she would stifle a yawn. He sat for two hours until finally she told him she must go because she had an appointment in town. He packed his Bibles and thanked her and prepared to leave, but in the doorway he stopped and wrung her hand and said that not on any of his trips had he met a lady as nice as her and he asked if he could come again. She had said she would always be happy to see him.

Joy had been standing in the road, apparently looking at something in the distance, when he came down the steps toward her, bent to the side with his heavy valise. He stopped where she was standing and confronted her directly. Mrs. Hopewell could not hear what he said but she trembled to think what Joy would say to him. She could see that after a minute Joy said something and that then the boy began to speak again, making an excited gesture with his free hand. After a minute Joy said something else at which the boy began to speak once more. Then to her amazement, Mrs. Hopewell saw the two of them walk off together, toward the gate. Joy had walked all the way to the gate with him and Mrs. Hopewell could not imagine what they had said to each other, and she had not yet dared to ask.

Mrs. Freeman was insisting upon her attention. She had moved from the refrigerator to the heater so that Mrs. Hopewell had to turn and face her in order to seem to be listening. "Glynese gone out with Harvey Hill again last night," she said. "She had this sty."

"Hill," Mrs. Hopewell said absently, "is that the one who works in the garage?"

"Nome, he's the one that goes to chiropracter school," Mrs. Freeman said. "She had this sty. Been had it two days. So she says when he brought her in the other night he says, 'Lemme get rid of that sty for you,' and she says, 'How?' and he says, 'You just lay yourself down acrost the seat of that car and I'll show you.' So she done it and he popped her neck. Kept on a-popping it several times until she made him quit. This morning," Mrs. Freeman said, "she ain't got no sty. She ain't got no traces of a sty."

"I never heard of that before," Mrs. Hopewell said.

"He ast her to marry him before the Ordinary,"[3] Mrs. Freeman went on, "and she told him she wasn't going to be married in no *office.*"

"Well, Glynese is a fine girl," Mrs. Hopewell said. "Glynese and Carramae are both fine girls."

"Carramae said when her and Lyman was married Lyman said it sure felt

---

3. Justice of the peace who performs the marriage ceremony in chambers rather than in public.

sacred to him. She said he said he wouldn't take five hundred dollars for being married by a preacher."

"How much would he take?" the girl asked from the stove.

"He said he wouldn't take five hundred dollars," Mrs. Freeman repeated.

"Well we all have work to do," Mrs. Hopewell said.

"Lyman said it just felt more sacred to him," Mrs. Freeman said. "The doctor wants Carramae to eat prunes. Says instead of medicine. Says them cramps is coming from pressure. You know where I think it is?"

"She'll be better in a few weeks," Mrs. Hopewell said.

"In the tube," Mrs. Freeman said. "Else she wouldn't be as sick as she is."

Hulga had cracked her two eggs into a saucer and was bringing them to the table along with a cup of coffee that she had filled too full. She sat down carefully and began to eat, meaning to keep Mrs. Freeman there by questions if for any reason she showed an inclination to leave. She could perceive her mother's eye on her. The first round-about question would be about the Bible salesman and she did not wish to bring it on. "How did he pop her neck?" she asked.

Mrs. Freeman went into a description of how he had popped her neck. She said he owned a '55 Mercury but that Glynese said she would rather marry a man with only a '36 Plymouth who would be married by a preacher. The girl asked what if he had a '32 Plymouth and Mrs. Freeman said what Glynese had said was a '36 Plymouth.

Mrs. Hopewell said there were not many girls with Glynese's common sense. She said what she admired in those girls was their common sense. She said that reminded her that they had had a nice visitor yesterday, a young man selling Bibles. "Lord," she said, "he bored me to death but he was so sincere and genuine I couldn't be rude to him. He was just good country people, you know," she said, "—just the salt of the earth."

"I seen him walk up," Mrs. Freeman said, "and then later—I seen him walk off," and Hulga could feel the slight shift in her voice, the slight insinuation, that he had not walked off alone, had he? Her face remained expressionless but the color rose into her neck and she seemed to swallow it down with the next spoonful of egg. Mrs. Freeman was looking at her as if they had a secret together.

"Well, it takes all kinds of people to make the world go 'round," Mrs. Hopewell said. "It's very good we aren't all alike."

"Some people are more alike than others," Mrs. Freeman said.

Hulga got up and stumped, with about twice the noise that was necessary, into her room and locked the door. She was to meet the Bible salesman at ten o'clock at the gate. She had thought about it half the night. She had started thinking of it as a great joke and then she had begun to see profound implications in it. She had lain in bed imagining dialogues for them that were insane on the surface but that reached below to depths that no Bible salesman would be aware of. Their conversation yesterday had been of this kind.

He had stopped in front of her and had simply stood there. His face was bony and sweaty and bright, with a little pointed nose in the center of it, and his look was different from what it had been at the dinner table. He was gazing at her with open curiosity, with fascination, like a child watching a new fantastic animal at the zoo, and he was breathing as if he had run a great distance to reach her. His gaze seemed somehow familiar but she could not think where she had been regarded with it before. For almost a minute he didn't say anything. Then on what seemed an insuck of breath, he whispered, "You ever ate a chicken that was two days old?"

The girl looked at him stonily. He might have just put this question up for consideration at the meeting of a philosophical association. "Yes," she presently replied as if she had considered it from all angles.

"It must have been mighty small!" he said triumphantly and shook all over with little nervous giggles, getting very red in the face, and subsiding finally into his gaze of complete admiration, while the girl's expression remained exactly the same.

"How old are you?" he asked softly.

She waited some time before she answered. Then in a flat voice she said, "Seventeen."

His smiles came in succession like waves breaking on the surface of a little lake. "I see you got a wooden leg," he said. "I think you're brave. I think you're real sweet."

The girl stood blank and solid and silent.

"Walk to the gate with me," he said. "You're a brave sweet little thing and I liked you the minute I seen you walk in the door."

Hulga began to move forward.

"What's your name?" he asked, smiling down on the top of her head.

"Hulga," she said.

"Hulga," he murmured, "Hulga. Hulga. I never heard of anybody name Hulga before. You're shy, aren't you, Hulga?" he asked.

She nodded, watching his large red hand on the handle of the giant valise.

"I like girls that wear glasses," he said. "I think a lot. I'm not like these people that a serious thought don't ever enter their heads. It's because I may die."

"I may die too," she said suddenly and looked up at him. His eyes were very small and brown, glittering feverishly.

"Listen," he said, "don't you think some people was meant to meet on account of what all they got in common and all? Like they both think serious thoughts and all?" He shifted the valise to his other hand so that the hand nearest her was free. He caught hold of her elbow and shook it a little. "I don't work on Saturday," he said. "I like to walk in the woods and see what Mother Nature is wearing. O'er the hills and far away. Pic-nics and things. Couldn't we go on a pic-nic tomorrow? Say yes, Hulga," he said and gave her a dying look as if he felt his insides about to drop out of him. He had even seemed to sway slightly toward her.

During the night she had imagined that she seduced him. She imagined that the two of them walked on the place until they came to the storage barn beyond the two back fields and there, she imagined, that things came to such a pass that she very easily seduced him and that then, of course, she had to reckon with his remorse. True genius can get an idea across even to an inferior mind. She imagined that she took his remorse in hand and changed it into a deeper understanding of life. She took all his shame away and turned it into something useful.

She set off for the gate at exactly ten o'clock, escaping without drawing Mrs. Hopewell's attention. She didn't take anything to eat, forgetting that food is usually taken on a picnic. She wore a pair of slacks and a dirty white shirt, and as an afterthought, she had put some Vapex on the collar of it since she did not own any perfume. When she reached the gate no one was there.

She looked up and down the empty highway and had the furious feeling that she had been tricked, that he had only meant to make her walk to the gate after the idea of him. Then suddenly he stood up, very tall, from behind a bush on the opposite embankment. Smiling, he lifted his hat which was new and wide-brimmed. He had not worn it yesterday and she wondered if he had bought it for the occasion. It was toast-colored with a red and white band around it and was slightly too large for him. He stepped from behind the bush still carrying the black valise. He had on the same suit and the same yellow socks sucked down in his shoes from walking. He crossed the highway and said, "I knew you'd come!"

The girl wondered acidly how he had known this. She pointed to the valise and asked, "Why did you bring your Bibles?"

He took her elbow, smiling down on her as if he could not stop. "You can never tell when you'll need the word of God, Hulga," he said. She had a moment in which she doubted that this was actually happening and then they began to climb the embankment. They went down into the pasture toward the woods. The boy walked lightly by her side, bouncing on his toes. The valise did not seem to be heavy today; he even swung it. They crossed half the pasture without saying anything and then, putting his hand easily on the small of her back, he asked softly, "Where does your wooden leg join on?"

She turned an ugly red and glared at him and for an instant the boy looked abashed. "I didn't mean you no harm," he said. "I only meant you're so brave and all. I guess God takes care of you."

"No," she said, looking forward and walking fast, "I don't even believe in God."

At this he stopped and whistled. "No!" he exclaimed as if he were too astonished to say anything else.

She walked on and in a second he was bouncing at her side, fanning with his hat. "That's very unusual for a girl," he remarked, watching her out of the corner of his eye. When they reached the edge of the wood, he put his hand on her back again and drew her against him without a word and kissed her heavily.

The kiss, which had more pressure than feeling behind it, produced that extra surge of adrenalin in the girl that enables one to carry a packed trunk out of a burning house, but in her, the power went at once to the brain. Even before he released her, her mind, clear and detached and ironic anyway, was regarding him from a great distance, with amusement but with pity. She had never been kissed before and she was pleased to discover that it was an unexceptional experience and all a matter of the mind's control. Some people might enjoy drain water if they were told it was vodka. When the boy, looking expectant but uncertain, pushed her gently away, she turned and walked on, saying nothing as if such business, for her, were common enough.

He came along panting at her side, trying to help her when he saw a root that she might trip over. He caught and held back the long swaying blades of thorn vine until she had passed beyond them. She led the way and he came breathing heavily behind her. Then they came out on a sunlit hillside, sloping softly into another one a little smaller. Beyond, they could see the rusted top of the old barn where the extra hay was stored.

The hill was sprinkled with small pink weeds. "Then you ain't saved?" he asked suddenly, stopping.

The girl smiled. It was the first time she had smiled at him at all. "In my economy," she said, "I'm saved and you are damned but I told you I didn't believe in God."

Nothing seemed to destroy the boy's look of admiration. He gazed at her now as if the fantastic animal at the zoo had put its paw through the bars and given him a loving poke. She thought he looked as if he wanted to kiss her again and she walked on before he had the chance.

"Ain't there somewheres we can sit down sometime?" he murmured, his voice softening toward the end of the sentence.

"In that barn," she said.

They made for it rapidly as if it might slide away like a train. It was a large two-story barn, cool and dark inside. The boy pointed up the ladder that led into the loft and said, "It's too bad we can't go up there."

"Why can't we?" she asked.

"Yer leg," he said reverently.

The girl gave him a contemptuous look and putting both hands on the ladder, she climbed it while he stood below, apparently awestruck. She pulled herself expertly through the opening and then looked down at him and said, "Well, come on if you're coming," and he began to climb the ladder, awkwardly bringing the suitcase with him.

"We won't need the Bible," she observed.

"You never can tell," he said, panting. After he had got into the loft, he was a few seconds catching his breath. She had sat down in a pile of straw. A wide sheath of sunlight, filled with dust particles, slanted over her. She lay back against a bale, her face turned away, looking out the front opening of the barn where hay was thrown from a wagon into the loft. The two pink-speckled hillsides lay back against a dark ridge of woods. The sky was cloudless and cold blue. The boy dropped down by her side and put one arm under her and the other over her and began methodically kissing her face, making little noises like a fish. He did not remove his hat but it was pushed far enough back not to interfere. When her glasses got in his way, he took them off of her and slipped them into his pocket.

The girl at first did not return any of the kisses but presently she began to and after she had put several on his cheek, she reached his lips and remained there, kissing him again and again as if she were trying to draw all the breath out of him. His breath was clear and sweet like a child's and the kisses were sticky like a child's. He mumbled about loving her and about knowing when he first seen her that he loved her, but the mumbling was like the sleepy fretting of a child being put to sleep by his mother. Her mind, throughout this, never stopped or lost itself for a second to her feelings. "You ain't said you loved me none," he whispered finally, pulling back from her. "You got to say that."

She looked away from him off into the hollow sky and then down at a black ridge and then down farther into what appeared to be two green swelling lakes. She didn't realize he had taken her glasses but this landscape could not seem exceptional to her for she seldom paid any close attention to her surroundings.

"You got to say it," he repeated. "You got to say you love me."

She was always careful how she committed herself. "In a sense," she began, "if you use the word loosely, you might say that. But it's not a word I use. I don't have illusions. I'm one of those people who see *through* to nothing."

The boy was frowning. "You got to say it. I said it and you got to say it," he said.

The girl looked at him almost tenderly. "You poor baby," she murmured. "It's just as well you don't understand," and she pulled him by the neck, face-down against her. "We are all damned," she said, "but some of us have taken off our blindfolds and see that there's nothing to see. It's a kind of salvation."

The boy's astonished eyes looked blankly through the ends of her hair. "Okay," he almost whined, "but do you love me or don'tcher?"

"Yes," she said and added, "in a sense. But I must tell you something. There mustn't be anything dishonest between us." She lifted his head and looked him in the eye. "I am thirty years old," she said. "I have a number of degrees."

The boy's look was irritated but dogged. "I don't care," he said. "I don't care a thing about what all you done. I just want to know if you love me or don'tcher?" and he caught her to him and wildly planted her face with kisses until she said, "Yes, yes."

"Okay then," he said, letting her go. "Prove it."

She smiled, looking dreamily out on the shifty landscape. She had seduced him without even making up her mind to try. "How?" she asked, feeling that he should be delayed a little.

He leaned over and put his lips to her ear. "Show me where your wooden leg joins on," he whispered.

The girl uttered a sharp little cry and her face instantly drained of color. The obscenity of the suggestion was not what shocked her. As a child she had sometimes been subject to feelings of shame but education had removed the last traces of that as a good surgeon scrapes for cancer; she would no more have felt it over what he was asking than she would have believed in his Bible. But she was as sensitive about the artificial leg as a peacock about his tail. No one ever touched it but her. She took care of it as someone else would his soul, in private and almost with her own eyes turned away. "No," she said.

"I known it," he muttered, sitting up. "You're just playing me for a sucker."

"Oh no no!" she cried. "It joins on at the knee. Only at the knee. Why do you want to see it?"

The boy gave her a long penetrating look. "Because," he said, "it's what makes you different. You ain't like anybody else."

She sat staring at him. There was nothing about her face or her round freezing-blue eyes to indicate that this had moved her; but she felt as if her heart had stopped and left her mind to pump her blood. She decided that for the first time in her life she was face to face with real innocence. This boy, with an instinct that came from beyond wisdom, had touched the truth about her. When after a minute, she said in a hoarse high voice, "All right," it was like surrendering to him completely. It was like losing her own life and finding it again, miraculously, in his.

Very gently he began to roll the slack leg up. The artificial limb, in a white sock and brown flat shoe, was bound in a heavy material like canvas and ended in an ugly jointure where it was attached to the stump. The boy's face and his voice were entirely reverent as he uncovered it and said, "Now show me how to take it off and on."

She took it off for him and put it back on again and then he took it off himself, handling it as tenderly as if it were a real one. "See!" he said with a delighted child's face. "Now I can do it myself!"

"Put it back on," she said. She was thinking that she would run away with him and that every night he would take the leg off and every morning put it back on again. "Put it back on," she said.

"Not yet," he murmured, setting it on its foot out of her reach. "Leave it off for a while. You got me instead."

She gave a cry of alarm but he pushed her down and began to kiss her again. Without the leg she felt entirely dependent on him. Her brain seemed to have stopped thinking altogether and to be about some other function that it was not very good at. Different expressions raced back and forth over her face. Every now and then the boy, his eyes like two steel spikes, would glance behind him where the leg stood. Finally she pushed him off and said, "Put it back on me now."

"Wait," he said. He leaned the other way and pulled the valise toward him and opened it. It had a pale blue spotted lining and there were only two Bibles in it. He took one of these out and opened the cover of it. It was hollow and contained a pocket flask of whiskey, a pack of cards, and a small blue box with printing on it. He laid these out in front of her one at a time in an evenly-spaced row, like one presenting offerings at the shrine of a goddess. He put the blue box in her hand. THIS PRODUCT TO BE USED ONLY FOR THE PREVENTION OF DISEASE, she read, and dropped it. The boy was unscrewing the top of the flask. He stopped and pointed, with a smile, to the deck of cards. It was not an ordinary deck but one with an obscene picture on the back of each card. "Take a swig," he said, offering her the bottle first. He held it in front of her, but like one mesmerized, she did not move.

Her voice when she spoke had an almost pleading sound. "Aren't you," she murmured, "aren't you just good country people?"

The boy cocked his head. He looked as if he were just beginning to understand that she might be trying to insult him. "Yeah," he said, curling his lip slightly, "but it ain't held me back none. I'm as good as you any day in the week."

"Give me my leg," she said.

He pushed it farther away with his foot. "Come on now, let's begin to have us a good time," he said coaxingly. "We ain't got to know one another good yet."

"Give me my leg!" she screamed and tried to lunge for it but he pushed her down easily.

"What's the matter with you all of a sudden?" he asked, frowning as he screwed the top on the flask and put it quickly back inside the Bible. "You just a while ago said you didn't believe in nothing. I thought you was some girl!"

Her face was almost purple. "You're a Christian!" she hissed. "You're a fine

Christian! You're just like them all—say one thing and do another. You're a perfect Christian, you're . . ."

The boy's mouth was set angrily. "I hope you don't think," he said in a lofty indignant tone, "that I believe in that crap! I may sell Bibles but I know which end is up and I wasn't born yesterday and I know where I'm going!"

"Give me my leg!" she screeched. He jumped up so quickly that she barely saw him sweep the cards and the blue box into the Bible and throw the Bible into the valise. She saw him grab the leg and then she saw it for an instant slanted forlornly across the inside of the suitcase with a Bible at either side of its opposite ends. He slammed the lid shut and snatched up the valise and swung it down the hole and then stepped through himself.

When all of him had passed but his head, he turned and regarded her with a look that no longer had any admiration in it. "I've gotten a lot of interesting things," he said. "One time I got a woman's glass eye this way. And you needn't to think you'll catch me because Pointer ain't really my name. I use a different name at every house I call at and don't stay nowhere long. And I'll tell you another thing, Hulga," he said, using the name as if he didn't think much of it, "you ain't so smart. I been believing in nothing every since I was born!" and then the toast-colored hat disappeared down the hole and the girl was left, sitting on the straw in the dusty sunlight. When she turned her churning face toward the opening, she saw his blue figure struggling successfully over the green speckled lake.

Mrs. Hopewell and Mrs. Freeman, who were in the back pasture, digging up onions, saw him emerge a little later from the woods and head across the meadow toward the highway. "Why, that looks like that nice dull young man that tried to sell me a Bible yesterday," Mrs. Hopewell said, squinting. "He must have been selling them to the Negroes back in there. He was so simple," she said, "but I guess the world would be better off if we were all that simple."

Mrs. Freeman's gaze drove forward and just touched him before he disappeared under the hill. Then she returned her attention to the evil-smelling onion shoot she was lifting from the ground. "Some can't be that simple," she said. "I know I never could."

1955

URSULA K. LE GUIN
b. 1929

Gender, social behavior, and art combine in the fiction of Ursula K. Le Guin to create model worlds, all with their own systems of organized belief. In doing so this author inquires more broadly and with more depth than is usual in science fiction. Traditionally, science fiction writers have been at their best when dealing with dystopian worlds, projecting alternative visions in which their satiric powers criticize contemporary tendencies gone bad in a nightmare future; utopias within this subgenre are more often declarative statements of what would be good and therefore less interesting and less engaging as art. Le Guin distinguishes herself by demonstrating a sincere interest in exploring the legitimacy of other styles of existence—not just what they are but how they work. Her utopian creations are tested against all we know not just about physical and mechanical science but about anthropology in general and gender relationships in particular.

Drawing on what she first learned from her anthropologist father and folklorist/ writer mother (Alfred L. and Theodora K. Kroeber), Le Guin has produced science fiction that shifts readers' interests from the pageantry of outer-space discovery and battle to the more subtle dimensions of human identity and communication. Foremost is the power of art. In "A Wizard of Earthsea" (1968) the power of naming something brings it into being; a similar creative effect is apparent in "She Unnames Them" (printed here), in which Eve revises Adam's masculine, typifying style by introducing an ethic representative of woman's feelings. Her novel *The Left Hand of Darkness* (1969) shows a human ethnologist investigating a world in which gender does not shape reality at all. In this society of hermaphrodites who experience sexual distinctions only for a short time during reproduction, such limitations as binary thinking disappear. Yet this is no simple utopia, for the author believes that any reality is a cultural rather than strictly scientific description—and that one description is superior to another only in its functional persuasiveness. Hence even her creatures in *The Left Hand of Darkness* need to overcome the restrictions of their society and develop secure identities capable of sharing love. This same appraisal informs her story "Schrödinger's Cat" (printed here), in which the famous Austrian physicist's great *Gedankenexperiment* (literally "thinking experiment," as opposed to a demonstration with physical matter) is examined in terms of its cultural implications not its scientific truth. A similarly complex understanding of socioeconomics informs the action of "The Dispossessed" (1974), in which a scientist compares visits to an outworn anarchistic utopia with a younger world whose capitalistic versus communistic rivalries are much like our own. Here, as is usual in her work, Le Guin dresses her thought with rich nuances of character and motivated behavior; the intelligence behind her work is always accessible in human terms—sometimes uncomfortably revealing terms, as apparent in the manner of her narrators in "She Unnames Them" and "Schrödinger's Cat."

Born in Berkeley, California, where her father taught at the University of California, Le Guin was raised in this academic environment before attending Radcliffe College (for an undergraduate degree in French) and Columbia University (for a master's degree in romance languages). Her longtime residence has been in Oregon, and the ecology of the Pacific Northwest figures as an element in her fiction as well as in the amazing amount and variety of her other work. In addition to many novels (often written in trilogies) she has written poetry, essays, children's books, and ecological statements and has collaborated on photographic and cinematic projects. As a science fictionist, she is one of the most highly honored writers in her field, a consistent winner of the subgenre's highest awards, including the Hugo and the Nebula several times.

Both texts are from *The Compass Rose* (1982).

Schrödinger's Cat[1]

As things appear to be coming to some sort of climax, I have withdrawn to this place. It is cooler here, and nothing moves fast.

On the way here I met a married couple who were coming apart. She had

1. The Austrian physicist Erwin Schrödinger (1887–1961) analogized a cat in a box to demonstrate his wave-mechanical approach to quantum theory.

pretty well gone to pieces, but he seemed, at first glance, quite hearty. While he was telling me that he had no hormones of any kind, she pulled herself together and, by supporting her head in the crook of her right knee and hopping on the toes of the right foot, approached us shouting, "Well what's *wrong* with a person trying to express themselves?" The left leg, the arms, and the trunk, which had remained lying in the heap, twitched and jerked in sympathy. "Great legs," the husband pointed out, looking at the slim ankle. "My wife has great legs."

A cat has arrived, interrupting my narrative. It is a striped yellow tom with white chest and paws. He has long whiskers and yellow eyes. I never noticed before that cats had whiskers above their eyes; is that normal? There is no way to tell. As he has gone to sleep on my knee, I shall proceed.

Where?

Nowhere, evidently. Yet the impulse to narrate remains. Many things are not worth doing, but almost anything is worth telling. In any case, I have a severe congenital case of *Ethica laboris puritanica*,[2] or Adam's Disease. It is incurable except by total decapitation. I even like to dream when asleep, and to try and recall my dreams: it assures me that I haven't wasted seven or eight hours just lying there. Now here I am, lying, here. Hard at it.

Well, the couple I was telling you about finally broke up. The pieces of him trotted around bouncing and cheeping, like little chicks, but she was finally reduced to nothing but a mass of nerves: rather like fine chicken wire, in fact, but hopelessly tangled.

So I came on, placing one foot carefully in front of the other, and grieving. This grief is with me still. I fear it is part of me, like foot or loin or eye, or may even be myself: for I seem to have no other self, nothing further, nothing that lies outside the borders of grief.

Yet I don't know what I grieve for: my wife? my husband? my children, or myself? I can't remember. Most dreams are forgotten, try as one will to remember. Yet later music strikes the note, and the harmonic rings along the mandolin strings of the mind, and we find tears in our eyes. Some note keeps playing that makes me want to cry; but what for? I am not certain.

The yellow cat, who may have belonged to the couple that broke up, is dreaming. His paws twitch now and then, and once he makes a small, suppressed remark with his mouth shut. I wonder what a cat dreams of, and to whom he was speaking just then. Cats seldom waste words. They are quiet beasts. They keep their counsel, they reflect. They reflect all day, and at night their eyes reflect. Overbred Siamese cats may be as noisy as little dogs, and then people say, "They're talking," but the noise is farther from speech than is the deep silence of the hound or the tabby. All this cat can say is meow, but maybe in his silences he will suggest to me what it is that I have lost, what I am grieving for. I have a feeling that he knows. That's why he came here. Cats look out for Number One.

It was getting awfully hot. I mean, you could touch less and less. The stove burners, for instance. Now I know that stove burners always used to get hot; that was their final cause, they existed in order to get hot. But they began to get hot without having been turned on. Electric units or gas rings, there

---

2. Puritan work ethic (Latin); a trait the narrator sees as a consequence of the biblical expulsion from the Garden of Eden ("Adam's Disease").

they'd be when you came into the kitchen for breakfast, all four of them glaring away, the air above them shaking like clear jelly with the heat waves. It did no good to turn them off, because they weren't on in the first place. Besides, the knobs and dials were also hot, uncomfortable to the touch.

Some people tried hard to cool them off. The favorite technique was to turn them on. It worked sometimes, but you could not count on it. Others investigated the phenomenon, tried to get at the root of it, the cause. They were probably the most frightened ones, but man is most human at his most frightened. In the face of the hot stove burners they acted with exemplary coolness. They studied, they observed. They were like the fellow in Michelangelo's *Last Judgment*,[3] who has clapped his hands over his face in horror as the devils drag him down to Hell—but only over one eye. The other eye is busy looking. It's all he can do, but he does it. He observes. Indeed, one wonders if Hell would exist, if he did not look at it. However, neither he, nor the people I am talking about, had enough time left to do much about it. And then finally of course there were the people who did not try to do or think anything about it at all.

When the water came out of the cold-water taps hot one morning, however, even people who had blamed it all on the Democrats began to feel a more profound unease. Before long, forks and pencils and wrenches were too hot to handle without gloves; and cars were really terrible. It was like opening the door of an oven going full blast, to open the door of your car. And by then, other people almost scorched your fingers off. A kiss was like a branding iron. Your child's hair flowed along your hand like fire.

Here, as I said, it is cooler; and, as a matter of fact, this animal is cool. A real cool cat. No wonder it's pleasant to pet his fur. Also he moves slowly, at least for the most part, which is all the slowness one can reasonably expect of a cat. He hasn't that frenetic quality most creatures acquired—all they did was ZAP and gone. They lacked presence. I suppose birds always tended to be that way, but even the hummingbird used to halt for a second in the very center of his metabolic frenzy, and hang, still as a hub, present, above the fuchsias—then gone again, but you knew something was there besides the blurring brightness. But it got so that even robins and pigeons, the heavy impudent birds, were a blur; and as for swallows, they cracked the sound barrier. You knew of swallows only by the small, curved sonic booms that looped about the eaves of old houses in the evening.

Worms shot like subway trains through the dirt of gardens, among the writhing roots of roses.

You could scarcely lay a hand on children, by then: too fast to catch, too hot to hold. They grew up before your eyes.

But then, maybe that's always been true.

I was interrupted by the cat, who woke and said meow once, then jumped down from my lap and leaned against my legs diligently. This is a cat who knows how to get fed. He also knows how to jump. There was a lazy fluidity to his leap, as if gravity affected him less than it does other creatures. As a matter of fact there were some localised cases, just before I left, of the failure

3. Magnificent fresco by the Italian Renaissance painter Michelangelo Buonarotti (1475–1564).

of gravity; but this quality in the cat's leap was something quite else. I am not yet in such a state of confusion that I can be alarmed by grace. Indeed, I found it reassuring. While I was opening a can of sardines, a person arrived.

Hearing the knock, I thought it might be the mailman. I miss mail very much, so I hurried to the door and said, "Is it the mail?"

A voice replied, "Yah!" I opened the door. He came in, almost pushing me aside in his haste. He dumped down an enormous knapsack he had been carrying, straightened up, massaged his shoulders, and said, "Wow!"

"How did you get here?"

He stared at me and repeated, "How?"

At this my thoughts concerning human and animal speech recurred to me, and I decided that this was probably not a man, but a small dog. (Large dogs seldom go yah, wow, how, unless it is appropriate to do so.)

"Come on, fella," I coaxed him. "Come, come on, that's a boy, good doggie!" I opened a can of pork and beans for him at once, for he looked half starved. He ate voraciously, gulping and lapping. When it was gone he said "Wow!" several times. I was just about to scratch him behind the ears when he stiffened, his hackles bristling, and growled deep in his throat. He had noticed the cat.

The cat had noticed him some time before, without interest, and was now sitting on a copy of *The Well-Tempered Clavier*[4] washing sardine oil off its whiskers.

"Wow!" the dog, whom I had thought of calling Rover, barked. "Wow! Do you know what that is? *That's Schrödinger's cat!*"

"No it's not, not any more; it's my cat," I said, unreasonably offended.

"Oh, well, Schrödinger's dead, of course, but it's his cat. I've seen hundreds of pictures of it. Erwin Schrödinger, the great physicist, you know. Oh, wow! To think of finding it here!"

The cat looked coldly at him for a moment, and began to wash its left shoulder with negligent energy. An almost religious expression had come into Rover's face. "It was meant," he said in a low, impressive tone. "Yah. It was *meant*. It can't be a mere coincidence. It's too improbable. Me, with the box; you, with the cat; to meet—here—now." He looked up at me, his eyes shining with happy fervor. "Isn't it wonderful?" he said. "I'll get the box set up right away." And he started to tear open his huge knapsack.

While the cat washed its front paws, Rover unpacked. While the cat washed its tail and belly, regions hard to reach gracefully, Rover put together what he had unpacked, a complex task. When he and the cat finished their operations simultaneously and looked at me, I was impressed. They had come out even, to the very second. Indeed it seemed that something more than chance was involved. I hoped it was not myself.

"What's that?" I asked, pointing to a protuberance on the outside of the box. I did not ask what the box was as it was quite clearly a box.

"The gun," Rover said with excited pride.

"The gun?"

"To shoot the cat."

"To shoot the cat?"

4. Music by the German preclassical composer Johann Christian Bach (1735–1782).

"Or to *not shoot* the cat. Depending on the photon."

"The photon?"

"Yah! It's Schrödinger's great Gedankenexperiment.[5] You see, there's a little emitter here. At Zero Time, five seconds after the lid of the box is closed, it will emit one photon. The photon will strike a half-silvered mirror. The quantum mechanical probability of the photon passing through the mirror is exactly one half, isn't it? So! If the photon passes through, the trigger will be activated and the gun will fire. If the photon is deflected, the trigger will not be activated and the gun will not fire. Now, you put the cat in. The cat is in the box. You close the lid. You go away! You stay away! What happens?" Rover's eyes were bright.

"The cat gets hungry?"

"The cat gets shot—or not shot," he said, seizing my arm, though not, fortunately, in his teeth. "But the gun is silent, perfectly silent. The box is soundproof. There is no way to know whether or not the cat has been shot, until you lift the lid of the box. There is *no* way! Do you see how central this is to the whole of quantum theory? Before Zero Time the whole system, on the quantum level or on our level, is nice and simple. But after Zero Time the whole system can be represented only by a linear combination of two waves. We cannot predict the behavior of the photon, and thus, once it has behaved, we cannot predict the state of the system it has determined. We cannot predict it! God plays dice with the world! So it is beautifully demonstrated that if you desire certainty, any certainty, you must create it yourself!"

"How?"

"By lifting the lid of the box, of course," Rover said, looking at me with sudden disappointment, perhaps a touch of suspicion, like a Baptist who finds he has been talking church matters not to another Baptist as he thought, but a Methodist, or even, God forbid, an Episcopalian. "To find out whether the cat is dead or not."

"Do you mean," I said carefully, "that until you lift the lid of the box, the cat has neither been shot nor not been shot?"

"Yah!" Rover said, radiant with relief, welcoming me back to the fold. "Or maybe, you know, both."

"But why does opening the box and looking reduce the system back to one probability, either live cat or dead cat? Why don't we get included in the system when we lift the lid of the box?"

There was a pause. "How?" Rover barked, distrustfully.

"Well, we would involve ourselves in the system, you see, the superposition of two waves. There's no reason why it should only exist *inside* an open box, is there? So when we came to look, there we would be, you and I, both looking at a live cat, and both looking at a dead cat. You see?"

A dark cloud lowered on Rover's eyes and brow. He barked twice in a subdued, harsh voice, and walked away. With his back turned to me he said in a firm, sad tone, "You must not complicate the issue. It is complicated enough."

"Are you sure?"

---

5. Thinking experiment (German, literal trans.); the intellectual demonstration of a theory, often making use of analogy.

He nodded. Turning, he spoke pleadingly. "Listen. It's all we have—the box. Truly it is. The box. And the cat. And they're here. The box, the cat, at last. Put the cat in the box. Will you? Will you let me put the cat in the box?"

"No," I said, shocked.

"Please. Please. Just for a minute. Just for half a minute! Please let me put the cat in the box!"

"Why?"

"I can't stand this terrible uncertainty," he said, and burst into tears.

I stood some while indecisive. Though I felt sorry for the poor son of a bitch, I was about to tell him, gently, No; when a curious thing happened. The cat walked over to the box, sniffed around it, lifted his tail and sprayed a corner to mark his territory, and then lightly, with that marvellous fluid case, leapt into it. His yellow tail just flicked the edge of the lid as he jumped, and it closed, falling into place with a soft, decisive click.

"The cat is in the box," I said.

"The cat is in the box," Rover repeated in a whisper, falling to his knees. "Oh, wow. Oh, wow. Oh, wow."

There was silence then: deep silence. We both gazed, I afoot, Rover kneeling, at the box. No sound. Nothing happened. Nothing would happen. Nothing would ever happen, until we lifted the lid of the box.

"Like Pandora,"[6] I said in a weak whisper. I could not quite recall Pandora's legend. She had let all the plagues and evils out of the box, of course, but there had been something else, too. After all the devils were let loose, something quite different, quite unexpected, had been left. What had it been? Hope? A dead cat? I could not remember.

Impatience welled up in me. I turned on Rover, glaring. He returned the look with expressive brown eyes. You can't tell me dogs haven't got souls.

"Just exactly what are you trying to prove?" I demanded.

"That the cat will be dead, or not dead," he murmured submissively. "Certainty. All I want is certainty. To know for *sure* that God *does* play dice with the world."[7]

I looked at him for a while with fascinated incredulity. "Whether he does, or doesn't," I said, "do you think he's going to leave you a note about it in the box?" I went to the box, and with a rather dramatic gesture, flung the lid back. Rover staggered up from his knees, gasping, to look. The cat was, of course, not there.

Rover neither barked, nor fainted, nor cursed, nor wept. He really took it very well.

"Where is the cat?" he asked at last.

"Where is the box?"

"Here."

"Where's here?"

"Here is now."

"We used to think so," I said, "but really we should use larger boxes."

He gazed about him in mute bewilderment, and did not flinch even when the roof of the house was lifted off just like the lid of a box, letting in the

---

6. In Greek mythology, the first mortal woman, who out of curiosity opened a box and released human ills into the world; another version has her losing all human blessings except hope.

7. American physicist Albert Einstein (1879–1955) stated that God *did not* play dice with the universe.

unconscionable, inordinate light of the stars. He had just time to breathe, "Oh, wow!"

I have identified the note that keeps sounding. I checked it on the mandolin before the glue melted. It is the note A, the one that drove the composer Schumann mad. It is a beautiful, clear tone, much clearer now that the stars are visible. I shall miss the cat. I wonder if he found what it was we lost?

1982

She Unnames Them

Most of them accepted namelessness with the perfect indifference with which they had so long accepted and ignored their names. Whales and dolphins, seals and sea otters consented with particular grace and alacrity, sliding into anonymity as into their element. A faction of yaks, however, protested. They said that "yak" sounded right, and that almost everyone who knew they existed called them that. Unlike the ubiquitous creatures such as rats or fleas who had been called by hundreds or thousands of different names since Babel,[1] the yaks could truly say, they said, that they had *a name*. They discussed the matter all summer. The councils of the elderly females finally agreed that though the name might be useful to others, it was so redundant from the yak point of view that they never spoke it themselves, and hence might as well dispense with it. After they presented the argument in this light to their bulls, a full consensus was delayed only by the onset of severe early blizzards. Soon after the beginning of the thaw their agreement was reached and the designation "yak" was returned to the donor.

Among the domestic animals, few horses had cared what anybody called them since the failure of Dean Swift's[2] attempt to name them from their own vocabulary. Cattle, sheep, swine, asses, mules, and goats, along with chickens, geese, and turkeys, all agreed enthusiastically to give their names back to the people to whom—as they put it—they belonged.

A couple of problems did come up with pets. The cats of course steadfastly denied ever having had any name other than those self-given, unspoken, effanineffably personal names which, as the poet named Eliot[3] said, they spend long hours daily contemplating—though none of the contemplators has ever admitted that what they contemplate is in fact their name, and some onlookers have wondered if the object of that meditative gaze might not in fact be the Perfect, or Platonic,[4] Mouse. In any case it is a moot point now. It was with the dogs, and with some parrots, lovebirds, ravens, and mynahs that the trouble arose. These verbally talented individuals insisted that their names were important to them, and flatly refused to part with them. But as soon as they understood that the issue was precisely one of individual choice, and that anybody who wanted to be called Rover, or Froufrou, or Polly, or

---

1. Biblical city where God determined people wouldn't speak just one language.
2. Anglo-Irish satirist Jonathan Swift (1667–1745), who in book IV of *Gulliver's Travels* (1726) invented horses who were smarter than people to mock human pretensions of higher intelligence.
3. T. S. Eliot (1888–1965), British poet (born in

America) and author of *Old Possum's Practical Book of Cats* (1939).
4. The Greek philosopher Plato (427–347 B.C.E.) posited that one perfect form existed in an ideal state to inform the many imperfect examples of it in the real world.

even Birdie in the personal sense, was perfectly free to do so, not one of them had the least objection to parting with the lower case (or, as regards German creatures, uppercase) generic appellations poodle, parrot, dog, or bird, and all the Linnaean[5] qualifiers that had trailed along behind them for two hundred years like tin cans tied to a tail.

The insects parted with their names in vast clouds and swarms of ephemeral syllables buzzing and stinging and humming and flitting and crawling and tunneling away.

As for the fish of the sea, their names dispersed from them in silence throughout the oceans like faint, dark blurs of cuttlefish ink, and drifted off on the currents without a trace.

None were left now to unname, and yet how close I felt to them when I saw one of them swim or fly or trot or crawl across my way or over my skin, or stalk me in the night, or go along beside me for a while in the day. They seemed far closer than when their names had stood between myself and them like a clear barrier: so close that my fear of them and their fear of me became one same fear. And the attraction that many of us felt, the desire to smell one another's smells, feel or rub or caress one another's scales or skin or feathers or fur, taste one another's blood or flesh, keep one another warm,— that attraction was now all one with the fear, and the hunter could not be told from the hunted, nor the eater from the food.

This was more or less the effect I had been after. It was somewhat more powerful than I had anticipated, but I could not now, in all conscience, make an exception for myself. I resolutely put anxiety away, went to Adam, and said, "You and your father lent me this—gave it to me, actually. It's been really useful, but it doesn't exactly seem to fit very well lately. But thanks very much! It's really been very useful."

It is hard to give back a gift without sounding peevish or ungrateful, and I did not want to leave him with that impression of me. He was not paying much attention, as it happened, and said only, "Put it down over there, OK?" and went on with what he was doing.

One of my reasons for doing what I did was that talk was getting us nowhere; but all the same I felt a little let down. I had been prepared to defend my decision. And I thought that perhaps when he did notice he might be upset and want to talk. I put some things away and fiddled around a little, but he continued to do what he was doing and to take no notice of anything else. At last I said, "Well, goodbye, dear. I hope the garden key turns up."

He was fitting parts together, and said without looking around, "OK, fine, dear. When's dinner?"

"I'm not sure," I said. "I'm going now. With the—" I hesitated, and finally said, "With them, you know," and went on. In fact I had only just then realized how hard it would have been to explain myself. I could not chatter away as I used to do, taking it all for granted. My words now must be as slow, as new, as single, as tentative as the steps I took going down the path away from the house, between the dark-branched, tall dancers motionless against the winter shining.

1982

---

5. Swedish botanist Carolus Linnaeus (1707–1778), who classified plants and animals by using a double name designating genus and species. "Uppercase": in German, all nouns are capitalized.

PAULE MARSHALL
b. 1929

Much of Paule Marshall's fiction explores the contrast between the Brooklyn of her childhood and her Caribbean heritage, specifically the Barbados from which her parents emigrated and to which her mother took her on visits. Such a heritage, at the crossroads of New World exploration and slave-trade exploitation, makes for a complex set of choices. How does one define oneself, her characters wonder: as Africans displaced to another hemisphere, as Americans in a newly formed multicultural society, or as Caribbeans whose identities are themselves a result of colonial forces?

Finding an identity apart from the trauma of racial oppression is a deeply psychological as well as artistic exercise. Marshall's early novels are noteworthy for giving women the power to define themselves, a power derived from their ability to verbalize their feelings. In her essay "Poets in the Kitchen" Marshall tells of how much she learned listening to her mother talking with friends and relatives—not just the subjects they covered but the rhythmic imperative of speech that liberated their powers of expression. When the two characters in "Reena" spend most of their story conversing, it is for this writer a sign of women gaining control of their thoughts and ultimately of their world. This is the oral tradition so evident in Marshall's fiction. The technique establishes Marshall as the earliest contributor to what critic Mary Helen Washington describes as "the renaissance of black women writers" that by the 1970s was flourishing with work from Gloria Naylor, Toni Morrison, Alice Walker, and Toni Cade Bambara as well.

In addition to its strong focus on the oral nature of storytelling, "Reena" reflects another important factor in Marshall's fiction, that of the autobiographical. By naming her narrator after herself and drawing so closely on her own background, Marshall invites the readers to accept her work as memoirs if they wish. Her career shows that the power to write fiction depends on the developed ability to work with one's place in the world, to understand it and employ it as the base of independence and self-sufficiency.

Brown Girl, Brownstones (1959), Marshall's first novel, traces a young woman's quest for assimilation in the context of her parents' immigrant limitations. Whereas earlier writers at times treat such conditions in terms of embracing survival and recording defeats, Marshall shows from the start how affirmation is possible by addressing spiritual rather than material concerns. Assimilation by itself can mean a surrender to materialism, a point made strongly in this first novel and reinforced in the stories of *Soul Clap Hands and Sing* (1961), where men's worldly success seems paltry compared to the inner life women can lose in the process. That a much more important goal can be achieved by a fundamental revolution in values emerges as the underlying theme of *The Chosen Place, the Timeless People* (1969), a novel that introduces mainland researchers to a supposedly inferior society in the Caribbean where multiple heritage and colonial domination are demonstrated in specifics of character, plot, and action. A similar contrast of values distinguishes *Praisesong for the Widow* (1983); in this novel Marshall returns to the Caribbean in a ritual journey to honor West Indian ancestors and reclaim what vestiges of African heritage they were able to maintain. In *Daughters* (1991) Marshall's confident protagonist, supported by a strong mother and good community, asserts herself politically, socially, and personally. This accomplishment completes the trend toward independence and self-sufficiency that began with the short fiction of *Reena and Other Stories* (1983) and is expressed so confidently in her novel *The Fisher King* (2000).

Marshall's professional career builds on both her fiction and her 1953 degree in English from Brooklyn College. After working as a journalist, she taught writing at Yale and Columbia. As background for both *The Chosen Place, the Timeless People* and *Praisesong for the Widow* Marshall spent time in Haiti. In addition to her fiction, she has published essays and poetry, and remains a leading spokesperson for literary and social issues.

The text is that of *Reena and Other Stories* (1983).

Reena

Like most people with unpleasant childhoods, I am on constant guard against the past—the past being for me the people and places associated with the years I served out my girlhood in Brooklyn. The places no longer matter that much since most of them have vanished. The old grammar school, for instance, P.S.[1] 35 ("Dirty 5's" we called it and with justification) has been replaced by a low, coldly functional arrangement of glass and Permastone which bears its name but has none of the feel of a school about it. The small, grudgingly lighted stores along Fulton Street, the soda parlor that was like a church with its stained-glass panels in the door and marble floor have given way to those impersonal emporiums, the supermarkets. Our house even, a brownstone relic whose halls smelled comfortingly of dust and lemon oil, the somnolent street upon which it stood, the tall, muscular trees which shaded it were leveled years ago to make way for a city housing project—a stark, graceless warren for the poor. So that now whenever I revisit that old section of Brooklyn and see these new and ugly forms, I feel nothing. I might as well be in a strange city.

But it is another matter with the people of my past, the faces that in their darkness were myriad reflections of mine. Whenever I encounter them at the funeral or wake, the wedding or christening—those ceremonies by which the past reaffirms its hold—my guard drops and memories banished to the rear of the mind rush forward to rout the present. I almost become the child again—anxious and angry, disgracefully diffident.

Reena was one of the people from that time, and a main contributor to my sense of ineffectualness then. She had not done this deliberately. It was just that whenever she talked about herself (and this was not as often as most people) she seemed to be talking about me also. She ruthlessly analyzed herself, sparing herself nothing. Her honesty was so absolute it was a kind of cruelty.

She had not changed, I was to discover in meeting her again after a separation of twenty years. Nor had I really. For although the years had altered our positions (she was no longer the lord and I the lackey) and I could even afford to forgive her now, she still had the ability to disturb me profoundly by dredging to the surface those aspects of myself that I kept buried. This time, as I listened to her talk over the stretch of one long night, she made vivid without knowing it what is perhaps the most critical fact of my existence—that definition of me, of her and millions like us, formulated by others to serve out their fantasies, a definition we have to combat at an unconscionable cost to the self and even use, at times, in order to survive; the cause of so much shame and rage as well as, oddly enough, a source of

1. Public School.

pride: simply, what it has meant, what it means, to be a black woman in America.

We met—Reena and myself—at the funeral of her aunt who had been my godmother and whom I had also called aunt, Aunt Vi, and loved, for she and her house had been, respectively, a source of understanding and a place of calm for me as a child. Reena entered the church where the funeral service was being held as though she, not the minister, were coming to officiate, sat down among the immediate family up front, and turned to inspect those behind her. I saw her face then.

It was a good copy of the original. The familiar mold was there, that is, and the configuration of bone beneath the skin was the same despite the slight fleshiness I had never seen there before; her features had even retained their distinctive touches: the positive set to her mouth, the assertive lift to her nose, the same insistent, unsettling eyes which when she was angry became as black as her skin—and this was total, unnerving, and very beautiful. Yet something had happened to her face. It was different despite its sameness. Aging even while it remained enviably young. Time had sketched in, very lightly, the evidence of the twenty years.

As soon as the funeral service was over, I left, hurrying out of the church into the early November night. The wind, already at its winter strength, brought with it the smell of dead leaves and the image of Aunt Vi there in the church, as dead as the leaves—as well as the thought of Reena, whom I would see later at the wake.

Her real name had been Doreen, a standard for girls among West Indians (her mother, like my parents, was from Barbados), but she had changed it to Reena on her twelfth birthday—"As a present to myself"—and had enforced the change on her family by refusing to answer to the old name. "Reena. With two e's!" she would say and imprint those e's on your mind with the indelible black of her eyes and a thin threatening finger that was like a quill.

She and I had not been friends through our own choice. Rather, our mothers, who had known each other since childhood, had forced the relationship. And from the beginning, I had been at a disadvantage. For Reena, as early as the age of twelve, had had a quality that was unique, superior, and therefore dangerous. She seemed defined, even then, all of a piece, the raw edges of her adolescence smoothed over; indeed, she seemed to have escaped adolescence altogether and made one dazzling leap from childhood into the very arena of adult life. At thirteen, for instance, she was reading Zola, Hauptmann, Steinbeck, while I was still in the thrall of the Little Minister and Lorna Doone.[2] When I could only barely conceive of the world beyond Brooklyn, she was talking of the Civil War in Spain, lynchings in the South, Hitler in Poland[3]—and talking with the outrage and passion of a revolutionary. I would try, I remember, to console myself with the thought that she was really an adult masquerading as a child, which meant that I could not possibly be her match.

For her part, Reena put up with me and was, by turns, patronizing and

2. I.e., staples of mature readership instead of children's literature. Émile Zola (1840–1902), French novelist. Gerhardt Hauptmann (1862–1946), German dramatist, novelist, and poet. John Steinbeck (1902–1968), American novelist. The Little Minister and Lorna Doone are characters of children's literature.

3. Important news events of the late 1930s.

impatient. I merely served as the audience before whom she rehearsed her ideas and the yardstick by which she measured her worldliness and knowledge.

"Do you realize that this stupid country supplied Japan with the scrap iron to make the weapons she's now using against it?" she had shouted at me once.

I had not known that.

Just as she overwhelmed me, she overwhelmed her family, with the result that despite a half dozen brothers and sisters who consumed quantities of bread and jam whenever they visited us, she behaved like an only child and got away with it. Her father, a gentle man with skin the color of dried tobacco and with the nose Reena had inherited jutting out like a crag from his nondescript face, had come from Georgia and was always making jokes about having married a foreigner—Reena's mother being from the West Indies. When not joking, he seemed slightly bewildered by his large family and so in awe of Reena that he avoided her. Reena's mother, a small, dry, formidably black woman, was less a person to me than the abstract principle of force, power, energy. She was alternately strict and indulgent with Reena and, despite the inconsistency, surprisingly effective.

They lived when I knew them in a cold-water railroad flat above a kosher[4] butcher on Belmont Avenue in Brownsville, some distance from us—and this in itself added to Reena's exotic quality. For it was a place where Sunday became Saturday, with all the stores open and pushcarts piled with vegetables and yard goods lined up along the curb, a crowded place where people hawked and spat freely in the streaming gutters and the men looked as if they had just stepped from the pages of the Old Testament with their profuse beards and long, black, satin coats.

When Reena was fifteen her family moved to Jamaica[5] in Queens and since, in those days, Jamaica was considered too far away for visiting, our families lost contact and I did not see Reena again until we were both in college and then only once and not to speak to. . . .

I had walked some distance and by the time I got to the wake, which was being held at Aunt Vi's house, it was well under way. It was a good wake. Aunt Vi would have been pleased. There was plenty to drink, and more than enough to eat, including some Barbadian favorites: coconut bread, pone made with the cassava root, and the little crisp codfish cakes that are so hot with peppers they bring tears to the eyes as you bite into them.

I had missed the beginning, when everyone had probably sat around talking about Aunt Vi and recalling the few events that had distinguished her otherwise undistinguished life. (Someone, I'm sure, had told of the time she had missed the excursion boat to Atlantic City[6] and had had her own private picnic—complete with pigeon peas and rice and fricassee chicken—on the pier at 42nd Street.) By the time I arrived, though, it would have been indiscreet to mention her name, for by then the wake had become—and this would also have pleased her—a celebration of life.

I had had two drinks, one right after the other, and was well into my third

---

4. Signifying food approved for consumption under Jewish dietary laws; a reminder that Brownsville was traditionally an Orthodox Jewish neighborhood.

5. An outlying part of New York City in the borough of Queens.

6. A seaside resort and amusement park in New Jersey.

when Reena, who must have been upstairs, entered the basement kitchen where I was. She saw me before I had quite seen her, and with a cry that alerted the entire room to her presence and charged the air with her special force, she rushed toward me.

"Hey, I'm the one who was supposed to be the writer, not you! Do you know, I still can't believe it," she said, stepping back, her blackness heightened by a white mocking smile. "I read both your books over and over again and I can't really believe it. My Little Paulie!"

I did not mind. For there was respect and even wonder behind the patronizing words and in her eyes. The old imbalance between us had ended and I was suddenly glad to see her.

I told her so and we both began talking at once, but Reena's voice overpowered mine, so that all I could do after a time was listen while she discussed my books, and dutifully answer her questions about my personal life.

"And what about you?" I said, almost brutally, at the first chance I got. "What've you been up to all this time?"

She got up abruptly. "Good Lord, in here's noisy as hell. Come on, let's go upstairs."

We got fresh drinks and went up to Aunt Vi's bedroom, where in the soft light from the lamps, the huge Victorian bed and the pink satin bedspread with roses of the same material strewn over its surface looked as if they had never been used. And, in a way, this was true. Aunt Vi had seldom slept in her bed or, for that matter, lived in her house, because in order to pay for it, she had had to work at a sleeping-in job which gave her only Thursdays and every other Sunday off.

Reena sat on the bed, crushing the roses, and I sat on one of the numerous trunks which crowded the room. They contained every dress, coat, hat, and shoe that Aunt Vi had worn since coming to the United States. I again asked Reena what she had been doing over the years.

"Do you want a blow by blow account?" she said. But despite the flippancy, she was suddenly serious. And when she began it was clear that she had written out the narrative in her mind many times. The words came too easily; the events, the incidents had been ordered in time, and the meaning of her behavior and of the people with whom she had been involved had been painstakingly analyzed. She talked willingly, with desperation almost. And the words by themselves weren't enough. She used her hands to give them form and urgency. I became totally involved with her and all that she said. So much so that as the night wore on I was not certain at times whether it was she or I speaking.

From the time her family moved to Jamaica until she was nineteen or so, Reena's life sounded, from what she told me in the beginning, as ordinary as mine and most of the girls we knew. After high school she had gone on to one of the free city colleges, where she had majored in journalism, worked part time in the school library, and, surprisingly enough, joined a houseplan. (Even I hadn't gone that far.) It was an all-Negro club, since there was a tacit understanding that Negro and white girls did not join each other's houseplans. "Integration, Northern style," she said, shrugging.

It seems that Reena had had a purpose and a plan in joining the group. "I thought," she said with a wry smile, "I could get those girls up off their complacent rumps and out doing something about social issues. . . . I couldn't get them to budge. I remember after the war when a Negro ex-soldier had his eyes gouged out by a bus driver down South I tried getting them to demonstrate on campus. I talked until I was hoarse, but to no avail. They were too busy planning the annual autumn frolic."

Her laugh was bitter but forgiving and it ended in a long, reflective silence. After which she said quietly, "It wasn't that they didn't give a damn. It was just, I suppose, that like most people they didn't want to get involved to the extent that they might have to stand up and be counted. If it ever came to that. Then another thing. They thought they were safe, special. After all, they had grown up in the North, most of them, and so had escaped the southern-style prejudice; their parents, like mine, were struggling to put them through college; they could look forward to being tidy little school-teachers, social workers, and lab technicians. Oh, they were safe!" The sarcasm scored her voice and then abruptly gave way to pity. "Poor things, they weren't safe, you see, and would never be as long as millions like themselves in Harlem, on Chicago's South Side,[7] down South, all over the place, were unsafe. I tried to tell them this—and they accused me of being oversensitive. They tried not to listen. But I would have held out and, I'm sure, even brought some of them around eventually if this other business with a silly boy hadn't happened at the same time. . . ."

Reena told me then about her first, brief, and apparently innocent affair with a boy she had met at one of the houseplan parties. It had ended, she said, when the boy's parents had met her. "That was it," she said and the flat of her hand cut into the air. "He was forbidden to see me. The reason? He couldn't bring himself to tell me, but I knew. I was too black.

"Naturally, it wasn't the first time something like that had happened. In fact, you might say that was the theme of my childhood. Because I was dark I was always being plastered with Vaseline so I wouldn't look ashy. Whenever I had my picture taken they would pile a whitish powder on my face and make the lights so bright I always came out looking ghostly. My mother stopped speaking to any number of people because they said I would have been pretty if I hadn't been so dark. Like nearly every little black girl, I had my share of dreams of waking up to find myself with long, blond curls, blue eyes, and skin like milk. So I should have been prepared. Besides, that boy's parents were really rejecting themselves in rejecting me.

"Take us"—and her hands, opening in front of my face as she suddenly leaned forward, seemed to offer me the whole of black humanity. "We live surrounded by white images, and white in this world is synonymous with the good, light, beauty, success, so that, despite ourselves sometimes, we run after that whiteness and deny our darkness, which has been made into the symbol of all that is evil and inferior. I wasn't a person to that boy's parents, but a symbol of the darkness they were in flight from, so that just as they—that boy, his parents, those silly girls in the houseplan—were running from me, I started running from them. . . ."

It must have been shortly after this happened when I saw Reena at a debate which was being held at my college. She did not see me, since she was one of the speakers and I was merely part of her audience in the crowded auditorium. The topic had something to do with intellectual freedom in the colleges (McCarthyism[8] was coming into vogue then) and aside from a Jewish

7. African American neighborhoods in New York City and Chicago, respectively.
8. Anticommunist investigations led by U.S. sen-ator Joseph McCarthy, Republican from Wisconsin from 1946 to 1957.

boy from City College, Reena was the most effective—sharp, provocative, her position the most radical. The others on the panel seemed intimidated not only by the strength and cogency of her argument but by the sheer impact of her blackness in their white midst.

Her color might have been a weapon she used to dazzle and disarm her opponents. And she had highlighted it with the clothes she was wearing: a white dress patterned with large blocks of primary colors I remember (it looked Mexican) and a pair of intricately wrought silver earrings—long and with many little parts which clashed like muted cymbals over the microphone each time she moved her head. She wore her hair cropped short like a boy's and it was not straightened like mine and the other Negro girls' in the audience, but left in its coarse natural state: a small forest under which her face emerged in its intense and startling handsomeness. I remember she left the auditorium in triumph that day, surrounded by a noisy entourage from her college—all of them white.

"We were very serious," she said now, describing the leftwing group she had belonged to then—and there was a defensiveness in her voice which sought to protect them from all censure. "We believed—because we were young, I suppose, and had nothing as yet to risk—that we could do something about the injustices which everyone around us seemed to take for granted. So we picketed and demonstrated and bombarded Washington with our protests, only to have our names added to the Attorney General's list for all our trouble. We were always standing on street corners handing out leaflets or getting people to sign petitions. We always seemed to pick the coldest days to do that." Her smile held long after the words had died.

"I, we all, had such a sense of purpose then," she said softly, and a sadness lay aslant the smile now, darkening it. "We were forever holding meetings, having endless discussions, arguing, shouting, theorizing. And we had fun. Those parties! There was always somebody with a guitar. We were always singing. . . ." Suddenly, she began singing—and her voice was sure, militant, and faintly self-mocking,

> "But the banks are made of marble
> With a guard at every door
> And the vaults are stuffed with silver
> That the workers sweated for . . ."[9]

When she spoke again the words were a sad coda to the song. "Well, as you probably know, things came to an ugly head with McCarthy reigning in Washington, and I was one of the people temporarily suspended from school."

She broke off and we both waited, the ice in our glasses melted and the drinks gone flat.

"At first, I didn't mind," she said finally. "After all, we were right. The fact that they suspended us proved it. Besides, I was in the middle of an affair, a real one this time, and too busy with that to care about anything else." She paused again, frowning.

"He was white," she said quickly and glanced at me as though to surprise either shock or disapproval in my face. "We were very involved. At one

9. A popular protest song among labor activists during the Great Depression of the 1930s.

point—I think just after we had been suspended and he started working—
we even thought of getting married. Living in New York, moving in the crowd
we did, we might have been able to manage it. But I couldn't. There were
too many complex things going on beneath the surface," she said, her voice
strained by the hopelessness she must have felt then, her hands shaping it
in the air between us. "Neither one of us could really escape what our color
had come to mean in this country. Let me explain. Bob was always, for some
odd reason, talking about how much the Negro suffered, and although I
would agree with him I would also try to get across that, you know, like all
people we also had fun once in a while, loved our children, liked making
love—that we were human beings, for God's sake. But he only wanted to
hear about the suffering. It was as if this comforted him and eased his own
suffering—and he did suffer because of any number of things: his own uncertainty, for one, his difficulties with his family, for another . . .

"Once, I remember, when his father came into New York, Bob insisted
that I meet him. I don't know why I agreed to go with him. . . ." She took a
deep breath and raised her head very high. "I'll never forget or forgive the
look on that old man's face when he opened his hotel-room door and saw
me. The horror. I might have been the personification of every evil in the
world. His inability to believe that it was his son standing there holding my
hand. His shock. I'm sure he never fully recovered. I know I never did. Nor
can I forget Bob's laugh in the elevator afterwards, the way he kept repeating:
'Did you see his face when he saw you? Did you? . . . ' He had used me, you
see. I had been the means, the instrument of his revenge.

"And I wasn't any better. I used him. I took every opportunity to treat him
shabbily, trying, you see, through him, to get at that white world which had
not only denied me, but had turned my own against me." Her eyes closed.
"I went numb all over when I understood what we were doing to, and with,
each other. I stayed numb for a long time."

As Reena described the events which followed—the break with Bob, her
gradual withdrawal from the left-wing group ("I had had it with them too. I
got tired of being 'their Negro,' their pet. Besides, they were just all talk,
really. All theories and abstractions. I doubt that, with all their elaborate
plans for the Negro and for the workers of the world, any of them had ever
been near a factory or up to Harlem")—as she spoke about her reinstatement
in school, her voice suggested the numbness she had felt then. It only stirred
into life again when she talked of her graduation.

"You should have seen my parents. It was really their day. My mother was
so proud she complained about everything: her seat, the heat, the speaker;
and my father just sat there long after everybody had left, too awed to move.
God, it meant so much to them. It was as if I had made up for the generations
his people had picked cotton in Georgia and my mother's family had cut cane
in the West Indies. It frightened me."

I asked her after a long wait what she had done after graduating.

"How do you mean, what I did. Looked for a job. Tell me, have you ever
looked for work in this man's city?"

"I know." I said, holding up my hand. "Don't tell me."

We both looked at my raised hand which sought to waive the discussion,
then at each other and suddenly we laughed, a laugh so loud and violent
with pain and outrage it brought tears.

"Girl," Reena said, the tears silver against her blackness. "You could put me blindfolded right now at the Times Building on 42nd Street and I would be able to find my way to every newspaper office in town. But tell me, how come white folks is so *hard?*"

"Just bo'n hard."

We were laughing again and this time I nearly slid off the trunk and Reena fell back among the satin roses.

"I didn't know there were so many ways of saying 'no' without ever once using the word," she said, the laughter lodged in her throat, but her eyes had gone hard. "Sometimes I'd find myself in the elevator, on my way out, and smiling all over myself because I thought I had gotten the job, before it would hit me that they had really said no, not yes. Some of those people in personnel had so perfected their smiles they looked almost genuine. The ones who used to get me, though, were those who tried to make the interview into an intimate chat between friends. They'd put you in a comfortable chair, offer you a cigarette, and order coffee. How I hated that coffee. They didn't know it— or maybe they did—but it was like offering me hemlock. . . .

" 'You think Christ had it tough?' " Her laughter rushed against the air which resisted it. "I was crucified five days a week and half-day on Saturday. I became almost paranoid. I began to think there might be something other than color wrong with me which everybody but me could see, some rare disease that had turned me into a monster.

"My parents suffered. And that bothered me most, because I felt I had failed them. My father didn't say anything but I knew because he avoided me more than usual. He was ashamed, I think, that he hadn't been able, as a man and as my father, to prevent this. My mother—well, you know her. In one breath she would try to comfort me by cursing them: 'But Gor blind them.' "—and Reena's voice captured her mother's aggressive accent—" 'if you had come looking for a job mopping down their floors they would o' hire you, the brutes. But mark my words, their time goin' come, cause God don't love ugly and he ain't stuck on pretty . . . ' And in the next breath she would curse me, 'Journalism! Journalism! Whoever heard of colored people taking up journalism. You must feel you's white or something so. The people is right to chuck you out their office. . . . ' Poor thing, to make up for saying all that she would wash my white gloves every night and cook cereal for me in the morning as if I were a little girl again. Once she went out and bought me a suit she couldn't afford from Lord and Taylor's. I looked like a Smith girl in blackface in it. . . . So guess where I ended up?"

"As a social investigator for the Welfare Department. Where else?"

We were helpless with laughter again.

"You too?"

"No" I said, "I taught, but that was just as bad."

"No," she said, sobering abruptly. "Nothing's as bad as working for Welfare. Do you know what they really mean by a social investigator? A spy. Someone whose dirty job it is to snoop into the corners of the lives of the poor and make their poverty more vivid by taking from them the last shred of privacy. 'Mrs. Jones, is that a new dress you're wearing?' 'Mrs. Brown, this kerosene heater is not listed in the household items. Did you get an authorization for it?' 'Mrs. Smith, is that a telephone I hear ringing under the sofa?' I was utterly demoralized within a month.

"And another thing. I thought I knew about poverty. I mean, I remember, as a child, having to eat soup made with those white beans the government used to give out free for days running, sometimes, because there was nothing else. I had lived in Brownsville, among all the poor Jews and Poles and Irish there. But what I saw in Harlem, where I had my case load, was different somehow. Perhaps because it seemed so final. There didn't seem to be any way to escape from those dark hallways and dingy furnished rooms. . . . All that defeat." Closing her eyes, she finished the stale whiskey and soda in her glass.

"I remember a client of mine, a girl my age with three children already and no father for them and living in the expensive squalor of a rooming house. Her bewilderment. Her resignation. Her anger. She could have pulled herself out of the mess she was in? People say that, you know, including some Negroes. But this girl didn't have a chance. She had been trapped from the day she was born in some small town down South.

"She became my reference. From then on and even now, whenever I hear people and groups coming up with all kinds of solutions to the quote Negro problem, I ask one question. What are they really doing for that girl, to save her or to save the children? . . . The answer isn't very encouraging."

It was some time before she continued, and then she told me that after Welfare she had gone to work for a private socialwork agency, in their publicity department, and had started on her master's in journalism at Columbia.[1] She also left home around this time.

"I had to. My mother started putting the pressure on me to get married. The hints, the remarks—and you know my mother was never the subtle type—her anxiety, which made me anxious about getting married after a while. Besides, it was time for me to be on my own."

In contrast to the unmistakably radical character of her late adolescence (her membership in the left-wing group, the affair with Bob, her suspension from college), Reena's life of this period sounded ordinary, standard—and she admitted it with a slightly self-deprecating, apologetic smile. It was similar to that of any number of unmarried professional Negro women in New York or Los Angeles or Washington: the job teaching or doing social work which brought in a fairly decent salary, the small apartment with kitchenette which they sometimes shared with a roommate; a car, some of them; membership in various political and social action organizations for the militant few like Reena; the vacations in Mexico, Europe, the West Indies, and now Africa; the occasional date. "The interesting men were invariably married," Reena said and then mentioned having had one affair during that time. She had found out he was married and had thought of her only as the perfect mistress. "The bastard," she said, but her smile forgave him.

"Women alone!" she cried, laughing sadly, and her raised opened arms, the empty glass she held in one hand made eloquent their aloneness. "Alone and lonely, and indulging themselves while they wait. The girls of the house-plan have reached their majority only to find that all those years they spent accumulating their degrees and finding the well-paying jobs in the hope that this would raise their stock have, instead, put them at a disadvantage. For the few eligible men around—those who are their intellectual and profes-

1. An Ivy League university in New York City, well known for its prestigious school of journalism.

sional peers, whom they can respect (and there are very few of them)—don't necessarily marry them, but younger women without the degrees and the fat jobs, who are no threat, or they don't marry at all because they are either queer or mother-ridden. Or they marry white women. Now, intellectually I accept this. In fact, some of my best friends are white women . . ." And again our laughter—that loud, searing burst which we used to cauterize our hurt mounted into the unaccepting silence of the room. "After all, our goal is a fully integrated society. And perhaps, as some people believe, the only solution to the race problem is miscegenation. Besides, a man should be able to marry whomever he wishes. Emotionally, though, I am less kind and understanding, and I resent like hell the reasons some black men give for rejecting us for them."

"We're too middle-class-oriented," I said. "Conservative."

"Right. Even though, thank God, that doesn't apply to me."

"Too threatening . . . castrating . . ."

"Too independent and impatient with them for not being more ambitious . . . contemptuous . . ."

"Sexually inhibited and unimaginative . . ."

"And the old myth of the excessive sexuality of the black woman goes out the window," Reena cried.

"Not supportive, unwilling to submerge our interests for theirs . . ."

"Lacking in the subtle art of getting and keeping a man . . ."

We had recited the accusations in the form and tone of a litany, and in the silence which followed we shared a thin, hopeless smile.

"They condemn us," Reena said softly but with anger, "without taking history into account. We are still, most of us, the black woman who had to be almost frighteningly strong in order for us all to survive. For, after all, she was the one whom they left (and I don't hold this against them; I understand) with the children to raise, who had to *make* it somehow or the other. And we are still, so many of us, living that history.

"You would think that they would understand this, but few do. So it's up to us. We have got to understand them and save them for ourselves. How? By being, on one hand, persons in our own right and, on the other, fully the woman and the wife. . . . Christ, listen to who's talking! I had my chance. And I tried. Very hard. But it wasn't enough."

The festive sounds of the wake had died to a sober murmur beyond the bedroom. The crowd had gone, leaving only Reena and myself upstairs and the last of Aunt Vi's closest friends in the basement below. They were drinking coffee. I smelled it, felt its warmth and intimacy in the empty house, heard the distant tapping of the cups against the saucers and voices muted by grief. The wake had come full circle: they were again mourning Aunt Vi.

And Reena might have been mourning with them, sitting there amid the satin roses, framed by the massive headboard. Her hands lay as if they had been broken in her lap. Her eyes were like those of someone blind or dead. I got up to go and get some coffee for her.

"You met my husband," she said quickly, stopping me.

"Have I?" I said, sitting down again.

"Yes, before we were married even. At an autograph party for you. He was free-lancing—he's a photographer—and one of the Negro magazines had sent him to cover the party."

As she went on to describe him I remembered him vaguely, not his face, but his rather large body stretching and bending with a dancer's fluidity and grace as he took the pictures. I had heard him talking to a group of people about some issue on race relations very much in the news then and had been struck by his vehemence. For the moment I had found this almost odd, since he was so fair skinned he could have passed for white.

They had met, Reena told me now, at a benefit show for a Harlem day nursery given by one of the progressive groups she belonged to, and had married a month afterward. From all that she said they had had a full and exciting life for a long time. Her words were so vivid that I could almost see them: she with her startling blackness and extraordinary force and he with his near-white skin and a militancy which matched hers; both of them moving among the disaffected in New York, their stand on political and social issues equally uncompromising, the line of their allegiance reaching directly to all those trapped in Harlem. And they had lived the meaning of this allegiance, so that even when they could have afforded a life among the black bourgeoisie of St. Albans or Teaneck,[2] they had chosen to live if not in Harlem so close that there was no difference.

"I—we—were so happy I was frightened at times. Not that anything would change between us, but that someone or something in the world outside us would invade our private place and destroy us out of envy. Perhaps this is what did happen. . . ." She shrugged and even tried to smile but she could not manage it. "Something slipped in while we weren't looking and began its deadly work.

"Maybe it started when Dave took a job with a Negro magazine. I'm not sure. Anyway, in no time, he hated it: the routine, unimaginative pictures he had to take and the magazine itself, which dealt only in unrealities: the high-society world of the black bourgeoisie and the spectacular strides Negroes were making in all fields—you know the type. Yet Dave wouldn't leave. It wasn't the money, but a kind of safety which he had never experienced before which kept him there. He would talk about free-lancing again, about storming the gates of the white magazines downtown, of opening his own studio but he never acted on any one of these things. You see, despite his talent—and he was very talented—he had a diffidence that was fatal.

"When I understood this I literally forced him to open the studio—and perhaps I should have been more subtle and indirect, but that's not my nature. Besides, I was frightened and desperate to help. Nothing happened for a time. Dave's work was too experimental to be commercial. Gradually, though, his photographs started appearing in the prestige camera magazines and money from various awards and exhibits and an occasional assignment started coming in.

"This wasn't enough somehow. Dave also wanted the big, gaudy commercial success that would dazzle and confound that white world downtown and force it to *see* him. And yet, as I said before, he couldn't bring himself to try—and this contradiction began to get to him after awhile.

"It was then, I think, that I began to fail him. I didn't know how to help, you see. I had never felt so inadequate before. And this was very strange and disturbing for someone like me. I was being submerged in his problems—and I began fighting against this.

"I started working again (I had stopped after the second baby). And I was

2. Middle-class areas outside Manhattan—St. Albans is in Queens; Teaneck is in New Jersey.

lucky because I got back my old job. And unlucky because Dave saw it as my way of pointing up his deficiencies. I couldn't convince him otherwise: that I had to do it for my own sanity. He would accuse me of wanting to see him fail, of trapping him in all kinds of responsibilities. . . . After a time we both got caught up in this thing, an ugliness came between us, and I began to answer his anger with anger and to trade him insult for insult.

"Things fell apart very quickly after that. I couldn't bear the pain of living with him—the insults, our mutual despair, his mocking, the silence. I couldn't subject the children to it any longer. The divorce didn't take long. And thank God, because of the children, we are pleasant when we have to see each other. He's making out very well, I hear."

She said nothing more, but simply bowed her head as though waiting for me to pass judgment on her. I don't know how long we remained like this, but when Reena finally raised her head, the darkness at the window had vanished and dawn was a still, gray smoke against the pane.

"Do you know," she said, and her eyes were clear and a smile had won out over pain, "I enjoy being alone. I don't tell people this because they'll accuse me of either lying or deluding myself. But I do. Perhaps, as my mother tells me, it's only temporary. I don't think so, though. I feel I don't ever want to be involved again. It's not that I've lost interest in men. I go out occasionally, but it's never anything serious. You see, I have all that I want for now."

Her children first of all, she told me, and from her description they sounded intelligent and capable. She was a friend as well as a mother to them, it seemed. They were planning, the four of them, to spend the summer touring Canada. "I will feel that I have done well by them if I give them, if nothing more, a sense of themselves and their worth and importance as black people. Everything I do with them, for them, is to this end. I don't want them ever to be confused about this. They must have their identifications straight from the beginning. No white dolls for them!"

Then her job. She was working now as a researcher for a small progressive news magazine with the promise that once she completed her master's in journalism (she was working on the thesis now) she might get a chance to do some minor reporting. And like most people, she hoped to write someday. "If I can ever stop talking away my substance," she said laughing.

And she was still active in any number of social action groups. In another week or so she would be heading a delegation of mothers down to City Hall "to give the mayor a little hell about conditions in the schools in Harlem." She had started an organization that was carrying on an almost door-to-door campaign in her neighborhood to expose, as she put it, "the blood suckers: all those slumlords and storekeepers with their fixed scales, the finance companies that never tell you the real price of a thing, the petty salesmen that leech off the poor. . . ." In May she was taking her two older girls on a nationwide pilgrimage to Washington to urge for a more rapid implementation of the school desegregation law.

"It's uncanny," she said, and the laugh which accompanied the words was warm, soft with wonder at herself, girlish even, and the air in the room which had refused her laughter before rushed to absorb this now. "Really uncanny. Here I am, practically middle-aged, with three children to raise by myself and with little or no money to do it, and yet I feel, strangely enough, as though life is just beginning—that it's new and fresh with all kinds of possibilities. Maybe it's because I've been through my purgatory and I can't ever be overwhelmed again. I don't know. Anyway, you should see me on evenings after I put the children to bed. I sit alone in the living room (I've repainted it and changed all the furniture since Dave's gone, so that it would at least look different)—I sit there making plans and all of them seem possible. The most important plan right now is Africa. I've already started saving the fare."

I asked her whether she was planning to live there permanently and she said simply, "I want to live and work there. For how long, for a lifetime, I can't say. All I know is that I have to. For myself and for my children. It is important that they see black people who have truly a place and history of their own and who are building for a new and, hopefully, more sensible world. And I must see it, get close to it, because I can never lose the sense of being a displaced person here in America because of my color. Oh, I know I should remain and fight not only for integration (even though, frankly, I question whether I want to be integrated into America as it stands now, with its complacency and materialism, its soullessness) but to help change the country into something better, sounder—if that is still possible. But I have to go to Africa . . .

"Poor Aunt Vi," she said after a long silence and straightened one of the roses she had crushed. "She never really got to enjoy her bed of roses what with only Thursdays and every other Sunday off. All that hard work. All her life. . . . Our lives have got to make more sense, if only for her."

We got up to leave shortly afterward. Reena was staying on to attend the burial, later in the morning, but I was taking the subway to Manhattan. We parted with the usual promise to get together and exchanged telephone numbers. And Reena did phone a week or so later. I don't remember what we talked about though.

Some months later I invited her to a party I was giving before leaving the country. But she did not come.

1983

DONALD BARTHELME
1931–1989

Born in Philadelphia, where his parents were attending college, Donald Barthelme was raised in Houston, Texas, where his father became a prominent architect. The author's own collegiate experience, as a reporter for and editor of the student newspaper at the University of Houston, influenced both his career and literary style. After army service he returned to work on the city newspaper, wrote publicity for the university, edited the school's quarterly magazine of the arts, *Forum*, and directed the Contemporary Arts Museum. During these years Barthelme developed a fascination with the mechanical workings of language, from the appearance of type on the page to finding verbal equivalents for nonverbal popular artifacts. When in 1962 he moved to New York to edit *Location*, a short-lived journal of literature and art, and started writing short stories and parodies for *The New Yorker*, Barthelme began to have a unique impact on literature through his recognition that language itself, rather than what language represents, could be the subject of fiction.

Lives, his narratives show, are influenced by the quality of language within which they are conducted. In today's world a material culture and a communications medium given to advertising and promotion feed each other in a frenzy of consumption; as in a shark's maw, everything is ingested, nothing is digested, with the result that meaning itself becomes a casualty of process. There is danger in letting fine-sounding words and phrases pass without questioning the motives that inform them—something that his engineers get away with in "Report" (collected in *Unspeakable Practices, Unnatural Acts,* 1968) when they propose to work on "realtime online computer-controlled wish evaporation" (a task they believe necessary in "meeting the rising expectations of the world's peoples, which are as you know rising entirely too fast"). Witty and satirical, Barthelme could be especially adept at making sophisticated philosophical points within mundane situations. "Me and Miss Mandible," from his first collection, *Come Back, Dr. Caligari* (1964), argues a postmodern understanding of semiotics from a sixth-grade classroom to which an adult has been mysteriously returned to suffer, with all his experience, in the company of twelve-year-olds. What he learns, and wishes he could teach the others now struggling through behavior molded by television and movies, is that "signs are signs, and that some of them are lies."

Barthelme's four novels move in the same direction as his ten volumes of short stories. *Snow White* (1967), like his early fiction, uses a preposterous situation—the fairy tale character living with seven small men in a contemporary Greenwich Village apartment—to show how modern life lacks heroism and romance. *The Dead Father* (1975) is more weighted with psychological issues, principally the power of fatherhood and how that power is absurdly clung to. Here the author began relying less on satirical references to current life and more on narrative statement itself. In the middle to late 1970s, Barthelme's fiction also became more comfortable in describing life as lived without the superimposition of defamiliarizing actions; *Paradise* (1986) reads almost conventionally. Yet as had happened so productively in such early work as "The Balloon" (printed here), Barthelme still wondered at existence. At his death he had completed a fanciful romance, *The King* (published posthumously in 1990); in it he recasts the situation of Britain in the early years of World War II, applying literally the Arthurian terms to which commentators of the time liked to allude.

The text is from *Unspeakable Practices, Unnatural Acts* (1968).

The Balloon

The balloon, beginning at a point on Fourteenth Street, the exact location of which I cannot reveal, expanded northward all one night, while people were sleeping, until it reached the Park. There, I stopped it; at dawn the northernmost edges lay over the Plaza;[1] the free-hanging motion was frivolous and gentle. But experiencing a faint irritation at stopping, even to protect the trees, and seeing no reason the balloon should not be allowed to expand upward, over the parts of the city it was already covering, into the "air space" to be found there, I asked the engineers to see to it. This expansion took place throughout the morning, soft imperceptible sighing of gas through the valves. The balloon then covered forty-five blocks north-south and an irregular area east-west, as many as six crosstown blocks on either side of the Avenue[2] in some places. That was the situation, then.

1. Grand Army Plaza, site of the Plaza Hotel (also called the Plaza), at the southeastern corner of Central Park in New York City, approximately 2.5 miles north of Fourteenth Street, the northern boundary of Greenwich Village.
2. Fifth Avenue.

But it is wrong to speak of "situations," implying sets of circumstances leading to some resolution, some escape of tension; there were no situations, simply the balloon hanging there—muted heavy grays and browns for the most part, contrasting with walnut and soft yellows. A deliberate lack of finish, enhanced by skillful installation, gave the surface a rough, forgotten quality; sliding weights on the inside, carefully adjusted, anchored the great, vari-shaped mass at a number of points. Now we have had a flood of original ideas in all media, works of singular beauty as well as significant milestones in the history of inflation, but at that moment there was only *this balloon*, concrete particular, hanging there.

There were reactions. Some people found the balloon "interesting." As a response this seemed inadequate to the immensity of the balloon, the suddenness of its appearance over the city; on the other hand, in the absence of hysteria or other societally-induced anxiety, it must be judged a calm "mature" one. There was a certain amount of initial argumentation about the "meaning" of the balloon; this subsided, because we have learned not to insist on meanings, and they are rarely even looked for now, except in cases involving the simplest, safest phenomena. It was agreed that since the meaning of the balloon could never be known absolutely, extended discussion was pointless, or at least less purposeful than the activities of those who, for example, hung green and blue paper lanterns from the warm gray underside, in certain streets, or seized the occasion to write messages on the surface, announcing their availability for the performance of unnatural acts, or the availability of acquaintances.

Daring children jumped, especially at those points where the balloon hovered close to a building, so that the gap between balloon and building was a matter of a few inches, or points where the balloon actually made contact, exerting an ever-so-slight pressure against the side of a building, so that balloon and building seemed a unity. The upper surface was so structured that a "landscape" was presented, small valleys as well as slight knolls, or mounds; once atop the balloon, a stroll was possible, or even a trip, from one place to another. There was pleasure in being able to run down an incline, then up the opposing slope, both gently graded, or in making a leap from one side to the other. Bouncing was possible, because of the pneumaticity of the surface, and even falling, if that was your wish. That all these varied motions, as well as others, were within one's possibilities, in experiencing the "up" side of the balloon, was extremely exciting for children, accustomed to the city's flat, hard skin. But the purpose of the balloon was not to amuse children.

Too, the number of people, children and adults, who took advantage of the opportunities described was not so large as it might have been: a certain timidity, lack of trust in the balloon, was seen. There was, furthermore, some hostility. Because we had hidden the pumps, which fed helium to the interior, and because the surface was so vast that the authorities could not determine the point of entry—that is, the point at which the gas was injected—a degree of frustration was evidenced by those city officers into whose province such manifestations normally fell. The apparent purposelessness of the balloon was vexing (as was the fact that it was "there" at all). Had we painted, in great letters, "LABORATORY TESTS PROVE" OR "18% MORE EFFECTIVE" on the sides of the balloon, this difficulty would have been circumvented. But I could not bear to do so. On the whole, these officers were remarkably tolerant, considering the dimensions of the anomaly, this tolerance being the result of, first, secret tests conducted by night that convinced them that little or nothing could be done in the way of removing or destroying the balloon, and, secondly, a public warmth that arose (not uncolored by touches of the aforementioned hostility) toward the balloon, from ordinary citizens.

As a single balloon must stand for a lifetime of thinking about balloons, so each citizen expressed, in the attitude he chose, a complex of attitudes. One man might consider that the balloon had to do with the notion *sullied*, as in the sentence *The big balloon sullied the otherwise clear and radiant Manhattan sky.* That is, the balloon was, in this man's view, an imposture, something inferior to the sky that had formerly been there, something interposed between the people and their "sky." But in fact it was January, the sky was dark and ugly; it was not a sky you could look up into, lying on your back in the street, with pleasure, unless pleasure, for you, proceeded from having been threatened, from having been misused. And the underside of the balloon was a pleasure to look up into, we had seen to that, muted grays and browns for the most part, contrasted with walnut and soft, forgotten yellows. And so, while this man was thinking *sullied*, still there was an admixture of pleasurable cognition in his thinking, struggling with the original perception.

Another man, on the other hand, might view the balloon as if it were part of a system of unanticipated rewards, as when one's employer walks in and says, "Here, Henry, take this package of money I have wrapped for you, because we have been doing so well in the business here, and I admire the way you bruise the tulips, without which bruising your department would not be a success, or at least not the success that it is." For this man the balloon might be a brilliantly heroic "muscle and pluck" experience, even if an experience poorly understood.

Another man might say, "Without the example of———, it is doubtful that———would exist today in its present form," and find many to agree with him, or to argue with him. Ideas of "bloat" and "float" were introduced, as well as concepts of dream and responsibility. Others engaged in remarkably detailed fantasies having to do with a wish either to lose themselves in the balloon, or to engorge it. The private character of these wishes, of their origins, deeply buried and unknown, was such that they were not much spoken of; yet there is evidence that they were widespread. It was also argued that what was important was what you felt when you stood under the balloon; some people claimed that they felt sheltered, warmed, as never before, while enemies of the balloon felt, or reported feeling, constrained, a "heavy" feeling.

Critical opinion was divided:

"monstrous pourings"

"harp"

XXXXXXX "certain contrasts with darker portions"

"inner joy"

"large, square corners"

"conservative eclecticism that has so far governed modern balloon design"

::::::: "abnormal vigor"

"warm, soft, lazy passages"

"Has unity been sacrificed for a sprawling quality?"

"Quelle catastrophe!"

"munching"

People began, in a curious way, to locate themselves in relation to aspects of the balloon: "I'll be at that place where it dips down into Forty-seventh Street almost to the sidewalk, near the Alamo Chile House," or, "Why don't we go stand on top, and take the air, and maybe walk about a bit, where it forms a tight, curving line with the façade of the Gallery of Modern Art—" Marginal intersections offered entrances within a given time duration, as well as "warm, soft, lazy passages" in which . . . But it is wrong to speak of "marginal intersections," each intersection was crucial, none could be ignored (as if, walking there, you might not find someone capable of turning your attention, in a flash, from old exercises to new exercises, risks and escalations). Each intersection was crucial, meeting of balloon and building, meeting of balloon and man, meeting of balloon and balloon.

It was suggested that what was admired about the balloon was finally this: that it was not limited, or defined. Sometimes a bulge, blister, or sub-section would carry all the way east to the river on its own initiative, in the manner of an army's movements on a map, as seen in a headquarters remote from the fighting. Then that part would be, as it were, thrown back again, or would withdraw into new dispositions; the next morning, that part would have made another sortie, or disappeared altogether. This ability of the balloon to shift its shape, to change, was very pleasing, especially to people whose lives were rather rigidly patterned, persons to whom change, although desired, was not available. The balloon, for the twenty-two days of its existence, offered the possibility, in its randomness, of mislocation of the self, in contradistinction to the grid of precise, rectangular pathways under our feet. The amount of specialized training currently needed, and the consequent desirability of long-term commitments, has been occasioned by the steadily growing importance of complex machinery, in virtually all kinds of operations; as this tendency increases, more and more people will turn, in bewildered inadequacy, to solutions for which the balloon may stand as a prototype, or "rough draft."

I met you under the balloon, on the occasion of your return from Norway; you asked if it was mine; I said it was. The balloon, I said, is a spontaneous autobiographical disclosure, having to do with the unease I felt at your absence, and with sexual deprivation, but now that your visit to Bergen has been terminated, it is no longer necessary or appropriate. Removal of the balloon was easy; trailer trucks carried away the depleted fabric, which is now stored in West Virginia, awaiting some other time of unhappiness, sometime, perhaps, when we are angry with one another.

1968

TONI MORRISON
b. 1931

The 1993 Nobel Laureate in literature, Toni Morrison is a novelist of great importance in her own right and has been the central figure in putting fiction by and about African American women at the forefront of the late-twentieth-century literary canon. Whereas the legacy of slavery had effaced a usable tradition, and critical stereotypes at times restricted such writers' range, Morrison's fiction serves as a model for reconstructing a culturally empowering past. She joins the great American tradition of self-invention: her own example and her editorial work have figured importantly in the careers of other writers, such as Toni Cade Bambara (included in this volume) and Gayl Jones.

Morrison was born in Lorain, Ohio, where much of her fiction is set (a departure from earlier African American narratives typically located in the rural South or urban North). Having earned a B.A. from Howard with a major in English and minor in classics, and an M.A. from Cornell University (with a thesis on suicide in the novels of Virginia Woolf and William Faulkner), Morrison began a teaching career in 1955 that reached from Texas Southern University back to Howard, where her students included the future activist Stokeley Carmichael and the future critic Houston A. Baker Jr. At this time she married Harold Morrison, a Jamaican architect, with whom she had two children before ending their marriage in 1964. Already writing, she took a job with the publishing firm of Random House and eventually settled in New York City, where she worked until 1983. During these same years she held visiting teaching appointments at institutions including Yale University and Bard College.

As a first novel, *The Bluest Eye* (1970) is uncommonly mature for its confident use of a variety of narrative voices. Throughout her career Morrison will be dedicated to constructing a practical cultural identity of both a race and a gender whose self-images have been obscured or denied by dominating forces, and in *The Bluest Eye* she already shows that narrative strategy is an important element in such construction. It is a girl's need to be loved that generates the novel's action, action that involves displaced and alienated affections (and eventually incestuous rape); it is the family's inability to produce a style of existence in which love can be born and thrive that leads to such a devastating fate for Morrison's protagonist. Love is also denied in *Sula* (1974), in which relationships extend in two directions: between contemporaries (Sula and her friend Nel) and with previous generations.

With *Song of Solomon* (1977) Morrison seeks more positive redemption of her characters. Turning away from his parents' loveless marriage, Milkman Dead makes a physical and mental journey to his ancestral roots. Here he discovers a more useful legacy in communal tales about Grandmother and Great-Grandfather, each long dead but infusing the local culture with emotionally sustaining lore. It is this lore that Milkman uses to learn how the spiritual guidance offered by his aunt Pilate eclipses the material concerns of his parents' world.

Allegory becomes an important strategy in *Tar Baby* (1981), drawing on the strong folk culture of Haiti where two contrasting persons form a troubled relationship based on their own distinct searches for and rejections of a heritage. Yet it is in a rebuilding of history, rather than allegory or myth, that Morrison achieves her great strength as a novelist in *Beloved* (1987), the winner of her first major award, the Pulitzer Prize. Set in the middle 1870s, when race relations in America were at their most crucial juncture (slavery having ended and the course of the South's Reconstruction not yet fully determined), this novel shows a mother (Sethe) being haunted and eventually destroyed by the ghost of a daughter (Beloved) whom she had killed eighteen years earlier rather than let her be taken by a vicious slavemaster. This novel is central to Morrison's canon because it involves so many important themes and techniques, from love and guilt to history's role in clarifying the past's influence on the present, all told in a style of magical realism that transforms (without deny-ing) more mundane facts.

Jazz (1992) finds Morrison reinforcing her strategy of narrative voice, here modeled on the progression of a jazz solo to demonstrate how improvisation with detail can change the nature of what is expressed. Present and past weave together in her char-acters' lives as the narrative seeks to understand the jealousies of love and the some-times macabre manifestations of hatred. *Paradise* (1988) takes a nineteenth-century utopia and reexamines its ideals in the face of 1970s realities—a reminder of how neither past nor present can be insulated from the other.

Presently serving as the prestigious Golheen Professor of the Humanities at Prince-ton University, Morrison has moved easily into the role of spokesperson for literary issues. Together with her Nobel lecture, her essays collected as *Playing in the Dark: Whiteness and the Literary Imagination* (1992) challenge stereotypes in white critical thinking about black literature. Her short story "Recitatif," written for the 1983 anthology edited by Amiri and Amina Baraka, *Confirmation,* directly addresses the issues of individual and family, past and present, and race and its effacements that motivate the larger sense of her work. A *recitatif* is a vocal performance in which a narrative is not stated but sung. In her work Morrison's voice sings proudly of a past that in the artistic nature of its reconstruction puts all Americans in touch with a more positively usable heritage.

The text is that printed in *Confirmation* (1983), edited by Amiri and Amina Baraka.

Recitatif

My mother danced all night and Roberta's was sick. That's why we were taken to St. Bonny's. People want to put their arms around you when you tell them you were in a shelter, but it really wasn't bad. No big long room with one hundred beds like Bellevue.[1] There were four to a room, and when Roberta and me came, there was a shortage of state kids, so we were the only ones assigned to 406 and could go from bed to bed if we wanted to. And we wanted to, too. We changed beds every night and for the whole four months we were there we never picked one out as our own permanent bed.

It didn't start out that way. The minute I walked in and the Big Bozo introduced us, I got sick to my stomach. It was one thing to be taken out of your own bed early in the morning—it was something else to be stuck in a strange place with a girl from a whole other race. And Mary, that's my mother, she was right. Every now and then she would stop dancing long enough to tell me something important and one of the things she said was that they never washed their hair and they smelled funny. Roberta sure did. Smell funny, I mean. So when the Big Bozo (nobody ever called her Mrs. Itkin, just like nobody ever said St. Bonaventure)—when she said, "Twyla, this is Roberta. Roberta, this is Twyla. Make each other welcome." I said, "My mother won't like you putting me in here."

"Good," said Bozo. "Maybe then she'll come and take you home."

How's that for mean? If Roberta had laughed I would have killed her, but she didn't. She just walked over to the window and stood with her back to us.

---

1. Bellevue Hospital in New York City is known for its psychiatric ward. St. Bonaventure's offers the services of a youth shelter and school.

"Turn around," said the Bozo. "Don't be rude. Now Twyla. Roberta. When you hear a loud buzzer, that's the call for dinner. Come down to the first floor. Any fights and no movie." And then, just to make sure we knew what we would be missing, *The Wizard of Oz.*"[2]

Roberta must have thought I meant that my mother would be mad about my being put in the shelter. Not about rooming with her, because as soon as Bozo left she came over to me and said, "Is your mother sick too?"

"No," I said. "She just likes to dance all night."

"Oh," she nodded her head and I liked the way she understood things so fast. So for the moment it didn't matter that we looked like salt and pepper standing there and that's what the other kids called us sometimes. We were eight years old and got F's all the time. Me because I couldn't remember what I read or what the teacher said. And Roberta because she couldn't read at all and didn't even listen to the teacher. She wasn't good at anything except jacks, at which she was a killer: pow scoop pow scoop pow scoop.

We didn't like each other all that much at first, but nobody else wanted to play with us because we weren't real orphans with beautiful dead parents in the sky. We were dumped. Even the New York City Puerto Ricans and the upstate Indians ignored us. All kinds of kids were in there, black ones, white ones, even two Koreans. The food was good, though. At least I thought so. Roberta hated it and left whole pieces of things on her plate: Spam, Salisbury steak—even jello with fruit cocktail in it, and she didn't care if I ate what she wouldn't. Mary's idea of supper was popcorn and a can of Yoo-Hoo.[3] Hot mashed potatoes and two weenies was like Thanksgiving for me.

It really wasn't bad, St. Bonny's. The big girls on the second floor pushed us around now and then. But that was all. They wore lipstick and eyebrow pencil and wobbled their knees while they watched TV. Fifteen, sixteen, even, some of them were. They were put-out girls, scared runaways most of them. Poor little girls who fought their uncles off but looked tough to us, and mean. God did they look mean. The staff tried to keep them separate from the younger children, but sometimes they caught us watching them in the orchard where they played radios and danced with each other. They'd light out after us and pull our hair or twist our arms. We were scared of them, Roberta and me, but neither of us wanted the other one to know it. So we got a good list of dirty names we could shout back when we ran from them through the orchard. I used to dream a lot and almost always the orchard was there. Two acres, four maybe, of these little apple trees. Hundreds of them. Empty and crooked like beggar women when I first came to St. Bonny's but fat with flowers when I left. I don't know why I dreamt about that orchard so much. Nothing really happened there. Nothing all that important, I mean. Just the big girls dancing and playing the radio. Roberta and me watching. Maggie fell down there once. The kitchen woman with legs like parentheses. And the big girls laughed at her. We should have helped her up, I know, but we were scared of those girls with lipstick and eyebrow pencil. Maggie couldn't talk. The kids said she had her tongue cut out, but I think she was just born that way: mute. She was old and sandy-colored and she worked in the kitchen. I don't know if she was nice or not. I just remem-

2. The famous children's book published in 1900 by American writer L. Frank Baum (1856–1919); it was made into a film in 1939.
3. A chocolate soft drink.

ber her legs like parentheses and how she rocked when she walked. She worked from early in the morning till two o'clock, and if she was late, if she had too much cleaning and didn't get out till two-fifteen or so, she'd cut through the orchard so she wouldn't miss her bus and have to wait another hour. She wore this really stupid little hat—a kid's hat with ear flaps—and she wasn't much taller than we were. A really awful little hat. Even for a mute, it was dumb—dressing like a kid and never saying anything at all.

"But what about if somebody tries to kill her?" I used to wonder about that. "Or what if she wants to cry? Can she cry?"

"Sure," Roberta said. "But just tears. No sounds come out."

"She can't scream?"

"Nope. Nothing."

"Can she hear?"

"I guess."

"Let's call her," I said. And we did.

"Dummy! Dummy!" She never turned her head.

"Bow legs! Bow legs!" Nothing. She just rocked on, the chin straps of her baby-boy hat swaying from side to side. I think we were wrong. I think she could hear and didn't let on. And it shames me even now to think there was somebody in there after all who heard us call her those names and couldn't tell on us.

We got along all right, Roberta and me. Changed beds every night, got F's in civics and communication skills and gym. The Bozo was disappointed in us, she said. Out of 130 of us state cases, 90 were under twelve. Almost all were real orphans with beautiful dead parents in the sky. We were the only ones dumped and the only ones with F's in three classes including gym. So we got along—what with her leaving whole pieces of things on her plate and being nice about not asking questions.

I think it was the day before Maggie fell down that we found out our mothers were coming to visit us on the same Sunday. We had been at the shelter twenty-eight days (Roberta twenty-eight and a half) and this was their first visit with us. Our mothers would come at ten o'clock in time for chapel, then lunch with us in the teachers' lounge. I thought if my dancing mother met her sick mother it might be good for her. And Roberta thought her sick mother would get a big bang out of a dancing one. We got excited about it and curled each other's hair. After breakfast we sat on the bed watching the road from the window. Roberta's socks were still wet. She washed them the night before and put them on the radiator to dry. They hadn't, but she put them on anyway because their tops were so pretty—scalloped in pink. Each of us had a purple construction-paper basket that we had made in craft class. Mine had a yellow crayon rabbit on it. Roberta's had eggs with wiggly lines of color. Inside were cellophane grass and just the jelly beans because I'd eaten the two marshmallow eggs they gave us. The Big Bozo came herself to get us. Smiling she told us we looked very nice and to come downstairs. We were so surprised by the smile we'd never seen before, neither of us moved.

"Don't you want to see your mommies?"

I stood up first and spilled the jelly beans all over the floor. Bozo's smile disappeared while we scrambled to get the candy up off the floor and put it back in the grass.

She escorted us downstairs to the first floor, where the other girls were lining up to file into the chapel. A bunch of grown-ups stood to one side. Viewers mostly. The old biddies who wanted servants and the fags who wanted company looking for children they might want to adopt. Once in a while a grandmother. Almost never anybody young or anybody whose face wouldn't scare you in the night. Because if any of the real orphans had young relatives they wouldn't be real orphans. I saw Mary right away. She had on those green slacks I hated and hated even more now because didn't she know we were going to chapel? And that fur jacket with the pocket linings so ripped she had to pull to get her hands out of them. But her face was pretty—like always, and she smiled and waved like she was the little girl looking for her mother—not me.

I walked slowly, trying not to drop the jelly beans and hoping the paper handle would hold. I had to use my last Chiclet because by the time I finished cutting everything out, all the Elmer's was gone. I am left-handed and the scissors never worked for me. It didn't matter, though; I might just as well have chewed the gum. Mary dropped to her knees and grabbed me, mashing the basket, the jelly beans, and the grass into her ratty fur jacket.

"Twyla, baby. Twyla, baby!"

I could have killed her. Already I heard the big girls in the orchard the next time saying, "Twyyyyyla, baby!" But I couldn't stay mad at Mary while she was smiling and hugging me and smelling of Lady Esther dusting powder. I wanted to stay buried in her fur all day.

To tell the truth I forgot about Roberta. Mary and I got in line for the traipse into chapel and I was feeling proud because she looked so beautiful even in those ugly green slacks that made her behind stick out. A pretty mother on earth is better than a beautiful dead one in the sky even if she did leave you all alone to go dancing.

I felt a tap on my shoulder, turned, and saw Roberta smiling. I smiled back, but not too much lest somebody think this visit was the biggest thing that ever happened in my life. Then Roberta said, "Mother, I want you to meet my roommate, Twyla. And that's Twyla's mother."

I looked up it seemed for miles. She was big. Bigger than any man and on her chest was the biggest cross I'd ever seen. I swear it was six inches long each way. And in the crook of her arm was the biggest Bible ever made.

Mary, simple-minded as ever, grinned and tried to yank her hand out of the pocket with the raggedy lining—to shake hands, I guess. Roberta's mother looked down at me and then looked down at Mary too. She didn't say anything, just grabbed Roberta with her Bible-free hand and stepped out of line, walking quickly to the rear of it. Mary was still grinning because she's not too swift when it comes to what's really going on. Then this light bulb goes off in her head and she says "That bitch!" really loud and us almost in the chapel now. Organ music whining; the Bonny Angels singing sweetly. Everybody in the world turned around to look. And Mary would have kept it up—kept calling names if I hadn't squeezed her hand as hard as I could. That helped a little, but she still twitched and crossed and uncrossed her legs all through service. Even groaned a couple of times. Why did I think she would come there and act right? Slacks. No hat like the grandmothers and viewers, and groaning all the while. When we stood for hymns she kept her mouth shut. Wouldn't even look at the words on the page. She actually reached in her purse for a mirror to check her lipstick. All I could think of was that she really needed to be killed. The sermon lasted a year, and I knew the real orphans were looking smug again.

We were supposed to have lunch in the teachers' lounge, but Mary didn't bring anything, so we picked fur and cellophane grass off the mashed jelly beans and ate them. I could have killed her. I sneaked a look at Roberta. Her mother had brought chicken legs and ham sandwiches and oranges and a whole box of chocolate-covered grahams. Roberta drank milk from a thermos while her mother read the Bible to her.

Things are not right. The wrong food is always with the wrong people. Maybe that's why I got into waitress work later—to match up the right people with the right food. Roberta just let those chicken legs sit there, but she did bring a stack of grahams up to me later when the visit was over. I think she was sorry that her mother would not shake my mother's hand. And I liked that and I liked the fact that she didn't say a word about Mary groaning all the way through the service and not bringing any lunch.

Roberta left in May when the apple trees were heavy and white. On her last day we went to the orchard to watch the big girls smoke and dance by the radio. It didn't matter that they said, "Twyyyyyla, baby." We sat on the ground and breathed. Lady Esther. Apple blossoms. I still go soft when I smell one or the other. Roberta was going home. The big cross and the big Bible was coming to get her and she seemed sort of glad and sort of not. I thought I would die in that room of four beds without her and I knew Bozo had plans to move some other dumped kid in there with me. Roberta promised to write every day, which was really sweet of her because she couldn't read a lick so how could she write anybody. I would have drawn pictures and sent them to her but she never gave me her address. Little by little she faded. Her wet socks with the pink scalloped tops and her big serious-looking eyes— that's all I could catch when I tried to bring her to mind.

I was working behind the counter at the Howard Johnson's on the Thruway just before the Kingston exit. Not a bad job. Kind of a long ride from New-burgh,[4] but okay once I got there. Mine was the second night shift—eleven to seven. Very light until a Greyhound checked in for breakfast around six-thirty. At that hour the sun was all the way clear of the hills behind the restaurant. The place looked better at night—more like shelter—but I loved it when the sun broke in, even if it did show all the cracks in the vinyl and the speckled floor looked dirty no matter what the mop boy did.

It was August and a bus crowd was just unloading. They would stand around a long while: going to the john, and looking at gifts and junk-for-sale machines, reluctant to sit down so soon. Even to eat. I was trying to fill the coffee pots and get them all situated on the electric burners when I saw her. She was sitting in a booth smoking a cigarette with two guys smothered in head and facial hair. Her own hair was so big and wild I could hardly see her face. But the eyes. I would know them anywhere. She had on a powder-blue halter and shorts outfit and earrings the size of bracelets. Talk about lipstick and eyebrow pencil. She made the big girls look like nuns. I couldn't get off the counter until seven o'clock, but I kept watching the booth in case they got up to leave before that. My replacement was on time for a change, so I counted and stacked my receipts as fast as I could and signed off. I

---

4. A community eighty miles north of New York City.

walked over to the booth, smiling and wondering if she would remember me. Or even if she wanted to remember me. Maybe she didn't want to be reminded of St. Bonny's or to have anybody know she was ever there. I know I never talked about it to anybody.

I put my hands in my apron pockets and leaned against the back of the booth facing them.

"Roberta? Roberta Fisk?"

She looked up. "Yeah?"

"Twyla."

She squinted for a second and then said, "Wow."

"Remember me?"

"Sure. Hey. Wow."

"It's been a while," I said, and gave a smile to the two hairy guys.

"Yeah. Wow. You work here?"

"Yeah," I said. "I live in Newburgh."

"Newburgh? No kidding?" She laughed then a private laugh that included the guys but only the guys, and they laughed with her. What could I do but laugh too and wonder why I was standing there with my knees showing out from under that uniform. Without looking I could see the blue and white triangle on my head, my hair shapeless in a net, my ankles thick in white oxfords. Nothing could have been less sheer than my stockings. There was this silence that came down right after I laughed. A silence it was her turn to fill up. With introductions, maybe, to her boyfriends or an invitation to sit down and have a Coke. Instead she lit a cigarette off the one she'd just finished and said, "We're on our way to the Coast. He's got an appointment with Hendrix." She gestured casually toward the boy next to her.

"Hendrix?[5] Fantastic," I said. "Really fantastic. What's she doing now?"

Roberta coughed on her cigarette and the two guys rolled their eyes up at the ceiling.

"Hendrix. Jimi Hendrix, asshole. He's only the biggest—Oh, wow. Forget it."

I was dismissed without anyone saying goodbye, so I thought I would do it for her.

"How's your mother?" I asked. Her grin cracked her whole face. She swallowed. "Fine," she said. "How's yours?"

"Pretty as a picture," I said and turned away. The backs of my knees were damp. Howard Johnson's really was a dump in the sunlight.

James is as comfortable as a house slipper. He liked my cooking and I liked his big loud family. They have lived in Newburgh all of their lives and talk about it the way people do who have always known a home. His grandmother is a porch swing older than his father and when they talk about streets and avenues and buildings they call them names they no longer have. They still call the A & P[6] Rico's because it stands on property once a mom and pop store owned by Mr. Rico. And they call the new community college Town Hall because it once was. My mother-in-law puts up jelly and cucumbers and buys butter wrapped in cloth from a dairy. James and his father talk

---

5. Jimi Hendrix (1942–1970), American musician and rock music star.   6. Supermarket, part of a national chain.

about fishing and baseball and I can see them all together on the Hudson in a raggedy skiff. Half the population of Newburgh is on welfare now, but to my husband's family it was still some upstate paradise of a time long past. A time of ice houses and vegetable wagons, coal furnaces and children weeding gardens. When our son was born my mother-in-law gave me the crib blanket that had been hers.

But the town they remembered had changed. Something quick was in the air. Magnificent old houses, so ruined they had become shelter for squatters and rent risks, were bought and renovated. Smart IBM people[7] moved out of their suburbs back into the city and put shutters up and herb gardens in their backyards. A brochure came in the mail announcing the opening of a Food Emporium. Gourmet food it said—and listed items the rich IBM crowd would want. It was located in a new mall at the edge of town and I drove out to shop there one day—just to see. It was late in June. After the tulips were gone and the Queen Elizabeth roses were open everywhere. I trailed my cart along the aisle tossing in smoked oysters and Robert's sauce and things I knew would sit in my cupboard for years. Only when I found some Klondike ice cream bars did I feel less guilty about spending James's fireman's salary so foolishly. My father-in-law ate them with the same gusto little Joseph did.

Waiting in the check-out line I heard a voice say, "Twyla!"

The classical music piped over the aisles had affected me and the woman leaning toward me was dressed to kill. Diamonds on her hand, a smart white summer dress. "I'm Mrs. Benson," I said.

"Ho. Ho. The Big Bozo," she sang.

For a split second I didn't know what she was talking about. She had a bunch of asparagus and two cartons of fancy water.

"Roberta!"

"Right."

"For heaven's sake. Roberta."

"You look great," she said.

"So do you. Where are you? Here? In Newburgh?"

"Yes. Over in Annandale."

I was opening my mouth to say more when the cashier called my attention to her empty counter.

"Meet you outside." Roberta pointed her finger and went into the express line.

I placed the groceries and kept myself from glancing around to check Roberta's progress. I remembered Howard Johnson's and looking for a chance to speak only to be greeted with a stingy "wow." But she was waiting for me and her huge hair was sleek now, smooth around a small, nicely shaped head. Shoes, dress, everything lovely and summery and rich. I was dying to know what happened to her, how she got from Jimi Hendrix to Annandale, a neighborhood full of doctors and IBM executives. Easy, I thought. Everything is so easy for them. They think they own the world.

"How long," I asked her. "How long have you been here?"

"A year. I got married to a man who lives here. And you, you're married too, right? Benson, you said."

7. High-salaried employees of the International Business Machine Corporation, headquartered in the suburbs of New York City.

"Yeah. James Benson."

"And is he nice?"

"Oh, is he nice?"

"Well, is he?" Roberta's eyes were steady as though she really meant the question and wanted an answer.

"He's wonderful, Roberta. Wonderful."

"So you're happy."

"Very."

"That's good," she said and nodded her head. "I always hoped you'd be happy. Any kids? I know you have kids."

"One. A boy. How about you?"

"Four."

"Four?"

She laughed. "Step kids. He's a widower."

"Oh."

"Got a minute? Let's have a coffee."

I thought about the Klondikes melting and the inconvenience of going all the way to my car and putting the bags in the trunk. Served me right for buying all that stuff I didn't need. Roberta was ahead of me.

"Put them in my car. It's right here."

And then I saw the dark blue limousine.

"You married a Chinaman?"

"No," she laughed. "He's the driver."

"Oh, my. If the Big Bozo could see you now."

We both giggled. Really giggled. Suddenly, in just a pulse beat, twenty years disappeared and all of it came rushing back. The big girls (whom we called gar girls—Roberta's misheard word for the evil stone faces described in a civics class) there dancing in the orchard, the ploppy mashed potatoes, the double weenies, the Spam with pineapple. We went into the coffee shop holding on to one another and I tried to think why we were glad to see each other this time and not before. Once, twelve years ago, we passed like strangers. A black girl and a white girl meeting in a Howard Johnson's on the road and having nothing to say. One in a blue and white triangle waitress hat—the other on her way to see Hendrix. Now we were behaving like sisters separated for much too long. Those four short months were nothing in time. Maybe it was the thing itself. Just being there, together. Two little girls who knew what nobody else in the world knew—how not to ask questions. How to believe what had to be believed. There was politeness in that reluctance and generosity as well. Is your mother sick too? No, she dances all night. Oh—and an understanding nod.

We sat in a booth by the window and fell into recollection like veterans.

"Did you ever learn to read?"

"Watch." She picked up the menu. "Special of the day. Cream of corn soup. Entrées. Two dots and a wriggly line. Quiche. Chef salad, scallops . . ."

I was laughing and applauding when the waitress came up.

"Remember the Easter baskets?"

"And how we tried to *introduce* them?"

"Your mother with that cross like two telephone poles."

"And yours with those tight slacks."

We laughed so loudly heads turned and made the laughter harder to suppress.

"What happened to the Jimi Hendrix date?"

Roberta made a blow-out sound with her lips.

"When he died I thought about you."

"Oh, you heard about him finally?"

"Finally. Come on, I was a small-town country waitress."

"And I was a small-town country dropout. God, were we wild. I still don't know how I got out of there alive."

"But you did."

"I did. I really did. Now I'm Mrs. Kenneth Norton."

"Sounds like a mouthful."

"It is."

"Servants and all?"

Roberta held up two fingers.

"Ow! What does he do?"

"Computers and stuff. What do I know?"

"I don't remember a hell of a lot from those days, but Lord, St. Bonny's is as clear as daylight. Remember Maggie? The day she fell down and those gar girls laughed at her?"

Roberta looked up from her salad and stared at me. "Maggie didn't fall," she said.

"Yes, she did. You remember."

"No, Twyla. They knocked her down. Those girls pushed her down and tore her clothes. In the orchard."

"I don't—that's not what happened."

"Sure it is. In the orchard. Remember how scared we were?"

"Wait a minute. I don't remember any of that."

"And Bozo was fired."

"You're crazy. She was there when I left. You left before me."

"I went back. You weren't there when they fired Bozo."

"What?"

"Twice. Once for a year when I was about ten, another for two months when I was fourteen. That's when I ran away."

"You ran away from St. Bonny's?"

"I had to. What do you want? Me dancing in that orchard?"

"Are you sure about Maggie?"

"Of course I'm sure. You've blocked it, Twyla. It happened. Those girls had behavior problems, you know."

"Didn't they, though. But why can't I remember the Maggie thing?"

"Believe me. It happened. And we were there."

"Who did you room with when you went back?" I asked her as if I would know her. The Maggie thing was troubling me.

"Creeps. They tickled themselves in the night."

My ears were itching and I wanted to go home suddenly. This was all very well but she couldn't just comb her hair, wash her face and pretend everything was hunky-dory. After the Howard Johnson's snub. And no apology. Nothing.

"Were you on dope or what that time at Howard Johnson's?" I tried to make my voice sound friendlier than I felt.

"Maybe, a little. I never did drugs much. Why?"

"I don't know; you acted sort of like you didn't want to know me then."

"Oh, Twyla, you know how it was in those days: black—white. You know how everything was."

But I didn't know. I thought it was just the opposite. Busloads of blacks and whites came into Howard Johnson's together. They roamed together then: students, musicians, lovers, protesters. You got to see everything at Howard Johnson's and blacks were very friendly with whites in those days. But sitting there with nothing on my plate but two hard tomato wedges wondering about the melting Klondikes it seemed childish remembering the slight. We went to her car, and with the help of the driver, got my stuff into my station wagon.

"We'll keep in touch this time," she said.

"Sure," I said. "Sure. Give me a call."

"I will," she said, and then just as I was sliding behind the wheel, she leaned into the window. "By the way. Your mother. Did she ever stop dancing?"

I shook my head. "No. Never."

Roberta nodded.

"And yours? Did she ever get well?"

She smiled a tiny sad smile. "No. She never did. Look, call me, okay?"

"Okay," I said, but I knew I wouldn't. Roberta had messed up my past somehow with that business about Maggie. I wouldn't forget a thing like that. Would I?

Strife came to us that fall. At least that's what the paper called it. Strife. Racial strife. The word made me think of a bird—a big shrieking bird out of 1,000,000,000 B.C. Flapping its wings and cawing. Its eye with no lid always bearing down on you. All day it screeched and at night it slept on the rooftops. It woke you in the morning and from the *Today* show to the eleven o'clock news it kept you an awful company. I couldn't figure it out from one day to the next. I knew I was supposed to feel something strong, but I didn't know what, and James wasn't any help. Joseph was on the list of kids to be transferred from the junior high school to another one at some far-out-of-the-way place and I thought it was a good thing until I heard it was a bad thing. I mean I didn't know. All the schools seemed dumps to me, and the fact that one was nicer looking didn't hold much weight. But the papers were full of it and then the kids began to get jumpy. In August, mind you. Schools weren't even open yet. I thought Joseph might be frightened to go over there, but he didn't seem scared so I forgot about it, until I found myself driving along Hudson Street out there by the school they were trying to integrate and saw a line of women marching. And who do you suppose was in line, big as life, holding a sign in front of her bigger than her mother's cross? MOTHERS HAVE RIGHTS TOO! it said.

I drove on, and then changed my mind. I circled the block, slowed down, and honked my horn.

Roberta looked over and when she saw me she waved. I didn't wave back, but I didn't move either. She handed her sign to another woman and came over to where I was parked.

"Hi."

"What are you doing?"

"Picketing. What's it look like?"

"What for?"

"What do you mean 'What for?' They want to take my kids and send them out of the neighborhood. They don't want to go."

"So what if they go to another school? My boy's being bussed too, and I don't mind. Why should you?"

"It's not about us, Twyla. Me and you. It's about our kids."

"What's more *us* than that?"

"Well, it is a free country."

"Not yet, but it will be."

"What the hell does that mean? I'm not doing anything to you."

"You really think that?"

"I know it."

"I wonder what made me think you were different."

"I wonder what made me think you were different."

"Look at them," I said. "Just look. Who do they think they are? Swarming all over the place like they own it. And now they think they can decide where my child goes to school. Look at them, Roberta. They're Bozos."

Roberta turned around and looked at the women. Almost all of them were standing still now, waiting. Some were even edging toward us. Roberta looked at me out of some refrigerator behind her eyes. "No, they're not. They're just mothers."

"And what am I? Swiss cheese?"

"I used to curl your hair."

"I hated your hands in my hair."

The women were moving. Our faces looked mean to them of course and they looked as though they could not wait to throw themselves in front of a police car, or better yet, into my car and drag me away by my ankles. Now they surrounded my car and gently, gently began to rock it. I swayed back and forth like a sideways yo-yo. Automatically I reached for Roberta, like the old days in the orchard when they saw us watching them and we had to get out of there, and if one of us fell the other pulled her up and if one of us was caught the other stayed to kick and scratch, and neither would leave the other behind. My arm shot out of the car window but no receiving hand was there. Roberta was looking at me sway from side to side in the car and her face was still. My purse slid from the car seat down under the dashboard. The four policemen who had been drinking Tab[8] in their car finally got the message and strolled over, forcing their way through the women. Quietly, firmly they spoke. "Okay, ladies. Back in line or off the streets."

Some of them went away willingly; others had to be urged away from the car doors and the hood. Roberta didn't move. She was looking steadily at me. I was fumbling to turn on the ignition, which wouldn't catch because the gearshift was still in drive. The seats of the car were a mess because the swaying had thrown my grocery coupons all over it and my purse was sprawled on the floor.

---

8. A carbonated diet soft drink.

"Maybe I am different now, Twyla. But you're not. You're the same little state kid who kicked a poor old black lady when she was down on the ground. You kicked a black lady and you have the nerve to call me a bigot."

The coupons were everywhere and the guts of my purse were bunched under the dashboard. What was she saying? Black? Maggie wasn't black.

"She wasn't black," I said.

"Like hell she wasn't, and you kicked her. We both did. You kicked a black lady who couldn't even scream."

"Liar!"

"You're the liar! Why don't you just go on home and leave us alone, huh?"

She turned away and I skidded away from the curb.

The next morning I went into the garage and cut the side out of the carton our portable TV had come in. It wasn't nearly big enough, but after a while I had a decent sign: red spray-painted letters on a white background—AND SO DO CHILDREN * * * *. I meant just to go down to the school and tack it up somewhere so those cows on the picket line across the street could see it, but when I got there, some ten or so others had already assembled—protesting the cows across the street. Police permits and everything. I got in line and we strutted in time on our side while Roberta's group strutted on theirs. That first day we were all dignified, pretending the other side didn't exist. The second day there was name calling and finger gestures. But that was about all. People changed signs from time to time, but Roberta never did and neither did I. Actually my sign didn't make sense without Roberta's. "And so do children what?" one of the women on my side asked me. Have rights, I said, as though it was obvious.

Roberta didn't acknowledge my presence in any way and I got to thinking maybe she didn't know I was there. I began to pace myself in the line, jostling people one minute and lagging behind the next, so Roberta and I could reach the end of our respective lines at the same time and there would be a moment in our turn when we would face each other. Still, I couldn't tell whether she saw me and knew my sign was for her. The next day I went early before we were scheduled to assemble. I waited until she got there before I exposed my new creation. As soon as she hoisted her MOTHERS HAVE RIGHTS TOO I began to wave my new one, which said, HOW WOULD YOU KNOW? I know she saw that one, but I had gotten addicted now. My signs got crazier each day, and the women on my side decided that I was a kook. They couldn't make heads or tails out of my brilliant screaming posters.

I brought a painted sign in queenly red with huge black letters that said, IS YOUR MOTHER WELL? Roberta took her lunch break and didn't come back for the rest of the day or any day after. Two days later I stopped going too and couldn't have been missed because nobody understood my signs anyway.

It was a nasty six weeks. Classes were suspended and Joseph didn't go to anybody's school until October. The children—everybody's children—soon got bored with that extended vacation they thought was going to be so great. They looked at TV until their eyes flattened. I spent a couple of mornings tutoring my son, as the other mothers said we should. Twice I opened a text from last year that he had never turned in. Twice he yawned in my face. Other mothers organized living room sessions so the kids would keep up. None of the kids could concentrate so they drifted back to *The Price Is Right* and *The Brady Bunch.*[9] When the school finally opened there were fights once or twice and some sirens roared through the streets every once in a while. There were a lot of photographers from Albany. And just when ABC was about to send up a news crew, the kids settled down like nothing in the world had happened. Joseph hung my HOW WOULD YOU KNOW? sign in his bedroom. I don't know what became of AND SO DO CHILDREN * * * *. I think my father-in-law cleaned some fish on it. He was always puttering around in our garage. Each of his five children lived in Newburgh and he acted as though he had five extra homes.

I couldn't help looking for Roberta when Joseph graduated from high school, but I didn't see her. It didn't trouble me much what she had said to me in the car. I mean the kicking part. I know I didn't do that, I couldn't do that. But I was puzzled by her telling me Maggie was black. When I thought about it I actually couldn't be certain. She wasn't pitch-black, I knew, or I would have remembered that. What I remember was the kiddie hat, and the semicircle legs. I tried to reassure myself about the race thing for a long time until it dawned on me that the truth was already there, and Roberta knew it. I didn't kick her; I didn't join in with the gar girls and kick that lady, but I sure did want to. We watched and never tried to help her and never called for help. Maggie was my dancing mother. Deaf, I thought, and dumb. Nobody inside. Nobody who would hear you if you cried in the night. Nobody who could tell you anything important that you could use. Rocking, dancing, swaying as she walked. And when the gar girls pushed her down, and started roughhousing, I knew she wouldn't scream, couldn't—just like me—and I was glad about that.

We decided not to have a tree, because Christmas would be at my mother-in-law's house, so why have a tree at both places? Joseph was at SUNY New Paltz[1] and we had to economize, we said. But at the last minute, I changed my mind. Nothing could be that bad. So I rushed around town looking for a tree, something small but wide. By the time I found a place, it was snowing and very late. I dawdled like it was the most important purchase in the world and the tree man was fed up with me. Finally I chose one and had it tied onto the trunk of the car. I drove away slowly because the sand trucks were not out yet and the streets could be murder at the beginning of a snowfall. Downtown the streets were wide and rather empty except for a cluster of people coming out of the Newburgh Hotel. The one hotel in town that wasn't built out of cardboard and Plexiglas. A party, probably. The men huddled in the snow were dressed in tails and the women had on furs. Shiny things glittered from underneath their coats. It made me tired to look at them. Tired, tired, tired. On the next corner was a small diner with loops and loops of paper bells in the window. I stopped the car and went in. Just for a cup of coffee and twenty minutes of peace before I went home and tried to finish everything before Christmas Eve.

"Twyla?"

There she was. In a silvery evening gown and dark fur coat. A man and

---

9. Respectively, a popular television game show and situation comedy.

1. A campus in the State University of New York system.

another woman were with her, the man fumbling for change to put in the cigarette machine. The woman was humming and tapping on the counter with her fingernails. They all looked a little bit drunk.

"Well. It's you."

"How are you?"

I shrugged. "Pretty good. Frazzled. Christmas and all."

"Regular?" called the woman from the counter.

"Fine," Roberta called back and then, "Wait for me in the car."

She slipped into the booth beside me. "I have to tell you something, Twyla. I made up my mind if I ever saw you again, I'd tell you."

"I'd just as soon not hear anything, Roberta. It doesn't matter now, anyway."

"No," she said. "Not about that."

"Don't be long," said the woman. She carried two regulars to go and the man peeled his cigarette pack as they left.

"It's about St. Bonny's and Maggie."

"Oh, please."

"Listen to me. I really did think she was black. I didn't make that up. I really thought so. But now I can't be sure. I just remember her as old, so old. And because she couldn't talk—well, you know, I thought she was crazy. She'd been brought up in an institution like my mother was and like I thought I would be too. And you were right. We didn't kick her. It was the gar girls. Only them. But, well, I wanted to. I really wanted them to hurt her. I said we did it, too. You and me, but that's not true. And I don't want you to carry that around. It was just that I wanted to do it so bad that day—wanting to is doing it."

Her eyes were watery from the drinks she'd had, I guess. I know it's that way with me. One glass of wine and I start bawling over the littlest thing.

"We were kids, Roberta."

"Yeah. Yeah. I know, just kids."

"Eight."

"Eight."

"And lonely."

"Scared, too."

She wiped her cheeks with the heel of her hand and smiled. "Well, that's all I wanted to say."

I nodded and couldn't think of any way to fill the silence that went from the diner past the paper bells on out into the snow. It was heavy now. I thought I'd better wait for the sand trucks before starting home.

"Thanks, Roberta."

"Sure."

"Did I tell you? My mother, she never did stop dancing."

"Yes. You told me. And mine, she never got well." Roberta lifted her hands from the tabletop and covered her face with her palms. When she took them away she really was crying. "Oh shit, Twyla. Shit, shit, shit. What the hell happened to Maggie?"

1983

JOHN UPDIKE
b. 1932

"To transcribe middleness with all its grits, bumps and anonymities, in its fullness of satisfaction and mystery: is it possible . . . or worth doing?" John Updike's novels and stories give a positive answer to the question he asks in his early memoir, *The Dogwood Tree: A Boyhood*; for he is arguably the most significant transcriber, or creator rather, of "middleness" in American writing since William Dean Howells (about whom he has written appreciatively). Falling in love in high school, meeting a college roommate, going to the eye doctor or dentist, eating supper on Sunday night, visiting your mother with your wife and son—these activities are made to yield up their possibilities to a writer as responsively curious in imagination and delicately precise in his literary expression as Updike has shown himself to be.

Born in Shillington, Pennsylvania, John Updike was an only child. He was gifted at drawing and caricature, and after graduating summa cum laude from Harvard in 1954, he spent a year studying art in England, then returned to America and went to work for *The New Yorker*, where his first stories appeared and to which he is still a regular contributor. When later in the 1950s he left the magazine, he also left New York City and with his wife and children settled in Ipswich, Massachusetts. There he pursued "his solitary trade as methodically as the dentist practiced his," resisting the temptations of university teaching as successfully as the blandishments of media talk shows. Like Howells, his ample production has been achieved through dedicated, steady work; his books are the fruit of patience, leisure, and craft.

Since 1958 when his first novel, *The Poorhouse Fair*, appeared, Updike has published not only many novels and stories but also six books of poetry, a play, and a vast store of book reviews and other prose writings. He is most admired by some readers as the author of the "Olinger" stories about life in an imaginary Pennsylvania town that takes on its colors from the real Shillington of his youth. The heroes of these stories are adolescents straining to break out of their fast-perishing environments, as they grow up and as their small town turns into something else. Updike treats them with a blend of affection and ironic humor that is wonderfully assured in its touch, although his sense of place, of growing up during the Depression and the years of World War II, is always vividly present. Like Howells (whose fine memoir of his youthful days in Ohio, *A Boy's Town*, is an ancestor of Updike's *The Dogwood Tree*) he shows how one's spirit takes on its coloration from the material circumstances—houses, clothes, landscape, food, parents—one is bounded by.

This sense of place, which is also a sense of life, is found in the stories and in the novels too, although Updike has found it harder to invent convincing forms in which to tell longer tales. His most ambitious novel is probably *The Centaur* (1964), memorable for its portrayal of three days of confusion and error in the life of an American high school teacher seen through his son's eyes, but the book is also burdened with an elaborate set of mythical trappings that seem less than inevitable. *Couples* (1968), a novel that gained him a good deal of notoriety as a chronicler of sexual relationships, marital and adulterous, is jammed with much interesting early-1960s lore about suburban life but seems uncertain whether it is an exercise in realism or a creative fantasy, as does *Marry Me* (1976).

It is in the four "Rabbit" novels that Updike found his most congenial and engaging subject for longer fiction. In each book he has managed to render the sense of an era—the 1950s in *Rabbit, Run*; the late 1960s in *Rabbit Redux*; the great gasoline crisis of 1979 in *Rabbit Is Rich*; the end of the Reagan era (and the end of Rabbit) in *Rabbit at Rest* (1990)—through the eyes of a hero who both is and is not like his creator. Harry "Rabbit" Angstrom, ex–high school basketball star, a prey to nostalgia and in love with his own past, perpetually lives in a present he can't abide. *Rabbit, Run* shows him trying to escape from his town, his job, his wife, and his child by a series of disastrously sentimental and humanly irresponsible actions; yet Updike makes us feel Rabbit's yearnings even as we judge the painful consequences of yielding to them. Ten years later the fading basketball star has become a fortyish, dispirited printer with a wayward wife and a country that is both landing on the moon and falling to pieces. *Rabbit Redux* is masterly in presenting a small town rotting away from its past certainties; it also attempts to deal with the Vietnam War and the black revolution. *Rabbit Is Rich* is a more gentle, sadder chronicling of the hero's settling into grandfatherhood as he draws ever closer to death; while *Rabbit at Rest*, the longest and richest of the four novels, brings him to a moving conclusion; indeed, Rabbit himself is worthy of a generational coda, one presented in the reflections of his son and illegitimate daughter in "Rabbit Remembered," collected in *Licks of Love* (2000). In *Roger's Version* (1986) and *S* (1988) Updike has adopted—or permitted his protagonists to adopt—a more broadly, sometimes a harsher, satiric view of contemporary religion, computer technology, feminism, and other forms of "liberation." Still, for all his virtuosity as a novelist, his best work may be found in the stories and in his short novel *Of the Farm* (1965). In "Separating" (printed here) the boy from "The Happiest I've Been" has grown up, married, and fathered children and is now about to leave them as he moves into divorce. It is a beautiful example of Updike's careful, poised sense of how things work, a sense that can also be observed in the poem "Dog's Death" and in his memoir *Self-Consciousness* (1989).

Near the end of "The Dogwood Tree" he summarized his boyish dream of becoming an artist:

> He saw art—between drawing and writing he ignorantly made no distinction— as a method of riding a thin pencil out of Shillington, out of time altogether, into an infinity of unseen and even unborn hearts. He pictured this infinity as radiant. How innocent!

Most writers would name that innocence only to deplore it. Updike maintains instead that, as with the Christian faith he still professes, succeeding years have given him no better assumptions with which to replace it. In any case, his fine sense of fact has protected him from fashionable extravagances in black humor and experimental narratives, while enabling him to be both a satirist and a celebrator of our social and domestic conditions. In recent years, he has allowed a fabulative, almost magical atmosphere to appear in some works, as with his 2000 novel, *Gertrude and Claudius*. Yet even here, as he does in the generational family saga based on spiritual perceptions, *In the Beauty of the Lilies* (1996), John Updike remains our era's most sensitive craftsman of personal and societal manners.

The text is that of *The New Yorker*, June 23, 1975.

Separating

The day was fair. Brilliant. All that June the weather had mocked the Maples' internal misery with solid sunlight—golden shafts and cascades of green in which their conversations had wormed unseeing, their sad murmuring selves the only stain in Nature. Usually by this time of the year they had acquired tans; but when they met their elder daughter's plane on her return from a year in England they were almost as pale as she, though Judith was too dazzled by the sunny opulent jumble of her native land to notice. They did not spoil her homecoming by telling her immediately. Wait a few days, let her recover from jet lag, had been one of their formulations, in that string of gray dialogues—over coffee, over cocktails, over Cointreau—that had shaped the strategy of their dissolution, while the earth performed its annual stunt of renewal unnoticed beyond their closed windows. Richard had thought to leave at Easter; Joan had insisted they wait until the four children were at last assembled, with all exams passed and ceremonies attended, and the bauble of summer to console them. So he had drudged away, in love, in dread, repairing screens, getting the mowers sharpened, rolling and patching their new tennis court.

The court, clay, had come through its first winter pitted and windswept bare of redcoat. Years ago the Maples had observed how often, among their friends, divorce followed a dramatic home improvement, as if the marriage were making one last twitchy effort to live; their own worst crisis had come amid the plaster dust and exposed plumbing of a kitchen renovation. Yet, a summer ago, as canary-yellow bulldozers gaily churned a grassy, daisy-dotted knoll into a muddy plateau, and a crew of pigtailed young men raked and tamped clay into a plane, this transformation did not strike them as ominous, but festive in its impudence; their marriage could rend the earth for fun. The next spring, waking each day at dawn to a sliding sensation as if the bed were being tipped, Richard found the barren tennis court, its net and tapes still rolled in the barn, an environment congruous with his mood of purposeful desolation, and the crumbling of handfuls of clay into cracks and holes (dogs had frolicked on the court in a thaw; rivulets had evolved trenches) an activity suitably elemental and interminable. In his sealed heart he hoped the day would never come.

Now it was here. A Friday. Judith was reacclimated; all four children were assembled, before jobs and camps and visits again scattered them. Joan thought they should be told one by one. Richard was for making an announcement at the table. She said, "I think just making an announcement is a cop-out. They'll start quarrelling and playing to each other instead of focussing. They're each individuals, you know, not just some corporate obstacle to your freedom."

"O.K., O.K. I agree." Joan's plan was exact. That evening, they were giving Judith a belated welcome-home dinner, of lobster and champagne. Then, the party over, they, the two of them, who nineteen years before would push her in a baby carriage along Tenth Street to Washington Square,[1] were to walk her out of the house, to the bridge across the salt creek, and tell her, swearing her to secrecy. Then Richard Jr., who was going directly from work to a rock concert in Boston, would be told, either late when he returned on the train or early Saturday morning before he went off to his job; he was seventeen and employed as one of a golf-course maintenance crew. Then the two younger children, John and Margaret, could, as the morning wore on, be informed.

"Mopped up, as it were," Richard said.

"Do you have any better plan? That leaves you the rest of Saturday to answer any questions, pack, and make your wonderful departure."

"No," he said, meaning he had no better plan, and agreed to hers, though it had an edge of false order, a plea for control in the semblance of its

---

1. In Greenwich Village, an area in lower Manhattan, New York City.

achievement, like Joan's long chore lists and financial accountings and, in the days when he first knew her, her too copious lecture notes. Her plan turned one hurdle for him into four—four knife-sharp walls, each with a sheer blind drop on the other side.

All spring he had been morbidly conscious of insides and outsides, of barriers and partitions. He and Joan stood as a thin barrier between the children and the truth. Each moment was a partition, with the past on one side and the future on the other, a future containing this unthinkable *now*. Beyond four knifelike walls a new life for him waited vaguely. His skull cupped a secret, a white face, a face both frightened and soothing, both strange and known, that he wanted to shield from tears, which he felt all about him, solid as the sunlight. So haunted, he had become obsessed with battening down the house against his absence, replacing screens and sash cords, hinges and latches—a Houdini[2] making things snug before his escape.

The lock. He had still to replace a lock on one of the doors of the screened porch. The task, like most such, proved more difficult than he had imagined. The old lock, aluminum frozen by corrosion, had been deliberately rendered obsolete by manufacturers. Three hardware stores had nothing that even approximately matched the mortised hole its removal (surprisingly easy) left. Another hole had to be gouged, with bits too small and saws too big, and the old hole fitted with a block of wood—the chisels dull, the saw rusty, his fingers thick with lack of sleep. The sun poured down, beyond the porch, on a world of neglect. The bushes already needed pruning, the windward side of the house was shedding flakes of paint, rain would get in when he was gone, insects, rot, death. His family, all those he would lose, filtered through the edges of his awareness as he struggled with screw holes, splinters, opaque instructions, minutiae of metal.

Judith sat on the porch, a princess returned from exile. She regaled them with stories of fuel shortages, of bomb scares in the Underground, of Pakistani workmen loudly lusting after her as she walked past on her way to dance school. Joan came and went, in and out of the house, calmer than she should have been, praising his struggles with the lock as if this were one more and not the last of their chain of shared chores. The younger of his sons, John, now at fifteen suddenly, unwittingly handsome, for a few minutes held the rickety screen door while his father clumsily hammered and chiselled, each blow a kind of sob in Richard's ears. His younger daughter, having been at a slumber party, slept on the porch hammock through all the noise— heavy and pink, trusting and forsaken. Time, like the sunlight, continued relentlessly; the sunlight slowly slanted. Today was one of the longest days. The lock clicked, worked. He was through. He had a drink; he drank it on the porch, listening to his daughter. "It was so sweet," she was saying, "during the worst of it, how all the butcher's and bakery shops kept open by candlelight. They're all so plucky and cute. From the papers, things sounded so much worse here—people shooting people in gas lines, and everybody freezing."

Richard asked her, "Do you still want to live in England forever?" *Forever:* the concept, now a reality upon him, pressed and scratched at the back of his throat.

2. Harry Houdini (1874–1926), American magician and escape artist.

"No," Judith confessed, turning her oval face to him, its eyes still childishly far apart, but the lips set as over something succulent and satisfactory. "I was anxious to come home. I'm an American." She was a woman. They had raised her; he and Joan had endured together to raise her, alone of the four. The others had still some raising left in them. Yet it was the thought of telling Judith—the image of her, their first baby, walking between them arm in arm to the bridge—that broke him. The partition between himself and the tears broke. Richard sat down to the celebratory meal with the back of his throat aching; the champagne, the lobster seemed phases of sunshine; he saw them and tasted them through tears. He blinked, swallowed, croakily joked about hay fever. The tears would not stop leaking through; they came not through a hole that could be plugged but through a permeable spot in a membrane, steadily, purely, endlessly, fruitfully. They became, his tears, a shield for himself against these others—their faces, the fact of their assembly, a last time as innocents, at a table where he sat the last time as head. Tears dropped from his nose as he broke the lobster's back; salt flavored his champagne as he sipped it; the raw clench at the back of his throat was delicious. He could not help himself.

His children tried to ignore his tears. Judith on his right, lit a cigarette, gazed upward in the direction of her too energetic, too sophisticated exhalation; on her other side, John earnestly bent his face to the extraction of the last morsels—legs, tail segments—from the scarlet corpse. Joan, at the opposite end of the table, glanced at him surprised, her reproach displaced by a quick grimace, of forgiveness, or of salute to his superior gift of strategy. Between them, Margaret, no longer called Bean, thirteen and large for her age, gazed from the other side of his pane of tears as if into a shopwindow at something she coveted—at her father, a crystalline heap of splinters and memories. It was not she, however, but John who, in the kitchen, as they cleared the plates and carapaces away, asked Joan the question: *"Why is Daddy crying?"*

Richard heard the question but not the murmured answer. Then he heard Bean cry, "Oh, no-oh!"—the faintly dramatized exclamation of one who had long expected it.

John returned to the table carrying a bowl of salad. He nodded tersely at his father and his lips shaped the conspiratorial words "She told."

"Told what?" Richard asked aloud, insanely.

The boy sat down as if to rebuke his father's distraction with the example of his own good manners and said quietly, "The separation."

Joan and Margaret returned; the child, in Richard's twisted vision, seemed diminished in size, and relieved, relieved to have had the boogeyman at last proved real. He called out to her—the distances at the table had grown immense—"You knew, you always knew," but the clenching at the back of his throat prevented him from making sense of it. From afar he heard Joan talking, levelly, sensibly, reciting what they had prepared: it was a separation for the summer, an experiment. She and Daddy both agreed it would be good for them; they needed space and time to think; they liked each other but did not make each other happy enough, somehow.

Judith, imitating her mother's factual tone, but in her youth off-key, too cool, said, "I think it's silly. You should either live together or get divorced."

Richard's crying, like a wave that has crested and crashed, had become tumultuous; but it was overtopped by another tumult, for John, who had been so reserved, now grew larger and larger at the table. Perhaps his younger sister's being credited with knowing set him off. "Why didn't you *tell* us?" he asked, in a large round voice quite unlike his own. "You should have *told* us you weren't getting along."

Richard was startled into attempting to force words through his tears. "We *do* get along, that's the trouble, so it doesn't show even to us—" "That we do not love each other" was the rest of the sentence; he couldn't finish it.

Joan finished for him, in her style. "And we've always, *especially,* loved our children."

John was not mollified. "What do you care about *us?*" he boomed. "We're just little things you *had.*" His sisters' laughing forced a laugh from him, which he turned hard and parodistic: "Ha ha *ha.*" Richard and Joan realized simultaneously that the child was drunk, on Judith's homecoming champagne. Feeling bound to keep the center of the stage, John took a cigarette from Judith's pack, poked it into his mouth, let it hang from his lower lip, and squinted like a gangster.

"You're not little things we had," Richard called to him. "You're the whole point. But you're grown. Or almost."

The boy was lighting matches. Instead of holding them to his cigarette (for they had never seen him smoke; being "good" had been his way of setting himself apart), he held them to his mother's face, closer and closer, for her to blow out. Then he lit the whole folder—a hiss and then a torch, held against his mother's face. Prismed by tears, the flame filled Richard's vision; he didn't know how it was extinguished. He heard Margaret say, "Oh stop showing off," and saw John, in response, break the cigarette in two and put the halves entirely into his mouth and chew, sticking out his tongue to display the shreds to his sister.

Joan talked to him, reasoning—a fountain of reason, unintelligible. "Talked about it for years . . . our children must help us . . . Daddy and I both want . . ." As the boy listened, he carefully wadded a paper napkin into the leaves of his salad, fashioned a ball of paper and lettuce, and popped it into his mouth, looking around the table for the expected laughter. None came. Judith said, "Be mature," and dismissed a plume of smoke.

Richard got up from this stifling table and led the boy outside. Though the house was in twilight, the outdoors still brimmed with light, the long waste light of high summer. Both laughing, he supervised John's spitting out the lettuce and paper and tobacco into the pachysandra.[3] He took him by the hand—a square gritty hand, but for its softness a man's. Yet, it held on. They ran together up into the field, past the tennis court. The raw banking left by the bulldozers was dotted with daisies. Past the court and a flat stretch where they used to play family baseball stood a soft green rise glorious in the sun, each weed and species of grass distinct as illumination on parchment. "I'm sorry, so sorry," Richard cried. "You were the only one who ever tried to help me with all the goddam jobs around this place."

Sobbing, safe within his tears and the champagne, John explained, "It's not just the separation, it's the whole crummy year, I *hate* that school, you can't make any friends, the history teacher's a scud."[4]

---

3. Green, leafy plant, frequently used as ground-cover.

4. Disagreeable, objectionable person.

They sat on the crest of the rise, shaking and warm from their tears but easier in their voices, and Richard tried to focus on the child's sad year—the weekdays long with homework, the weekends spent in his room with model airplanes, while his parents murmured down below, nursing their separation. How selfish, how blind, Richard thought; his eyes felt scoured. He told his son, "We'll think about getting you transferred. Life's too short to be miserable."

They had said what they could, but did not want the moment to heal, and talked on, about the school, about the tennis court, whether it would ever again be as good as it had been that first summer. They walked to inspect it and pressed a few more tapes more firmly down. A little stiltedly, perhaps trying to make too much of the moment, to prolong it, Richard led the boy to the spot in the field where the view was best, of the metallic blue river, the emerald marsh, the scattered islands velvet with shadow in the low light, the white bits of beach far away. "See," he said. "It goes on being beautiful. It'll be here tomorrow."

"I know," John answered, impatiently. The moment had closed.

Back in the house, the others had opened some white wine, the champagne being drunk, and still sat at the table, the three females, gossiping. Where Joan sat had become the head. She turned, showing him a tearless face, and asked, "All right?"

"We're fine," he said, resenting it, though relieved, that the party went on without him.

In bed she explained, "I couldn't cry I guess because I cried so much all spring. It really wasn't fair. It's your idea, and you made it look as though I was kicking you out."

"I'm sorry," he said. "I couldn't stop. I wanted to but couldn't."

"You *didn't* want to. You loved it. You were having your way, making a general announcement."

"I love having it over," he admitted. "God, those kids were great. So brave and funny." John, returned to the house, had settled to a model airplane in his room, and kept shouting down to them, "I'm O.K. No sweat." "And the way," Richard went on, cozy in his relief, "they never questioned the reasons we gave. No thought of a third person. Not even Judith."

"That *was* touching," Joan said.

He gave her a hug. "You were great too. Thank you." Guiltily, he realized he did not feel separated.

"You still have Dickie to do," she told him. These words set before him a black mountain in the darkness; its cold breath, its near weight affected his chest. Of the four children Dickie was most nearly his conscience. Joan did not need to add, "That's one piece of your dirty work I won't do for you."

"I know. I'll do it. You go to sleep."

Within minutes, her breathing slowed, became oblivious and deep. It was quarter to midnight. Dickie's train from the concert would come in at one-fourteen. Richard set the alarm for one. He had slept atrociously for weeks. But whenever he closed his lids some glimpse of the last hours scorched them—Judith exhaling toward the ceiling in a kind of aversion, Bean's mute staring, the sunstruck growth of the field where he and John had rested. The mountain before him moved closer, moved within him; he was huge, momentous. The ache at the back of his throat felt stale. His wife slept as if slain beside him. When, exasperated by his hot lids, his crowded heart, he rose from bed and dressed, she awoke enough to turn over. He told her then, "If I could undo it all, I would."

"Where would you begin?" she asked. There was no place. Giving him courage, she was always giving him courage. He put on shoes without socks in the dark. The children were breathing in their rooms, the downstairs was hollow. In their confusion they had left lights burning. He turned off all but one, the kitchen overhead. The car started. He had hoped it wouldn't. He met only moonlight on the road; it seemed a diaphanous companion, flickering in the leaves along the roadside, haunting his rearview mirror like a pursuer, melting under his headlights. The center of town, not quite deserted, was eerie at this hour. A young cop in uniform kept company with a gang of T-shirted kids on the steps of the bank. Across from the railroad station, several bars kept open. Customers, mostly young, passed in and out of the warm night, savoring summer's novelty. Voices shouted from cars as they passed; an immense conversation seemed in progress. Richard parked and in his weariness put his head on the passenger seat, out of the commotion and wheeling lights. It was as when, in the movies, an assassin grimly carries his mission through the jostle of a carnival—except the movies cannot show the precipitous, palpable slope you cling to within. You cannot climb back down; you can only fall. The synthetic fabric of the car seat, warmed by his cheek, confided to him an ancient, distant scent of vanilla.

A train whistle caused him to lift his head. It was on time; he had hoped it would be late. The slender drawgates descended. The bell of approach tingled happily. The great metal body, horizontally fluted, rocked to a stop, and sleepy teen-agers disembarked, his son among them. Dickie did not show surprise that his father was meeting him at this terrible hour. He sauntered to the car with two friends, both taller than he. He said "Hi" to his father and took the passenger's seat with an exhausted promptness that expressed gratitude. The friends got into the back, and Richard was grateful; a few more minutes' postponement would be won by driving them home.

He asked, "How was the concert?"

"Groovy," one boy said from the back seat.

"It bit," the other said.

"It was O.K.," Dickie said, moderate by nature, so reasonable that in his childhood the unreason of the world had given him headaches, stomach aches, nausea. When the second friend had been dropped off at his dark house, the boy blurted, "Dad, my eyes are killing me with hay fever! I'm out there cutting that mothering grass all day!"

"Do we still have those drops?"

"They didn't do any good last summer."

"They might this." Richard swung a U-turn on the empty street. The drive home took a few minutes. The mountain was here, in his throat. "Richard," he said, and felt the boy, slumped and rubbing his eyes, go tense at his tone, "I didn't come to meet you just to make your life easier. I came because your mother and I have some news for you, and you're a hard man to get ahold of these days. It's sad news."

"That's O.K." The reassurance came out soft, but quick, as if released from the tip of a spring.

Richard had feared that his tears would return and choke him, but the boy's manliness set an example, and his voice issued forth steady and dry. "It's sad news, but it needn't be tragic news, at least for you. It should have no practical effect on your life, though it's bound to have an emotional effect. You'll work at your job, and go back to school in September. Your mother and I are really proud of what you're making of your life; we don't want that to change at all."

"Yeah," the boy said lightly, on the intake of his breath, holding himself up. They turned the corner; the church they went to loomed like a gutted fort. The home of the woman Richard hoped to marry stood across the green. Her bedroom light burned.

"Your mother and I," he said, "have decided to separate. For the summer. Nothing legal, no divorce yet. We want to see how it feels. For some years now, we haven't been doing enough for each other, making each other as happy as we should be. Have you sensed that?"

"No," the boy said. It was an honest, unemotional answer: true or false in a quiz.

Glad for the factual basis, Richard pursued, even garrulously, the details. His apartment across town, his utter accessibility, the split vacation arrangements, the advantages to the children, the added mobility and variety of the summer. Dickie listened, absorbing. "Do the others know?"

Richard described how they had been told.

"How did they take it?"

"The girls pretty calmly. John flipped out; he shouted and ate a cigarette and made a salad out of his napkin and told us how much he hated school."

His brother chuckled. "He did?"

"Yeah. The school issue was more upsetting for him than Mom and me. He seemed to feel better for having exploded."

"He did?" The repetition was the first sign that he was stunned.

"Yes. Dickie, I want to tell you something. This last hour, waiting for your train to get in, has been about the worst of my life. I hate this. *Hate* it. My father would have died before doing it to me." He felt immensely lighter, saying this. He had dumped the mountain on the boy. They were home. Moving swiftly as a shadow, Dickie was out of the car, through the bright kitchen. Richard called after him, "Want a glass of milk or anything?"

"No thanks."

"Want us to call the course tomorrow and say you're too sick to work?"

"No, that's all right." The answer was faint, delivered at the door to his room; Richard listened for the slam of a tantrum. The door closed normally. The sound was sickening.

Joan had sunk into that first deep trough of sleep and was slow to awake. Richard had to repeat, "I told him."

"What did he say?"

"Nothing much. Could you go say good night to him? Please."

She left their room, without putting on a bathrobe. He sluggishly changed back into his pajamas and walked down the hall. Dickie was already in bed, Joan was sitting beside him, and the boy's bedside clock radio was murmuring music. When she stood, an inexplicable light—the moon?—outlined her body through the nightie. Richard sat on the warm place she had indented on the child's narrow mattress. He asked him, "Do you want the radio on like that?"

"It always is."

"Doesn't it keep you awake? It would me."

"No."

"Are you sleepy?"

"Yeah."

"Good. Sure you want to get up and go to work? You've had a big night."

"I want to."

Away at school this winter he had learned for the first time that you can go short of sleep and live. As an infant he had slept with an immobile, sweating intensity that had alarmed his babysitters. As the children aged, he became the first to go to bed, earlier for a time than his younger brother and sister. Even now, he would go slack in the middle of a television show, his sprawled legs hairy and brown. "O.K. Good boy. Dickie, listen. I love you so much, I never knew how much until now. No matter how this works out, I'll always be with you. Really."

Richard bent to kiss an averted face but his son, sinewy, turned and with wet cheeks embraced him and gave him a kiss, on the lips, passionate as a woman's. In his father's ear he moaned one word, the crucial, intelligent word: *"Why?"*

Why. It was a whistle of wind in a crack, a knife thrust, a window thrown open on emptiness. The white face was gone, the darkness was featureless. Richard had forgotten why.

1975

PHILIP ROTH
b. 1933

From the moment Philip Roth's collection of stories *Goodbye, Columbus* won the Houghton Mifflin Literary Fellowship for 1959, his career has received the ambiguous reward of much anxious concern, directed at it by critics and centered on whether he would develop the promise displayed in this first book. Ten years later, with *Portnoy's Complaint*, Roth became overnight the famous author of a "dirty" best-seller, yet his success only made his critics more uneasy. Was this gifted portrayer of Jewish middle-class life really more interested in scoring points off caricatures than in creating and exploring characters? Did his very facility with words inhibit the exercise of deeper sympathies and more humanly generous purposes?

Roth grew up in Newark, New Jersey, attended the branch of Rutgers University there, graduated from Bucknell University, took an M.A. in English literature at the University of Chicago, then served in the army. Over the years he has taught at a number of universities while receiving many awards and fellowships. Like John Barth, another "university" writer, Roth is an ironic humorist, although the impulse behind his early stories is darker and less playful. *Goodbye, Columbus* is about Jews on the verge of being or already having been assimilated into the larger American culture, and the stories confidently take the measure of their embattled heroes, as in "The Conversion of the Jews" or "Epstein" or the long title story. "Defender of the Faith" (printed here), arguably the best piece in the collection, is distinguished for the way Roth explores rather than exploits the conflict between personal feelings and religious loyalties as they are felt by Nathan Marx, a U.S. Army sergeant in a Missouri training company near the end of World War II. Throughout *Goodbye, Columbus* the narrator's voice is centrally important: in some stories it is indistinguishable from that of a campus wiseguy; in others it reaches out to a calmer and graver sense of disparities between promises and performance.

Roth's first two novels, *Letting Go* (1962) and *When She Was Good* (1967), markedly extended the territory charted in *Goodbye, Columbus* and showed him eager and equipped to write about people other than Jews. *Letting Go* is conventional in technique and in its subjects—love, marriage, university life—but Roth's easy mastery of the look and feel of places and things is everywhere evident. F. Scott Fitzgerald is the American writer whose presence in these early novels is most strongly felt; in particular, the section from *Letting Go* told in the first person by a graduate student in English betrays its indebtedness to Fitzgerald's Nick Carraway, the narrator of *The Great Gatsby*. This Fitzgeraldian atmosphere, with its nostalgic presentation of adolescence and early romantic visions, is even more evident in *When She Was Good*, which is strong in its rendering of middle-American living rooms and kitchens, the flushed atmosphere of late-night 1950s sex in parked cars, or the lyrics of popular songs—bits of remembered trivia that Roth, like his predecessor, has a genius for bringing to life.

The less-than-overwhelming reception of his second novel probably helped Roth move away from relatively sober realism; certainly *Portnoy's Complaint* (1969) is a louder and more virtuoso performance than the earlier books. Alexander Portnoy's recollections of early childhood miseries are really a pretext for Roth to perform a succession of clever numbers in the inventive mode of a stand-up comic. Memories of growing up in New Jersey, listening to radio programs, playing softball, ogling girls at the ice-skating rink, or (most sensationally) masturbating in outlandish ways add up to an entertaining narrative that is sometimes crude but more often delicate and precise.

After *Portnoy* Roth moved toward fantasy and further showmanly operations: *Our Gang* (1970) attempted to do for Richard Nixon and his associates what actual events were to do one better; *The Breast* (1971) is a rather unamusing fable about a man's metamorphosis into that object; *The Great American Novel* (1973) threatened to sink under its weight of baseball lore dressed up in tall tales and sick jokes. But in *My Life as a Man* (1974) and *The Professor of Desire* (1977) he returned to matters that have traditionally preoccupied the social novelist and that inform his own best work: marriage, divorce, the family, being a Jew, and being psychoanalyzed—the pressures of civilization and the resultant individual discontents.

His finest work is to be found in the Zuckerman trilogy (*Zuckerman Bound*, 1985) and its successor, *The Counterlife* (1987). In these novels Roth created a hero-as-novelist whose experience parallels in important ways his creator's. A scandalous novel, "Carnovsky," refers to *Portnoy's Complaint*; a critic named Milton Appel is a stand-in for the real critic Irving Howe, who once subjected Roth's work to hostile criticism. Yet for all the dangers of self-pity or self-absorption such autobiographical reference involves, the novels add up to something much deeper, more comic and touching, than self-advertisement and complaint. Scenes like the death of Zuckerman's father in a Florida hospital and the subsequent return of the son to the vanished Newark where he grew up are moving expressions of the generous purposes and human sympathies we find in Roth's work at its best. And those purposes and sympathies are also evident in his autobiographical writing: in *The Facts* (1988) and especially in *Patrimony* (1991), a poignant memoir of his father.

In the 1990s and into the twenty-first century, Roth has developed his art of impersonation into sometimes excessive and audacious forms. *Operation Shylock* (1993) poses a presumably real Philip Roth who encounters an impostor; *Sabbath's Theater* (1995) recasts his typical protagonist as a puppeteer who manipulates women much the same way; *American Pastoral* (1997) brings back Nathan Zuckerman for a high school reunion and the investigation of a "more ordinary" classmate's life. Zuckerman remains on hand for *I Married a Communist* (1998) and *The Human Stain* (2000), while David Kepesh (who had turned into a female breast in the author's much earlier fantasy) reappears as a professor who seduces his students in *The Dying Animal* (2001). Throughout, Roth's emphasis remains on invention, reminding readers that the writerly self is a virtually inexhaustible resource for the imagination.

The text is that printed in *Goodbye, Columbus* (1959).

Defender of the Faith

In May of 1945, only a few weeks after the fighting had ended in Europe, I was rotated back to the States, where I spent the remainder of the war with a training company at Camp Crowder, Missouri. We had been racing across Germany so swiftly during the late winter and spring that when I boarded the plane that drizzly morning in Berlin, I couldn't believe our destination lay to the west. My mind might inform me otherwise, but there was an inertia of the spirit that told me we were flying to a new front where we would disembark and continue our push eastward—eastward until we'd circled the globe, marching through villages along whose twisting, cobbled streets crowds of the enemy would watch us take possession of what up till then they'd considered their own. I had changed enough in two years not to mind the trembling of the old people, the crying of the very young, the uncertain fear in the eyes of the once-arrogant. After two years I had been fortunate enough to develop an infantryman's heart which, like his feet, at first aches and swells, but finally grows horny enough for him to travel the weirdest paths without feeling a thing.

Captain Paul Barrett was to be my C. O. at Camp Crowder. The day I reported for duty he came out of his office to shake my hand. He was short, gruff, and fiery, and indoors or out he wore his polished helmet liner[1] down on his little eyes. In Europe he had received a battlefield commission and a serious chest wound, and had been returned to the States only a few months before. He spoke easily to me, but was, I thought, unnecessarily abusive towards the troops. At the evening formation, he introduced me.

"Gentlemen," he called. "Sergeant Thurston, as you know, is no longer with this Company. Your new First Sergeant is Sergeant Nathan Marx here. He is a veteran of the European theater and consequently will take no shit."

I sat up late in the orderly room that evening, trying halfheartedly to solve the riddle of duty rosters, personnel forms, and morning reports. The CQ[2] slept with his mouth open on a mattress on the floor. A trainee stood reading the next day's duty roster, which was posted on the bulletin board directly inside the screen door. It was a warm evening and I could hear the men's radios playing dance music over in the barracks.

The trainee, who I knew had been staring at me whenever I looked groggily into the forms, finally took a step in my direction.

"Hey, Sarge—we having a G.I. party tomorrow night?" A G.I. party is a barracks-cleaning.

---

1. Plastic liner worn under a helmet to prevent chafing and bruising.

2. Noncommissioned officer in charge of quarters at night or on weekends.

"You usually have them on Friday nights?"

"Yes," and then he added mysteriously, "that's the whole thing."

"Then you'll have a G.I. party."

He turned away and I heard him mumbling. His shoulders were moving and I wondered if he was crying.

"What's your name, soldier?" I asked.

He turned, not crying at all. Instead his green-speckled eyes, long and narrow, flashed like fish in the sun. He walked over to me and sat on the edge of my desk.

He reached out a hand. "Sheldon," he said.

"Stand on your own two feet, Sheldon."

Climbing off the desk, he said, "Sheldon Grossbart." He smiled wider at the intimacy into which he'd led me.

"You against cleaning the barracks Friday night, Grossbart? Maybe we shouldn't have G.I. parties—maybe we should get a maid." My tone startled me: I felt like a Charlie McCarthy, with every top sergeant I had ever known as my Edgar Bergen.[3]

"No, Sergeant." He grew serious, but with a seriousness that seemed only to be the stifling of a smile. "It's just G.I. parties on Friday night, of all nights . . ."

He slipped up to the corner of the desk again—not quite sitting, but not quite standing either. He looked at me with those speckled eyes flashing and then made a gesture with his hand. It was very slight, no more than a rotation back and forth of the wrist, and yet it managed to exclude from our affairs everything else in the orderly room, to make the two of us the center of the world. It seemed, in fact, to exclude everything about the two of us except our hearts. "Sergeant Thurston was one thing," he whispered, an eye flashing to the sleeping CQ, "but we thought with you here, things might be a little different."

"We?"

"The Jewish personnel."

"Why?" I said, harshly.

He hesitated a moment, and then, uncontrollably, his hand went up to his mouth. "I mean . . ." he said.

"What's on your mind?" Whether I was still angry at the "Sheldon" business or something else, I hadn't a chance to tell—but clearly I was angry.

". . . we thought you . . . Marx, you know, like Karl Marx. The Marx brothers. Those guys are all . . . M-A-R-X, isn't that how you spell it, Sergeant?"

"M-A-R-X."

"Fishbein said—" He stopped. "What I mean to say, Sergeant—" His face and neck were red, and his mouth moved but no words came out. In a moment, he raised himself to attention, gazing down at me. It was as though he had suddenly decided he could expect no more sympathy from me than from Thurston, the reason being that I was of Thurston's faith and not his. The young man had managed to confuse himself as to what my faith really was, but I felt no desire to straighten him out. Very simply, I didn't like him.

When I did nothing but return his gaze, he spoke, in an altered tone. "You

---

3. A ventriloquist who, with Charlie McCarthy, his dummy, was a popular radio comedian.

see, Sergeant," he explained to me, "Friday nights, Jews are supposed to go to services."

"Did Sergeant Thurston tell you you couldn't go to them when there was a G.I. party?"

"No."

"Did he say you had to stay and scrub the floors?"

"No, Sergeant."

"Did the Captain say you had to stay and scrub the floors?"

"That isn't it, Sergeant. It's the other guys in the barracks." He leaned toward me. "They think we're goofing off. But we're not. That's when Jews go to services, Friday night. We have to."

"Then go."

"But the other guys make accusations. They have no right."

"That's not the Army's problem, Grossbart. It's a personal problem you'll have to work out yourself."

"But it's un*fair*."

I got up to leave. "There's nothing I can do about it," I said.

Grossbart stiffened in front of me. "But this is a matter of *religion*, sir."

"Sergeant."

"I mean 'Sergeant,' " he said, almost snarling.

"Look, go see the chaplain. The I.G.[4] You want to see Captain Barrett, I'll arrange an appointment."

"No, no. I don't want to make trouble, Sergeant. That's the first thing they throw up to you. I just want my rights!"

"Damn it, Grossbart, stop whining. You have your rights. You can stay and scrub floors or you can go to *shul*[5]—"

The smile swam in again. Spittle gleamed at the corners of his mouth. "You mean church, Sergeant."

"I mean *shul*, Grossbart!" I walked past him and outside. Near me I heard the scrunching of a guard's boots on gravel. In the lighted windows of the barracks the young men in T-shirts and fatigue pants were sitting on their bunks, polishing their rifles. Suddenly there was a light rustling behind me. I turned and saw Grossbart's dark frame fleeing back to the barracks, racing to tell his Jewish friends that they were right—that like Karl and Harpo, I was one of them.

The next morning, while chatting with the Captain, I recounted the incident of the previous evening, as if to unburden myself of it. Somehow in the telling it seemed to the Captain that I was not so much explaining Grossbart's position as defending it.

"Marx, I'd fight side by side with a nigger if the fellow proved to me he was a man. I pride myself," the Captain said looking out the window, "that I've got an open mind. Consequently, Sergeant, nobody gets special treatment here, for the good *or* the bad. All a man's got to do is prove himself. A man fires well on the range, I give him a weekend pass. He scores high in PT, he gets a weekend pass. He *earns* it." He turned from the window and pointed a finger at me. "You're a Jewish fellow, am I right, Marx?"

---

4. Inspector general, who, apart from the chaplain, provided the only route by which complaints
could be registered.
5. Synagogue.

"Yes, sir."

"And I admire you. I admire you because of the ribbons on your chest, not because you had a hem stitched on your dick before you were old enough to even know you had one. I judge a man by what he shows me on the field of battle, Sergeant. It's what he's got *here*," he said, and then, though I expected he would point to his heart, he jerked a thumb towards the buttons straining to hold his blouse across his belly. "Guts," he said.

"Okay, sir, I only wanted to pass on to you how the men felt."

"Mr. Marx, you're going to be old before your time if you worry about how the men feel. Leave that stuff to the Chaplain—pussy, the clap, church picnics with the little girls from Joplin, that's all his business, not yours. Let's us train these fellas to shoot straight. If the Jewish personnel feels the other men are accusing them of goldbricking . . . well, I just don't know. Seems awful funny how suddenly the Lord is calling so loud in Private Grossman's ear he's just got to run to church."

"Synagogue," I said.

"Synagogue is right, Sergeant. I'll write that down for handy reference. Thank you for stopping by."

That evening, a few minutes before the company gathered outside the orderly room for the chow formation, I called the CQ, Corporal Robert LaHill, in to see me. LaHill was a dark burly fellow whose hair curled out of his clothes wherever it could. He carried a glaze in his eyes that made one think of caves and dinosaurs. "LaHill," I said, "when you take the formation, remind the men that they're free to attend church services *whenever* they are held, provided they report to the orderly room before they leave the area."

LaHill didn't flicker; he scratched his wrist, but gave no indication that he'd heard or understood.

"LaHill," I said, "*church*. You remember? Church, priest, Mass, confession . . ."

He curled one lip into a ghastly smile; I took it for a signal that for a second he had flickered back up into the human race.

"Jewish personnel who want to attend services this evening are to fall out in front of the orderly room at 1900." And then I added, "By order of Captain Barrett."

A little while later, as a twilight softer than any I had seen that year dropped over Camp Crowder, I heard LaHill's thick, inflectionless voice outside my window: "Give me your ears, troopers. Toppie says for me to tell you that at 1900 hours all Jewish personnel is to fall out in front here if they wants to attend the Jewish Mass."

At seven o'clock, I looked out of the orderly-room window and saw three soldiers in starched khakis standing alone on the dusty quadrangle. They looked at their watches, and fidgeted while they whispered back and forth. It was getting darker, and alone on the deserted field they looked tiny. When I walked to the door I heard the noises of the G.I. party coming from the surrounding barracks—bunks being pushed to the wall, faucets pounding water into buckets, brooms whisking at the wooden floors. In the windows big puffs of cloth moved round and round, cleaning the dirt away for Saturday's inspection. I walked outside and the moment my foot hit the ground

I thought I heard Grossbart, who was now in the center, call to the other two, "Ten-*hut!*" Or maybe when they all three jumped to attention, I imagined I heard the command.

At my approach, Grossbart stepped forward. "Thank you, sir," he said.

"Sergeant, Grossbart," I reminded him. "You call officers 'Sir.' I'm not an officer. You've been in the Army three weeks—you know that."

He turned his palms out at his sides to indicate that, in truth, he and I lived beyond convention. "Thank you, anyway," he said.

"Yes," the tall boy behind him said. "Thanks a lot."

And the third whispered, "Thank you," but his mouth barely fluttered so that he did not alter by more than a lip's movement, the posture of attention.

"For what?" I said.

Grossbart snorted, happily. "For the announcement before. The Corporal's announcement. It helped. It made it . . ."

"Fancier." It was the tall boy finishing Grossbart's sentence.

Grossbart smiled. "He means formal, sir. Public," he said to me. "Now it won't seem as though we're just taking off, goldbricking, because the work has begun."

"It was by order of Captain Barrett," I said.

"Ahh, but you pull a little weight . . ." Grossbart said. "So we thank you." Then he turned to his companions. "Sergeant Marx, I want you to meet Larry Fishbein."

The tall boy stepped forward and extended his hand. I shook it. "You from New York?" he asked.

"Yes."

"Me too." He had a cadaverous face that collapsed inward from his cheekbone to his jaw, and when he smiled—as he did at the news of our communal attachment—revealed a mouthful of bad teeth. He blinked his eyes a good deal, as though he were fighting back tears. "What borough?" he asked.

I turned to Grossbart. "It's five after seven. What time are services?"

"*Shul,*" he smiled, "is in ten minutes. I want you to meet Mickey Halpern. This is Nathan Marx, our Sergeant."

The third boy hopped forward. "Private Michael Halpern." He saluted.

"Salute officers, Halpern." The boy dropped his hand, and in his nervousness checked to see if his shirt pockets were buttoned on the way down.

"Shall I march them over, sir?" Grossbart asked, "or are you coming along?"

From behind Grossbart, Fishbein piped up. "Afterwards they're having refreshments. A Ladies' Auxiliary from St. Louis, the rabbi told us last week."

"The chaplain," whispered Halpern.

"You're welcome to come along," Grossbart said.

To avoid his plea, I looked away, and saw, in the windows of the barracks, a cloud of faces staring out at the four of us.

"Look, hurry out of here, Grossbart."

"Okay, then," he said. He turned to the others. "Double time, *march!*" and they started off, but ten feet away Grossbart spun about, and running backwards he called to me, "Good *shabus,*[6] sir." And then the three were swallowed into the Missouri dusk.

6. Sabbath.

Even after they'd disappeared over the parade grounds, whose green was now a deep twilight blue, I could hear Grossbart singing the double-time cadence, and as it grew dimmer and dimmer it suddenly touched some deep memory—as did the slant of light—and I was remembering the shrill sounds of a Bronx playground, where years ago, beside the Grand Concourse,[7] I had played on long spring evenings such as this. Those thin fading sounds . . . It was a pleasant memory for a young man so far from peace and home, and it brought so very many recollections with it that I began to grow exceedingly tender about myself. In fact, I indulged myself to a reverie so strong that I felt within as though a hand had opened and was reaching down inside. It had to reach so very far to touch me. It had to reach past those days in the forests of Belgium and the dying I'd refused to weep over; past the nights in those German farmhouses whose books we'd burned to warm us, and which I couldn't bother to mourn; past those endless stretches when I'd shut off all softness I might feel for my fellows, and managed even to deny myself the posture of a conqueror—the swagger that I, as a Jew, might well have worn as my boots whacked against the rubble of Münster, Braunschweig, and finally Berlin.

But now one night noise, one rumor of home and time past, and memory plunged down through all I had anesthetized and came to what I suddenly remembered to be myself. So it was not altogether curious that in search of more of me I found myself following Grossbart's tracks to Chapel No. 3 where the Jewish services were being held.

I took a seat in the last row, which was empty. Two rows in front sat Grossbart, Fishbein, and Halpern, each holding a little white dixie cup. Fishbein was pouring the contents of his cup into Grossbart's, and Grossbart looked mirthful as the liquid drew a purple arc between his hand and Fishbein's. In the glary yellow light, I saw the chaplain on the pulpit chanting the first line of the responsive reading. Grossbart's prayerbook remained closed on his lap; he swished the cup around. Only Halpern responded in prayer. The fingers of his right hand were spread wide across the cover of the book, and his cap was pulled down low onto his brow so that it was round like a *yarmulke*[8] rather than long and pointed. From time to time, Grossbart wet his lips at the cup's edge; Fishbein, his long yellow face, a dying light bulb, looked from here to there, leaning forward at the neck to catch sight of the faces down the row, in front—then behind. He saw me and his eyelids beat a tattoo. His elbow slid into Grossbart's side, his neck inclined towards his friend, and then, when the congregation responded, Grossbart's voice was among them. Fishbein looked into his book now too; his lips, however, didn't move.

Finally it was time to drink the wine. The chaplain smiled down at them as Grossbart swigged in one long gulp, Halpern sipped, meditating, and Fishbein faked devotion with an empty cup.

At last the chaplain spoke: "As I look down amongst the congregation—" he grinned at the word, "this night, I see many new faces, and I want to welcome you to Friday night services here at Camp Crowder. I am Major Leo Ben Ezra, your chaplain . . ." Though an American, the chaplain spoke English very deliberately, syllabically almost, as though to communicate,

---

7. Bronx, New York, avenue.   8. Skullcap.

above all, to the lip-readers in the audience. "I have only a few words to say before we adjourn to the refreshment room where the kind ladies of the Temple Sinai, St. Louis, Missouri, have a nice setting for you."

Applause and whistling broke out. After a momentary grin, the chaplain raised his palms to the congregation, his eyes flicking upward a moment, as if to remind the troops where they were and Who Else might be in attendance. In the sudden silence that followed, I thought I heard Grossbart's cackle—"Let the goyim[9] clean the floors!" Were those the words? I wasn't sure, but Fishbein, grinning, nudged Halpern. Halpern looked dumbly at him, then went back to his prayerbook, which had been occupying him all through the rabbi's talk. One hand tugged at the black kinky hair that stuck out under his cap. His lips moved.

The rabbi continued. "It is about the food that I want to speak to you for a moment. I know, I know, I know," he intoned, wearily, "how in the mouths of most of you the trafe[1] food tastes like ashes. I know how you gag, some of you, and how your parents suffer to think of their children eating foods unclean and offensive to the palate. What can I tell you? I can only say close your eyes and swallow as best you can. Eat what you must to live and throw away the rest. I wish I could help more. For those of you who find this impossible, may I ask that you try and try, but then come to see me in private where, if your revulsion is such, we will have to seek aid from those higher up."

A round of chatter rose and subsided; then everyone sang "Ain Kelohanoh," after all those years I discovered I still knew the words.

Suddenly, the service over, Grossbart was upon me. "Higher up? He means the General?"

"Hey, Shelly," Fishbein interrupted, "he means God." He smacked his face and looked at Halpern. "How high can you go!"

"Shhh!" Grossbart said. "What do you think, Sergeant?"

"I don't know. You better ask the chaplain."

"I'm going to. I'm making an appointment to see him in private. So is Mickey."

Halpern shook his head. "No, no, Sheldon . . ."

"You have rights, Mickey. They can't push us around."

"It's okay. It bothers my mother, not me . . ."

Grossbart looked at me. "Yesterday he threw up. From the hash. It was all ham and God knows what else."

"I have a cold—that was why," Halpern said. He pushed his *yamalkah* back into a cap.

"What about you, Fishbein?" I asked. "You kosher too?"

He flushed, which made the yellow more gray than pink. "A little. But I'll let it ride. I have a very strong stomach. And I don't eat a lot anyway . . ." I continued to look at him, and he held up his wrist to re-enforce what he'd just said. His watch was tightened to the last hole and he pointed that out to me. "So I don't mind."

"But services are important to you?" I asked him.

He looked at Grossbart. "Sure, sir."

"Sergeant."

---

9. Gentiles.   1. Unkosher—unfit to eat.

"Not so much at home," said Grossbart, coming between us, "but away from home it gives one a sense of his Jewishness."

"We have to stick together," Fishbein said.

I started to walk towards the door; Halpern stepped back to make way for me.

"That's what happened in Germany," Grossbart was saying, loud enough for me to hear. "They didn't stick together. They let themselves get pushed around."

I turned. "Look, Grossbart, this is the Army, not summer camp."

He smiled. "So?" Halpern tried to sneak off, but Grossbart held his arm. "So?" he said again.

"Grossbart," I asked, "how old are you?"

"Nineteen."

"And you?" I said to Fishbein.

"The same. The same month even."

"And what about him?" I pointed to Halpern, who'd finally made it safely to the door.

"Eighteen," Grossbart whispered. "But he's like he can't tie his shoes or brush his teeth himself. I feel sorry for him."

"I feel sorry for all of us, Grossbart, but just act like a man. Just don't overdo it."

"Overdo what, sir?"

"The sir business. Don't overdo that," I said, and I left him standing there. I passed by Halpern but he did not look up. Then I was outside, black surrounded me—but behind I heard Grossbart call, "Hey, Mickey, *liebschen*,[2] come on back. Refreshments!"

Liebschen! My grandmother's word for me!

One morning, a week later, while I was working at my desk, Captain Barrett shouted for me to come into his office. When I entered, he had his helmet liner squashed down so that I couldn't even see his eyes. He was on the phone, and when he spoke to me, he cupped one hand over the mouthpiece.

"Who the fuck is Grossbart?"

"Third platoon, Captain," I said. "A trainee."

"What's all this stink about food? His mother called a goddam congressman about the food . . ." He uncovered the mouthpiece and slid his helmet up so I could see the curl of his bottom eyelash. "Yes, sir," he said into the phone. "Yes, sir. I'm still here, sir. I'm asking Marx here right now . . ."

He covered the mouthpiece again and looked back to me. "Lightfoot Harry's on the phone," he said, between his teeth. "This congressman calls General Lyman who calls Colonel Sousa who calls the Major who calls me. They're just dying to stick this thing on me. What's a matter," he shook the phone at me, "I don't feed the troops? What the hell is this?"

"Sir, Grossbart is strange . . ." Barrett greeted that with a mockingly indulgent smile. I altered my approach. "Captain, he's a very orthodox Jew and so he's only allowed to eat certain foods."

2. Darling.

"He throws up, the congressman said. Every time he eats something his mother says he throws up!"

"He's accustomed to observing the dietary laws, Captain."

"So why's his old lady have to call the White House!"

"Jewish parents, sir, they're apt to be more protective than you expect. I mean Jews have a very close family life. A boy goes away from home, sometimes the mother is liable to get very upset. Probably the boy *mentioned* something in a letter and his mother misinterpreted."

"I'd like to punch him one right in the mouth. There's a goddam war on and he wants a silver platter!"

"I don't think the boy's to blame, sir. I'm sure we can straighten it out by just asking him. Jewish parents worry—"

"*All* parents worry, for Christ sake. But they don't get on their high horse and start pulling strings—"

I interrupted, my voice higher, tighter than before. "The home life, Captain, is so very important . . . but you're right, it may sometimes get out of hand. It's a very wonderful thing, Captain, but because it's so close, this kind of thing—"

He didn't listen any longer to my attempt to present both myself and Lightfoot Harry with an explanation for the letter. He turned back to the phone. "Sir?" he said. "Sir, Marx here tells me Jews have a tendency to be pushy. He says he thinks he can settle it right here in the Company . . . Yes, sir . . . I *will* call back, sir, soon as I can . . ." He hung up. "Where are the men, Sergeant?"

"On the range."

With a whack on the top, he crushed his helmet over his eyes, and charged out of his chair. "We're going for a ride."

The Captain drove and I sat beside him. It was a hot spring day and under my newly starched fatigues it felt as though my armpits were melting down onto my sides and chest. The roads were dry and by the time we reached the firing range, my teeth felt gritty with dust though my mouth had been shut the whole trip. The Captain slammed the brakes on and told me to get the hell out and find Grossbart.

I found him on his belly, firing wildly at the 500 feet target. Waiting their turns behind him were Halpern and Fishbein. Fishbein, wearing a pair of rimless G.I. glasses I hadn't seen on him before, gave the appearance of an old peddler who would gladly have sold you the rifle and cartridges that were slung all over him. I stood back by the ammo boxes, waiting for Grossbart to finish spraying the distant targets. Fishbein straggled back to stand near me.

"Hello, Sergeant Marx."

"How are you?" I mumbled.

"Fine, thank you. Sheldon's really a good shot."

"I didn't notice."

"I'm not so good, but I think I'm getting the hang of it now . . . Sergeant, I don't mean to, you know, ask what I shouldn't . . ." The boy stopped. He was trying to speak intimately but the noise of the shooting necessitated that he shout at me.

"What is it?" I asked. Down the range I saw Captain Barrett standing up in the jeep, scanning the line for me and Grossbart.

"My parents keep asking and asking where we're going. Everybody says the Pacific. I don't care, but my parents . . . If I could relieve their minds I think I could concentrate more on my shooting."

"I don't know where, Fishbein. Try to concentrate anyway."

"Sheldon says you might be able to find out—"

"I don't know a thing, Fishbein. You just take it easy, and don't let Sheldon—"

"*I'm* taking it easy, Sergeant. It's at home—"

Grossbart had just finished on the line and was dusting his fatigues with one hand. I left Fishbein's sentence in the middle.

"Grossbart, the Captain wants to see you."

He came toward us. His eyes blazed and twinkled. "Hi!"

"Don't point that goddam rifle!"

"I wouldn't shoot you, Sarge." He gave me a smile wide as a pumpkin as he turned the barrel aside.

"Damn you, Grossbart—this is no joke! Follow me."

I walked ahead of him and had the awful suspicion that behind me Grossbart was *marching*, his rifle on his shoulder, as though he were a one-man detachment.

At the jeep he gave the Captain a rifle salute. "Private Sheldon Grossbart, sir."

"At ease, Grossman." The Captain slid over to the empty front seat, and crooking a finger, invited Grossbart closer.

"Bart, sir. Sheldon Gross*bart*. It's a common error." Grossbart nodded to me—*I understand*, he indicated. I looked away, just as the mess truck pulled up to the range, disgorging a half dozen K.P.'s with rolled-up sleeves. The mess sergeant screamed at them while they set up the chow line equipment.

"Grossbart, your mama wrote some congressman that we don't feed you right. Do you know that?" the Captain said.

"It was my father, sir. He wrote to Representative Franconi that my religion forbids me to eat certain foods."

"What religion is that, Grossbart?"

"Jewish."

"Jewish, *sir*," I said to Grossbart.

"Excuse me, sir. 'Jewish, sir.' "

"What have you been living on?" the Captain asked. "You've been in the Army a month already. You don't look to me like you're falling to pieces."

"I eat because I have to, sir. But Sergeant Marx will testify to the fact that I don't eat one mouthful more than I need to in order to survive."

"Marx," Barrett asked, "is that so?"

"I've never seen Grossbart eat, sir," I said.

"But you heard the rabbi," Grossbart said. "He told us what to do, and I listened."

The Captain looked at me. "Well, Marx?"

"I still don't know what he eats and doesn't eat, sir."

Grossbart raised his rifle, as though to offer it to me. "But, Sergeant—"

"Look, Grossbart, just answer the Captain's questions!" I said sharply.

Barrett smiled at me and I resented it. "All right, Grossbart," he said, "What is it you want? The little piece of paper? You want out?"

"No, sir. Only to be allowed to live as a Jew. And for the others, too."

"What others?"

"Fishbein, sir, and Halpern."

"They don't like the way we serve either?"

"Halpern throws up, sir. I've seen it."

"I thought *you* threw up."

"Just once, sir. I didn't know the sausage was sausage."

"We'll give menus, Grossbart. We'll show training films about the food, so you can identify when we're trying to poison you."

Grossbart did not answer. Out before me, the men had been organized into two long chow lines. At the tail end of one I spotted Fishbein—or rather, his glasses spotted me. They winked sunlight back at me like a friend. Halpern stood next to him, patting inside his collar with a khaki handkerchief. They moved with the line as it began to edge up towards the food. The mess sergeant was still screaming at the K.P.'s, who stood ready to ladle out the food, bewildered. For a moment I was actually terrorized by the thought that somehow the mess sergeant was going to get involved in Grossbart's problem.

"Come over here, Marx," the Captain said to me. "Marx, you're a Jewish fella, am I right?"

I played straight man. "Yes, sir."

"How long you been in the Army? Tell this boy."

"Three years and two months."

"A year in combat, Grossbart. Twelve goddam months in combat all through Europe. I admire this man," the Captain said, snapping a wrist against my chest. But do you hear him peeping about the food? Do you? I want an answer, Grossbart. Yes or no."

"No, sir."

"And why not? He's a Jewish fella."

"Some things are more important to some Jews than other things to other Jews."

Barrett blew up. "Look, Grossbart, Marx here is a good man, a goddam *hero*. When you were sitting on your sweet ass in high school, Sergeant Marx was killing Germans. Who does more for the Jews, you by throwing up over a lousy piece of sausage, a piece of firstcut meat—or Marx by killing those Nazi bastards? If I was a Jew, Grossbart, I'd kiss this man's feet. He's a goddam hero, you know that? And *he* eats what we give him. Why do you have to cause trouble is what I want to know! What is it you're buckin' for, a discharge?"

"No, sir."

"I'm talking to a *wall*! Sergeant, get him out of my way." Barrett pounced over to the driver's seat. "I'm going to see the chaplain!" The engine roared, the jeep spun around, and then, raising a whirl of dust, the Captain was headed back to camp.

For a moment, Grossbart and I stood side by side, watching the jeep. Then he looked at me and said, "I don't want to start trouble. That's the first thing they toss up to us."

When he spoke I saw that his teeth were white and straight, and the sight of them suddenly made me understand that Grossbart actually did have parents: that once upon a time someone had taken little Sheldon to the dentist. He was someone's son. Despite all the talk about his parents, it was hard to believe in Grossbart as a child, an heir—as related by blood to anyone, mother, father, or, above all, to me. This realization led me to another.

"What does your father do, Grossbart?" I asked, as we started to walk back towards the chow line.

"He's a tailor."

"An American?"

"Now, yes. A son in the Army," he said, jokingly.

"And your mother?" I asked.

He winked. "A *ballabusta*[3]—she practically sleeps with a dustcloth in her hand."

"She's also an immigrant?"

"All she talks is Yiddish, still."

"And your father too?"

"A little English. 'Clean,' 'Press,' 'Take the pants in . . . ' That's the extent of it. But they're good to me . . ."

"Then, Grossbart—" I reached out and stopped him. He turned towards me and when our eyes met his seemed to jump back, shiver in their sockets. He looked afraid. "Grossbart, then you were the one who wrote that letter, weren't you?"

It took only a second or two for his eyes to flash happy again. "Yes." He walked on, and I kept pace. "It's what my father *would* have written if he had known how. It was his name, though. *He* signed it. He even mailed it. I sent it home. For the New York postmark."

I was astonished, and he saw it. With complete seriousness, he thrust his right arm in front of me. "Blood is blood, Sergeant," he said, pinching the blue vein in his wrist.

"What the hell *are* you trying to do, Grossbart? I've seen you eat. Do you know that? I told the Captain I don't know what you eat, but I've seen you eat like a hound at chow."

"We work hard, Sergeant. We're in training. For a furnace to work, you've got to feed it coal."

"If you wrote the letter, Grossbart, then why did you say you threw up all the time?"

"I was really talking about Mickey there. But he would never write, Sergeant, though I pleaded with him. He'll waste away to nothing if I don't help. Sergeant, I used my name, my father's name, but it's Mickey and Fishbein too I'm watching out for."

"You're a regular Messiah,[4] aren't you?"

We were at the chow line now.

"That's a good one, Sergeant." He smiled. "But who knows? Who can tell? Maybe you're the Messiah . . . a little bit. What Mickey says is the Messiah is a collective idea. He went to Yeshivah,[5] Mickey, for a while. He says *together* we're the Messiah. Me a little bit, you a little bit . . . You should hear that kid talk, Sergeant, when he gets going."

"Me a little bit, you a little bit. You'd like to believe that, wouldn't you, Grossbart? That makes everything so clean for you."

---

3. Good housekeeper.
4. The deliverer who will rule over the people of

Israel at the end of time.
5. Jewish institution of learning.

"It doesn't seem too bad a thing to believe, Sergeant. It only means we should all give a little, is all . . ."

I walked off to eat my rations with the other noncoms.

Two days later a letter addressed to Captain Barrett passed over my desk. It had come through the chain of command—from the office of Congressman Franconi, where it had been received, to General Lyman, to Colonel Sousa, to Major Lamont, to Captain Barrett. I read it over twice while the Captain was at the officers' mess. It was dated May 14th, the day Barrett had spoken with Grossbart on the rifle range.

Dear Congressman:

First let me thank you for your interest in behalf of my son, Private Sheldon Grossbart. Fortunately, I was able to speak with Sheldon on the phone the other night, and I think I've been able to solve our problem. He is, as I mentioned in my last letter, a very religious boy, and it was only with the greatest difficulty that I could persuade him that the religious thing to do— what God Himself would want Sheldon to do—would be to suffer the pangs of religious remorse for the good of his country and all mankind. It took some doing, Congressman, but finally he saw the light. In fact, what he said (and I wrote down the words on a scratch pad so as never to forget), what he said was, "I guess you're right, Dad. So many millions of my fellow Jews gave up their lives to the enemy, the least I can do is live for a while minus a bit of my heritage so as to help end this struggle and regain for all the children of God dignity and humanity." That, Congressman, would make any father proud.

By the way, Sheldon wanted me to know—and to pass on to you—the name of a soldier who helped him reach this decision: SERGEANT NATHAN MARX. Sergeant Marx is a combat veteran who is Sheldon's First Sergeant. This man has helped Sheldon over some of the first hurdles he's had to face in the Army, and is in part responsible for Sheldon's changing his mind about the dietary laws. I know Sheldon would appreciate any recognition Marx could receive.

Thank you and good luck. I look forward to seeing your name on the next election ballot.

Respectfully,

Samuel E. Grossbart

Attached to the Grossbart communiqué was a communiqué addressed to General Marshall Lyman, the post commander, and signed by Representative Charles E. Franconi of the House of Representatives. The communiqué informed General Lyman that Sergeant Nathan Marx was a credit to the U.S. Army and the Jewish people.

What was Grossbart's motive in recanting? Did he feel he'd gone too far? Was the letter a strategic retreat—a crafty attempt to strengthen what he considered our alliance? Or had he actually changed his mind, via an imaginary dialogue between Grossbart *père* and *fils?* I was puzzled, but only for a few days—that is, only until I realized that whatever his reasons, he had actually decided to disappear from my life: he was going to allow himself to become just another trainee. I saw him at inspection but he never winked; at chow formations but he never flashed me a sign; on Sundays, with the other trainees, he would sit around watching the noncoms' softball team, for whom I pitched, but not once did he speak an unnecessary or unusual word to me. Fishbein and Halpern retreated from sight too, at Grossbart's command I was sure. Apparently he'd seen that wisdom lay in turning back before he plunged us over into the ugliness of privilege undeserved. Our separation allowed me to forgive him our past encounters, and, finally, to admire him for his good sense.

Meanwhile, free of Grossbart, I grew used to my job and my administrative tasks. I stepped on a scale one day and discovered I had truly become a noncombatant: I had gained seven pounds. I found patience to get past the first three pages of a book. I thought about the future more and more, and wrote letters to girls I'd known before the war—I even got a few answers. I sent away to Columbia for a Law School catalogue. I continued to follow the war in the Pacific, but it was not my war and I read of bombings and battles like a civilian. I thought I could see the end in sight and sometimes at night I dreamed that I was walking on the streets of Manhattan—Broadway, Third Avenue, and 116th Street, where I had lived those three years I'd attended Columbia College. I curled myself around these dreams and I began to be happy.

And then one Saturday when everyone was away and I was alone in the orderly room reading a month-old copy of *The Sporting News*, Grossbart reappeared.

"You a baseball fan, Sergeant?"

I looked up. "How are you?"

"Fine," Grossbart said. "They're making a soldier out of me."

"How are Fishbein and Halpern?"

"Coming along," he said. "We've got no training this afternoon. They're at the movies."

"How come you're not with them?"

"I wanted to come over and say hello."

He smiled—a shy, regular-guy smile, as though he and I well knew that our friendship drew its sustenance from unexpected visits, remembered birthdays, and borrowed lawnmowers. At first it offended me, and then the feeling was swallowed by the general uneasiness I felt at the thought that everyone on the post was locked away in a dark movie theater and I was here alone with Grossbart. I folded my paper.

"Sergeant," he said, "I'd like to ask a favor. It is a favor and I'm making no bones about it."

He stopped, allowing me to refuse him a hearing—which, of course, forced me into a courtesy I did not intend. "Go ahead."

"Well, actually it's two favors."

I said nothing.

"The first one's about these rumors. Everybody says we're going to the Pacific."

"As I told your friend Fishbein, I don't know. You'll just have to wait to find out. Like everybody else."

"You think there's a chance of any of us going East?"

"Germany," I said, "maybe."

"I meant New York."

"I don't think so, Grossbart. Offhand."

"Thanks for the information, Sergeant," he said.

"It's not information, Grossbart. Just what I surmise."

"It certainly would be good to be near home. My parents . . . you know." He took a step towards the door and then turned back. "Oh the other thing. May I ask the other?"

"What is it?"

"The other thing is—I've got relatives in St. Louis and they say they'll give me a whole Passover dinner if I can get down there. God, Sergeant, that'd mean an awful lot to me."

I stood up. "No passes during basic, Grossbart."

"But we're off from now till Monday morning, Sergeant. I could leave the post and no one would even know."

"I'd know. You'd know."

"But that's all. Just the two of us. Last night I called my aunt and you should have heard her. 'Come, come,' she said. 'I got gefilte fish, *chrain*,[6] the works!' Just a day, Sergeant, I'd take the blame if anything happened."

"The captain isn't here to sign a pass."

"You could sign."

"Look, Grossbart—"

"Sergeant, for two months practically I've been eating *trafe* till I want to die."

"I thought you'd made up your mind to live with it. To be minus a little bit of heritage."

He pointed a finger at me. "You!" he said. "That wasn't for you to read!"

"I read it. So what."

"That letter was addressed to a congressman."

"Grossbart, don't feed me any crap. You *wanted* me to read it."

"Why are you persecuting me, Sergeant?"

"Are you kidding!"

"I've run into this before," he said, "but never from my own!"

"Get out of here, Grossbart! Get the hell out of my sight!"

He did not move. "Ashamed, that's what you are. So you take it out on the rest of us. They say Hitler himself was half a Jew. Seeing this, I wouldn't doubt it!"

"What are you trying to do with me, Grossbart? What are you after? You want me to give you special privileges, to change the food, to find out about your orders, to give you weekend passes."

"You even talk like a goy!" Grossbart shook his fist. "Is this a weekend pass I'm asking for? Is a Seder[7] sacred or not?"

Seder! It suddenly occurred to me that Passover had been celebrated weeks before. I confronted Grossbart with the fact.

"That's right," he said. "Who says no? A month ago, and *I* was in the field eating hash! And now all I ask is a simple favor—a Jewish boy I thought would understand. My aunt's willing to go out of her way—to make a Seder a month later—" He turned to go, mumbling.

"Come back here!" I called. He stopped and looked at me. "Grossbart, why

---

6. Horseradish.
7. Ceremonial dinner on the first evening of Passover.

can't you be like the rest? Why do you have to stick out like a sore thumb?
Why do you beg for special treatment?"

"Because I'm a Jew, Sergeant. I *am* different. Better, maybe not. But different."

"This is a war, Grossbart. For the time being *be* the same."

"I refuse."

"What?"

"I refuse. I can't stop being me, that's all there is to it." Tears came to his
eyes. "It's a hard thing to be a Jew. But now I see what Mickey says—it's a
harder thing to stay one." He raised a hand sadly toward me. "Look at you."

"Stop crying!"

"Stop this, stop that, stop the other thing! You stop, Sergeant. Stop closing
your heart to your own!" And wiping his face with his sleeve, he ran out the
door. "The least we can do for one another . . . the least . . ."

An hour later I saw Grossbart headed across the field. He wore a pair of
starched khakis and carried only a little leather ditty bag. I went to the door
and from the outside felt the heat of the day. It was quiet—not a soul in
sight except over by the mess hall four K.P.'s sitting round a pan, sloped
forward from the waists, gabbing and peeling potatoes in the sun.

"Grossbart!" I called.

He looked toward me and continued walking.

"Grossbart, get over here!"

He turned and stepped into his long shadow. Finally he stood before me.

"Where are you going?" I said.

"St. Louis. I don't care."

"You'll get caught without a pass."

"So I'll get caught without a pass."

"You'll go to the stockade."

"I'm in the stockade." He made an about-face and headed off.

I let him go only a step: "Come back here," I said, and he followed me
into the office, where I typed out a pass and signed the Captain's name and
my own initials after it.

He took the pass from me and then, a moment later, he reached out and
grabbed my hand. "Sergeant, you don't know how much this means to me."

"Okay. Don't get in any trouble."

"I wish I could show you how much this means to me."

"Don't do me any favors. Don't write any more congressmen for citations."

Amazingly, he smiled. "You're right. I won't. But let me do something."

"Bring me a piece of that gefilte fish. Just get out of here."

"I will! With a slice of carrot and a little horseradish. I won't forget."

"All right. Just show your pass at the gate. And don't tell *anybody*."

"I won't. It's a month late, but a good Yom Tov to you."

"Good Yom Tov,[8] Grossbart," I said.

"You're a good Jew, Sergeant. You like to think you have a hard heart, but
underneath you're a fine decent man. I mean that."

Those last three words touched me more than any words from Grossbart's
mouth had the right to. "All right, Grossbart. Now call me 'sir' and get the
hell out of here."

He ran out the door and was gone. I felt very pleased with myself—it was

8. Praise the day.

a great relief to stop fighting Grossbart. And it had cost me nothing. Barrett would never find out, and if he did, I could manage to invent some excuse. For a while I sat at my desk, comfortable in my decision. Then the screen door flew back and Grossbart burst in again. "Sergeant!" he said. Behind him I saw Fishbein and Halpern, both in starched khakis, both carrying ditty bags exactly like Grossbart's.

"Sergeant, I caught Mickey and Larry coming out of the movies. I almost missed them."

"Grossbart, did I say tell no one?"

"But my aunt said I could bring friends. That I should, in fact."

"I'm the Sergeant, Grossbart—not your aunt!"

Grossbart looked at me in disbelief; he pulled Halpern up by his sleeve. "Mickey, tell the Sergeant what this would mean to you."

"Grossbart, for God's sake, spare us—"

"Tell him what you told me, Mickey. How much it would mean."

Halpern looked at me and, shrugging his shoulders, made his admission. "A lot."

Fishbein stepped forward without prompting. "This would mean a great deal to me and my parents, Sergeant Marx."

"No!" I shouted.

Grossbart was shaking his head. "Sergeant, I could see you denying me, but how you can deny Mickey, a Yeshivah boy, that's beyond me."

"I'm not denying Mickey anything. You just pushed a little too hard, Grossbart. *You* denied him."

"I'll give him my pass, then," Grossbart said. "I'll give him my aunt's address and a little note. At least let him go."

In a second he had crammed the pass into Halpern's pants' pocket. Halpern looked at me, Fishbein too. Grossbart was at the door, pushing it open. "Mickey, bring me a piece of gefilte fish at least." And then he was outside again.

The three of us looked at one another and then I said, "Halpern, hand that pass over."

He took it from his pocket and gave it to me. Fishbein had now moved to the doorway, where he lingered. He stood there with his mouth slightly open and then pointed to himself. "And me?" he asked.

His utter ridiculousness exhausted me. I slumped down in my seat and I felt pulses knocking at the back of my eyes. "Fishbein," I said, "you understand I'm not trying to deny you anything, don't you? If it was my Army I'd serve gefilte fish in the mess hall. I'd sell kugel[9] in the PX, honest to God."

Halpern smiled.

"You understand, don't you, Halpern?"

"Yes, Sergeant."

"And you, Fishbein? I don't want enemies. I'm just like you—I want to serve my time and go home. I miss the same things you miss."

"Then, Sergeant," Fishbein interrupted, "Why don't you come too?"

"Where?"

"To St. Louis. To Shelley's aunt. We'll have a regular Seder. Play hide-the-matzah." He gave a broad, black-toothed smile.

9. Baked pudding of noodles or potatoes.

I saw Grossbart in the doorway again, on the other side of the screen.

"Pssst!" He waved a piece of paper. "Mickey, here's the address. Tell her I couldn't get away."

Halpern did not move. He looked at me and I saw the shrug moving up his arms into his shoulders again. I took the cover off my typewriter and made out passes for him and Fishbein. "Go," I said, "the three of you."

I thought Halpern was going to kiss my hand.

That afternoon, in a bar in Joplin, I drank beer and listened with half an ear to the Cardinal game. I tried to look squarely at what I'd become involved in, and began to wonder if perhaps the struggle with Grossbart wasn't as much my fault as his. What was I that I had to *muster* generous feelings? Who was I to have been feeling so grudging, so tight-hearted? After all, I wasn't being asked to move the world. Had I a right, then, or a reason, to clamp down on Grossbart, when that meant clamping down on Halpern, too? And Fishbein, that ugly agreeable soul, wouldn't he suffer in the bargain also? Out of the many recollections that had tumbled over me these past few days, I heard from some childhood moment my grandmother's voice: "What are you making a *tsimas?*"[1] It was what she would ask my mother when, say, I had cut myself with a knife and her daughter was busy bawling me out. I would need a hug and a kiss and my mother would moralize! But my grandmother knew—mercy overrides justice. I should have known it, too. Who was Nathan Marx to be such a pennypincher with kindness? Surely, I thought, the Messiah himself—if he should ever come—won't niggle over nickels and dimes. God willing, he'll hug and kiss.

The next day, while we were playing softball over on the Parade Grounds, I decided to ask Bob Wright, who was noncom in charge over at Classification and Assignment, where he thought our trainees would be sent when their cycle ended in two weeks. I asked casually, between innings, and he said, "They're pushing them all into the Pacific. Shulman cut the orders on your boys the other day."

The news shocked me, as though I were father to Halpern, Fishbein, and Grossbart.

That night I was just sliding into sleep when someone tapped on the door. "What is it?"

"Sheldon."

He opened the door and came in. For a moment I felt his presence without being able to see him. "How was it?" I asked, as though to the darkness.

He popped into sight before me. "Great, Sergeant." I felt my springs sag; Grossbart was sitting on the edge of the bed. I sat up.

"How about you?" he asked. "Have a nice weekend?"

"Yes."

He took a deep paternal breath. "The others went to sleep . . ." We sat silently for a while, as a homey feeling invaded my ugly little cubicle: the door was locked, the cat out, the children safely in bed.

"Sergeant, can I tell you something? Personal?"

I did not answer and he seemed to know why. "Not about me. About

---

1. Fuss (Yiddish, literal trans.); here a side dish made of mixed cooked vegetables and fruit.

Mickey. Sergeant, I never felt for anybody like I feel for him. Last night I heard Mickey in the bed next to me. He was crying so, it could have broken your heart. Real sobs."

"I'm sorry to hear that."

"I had to talk to him to stop him. He held my hand, Sergeant—he wouldn't let it go. He was almost hysterical. He kept saying if he only knew where we were going. Even if he knew it *was* the Pacific, that would be better than nothing. Just to know."

Long ago, someone had taught Grossbart the sad law that only lies can get the truth. Not that I couldn't believe in Halpern's crying—his eyes *always* seemed red-rimmed. But, fact or not, it became a lie when Grossbart uttered it. He was entirely strategic. But then—it came with the force of indictment—so was I! There are strategies of aggression, but there are strategies of retreat, as well. And so, recognizing that I myself, had been without craft and guile, I told him what I knew. "It is the Pacific."

He let out a small gasp, which was not a lie. "I'll tell him. I wish it was otherwise."

"So do I."

He jumped on my words. "You mean you think you could do something? A change maybe?"

"No, I couldn't do a thing."

"Don't you know anybody over at C & A?"

"Grossbart, there's nothing I can do. If your orders are for the Pacific then it's the Pacific."

"But Mickey."

"Mickey, you, me—everybody, Grossbart. There's nothing to be done. Maybe the war'll end before you go. Pray for a miracle."

"But—"

"Good night, Grossbart." I settled back, and was relieved to feel the springs upbend again as Grossbart rose to leave. I could see him clearly now; his jaw had dropped and he looked like a dazed prizefighter. I noticed for the first time a little paper bag in his hand.

"Grossbart"—I smiled—"my gift?"

"Oh, yes, Sergeant. Here, from all of us." He handed me the bag. "It's egg roll."

"Egg roll?" I accepted the bag and felt a damp grease spot on the bottom. I opened it, sure that Grossbart was joking.

"We thought you'd probably like it. You know, Chinese egg roll. We thought you'd probably have a taste for—"

"Your aunt served egg roll?"

"She wasn't home."

"Grossbart, she invited you. You told me she invited you and your friends."

"I know. I just reread the letter. *Next* week."

I got out of bed and walked to the window. It was black as far off as I could see. "Grossbart," I said. But I was not calling him.

"What?"

"What are you, Grossbart? Honest to God, what are you?"

I think it was the first time I'd asked him a question for which he didn't have an immediate answer.

"How can you do this to people?" I asked.

"Sergeant, the day away did us all a world of good. Fishbein, you should see him, he *loves* Chinese food."

"But the Seder," I said.

"We took second best, Sergeant."

Rage came charging at me. I didn't sidestep—I grabbed it, pulled it in, hugged it to my chest.

"Grossbart, you're a liar! You're a schemer and a crook! You've got no respect for anything! Nothing at all! Not for me, for the truth, not even for poor Halpern! You use us all—"

"Sergeant, Sergeant, I feel for Mickey, honest to God, I do. I *love* Mickey. I try—"

"You try! You feel!" I lurched towards him and grabbed his shirt front. I shook him furiously. "Grossbart, get out. Get out and stay the hell away from me! Because if I see you, I'll make your life miserable. *You understand that?*"

"Yes."

I let him free, and when he walked from the room I wanted to spit on the floor where he had stood. I couldn't stop the fury from rising in my heart. It engulfed me, owned me, till it seemed I could only rid myself of it with tears or an act of violence. I snatched from the bed the bag Grossbart had given me and with all my strength threw it out the window. And the next morning, as the men policed the area around the barracks, I heard a great cry go up from one of the trainees who'd been anticipating only this morning handful of cigarette butts and candy wrappers. "Egg roll!" he shouted. "Holy Christ, Chinese goddam egg roll!"

A week later when I read the orders that had come down from C & A I couldn't believe my eyes. Every single trainee was to be shipped to Camp Stoneham, California, and from there to the Pacific. Every trainee but one: Private Sheldon Grossbart was to be sent to Fort Monmouth, New Jersey. I read the mimeographed sheet several times. Dee, Farrell, Fishbein, Fuselli, Fylypowycz, Glinicki, Gromke, Gucwa, Halpern, Hardy, Helebrandt . . . right down to Anton Zygadlo, all were to be headed West before the month was out. All except Grossbart. He had pulled a string and I wasn't it.

I lifted the phone and called C & A.

The voice on the other end said smartly, "Corporal Shulman, sir."

"Let me speak to Sergeant Wright."

"Who is this calling, sir?"

"Sergeant Marx."

And to my surprise, the voice said, *"Oh."* Then: "Just a minute, Sergeant."

Shulman's *oh* stayed with me while I waited for Wright to come to the phone. Why *oh?* Who was Shulman? And then, so simply, I knew I'd discovered the string Grossbart had pulled. In fact, I could hear Grossbart the day he'd discovered Shulman, in the PX, or the bowling alley, or maybe even at services. "Glad to meet you. Where you from? Bronx? Me too. Do you know so-and-so? And so-and-so? Me too! You work at C & A? Really? Hey, how's chances of getting East? Could you do something? Change something? Swindle, cheat, lie? We gotta help each other, you know . . . if the Jews in Germany . . ."

At the other end Bob Wright answered. "How are you, Nate? How's the pitching arm?"

"Good. Bob, I wonder if you could do me a favor." I heard clearly my own words and they so reminded me of Grossbart that I dropped more easily than I could have imagined into what I had planned. "This may sound crazy, Bob, but I got a kid here on orders to Monmouth who wants them changed. He had a brother killed in Europe and he's hot to go to the Pacific. Says he'd feel like a coward if he wound up stateside. I don't know, Bob, can anything be done? Put somebody else in the Monmouth slot?"

"Who?" he asked cagily.

"Anybody. First guy on the alphabet. I don't care. The kid just asked if something could be done."

"What's his name?"

"Grossbart, Sheldon."

Wright didn't answer.

"Yeah," I said, "he's a Jewish kid, so he thought I could help him out. You know."

"I guess I can do something," he finally said. "The Major hasn't been around here for weeks—TDY[2] to the golf course. I'll try, Nate that's all I can say."

"I'd appreciate it, Bob. See you Sunday," and I hung up, perspiring.

And the following day the corrected orders appeared: Fishbein, Fuselli, Fylypowycz, Glinicki, Grossbart, Gucwa, Halpern, Hardy . . . Lucky Private Harley Alton was to go to Fort Monmouth, New Jersey, where for some reason or other, they wanted an enlisted man with infantry training.

After chow that night I stopped back at the orderly room to straighten out the guard duty roster. Grossbart was waiting for me. He spoke first.

"You son of a bitch!"

I sat down at my desk and while he glared down at me I began to make the necessary alterations in the duty roster.

"What do you have against me?" he cried. "Against my family? Would it kill you for me to be near my father, God knows how many months he has left to him."

"Why?"

"His heart," Grossbart said. "He hasn't had enough troubles in a lifetime, you've got to add to them. I curse the day I ever met you, Marx! Shulman told me what happened over there. There's no limit to your anti-Semitism, is there! The damage you've done here isn't enough. You have to make a special phone call! You really want me dead!"

I made the last few notations in the duty roster and got up to leave. "Good night, Grossbart."

"You owe me an explanation!" He stood in my path.

"Sheldon, you're the one who owes explanations."

He scowled. "To you?"

"To me, I think so, yes. Mostly to Fishbein and Halpern."

"That's right, twist things around. I owe nobody nothing, I've done all I could do for them. Now I think I've got the right to watch out for myself."

"For each other we have to learn to watch out, Sheldon. You told me yourself."

"You call this watching out for me, what you did?"

2. Temporary Duty, an army orders term used ironically here.

"No. For all of us."

I pushed him aside and started for the door. I heard his furious breathing behind me, and it sounded like steam rushing from the engine of his terrible strength.

"You'll be all right," I said from the door. And, I thought, so would Fishbein and Halpern be all right, even in the Pacific, if only Grossbart could continue to see in the obsequiousness of the one, the soft spirituality of the other, some profit for himself.

I stood outside the orderly room, and I heard Grossbart weeping behind me. Over in the barracks, in the lighted windows, I could see the boys in their T-shirts sitting on their bunks talking about their orders, as they'd been doing for the past two days. With a kind of quiet nervousness, they polished shoes, shined belt buckles, squared away underwear, trying as best they could to accept their fate. Behind me, Grossbart swallowed hard, accepting his. And then, resisting with all my will an impulse to turn and seek pardon for my vindictiveness, I accepted my own.

1959

AMIRI BARAKA (LEROI JONES)
b. 1934

When in 1967 LeRoi Jones assumed the Bantuized Muslim name Amiri Baraka (meaning Prince, a Blessed One), he was undergoing one of several changes in his progression as a maker of literature. Born Everett Leroy Jones, he was the child of middle-class African American parents in Newark, New Jersey, where his scholastic abilities took him to the best schools available; as Baraka recalls in his autobiography, his classmates were more often white suburbanites than inner-city children of his own race. The stylizing "LeRoi" was undertaken during his undergraduate years at Howard University (a traditionally African American institution), to which he had transferred from the mostly white campus of Rutgers University (where he had won a scholarship). After leaving Howard in 1954 and serving in the U.S. Air Force, from which he was discharged for unapproved political activities, Jones moved to New York City's Greenwich Village and became prominent on the avant-garde poetry scene. His friends were white innovators—Gilbert Sorrentino, Diane DiPrima, and Frank O'Hara among them—with whom he worked on the magazine *Kulchur* in addition to editing and publishing his own journal, *Yugen.* Married to Hettie Cohen, he began an interracial family and wrote record reviews for mainstream jazz magazines.

Jones was well established in the more intellectually elite quarters of New York's world of poetry, art, and music when *Dutchman* was produced in 1964. That it won an Obie (as one of the year's best Off-Broadway plays) seemed appropriate for a work by someone on the cutting edge of literature. Yet as racial tensions mounted, with the assassination of Medgar Evers; fatal church bombings in Alabama; and the murder of civil rights workers James Chaney, Andrew Goodman, and Michael Schwerner in Mississippi; Jones's life underwent major changes as well. In 1965, following the assassination of Malcolm X, he left his wife and children and moved to Harlem, where as a newly declared black cultural nationalist he founded the Black Arts Repetory

Theater, dedicated to taking socially militant drama directly to the people it concerned. At this time his drama itself assumed the spokesmanship role expressed by his character Clay in *Dutchman*. Such works as *The Baptism* and *The Toilet* (1967) are physically assaultive in their dramaturgy; in the latter the stage set is a realistically constructed public lavatory, where among the uncleaned urinals a student is harassed and beaten as a vehicle of the play's narrative exposition. *Four Black Revolutionary Plays* (1969) collects similarly harsh works and includes as well the author's comments on a play that because of its explosiveness could not be printed in an America only recently disrupted by assassinations and urban rioting (*J-E-L-L-O*, in which Rochester, the comically beloved servant of Jack Benny's popular radio and television show, kills Benny and his family; the Jell-O Food Company, Benny's longtime sponsor, refused to let its name be used). By 1970 Amiri Baraka, as he asked to be called, had moved to Newark; married Sylvia Robinson (who became Amina Baraka); and begun work toward electing Kenneth Gibson as the city's first black mayor, a consequence of the author having been convicted of incitement to riot on the evidence of his poetry. The conviction was overturned on appeal. Yet even with Gibson in control, Baraka was not happy with the quality of African-American life in the city and soon parted with both the mayor and black nationalism in favor of third world Marxism.

Poetry as a vehicle of popular encouragement remains central to Baraka's belief. He may well have agreed with the originally convicting judge that his poem could motivate people to act (whether such culpability had been proven in legal form is another matter). As opposed to his very first work, which conveyed a personal anguish for which the poet projected no political situation ("I am inside someone / who hates me, I look / out from his eyes") and whose collective title conveys little hope other than in the act of expression (*Preface to a Twenty Volume Suicide Note*, 1961), his later work is replete with exhortations, capitalized imperatives for action, and chant-like repetitions designed to arouse a fury for action and then direct it toward the achievement of specific social goals. Much like his drama, this poetry is overtly presentational, showing what the reader needs to think about and then providing the stimulus to act. Yet all the while the personal nature of Baraka stands behind it, making clear that a deep and complex imagination has been brought to bear on the issues.

Since the 1980s Baraka has taught in the African Studies Department at the State University of New York, Stony Brook. In addition to poetry and drama, he continues to write essays on social subjects and on jazz. Thanks to its availability on videocassette, the original stage presentation of *Dutchman* remains an important part of his writer's reputation. From the same era that produced Edward Albee's equally riveting *The Zoo Story* (the first American staging of which was in 1960), this play reflects the personally felt violence tearing at the major social issues of the day. Clay, not uncomfortably confined in his establishment suit, seems much like a younger Everett Leroy Jones, who had gone on to achieve such success in the white world of avant-garde poetry and esoteric art and music. Yet there is another person ready to burst out from Clay's restrained identity, a person who from his speeches here suggests the figure who would soon become Amiri Baraka. Without an enabling program for such beliefs, as the play shows, such spokespersons are taken out of the way in favor of the next victim. Baraka's ever-fluid sense of development eludes any such entrapment.

Dutchman[1]

CHARACTERS

CLAY, twenty-year-old Negro
LULA, thirty-year-old white woman
RIDERS OF COACH, white and black
YOUNG NEGRO
CONDUCTOR

In the flying underbelly of the city. Steaming hot, and summer on top, outside. Underground. The subway heaped in modern myth.

Opening scene is a man sitting in a subway seat, holding a magazine but looking vacantly just above its wilting pages. Occasionally he looks blankly toward the window on his right. Dim lights and darkness whistling by against the glass. (Or paste the lights, as admitted props, right on the subway windows. Have them move, even dim and flicker. But give the sense of speed. Also stations, whether the train is stopped or the glitter and activity of these stations merely flashes by the windows.)

The man is sitting alone. That is, only his seat is visible, though the rest of the car is outfitted as a complete subway car. But only his seat is shown. There might be, for a time, as the play begins, a loud scream of the actual train. And it can recur throughout the play, or continue on a lower key once the dialogue starts.

The train slows after a time, pulling to a brief stop at one of the stations. The man looks idly up, until he sees a woman's face staring at him through the window; when it realizes that the man has noticed the face, it begins very premeditatedly to smile. The man smiles too, for a moment, without a trace of self-consciousness. Almost an instinctive though undesirable response. Then a kind of awkwardness or embarrassment sets in, and the man makes to look away, is further embarrassed, so he brings back his eyes to where the face was, but by now the train is moving again, and the face would seem to be left behind by the way the man turns his head to look back through the other windows at the slowly fading platform. He smiles then; more comfortably confident, hoping perhaps that his memory of this brief encounter will be pleasant. And then he is idle again.

Scene I

Train roars. Lights flash outside the windows.

LULA *enters from the rear of the car in bright, skimpy summer clothes and sandals. She carries a net bag full of paper books, fruit, and other anonymous articles. She is wearing sunglasses, which she pushes up on her forehead from time to time.* LULA *is a tall, slender, beautiful woman with long red hair hanging straight down her back, wearing only loud lipstick in somebody's good taste. She is eating an apple, very daintily. Coming down the car toward* CLAY.

1. From *Dutchman and The Slave* (1964).

She stops beside CLAY's *seat and hangs languidly from the strap, still managing to eat the apple. It is apparent that she is going to sit in the seat next to* CLAY, *and that she is only waiting for him to notice her before she sits.*

CLAY *sits as before, looking just beyond his magazine, now and again pulling the magazine slowly back and forth in front of his face in a hopeless effort to fan himself. Then he sees the woman hanging there beside him and he looks up into her face, smiling quizzically.*

LULA   Hello.

CLAY   Uh, hi're you?

LULA   I'm going to sit down. . . . O.K.?

CLAY   Sure.

LULA   [*Swings down onto the seat, pushing her legs straight out as if she is very weary*]   Oooof! Too much weight.

CLAY   Ha, doesn't look like much to me. [*Leaning back against the window, a little surprised and maybe stiff*]

LULA   It's so anyway. [*And she moves her toes in the sandals, then pulls her right leg up on the left knee, better to inspect the bottoms of the sandals and the back of her heel. She appears for a second not to notice that* CLAY *is sitting next to her or that she has spoken to him just a second before.* CLAY *looks at the magazine, then out the black window. As he does this, she turns very quickly toward him*] Weren't you staring at me through the window?

CLAY   [*Wheeling around and very much stiffened*]   What?

LULA   Weren't you staring at me through the window? At the last stop?

CLAY   Staring at you? What do you mean?

LULA   Don't you know what staring means?

CLAY   I saw you through the window . . . if that's what it means. I don't know if I was staring. Seems to me you were staring through the window at me.

LULA   I was. But only after I'd turned around and saw you staring through that window down in the vicinity of my ass and legs.

CLAY   Really?

LULA   Really. I guess you were just taking those idle potshots. Nothing else to do. Run your mind over people's flesh.

CLAY   Oh boy. Wow, now I admit I was looking in your direction. But the rest of that weight is yours.

LULA   I suppose.

CLAY   Staring through train windows is weird business. Much weirder than staring very sedately at abstract asses.

LULA   That's why I came looking through the window . . . so you'd have more than that to go on. I even smiled at you.

CLAY   That's right.

LULA   I even got into this train, going some other way than mine. Walked down the aisle . . . searching you out.

CLAY   Really? That's pretty funny.

LULA   That's pretty funny. . . . God, you're dull.

CLAY   Well, I'm sorry, lady, but I really wasn't prepared for party talk.

LULA   No, you're not. What are you prepared for? [*Wrapping the apple core in a Kleenex and dropping it on the floor*]

CLAY [*Takes her conversation as pure sex talk. He turns to confront her squarely with this idea*] I'm prepared for anything. How about you?

LULA [*Laughing loudly and cutting it off abruptly*] What do you think you're doing?

CLAY What?

LULA You think I want to pick you up, get you to take me somewhere and screw me, huh?

CLAY Is that the way I look?

LULA You look like you been trying to grow a beard. That's exactly what you look like. You look like you live in New Jersey with your parents and are trying to grow a beard. That's what. You look like you've been reading Chinese poetry and drinking lukewarm sugarless tea. [*Laughs, uncrossing and recrossing her legs*] You look like death eating a soda cracker.

CLAY [*Cocking his head from one side to the other, embarrassed and trying to make some comeback, but also intrigued by what the woman is saying . . . even the sharp city coarseness of her voice, which is still a kind of gentle sidewalk throb*] Really? I look like all that?

LULA Not all of it. [*She feints a seriousness to cover an actual somber tone*] I lie a lot. [*Smiling*] It helps me control the world.

CLAY [*Relieved and laughing louder than the humor*] Yeah, I bet.

LULA But it's true, most of it, right? Jersey? Your bumpy neck?

CLAY How'd you know all that? Huh? Really, I mean about Jersey . . . and even the beard. I met you before? You know Warren Enright?

LULA You tried to make it with your sister when you were ten. [CLAY *leans back hard against the back of the seat, his eyes opening now, still trying to look amused*] But I succeeded a few weeks ago. [*She starts to laugh again*]

CLAY What're you talking about? Warren tell you that? You're a friend of Georgia's?

LULA I told you I lie. I don't know your sister. I don't know Warren Enright.

CLAY You mean you're just picking these things out of the air?

LULA Is Warren Enright a tall skinny black black boy with a phony English accent?

CLAY I figured you knew him.

LULA But I don't. I just figured you would know somebody like that. [*Laughs*]

CLAY Yeah, yeah.

LULA You're probably on your way to his house now.

CLAY That's right.

LULA [*Putting her hand on* CLAY'*s closest knee, drawing it from the knee up to the thigh's hinge, then removing it, watching his face very closely, and continuing to laugh, perhaps more gently than before*] Dull, dull, dull. I bet you think I'm exciting.

CLAY You're O.K.

LULA Am I exciting you now?

CLAY Right. That's not what's supposed to happen?

LULA How do I know? [*She returns her hand, without moving it, then takes it away and plunges it in her bag to draw out an apple*] You want this?

CLAY Sure.

LULA [*She gets one out of the bag for herself*] Eating apples together is always the first step. Or walking up uninhabited Seventh Avenue in the twenties[2] on weekends. [*Bites and giggles, glancing at Clay and speaking in loose sing-song*] Can get you involved . . . boy! Get us involved. Um-huh. [*Mock seriousness*] Would you like to get involved with me, Mister Man?

CLAY [*Trying to be as flippant as* LULA, *whacking happily at the apple*]   Sure. Why not? A beautiful woman like you. Huh, I'd be a fool not to.

LULA   And I bet you're sure you know what you're talking about. [*Taking him a little roughly by the wrist, so he cannot eat the apple, then shaking the wrist*] I bet you're sure of almost everything anybody ever asked you about . . . right? [*Shakes his wrist harder*] Right?

CLAY   Yeah, right. . . . Wow, you're pretty strong, you know? Whatta you, a lady wrestler or something?

LULA   What's wrong with lady wrestlers? And don't answer because you never knew any. Huh. [*Cynically*] That's for sure. They don't have any lady wrestlers in that part of Jersey. That's for sure.

CLAY   Hey, you still haven't told me how you know so much about me.

LULA   I told you I didn't know anything about *you* . . . you're a well-known type.

CLAY   Really?

LULA   Or at least I know the type very well. And your skinny English friend too.

CLAY   Anonymously?

LULA [*Settles back in seat, single-mindedly finishing her apple and humming snatches of rhythm and blues song*]   What?

CLAY   Without knowing us specifically?

LULA   Oh boy. [*Looking quickly at* CLAY] What a face. You know, you could be a handsome man.

CLAY   I can't argue with you.

LULA [*Vague, off-center response*]   What?

CLAY [*Raising his voice, thinking the train noise has drowned part of his sentence*]   I can't argue with you.

LULA   My hair is turning gray. A gray hair for each year and type I've come through.

CLAY   Why do you want to sound so old?

LULA   But it's always gentle when it starts. [*Attention drifting*] Hugged against tenements, day or night.

CLAY   What?

LULA [*Refocusing*]   Hey, why don't you take me to that party you're going to?

CLAY   You must be a friend of Warren's to know about the party.

LULA   Wouldn't you like to take me to the party? [*Imitates clinging vine*] Oh, come on, ask me to your party.

CLAY   Of course I'll ask you to come with me to the party. And I'll bet you're a friend of Warren's.

LULA   Why not be a friend of Warren's? Why not? [*Taking his arm*] Have you asked me yet?

CLAY   How can I ask you when I don't know your name?

LULA   Are you talking to my name?

CLAY   What is it, a secret?

---

2. The Chelsea neighborhood of New York City, famous for its underground arts scene.

LULA I'm Lena the Hyena.

CLAY The famous woman poet?

LULA Poetess! The same!

CLAY Well, you know so much about me . . . what's my name?

LULA Morris the Hyena.

CLAY The famous woman poet?

LULA The same. [*Laughing and going into her bag*] You want another apple?

CLAY Can't make it, lady. I only have to keep one doctor away a day.

LULA I bet your name is . . . something like . . . uh, Gerald or Walter. Huh?

CLAY God, no.

LULA Lloyd, Norman? One of those hopeless colored names creeping out of New Jersey. Leonard? Gag. . . .

CLAY Like Warren?

LULA Definitely. Just exactly like Warren. Or Everett.[3]

CLAY Gag. . . .

LULA Well, for sure, it's not Willie.

CLAY It's Clay.

LULA Clay? Really? Clay what?

CLAY Take your pick. Jackson, Johnson, or Williams.

LULA Oh, really? Good for you. But it's got to be Williams. You're too pretentious to be a Jackson or Johnson.

CLAY Thass right.

LULA But Clay's O.K.

CLAY So's Lena.

LULA It's Lula.

CLAY Oh?

LULA Lula the Hyena.

CLAY Very good.

LULA [*Starts laughing again*] Now you say to me, "Lula, Lula, why don't you go to this party with me tonight?" It's your turn, and let those be your lines.

CLAY Lula, why don't you go to this party with me tonight, Huh?

LULA Say my name twice before you ask, and no huh's.

CLAY Lula, Lula, why don't you go to this party with me tonight?

LULA I'd like to go, Clay, but how can you ask me to go when you barely know me?

CLAY That is strange, isn't it?

LULA What kind of reaction is that? You're supposed to say, "Aw, come on, we'll get to know each other better at the party."

CLAY That's pretty corny.

LULA What are you into anyway? [*Looking at him half sullenly but still amused*] What thing are you playing at, Mister? Mister Clay Williams? [*Grabs his thigh, up near the crotch*] What are *you* thinking about?

CLAY Watch it now, you're gonna excite me for real.

LULA [*Taking her hand away and throwing her apple core through the window*] I bet. [*She slumps in the seat and is heavily silent*]

CLAY I thought you knew everything about me? What happened? [LULA

---

3. Baraka was born in Newark, New Jersey, as Everett Leroy Jones.

looks at him, then looks slowly away, then over where the other aisle would be. Noise of the train. She reaches in her bag and pulls out one of the paper books. She puts it on her leg and thumbs the pages listlessly. CLAY *cocks his head to see the title of the book. Noise of the train.* LULA *flips pages and her eyes drift. Both remain silent]* Are you going to the party with me, Lula?

LULA [*Bored and not even looking*] I don't even know you.

CLAY You said you know my type.

LULA [*Strangely irritated*] Don't get smart with me, Buster. I know you like the palm of my hand.

CLAY The one you eat the apples with?

LULA Yeh. And the one I open doors late Saturday evening with. That's my door. Up at the top of the stairs. Five flights. Above a lot of Italians and lying Americans. And scrape carrots with. Also . . . [*Looks at him*] the same hand I unbutton my dress with, or let my skirt fall down. Same hand. Lover.

CLAY Are you angry about anything? Did I say something wrong?

LULA Everything you say is wrong. [*Mock smile*] That's what makes you so attractive. Ha. In that funnybook jacket with all the buttons. [*More animate, taking hold of his jacket*] What've you got that jacket and tie on in all this heat for? And why're you wearing a jacket and tie like that? Did your people ever burn witches or start revolutions over the price of tea? Boy, those narrow-shoulder clothes come from a tradition you ought to feel oppressed by. A three-button suit. What right do you have to be wearing a three-button suit and striped tie? Your grandfather was a slave, he didn't go to Harvard.

CLAY My grandfather was a night watchman.

LULA And you went to a colored college where everybody thought they were Averell Harriman.[4]

CLAY All except me.

LULA And who did you think you were? Who do you think you are now?

CLAY [*Laughs as if to make light of the whole trend of the conversation*] Well, in college I thought I was Baudelaire.[5] But I've slowed down since.

LULA I bet you never once thought you were a black nigger. [*Mock serious, then she howls with laughter.* CLAY *is stunned but after initial reaction, he quickly tries to appreciate the humor.* LULA *almost shrieks*] A black Baudelaire.

CLAY That's right.

LULA Boy, are you corny. I take back what I said before. Everything you say is not wrong. It's perfect. You should be on television.

CLAY You act like you're on television already.

LULA That's because I'm an actress.

CLAY I thought so.

LULA Well, you're wrong. I'm no actress. I told you I always lie. I'm nothing, honey, and don't you ever forget it. [*Lighter*] Although my mother was a Communist. The only person in my family ever to amount to anything.

4. American cabinet member, ambassador, and governor of New York, who was born into a wealthy and prominent family (1891–1986).

5. Charles Baudelaire (1821–1867), French poet known for his images of sensuality and evil.

CLAY   My mother was a Republican.

LULA   And your father voted for the man rather than the party.

CLAY   Right!

LULA   Yea for him. Yea, yea for him.

CLAY   Yea!

LULA   And yea for America where he is free to vote for the mediocrity of his choice! Yea!

CLAY   Yea!

LULA   And yea for both your parents who even though they differ about so crucial a matter as the body politic still forged a union of love and sacrifice that was destined to flower at the birth of the noble Clay . . . what's your middle name?

CLAY   Clay.

LULA   A union of love and sacrifice that was destined to flower at the birth of the noble Clay Clay Williams. Yea! And most of all yea yea for you, Clay Clay. The Black Baudelaire! Yes! [*And with knifelike cynicism*] My Christ. My Christ.

CLAY   Thank you, ma'am.

LULA   May the people accept you as a ghost of the future. And love you, that you might not kill them when you can.

CLAY   What?

LULA   You're a murderer, Clay, and you know it. [*Her voice darkening with significance*] You know goddamn well what I mean.

CLAY   I do?

LULA   So we'll pretend the air is light and full of perfume.

CLAY   [*Sniffing at her blouse*]   It is.

LULA   And we'll pretend that people cannot see you. That is, the citizens. And that you are free of your own history. And I am free of my history. We'll pretend that we are both anonymous beauties smashing along through the city's entrails. [*She yells as loud as she can*] GROOVE!

        [*Black*]

Scene II

Scene is the same as before, though now there are other seats visible in the car. And throughout the scene other people get on the subway. There are maybe one or two seated in the car as the scene opens, though neither CLAY *nor* LULA *notices them.* CLAY's *tie is open.* LULA *is hugging his arm.*

CLAY   The party!

LULA   I know it'll be something good. You can come in with me, looking casual and significant. I'll be strange, haughty, and silent, and walk with long slow strides.

CLAY   Right.

LULA   When you get drunk, pat me once, very lovingly on the flanks, and I'll look at you cryptically, licking my lips.

CLAY   It sounds like something we can do.

LULA   You'll go around talking to young men about your mind, and to old men about your plans. If you meet a very close friend who is also with someone like me, we can stand together, sipping our drinks and exchanging codes of lust. The atmosphere will be slithering in love and half-love and very open moral decision.

CLAY   Great. Great.

LULA   And everyone will pretend they don't know your name, and then . . . [*She pauses heavily*] later, when they have to, they'll claim a friendship that denies your sterling character.

CLAY   [*Kissing her neck and fingers*]   And then what?

LULA   Then? Well, then we'll go down the street, late night, eating apples and winding very deliberately toward my house.

CLAY   Deliberately?

LULA   I mean, we'll look in all the shop windows, and make fun of the queers. Maybe we'll meet a Jewish Buddhist and flatten his conceits over some very pretentious coffee.

CLAY   In honor of whose God?

LULA   Mine.

CLAY   Who is . . . ?

LULA   Me . . . and you?

CLAY   A corporate Godhead.

LULA   Exactly. Exactly. [*Notices one of the other people entering*]

CLAY   Go on with the chronicle. Then what happens to us?

LULA   [*A mild depression, but she still makes her description triumphant and increasingly direct*]   To my house, of course.

CLAY   Of course.

LULA   And up the narrow steps of the tenement.

CLAY   You live in a tenement?

LULA   Wouldn't live anywhere else. Reminds me specifically of my novel form of insanity.

CLAY   Up the tenement stairs.

LULA   And with my apple-eating hand I push open the door and lead you, my tender big-eyed prey, into my . . . God, what can I call it . . . into my hovel.

CLAY   Then what happens?

LULA   After the dancing and games, after the long drinks and long walks, the real fun begins.

CLAY   Ah, the real fun. [*Embarrassed, in spite of himself*] Which is . . . ?

LULA   [*Laughs at him*]   Real fun in the dark house. Hah! Real fun in the dark house, high up above the street and the ignorant cowboys. I lead you in, holding your wet hand gently in my hand . . .

CLAY   Which is not wet?

LULA   Which is dry as ashes.

CLAY   And cold?

LULA   Don't think you'll get out of your responsibility that way. It's not cold at all. You Fascist! Into my dark living room. Where we'll sit and talk endlessly, endlessly.

CLAY   About what?

LULA   About what? About your manhood, what do you think? What do you think we've been talking about all this time?

CLAY   Well, I didn't know it was that. That's for sure. Every other thing in the world but that. [*Notices another person entering, looks quickly, almost involuntarily up and down the car, seeing the other people in the car*] Hey, I didn't even notice when those people got on.

LULA   Yeah, I know.

CLAY   Man, this subway is slow.

LULA   Yeah, I know.

CLAY   Well, go on. We were talking about my manhood.

LULA   We still are. All the time.

CLAY   We were in your living room.

LULA   My dark living room. Talking endlessly.

CLAY   About my manhood.

LULA   I'll make you a map of it. Just as soon as we get to my house.

CLAY   Well, that's great.

LULA   One of the things we do while we talk. And screw.

CLAY   [*Trying to make his smile broader and less shaky*]   We finally got there.

LULA   And you'll call my rooms black as a grave. You'll say, "This place is like Juliet's tomb."[6]

CLAY   [*Laughs*]   I might.

LULA   I know. You've probably said it before.

CLAY   And is that all? The whole grand tour?

LULA   Not all. You'll say to me very close to my face, many, many times, you'll say, even whisper, that you love me.

CLAY   Maybe I will.

LULA   And you'll be lying.

CLAY   I wouldn't lie about something like that.

LULA   Hah. It's the only kind of thing you will lie about. Especially if you think it'll keep me alive.

CLAY   Keep you alive? I don't understand.

LULA   [*Bursting out laughing, but too shrilly*]   Don't understand? Well, don't look at me. It's the path I take, that's all. Where both feet take me when I set them down. One in front of the other.

CLAY   Morbid. Morbid. You sure you're not an actress? All that self-aggrandizement.

LULA   Well, I told you I wasn't an actress . . . but I also told you I lie all the time. Draw your own conclusions.

CLAY   Morbid. Morbid. You sure you're not an actress? All scribed? There's no more?

LULA   I've told you all I know. Or almost all.

CLAY   There's no funny parts?

LULA   I thought it was all funny.

CLAY   But you mean peculiar, not ha-ha.

LULA   You don't know what I mean.

CLAY   Well, tell me the almost part then. You said almost all. What else? I want the whole story.

LULA   [*Searching aimlessly through her bag. She begins to talk breathlessly, with a light and silly tone*]   All stories are whole stories. All of 'em. Our whole story . . . nothing but change. How could things go on like that forever? Huh? [*Slaps him on the shoulder, begins finding things in her bag, taking them out and throwing them over her shoulder into the aisle*] Except I do go on as I do. Apples and long walks with deathless intelligent lovers. But you mix it up. Look out the window, all the time. Turning pages. Change change change. Till, shit, I don't know you. Wouldn't, for

---

6. A scene in Shakespeare's *Romeo and Juliet.*

that matter. You're too serious. I bet you're even too serious to be psychoanalyzed. Like all those Jewish poets from Yonkers, who leave their mothers looking for other mothers, or others' mothers, on whose baggy tits they lay their fumbling heads. Their poems are always funny, and all about sex.

CLAY   They sound great. Like movies.

LULA   But you change. [*Blankly*] And things work on you till you hate them. [*More people come into the train. They come closer to the couple, some of them not sitting, but swinging drearily on the straps, staring at the two with uncertain interest*]

CLAY   Wow. All these people, so suddenly. They must all come from the same place.

LULA   Right. That they do.

CLAY   Oh? You know about them too?

LULA   Oh yeah. About them more than I know about you. Do they frighten you?

CLAY   Frighten me? Why should they frighten me?

LULA   'Cause you're an escaped nigger.

CLAY   Yeah?

LULA   'Cause you crawled through the wire and made tracks to my side.

CLAY   Wire?

LULA   Don't they have wire around plantations?

CLAY   You must be Jewish. All you can think about is wire. Plantations didn't have any wire. Plantations were big open whitewashed places like heaven, and everybody on 'em was grooved to be there. Just strummin' and hummin' all day.

LULA   Yes, yes.

CLAY   And that's how the blues was born.

LULA   Yes, yes. And that's how the blues was born. [*Begins to make up a song that becomes quickly hysterical. As she sings she rises from her seat, still throwing things out of her bag into the aisle, beginning a rhythmical shudder and twistlike wiggle, which she continues up and down the aisle, bumping into many of the standing people and tripping over the feet of those sitting. Each time she runs into a person she lets out a very vicious piece of profanity, wiggling and stepping all the time*] And that's how the blues was born. Yes. Yes. Son of a bitch, get out of the way. Yes. Quack. Yes. Yes. And that's how the blues was born. Ten little niggers sitting on a limb, but none of them ever looked like him. [*Points to* CLAY, *returns toward the seat, with her hands extended for him to rise and dance with her*] And that's how blues was born. Yes. Come on, Clay. Let's do the nasty. Rub bellies. Rub bellies.

CLAY   [*Waves his hands to refuse. He is embarrassed, but determined to get a kick out of the proceedings*]   Hey, what was in those apples? Mirror, mirror on the wall, who's the fairest one of all? Snow White, baby, and don't you forget it.

LULA   [*Grabbing for his hands, which he draws away*]   Come on, Clay. Let's rub bellies on the train. The nasty. The nasty. Do the gritty grind, like your ol' rag-head mammy. Grind till you lose your mind. Shake it, shake it, shake it, shake it! OOOOweeee! Come on, Clay. Let's do the choo-choo train shuffle, the navel scratcher.

CLAY   Hey, you coming on like the lady who smoked up her grass skirt.

LULA [*Becoming annoyed that he will not dance, and becoming more ani-mated as if to embarrass him still further*]   Come on, Clay . . . let's do the thing. Uhh! Uhh! Clay! Clay! You middle-class black bastard. Forget your social-working mother for a few seconds and let's knock stomachs. Clay, you liver-lipped white man. You would-be Christian. You ain't no nigger, you're just a dirty white man. Get up, Clay. Dance with me, Clay.

CLAY   Lula! Sit down, now. Be cool.

LULA [*Mocking him, in wild dance*]   Be cool. Be cool. That's all you know . . . shaking that wildroot cream-oil on your knotty head, jackets button-ing up to your chin, so full of white man's words. Christ. God. Get up and scream at these people. Like scream meaningless shit in these hope-less faces. [*She screams at people in train, still dancing*] Red trains cough Jewish underwear for keeps! Expanding smells of silence. Gravy snot whistling like sea birds. Clay. Clay, you got to break out. Don't sit there dying the way they want you to die. Get up.

CLAY   Oh, sit the fuck down. [*He moves to restrain her*] Sit down, goddamn it.

LULA [*Twisting out of his reach*]   Screw yourself, Uncle Tom.[7] Thomas Woolly-head. [*Begins to dance a kind of jig, mocking* CLAY *with loud forced humor*] There is Uncle Tom . . . I mean, Uncle Thomas Woolly-Head. With old white matted mane. He hobbles on his wooden cane. Old Tom. Old Tom. Let the white man hump his ol' mama, and he jes' shuffle off in the woods and hide his gentle gray head. Ol' Thomas Woolly-Head. [*Some of the other riders are laughing now. A* DRUNK *gets up and joins* LULA *in her dance, singing, as best he can, her "song."* CLAY *gets up out of his seat and visibly scans the faces of the other riders*]

CLAY   Lula! Lula! [*She is dancing and turning, still shouting as loud as she can. The* DRUNK *too is shouting, and waving his hands wildly*] Lula . . . you dumb bitch. Why don't you stop it? [*He rushes half stumbling from his seat, and grabs one of her flailing arms*]

LULA   Let me go! You black son of a bitch. [*She struggles against him*] Let me go! Help! [CLAY *is dragging her towards her seat, and the* DRUNK *seeks to interfere. He grabs* CLAY *around the shoulders and begins wrestling with him.* CLAY *clubs the drunk to the floor without releasing* LULA, *who is still screaming.* CLAY *finally gets her to the seat and throws her into it*]

CLAY   Now you shut the hell up. [*Grabbing her shoulders*] Just shut up. You don't know what you're talking about. You don't know anything. So just keep your stupid mouth closed.

LULA   You're afraid of white people. And your father was. Uncle Tom Big Lip!

CLAY [*Slaps her as hard as he can, across the mouth.* LULA's *head bangs against the back of the seat. When she raises it again,* CLAY *slaps her again*]   Now shut up and let me talk. [*He turns toward the other riders, some of whom are sitting on the edge of their seats. The* DRUNK *is on one knee, rubbing his head, and singing softly the same song. He shuts up too when he sees* CLAY *watching him. The others go back to newspapers or stare out the*

---

7. Character in the novel *Uncle Tom's Cabin* (1852) by American writer Harriet Beecher Stowe (1811–1896), stereotyped in popular culture as a compliant slave.

windows] Shit, you don't have any sense, Lula, nor feelings either. I could murder you now. Such a tiny ugly throat. I could squeeze it flat, and watch you turn blue, on a humble. For dull kicks. And all these weak-faced ofays squatting around here, staring over their papers at me. Murder them too. Even if they expected it. That man there . . . [*Points to a* WELL-DRESSED MAN] I could rip that *Times* right out of his hand, as skinny and middle-classed as I am, I could rip that paper out of his hand and just as easily rip out his throat. It takes no great effort. For what? To kill you soft idiots? You don't understand anything but luxury.

LULA   You fool!

CLAY   [*Pushing her against the seat*]   I'm not telling you again, Tallulah Bankhead! Luxury. In your face and your fingers. You telling me what I ought to do. [*Sudden scream frightening the whole coach*] Well, don't! Don't you tell me anything! If I'm a middle-class fake white man . . . let me be. And let me be in the way I want. [*Through his teeth*] I'll rip your lousy breasts off! Let me be who I feel like being. Uncle Tom. Thomas. Whoever. It's none of your business. You don't know anything except what's there for you to see. An act. Lies. Device. Not the pure heart, the pumping black heart. You don't ever know that. And I sit here, in this buttoned-up suit, to keep myself from cutting all your throats. I mean wantonly. You great liberated whore! You fuck some black man, and right away you're an expert on black people. What a lotta shit that is. The only thing you know is that you come if he bangs you hard enough. And that's all. The belly rub? You wanted to do the belly rub? Shit, you don't even know how. You don't know how. That ol' dipty-dip shit you do, rolling your ass like an elephant. That's not my kind of belly rub. Belly rub is not Queens.[8] Belly rub is dark places, with big hats and overcoats held up with one arm. Belly rub hates you. Old bald-headed four-eyed ofays popping their fingers . . . and don't know yet what they're doing. They say, "I love Bessie Smith."[9] and don't even understand that Bessie Smith is saying, "Kiss my ass, kiss my black unruly ass." Before love, suffering, desire, anything you can explain, she's saying, and very plainly, "Kiss my black ass." And if you don't know that, it's you that's doing the kissing.

Charlie Parker?[1] Charlie Parker. All the hip white boys scream for Bird. And Bird saying, "Up your ass, feeble-minded ofay! Up your ass." And they sit there talking about the tortured genius of Charlie Parker. Bird would've played not a note of music if he just walked up to East Sixty-seventh Street[2] and killed the first ten white people he saw. Not a note! And I'm the great would-be poet. Yes. That's right! Poet. Some kind of bastard literature . . . all it needs is a simple knife thrust. Just let me bleed you, you loud whore, and one poem vanished. A whole people of neurotics, struggling to keep from being sane. And the only thing that would cure the neurosis would be your murder. Simple as that. I mean if I murdered you, then other white people would begin to understand

---

8. At the time the borough of New York City most representative of middle-class, white, suburban culture.
9. American blues singer (1894–1937) who died of injuries after being refused treatment in a white hospital.

1. American jazz musician (1920–1955) nicknamed "Bird," famous as an innovator of the bebop style.
2. A wealthy, exclusive neighborhood, fifteen blocks north of the Fifty-Second Street jazz clubs in New York City.

me. You understand? No. I guess not. If Bessie Smith had killed some white people she wouldn't have needed that music. She could have talked very straight and plain about the world. No metaphors. No grunts. No wiggles in the dark of her soul. Just straight two and two are four. Money. Power. Luxury. Like that. All of them. Crazy niggers turning their backs on sanity. When all it needs is that simple act. Murder. Just murder! Would make us all sane. [*Suddenly weary*] Ahhh. Shit. But who needs it? I'd rather be a fool. Insane. Safe with my words, and no deaths, and clean, hard thoughts, urging me to new conquests. My people's madness. Hah! That's a laugh. My people. They don't need me to claim them. They got legs and arms of their own. Personal insanities. Mirrors. They don't need all those words. They don't need any defense. But listen, though, one more thing. And you tell this to your father, who's probably the kind of man who needs to know at once. So he can plan ahead. Tell him not to preach so much rationalism and cold logic to these niggers. Let them alone. Let them sing curses at you in code and see your filth as simple lack of style. Don't make the mistake, through some irresponsible surge of Christian charity, of talking too much about the advantages of Western rationalism, or the great intellectual legacy of the white man, or maybe they'll begin to listen. And then, maybe one day, you'll find they actually do understand exactly what you are talking about, all these fantasy people. All these blues people. And on that day, as sure as shit, when you really believe you can "accept" them into your fold, as half-white trusties late of the subject peoples. With no more blues, except the very old ones, and not a watermelon in sight, the great missionary heart will have triumphed, and all of those ex-coons will be stand-up Western men, with eyes for clean hard useful lives, sober, pious and sane, and they'll murder you. They'll murder you, and have very rational explanations. Very much like your own. They'll cut your throats, and drag you out to the edge of your cities so the flesh can fall away from your bones, in sanitary isolation.

LULA [*Her voice takes on a different, more businesslike quality*]   I've heard enough.

CLAY [*Reaching for his books*]   I bet you have. I guess I better collect my stuff and get off this train. Looks like we won't be acting out that little pageant you outlined before.

LULA   No. We won't. You're right about that, at least. [*She turns to look quickly around the rest of the car*] All right! [*The others respond*]

CLAY [*Bending across the girl to retrieve his belongings*]   Sorry, baby, I don't think we could make it. [*As he is bending over her, the girl brings up a small knife and plunges it into* CLAY's *chest. Twice. He slumps across her knees, his mouth working stupidly*]

LULA   Sorry is right. [*Turning to the others in the car who have already gotten up from their seats*] Sorry is the rightest thing you've said. Get this man off me! Hurry, now! [*The others come and drag* CLAY's *body down the aisle*] Open the door and throw his body out. [*They throw him off*] And all of you get off at the next stop. [LULA *busies herself straightening her things. Getting everything in order. She takes out a notebook and makes a quick scribbling note. Drops it in her bag. The train apparently stops and all the others get off, leaving her alone in the coach.*]

Very soon a YOUNG NEGRO of about twenty comes into the coach, with a
couple of books under his arm. He sits a few seats in back of LULA. When
he is seated she turns and gives him a long slow look. He looks up from his
book and drops the book on his lap. Then an OLD NEGRO CONDUCTOR comes
into the car, doing a sort of restrained soft shoe, and half mumbling the
words of some song. He looks at THE YOUNG MAN, briefly, with a quick
greeting]

CONDUCTOR.   Hey, brother!

YOUNG MAN   Hey. [The CONDUCTOR continues down the aisle with his little
dance and the mumbled song. LULA turns to stare at him and follows his
movements down the aisle. The CONDUCTOR tips his hat when he reaches
her seat, and continues out the car]

CURTAIN

1964

An Agony. As Now.

I am inside someone
who hates me. I look
out from his eyes. Smell
what fouled tunes come in
to his breath. Love his   5
wretched women.

Slits in the metal, for sun. Where
my eyes sit turning, at the cool air
the glance of light, or hard flesh
rubbed against me, a woman, a man,   10
without shadow, or voice, or meaning.

This is the enclosure (flesh,
where innocence is a weapon. An
abstraction. Touch. (Not mine,
Or yours, if you are the soul I had   15
and abandoned when I was blind and had
my enemies carry me as a dead man
(if he is beautiful, or pitied.

It can be pain. (As now, as all his
flesh hurts me.) It can be that. Or   20
pain. As when she ran from me into
that forest.
          Or pain, the mind
silver spiraled whirled against the
sun, higher than even old men thought   25
God would be. Or pain. And the other. The
yes. (Inside his books, his fingers. They
are withered yellow flowers and were never

beautiful.) The yes. You will, lost soul, say
'beauty.' Beauty, practiced, as the tree. The   30
slow river. A white sun in its wet sentences.

Or, the cold men in their gale. Ecstasy. Flesh
or soul. The yes. (Their robes blown. Their bowls
empty. They chant at my heels, not at yours.) Flesh
or soul, as corrupt. Where the answer moves too quickly.   35
Where the God is a self, after all.)

Cold air blown through narrow blind eyes. Flesh,
white hot metal. Glows as the day with its sun.
It is a human love, I live inside. A bony skeleton
you recognize as words or simple feeling.   40

But it has no feeling. As the metal, is hot, it is not,
given to love.

It burns the thing
inside it. And that thing
screams.   45

1964

A Poem for Willie Best[1]

I

The face sings, alone
at the top
           of the body. All
flesh, all song, aligned. For hell
is silent, at those cracked lips   5
flakes of skin and mind
twist and whistle softly
as they fall.
           It was your own death
you saw. Your own face, stiff   10
and raw. This
without sound, or
movement. Sweet afton, the
dead beggar bleeds
yet. His blood, for a time   15
alive, and huddled in a door
way, struggling to sing. Rain
washes it into cracks. Pits
whose bottoms are famous. Whose sides
are innocent broadcasts   20
of another life.

---

1. Willie Best was a negro character actor whose Hollywood name was Sleep'n'eat [Baraka's note].

II

At this point, neither
front nor back. A point, the
dimensionless line. The top
of a head, seen from Christ's   25
heaven, stripped of history
or desire.
               Fixed, perpendicular
to shadow. (Even speech, vertical,
leaves no trace. Born in to death   30
held fast to it, where
the lover spreads his arms, the line
he makes to threaten Gods with history.
The fingers stretch to emptiness. At
each point, after flesh, even light   35
is speculation. But an end, his end,
failing a beginning.

2

A cross. The gesture, symbol, line
arms held stiff, nailed stiff, with
no sign, of what gave them strength.   40
The point, become a line, a cross, or
the man, and his material, driven in
the ground. If the head rolls back
and the mouth opens, screamed into
existence, there will be perhaps   45
only the slightest hint of movement
a smear; no help will come. No one
will turn to that station again.

III

At a cross roads, sits the
player. No drum, no umbrella, even   50
though it's raining. Again, and we
are somehow less miserable because
here is a hero, used to being wet.
One road is where you are standing now
(reading this, the other, crosses then   55
rushes into a wood.
                   5 lbs neckbones.
                   5 lbs hog innards.
                   10 bottles cheap wine.
                                   (the contents   60
of a paper bag, also shoes, with holes
for the big toe, and several rusted
knives. This is a literature, of
symbols. And it is his gift, as the
bag is.   65

(The contents
again, holy saviours,
                    300 men on horseback
                    75 bibles
                    the quietness   70
of a field. A rich
man, though wet through
by the rain.
            I said,
                    47 howitzers   75
                    7 polished horse jaws
                    a few trees being waved
softly back under
the black night
                    All this should be   80
invested.

IV

Where
ever,
        he has gone. Who ever
mourns   85
or sits silent
to remember

There is nothing of pity
here. Nothing
of sympathy.   90

V

This is the dance of the raised
leg. Of the hand on the knee
quickly.
            As a dance it punishes
speech. 'The house burned. The   95
old man killed.'
                As a dance it
is obscure.

VI

This is the song
of the highest C.   100
                    The falsetto. An elegance
that punishes silence. This is the song
of the toes pointed inward, the arms swung, the
hips, moved, for fucking, slow, from side
to side. He is quoted   105
saying, "My father was

never a jockey,
                but
    he did teach me
                    how to ride."   110

VII

The balance.
                (Rushed in, swarmed of dark, cloaks,
and only red lights pushed a message
to the street. Rub.
                    This is the lady,   115
I saw you with.
This is your mother.
This is the lady I wanted
some how to sleep with.
                    As a dance, or   120
our elegant song. Sun red and grown
from trees, fences, mud roads in dried out
river beds. This is for me, with no God
but what is given. Give me
                      Something more   125
than what is here. I must tell you
my body hurts.

The balance.
                  Can you hear? Here
I am again. Your boy, dynamite. Can   130
you hear? My soul is moved. The soul
you gave me. I say, my soul, and it
is moved. That soul
you gave me.
                  Yes, I'm sure   135
this is the lady. You
slept with her. Witness, your boy,
here, dynamite. Hear?
                  I mean
can you?   140
The balance.
                He was tired of losing. (And
his walking buddies tired
of walking.
                Bent slightly,   145
at the waist. Left hand low, to flick
quick showy jabs ala Sugar.[2] The right
cocked, to complete,
                  any combination.
                He was   150
tired of losing, but he was fighting
a big dumb "farmer."
                Such a blue bright

---

2. Sugar Ray Robinson, a boxer.

afternoon, and only a few hundred yards
from the beach. He said, I'm tired   155
of losing.
            "I *got* ta cut'cha."

VIII

A renegade
behind the mask. And even
the mask, a renegade   160
disguise. Black skin
and hanging lip.
                        Lazy
                        Frightened
                        Thieving   165
                        Very potent sexually
                        Scars
                        Generally inferior
                                    (but natural
rhythms.   170

His head is
at the window. The only
part
        that sings.
(The word he used   175
            (we are passing St. Mark's place
            and those crazy jews who fuck)
                                        to provoke
in neon, still useful
in the rain,   180
            to provoke
some meaning, where before
there was only hell. I said
silence, at his huddled blood.
                        It is an obscene invention.   185
                        A white sticky discharge.
                        "Jism," in white chalk
                        on the back of Angel's garage.
                        Red jackets with the head of
                        Hobbes[3] staring into space. "Jasm"   190
                        the name the leader took, had it
                        stenciled on his chest.
                                        And he sits
wet at the crossroads, remembering distinctly
each weightless face that eases by. (Sun at   195
the back door, and that hideous mindless grin.
                                    (Hear?

                                                        1964

---

3. Thomas Hobbes (1588–1679), English philosopher who believed a "social contract" was necessary between rulers and the ruled. Here he
represents the Western, white, materialist tradition.

Will They Cry When You're Gone, You Bet

You leave dead friends in
a desert. But they've deserted
you, and them-
selves, and are leaving
themselves,   5
in the foot paths
of madmen and saints
enough sense to get away
from the dryness and uselessness
of such relaxation, dying in the dry   10
light, sand packed in their mouths
eyes burning, white women serenade them
in mystic deviousness, which is another
way of saying they're seeing things, which
are not really there, except for them,   15
never to find an oasis, even bitter water
which we get used to, is better than
white drifting fairies, muses, singing
to us, in calm tones, about how it is better to die
etcetera, than go off from them, how it is better to   20
lie in the cruel sun with your eyes turning to dunes
than leave them alone in that white heat,

1969

N. SCOTT MOMADAY
b. 1934

"In a certain sense," writes N. Scott Momaday in *The Man Made of Words*, "we are all made of words; . . . our most essential being consists in language. It is the element in which we think and dream and act, in which we live our daily lives." Since the publication of his Pulitzer Prize–winning novel *House Made of Dawn* (1968), Momaday's writing has crossed boundaries of language, form, and genre, thereby creating for Momaday himself, through will and imagination, an American Indian identity in words.

Navarre Scott Momaday was born at the Kiowa and Comanche Indian Hospital in Lawton, Oklahoma, the only child of Al Momaday, a Kiowa, and Natachee Scott, who was part Cherokee. He spent most of his early years in New Mexico and Arizona, moving in 1946 to Jemez Pueblo in New Mexico's Rio Grande Valley. There his parents, both artists and teachers, took jobs at a small day school. Growing up on reservations, including those of the Navajo and the Apache, Momaday experienced the rhythms of traditional tribal life, but saw, too, the changes wrought by postwar material culture, and their human costs—the alcoholism, unemployment, and personal disintegration that mark the life of Abel, the returning veteran in *House Made of Dawn*. Early on, Momaday's mother instilled in him the value of a bicultural education that would open the future without closing off his native heritage. Momaday attended reservation, public, and mission schools, then graduated from military high school in Virginia and the University of New Mexico. He received his Ph.D. in 1963 from Stanford University, where his mentor in American and English literature was the poet and critic Yvor Winters. Since then his teaching career has taken him to Santa Barbara, Berkeley, the University of Moscow, Stanford, and the University of Arizona.

What some scholars call the "Native American Renaissance" is usually said to have begun with the publication of *House Made of Dawn* in 1968 and its reception of the Pulitzer Prize the following year. And, indeed, from 1968 to the present, Native American writers have published a substantial body of fine poetry, fiction, and autobiography, gaining considerable notice both in the United States and abroad.

Over the decades since the publication of *House Made of Dawn,* Momaday has published two more novels, *The Ancient Child* (1989) and *In the Bear's House* (1999); four volumes of poems, *Angle of Geese and Other Poems* (1974), *Before an Old Painting of the Crucifixion, Carmel Mission, June 1960* (1975), and *The Gourd Dancer* (1976); stories and poems in *In the Presence of the Sun* (1992); and three works of autobiography, *The Journey to Tai-me* (1967, privately published), *The Way to Rainy Mountain* (1969), and *The Names: A Memoir* (1976) as well as critical works. His deliberate engagement with a variety of forms—oral and written poetry, prose fiction and nonfiction, autobiography, legend, history, photography, painting—all "forms of discovery," in Winters's words, has helped him to lay claim to his Kiowa past.

Momaday's idea of the past as a journey is consciously expressed in *The Journey of Tai-me.* This work relates the story of the Sun Dance—a ceremony for spiritual guidance and power performed by many Plains Indian groups that his grandmother Aho saw outlawed in the late 1800s—to his revelatory memory on journeying to Oklahoma to see the sacred Tai-me bundle: "I became more keenly aware of myself as someone who had walked through time and in whose blood there is something inestimably old and undying. It was as if I had remembered something that happened two hundred years ago. I meant then to seek after the source of my memory and myself." In *The Way to Rainy Mountain* (1969), Momaday undertakes this search, collecting, with his father as translator, Kiowa tales and myths and clustering them with brief, loose historical commentaries and personal family stories. What seem to be fragments come together in a complex structure—twenty-four "quintessential novels," divided into three sections, framed by poems and prose pieces—that follow the Kiowa from emergence through maturity to decline as a Plains Indian culture. Central to *Rainy Mountain,* and to all of Momaday's writing, is the land, the focal point of memory, the defining place for Kiowa culture. The same rootedness that defines Momaday's ancestors gives his work its conjuring power, a power that comes from distilling in words and pictures, as Momaday writes, "the glare of noon and all the colors of the dawn and dusk."

The text is from *The Way to Rainy Mountain* (1969).

From The Way to Rainy Mountain

Headwaters

Noon in the intermountain plain:
There is scant telling of the marsh—
A log, hollow and weather-stained,
An insect at the mouth, and moss—
Yet waters rise against the roots,   5
Stand brimming to the stalks. What moves?

What moves on this archaic force
Was wild and welling at the source.

Introduction

A single knoll rises out of the plain in Oklahoma, north and west of the Wichita Range. For my people, the Kiowas,[1] it is an old landmark, and they gave it the name Rainy Mountain. The hardest weather in the world is there. Winter brings blizzards, hot tornadic winds arise in the spring, and in summer the prairie is an anvil's edge. The grass turns brittle and brown, and it cracks beneath your feet. There are green belts along the rivers and creeks, linear groves of hickory and pecan, willow and witch hazel. At a distance in July or August the steaming foliage seems almost to writhe in fire. Great green and yellow grasshoppers are everywhere in the tall grass, popping up like corn to sting the flesh, and tortoises crawl about on the red earth, going nowhere in the plenty of time. Loneliness is an aspect of the land. All things in the plain are isolate; there is no confusion of objects in the eye, but *one* hill or *one* tree or *one* man. To look upon that landscape in the early morning, with the sun at your back, is to lose the sense of proportion. Your imagination comes to life, and this, you think, is where Creation was begun.

I returned to Rainy Mountain in July. My grandmother had died in the spring, and I wanted to be at her grave. She had lived to be very old and at last infirm. Her only living daughter was with her when she died, and I was told that in death her face was that of a child.

I like to think of her as a child. When she was born, the Kiowas were living the last great moment of their history. For more than a hundred years they had controlled the open range from the Smoky Hill River to the Red, from the headwaters of the Canadian to the fork of the Arkansas and Cimarron. In alliance with the Comanches, they had ruled the whole of the southern Plains. War was their sacred business, and they were among the finest horsemen the world has ever known. But warfare for the Kiowas was preeminently a matter of disposition rather than of survival, and they never understood the grim, unrelenting advance of the U.S. Cavalry. When at last, divided and ill-provisioned, they were driven onto the Staked Plains in the cold rains of autumn, they fell into panic. In Palo Duro Canyon[2] they abandoned their crucial stores to pillage and had nothing then but their lives. In order to save themselves, they surrendered to the soldiers at Fort Sill[3] and were imprisoned in the old stone corral that now stands as a military museum. My grandmother was spared the humiliation of those high gray walls by eight or ten years, but she must have known from birth the affliction of defeat, the dark brooding of old warriors.

Her name was Aho, and she belonged to the last culture to evolve in North America. Her forebears came down from the high country in western Montana nearly three centuries ago. They were a mountain people, a mysterious tribe of hunters whose language has never been positively classified in any major group. In the late seventeenth century they began a long migration to

---

1. The Kiowa were a mobile hunting and gathering people of the Southern Plains.
2. On the Staked Plains, or the Texas Panhandle, that part of the state jutting north between New

Mexico and Oklahoma.
3. U.S. cavalry fort in Oklahoma and site of the Kiowa-Comanche Agency.

the south and east. It was a journey toward the dawn, and it led to a golden age. Along the way the Kiowas were befriended by the Crows, who gave them the culture and religion of the Plains. They acquired horses, and their ancient nomadic spirit was suddenly free of the ground. They acquired Tai-me,[4] the sacred Sun Dance doll, from that moment the object and symbol of their worship, and so shared in the divinity of the sun. Not least, they acquired the sense of destiny, therefore courage and pride. When they entered upon the southern Plains they had been transformed. No longer were they slaves to the simple necessity of survival; they were a lordly and dangerous society of fighters and thieves, hunters and priests of the sun. According to their origin myth, they entered the world through a hollow log. From one point of view, their migration was the fruit of an old prophecy, for indeed they emerged from a sunless world.

Although my grandmother lived out her long life in the shadow of Rainy Mountain, the immense landscape of the continental interior lay like memory in her blood. She could tell of the Crows, whom she had never seen, and of the Black Hills, where she had never been. I wanted to see in reality what she had seen more perfectly in the mind's eye, and traveled fifteen hundred miles to begin my pilgrimage.

Yellowstone, it seemed to me, was the top of the world, a region of deep lakes and dark timber, canyons and waterfalls. But, beautiful as it is, one might have the sense of confinement there. The skyline in all directions is close at hand, the high wall of the woods and deep cleavages of shade. There is a perfect freedom in the mountains, but it belongs to the eagle and the elk, the badger and the bear. The Kiowas reckoned their stature by the distance they could see, and they were bent and blind in the wilderness.

Descending eastward, the highland meadows are a stairway to the plain. In July the inland slope of the Rockies is luxuriant with flax and buckwheat, stonecrop and larkspur. The earth unfolds and the limit of the land recedes. Clusters of trees, and animals grazing far in the distance, cause the vision to reach away and wonder to build upon the mind. The sun follows a longer course in the day, and the sky is immense beyond all comparison. The great billowing clouds that sail upon it are shadows that move upon the grain like water, dividing light. Farther down, in the land of the Crows and Blackfeet, the plain is yellow. Sweet clover takes hold of the hills and bends upon itself to cover and seal the soil. There the Kiowas paused on their way; they had come to the place where they must change their lives. The sun is at home on the plains. Precisely there does it have the certain character of a god. When the Kiowas came to the land of the Crows, they could see the dark lees of the hills at dawn across the Bighorn River, the profusion of light on the grain shelves, the oldest deity ranging after the solstices. Not yet would they veer southward to the caldron of the land that lay below; they must wean their blood from the northern winter and hold the mountains a while longer in their view. They bore Tai-me in procession to the east.

A dark mist lay over the Black Hills, and the land was like iron. At the top of a ridge I caught sight of Devil's Tower upthrust against the gray sky as if in the birth of time the core of the earth had broken through its crust and

4. The sacred being who aids the Kiowa in times of trouble; this being is embodied in the holy doll central to Kiowa ritual.

the motion of the world was begun. There are things in nature that engender an awful quiet in the heart of man; Devil's Tower is one of them. Two centuries ago, because they could not do otherwise, the Kiowas made a legend at the base of the rock. My grandmother said:

> Eight children were there at play, seven sisters and their brother. Suddenly the boy was struck dumb; he trembled and began to run upon his hands and feet. His fingers became claws, and his body was covered with fur. Directly there was a bear where the boy had been. The sisters were terrified; they ran, and the bear after them. They came to the stump of a great tree, and the tree spoke to them. It bade them climb upon it, and as they did so it began to rise into the air. The bear came to kill them, but they were just beyond its reach. It reared against the tree and scored the bark all around with its claws. The seven sisters were borne into the sky, and they became the stars of the Big Dipper.

From that moment, and so long as the legend lives, the Kiowas have kinsmen in the night sky. Whatever they were in the mountains, they could be no more. However tenuous their well-being, however much they had suffered and would suffer again, they had found a way out of the wilderness.

My grandmother had a reverence for the sun, a holy regard that now is all but gone out of mankind. There was a wariness in her, and an ancient awe. She was a Christian in her later years, but she had come a long way about, and she never forgot her birthright. As a child she had been to the Sun Dances; she had taken part in those annual rites, and by them she had learned the restoration of her people in the presence of Tai-me. She was about seven when the last Kiowa Sun Dance was held in 1887 on the Washita River above Rainy Mountain Creek. The buffalo were gone. In order to consummate the ancient sacrifice—to impale the head of a buffalo bull upon the medicine tree—a delegation of old men journeyed into Texas, there to beg and barter for an animal from the Goodnight herd. She was ten when the Kiowas came together for the last time as a living Sun Dance culture. They could find no buffalo; they had to hang an old hide from the sacred tree. Before the dance could begin, a company of soldiers rode out from Fort Sill under orders to disperse the tribe. Forbidden without cause the essential act of their faith,[5] having seen the wild herds slaughtered and left to rot upon the ground, the Kiowas backed away forever from the medicine tree. That was July 20, 1890, at the great bend of the Washita. My grandmother was there. Without bitterness, and for as long as she lived, she bore a vision of deicide.

Now that I can have her only in memory, I see my grandmother in the several postures that were peculiar to her: standing at the wood stove on a winter morning and turning meat in a great iron skillet; sitting at the south window, bent above her beadwork, and afterwards, when her vision failed, looking down for a long time into the fold of her hands; going out upon a cane, very slowly as she did when the weight of age came upon her; praying. I remember her most often at prayer. She made long, rambling prayers out of suffering and hope, having seen many things. I was never sure that I had the right to hear, so exclusive were they of all mere custom and company.

---

5. From the 1880s on, the U.S. government sought to ban all "heathenish" practices among Native American peoples in a continuing effort to Christianize and "civilize" them.

The last time I saw her she prayed standing by the side of her bed at night, naked to the waist, the light of a kerosene lamp moving upon her dark skin. Her long, black hair, always drawn and braided in the day, lay upon her shoulders and against her breasts like a shawl. I do not speak Kiowa, and I never understood her prayers, but there was something inherently sad in the sound, some merest hesitation upon the syllables of sorrow. She began in a high and descending pitch, exhausting her breath to silence; then again and again—and always the same intensity of effort, of something that is, and is not, like urgency in the human voice. Transported so in the dancing light among the shadows of her room, she seemed beyond the reach of time. But that was illusion; I think I knew then that I should not see her again.

Houses are like sentinels in the plain, old keepers of the weather watch. There, in a very little while, wood takes on the appearance of great age. All colors wear soon away in the wind and rain, and then the wood is burned gray and the grain appears and the nails turn red with rust. The windowpanes are black and opaque; you imagine there is nothing within, and indeed there are many ghosts, bones given up to the land. They stand here and there against the sky, and you approach them for a longer time than you expect. They belong in the distance; it is their domain.

Once there was a lot of sound in my grandmother's house, a lot of coming and going, feasting and talk. The summers there were full of excitement and reunion. The Kiowas are a summer people; they abide the cold and keep to themselves, but when the season turns and the land becomes warm and vital they cannot hold still; an old love of going returns upon them. The aged visitors who came to my grandmother's house when I was a child were made of lean and leather, and they bore themselves upright. They wore great black hats and bright ample shirts that shook in the wind. They rubbed fat upon their hair and wound their braids with strips of colored cloth. Some of them painted their faces and carried the scars of old and cherished enmities. They were an old council of warlords, come to remind and be reminded of who they were. Their wives and daughters served them well. The women might indulge themselves; gossip was at once the mark and compensation of their servitude. They made loud and elaborate talk among themselves, full of jest and gesture, fright and false alarm. They went abroad in fringed and flowered shawls, bright beadwork and German silver. They were at home in the kitchen, and they prepared meals that were banquets.

There were frequent prayer meetings, and great nocturnal feasts. When I was a child I played with my cousins outside, where the lamplight fell upon the ground and the singing of the old people rose up around us and carried away into the darkness. There were a lot of good things to eat, a lot of laughter and surprise. And afterwards, when the quiet returned, I lay down with my grandmother and could hear the frogs away by the river and feel the motion of the air.

Now there is a funeral silence in the rooms, the endless wake of some final word. The walls have closed in upon my grandmother's house. When I returned to it in mourning, I saw for the first time in my life how small it was. It was late at night, and there was a white moon, nearly full. I sat for a long time on the stone steps by the kitchen door. From there I could see out across the land; I could see the long row of trees by the creek, the low light upon the rolling plains, and the stars of the Big Dipper. Once I looked at the moon and caught sight of a strange thing. A cricket had perched upon the handrail, only a few inches away from me. My line of vision was such that the creature filled the moon like a fossil. It had gone there, I thought, to live and die, for there, of all places, was its small definition made whole and eternal. A warm wind rose up and purled like the longing within me.

The next morning I awoke at dawn and went out on the dirt road to Rainy Mountain. It was already hot, and the grasshoppers began to fill the air. Still, it was early in the morning, and the birds sang out of the shadows. The long yellow grass on the mountain shone in the bright light, and a scissortail hied above the land. There, where it ought to be, at the end of a long and legendary way, was my grandmother's grave. Here and there on the dark stones were ancestral names. Looking back once, I saw the mountain and came away.

IV

They lived at first in the mountains. They did not yet know of Tai-me, but this is what they knew: There was a man and his wife. They had a beautiful child, a little girl whom they would not allow to go out of their sight. But one day a friend of the family came and asked if she might take the child outside to play. The mother guessed that would be all right, but she told the friend to leave the child in its cradle and to place the cradle in a tree. While the child was in the tree, a redbird came among the branches. It was not like any bird that you have seen; it was very beautiful, and it did not fly away. It kept still upon a limb, close to the child. After a while the child got out of its cradle and began to climb after the redbird. And at the same time the tree began to grow taller, and the child was borne up into the sky. She was then a woman, and she found herself in a strange place. Instead of a redbird, there was a young man standing before her. The man spoke to her and said: "I have been watching you for a long time, and I knew that I would find a way to bring you here. I have brought you here to be my wife." The woman looked all around; she saw that he was the only living man there. She saw that he was the sun.

There the land itself ascends into the sky. These mountains lie at the top of the continent, and they cast a long rain shadow on the sea of grasses to the east. They arise out of the last North American wilderness, and they have wilderness names: Wasatch, Bitterroot, Bighorn, Wind River.

I have walked in a mountain meadow bright with Indian paintbrush, lupine, and wild buckwheat, and I have seen high in the branches of a lodgepole pine the male pine grosbeak, round and rose-colored, its dark, striped wings nearly invisible in the soft, mottled light. And the uppermost branches of the tree seemed very slowly to ride across the blue sky.

XIII

If an arrow is well made, it will have tooth marks upon it. That is how you know. The Kiowas made fine arrows and straightened them in their teeth. Then they drew them to the bow to see if they were straight. Once there was a man and his wife. They were alone at night in their tipi. By the light of the fire the man was making arrows. After a while he caught sight of something. There was a small opening in the tipi where two hides were sewn together. Someone was there on the outside, looking in. The man went on with his work, but he said to his wife: "Someone is standing outside. Do not be afraid. Let us talk easily, as of ordinary things." He took up an arrow and straightened it in his teeth; then, as it was right for him to do, he drew it to the bow and took aim, first in this direction and then in that. And all the while he was talking, as if to his wife. But this is how he spoke: "I know that you are there on the outside, for I can feel your eyes upon me. If you are a Kiowa, you will understand what I am saying, and you will speak your name." But there was no answer, and the man went on in the same way, pointing the arrow all around. At last his aim fell upon the place where his enemy stood, and he let go of the string. The arrow went straight to the enemy's heart.

The old men were the best arrow-makers, for they could bring time and patience to their craft. The young men—the fighters and hunters—were willing to pay a high price for arrows that were well made.

When my father was a boy, an old man used to come to Mammedaty's[6] house and pay his respects. He was a lean old man in braids and was impressive in his age and bearing. His name was Cheney, and he was an arrowmaker. Every morning, my father tells me, Cheney would paint his wrinkled face, go out, and pray aloud to the rising sun. In my mind I can see that man as if he were there now. I like to watch him as he makes his prayer. I know where he stands and where his voice goes on the rolling grasses and where the sun comes up on the land. There, at dawn, you can feel the silence. It is cold and clear and deep like water. It takes hold of you and will not let you go.

XVII

Bad women are thrown away. Once there was a handsome young man. He was wild and reckless, and the chief talked to the wind about him. After that, the man went hunting. A great whirlwind passed by, and he was blind. The Kiowas have no need

In the Kiowa calendars[7] there is graphic proof that the lives of women were hard, whether they were "bad women" or not. Only the captives, who were slaves, held lower status. During the Sun Dance of 1843, a man stabbed his wife in the breast

6. Momaday's paternal grandfather.
7. The Kiowa recorded their history in pictures that functioned as calendars.

of a blind man; they left him alone with his wife and child. The winter was coming on and food was scarce. In four days the man's wife grew tired of caring for him. A herd of buffalo came near, and the man knew the sound. He asked his wife to hand him a bow and an arrow. "You must tell me," he said, "when the buffalo are directly in front of me." And in that way he killed a bull, but his wife said that he had missed. He asked for another arrow and killed another bull, but again his wife said that he had missed. Now the man was a hunter, and he knew the sound an arrow makes when it strikes home, but he said nothing. Then his wife helped herself to the meat and ran away with her child. The man was blind; he ate grass and kept himself alive. In seven days a band of Kiowas found him and took him to their camp. There in the firelight a woman was telling a story. She told of how her husband had been killed by enemy warriors. The blind man listened, and he knew her voice. That was a bad woman. At sunrise they threw her away.

because she accepted Chief Dohasan's invitation to ride with him in the ceremonial procession. And in the winter of 1851–52, Big Bow stole the wife of a man who was away on a raiding expedition. He brought her to his father's camp and made her wait outside in the bitter cold while he went in to collect his things. But his father knew what was going on, and he held Big Bow and would not let him go. The woman was made to wait in the snow until her feet were frozen.

Mammedaty's grandmother, Kau-au-ointy,[8] *was a Mexican captive, taken from her homeland when she was a child of eight or ten years. I never knew her, but I have been to her grave at Rainy Mountain.*

> KAU-AU-OINTY
> BORN 1834
> DIED 1929
> AT REST

She raised a lot of eyebrows, they say, for she would not play the part of a Kiowa woman. From slavery she rose up to become a figure in the tribe. She owned a great herd of cattle, and she could ride as well as any man. She had blue eyes.

XXIV

East of my grandmother's house, south of the pecan grove, there is buried a woman in a beautiful dress. Mammedaty used to know where she is buried, but now no one knows. If you stand on the front porch of the house and look eastward towards Carnegie, you know that the woman is buried somewhere within the range of your vision. But her grave is unmarked. She was buried in a cabinet, and she wore a beautiful dress.

Aho's high moccasins are made of softest, cream-colored skins. On each instep there is a bright disc of beadwork—an eight-pointed star, red and pale blue on a white field— and there are bands of beadwork at the soles and ankles. The flaps of the leggings are wide and richly ornamented with blue and red and green and white and lavender beads.

---

8. Momaday's great-great grandmother.

How beautiful it was! It was one of those fine buckskin dresses, and it was decorated with elk's teeth and beadwork. That dress is still there, under the ground.

East of my grandmother's house the sun rises out of the plain. Once in his life a man ought to concentrate his mind upon the remembered earth, I believe. He ought to give himself up to a particular landscape in his experience, to look at it from as many angles as he can, to wonder about it, to dwell upon it. He ought to imagine that he touches it with his hands at every season and listens to the sounds that are made upon it. He ought to imagine the creatures there and all the faintest motions of the wind. He ought to recollect the glare of noon and all the colors of the dawn and dusk.

Epilogue

During the first hours after midnight on the morning of November 13, 1833, it seemed that the world was coming to an end. Suddenly the stillness of the night was broken; there were brilliant flashes of light in the sky, light of such intensity that people were awakened by it. With the speed and density of a driving rain, stars were falling in the universe. Some were brighter than Venus; one was said to be as large as the moon.

That most brilliant shower of Leonid meteors has a special place in the memory of the Kiowa people. It is among the earliest entries in the Kiowa calendars, and it marks the beginning as it were of the historical period in the tribal mind. In the preceding year Tai-me had been stolen by a band of Osages, and although it was later returned, the loss was an almost unimaginable tragedy; and in 1837 the Kiowas made the first of their treaties[9] with the United States. The falling stars seemed to image the sudden and violent disintegration of an old order.

But indeed the golden age of the Kiowas had been short-lived, ninety or a hundred years, say, from about 1740. The culture would persist for a while in decline, until about 1875, but then it would be gone, and there would be very little material evidence that it had ever been. Yet it is within the reach of memory still, though tenuously now, and moreover it is even defined in a remarkably rich and living verbal tradition which demands to be preserved for its own sake. The living memory and the verbal tradition which transcends it were brought together for me once and for all in the person of Ko-sahn.

A hundred-year-old woman came to my grandmother's house one afternoon in July. Aho was dead; Mammedaty had died before I was born. There were very few Kiowas left who could remember the Sun Dances; Ko-sahn was one of them; she was a grown woman when my grandparents came into the world. Her body was twisted and her face deeply lined with age. Her thin

---

9. This treaty provided for the passage of settlers through Kiowa and Comanche lands.

white hair was held in place by a cap of black netting, though she wore braids as well, and she had but one eye. She was dressed in the manner of a Kiowa matron, a dark, full-cut dress that reached nearly to the ankles, full, flowing sleeves, and a wide, apron-like sash. She sat on a bench in the arbor so concentrated in her great age that she seemed extraordinarily small. She was quiet for a time—she might almost have been asleep—and then she began to speak and to sing. She spoke of many things, and once she spoke of the Sun Dance:

> My sisters and I were very young; that was a long time ago. Early one morning they came to wake us up. They had brought a great buffalo in from the plain. Everyone went out to see and to pray. We heard a great many voices. One man said that the lodge was almost ready. We were told to go there, and someone gave me a piece of cloth. It was very beautiful. Then I asked what I ought to do with it, and they said that I must tie it to the Tai-me tree. There were other pieces of cloth on the tree, and so I put mine there as well.
>
> When the lodge frame was finished, a woman—sometimes a man— began to sing. It was like this:
>
>> Everything is ready.
>> Now the four societies must go out.
>> They must go out and get the leaves,
>>   the branches for the lodge.
>
> And when the branches were tied in place, again there was singing:
>
>> Let the boys go out.
>> Come on, boys, now we must get the earth.
>
> The boys began to shout. Now they were not just ordinary boys, not all of them; they were those for whom prayers had been made, and they were dressed in different ways. There was an old, old woman. She had something on her back. The boys went out to see. The old woman had a bag full of earth on her back. It was a certain kind of sandy earth. That is what they must have in the lodge. The dancers must dance upon the sandy earth. The old woman held a digging tool in her hand. She turned towards the south and pointed with her lips. It was like a kiss, and she began to sing:
>
>> We have brought the earth.
>> Now it is time to play;
>> As old as I am, I still have the feeling of play.
>
> That was the beginning of the Sun Dance. The dancers treated themselves with buffalo medicine, and slowly they began to take their steps. . . . And all the people were around, and they wore splendid things— beautiful buckskin and beads. The chiefs wore necklaces, and their pendants shone like the sun. There were many people, and oh, it was beautiful! That was the beginning of the Sun Dance. It was all for Tai-me, you know, and it was a long time ago.

It was—all of this and more—a quest, a going forth upon the way to Rainy Mountain. Probably Ko-sahn too is dead now. At times, in the quiet of evening, I think she must have wondered, dreaming, who she was. Was she become in her sleep that old purveyor of the sacred earth, perhaps, that ancient one who, old as she was, still had the feeling of play? And in her mind, at times, did she see the falling stars?

Rainy Mountain Cemetery

Most is your name the name of this dark stone.
Deranged in death, the mind to be inheres
Forever in the nominal unknown,
The wake of nothing audible he hears
Who listens here and now to hear your name.   5

The early sun, red as a hunter's moon,
Runs in the plain. The mountain burns and shines;
And silence is the long approach of noon
Upon the shadow that your name defines—
And death this cold, black density of stone.   10

1969

GERALD VIZENOR
b. 1934

No writer combines Native American materials with contemporary literary strategy more provocatively than does Gerald Vizenor. Born in Minneapolis, Minnesota, of mixed French and Chippewa descent, Vizenor (like many practitioners of innovative writing) has held a wide variety of jobs. With a college education in child development and psychology supplemented by graduate work in anthropology, library science, and Asian studies, he worked professionally in social services and journalism between 1962 and 1967. During these years he began writing in ways quite different from then-current literary practice, transforming the traditional haiku form of Japanese poetry into an evocation of Ojibway songs and stories.

By 1970 he was sufficiently published to win a teaching position at Lake Forest College in Illinois; since then he has taught at other universities, presently at the University of California at Berkeley. Like other writers striving to establish new forms, he pursued publication through small literary presses and via the Fiction Collective, an organization of writers (first based in New York but later shifting to Boulder, Colorado, and points west) who found commercial houses uninterested in publishing experimental work. Where colleagues in the Fiction Collective (such as Clarence Major and Ronald Sukenick) turned to popular culture (including blues music and jazz improvisation) for expressive strategies, Vizenor looked to tribal heritage and practice. Especially valuable were beliefs in narrative as an ongoing process and in the multiform shapes of the trickster character, whose shape-changing and disruptive behavior he found helpful for turning discourse in unconventional directions.

Vizenor's earliest work was in poetry, but his fascination with shape-changing finds its most productive form in fiction. Beginning with *Darkness in Saint Louis Bearheart* (1978) and continuing through *Griever: An American Monkey King in China* (1987),

The Trickster of Liberty (1988), *The Heirs of Columbus* (1991), *Dead Voices* (1992), *Hotline Healers* (1997) and *Chancers* (2000), Vizenor circles the globe and presents a wide variety of protagonists whose one point in common is their success at playing the trickster's role. In tribal lore a trickster disrupts visions of reality to show how much of human existence dwells on the borders, at the crossroads between worlds; exploiting such an ability to straddle borders allows characters to flourish who would otherwise be marginalized out of culturally acknowledged existence. In *Griever* the author employs a variation of this figure from Chinese mythology, the Monkey King, as a way of letting his mixed-blood Native American protagonist overcome the narrowly defined bureaucracy that would otherwise restrict his teaching career and personal life in modern-day China. "Almost Browne" (printed here), portrays a similar figure finding insight in the principle that meaning itself is empty of anything other than what people put into it. Browne's world, therefore, is not meaningless, but rather triumphs as an eminently personal construction, continually reorienting himself to society not to instill an awareness of appropriate behavior but rather to make the disjunction and instability of his own life an acceptable norm. As Vizenor writes in "The People Named the Chippewa" (1984), "The Trickster is comic in the sense that he does not reclaim idealistic ethics, but survives as a part of the natural world; he represents a spiritual balance in a comic drama rather than the romantic eliminations of human contradiction and evil."

The text is that of *Landfill Meditations: Crossblood Stories* (1991).

Almost Browne

Almost Browne was born on the White Earth Indian Reservation in Minnesota. Well, he was *almost* born there; that much is the absolute truth about his birth. Almost, you see, is a crossblood and he was born on the road; his father is tribal and his mother is blonde.

Marthie Jean Peterson and Hare Browne met on the dock at Sugar Bush Lake. He worked for the conservation department on the reservation, and she was there on vacation with her parents. Marthie Jean trusted her heart and proposed in the back of an aluminum boat. Hare was silent, but they were married that year at the end of the wild rice season.

Hare and Marthie had been in the cities over the weekend with her relatives. The men told stories about fish farms, construction, the weather, and automobiles, and the women prepared five meals that were eaten in front of the television set in the amusement room.

Marthie loved fish sticks and baloney, but most of all she loved to eat orange Jell-O with mayonnaise. She had just finished a second bowl when she felt the first birth pain.

"Hare, your son is almost here," she whispered in his ear. Marthie did not want her parents to know about the pain; naturally, they never would have allowed her to return to the reservation in labor.

Marthie never forgot anything; even as a child she could recite the state capitals. She remembered birthdates and presidents, but that afternoon she packed two baloney sandwiches and forgot her purse. She was on the road in labor with no checkbook, no money, no proof of identity. She was in love and trusted her heart.

The leaves had turned earlier than usual that autumn, and the silent crows bounced on the cold black road a few miles this side of the reservation border. Ahead, the red sumac burned on the curve.

Hare was worried that the crows would not move in time, so he slowed down and honked the horn. The crows circled a dead squirrel. He honked again, but the crows were too wise to be threatened. The engine wheezed, lurched three times, and then died on the curve in the light of the sumac.

Almost earned his nickname in the back seat of that seventeen-year-old hatchback; he was born on the road, almost on the reservation. His father pushed the car around the curve, past the crows and red sumac, about a half a mile to a small town. There, closer to the reservation border, he borrowed two gallons of gas from the station manager and hurried to the hospital on the White Earth Reservation.

The hatchback thundered over the unpaved government road; a wild bloom of brown dust covered the birch on the shoulders. The dust shrouded the red arrow to the resort at Sugar Bush Lake. The hospital was located at the end of the road near the federal water tower.

Wolfie Wight, the reservation medical doctor, opened the hatchback and reached into the dust. Her enormous head, wide grin, and hard pink hands frightened the crossblood infant in the back seat.

Almost was covered with dust, darker at birth than he has ever been since then. Wolfie laughed when the child turned white in his first bath. He was weighed and measured, and a tribal nurse listened to his heartbeat. Later, the doctor raised her enormous black fountain pen over the birth certificate and asked the parents, "Where was your child born?"

"White Earth," shouted the father.

"Hatchback?" The doctor smiled.

"White Earth," he answered, uncertain of his rights.

"Hatchback near the reservation?"

"White Earth," said the father a third time.

"Almost White Earth," said the doctor.

"White Earth," he repeated, determined that the birth of his son would be recorded on the reservation. He was born so close to the border, and he never touched the earth outside the reservation.

"Indeed, Almost Browne," said the doctor, and printed that name on the birth certificate. Wolfie recorded the place of birth as "Hatchback at White Earth" and signed the certificate with a flourish. "One more trail-born half-breed with a new name," she told the nurse. The nurse was silent; she resisted medical humor about tribal people.

Almost was born to be a tribal trickster. He learned to walk and talk in the wild brush; he listened to birds, water, lightning, the crack of thunder and ice, the turn of seasons; and he moved with animals in dreams. But he was more at home on cracked polyvinyl chloride in the back seats of cars, a natural outcome of his birth in a used hatchback.

Almost told a blonde anthropologist one summer that he was born in the bottom of a boat and learned how to read in limousines; she was amused and recorded his stories in narrow blue notebooks. They sat in the back seat of an abandoned car.

"I grew up with mongrels," he told the anthropologist. "We lived in seven cars, dead ones, behind the house. One car, the brown one, that was my observatory. That's where I made the summer star charts."

"Indian constellations?" asked the anthropologist.

"Yes, the stars that moved in the sunroof," he explained. "I marked the stars on cards, the bright ones that came into the sunroof got names."

"What were the names?" asked the anthropologist.

"The sunroof stars."

"The names of the constellations?"

"We had nicknames," he answered.

"What were the names?"

"The sunroof charts were like cartoon pictures."

"What names?"

"Moths are on one chart."

"What are the other names?"

"Mosquitoes, white lies, pure gumption, private jones."

"Those are constellations?"

"The sunroof charts are named after my dogs," he said and called the mongrels into the back seat. White Lies licked the blond hair on the arms of the anthropologist.

Almost learned how to read from books that had been burned in a fire at the reservation library. The books were burned on the sides. He read the centers of the pages and imagined the stories from the words that were burned.

Almost had one close friend; his nickname was Drain. They were so close that some people thought they must be brothers. The two were born on the same day near the same town on the reservation border. Drain lived on a farm, the fifth son of white immigrants.

Drain was a reservation consumer, because he believed the stories he heard about the tribe. He became what he heard, and when the old men told him to shout, he shouted; he learned to shout at shadows and thunderstorms.

Almost told stories that made the tribe seem more real; he imagined a trickster world of chance and transformation. Drain listened and consumed the adventures. The two were inseparable; one the crossblood trickster, the other a white consumer. Together, the reservation became their paradise in stories.

Almost never attended school; well, he almost never attended. He lived on the border between two school districts, one white and the other tribal. When he wanted to use the machines in school, the microscopes, lathes, and laboratories, he would attend classes, but not more than two or three times a month. Each school thought he attended the other, and besides, no one cared that much where he lived or what he learned.

Almost learned four natural deals about life from his grandmother; he learned to see the wild world as deals between memories and tribal stories. The first deal, she told him, was chance, where things just happen and that becomes the deal with animals and their languages; words were pictures in the second natural deal; the third deal, she said, was to eat from the real world, not from the pictures on menus; and the last deal, she told him, was to liberate his mind with trickster stories.

"In natural deals," he explained to his best friend, "we act, bargain, agree, deliver, and remember that birds never eat monarchs in our stories."

"What monarchs?" asked Drain.

"The milkweed butterflies."

"So, what's the deal?"

"We're the deal in our stories."

"Some deal," moaned Drain.

"The deal is that whites are fleas and the tribes are the best dealers," said

Almost. "Indians are the tricksters, we are the rabbits, and when we get excited, our ears heat up and the white fleas breed."

Almost converted a reservation station wagon into a bookmobile; he sold books from a rack that unfolded out of the back. The books, however, were not what most people expected, not even in trickster stories, and he needed a loan to expand his business.

"We're almost a bookstore," said Almost.

"Blank books?" shouted Wolfie. "You can't sell books on a reservation, people don't read here, not even blank ones."

"Some of them are burned," said Almost.

"You're crazy, blank and burned books," said the doctor, "but you do have gumption, that much is worth a loan." She polished her black pen on the sleeve of her white coat and signed a check to the crossblood.

Almost the whole truth:

Almost is my name, my real name, believe that or not, because my father ran out of money and then out of gas on the way back. I was born in the back seat of a beatup reservation car, almost white, almost on the reservation, and almost a real person.

White Jaws, the government doctor who got her cold hands on my birth certificate, gave me my name. Imagine, if we had run out of gas ten miles earlier, near a white hospital, my name might be Robert, or how about Truman? Instead, White Jaws made me Almost.

Listen, there must be something to learn in public schools, but not by me. My imagination stopped at the double doors; being inside a school was like a drain on my brain. So, my chance to learn came in bad nature and white books. Not picture nature in a dozen bird names, but road kills, white pine in eagle nests, fleas in rabbit ears, the last green flies in late autumn, and moths that whisper, whisper at the mirror. Nature voices, crows in the poplars, not plastic bird mobiles over a baby crib. So, nature was my big book, imagination was my teacher.

Classrooms were nothing more than parking lots to me, places to park a mind rather than drive a mind wild in the glorious woods, through the dangerous present in the winter when the whole real world struggles to survive. For me, double doors and desks are the end of imagination, the end of animals, the end of nature, and the end of the tribes. I might never have entered the book business if I had been forced to attend a white school.

The truth is, I almost got into the book business before my time. A blonde anthropology student started a library on the reservation and she put me in charge of finding and sorting books. I found hundreds of books that summer, what a great time, books were like chance meetings, but the whole thing burned down before I learned how to read. The anthropologist told me not to use my finger on the page but we never practiced in any real books. She talked and talked and then when the building burned down she drove back home to the city. People always come here with some other place in mind.

Drain, he's my best friend, said it was a good thing the library burned because most of the stuff in there was worthless digest books that nobody wanted to read in the first place. Drain is a white farm kid who lives on the other side of the road, on the white side of the road, outside the reservation. He learned how to read in another language before he went to school.

I actually taught myself how to read with almost whole books, and that's the truth. I'd read with my finger first, word for word out loud right down to the burned parts and then I'd picture the rest, or imagine the rest of the words on the page. The words became more real in my imagination. From the words in pictures I turned back to the words on the center of the page. Finally, I could imagine the words and read the whole page, printed or burned.

Listen, there are words almost everywhere. I realized that in a chance moment. Words are in the air, in our blood, words were always there, way before my burned book collection in the back seat of a car. Words are in snow, trees, leaves, wind, birds, beaver, the sound of ice cracking; words are in fish and mongrels, where they've been since we came to this place with the animals. My winter breath is a word, we are words, real words, and the mongrels are their own words. Words are crossbloods too, almost whole right down to the cold printed page burned on the sides.

Drain never thought about real words because he found them in books, nowhere else. He taught me how to read better, and I showed him how to see real words where we lived, and the words that were burned on the pages of my books. Words burned but never dead. It was my idea to open a bookstore with blank books, a mobile bookstore.

Doctor Wolfie gave us a loan, so we packed up and drove to the city, where we started our blank book business near the university. Drain somehow knew the city like the back of his hand. I told him that was the same as finding words in animals. Everything was almost perfect; we were making good money on the street and going to parties with college students, but then the university police arrested us for false advertising, fraud, and trading on the campus without a permit. The car wasn't registered, and we didn't have a license. I think that was the real problem.

Drain played Indian because the judge said he would drop the charges if we went straight back to the reservation where we belonged and learned a useful trade.

"Almost Browne, that's my real name," I told the judge. "I was almost born in the city." The judge never even smiled. These men who rule words from behind double doors and polished benches miss the best words in the language, they miss the real words. They never hear the real words in court, not even the burned words. No one would ever bring real words to court.

Drain was bold and determined in the city. He drove right onto campus, opened the back of the station wagon, unfolded our book rack, and we were in business. That's how it happened, but the judge was not even listening. Wait, we played a shaman drum tape on a small recorder perched on the top of the car. The tape was old; the sound crackled like a pine fire, we told the judge.

Professor Monte Franzgomery was always there, every day. He would dance a little to the music, and he helped us sell blank books to college students. "Listen to that music," he shouted at the students. "That's real music, ethnic authenticity at the very threshold of civilization." That old professor shouted that we were real too, but we were never sure about him because he talked too much. We knew we were on the threshold of something big when we sold out our whole stock in a week, more than a hundred blank books in a week.

Monte said our blank books made more sense to him than anything he had ever read. This guy was really cracked. Our books were blank except on one page there was an original tribal pictomyth painted by me in green ink, a different pictomyth on a different page in every blank book. Yes, pictomyths, stories that are imagined about a picture, about memories. So, even our blank books had a story. I think those college students were tired of books filled with words behind double doors that never pictured anything. Our blank books said everything, whatever you could imagine in a picture. One pictomyth was almost worth a good story in those days.

Well, we were almost on our way to a fortune at the university when the police burned our blank books. Not really, but a ban on the sale of blank books is almost as bad as burning a book with print.

So, now we're back on the reservation in the mail-order business, a sovereign tribal blank book business in an abandoned car. Our business has been brisk, almost as good as it was at the university; better yet, there's no overhead in the back seat of a station wagon on the reservation. Listen, last week the best edition of our blank books was adopted in a cinema class at the University of California in Santa Cruz. Blank books are real popular on the coast.

Monte promised that he would use our blank books in his seminar on romantic literature. He told a newspaper reporter, when we were arrested, that the pictomyths were a "spontaneous overflow of powerful feelings."

Drain said we should autograph our blank books, a different signature on each book. I told him the pictomyths were enough. No, he said, the consumer wants something new, something different from time to time. The stories in the pictomyths are what's new, I told him. He was right, and we agreed. I made pictures and he signed the books. He even signed the names of tribal leaders, presidents, and famous authors.

Later, we published oversized blank books, and a miniature edition of blank books. Drain bought a new car, we did almost everything with blank books. We even started a blank book library on the reservation, but that's another story for another time.

1991

STEPHEN DIXON
b. 1936

Stephen Dixon's short stories often begin where narratives by others would end. Consider the opening line of "Mac in Love," the first story in his initial collection, *No Relief* (1976): "She said 'You're crazy, Mac,' and shut the door." Or the opening of "14 Stories," the title work of Dixon's 1980 collection: "Eugene Randall held the gun in front of his mouth and fired." Or later in the same volume, where "The Signing" begins: "My wife dies. Now I'm alone. I kiss her hands and leave the hospital room." Each could be the final line of a traditional short story. But for Dixon such lines are beginnings, a challenge to continue writing just where most narratives would stop.

Others of Dixon's stories are even more minimal. Many start with flat, present-tense statements that are immediately modified or retracted. Occasionally the author begins with the conjunction of just two elements, such as a man walking past a window in which he can see a baby being held, out of which he generates a complete narrative. Or Dixon will eliminate expected material, as in his story "Said" (from his 1989 collection *Love and Will*), where *what* the arguing couple actually said is omitted in favor of an all-too-revealing rhythm of "he saids" and "she saids."

The motive for such writing is evident from literary theory of the time, which suggested that even in its great variety fiction had become exhausted. Dixon's inventions show that something can be made of nothing, or almost nothing, and hence that fiction is inexhaustible. Yet, always, Dixon keeps his action strictly within the bounds of recognizable life, as in "Time to Go" (from his 1984 collection of that title; printed here). A parent does not usually accompany a son who is shopping for an engagement present, much less when the engaged couple buys their wedding rings; but what would happen if one did? The presence of the father in this story is typically Dixonesque, for the situation produces inherent complexities far beyond anything extraneous references could add.

Dixon, whose father was a dentist and whose mother worked in interior design, was born and raised in New York City. Unhappy with predental courses at the City College of New York, he switched to a curriculum that prepared him for a reporter's job with a news service in Washington, D.C., where he worked for two years after graduation covering the U.S. Senate and House. Returning to New York, he began writing fiction in the early 1960s, taking numerous diverse jobs (technical writing, department store sales, tour leader, waiter, bartender, school bus driver, artist's model, counterman, dishwasher, radio news editor) to support himself. In 1980 he assumed a professorship in the Writing Seminars at Johns Hopkins University, where he continues to teach. With his wife, Anne Frydman (who teaches and translates Russian), and their two daughters, Dixon maintains a home in Baltimore and summers in Maine, but also keeps an apartment in New York City, an environment still central to his work.

There is an urban energy that propels Dixon's writing well past its minimal needs for subject matter, and this compulsive energy characterizes his novels as well. His first, *Work* (1977), shows a narrator struggling through the rules that complicate his job as a bartender; indeed, the rules themselves structure his narrative. *Too Late* (1978) and *Fall & Rise* (1985) make the most of similarly miniature experiences: protagonists respectively wrought with anxiety following a mate's failure to return home after leaving a movie and journeying through the nighttime city to meet again a woman encountered at a party earlier that evening. Dixon's most developed novels have unusual formats. His massive and multifaceted work *Frog* (1991) treats one character by means of interrelated stories and novels; *Interstate* (1995) comprises eight self-contained narratives, each giving a different version of a terrifying incident during an automobile trip; *Gould* (1996) is a novel in two parts, the first tracing a character's life through the stories of abortions undertaken by women living with him, the second narrating his one relationship that did not result in a terminated pregnancy. *30* (1999) reads as short stories but is subtitled "Pieces of a Novel," Dixon's farewell to his character Gould *I.* (2002) is a novel per se, in which the first person is developed as a protagonist.

Dixon's work has been compared to Samuel Beckett's for his spare, ongoing, self-consuming energy. Yet unlike some of Beckett's abstract situations, Dixon's characters and their problems are quite familiar. Not existing to demonstrate universal philosophical absurdities, they simply wish to avoid mistakes and do as well as they can. They struggle with conditions more suitable for closure than for possibility, and many times their sincerity proves their undoing. Yet they all persist, and in that effort they provide narrative motivation.

The text is the title story in Dixon's 1984 collection *Time to Go*.

Time to Go

My father follows me on the street. He says "Don't go into that store and don't go into the next one you might want to go into either. Go into none, that's what I'm saying." But I stand in front of the door of the jewelry store I heard was the best in the city and am buzzed in. My father's right behind me, and I nod to the guard and say to the saleswoman after she says "Can I help you?" "Yes, I'm looking for a necklace—amber—I mean jade. I always get the two mixed up. But jade's what I want: long-lasting, forever, is the symbol, right? This might sound funny, but I want to present the necklace to my wife-to-be as a prenuptial gift."

"Doesn't sound funny to me and you've come to the right store." She takes out a tray of jade necklaces. All have gold around or in them, and when I ask the price of two of them, are too expensive.

"I don't want any gold in them, except maybe for the clasp, and these are way too expensive for me."

"Much too expensive," my father says.

"I'll show you some a little lower in price."

"Much lower in price," my father says.

"Maybe a little lower than even that," I say.

She puts away the tray she was about to show me and takes out a third tray.

"These seem darker than I want—to go with her blue eyes and kind of pale skin I mean—but how much is this one?"

"You can pick it up," she says. "Jade doesn't bite."

"Just the price," my father says. "But go on, pick it up. You'll see how jade's as cold to feel as it is to look at."

I pick it up. "It feels nice, just the right weight, and seems"—holding it out—"the right size for her neck."

"Is she around my height?"

"Five-five."

"Then exactly my height and this is the size I'd wear."

"I'm sure it's still too expensive for me."

She looks at the tag on it, which seems to be in code: $412 \times T +$. "It goes for three-fifty but I'll make it two-seventy-five for you."

"Way out of my range."

"What is your range?"

"You're going to wind up with crap," my father says, "pure crap. If you have to buy a necklace, go somewhere else. I bet you can get this one for a hundred any other place."

"Around a hundred, hundred-twenty-five," I tell her.

"Let me show you these then."

"Here we go again," my father says.

"I have to get her something, don't I?" I tell him. "And I want to, because she wants something she can always wear, treasure—that'll remind her of me. That's what she said."

"Fine, but what's she getting you?"

"How do I know? I hope nothing. I don't want anything. That's what I told her."

"Oh, you don't want anything to remind you of her?"

"She'll remind me of her. I have her, that's enough, and besides I don't like jewelry."

"You thinkers: all so romantic and impractical. I wouldn't get her anything if she isn't getting you anything. Listen, I like her, don't misunderstand me: she's a fine attractive girl and you couldn't get better if you tried for ten more years. But tit for tat I say. He who gives, receives, and one should be a receiver and giver both."

"You're not getting my point. She wants something and I don't. I accept that and I wish you would."

"Sucker," he says. "All my boys are suckers. None of them took after me."

"Some people might say that was an improvement."

"Stupid people might, just as stupid people might make jokes like you just did. If you took after me you would've been married sooner, had almost grown-up children, a much better job, three times as much income and been much much happier because your happiness would've been going on longer."

"Look at this batch," the saleswoman says, putting another tray of jade necklaces on the counter. I see one I like. A light green, smaller beads, nicely strung with string, no gold on it except the clasp. I hold it up. "I like this one."

"Hedge, hedge," my father says. "Then ask the price and offer her half."

"How much is it?" I ask her.

"A hundred-ten."

"Fifty-five or sixty—quick," my father says.

"Sounds fair, and this is the first one I really feel good about."

"That's the only way to buy. Janine," she says to a younger saleswoman, "would you try this on for this gentleman?"

Janine comes over, smiles and says hello to me, undoes the top two buttons of her blouse and starts on the third.

"It's not necessary," I say.

"Don't worry," the older woman says. "That's as far as I'll let her go for that price."

Janine holds the necklace to her neck and the older woman clasps it behind her. "Feels wonderful," Janine says, rolling the beads between her fingers. "This is the one I'd choose of this box—maybe even out of all the boxes despite the more expensive ones."

"Who are you working for, him or me?"

"No, it really feels great."

"Don't fall for their patter," my father says. "Sixty-five—go no higher. She says seventy-five, say 'Look, I'm a little short what with all my wedding expenses and all, can't you take the sixty-five—the most seventy?' But you got to give them an excuse for accepting your offer, and no crying."

"How much is this one again?" I ask her.

"One-ten," the older woman says, "but I'll make it a hundred."

"That's just fine. I didn't mean to bargain down, but if you say it's a hundred, fine, I'll take it."

"Idiot," my father says. "You could've had it for seventy easy."

"Terrific. Janine, wrap it up special as a prewedding gift. Cash or charge, sir?"

"You'll take a check?"

"Janine, I don't know this guy, so check his references. If they're okay, let him pay by check. Thank you, sir. What about calling Michaels now?" she says to a man at the end of the counter and they go in back. I take out my wallet.

My father sits in a chair next to the guard. "My son," he says to him. "Nothing like me. Never learned anything I ever taught him and I tried hard as I could. He could've been much more successful if he'd listened. But he was stubborn. All my children were stubborn. Neither of my girls had the beauty of their mother and none of my sons the brains of their dad. Health you'd think they'd have had at least, but they didn't even have that. Oh, this one, he's healthy enough—strong as an ox. But two I lost to diseases, boy and a girl, and both in their twenties, which was hard for my wife and I to take, before I went myself. So, there you have it. And I hope his bride likes his present. He's paying enough. Though why he doesn't insist on getting something in return—hint on it at least if he doesn't want to insist—or at least insist her family pay for the wedding, is a mystery as much to you as to me. To everyone including his bride, who I admire—don't think I was just buttering him up there—he says he's too old to have anyone but him pay for the wedding, and she makes it worse by praising him for what she calls his integrity. Make sense to you? Doesn't to me. Since to me integrity is great in its place but is best when it pays. All of which is why I hound him the way I do—for his benefit and his only. So. Think it'll stay as nice out as it is? Ah, what's the difference?"

I get off the train from Baltimore, get on the subway for upper Broadway, suddenly my father's in the car standing beside me. "Welcome home," he says. "You still going through with giving her that present and making the wedding all by yourselves? Anything you say. I won't interfere. I can only tell you once, maybe three times, then you have to finish digging your own grave."

"If that's really the last time, fine by me," and I go back to reading my book.

"Just like when you were a boy. You didn't like what I said, you pretended I wasn't there. But I'm here all right. And the truth is, in spite of all the mistakes you made with your life and are still making, I'm wishing you all the luck in the world. You were okay to me at the end—I won't deny it. I can't—who could I to?—the way you took care of me when I was sick—so I suppose I should be a little better to you now. Am I right? So do you want to be not only family now but good friends? If so, let's shake like friends. We kissed a lot when you were young—in fact, right to when I went and then you to me a few seconds after that, which I don't think if the tables were turned you would've got from me—but for a first time let's just shake."

The car's crowded. Late afternoon Christmas shoppers returning home but not the rush hour riders yet. I'm squeezed right up to him. "Look," I say, "we can talk but don't remind me of how sick you were. I don't want to think of it now. I will say I respected you for a lot of things in your life, especially the way you took the discomfort and pain then, something I told you a number of times but I think you were too out of it to understand me. But you also have to realize, and which I maybe didn't tell you, how much you screwed me up, and I allowed you to screw me up—whatever the causes or combination of them. I've worked out a lot of it, I'll try to work out the rest, but no real complaints from me for anything now for I'm going through absolutely the best time in my life."

"Good, we're friends," and he shakes my hand.

I get off at Magna's stop. Today began my school's winter break. I head for the revolving exit gate at the end of the platform. A boy of about sixteen's between me and the woman exiting in front of him. But he's hesitating, looking around and behind him, at me, the downtown platform across the tracks, the woman who's now through the gate and walking upstairs, back at me sullenly. I don't know whether to walk around him or go to the other end of the platform and the main exit. Maybe I'm wrong. He might just be an angry kid who's hesitating now because he doesn't know which exit to take, this or the main one. I walk past him but keep my eyes on him. As I'm stepping backwards into the gate he turns to me, sticks his left hand into his side jacket pocket and thrusts it at me, clamps his other hand on my shoulder and says "Give me all your money." I say "What? What?" and push backwards and revolve around the gate to the other side and he has to pull his hand away or get it caught between the bars.

"Hey, wait," and he revolves around the gate after me, rips the satchel off my shoulder and runs upstairs. It has the necklace, my writings, student papers, a framed drawing I bought for Magna, some clothing. The boy's already gone. I yell upstairs "Police, police, catch that kid with my satchel—a canvas one," as I chase after him. On the sidewalk I say to that woman "Did you see a boy running past?" and she says "Who?" but he's nowhere around. A police car's across the street and I run to it. The policemen are in a luncheonette waiting for their takeout order. I go in, say "I'm not going to sound sensible to you, believe me, but I was just robbed, he might've had a gun or knife in his pocket, a kid, boy, around sixteen with a gray ski cap on his head with the word 'ski' on it, down in the subway exit there, he took my satchel with some valuable things in it and then ran upstairs. I'm sure if we—" "Come with us," one of them says and we rush outside and are getting in their car when the counterman raps on the luncheonette window and holds up their bag of food. "Later," the policeman shouts out his window as we drive off.

We drive around and don't find the boy. The policeman says "There are so many young thieves wearing the outfit you described. Parka jacket, fancy running sneakers, hat sort of extra tall and squeezed on top, sometimes with a pompom, sometimes not. Tough luck about your necklace and painting though."

"I could've told you," my father says, seated beside me. "Fact is, I told you—a thousand times about how to be wise in New York, but you always got your own ideas. You think I'd ever exit through a revolving gate when there's no token booth there, even in what they call the better days? That's where they leap on you, trap you against the gate on either side or on the stairs leaving it, but you never want to play it safe. Now you've lost everything. Well, you still got your life and it's not that I have no sympathy for you over what happened, but it seems you were almost asking for it it could've been so easily avoided."

"Lay off me, will you? I already feel bad enough." I get out of the car in front of Magna's building. "Thanks, officers."

"As I say," my father says, going in with me, "I can understand how you feel. But this one time, since your life depends on it, I wish you'd learn from your mistake."

I go upstairs and tell Magna about the robbery. My father sits on the daybed she uses as a couch. "Every week closer to the wedding she gets more radiant," he says. "You got yourself one hell of a catch. She's smart, she's good, she has wonderful parents and she's also beautiful. I don't know how you rate it but I'm glad you did."

"It had your special present in it," I tell her, "plus some drawing for you I know he's going to just throw away. I won't tell you what the special gift is. I'll try to get something like it or close to it. God, I could have killed that kid."

"That wouldn't have helped," she says.

"It certainly wouldn't've," my father says. "Because in the process you could've got killed in his place, and those kids always got ones working with them or friends for revenge. This is what I tell you and hope you'll remember for all time: stay out of other people's business, and if something like a robbery happens to you, shut your mouth and give everything you have. Twice I got held up by gunmen in my dental office and both times my advice worked. They not only didn't harm me but gave me back my empty wallet."

Magna and I go to the Marriage License Bureau. The line for applications extends into the hallway. "I hate lines," my father says. "I've always avoided them by calling before to see what time the place opens and then trying to be the first one there."

"It looks like the line for food stamps," the woman in front of us says to her mate.

"To me like the one for Welfare," another woman says.

"Unemployment insurance," Magna says to me. "I've been on them. Didn't want to but had no choice. Have you?"

"Him?" my father says. "Oh, he was too pure to take unemployment. He deserved it too but you know what he did? Refused to even go down to sign up for it. He was living home then and I told him he was crazy. I said 'I always want you to have a job, but if you're fired from one or laid off, well, you paid for that insurance, so take it.' But him? Always too damn pure. That can work against you as much as it can for. Must've got that trait from his mother, because he certainly didn't get that way from me."

"I could have got unemployment a few times," I say to her, "but I always had some money saved and so thought I'd live off it and write at the same time. To sort of use the time break to produce some writing that might earn me some money but not intentionally to make me money—"

"There he goes again with his purity bent. Look, I never encouraged my children to take anything that wasn't theirs. Oh, maybe by my actions I occasionally did, but I never encouraged them personally to take like that. But he wouldn't listen about that insurance. We had terrible fights over it. Of course he never would've had to reject or accept any unemployment insurance if he'd've become the dentist I wanted him to. I pleaded with all my sons to and each one in turn broke my heart. But he out of all of them had the brains and personality for it and he could've worked alongside me for a few years and then bought me out of my practice. I would've even given him the practice for nothing if that's what it took to get him to become a dentist, though with maybe him contributing to my support a little each month, mine and his mother's."

"I wasn't good in the sciences," I say to him. "I told you that and offered my grades as proof over and over again. I used to almost regurgitate every time I went into the chemistry building and biology labs. I tried. I was predent for more than two years."

"Regurgitate. See the words he uses? No, you didn't want to become a dentist because I was one. You wanted to go into the arts. To be an artiste. The intelligentsia you wanted to belong to. Well, now you're able to make a decent living off it teaching, but for how many years you practically starved? You almost broke my heart then, seeing you struggle like that for so long, though you still have time to become one. Dentists average even more money than doctors today."

"Next," the clerk says.

Magna gives her our blood tests results. She gives us the application to fill out.

"Can we come right up to the front of the line after we fill it out?" I say.

"You have to go to the back," she says.

"Why aren't there two lines as there are supposed to be? Why's the other window closed?"

"We're a little shorthanded today. You think I like it? It's double my usual load."

"There are three people typing over there and two putting away things in files. Why not get one of them to man the other window till this line's a little relieved?"

"Shh, don't make trouble," my father says. "You can't avoid the situation, accept it. It's the city."

"I'm not the supervisor," she says, "and the supervisor can't just tell someone to do something when it's not that person's job. Next," she says to the couple behind us.

Magna pulls me away. "Wherever we are," she says, "I can always count on you to try to improve things."

"Am I wrong?"

"You'd think at the Marriage Bureau you'd tone it down a little, but no real harm. It'd be too laughable for us to break up down here."

"He was always like that," my father says. "Always a protester, a rebel. Nothing was ever good enough in life for him. He'd see a Broadway play that maybe the whole world thought was great and which'd win all the prizes, he'd say it could've been much better. Books, politics, his schools, the banks—whatever, always the same. I told him plenty of times to run for mayor of this city, then governor, then president. He never took me seriously. I suppose all that does mean he's thinking or his heart's mostly in the right place, but sometimes he can get rude with people with all those changes of his he wants. He doesn't have the knack to let things roll off him as I did. Maybe that's good. I couldn't live with it if that was me. You'll have troubles with him, young lady."

We go to the Diamond Center for wedding bands. "How'd you find us?" the man behind the counter says.

"We saw all the stores and didn't know which one to choose," I say. "So I asked this man who looked as if he worked in the area 'Any one place carry only gold wedding bands?' He said 'Nat Sisler's,' who I suppose, from the photo there, is you, '4 West, down the middle aisle on the right. There are forty other booths there but you won't miss his. He's got the biggest sign.' "

"Just like me on both my office windows," my father says. "Biggest the city allowed for a dentist. If they'd allowed me to have signs to cover my entire window, I would've."

"Too bad you don't know this man's name," Nat says. "We always like to thank the people who refer customers to us. But he was right. We've nineteen-hundred different rings, so I promise you won't walk away from here without finding one you like. Anything particular you looking for?"

"Something very simple," I say.

He holds up his ring finger. "Nothing more simple and comfortable than this one. I've been wearing it without taking it off once for forty-five years."

"That's amazing," Magna says. "Not once?"

"I can't. I've gained sixty pounds since I got married and my finger's grown around it. Maybe he'll have better luck with his weight. He's so slim now, he probably will."

"More patter," my father says. "Then when you're off-guard they knock you over the head with the price. But remember: this is the Diamond Center. The bargaining's built into the price. Here they think it's almost a crime not to, so this time whatever price he quotes, cut him in half."

"Single or double-ring ceremony?" Nat says.

"Double," Magna says, "and identical rings."

"Better yet," my father says. "For two rings you have even greater bargaining power. Cut him more than half."

Nat brings out a tray of rings. "What do you do?" he asks me. "You look like a doctor."

"I teach at a university."

"So you are a doctor, but of philosophy."

"I barely got my B.A. I write, so I teach writing. She's the doctor of philosophy."

"Oh yeah?" he says while Magna's looking at the rings.

"Turn your ears off," my father says. "Next he's going to tell you you're a handsome couple, how great marriage can be, wish you all the luck and success there is, which you'll need, he'll say—all that stuff. Though they love bargaining down here, they love making money more, so act businesslike. Ask him right off what the price of this is and then that. Tell him it seems high even if you don't think it is. Tell him you're a teacher at the lowest level. Tell him you make almost zero from your writing and that she won't be teaching next year, so you'll have to support you both. Tell him any other time but this you might have the money to pay what he's asking, but now, even if it is something as sacred as marriage, you're going to have to ask him to cut the price more than half. And being there are two rings you're buying—"

"What do you think of this one?" Magna asks me. It looks nice. It fits her finger.

"You have one like this in my size?" I say.

"That's an awfully big finger you have there," Nat says, holding my ring finger up. He puts several ring sizers on my finger before one fits. "Ten and a half. We'd have to make it on order. When's the wedding date?"

"Ask him how much first," my father says, "ask him how much."

"The fourteenth," Magna says. "But I'm sure these will be much higher than we planned to pay."

"That a girl," my father says.

"Hey," I say. "You'll be wearing it every day of your life, you say, so get what you want. I happen to like it."

"How much are they?" she asks Nat.

He puts the ring she wants on a scale. "Seventy-two dollars. Let's say seventy. The professor's, being a much larger size—and they're both seamless, I want you to know. That means they won't break apart unexpectedly and is the best kind of craftsmanship you can get—is eighty-five."

"Sounds okay to me," I say.

"Oh my God," my father says. "I won't even say what I think."

We go to the apartment of a rabbi someone told us about. His wife says "What would you like to drink? We've scotch, vodka, white wine, ginger ale—"

"Scotch on the rocks for me," I say.

"Same for me, thanks," Magna says.

"So," the rabbi says when we all get our drinks, "to your health, a long life, and especially to your marriage," and we click glasses and drink. He shows us the certificate we'll get at the end of the ceremony. "On the cover—I don't know if you can read it—but it says 'marriage' in Hebrew."

"It's a little bit gaudy for me," I say. "You don't have one with fewer frills? Oh, I guess it's not important."

"It is so important," my father says. "That certificate will end up meaning more to you than your license. And it's beautifully designed—good enough to frame and hang—but of course not good enough for you."

"You'll have to provide two glasses for the ceremony," the rabbi says. "One with the red wine in it you'll both be drinking from."

"Dry or sweet?" Magna says.

"What a question," my father says. "Sweet, sweet."

"Whichever you choose," the rabbi says. "You'll be the ones drinking it."

"A modern rabbi," my father says. "Well, better than a modern judge. Ask him what synagogue he represents."

"By the way," I say, "do you have a congregation? George said he thought you'd given that up."

"Right now," he says, "I'm marketing a wonderful little device that could save the country about five hundred thousand barrels of oil a month, if the public would just accept it. I got tired of preaching, but I'll get back to it one day."

"What he's not saying," his wife says, "is that this gadget will only cost three and a half dollars retail, plus a slight installation fee, and will save every apartment and home owner about fifty dollars a month during the winter. The oil companies hate him for it."

"I wouldn't go that far," he says, "but I will say I haven't made any friends in the oil industry. But the effectiveness of the device has been proven, it'll last without repairs for up to fifteen years, and someone has to market it, so it's almost been like a crusade with me to get it into every oil user's home. Wait, I'll show it to you."

"Wait'll he comes around to telling you the cost of his ceremony," my father says.

"The other glass," I say, after we've passed the device around. "Is that the one I'm supposed to break with my foot?"

"Scott has the most brilliant interpretation of it during the ceremony you'll ever want to hear," his wife says. "I've heard it a dozen times and each time I'm completely absorbed. Actually, except for the exchange of vows, I'd call it the highlight of the ceremony."

"Would you mind if we don't have the breaking of the glass? We've already decided on this. To us it represents the breaking of the hymen—"

"That's just one interpretation," he says, "and not the one I give. Mine's about the destruction of the temples and other things. I use biblical quotes."

"Wait wait wait," my father says. "Did I hear you don't want to break the glass?"

"It's also just a bit too theatrical for me," I say to the rabbi. "Just isn't my style."

"Isn't your style?" my father says. "It goes back two thousand years—maybe even three. You have to break the glass. I did with your mother and her father and mine with our mothers and their fathers with our grandmothers and so on. A marriage isn't a marriage without it. It's the one thing you have to do for me of anything I ask."

"I can wrap a lightbulb in newspaper if it's only that you're concerned a regular glass might cut your foot," the rabbi says. "But if you don't want it."

"If they don't, they don't," his wife says.

"We don't," Magna says, "but thank you."

"Then no second glass," he says. "It's your day."

"That's it," my father says. "Now you've really made me mad. That she's on your side in this—well, you must've forced it on her. Or maybe not. Anyway, I'm tired of complaining. From the man's point you'll be missing the best part of the ceremony, not the second best. I won't even begin to advise you about anything about the rabbi's fee."

"I know what your advice will be," I say, "and I don't want to bargain with him, is that so bad? Because what's he going to charge—a hundred-fifty? two hundred? So how much can I cut off it—fifty, seventy-five? What's fifty anyway? What's a hundred? And he's a professional. A professional should not only do his work well but know what to charge. You always let your patients cut your dental fees in half?"

"If I thought they'd go somewhere else, sure. Because if I wasn't working on them I'd be sitting around earning nothing in that time. But if your rabbi asks four hundred?"

"He won't. You can see he's a fair guy. And I'm not a complete jerk. If I think his fee's way out of line, I'll tell him."

"That's not the way to do it, but do what you want. I've said it a hundred times to you and now I'll say it a last time. Do what you want because you will anyway. But I'll tell you something else. Your mother didn't give you three thousand dollars of my insurance policy benefit to just piss away."

"That money was nine years ago. I didn't ask for a cent of it but she thought I deserved it because of the four years I helped her with you. And I used it to good purpose. I lived off it and worked hard on what I wanted to work on for one entire year."

"Oh, just pay anything he asks no matter how high. In fact, when he says his fee, say 'No, it's too little,' and double him. That's the kind of schmo I sometimes think you can be."

We're being married in Magna's apartment. The rabbi's talking about what the sharing of the wine means. My mother's there. My brother and sister and their spouses. My nieces and an uncle and aunt. Magna's parents and cousins and her uncle and aunts. A few of our friends and their children. My father. He looks tired and ill. He's dressed for the wedding, has on his best suit, though it needs to be pressed. He sits down on the piano bench he's so tired. The rabbi pronounces us married. I'm crying. Magna smiles and starts to cry. My mother says "What is this? You're not supposed to be crying, but go ahead. Tears of happiness."

"Kiss the bride," my sister says. I kiss Magna. Then I kiss my mother and Magna's mother and shake Magna's father's hand while I kiss his cheek. I kiss Magna again and then my sister and brother and brother's wife and my nieces and aunt and uncle and Magna's aunts and uncle. Then our friends and Magna's female cousin and I shake the hand of her male cousin and say "Oh what the hell," and kiss his cheek and the cheek of my sister's husband and the rabbi's cheek too. I look over to the bench. My father's crying. His head's bent way over and he dabs his eyes with old tissues. He starts making loud sobbing noises. "Excuse me," I say and I go over to him, get on my knees, put my arms around his lower legs and my head on his thighs. He's sitting up straight now and pats my head. "My boy," he says. "You're a good sweet kid. I'm actually having a great time. And there was no real harm meant between us and never was, am I right? Sure, we got angry as hell at one another lots of times, but I've always had a special feeling for you deep down. It's true, you don't have to believe me, but it's true. And I'm so happy for you. I'm crying because I'm that happy. I'm also crying because I think it's wonderful you're all together today and so happy, and I'm glad I'm here. Your other sister and brother, it'd be grand if they were here too." I look around for them. "Maybe they couldn't find the right clothes," I say. I get on one knee and hug him with my cheek pressed against his and then he disappears.

1984

RUDOLFO A. ANAYA
b. 1937

Llano is the Spanish adjective meaning "plain, simple, even, smooth, level"; as a noun, its feminine form (*llana*) indicates a "mason's trowel," while the masculine, *llano*, describes the condition of plain, flat ground. It was in the village of Pastura, on the eastern *llanos* of New Mexico, that Rudolfo Anaya was born on October 30, 1937. This high, arid, windy landscape figures in much of Anaya's fiction, suggesting the way that nature's trowel works incessantly to level out human effort. As a Hispanic American, the author can trace his ancestry back through four centuries of activity in this region. As critic Margarite Fernández Olmos indicates, his parents' backgrounds combined both sides of the region's rural life: his mother's family were farmers growing crops and raising pigs, sheep, and cows in the Puerto de Luna valley, while his father was a free-ranging *vaquero*, a cowboy whose own family tradition was to work with cattle herds in the open rather than settling the land. After Anaya's father was killed in an accident, his mother married another *vaquero*, who helped raise his step-son with an understanding of both farming and ranching lifestyles. When still a small child, Anaya moved with his family to the town of Santa Rosa, New Mexico—"the social hub of the surrounding rural communities," as Olmos describes it, where on busy Highway 66 Anaya could witness the transcontinental link between East Coast and West Coast cultures. Yet the nearby Pescos River and its opportunities for hunting and fishing let the author grow up in close proximity to nature, an experience he would appreciate for its spiritual dimensions. By age fifteen, he and his family joined the urban migration that had begun in the years following World War II and moved to a *barrio* (Hispanic neighborhood) in Albuquerque. Here he learned the ways of big cities, another influence on his subsequent fiction. But it was an accident more typical of rural life that directed his interests to literature: while diving into an irrigation ditch that he and his friends were using as a swimming hole, Anaya fractured two vertebrae in his neck and spent much of his seventeenth year recovering in a world of books and meditation. After a false start in business school, he became an English major at the University of New Mexico, where he began writing fiction (for himself) and went on to earn two M.A. degrees in English and in counseling, allowing him to work as a high school teacher and guidance counselor.

Bless Me, Ultima (1972) was Anaya's first novel, published to acclaim within the just-emerging network of the Chicano arts movement that would eventually include recognition of such writers as Rolando Hinjosa, Estella Portillo, Bernice Zamora, and Ricardo Sánchez. As a result of its success, Anaya was appointed to a professorship at the University of New Mexico, where he taught until achieving emeritus status in 1993. In the novel, Ultima is a practitioner of folk-healing arts developed by women who serves as mentor to the boy Antonio, who in the coming-of-age tradition of the *bildingsroman* (*David Copperfield, A Portrait of the Artist as a Young Man, The Magic Mountain*) must make the choices that will define his adult life. In Antonio's case, these conflicts reflect the alternatives of Anaya's own boyhood: farming one's land or wandering as a *vaquero*, taking one's cultural lead from the Hispanic or the Anglo, and sorting out the gender biases in competing systems of religious belief. *Heart of Aztlán* (1976) and *Tortuga* (1979) complete what critics describe as Anaya's initial Chicano trilogy of novels, as the narrative action shifts from the countryside to the city and then to the experiences of a teenager recovering from a paralyzing accident. In all three works the author blends the modern with the ancient, the formalities of culture with folklorish roots, and the plainly discursive with the richly allegorical, producing narratives that proceed on many different levels all at one time.

"The Christmas Play," collected in *The Silence of the Llano* (1982), displays Anaya's characteristic literary techniques, including the mix of Hispanic and Anglo references that helps create the Chicano experience—a condition of living in the borderland area that until 1848 was part of Mexico and that today retains many aspects of Mexican culture, including the Hispanic, Indian, and *mestizo* (mixed race). In recent years his writing has expanded from autobiography to a more general social vision of Chicano life. *Alburquque* (1992)—the title reflects the original spelling of the city—follows the quest of a young boxer who must look beyond his adoptive family to finds his roots. With *Zia Summer* (1995) Anaya writes a full-fledged detective novel, introducing a private eye named Sonny Baca who seeks the murderer of a prominent politician's wife by sorting through the type of social and ethnic issues the author had treated previously in a more personal manner.

Other Sonny Baca novels have followed, all of them set in the city that he continues to name according to its original Spanish spelling, a reminder of how far the largest city in New Mexico has come from its days as a frontier outpost (while retaining its mix of Spanish, Native American, and *mestizo* cultures).

The text is from Anaya's *The Silence of the Llano* (1982).

The Christmas Play

It was the day before Christmas vacation and the schoolhouse was quiet, like a tomb frozen by winter. The buses didn't come in because of the blizzard, and even most of the town kids stayed home. But Horse and Bones and the rest of the gang from Los Jaros were there. They were the dumbest kids in school, but they never missed a single day. Hell could freeze over but they would still come marching across the tracks, wrestling, kicking at each other, stomping into the classrooms where they fidgeted nervously all day and made things miserable for their teachers.

"Where are the girls?" Bones sniffed the wind wildly and plunked into a frozen desk.

"They didn't come," I answered.

"Why?"

"¡Chingada!"[1]

"What about the play?"

"I don't know," I said and pointed to the hall where Miss Violet conferred with the other teachers who had come to school. They all wore their sweaters and shivered. Downstairs the furnace groaned and made the steam radiators ping, but it was still cold.

"No play. Shit!" Abel groaned.

Miss Violet came in. "What did you say, Abel?"

"No play. Shucks."

"We can still have a play." Miss Violet sat down and we gathered around her. "If the boys play the parts. . . ."

We all looked at each other. The girls had set up all the stuff in the auditorium; and they had, with Miss Violet's help, composed the story about the Three Wise Men. Originally we just stood around and acted like shepherds, but now we would have to do everything because the girls stayed home.

"Yeahhhhhh!" Horse breathed on Miss Violet.

"The other teachers don't have much to do, with so many kids absent," she turned away from the inquisitive Horse, "and they would like to come to our play. . . ."

"Aghhhh, nooooo," Bones growled.

"We have to read all the parts," Lloyd said. He was carefully picking at his nose.

"We could practice all morning," Miss Violet said. She looked at me.

"I think it's a great idea," Red nodded his head vigorously. He always tried to help the teacher.

"¡A la veca!"[2]

"What does that mean?" Miss Violet asked.

"It means okay!"

So the rest of the morning we sat around reading the parts for the play. It was hard because the kids from Los Jaros couldn't read. After lunch we went to the auditorium for one quick practice before the other teachers came in with their classes. Being on stage scared us and some of the boys began to back down. Bones climbed up a stage rope and perched on a beam near the ceiling. He refused to come down and be in the play.

---

1. Fucker (Spanish).   2. Okay (Spanish).

"Booooooooo-enz!" Miss Violet called. "Come down!"

Bones snapped down at her like a cornered dog. "The play is for sissies!" he shouted.

Horse threw a chunk of two-by-four at him and almost clobbered him. The board fell and hit the Kid and knocked him out cold. It was funny because although he turned white and was out, his legs kept going, like he was racing someone across the bridge. Miss Violet worked frantically to revive him. She was very worried.

"Here." Red had gone for water which he splashed on the Kid's face. The Kid groaned and opened his eyes.

"¡Cabrón Caballo!"³ he cursed.

The rest of us were either putting on the silly robes and towels to make us look like shepherds, or wandering around the stage. Someone tipped the Christ Child over and it lost its head.

"There ain't no such thing as virgin birth," Florence said, looking down at the decapitated doll. He looked like a madman, with his long legs sticking out beneath the short robe and his head wound in a turban.

"You're all a bunch of sissies!" Bones shouted from above. Horse aimed the two-by-four again but Miss Violet stopped him in time.

"Go put the head on the doll," she said.

"I gotta go to the bathroom," Abel said. He held the front of his pants.

Miss Violet nodded her head slowly, closed her eyes and said, "No."

"You could be sued for not letting him go," Lloyd said in his girlish voice. He was chewing a Tootsie Roll. Chocolate dripped down the sides of his mouth and made him look evil.

"I could be tried for murder!" Miss Violet reached for Lloyd, but he ducked and disappeared behind one of the cardboard cows by the manger.

"Come on you guys, let's cooperate!" Red shouted. He had been busy trying to get everyone to stand in their places. We had decided to make everyone stand in one place during the play. It would be easier that way. Only the kings would step forth to the manger and offer their gifts.

"Places! Places!" Miss Violet shouted. "Joseph?" she called and I stepped forward. "Mary?" Who is Mary?"

"Horse!" Red answered.

"No! No! No!" Horse cried. We chased him down on the stage and knocked over a lot of props, but we finally got the beautiful robe on him.

"Horse is a virgin!" Bones called.

"Aghhhhh! ¡Cabrón!"⁴ Horse started up the rope but we pulled him down.

"Horse! Horse!" Miss Violet tried to subdue him. "It's only for a little while. And no one will know. Here." She put a heavy veil on his head and tied it around his face so that it covered all except his eyes.

"Naggggggh!" Horse screamed. It was awful to hear him cry, like he was in pain.

"I'll give you an A," Miss Violet said in exasperation. That made Horse think. He had never gotten an A in anything in his life.

"An A," he muttered, his large horse jaws working as he weighed the disgrace of his role for the grade. "Okay," he said finally, "Okay. But remember, you said an A."

"I'll be your witness," Lloyd said from behind the cow.

---

3. Fag horse (Spanish).   4. Fag (Spanish).

"Horse is a virgin!" Bones sang, and Horse quit the job and we had to persuade him all over again.

"Bones is just jealous," Red convinced him.

"Come down!" Miss Violet yelled at Bones.

"Gimme an A," Bones growled.

"All right," she agreed.

He thought awhile, then yelled, "No, gimme two A's!"

"Go to. . . ." She stopped herself and said, "Stay up there. But if you fall and break your neck it's not my fault!"

"You could be sued by his family for saying that," Lloyd said. He wiped his mouth and the chocolate spread all over his face.

"I got to pee. . . ." Abel groaned.

"Horse, kneel here." Horse was to kneel by the manger and I stood at his side, with one hand on his shoulder. When I put my arm around his shoulder, Horse's lips sputtered and I thought he would bolt. His big horse-eyes looked up at me nervously. One of the cardboard donkeys kept tipping over and hitting Horse; this only served to make him more nervous. Some of the kids were stationed behind the cardboard animals to keep them up, and they giggled and kept looking around the edges at each other. They started a spit-wad game and that made Miss Violet angry.

"Please behave!" she shouted, "pleeeeeeee-z!" The Vitamin Kid had recovered and was running around the stage. She collared him and made him stand in one spot. "Kings here," she said. I guess someone had put the robe on the Kid when he was knocked out, because otherwise no one could have held him long enough to slip the robe on.

"Does everybody have copies of the play?" Red shouted. "If you have to look at the lines, keep the script hidden so the audience doesn't see. . . ."

"I can seeeeeee. . . ." It was Bones. He leaned to look down at Florence's copy of the play and almost fell off the rafter. We all gasped, but he recovered. Then he bragged, "Tarzuuuuuuun, king of the jungle!" And he started calling elephants like Tarzan does in the movie, "Aghhh-uhhhh-uhhhh-uhhhhhhhhh. . . ."

"¡Cabrón!"

"¡Chingada!"

Everyone was laughing.

"Bones," Miss Violet pleaded. I thought she was going to cry. "Please come down."

"I ain't no sissy!" he snarled.

"You know, I'm going to have to report you to the principal. . . ."

Bones laughed. He had been spanked so many times by the principal that it didn't mean anything anymore. They had become almost like friends, or like enemies who respected each other. Now when Bones was sent in for misbehaving he said the principal just made him sit. Then, Bones said, the principal very slowly lit a cigarette and smoked it, blowing rings of smoke in Bones' face all the while. Bones liked it. I guess they both got a satisfaction out of it. When the cigarette was gone and its light crushed in the ashtray, Bones was excused. Then Bones went back to the room and told the teacher he had really gotten it this time and he promised to be a good boy and not break any rules. But five minutes later he broke a rule, and of course he couldn't help it because they said his brother who worked at the meat market had brought Bones up on raw meat.

"I ain't got page five," Abel cried. His face was red and he looked sick.

"You don't need page five, your lines are on page two," Red told him. He was very good about helping Miss Violet; I only wished I could help more. But the kids wouldn't listen to me because I wasn't big like Red, and besides there I was stuck with my arm around Horse.

"Florence by the light. . . ." Tall, angelic Florence moved under the light bulb that was the star of the east. When the rest of the lights were turned off the light bulb behind Florence would be the only light. "Watch your head. . . ."

"Everybody ready?" The three wise men were ready. Samuel, Florence, and the Kid. Horse and I were ready. The fellows holding up the cardboard animals were ready, and Red was ready.

"Here they come," Miss Violet whispered. She stepped into the wings.

I glanced up and saw the screaming horde of first graders rushing down the aisle to sit in the front rows. The fourth and fifth graders sat behind them. Their teachers looked at the stage, shook their heads and left, closing the doors behind them. The audience was all ours.

"I got to pee," Abel whispered.

"Shhhhhh," Miss Violet coaxed, "everybody quiet." She hit the light switch and the auditorium darkened. Only the star of the east shone on the stage. Miss Violet whispered for Red to begin. He stepped to the center of the stage and began his narration.

"**The First Christmas!**" he announced loudly. He was a good reader.

"Hey, it's Red!" someone in the audience shouted, and everybody giggled. I'm sure Red blushed, but he went on; he wasn't ashamed of stuff like that.

"I got to . . ." Abel moaned.

Lloyd began to unwrap another Tootsie Roll and the cow he was holding teetered. "The cow's moving," someone in the first row whispered. Horse glanced nervously behind me. I was afraid he would run. He was trembling.

". . . And they were led by the star of the east . . ." and here Red pointed to the light bulb. The kids went wild with laughter. ". . . So they journeyed that cold night until they came to the town of Bethlehem. . . ."

"Abel peed!" Bones called from above. We turned and saw the light of the east reflecting off a golden pool at Abel's feet. Abel looked relieved.

"¡A la veca!"

"¡Puto!"[5]

"How nasty," Lloyd scoffed. He turned and spit a mouthful of chewed-up Tootsie Roll. It landed on Maxie who was holding up a cardboard donkey behind us.

Maxie got up, cleaning himself. The donkey toppled over. "¡Jodido!"[6] he cursed Lloyd and shoved him. Lloyd fell over his cow.

"You could be sued for that," he threatened from the floor.

"Boys! Boys!" Miss Violet called excitedly from the dark.

I felt Horse's head tossing at the excitement. I clamped my arms down to hold him, and he bit my hand.

"¡Ay!"

---

5. Fag (Spanish).   6. Fucker (Spanish).

"... And there in a manger, they found the babe. ..." Red turned and nodded for me to speak.

"I am Joseph!" I said as loud as I could, trying to ignore the sting of the horse bite, "and this is the baby's mother. ..."

"Damn you!" Horse cursed when I said that. He jumped up and let me have a hard fist in the face.

"It's Horse!" the audience squealed. He had dropped the veil, and he stood there trembling, like a trapped animal.

"Horse the virgin!" Bones called.

"Boys, Bowoooo-oizz!" Miss Violet pleaded.

"............AndthethreekingsbroughtgiftstotheChristchild. ...." Red was reading very fast to try to get through the play, because everything was really falling apart on the stage.

The audience wasn't helping either, because they kept shouting, "Is that you, Horse?" or "Is that you, Tony?"

The Kid stepped up with the first gift. "I bring, I bring. ..." He looked at his script but he couldn't read.

"Incense." I whispered.

"¿Qué?"[7]

"Incense," I repeated. Miss Violet had rearranged Horse's robe and pushed him back to kneel by me. My eyes were watering from his blow.

"In-sense," the Kid said and he threw the crayon box we were using for incense right into the manger and busted the doll's head again. The round head just rolled out into the center of the stage where Red stood and he looked down at it with a puzzled expression on his face.

Then the Kid stepped back and slipped on Abel's pee. He tried to get up and run, but that only made it worse. He kept slipping and getting up, and slipping and getting up, and all the while the audience had gone wild with laughter and hysteria.

"... Andthesecondwisemanbroughtmyrrh!" Red shouted above the din.

"Meerrr, merrrrda, mierda!" [8] Bones cried like a monkey.

"I bring myra," Samuel said.

"Myra!" someone in the audience shouted, and all the fifth graders turned to look at a girl named Myra. All the boys said she sat on her wall at home after school and showed her panties to those who wanted to see.

"Hey, Horse!"

"¡Chingada!" the Horse said, working his teeth nervously. He stood up and I pushed and he knelt again.

The Kid was holding on to Abel, trying to regain his footing, and Abel just stood very straight and said, "I had to."

"And the third wise man brought gold!" Red shouted triumphantly. We were nearing the end.

Florence stepped forward, bowed low and handed an empty cigar box to Horse. "For the virgin," he grinned.

"¡Cabrón!" The Horse jumped up and shoved Florence across the stage, and at the same time a blood-curdling scream filled the air and Bones came sailing through the air and landed on Horse.

7. What (Spanish)?   8. Shit (Spanish).

Florence must have hit the light bulb as he went back because there was a pop and darkness as the light of the east went out.

" . . . **And that's how it was on the first Christmas!**" I heard brave Red call out above the confusion and free-for-all on stage and the howling of the audience. The bell rang and everybody ran out shouting, "Merry Christmas!" "Merry Christmas!" "¡Chingada!"

In a very few moments the auditorium was quiet. Only Red and I and Miss Violet remained on the stage. My ears were ringing, like when I stood under the railroad bridge while a train went by overhead. For the first time since we came in it was quiet in the auditorium. Overhead the wind continued to blow. The blizzard had not died out.

"What a play," Miss Violet laughed, "my Lord, what a play!" She sat on a crate in the middle of the jumbled mess and laughed. Then she looked up at the empty beam and called, "Bones, come down!" Her voice echoed in the lonely auditorium. Red and I stood quietly by her.

"Shall we start putting the things away?" Red finally asked. Miss Violet looked up at us and nodded with a smile. We straightened up the stage as best we could. While we worked we felt the wind of the blizzard increase, and the skylight of the auditorium grew dark with snow.

"I think that's about all we can do," Miss Violet said. "The storm seems to be getting worse. . . ."

We put on our jackets, closed the auditorium door and walked down the big, empty hall. The janitor must have turned off the furnace, because there was no noise.

"This place is like a tomb," Miss Violet shivered.

It was like a tomb. Without the kids the schoolhouse was a giant, quiet tomb with the moaning wind crying around its edges. It was strange how everything had been so full of life and funny and in a way sad, and now everything was quiet. Our footsteps echoed in the hall.

1982

THOMAS PYNCHON
b. 1937

Thomas Pynchon has managed to remain the most private of contemporary American writers, without so much as a photograph of him in circulation. A few facts are known: born on Long Island, graduated from Cornell University (where he was a student in Vladimir Nabokov's course) in the late 1950s, served a term in the navy, and now lives—it is said—in southern, or is it northern, California. Beyond that, silence, which has been broken only by five strange and distinctive novels, plus a few short stories.

"Entropy," one of Pynchon's first publications (1960), is printed here as an introduction to his work. Its thematics of an elusive order within radical disorder anticipates his first novel, particularly in its reference to modern physics. As for *V.* (1963) itself, this complex work cannot be understood by reference to convenient fictional signposts. Although it showed an indebtedness to Faulkner and Joyce (an indebtedness shared by most ambitious American novelists), Pynchon's style was already wholly his own. In writing that was by turns labyrinthine, eloquent, and colloquial, he showed a particular fondness for imitating other styles and writing. But these imitations and parodies instead of disparaging or minimizing their subjects radiated a generous spirit of exuberance that extended to the many characters who inhabit V. and whose individual paranoias—Pynchon's word to characterize the human attempt to make connections between events—propel them into unbelievably complicated and absurd plots. The interest of V. was largely in the remarkably unending inventiveness with which Pynchon developed those plots, which might involve anything from diplomatic spy stories in nineteenth-century Africa to the bombing of Malta during World War II to surgical reconstruction of a young woman's nose, or a hunt for alligators in the sewers of New York City.

The comic talent shown in various New York episodes from V. was also evident in The Crying of Lot 49 (1966). This short, perfectly controlled novel teases us and itself with questions about the meaning of our American heritage, as embodied in the form of the mysterious legacy left to its heroine, Oedipa Maas. (The jokey yet portentous name exemplifies Pynchon's teasing way of playing at "significance.") What is the connection between this legacy and the mysterious alternative to the U.S. Postal System on which Oedipa believes she has stumbled? Is there a secret network of alienated citizens carrying on their lives outside the ordinary systems and institutions of American life? Or is it all Oedipa's delusion, her private paranoia? These questions are considered through a style that continually surprises and unsettles us, though it is less discontinuous than V.'s. In Pynchon's world everything serious has its silly aspects (the Marx Brothers, among countless other comic acts, are in the background), while bits of trivia and foolery are suddenly elevated, through the style, into objects of sublime contemplation—as at the novel's end, when Oedipa thinks of "squatters" who

> slept in junkyards in the stripped shells of wrecked Plymouths, or even, daring, spent the night up some pole in a lineman's tent like caterpillars, swung among a web of telephone wires, living in the very copper rigging and secular miracle of communication, untroubled by the dumb voltages flickering their miles, the night long, in the thousands of unheard messages.

Here his sentences enact the daring freedom he admires, in contrast to the institutions of a technological society.

Pynchon's longest and most daring and exhaustive effort came with the publication, in 1973, of Gravity's Rainbow. This encyclopedic fantasy operates through brilliant improvisations, tall tales, obscene parables, and burlesque stage routines, all of which work together into a story of supersonic capabilities and annihilative retributions. A huge cast of characters, each with a crazy name and a plot to unravel, is located all over the map, but mainly in World War II London and in postwar Germany. As the four main and the countless subsidiary plots take shape, characters—and the reader as well—attempt to "read" the messages flickering, the dumb intent to communicate, in the most casual as well as the most portentous sign. Pynchon's knowingness and fascination with popular culture are overwhelmingly evident in Gravity's Rainbow as is his preoccupation with the lore of theoretical science, of obscure historical tales, and of contemporary comic books. No one denies the formidably encyclopedic nature of this astonishing effort; the question is, as Warner Berthoff has asked it, whether that effort may not also be "encyclopedically monotonous and static." More readers begin Gravity's Rainbow than finish it.

After 1973, except for the publication in 1984 of some of his early stories (in Slow Learner), all was silent on the Pynchon front until Vineland appeared in 1990, followed by *Mason & Dixon* in 1997. *Vineland* is wonderful on the California terrain and has much free-wheeling and funny inventiveness; at other times Pynchon seems to be flogging his material and repeating himself. *Mason & Dixon*, about the plotters of the line that would differentiate the American North and South, is written in the manner of his more ambitious works, a massive "mega-novel" that by its very excesses of character, plot, and references to history (arcane and otherwise) seeks to overwhelm the reader with its display of authority. But although there is still no consensus on his stature as an enduring American writer, there is general recognition of the quirky, uncanny exactitude of his imagination. Pynchon's theatrical spellbindings as a man of metaphor, his feats of association (in Robert Frost's phrase), are employed on subjects—like the rocket in *Gravity's Rainbow*—that were thought to be beyond words. For daring, wit, and exuberance, there is no contemporary writer who excels him.

The text is that printed in *Slow Learner* (1984).

Entropy

> Boris has just given me a summary of his views. He is a weather prophet. The weather will continue bad, he says. There will be more calamities, more death, more despair. Not the slightest indication of a change anywhere . . . We must get into step, a lockstep toward the prison of death. There is no escape. The weather will not change.
>
> —*Tropic of Cancer*[1]

Downstairs, Meatball Mulligan's lease-breaking party was moving into its 40th hour. On the kitchen floor, amid a litter of empty champagne fifths, were Sandor Rojas and three friends, playing spit in the ocean and staying awake on Heidseck[2] and benzedrine pills. In the living room Duke, Vincent, Krinkles and Paco sat crouched over a 15-inch speaker which had been bolted into the top of a wastepaper basket, listening to 27 watts' worth of *The Heroes' Gate at Kiev.*[3] They all wore hornrimmed sunglasses and rapt expressions, and smoked funny-looking cigarettes which contained not, as you might expect, tobacco, but an adulterated form of *cannabis sativa.*[4] This group was the Duke di Angelis quartet. They recorded for a local label called Tambú and had to their credit one 10" LP entitled *Songs of Outer Space.* From time to time one of them would flick the ashes from his cigarette into the speaker cone to watch them dance around. Meatball himself was sleeping over by the window, holding an empty magnum to his chest as if it were a teddy bear. Several government girls, who worked for people like the State Department and NSA, had passed out on couches, chairs and in one case the bathroom sink.

This was in early February of '57 and back then there were a lot of American expatriates around Washington, D.C., who would talk, every time they met you, about how someday they were going to go over to Europe for real but right now it seemed they were working for the government. Everyone

---

1. Novel (1934) by American writer Henry Miller (1891–1980).
2. A very dry champagne.
3. Music by the Russian composer Modest Mus-

sorgsky (1839–1881) from his *Pictures at an Exhibition.*
4. Marijuana.

saw a fine irony in this. They would stage, for instance, polyglot parties where the newcomer was sort of ignored if he couldn't carry on simultaneous conversations in three or four languages. They would haunt Armenian delicatessens for weeks at a stretch and invite you over for bulghour and lamb in tiny kitchens whose walls were covered with bullfight posters. They would have affairs with sultry girls from Andalucía or the Midi[5] who studied economics at Georgetown. Their Dôme was a collegiate Rathskeller out on Wisconsin Avenue called the Old Heidelberg and they had to settle for cherry blossoms instead of lime trees when spring came, but in its lethargic way their life provided, as they said, kicks.

At the moment, Meatball's party seemed to be gathering its second wind. Outside there was rain. Rain splatted against the tar paper on the roof and was fractured into a fine spray off the noses, eyebrows and lips of wooden gargoyles under the eaves, and ran like drool down the windowpanes. The day before, it had snowed and the day before that there had been winds of gale force and before that the sun had made the city glitter bright as April, though the calendar read early February. It is a curious season in Washington, this false spring. Somewhere in it are Lincoln's Birthday and the Chinese New Year, and a forlornness in the streets because cherry blossoms are weeks away still and, as Sarah Vaughan has put it, spring will be a little late this year. Generally crowds like the one which would gather in the Old Heidelberg on weekday afternoons to drink Würtzburger and to sing Lili Marlene (not to mention The Sweetheart of Sigma Chi) are inevitably and incorrigibly Romantic. And as every good Romantic knows, the soul (*spiritus, ruach, pneuma*) is nothing, substantially, but air; it is only natural that warpings in the atmosphere should be recapitulated in those who breathe it. So that over and above the public components—holidays, tourist attractions—there are private meanderings, linked to the climate as if this spell were a *stretto* passage in the year's fugue: haphazard weather, aimless loves, unpredicted commitments: months one can easily spend *in* fugue, because oddly enough, later on, winds, rains, passions of February and March are never remembered in that city, it is as if they had never been.

The last bass notes of *The Heroes' Gate* boomed up through the floor and woke Callisto from an uneasy sleep. The first thing he became aware of was a small bird he had been holding gently between his hands, against his body. He turned his head sidewise on the pillow to smile down at it, at its blue hunched-down head and sick, lidded eyes, wondering how many more nights he would have to give it warmth before it was well again. He had been holding the bird like that for three days: it was the only way he knew to restore its health. Next to him the girl stirred and whimpered, her arm thrown across her face. Mingled with the sounds of the rain came the first tentative, querulous morning voices of the other birds, hidden in philodendrons and small fan palms: patches of scarlet, yellow and blue laced through this Rousseau[6]-like fantasy, this hothouse jungle it had taken him seven years to weave together. Hermetically sealed, it was a tiny enclave of regularity in the city's chaos, alien to the vagaries of the weather, of national politics, of any civil disorder. Through trial-and-error Callisto had perfected its ecological bal-

---

5. Regions of Spain and France, respectively.
6. Henri Rousseau (1844–1910), French primitive painter of exotic landscapes.

ance, with the help of the girl its artistic harmony, so that the swayings of its plant life, the stirrings of its birds and human inhabitants were all as integral as the rhythms of a perfectly-executed mobile. He and the girl could no longer, of course, be omitted from that sanctuary; they had become necessary to its unity. What they needed from outside was delivered. They did not go out.

"Is he all right," she whispered. She lay like a tawny question mark facing him, her eyes suddenly huge and dark and blinking slowly. Callisto ran a finger beneath the feathers at the base of the bird's neck; caressed it gently. "He's going to be well, I think. See: he hears his friends beginning to wake up." The girl had heard the rain and the birds even before she was fully awake. Her name was Aubade: she was part French and part Annamese, and she lived on her own curious and lonely planet, where the clouds and the odor of poincianas, the bitterness of wine and the accidental fingers at the small of her back or feathery against her breasts came to her reduced inevitably to the terms of sound: of music which emerged at intervals from a howling darkness of discordancy. "Aubade," he said, "go see." Obedient, she arose; padded to the window, pulled aside the drapes and after a moment said: "It is 37. Still 37." Callisto frowned. "Since Tuesday, then," he said. "No change." Henry Adams,[7] three generations before his own, had stared aghast at Power; Callisto found himself now in much the same state over Thermodynamics, the inner life of that power, realizing like his predecessor that the Virgin and the dynamo stand as much for love as for power; that the two are indeed identical; and that love therefore not only makes the world go round but also makes the boccie ball spin, the nebula precess. It was this latter or sidereal element which disturbed him. The cosmologists had predicted an eventual heat-death for the universe (something like Limbo: form and motion abolished, heat-energy identical at every point in it); the meteorologists, day-to-day, staved it off by contradicting with a reassuring array of varied temperatures.

But for three days now, despite the changeful weather, the mercury had stayed at 37 degrees Fahrenheit. Leery at omens of apocalypse, Callisto shifted beneath the covers. His fingers pressed the bird more firmly, as if needing some pulsing or suffering assurance of an early break in the temperature.

It was that last cymbal crash that did it. Meatball was hurled wincing into consciousness as the synchronized wagging of heads over the wastebasket stopped. The final hiss remained for an instant in the room, then melted into the whisper of rain outside. "Aarrgghh," announced Meatball in the silence, looking at the empty magnum. Krinkles, in slow motion, turned, smiled and held out a cigarette. "Tea time, man," he said. "No, no," said Meatball. "How many times I got to tell you guys. Not at my place. You ought to know, Washington is lousy with Feds." Krinkles looked wistful. "Jeez, Meatball," he said, "you don't want to do nothing no more." "Hair of dog," said Meatball. "Only hope. Any juice left?" He began to crawl toward the kitchen. "No champagne, I don't think," Duke said. "Case of tequila behind the icebox." They put on an Earl Bostic[8] side. Meatball paused at the kitchen door, glow-

---

7. American historian and man of letters (1838–1918) whose writings explore the nature of power, cultural figurations of which ranged from the Virgin Mary to the modern dynamo engine.

8. American jazz musician (1913–1965) who popularized his music by recording rhythm and blues material.

ering at Sandor Rojas. "Lemons," he said after some thought. He crawled to the refrigerator and got out three lemons and some cubes, found the tequila and set about restoring order to his nervous system. He drew blood once cutting the lemons and had to use two hands squeezing them and his foot to crack the ice tray but after about ten minutes he found himself, through some miracle, beaming down into a monster tequila sour. "That looks yummy," Sandor Rojas said. "How about you make me one." Meatball blinked at him. *"Kitchi lofass a shegithe,"*[9] he replied automatically, and wandered away into the bathroom. "I say," he called out a moment later to no one in particular. "I say, there seems to be a girl or something sleeping in the sink." He took her by the shoulders and shook. "Wha," she said. "You don't look too comfortable," Meatball said. "Well," she agreed. She stumbled to the shower, turned on the cold water and sat down crosslegged in the spray. "That's better," she smiled.

"Meatball," Sandor Rojas yelled from the kitchen. "Somebody is trying to come in the window. A burglar, I think. A second-story man." "What are you worrying about," Meatball said. "We're on the third floor." He loped back into the kitchen. A shaggy woebegone figure stood out on the fire escape, raking his fingernails down the windowpane. Meatball opened the window. "Saul," he said.

"Sort of wet out," Saul said. He climbed in, dripping. "You heard, I guess."

"Miriam left you," Meatball said, "or something, is all I heard."

There was a sudden flurry of knocking at the front door. "Do come in," Sandor Rojas called. The door opened and there were three coeds from George Washington, all of whom were majoring in philosophy. They were each holding a gallon of Chianti. Sandor leaped up and dashed into the living room. "We heard there was a party," one blonde said. "Young blood," Sandor shouted. He was an ex-Hungarian freedom fighter who had easily the worst chronic case of what certain critics of the middle class have called Don Giovannism in the District of Columbia. *Purche porti la gonnella, voi sapete quel che fa.*[1] Like Pavlov's dog: a contralto voice or a whiff of Arpège and Sandor would begin to salivate. Meatball regarded the trio blearily as they filed into the kitchen; he shrugged. "Put the wine in the icebox," he said, "and good morning."

Aubade's neck made a golden bow as she bent over the sheets of foolscap, scribbling away in the green murk of the room. "As a young man at Princeton," Callisto was dictating, nestling the bird against the gray hairs of his chest, "Callisto had learned a mnemonic device for remembering the Laws of Thermodynamics: you can't win, things are going to get worse before they get better, who says they're going to get better. At the age of 54, confronted with Gibbs'[2] notion of the universe, he suddenly realized that undergraduate cant had been oracle, after all. That spindly maze of equations became, for him, a vision of ultimate, cosmic heat-death. He had known all along, of course, that nothing but a theoretical engine or system ever runs at 100% efficiency; and about the theorem of Clausius, which states that the entropy of an isolated system always continually increases. It was not, however, until Gibbs and Boltzmann[3] brought to this principle the methods of statistical

9. Little horse prick in your asshole (Hungarian).
1. If you wear a shirt, you know what to do (Italian).
2. Josiah Willard Gibbs (1839–1903), American

physicist and chemist, a founder of statistical mechanics.
3. Ludwig Boltzmann (1844–1906), Austrian physicist who studied how atoms determine visual

mechanics that the horrible significance of it all dawned on him: only then did he realize that the isolated system—galaxy, engine, human being, culture, whatever—must evolve spontaneously toward the Condition of the More Probable. He was forced, therefore, in the sad dying fall of middle age, to a radical reëvaluation of everything he had learned up to then; all the cities and seasons and casual passions of his days had now to be looked at in a new and elusive light. He did not know if he was equal to the task. He was aware of the dangers of the reductive fallacy and, he hoped, strong enough not to drift into the graceful decadence of an enervated fatalism. His had always been a vigorous, Italian sort of pessimism: like Machiavelli, he allowed the forces of *virtù* and *fortuna*[4] to be about 50/50; but the equations now introduced a random factor which pushed the odds to some unutterable and indeterminate ratio which he found himself afraid to calculate." Around him loomed vague hothouse shapes; the pitifully small heart fluttered against his own. Counterpointed against his words the girl heard the chatter of birds and fitful car honkings scattered along the wet morning and Earl Bostic's alto rising in occasional wild peaks through the floor. The architectonic purity of her world was constantly threatened by such hints of anarchy: gaps and excrescences and skew lines, and a shifting or tilting of planes to which she had continually to readjust lest the whole structure shiver into a disarray of discrete and meaningless signals. Callisto had described the process once as a kind of "feedback": she crawled into dreams each night with a sense of exhaustion, and a desperate resolve never to relax that vigilance. Even in the brief periods when Callisto made love to her, soaring above the bowing of taut nerves in haphazard double-stops would be the one singing string of her determination.

"Nevertheless," continued Callisto, "he found in entropy or the measure of disorganization for a closed system an adequate metaphor to apply to certain phenomena in his own world. He saw, for example, the younger generation responding to Madison Avenue with the same spleen his own had once reserved for Wall Street: and in American 'consumerism' discovered a similar tendency from the least to the most probable, from differentiation to sameness, from ordered individuality to a kind of chaos. He found himself, in short, restating Gibbs' prediction in social terms, and envisioned a heat-death for his culture in which ideas, like heat-energy, would no longer be transferred, since each point in it would ultimately have the same quantity of energy; and intellectual motion would, accordingly, cease." He glanced up suddenly. "Check it now," he said. Again she rose and peered out at the thermometer. "37," she said. "The rain has stopped." He bent his head quickly and held his lips against a quivering wing. "Then it will change soon," he said, trying to keep his voice firm.

Sitting on the stove Saul was like any big rag doll that a kid has been taking out some incomprehensible rage on. "What happened," Meatball said. "If you feel like talking, I mean."

"Of course I feel like talking," Saul said. "One thing I did, I slugged her."

"Discipline must be maintained."

"Ha, ha. I wish you'd been there. Oh Meatball, it was a lovely fight. She ended up throwing a *Handbook of Chemistry and Physics* at me, only it missed

---

properties of matter. Rudolf Clausius (1822–1888), German physicist, developer of the science of thermodynamics.

4. Nicolo Machiavelli (1469–1527), Florentine statesman and writer on government, contrasted virtuous behavior (*virtù*) with good luck (*fortuna*).

and went through the window, and when the glass broke I reckon something in her broke too. She stormed out of the house crying, out in the rain. No raincoat or anything."

"She'll be back."

"No."

"Well!" Soon Meatball said: "It was something earthshattering, no doubt. Like who is better, Sal Mineo or Ricky Nelson."[5]

"What it was about," Saul said, "was communication theory. Which of course makes it very hilarious."

"I don't know anything about communication theory."

"Neither does my wife. Come right down to it, who does? That's the joke."

When Meatball saw the kind of smile Saul had on his face he said: "Maybe you would like tequila or something."

"No. I mean, I'm sorry. It's a field you can go off the deep end in, is all. You get where you're watching all the time for security cops: behind bushes, around corners. MUFFET is top secret."

"Wha."

"Multi-unit factorial field electronic tabulator."

"You were fighting about that."

"Miriam has been reading science fiction again. That and *Scientific American*. It seems she is, as we say, bugged at this idea of computers acting like people. I made the mistake of saying you can just as well turn that around, and talk about human behavior like a program fed into an IBM machine."

"Why not," Meatball said.

"Indeed, why not. In fact it is sort of crucial to communication, not to mention information theory. Only when I said that she hit the roof. Up went the balloon. And I can't figure out *why*. If anybody should know why, I should. I refuse to believe the government is wasting taxpayers' money on me, when it has so many bigger and better things to waste it on."

Meatball made a moue. "Maybe she thought you were acting like a cold, dehumanized amoral scientist type."

"My god," Saul flung up an arm. "Dehumanized. How much more human can I get? I worry, Meatball, I do. There are Europeans wandering around North Africa these days with their tongues torn out of their heads because those tongues have spoken the wrong words. Only the Europeans thought they were the right words."

"Language barrier," Meatball suggested.

Saul jumped down off the stove. "That," he said, angry, "is a good candidate for sick joke of the year. No, ace, it is *not* a barrier. If it is anything it's a kind of leakage. Tell a girl: 'I love you.' No trouble with two-thirds of that, it's a closed circuit. Just you and she. But that nasty four-letter word in the middle, *that's* the one you have to look out for. Ambiguity. Redundance. Irrelevance, even. Leakage. All this is noise. Noise screws up your signal, makes for disorganization in the circuit."

Meatball shuffled around. "Well, now, Saul," he muttered, "you're sort of, I don't know, expecting a lot from people. I mean, you know. What it is is, most of the things we say, I guess, are mostly noise."

---

5. Contemporary figures from film and television who were icons of bad and good teenage behavior, respectively.

"Ha! Half of what you just said, for example."

"Well, you do it too."

"I know." Saul smiled grimly. "It's a bitch, ain't it."

"I bet that's what keeps divorce lawyers in business. Whoops."

"Oh I'm not sensitive. Besides," frowning, "you're right. You find I think that most 'successful' marriages—Miriam and me, up to last night—are sort of founded on compromises. You never run at top efficiency, usually all you have is a minimum basis for a workable thing. I believe the phrase is Togetherness."

"Aarrgghh."

"Exactly. You find that one a bit noisy, don't you. But the noise content is different for each of us because you're a bachelor and I'm not. Or wasn't. The hell with it."

"Well sure," Meatball said, trying to be helpful, "you were using different words. By 'human being' you meant something that you can look at like it was a computer. It helps you think better on the job or something. But Miriam meant something entirely—"

"The hell with it."

Meatball fell silent. "I'll take that drink," Saul said after a while.

The card game had been abandoned and Sandor's friends were slowly getting wasted on tequila. On the living room couch, one of the coeds and Krinkles were engaged in amorous conversation. "No," Krinkles was saying, "no, I can't put Dave *down*. In fact I give Dave a lot of credit, man. Especially considering his accident and all." The girl's smile faded. "How terrible," she said. "What accident?" "Hadn't you heard?" Krinkles said. "When Dave was in the army, just a private E-2, they sent him down to Oak Ridge on special duty. Something to do with the Manhattan Project.[6] He was handling hot stuff one day and got an overdose of radiation. So now he's got to wear lead gloves all the time." She shook her head sympathetically. "What an awful break for a piano player."

Meatball had abandoned Saul to a bottle of tequila and was about to go to sleep in a closet when the front door flew open and the place was invaded by five enlisted personnel of the U.S. Navy, all in varying stages of abomination. "This is the place," shouted a fat, pimply seaman apprentice who had lost his white hat. "This here is the hoorhouse that chief was telling us about." A stringylooking 3rd class boatswain's mate pushed him aside and cased the living room. "You're right, Slab," he said. "But it don't look like much, even for Stateside. I seen better tail in Naples, Italy." "How much, hey," boomed a large seaman with adenoids, who was holding a Mason jar full of white lightning. "Oh, my god," said Meatball.

Outside the temperature remained constant at 37 degrees Fahrenheit. In the hothouse Aubade stood absently caressing the branches of a young mimosa, hearing a motif of sap-rising, the rough and unresolved anticipatory theme of those fragile pink blossoms which, it is said, insure fertility. That music rose in a tangled tracery: arabesques of order competing fugally with the improvised discords of the party downstairs, which peaked sometimes in cusps and ogees of noise. That precious signal-to-noise ratio, whose delicate balance required every calorie of her strength, seesawed inside the small

6. The research that developed the atomic bomb for use at the end of World War II.

tenuous skull as she watched Callisto, sheltering the bird. Callisto was trying to confront any idea of the heat-death now, as he nuzzled the feathery lump in his hands. He sought correspondences. Sade, of course. And Temple Drake, gaunt and hopeless in her little park in Paris, at the end of *Sanctuary*.[7] Final equilibrium. *Nightwood*.[8] And the tango. Any tango, but more than any perhaps the sad sick dance in Stravinsky's *L'Histoire du Soldat*.[9] He thought back: what had tango music been for them after the war, what meanings had he missed in all the stately coupled automatons in the *cafés-dansants*,[1] or in the metronomes which had ticked behind the eyes of his own partners? Not even the clean constant winds of Switzerland could cure the *grippe espagnole*:[2] Stravinsky had had it, they all had had it. And how many musicians were left after Passchendaele, after the Marne?[3] It came down in this case to seven: violin, double-bass. Clarinet, bassoon. Cornet, trombone. Tympani. Almost as if any tiny troupe of saltimbanques had set about conveying the same information as a full pit-orchestra. There was hardly a full complement left in Europe. Yet with violin and tympani Stravinsky had managed to communicate in that tango the same exhaustion, the same airlessness one saw in the slicked-down youths who were trying to imitate Vernon Castle, and in their mistresses, who simply did not care. *Ma maîtresse*.[4] Celeste. Returning to Nice after the second war he had found that café replaced by a perfume shop which catered to American tourists. And no secret vestige of her in the cobblestones or in the old pension next door; no perfume to match her breath heavy with the sweet Spanish wine she always drank. And so instead he had purchased a Henry Miller[5] novel and left for Paris, and read the book on the train so that when he arrived he had been given at least a little forewarning. And saw that Celeste and the others and even Temple Drake were not all that had changed. "Aubade," he said, "my head aches." The sound of his voice generated in the girl an answering scrap of melody. Her movement toward the kitchen, the towel, the cold water, and his eyes following her formed a weird and intricate canon; as she placed the compress on his forehead his sigh of gratitude seemed to signal a new subject, another series of modulations.

"No," Meatball was still saying, "no, I'm afraid not. This is not a house of ill repute. I'm sorry, really I am." Slab was adamant. "But the chief said," he kept repeating. The seaman offered to swap the moonshine for a good piece. Meatball looked around frantically, as if seeking assistance. In the middle of the room, the Duke di Angelis quartet were engaged in a historic moment. Vincent was seated and the others standing: they were going through the motions of a group having a session, only without instruments. "I say," Meatball said. Duke moved his head a few times, smiled faintly, lit a cigarette, and eventually caught sight of Meatball. "Quiet, man," he whispered. Vincent began to fling his arms around, his fists clenched; then, abruptly, was still, then repeated the performance. This went on for a few minutes while Meatball sipped his drink moodily. The navy had withdrawn to the kitchen.

7. Sexually notorious novel published in 1931 by American writer William Faulkner (1897–1962).
8. Novel published in 1936 by American expatriate writer Djuna Barnes (1892–1982).
9. A 1918 work by the Russian composer Igor Stravinsky (1882–1971).
1. Café dancers (French).

2. Spanish flu (Spanish).
3. Battle sites in World War I noted for their extremely high casualties.
4. My mistress (French).
5. Miller was famous for his strongly sexual novels written in Paris during the 1930s.

Finally at some invisible signal the group stopped tapping their feet and Duke grinned and said, "At least we ended together."

Meatball glared at him. "I say," he said. "I have this new conception, man," Duke said. "You remember your namesake. You remember Gerry."

"No," said Meatball. "I'll remember April, if that's any help."

"As a matter of fact," Duke said, "it was Love for Sale. Which shows how much you know. The point is, it was Mulligan, Chet Baker[6] and that crew, way back then, out yonder. You dig?"

"Baritone sax," Meatball said. "Something about a baritone sax."

"But no piano, man. No guitar. Or accordion. You know what that means."

"Not exactly," Meatball said.

"Well first let me just say, that I am no Mingus, no John Lewis.[7] Theory was never my strong point. I mean things like reading were always difficult for me and all—"

"I know," Meatball said drily. "You got your card taken away because you changed key on Happy Birthday at a Kiwanis Club picnic."

"Rotarian. But it occurred to me, in one of these flashes of insight, that if that first quartet of Mulligan's had no piano, it could only mean one thing."

"No chords," said Paco, the baby-faced bass.

"What he is trying to say," Duke said, "is no root chords. Nothing to listen to while you blow a horizontal line. What one does in such a case is, one *thinks* the roots."

A horrified awareness was dawning on Meatball. "And the next logical extension," he said.

"Is to think everything," Duke announced with simple dignity. "Roots, line, everything."

Meatball looked at Duke, awed. "But," he said.

"Well," Duke said modestly, "there are a few bugs to work out."

"But," Meatball said.

"Just listen," Duke said. "You'll catch on." And off they went again into orbit, presumably somewhere around the asteroid belt. After a while Krinkles made an embouchure and started moving his fingers and Duke clapped his hand to his forehead. "Oaf!" he roared. "The new head we're using, you remember, I wrote last night?" "Sure," Krinkles said, "the new head. I come in on the bridge. All your heads I come in then." "Right," Duke said. "So why—" "Wha," said Krinkles, "16 bars, I wait, I come in—" "16?" Duke said. "No. No, Krinkles. Eight you waited. You want me to sing it? A cigarette that bears a lipstick's traces, an airline ticket to romantic places." Krinkles scratched his head. "These Foolish Things, you mean." "Yes," Duke said, "yes, Krinkles. Bravo." "Not I'll Remember April," Krinkles said. "*Minghe morte,*"[8] said Duke. "I *figured* we were playing it a little slow," Krinkles said. Meatball chuckled. "Back to the old drawing board," he said. "No, man," Duke said, "back to the airless void." And they took off again, only it seemed Paco was playing in G sharp while the rest were in E flat, so they had to start all over.

In the kitchen two of the girls from George Washington and the sailors

6. The American jazz musicians Gerry Mulligan (1927–1996) and Chet Baker (1929–1988) became famous in 1952 for their revolutionary pianoless quartet.

7. Jazz musicians noted for their compositions based in musical theory.

8. Dead prick (Italian).

were singing Let's All Go Down and Piss on the Forrestal.[9] There was a two-handed, bilingual *morra* game on over by the icebox. Saul had filled several paper bags with water and was sitting on the fire escape, dropping them on passersby in the street. A fat government girl in a Bennington sweatshirt, recently engaged to an ensign attached to the Forrestal, came charging into the kitchen, head lowered, and butted Slab in the stomach. Figuring this was as good an excuse for a fight as any, Slab's buddies piled in. The *morra* players were nose-to-nose, screaming *trois, sette*[1] at the tops of their lungs. From the shower the girl Meatball had taken out of the sink announced that she was drowning. She had apparently sat on the drain and the water was now up to her neck. The noise in Meatball's apartment had reached a sustained, ungodly crescendo.

Meatball stood and watched, scratching his stomach lazily. The way he figured, there were only about two ways he could cope: (a) lock himself in the closet and maybe eventually they would all go away, or (b) try to calm everybody down, one by one. (a) was certainly the more attractive alternative. But then he started thinking about that closet. It was dark and stuffy and he would be alone. He did not feature being alone. And then this crew off the good ship Lollipop[2] or whatever it was might take it upon themselves to kick down the closet door, for a lark. And if that happened he would be, at the very least, embarrassed. The other way was more a pain in the neck, but probably better in the long run.

So he decided to try and keep his lease-breaking party from deteriorating into total chaos: he gave wine to the sailors and separated the *morra* players; he introduced the fat government girl to Sandor Rojas, who would keep her out of trouble; he helped the girl in the shower to dry off and get into bed; he had another talk with Saul; he called a repairman for the refrigerator, which someone had discovered was on the blink. This is what he did until nightfall, when most of the revellers had passed out and the party trembled on the threshold of its third day.

Upstairs Callisto, helpless in the past, did not feel the faint rhythm inside the bird begin to slacken and fail. Aubade was by the window, wandering the ashes of her own lovely world; the temperature held steady, the sky had become a uniform darkening gray. Then something from downstairs—a girl's scream, an overturned chair, a glass dropped on the floor, he would never know what exactly—pierced that private time-warp and he became aware of the faltering, the constriction of muscles, the tiny tossings of the bird's head; and his own pulse began to pound more fiercely, as if trying to compensate. "Aubade," he called weakly, "he's dying." The girl, flowing and rapt, crossed the hothouse to gaze down at Callisto's hands. The two remained like that, poised, for one minute, and two, while the heartbeat ticked a graceful diminuendo down at last into stillness. Callisto raised his head slowly. "I held him," he protested, impotent with the wonder of it, "to give him the warmth of my body. Almost as if I were communicating life to him, or a sense of life. What has happened? Has the transfer of heat ceased to work? Is there no more . . ." He did not finish.

9. Aircraft carrier in the U.S. Navy.
1. *"Morra"*: finger game originally played by Italians. The commands are numbers; here, three (*trois*, French) and seven (*sette*, Italian).

2. The subject of film and song popularized in the 1930s by the American child actress Shirley Temple.

"I was just at the window," she said. He sank back, terrified. She stood a moment more, irresolute; she had sensed his obsession long ago, realized somehow that that constant 37 was now decisive. Suddenly then, as if seeing the single and unavoidable conclusion to all this she moved swiftly to the window before Callisto could speak; tore away the drapes and smashed out the glass with two exquisite hands which came away bleeding and glistening with splinters; and turned to face the man on the bed and wait with him until the moment of equilibrium was reached, when 37 degrees Fahrenheit should prevail both outside and inside, and forever, and the hovering, curious dominant of their separate lives should resolve into a tonic of darkness and the final absence of all motion.

1984

RAYMOND CARVER
1938–1988

Minimal fiction; designer fiction; even "dirty fiction," a phrase the British magazine *Granta* used to characterize the new style of American writing that was supposedly polluting the realistic short story with unconventional, irrealistic techniques—these were terms tossed around by critics of an abruptly new style of work that at times seemed to dominate the 1980s. Popularized by Bobbie Ann Mason, Ann Beattie, Frederick Barthelme, and Barry Hannah as well, its chief practitioner was a master of fine arts graduate from the University of Iowa's Writers Workshop, Raymond Carver, whose collections *Will You Please Be Quiet, Please?* (1976), *What We Talk about When We Talk about Love* (1981), and *Cathedral* (1983) set the most imitated style of their generation. Moved to put some order to these many definitions, writer John Barth—whose nonrealistic, innovative work had helped characterize the writing of the decades before—coined the term Post-Alcoholic Blue-Collar Minimalist Hyperrealism to describe the school Carver may have inadvertently founded. A recovering alcoholic, Carver had also worked as a janitor, sawmill hand, delivery person, and sales representative, suggesting the profile Barth had in mind. But more pertinent to the style of his fiction was his training at Iowa and teaching in creative writing programs at universities around the country. By the time of his death, his became the most accepted style in such academic programs and in the literary magazines they generated.

This style's success is important. With conventions of literary realism having been challenged and theorists questioning all such previously stable assumptions, readers of Barth, Donald Barthelme, Kurt Vonnegut, and other such experimenters may have felt that simple realism was no longer an up-to-date way in which to write. Raymond Carver proved that it was, and that previous challenges to realistic tradition had only made it all the more effective, especially when those challenges are incorporated in the new style. Carver's patient narration does not strive for a reader's suspension of disbelief. Rather, as in the introduction of the bizarre situation experienced in "Cathedral" (printed here), its plain, even flat statement presents matter unadorned by devices meant to persuade or convince. So a blind man wants to learn what the architecture of a cathedral suggests? Here it is, Carver's story says: what you see is what there is; take it or leave it; if you are blind, he will help you feel your way through, but never as a direction to meaning, only to an apprehension of the facts. Carver's characters are usually working-class people somewhat down on their luck. Often, alcohol figures in their lives, less as a stimulant than as a further depressant. Totally unexceptional, their failures, like their hopes, are small, even puny. But from such stripped down essentials the author is able to write in a plain, simple manner, sticking to the absolute minimum so that no one can accuse him of trying to create illusions.

Much was made of Raymond Carver's alcoholism and recovery. He made no apologies for his hard, sometimes abusive life, the rigors of which contributed to ill health and an early death. His stories and poems have the same quiet toughness to them, not flamboyant in confrontation with life's meanness but dedicated to holding on against time's slowly destructive friction with a grittiness all their own.

The text is from *Cathedral* (1983).

Cathedral

This blind man, an old friend of my wife's, he was on his way to spend the night. His wife had died. So he was visiting the dead wife's relatives in Connecticut. He called my wife from his in-laws'. Arrangements were made. He would come by train, a five-hour trip, and my wife would meet him at the station. She hadn't seen him since she worked for him one summer in Seattle ten years ago. But she and the blind man had kept in touch. They made tapes and mailed them back and forth. I wasn't enthusiastic about his visit. He was no one I knew. And his being blind bothered me. My idea of blindness came from the movies. In the movies, the blind moved slowly and never laughed. Sometimes they were led by seeing-eye dogs. A blind man in my house was not something I looked forward to.

That summer in Seattle she had needed a job. She didn't have any money. The man she was going to marry at the end of the summer was in officers' training school. He didn't have any money, either. But she was in love with the guy, and he was in love with her, etc. She'd seen something in the paper: HELP WANTED—*Reading to Blind Man*, and a telephone number. She phoned and went over, was hired on the spot. She'd worked with this blind man all summer. She read stuff to him, case studies, reports, that sort of thing. She helped him organize his little office in the county social-service department. They'd become good friends, my wife and the blind man. How do I know these things? She told me. And she told me something else. On her last day in the office, the blind man asked if he could touch her face. She agreed to this. She told me he touched his fingers to every part of her face, her nose— even her neck! She never forgot it. She even tried to write a poem about it. She was always trying to write a poem. She wrote a poem or two every year, usually after something really important had happened to her.

When we first started going out together, she showed me the poem. In the poem, she recalled his fingers and the way they had moved around over her face. In the poem, she talked about what she had felt at the time, about what went through her mind when the blind man touched her nose and lips. I can remember I didn't think much of the poem. Of course, I didn't tell her that. Maybe I just don't understand poetry. I admit it's not the first thing I reach for when I pick up something to read.

Anyway, this man who'd first enjoyed her favors, the officer-to-be, he'd been her childhood sweetheart. So okay. I'm saying that at the end of the summer she let the blind man run his hands over her face, said goodbye to him, married her childhood etc., who was now a commissioned officer, and she moved away from Seattle. But they'd kept in touch, she and the blind man. She made the first contact after a year or so. She called him up one night from an Air Force base in Alabama. She wanted to talk. They talked. He asked her to send him a tape and tell him about her life. She did this. She sent the tape. On the tape, she told the blind man about her husband and about their life together in the military. She told the blind man she loved her husband but she didn't like it where they lived and she didn't like it that he was a part of the military-industrial thing. She told the blind man she'd written a poem and he was in it. She told him that she was writing a poem about what it was like to be an Air Force officer's wife. The poem wasn't finished yet. She was still writing it. The blind man made a tape. He sent her the tape. She made a tape. This went on for years. My wife's officer was posted to one base and then another. She sent tapes from Moody AFB,[1] McGuire, McConnell, and finally Travis, near Sacramento, where one night she got to feeling lonely and cut off from people she kept losing in that moving-around life. She got to feeling she couldn't go it another step. She went in and swallowed all the pills and capsules in the medicine chest and washed them down with a bottle of gin. Then she got into a hot bath and passed out.

But instead of dying, she got sick. She threw up. Her officer—why should he have a name? he was the childhood sweetheart, and what more does he want?—came home from somewhere, found her, and called the ambulance. In time, she put it all on a tape and sent the tape to the blind man. Over the years, she put all kinds of stuff on tapes and sent the tapes off lickety-split. Next to writing a poem every year, I think it was her chief means of recreation. On one tape, she told the blind man she'd decided to live away from her officer for a time. On another tape, she told him about her divorce. She and I began going out, and of course she told her blind man about it. She told him everything, or so it seemed to me. Once she asked me if I'd like to hear the latest tape from the blind man. This was a year ago. I was on the tape, she said. So I said okay, I'd listen to it. I got us drinks and we settled down in the living room. We made ready to listen. First she inserted the tape into the player and adjusted a couple of dials. Then she pushed a lever. The tape squeaked and someone began to talk in this loud voice. She lowered the volume. After a few minutes of harmless chitchat, I heard my own name in the mouth of this stranger, this blind man I didn't even know! And then this: "From all you've said about him, I can only conclude—" But we were interrupted, a knock at the door, something, and we didn't ever get back to the tape. Maybe it was just as well. I'd heard all I wanted to.

Now this same blind man was coming to sleep in my house.

"Maybe I could take him bowling," I said to my wife. She was at the draining board doing scalloped potatoes. She put down the knife she was using and turned around.

"If you love me," she said, "you can do this for me. If you don't love me, okay. But if you had a friend, any friend, and the friend came to visit, I'd make him feel comfortable." She wiped her hands with the dish towel.

"I don't have any blind friends," I said.

1. Air force base. Names of other air force bases follow.

"You don't have *any* friends," she said. "Period. Besides," she said, "goddam it, his wife's just died! Don't you understand that? The man's lost his wife!"

I didn't answer. She'd told me a little about the blind man's wife. Her name was Beulah. Beulah! That's a name for a colored woman.

"Was his wife a Negro?" I asked.

"Are you crazy?" my wife said. "Have you just flipped or something?" She picked up a potato. I saw it hit the floor, then roll under the stove. "What's wrong with you?" she said. "Are you drunk?"

"I'm just asking," I said.

Right then my wife filled me in with more detail than I cared to know. I made a drink and sat at the kitchen table to listen. Pieces of the story began to fall into place.

Beulah had gone to work for the blind man the summer after my wife had stopped working for him. Pretty soon Beulah and the blind man had themselves a church wedding. It was a little wedding—who'd want to go to such a wedding in the first place?—just the two of them, plus the minister and the minister's wife. But it was a church wedding just the same. It was what Beulah had wanted, he'd said. But even then Beulah must have been carrying the cancer in her glands. After they had been inseparable for eight years— my wife's word, *inseparable*—Beulah's health went into a rapid decline. She died in a Seattle hospital room, the blind man sitting beside the bed and holding on to her hand. They'd married, lived and worked together, slept together—had sex, sure—and then the blind man had to bury her. All this without his having ever seen what the goddamned woman looked like. It was beyond my understanding. Hearing this, I felt sorry for the blind man for a little bit. And then I found myself thinking what a pitiful life this woman must have led. Imagine a woman who could never see herself as she was seen in the eyes of her loved one. A woman who could go on day after day and never receive the smallest compliment from her beloved. A woman whose husband could never read the expression on her face, be it misery or something better. Someone who could wear makeup or not—what difference to him? She could, if she wanted, wear green eye-shadow around one eye, a straight pin in her nostril, yellow slacks and purple shoes, no matter. And then to slip off into death, the blind man's hand on her hand, his blind eyes streaming tears—I'm imagining now—her last thought maybe this: that he never even knew what she looked like, and she on an express to the grave. Robert was left with a small insurance policy and half of a twenty-peso Mexican coin. The other half of the coin went into the box with her. Pathetic.

So when the time rolled around, my wife went to the depot to pick him up. With nothing to do but wait—sure, I blamed him for that—I was having a drink and watching the TV when I heard the car pull into the drive. I got up from the sofa with my drink and went to the window to have a look.

I saw my wife laughing as she parked the car. I saw her get out of the car and shut the door. She was still wearing a smile. Just amazing. She went around to the other side of the car to where the blind man was already starting to get out. This blind man, feature this, he was wearing a full beard! A beard on a blind man! Too much, I say. The blind man reached into the back seat and dragged out a suitcase. My wife took his arm, shut the car door, and, talking all the way, moved him down the drive and then up the steps to the front porch. I turned off the TV. I finished my drink, rinsed the glass, dried my hands. Then I went to the door.

My wife said, "I want you to meet Robert. Robert, this is my husband. I've told you all about him." She was beaming. She had this blind man by his coat sleeve.

The blind man let go of his suitcase and up came his hand.

I took it. He squeezed hard, held my hand, and then he let it go.

"I feel like we've already met," he boomed.

"Likewise," I said. I didn't know what else to say. Then I said, "Welcome. I've heard a lot about you." We began to move then, a little group, from the porch into the living room, my wife guiding him by the arm. The blind man was carrying his suitcase in his other hand. My wife said things like, "To your left here, Robert. That's right. Now watch it, there's a chair. That's it. Sit down right here. This is the sofa. We just bought this sofa two weeks ago."

I started to say something about the old sofa. I'd liked that old sofa. But I didn't say anything. Then I wanted to say something else, small-talk, about the scenic ride along the Hudson. How going *to* New York, you should sit on the right-hand side of the train, and coming *from* New York, the left-hand side.

"Did you have a good train ride?" I said. "Which side of the train did you sit on, by the way?"

"What a question, which side!" my wife said. "What's it matter which side?" she said.

"I just asked," I said.

"Right side," the blind man said. "I hadn't been on a train in nearly forty years. Not since I was a kid. With my folks. That's been a long time. I'd nearly forgotten the sensation. I have winter in my beard now," he said. "So I've been told, anyway. Do I look distinguished, my dear?" the blind man said to my wife.

"You look distinguished, Robert," she said. "Robert," she said. "Robert, it's just so good to see you."

My wife finally took her eyes off the blind man and looked at me. I had the feeling she didn't like what she saw. I shrugged.

I've never met, or personally known, anyone who was blind. This blind man was late forties, a heavy-set, balding man with stooped shoulders, as if he carried a great weight there. He wore brown slacks, brown shoes, a light-brown shirt, a tie, a sports coat. Spiffy. He also had this full beard. But he didn't use a cane and he didn't wear dark glasses. I'd always thought dark glasses were a must for the blind. Fact was, I wished he had a pair. At first glance, his eyes looked like anyone else's eyes. But if you looked close, there was something different about them. Too much white in the iris, for one thing, and the pupils seemed to move around in the sockets without his knowing it or being able to stop it. Creepy. As I stared at his face, I saw the left pupil turn in toward his nose while the other made an effort to keep in one place. But it was only an effort, for that eye was on the roam without his knowing it or wanting it to be.

I said, "Let me get you a drink. What's your pleasure? We have a little of everything. It's one of our pastimes."

"Bub, I'm a Scotch man myself," he said fast enough in this big voice.

"Right," I said. Bub! "Sure you are. I knew it."

He let his fingers touch his suitcase, which was sitting alongside the sofa. He was taking his bearings. I didn't blame him for that.

"I'll move that up to your room," my wife said.

"No, that's fine," the blind man said loudly. "It can go up when I go up."

"A little water with the Scotch?" I said.

"Very little," he said.

"I knew it," I said.

He said, "Just a tad. The Irish actor, Barry Fitzgerald?[2] I'm like that fellow. When I drink water, Fitzgerald said, I drink water. When I drink whiskey, I drink whiskey." My wife laughed. The blind man brought his hand up under his beard. He lifted his beard slowly and let it drop.

I did the drinks, three big glasses of Scotch with a splash of water in each. Then we made ourselves comfortable and talked about Robert's travels. First the long flight from the West Coast to Connecticut, we covered that. Then from Connecticut up here by train. We had another drink concerning that leg of the trip.

I remembered having read somewhere that the blind didn't smoke because, as speculation had it, they couldn't see the smoke they exhaled. I thought I knew that much and that much only about blind people. But this blind man smoked his cigarette down to the nubbin and then lit another one. This blind man filled his ashtray and my wife emptied it.

When we sat down at the table for dinner, we had another drink. My wife heaped Robert's plate with cube steak, scalloped potatoes, green beans. I buttered him up two slices of bread. I said, "Here's bread and butter for you." I swallowed some of my drink. "Now let us pray," I said, and the blind man lowered his head. My wife looked at me, her mouth agape. "Pray the phone won't ring and the food doesn't get cold," I said.

We dug in. We ate everything there was to eat on the table. We ate like there was no tomorrow. We didn't talk. We ate. We scarfed. We grazed that table. We were into serious eating. The blind man had right away located his foods, he knew just where everything was on his plate. I watched with admiration as he used his knife and fork on the meat. He'd cut two pieces of meat, fork the meat into his mouth, and then go all out for the scalloped potatoes, the beans next, and then he'd tear off a hunk of buttered bread and eat that. He'd follow this up with a big drink of milk. It didn't seem to bother him to use his fingers once in a while, either.

We finished everything, including half a strawberry pie. For a few moments, we sat as if stunned. Sweat beaded on our faces. Finally, we got up from the table and left the dirty plates. We didn't look back. We took ourselves into the living room and sank into our places again. Robert and my wife sat on the sofa. I took the big chair. We had us two or three more drinks while they talked about the major things that had come to pass for them in the past ten years. For the most part, I just listened. Now and then I joined in. I didn't want him to think I'd left the room, and I didn't want her to think I was feeling left out. They talked of things that had happened to them—to them!—these past ten years. I waited in vain to hear my name on my wife's sweet lips: "And then my dear husband came into my life"—something like that. But I heard nothing of the sort. More talk of Robert. Robert had done a little of everything, it seemed, a regular blind jack-of-all-trades. But most

2. Noted for his stock characterizations of Irish figures (often priests) in American films of the 1940s and 1950s.

recently he and his wife had had an Amway[3] distributorship, from which, I gathered, they'd earned their living, such as it was. The blind man was also a ham radio operator. He talked in his loud voice about conversations he'd had with fellow operators in Guam, in the Philippines, in Alaska, and even in Tahiti. He said he'd have a lot of friends there if he ever wanted to go visit those places. From time to time, he'd turn his blind face toward me, put his hand under his beard, ask me something. How long had I been in my present position? (Three years.) Did I like my work? (I didn't.) Was I going to stay with it? (What were the options?) Finally, when I thought he was beginning to run down, I got up and turned on the TV.

My wife looked at me with irritation. She was heading toward a boil. Then she looked at the blind man and said, "Robert, do you have a TV?"

The blind man said, "My dear, I have two TVs. I have a color set and a black-and-white thing, an old relic. It's funny, but if I turn the TV on, and I'm always turning it on, I turn on the color set. It's funny, don't you think?"

I didn't know what to say to that. I had absolutely nothing to say to that. No opinion. So I watched the news program and tried to listen to what the announcer was saying.

"This is a color TV," the blind man said. "Don't ask me how, but I can tell."

"We traded up a while ago," I said.

The blind man had another taste of his drink. He lifted his beard, sniffed it, and let it fall. He leaned forward on the sofa. He positioned his ashtray on the coffee table, then put the lighter to his cigarette. He leaned back on the sofa and crossed his legs at the ankles.

My wife covered her mouth, and then she yawned. She stretched. She said, "I think I'll go upstairs and put on my robe. I think I'll change into something else. Robert, you make yourself comfortable," she said.

"I'm comfortable," the blind man said.

"I want you to feel comfortable in this house," she said.

"I am comfortable," the blind man said.

After she'd left the room, he and I listened to the weather report and then to the sports roundup. By that time, she'd been gone so long I didn't know if she was going to come back. I thought she might have gone to bed. I wished she'd come back downstairs. I didn't want to be left alone with a blind man. I asked him if he wanted another drink, and he said sure. Then I asked if he wanted to smoke some dope with me. I said I'd just rolled a number. I hadn't, but I planned to do so in about two shakes.

"I'll try some with you," he said.

"Damn right," I said. "That's the stuff."

I got our drinks and sat down on the sofa with him. Then I rolled us two fat numbers. I lit one and passed it. I brought it to his fingers. He took it and inhaled.

"Hold it as long as you can," I said. I could tell he didn't know the first thing.

My wife came back downstairs wearing her pink robe and her pink slippers.

"What do I smell?" she said.

---

3. A retail sales business operated by taking orders at home.

"We thought we'd have us some cannabis," I said.

My wife gave me a savage look. Then she looked at the blind man and said, "Robert, I didn't know you smoked."

He said, "I do now, my dear. There's a first time for everything. But I don't feel anything yet."

"This stuff is pretty mellow," I said. "This stuff is mild. It's dope you can reason with," I said. "It doesn't mess you up."

"Not much it doesn't, bub," he said, and laughed.

My wife sat on the sofa between the blind man and me. I passed her the number. She took it and toked and then passed it back to me. "Which way is this going?" she said. Then she said, "I shouldn't be smoking this. I can hardly keep my eyes open as it is. That dinner did me in. I shouldn't have eaten so much."

"It was the strawberry pie," the blind man said. "That's what did it," he said, and he laughed his big laugh. Then he shook his head.

"There's more strawberry pie," I said.

"Do you want some more, Robert?" my wife said.

"Maybe in a little while," he said.

We gave our attention to the TV. My wife yawned again. She said, "Your bed is made up when you feel like going to bed, Robert. I know you must have had a long day. When you're ready to go to bed, say so." She pulled his arm. "Robert?"

He came to and said, "I've had a real nice time. This beats tapes, doesn't it?"

I said, "Coming at you," and I put the number between his fingers. He inhaled, held the smoke, and then let it go. It was like he'd been doing it since he was nine years old.

"Thanks, bub," he said. "But I think this is all for me. I think I'm beginning to feel it," he said. He held the burning roach out for my wife.

"Same here," she said. "Ditto. Me, too." She took the roach and passed it to me. "I may just sit here for a while between you two guys with my eyes closed. But don't let me bother you, okay? Either one of you. If it bothers you, say so. Otherwise, I may just sit here with my eyes closed until you're ready to go to bed," she said. "Your bed's made up, Robert, when you're ready. It's right next to our room at the top of the stairs. We'll show you up when you're ready. You wake me up now, you guys, if I fall asleep." She said that and then she closed her eyes and went to sleep.

The news program ended. I got up and changed the channel. I sat back down on the sofa. I wished my wife hadn't pooped out. Her head lay across the back of the sofa, her mouth open. She'd turned so that her robe had slipped away from her legs, exposing a juicy thigh. I reached to draw her robe back over her, and it was then that I glanced at the blind man. What the hell! I flipped the robe open again.

"You say when you want some strawberry pie," I said.

"I will," he said.

I said, "Are you tired? Do you want me to take you up to your bed? Are you ready to hit the hay?"

"Not yet," he said. "No, I'll stay up with you, bub. If that's all right. I'll stay up until you're ready to turn in. We haven't had a chance to talk. Know what I mean? I feel like me and her monopolized the evening." He lifted his beard and he let it fall. He picked up his cigarettes and his lighter.

"That's all right," I said. Then I said, "I'm glad for the company."

And I guess I was. Every night I smoked dope and stayed up as long as I could before I fell asleep. My wife and I hardly ever went to bed at the same time. When I did go to sleep, I had these dreams. Sometimes I'd wake up from one of them, my heart going crazy.

Something about the church and the Middle Ages was on the TV. Not your run-of-the-mill TV fare. I wanted to watch something else. I turned to the other channels. But there was nothing on them, either. So I turned back to the first channel and apologized.

"Bub, it's all right," the blind man said. "It's fine with me. Whatever you want to watch is okay. I'm always learning something. Learning never ends. It won't hurt me to learn something tonight. I got ears," he said.

We didn't say anything for a time. He was leaning forward with his head turned at me, his right ear aimed in the direction of the set. Very disconcerting. Now and then his eyelids drooped and then they snapped open again. Now and then he put his fingers into his beard and tugged, like he was thinking about something he was hearing on the television.

On the screen, a group of men wearing cowls was being set upon and tormented by men dressed in skeleton costumes and men dressed as devils. The men dressed as devils wore devil masks, horns, and long tails. This pageant was part of a procession. The Englishman who was narrating the thing said it took place in Spain once a year. I tried to explain to the blind man what was happening.

"Skeletons," he said. "I know about skeletons," he said, and he nodded.

The TV showed this one cathedral. Then there was a long, slow look at another one. Finally, the picture switched to the famous one in Paris, with its flying buttresses and its spires reaching up to the clouds. The camera pulled away to show the whole of the cathedral rising above the skyline.

There were times when the Englishman who was telling the thing would shut up, would simply let the camera move around over the cathedrals. Or else the camera would tour the countryside, men in fields walking behind oxen. I waited as long as I could. Then I felt I had to say something. I said, "They're showing the outside of this cathedral now. Gargoyles. Little statues carved to look like monsters. Now I guess they're in Italy. Yeah, they're in Italy. There's paintings on the walls of this one church."

"Are those fresco paintings, bub?" he asked, and he sipped from his drink.

I reached for my glass. But it was empty. I tried to remember what I could remember. "You're asking me are those frescoes?" I said. "That's a good question. I don't know."

The camera moved to a cathedral outside Lisbon. The differences in the Portuguese cathedral compared with the French and Italian were not that great. But they were there. Mostly the interior stuff. Then something occurred to me, and I said, "Something has occurred to me. Do you have any idea what a cathedral is? What they look like, that is? Do you follow me? If somebody says cathedral to you, do you have any notion what they're talking about? Do you know the difference between that and a Baptist church, say?"

He let the smoke dribble from his mouth. "I know they took hundreds of workers fifty or a hundred years to build," he said. "I just heard the man say that, of course. I know generations of the same families worked on a cathedral. I heard him say that, too. The men who began their life's work on them, they never lived to see the completion of their work. In that wise, bub, they're no different from the rest of us, right?" He laughed. Then his eyelids drooped again. His head nodded. He seemed to be snoozing. Maybe he was imagining himself in Portugal. The TV was showing another cathedral now. This one was in Germany. The Englishman's voice droned on. "Cathedrals," the blind man said. He sat up and rolled his head back and forth. "If you want the truth, bub, that's about all I know. What I just said. What I heard him say. But maybe you could describe one to me? I wish you'd do it. I'd like that. If you want to know, I really don't have a good idea."

I stared hard at the shot of the cathedral on the TV. How could I even begin to describe it? But say my life depended on it. Say my life was being threatened by an insane guy who said I had to do it or else.

I stared some more at the cathedral before the picture flipped off into the countryside. There was no use. I turned to the blind man and said, "To begin with, they're very tall." I was looking around the room for clues. "They reach way up. Up and up. Toward the sky. They're so big, some of them, they have to have these supports. To help hold them up, so to speak. These supports are called buttresses. They remind me of viaducts, for some reason. But maybe you don't know viaducts, either? Sometimes the cathedrals have devils and such carved into the front. Sometimes lords and ladies. Don't ask me why this is," I said.

He was nodding. The whole upper part of his body seemed to be moving back and forth.

"I'm not doing so good, am I?" I said.

He stopped nodding and leaned forward on the edge of the sofa. As he listened to me, he was running his fingers through his beard. I wasn't getting through to him, I could see that. But he waited for me to go on just the same. He nodded, like he was trying to encourage me. I tried to think what else to say. "They're really big," I said. "They're massive. They're built of stone. Marble, too, sometimes. In those olden days, when they built cathedrals, men wanted to be close to God. In those olden days, God was an important part of everyone's life. You could tell this from their cathedral-building. I'm sorry," I said, "but it looks like that's the best I can do for you. I'm just no good at it."

"That's all right, bub," the blind man said. "Hey, listen. I hope you don't mind my asking you. Can I ask you something? Let me ask you a simple question, yes or no. I'm just curious and there's no offense. You're my host. But let me ask if you are in any way religious? You don't mind my asking?"

I shook my head. He couldn't see that, though. A wink is the same as a nod to a blind man. "I guess I don't believe in it. In anything. Sometimes it's hard. You know what I'm saying?"

"Sure, I do," he said.

"Right," I said.

The Englishman was still holding forth. My wife sighed in her sleep. She drew a long breath and went on with her sleeping.

"You'll have to forgive me," I said. "But I can't tell you what a cathedral looks like. It just isn't in me to do it. I can't do any more than I've done."

The blind man sat very still, his head down, as he listened to me.

I said, "The truth is, cathedrals don't mean anything special to me. Nothing. Cathedrals. They're something to look at on late-night TV. That's all they are."

It was then that the blind man cleared his throat. He brought something up. He took a handkerchief from his back pocket. Then he said, "I get it, bub. It's okay. It happens. Don't worry about it," he said. "Hey, listen to me. Will you do me a favor? I got an idea. Why don't you find us some heavy paper? And a pen. We'll do something. We'll draw one together. Get us a pen and some heavy paper. Go on, bub, get the stuff," he said.

So I went upstairs. My legs felt like they didn't have any strength in them. They felt like they did after I'd done some running. In my wife's room, I looked around. I found some ballpoints in a little basket on her table. And then I tried to think where to look for the kind of paper he was talking about.

Downstairs, in the kitchen, I found a shopping bag with onion skins in the bottom of the bag. I emptied the bag and shook it. I brought it into the living room and sat down with it near his legs. I moved some things, smoothed the wrinkles from the bag, spread it out on the coffee table.

The blind man got down from the sofa and sat next to me on the carpet.

He ran his fingers over the paper. He went up and down the sides of the paper. The edges, even the edges. He fingered the corners.

"All right," he said. "All right, let's do her."

He found my hand, the hand with the pen. He closed his hand over my hand. "Go ahead, bub, draw," he said. "Draw. You'll see. I'll follow along with you. It'll be okay. Just begin now like I'm telling you. You'll see. Draw," the blind man said.

So I began. First I drew a box that looked like a house. It could have been the house I lived in. Then I put a roof on it. At either end of the roof, I drew spires. Crazy.

"Swell," he said. "Terrific. You're doing fine," he said. "Never thought anything like this could happen in your lifetime, did you, bub? Well, it's a strange life, we all know that. Go on now. Keep it up."

I put in windows with arches. I drew flying buttresses. I hung great doors. I couldn't stop. The TV station went off the air. I put down the pen and closed and opened my fingers. The blind man felt around over the paper. He moved the tips of his fingers over the paper, all over what I had drawn, and he nodded.

"Doing fine," the blind man said.

I took up the pen again, and he found my hand. I kept at it. I'm no artist. But I kept drawing just the same.

My wife opened up her eyes and gazed at us. She sat up on the sofa, her robe hanging open. She said, "What are you doing? Tell me, I want to know."

I didn't answer her.

The blind man said, "We're drawing a cathedral. Me and him are working on it. Press hard," he said to me. "That's right. That's good," he said. "Sure. You got it, bub. I can tell. You didn't think you could. But you can, can't you? You're cooking with gas now. You know what I'm saying? We're going to really have us something here in a minute. How's the old arm?" he said. "Put some people in there now. What's a cathedral without people?"

My wife said, "What's going on? Robert, what are you doing? What's going on?"

"It's all right," he said to her. "Close your eyes now," the blind man said to me.

I did it. I closed them just like he said.

"Are they closed?" he said. "Don't fudge."

"They're closed," I said.

"Keep them that way," he said. He said, "Don't stop now. Draw."

So we kept on with it. His fingers rode my fingers as my hand went over the paper. It was like nothing else in my life up to now.

Then he said, "I think that's it. I think you got it," he said. "Take a look. What do you think?"

But I had my eyes closed. I thought I'd keep them that way for a little longer. I thought it was something I ought to do.

"Well?" he said. "Are you looking?"

My eyes were still closed. I was in my house. I knew that. But I didn't feel like I was inside anything.

"It's really something," I said.

1983

ISHMAEL REED
b. 1938

Ishmael Reed's love-hate affair with American popular culture has led him to both literary successes and entanglements with sociocultural obstacles. On the positive side, his appreciation of African American rich artistry, including such only-in-America items as jazz, rhythm and blues, detective novels, comic books, and the rich blend of multicultures and their unique vernaculars, has enabled him to champion a truly native literature apart from the standards imposed (in a colonial manner) from European culture. Perhaps partly in recognition of this versatility, Reed was awarded a Macarthur Foundation "genius" fellowship. Negatively, his unbounded sense of satire has managed to offend almost every interest group in the profession of literature from feminists to creative writing program teachers of poetry. In the chapter printed here from his novel *The Last Days of Louisiana Red* (1974), Reed offers a humorous critique of a presumed ally, someone who teaches African American literature. The text being taught, Richard Wright's *Native Son* (1940), is one of the most important novels in American literature. Yet Reed objects to the stereotyping that this very success makes possible. So too for his character Minnie the Moocher from this same novel. The satire is especially cutting in naming the novel's chief feminist after a figure in bandleader Cab Calloway's song from the 1940s, an era of popular culture heavy with now-abhorrent sexual caricatures; it is effective, however, because of the way Reed shows how people like Minnie cooperate with their own oppression by maintaining forces of exclusion. It is to Reed's credit that he uses history and folklore to subvert such exclusionary processes, just as his novel employs figures from classic radio comedy such as Amos and Andy and their friend Kingfish to undermine ideas that when stated by others pass for the logic of a black bourgeoisie.

Reed draws a good picture of himself in the biographical note to his second novel, *Yellow Back Radio Broke-Down* (1969):

Ishmael Reed was born in Chattanooga, Tennessee, on February 22, 1938. Chattanooga built a monument to every Confederate soldier killed in the Civil War, so Ishmael Reed spent his early years bumping into stone. He grew up in Buffalo, New York, where "polack" is scribbled on the bust of Chopin in Humboldt Park.

Ishmael Reed attended the University of Buffalo and left after receiving rude phone calls from an anti-Gnostic bursar. At 20 he was stranded in North Platte, Nebraska. Buffalo Bill once had a drink there. He has taught American fiction at the University of California at Berkeley, and the University of Washington at Seattle.

He startled the scientific community by making his home in New York City. Ishmael Reed has been buffaloed by many aspects of American society, which makes him uniquely qualified to write about the West.

Yellow Back Radio Broke-Down is indeed about the West, but a West in which a band of cowboy rustlers is confronted by the pope in a helicopter. Similar anachronisms distinguish Reed's other novels, including the Egyptology and Haitian hoodoo of *Mumbo Jumbo* (1972), in which West Indian religion is employed for its imaginative resources, and the Civil War slave narrative of *Flight to Canada* (1976). Subsequent novels lampoon contemporary politics, including political correctness; notable among these are *Reckless Eyeballing* (1986) and *Japanese by Spring* (1993).

Most of Ishmael Reed's literary methods are evident in *The Last Days of Louisiana Red*. Hoodoo is present in the folklore practices of Papa LaBas and his Solid Gumbo Works, an enterprise that much like this native religion draws on the spiritual nature of life, especially in contrast to the materialism of its rivals, Louisiana Red and the Moochers. It is set in a Berkeley, California, rife with early 1970s turbulence, including a university curriculum destabilized by an intellectual who, in the chapter printed here, dreams he has become the character Mary Dalton in Richard Wright's *Native Son,* a novel in which a young, rich white woman is inadvertently killed by her family's physically intimidating black chauffeur, Bigger Thomas. Sexual, racial, intellectual, and religious issues are thrown together in a mixed bag of popular references, all of which Reed shakes up and displays in fresh new postures. Like all good satirists, he exposes his subjects' weaknesses by emphasizing problems in their own terms.

Reed's poetry is an even more direct introduction to his general literary activity, for here is seen the blending of popular forms from many different cultures that to him constitutes truly American expression. His "Neo-HooDoo Manifesto," presented as a poem, is in fact a program for what Reed would write himself and help others publish (via his *Yardbird Reader* series of books and anthologies produced with the Before Columbus Foundation). His message is that a rich culture, an original culture, exists within the very forms older European standards disallow as lowbrow. He catalogs a wide range of popular entertainment figures and devises a poetic language that employs the power of expression so evident in the rhythms of such music. His editing and anthologizing and small press productions have called on the resources of not just African American writers but of Chinese Americans, Japanese Americans, white Americans of various ethnic backgrounds, and Native Americans, the blending of which into non-Eurocentric aesthetic forms is unique to America.

From The Last Days of Louisiana Red[1]

Chapter 36

[MARY DALTON'S DREAM]

He was a blonde. He lay in the bed, tossing and turning. His room. What was that odor? The pungent odor of middle-class perfume making the air misty. He didn't feel right. His hair. What on earth was the matter with his hair? It was long and was covering the pillow. The pillows? They had a flower print and were pink. Pink? He rose in his bed and his breasts jiggled. BREASTS? THE BREASTS?? He looked back into the mirror next to the bed and his mouth made a black hollow hole of horror. "O MY GOD. MY GOD." He was a woman. You know what he said next, don't you, reader? He's from New York and so . . . you guessed it! "Kafka.[2] Pure Kafka," he said. A feeling crept over him. Tingly. What could he do? He felt like screaming, but he couldn't scream. Was that someone coming down the hall? He ran and jumped back into the bed, pulled the covers up to his neck and pretended to be asleep. Someone *was* coming down the hall. They stood for a moment outside in the hall. And then the knob slowly turned. Someone was now in the room; a dark foreboding shadow crept to the foot of the bed. A giant colored man—an Olmec-headed[3] giant wearing a chauffeur's cap. Max started to really scream this time.

"Please, Ms. Dalton,[4] you will wake the whole house," the figure says. *Look at that white bitch laying there. Sloppy drunk. Probably wants some peter too. That's all they think about anyway. I'll fuck her into a cunt energy crisis she mess with me. That's probably what she wont. Been hittin on me all night. Probably pretending to be drunk. Wonts to see how far I go. I know Jan ain't gettin any. One simple dude. Tried to give me that old PROGRESSIVE LABOR[5] line. Who don't know that? Who don't know that old simple ass mutherfuckin bullshit? Them mens was working at the Ford plant. Had some good jobs too. Then here come this Progressive Labor bullshit and them niggers lost they job after it was over. Ha! When is this bitch going to go to sleep? I wont to take that dark blue Buick with steel spoke wheels over to the South Side. Man, will them mo'fugs be mad when they see. Think I'm a pimp. Then I'll go up to the counter and roll out my 75 dollars. Man, they think I'm one of them pimps. Then I go get me some rangs. Lots of them. Have them all shining on my fingers. Shining. Justa shining. Gee. Bet I could have me plenty ol stankin bitches. Commisstee. That shit ain't nothing but some bunk. Roosia. Shhhhhhit. Started to bust that mo'fug Jan right in the mouf. Must be a sissy. . . . The door opens and in comes a woman tapping a cane. Ahhhhshitt. Here come that other old crazy white woman down the hall. Look like Ms. Mary trying to say something. I better do something quick.*

1. The text is that of *The Last Days of Louisiana Red* (1974).
2. Franz Kafka (1883–1924), Austrian-Czech author of *The Metamorphosis*, in which the protagonist awakes to find himself turned into a giant insect.
3. A cultural characteristic of the ancient Indian peoples of what is now Tabasco and Veracruz in Mexico.
4. The character murdered by Bigger Thomas in *Native Son* (1940), a novel by the American writer Richard Wright (1908–1960).
5. A Marxist magazine and political party active in the United States beginning in the 1930s.

Max finally realized the situation. He made a futile effort to move his lips. "Bigggg. Biggggggg." Meanwhile the cane tapping comes closer to the door. Bigger picks up the pillow and starts towards Mary Dalton when—

Max wakes up from the nightmare.

There was some bamming at the door real rough. Bam! Bam! Bam! Bam! Bam, Bam! Max leaped out of his dream and rushed to the door. Who could this be bamming at his door this time of night? The woman, trembling, rushed into the room.

"What do you want? I told you to never come here."

She wriggled out of her raincoat, then nervously wrung out a match after lighting a cigarette. She plopped down in a chair and drew her breath. It was Lisa, stripped of her Nanny's rags, sharp, voluptuous.

"It's LaBas. He called. He wants to talk about Ed's killing. Suppose he starts to ask me a lot of questions? You know I can't stand up under a lot of questions."

"You fool. You come here for that? I told you never to contact me here on this assignment."

"Look, you've only been here for a few years. I've been here more than ten, ever since his wife Ruby left. I've worked on that household and put my conjure all over the place. Then they sent you in to begin this organization to add to Ed's problems. Just as I had worked hard to prepare Minnie to do that. We've done enough damage to that family. When will it end?"

"It will end when Solid Gumbo Works has folded."

"I can't wait any longer. Since Wolf was killed, she's brought those Moochers into the household. I have to shuffle about like Hattie McDaniel[6] to take care of their needs. They write slogans all over the walls and sleep on stained mattresses. They leave rings in the bathtub. They've been up all night with the mimeograph machine, trying to free Kingfish and Andy."[7]

"Yes, I know," Max said. "I wrote the copy."

"I have to fix breakfast and clean up their mess. You know how Moochers are, never clean up after themselves, always expect someone else to do their cleaning for them. I told you not to draw the girl into that organization. I was doing O.K. All I needed was some more time."

"You were taking too long. Besides, the Moochers provided us with the numbers to wear down Solid Gumbo Works."

"Well, I still maintain that if it had been left to me, I would have put her on Ed. I never did go along with his killing."

"It was necessary. You know that. If we hadn't butchered him that night, he would have discovered the cure for heroin addiction. That was the industrial secret you passed on to me; the papers of his you Xeroxed. We had to do it. If he had found a legitimate cure, our quack operation would have shut down: the southern mailhouse empire we built would shut down. Heroin, jukeboxes, our black record company in the east, The House of Cocaine. Everybody would have been asking for Ed's Gumbo. Wasn't it enough that he found a cure for cancer?"

---

6. An actress portraying African American maids in American films of the 1940s and 1950s.

7. African American characters in the radio and television comedy show of the 1940s and 1950s.

"You thought you'd gotten rid of that threat when you killed that Chinese acupuncturist, but Ed found different means."

"You always respected him a bit, didn't you?"

"He was a man. Ed was a hard-working man. Sometimes I wanted to tell him who I was, where I was from, and what was wrong with me. That I had been sent into his house to train his child to drive him crazy."

"You can't quit. I received orders from Louisiana Red that we have one more job. You think you have problems. Do you think I like posing as a visiting lecturer at the University of California at Berkeley? The way the women in the English Department office whisper about my lack of potency and sometimes refuse to file for my office post box.

"Do you think that I enjoy it when they refuse to mimeograph copies of lecture notes for my students? Why, this campus reminds me of the set of I Was a Teenage Werewolf.[8] If Louisiana Red hadn't promised me this one-million-dollar retirement money, I never would have taken care of this assignment. I was doing all right with my New York industrial spy firm. But you, you have to stay until it's over. They have you where they want you."

"I'm leaving."

Max pulls out a sheet of paper from a desk drawer. "You know that Louisiana Red doesn't play. They will get to you through your police record. You are a fugitive from justice, you know, you bag woman. (Reads) 'Real name: The Hammerhead Shark.' The title you picked up in that caper when you hit a man on the head with a hammer, put a hex on a congressman, double-crossed Jack Johnson, stabbed Martin Luther King, brought charges against Father Divine, brought down Sam Cooke in a blaze of gunfire and bad-mouthed Joe Louis.[9] They know your penchant for Coon-Can and about your scar too. Not only are the law enforcement bureaus after you, but you know the consequences of crossing the Louisiana Red Corporation."

"I'm not frightened any more. I've sent a message to the Red Rooster and told him that I want out, Max."

"I've thought about leaving myself."

"You have? Why, Max, we can leave together, go to Reno; why, I can get a job as a waitress, you can deal blackjack."

"But they'll follow us."

"Not if we move fast enough."

"Maybe we ought to. You know how I missed you during those long days. When you couldn't be with me in my arms. How we had to limit ourselves to meeting every other Thursday, your day off. There must be thousands of us all over the country, meeting like this out of public view.

"Yes, my dearest, the American underground of Desire, the name of the first American slaver; we know each other on the street and recognize each other's signals. How we pay subscriptions to our propaganda organs which convince the public that it's only the Jim Brown and Racquel Welch[1] bed-

8. Popular American film of the 1950s.
9. Popular figures from African American culture. Johnson (1878–1946), first black heavyweight champion of the world. King (1929–1968), civil rights leader. Father Divine, born George Baker

(1877–1965), American religious leader. Cooke (1935–1964), popular singer. Louis (1914–1981), world heavyweight champion.
1. Current film stars, respectively African American and white.

room scene that's the problem. We rule America, all of it, my Nanny and me. The 'Every Other Thursday Society.' Yes, I want to leave, Lisa. My cover is getting to me."

"I don't understand."

"That book I'm doing—the one on Richard Wright's book." He rushes to the bar, makes a drink and gulps it down. Then he slams the empty glass on the bar. "It's getting to me. I'm having these dreams. Just before you knocked on the door, I had one. I was the murder victim and this big brute was coming towards me with a pillow."

"That dream will come true if you won't move over to the wall."

The startled couple turned around to see the gunman standing in the doorway.

"Son of a bitch. So you were going to take it on the lam and leave me stranded now that the assignment has heated up."

"T, take it easy, have a drink."

"No thanks, I'm not thirsty. Here I have been playing the fool for these past years, helping you set up Ed Yellings, and now you are going to drop me. Years of swallowing my pride and acting like a kookie rookie when all along you two were carrying on. I'm finished with this assignment. I feel sick about what has happened to Minnie. She wants more power now than Marie Laveau,[2] and you two did it to her. I'm going to call the Director of Louisiana Red Corporation, the Red Rooster, and tell him everything I know about you two. You see, it's all over. That's what I came up here to tell you about."

"What's all over?" Lisa says. "You don't make sense."

"About an hour ago Minnie busted George Kingfish Stevens and Andy Brown out of jail and then commandeered an airplane after miraculously evading San Francisco security, which was as tight as a drum. You don't have anything else to use against Solid Gumbo Works because Minnie has been shot."

"Shot," both Lisa and Max exclaim.

"Yes, she was shot by a passenger. The poor child was rushed to a New York hospital. It sickens me, my part in this whole thing."

He walks over to the telephone and dials.

"Hello, operator, give me Louisiana Red Corporation in New Orleans, person to person to the Red Rooster, the number is area code 504—" but before he could say anything Max lunged for him and with incredible strength wrestled him to the floor. The gun went off, killing T Feeler.

"Max, let's get out of here. We really must go now."

Max slowly looked up from where he knelt over the corpse. "Who you callin Max, bitch? I'll whip you into bad health."

"Max, what's the matter with you? Why are you talking that way?"

"I'm gone fix you good. Killing you won't count. Not even the best critics will notice it. I'm going to kill you." He walks towards her. She screams.

"Max! Stop!"

"Max? Who Max? I'm Bigger," Max growls.

1974

---

2. Quasi-legendary hoodoo worker in old New Orleans.

Neo-HooDoo Manifesto[1]

Neo-HooDoo is a "Lost American Church" updated. Neo-HooDoo is the music of James Brown without the lyrics and ads for Black Capitalism. Neo-HooDoo is the 8 basic dances of 19-century New Orleans' *Place Congo*—the Calinda the Bamboula the Chacta the Babouille the Conjaille the Juba the Congo and the VooDoo—modernized into the Philly Dog, the Hully Gully, the Funky Chicken, the Popcorn, the Boogaloo and the dance of great American choreographer Buddy Bradley.

Neo-HooDoos would rather "shake that thing" than be stiff and erect. (There were more people performing a Neo-HooDoo sacred dance, the Boogaloo, at Woodstock than chanting Hare Krishna . . . Hare Hare!) All so-called "Store Front Churches" and "Rock Festivals"[2] receive their matrix in the HooDoo rites of Marie Laveau conducted at New Orleans' Lake Pontchartrain, and Bayou St. John in the 1880's. The power of HooDoo challenged the stability of civil authority in New Orleans and was driven underground where to this day it flourishes in the Black ghettos throughout the country. Thats why in Ralph Ellison's[3] modern novel *Invisible Man* New Orleans is described as "The Home of Mystery." "Everybody from New Orleans got that thing," Louis Armstrong[4] said once.

HooDoo is the strange and beautiful "fits" the Black slave Tituba gave the children of Salem.[5] (Notice the arm waving ecstatic females seemingly possessed at the "Pentecostal," "Baptist," and "Rock Festivals," [all fronts for Neo-HooDoo]). The reason that HooDoo isn't given the credit it deserves in influencing American Culture is because the students of that culture both "overground" and "underground" are uptight closet Jeho-vah revisionists. They would assert the American and East Indian and Chinese thing before they would the Black thing. Their spiritual leaders Ezra Pound and T. S. Eliot[6] hated Africa and "Darkies." In Theodore Roszak's book *The Making of a Counter Culture*[7]—there is barely any mention of the Black influence on this culture even though its members dress like Blacks talk like Blacks walk like Blacks, gesture like Blacks wear Afros and indulge in Black music and dance (Neo-HooDoo).

Neo-HooDoo is sexual, sensual and digs the old "heathen" good good loving. An early American HooDoo song says:

> *Now lady I ain't no mill man*
> *Just the mill man's son*
> *But I can do your grinding*
> *till the mill man comes*

---

1. From *Conjure* (1972).
2. Massively attended concerts, often outdoors, popular in the 1960s and 1970s. "Store Front Churches": small churches with improvised sites in neighborhood shops.
3. African American writer (1914–1994).
4. American jazz musician and vocalist (1900–

1971).
5. A town in Massachusetts that was the site of witchcraft hysteria in 1692.
6. Pound (1885–1972) and Eliot (1888–1965) were modernist American poets.
7. A 1969 study of contemporary young people's revolt against establishment codes and traditions.

Which doesn't mean that women are treated as "sexual toys" in Neo-HooDoo or as one slick Jeho-vah Revisionist recently said, "victims of a raging hormone imbalance." Neo-HooDoo claims many women philosophers and theoreticians which is more than ugh religions Christianity and its offspring Islam can claim. When our theoretician Zora Neale Hurston[8] asked a *Mambo* (a female priestess in the Haitian VooDoo) a definition of VooDoo the Mambo lifted her skirts and exhibited her Erzulie Seal, her Isis seal. Neo-HooDoo identifies with Julia Jackson[9] who stripped HooDoo of its oppressive Catholic layer—Julia Jackson said when asked the origin of the amulets and talismans in her studio, "I make all my own stuff. It saves money and it's as good. People who has to buy their stuff ain't using their heads."

Neo-HooDoo is not a church for egotripping—it takes its "organization" from Haitian VooDoo of which Milo Rigaud wrote:

Unlike other established religions, there is no hierarchy of bishops, archbishops, cardinals, or a pope in VooDoo. Each oum'phor is a law unto itself, following the traditions of VooDoo but modifying and changing the ceremonies and rituals in various ways. Secrets of VooDoo.

Neo-HooDoo believes that every man is an artist and every artist a priest. You can bring your own creative ideas to Neo-HooDoo. Charlie "Yardbird (Thoth)" Parker[1] is an example of the Neo-HooDoo artist as an innovator and improvisor.

In Neo-HooDoo, Christ the landlord deity ("render unto Caesar") is on probation. This includes "The Black Christ" and "The Hippie Christ." Neo-HooDoo tells Christ to get lost. (Judas Iscariot holds an honorary degree from Neo-HooDoo.)

Whereas at the center of Christianity lies the graveyard the organ-drone and the cross, the center of Neo-HooDoo is the drum the anhk and the Dance. So Fine, Barefootin, Heard it Through the Grapevine,[2] are all Neo-HooDoos.

Neo-HooDoo has "seen a lot of things in this old world."

Neo-HooDoo borrows from Ancient Egyptians (ritual accessories of Ancient Egypt are still sold in the House of Candles and Talismans on Stanton Street in New York, the Botanical Gardens in East Harlem, and Min and Mom on Haight Street in San Francisco, examples of underground centers found in ghettos throughout America).

Neo-HooDoo borrows from Haiti Africa and South America. Neo-HooDoo comes in all styles and moods.

---

8. American fiction writer, poet, and folklorist (1891–1960).
9. American sculptor (b. 1936).
1. American jazz musician (1920–1955), pioneer of the bebop style of modern jazz.
2. Popular rock 'n' roll and rhythm-and-blues songs that inspired new dances.

Louis Jordon Nellie Lutcher John Lee Hooker Ma Rainey Dinah Washington
the Temptations Ike and Tina Turner Aretha Franklin Muddy Waters Otis
Redding Sly and the Family Stone B. B. King Junior Wells Bessie Smith Jelly
Roll Morton Ray Charles Jimi Hendrix Buddy Miles the 5th Dimension the
Chambers Brothers Etta James and acolytes Creedence Clearwater Revival
the Flaming Embers Procol Harum are all Neo-HooDoos. Neo-HooDoo
never turns down pork. In fact Neo-HooDoo is the Bar-B-Cue of Amerika.
The Neo-HooDoo cuisine is Geechee Gree Gree Verta Mae's *Vibration
Cooking*.[3] (Ortiz Walton's Neo-HooDoo Jass Band performs at the Native
Son Restaurant in Berkeley, California. Joe Overstreet's[4] Neo-HooDoo
exhibit will happen at the Berkeley Gallery Sept. 1, 1970 in Berkeley.)

Neo-HooDoo ain't Negritude.[5] Neo-HooDoo never been to France. Neo-
HooDoo is "your Mama" as Larry Neal[6] said. Neo-HooDoos Little Richard
and Chuck Berry nearly succeeded in converting the Beatles.[7] When the
Beatles said they were more popular than Christ they seemed astonished at
the resulting outcry. This is because although they could feebly through
amplification and technological sham 'mimic' (as if Little Richard and Chuck
Berry were Loa [Spirits] practicing ventriloquism on their "Horses") the
Beatles failed to realize that they were conjuring the music and ritual
(although imitation) of a Forgotten Faith, a traditional enemy of Christianity
which Christianity the Cop Religion has had to drive underground each time
they meet. Neo-HooDoo now demands a rematch, the referees were bribed
and the adversary had resin on his gloves.

The Vatican Forbids Jazz Masses in Italy
*Rome, Aug. 6 (UPI)—The Vatican today barred jazz and popular music from
masses in Italian churches and forbade young Roman Catholics to change
prayers or readings used on Sundays and holy days.*

It said such changes in worship were "eccentric and arbitrary."

*A Vatican document distributed to all Italian bishops did not refer to similar
experimental masses elsewhere in the world, although Pope Paul VI and other
high-ranking churchmen are known to dislike the growing tendency to deviate
from the accepted form of the mass.*

*Some Italian churches have permitted jazz masses played by combos while
youthful worshipers sang such songs as "We Shall Overcome."*

*Church leaders two years ago rebuked priests who permitted such experi-
ments. The New York Times, August 7, 1970.*

Africa is the home of the Ioa (Spirits) of Neo-HooDoo although we are
building our own American "pantheon." Thousands of "Spirits" (Ka) who
would laugh at Jeho-vah's fury concerning "false idols" (translated everybody else's religion) or "fetishes." Moses, Jeho-vah's messenger and zom-

---

3. This paragraph lists a mélange of contemporary
popular musicians and musical groups from a wide
range of musical styles, including the blues, jazz,
rock 'n' roll, and Motown.
4. Joseph Overstreet (b. 1934), American painter.
5. A 20th-century literary school of poetry written
in French by African authors.

6. Music critic, theoretician of African American
literature, and anthologist (1937–1981).
7. British rock group of the 1960s and 1970s. Little Richard (b. 1935) and Chuck Berry (b. 1926),
African American rhythm-and-blues artists who
had a formative influence on the Beatles.

bie swiped the secrets of VooDoo from old Jethro but nevertheless ended up with a curse. (Warning, many White "Black delineators" who practiced HooDoo VooDoo for gain and did not "feed" the Black Spirits of HooDoo ended up tragically. Bix Beiderbecke and Irene Castle (who exploited Black Dance in the 1920s and relished in dressing up as a Nun) are examples of this tragic tendency.

Moses had a near heart attack when he saw his sons dancing nude before the Black Bull God Apis. They were dancing to a "heathen sound" that Moses had "heard before in Egypt" (probably a mixture of Sun Ra and Jimmy Reed[8] played in the nightclub district of ancient Egypt's "The Domain of Osiris"—named after the god who enjoyed the fancy footwork of the pigmies).

The continuing war between Moses and his "Sons" was recently acted out in Chicago in the guise of an American "trial."

I have called Jeho-vah (most likely Set the Egyptian Sat-on [a pun on the fiend's penalty] Satan) somewhere "a party-pooper and hater of dance." Neo-HooDoos are detectives of the metaphysical about to make a pinch. We have issued warrants for a god arrest. If Jeho-vah reveals his real name he will be released on his own recognizance de-horned and put out to pasture.

A dangerous paranoid pain-in-the-neck a CopGod from the git-go, Jeho-vah was the successful law and order candidate in the mythological relay of the 4th century A.D. Jeho-vah is the God of punishment. The H-Bomb is a typical Jeho-vah "miracle." Jeho-vah is why we are in Vietnam.[9] He told Moses to go out and "subdue" the world.

There has never been in history another such culture as the Western civilization—a culture which has practiced the belief that the physical and social environment of man is subject to rational manipulation and that history is subject to the will and action of man; whereas central to the traditional cultures of the rivals of Western civilization, those of Africa and Asia, is a belief that it is environment that dominates man. The Politics of Hysteria, *Edmund Stillman and William Pfaff.*

"Political leaders" are merely altar boys from Jeho-vah. While the targets of some "revolutionaries" are laundramats and candy stores, Neo-HooDoo targets are TV the museums the symphony halls and churches art music and literature departments in Christianizing (education I think they call it!) universities which propogate the Art of Jeho-vah—much Byzantine Middle Ages Renaissance painting of Jeho-vah's "500 years of civilization" as Nixon[1] put it are Jeho-vah propaganda. Many White revolutionaries can only get together with 3rd world people on the most mundane 'political' level because

8. Blues musician from the 1950s (1925–1976). Sun Ra (1914–1993), an avant-garde jazz musician of the 1950s.
9. The war in Vietnam was being waged at the time this essay was written.
1. Richard Nixon (1913–1994) was president of the United States at the time this essay was written.

they are of Jeho-vah's party and don't know it. How much Black music do so-called revolutionary underground radio stations play. On the other hand how much Bach?

Neo-HooDoos are Black Red (Black Hawk an American Indian was an early philosopher of the HooDoo Church) and occasionally White (Mademoiselle Charlotte is a Haitian Loa [Spirit]).

Neo-HooDoo is a litany seeking its text
Neo-HooDoo is a Dance and Music closing in on its words
Neo-HooDoo is a Church finding its lyrics
Cecil Brown Al Young Calvin Hernton
David Henderson Steven Cannon Quincy Troupe
Ted Joans Victor Cruz N. H. Pritchard Ishmael Reed
Lennox Raphael Sarah Fabio Ron Welburn[2] are Neo-
HooDoo's "Manhattan Project" of writing . . .

A Neo-HooDoo celebration will involve the dance music
and poetry of Neo-HooDoo and whatever ideas the
participating artists might add. A Neo-HooDoo seal
is the Face of an Old American Train.
Neo-HooDoo signs are everywhere!
Neo-HooDoo is the Now Locomotive swinging
up the Tracks of the American Soul.

Almost 100 years ago HooDoo was forced to say
Goodbye to America. Now HooDoo is
back as Neo-HooDoo
You can't keep a good church down!

1972

2. These lines list contemporary multicultural writers.

TONI CADE BAMBARA
1939–1995

"Her writing is woven, aware of its music, its overlapping waves of scenic action, so clearly on its way," Toni Morrison wrote about editing the work of her friend Toni Cade Bambara, "like a magnet collecting details in its wake, each of which is essential to the final effect." In her preface to the posthumous collection of fiction, essays, and conversations titled *Deep Sightings and Rescue Missions* (1996), Morrison describes Bambara as an "ever vocal woman," and it is the remarkable presence of living voice that distinguishes the stories collected in *Gorilla, My Love* (1972) and *The Sea Birds Are Still Alive* (1977) and Bambara's novels, *The Salt Eaters* (1981) and the posthumously published *Those Bones Are Not My Child* (1999).

Born and raised in New York City, Toni Cade Bambara was as much a social activist as a writer. She worked in organizations dedicated to the most practical of day-to-day benefits for minority city dwellers and also traveled to Cuba and Vietnam to lobby for revised national politics. She spent the last fifteen years of her professional life working on television documentaries, including *The Bombing of Orange Avenue* (about the Philadelphia police department's deadly assault on the MOVE organization). Yet it is for her short stories that she will be remembered, particularly the first-person narratives of her women storytellers about their experiences in the black community. Like herself, her protagonists are activists in their societies, societies that in their flux demand creative readjustment at every stage. Such is the dynamic of "Medley" (printed here), in which a culture's music indexes the pace and rhythms of its social existence. As in this story, Bambara's plots are always moving, existing in a state of being "on their way" toward an imperatively stated conclusion, as Toni Morrison has said of this writer's prose style.

As her novel, *The Salt Eaters,* shows, Bambara was sensitive to the role storytelling plays in healthy communities. Here, when an activist is frustrated over divisiveness in the people she wishes to help, a traditional healer comes to the rescue with her tales of folk values. Life is change, Bambara understood; the fluid nature of language itself teaches that there is no stable, secure place beyond the voice's constant ability to reinvent itself. Hence Bambara meant to be of service herself in editing *Tales and Stories of Black Folks* (1971), an anthology that provides ample evidence for how African Americans not only created their own folk legends but adapted European and African materials to their own uniquely American ends. In this writer's fiction readers can see the same process taking place, a joyful embrace of voice as the most personal statement possible in a world dependent on self-invention for survival.

The text is that of *The Sea Birds Are Still Alive* (1977).

Medley

I could tell the minute I got in the door and dropped my bag, I wasn't staying. Dishes piled sky-high in the sink looking like some circus act. Glasses all ghosty on the counter. Busted tea bags, curling canteloupe rinds, white cartons from the Chinamen, green sacks from the deli, and that damn dog creeping up on me for me to wrassle his head or kick him in the ribs one. No, I definitely wasn't staying. Couldn't even figure why I'd come. But picked my way to the hallway anyway till the laundry-stuffed pillowcases stopped me. Larry's bass blocking the view to the bedroom.

"That you, Sweet Pea?"

"No, man, ain't me at all," I say, working my way back to the suitcase and shoving that damn dog out the way. "See ya round," I holler, the door slamming behind me, cutting off the words abrupt.

Quite naturally sitting cross-legged at the club, I embroider a little on the homecoming tale, what with an audience of two crazy women and a fresh bottle of Jack Daniels.[1] Got so I could actually see shonuff toadstools growing in the sink. Canteloupe seeds sprouting in the muck. A goddamn compost heap breeding near the stove, garbage gardens on the grill.

1. A potent brand of Tennessee sour mash whisky.

"Sweet Pea, you oughta hush, cause you can't possibly keep on lying so," Pot Limit's screaming, tears popping from her eyes. "Lawd hold my legs, cause this liar bout to kill me off."

"Never mind about Larry's housekeeping, girl," Sylvia's soothing me, sloshing perfectly good bourbon all over the table. "You can come and stay with me till your house comes through. It'll be like old times at Aunt Merriam's."

I ease back into the booth to wait for the next set. The drummer's fooling with the equipment, tapping the mikes, hoping he's watched, so I watch him. But feeling worried in my mind about Larry, cause I've been through days like that myself. Cold cream caked on my face from the day before, hair matted, bathrobe funky, not a clean pair of drawers to my name. Even the emergency ones, the draggy cotton numbers stuffed way in the back of the drawer under the scented paper gone. And no clean silverware in the box and the last of the paper cups gone too. Icebox empty cept for a rock of cheese and the lone water jug that ain't even half full that's how anyhow the thing's gone on. And not a clue as to the next step. But then Pot Limit'll come bamming on the door to say So-and-so's in town and can she have the card table for a game. Or Sylvia'll send a funny card inviting herself to dinner and even giving me the menu. Then I zoom through that house like a manic work brigade till me and the place ready for white-glove inspection. But what if some somebody or other don't intervene for Larry, I'm thinking.

The drummer's messin round on the cymbals, head cocked to the side, rings sparkling. The other dudes are stepping out from behind the curtain. The piano man playing with the wah-wah doing splashy, breathy science fiction stuff. Sylvia checking me out to make sure I ain't too blue. Blue got hold to me, but I lean foward out of the shadows and babble something about how off the bourbon tastes these days. Hate worryin Sylvia, who is the kind of friend who bleeds at the eyes with your pain. I drain my glass and hum along with the opening riff of the guitar and I keep my eyes strictly off the bass player, whoever he is.

Larry Landers looked more like a bass player than ole Mingus himself. Got these long arms that drape down over the bass like they were grown special for that purpose. Fine, strong hands with long fingers and muscular knuckles, the dimples deep black at the joints. His calluses so other-colored and hard, looked like Larry had swiped his grandmother's tarnished thimbles to play with. He'd move in on that bass like he was going to hump it or something, slide up behind it as he lifted it from the rug, all slinky. He'd become one with the wood. Head dipped down sideways bobbing out the rhythm, feet tapping, legs jiggling, he'd look good. Thing about it, though, ole Larry couldn't play for shit. Couldn't never find the right placement for the notes. Never plucking with enough strength, despite the perfectly capable hands. Either you didn't hear him at all or what you heard was off. The man couldn't play for nuthin is what I'm saying. But Larry Landers was baad in the shower, though.

He'd soap me up and down with them great, fine hands, doing a deep bass walking in the back of his mouth. And I'd just have to sing, though I can't sing to save my life. But we'd have one hellafyin musical time in the shower, lemme tell you. "Green Dolphin Street"[2] never sounded like nuthin till Larry

---

2. Song made into a modern jazz classic by the Miles Davis Quintet and other groups.

bopped out them changes and actually made me sound good. On "My Funny Valentine"[3] he'd do a whizzing sounding bow thing that made his throat vibrate real sexy and I'd cutesy up the introduction, which is, come to think of it, my favorite part. But the main number when the hot water started running out was "I Feel Like Making Love." That was usually the wind up of our repertoire cause you can imagine what that song can do to you in the shower and all.

Got so we spent a helluva lotta time in the shower. Just as well, cause didn't nobody call Larry for gigs. He a nice man, considerate, generous, baad in the shower, and good taste in music. But he just wasn't nobody's bass player. Knew all the stances, though, the postures, the facial expressions, had the choreography down. And right in the middle of supper he'd get some Ron Carter[4] thing going in his head and hop up from the table to go get the bass. Haul that sucker right in the kitchen and do a number in dumb show, all the playing in his throat, the acting with his hands. But that ain't nuthin. I mean that can't get it. I can impersonate Betty Carter[5] if it comes to that. The arms crooked just so, the fingers popping, the body working, the cap and all, the teeth, authentic. But I got sense enough to know I ain't nobody's singer. Actually, I am a mother, though I'm only just now getting it together. And too, I'm an A-1 manicurist.

Me and my cousin Sinbad come North working our show in cathouses at first. Set up a salon right smack in the middle of Miz Maybry's Saturday traffic. But that wasn't no kind of life to be bringing my daughter into. So I parked her at a boarding school till I could make some other kind of life. Wasn't no kind of life for Sinbad either, so we quit.

Our first shop was a three-chair affair on Austin. Had a student barber who could do anything—blow-outs, do's, corn rows, weird cuts, afros, press and curl, whatever you wanted. Plus he din't gab you to death. And he always brought his sides and didn't blast em neither. He went on to New York and opened his own shop. Was a bootblack too then, an old dude named James Noughton, had a crooked back and worked at the post office at night, and knew everything about everything, read all the time.

"Whatcha want to know about Marcus Garvey,[6] Sweet Pea?"

If it wasn't Garvey, it was the rackets or the trucking industry or the flora and fauna of Greenland or the planets or how the special effects in the disaster movies were done. One Saturday I asked him to tell me about the war, cause my nephew'd been drafted and it all seemed so wrong to me, our men over there in Nam fighting folks who fighting for the same things we are, to get that blood-sucker off our backs.

Well, what I say that for. Old dude gave us a deep knee bend, straight up eight-credit dissertation on World Wars I and II—the archduke getting offed, Africa cut up like so much cake, Churchill and his cigars, Gabriel Heatter on the radio, Hitler at the Olympics igging Owens, Red Cross doing Bloods dirty refusing donuts and bandages, A. Philip Randolph scaring the white folks to death, Mary McLeod Bethune[7] at the White House, Liberty Bond

---

3. Modern jazz classic, popular among trumpet players.
4. Contemporary jazz bassist (b. 1937).
5. Contemporary jazz singer (b. 1930).

6. American black nationalist leader (1887–1940).
7. American educator and founder of the National Council of Negro Women (1875–1955). Jesse

drives, the Russian front, frostbite of the feet, the Jew stiffs, the gypsies no one mourned . . . the whole johnson. Talked straight through the day, Miz Mary's fish dinner growing cold on the radiator, his one and only customer walking off with one dull shoe. Fell out exhausted, his shoe rag limp in his lap, one arm draped over the left foot platform, the other clutching his heart. Took Sinbad and our cousin Pepper to get the old man home. I stayed with him all night with the ice pack and a fifth of Old Crow.[8] He liked to die.

After while trade picked up and with a better class of folk too. Then me and Sinbad moved to North and Gaylord and called the shop Chez Sinbad. No more winos stumbling in or deadbeats wasting my time talking raunchy shit. The paperboy, the numbers man, the dudes with classier hot stuff coming in on Tuesday mornings only. We did up the place nice. Light globes from a New Orleans whorehouse, Sinbad likes to lie. Brown-and-black-and-silver-striped wallpaper. Lots of mirrors and hanging plants. Them old barber chairs spruced up and called antiques and damn if someone didn't buy one off us for eight hundred, cracked me up.

I cut my schedule down to ten hours in the shop so I could do private sessions with the gamblers and other business men and women who don't like sitting around the shop even though it's comfy, specially my part. Got me a cigar showcase with a marble top for serving coffee in clear glass mugs with heatproof handles too. My ten hours in the shop are spent leisurely. And my twenty hours out are making me a mint. Takes dust to be a mother, don't you know.

It was a perfect schedule once Larry Landers came into my life. He part-timed at a record shop and bartended at Topp's on the days and nights I worked at the shops. That gave us most of Monday and Wednesdays to listen to sides and hit the clubs. Gave me Fridays all to myself to study in the library and wade through them college bulletins and get to the museum and generally chart out a routine for when Debbie and me are a team. Sundays I always drive to Delaware to see her, and Larry detours to D.C. to see his sons. My bankbook started telling me I was soon going to be a full-time mama again and a college girl to boot, if I can ever talk myself into doing a school thing again, old as I am.

Life with Larry was cool. Not just cause he wouldn't hear about me going halves on the bills. But cause he was an easy man to be easy with. He liked talking softly and listening to music. And he liked having folks over for dinner and cards. Larry a real nice man and I liked him a lot. And I liked his friend Hector, who lived in the back of the apartment. Ole moon-face Hector went to school with Larry years ago and is some kind of kin. And they once failed in the funeral business together and I guess those stories of them times kinda keep them friends.

The time they had to put Larry's brother away is their best story, Hector's story really, since Larry got to play a little grief music round the edges. They decided to pass up a church service, since Bam was such a treacherous desperado wouldn't nobody want to preach over his body and wouldn't

Owens (1913–1980), black track and field star. Chancellor Adolf Hitler (1889–1945), representing Germany as host of the 1936 Olympic Games, refused to honor Owens, who had won four gold medals. Randolph (1889–1979), American labor leader and organizer of the Brotherhood of Sleeping Car Porters.
8. A common brand of whisky.

nobody want to come to hear no lies about the dearly departed untimely ripped or cut down or whatever. So Hector and Larry set up some kind of pop stand awning right at the gravesite, expecting close blood only. But seems the whole town turned out to make sure ole evil, hell-raising Bam was truly dead. Dudes straight from the barber chair, the striped ponchos blowing like wings, fuzz and foam on they face and all, lumbering up the hill to the hole taking bets and talking shit, relating how Ole Crazy Bam had shot up the town, shot up the jail, shot up the hospital pursuing some bootlegger who'd come up one keg short of the order. Women from all around come to demand the lid be lifted so they could check for themselves and be sure that Bam was stone cold. No matter how I tried I couldn't think of nobody bad enough to think on when they told the story of the man I'd never met.

Larry and Hector so bent over laughing bout the funeral, I couldn't hardly put the events in proper sequence. But I could surely picture some neighbor lady calling on Larry and Bam's mama reporting how the whole town had turned out for the burying. And the mama snatching up the first black thing she could find to wrap around herself and make an appearance. No use passing up a scene like that. And Larry prancing round the kitchen being his mama. And I'm too stunned to laugh, not at somebody's mama, and somebody's brother dead. But him and Hector laughing to beat the band and I can't help myself.

Thing about it, though, the funeral business stories are Hector's stories and he's not what you'd call a good storyteller. He never gives you the names, so you got all these he's and she's floating around. And he don't believe in giving details, so you got to scramble to paint your own pictures. Toward the end of that particular tale of Bam, all I could picture was the townspeople driving a stake through the dead man's heart, then hurling that coffin into the hole right quick. There was also something in that story about the civil rights workers wanting to make a case cause a white cop had cut Bam down. But looked like Hector didn't have a hold to that part of the story, so I just don't know.

Stories are not Hector's long suit. But he is an absolute artist on windows. Ole Moon-Face can wash some windows and make you cry about it too. Makes these smooth little turns out there on that little bitty sill just like he wasn't four stories up without a belt. I'd park myself at the breakfast counter and thread the new curtains on the rods while Hector mixed up the vinegar solution real chef-like. Wring out the rags just so, scrunch up the newspapers into soft wads that make you think of cat's paws. Hector was a cat himself out there on the sill, making these marvelous circles in the glass, rubbing the hardhead spots with a strip of steel wool he had pinned to his overalls.

Hector offered to do my car once. But I put a stop to that after that first time. My windshield so clear and sparkling felt like I was in an accident and heading over the hood, no glass there. But it was a pleasure to have coffee and watch Hector. After while, though, Larry started hinting that the apartment wasn't big enough for four. I agreed, thinking he meant Earl had to go. Come to find Larry meant Hector, which was a real drag. I love to be around people who do whatever it is they do with style and care.

Larry's dog's named Earl P. Jessup Bowers, if you can get ready for that. And I should mention straightaway that I do not like dogs one bit, which is why I was glad when Larry said somebody had to go. Cats are bad enough.

Horses are a total drag. By the age of nine I was fed up with all that noble horse this and noble horse that. They got good PR,[9] horses. But I really can't use em. Was a fire once when I was little and some dumb horse almost burnt my daddy up messin around, twisting, snorting, broncing, rearing up, doing everything but comin on out the barn like even the chickens had sense enough to do. I told my daddy to let that horse's ass burn. Horses be as dumb as cows. Cows just don't have good press agents at all.

I used to like cows when I was real little and needed to hug me something bigger than a goldfish. But don't let it rain, the dumbbells'll fall right in a ditch and you break a plow and shout yourself hoarse trying to get them fools to come up out the ditch. Chipmunks I don't mind when I'm at the breakfast counter with my tea and they're on their side of the glass doing Disney things in the yard. Blue jays are law-and-order birds, thoroughly despicable. And there's one prize fool in my Aunt Merriam's yard I will one day surely kill. He tries to "whip whip whippoorwill" like the Indians do in the Fort This or That movies when they're signaling to each other closing in on George Montgomery but don't never get around to wiping that sucker out. But dogs are one of my favorite hatreds. All the time woofing, bolting down their food, slopping water on the newly waxed linoleum, messin with you when you trying to read, chewin on the slippers.

Earl P. Jessup Bowers was an especial drag. But I could put up with Earl when Hector was around. Once Hector was gone and them windows got cloudy and gritty, I was through. Kicked that dog every chance I got. And after thinking what it meant, how the deal went down, place too small for four and it was Hector not Earl—I started moving up my calendar so I could get out of there. I ain't the kind of lady to press no ultimatum on no man. Like "Chose, me or the dog." That's unattractive. Kicking Hector out was too. An insult to me, once I got to thinking on it. Especially since I had carefully explained from jump street to Larry that I got one item on my agenda, making a home for me and my kid. So if anybody should've been given walking papers, should've been me.

Anyway. One day Moody comes waltzing into Chez Sinbad's and tips his hat. He glances at his nails and glances at me. And I figure here is my house in a green corduroy suit. Pot Limit had just read my cards and the jack of diamonds kept coming up on my resource side. Sylvia and me put our heads together and figure it got to be some gambler or hustler who wants his nails done. What other jacks do I know to make my fortune? I'm so positive about Moody, I whip out a postcard from the drawer where I keep the emeries and write my daughter to start packing.

"How much you make a day, Miss Lady?"

"Thursdays are always good for fifty," I lie.

He hands me fifty and glances over at Sinbad, who nods that it's cool. "I'd like my nails done at four-thirty. My place."

"Got a customer at that time, Mr. Moody, and I like to stay reliable. How bout five-twenty?"

He smiles a slow smile and glances at Sinbad, who nods again, everything's

9. Public relations; here suggesting a good image, good reputation.

cool. "Fine," he says. "And do you think you can manage a shave without cutting a person's throat?"

"Mr. Moody, I don't know you well enough to have just cause. And none of your friends have gotten to me yet with that particular proposition. Can't say what I'm prepared to do in the future, but for now I can surely shave you real careful-like."

Moody smiles again, then turns to Sinbad, who says it's cool and he'll give me the address. This look-nod dialogue burns my ass. That's like when you take a dude to lunch and pay the check and the waiter's standing there with *your* money in his paws asking *the dude* was everything all right and later for *you*. Shit. But I take down Moody's address and let the rest roll off me like so much steaming lava. I start packing up my little alligator case—buffer, batteries, clippers, emeries, massager, sifter, arrowroot and cornstarch, clear sealer, magnifying glass, and my own mixture of green and purple pigments.

"Five-twenty ain't five-twenty-one, is it, Miss Lady?"

"Not in my book," I say, swinging my appointment book around so he can see how full it is and how neatly the times are printed in. Course I always fill in phony names case some creep starts pressing me for a session.

For six Thursdays running and two Monday nights, I'm at Moody's bending over them nails with a miner's light strapped to my forehead, the magnifying glass in its stand, nicking just enough of the nails at the sides, tinting just enough with the color so he can mark them cards as he shuffles. Takes an hour to do it proper. Then I sift my talc concoction and brush his hands till they're smooth. Them cards move around so fast in his hands, he can actually tell me he's about to deal from the bottom in the next three moves and I miss it and I'm not new to this. I been a gambler's manicurist for more years than I care to mention. Ten times he'll cut and each time the same fifteen cards in the top cut and each time in exactly the same order. Incredible.

Now, I've known hands. My first husband, for instance. To see them hands work their show in the grandstands, at a circus, in a parade, the pari-mutuels—artistry in action. We met on the train. As a matter of fact, he was trying to burgle my bag. Some story to tell the grandchildren, hunh? I had to get him straight about robbing from folks. I don't play that. Ya gonna steal, hell, steal back some of them millions we got in escrow is my opinion. We spent three good years on the circuit. Then credit cards moved in. Then choke-and-grab muggers killed the whole tradition. He was reduced to a mere shell of his former self, as they say, and took to putting them hands on me. I try not to think on when things went sour. Try not to think about them big slapping hands, only of them working hands. Moody's working hands were something like that, but even better. So I'm impressed and he's impressed. And he pays me fifty and tips me fifty and shuts up when I shave him and keeps his hands off my lovely person.

I'm so excited counting up my bread, moving up the calendar, making impulsive calls to Delaware and the two of us squealing over the wire like a coupla fools, that what Larry got to say about all these goings-on just rolls off my back like so much molten lead.

"Well, who be up there while he got his head in your lap and you squeezing his goddamn blackheads?"

"I don't squeeze his goddamn blackheads, Larry, on account of he don't have no goddamn blackheads. I give him a shave, a steam, and an egg-white face mask. And when I'm through, his face is as smooth as his hands."

"I'll bet," Larry says. That makes me mad cause I expect some kind of respect for my work, which is better than just good.

"And he doesn't have his head in my lap. He's got a whole barbershop set up on his solarium."

"His what?" Larry squinting at me, raising the wooden spoon he stirring the spaghetti with, and I raise the knife I'm chopping the onions with. Thing about it, though, he don't laugh. It's funny as hell to me, but Larry got no sense of humor sometimes, which is too bad cause he's a lotta fun when he's laughing and joking.

"It's not a bedroom. He's got this screened-in sun porch where he raises African violets and—"

"Please, Sweet Pea. Why don't you quit? You think I'm dumb?"

"I'm serious. I'm serious and I'm mad cause I ain't got no reason to lie to you whatever was going on, Larry." He turns back to the pot and I continue working on the sauce and I'm pissed off cause this is silly. "He sits in the barber chair and I shave him and give him a manicure."

"What else you be giving him? A man don't be paying a good-looking woman to come to his house and all and don't—"

"Larry, if you had the dough and felt like it, wouldn't you pay Pot Limit to come read your cards? And couldn't you keep your hands to yourself and she a good-looking woman? And couldn't you see yourself paying Sylvia to come and cook for you and no funny stuff, and she's one of the best-looking women in town?"

Larry cooled out fast. My next shot was to bring up the fact that he was insulting my work. Do I go around saying the women who pass up Bill the bartender and come to him are after his joint? No, cause I respect the fact that Larry Landers mixes the best piña coladas this side of Barbados. And he's flashy with the blender and the glasses and the whole show. He's good and I respect that. But he cooled out so fast I didn't have to bring it up. I don't believe in overkill, besides I like to keep some things in reserve. He cooled out so fast I realized he wasn't really jealous. He was just going through one of them obligatory male numbers, all symbolic, no depth.

Like the time this dude came into the shop to talk some trash and Sinbad got his ass on his shoulders, talking about the dude showed no respect for him cause for all he knew I could be Sinbad's woman. And me arguing that since that ain't the case, what's the deal? I mean why get hot over what if if what if ain't. Men are crazy. Now there is Sinbad, my blood cousin who grew up right in the same house like a brother damn near, putting me through simple-ass changes like that. Who's got time for grand opera and comic strips, I'm trying to make a life for me and my kid. But men are like that. Gorillas, if you know what I mean.

Like at Topp's sometimes. I'll drop in to have a drink with Larry when he's on the bar and then I leave. And maybe some dude'll take it in his head to walk me to the car. That's cool. I lay it out right quick that me and Larry are a we and then we take it from there, just two people gassing in the summer breeze and that's just fine. But don't let some other dude holler over something like "Hey, man, can you handle all that? Why don't you step aside, junior, and let a man . . ." and blah-de-da-de-dah. They can be the best of friends or total strangers just kidding around, but right away they two gorillas pounding on their chest, pounding on their chest and talking over my head, yelling over the tops of cars just like I'm not a person with some say-so in the matter. It's a man-to-man ritual that ain't got nothing to do with me. So I just get in my car and take off and leave them to get it on if they've a mind to. They got it.

But if one of the gorillas is a relative, or a friend of mine, or a nice kinda man I got in mind for one of my friends, I will stick around long enough to shout em down and point out that they are some ugly gorillas and are showing no respect for me and therefore owe me an apology. But if they don't fit into one of them categories, I figure it ain't my place to try to develop them so they can make the leap from gorilla to human. If their own mamas and daddies didn't care whether they turned out to be amoebas or catfish or whatever, it ain't my weight. I got my own weight. I'm a mother. So they got it.

Like I use to tell my daughter's daddy, the key to getting along and living with other folks is to keep clear whose weight is whose. His drinking, for instance, was not my weight. And him waking me up in the night for them long, rambling, ninety-proof monologues bout how the whole world's made up of victims, rescuers, and executioners and I'm the dirty bitch cause I ain't rescuing him fast enough to suit him. Then got so I was the executioner, to hear him tell it. I don't say nuthin cause my philosophy of life and death is this—I'll go when the wagon comes, but I ain't going out behind somebody else's shit. I arranged my priorities long ago when I jumped into my woman stride. Some things I'll go off on. Some things I'll hold my silence and wait it out. Some things I just bump off, cause the best solution to some problems is to just abandon them.

But I struggled with Mac, Debbie's daddy. Talked to his family, his church, AA, hid the bottles, threatened the liquor man, left a good job to play nurse, mistress, kitten, buddy. But then he stopped calling me Dahlin and started calling me Mama. I don't play that. I'm my daughter's mama. So I split. Did my best to sweeten them last few months, but I'd been leaving for a long time.

The silliest thing about all of Larry's grumblings back then was Moody had no eyes for me and vice versa. I just like the money. And I like watching him mess around with the cards. He's exquisite, dazzling, stunning shuffling, cutting, marking, dealing from the bottom, the middle, the near top. I ain't never seen nothing like it, and I seen a whole lot. The thing that made me mad, though, and made me know Larry Landers wasn't ready to deal with no woman full grown was the way he kept bringing it up, always talking about what he figured was on Moody's mind, like what's on my mind don't count. So I finally did have to use up my reserves and point out to Larry that he was insulting my work and that I would never dream of accusing him of not being a good bartender, of just being another pretty face, like they say.

"You can't tell me he don't have eyes," he kept saying.

"What about my eyes? Don't my eyes count?" I gave it up after a coupla tries. All I know is, Moody wasn't even thinking about me. I was impressed with his work and needed the trade and vice versa.

One time, for instance, I was doing his hands on the solarium and thought

I saw a glint of metal up under his jacket. I rearranged myself in the chair so I could work my elbow in there to see if he was carrying heat. I thought I was being cool about it.

"How bout keeping your tits on your side of the table, Miss Lady."

I would rather he think anything but that. I would rather he think I was clumsy in my work even. "Wasn't about tits, Moody. I was just trying to see if you had a holster on and was too lazy to ask."

"Would have expected you too. You a straight-up, direct kind of person." He opened his jacket away with the heel of his hand, being careful with his nails. I liked that.

"It's not about you," he said quietly, jerking his chin in the direction of the revolver. "Had to transport some money today and forgot to take it off. Sorry."

I gave myself two demerits. One for the tits, the other for setting up a situation where he wound up telling me something about his comings and goings. I'm too old to be making mistakes like that. So I apologized. Then gave myself two stars. He had a good opinion of me and my work. I did an extra-fine job on his hands that day.

Then the house happened. I had been reading the rental ads and For Sale columns for months and looking at some awful, tacky places. Then one Monday me and Sylvia lucked up on this cute little white-brick job up on a hill away from the street. Lots of light and enough room and not too much yard to kill me off. I paid my money down and rushed them papers through. Got back to Larry's place all excited and found him with his mouth all poked out.

Half grumbling, half proposing, he hinted around that we all should live at his place like a family. Only he didn't quite lay it out plain in case of rejection. And I'll tell you something, I wouldn't want to be no man. Must be hard on the heart always having to get out there, setting yourself up to be possibly shot down, approaching the lady, calling, the invitation, the rap. I don't think I could handle it myself unless everybody was just straight up at all times from day one till the end. I didn't answer Larry's nonproposed proposal cause it didn't come clear to me till after dinner. So I just let my silence carry whatever meaning it will. Ain't nuthin too much changed from the first day he came to get me from my Aunt Merriam's place. My agenda is still to make a home for my girl. Marriage just ain't one of the things on my mind no more, not after two. Got no regrets or bad feelings about them husbands neither. Like the poem says, when you're handed a lemon, make lemonade, honey, make lemonade. That's Gwen Brooks'[1] motto, that's mine too. You get a lemon, well, just make lemonade.

"Going on the road next week," Moody announces one day through the steam towel. "Like you to travel with me, keep my hands in shape. Keep the women off my neck. Check the dudes at my back. Ain't asking you to carry heat or money or put yourself in no danger. But I could use your help." He pauses and I ease my buns into the chair, staring at the steam curling from the towel.

"Wicked schedule though—Mobile, Birmingham, Sarasota Springs, Jacksonville, then Puerto Rico and back. Can pay you two thousand and

---

1. Gwendolyn Brooks (1917–2000), American poet, novelist, and autobiographer.

expenses. You're good, Miss Lady. You're good and you got good sense. And while I don't believe in nothing but my skill and chance, I gotta say you've brought me luck. You a lucky lady, Miss Lady."

He raises his hands and cracks his knuckles and it's like the talking towel has eyes as well cause damn if he ain't checking his cuticles.

"I'll call you later, Moody," I manage to say, mind reeling. With two thousand I can get my stuff out of storage, and buy Debbie a real nice bedroom set, pay tuition at the college too and start my three-credit-at-a-time grind.

Course I never dreamed the week would be so unnerving, exhausting, constantly on my feet, serving drinks, woofing sisters, trying to distract dudes, keeping track of fifty-leven umpteen goings on. Did have to carry the heat on three occasions and had to do a helluva lotta driving. Plus was most of the time holed up in the hotel room close to the phone. I had pictured myself lazying on the beach in Florida dreaming up cruises around the world with two matching steamer trunks with the drawers and hangers and stuff. I'd pictured traipsing through the casinos in Puerto Rico ordering chicken salad and coffee liqueur and tipping the croupiers with blue chips. Shit no. Was work. And I sure as hell learned how Moody got his name. Got so we didn't even speak, but I kept those hands in shape and his face smooth and placid. And whether he won, lost, broke even, or got wiped out, I don't even know. He gave me my money and took off for New Orleans. That trip liked to kill me.

"You never did say nothing interesting about Moody," Pot Limit says insinuatingly, swinging her legs in from the aisle cause ain't nobody there to snatch so she might as well sit comfortable.

"Yeah, she thought she'd put us off the trail with a rip-roaring tale about Larry's housekeeping."

They slapping five and hunching each other and making a whole lotta noise, spilling Jack Daniels on my turquoise T-straps from Puerto Rico.

"Come on, fess up, Sweet Pea," they crooning. "Did you give him some?"

"Ahhh, yawl bitches are tiresome, you know that?"

"Naaw, naaw," say Sylvia, grabbing my arm. "You can tell us. We wantta know all about the trip, specially the nights." She winks at Pot Limit.

"Tell us about this Moody man and his wonderful hands one more time, cept we want to hear how the hands feel on the flesh, honey." Pot Limit doing a bump and grind in the chair that almost makes me join in the fun, except I'm worried in my mind about Larry Landers.

Just then the piano player comes by and leans over Sylvia, blowing in her ear. And me and Pot Limit mimic the confectionary goings-on. And just as well, cause there's nothin to tell about Moody. It wasn't a movie after all. And in real life the good-looking gambler's got cards on his mind. Just like I got my child on my mind. Onliest thing to say about the trip is I'm five pounds lighter, not a shade darker, but two thousand closer toward my goal.

"Ease up," Sylvia says, interrupting the piano player to fuss over me. Then the drummer comes by and eases in on Pot Limit. And I ease back into the shadows of the booth to think Larry over.

I'm staring at the entrance half expecting Larry to come into Topps, but it's not his night. Then too, the thing is ended if I'd only know it. Larry the kind of man you're either living with him or you're out. I for one would've liked us to continue, me and Debbie in our place, him and Earl at his. But he got so grumpy the time I said that, I sure wasn't gonna bring it up again. Got grumpy in the shower too, got so he didn't want to wash my back.

But that last night fore I left for Birmingham, we had us one crazy musical time in the shower. I kept trying to lure him into "Maiden Voyage," which I really can't do without back-up, cause I can't sing all them changes. After while he come out from behind his sulk and did a Jon Lucien combination on vocal and bass, alternating the sections, eight bars of singing words, eight bars of singing bass. It was baad. Then he insisted on doing "I Love You More Today Than Yesterday." And we like to break our arches, stomping out the beat against the shower mat.

The bathroom was all steamy and we had the curtains open so we could see the plants and watch the candles burning. I had bought us a big fat cake of sandalwood soap and it was matching them candles scent for scent. Must've been two o'clock in the morning and looked like the hot water would last forever and ever and ever. Larry finally let go of the love songs, which were making me feel kinda funny cause I thought it was understood that I was splitting, just like he'd always made it clear either I was there or nowhere.

Then we hit on a tune I don't even know the name of cept I like to scat and do my thing Larry calls Swahili wailing. He laid down the most intricate weaving, walking, bopping, strutting bottom to my singing I ever heard. It inspired me. Took that melody and went right on out that shower, them candles bout used up, the fatty soap long since abandoned in the dish, our bodies barely visible in the steamed-up mirrors walling his bathroom. Took that melody right on out the room and out of doors and somewhere out this world. Larry changing instruments fast as I'm changing moods, colors. Took an alto solo and gave me a rest, worked an intro up on the piano playing the chords across my back, drove me all up into the high register while he weaved in and out around my head on a flute sounding like them chilly pipes of the Andes.[2] And I was Yma Sumac[3] for one minute there, up there breathing some rare air and losing my mind, I was so high on just sheer music. Music and water, the healthiest things in the world. And that hot water pounding like it was part of the group with a union card and all. And I could tell that if that bass could've fit in the tub, Larry would've dragged that bad boy in there and played the hell out of them soggy strings once and for all.

I dipped way down and reached way back for snatches of Jelly Roll Morton's "Deep Creek Blues"[4] and Larry so painful, so stinging on the bass, could make you cry. Then I'm racing fast through Bessie and all the other Smith singers, Mildred Bailey, Billie and imitators, Betty Roche, Nat King Cole vintage 46, a little Joe Carroll, King Pleasure, some Babs.[5] Found myself pulling lines out of songs I don't even like, but ransacked songs just for the meaningful lines or two cause I realized we were doing more than just making music together, and it had to be said just how things stood.

Then I was off again and lost Larry somewhere down there doing scales, sound like. And he went back to that first supporting line that had drove me up into the Andes. And he stayed there waiting for me to return and do some more Swahili wailing. But I was elsewhere and liked it out there and ignored

---

2. Mountain range in South America. "Chilly pipes": i.e., Chilean folk music.
3. Peruvian singer popular with American audiences in the 1950s.

4. Dixieland jazz classic of the 1920s.
5. Blues and jazz musicians of the 1920s, 1930s, and 1940s.

the fact that he was aiming for a wind-up of "I Love You More Today Than Yesterday." I sang myself out till all I could ever have left in life was "Brown Baby" to sing to my little girl. Larry stayed on the ground with the same supporting line, and the hot water started getting funny and I knew my time was up. So I came crashing down, jarring the song out of shape, diving back into the melody line and somehow, not even knowing what song each other was doing, we finished up together just as the water turned cold.

1977

MAXINE HONG KINGSTON
b. 1940

Maxine Hong Kingston was born in Stockton, California, to parents who had emigrated from China. Before they emigrated, Kingston's father was a schoolteacher and a poet; her mother was a rural doctor in a profession consisting almost entirely of men. In America they took on quite different identities: her father, at times unemployed, worked in a gambling house and a laundry; her mother raised six children, of whom Kingston was the eldest.

Kingston graduated from the University of California at Berkeley, studying there in the turbulent middle sixties. Her debut as a writer was auspicious: in 1976, an unknown, she published her first and most widely read book, *The Woman Warrior*, and was catapulted to literary fame. Subtitled "Memoirs of a Girlhood among Ghosts," it draws on autobiographical fact and combines it with legends, especially Asian ones, to make a distinct imaginative creation. Reviews of the book, almost universally laudatory, emphasized its poetic and lyric beauty. *The Woman Warrior* is about the cultural conflicts Americans of Chinese descent must confront. Still, what remains in the mind is its quality of vivid particularity, as for example at the beginning of "Shaman," the book's third section:

> Once in a long while, four times so far for me, my mother brings out the metal tube that holds her medical diploma. On the tube are gold circles crossed with seven red lines each—"joy" ideographs in abstract. There are also little flowers that look like gears for a gold machine. . . . When I open it the smell of China flies out, a thousand-year-old bat flying heavy-handed out of the Chinese caverns where bats are as white as dust, a smell that comes from long ago, far back in my brain.

Although *The Woman Warrior* received the National Book Critics' Circle award for general nonfiction, there is nothing "general" in the sensuous density of its reference.

The importance of storytelling to Kingston's enterprise in *The Woman Warrior* and its successor, *China Men* (1980), cannot be overemphasized. In an interview with Bill Moyers on public television, Kingston said that her attempt was to push the account toward "form" by giving it a "redemptive" meaning, making it a "beautiful" story rather than a sordid one. As is the case typically with her practice as a writer, her effort is to mediate between present and past: "I think that my stories have a constant breaking in and out of the present and past. So the reader might be walking along very well in the present, but the past breaks through and changes and enlightens the present and vice versa."

Kingston had originally conceived of *The Woman Warrior* and *China Men* as one long book, but decided to preserve an overall division by gender: *Warrior* is about her female antecedents; while *China Men,* which won the 1980 National Book Award for nonfiction, deals with her relation to her father and complements that relation by providing epiclike biographies of earlier male forebears, especially those Chinese who came to America and worked on building the railroads. In a final section, she writes about her brother who served in the U.S. Navy during the Vietnam War. Interestingly enough, as she said in the interview with Moyers, her father annotated both of these memoir-meditations, thus carrying further the conversation between the generations.

Tripmaster Monkey (1989), presented more deliberately as a novel, is an exercise as excessive as the young fifth-generation American hero, Wittman Ah Sing, who is portrayed there. Subtitled "His Fake Book," the novel is an extended, picaresque account of Wittman's adventures as an aspiring playwright who imagines himself to be an incarnation of the legendary Monkey King—a trickster hero said to have brought the Buddha's teaching to China. Combining magic, realism, and black humor, *Tripmaster Monkey* is about a young male's search for a community in America. Although Kingston's myth-laden narratives have been called "exotic," she dislikes the word, since she has dedicated her art to exploring what it means to be a human being in American society. In fact, she thinks of her books as more American than Chinese, sees William Carlos Williams's *In the American Grain* as a true prose predecessor, and probably would not be unhappy to think of the hero of *Tripmaster Monkey* as a later, different version of Huck Finn or Augie March. As critic Jennie Wang explains in even larger dimensions, Kingston's Wittman Ah Sing is "the maker/magician created in the wake of James Joyce's 'bygmester,' conceived in the mind's fancy of a metafictionist," who joins in his multiculturalism both American and postmodern ambitions.

The text is from *Tripmaster Monkey* (1989).

From Tripmaster Monkey

1. Trippers and Askers

Maybe it comes from living in San Francisco, city of clammy humors and foghorns that warn and warn—omen, o-o-men, o dolorous omen, o dolors of omens—and not enough sun, but Wittman Ah Sing considered suicide every day. Entertained it. There slid beside his right eye a black gun. He looked side-eyed for it. Here it comes. He actually crooked his trigger finger and—bang!—his head breaks into pieces that fly far apart in the scattered universe. Then blood, meat, disgusting brains, mind guts, but he would be dead already and not see the garbage. The mouth part of his head would remain attached. He groaned. Hemingway had done it in the mouth. Wittman was not el pachuco loco.[1] Proof: he could tell a figment from a table. Or a tree. Being outdoors, in Golden Gate Park, he stepped over to a tree and knock-knocked on it, struck a match on it. Lit a cigarette. Whose mind is it that doesn't suffer a loud takeover once in a while? He was aware of the run of his mind, that's all. He was not making plans to do himself in, and no more willed these seppuku[2] movies—no more conjured up that gun—than

1. Flashily dressed crazy person (Mexican Spanish slang).   2. Japanese form of ritual suicide.

built this city. His cowboy boots, old brown Wellingtons, hit its pavements hard. Anybody serious about killing himself does the big leap off the Golden Gate. The wind or shock knocks you out before impact. Oh, long before impact. So far, two hundred and thirty-five people, while taking a walk alone on the bridge—a mere net between you and the grabby ocean—had heard a voice out of the windy sky—Laurence Olivier[3] asking them something: "To be or not to be?" And they'd answered, "Not to be," and climbed on top of the railing, fingers and toes roosting on the cinnabarine steel. They take the side of the bridge that faces land. And the City. The last city. Feet first. Coit Tower giving you the finger all the way down. Wittman would face the sea. And the setting sun. Dive. But he was not going to do that. Strange. These gun pictures were what was left of his childhood ability to see galaxies. Glass cosmospheres there had once been, and planets with creatures, such doings, such colors. None abiding. In the *Chronicle,* a husband and wife, past eighty, too old to live, had shot each other with a weak gun, and had had to go to a doctor to have the bullets prized out of their ears. And a Buddhist had set fire to himself and burned to death on purpose;[4] his name was Quang Duc. Quang Duc. Remember. In the cremations along the Ganges, the mourners stay with the burning body until its head pops. Pop.

Today Wittman was taking a walk on a path that will lead into the underpass beneath the gnarly trees. In fact, the park didn't look half bad in the fog beginning to fall, dimming the hillocks that domed like green-grey moons rising or setting. He pulled the collar of his pea coat higher and dragged on his cigarette. He had walked this far into the park hardly seeing it. He ought to let it come in, he decided. He would let it all come in. An old white woman was sitting on a bench selling trivets "@ ½ dollar ea.," which a ducky and a bunny pointed out with gloved fingers. She lifted her head and turned her face toward Wittman's; her hands were working one more trivet out of yarn and bottlecaps. Not eyelids exactly but like skin flaps or membranes covered her eye sockets and quivered from the empty air in the holes or with efforts to see. Sockets wide open. He looked at her thick feet chapped and dirty in zoris.[5] Their sorry feet is how you can tell crazy people who have no place to go and walk everywhere.

Wittman turned his head, and there on the ground were a pigeon and a squatting man, both puking. He looked away so that he would not himself get nauseated. Pigeons have milk sacs in their throats. Maybe this one was disgorging milk because last night a wind had blown in from the ocean and blown its squabs out of their nest, and it was milking itself. Or does that happen in the spring? But in California in the fall as well? The man was only a vomiting drunk. This walk was turning out to be a Malte Laurids Brigge[6] walk. There was no helping that. There is no helping what you see when you let it all come in; he hadn't been in on building any city. It was already cold, soon the downside of the year. He walked into the tunnel.

---

3. British actor (1907–1989) who starred in film of Shakespeare's *Hamlet.*
4. During the Vietnam War several Buddhist monks sacrificed themselves to protest government policy.

5. Sandals.
6. A protagonist of Austrian poet Rainer Maria Rilke (1875–1926) who rises from abject misery to eternal bliss.

Heading toward him from the other end came a Chinese dude from China, hands clasped behind, bow-legged, loose-seated, out on a stroll—that walk they do in kung fu movies when they are full of contentment on a sunny day. As luck would have it, although there was plenty of room, this dude and Wittman tried to pass each other both on the same side, then both on the other, sidestepping like a couple of basketball stars. Wittman stopped dead in his tracks, and shot the dude a direct stink-eye. The F.O.B.[7] stepped aside. Following, straggling, came the poor guy's wife. She was coaxing their kid with sunflower seeds, which she cracked with her gold tooth and held out to him. "Ho sick, la. Ho sick," she said. "Good eating. Good eats." Her voice sang, rang, banged in the echo-chamber tunnel. Mom and shamble-legged kid were each stuffed inside of about ten homemade sweaters. Their arms stuck out fatly. The mom had on a nylon or rayon pantsuit. ("Ny-lon ge. Mm lon doc." "Nylon-made. Lasts forever.") "No!" said the kid. Echoes of "No!" Next there came scrabbling an old lady with a cane. She also wore one of those do-it-yourself pantsuit outfits. On Granny's head was a cap with a pompon that matched everybody's sweaters. The whole family taking a cheap outing on their day off. Immigrants. Fresh Off the Boats out in public. Didn't know how to walk together. Spitting seeds. So uncool. You wouldn't mislike them on sight if their pants weren't so highwater, gym socks white and noticeable. F.O.B. fashions—highwaters or puddlecuffs. Can't get it right. Uncool. Uncool. The tunnel smelled of mothballs—F.O.B. perfume.

On the tunnel ceiling, some tall paint-head had sprayed, "I love my skull." And somebody else had answered, "But oh you kidney!" This straighter person had prime-coated in bone-white a precise oval on the slope of the wall, and lettered in neat black, "But oh you kidney!"

He would avoid the Academy of Sciences, especially the North American Hall. Coyotes and bobcats dead behind glass forever. Stuffed birds stuffed inside their pried-open mouths. He was never going to go in there again. Claustro. Dark except for the glow of fake suns on the "scenes." Funeral-parlor smell seeping through the sealant.

Don't go into the Steinhart Aquarium either. Remember *The Lady from Shanghai*?[8] The seasick cameras shoot through and around the fishtanks at Orson Welles and Rita Hayworth saying goodbye. The fish are moving, unctuously moving.

No Oriental Tea Garden either. "Oriental." Shit.

On the paths where no other human being was wending, he stepped over and between fallen trees into sudden fens of ferns and banana trees with no bananas. A wild strawberry—someone had been wounded and bled a drop here—said, "Eat me," but he didn't obey, maybe poison. How come ripe when it isn't even spring? There were no flowers in the Shakespeare Garden, its plants gone indistinguishably to leaf and twig.

Long before Ocean Beach and the Great Highway, he turned back into the woods. Eucalyptus, pine, and black oak—those three trees together is how you tell that you're in Northern California and not Los Angeles. The

---

7. Fresh off the boat; derogatory term for persons showing their recent-immigrant status.
8. Orson Welles directed and starred in this 1948 film, in which the title character is not Chinese but White Russian, played by the actress Rita Hayworth.

last time he had walked along the ocean, he ended up at the zoo. Aquarium and dank zoo on the same day. "Fu-li-sah-kah Soo." He said "Fleishhacker Zoo" to himself in Chinatown language, just to keep a hand in, so to speak, to remember and so to keep a while longer words spoken by the people of his brief and dying culture. At Fu-li-sah-kah Soo, he once saw a monkey catch a flying pigeon and tear it up. In another cage, a tiger backed up to its wading pool and took a dump in it. The stained polar bears make you want to throw things at them and to bite into an eraser.

If it were Sunday, football roars would be rising out of Kezar Stadium, and everywhere you walk, in the woods, along the Chain of Lakes, at the paddock of buffaloes, you'd hear the united voice of the crowd, and the separate loudspeaker voice of the announcer doing the play-by-play. Football season. Good thing that when he was in school, an American of Japanese Ancestry had played on the Cal football team, and there had been a couple of A.J.A. pompon girls too. Otherwise, his manhood would have been even more totally destroyed than it was.

Having lost track of his whereabouts, Wittman was surprised by a snowy glass palace—the Conservatory—that coalesced out of the fog. A piece had sharded off and was floating to the right of the spire on top of the cupola— the day moon. Up the stairs to this fancy hothouse (built with Crocker[9] money), where unlikely roses and cacti grow, climbed a man and a dog. They were the same color and leanness, the dog a Doberman pinscher. "Bitch. You fucking bitch." The man was scolding the dog, the two of them walking fast, the dog pulling forward and the man pulling the short new chain taut. "Who do you think you are, bitch? Huh, bitch? You listening to me? Who the fuck do you think you are?" The man had plucked his eyebrows into the shapes of tadpoles, the same definition as the dog's, which were light tan. The dog wore a shame look on its face, and its legs were bending with straint. "Bitch animal," said the man, who looked nowhere but at his dog. "How could you, huh, bitch? Huh? You listening to me?" A yank on the choke- chain. "You hear me? You cuntless bitch."

Along a side path came another Black man, this one pushing a shopping cart transporting one red apple and a red bull from Tijuana. It was time, Wittman thought, to stop letting it all come in.

"Newspaper, sir?" said the man with the red bull. "Newspaper. Ten cents." He was holding out a folded page of newspaper. He was embracing an arm- load of these folios and quartos. Wittman had dimes in his pocket, so bought one. The man thanked him, and specially gave him a color insert from last Sunday's paper. He must be illiterate and not know that newspapers come out new every day.

Some children were climbing rocks. A little girl, who was at the top of the pile, jumped off, saying, "Don't tell *me* your personal problems." She talked like that because she copied women. "I got problems of my *own*," she said. The kid was ruined already. A shot of hate went from him to her that ought to have felled her, but up she climbed again. Wittman tossed his smoke and headed for an exit from the park.

Under a bush was a rag that had been squirted with blue paint. That rag

9. The Crocker Bank of California is noteworthy for having endowed many public buildings.

had sucked a boy's breath and eaten up his brain cells. His traitorous hand that should have torn the rag away had pressed it against his face, smeared him blue, and made him drag in the fumes.

Wittman stood at the bus stop on the corner of Arguello and Fulton. He was avoiding the corner where the grizzly bear on one rock and the mountain lion with tensed shoulders on the opposite rock look down at you. The Muni bus came along on the cables not too much later. Continue. "I can't go on, I go on." "I can't go on comma I go on." Wow.

On the ride downtown, for quite a while—the spires of St. Ignatius to the left and the dome of City Hall straight ahead as if rising out of the center of the street—San Francisco seemed to be a city in a good dream. Past the gilded gates of the Opera House and Civic Auditorium. Past the Orpheum, once "the best vaudeville house in the West"; on the evening of the day of the Earthquake and Fire, its actors went to the park and sang an act from *Carmen*. In 1911, Count Ilya Tolstoy, *the* Tolstoy's son, lectured in the Orpheum on "Universal Peace." Wittman had heard the orotund voice of Lowell Thomas intone, "THIS IS CINERAMA!" The Embassy, the Golden Gate, U. A. Cinema, the Paramount, the Warfield, the St. Francis, the Esquire. Then the neighborhood of the Curran, the Geary, and the Marines Memorial, where he had seen the Actor's Workshop do *King Lear* with Michael O'Sullivan as Lear—"Blow, winds, and crack your cheeks."[1] Out the bus window, he kept spotting people who offended him in their postures and gestures, their walks, their nose-blowing, their clothes, their facial expressions. Normal humanity, mean and wrong. He was a convict on a locked bus staring at the sights on the way from county jail to San Quentin. Breathe shallow so as not to smell the other passengers. It's true, isn't it, that molecules break off and float about, and go up your nose, and that's how you smell? Always some freak riding the Muni. And making eye contact. Wittman was the only passenger sitting on a crosswise seat in front; the other passengers, facing forward, were looking at him. Had he spoken aloud? They're about to make sudden faces, like in *El*.[2] *Who, if I cried out, would hear me among the angels' hierarchies?* All right, then, all right. Out of a pocket, he took his Rilke. For such gone days, he carried *The Notebooks of Malte Laurids Brigge* in his pea coat—and read out loud to his fellow riders: " 'My father had taken me with him to Urnekloster. . . . There remains whole in my heart, so it seems to me, only that large hall in which we used to gather for dinner every evening at seven o'clock. I never saw this room by day; I do not even remember whether it had windows or on what they looked out; always, whenever the family entered, the candles were burning in the ponderous branched candlesticks, and in a few minutes one forgot the time of day and all that one had seen outside. This lofty and, as I suspect, vaulted chamber was stronger than everything else. With its darkening height, with its never quite clarified corners, it sucked all images out of one without giving one any definite substitute for them. One sat there as if dissolved; entirely without will, without consciousness, without desire, without defence. One was like a vacant spot. I remember that at first this annihilating state almost caused

---

1. A deliberately wild mixture of high and low cultural productions, from French opera to Russian literary spokespersons to cinematic gimmicks of 1950s popular films and avant-garde acting methods for Shakespearean tragedy.
2. *El Cid* (c. 1140), an epic written in Old Spanish.

me nausea; it brought on a kind of sea-sickness which I only overcame by stretching out my leg until I touched with my foot the knee of my father who sat opposite me. It did not strike me until afterwards that he seemed to understand, or at least to tolerate, this singular behavior, although there existed between us an almost cool relationship which would not account for such a gesture. Nevertheless it was this slight contact that gave me strength to support the long repasts. And after a few weeks of spasmodic endurance, I became, with the almost boundless adaptability of a child, so inured to the eeriness of these gatherings, that it no longer cost me effort to sit at table for two hours; now these hours passed comparatively swiftly, for I occupied myself in observing those present.' " Some of those present on the Muni were looking at the reader, some had closed their eyes, some looked out the window, everyone perhaps listening.

" 'My grandfather called them "the family," and I also heard the others use the same term, which was entirely arbitrary.' " Wittman read on, reading the descriptions of the four persons at table. The bus driver did not tell him to shut up, and he got to the good part: " 'The meal dragged along as usual, and we had just reached the dessert when my eye was caught and carried along by a movement going on, in the half-darkness, at the back of the room. In that quarter a door which I had been told led to the mezzanine floor, had opened little by little, and now, as I looked on with a feeling entirely new to me of curiosity and consternation, there stepped into the darkness of the doorway a slender lady in a light-colored dress, who came slowly toward us. I do not know whether I made any movement or any sound; the noise of a chair being overturned forced me to tear my eyes from that strange figure, and I caught sight of my father, who had jumped up now, his face pale as death, his hands clenched by his sides, going toward the lady. She, meantime, quite untouched by this scene, moved toward us, step by step, and was already not far from the Count's place, when he rose brusquely and, seizing my father by the arm, drew him back to the table and held him fast, while the strange lady, slowly and indifferently, traversed the space now left clear, step by step, through an indescribable stillness in which only a glass clinked trembling somewhere, and disappeared through a door in the opposite wall of the dining-hall.' "

None of the passengers was telling Wittman to cool it. It was pleasant, then, for them to ride the bus while Rilke shaded and polished the City's greys and golds. Here we are, Walt Whitman's "classless society" of "everyone who could read or be read to." Will one of these listening passengers please write to the City Council and suggest that there always be a reader on this route? Wittman has begun a someday tradition that may lead to a job as a reader riding the railroads throughout the West. On the train through Fresno—Saroyan; through the Salinas Valley—Steinbeck; through Monterey—*Cannery Row*; along the Big Sur ocean—Jack Kerouac;[3] on the way to Weed—*Of Mice and Men*; in the Mother Lode—Mark Twain and Robert Louis Stevenson, who went on a honeymoon in *The Silverado Squatters*; *Roughing It* through Calaveras County and the Sacramento Valley; through the redwoods—John Muir; up into the Rockies—*The Big Rock Candy Mountain* by Wallace Stegner. Hollywood and San Elmo with John Fante. And all

3. American novelist (1922–1959), famous for his *On the Road*.

of the Central Valley on the Southern Pacific with migrant Carlos Bulosan, *America Is in the Heart*. What a repertoire.[4] A lifetime reading job. And he had yet to check out Gertrude Atherton, and Jack London of Oakland, and Ambrose Bierce of San Francisco. And to find "Relocation" Camp diaries to read in his fierce voice when the train goes through Elk Grove and other places where the land once belonged to the A.J.A.s. He will refuse to be a reader of racist Frank Norris. He won't read Bret Harte either, in revenge for that Ah Sin[5] thing. Nor *Ramona* by Helen Hunt Jackson, in case it turned out to be like *Gone with the Wind*. Travelers will go to the reading car to hear the long novels of the country they were riding through for hours and for days. A fool for literature, the railroad reader of the S.P.[6] is getting his start busting through reader's block on the Muni. Wittman's talent was that he could read while riding without getting carsick.

The ghost of Christine Brahe[7] for the third and last time walked through the dining hall. The Count and Malte's father raised their heavy wine-glasses "to the left of the huge silver swan filled with narcissus," Rilke's ancestral tale came to a close, and the bus came to the place for Wittman to get off. He walked through the Stockton Street tunnel—beneath the Tunnel Top Bar on Bush and Burill, where Sam Spade's partner, Miles Archer, was done in by Brigid O'Shaughnessy[8]—and emerged in Chinatown. At a payphone— this was not the phone booth with the chinky-chinaman corny horny roof— he thought about whether he needed to make any calls. He had a couple more dimes. What the hell. He dropped one into the slot and dialed information for the number of the most ungettable girl of his acquaintance.

So, that very afternoon it happened that: It was September again, which used to be the beginning of the year, and Wittman Ah Sing, though not a student anymore, nevertheless was having cappuccino in North Beach with a new pretty girl. The utter last of summer's air lifted the Cinzano scallops of the table umbrella, and sun kept hitting beautiful Nanci Lee in the hair and eyes. In shade, Wittman leaned back and glowered at her. He sucked shallow on his cigarette and the smoke clouded out thick over his face, made his eyes squint. He also had the advantage of the backlighting, his hair all haloed, any zits and pores shadowed. She, on her side, got to watch the sun go down. A summer and a year had gone by since graduation from Berkeley. Somebody's favorite tune was "Moscow Nights," and balalaikas kept trembling out of the jukebox.

"You," he said. "You're from L.A., aren't you? Why didn't you go back there?" Well, the place that a Chinese holds among other Chinese—in a community somewhere—matters. It was a very personal question he was asking her. It would pain a true Chinese to admit that he or she did not have a community, or belonged at the bottom or the margin.

People who have gone to college—people their age with their at-tee-tood— well, there are reasons—people who wear black turtleneck sweaters have no place. You don't easily come home, come back to Chinatown, where they

---

4. This paragraph is an extensive list of authors who have written in the English language about California and the American West along with some titles of their works.
5. A character in Harte's 1870 poem "The Heathen Chinee," which helped establish Chinese ste-

reotypes in the American consciousness.
6. Southern Pacific Railway.
7. Character in Rilke's *The Notebooks of Malte Laurids Brigge* (1910).
8. References to locales and characters of detective novels.

give you stink-eye and call you a saang-hsü lo, a whisker-growing man,[9] Beatnik.

Nanci brought her coffee cup up to her mouth, bouging to catch the rim, and looked warily, he hoped, at him over it. Beautiful and shy, what a turn-on she is. She took a cigarette out of her purse, and held it in front of that mouth until he lit it. "Yes, I'm from Los Angeles," she said, answering one of his questions. Pause. Take a beat. "I'm going back down there soon. To audition. I'm on my way." Pause yet another beat or two. "Why don't you go back to Sacramento?"

Unfair. No fair. L.A. is wide, flat, new. Go through the flashing arch, and there you are: Chinatownland. Nothing *to* going back to L.A. Cecil B. DeMille rebuilds it new ahead of you as you approach it and approach it on the freeway, whether 101 or over the grapevine.[1] But, say, you stake a claim to San Francisco as your home place. . . .

"Golden Gate Park was wild today. I fought my way out. Lucky." He blew smoke hard between clenched teeth. "The paint-heads were cutting loose out of their minds, and messing with my head. Through the pines and eucalyptus, I could smell the natural-history museum. They may have let those trees grow to hide the funeral-parlor smell, which seeps through the sealant. You got claustro, you got fear of the dark, you keep out of museums of natural history; every kind of phobia lets you have it. It's too quiet, the ursus horribilus[2] propped up on its hind legs; his maw is open but no roar. I don't like walking in the dark with fake suns glowing on the 'scenes.' Pairs of cat-eye marbles look at you from bobcat heads and coyote heads. Freak me out. The male animals are set in hunting poses, and the female ones in nursing poses. Dead babies. There's a lizard coming out of a dinosaur's tail. Stiffs. Dead behind glass forever. Stuffed birds stuffed inside pried-open mouths. 'Taxidermy' means the ordering of skin. Skin arrangements. If you're at my bedside when I die, Nanci, please, don't embalm me. I don't want some mortician who's never met me to push my face into a serene smile. They try to make the buffaloes and deer more natural by balding a patch of hair, omitting a toenail, breaking a horn. I paid my way out of the park. I saw the pattern: twice, there were people refashioning and selling castoffs. Flotsam and jetsam selling flotsam and jetsam. I bought this insert from last Sunday's paper."

Nanci took the paper from him, and folded it into a hat. She put it on Wittman's head. She was not squeamish to touch what a dirty stranger had touched, nor to touch this hairy head before her. He was at a party. He took off the hat, and with a few changes of folds, origamied it into a popgun. He whopped it through the air, it popped good.

"In Sacramento, I don't belong. Don't you wonder how I have information about you and L.A., your town? And how come you have information about me? You have committed to memory that I have family in Sacramento." And, yes, a wondering—a wonderfulness—did play in her eyes and on her face. Two invisible star points dinted her cheeks with dimples; an invisible kung fu knight was poking her cheeks with the points of a silver shuriken.[3] "And I bet you know what I studied. And whether I'm rich boy or poor boy. What

9. Derogatory Chinese slang for a white man.
1. Interstate 5. De Mille (1881–1959), director of lavish Hollywood film epics.

2. Grizzly bear.
3. A throwing-star weapon.

my family is—Lodi grocery or Watsonville farmer, Castroville artichoke or
Oakland restaurant or L.A. rich."[4] Smart was what he was. Scholarship
smart.

"No," she said. "I don't know much about you."

No, she wouldn't. She was no China Man the way he was China Man. A
good-looking chick like her floats above it all. He, out of it, knows ugly and
knows Black, and also knows fat, and funny-looking. Yeah, he knows fat too,
though he's tall and skinny. She's maybe only part Chinese—Lee could be
Black or white Southern, Korean, Scotsman, anything—and also rich. Nanci
Lee and her highborn kin, rich Chinese-Americans of Orange County,[5]
where the most Chinese thing they do is throw the headdress ball. No, he
hadn't exactly captured her fancy and broken her heart. When the rest of
them shot the shit about him, she hadn't paid attention. Though she should
have; he was more interesting than most, stood out, tall for one thing, long
hair for another, dressed in Hamlet's night colors for another. Sly-eyed, he
checked himself out in the plate-glass window. The ends of his moustache
fell below his bearded jawbone. He had tied his hair back, braided loose,
almost a queue but not a slave queue, very hip, like a samurai whose hair
has gotten slightly undone in battle. Like Kyuzu, terse swordsman in *Seven
Samurai*.[6] A head of his time, ha ha. He was combat-ready, a sayonara soldier
sitting on his red carpet beside the palace moat and digging the cherry blossoms in their significant short bloom.

"You must not have been in on the Chinese gossip," he said, counting on
what would hurt her, that at school she had been left out by the main Chinese. (They left everybody out.)

"Let me tell you about where I was born," he said. She was, in a way,
asking for the story of his life, wasn't she? Yeah, she was picking up okay.

"Chinatown?" she guessed. Is that a sneer on her face? In her voice? Is
she stereotypecasting him? Is she showing him the interest of an anthropologist, or a tourist? No, guess not.

"Yes. Yes, wherever I appear, there, there it's Chinatown. But not that
Chinatown." He chinned in its direction. "I was born backstage in vaudeville.
Yeah, I really was. No kidding. They kept me in an actual theatrical trunk—
wallpaper lining, greasepaint, and mothball smells, paste smell. The lid they
braced with a cane. My mother was a Flora Dora girl. To this day, they call
her Ruby Long Legs, all alliteration the way they say it."

Yes, when she came near the trunk, a rubescence had filled the light and
air, and he'd tasted strawberry jam and smelled and seen clouds of cotton
candy. Wittman really does have show business in his blood. He wasn't lying
to impress Nanci. He was taking credit for the circumstances of his birth,
such as his parents. Parents are gifts; they're part of the life-which-happens-
to-one. He hadn't yet done enough of the life-which-one-has-to-make. Commit more experience, Wittman. *It is true you were an actor's child, and when
your people played they wanted to be seen. . . .*

"She did the blackbottom and the Charleston in this act, Doctor Ng and
the Flora Dora Girls. Only, after a couple of cities, Doctor Ng changed it to
Doctor Woo and the Chinese Flora Dora Girls so that the low fawn gwai[7]

---

4. Towns and cities in California.
5. Middle-class suburb near Los Angeles.
6. A 1954 film by the Japanese director Akira

Kurosawa.
7. Derogatory Chinese slang for white people.

would have no problem reading the flyers. 'Woo' easier in the Caucasian mouth. Not broke the mouth, grunting and gutturating and hitting the tones. 'Woo' sounds more classy anyway, the dialect of a better-class village. 'Woo' good for white ear. A class act. You know?" Of course, she did not know; he rubbed it in, how much she did not know about her own. "Doctor Woo's Chinese Flora Dora Jitter and June Bug Girls were boogie-woogying and saluting right through World War II. Yeah, within our lifetimes."

"What *was* the blackbottom?" she asked.

For her, he danced his forefingers like little legs across the tabletop. (Like Charlie Chaplin doing the Oceana Roll with dinner rolls on forks in *The Gold Rush*.) " 'Hop down front and then you doodle back. Mooch to your left and then you mooch to your right. Hands on your hips and do the mess around. Break a leg and buckle near the ground. Now that's the Old Black Bottom.' " She laughed to see one finger-leg buckle and kick, buckle and kick, then straighten up, and the other finger-leg buckle and kick all the way across and off the table. Knuckle-knees.

O Someday Girl, find him and admire him for his interests. And dig his allusions. And laugh sincerely at his jokes. And were he to take up dandy ways, for example, why, remark on his comeliness in a cravat. Say "He's beau," without his having to point out the cravat.

But at the moment, this Nanci was smiling one of those Anne Bancroft— Tuesday Weld sneer-smiles, and he went on talking. In case she turns out to be the one he ends up with, he better tell her his life from the beginning. "You have to imagine Doctor Woo in white tie, top hat, tails—his Dignity. He called that outfit his Dignity. 'What shall I wear? I shall wear my Dignity,' he used to say, and put on his tux. 'I'm attending that affair dressed in my Dignity.' 'My Dignity is at the cleaner's.' 'My Dignity will see me out,' which means he'll be buried in it. Doctor Woo did sleight of hand, and he did patter song. He also did an oriental turn. Do you want to hear a Doctor Woo joke? No, wait. Wait. Never mind. Some other time. Later. It'd bring you down. He rip-rapped about sweet-and-sour eyes and chop-suey dis and dat, and white people all alikee. Yeah, old Doc Woo did a racist turn." (What Wittman wanted to say was, "Old Doc Woo milked the tit of stereotype," but he went shy.) "The audience loved it. Not one show-girl caught him up on it." Wittman made lemon eyes, and quince mouth, and Nanci laughed. He scooped up shreds of nervous paper napkins, his and hers, wadded them into a ball—held it like a delicate egg between thumb and forefinger—palm empty—see?—and out of the fist, he tugged and pulled a clean, whole napkin—opened the hand, no scraps. Come quick, your majesty. Simple Simon is making the princess laugh; she will have to marry him. "During intermissions and after the show, we sold Doctor Woo's Wishes Come True Medicine. The old healing-powers-and-aphrodisiacs-of-the-East scam. I'm dressed as a monkey. I'm running around in the crowd handing up jars and bottles and taking in the money. Overhead Doc Woo is giving the pitch and jam: 'You hurt? You tired? Ah, tuckered out? Where you ache? This medicine for you. Ease you sprain, ease you pain. What you wish? You earn enough prosperity? Rub over here. Tired be gone. Hurt no more. Guarantee! Also protect against accidental bodily harm. And the Law. Smell. Breathe in deep. Free whiff. Drop three drops—four too muchee, I warn you—into you lady's goblet, and she be you own lady. Make who you love love you back. Hold you true love true to you. Guarantee! Guarantee!' We sold a line of products: those pretty silver beebees—remember them?—for when you have a tummy ache?—and Tiger Balm, which he bought in Chinatown and sold at a markup—cheaper for Chinese customers, of course. The Deet Dah Jow, we mixed ourselves. I use it quite often." "Deet Dah Jow" means "Fall Down and Beaten Up Alcohol." Medicine for the Fallen Down and Beaten Up. Felled and Beaten.

"When I smell Mahn Gum Yow," said Nanci, saying "Ten Thousand Gold Pieces Oil" very prettily, high-noting "gum," "I remember being sick in bed with the t.v. on. I got to play treasure trove with the red tins. I liked having a collection of gold tigers—they used to be raised, embossed—they're flat now—with emerald eyes and red tongues. I thought Tiger Balm was like Little Black Sambo's tiger butter. That in India the tigers chase around the palm tree until they churn into butter. And here they churn into ointment."

May this time be the first and only time she charms with this tale, and he its inspiration. "Yeah," he said. "Yeah. Yeah."

He continued. Onward. "Backstage old Doc Woo used to peptalk the Flora Dora girls about how they weren't just entertaining but doing public service like Ng Poon Chew and Wellington Koo, credits to our race. Show the bok gwai that Chinese-Ah-mei-li-cans are human jess likee anybody elsoo, dancing, dressed civilized, telling jokes, getting boffo laffs. We got rhythm. We got humor." Oh, god, he was so glad. He had not lost it, then—the mouth—to send the day high.

Nanci said, "You aren't making this up, are you?"

"Hey, you don't believe me? I haven't given you anything but facts. So I don't have an imagination. It's some kind of retardation. So I am incapable of making things up. My mother's name is Ruby, and my father is Zeppelin Ah Sing. He was a Stagedoor Johnny, then a backstage electrician, then emcee on stage. To get Mom to marry him, he bought out the front row of seats for entire runs. He loved her the best when she was on stage as Ruby Long Legs; and she loved him best leading his Army buddies in applause. They got married in Carson City, which is open for weddings twenty-four hours a day.

"To this day, whenever they go gambling at State Line, they start divorce proceedings. To keep up the *ro*mance. My parents are free spirits—I'm a descendant of free spirits. He left her and me for World War II. My aunties, the showgirls, said I was a mad baby from the start. Yeah. Mad baby and mad man." Come on, Nanci. The stars in a white girl's eyes would be glittering and popping by now.

"Uh-huh. Uh-huh," she said. "Uh-huh."

"You should have seen me in my Baby Uncle Sam outfit. The striped pants had an open seam in the back, so if I could grow a tail, it would come out of there. Sure, the costume came off of a circus monkey or a street-dancing monkey. You want details? I can impart details to you." She wasn't bored out of her mind anyway. Please be patient. Are you the one I can tell my whole life to? From the beginning to this moment? Using words that one reads and thinks but never gets to hear and say? "Think back as far as you can," he said. "First it's dark, right? But a warm, close dark, not a cold outer-space dark." A stupid girl would think he knew her personal mind. "Then you made out a slit of light, and another, and another—a zoetrope—faster and faster, until all the lights combined. And you had: consciousness. Most people's lights turn on by degrees like that. (When you come across 'lights' in books, like the Donner Party[8] ate lights, do you think 'lights' means the eyes or the brains?) I got zapped all at once. That may account for why I'm uncommon. I saw: all of a sudden, curtains that rose and rose, and on the other side of them, lights, footlights and overheads, and behind them, the dark, but different from the previous dark. Rows of lights, like teeth, uppers and lowers, and the mouth wide open laughing—and either I was inside it standing on the tongue, or I was outside, looking into a mouth, and inside the mouth were many, many strangers. All looking at me. *For a while they looked at me, wondering at my littleness.* And pointing at me and saying, 'Aaah.' Which is my name, do you see? Then one big light blasted me. It was a spotlight or a floodlight, and I thought that it had dissolved me into light, but it hadn't, of course. I made out people breathing—expecting something. They wanted an important thing to happen. If I opened my mouth, whatever it was that was pouring into my ears and eyes and my skin would shout out of my mouth. I opened my mouth for it to happen. But somebody swooped me up—arms caught me—and carried me back into the wings. Sheepcrooked m'act.". . . *a door had swung open before you, and now you were among the alembics in the firelight. . . . Your theater came into being.*

Yes, this flight, this rush, the oncoming high. He had talked his way—here—once more. Good and bad, the world was exactly as it should be. The sidewalk trees were afire in leaf-flames. And the most beyond girl in the world was listening to him. The air which contained all this pleasure was as clear as mescaline and he was straight. The sun was out which shines golden like this but three times a San Francisco autumn.

"When I was a child," said Nanci—*her* turn to talk about *her* kiddiehood—"I had a magic act too. But it wasn't an act. I didn't have an audience; it was secret. I believed I could make things appear and disappear by taking every step I had seen the magician take at my birthday party. I sprinkled salt on a hanky to make a dime appear." She opened a paper napkin, and shook salt into it. What's this? She doing geisha shtick for me? "I tied the corners together and said my magic words. Then undid the knot, and blew the salt." She made kiss-me lips, and blew. The wind is driving snow off of a silver pond. The wind is driving a snowcloud across the full moon. "I didn't find a dime then either. What step did I do wrong—not enough salt, too much salt? Didn't I tie the knot right? It has to be a seventh birthday?" She giggled, looked at him to help her out, to sympathize with her gullibility or to laugh at her joking. Doesn't she know that all magic acts you have to cheat, the missing step is cheating? You're not the only one, Wittman, who fooled with magic, and not the only one who refuses to work for money. And also not the only one to talk. She had to talk too, make this a conversation. In those days, women did not speak as much as men. Even among the educated and Bohemian, a man talked out his dreams and plans while a girl thought whether she would be able to adapt herself to them. Girls gave one another critiques on how adaptable they were. The artistic girls had dead-white lips and aborigine eyes, and they wore mourning colors. There were two wake-robins, Diane Wakoski and Lenore Kandell;[9] the latter wailed out sex-challenge poems larger and louder than the men, who were still into cool.

---

8. A group of pioneers who were stranded in a mountain pass in California's Sierra Nevada mountains during the winter of 1846–47; some of the survivors resorted to cannibalism.
9. Contemporary American feminist poets.

"Why did you ask me out?" asked Nanci.

Because you're beautiful, he thought, and maybe I love you; I need to get it on with a Chinese-American chick. He said, "I wanted to find out if the most beautiful girl of all my school days would come to me." There. Said. Would come to me. Intimate. He let her know that he used to be—and still was—in her thrall. "I'm calling you up," he had said on the phone, "to celebrate the first anniversary of our graduation. Come tell me, have you found out, 'Is there life after Berkeley?' " "I told you—we're having a reunion, a party for me."

"Shouldn't we be at Homecoming, then, with everyone else?"

What? Buy her a lion-head chrysanthemum, pin it on her tweed lapel? Do the two of us have to walk again past the fraternities on College Avenue, and admire their jungle-bunny house decorations? The Jew Guais too with Greek letters—Sammies—and Yom Kippur banners. Yeah, there were a Chinese fraternity and sorority, but if you were bone-proud, you didn't have anything to do with SOP sisters and the Pineapple Pies. Nor the Christian house, which let anybody in. The crowd let the city and county sawhorses route them, governments too co-operating with football. He was always walking alone in the opposite direction but ending up at Strawberry Canyon—the smell of eucalyptus in the cold air breaks your heart—among the group looking down into the stadium for free. Only he was up here for the walk, awaiting a poem to land on him, to choose him, walking to pace the words to the rhythm of his own stride. And there was all this football interference. The Cal Marching Band, the drum booming, and the pompon girls kneeling and rotating an arm with pompons in the air, and the teams running toward each other with the crowd going oo-oo-OO-OH! How do all those people know you're supposed to stand and yell that yell at kickoff? The reason he didn't like going to football games was the same reason he didn't like going to theater: he wanted to be playing. Does his inability at cheers have to do with being Chinese? He ought to be in Paris, where everything is dark and chic.

"The Big Game soon," she said.

"Weren't you an Oski Doll? You were an Oski Doll, weren't you?"

"Come on. It was an honor to be an Oski Doll. It's based on scholarship too, you know? It's a good reference. Some of us Oski Dolls helped integrate the rooting section from you boys."

" 'Here we go, Bears, here we go.' 'We smell roses.' 'All hail Blue and Gold; thy colors unfold.' 'Block that kick, hey.' 'Hold that line, hey.' 'The Golden Bear is ever watching.' "

"See? You did participate."

"Well, yeah, I went to the Big Game once. Stanford won." But most of the time I was participating in the big dread. "Those songs and cheers will stick in the head forever, huh?"

"I know your motive for wanting to see me," she said. "You want to know how you were seen. What your reputation was. What people thought of you. You care what people think of you. You're interested in my telling you."

He looked at the bitten nails of the fingers that held her cigarette and of her other fingers, both hands; they put him at ease. "Yes, if you want to tell me, go ahead."

"Well, let me think back," she said, as if school had been long ago and not interesting anymore. "It seems to me you were a conservative."

No. No. No. He had been wild. Maybe she thought it flattered a Chinese man to be called temperate? Safe. What about his white girlfriends? What about his Black girlfriend? His play-in-progress? That he read aloud on afternoons on the Terrace and at the Mediterraneum (called The Piccolo by those hip to the earlier Avenue scene). There had been no other playwright. Of whatever color. He was the only one. She hadn't cared for his poem in *The Occident?*

"Conservative like F.O.B.? Like Fresh Off the Boat?" He insulted her with translation; she was so banana,[1] she needed a translation. "Conservative like engineering major from Fresno with a slide rule on his belt? Like dental student from Stockton? Like pre-optometry majors from Gilroy and Vallejo and Lodi?" But I'm an artist, an artist of all the Far Out West. "Feh-see-no. Soo-dock-dun," he said, like an old Chinese guy bopping out a list poem. "Gi-loy. Wah-lay-ho. Lo-di." But hadn't he already done for her a catalog of places? Repeating himself already. One of his rules for maintaining sincerity used to be: Never tell the same story twice. He changed that to: Don't say the same thing in the same way to the same person twice. Better to be dead than boring.

"I mean quiet," she said and did not elaborate, poured more espresso out of her individual carafe, sipped it, smoked. She wasn't deigning to go on. No examples. He had talked for four years, building worlds, inventing selves, and she had not heard. The gold went out of the day. He came crashing down. He must have been feeling good only because the sun was out amid grey weeks. (In the plague year, according to Defoe,[2] the people's moods were much affected by the weather.)

"Well?" she said, pushing away from the table, her shoulders up, like a forties movie girl being hugged. "I have an appointment at three-thirty." As if she had come to the City for that important appointment and incidentally might as well have met with him too, a former classmate, after all. But there was no guile on her face, which seemed always uplifted. Was she joyful, or was that curve the way her mouth naturally grew? The way some cats and dogs have smile markings. Yeah, it was not a smile but a smile marking.

"Hey, wait a minute," he said, and grabbed her hand, held hands with her, a sudden endearment achieved right smack through force fields. "Let's go for a walk. Come for a walk with me. I live near here. Yeah, I do. Let me show you where I live."

Since she, in truth, did not have an appointment, she agreed to go with him. Finding digs, having digs, arranging them interested each of them very much. *God's solitaries in their caves and bare retreats.*[3]

"Let's walk," he said, stubbing out his cigarette. Let's amble the blue North Beach streets as the evening sun goes down into the far grey water.

Though they walked through the land of the wasted, no Malte sights popped out to hurt him, she dispelling them. By day, the neon was not coursing through its glass veins. The dancing girl in spangles and feathers had flown out of her cage, which hung empty over the street. Nobody barked and hustled at the doorways to acts and shows. The day-folks, wheeling babies, wheeling grandpas, holding children by the hand, were shopping for dinner

1. Slang for an Americanized Chinese person: yellow-skinned but white inside.
2. Daniel Defoe (1660?–1731), English author of

A Journal of the Plague Year (1722).
3. From Rilke's *Notebooks.*

at the grocery stores and the bakery, dropping by the shoe repair. Oh, the smell of the focaccia ovens—O Home. A florist with white moustachios jay-walked through traffic with armsful of leonine football chrysanthemums. Behind glass, at the all-day-all-night place on the pie-wedge corner, poets, one to a table, were eating breakfast. The Co-Existence Bagel Shop was gone. The old guys, *Seventh Seal*[4] knights, had played chess with Death and lost. The Bagel Shop, Miss Smith's Tea Room, Blabbermouth Night at The Place—all of a gone time. Out from the open door of La Bodega, a folksy guitar sweetened the air. The guitar was being passed around, and each played the tune he knew. You should have been there the night Segovia[5] dropped by and played flamenco. Wittman musefully sang as if to himself a Mose Allison riff.

> *A young ma-a-an*
> *ain't nothin' in this world today.*
> *Because the ol' men's*
> *got all the money.*[6]

The air of the City is so filled with poems, you have to fight becoming imbued with the general romanza. Nanci's long black hair and long black skirt skirled with the afternoon breezes. The leather of her shoulder bag strapped a breast. Her arms and outstretching legs were also long and black; she wore a leotard and tights like an old-fashioned Beat chick but, honestly, a dancer, dance togs for a good reason. Here he was: Wittman Ah Sing profiling down the street with a beautiful almost-girlfriend, clipping along, alongside, keeping up with him, the two of them making the scene on the Beach, like cruising in the gone Kerouac time of yore.

He ducked into the bookstore. She followed right on in. She stood beside him, browsing the rack of quarterlies, quite a few brave Volume I Number Ones. There were homemade books too, mimeo jobs, stencils, and small-press poetry that fit neat in the hand. On the top rack—right inside the door at eye level for all to see coming in or going out—was: an artistic avant-garde far-out new magazine that had published—in print—a scene from his play-in-progress—the lead-off piece—with his byline—right inside the front cover. He could reach over and hand it to her, but it would be more perfect if she happened to pick it out herself, come upon his premiere on her own, and be impressed. (F. Scott Fitzgerald, trying to impress Sheilah Graham,[7] had driven to every bookstore in L.A., but could not find a copy of any of his books.)

Wittman went downstairs to the cool basement, where among the book-shelves were chairs and tables with ashtrays. He had first come to this place when he was a high-school kid on one of his escapes from Sacramento, Second City to Big City. No *No Free Reading* sign. No *No Smoking*. You didn't have to buy a book; you could read for nothing. You had a hangout where you didn't have to spend money. Quiet. All the radios in Chinatown blaring out the ball game, but here, we don't care about the World Series.

4. A 1957 film by the Swedish director Ingmar Bergman (b. 1918).
5. Andrés Segovia (1893–1987), Spanish classical guitarist.

6. From "Back Country Suite" (1957) by jazz musician Mose Allison (b. 1927).
7. British writer. Fitzgerald (1896–1940), American novelist and short story writer.

He hadn't known the City Lights Pocket Book Shop was famous until the *Howl* trial,[8] which he had cut school to attend. "Shig" Shigeyoshi Murao was the one charged with selling an obscene book. The muster of famous poets had blown Wittman away—everybody friends with everybody else, a gang of poets. He, poor monkey, was yet looking for others of his kind.

There had been a Chinese-American guy who rode with Jack and Neal.[9] His name was Victor Wong, and he was a painter and an actor. Wittman had maybe seen him, or someone Chinese with the asymmetrical face of a character actor; he wore a white t-shirt with paint streaks and "hand-tooled leather shoes." Victor Wong, who went to the cabin in Bixby Canyon with Jack Duluoz and Neal/Cody. All this written up in *Big Sur*,[1] where Jack calls Victor Wong Arthur Ma ("Little Chinese buddy Arthur Ma." Shit.), and flips out of his gourd walking in the moonless night above the wild ocean that rants for his life. Jack hangs on to the side of the mountain and listens and shouts back and sings. "Mien Mo Big Sur killer mountain for singing madly in." It would have been better if Victor/Arthur had been a writing man like the rest of them, but anyway he talked a lot and was good at hallucinations. "Little Arthur Ma [yet again "little"!] who never goes anywhere without his drawing paper and his Yellowjacket felt tips of all colors, red, blue, yellow, green, black, he draws marvelous subconscious glurbs and can also do excellent objective scenes or anything he wants on to cartoons—." They stay up all night, and Arthur Ma keeps making it up; he's not one of those storytellers who has to rehearse in the bathroom. Wittman had not gone up to the man with the character actor's face—one eye big, one eye small—and grabbed him by the arm and introduced himself. The poets at Big Sur fall asleep but not Arthur, who stays awake with Jack, the two of them yelling till dawn. ". . . and Arthur Ma suddenly yells: 'Hold still you buncha bastards, I got a hole in my eye.' "

It would be nice were Nanci to walk down the pine-slab steps and say, "Oh, you're published. Why didn't you tell me? Will you autograph a copy for me?" Holding his words to her bosom.

Girls in my native land. May the loveliest of you on an afternoon in summer in the darkened library find herself the little book that Jan des Tournes[2] printed in 1556. May she take the cooling, glossy volume out with her into the murmurous orchard, or yonder to the phlox, in whose oversweet fragrance there lies a sediment of sheer sweetness.

She was two aisles away browsing through the French and German shelves. The Europeans made books with creme linen paper; the soft covers were not illustrated except for a sharp line of vermillion trim. When you slice the pages open with your paperknife, the book will have flossy raggedy edges. You feel like owning books like that. Remember Phoebe Weatherfield Caulfield asking Holden[3] to name one thing he liked a lot? "Name one thing." "One thing I like a lot, or one thing I just like?" "You like a lot." Wittman

8. Some of the sellers of this 1956 book-length poem by Allen Ginsberg (1926–1997) were prosecuted for obscenity. "City Lights": San Francisco bookstore owned by poet Lawrence Ferlinghetti (b. 1919).
9. Neal Cassady, American writer who is the basis for several of Kerouac's characters, especially Dean

Moriarty of *On the Road* (1957).
1. Kerouac's 1962 novel.
2. Jean des Tournes (fl. 1550), French printer of editions of Dante and Petrarch.
3. Characters in *The Catcher in the Rye* (1951), by American novelist and short story writer J. D. Salinger (b. 1919).

liked a lot this poky hole in the San Francisco underground earth. He will not point out to Nanci what's so good about it. Spoil it to make a big deal. She had to take a liking of her own accord. He took his own sweet time, testing her scanning and skimming of foreign lit.

But the next time he looked her way, she was talking to a couple of Black guys, laughing, carrying on in French. Maybe they had met before, or maybe she let herself be picked up. There was something Black about her too, come to think of it; it was in a fullness of the mouth, and a wildness in her clothes, and something about her dry hair. "Très joli.⁴ Ahh, très joli. Oo-la-la, très joli." So, people really do say "Oo-la-la." She and they were mutually delighting in something. These black French must have lately arrived from one of those colonial places. Their faces were not chary and wary; they were not "friendly," or "bad," or "loose." Their long hands and fingers wafted through a gentler atmosphere. Give them a few more weeks among the Amerikans; we'll show them how far très joli manners get them, and how much respect with *Saturday Review*⁵ tucked under the arm. They'll tighten up their act. Turn complicated. He squeezed past them; they easily stepped aside, gave him no trouble. Let's go already, Nanci. Wittman gave a jerk of his head— ¡Vamos! ¡Andalay!⁶—and, surprisingly, she said her adieux and followed him up the stairs. You would think only homely girls obey like that.

"Wait," she called. "I'll be right with you." She paid for a book. "See?" she said. "Beckett."⁷

"Ah, Bik Giht," he said, Chinatown having a pronunciation because of Beckett Street and not because of absurdity. Of course not.

"I'm looking for audition pieces," said Nanci as they walked along. "The speeches of just about any Beckett man make sense—more sense—coming from a woman. A minority woman. It doesn't matter what a Beckett character looks like. I won't play an oriental prostitute, and I won't speak broken English. No matter what. I can't. I won't. I'll be too old to play an ingenue? I'm a leading lady. I am the leading-lady type. No ching-chong chinaman for me."

What did she say? She said "ching-chong chinaman." She can bear to say that. God, she's tough. He had to get tougher. His head and bod were going through contortions from merely hearing that. Did I hear wrong? Hallucinating again? She mean me? Who you talking to? You talking to me, girl? You talking *about* me? Am I too paranoid, or what? She hadn't called me a name, had she? Someone called her that? Who called her that? Who she quoting? Was he hearing English wrong like any greenhorn F.O.B.? Now he was laughing nervously—the Chinese laugh—the giggle—lest it be a joke— that please-let-it-be-a-joke giggle. That betraying Chinese giggle trebled out of him. Where he'd almost gone deaf, she had said, "No ching-chong chinaman for me." She meant she refused to read a grotesque whose bucktoof mouth can't make intelligent American sounds. As if this language didn't belong to us. Well, the ugly is ugly no matter whose beautiful mouth it comes out of. She shouldn't wreck her mouth, and her voice, and her face, and her soul by repeating scurrilities.

"For my classical, I'll do Rosalind or Portia. Then when I'm older, anybody

---

4. Very pretty (French).
5. Eminent weekly magazine reviewing literature and the arts.
6. Hurry up! Move along! (Spanish).
7. Samuel Beckett (1906–1989), Irish writer who lived in France and wrote in English and French.

can be the queen." Anybody. Her. A leading lady. Why not? Who has more in common with a Shakespeare queen—a country-fair beauty starlet or Leontyne Price? Medea and Cleopatra and Clytemnestra and the statue lady from *Winter's Tale* are not blondies. Nor, it so happened, were any of the people walking by them on the street, nor are most people in the world.

"I don't like *Flower Drum Song*,"[8] she said. Wittman didn't either—a bunch of A.J.A.s and "Eurasians" playing weird Chinese. Not that Chinese have to play Chinese. Chineseness does not come to an actor through genetic memory. The well-trained actor observes humanity and the text.

"Oh, I'm so sorry," said Nanci, "that I took my grandmother to see *The World of Suzie Wong*[9] for the scenes of Hong Kong. I'm so sorry. Wittman? I've been to New York and Hollywood. I look a bit dark. They're overt, you know? They say, 'You don't *look* oriental.' I walk in, they can tell about me. They read me, then they say, 'You don't sound right. You don't sound the way you look. You don't look the way you talk. Too distracting.' I'm wearing my high heels, and walking elegant, you know? The a.d. hands me the script, and tells me I have to take my shoes off. It's a cold reading, but I know what my part will be—an oriental peasant. You only need high heels for the part of the oriental prostitute. A good-looking talented actor, who's gotten his callback, who's been cast maybe, says my cue, which is 'Hey, there, mama-san.' And I have to say, I have to say, you know, something stupid. I have to speak in a way I've worked hard not to speak like. I stand there barefoot saying a line like—like that. And the director says, 'Can't you act more oriental? Act oriental.' I haven't been making rounds for a while." Oh, no, Nanci, don't lose the will to audition.

Wittman, now's your chance to whip out your Rilke, and give her his sympathy: *Let us be honest about it, then; we have no theatre, any more than we have God: for this, community is needed. . . . Had we a theatre, would you, tragic one, stand there again and again and again—so slight, so bare, so without pretext of a role. . . .*

"Wittman?" she said, laying a hand on his arm. "I performed twice as a crowd member. Once in a movie, and once on t.v. While the make-up lady was shading my nose, she said, 'I'm going to give you a cute Irish nose.' I'm tilted back in the chair, and holding my face steady. I don't reply. I don't want to get her mad so she makes me up ugly. And I wanted to see what I'd look like with my nose upturned. She shadowed the nostrils, and put white make-up down the length, ending with a diamond on the tip. The other show I was in, we had a male make-up artist—bitchy gay?—who finished my face without talking to me. Then he says, 'There's just so much we can do about those eyes.'" Those eyes were now downcast with mortification and tears. Oh, baby, what can I do to defend you against—cosmetologists. "They were trying to give me advice? For my own good? They didn't mean to hurt me."

"Yes, they did. They hurt you."

"Yes. I should have done my own make-up."

"It's no fair," said Wittman, who would not put his arm around her shoulder or waist. This called for a higher level of comforting. Help her out by thinking up a piece for her to do without insult. He ought to tell her that

---

8. A 1961 Broadway musical by Richard Rodgers and Oscar Hammerstein.

9. A 1960 film about an Asian prostitute (played by Nancy Kwan).

her face was perfectly lovely. But he was annoyed at her for talking about her face so much. Her nickname in college had been The Face. "How about the girl in *The Seven Year Itch?*"[1] he suggested. "Yeah, that's what the script says—The Girl. Not The White Girl. The Girl. She's just a girl in New York on her own. No family from the old country camping in her apartment."

"I hate *The Seven Year Itch*. I loathe it."

"Just testing. I was testing you. You passed." Therefore, thou art mine, sought and found.

"But you're right. She could very well look like me. There isn't any reason why she shouldn't look like me. Wittman?" She had his sleeve in her fingers, and pulled at it for them to stop walking so fast. "I was thinking of *Krapp's Last Tape*.[2] I could do it by myself, no other face up there to compare mine to. A director doesn't have to match me. My lost love who's beside me in the boat could be a male nurse. 'We lay there without moving but under us all moved, and moved us, gently, up and down, and from side to side.' When Krapp says, 'Let me in,' I, a woman, could mean: Open your eyes, and let me into your eyes."

Why hadn't he thought of that? She must think him ill-read and a dried-up intellectual not to have seen the sensuality in Beckett. "You're resorting to Krapp, Nanci, because of being left out of the Hogan Tyrone Loman Big Daddy family. And whatever the names of those families were in *Seven Brides for Seven Brothers*.[3] Seven white brides for seven white brothers. They took a perfectly good pro-miscegenation legend and wrote fourteen principal parts for Caucasians. I know legends about seven Chinese brothers named Juan; they were part of a nation of one hundred and eight heroes and heroines. What I'm going to do, I've got to wrest the theater back for you. Those Juans were hermanos chinos.

"I understand your agony, Nanci," he said. "The most important tradition in my high school was the senior play. My year they did *The Barretts of Wimpole Street*.[4] The student who won the most Willie Awards was supposed to play the lead. In the U.K., 'willie' means 'weenie'; in Sacramento, it means 'talent.' I was the man of a thousand faces and got my Willies for winning talent shows. Robert Browning, tall, thin, sensitive, dark, melancholy—that's me, let me count the ways. But the drama coach held auditions. Then he told me, I'm the emcee for the evening, the 'host'; I warm up the audience, talk to them entr'acte, do my stand-up shtick, whatever I like, do my magic act, my ventriloquist act, throw my voice, 'Help. Help. Let me out.' I'd be featured. Very special, my spot. The way they staged *The Barretts of Wimpole Street* was Wilderesque, with an important *Our Town*[5] stage manager character played by me. I look like Frank Craven, who had Chinese eyes and a viewpoint from the outskirts of Grover's Corners, U.S.A. I did my medley of soliloquies, Hamlet, Richard III, Macbeth, Romeo. No Juliet. I did my bearded Americans, Walt Whitman and John Muir, guys with a lot of facial hair to cover up my face and my race. Mark Twain: ' . . . a white to make a body sick, a white to make a body's flesh crawl—a tree-toad white, a fish-belly white.' Between *Barretts*, I also did great movie lines. 'Philip. Give me

1. A 1955 film starring Marilyn Monroe.
2. A 1957 play by Samuel Beckett.
3. A 1954 film based on a Broadway musical.
4. A 1930s drama and film depicting the lives of

19th-century British poets Elizabeth Barrett Browning and Robert Browning.
5. A 1938 play by American dramatist Thornton Wilder (1897–1975).

the letter, Philip.' 'Last night I dreamt I went to Manderley again.' 'As God is my witness, I'll never be hungry again. Chomp chomp.' 'The calla lilies are in bloom. Such a strange flowah.' "

Nanci guessed the actress whom each of those lines belonged to. " 'Maybe you found someone you like betta,' " she said. "Mae Clarke before James Cagney shoves the grapefruit in her kisser. 'I'd rather have his one arm around me than be in the two arms of another man.' "

"I know. I know. That movie where Linda Darnell and the British flyer and Tab Hunter are marooned on an island of desire. The British flyer has one arm, and Tab Hunter has the two arms but doesn't get the girl."

"No. Thelma Ritter says it to Marilyn Monroe in *The Misfits*."[6]

"Nanci, I think we're on to something. That line is so meaningful, they've used it in two movies. It's what you call a perennial favorite. Women have all the good lines. I almost turned into a Mei Lan Fang[7] androgyne doing those lines single-handed. I'm ruined for ensemble work. I haven't been on the stage since."

Grant Avenue, or Du Pont Gai—they/we call it Du Pont Gai—changed from North Beach to Chinatown. That factory which baked the Beatnik fortune cookies for the Actor's Workshop benefit should be situated at this border. You can't pick out just exactly which Italian store or Chinese store or red or red-white-and-green festooning it is that demarcates the change, but suddenly or gradually—depending on how closely you're keeping a lookout—you are in the flak and flash of Chinatown. Autumn was here: A red banner strung above the street announced the Double Ten parade and its sponsors, the Chinese-American Anti-Communist League and the Six Companies. They'll leave the banner up there all this month before Double Ten and afterwards into winter. To show Immigration and HUAC that we Chinese-Americans, super Americans, we too better dead than red-hot communists. Neither Wittman nor Nanci had plans to observe Double Ten.[8] They had no idea how you go about doing that since nobody they knew showed much interest. It seemed like a fake holiday. A woody station wagon[9] with Ohio plates drove slowly by. Painted across it was: "North Beach or Bust." Poor bastards. Too late. They had crossed the country to join the Beatniks.

"I'm writing a play for you, Nanci," said Wittman. Wait for me while I write for you a theater; I will plant and grow for you a pear garden. Then she did look at him—he's wonderful. She stopped in her tracks to look up at him. She took his upper arm with her two hands. "I'll write you a part," he said, "where the audience learns to fall in love with you for your ochery skin and round nose and flat profile and slanty eyes, and your bit of an accent."

She made a pouty mouth. They walked on, she still holding his arm with both hands. Nanci, as a matter of fact, had a pointy nose with a bridge, where her dark glasses had a place to sit. Even Marilyn Monroe, blonde, dead, had not been able to get away with a round nose. Rhinoplasty. Nanci looked good. When the directors tell her, "You don't look Chinese," they mean: too pretty for a Chinese. She had represented Cal at the intercollegiate (Chinese) beauty-personality-good-grades contest at U.C.L.A.

---

6. A 1961 film written by Arthur Miller (b. 1915).
7. Mei Lan Fang (1894–1961), Beijing opera star.
8. I.e., October 10; National Day of the People's Republic of China.
9. Wood-paneled station wagon, popular with surfers.

What theater do we have besides beauty contests? Do we have a culture that's not these knickknacks we sell to the bok gwai? If Chinese-American culture is not knickknackatory—look at it—backscratcher swizzle sticks, pointed chopsticks for the hair, Jade East aftershave in a Buddha-shape bottle, the head screws off and you pour lotion out of its neck—then what is it? No other people sell out their streets like this. Tourists can't buy up J-town. Wait a goddamn minute. *We* don't make Jade East. It's one of your hakujin[1] products by Swank. Would we do that to you? Make Jesus-on-the-cross bottles, so every morning, all over the country, hairy men twist his head off, and pour this green stuff out of his neck? So what do we have in the way of a culture besides Chinese hand laundries? You might make a joke on that— something about 'What's the difference between a Chinese hand laundry and a French laundry?' Where's our jazz? Where's our blues? Where's our ain't-taking-no-shit-from-nobody street-strutting language? I want so bad to be the first bad-jazz China Man bluesman of America. Of all the music on the airwaves, there's one syllable that sounds like ours. It's in that song by the Coasters. "It'll take an ocean of calamine lotion. Poison iv-ee-eeee-ee." No, not the ivy part. It's where they sing, "Aro-ou-ound-aaaaa-ah." Right there, that's a Chinese opera run. A Coaster must have been among those Black guys you see at the Chinese movies and at dojos[2] seeking kung fu power.

Wittman and Nanci toned down any show-off in their walks. Chinese like for young people to look soo-mun or see-mun.[3] Proper. Well turned out. Decorous. Kempt. The Ivy League look is soo-mun. Clean-cut all-American. For girls: sprayed, fixed hair—hair helmet—and they should have a jade heart at their throat always. Wittman was glad Nanci was wearing a defiant black leotard. If they were Japanese and walking through J-town in their grubbies, the Issei,[4] who have a word for every social condition, would call them "yogore." (Zato-Ichi the Blind Swordsman, who flicked his snot into the haw-haw-haw mouth of a villain, is yogore. He'd be rolling the snotball all the time he's pretending to be putting up with their taunts.) Wittman went up Jackson Street (Dik-son Gai), sort of herding Nanci, turned her at the corner, guided her across the street by leaning toward her or leading away. Strange the way a man has to walk with a woman. She follows his lead like they're dancing, she wasn't even a wife or girlfriend. Did you hear what Jack Kennedy said to his media advisers, who told him that in pictures Jackie isn't walking beside him enough? He said, "She will just have to walk faster." (It is not a Chinese custom for women to walk behind men. That's a base stereotype.) No, Wittman didn't want to slow down for anybody either, become an inclining, compliant owned man. Husbands walk differently from single guys. He unlocked the door of his building, having to reach in through the security bars for a somewhat hidden lock. Nanci went right on in. They climbed the many steps and landings, she ahead, and he behind thinking, "Pomegranates." They didn't run into anybody in the hallways, all decent people at work, their doors shut, rows of jailhouse-green doors.

"My ah-pok-mun," he said, opening the door wide to his roomland, switch-

1. Japanese slang for white people.
2. Martial arts studios.
3. To look like a scholar or a gentleman (Chinese).
4. First-generation Japanese American.

ing on the overhead light, which also switched on the desk lamp. "Come in. Come in," turning his desk chair around for his guest. "Welcome to my pok-mun. Sit. Sit." He dumped the fullness of his ashtray into the trash and set the ashtray next to his mattress on the floor. "For sitting furniture, I don't have but the one chair." She hung her suede jacket over the back of it, and sat down. Sweeping open his invisible magician's cape, he presented: his roomland, his boxes of papers, his table, which was desk and dining table, his hotplate on a crate, which was a cupboard for foodstuffs such as instant coffee and Campbell's Soup, edible out of the can. (Cook like a Mexicano: Put the tortilla directly on the burner, flipflop, ready to eat. So you get burner rings on your tortilla, but fast and nongreasy.) He quoted to her some Beat advice: " 'How many things do you own?' 'Fifteen.' 'Too many.' " No rug here. No sofa here. Never own a rug or a sofa. And thus be free. " 'What's the use of living if I can't make paradise in my own roomland?' " Peter Orlovsky was another one good at how to live. She laughed but did not give him the next lines, which are: "For this drop of time upon my eyes / like the endurance of a red star on a cigarette / makes me feel life splits faster than scissors."

Good thing the typewriter crouched, ready, on the table—his grand piano—that faces the window, where you look out at another pok-mun. If he was going to bring people up here, he ought to have been a painter. Painters have something to show for their work—an easel with the painting they're working on like a billboard all sunny under the skylight, their food composed into still-lifes, their favorite colors everywhere. They get to wear their palette on their grey sweatshirts, and spatters and swipes on their blue jeans. He sat down on the mattress, straightened out his sleeping bag, bed made.

"So this is where you live," Nanci said, looking down into one of his cartons, not touching the poems, just looking.

"See that trunk over there?" He pointed at it with the toe of his boot. Books, papers, his coffee cup sat on its lid; a person could sit on it too, and it becomes a second chair.

"That's the trunk I told you about. Proof, huh? Evidence. It exists. It *became* a theatrical trunk; it used to be a Gold Mountain trunk." It was big enough for crossing oceans, all right. It would take a huge man to hoist it onto his back. The hasps and clasps were rusty (with salt sea air), and the leather straps were worn. Big enough to carry all you own to a new land and never come back, enough stuff to settle the Far West with. And big enough to hold all the costumes for the seventy-two transformations of the King of the Monkeys in a long run of *The Journey to the West* in its entirety. "My great-great-grandfather came to America with that trunk."

"Yes," said Nanci, "I recognize it." Every family has a Gold Mountain trunk in their attic or basement.

"I can't die until I fill it with poems and play-acts," said Wittman.

"Would you like to read me a poem?" asked Nanci.

Oh, yes. Yes, I would. My name is Wittman Ah Sing, but you may call me Bold. When you get to know me better, you may call me Bolder, and I'll show you like Emily Dickinson secret poems in the false bottom of my Gold Mountain theater trunk. Oh, too guest-happy.

He rummaged through a carton for a poem that had made him feel like a genius when he made it. "New poems. New green poems. Haven't gone over this batch. Too green. Need one or two more drafts, make fair copies." Oh, shut up. Take one up at random. Any old poem.

Remember when everyone you fell in love with read poems and listened to poems? Love poetry has gone. And thou? Where went thou?

He put on his intellectual's glasses with the heavy black rims, scowled, made no eye contact. Oh, no—a poem—nah, a paragraph—that had been forced on speed, and coffee jacking the bennies up higher, then grass to smooth out the jaw-grinding jangles—does it show? A poem on beanie weenies, when he was a frijoles[5] head—from his Making a Living series, a cycle of useful poetry—well, prose poems, actually—Gig Poems. Wishing he had a chance to re-do it, explain, he read aloud to Nanci something like this: Should a window-washing poet climb over the edge of a skyscraper, one leg at a time, onto his swing, and unclutch the ropes, may the tilted City hold still. Don't look down those paned streets. In view of the typing pools, he makes a noose, and tests the slide of it, and the dingle dangle of it. Yes? Yes? No? No? Yes? No? Hey, look—sky doggies. Up here—a stampede of longhorns. Point the rope like a wand, whirl a Möbius strip, outline a buffalo. Shoot la riata sideways over the street, overhead at the helicopters, jump in and out of it, and lassoo one of those steers. It drags the poet right off the plank—but the harness holds! Hey, you pretty girls of the typing pool, give me a big pantomime hand. Can't hear the clap-clap, but it's applause, and it's mine. Kisses blow through glass. Their impact knocks me off again, falling far down, and down as the pulley runs, and brakes. I vow: I will make of my scaffold, a stage.

The poet—the one in real life, not the one in the poem—wouldn't mind, when the poem ends, if his listening lady were to pay him a compliment. Such as agreeing, yes, let's transfigure every surface of the City with theater. Such as saying, "Did you on purpose make the line that tells about the tilted City bevel upsettingly—the verb fulcrumming a lot more phrases on one end than the other?" He'd love her for such particular appreciation. At least, praise him on the utilitarian level. From out of my head into the world. The window-washer was using newspapers and water, the chemicals in newsprint as good as Windex spray. Also, you can get rich by contracting with the owners of buildings for window-washing services a year in advance. Charge thousands, but pay the window-washers minimum wage by the hour. The kind of men you hire, whatever you pay them, they think it's a lot.

Nanci made no move to show that she heard that the poem was over. Give her a love story, Wittman. He ought to have read her the one about how this broken-hearted guy had long ago stashed in his *Physicians' Desk Reference* the last letter, unread, from the ex-love of his life, written upon taking her leave of him. A lifetime later, an envelope falls out of the *P.D.R.* . . . . (No, he wasn't a doctor. Each head had his own *P.D.R.* to identify street pills, and their effects and side effects, that is, trips and side trips.)

"Want to hear another one?" he asked.

"Okay," she said.

He reached into the poem box beside the black curve of her calf. His arm could graze its black length. But a true poet can't love up a woman who

5. Beans (Spanish).

doesn't get that he's a poet. He can't touch her until she feels his poetry. Japanese have a custom where the host leaves a piece of art about, and the guest may notice it. The carton was labeled The International Nut Corporation, 100 Phoenix Ave., Lowell, Mass. His soul chick would notice it, and say, "Did you make a pilgrimage to Kerouac's town and his city?" Then he grabs her leg.

"What do you want to hear? How about one of my railroad cantos? A land chantey, the worker-poet as chanteyman? How's about a dueling sequence? 'The Dueling Mammy,' ha ha. Loss poems? You need a revenge sonnet? I've got twenty-eight sonnets now. I have one hundred and twenty-six sonnets to go to catch up with Shakespeare, who finished everything at the age of forty-five. I'm twenty-three. You too, right?"

She nodded, crossing one of those legs over the other. She folded her arms under her breasts.

He read to her about the ineluctable goingness of railroad tracks. Then he gave her the poet's intense stare, holding her eyes until she spoke. "Lovely," she said. "Sweet."

But he did not want to be sweet and lovely.

He dug deeper into the poem box, letting the ashes of his cigarette fall right on in. He took hold of a bane poem. Standing up, as if on platform, he read to her about mongoloids. " 'What's wrong with the baby, doctor?' 'Is it deformed?' 'Is it Chinese?!' Interbang?! Interbang!? 'But *we're* Chinese.' 'He's *supposed* to look like that!?' 'How can you tell if it's defective or if it's Chinese?!' 'Look at its little eyes.' 'Its tongue's too long.' 'Yellow skin *and* yellow jaundice?!' 'It's mongoloid?!' 'It's mongoloid!' 'It's an idiot?!' 'It's a mongolian idiot!' 'They're affectionate.' 'No, they bite.' 'Do they drool?!' 'All babies drool.' 'Can they be house-broken?!' 'Let's put it in a home.' The chorus goes like this: 'Gabble gobble. One of us. One of us.' " Wittman opened his eyes as wide as they got and looked into Nanci's—epicanthic eyes meeting epicanthic eyes. Fingers wiggling to communicate. " 'Look at it cry!' 'Is that a cleft palate in there? And a giraffe tongue?!' 'It's got a wee penis.' 'All babies have a small penis.' 'Unlike apes, mongoloids do not turn dangerous to their keepers at puberty.' " Wittman played like he was sitting with the other mongoloid children on the go-around in the playground at the home. Their arms and chins hang over the top railing, a head lolls. A club foot gives the earth a kick, and they go around and around and around. Reading in the manner of Charles Laughton as the Hunchback of Notre Dame (who grunted and snorted in some scenes, and in others discoursed fluently on the nature of man) and like Helen Keller, he stuttered out, " 'Wa-wa-wa-water? Gabble gobble, one of us.' "

No coward, Wittman asked Nanci, "How do you like my work?" Straight out. Asking for it. I can take it.

"You sound black," she said. "I mean like a Black poet. Jive. Slang. Like LeRoi Jones.[6] Like . . . like Black."

He slammed his hand—a fist with a poem in it—down on the desk—fistful of poem. He spit in his genuine brass China Man spittoon, and jumped up on top of the desk, squatted there, scratching. "Monkey see, monkey do?" he said. "Huh? Monkey see, monkey do?" Which sounds much uglier if you

---

6. Now known as Amiri Baraka (b. 1934), American poet, essayist, dramatist, and fiction writer.

know Chinese. "Monkey shit, monkey belly." "A lot you know," he said. "A lot you know about us monkeys." She got up and stood behind her chair. He sprang from the desk onto the chair, and from the chair to the mattress, and from the mattress up to the desk again, dragging his long arms and heavy knuckles. His head turned from side to side like a quick questioning monkey, then slower, like an Indian in a squat, waggling his head meaning yes-and-no. He picked a flea from behind an ear—is this a flea?—or is it the magic pole in its toothpick state that the King of the Monkeys keeps hidden behind his ear? He bit it. "Monkey see. Monkey do. What you do in fleaman's pok-mun?" She didn't answer him. He picked up loose papers with one hand and looked at them, scratched his genitals with the other hand, smelled hands and pages, nibbled the pages. " 'Black?' " he hatefully imitated her. " 'Jive.' " He let drop the papers, nudged one farther with his toe, and wiped his fingers on his moustache. "That bad, huh?" He lifted a page and turned it, examined it back and front. Upside down and sideways. " 'LeRoi Jones?!' " He recoiled from it, dropped it over the edge of the desk, and leaned way over to watch it fall. Keeping an eye on it, he picked up another sheet and sniffed it. "Too Black. If you can't say something nice, don't say anything at all. That's my motto." He wadded it up and threw it over his shoulder. He jumped on top of the trunk, scrunching and scattering the whole shit pile, then pounced on a page, and returned with it to the desk. "This is it! Here's one you'll like. That is, likee. Guarantee. Ah. I mean, aiya. 'Wokking on da Waywoad. Cent-ing da dollahs buck home to why-foo and biby. No booty-full Ah-mei-li-can gal-low fo me. Aiya. Aiya.' " He wiped his eyes with the paper, crushed it, and pitched the wad at the window, which was shut. Sorting papers into two piles, he said, "Goot po-yum. Goot. Goot. No goot. No goot. Goot. No goot." He tasted one, grimaced. "No goot." Breaking character, he said, "Now, if I were speaking in a French accent, you would think it charming. Honk-honk-ho-onk." He did the Maurice Chevalier laugh, which isn't really a laugh, is it? He started new piles. "Angry po-yum." "Sad po-yum." "Goot and angry." "Angry." "Angry." "Imitation of Blacks." He threw some to the floor. "Angry too muchee. Sad. Angry sad. No goot. Angry no goot. Sad. Sad. Sad."

"Please don't freak out," Nanci requested, standing behind the chair.

"I am not freaking out," Wittman said. "I've got to tell you the real truth. No lie. Listen, Lois. Underneath these glasses"—ripping the glasses off, wiping them on his sleeve, which he pulled out over his hand, so it looked like one hand was missing—"I am really: the present-day U.S.A. incarnation of the King of the Monkeys." He unbuttoned his blue chambray workshirt, which he wore on top of his black turtleneck. "Promise me you won't blab this all over the front page of the *Chron*. You'd like a scoop, I know, but I'm trusting you to keep our secret. For the sake of the world."

Now, if Nanci were the right girl for him, she would have said, "Dear monkey. Dear, dear old monkey. Poor monkey." She could scratch his head and under his chin, laugh at his antics, saying, "Poor dear monkey, what's to become of you?" and have him eating out of her hand. "Dear monkey. Poor poor monkey. You do have such an endearing Chinese giggle."

But who could be the right consoling girl for him? Nanci was getting into her jacket and finding her purse. How fucked up he is.

She hurried for the door, and got it open. She turned in the doorway, and said, "An actress says other people's words. I'm an actress; I know about saying other people's words. You scare me. A poet saying his own words. I don't like watching." She held up her hand, "Ciao," closed her fingers, and shut the door.

Alone, Wittman jumped off the table to the mattress, trampolined off that to the Gold Mountain trunk and onto the chair. Keep up the mood, not in liege to her. Elongating his chimp-like torso, he stretched for a look at himself in the built-in mirror on the door. He ruffled out his hair. Sao mang mang mang-key maw-lau. Skinny skinny monkey. "Bee-e-een!" he yelled, loud enough for her to hear. "Bee-e-een!" which is what Monkey yells when he changes. He whipped around and began to type like mad. Action. At work again.

And again whammed into the block question: Does he announce now that the author is—Chinese? Or, rather, Chinese-American? And be forced into autobiographical confession. Stop the music—I have to butt in and introduce myself and my race. "Dear reader, all these characters whom you've been identifying with—Bill, Brooke, and Annie—are Chinese—and I am too." The fiction is spoiled. You who read have been suckered along, identifying like hell, only to find out that you'd been getting a peculiar, colored, slanted p.o.v. "Call me Ishmael." See? You pictured a white guy, didn't you? If Ishmael were described—ochery ecru amber umber skin—you picture a *tan* white guy. Wittman wanted to spoil all those stories coming out of and set in New England Back East—to blacken and to yellow Bill, Brooke, and Annie. A new rule for the imagination: The common man has Chinese looks. From now on, whenever you read about those people with no surnames, color them with black skin or yellow skin. Wittman made an end run, evaded the block. By writing a play, he didn't need descriptions that racinated anybody. The actors will walk out on stage and their looks will be self-evident. They will speak dialects and accents, which the audience will get upon hearing. No need for an unreadable orthography such as Mark Twain's insultingly dumb dis and dat misspelling and apostrophying. Yes, the play's the thing.

It is ridiculous. Here I sit in my little room, I, Brigge, who have grown to be 28 years old and of whom no one knows. I sit here and am nothing. And nevertheless this nothing begins to think and think, five flights up, on a grey Parisian afternoon, these thoughts: . . .

A long time ago, before the blackbottom, a band of ancestors with talent left their music house, which was the largest hut in Ancient Wells, a place, and sailed a music boat a-roving the rivers of China. They beat the big drum hard, which vibrated in stomachs and diaphragms for miles around. An audience gathered on the riverbank, and saw the red swan boat come floating on strains of mandolin and flute. Between red wings, got up in the style of putting-on-a-show, rode the players. To the knocking of the wood fish drums—dok-dok-dok—the singer lifted his skylark voice over water and fields. He threw out ropes, and their audience pulled them to shore. Party time again. Let musicians rule. Play a—what kind of music?—how does it go?—and make the world spin in the palm of your hand.

Our Wittman is going to work on his play for the rest of the night. If you want to see whether he will get that play up, and how a poor monkey makes a living so he can afford to spend the weekday afternoon drinking coffee and hanging out, go on to the next chapter.

1989

DIANE GLANCY
b. 1941

"The cold made the noises travel," notes a character in Diane Glancy's novel *Pushing the Bear* (1996). "Voices from across the field. If I open my mouth, sometimes the faraway sounds enter. I can chew the sounds." With such material qualities of language Glancy tells the story of the Trail of Tears, the nine-hundred-mile forced journey of the Cherokee people in 1837–38, from their home in Georgia to a bitter exile in the newly created Indian Territory of Oklahoma.

Since publishing her first collection of fiction, *Trigger Dance* (1990), Diane Glancy has endowed her narratives with a rich physicality that energizes her three-fold themes. First, a mixed heritage from her Cherokee mother and her father of English and German descent lets her be inside and outside the Native American tradition; her characters often share this complex background, and their stories are energized by the alternating attractions and repulsions they feel. Second, as an academic, Glancy has observed the commodification of native American culture; in "Jack Wilson or Wovoka and Christ My Lord" (printed here), she plays this practice against the feelings any woman, American Indian or not, might experience in such a situation. Finally, the author extends her vision to include not only issues of culture and gender but of age, as "Polar Breath" so tellingly portrays as Winter's presence in the life of an old, widowed woman. *Firesticks* (1993), the collection from which these two stories are taken, alternates brief narratives of contemporary Native American culture with fragments from the life of a middle-aged woman who judges her existence against the history and lore of her own mixed heritage, a circumstance that the alternating stories particularize in strongly physical detail.

Born in Kansas City and educated at the University of Missouri and at the University of Iowa's Writers Workshop, Glancy teaches at Macalaster College in St. Paul, Minnesota. She has written poetry and essays as well as fiction and is recognized as an author not just of Native American interest but sufficiently broad to appeal to science fiction readers and activists for the environment. Her commitment is to American Indian cultures as continuing, ever-adapting sets of practices and beliefs that maintain their vitality by interacting with the larger world. Conditions change; to revitalize traditional ways can have baleful and unforeseen effects, as in the late nineteenth century when the Paiute prophet, Wovoka—named in the title of the first story below—inspired the messianic movement that became known as the Ghost Dance religion. It was fear of Ghost Dancers that ultimately led to the U.S. Army's massacre of Minneconjoux Sioux in 1890. Is it the case that all religious leaders promise the impossible? Can any prophetic religion escape misinterpretation? These questions and others, considered from the viewpoint of a strong woman familiar with more than one culture, characterize Glancy's complex, nuanced writings.

The texts are from *Firesticks* (1993).

Jack Wilson or Wovoka[1] and Christ My Lord

Native American heritage is something I don't like to get into. You see I have as much white blood as red. I shouldn't be talking but it's hard to be

---

1. Paiute prophet (1856–1932) whose visions inspired a religion that anticipated the restoration of traditional ways, the return of the honored Indian dead, and the nonviolent disappearance of the whites. Ghost dancing at the Pine Ridge was perceived by the reservation's Indian agent as potentially insurrectionary. The agent, a U.S. government employee, called for troops; the Seventh Cavalry (Custer's former regiment) was sent in; and late in 1890, a series of circumstances led to the massacre at Wounded Knee.

quiet. Not really that either because it was years before I started saying what I thought. The fact that I had opinions that mattered took me from Oklahoma to Minnesota to realize.

I remember in school being small and brown. Someone would mention the freckles on my face. Pecan-Face would have been my Indian name if I had one. I also knew my hide was transparent. It's true though no one told me to my face. It's one of those things you just know. Every feeling I ever had showed. I remember my face burning in class with shame. I think it was because of my Indian heritage. I think it's influenced everything I do. Yet I'm also white. I want you to remember that.

Now this is what I have against Indians. I don't think they care for the land they say they care for. I think they're irresponsible. They only care about their good times. High hooters. Rooty fluters. Ghosters. Who thought they could chase away the white man. Thought they could call back buffalo. Thought they could return the ancestors. Handle firewater. Handle a bigger than.

Oh I know, be generous. Their culture was ripped off, then they're expected to be kind to the earth. We expect them to do more with less.

We had a Native American Awareness week at our college and I invited a speaker. This Indian poet dude. I saw right away I was invisible to him. Women are short-skirters or nothing to the accoutrements in his head. His attitude you see. Warrior and squaw. I saw him look at all the girls.

On the phone he had told me how he had dried out and I thought he would be a good speaker for the students and maybe he had you see but not enough to know in the meantime I raised the children took the warbonnet raised the tomahawk and went after the great reservation nothingness that licked us up and down and all over just when it wanted to. And he read about his warrior sons when he had no children. Had not been a father. Said his own father left him and his stepfather beat him and he had a hundred reasons and I'm sure all true but he annoyed me with his superior-ass stance in front of everyone. And I the one who invited him was invisible too.

I sat there on the front row thinking I mattered too. I remembered the time I walked down the road on the old place and a bird sang on a wire. Someone said don't you hear what that bird is saying and you know I did. I don't know exactly what in words but in his language he said I was visible in the invisibility I would feel. I knew already what he meant.

So the bird had told me I was pretty but not in the meaning you think of. Not exactly spiritual either. But in presence. Substance. That something visible. So while the poet looked at a young girl and asked to be kissing cousins, asked almost in front of everyone to touch her sweet brown hide and I the one who invited him remembered what the bird had said while I listened to the Indian guy say he wanted to be a teacher because girls wore short skirts. And I thought that's an Indian for you. Or maybe just a man. And I thought what tough-guy learned responses that he maybe didn't even think about but that's the way he was the old way and that's how he would be.

I believe in being generous up to a point and then I think to say things like they are.

Well you have that buck warrior probably promising more than he could deliver up there jabbering about his life and his firewater fleamarket days along the bar-rails of life and I thought this is the heritage I received from my forefathers? This is the message we pass to the young? Like it was a piece of licorice or a black snake twirling up our leg. Well he'd had a good time at least til it caught up with him.

While I was given by the just God the role of wife mother the other lesser not mattering one. I was given myself to be responsible. Not a card-carrying Indian. Not a card-carrying White. But schoolteacher, provider, minority, and everything nobody else wanted to be. An Indian because I wasn't White. An Indian because I could synthesize the fragments and live with hurt. Yipes.

Me and all the runny-nosed reservation children suffering alcoholism poverty want closed-mindedness growing up to engender the same in their own.

I'm getting rid of my grumpiness.

But it was in church this white guy minister fundamentalist who ran his church like a battleship and allowed no women on his pews without a hat this very opposite of the Indian dude said Christ made us whole well we could walk over any pitfall and not fall or if by strange chance we fell of our own accord you see not his of course Christ's that we could get up rise to our feet and go on as if we hadn't fallen at all and I thought I wanted to be able to do that so I went to the altar without making a sound while everyone else was howling Jesus like the baboon in the zoo in Tulsa and I wanted to go on by myself without anyone holding me up you know by the shirt collar or ankle straps or shoestrings on my keds and well it worked I just went on through my life praising Jesus and raising my communion cup to him saying glory hallelujah being now another bird myself on the wire on the old place giving out words of life that would last through all the days and would usher into the hereafter as if it were a cool theater on a hot Oklahoma day and the nickel to get in was Christ and you had it too and all that mattered was you and he.

It probably wouldn't work for everyone. In the end it may not matter. God may not care what he is called whether male or female because he is spirit and in the hereafter we are neither either.

Yet I still think there will be intercourse. Does not Christ do all this talk about his longing for his bride? I maybe be straying but there's some sort of fucking we're not accustomed to yet, but will grow to like, I'm sure. You know how that's supposed to be and in the end really it turns out all right because you end up wanting it about the time he doesn't.

And the Indian intellectuals write their surreal coyote tales. He is now she eating at trendy restaurants wearing high-top tennies and who knows what. The changing surviving ole Coyote finally teaches in the end that there's no ultimate reality no foundation and whatever he/she believes is true and the "heesh" eats away at the foundation the thought there is anything solid like the Rock of Ages under our feet. Well he denies that final authority yes he does and is proud of it.

We had another speaker at Native American week who told stories that didn't have a lot to do with what we would call ordinary life and he probably had the same attitudes as the other dude just hid them off better but he told a story of prophecy of how the white man would come and use up even the stars. But one star was saved for us and he snapped a cottonwood twig right in two and there was a star something the way you cut an apple crossways and there's a star just our slice of heaven right there in an apple.

And he told this story although it was a story that could only be told when there's snow on the ground. But you know they'd had a sweat and prayed that morning and it snowed that very hour yes it did and he talked about Indian spirituality and how it called snow down from the heavens but what happened still in the rest of the world the hunger disease injustice he could do nothing about but we had snow that morning and he told the story. This other world in the midst of our own dark one. A star from another place and it was ours yes because we held the broken twig of cottonwood in our hand.

I don't know why my white husband was surprised that I wanted a divorce there were times I started crying and couldn't stop. Yet I didn't want to be without that support invisible as it was from time to time most of the time really if I'd look at it with square eyes. But once you have children if he's willing to stay you usually let him empty as the house is even with him in it. We never had enough of the other and just burrowed into ourselves. This living is just surprising isn't it? The absoluteness of it you see no matter what Coyote says.

Yet you know somewhere say Tucumcari there's this Indian dude riding down the street with his easy-rider cycle his headband and black silky hair streaming like crows in the night air or black fish deep in the river and he's about as stable as that April snowfall but you look at him anyway and say that's part of my heritage. It's nothing you can stand on no nor even put your finger on but it sure does make a show.

Yet he's so full of metal he couldn't get through the detector-booth in an airport. Can't fly really so heavy with his heritage but I remember sitting on a runway once in a plane looking through the little opening that's supposed to be a window and I saw a plane rushing ahead of us on the runway to take off lifting in that exhaust smoke and noise and jittering our own plane on the runway behind it as it lifted there right in the air ahead of us like a cross with its arms outstretched.

1993

Polar Breath

Now she was an old woman with a cat, who had spent her life raising children and living with a man she didn't love. She hadn't been anywhere but on her own place. She was an exile in herself. For her, pleasure was her house in its cluttered order with all the rowdiness out.

She leased her field and makeshift barn. She didn't even have to feed the animals anymore. She could be at peace, but the spirits wouldn't let her. They stayed in the woods during the day. They camped outside her house at night.

She would spend the afternoon ironing, remaking a dress to wear another year. All she asked was to have the day to herself while her cat slept on the papers and scraps of material in the brown chair by the east window.

From the kitchen window, she watched a red squirrel dig in the hard ground. Once in a while it stood on its hind legs to make sure no one came. Then it rooted again. Finally it found the nut and sat chewing.

She saw the old tree wrapped in its gross bark, its eyes where branches had been. Across the field, traffic moved on the highway. She could hear the trucks at night. From the upstairs window she could even see their lights pass like a shooting-gallery across the field. They stirred no desire in her to travel.

Beyond the kitchen window there was the bush, the garden and grape arbor, the white fields and a neighbor's barn. Beyond that, a church with its steeple. Then sky above it, without its lack of conformity, pale as the ground.

She watched the squirrel again. Chewing with quick bites, then running up the tree. What bothered squirrels? She saw one sometimes on the road, run over by a car. But that was all. Maybe cars were their natural predator. Tan Buicks.

She nibbled a cracker at the sink. The squirrel was back again. The wind blew backward against its fur. Its tail bushed out like a cape. She pushed some kettles and jars out of her way. On the floor, a pail of water seemed to have a thin film of ice.

The week before, she had driven her old car out of the shed and gone to the grocer in town. She could last a long time without getting out again. It seemed the old furnace ran constantly now, if she'd let it. The thermometer outside fell below zero. The spirits wouldn't stay in the woods anymore. They'd come and sit around her flue and chimney.

Now three blue jays sat in the bush. She wondered if the spirits were near, but she didn't see them. Farther away, there was only the tree looking at her. She finished the crumbs of her cornbread at the sink, and stuck the image of the birds on the walls of her head. She would keep the world as it should be. Even if the spirits ran around her house in the freezing gusts of wind.

She had pictures of her children on a table by the window where the cat slept. Her son and two daughters. She even had a picture of her husband though she'd seen enough of him. He sat there in his green-and-orange plaid shirt, with his bear-claw and his black hair slicked back. He smiled like he was still sitting in his icehouse on the lake. She had taken his stamp collection and pasted some of the stamps on the frame. She'd papered the cellar shelves with the rest. Her son was mad at her for it, but now she could do what she liked.

Once in a while she still woke in the mornings with the stale thought of him on her mind. He must have sneaked around inside her during the night, climbing the mattress coils of her brain.

Out the back window she saw her barn, leaning slightly toward the south, still mostly white, but the red underneath was bleeding through. In another summer or two, the barn would be rust.

She thought of the black-and-white check dress she worked on. It was probably ten years old and she wanted to change the sleeves. The flannel had worn thin at her neck. She would turn the collar around and it would be a new dress. Maybe she'd tighten the waist and sew on new buttons. Yes, that's what she'd do. It would take several days.

She looked through the patches of frost on the kitchen window and saw that the bird-feeder was empty. Why hadn't she noticed? Maybe that's what the blue jays had been waiting for, their blue tails striped with black like tire-marks on a small, plowed field.

She went to the cellar for birdseed and she also got a jar of her pickles. She liked the close-darkness of the cellar under the kitchen. Sometimes she didn't even turn on the light because she knew where everything was.

Back in the kitchen she got her coat and galoshes. She put a scarf around her head and found her gloves. Her cat came into the kitchen to go with her. He wouldn't go out anymore by himself. Other cats bothered him and he was too old to fight. He let them have their way in his territory, even when she shamed him.

The two of them found their way through the clutter in the kitchen. She unbolted the door and they walked through the snowy yard to the bush at the west of the house. She poured birdseed into the feeder. What were those funny tracks? Her cat stayed by the tree smelling them. Ah! She knew. The spirits in raccoon-feet to camouflage their sneaking around her house. Could it really be them? Were they already brave enough to come to her house in daylight?

Inside again, she noticed the feeder was crooked. Would the birds fall off while they tried to eat? She got a string and some old scissors from the drawers. Maybe the bush had shifted with snow, or grown one-sided over the summer. She clipped the shorter string and tied the feeder to the branch with a longer string.

The birds chattered in the fir trees by the front corner of the house, dusting the yard with more snow. Maybe they made all that noise to comfort one another in the cold. She wished she could gather them all into her house. Why didn't their little bodies freeze like ice-cubes? What kept them warm? Their little hearts beating fiercely like an old coal stove? How many shovels had she shucked into one of them?

She saw her neighbor pouring a bucket on his garden rows. Probably sheep manure. He was far away but he waved at her and the howl of his black dog broke the cold. Her cat looked up, alarmed.

On the edge of her garden she found a cob emptied of its corn. It sparkled on one end with frost. She looked at the muffin-tin shape. The honeycomb openings where the kernels had gone. She decided the spirits left it there. Everytime she moved they snipped another detail from the world. They had taken enough from her. Now she was getting parts of it back, sucking them deep within herself. She felt her bowels rumble. The thick branches of the bush stitched a net for her. The empty garden rows. All of them growing like frozen vines around her. Maybe she'd disappear into them someday.

Inside the house once more, she wiped a place to look through the window. Her cat would be scratching at the door soon. She lit the stove and boiled water for tea. She saw that the wet teabag looked like birdseed. She turned the furnace down even farther when it came on. She didn't want to call the gas truck yet. She would wear her coat and scarf, her galoshes and gloves in the house.

Where was her needle? She needed to work her fingers. They felt blue and cold. She'd sew a bright pocket on the dress she was working on. A pocket to help her remember everything she saw. Things she noticed, thoughts she wanted to store in her head. The bush with the blue gas-flame of the blue jay's heads. The pattern of frost growing on the windows. How it covered the glass like ancient cave markings or the scribblings of a child. No, it wasn't the frost at all. It was the spirits that got loose when it was cold. The north wind opened up a highway and they slipped right down to the Great Lakes from the north. Hadn't she seen them after her husband died last winter? Hadn't she heard his ice-fishing decoys rattle one night? Weren't the spirits a pale blue when she looked from the window, floating around the house like manta rays? Their graceful edges undulating in the dim light from the window. Now they were wrapping her house in cellophane. She knew it as she stood at the sink looking out. Something scratched the door and it startled her, but she remembered it was the cat and she let him in.

She knew another secret. They had been in her house. They could walk across the floor without creaking. They could sit on her roof and she'd never know it. Stingrays with their blue-finger edges. Devilfish! She whacked the counter with her broom. The cat ran.

They were coming to take her too. She panicked at the sink. She saw her husband in his icehouse fishing in winter. She felt like she was walking barefoot across the ice to him. She fought to hold to the counter. But she was shuffling across the lake. The drift of cold fog across the ice was like a line of old people. Inside her head, birds flew from the wall. They banged at the windows to get out. Up the road, the church steeple hung like a telephone pole pulled crooked by its wires after an ice storm. How long had she been there? The room circled like the round hole in the ice. She felt the tight hole around her chest. There was something hurting her ankles. She was tangled in the fishing line that went down into the cold, dark hole below her. Now the sun shined its wicked and beautiful pattern on the kitchen window. The cold fog still shuffled across the lake. Something knocked the old cans and kettles from the counter to the floor. She was walking up the road now. Wasn't the afternoon light through the window-frost like a church? How many years had she sung hymns up the road? The little tendrils of the ice like petroglyphs? She heard her children drawing in the frost on the windows. She reached for the finger she saw at the glass. But the ice-hole burped like her old husband in his chair and the frigid water closed her up.

1993

GLORIA ANZALDÚA
1942–2004

The term *Chicano* was originally pejorative, used on both sides of the border to identify Mexican Americans of the lowest social class. Just as the once demeaning label *black* was appropriated and revalued by African Americans during the civil rights, black power, and black arts movements of the 1960s, so *Chicano* was embraced by Hispanic activists as a badge of pride, especially among university students and farm workers. By 1987, when the first edition of Gloria Anzaldúa's *Borderlands/La Frontera: The New Mestiza* appeared, two more politically sensitive terms had been added to the sociocultural lexicon: *Chicana,* specifically identifying Mexican American women, particularly in light of their announced aims and the general interests of the Chicano movement, and *mestiza,* describing Chicana women who are especially concerned with a heritage that is both Chicana and native American. Together with Cherríe Moraga, her co-editor on *This Bridge Called My Back: Writings by Radical Women of Color* (1981), Anzaldúa emerged as a pioneer in both the writing and the study of Chicana literature.

The daughter of ranchers in Jesus Maria of the Valley, Texas, Gloria Anzaldúa labored as a migrant fieldworker before earning a B.A. from Pan American University (1969) and an M.A. from the University of Texas at Austin (1973); she did further graduate study at the University of California at Santa Cruz. She taught creative writing, Chicano studies, and feminist studies at major universities from Texas to California. As a writer, she published a novel, *La Prieta* (Spanish for "the dark one," 1997), other anthologies, and a series of children's books, the most notable of which—*Prietita and the Ghost Woman/Prietita y La Llorona* (1996)—introduces young readers to an important figure in Chicana culture.

La Llorona is one of the three principal representations of women in Mexican culture: *La Virgen de Guadalupe*, a vision of the Virgin Mary who appeared to an Indian, Juan Diego, in 1531 on a hillside outside Mexico City that was sacred to the worship of Tonantzín, the Indian "Mother of Heaven"; *La Chingada*, incorrectly translated as "The Raped One" but whom Anzaldúa insists be accurately identified as "The Fucked One," the deposed Aztec princess (also known as La Malinche, Doña Marina, and Malintzín Tenepal) who served as the translator for and lover of the Spanish military leader Hernan Cortés during his consolidation of colonial power between 1519 and 1522; and *La Llorona*, "The Woman Who Cries," a spurned mistress of Mexican legend who drowned her children and was fated to eternally seek their recovery. Each of these representations metaphorically controls a narrow realm of possibility for Chicanas. At the core of Anzaldúa's work is the belief that because metaphors structure the way we think, the metaphorical influences of these types of

women must be reshaped so that Chicanas can escape the binary constraint of being judged as either a virgin or a whore (and nothing else). *Borderlands/La Frontera* is Anzaldúa's most comprehensive effort toward that restructuring.

Although written mainly in English, the personal essays and narrative poem printed here reflect another key part of Anzaldúa's art: not only did she wish to write in Spanish from time to time but she did not always translate that Spanish into English. When she did not provide such a translation in a piece that is primarily in English, it was because she wanted to speak directly to those who either could not or chose not to communicate in English. This practice, much like her blending of fiction, poetry, social commentary, and personal memoir, helps create the richness of narrative that characterizes her work.

The text is from the second edition of *Borderlands/La Frontera* (1999).

La conciencia de la mestiza/Towards a New Consciousness

> *Por la mujer de mi raza*
> *hablará el espíritu.*[1]

José Vasconcelos, Mexican philosopher, envisaged *una raza mestiza, una mezcla de razas afines, una raza de color—la primera raza síntesis del globo.* He called it a cosmic race, *la raza cósmica*, a fifth race embracing the four major races of the world.[2] Opposite to the theory of the pure Aryan,[3] and to the policy of racial purity that white America practices, his theory is one of inclusivity. At the confluence of two or more genetic streams, with chromosomes constantly "crossing over," this mixture of races, rather than resulting in an inferior being, provides hybrid progeny, a mutable, more malleable species with a rich gene pool. From this racial, ideological, cultural and

---

1. "This is my own 'take off' on Jose Vasconcelos' idea. José Vasconcelos, *La Raza Cósmica: Misión de la Raza Ibero-Americana* (México: Aguilar S.A. de Ediciones, 1961)" [Anzaldúa's note]. José Vas-

concelos (1882–1959) was a Mexican philosopher.
2. Vasconcelos [Anzaldúa's note].
3. Nazi misnomer for Caucasians of non-Jewish descent.

biological cross-pollinization, an "alien" consciousness is presently in the making—a new *mestiza* consciousness, *una conciencia de mujer*. It is a consciousness of the Borderlands.

Una lucha de fronteras/A *Struggle of Borders*

Because I, a *mestiza*,
continually walk out of one culture
and into another,
because I am in all cultures at the same time,
alma entre dos mundos, tres, cuatro,
me zumba la cabeza con lo contradictorio.
Estoy norteada por todas las voces que me hablan
simultáneamente.

The ambivalence from the clash of voices results in mental and emotional states of perplexity. Internal strife results in insecurity and indecisiveness. The *mestiza's* dual or multiple personality is plagued by psychic restlessness.

In a constant state of mental nepantilism, an Aztec[4] word meaning torn between ways, *la mestiza* is a product of the transfer of the cultural and spiritual values of one group to another. Being tricultural, monolingual, bilingual, or multilingual, speaking a patois, and in a state of perpetual transition, the *mestiza* faces the dilemma of the mixed breed: which collectivity does the daughter of a darkskinned mother listen to?

El choque de un alma atrapado entire el mundo del espíritu y el mundo de la técnica a veces la deja entullada. Cradled in one culture, sandwiched between two cultures, straddling all three cultures and their value systems, *la mestiza* undergoes a struggle of flesh, a struggle of borders, an inner war. Like all people, we perceive the version of reality that our culture communicates. Like others having or living in more than one culture, we get multiple, often opposing messages. The coming together of two self-consistent but habitually incompatible frames of reference[5] causes *un choque,* a cultural collision.

Within us and within *la cultura chicana,* commonly held beliefs of the white culture attack commonly held beliefs of the Mexican culture, and both attack commonly held beliefs of the indigenous culture. Subconsciously, we see an attack on ourselves and our beliefs as a threat and we attempt to block with a counterstance.

But it is not enough to stand on the opposite river bank, shouting questions, challenging patriarchal, white conventions. A counterstance locks one into a duel of oppressor and oppressed; locked in mortal combat, like the cop and the criminal, both are reduced to a common denominator of violence. The counterstance refutes the dominant culture's views and beliefs, and, for this, it is proudly defiant. All reaction is limited by, and dependent on, what it is reacting against. Because the counterstance stems from a problem with authority—outer as well as inner—it's a step towards liberation from cultural domination. But it is not a way of life. At some point, on our

---

4. A precolonial people of Mexico with a highly developed civilization.
5. Arthur Koestler [(1905–1983), Hungarian-born writer active in Germany and Britain] termed this term "bisociation." Albert Rothenberg, *The Creative Process in Art, Science, and Other Fields* (Chicago, IL: University of Chicago Press, 1979), 12 [Anzaldúa's note].

way to a new consciousness, we will have to leave the opposite bank, the split between the two mortal combatants somehow healed so that we are on both shores at once and, at once, see through serpent and eagle[6] eyes. Or perhaps we will decide to disengage from the dominant culture, write it off altogether as a lost cause, and cross the border into a wholly new and separate territory. Or we might go another route. The possibilities are numerous once we decide to act and not react.

A Tolerance for Ambiguity

These numerous possibilities leave *la mestiza* floundering in uncharted seas. In perceiving conflicting information and points of view, she is subjected to a swamping of her psychological borders. She has discovered that she can't hold concepts or ideas in rigid boundaries. The borders and walls that are supposed to keep the undesirable ideas out are entrenched habits and patterns of behavior; these habits and patterns are the enemy within. Rigidity means death. Only by remaining flexible is she able to stretch the psyche horizontally and vertically. *La mestiza* constantly has to shift out of habitual formations; from convergent thinking, analytical reasoning that tends to use rationality to move toward a single goal (a Western mode), to divergent thinking,[7] characterized by movement away from set patterns and goals and toward a more whole perspective, one that includes rather than excludes.

The new *mestiza* copes by developing a tolerance for contradictions, a tolerance for ambiguity. She learns to be an Indian in Mexican culture, to be Mexican from an Anglo point of view. She learns to juggle cultures. She has a plural personality, she operates in a pluralistic mode—nothing is thrust out, the good the bad and the ugly, nothing rejected, nothing abandoned. Not only does she sustain contradictions, she turns the ambivalence into something else.

She can be jarred out of ambivalence by an intense, and often painful, emotional event which inverts or resolves the ambivalence. I'm not sure exactly how. The work takes place underground—subconsciously. It is work that the soul performs. That focal point or fulcrum, that juncture where the *mestiza* stands, is where phenomena tend to collide. It is where the possibility of uniting all that is separate occurs. This assembly is not one where severed or separated pieces merely come together. Nor is it a balancing of opposing powers. In attempting to work out a synthesis, the self has added a third element which is greater than the sum of its severed parts. That third element is a new consciousness—a *mestiza* consciousness—and though it is a source of intense pain, its energy comes from continual creative motion that keeps breaking down the unitary aspect of each new paradigm.

En unas pocas centurias, the future will belong to the *mestiza*. Because the future depends on the breaking down of paradigms, it depends on the straddling of two or more cultures. By creating a new mythos—that is, a change in the way we perceive reality, the way we see ourselves, and the ways we behave—*la mestiza* creates a new consciousness.

---

6. Female and male, respectively; a binarism in traditional Mexican culture.
7. In part, I derive my definitions for "convergent" and "divergent" thinking from Rothenberg, 12–13 [Anzaldúa's note].

The work of *mestiza* consciousness is to break down the subject-object duality that keeps her a prisoner and to show in the flesh and through the images in her work how duality is transcended. The answer to the problem between the white race and the colored, between males and females, lies in healing the split that originates in the very foundation of our lives, our culture, our languages, our thoughts. A massive uprooting of dualistic thinking in the individual and collective consciousness is the beginning of a long struggle, but one that could, in our best hopes, bring us to the end of rape, of violence, of war.

La encrucijada/*The Crossroads*

A chicken is being sacrificed
    at a crossroads, a simple mound of earth
a mud shrine for *Eshu*,
    Yoruba[8] god of indeterminacy,
who blesses her choice of path.
    She begins her journey.

Su cuerpo es una bocacalle. La mestiza has gone from being the sacrificial goat to becoming the officiating priestess at the crossroads.

As a *mestiza* I have no country, my homeland cast me out; yet all countries are mine because I am every woman's sister or potential lover. (As a lesbian I have no race, my own people disclaim me; but I am all races because there is the queer of me in all races.) I am cultureless because, as a feminist, I challenge the collective cultural/religious male-derived beliefs of Indo-Hispanics and Anglos; yet I am cultured because I am participating in the creation of yet another culture, a new story to explain the world and our participation in it, a new value system with images and symbols that connect us to each other and to the planet. *Soy un amasamiento*, I am an act of kneading, of uniting and joining that not only has produced both a creature of darkness and a creature of light, but also a creature that questions the definitions of light and dark and gives them new meanings.

We are the people who leap in the dark, we are the people on the knees of the gods. In our very flesh, (r)evolution works out the clash of cultures. It makes us crazy constantly, but if the center holds, we've made some kind of evolutionary step forward. *Nuestra alma el trabajo*, the opus, the great alchemical work; spiritual *mestizaje*, a "morphogenesis,"[9] an inevitable unfolding. We have become the quickening serpent movement.

Indigenous like corn, like corn, the *mestiza* is a product of crossbreeding, designed for preservation under a variety of conditions. Like an ear of corn—a female seed-bearing organ—the *mestiza* is tenacious, tightly wrapped in the husks of her culture. Like kernels she clings to the cob; with thick stalks

---

8. Large ethnic group of southwest Nigeria and southeast Benin, in Africa.
9. "To borrow from chemist Ilya Prigogine's theory of 'dissipative structures.' Prigogine discovered that substances interact not in predictable ways as it was taught in science, but in different and fluctuating ways to produce new and more complex structures, a kind of birth he called 'morphogenesis,' which created unpredictable innovations. Harold Gilliam, 'Searching for a New World View,' *This World* (January, 1981), 23" [Anzaldúa's note]. Ilya Prigogine (b. 1917), Russian-born Belgian physical chemist active in the United States.

and strong brace roots, she holds tight to the earth—she will survive the crossroads.

Lavando y remojando el maíz en agua de cal, despojando el pellejo. Moliendo, mixteando, amasando, haciendo tortillas de masa.[1] She steeps the corn in lime, it swells, softens. With stone roller on *metate*, she grinds the corn, then grinds again. She kneads and moulds the dough, pats the round balls into *tortillas*.

> We are the porous rock in the stone *metate*
> squatting on the ground.
> We are the rolling pin, *el maíz y agua,*
> *la masa harina. Somos el amasijo.*
> *Somos lo molido en el metate.*
> We are the *comal* sizzling hot,
> the hot *tortilla*, the hungry mouth.
> We are the coarse rock.
> We are the grinding motion,
> the mixed potion, *somos el molcajete.*
> We are the pestle, the *comino, ajo, pimienta,*
> We are the *chile colorado,*
> the green shoot that cracks the rock.
> We will abide.

El camino de la mestiza/*The Mestiza Way*

Caught between the sudden contraction, the breath sucked in and the endless space, the brown woman stands still, looks at the sky. She decides to go down, digging her way along the roots of trees. Sifting through the bones, she shakes them to see if there is any marrow in them. Then, touching the dirt to her forehead, to her tongue, she takes a few bones, leaves the rest in their burial place.

She goes through her backpack, keeps her journal and address book, throws away the muni-bart metromaps. The coins are heavy and they go next, then the greenbacks flutter through the air. She keeps her knife, can opener and eyebrow pencil. She puts bones, pieces of bark, *hierbas*, eagle feather, snakeskin, tape recorder, the rattle and drum in her pack and she sets out to become the complete *tolteca*.[2]

Her first step is to take inventory. *Despojando, desgranando, quitando paja.* Just what did she inherit from her ancestors? This weight on her back—which is the baggage from the Indian mother, which the baggage from the Spanish father, which the baggage from the Anglo?

Pero es difícil differentiating between *lo heredado, lo adquirido, lo impuesto.* She puts history through a sieve, winnows out the lies, looks at the forces that we as a race, as women, have been a part of. *Luego bota lo que no vale, los desmientos, los desencuentros, el embrutecimiento. Aguarda el*

---

1. *Tortillas de masa harina:* corn tortillas are of two types, the smooth uniform ones made in a tortilla press and usually bought at a tortilla factory or supermarket, and *gorditas*, made by mixing *masa* with lard or shortening or butter (my mother some-times puts in bits of bacon or chicharones [Anzaldúa's note].

2. Female member of the ancient Toltec group of Nahuatl Indians who lived in Mexico before the Aztecs.

juicio, bondo y enraízado, de la gente antigua. This step is a conscious rupture with all oppressive traditions of all cultures and religions. She communicates that rupture, documents the struggle. She reinterprets history and, using new symbols, she shapes new myths. She adopts new perspectives toward the darkskinned, women and queers. She strengthens her tolerance (and intolerance) for ambiguity. She is willing to share, to make herself vulnerable to foreign ways of seeing and thinking. She surrenders all notions of safety of the familiar. Deconstruct, construct. She becomes a *nahual*, able to transform herself into a tree, a coyote, into another person. She learns to transform the small "I" into the total Self. *Se hace moldeadora de su alma. Según la concepción que tiene de sí misma, así será.*

Que no se nos olviden los hombres

> *"Tú no sirves pa'nada—*
> you're good for nothing.
> *Eres pura vieja."*

"You're nothing but a woman" means you are defective. Its opposite is to be *un macho*. The modern meaning of the word "machismo," as well as the concept, is actually an Anglo invention. For men like my father, being "macho" meant being strong enough to protect and support my mother and us, yet being able to show love. Today's macho has doubts about his ability to feed and protect his family. His "machismo" is an adaptation to oppression and poverty and low self-esteem. It is the result of hierarchical male dominance. The Anglo, feeling inadequate and inferior and powerless, displaces or transfers these feelings to the Chicano by shaming him. In the Gringo world, the Chicano suffers from excessive humility and self-effacement, shame of self and self-deprecation. Around Latinos he suffers from a sense of language inadequacy and its accompanying discomfort; with Native Americans he suffers from a racial amnesia which ignores our common blood, and from guilt because the Spanish part of him took their land and oppressed them. He has an excessive compensatory hubris when around Mexicans from the other side. It overlays a deep sense of racial shame.

The loss of a sense of dignity and respect in the macho breeds a false machismo which leads him to put down women and even to brutalize them. Coexisting with his sexist behavior is a love for the mother which takes precedence over that of all others. Devoted son, macho pig. To wash down the shame of his acts, of his very being, and to handle the brute in the mirror, he takes to the bottle, the snort, the needle, and the fist.

Though we "understand" the root causes of male hatred and fear, and the subsequent wounding of women, we do not excuse, we do not condone, and we will no longer put up with it. From the men of our race, we demand the admission/acknowledgment/disclosure/testimony that they wound us, violate us, are afraid of us and of our power. We need them to say they will begin to eliminate their hurtful put-down ways. But more than the words, we demand acts. We say to them: We will develop equal power with you and those who have shamed us.

It is imperative that *mestizas* support each other in changing the sexist elements in the Mexican-Indian culture. As long as woman is put down, the Indian and the Black in all of us is put down. The struggle of the *mestiza* is above all a feminist one. As long as *los hombres* think they have to *chingar mujeres* and each other to be men, as long as men are taught that they are superior and therefore culturally favored over *la mujer*, as long as to be a *vieja* is a thing of derision, there can be no real healing of our psyches. We're halfway there—we have such love of the Mother, the good mother. The first step is to unlearn the *puta/virgen* dichotomy and to see *Coatlalopeuh-Coatlicue* in the Mother, *Guadalupe.*[3]

Tenderness, a sign of vulnerability, is so feared that it is showered on women with verbal abuse and blows. Men, even more than women, are fettered to gender roles. Women at least have had the guts to break out of bondage. Only gay men have had the courage to expose themselves to the woman inside them and to challenge the current masculinity. I've encountered a few scattered and isolated gentle straight men, the beginnings of a new breed, but they are confused, and entangled with sexist behaviors that they have not been able to eradicate. We need a new masculinity and the new man needs a movement.

Lumping the males who deviate from the general norm with man, the oppressor, is a gross injustice. *Asombra pensar que nos hemos quedado en ese pozo oscuro donde el mundo encierra a las lesbianas. Asombra pensar que hemos, como femenistas y lesbianas, cerrado nuestros corazónes a los hombres, a nuestros hermanos los jotos, desheredados y marginales como nosotros.* Being the supreme crossers of cultures, homosexuals have strong bonds with the queer white, Black, Asian, Native American, Latino, and with the queer in Italy, Australia and the rest of the planet. We come from all colors, all classes, all races, all time periods. Our role is to link people with each other—the Blacks with Jews with Indians with Asians with whites with extraterrestrials. It is to transfer ideas and information from one culture to another. Colored homosexuals have more knowledge of other cultures; have always been at the forefront (although sometimes in the closet) of all liberation struggles in this country; have suffered more injustices and have survived them despite all odds. Chicanos need to acknowledge the political and artistic contributions of their queer. People, listen to what your *jotería* is saying.

The *mestizo* and the queer exist at this time and point on the evolutionary continuum for a purpose. We are a blending that proves that all blood is intricately woven together, and that we are spawned out of similar souls.

Somos una gente

Hay tantísimas fronteras
que dividen a la gente,
pero por cada frontera
existe también un puente.
—Gina Valdés[4]

---

3. The Virgin of Guadalupe, patron saint of Mexico. In matriarchal Olmec culture, Coatl was a figuration of the sacred womb from which all things were born and to which they returned. Coatlicue is the Meso-American serpent that is half male, half female.

4. Gina Valdés, *Puentes y Fronteras: Coplas Chicanas* (Los Angeles, CA: Castle Lithograph, 1982), 2 [Anzaldúa's note].

Divided Loyalties. Many women and men of color do not want to have any dealings with white people. It takes too much time and energy to explain to the downwardly mobile, white middle-class women that it's okay for us to want to own "possessions," never having had any nice furniture on our dirt floors or "luxuries" like washing machines. Many feel that whites should help their own people rid themselves of race hatred and fear first. I, for one, choose to use some of my energy to serve as mediator. I think we need to allow whites to be our allies. Through our literature, art, *corridos*, and folktales we must share our history with them so when they set up committees to help Big Mountain *Navajos* or the Chicano farmworkers or *los Nicaragüenses*[5] they won't turn people away because of their racial fears and ignorances. They will come to see that they are not helping us but following our lead.

Individually, but also as a racial entity, we need to voice our needs. We need to say to white society: We need you to accept the fact that Chicanos are different, to acknowledge your rejection and negation of us. We need you to own the fact that you looked upon us as less than human, that you stole our lands, our personhood, our self-respect. We need you to make public restitution: to say that, to compensate for your own sense of defectiveness, you strive for power over us, you erase our history and our experience because it makes you feel guilty—you'd rather forget your brutish acts. To say you've split yourself from minority groups, that you disown us, that your dual consciousness splits off parts of yourself, transferring the "negative" parts onto us. (Where there is persecution of minorities, there is shadow projection. Where there is violence and war, there is repression of shadow.) To say that you are afraid of us, that to put distance between us, you wear the mask of contempt. Admit that Mexico is your double, that she exists in the shadow of this country, that we are irrevocably tied to her. Gringo, accept the doppelganger[6] in your psyche. By taking back your collective shadow the intracultural split will heal. And finally, tell us what you need from us.

By Your True Faces We Will Know You

I am visible—see this Indian face—yet I am invisible. I both blind them with my beak nose and am their blind spot. But I exist, we exist. They'd like to think I have melted in the pot. But I haven't, we haven't.

The dominant white culture is killing us slowly with its ignorance. By taking away our self-determination, it has made us weak and empty. As a people we have resisted and we have taken expedient positions, but we have never been allowed to develop unencumbered—we have never been allowed to be fully ourselves. The whites in power want us people of color to barricade ourselves behind our separate tribal walls so they can pick us off one at a time with their hidden weapons; so they can whitewash and distort history. Ignorance splits people, creates prejudices. A misinformed people is a subjugated people.

5. Nicaraguans; here a reference to the Sandinista government, which was opposed covertly by the United States in the 1980s. "Big Mountain Navajos": Dineh people of Big Mountain, Arizona, forcibly removed in a land dispute with energy companies in 1997. "Farmworkers": members of the United Farm Workers, a union founded in 1962.
6. Other-goer (German); reference to the ghost of a living person.

Before the Chicano and the undocumented worker and the Mexican from the other side can come together, before the Chicano can have unity with Native Americans and other groups, we need to know the history of their struggle and they need to know ours. Our mothers, our sisters and brothers, the guys who hang out on street corners, the children in the playgrounds, each of us must know our Indian lineage, our afro-*mestizaje*, our history of resistance.

To the immigrant *mexicano* and the recent arrivals we must teach our history. The 80 million *mexicanos* and the Latinos from Central and South America must know of our struggles. Each one of us must know basic facts about Nicaragua, Chile and the rest of Latin America. The Latinoist movement (Chicanos, Puerto Ricans, Cubans and other Spanish-speaking people working together to combat racial discrimination in the marketplace) is good but it is not enough. Other than a common culture we will have nothing to hold us together. We need to meet on a broader communal ground.

The struggle is inner: Chicano, *indio*, American Indian, *mojado, mexicano*, immigrant Latino, Anglo in power, working class Anglo, Black, Asian—our psyches resemble the bordertowns and are populated by the same people. The struggle has always been inner, and is played out in the outer terrains. Awareness of our situation must come before inner changes, which in turn come before changes in society. Nothing happens in the "real" world unless it first happens in the images in our heads.

El día de la Chicana

I will not be shamed again
Nor will I shame myself.

I am possessed by a vision: that we Chicanas and Chicanos have taken back or uncovered our true faces, our dignity and self-respect. It's a validation vision.

Seeing the Chicana anew in light of her history. I seek an exoneration, a seeing through the fictions of white supremacy, a seeing of ourselves in our true guises and not as the false racial personality that has been given to us and that we have given to ourselves. I seek our woman's face, our true features, the positive and the negative seen clearly, free of the tainted biases of male dominance. I seek new images of identity, new beliefs about ourselves, our humanity and worth no longer in question.

Estamos viviendo en la noche de la Raza, un tiempo cuando el trabajo se hace a lo quieto, en lo oscuro. El día cuando aceptamos tal y como somos y para donde vamos y porque—ese día será el día de la Raza. Yo tengo el compromiso de expresar mi visión, mi sensibilidad, mi percepción de la revalidación de la gente mexicana, su mérito, estimación, honra, aprecio, y validez.

On December 2nd when my sun goes into my first house, I celebrate *el día de la Chicana y el Chicano:* On that day I clean my altars, light my *Coatlalopeuh* candle, burn sage and copal,[7] take *el baño para espantar basura;* sweep my house. On that day I bare my soul, make myself vulnerable to

---

7. Fossilized resin from tropical trees.

friends and family by expressing my feelings. On that day I affirm who we are.

On that day I look inside our conflicts and our basic introverted racial temperament. I identify our needs, voice them. I acknowledge that the self and the race have been wounded. I recognize the need to take care of our personhood, of our racial self. On that day I gather the splintered and disowned parts of *la gente mexicana* and hold them in my arms. *Todas las partes de nosotros valen.*

On that day I say, "Yes, all you people wound us when you reject us. Rejection strips us of self-worth; our vulnerability exposes us to shame. It is our innate identity you find wanting. We are ashamed that we need your good opinion, that we need your acceptance. We can no longer camouflage our needs, can no longer let defenses and fences sprout around us. We can no longer withdraw. To rage and look upon you with contempt is to rage and be contemptuous of ourselves. We can no longer blame you, nor disown the white parts, the male parts, the pathological parts, the queer parts, the vulnerable parts. Here we are weaponless with open arms, with only our magic. Let's try it our way, the *mestiza* way, the Chicana way, the woman way."

On that day, I search for our essential dignity as a people, a people with a sense of purpose—to belong and contribute to something greater than our *pueblo*. On that day I seek to recover and reshape my spiritual identity. *¡Anímate! Raza, a celebrar el día de la Chicana.*

El retorno

All movements are accomplished in six stages,
and the seventh brings return.
        —I Ching[8]

Tanto tiempo sin verte casa mía,
mi cuna, mi bondo nido de la huerta.
        —"Soledad"[9]

I stand at the river, watch the curving, twisting serpent, a serpent nailed to the fence where the mouth of the Rio Grande empties into the Gulf.

I have come back. *Tanto dolor me costó el alejamiento.* I shade my eyes and look up. The bone beak of a hawk slowly circling over me, checking me out as potential carrion. In its wake a little bird flickering its wings, swimming sporadically like a fish. In the distance the expressway and the slough of traffic like an irritated sow. The sudden pull in my gut, *la tierra, los aguaceros.* My land, *el viento soplando la arena, el lagartijo debajo de un nopalito. Me acuerdo como era antes. Una región desértica de vasta llanuras, costeras de baja altura, de escasa lluvia, de chaparrales formados por mesquites y huizaches.* If I look real hard I can almost see the Spanish fathers who were called "the cavalry of Christ" enter this valley riding their *burros*, see the clash of cultures commence.

8. "Richard Wilhelm, *The I Ching or Book of Changes*, trans. Cary F. Baynes (Princeton: Princeton University Press, 1950), 98" [Anzaldúa's note]. Central text of Confucianism dating from the first millennium B.C.E.
9. *Soledad* is sung by the group Haciendo Punto en Otro Son [Anzaldúa's note].

Tierra natal. This is home, the small towns in the Valley, *los pueblitos* with chicken pens and goats picketed to mesquite shrubs. *En las colonias* on the other side of the tracks, junk cars line the front yards of hot pink and lavender-trimmed houses—Chicano architecture we call it, self-consciously. I have missed the TV shows where hosts speak in half and half, and where awards are given in the category of Tex-Mex music. I have missed the Mexican cemeteries blooming with artificial flowers, the fields of aloe vera and red pepper, rows of sugar cane, of corn hanging on the stalks, the cloud of *polvareda* in the dirt roads behind a speeding pickup truck, *el sabor de tamales de rez y venado* I have missed *la yegua colorada* gnawing the wooden gate of her stall, the smell of horse flesh from Carito's corrals. *Hecho menos las noches calientes sin aire, noches de linternas y lechuzas* making holes in the night.

I still feel the old despair when I look at the unpainted, dilapidated, scrap lumber houses consisting mostly of corrugated aluminum. Some of the poorest people in the U.S. live in the Lower Rio Grande Valley, and arid and semi-arid land of irrigated farming, intense sunlight and heat, citrus groves next to chaparral and cactus. I walk through the elementary school I attended so long ago, that remained segregated until recently. I remember how the white teachers used to punish us for being Mexican.

How I love this tragic valley of South Texas, as Ricardo Sánchez, calls it; this borderland between the Nueces and the Rio Grande.[1] This land has survived possession and ill-use by five countries: Spain, Mexico, the Republic of Texas, the U.S., the Confederacy,[2] and the U.S. again. It has survived Anglo-Mexican blood feuds, lynchings, burnings, rapes, pillage.

Today I see the Valley still struggling to survive. Whether it does or not, it will never be as I remember it. The borderlands depression that was set off by the 1982 peso devaluation in Mexico resulted in the closure of hundreds of Valley businesses. Many people lost their homes, cars, land. Prior to 1982, U.S. store owners thrived on retail sales to Mexicans who came across the border for groceries and clothes and appliances. While goods on the U.S. side have become 10, 100, 1000 times more expensive for Mexican buyers, goods on the Mexican side have become 10, 100, 1000 times cheaper for Americans. Because the Valley is heavily dependent on agriculture and Mexican retail trade, it has the highest unemployment rates along the entire border region; it is the Valley that has been hardest hit.[3]

"It's been a bad year for corn," my brother, Nune, says. As he talks, I remember my father scanning the sky for a rain that would end the drought, looking up into the sky, day after day, while the corn withered on its stalk.

1. Rivers in southern Texas. Sánchez (1941–1995), Chicano poet, educator, and activist.
2. I.e., the Confederate States of America, made up of eleven southern states (including Texas) that seceded from the union at the start of the U.S. Civil War (1861–65). After it won independence from Mexico (1836) and before it was admitted as a state to the United States (1845), Texas was a republic.
3. Out of the twenty-two border countries in the four border states, Hidalgo County (named for Father Hidalgo who was shot in 1810 after instigating Mexico's revolt against Spanish rule under the banner of *la Virgen de Guadalupe*) is the most poverty-stricken county in the nation as well as the largest home base (along with Imperial in California) for migrant farmworkers. It was here I was born and raised. I am amazed that both it and I have survived [Anzaldúa's note].

My father has been dead for 29 years, having worked himself to death. The life span of a Mexican farm laborer is 56—he lived to be 38. It shocks me that I am older than he. I, too, search the sky for rain. Like the ancients, I worship the rain god and the maize goddess, but unlike my father I have recovered their names. Now for rain (irrigation) one offers not a sacrifice of blood, but of money.

"Farming is in a bad way," my brother says. "Two to three thousand small and big farmers went bankrupt in this country last year. Six years ago the price of corn was $8.00 per hundred pounds," he goes on. "This year it is $3.90 per hundred pounds." And, I think to myself, after taking inflation into account, not planting anything puts you ahead.

I walk out to the back yard, stare at *los rosales de mamá*. She wants me to help her prune the rose bushes, dig out the carpet grass that is choking them. *Mamagrande Ramona también tenía rosales*. Here every Mexican grows flowers. If they don't have a piece of dirt, they use car tires, jars, cans, shoe boxes. Roses are the Mexican's favorite flower. I think, how symbolic—thorns and all.

Yes, the Chicano and Chicana have always taken care of growing things and the land. Again I see the four of us kids getting off the school bus, changing into our work clothes, walking into the field with Papi and Mami, all six of us bending to the ground. Below our feet, under the earth lie the watermelon seeds. We cover them with paper plates, putting *terremotes* on top of the plates to keep them from being blown away by the wind. The paper plates keep the freeze away. Next day or the next, we remove the plates, bare the tiny green shoots to the elements. They survive and grow, give fruit hundreds of times the size of the seed. We water them and hoe them. We harvest them. The vines dry, rot, are plowed under. Growth, death, decay, birth. The soil prepared again and again, impregnated, worked on. A constant changing of forms, *renacimientos de la tierra madre*.

> This land was Mexican once
> was Indian always
> and is.
> And will be again.

1987

How to Tame a Wild Tongue

"We're going to have to control your tongue," the dentist says, pulling out all the metal from my mouth. Silver bits plop and tinkle into the basin. My mouth is a motherlode.

The dentist is cleaning out my roots. I get a whiff of the stench when I gasp. "I can't cap that tooth yet, you're still draining," he says.

"We're going to have to do something about your tongue," I hear the anger rising in his voice. My tongue keeps pushing out the wads of cotton, pushing back the drills, the long thin needles. "I've never seen anything as strong or as stubborn," he says. And I think, how do you tame a wild tongue, train it to be quiet, how do you bridle and saddle it? How do you make it lie down?

> "Who is to say that robbing a people of
> its language is less violent than war?"
> —Ray Gwyn Smith[1]

I remember being caught speaking Spanish at recess—that was good for three licks on the knuckles with a sharp ruler. I remember being sent to the corner of the classroom for "talking back" to the Anglo teacher when all I was trying to do was tell her how to pronounce my name. "If you want to be American, speak 'American.' If you don't like it, go back to Mexico where you belong."

"I want you to speak English. *Pa'hallar buen trabajo tienes que saber hablar el inglés bien. Qué vale toda tu educación si todavía hablas inglés con un* 'accent,'" my mother would say, mortified that I spoke English like a Mexican. At Pan American University, I, and all Chicano students were required to take two speech classes. Their purpose: to get rid of our accents.

Attacks on one's form of expression with the intent to censor are a violation of the First Amendment. *El Anglo con cara de inocente nos arrancó la lengua.* Wild tongues can't be tamed, they can only be cut out.

Overcoming the Tradition of Silence

> *Ahogadas, escupimos el oscuro.*
> *Peleando con nuestra propia sombra*
> *el silencio nos sepulta.*

En boca cerrada no entran moscas. "Flies don't enter a closed mouth" is a saying I kept hearing when I was a child. *Ser habladora* was to be a gossip and a liar, to talk too much. *Muchachitas bien criadas,* well-bred girls don't answer back. *Es una falta de respeto* to talk back to one's mother or father. I remember one of the sins I'd recite to the priest in the confession box the few times I went to confession: talking back to my mother, *hablar pa' 'trás, repelar. Hocicona, repelona, chismosa,* having a big mouth, questioning, carrying tales are all signs of being *mal criada.* In my culture they are all words that are derogatory if applied to women—I've never heard them applied to men.

The first time I heard two women, a Puerto Rican and a Cuban, say the word "*nosotras,*" I was shocked. I had not known the word existed. Chicanas use *nosotros* whether we're male or female. We are robbed of our female being by the masculine plural. Language is a male discourse.

> And our tongues have become
> dry   the wilderness has
> dried out our tongues   and

1. Ray Gwyn Smith [(b. 1944), Welsh painter and art educator active in the United States], *Moorland Is Cold Country,* unpublished book [Anzaldúa's note].

we have forgotten speech.
—Irena Klepfisz[2]

Even our own people, other Spanish speakers *nos quieren poner candados en la boca.* They would hold us back with their bag of *reglas de academia.*

Oyé como ladra: el lenguaje de la frontera

Quien tiene boca se equivoca.
—Mexican saying

"*Pocho,*[3] cultural traitor, you're speaking the oppressor's language by speaking English, you're ruining the Spanish language," I have been accused by various Latinos and Latinas. Chicano Spanish is considered by the purist and by most Latinos deficient, a mutilation of Spanish.

But Chicano Spanish is a border tongue which developed naturally. Change, *evolución, enriquecimiento de palabras nuevas por invención o adopción* have created variants of Chicano Spanish, *un nuevo, lenguaje. Un lenguaje que corresponde a un modo de vivir.* Chicano Spanish is not incorrect, it is a living language.

For a people who are neither Spanish nor live in a country in which Spanish is the first language; for a people who live in a country in which English is the reigning tongue but who are not Anglo; for a people who cannot entirely identify with either standard (formal, Castillian) Spanish nor standard English, what recourse is left to them but to create their own language? A language which they can connect their identity to, one capable of communicating the realities and values true to themselves—a language with terms that are neither *español ni inglés,* but both. We speak a patois, a forked tongue, a variation of two languages.

Chicano Spanish sprang out of the Chicanos' need to identify ourselves as a distinct people. We needed a language with which we could communicate with ourselves, a secret language. For some of us, language is a homeland closer than the Southwest—for many Chicanos today live in the Midwest and the East. And because we are a complex, heterogeneous people, we speak many languages. Some of the languages we speak are:

1. Standard English
2. Working class and slang English
3. Standard Spanish
4. Standard Mexican Spanish
5. North Mexican Spanish dialect
6. Chicano Spanish (Texas, New Mexico, Arizona and California have regional variations)
7. Tex-Mex
8. *Pachuco* (called *caló*)

My "home" tongues are the languages I speak with my sister and brothers, with my friends. They are the last five listed, with 6 and 7 being closest to

---

2. Irena Klepfisz [(b. 1941), North American critic], *"Di rayze aheym / The Journey Home,"* in *The Tribe of Dina: A Jewish Women's Anthology,* Melanie Kaye/Kantrowitz and Irena Klepfisz, eds. (Montpelier, VT: Sinister Wisdom Books, 1986), 49 [Anzaldúa's note].

3. An anglicized Mexican or American of Mexican origin who speaks Spanish with an accent characteristic of North Americans and who distorts and reconstructs the language according to the influence of English. Anzaldúa offers a definition later in this selection.

my heart. From school, the media and job situations, I've picked up standard and working class English. From Mamagrande Locha and from reading Spanish and Mexican literature, I've picked up Standard Spanish and Standard Mexican Spanish. From *los recién llegados*, Mexican immigrants, and *braceros*, I learned the North Mexican dialect. With Mexicans I'll try to speak either Standard Mexican Spanish or the North Mexican dialect. From my parents and Chicanos living in the Valley,[4] I picked up Chicano Texas Spanish, and I speak it with my mom; younger brother (who married a Mexican and who rarely mixes Spanish with English), aunts and older relatives.

With Chicanas from *Nuevo México* or *Arizona* I will speak Chicano Spanish a little, but often they don't understand what I'm saying. With most California Chicanas I speak entirely in English (unless I forget). When I first moved to San Francisco, I'd rattle off something in Spanish, unintentionally embarrassing them. Often it is only with another Chicana *tejana* that I can talk freely.

Words distorted by English are known as anglicisms or *pochismos*. The *pocho* is an anglicized Mexican or American of Mexican origin who speaks Spanish with an accent characteristic of North Americans and who distorts and reconstructs the language according to the influence of English.[5] Tex-Mex, or Spanglish, comes most naturally to me. I may switch back and forth from English to Spanish in the same sentence or in the same word. With my sister and my brother Nune and with Chicano *tejano* contemporaries I speak in Tex-Mex.

From kids and people my own age I picked up *Pachuco*. *Pachuco* (the language of the zoot suiters) is a language of rebellion, both against Standard Spanish and Standard English. It is a secret language. Adults of the culture and outsiders cannot understand it. It is made up of slang words from both English and Spanish. *Ruca* means girl or woman, *vato* means guy or dude, *chale* means no, *simón* means yes, *churo* is sure, talk is *periquiar, pigionear* means petting, *que gacho* means how nerdy, *ponte águila* means watch out, death is called *la pelona*. Through lack of practice and not having others who can speak it, I've lost most of the *Pachuco* tongue.

Chicano Spanish

Chicanos, after 250 years of Spanish/Anglo colonization have developed significant differences in the Spanish we speak. We collapse two adjacent vowels into a single syllable and sometimes shift the stress in certain words such as *maíz/maiz, cohete/cuete*. We leave out certain consonants when they appear between vowels: *lado/lao, mojado/mojao*. Chicanos from South Texas pronounced *f* as *j* as in *jue* (*fue*). Chicanos use "archaisms," words that are no longer in the Spanish language, words that have been evolved out. We say *semos, truje, haiga, ansina*, and *naiden*. We retain the "archaic" *j*, as in *jalar*, that derives from an earlier *h*, (the French *halar* or the Germanic *halon* which was lost to standard Spanish in the 16th century), but which is still found in several regional dialects such as the one spoken in South Texas.

4. I.e., of the Rio Grande River in southern Texas, bordering Mexico.
5. R. C. Ortega, *Dialectología Del Barrio*, trans. Hortencia S. Alwan (Los Angeles, CA: R. C. Ortega Publisher & Bookseller, 1977), 132 [Anzaldúa's note].

(Due to geography, Chicanos from the Valley of South Texas were cut off linguistically from other Spanish speakers. We tend to use words that the Spaniards brought over from Medieval Spain. The majority of the Spanish colonizers in Mexico and the Southwest came from Extremadura—Hernán Cortés' was one of them—and Andalucía.[6] Andalucians pronounce *ll* like a *y*, and their *d*'s tend to be absorbed by adjacent vowels: *tirado* becomes *tirao*. They brought *el lenguaje popular, dialectos y regionalismos*.)[7]

Chicanos and other Spanish speakers also shift *ll* to *y* and *z* to *s*.[8] We leave out initial syllables, saying *tar* for *estar*, *toy* for *estoy*; *hora* for *ahora* (*cubanos* and *puertorriqueños* also leave out initial letters of some words.) We also leave out the final syllable such as *pa* for *para*. The intervocalic *y*, the *ll* as in *tortilla, ella, botella*, gets replaced by *tortia* or *tortiya, ea, botea*. We add an additional syllable at the beginning of certain words: *atocar* for *tocar*, *agastar* for *gastar*. Sometimes we'll say *lavaste las vacijas*, other times *lavates* (substituting the *ates* verb endings for the *aste*).

We use anglicisms, words borrowed from English: *bola* from ball, *carpeta* from carpet, *máchina de lavar* (instead of *lavadora*) from washing machine. Tex-Mex argot, created by adding a Spanish sound at the beginning or end of an English word such as *cookiar* for cook, *watchar* for watch, *parkiar* for park, and *rapiar* for rape, is the result of the pressures on Spanish speakers to adapt to English.

We don't use the word *vosotros/as* or its accompanying verb form. We don't say *claro* (to mean yes), *imagínate*, or *me emociona*, unless we picked up Spanish from Latinas, out of a book, or in a classroom. Other Spanish-speaking groups are going through the same, or similar, development in their Spanish.

Linguistic Terrorism

Deslenguadas. Somos los del español deficiente. We are your linguistic nightmare, your linguistic aberration, your linguistic *mestizaje*, the subject of your *burla*. Because we speak with tongues of fire we are culturally crucified. Racially, culturally and linguistically *somos huérfanos*—we speak an orphan tongue.

Chicanas who grew up speaking Chicano Spanish have internalized the belief that we speak poor Spanish. It is illegitimate, a bastard language. And because we internalize how our language has been used against us by the dominant culture, we use our language differences against each other.

Chicana feminists often skirt around each other with suspicion and hesitation. For the longest time I couldn't figure it out. Then it dawned on me. To be close to another Chicana is like looking into the mirror. We are afraid of what we'll see there. *Pena*. Shame. Low estimation of self. In childhood we are told that our language is wrong. Repeated attacks on our native tongue diminish our sense of self. The attacks continue throughout our lives.

Chicanas feel uncomfortable talking in Spanish to Latinas, afraid of their censure. Their language was not outlawed in their countries. They had a

---

6. Region in southern Spain. Extremadura is a city in central Spain. Cortés (1485–1547), Spanish soldier and explorer active in Mexico.

7. Eduardo Hernandéz-Chávez, Andrew D. Cohen, and Anthony F. Beltramo, *El Lenguaje de los Chicanos: Regional and Social Characteristics of Language Used by Mexican Americans* (Arlington, VA: Center for Applied Linguistics, 1975), 39 [Anzaldúa's note].

8. Hernandéz-Chávez, xvii [Anzaldúa's note].

whole lifetime of being immersed in their native tongue; generations, centuries in which Spanish was a first language, taught in school, heard on radio and TV, and read in the newspaper.

If a person, Chicana or Latina, has a low estimation of my native tongue, she also has a low estimation of me. Often with *mexicanas y latinas* we'll speak English as a neutral language. Even among Chicanas we tend to speak English at parties or conferences. Yet, at the same time, we're afraid the other will think we're *agringadas* because we don't speak Chicano Spanish. We oppress each other trying to out-Chicano each other, vying to be the "real" Chicanas, to speak like Chicanos. There is no one Chicano language just as there is no one Chicano experience. A monolingual Chicana whose first language is English or Spanish is just as much a Chicana as one who speaks several variants of Spanish. A Chicana from Michigan or Chicago or Detroit is just as much a Chicana as one from the Southwest. Chicano Spanish is as diverse linguistically as it is regionally.

By the end of this century, Spanish speakers will comprise the biggest minority group in the U.S., a country where students in high schools and colleges are encouraged to take French classes because French is considered more "cultured." But for a language to remain alive it must be used.[9] By the end of this century English, and not Spanish, will be the mother tongue of most Chicanos and Latinos.

So, if you want to really hurt me, talk badly about my language. Ethnic identity is twin skin to linguistic identity—I am my language. Until I can take pride in my language, I cannot take pride in myself. Until I can accept as legitimate Chicano Texas Spanish, Tex-Mex and all the other languages I speak, I cannot accept the legitimacy of myself. Until I am free to write bilingually and to switch codes without having always to translate, while I still have to speak English or Spanish when I would rather speak Spanglish, and as long as I have to accommodate the English speakers rather than having them accommodate me, my tongue will be illegitimate.

I will no longer be made to feel ashamed of existing. I will have my voice: Indian, Spanish, white. I will have my serpent's tongue—my woman's voice, my sexual voice, my poet's voice. I will overcome the tradition of silence.

> My fingers
> move sly against your palm
> Like women everywhere, we speak in code. . . .
> —Melanie Kaye/Kantrowitz[1]

"Vistas," corridos, y comida: My Native Tongue

In the 1960s, I read my first Chicano novel. It was *City of Night* by John Rechy[2] a gay Texan, son of a Scottish father and a Mexican mother. For days I walked around in stunned amazement that a Chicano could write and could get published. When I read *I Am Joaquín*[3] I was surprised to see a bilingual

9. Irena Klepfisz, "Secular Jewish Identity: Yidish-kayt in America," in *The Tribe of Dina*, Kaye/Kantrowitz, eds., 43 [Anzaldúa's note].
1. Melanie Kaye/Kantrowitz, "Sign," in *We Speak in Code: Poems and Other Writings* (Pittsburgh, PA: Motheroot Publications, Inc., 1980), 85 [Anzaldúa's note].

2. American novelist (b. 1934). The book was published in 1963.
3. Rodolfo Gonzales [(b. 1928), Chicano novelist], *I Am Joaquín/Yo Soy Joaquín* (New York, NY: Bantam Books, 1972). It was first published in 1967 [Anzaldúa's note].

book by a Chicano in print. When I saw poetry written in Tex-Mex for the first time, a feeling of pure joy flashed through me. I felt like we really existed as a people. In 1971, when I started teaching High School English to Chicano students, I tried to supplement the required texts with works by Chicanos, only to be reprimanded and forbidden to do so by the principal. He claimed that I was supposed to teach "American" and English literature. At the risk of being fired, I swore my students to secrecy and slipped in Chicano short stories, poems, a play. In graduate school, while working toward a Ph.D., I had to "argue" with one advisor after the other, semester after semester, before I was allowed to make Chicano literature an area of focus.

Even before I read books by Chicanos or Mexicans, it was the Mexican movies I saw at the drive-in—the Thursday night special of $1.00 a carload—that gave me a sense of belonging. "*Vámonos a las vistas*," my mother would call out and we'd all—grandmother, brothers, sister and cousins—squeeze into the car. We'd wolf down cheese and bologna white bread sandwiches while watching Pedro Infante in melodramatic tear-jerkers like *Nosotros los pobres*,[4] the first "real" Mexican movie (that was not an imitation of European movies). I remember seeing *Cuando los hijos se van*[5] and surmising that all Mexican movies played up the love a mother has for her children and what ungrateful sons and daughters suffer when they are not devoted to their mothers. I remember the singing-type "westerns" of Jorge Negrete and Miguel Aceves Mejía.[6] When watching Mexican movies, I felt a sense of homecoming as well as alienation. People who were to amount to something didn't go to Mexican movies, or *bailes* or tune their radios to *bolero*, *rancherita*, and *corrido* music.

The whole time I was growing up, there was *norteño* music sometimes called North Mexican border music, or Tex-Mex music, or Chicano music, or *cantina* (bar) music. I grew up listening to *conjuntos*, three- or four-piece bands made up of folk musicians playing guitar, *bajo sexto*,[7] drums and button accordion, which Chicanos had borrowed from the German immigrants who had come to Central Texas and Mexico to farm and build breweries. In the Rio Grande Valley, Steve Jordan and Little Joe Hernández were popular, and Flaco Jiménez[8] was the accordion king. The rhythms of Tex-Mex music are those of the polka, also adapted from the Germans, who in turn had borrowed the polka from the Czechs and Bohemians.

I remember the hot, sultry evenings when *corridos*—songs of love and death on the Texas-Mexican borderlands—reverberated out of cheap amplifiers from the local *cantinas* and wafted in through my bedroom window.

Corridos first became widely used along the South Texas/Mexican border during the early conflict between Chicanos and Anglos. The *corridos* are usually about Mexican heroes who do valiant deeds against the Anglo oppressors. Pancho Villa's[9] song, "*La cucaracha*," is the most famous one. *Corridos* of John F. Kennedy and his death are still very popular in the Valley. Older

---

4. A 1947 film. Infante (1917–1957), Mexican film actor and singer.
5. A 1941 film.
6. Mexican singer and film actor (b. 1916). Negrete (1911–1953), Mexican singing actor.
7. Twelve-string guitar tuned one octave lower

than normal.
8. Mexican American musicians. Esteban Jordán (b. 1939). José María De Leon Hérnandez (1940). Leonardo Jiménez (b. 1939).
9. Villa (ca. 1877–1923), born Doroteo Arango, Mexican revolutionary leader.

Chicanos remember Lydia Mendoza, one of the great border *corrido* singers who was called *la Gloria de Tejas*.[1] Her *"El tango negro,"* sung during the Great Depression, made her a singer of the people. The everpresent *corridos* narrated one hundred years of border history, bringing news of events as well as entertaining. These folk musicians and folk songs are our chief cultural mythmakers, and they made our hard lives seem bearable.

I grew up feeling ambivalent about our music. Country-western and rock-and-roll had more status. In the 50s and 60s, for the slightly educated and *agringado* Chicanos, there existed a sense of shame at being caught listening to our music. Yet I couldn't stop my feet from thumping to the music, could not stop humming the words, nor hide from myself the exhilaration I felt when I heard it.

There are more subtle ways that we internalize identification, especially in the forms of images and emotions. For me food and certain smells are tied to my identity, to my homeland. Woodsmoke curling up to an immense blue sky; woodsmoke perfuming my grandmother's clothes, her skin. The stench of cow manure and the yellow patches on the ground; the crack of a .22 rifle and the reek of cordite. Homemade white cheese sizzling in a pan, melting inside a folded *tortilla*. My sister Hilda's hot, spicy *menudo*[2] *chile colorado* making it deep red, pieces of *panza* and hominy floating on top. My brother Carito barbecuing *fajitas* in the backyard. Even now and 3,000 miles away, I can see my mother spicing the ground beef, pork and venison with *chile*. My mouth salivates at the thought of the hot steaming *tamales* I would be eating if I were home.

Si le preguntas a mi mamá, "¿Qué eres?"

"Identity is the essential core of who
we are as individuals, the conscious
experience of the self inside."
—Kaufman[3]

Nosotros los Chicanos straddle the borderlands. On one side of us, we are constantly exposed to the Spanish of the Mexicans, on the other side we hear the Anglos' incessant clamoring so that we forget our language. Among ourselves we don't say *nosotros los americanos, o nosotros los españoles, o nosotros los hispanos*. We say *nosotros los mexicanos* (by *mexicanos* we do not mean citizens of Mexico; we do not mean a national identity, but a racial one). We distinguish between *mexicanos del otro lado* and *mexicanos de este lado*. Deep in our hearts we believe that being Mexican has nothing to do with which country one lives in. Being Mexican is a state of soul—not one of mind, not one of citizenship. Neither eagle nor serpent,[4] but both. And like the ocean, neither animal respects borders.

1. Mendoza (b. 1916), Mexican American singer, songwriter, and musician.
2. Mexican soup made of simmered tripe, onion, garlic, chili, and hominy.
3. Gershen Kaufman [(b. 1943), American psychologist], *Shame: The Power of Caring* (Cambridge: Schenkman Books, Inc. 1980), 68. This book was instrumental in my understanding of shame [from Anzaldúa's note].
4. Male and female, respectively, cultural figurations.

> Dime con quien andas y te diré quien eres.
> (Tell me who your friends are and I'll tell you who
> you are.)
> —Mexican saying

Si le preguntas a mi mamá, "¿Qué eres?" te dirá, "Soy mexicana." My brothers and sister say the same. I sometimes will answer *"soy mexicana"* and at others will say *"soy Chicana" o "soy tejana."* But I identified as *"Raza"* before I ever identified as *"mexicana"* or "Chicana."

As a culture, we call ourselves Spanish when referring to ourselves as a linguistic group and when copping out. It is then that we forget our predominant Indian genes. We are 70 to 80% Indian.[5] We call ourselves Hispanic[6] or Spanish-American or Latin American or Latin when linking ourselves to other Spanish-speaking peoples of the Western hemisphere and when copping out. We call ourselves Mexican-American[7] to signify we are neither Mexican nor American, but more the noun "American" than the adjective "Mexican" (and when copping out).

Chicanos and other people of color suffer economically for not acculturating. This voluntary (yet forced) alienation makes for psychological conflict, a kind of dual identity—we don't identify with the Anglo-American cultural values and we don't totally identify with the Mexican cultural values. We are a synergy of two cultures with various degrees of Mexicanness or Angloness. I have so internalized the borderland conflict that sometimes I feel like one cancels out the other and we are zero, nothing, no one. *A veces no soy nada ni nadie. Pero hasta cuando no lo soy, lo soy.*

When not copping out, when we know we are more than nothing, we call ourselves Mexican, referring to race and ancestry; *mestizo* when affirming both our Indian and Spanish (but we hardly ever own our Black ancestry); Chicano when referring to a politically aware people born and/or raised in the U.S.; *Raza* when referring to Chicanos; *tejanos* when we are Chicanos from Texas.

Chicanos did not know we were a people until 1965 when Cesar Chavez[8] and the farmworkers united and *I Am Joaquín* was published and *la Raza Unida*[9] party was formed in Texas. With that recognition, we became a distinct people. Something momentous happened to the Chicano soul—we became aware of our reality and acquired a name and a language (Chicano Spanish) that reflected that reality. Now that we had a name, some of the fragmented pieces began to fall together—who we were, what we were, how we had evolved. We began to get glimpses of what we might eventually become.

Yet the struggle of identities continues, the struggle of borders is our reality still. One day the inner struggle will cease and a true integration take place. In the meantime, *tenemos que hacerla lucha. ¿Quién está protegiendo los ranchos de mi gente? ¿Quién está tratando de cerrar la fisura entre la india y*

---

5. John R. Chávez [(b. 1949), American scholar and educator], *The Lost Land: The Chicano Images of the Southwest* (Albuquerque, NM: University of New Mexico Press, 1984), 88–90 [from Anzaldúa's note].
6. "Hispanic" is derived from Hispanis (*España,* a name given to the Iberian Peninsula in ancient times when it was a part of the Roman Empire) and is a term designated by the U.S. government to make it easier to handle us on paper [Anzaldúa's note].
7. The Treaty of Guadalupe Hidalgo created the Mexican-American in 1848 [Anzaldúa's note].
8. Chicano union organizer (b. 1927).
9. In America *La Raza Unida* party is known as the United Farm Workers; it was founded in 1962.

el blanco en nuestra sangre? El Chicano, sí, el Chicano que anda como un ladrón en su propia casa.[1]

Los Chicanos, how patient we seem, how very patient. There is the quiet of the Indian about us. We know how to survive. When other races have given up their tongue, we've kept ours. We know what it is to live under the hammer blow of the dominant *norteamericano* culture. But more than we count the blows, we count the days the weeks the years the centuries the eons until the white laws and commerce and customs, will rot in the deserts they've created, lie bleached. *Humildes* yet proud, *quietos* yet wild, *nosotros los mexicanos* Chicanos will walk by the crumbling ashes as we go about our business. Stubborn, persevering, impenetrable as stone, yet possessing a malleability that renders us unbreakable, we, the *mestizas* and *mestizos*, will remain.

1987

El sonavabitche

(for Aishe Berger)

Car flowing down a lava of highway
just happened to glance out the window
in time to see brown faces bent backs
like prehistoric boulders in a field
so common a sight no one   5
notices
blood rushes to my face
twelve years I'd sat on the memory
the anger scorching me
my throat so tight I can   10
barely get the words out.

I got to the farm
in time to hear the shots
ricochet off barn,
spit into the sand,   15
in time to see tall men in uniforms
thumping fists on doors
metallic voices yelling Halt!
their hawk eyes constantly shifting.

When I hear the words, *"Corran muchachos"*[1]   20
I run back to the car, ducking,
see the glistening faces, arms outflung,

1. Anglos, in order to alleviate their guilt for dispossessing the Chicano, stressed the Spanish part of us and perpetrated the myth of the Spanish Southwest. We have accepted the fiction that we are Hispanic, that is Spanish, in order to accommodate ourselves to the dominant culture and its abhorrence of Indians. Chávez, 88–91 [Anzaldúa's note].

1. "Run boys" [Anzaldúa's note].

of the *mexicanos* running headlong
through the fields
kicking up clouds of dirt   25

see them reach the tree line
foliage opening, swishing closed behind them.
I hear the tussling of bodies, grunts, panting
squeak of leather squawk of walkie-talkies
sun reflecting off gunbarrels   30
    the world a blinding light
    a great buzzing in my ears
    my knees like aspens in the wind.
    I see that wide cavernous look of the hunted
    the look of hares   35
    thick limp blue-black hair
    The bare heads humbly bent
    of those who do not speak
    the ember in their eyes extinguished.

I lean on the shanty wall of that migrant camp   40
north of Muncie, Indiana.
Wets, a voice says.
I turn to see a Chicano pushing
the head of his *muchachita*[2]
back into the *naguas*[3] of the mother   45
a tin plate face down on the floor
tortillas scattered around them.
His other hand signals me over.
He too is from *el valle de Tejas*[4]
I had been his kid's teacher.   50
I'd come to get the grower
to fill up the sewage ditch near the huts
saying it wouldn't do for the children
to play in it.
    Smoke from a cooking fire and   55
    shirtless *niños* gather around us.

    Mojados[5] he says again,
leaning on his chipped Chevy station wagon
Been here two weeks
about a dozen of them.   60
The *sonavabitche* works them
from sunup to dark—15 hours sometimes.
Como mulas los trabaja[6]
no saben como hacer la perra.[7]
Last Sunday they asked for a day off   65
wanted to pray and rest,

---

2. Little girl [Anzaldúa's note].
3. Skirt [Anzaldúa's note].
4. Rio Grande Valley in Texas [Anzaldúa's note].
5. Wetbacks, undocumented workers, illegal immigrants from Mexico and parts south

[Anzaldúa's note].
6. He works them like mules [Anzaldúa's note].
7. They don't know how to make the work easier for themselves [Anzaldúa's note].

write letters to their *familias*.
¿Y sabes lo que hizo el sonavabitche?[8]
He turns away and spits.
Says he has to hold back half their wages 70
that they'd eaten the other half:
sack of beans, sack of rice, sack of flour.
Frijoleros sí lo son[9] but no way
could they have eaten that many *frijoles*.
I nod. 75

Como le dije, son doce[1]—started out 13
five days packed in the back of a pickup
boarded up tight
fast cross-country run no stops
except to change drivers, to gas up 80
no food they pissed into their shoes—
those that had *guaraches*[2]
slept slumped against each other
sabe Dios[3] where they shit.
One smothered to death on the way here 85

Miss, you should've seen them when they
stumbled out.
First thing the *sonavabitche* did was clamp
a handkerchief over his nose
then ordered them stripped 90
hosed them down himself
in front of everybody.
They hobbled about
learning to walk all over again.
Flacos con caras de viejos[4] 95
aunque la mita'eran jóvenes.[5]

Como le estaba diciendo[6]
today was payday.
You saw them, *la migra*[7] came busting in
waving their *pinche pistolas.*[8] 100
Said someone made a call,
what you call it? Anonymous.
Guess who? That *sonavabitche*, who else?
Done this three times since we've been coming here
Sepa Dios how many times in between. 105
Wets, free labor, *esclavos.*[9]
Pobres jijos de la Chingada.[1]

---

8. And you know what the son of a bitch did? [Anzaldúa's note].
9. Bean eaters they are [Anzaldúa's note].
1. Like I told you, they're 12 [Anzaldúa's note].
2. Sandals [Anzaldúa's note].
3. God knows [Anzaldúa's note].
4. Skinny with old faces [Anzaldúa's note].
5. Though half were youths [Anzaldúa's note].
6. As I was telling you [Anzaldúa's note].
7. Slang for immigration officials [Anzaldúa's note].
8. Guns [Anzaldúa's note].
9. Slaves [Anzaldúa's note].
1. "Poor sons of the fucked one" [Anzaldúa's note]. *La Chingada* is the preferred Chicana term for *La Malinche* or *Malintzin,* the deposed Aztec princess who served Hernan Cortés as translator and became his lover during the Spanish Conquest of Mexico (1519–22).

This the last time we work for him
no matter how *fregados*[2] we are
he said, shaking his head,   110
spitting at the ground.
Vámonos, mujer, empaca el mugrero.[3]

He hands me a cup of coffee,
half of it sugar, half of it milk
my throat so dry I even down the dregs.   115
It has to be done.
Steeling myself
I take that walk to the big house.

Finally the big man lets me in.
How about a drink? I shake my head.   120
He looks me over, opens his eyes wide
and smiles, says how sorry he is immigration[4]
is getting so tough
a poor Mexican can't make a living
and they sure do need the work.   125
My throat so thick the words stick.
He studies me, then says,
Well, what can I do you for?
I want two weeks wages
including two Saturdays and Sundays,   130
minimum wage, 15 hours a day.
I'm more startled than he.
Whoa there, sinorita,
wets work for whatever you give them
the season hasn't been good.   135
Besides most are halfway to Mexico by now.
Two weeks wages, I say,
the words swelling in my throat.

Miss uh what did you say your name was?
I fumble for my card.   140
You can't do this,
I haven't broken no law,
his lidded eyes darken, I step back.
I'm leaving in two minutes and I want cash
the whole amount right here in my purse   145
when I walk out.
No hoarseness, no trembling.
It startled both of us.

You want me telling every single one
of your neighbors what you've been doing   150
all these years? The mayor, too?

---

2. Poor, beaten, downtrodden, in need
[Anzaldúa's note].
3. Let's go, woman, pack our junk [Anzaldúa's
note].
4. The U.S. Immigration and Naturalization Service.

Maybe make a call to Washington?
Slitted eyes studied the card again.
They had no cards, no papers.
I'd seen it over and over.   155
Work them, then turn them in before paying them.

    Well, now, he was saying,
    I know we can work something out,
    a sweet young thang like yourself.
    Cash, I said. I didn't know anyone in D.C.   160
now I didn't have to.
You want to keep it for yourself?
That it? His eyes were pin pricks.
Sweat money, Mister, blood money,
not my sweat, but same blood.   165
Yeah, but who's to say you won't abscond with it?
If I ever hear that you got illegals on your land
even a single one, I'm going to come here
in broad daylight and have you
hung by your balls.   170
He walks slowly to his desk.
Knees shaking, I count every bill
taking my time.

1987

BARRY HANNAH
b. 1942

Many Americans who have written fiction about the Vietnam War, among them Philip
Caputo, Tim O'Brien, William Crawford Woods, and James Park Sloan, say that just
as the conflict itself broke all previous conventions of warfare so too did fiction about
it move beyond standard narrative forms. Although he did not serve in Vietnam, Barry
Hannah thinks that it was as important as the Civil War in shaping the southern view
of two centuries of American military vision and was as well the signal event of his
generation. In treating Vietnam, he expresses the war's particular nature by fore-
grounding the highly stylized language of his narrator-monologist. Though there is
action aplenty in "Midnight and I'm Not Famous Yet" (printed here), the piece's true
focus is on how the narrator maintains an energetic lingo that keeps well ahead of
events both in Vietnam and at home, no matter how bizarre the activity.

    Hannah was born in Meridian, Mississippi; and his first novel, *Geronimo Rex*
(1972), can be read as a sensitive coming-of-age narrative about a southern adolescence. In college, Hannah's interests and experiences become self-consciously literary. Following undergraduate work at Mississippi College he went on to earn master
of arts and master of fine arts degrees at the University of Arkansas, followed at once
(in 1967) with a series of academic appointments at Clemson University; Middlebury
College; and the universities of Alabama, Iowa, Mississippi, and Montana. During

the 1970s such creative writing programs put much emphasis on uniqueness of voice and the stories collected in *Airships* (1978) show his ability to create colorful story-tellers. The protagonist of "Midnight and I'm Not Famous Yet," stumbling into pre-posterous incidents both on the streets of Saigon and in the field, is never at a loss for words. Instead, he floods these unlikely events with a great wash of exuberant language, carrying the reader beyond this little part of the war into an even more amazing relationship that develops after his return to Mississippi. In Hannah's third novel, *Ray* (1980), one finds the author's typical protagonist: an abuser of alcohol, drugs, and marriage, his Vietnam experience melding with fantasies of the Civil War, all of which would end his life did he not take such pleasure in abject misery. *Yonder Stands Your Orphan* (2001) includes another Vietnam vet in its cast of characters, but only as a part of the author's contemporary oddball mix.

Grotesqueries predominate in Hannah's fiction, but his narrators' flamboyance always salvages enough creative energy to get the story told. A writer-in-residence by profession, Hannah has flourished in the context of university writing programs, which have a strong supporting community of readings and café life and which seem these stories' natural environment.

The text is that printed in *Airships* (1978).

Midnight and I'm Not Famous Yet

I was walking around Gon[1] one night, and this C-man—I saw him open the window, and there was a girl in back of him, so I thought it was all right—peeled down on me and shot the back heel off my boot. Nearest I came to getting mailed home when I was there. A jeep came by almost instantly with a thirty cal mounted, couple of allies in it. I pointed over to the window. They shot out about a box and a half on the apartment, just about burned out the dark slot up there. As if the dude was hanging around digging the weather after he shot me. There were shrieks in the night, etc. But then a man opened the bottom door and started running in the street. This ARVN[2] fellow knocked the shit out of his buddy's head turning the gun to zap the running man. Then I saw something as the dude hit a light. He was fat. I never saw a fat Cong.[3] So I screamed out in Vietnamese. He didn't shoot. I took out my machine pistol and ran after the man, who was up the street by now, and I was hobbling without a heel on my left boot.

Some kind of warm nerve sparklers were getting all over me. I believe in magic, because, million-to-one odds, it was Ike "Tubby" Wooten, from Red-wood, a town just north of Vicksburg. He was leaning on a rail, couldn't run anymore. He was wearing the uniform of our Army with a patch on it I didn't even know what was. Old Tubby would remember me. I was the joker at our school. I once pissed in a Dixie cup and eased three drops of it on the library radiator. But Tubby was so serious, reading some photo magazine. He peeped up and saw me do it, then looked down quickly. When the smell came over the place, he asked me, Why? What do you want? What profit is there in that? I guess I just giggled. Sometimes around midnight I'd wake up and think of his questions, and it disturbed me that there was no answer. I giggled

1. I.e., Saigon, capital of South Vietnam.
2. Army of the Republic of Vietnam (South Vietnam, America's ally).

3. Vietcong, guerrilla force allied with Communist North Vietnam.

my whole youth away. Then I joined the Army. So I thought it was fitting I'd play a Nelda on him now. A Nelda was invented by a corporal when they massacred a patrol up north on a mountain and he was the only one left. The NVA[4] ran all around him and he had this empty rifle hanging on him. They spared him.

"I'm a virgin! Spare me!"

"You, holding the gun? Did you say you were a virgin?" said poor Tubby, trying to get air.

"I am a virgin," I said, which was true, but hoping to get a laugh, anyway.

"And a Southern virgin. A captain. Please to God, don't shoot me," that fat boy said. "I was cheating on my wife for the first time. The penalty shouldn't be death."

"Why'd you run from the house, Tubby?"

"You know me." Up the street they had searchlights moved up all over the apartment house. They shot about fifty rounds into the house. They were shooting tracers now. It must've lit up my face; then a spotlight went by us.

"Bobby Smith," said Tubby. "My God, I thought you were God."

"I'm not. But it seems holy. Here we are looking at each other."

"Aw, Bobby, they were three beautiful girls. I'd never have done the thing with one, but there were *three*." He was a man with a small pretty face laid around by three layers of jowl and chin. "I heard the machine gun and the guilt struck me. I had to get out. So I just ran."

"Why're you in Nam, anyway?"

"I joined. I wasn't getting anything done but being in love with my wife. That wasn't doing America any good."

"What's that patch on you?"

"Photography." He lifted his hands to hold an imaginary camera. "I'm with the Big Red.[5] I've done a few things out of helicopters."

"You want to see a ground unit? With me. Or does Big Red own you?"

"I have no idea. There hasn't been much to shoot. Some smoking villages. A fire in a bamboo forest. I'd like to see a face."

"You got any pictures of Vicksburg?"

"Oh, well, a few I brought over."

The next day I found out he was doing idlework and Big Red didn't care where he was, so I got him over in my unit. I worried about his weight, etc., and the fact he might be killed. But the boys liked a movie-cameraist being along and I wanted to see the pictures from Vicksburg. It was nice to have Tubby alongside. He was hometown, such as he was. Before we flew out north, he showed me what he had. There was a fine touch in his pictures. There was a cute little Negro on roller skates, and an old woman on a porch, a little boy sleeping in a speedboat with the river in the background. Then there was a blurred picture of his wife naked, just moving through the kitchen, nothing sexy. The last picture was the best. It was John Whitelaw about to crack a golf ball. Tubby had taken it at Augusta, at the Masters. I used to live about five houses away from the Whitelaws. John had his mouth open and his arms, the forearm muscles, were bulked up plain as wires.

John was ten years older than me, but I knew about him. John Whitelaw

---

4. North Vietnamese Army.
5. I.e., the principal U.S. Army combat division in Vietnam.

was our only celebrity since the Civil War. In the picture he wore spectacles. It struck me as something deep, brave, mighty and, well, modern; he had to have the eyeglasses on him to see the mighty thing he was about to do. Maybe I sympathized too much, since I have to wear glasses too, but I thought this picture was worthy of a statue. Tubby had taken it in a striking gray-and-white grain. John seemed to be hitting under a heroic deficiency. You could see the sweat droplets on his neck. His eyes were in agony. But the thing that got me was that John Whitelaw *cared* so much about what he was doing. It made me love America to know he was in it, and I hadn't loved anything for nigh three years then. Tubby was talking about all this "our country" eagle and stars mooky and had seen all the war movies coming over on the boat. I never saw a higher case of fresh and crazy in my life.

But the picture of John at Augusta, it moved me. It was a man at work and play at the same time, doing his damnedest. And Whitelaw was a beautiful man. They pass that term "beautiful" around like pennies nowadays, but I saw him in the flesh once. It was fall in Baton Rouge, around the campus of LSU. He was getting out of a car with a gypsyish girl on his hand. I was ten, I guess, and he was twenty. We were down for a ball game, Mississippi vs. Louisiana, a classic that makes you goo-goo eyed when you're a full-grown man if your heart's in Dixie, etc. At ten, it's Ozville. So in the middle of it, this feeling, I saw Whitelaw and his woman. My dad stopped the car.

"Wasn't that Johnny Whitelaw?" he asked my grandfather.

"You mean that little peacock who left football for golf? He ought to be quarterbacking. Ole Miss right now. It wouldn't be no contest," said my grandfather.

I got my whole idea of what a woman should look like that day . . . and what a man should be. The way John Whitelaw looked, it sort of rebuked yourself ever hoping to call yourself a man. The girl he was with woke up my clammy little dreams about, not even sex, but the perfect thing—it was something like her. As for Whitelaw, his face was curled around by that wild hair the color of beer; his chest was deep, just about to bust out of that collar and bow tie.

"That girl he had, she had a drink in her hand. You could hardly see her for her hair," said grandfather.

"Johnny got him something Cajun,"[6] said my father.

Then my grandfather turned around, looking at me like I was a crab who could say a couple of words. "You look like your mother, but you got gray eyes. What's wrong? You have to take a leak?"

Nothing was wrong with me. I'd just seen John Whitelaw and his girl, that was all.

Tubby had jumped a half-dozen times at Fort Bragg, but he had that heavy box harnessed on him now and I knew he was going down fast and better know how to hit. I explained to him. I went off the plane four behind him, cupping a joint. I didn't want Tubby seeing me smoking grass, but it's just about the only way to get down. If the Cong saw the plane, you'd fall into a barbecue. They've killed a whole unit before, using shotguns and flame bul-

---

6. Residents of southwestern Louisiana who are descended from French-speaking immigrants removed from Canada in 1755 (properly, *Acadian*).

lets, just like your ducks floating in. You hear a lot of noise going in with a whole unit in the air like this. We start shooting about a hundred feet from the ground. If you ever hear one bullet pass you, you get sick thinking there might be a lot of them. All you can do is point your gun down and shoot it all out. You can't reload. You never hit anything. There's a sharpshooter, McIntire, who killed a C shooting from his chute, but that's unlikely. They've got you like a gallery of rabbits if they're down there.

I saw Tubby sinking fast over the wrong part of the field. I had two chutes out, so I cut one off and dropped over toward him, pulling on the left lines so hard I almost didn't have a chute at all for a while. I got level with him and he looked over, pointing down. He was doing his arm up and down. Could have been farmers or just curious rubbernecks down in the field, but there were about ten of them grouped up together, holding things. They weren't shooting, though. I was carrying an experimental gun, me and about ten of my boys. It was a big, light thing; really, it was just a launcher. There were five shells in it, bigger than shotgun shells. If you shot one of them, it was supposed to explode on impact and burn out everything in a twenty-five-yard radius. It was a mean little mother of phosphorus, is what it was. I saw the boys shooting them down into the other side of the field. This stuff would take down a whole tree and you'd chute into a quiet smoking bare area.

I don't know. I don't like a group waiting on me when I jump out of a plane. I almost zapped them, but they weren't throwing anything up. Me and Tubby hit the ground about the same time. They were farmers. I talked to them. They said there were three Cong with them until we were about a hundred feet over. The Cong knew we had the phosphorus shotgun and showed ass, loping out to the woods fifty yards to the north when me and Tubby were coming in.

Tubby took some film of the farmers. All of them had thin chin beards and soft hands because their wives did most of the work. They essentially just lay around and were hung with philosophy, and actually were pretty happy. Nothing had happened around here until we jumped in. These were fresh people. I told them to get everybody out of the huts because we were going to have a thing in the field. It was a crisis point. A huge army of NVA was coming down and they just couldn't avoid us if they wanted to have any run of the valley five miles south. We were there to harass the front point of the army, whatever it was like.

"We're here to check their advance," Tubby told the farmers.

Then we all collected in the woods, five hundred and fifty souls, scared out of mind. What we had going was we knew the NVA general bringing them down was not too bright. He went to the Sorbonne and we had this report from his professor: "Li Dap speaks French very well and had studied Napoleon before he got to me. He knows Robert Lee and the strategy of Jeb Stuart, whose daring circles around an immense army captured his mind. Li Dap wants to be Jeb Stuart. I cannot imagine him in command of more than five hundred troops."

And what we knew stood up. Li Dap had tried to circle left with twenty thousand and got the hell kicked out of him by idle Navy guns sitting outside Gon. He just wasn't very bright. He had half his army climbing around these bluffs, no artillery or air force with them, and it was New Year's Eve for our side.

"So we're here just to kill the edge of their army?" said Tubby.

"That's what I'm here for, why I'm elected. We kill more C's than anybody else in the Army."

"But what if they take a big run at you, all of them?" said Tubby.

"There'll be lots of cooking."

We went out in the edge of the woods and I glassed the field. It was almost night. I saw two tanks come out of the other side and our pickets running back. Pock, pock, pock from the tanks. Then you saw this white glare on one tank where somebody on our team had laid on with one of the phosphorus shotguns. It got white and throbbing, like a little star, and the gun wilted off of it. The other tank ran off a gully into a hell of a cow pond. You wouldn't have known it was that deep. It went underwater over the gun, and they let off the cannon when they went under, raising the water in a spray. It was the silliest-looking thing. Some of them got out and a sergeant yelled for me to come up. It was about a quarter mile out there. Tubby got his camera, and we went out with about fifteen troops.

At the edge of the pond, looking into flashlights, two tankmen sat, one tiny, the other about my size. They were wet, and the big guy was mad. Lot of the troops were chortling, etc. It was awfully damned funny, if you didn't happen to be one of the C-men in the tank.

"Of all the fuck-ups. This is truly saddening." The big guy was saying something like that. I took a flashlight and looked him over. Then I didn't believe it. I told Tubby to get a shot of the big cursing one. Then they brought them on back. I told the boys to tie up the big one and carry him in.

I sat on the ground, talking to Tubby.

"Its so quiet. You'd think they'd be shelling us," he said.

"We're spread out too good. They don't have much ammo now. They really galloped down here. That's the way Li Dap does it. Their side's got big trouble now. And, Tubby, me and you are famous."

"Me, what?"

"You took his picture. You can get some more, more arty angles on him tomorrow."

"Him?"

"It's Li Dap himself. He was in the tank in the pond."

"No. Their general?"

"You want me to go prove it?"

We walked over. They had him tied around a tree. His hands were above his head and he was sitting down. I smelled some hash in the air. The guy who was blowing it was a boy from Detroit I really liked, and I hated to come down on him, but I really beat him up. He never got a lick in. I kicked his rump when he was crawling away and some friends picked him up. You can't have lighting up that shit at night on the ground. Li Dap was watching the fight, still cursing.

"Asshole of the mountains." He was saying something like that. "Fortune's ninny."

"Hi, General. My French isn't so good. You speak English. Honor us."

He wouldn't say anything.

"You have a lot of courage, running out front with the tanks." There were some snickers in the bush, but I cut them out quick. We had a real romantic here and I didn't want him laughed at. He wasn't hearing much, though. About that time two of their rockets flashed into the woods. They went off in the treetops and scattered.

"It was worthy of Patton," I said. "You had some bad luck. But we're glad you made it alive."

"Kiss my ass."

"You want your hands free? Oliver, get his ropes off the tree." The guy I beat up cut him off the tree.

"You scared us very deeply. How many tanks do you have over there?"

"Nonsense," he said.

"What do you have except for a few rockets?"

"I have no credence in the phosphorus gun."

"Your men saw us use them when we landed."

"I had no credence."

"So you just came out to see."

"I say to them never to fear the machine when the cause is just. To throw oneself past the technology tricks of the monsters and into his soft soul."

"And there you will win, huh?"

"Of course. It is our country." He smiled at me. "It's relative to your war in the nineteenth century. The South had slavery. The North must purge it so that it is a healthy region of our country.

"You were out in the tank as an example to your men?"

"Yes!"

All this hero needed was a plumed hat.

"Sleep well," I said, and told Oliver to get him a blanket and feed him, and feed the tiny gunner with him.

When we got back to my dump, I walked away for a while, not wanting to talk with Tubby. I started crying. It started with these hard sobs coming up like rocks in my throat. I started looking out at forever, across the field. They shot up three more rockets from the woods below the hill. I waited for the things to land on us. They fell on the top of trees, nothing near me, but there was some howling off to the right. Somebody had got some shrapnel.

I'd killed so many gooks. I'd killed them with machine guns, mortars, howitzers, knives, wire, me and my boys. My boys loved me. They were lying all around me, laying this great cloud of trust on me. The picture of John Whitelaw about to hit that ball at Augusta was jammed in my head. There was such care in his eyes, and it was only a golf ball, a goddamned piece of nothing. But it was wonderful and peaceful. Nobody was being killed. Whitelaw had the right. He had the beloved American right to the pursuit of happiness. The tears were out of my jaws then. Here we shot each other up. All we had going was the pursuit of horror. It seemed to me my life had gone straight from teen-age giggling to horror. I had never had time to be but two things, a giggler and a killer.

Christ, I was crying for myself. I had nothing for the other side, understand that. North Vietnam was a land full of lousy little Commie robots, as far as I knew. A place of the worst propaganda and hypocrisy. You should have read some of their agitprop around Gon, talking about freedom and throwing off the yoke, etc. The gooks went for Communism because they were so ignorant and had nothing to lose. The South Vietnamese, too. I couldn't believe we had them as allies. They were such a pretty and uniformly indecent people. I once saw a little taxi boy, a kid is all, walk into a Medevac with one arm and a hand blown off by a mine he'd picked up. These housewives were walking behind him in the street, right in the middle of Gon. Know what they were doing? They were laughing. They thought it was the most hysterical misadventure they'd ever seen. These people were on our side. These were our friends and lovers. That happened early when I got there. I was a virgin when I got to Nam and stayed a virgin, through a horde of B-girls, the most base and luscious-lipped hustlers. Because I did not want to mingle with this race.

In an ARVN hospital tent you see the hurt officers lined up in front of a private who's holding his guts with his hands. They'll treat the officer with a bad pimple before they treat the dying private. We're supposed to be shaking hands with these people. Why can't we be fighting for some place like England? When you train yourself to blow gooks away, like I did, something happens, some kind of popping returning dream of murder-with-a-smile.

I needed a way. I was sick. In another three months I'd be zapping orphanages.

"Bobby, are you all right?" said Tubby, waddling out to the tree I was hanging on.

"I shouldn't ever've seen that picture of John Whitelaw. I shouldn't've."

"Do you really think we'll be famous?" Tubby got an enchanted look on him, sort of dumb angel look in that small pretty face amid the fat rolls. It was about midnight. There was a fine Southern moon lighting up the field. You could see every piece of straw out there. Tubby, by my ass, had the high daze on him. He'd stepped out here in the boonies and put down his foot in Ozville.

"This'll get me Major, anyhow. Sure. Fame. Both of us," I said.

Tubby said: "I tried to get nice touches in with the light coming over his face. These pictures could turn out awfully interesting. I was thinking about the cover of *Time* or *Newsweek*."

"It'll change your whole life, Tubby," I said.

Tubby was just about to die for love of fate. He was shivering.

I started enjoying the field again. This time the straws were waving. It was covered with rushing little triangles, these sort of toiling dots. Our side opened up. All the boys came up to join within a minute and it was a sheet of lightning rolling back and forth along the outside of the woods. I could see it all while I was walking back to the radio. I mean humping low. Tubby must've been walking straight up. He took something big right in the square of his back. It rolled him up twenty feet in front of me. He was dead and smoking when I made it to him.

"C'mon, I've got to get the pictures," he said.

I think he was already dead.

I got my phosphorus shotgun. Couldn't think of anything but the radio and getting it over how we were being hit, so we could get dragons—helicopters with fifty cals—in quick. The dragons are nice. They've got searchlights, and you put two of them over a field like we were looking at, they'd clean it out in half an hour. So I made it to the radio and the boys had already called the dragons in, everything was fine. Only we had to hold them for an hour and a half until the dragons got there. I humped up front. Every now and then you'd see somebody use one of the experimental guns. The bad thing was that it lit up the gunner too much at night, too much shine out of the muzzle. I took note of that to tell them when we got back. But the gun really smacked the gook assault. It was good for about seventy-five yards and hit wth a huge circle burn about the way they said it would. The gook's first force was knocked off. You could see men who were still burning running back through the straw, hear them screaming.

I don't remember too well. I was just loitering near the radio, a few fires out in the field, everything mainly quiet. Copters on the way. I decided to go take a look at Li Dap. I thought it was our boys around him, though I didn't know why. They were wearing green and standing up plain as day. There was Oliver, smoking a joint. His rifle was on the ground. The NVA were all around him and he hadn't even noticed. There were so many of them—twenty or so—they were clanking rifles against each other. One of them was going up behind Oliver with a bayonet, just about on him. If I'd had a carbine like usual, I could've taken the bayoneteer off and at least five of the others. Oliver and Li Dap might've ducked and survived.

But I couldn't pick and choose. I hardly even thought. The barrel of the shotgun was up and I pulled on the trigger, aiming at the bayoneteer.

I burned them all up.

Nobody even made a squeak.

There was a flare and they were gone.

Some of my boys rushed over with guns. All they were good for was stomping out the little fires on the edges.

When we got back, I handed over Tubby's pictures. The old man was beside himself over my killing a general, a captured general. He couldn't understand what kind of laxity I'd allowed to let twenty gooks come up on us like that. They thought I might have a court-martial, and I was under arrest for a week. The story got out to UPI and they were saying things like "atrocity," with my name spelled all over the column.

But it was dropped and I was pulled out and went home a lieutenant.

That's all right. I've got four hundred and two boys out there—the ones that got back—who love me and know the truth, who love me *because* they know the truth.

It's Tubby's lost fame I dream about.

The Army confiscated the roll and all his pictures. I wrote the Pentagon a letter asking for a print and waited two years here in Vicksburg without even a statement they received the note. I see his wife, who's remarried and is fat herself now, at the discount drugstore every now and then. She has the look of a kind of hopeless cheer. I got a print from the Pentagon when the war was over and it didn't matter. Li Dap looked wonderful—strained, abused and wild, his hair flying over his eyes while he's making a statement full of conviction.

It made me start thinking of faces again.

Since I've been home I've crawled in bed with almost anything that would have me. I've slept with high-school teachers, Negroes and, the other night, my own aunt. It made her smile. All those years of keeping her body in trim came to something, the big naughty surprise that the other women look for in religion, God showing up and killing their neighbors, sparing them. But she knows a lot about things and I think I'll be in love with her.

We were at the John Whitelaw vs. Whitney Maxwell playoff together. It was a piece of wonder. I felt thankful to the wind or God or whoever who brought that fine contest near enough by. When they hit the ball, the sound traveled like a rifle snap out over the bluffs. When it was impossible to hit the ball, that is exactly when they hit it.

My aunt grabbed hold of my fingers when the tension was almost up to a roar. The last two holes. Ah, John lost. I looked over the despondency of the home crowd.

Fools! Fools! I thought. Love it! Love the loss as well as the gain. Go home and dig it. Nobody was killed. We saw victory and defeat, and they were both wonderful.

1978

ALICE WALKER
b. 1944

Of the two daughters at odds over family heirlooms in the story "Everyday Use" (printed here), Alice Walker resembles each one. Like the burned Maggie, she spent a childhood even more limited than her family's rural poverty dictated, for as a little girl she was shot in the eye with a BB gun; the disfigurement plagued her until it was corrected during her college years. Like Dee, she was able to attend college—first Spelman College and then Sarah Lawrence College on a scholarship—and acquire urban sophistications from the North. Many of Walker's characters become adept in the new cultural language of Black Arts and black power to which the author herself contributed as a young writer—and all of them are subjected to the same dismay Dee's mother feels at having to rule against this daughter's wishes. Like the mother, therefore, Walker is given to seeing both sides of a situation; and when it comes to making a choice between her characters' opposing positions, she tends to be self-critical of her own personality first and extremely sparing in her judgment of others.

From her birthplace in Eatonton, Georgia, Walker gained a thorough understanding of the rural South, an understanding she employs when evaluating the importance of Flannery O'Connor, an older white writer who lived in nearby Milledgeville. As her essay "Beyond the Peacock" shows, Walker's own eminence as a writer invites readers to see the region and its heritage in a different perspective, as visitors' habits of romanticizing how the bricks of the O'Connor home were handmade on the site by slaves as contrasted to the author's pained awareness of how the slaves surely suffered in the process. That O'Connor's work survives and even profits by such critical reexamination speaks again for Walker's sense of balance. As a child of share-croppers educated at a sophisticated northern college, Walker is able to weigh human and artistic concerns in a way that lets Flannery O'Connor be read for the complex writer she is.

After college Walker returned to the South, first to work against segregation in the civil rights movement and then to begin her teaching career at Jackson State College in Mississippi. Her first novel, *The Third Life of Grange Copeland* (1970), follows its protagonist through three generations of domestic experience. In *Meridian* (1976) Walker changes her narrative approach to encompass fragmentary recollections of the 1960s among characters trying to make sense of their recent past. This novel reflects many of the topics treated in the author's short story collection, *In Love & Trouble* (1973), in which a range of African American women almost always have unhappy relationships with men. Walker's third novel, *The Color Purple* (1982), makes her strongest narrative statement, formulated as it is from what she calls a "womanist" (as opposed to strictly feminist) perspective. This approach draws on the black folk expression "womanish," which in a mother-to-daughter context signifies a call to adult, mature, responsible (and courageous) behavior. Such behavior is beneficial to both women and men, and is necessary, Walker argues, for the survival of all African Americans by keeping creativity alive. Both the plot and the stylistic nature of *The Color Purple* show how this happens, as the young black woman Celie draws on her sister's letters (written from Africa) for her own letters that she writes to God. Though Celie's life by any other terms could be considered disastrous (including rape, incest, and the killing of her babies by her father and both physical and psychological abuse by her husband), her ability to express herself and act successfully gives her status as an individual in the world. To everything that will listen, Celie says "I am here."

Walker's work has continued with other novels, short stories, collections of poetry, and several important volumes of essays. In "The Same River Twice" (1996) she wrote about how the filming of *The Color Purple* both challenged and changed her life. As a sociocultural critic, she has examined the atrocity of female genital mutilation in parts of Africa, incorporating her conclusions in her novel *Possessing the Secret of Joy* (1992), and as a literary critic has spoken for a richer and more complete understanding of Zora Neale Hurston, whose employment of folk materials in narrative anticipates Walker's own. Throughout her career she speaks for the need for strength from African American women, and her writing is ever conscious of providing workable models for such strength being achieved.

The text is from *In Love & Trouble* (1973).

Everyday Use

For Your Grandmama

I will wait for her in the yard that Maggie and I made so clean and wavy yesterday afternoon. A yard like this is more comfortable than most people know. It is not just a yard. It is like an extended living room. When the hard clay is swept clean as a floor and the fine sand around the edges lined with tiny, irregular grooves, anyone can come and sit and look up into the elm tree and wait for the breezes that never come inside the house.

Maggie will be nervous until after her sister goes: she will stand hopelessly in corners, homely and ashamed of the burn scars down her arms and legs, eyeing her sister with a mixture of envy and awe. She thinks her sister has held life always in the palm of one hand, that "no" is a word the world never learned to say to her.

You've no doubt seen those TV shows where the child who has "made it" is confronted, as a surprise, by her own mother and father, tottering in weakly from backstage. (A pleasant surprise, of course: What would they do if parent and child came on the show only to curse out and insult each other?) On TV mother and child embrace and smile into each other's faces. Sometimes the mother and father weep, the child wraps them in her arms and leans across the table to tell how she would not have made it without their help. I have seen these programs.

Sometimes I dream a dream in which Dee and I are suddenly brought together on a TV program of this sort. Out of a dark and soft-seated limousine I am ushered into a bright room filled with many people. There I meet a smiling, gray, sporty man like Johnny Carson who shakes my hand and tells me what a fine girl I have. Then we are on the stage and Dee is embracing me with tears in her eyes. She pins on my dress a large orchid, even though she has told me once that she thinks orchids are tacky flowers.

In real life I am a large, big-boned woman with rough, man-working hands. In the winter I wear flannel nightgowns to bed and overalls during the day. I can kill and clean a hog as mercilessly as a man. My fat keeps me hot in zero weather. I can work outside all day, breaking ice to get water for washing; I can eat pork liver cooked over the open fire minutes after it comes steaming from the hog. One winter I knocked a bull calf straight in the brain between the eyes with a sledge hammer and had the meat hung up to chill before nightfall. But of course all this does not show on television. I am the way my daughter would want me to be: a hundred pounds lighter, my skin like an uncooked barley pancake. My hair glistens in the hot bright lights. Johnny Carson has much to do to keep up with my quick and witty tongue.

But that is a mistake. I know even before I wake up. Who ever knew a Johnson with a quick tongue? Who can even imagine me looking a strange white man in the eye? It seems to me I have talked to them always with one foot raised in flight, with my head turned in whichever way is farthest from them. Dee, though. She would always look anyone in the eye. Hesitation was no part of her nature.

"How do I look, Mama?" Maggie says, showing just enough of her thin body enveloped in pink skirt and red blouse for me to know she's there, almost hidden by the door.

"Come out into the yard," I say.

Have you ever seen a lame animal, perhaps a dog run over by some careless person rich enough to own a car, sidle up to someone who is ignorant enough to be kind to them? That is the way my Maggie walks. She has been like this, chin on chest, eyes on ground, feet in shuffle, ever since the fire that burned the other house to the ground.

Dee is lighter than Maggie, with nicer hair and a fuller figure. She's a woman now, though sometimes I forget. How long ago was it that the other house burned? Ten, twelve years? Sometimes I can still hear the flames and feel Maggie's arms sticking to me, her hair smoking and her dress falling off her in little black papery flakes. Her eyes seemed stretched open, blazed open by the flames reflected in them. And Dee. I see her standing off under the sweet gum tree she used to dig gum out of; a look of concentration on her face as she watched the last dingy gray board of the house fall in toward the red-hot brick chimney. Why don't you do a dance around the ashes? I'd wanted to ask her. She had hated the house that much.

I used to think she hated Maggie, too. But that was before we raised the money, the church and me, to send her to Augusta to school. She used to read to us without pity; forcing words, lies, other folks' habits, whole lives upon us two, sitting trapped and ignorant underneath her voice. She washed us in a river of make-believe, burned us with a lot of knowledge we didn't necessarily need to know. Pressed us to her with the serious way she read, to shove us away at just the moment, like dimwits, we seemed about to understand.

Dee wanted nice things. A yellow organdy dress to wear to her graduation from high school; black pumps to match a green suit she'd made from an old suit somebody gave me. She was determined to stare down any disaster in her efforts. Her eyelids would not flicker for minutes at a time. Often I fought off the temptation to shake her. At sixteen she had a style of her own: and knew what style was.

I never had an education myself. After second grade the school was closed down. Don't ask me why: in 1927 colored asked fewer questions than they do now. Sometimes Maggie reads to me. She stumbles along good-naturedly but can't see well. She knows she is not bright. Like good looks and money, quickness passed her by. She will marry John Thomas (who has mossy teeth in an earnest face) and then I'll be free to sit here and I guess just sing church songs to myself. Although I never was a good singer. Never could carry a tune. I was always better at a man's job. I used to love to milk till I was hooked in the side in '49. Cows are soothing and slow and don't bother you, unless you try to milk them the wrong way.

I have deliberately turned my back on the house. It is three rooms, just like the one that burned, except the roof is tin; they don't make shingle roofs any more. There are no real windows, just some holes cut in the sides, like the portholes in a ship, but not round and not square, with rawhide holding the shutters up on the outside. This house is in a pasture, too, like the other one. No doubt when Dee sees it she will want to tear it down. She wrote me once that no matter where we "choose" to live, she will manage to come see us. But she will never bring her friends. Maggie and I thought about this and Maggie asked me, "Mama, when did Dee ever *have* any friends?"

She had a few. Furtive boys in pink shirts hanging about on washday after school. Nervous girls who never laughed. Impressed with her they worshiped the well-turned phrase, the cute shape, the scalding humor that erupted like bubbles in lye. She read to them.

When she was courting Jimmy T she didn't have much time to pay to us, but turned all her faultfinding power on him. He *flew* to marry a cheap city girl from a family of ignorant flashy people. She hardly had time to recompose herself.

When she comes I will meet—but there they are!

Maggie attempts to make a dash for the house, in her shuffling way, but I stay her with my hand. "Come back here," I say. And she stops and tries to dig a well in the sand with her toe.

It is hard to see them clearly through the strong sun. But even the first glimpse of leg out of the car tells me it is Dee. Her feet were always neat-looking, as if God himself had shaped them with a certain style. From the other side of the car comes a short, stocky man. Hair is all over his head a foot long and hanging from his chin like a kinky mule tail. I hear Maggie suck in her breath. "Uhnnnh," is what it sounds like. Like when you see the wriggling end of a snake just in front of your foot on the road. "Uhnnnh."

Dee next. A dress down to the ground, in this hot weather. A dress so loud it hurts my eyes. There are yellows and oranges enough to throw back the light of the sun. I feel my whole face warming from the heat waves it throws out. Earrings gold, too, and hanging down to her shoulders. Bracelets dangling and making noises when she moves her arm up to shake the folds of the dress out of her armpits. The dress is loose and flows, and as she walks closer, I like it. I hear Maggie go "Uhnnnh" again. It is her sister's hair. It stands straight up like the wool on a sheep. It is black as night and around the edges are two long pigtails that rope about like small lizards disappearing behind her ears.

"Wa-su-zo-Tean-o!" she says, coming on in that gliding way the dress makes her move. The short stocky fellow with the hair to his navel is all grinning and he follows up with "Asalamalakim, my mother and sister!" He moves to hug Maggie but she falls back, right up against the back of my chair. I feel her trembling there and when I look up I see the perspiration falling off her chin.

"Don't get up," says Dee. Since I am stout it takes something of a push. You can see me trying to move a second or two before I make it. She turns, showing white heels through her sandals, and goes back to the car. Out she peeks next with a Polaroid. She stoops down quickly and lines up picture after picture of me sitting there in front of the house with Maggie cowering behind me. She never takes a shot without making sure the house is included. When a cow comes nibbling around the edge of the yard she snaps it and me and Maggie *and* the house. Then she puts the Polaroid in the back seat of the car, and comes up and kisses me on the forehead.

Meanwhile Asalamalakim is going through motions with Maggie's hand. Maggie's hand is as limp as a fish, and probably as cold, despite the sweat, and she keeps trying to pull it back. It looks like Asalamalakim wants to shake hands but wants to do it fancy. Or maybe he don't know how people shake hands. Anyhow, he soon gives up on Maggie.

"Well," I say. "Dee."

"No, Mama," she says. "Not 'Dee,' Wangero Leewanika Kemanjo!"

"What happened to 'Dee'?" I wanted to know.

"She's dead," Wangero said. "I couldn't bear it any longer, being named after the people who oppress me."

"You know as well as me you was named after your aunt Dicie," I said. Dicie is my sister. She named Dee. We called her "Big Dee" after Dee was born.

"But who was *she* named after?" asked Wangero.

"I guess after Grandma Dee," I said.

"And who was she named after?" asked Wangero.

"Her mother," I said, and saw Wangero was getting tired. "That's about as far back as I can trace it," I said. Though, in fact, I probably could have carried it back beyond the Civil War through the branches.

"Well," said Asalamalakim, "there you are."

"Uhnnnh," I heard Maggie say.

"There I was not," I said, "before 'Dicie' cropped up in our family, so why should I try to trace it that far back?"

He just stood there grinning, looking down on me like somebody inspecting a Model A car. Every once in a while he and Wangero sent eye signals over my head.

"How do you pronounce this name?" I asked.

"You don't have to call me by it if you don't want to," said Wangero.

"Why shouldn't I?" I asked. "If that's what you want us to call you, we'll call you."

"I know it might sound awkward at first," said Wangero.

"I'll get used to it," I said. "Ream it out again."

Well, soon we got the name out of the way. Asalamalakim had a name twice as long and three times as hard. After I tripped over it two or three times he told me to just call him Hakim-a-barber. I wanted to ask him was he a barber, but I didn't really think he was, so I didn't ask.

"You must belong to those beef-cattle peoples down the road," I said. They said "Asalamalakim" when they met you, too, but they didn't shake hands. Always too busy: feeding the cattle, fixing the fences, putting up salt-lick shelters, throwing down hay. When the white folks poisoned some of the herd the men stayed up all night with rifles in their hands. I walked a mile and a half just to see the sight.

Hakim-a-barber said, "I accept some of their doctrines, but farming and raising cattle is not my style." (They didn't tell me, and I didn't ask, whether Wangero (Dee) had really gone and married him.)

We sat down to eat and right away he said he didn't eat collards and pork was unclean. Wangero, though, went on through the chitlins and corn bread, the greens and everything else. She talked a blue streak over the sweet potatoes. Everything delighted her. Even the fact that we still used the benches her daddy made for the table when we couldn't afford to buy chairs.

"Oh, Mama!" she cried. Then turned to Hakim-a-barber. "I never knew how lovely these benches are. You can feel the rump prints," she said, running her hands underneath her and along the bench. Then she gave a sigh and her hand closed over Grandma Dee's butter dish. "That's it!" she said. "I knew there was something I wanted to ask you if I could have." She jumped up from the table and went over in the corner where the churn stood, the milk in it clabber by now. She looked at the churn and looked at it.

"This churn top is what I need," she said. "Didn't Uncle Buddy whittle it out of a tree you all used to have?"

"Yes," I said.

"Uh huh," she said happily. "And I want the dasher, too."

"Uncle Buddy whittle that, too?" asked the barber.

Dee (Wangero) looked up at me.

"Aunt Dee's first husband whittled the dash," said Maggie so low you almost couldn't hear her. "His name was Henry, but they called him Stash."

"Maggie's brain is like an elephant's," Wangero said, laughing. "I can use the churn top as a centerpiece for the alcove table," she said, sliding a plate over the churn, "and I'll think of something artistic to do with the dasher."

When she finished wrapping the dasher the handle stuck out. I took it for a moment in my hands. You didn't even have to look close to see where hands pushing the dasher up and down to make butter had left a kind of sink in the wood. In fact, there were a lot of small sinks; you could see where thumbs and fingers had sunk into the wood. It was beautiful light yellow wood, from a tree that grew in the yard where Big Dee and Stash had lived.

After dinner Dee (Wangero) went to the trunk at the foot of my bed and started rifling through it. Maggie hung back in the kitchen over the dishpan. Out came Wangero with two quilts. They had been pieced by Grandma Dee and then Big Dee and me had hung them on the quilt frames on the front porch and quilted them. One was in the Lone Star pattern. The other was Walk Around the Mountain. In both of them were scraps of dresses Grandma Dee had worn fifty and more years ago. Bits and pieces of Grandpa Jarrell's Paisley shirts. And one teeny faded blue piece, about the size of a penny matchbox, that was from Great Grandpa Ezra's uniform that he wore in the Civil War.

"Mama," Wangero said sweet as a bird. "Can I have these old quilts?"

I heard something fall in the kitchen, and a minute later the kitchen door slammed.

"Why don't you take one or two of the others?" I asked. "These old things was just done by me and Big Dee from some tops your grandma pieced before she died."

"No," said Wangero. "I don't want those. They are stitched around the borders by machine."

"That'll make them last better," I said.

"That's not the point," said Wangero. "These are all pieces of dresses Grandma used to wear. She did all this stitching by hand. Imagine!" She held the quilts securely in her arms, stroking them.

"Some of the pieces, like those lavender ones, come from old clothes her mother handed down to her," I said, moving up to touch the quilts. Dee (Wangero) moved back just enough so that I couldn't reach the quilts. They already belonged to her.

"Imagine!" she breathed again, clutching them closely to her bosom.

"The truth is," I said, "I promised to give them quilts to Maggie, for when she marries John Thomas."

She gasped like a bee had stung her.

"Maggie can't appreciate these quilts!" she said. "She'd probably be backward enough to put them to everyday use."

"I reckon she would," I said. "God knows I been saving 'em for long enough with nobody using 'em. I hope she will!" I didn't want to bring up how I had offered Dee (Wangero) a quilt when she went away to college. Then she had told me they were old-fashioned, out of style.

"But they're *priceless!*" she was saying now, furiously; for she has a temper. "Maggie would put them on the bed and in five years they'd be in rags. Less than that!"

"She can always make some more," I said. "Maggie knows how to quilt."

Dee (Wangero) looked at me with hatred. "You just will not understand. The point is these quilts, *these* quilts!"

"Well," I said, stumped. "What would *you* do with them?"

"Hang them," she said. As if that was the only thing you *could* do with quilts.

Maggie by now was standing in the door. I could almost hear the sound her feet made as they scraped over each other.

"She can have them, Mama," she said, like somebody used to never winning anything, or having anything reserved for her. "I can 'member Grandma Dee without the quilts."

I looked at her hard. She had filled her bottom lip with checkerberry snuff and it gave her a face a kind of dopey, hangdog look. It was Grandma Dee and Big Dee who taught her how to quilt herself. She stood there with her scarred hands hidden in the folds of her skirt. She looked at her sister with something like fear but she wasn't mad at her. This was Maggie's portion. This was the way she knew God to work.

When I looked at her like that something hit me in the top of my head and ran down to the soles of my feet. Just like when I'm in church and the spirit of God touches me and I get happy and shout. I did something I never had done before: hugged Maggie to me, then dragged her on into the room, snatched the quilts out of Miss Wangero's hands and dumped them into Maggie's lap. Maggie just sat there on my bed with her mouth open.

"Take one or two of the others," I said to Dee.

But she turned without a word and went out to Hakim-a-barber.

"You just don't understand," she said, as Maggie and I came out to the car.

"What don't I understand?" I wanted to know.

"Your heritage," she said. And then she turned to Maggie, kissed her, and said, "You ought to try to make something of yourself, too, Maggie. It's really a new day for us. But from the way you and Mama still live you'd never know it."

She put on some sunglasses that hid everything above the tip of her nose and her chin.

Maggie smiled; maybe at the sunglasses. But a real smile, not scared. After we watched the car dust settle I asked Maggie to bring me a dip of snuff. And then the two of us sat there just enjoying, until it was time to go in the house and go to bed.

1973

ANNIE DILLARD
b. 1945

Annie Dillard was born in Pittsburgh, Pennsylvania; was educated at Hollins College, Virginia; and has taught creative writing at Western Washington University and Wesleyan University. She has lived in the Blue Ridge Mountains of the Appalachian chain and among the Cascades of the Pacific Northwest; it is the soltitude and close attention to nature and one's own thoughts prompted by rural life in these regions that motivate her writing, which among her generation is stylistically unique. She is deeply meditative, even spiritual, yet she can express herself in a swinging rhythm that sweeps up poetic insight and religious references with the same joyful ease of describing nature at play. *Pilgrim at Tinker Creek* (1974) follows the progress of the seasons as the author lives a quiet, closely observant life in the seclusion of Virginia's Roanoke Valley. Nature is studied, but so are books of a widely ranging theological, philosophical, and scientific nature. The author's subject is nothing less than cosmic, a search for understanding how beauty and violence form necessary parts of the world as we know it. Nature, like human life itself, is both generously productive and violently destructive, equally inclusive and isolative. These tensions reinforce the thoughts Dillard examines: her own, and also those of writers who have formed our intellectual heritage. In this way her work resembles Thoreau's in *Walden*, particularly in its appreciation of nature's cyclic patterns. More like Thoreau's friend, Emerson, however, Dillard directs her thoughts to metaphysical ends, joining a tradition reaching back to Puritan poetry and sermons. "Holy the Firm" (1977) takes Dillard's metaphysical talents to their fullest form of expression. That a little girl has been horribly burned is all too immediately real, and the author can experience the terror of her suffering in vividly personal terms. Yet even more compelling are Dillard's wide-ranging and deeply probing meditations on the ultimate meaning of such a terrible event, that such innocence should be subjected to such disfigurement and pain. As critic Wendy Lesser noted about the author's similar work "For the Time Being" (1999), Dillard excels with "the conjunction of seemingly disparate facts that eventually add up to a complex whole."

Elsewhere in Dillard's canon are lighter subjects, such as the status of the contemporary novel (*Living by Fiction*, 1982) and accounts of picturesque travel (*Teaching a Stone to Talk*, 1982). The author has written about meeting Chinese writers, reminisced about her childhood, and studied the processes in her own work. In 1992 she published a novel, *The Living*, an historical narrative set in the Pacific Northwest that is as much about the landscape as its people. As the critic Ihab Hassan has said of Dillard's success in "Holy the Firm," "Her language is as textured as her perception, an Orphic poetry with terrors small and near at hand; her path is that of the solitary wanderer, in the wilderness of the Cascades or Blue Ridge Mountains, living in a rough cabin to 'study hard things.' "

The text is that printed in *The Annie Dillard Reader* (1994).

Holy the Firm

I live on northern Puget Sound, in Washington State, alone.

There is a spider in the bathroom with whom I keep a sort of company. Her little outfit always reminds me of a certain moth I helped to kill. The spider herself is of uncertain lineage, bulbous at the abdomen and drab. Her six-inch mess of a web works, works somehow, works miraculously, to keep her alive and me amazed. The web itself is in a corner behind the toilet, connecting tile wall to tile wall and floor, in a place where there is, I would have thought, scant traffic. Yet under the web are sixteen or so corpses she has tossed to the floor.

The corpses appear to be mostly sow bugs, those little armadillo creatures who live to travel flat out in houses, and die round. There is also a new shred of earwig, three old spider skins, crinkled and clenched, and two moth bodies, wingless and huge and empty, moth bodies I drop to my knees to see.

Today the earwig shines darkly and gleams, what there is of him: a dorsal curve of thorax and abdomen, and a smooth pair of cerci, by which I knew his name. Next week, if the other bodies are any indication, he will be shrunken and gray, webbed to the floor with dust. The sow bugs beside him are hollow and empty of color, fragile, a breath away from brittle fluff. The spider skins lie on their sides, translucent and ragged, their legs drying in knots. And the moths, the empty moths, stagger against each other, headless, in a confusion of arcing strips of chitin like peeling varnish, like a jumble of buttresses for cathedral domes, like nothing resembling moths, so that I should hesitate to call them moths, except that I have had some experience with the figure Moth reduced to a nub.

Two years ago I was camping alone in the Blue Ridge Mountains in Virginia. I had hauled myself and gear up there to read, among other things, James Ramsey Ullman's *The Day on Fire,* a novel about Rimbaud[1] that had made me want to be a writer when I was sixteen; I was hoping it would do it again. So I read, lost, every day sitting under a tree by my tent, while warblers swung in the leaves overhead and bristle worms trailed their inches over the twiggy dirt at my feet; and I read every night by candlelight, while barred owls called in the forest and pale moths massed round my head in the clearing, where my light made a ring.

Moths kept flying into the candle. They hissed and recoiled, lost upside down in the shadows among my cooking pans. Or they singed their wings and fell, and their hot wings, as if melted, stuck to the first thing they touched—a pan, a lid, a spoon—so that the snagged moths could flutter only in tiny arcs, unable to struggle free. These I could release by a quick flip with a stick; in the morning I would find my cooking stuff gilded with torn flecks of moth wings, triangles of shiny dust here and there on the aluminum. So I read, and boiled water, and replenished candles, and read on.

One night a moth flew into the candle, was caught, burned dry, and held. I must have been staring at the candle, or maybe I looked up when a shadow crossed my page; at any rate, I saw it all. A golden female moth, a biggish one with a two-inch wingspan, flapped into the fire, dropped her abdomen into the wet wax, stuck, flamed, frazzled, and fried in a second. Her moving wings ignited like tissue paper, enlarging the circle of light in the clearing and creating out of the darkness the sudden blue sleeves of my sweater, the green leaves of jewelweed by my side, the ragged red trunk of a pine. At once the light contracted again and the moth's wings vanished in a fine, foul smoke. At the same time her six legs clawed, curled, blackened, and ceased, disappearing utterly. And her head jerked in spasms, making a spattering noise; her antennae crisped and burned away, and her heaving mouth parts crackled like pistol fire. When it was all over, her head was, so far as I could determine, gone, gone the long way of her wings and legs. Had she been new, or old? Had she mated and laid her eggs, had she done her work? All that was left was the glowing horn shell of her abdomen and thorax—a fraying, partially collapsed gold tube jammed upright in the candle's round pool.

And then this moth essence, this spectacular skeleton, began to act as a wick. She kept burning. The wax rose in the moth's body from her soaking abdomen to her thorax to the jagged hole where her head should be, and widened into flame, a saffron-yellow flame that robed her to the ground like any immolating monk. That candle had two wicks, two flames of identical height, side by side. The moth's head was fire. She burned for two hours, until I blew her out.

She burned for two hours without changing, without bending or leaning— only glowing within, like a building fire glimpsed through silhouetted walls, like a hollow saint, like a flame-faced virgin gone to God, while I read by her light, kindled, while Rimbaud in Paris burned out his brains in a thousand poems, while night pooled wetly at my feet.

---

1. Arthur Rimbaud (1854–1891), French poet noted for his sometimes morbid introspection.

And that is why I believe those hollow crisps on the bathroom floor are moths. I think I know moths, and fragments of moths, and chips and tatters of utterly empty moths, in any state. How many of you, I asked the people in my class, which of you want to give your lives and be writers? I was trembling from coffee, or cigarettes, or the closeness of faces all around me. (Is this what we live for? I thought; is this the only final beauty: the color of any skin in any light, and living, human eyes?) All hands rose to the question. (You, Nick? Will you? Margaret? Randy? Why do I want them to mean it?) And then I tried to tell them what the choice must mean: you can't be anything else. You must go at your life with a broadax. . . . They had no idea what I was saying. (I have two hands, don't I? And all this energy, for as long as I can remember. I'll do it in the evenings, after skiing, or on the way home from the bank, or after the children are asleep. . . .) They thought I was raving again. It's just as well.

There is a gold cat here, named Small, who sleeps on my legs. In the morning I joke to her blank face: Do you remember last night? Do you remember? I throw her out before breakfast.

I have three candles on the table, which I disentangle from the plants and light when visitors come. Small usually avoids them, although once she came too close and her tail caught fire; I rubbed it out before she noticed. The flames move light over everyone's skin, draw light to the surface of the faces of my friends. When the people leave I never blow the candles out, and after I'm asleep they flame and burn.

The Cascade range, in these high latitudes, backs almost into the water. There is only a narrow strip, an afterthought of foothills and farms sixty miles wide, between the snowy mountains and the sea. The mountains wall well. The rest of the country—most of the rest of the planet, in some very real sense, excluding a shred of British Columbia's coastline and the Alaskan islands—is called, and profoundly felt to be, simply "East of the Mountains." I've been there.

I came here to study hard things—rock mountain and salt sea—and to temper my spirit on their edges. "Teach me thy ways, O Lord" is, like all prayers, a rash one, and one I cannot but recommend. These mountains—Mount Baker and the Sisters and Shuksan, the Canadian Coastal Range and the Olympics on the peninsula—are surely the edge of the known and comprehended world. They are high. That they bear their own unimaginable masses and weathers aloft, holding them up in the sky for anyone to see plain, makes them, as Chesterton[2] said of the Eucharist, only the more mysterious by their very visibility and absence of secrecy. They are the western rim of the real, if not considerably beyond it. If the Greeks had looked at Mount Baker all day, their large and honest art would have broken, and they would have gone fishing, as these people do. And as perhaps I one day shall.

But the mountains are, incredibly, east. When I first came here I faced east and watched the mountains, thinking: These are the Ultima Thule, the final westering, the last serrate margin of time. Since they are, incredibly, east, I must be no place at all. But the sun rose over the snowfields and woke me where I lay, and I rose and cast a shadow over someplace, and thought:

2. G. K. Chesterton (1874–1936), English novelist, essayist, poet, and journalist.

There is, God help us, more. So gathering my bowls and spoons, and turning my head, as it were, I moved to face west, relinquishing all hope of sanity, for what is more.

And what is more is islands: sea, and unimaginably solid islands, and sea, and a hundred rolling skies. You spill your breath. Nothing holds; the whole show rolls. I can imagine Virginias no less than Pacifics. Inland valley, pool, desert, plain—it's all a falling sheaf of edges, like a quick-flapped deck of cards, like a dory or a day launched all unchristened, lost at sea. Land is a poured thing and time a surface film lapping and fringeing at fastness, at a hundred hollow and receding blues. Breathe fast: we're backing off the rim.

Here is the fringey edge where elements meet and realms mingle, where time and eternity spatter each other with foam. The salt sea and the islands, molding and molding, row upon rolling row, don't quit; nor do winds end nor skies cease from spreading in curves. The actual percentage of landmass to sea in the Sound equals that of the rest of the planet: we have less time than we knew. Time is eternity's pale interlinear, as the islands are the sea's. We have less time than we knew and that time buoyant, and cloven, lucent, and missile, and wild.

The room where I live is plain as a skull, a firm setting for windows. A nun lives in the fires of the spirit, a thinker lives in the bright wick of the mind, an artist lives jammed in the pool of materials. (Or, a nun lives, thoughtful and tough, in the mind, a nun lives, with that special poignancy peculiar to religious, in the exile of materials; and a thinker, who would think of something, lives in the clash of materials, and in the world of spirit where all long thoughts must lead; and an artist lives in the mind, that warehouse of forms, and an artist lives, of course, in the spirit. So.) But this room is a skull, a fire tower, wooden, and empty. Of itself it is nothing, but the view, as they say, is good.

Since I live in one room, one long wall of which is glass, I am myself, at everything I do, a backdrop to all the landscape's occasions, to all its weathers, colors, and lights. From the kitchen sink, and from my bed, and from the table, the couch, the hearth, and the desk, I see land and water, islands, sky.

The land is complex and shifting: the eye leaves it. There is a white Congregationalist church among Douglas firs; there is a green pasture between two yellow fallow fields; there are sheep bent over beneath some alders, and beside them a yard of running brown hens. But everything in the landscape points to sea. The land's progress of colors leads the eye up a distant hill, a sweeping big farm of a hill whose yellow pastures bounce light all day from a billion stems and blades; and down the hill's rim drops a dark slope of fir forest, a slant your eye rides down to the point, the dark sliver of land that holds the bay. From this angle you see the bay cut a crescent; your eye flies up the black beach to the point, or slides down the green firs to the point, and the point is an arrow pointing over and over, with its log-strewn beach, its gray singleness, and its recurved white edging of foam, to sea: to the bright sound, the bluing of water with distance at the world's rim, and on it the far blue islands, and over these lights the light clouds.

You can't picture it, can you? Neither can I. Oh, the desk is yellow, the oak table round, the ferns alive, the mirror cold, and I never have cared. I read. In the Middle Ages, I read, "the idea of a thing which a man framed for himself was always more real to him than the actual thing itself." Of course. I am in my Middle Ages; the world at my feet, the world through the window, is an illuminated manuscript whose leaves the wind takes, one by one, whose painted illuminations and halting words draw me, one by one, and I am dazzled in days and lost.

There is, in short, one country, one room, one enormous window, one cat, one spider, and one person: but I am hollow. And, for now, there are the many gods of mornings and the many things to give them for their work—lungs and heart, muscle, nerve, and bone—and there is the no-man's-land of many things wherein they dwell, and from which I seek to call them, in work that's mine.

Nothing is going to happen in this book. There is only a little violence here and there in the language, at the corner where eternity clips time.

Day One

Every day is a god, each day is a god, and holiness holds forth in time. I worship each god, I praise each day splintered down, splintered down and wrapped in time like a husk, a husk of many colors spreading, at dawn fast over the mountains split.

I wake in a god. I wake in arms holding my quilt, holding me as best they can inside my quilt.

Someone is kissing me—already. I wake, I cry "Oh," I rise from the pillow. Why should I open my eyes?

I open my eyes. The god lifts from the water. His head fills the bay. He is Puget Sound, the Pacific; his breast rises from pastures; his fingers are firs; islands slide wet down his shoulders. Islands slip blue from his shoulders and glide over the water, the empty, lighted water like a stage.

Today's god rises, his long eyes flecked in clouds. He flings his arms, spreading colors; he arches, cupping sky in his belly; he vaults, vaulting and spread, holding all and spread on me like skin.

Under the quilt in my knees' crook is a cat. She wakes; she curls to bite her metal sutures. The day is real; already, I can feel it click, hear it clicking under my knees.

The day is real; the sky clicks securely in place over the mountains, locks round the islands, snaps slap on the bay. Air fits flush on farm roofs; it rises inside the doors of barns and rubs at yellow barn windows. Air clicks up my hand cloven into fingers and wells in my ears' holes, whole and entire. I call it simplicity, the way matter is smooth and alone.

I toss the cat. I stand and smooth the quilt. "Oh," I cry, "Oh!"

I read. Armenians, I read, salt their newborn babies. I check somewhere else: so did the Jews at the time of the prophets. They washed a baby in water, salted him, and wrapped him in cloths. When God promised to Aaron and all the Levites all the offerings Israel made to God, the first fruits and the firstling livestock, "all the best of the oil, and all the best of the wine," he said of this promise, "It is a covenant of salt forever." In the Roman Church baptism, the priest places salt in the infant's mouth.

I salt my breakfast eggs. All day long I feel created. I can see the blown dust on the skin on the back of my hand, the tiny trapezoids of chipped clay, moistened and breathed alive. There are some created sheep in the pasture below me, sheep set down here precisely, just touching their blue shadows hoof to hoof on the grass. Created gulls pock the air, rip great curved seams in the settled air: I greet my created meal, amazed.

I have been drawing a key to the islands I see from my window. Everyone told me a different set of names for them, until one day a sailor came and named them all with such authority that I believed him. So I penciled an outline of the horizon on a sheet of paper and labeled the lobes: Skipjack, Sucia, Saturna, Salt Spring, Bare Island. . . .

Today, November 18 and no wind, today a veil of air has lifted that I didn't know was there. I see a new island, a new wrinkle, the deepening of wonder, behind the blue translucence the sailor said is Salt Spring Island. I have no way of learning its name. I bring the labeled map to the table and pencil a new line. Call that: Unknown Island North; Water-Statue; Sky-Ruck; Newborn and Salted; Waiting for Sailor.

Henry Miller relates that Knut Hamsun[3] once said, in response to a questionnaire, that he wrote to kill time. This is funny in a number of ways. In a number of ways I kill myself laughing, looking out at islands. Startled, the yellow cat on the floor stares over her shoulder. She has carried in a wren, I suddenly see, a wren she has killed, whose dead wings points askew on the circular rug. It is time. Out with you both. I'm busy laughing, to kill time. I shoo the cat from the door, turn the wren over in my palm, and drop him from the porch, down to the winter-killed hair grass and sedge, where the cat may find him if she will, or crows, or beetles, or rain.

When I next look up from my coffee, there is a ruckus on the porch. The cat has dragged in a god, scorched. He is alive. I run outside. Save for his wings, he is a perfect, very small man. He is fair, thin-skinned in the cat's mouth, and kicking. His hair is on fire and stinks; his wingtips are blackened and seared. From the two soft flaps of the cat's tiger muzzle his body jerks, naked. One of his miniature hands pushes hard at her nose. He waves his thighs; he beats her face and the air with his smoking wings. I cannot breathe. I run at the cat to scare her; she drops him, casting at me an evil look, and runs from the porch.

The god lies gasping and perfect. He is no longer than my face. Quickly I snuff the smoldering fire in his yellow hair with a finger and thumb. In so doing I accidently touch his skull, brush against his hot skull, which is the size of a hazelnut, as the saying goes, warm-skinned and alive.

He rolls his colorless eyes toward mine: his long wings catch strength from the sun, and heave.

Later I am walking in the day's last light. The god rides barefoot on my shoulder, or astride it, or tugging or swinging on loops of my hair.

He is whistling at my ear; he is blowing a huge tune in my ear, a myth

---

3. Norwegian novelist (1859–1952), noted for his exploration of mystical forces in the human psyche. Miller (1891–1980), American novelist, noted for his frank treatment of sexual themes.

about November. He is heaping a hot hurricane into my ear, into my hair, an ignorant ditty calling things real, calling islands out of the sea, calling solid moss from curling rock, and ducks down the sky for the winter.

I see it! I see it all! Two islands, twelve islands, worlds, gather substance, gather the blue contours of time, and array themselves down distance, mute and hard.

I seem to see a road; I seem to be on a road, walking. I seem to walk on a blacktop road that runs over a hill. The hill creates itself, a powerful suggestion. It creates itself, thickening with apparently solid earth and waving plants, with houses and browsing cattle, unrolling wherever my eyes go, as though my focus were a brush painting in a world. I cannot escape the illusion. The colorful thought persists, this world, a dream forced into my ear and sent round my body on ropes of hot blood. If I throw my eyes past the rim of the hill to see the real—stars, where are they? something with wings, or loops?—I elaborate the illusion instead; I rough in a middle ground. I stitch the transparent curtain solid with bright phantom mountains, with thick clouds gliding just so over their shadows on green water, with blank, impenetrable sky. The dream fills in, like wind widening over a bay. Quickly I look to the flat dream's rim for a glimpse of that old deep . . . and, just as quickly, the blue slaps shut, the colors wrap everything out. There is not a chink. The sky is gagging on trees. I seem to be on a road, walking, greeting the hedgerows, the rose hips, apples, and thorn. I seem to be on a road walking, familiar with neighbors, high-handed with cattle, smelling the sea, and alone. Already, I know the names of things. I can kick a stone.

Time is enough, more than enough, and matter multiple and given. The god of today is a child, a baby new and filling the house, remarkably here in the flesh. He is day. He thrives in a cup of wind, landlocked and thrashing. He unrolls, revealing his shape an edge at a time, a smatter of content, footfirst: a word, a friend for coffee, a windshift, the shingling or coincidence of ideas. Today, November 18 and no wind, is clear. Terry Wean—who fishes, and takes my poetry course—could see Mount Rainier. He hauls his reef net gear from the bay; we talk on its deck while he hammers at shrunken knots. The Moores for dinner. In bed, I call to me my sad cat, I read.

The god of today is rampant and drenched. His arms spread, bearing moist pastures; his fingers spread, fingering the shore. He is time's live skin; he burgeons up from day like any tree. His legs spread crossing the heavens, flicking hugely, and flashing and arcing around the earth toward night.

This is the one world, bound to itself and exultant. It fizzes up in trees, trees heaving up streams of salt to their leaves. This is the one air, bitten by grackles; time is alone and in and out of mind. The god of today is a boy, pagan and fernfoot. His power is enthusiasm; his innocence is mystery. He sockets into everything that is, and that right holy. Loud as music, filling the grasses and skies, his day spreads rising at home in the hundred senses. He rises, new and surrounding; he *is* everything that is, wholly here and emptied—flung, and flowing, sowing, unseen, and flown.

Day Two

Into this world falls a plane.

The earth is a mineral speckle planted in trees. The plane snagged its wing on a tree, fluttered in a tiny arc, and struggled down.

I heard it go. The cat looked up. There was no reason: the plane's engine simply stalled after takeoff, and the light plane failed to clear the firs. It fell easily; one wing snagged on a fir top; the metal fell down through the air and smashed in the thin woods where cattle browse; the fuel exploded; and Julie Norwich seven years old burned off her face.

Little Julie mute in some room at Saint Joe's now, drugs dissolving into the sheets. Little Julie with her eyes naked and spherical, baffled. Can you scream without lips? Yes. But do children in long pain scream?

It is November 19 and no wind, and no hope of heaven, and no wish for heaven, since the meanest of people show more mercy than hounding and terrorist gods.

The airstrip, a cleared washboard affair on the flat crest of a low hill, is a few long fields distant from my house—up the road and through the woods, or across the sheep pasture and through the woods. A flight instructor told me once that when his students get cocky, when they think they know how to fly a plane, he takes them out here and makes them land on that field. You go over the wires and down, and along the strip and up before the trees, or vice versa, vice versa, depending on the wind. But the airstrip is not unsafe. Jesse's engine failed. The FAA[4] will cart the wreckage away, bit by bit, picking it out of the tree trunk, and try to discover just why that engine failed. In the meantime, the emergency siren has sounded, causing everyone who didn't see the plane go down to halt—Patty at her weaving, Jonathan slicing apples, Jan washing her baby's face—to halt, in pity and terror, wondering which among us got hit, by what bad accident, and why. The volunteer firemen have mustered; the fire trucks have come—stampeding Shuller's sheep—and gone, bearing burned Julie and Jesse her father to the emergency room in town, leaving the rest of us to gossip, fight grass fires on the airstrip, and pray, or wander from window to window, fierce.

So she is burned on her face and neck, Julie Norwich. The one whose teeth are short in a row, Jesse and Ann's oldest, red-kneed, green-socked, carrying cats.

I saw her only once. It was two weeks ago, under an English hawthorn tree, at the farm.

There are many farms in this neck of the woods, but only one we call "the farm"—the old Corcoran place, where Gus grows hay and raises calves: the farm, whose abandoned frame chicken coops ply the fields like longboats, like floating war canoes; whose clay driveway and grass footpaths are a tangle of orange calendula blossoms, ropes, equipment, and seeding grasses; the farm, whose canny heifers and bull calves figure the fences, run amok to the garden, and plant themselves suddenly black and white, up to their necks in green peas.

4. Federal Aviation Administration.

Between the gray farmhouse and the barn is the green grass farmyard, suitable for all projects. That day, sixteen of us were making cider. It was cold. There were piles of apples everywhere. We had filled our trucks that morning, climbing trees and shaking their boughs, dragging tarps heavy with apples, hauling bushels and boxes and buckets of apples, and loading them all back to the farm. Jesse and Ann, who are in their thirties, with Julie and the baby, whose name I forget, had driven down from the mountains that morning with a truckload of apples, loose, to make cider with us, fill their jugs, and drive back. I had not met them before. We all drank coffee on the farmhouse porch to warm us; we hosed jugs in the yard. Now we were throwing apples into a shredder and wringing the mash through pillowcases, staining our palms and freezing our fingers, and decanting the pails into seventy one-gallon jugs. And all this long day, Julie Norwich chased my cat, Small, around the farmyard and played with her, manhandled her, next to the porch under the hawthorn tree.

She was a thin child, pointy-chinned, yellow bangs and braids. She squinted, and when you looked at her she sometimes started laughing, as if you had surprised her at using some power she wasn't yet ready to show. I kept my eye on her, wondering if she was cold with her sweater unbuttoned and bony knees bare.

She would hum up a little noise for half-hour stretches. In the intervals, for maybe five minutes each, she was trying, very quietly, to learn to whistle. I think. Or she was practicing a certain concentrated face. But I think she was trying to learn to whistle, because sometimes she would squeak a little falsetto[5] note through an imitation whistle hole in her lips, as if that could fool anyone. And all day she was dressing and undressing the yellow cat, sticking it into a black dress, a black dress long and full as a nun's.

I was amazed at that dress. It must have been some sort of doll clothing she had dragged with her in the truck; I've never seen its kind before or since. A white collar bibbed the yoke of it like a guimpe. It had great black sleeves like wings. Julie scooped up the cat and rammed her into the cloth. I knew how she felt, exasperated, breaking her heart on a finger curl's width of skinny cat arm. I knew the many feelings she had sticking those furry arms through the sleeves. Small is not large: her limbs feel like bird bones strung in a sock. When Julie had the cat dressed in its curious habit, she would rock it like a baby doll. The cat blinked, upside down.

Once she whistled at it, or tried, blowing in its face; the cat poured from her arms and ran. It leapt across the driveway, lightfoot in its sleeves; its black dress pulled this way and that, dragging dust, bent up in back by its yellow tail. I was squeezing one end of a twisted pillowcase full of apple mash and looking over my shoulder. I watched the cat hurdle the driveway and vanish under the potting shed, cringing; I watched Julie dash after it without hesitation, seize it, hit its face, and drag it back to the tree, carrying it caught fast by either forepaw, so its body hung straight from its arms.

She saw me watching her and we exchanged a look, a very conscious and self-conscious look—because we look a bit alike and we both knew it; because she was still short and I grown; because I was stuck kneeling before

5. High-pitched sound expressed by constricting the throat.

the cider pail, looking at her sidewise over my shoulder; because she was carrying the cat so oddly, so that she had to walk with her long legs parted; because it was my cat, and she'd dressed it, and it looked like a nun; and because she knew I'd been watching her, and how fondly, all along. We were laughing.

We *looked* a bit alike. Her face is slaughtered now, and I don't remember mine. It is the best joke there is, that we are here, and fools—that we are sown into time like so much corn, that we are souls sprinkled at random like salt into time and dissolved here, spread into matter, connected by cells right down to our feet, and those feet likely to fell us over a tree root or jam us on a stone. The joke part is that we forget it. Give the mind two seconds alone, and it thinks it's Pythagoras.[6] We wake up a hundred times a day and laugh.

The joke of the world is less like a banana peel than a rake, the old rake in the grass, the one you step on, foot to forehead. It all comes together. In a twinkling. You have to admire the gag for its symmetry, accomplishing all with one right angle, the same right angle that accomplishes all philosophy. One step on the rake, and it's mind under matter once again. You wake up with a piece of tree in your skull. You wake up with fruit on your hands. You wake up in a clearing and see yourself, ashamed. You see your own face and it's seven years old and there's no knowing why, or where you've been since. We're tossed broadcast into time like so much grass, some ravening god's sweet hay. You wake up and a plane falls out of the sky.

That day was a god, too, the day we made cider and Julie played under the hawthorn tree. He must have been a heyday sort of god, a husbandman. He was spread under gardens, sleeping in time, an innocent old man scratching his head, thinking of pruning the orchard, in love with families.

Has he no power? Can the other gods carry time and its loves upside down like a doll in their blundering arms? As though we the people were playing house—when we are serious and do love—and not the gods? No, that day's god has no power. No gods have power to save. There are only days. The one great god abandoned us to days, to time's tumult of occasions, abandoned us to the gods of days, each brute and amok in his hugeness and idiocy.

Jesse, her father, had grabbed her clear of the plane this morning, and was hauling her off when the fuel blew. A gob of flung ignited vapor hit her face, or something flaming from the plane or fir tree hit her face. No one else was burned, or hurt in any way.

So this is where we are. Ashes, ashes, all fall down. How could I have forgotten? Didn't I see the heavens wiped shut just yesterday, on the road walking? Didn't I fall from the dark of the stars to these senselit and noisome days? The great ridged granite millstone of time is illusion, for only the good is real; the great ridged granite millstone of space is illusion, for God is spirit and worlds his flimsiest dreams: but the illusions are almost perfect, are apparently perfect for generations on end, and the pain is also, and undeniably, real. The pain within the millstones' pitiless turning is real, for our love for each other—for world and all the products of extension—is real, vaulting, insofar as it is love, beyond the plane of the stones' sickening churn

6. Greek philosopher and mathematician (6th century B.C.E.).

and arcing to the realm of spirit bare. And you can get caught holding one end of a love, when your father drops, and your mother; when a land is lost, or a time, and your friend blotted out, gone, your brother's body spoiled, and cold, your infant dead, and you dying: you reel out love's long line alone, stripped like a live wire loosing its sparks to a cloud, like a live wire loosed in space to longing and grief everlasting.

I sit at the window. It is a fool's lot, this sitting always at windows spoiling little blowy slips of paper and myself in the process. Shall I be old? Here comes Small, old sparrow-mouth, wanting my lap. Done. Do you have any earthly idea how young I am? Where's your dress, kitty? I suppose I'll outlive this wretched cat. Get another. Leave it my silver spoons, like old ladies you hear about. I prefer dogs.

So I read. Angels, I read, belong to nine different orders. Seraphs are the highest; they are aflame with love for God, and stand closer to him than the others. Seraphs love God; cherubs, who are second, possess perfect knowledge of him. So love is greater than knowledge; how could I have forgotten? The seraphs are born of a stream of fire issuing from under God's throne. They are, according to Dionysius[7] the Areopagite, "all wings," having, as Isaiah noted, six wings apiece, two of which they fold over their eyes. Moving perpetually toward God, they perpetually praise him, crying Holy, Holy, Holy. . . . But, according to some rabbinic writings, they can sing only the first "Holy" before the intensity of their love ignites them again and dissolves them again, perpetually, into flames. "Abandon everything," Dionysius told his disciple. "God despises ideas."

God despises everything, apparently. If he abandoned us, slashing creation loose at its base from any roots in the real; and if we in turn abandon everything—all these illusions of time and space and lives—in order to love only the real: then where are we? Thought itself is impossible, for subject can have no guaranteed connection with object, nor any object with God. Knowledge is impossible. We are precisely nowhere, sinking on an entirely imaginary ice floe, into entirely imaginary seas themselves adrift. Then we reel out love's long line alone toward a God less lovable than a grasshead, who treats us less well than we treat our lawns.

Of faith I have nothing, only of truth: that this one God is a brute and traitor, abandoning us to time, to necessity and the engines of matter unhinged. This is no leap; this is evidence of things seen: one Julie, one sorrow, one sensation bewildering the heart, and enraging the mind, and causing me to look at the world stuff appalled, at the blithering rock of trees in a random wind, at my hand like some gibberish sprouted, my fist opening and closing, so that I think: Have I once turned my hand in this circus, have I ever called it home?

Faith would be that God is self-limited utterly by his creation—a contraction of the scope of his will; that he bound himself to time and its hazards and haps as a man would lash himself to a tree for love. That God's works are as good as we make them. That God is helpless, our baby to bear, self-abandoned on the doorstep of time, wondered at by cattle and oxen. Faith would be that God moved and moves once and for all and "down," so to speak, like a diver, like a man who eternally gathers himself for a dive and

---

7. Roman monk and Christian theologian (6th century B.C.E.).

eternally is diving, and eternally splitting the spread of the water, and eternally drowned.

Faith would be, in short, that God has any willful connection with time whatsoever, and with us. For I know it as given that God is all good. And I take it also as given that whatever he touches has meaning, if only in his mysterious terms, the which I readily grant. The question is, then, whether God touches anything. Is anything firm, or is time on the loose? Did Christ descend once and for all to no purpose, in a kind of divine and kenotic suicide, or ascend once and for all, pulling his cross up after him like a rope ladder home? Is there—even if Christ holds the tip of things fast and stretches eternity clear to the dim souls of men—is there no link at the base of things, some kernel or air deep in the matrix of matter from which universe furls like a ribbon twined into time?

Has God a hand in this? Then it is a good hand. But has he a hand at all? Or is he a holy fire burning self-contained for power's sake alone? Then he knows himself blissfully as flame unconsuming, as all brilliance and beauty and power, and the rest of us can go hang. Then the accidental universe spins mute, obedient only to its own gross terms, meaningless, out of mind, and alone. The universe is neither contingent upon nor participant in the holy, in being itself, the real, the power play of fire. The universe is illusion merely, not one speck of it real, and we are not only its victims, falling always into or smashed by a planet slung by its sun, but also its captives, bound by the mineral-made ropes of our senses.

But how do we know—how could we know—that the real is there? By what freak chance does the skin of illusion ever split, and reveal to us the real, which seems to know us by name, and by what freak chance and why did the capacity to prehend it evolve?

I sit at the window, chewing the bones in my wrist. Pray for them: for Julie, for Jesse her father, for Ann her mother, pray. Who will teach us to pray? The god of today is a glacier. We live in his shifting crevasses, unheard. The god of today is delinquent, a barn-burner, a punk with a pittance of power in a match. It is late, a late time to be living. Now it is afternoon; the sky is appallingly clear. Everything in the landscape points to sea, and the sea is nothing; it is snipped from the real as a stuff without form, rising up the sides of islands and falling, mineral to mineral, salt.

Everything I see—the water, the log-wrecked beach, the farm on the hill, the bluff, the white church in the trees—looks overly distinct and shining. (What is the relationship of color to this sun, of sun to anything else?) It all looks staged. It all looks brittle and unreal, a skin of colors painted on glass, which if you prodded it with a finger would powder and fall. A blank sky, perfectly blended with all other sky, has sealed over the crack in the world where the plane fell, and the air has hushed the matter up.

If days are gods, then gods are dead, and artists pyrotechnic fools. Time is a hurdy-gurdy, a lampoon, and death's a bawd. We're beheaded by the nick of time. We're logrolling on a falling world, on time released from meaning and rolling loose, like one of Atalanta's[8] golden apples, a bauble flung and forgotten, lapsed, and the gods on the lam.

8. In Greek mythology, she offered to marry any man able to outrace her; her eventual husband distracted her by dropping three golden apples.

And now outside the window, deep on the horizon, a new thing appears, as if we needed a new thing. It is a new land blue beyond islands, hitherto hidden by haze and now revealed, and as dumb as the rest. I check my chart, my amateur penciled sketch of the skyline. Yes, this land is new, this spread blue spark beyond yesterday's new wrinkled line, beyond the blue veil a sailor said was Salt Spring Island. How long can this go on? But let us by all means extend the scope of our charts.

I draw it as I seem to see it, a blue chunk fitted just so beyond islands, a wag of graphite rising just here above another anonymous line, and here meeting the slope of Salt Spring: though whether this be headland I see or heartland, or the distance-blurred bluffs of a hundred bays, I have no way of knowing, or if it be island or main. I call it Thule, O Julialand, Time's Bad News; I name it Terror, the Farthest Limb of the Day, God's Tooth.

Day Three

I know only enough of God to want to worship him, by any means ready to hand. There is an anomalous specificity to all our experience in space, a scandal of particularity, by which God burgeons up or showers down into the shabbiest of occasions, and leaves his creation's dealings with him in the hands of purblind and clumsy amateurs. This is all we are and all we ever were; God *kann nicht anders.*[9] This process in time is history; in space, at such shocking random, it is mystery.

A blur of romance clings to notions of "publicans," "sinners," "the poor," "the people in the marketplace," "our neighbors," as though of course God should reveal himself, if at all, to these simple people, these Sunday school watercolor figures, who are so purely themselves in their tattered robes, who are single in themselves, while we now are various, complex, and full at heart. We are busy. So, I see now, were they. Who shall ascend into the hill of the Lord? or who shall stand in his holy place? There is no one but us. There is no one to send, nor a clean hand, nor a pure heart on the face of the earth, nor in the earth, but only us, a generation comforting ourselves with the notion that we have come at an awkward time, that our innocent fathers are all dead—as if innocence had ever been—and our children busy and troubled, and we ourselves unfit, not yet ready, having each of us chosen wrongly, made a false start, failed, yielded to impulse and the tangled comfort of pleasures, and grown exhausted, unable to seek the thread, weak, and involved. But there is no one but us. There never has been. There have been generations which remembered, and generations which forgot; there has never been a generation of whole men and women who lived well for even one day. Yet some have imagined well, with honesty and art, the detail of such a life, and have described it with such grace, that we mistake vision for history, dream for description, and fancy that life has devolved. So. You learn this studying any history at all, especially the lives of artists and visionaries; you learn it from Emerson,[1] who noticed that the meanness of our days is itself worth our thought; and you learn it, fitful in your pew, at church.

9. Cannot do otherwise (German).
1. Ralph Waldo Emerson (1803–1882), American essayist, philosopher, and poet.

There is one church here, so I go to it. On Sunday mornings I quit the house and wander down the hill to the white frame church in the firs. On a big Sunday there might be twenty of us there; often I am the only person under sixty, and feel as though I'm on an archaeological tour of Soviet Russia. The members are of mixed denominations; the minister is a Congregationalist, and wears a white shirt. The man knows God. Once, in the middle of the long pastoral prayer of intercession for the whole world—for the gift of wisdom to its leaders, for hope and mercy to the grieving and pained, succor to the oppressed, and God's grace to all—in the middle of this he stopped, and burst out, "Lord, we bring you these same petitions every week." After a shocked pause, he continued reading the prayer. Because of this, I like him very much. "Good morning!" he says after the first hymn and invocation, startling me witless every time, and we all shout back, "Good morning!"

The churchwomen all bring flowers for the altar; they haul in arrangements as big as hedges, of wayside herbs in season, and flowers from their gardens, huge bunches of foliage and blossoms as tall as I am, in vases the size of tubs, and the altar still looks empty, irredeemably linoleum, and beige. We had a wretched singer once, a guest from a Canadian congregation, a hulking blond girl with chopped hair and big shoulders, who wore tinted spectacles and a long lacy dress, and sang, grinning, to faltering accompaniment, an entirely secular song about mountains. Nothing could have been more apparent than that God loved this girl; nothing could more surely convince me of God's unending mercy than the continued existence on earth of the church.

The higher Christian churches—where, if anywhere, I belong—come at God with an unwarranted air of professionalism, with authority and pomp, as though they knew what they were doing, as though people in themselves were an appropriate set of creatures to have dealings with God. I often think of the set pieces of liturgy as certain words that people have successfully addressed to God without their getting killed. In the high churches they saunter through the liturgy like Mohawks along a strand of scaffolding who have long since forgotten their danger. If God were to blast such a service to bits, the congregation would be, I believe, genuinely shocked. But in the low churches you expect it any minute. This is the beginning of wisdom.

Today is Friday, November 20. Julie Norwich is in the hospital, burned; we can get no word of her condition. People released from burn wards, I read once, have a very high suicide rate. They had not realized, before they were burned, that life could include such suffering, nor that they personally could be permitted such pain. No drugs ease the pain of third-degree burns, because burns destroy skin: the drugs simply leak into the sheets. His disciples asked Christ about a roadside beggar who had been blind from birth, "Who did sin, this man or his parents, that he was born blind?" And Christ, who spat on the ground, made a mud of spittle and clay, plastered the mud over the man's eyes, and gave him sight, answered, "Neither hath this man sinned, nor his parents: but that the works of God should be made manifest in him." Really? If we take this answer to refer to the affliction itself—and not the subsequent cure—as "God's works made manifest," then we have, along with "Not as the world gives do I give unto you," two meager, baffling, and infuriating answers to one of the few questions worth asking, to wit, What in the Sam Hill is going on here?

The works of God made manifest? Do we really need more victims to remind us that we're all victims? Is this some sort of parade for which a conquering army shines up its terrible guns and rolls them down the streets for the people to see? Do we need blind men stumbling about, and little flamefaced children, to remind us what God can—and will—do?

I am drinking boiled coffee and watching the bay from the window. Almost all of the people who reef net have hauled their gear for the winter; the salmon runs are over, days are short. Still, boats come and go on the water—tankers, tugs and barges, rowboats and sails. There are killer whales if you're lucky, rafts of harlequin ducks if you're lucky, and every day the scoter and the solitary grebes. How many tons of sky can I see from the window? It is morning: morning! and the water clobbered with light. Yes, in fact, we do. We do need reminding, not of what God can do, but of what he cannot do, or will not, which is to catch time in its free fall and stick a nickel's worth of sense into our days. And we need reminding of what time can do, must only do: churn out enormities at random and beat them, with God's blessing, into our heads—that we are created, *created*, sojourners in a land we did not make, a land with no meaning of itself and no meaning we can make for it alone. Who are we to demand explanations of God? (And what monsters of perfection should we be if we did not?) We forget ourselves, picnicking; we forget where we are. There is no such thing as a freak accident. "God is at home," says Meister Eckhart,[2] "We are in the far country."

We are most deeply asleep at the switch when we fancy we control any switches at all. We sleep to time's hurdy-gurdy; we wake, if we ever wake, to the silence of God. And then, when we wake to the deep shores of light uncreated, then when the dazzling dark breaks over the far slopes of time, then it's time to toss things, like our reason, and our will; then it's time to break our necks for home.

There are no events but thoughts and the heart's hard turning, the heart's slow learning where to love and whom. The rest is merely gossip, and tales for other times. The god of today is a tree. He is a forest of trees or a desert, or a wedge from wideness down to a scatter of stars, stars like salt, low and dumb and abiding. Today's god said: shed. He peels from eternity always, spread; he winds into time like a rind. I am or seem to be on a road, walking. The hedges are just where they were. There is a corner, and a long hill, a glimpse of snow on the mountains, a slope planted in apple trees, and a store next to a pasture, where I am going to buy the communion wine.

How can I buy the communion wine? Who am I to buy the communion wine? Someone has to buy the communion wine. Having wine instead of grape juice was my idea, and of course I offered to buy it. Shouldn't I be wearing robes and, especially, a mask? Shouldn't I *make* the communion wine? Are there holy grapes, is there holy ground, is anything here holy? There are no holy grapes, there is no holy ground, nor is there anyone but us. I have an empty knapsack over my parka's shoulders; it is cold, and I'll

2. Johannes Eckhart (1260–1327), German theologian and mystic.

want my hands in my pockets. According to the Rule of St. Benedict,[3] I should say, Our hands in our pockets. "All things come of thee, O Lord, and of thine own have we given thee." There must be a rule for the purchase of communion wine. "Will that be cash, or charge?" All I know is that when I go to this store—to buy eggs, or sandpaper, broccoli, wood screws, milk—I like to tease a bit, if he'll let me, with the owners' son, two, whose name happens to be Chandler, and who himself likes to play in the big bins of nails.

And so, forgetting myself, thank God: Hullo. Hullo, short and relatively new. Welcome again to the land of the living, to time, this hill of beans. Chandler will have, as usual, none of it. He keeps his mysterious counsel. And I'm out on the road again, walking, my right hand forgetting my left. I'm out on the road again, walking, and toting a backload of God.

Here is a bottle of wine with a label, Christ with a cork. I bear holiness splintered into a vessel, very God of very God, the sempiternal silence personal and brooding, bright on the back of my ribs. I start up the hill.

The world is changing. The landscape begins to respond as a current upwells. It is starting to clack with itself, though nothing moves in space and there's no wind. It is starting to utter its infinite particulars, each overlapping and lone, like a hundred hills of hounds all giving tongue. The hedgerows are blackberry brambles, white snowberries, red rose hips, gaunt and clattering broom. Their leafless stems are starting to live visibly deep in their centers, as hidden as banked fires live, and as clearly as recognition, mute, shines forth from eyes. Above me the mountains are raw nerves, sensible and exultant; the trees, the grass, and the asphalt below me are living petals of mind, each sharp and invisible, held in a greeting or glance full perfectly formed. There is something stretched or jostling about the sky, which, when I study it, vanishes. Why are there all these apples in the world, and why so wet and transparent? Through all my clothing, through the pack on my back and through the bottle's glass, I feel the wine. Walking faster and faster, weightless, I feel the wine. It sheds light in slats through my rib cage, and fills the buttressed vaults of my ribs with light pooled and buoyant.

Each thing in the world is translucent, even the cattle, and moving, cell by cell. I remember this reality. Where has it been? I sail to the crest of the hill as if blown up the slope of a swell. I see, blasted, the bay transfigured below me, the saltwater bay, far down the hill past the road to my house, past the firs and the church and the sheep in the pasture: the bay and the islands on fire and boundless beyond it, catching alight the unraveling sky. Pieces of the sky are falling down. Everything, everything, is whole, and a parcel of everything else. I myself am falling down, slowly, or slowly lifting up. On the bay's stone shore are people among whom I float, real people, gathering of an afternoon, in the cells of whose skin stream thin colored waters in pieces, which give back the general flame.

Christ is being baptized. The one who is Christ is there, and the one who is John, and the dim other people standing on cobbles or sitting on beach logs back from the bay. These are ordinary people—if I am one now, if those are ordinary sheep singing a song in the pasture.

---

3. Italian monk (480–547) who founded the Benedictine order and its model monastic rule.

The two men are bare to the waist. The one walks him into the water, and holds him under. His hand is on his neck. Christ is coiled and white under the water, standing on stones.

He lifts from the water. Water beads on his shoulders. I see the water in balls as heavy as planets, a billion beads of water as weighty as worlds, and he lifts them up on his back as he rises. He stands wet in the water. Each one bead is transparent, and each has a world, or the same world, light and alive and apparent inside the drop: it is all there ever could be, moving at once, past and future, and all the people. I can look into any sphere and see people stream past me, and cool my eyes with colors and the sight of the world in spectacle perishing ever, and ever renewed. I do; I deepen into a drop and see all that time contains, all the faces and deeps of the worlds and all the earth's contents, every landscape and room, everything living or made or fashioned, all past and future stars, and especially faces, faces like the cells of everything, faces pouring past me talking, and going, and gone. And I am gone.

For outside it is bright. The surface of things outside the drops has fused. Christ himself and the others, and the brown warm wind, and hair, sky, the beach, the shattered water—all this has fused. It is the one glare of holiness; it is bare and unspeakable. There is no speech nor language; there is nothing, no one thing, nor motion, nor time. There is only this everything. There is only this everything. There is only this, and its bright and multiple noise.

I seem to be on a road, standing still. It is the top of the hill. The hedges are here, subsiding. My hands are in my pockets. There is a bottle of wine on my back, a California red. I see my feet. I move down the hill toward home.

You must rest now. I cannot rest you. For me there is, I am trying to tell you, no time.

There are a thousand new islands today, uncharted. They are salt stones on fire and dimming; I read by their light. Small the cat lies on my neck. In the bathroom the spider is working on yesterday's moth.

Esoteric Christianity, I read, posits a substance. It is a created substance, lower than metals and minerals on a "spiritual scale," and lower than salts and earths, occurring beneath salts and earths in the waxy deepness of planets, but never on the surface of planets where men could discern it; and it is in touch with the Absolute, at base. In touch with the Absolute! At base. The name of this substance is: Holy the Firm.

Holy the Firm: and is Holy the Firm in touch with metals and minerals? With salts and earths? Of course, and straight on up, till "up" ends by curving back. Does something that touched something that touched Holy the Firm in touch with the Absolute at base seep into groundwater, into grain; are islands rooted in it, and trees? Of course.

Scholarship has long distinguished between two strains of thought that proceed in the West from human knowledge of God. In one, the ascetic's metaphysic, the world is far from God. Emanating from God, and linked to him by Christ, the world is yet infinitely other than God, furled away from him like the end of a long banner falling. This notion makes, to my mind, a vertical line of the world, a great chain of burning. The more accessible and universal view, held by Eckhart and by many peoples in various forms, is scarcely different from pantheism: that the world is immanation, that God is in the thing, and eternally present here, if nowhere else. By these lights the world is flattened on a horizontal plane, singular, all here, crammed with heaven, and alone. But I know that it is not alone, nor singular, nor all. The notion of immanence needs a handle, and the two ideas themselves need a link, so that life can mean aught to the one, and Christ to the other.

For to immanence, to the heart, Christ is redundant and all things are one. To emanance, to the mind, Christ touches only the top, skims off only the top, as it were, the souls of men, the wheat grains whole, and lets the chaff fall where? To the world flat and patently unredeemed; to the entire rest of the universe, which is irrelevant and nonparticipant; to time and matter unreal, and so unknowable, an illusory, absurd, accidental, and over-elaborate stage.

But if Holy the Firm is "underneath salts," if Holy the Firm is matter at its dullest, Aristotle's[4] *materia prima,* absolute zero, and since Holy the Firm is in touch with the Absolute at base, then the circle is unbroken. And it is. Thought advances, and the world creates itself, by the gradual positing of, and belief in, a series of bright ideas. Time and space are in touch with the Absolute at base. Eternity sockets twice into time and space curves, bound and bound by idea. Matter and spirit are of a piece but distinguishable; God has a stake guaranteed in all the world. And the universe is real and not a dream, not a manufacture of the senses; subject may know object, knowledge may proceed, and Holy the Firm is in short the philosopher's stone.

These are only ideas, by the single handful. Lines, lines and their infinite points! Hold hands and crack the whip, and yank the Absolute out of there and into the light, God pale and astounded, spraying a spiral of salts and earths, God footloose and flung. And cry down the line to his passing white ear, "Old Sir! Do you hold space from buckling by a finger in its hole? O Old! Where is your other hand?" His right hand is clenching calm, round the exploding left hand of Holy the Firm.

How can people think that artists seek a name? A name, like a face, is something you have when you're not alone. There is no such thing as an artist: there is only the world, lit or unlit as the light allows. When the candle is burning, who looks at the wick? When the candle is out, who needs it? But the world without light is wasteland and chaos, and a life without sac-rifice is abomination.

What can any artist set on fire but his world? What can any people bring to the altar but all it has ever owned in the third towns or over the desolate plains? What can an artist use but materials, such as they are? What can he light but the short string of his gut, and when that's burned out, any muck ready to hand?

His face is flame like a seraph's, lighting the kingdom of God for the people to see; his life goes up in the works; his feet are waxen and salt. He is holy

4. Greek philosopher (384–322 B.C.E.) whose belief in prime matter (*materia prima*) held that, as opposed to Plato's idealism, particular objects held basic significance instead of being mere shad-ows of a perfect form.

and he is firm, spanning all the long gap with the length of his love, in flawed imitation of Christ on the cross stretched both ways unbroken and thorned. So must the work be also, in touch with, in touch with, in touch with; spanning the gap, from here to eternity, home.

Hoopla! All that I see arches, and light arches around it. The air churns out forces and lashes the marveling land. A hundred times through the fields and along the deep roads I've cried Holy. I see a hundred insects moving across the air, rising and falling. Chipped notes of birdsong descend from the trees, tuneful and broken; the notes pile about me like leaves. Why do these molded clouds make themselves overhead innocently changing, trailing their flat blue shadows up and down everything, and passing, and gone? Ladies and gentlemen! You are given insects, and birdsong, and a replenishing series of clouds. The air is buoyant and wholly transparent, scoured by grasses. The earth stuck through it is noisome, lighted, and salt. Who shall ascend into the hill of the Lord? or who shall stand in his holy place? "Whom shall I send," heard the first Isaiah, "and who will go for us?" And poor Isaiah, who happened to be standing there—and there was no one else—burst out, "Here am I; send me."

There is Julie Norwich. Julie Norwich is salted with fire. She is preserved like a salted fillet from all evil, baptized at birth into time and now into eternity, into the bladelike arms of God. For who will love her now, without a face, when women with faces abound, and people are so? People are reasoned, while God is mad. They love only beauty; who knows what God loves? Happy birthday, little one and wise: you got there early, the easy way. The world knew you before you knew the world. The gods in their boyish, brutal games bore you like a torch, a firebrand, recklessly over the heavens, to the glance of the one God, fathomless and mild, dissolving you into the sheets.

You might as well be a nun. You might as well be God's chaste bride, chased by plunderers to the high caves of solitude, to the heartless rooms empty of voices, and of warm limbs hooking your heart to the world. Look how he loves you! Are you bandaged now, or loose in a sterilized room? Wait till they hand you a mirror, if you can hold one, and know what it means. That skinlessness, that black shroud of flesh in strips on your skull, is your veil. There are two kinds of nun, out of the cloister or in. You can serve or you can sing, and wreck your heart in prayer, working the world's hard work. Forget whistling: you have no lips for that, or for kissing the face of a man or a child. Learn Latin, and it please my Lord, learn the foolish downward look called Custody of the Eyes.

And learn power, however sweet they call you, learn power, the smash of the holy once more, and signed by its name. Be victim to abruptness and seizures, events intercalated, swellings of heart. You'll climb trees. You won't be able to sleep, or need to, for the joy of it. Mornings, when light spreads over the pastures like wings, and fans a secret color into everything, and beats the trees senseless with beauty, so that you can't tell whether the beauty is *in* the trees—dazzling in cells like yellow sparks or green flashing waters—or *on* them—a transfiguring silver air charged with the wings' invisible motion; mornings, you won't be able to walk for the power of it: earth's too round. And by long and waking day—Sext, None, Vespers—when the grasses, living or dead, drowse while the sun reels, or lash in any wind, when sparrows hush and tides slack at the ebb, or flood up the beaches and cliff-

sides tangled with weed, and hay waits, and elsewhere people buy shoes—
then you kneel, clattering with thoughts, ill, or some days erupting, some
days holding the altar rail, gripping the brass-bolt altar rail, so you won't fly.
Do you think I don't believe this? You have no idea, none. And nights? Nights
after Compline under the ribs of Orion, nights in rooms at lamps or windows
like moths? Nights you see Deneb, one-eyed over the trees; you vanish into
the sheets, shrunken, your eyes bright as candles and as sightless, exhausted.
Nights Murzim, Arcturus, Aldebaran in the Bull: You cry: My father, my
father, the chariots of Israel, and the horsemen thereof! Held, held fast by
love in the world like the moth in wax, your life a wick, your head on fire
with prayer, held utterly, outside and in, you sleep alone, if you call that
alone, you cry God.

Julie Norwich; I know. Surgeons will fix your face. This will all be a dream,
an anecdote, something to tell your husband one night: I was burned. Or if
you're scarred, you're scarred. People love the good not much less than the
beautiful, and the happy as well, or even just the living, for the world of it
all, and heart's home. You'll dress your own children, sticking their arms
through the sleeves. Mornings you'll whistle, full of the pleasure of days, and
afternoons this or that, and nights cry love. So live. I'll be the nun for you.
I am now.

1977   1994

ANN BEATTIE
b. 1947

The American 1960s, a highly publicized decade, was bound to produce a writer who
would be held responsible for chronicling the fortunes of its young people, as they
grew up, got married and divorced, worked at different jobs and went to the same
parties. There is some truth in the claim that Ann Beattie, who graduated from high
school in 1965, is that writer; indeed she has picked up some of the mythical reputation that adheres to the film *The Big Chill* as somehow "representative" in its representation of late-sixties idealism and conviction gone flat or sour. Yet to stress
Beattie's importance as portraitist of a generation may be to do her a disservice, since
she is above all else a writer, and one with an unrepresentative, even idiosyncratic,
style. Her stories and novels should not be taken merely as vehicles for displaying
social attitudes and manners, but as mannerist compositions that need to be not only
looked at but listened to. Her style is too pronounced, too carefully contrived, to be
treated as a transparent medium through which "reality" is given us directly.

On its surface her life has been relatively uneventful, from growing up in a middle-
class suburb of Washington, D.C. ("an artsy little thing . . . you know, painting pictures, writing," as she put it), taking her undergraduate degree at American University,
then going on to graduate study for a time at the University of Connecticut. She soon
began to send stories to *The New Yorker* (one of her collections is dedicated to Roger
Angell, of that magazine) and after the usual spate of rejections had one accepted,
then others. By the time she was in her mid-twenties she had become a publishing
writer in the most sought-after place, and in 1976 on the verge of her thirtieth birth-

day she brought out simultaneously a collection of her stories, *Distortions,* and her first novel, *Chilly Scenes of Winter.*

The stories—some of them more experimental in style than her more recent work—are about transient, usually unsatisfactory relationships between people, married and single, male and female. Their work provides them with little pleasure or fulfillment; almost anything threatens to become "just a job." What they do best, and incessantly, is talk to each other about themselves, how they feel about their lives. In fact such talk is the essential ingredient in her fiction. As one of her more severe critics, Joseph Epstein, has pointed out, what she strives for in her writing is not "development of character, accounts of motivation or moral resolution" but rather "states of feeling." In stories from her second collection, *Secrets and Surprises* (1978), such as "A Reasonable Man," "Lawn Party," and "Weekend," feelings are talked around, hinted at, never quite said, but are the only "thing" that happens in the story. In "Weekend" (printed here) the happening has a force that is cumulative and disturbing.

Like many fiction writers, Beattie acknowledges the influence of Hemingway ("I sound like someone talking in *The Sun Also Rises,*" says a character in "The Lawn Party"), but her kinship with him is especially strong in that each uses language, exchanges between characters, to suggest—by all that is left unsaid in the spare, often dull sentences, the platitudinous conversations—that something interesting lies behind the words, that conversation. Hemingway manages in his best stories to make us feel the presence of something powerful behind the conventional words. Beattie's characters, decades later, yearn for there to be something real or interesting behind their banal words, but the poignancy of her comedy—she is frequently a comic writer—lies in the hint that, as the characters themselves half guess, there may be nothing much behind them. Something important got lost, back there in the sixties.

Of her seven novels, the most ambitious is *Falling in Place* (1980), which spreads the usual urban and suburban anomie over the usual Beattie cast of dispirited seekers after a better day. But the book comes to life—a rather chilling, comic life—when it focuses on a fifteen-year-old girl named Mary (whose favorite characterizing response to things is "Suck-O") and her younger brother, John Joel, a compulsive eater who loves violent comics but little else in the world. This twosome, who could give the most obnoxious of Flannery O'Connor's fictional children a run for their money, is observed with satiric verve, and although as a whole the book doesn't add up very satisfactorily, it contains a number of brilliant parts. Beattie is essentially a writer of scenes rather than a contriver of extended sequences, just as the people she writes about can only deal with life—and that just barely—a moment at a time.

Like her contemporary the short-fiction writer Raymond Carver, Beattie has many imitators, "minimalists" who try to prove that less is more and most often make the attempt with less than maximum talents. In fact, like all distinctive stylists, she cannot be imitated, only travestied. Her sharp, idiomatic humor, often operating so quietly the reader almost misses it, is an insurance against airlessness in her fiction. Now that she has fully developed her distinctive style, the question is whether she can avoid further bureaucratizing of it—continuing efficiently to turn out the same product—and move instead in directions new and surprising to her readers.

The text is that printed in *Secrets and Surprises* (1978).

Weekend

On Saturday morning Lenore is up before the others. She carries her baby into the living room and puts him in George's favorite chair, which tilts because its back legs are missing, and covers him with a blanket. Then she lights a fire in the fireplace, putting fresh logs on a few embers that are still glowing from the night before. She sits down on the floor beside the chair and checks the baby, who has already gone back to sleep—a good thing, because there are guests in the house. George, the man she lives with, is very hospitable and impetuous; he extends invitations whenever old friends call, urging them to come spend the weekend. Most of the callers are his former students—he used to be an English professor—and when they come it seems to make things much worse. It makes *him* much worse, because he falls into smoking too much and drinking and not eating, and then his ulcer bothers him. When the guests leave, when the weekend is over, she has to cook bland food: applesauce, oatmeal, puddings. And his drinking does not taper off easily anymore; in the past he would stop cold when the guests left, but lately he only tapers down from Scotch to wine, and drinks wine well into the week—a lot of wine, perhaps a whole bottle with his meal—until his stomach is much worse. He is hard to live with. Once when a former student, a woman named Ruth, visited them—a lover, she suspected—she overheard George talking to her in his study, where he had taken her to see a photograph of their house before he began repairing it. George had told Ruth that she, Lenore, stayed with him because she was simple. It hurt her badly, made her actually dizzy with surprise and shame, and since then, no matter who the guests are, she never feels quite at ease on the weekends. In the past she enjoyed some of the things she and George did with their guests, but since overhearing what he said to Ruth she feels that all their visitors have been secretly told the same thing about her. To her, though, George is usually kind. But she is sure that is the reason he has not married her, and when he recently remarked on their daughter's intelligence (she is five years old, a girl named Maria) she found that she could no longer respond with simple pride; now she feels spite as well, feels that Maria exists as proof of her own good genes. She has begun to expect perfection of the child. She knows this is wrong, and she has tried hard not to communicate her anxiety to Maria, who is already, as her kindergarten teacher says, "untypical."

At first Lenore loved George because he was untypical, although after she had moved in with him and lived with him for a while she began to see that he was not exceptional but a variation on a type. She is proud of observing that, and she harbors the discovery—her silent response to his low opinion of her. She does not know why he found her attractive—in the beginning he did—because she does not resemble the pretty, articulate young women he likes to invite, with their lovers or girl friends, to their house for the weekend. None of these young women have husbands; when they bring a man with them at all they bring a lover, and they seem happy not to be married. Lenore, too, is happy to be single—not out of conviction that marriage is wrong but because she knows that it would be wrong to be married to George if he thinks she is simple. She thought at first to confront him with what she had overheard, to demand an explanation. But he can weasel out of any corner. At best, she can mildly fluster him, and later he will only blame it on Scotch. Of course she might ask why he has all these women come to visit, why he devotes so little time to her or the children. To that he would say that it was the quality of the time they spent together that mattered, not the quantity. He has already said that, in fact, without being asked. He says things over and over so that she will accept them as truths. And eventually she does. She does not like to think long and hard, and when there is an answer—

even his answer—it is usually easier to accept it and go on with things. She goes on with what she has always done: tending the house and the children and George, when he needs her. She likes to bake and she collects art postcards. She is proud of their house, which was bought cheaply and improved by George when he was still interested in that kind of work, and she is happy to have visitors come there, even if she does not admire them or even like them.

Except for teaching a night course in photography at a junior college once a week, George has not worked since he left the university two years ago, after he was denied tenure. She cannot really tell if he is unhappy working so little, because he keeps busy in other ways. He listens to classical music in the morning, slowly sipping herbal teas, and on fair afternoons he lies outdoors in the sun, no matter how cold the day. He takes photographs, and walks alone in the woods. He does errands for her if they need to be done. Sometimes at night he goes to the library or goes to visit friends; he tells her that these people often ask her to come too, but he says she would not like them. This is true—she would not like them. Recently he has done some late-night cooking. He has always kept a journal, and he is a great letter writer. An aunt left him most of her estate, ten thousand dollars, and said in her will that he was the only one who really cared, who took the time, again and again, to write. He had not seen his aunt for five years before she died, but he wrote regularly. Sometimes Lenore finds notes that he has left for her. Once, on the refrigerator, there was a long note suggesting clever Christmas presents for her family that he had thought of while she was out. Last week he scotch-taped a slip of paper to a casserole dish that contained leftover veal stew, saying "This was delicious." He does not compliment her verbally, but he likes to let her know that he is pleased.

A few nights ago—the same night they got a call from Julie and Sarah, saying they were coming for a visit—she told him that she wished he would talk more, that he would confide in her.

"Confide what?" he said.

"You always take that attitude," she said. "You pretend that you have no thoughts. Why does there have to be so much silence?"

"I'm not a professor anymore," he said. "I don't have to spend every minute *thinking.*"

But he loves to talk to the young women. He will talk to them on the phone for as much as an hour; he walks with them through the woods for most of the day when they visit. The lovers the young women bring with them always seem to fall behind; they give up and return to the house to sit and talk to her, or to help with the preparation of the meal, or to play with the children. The young woman and George come back refreshed, ready for another round of conversation at dinner.

A few weeks ago one of the young men said to her, "Why do you let it go on?" They had been talking lightly before that—about the weather, the children—and then, in the kitchen, where he was sitting shelling peas, he put his head on the table and said, barely audibly, "Why do you let it go on?" He did not raise his head, and she stared at him, thinking that she must have imagined his speaking. She was surprised—surprised to have heard it, and surprised that he had said nothing after that, which made her doubt that he had spoken.

"Why do I let what go on?" she said.

There was a long silence. "Whatever this sick game is, I don't want to get involved in it," he said at last. "It was none of my business to ask. I understand that you don't want to talk about it."

"But it's really cold out there," she said. "What could happen when it's freezing out?"

He shook his head, the way George did, to indicate that she was beyond understanding. But she wasn't stupid, and she knew what might be going on. She had said the right thing, had been on the right track, but she had to say what she felt, which was that nothing very serious could be happening at that moment because they were walking in the woods. There wasn't even a barn on the property. She knew perfectly well that they were talking.

When George and the young woman had come back, he fixed hot apple juice, into which he trickled rum. Lenore was pleasant, because she was sure of what had not happened; the young man was not, because he did not think as she did. Still at the kitchen table, he ran his thumb across a pea pod as though it were a knife.

This weekend Sarah and Julie are visiting. They came on Friday evening. Sarah was one of George's students—the one who led the fight to have him rehired. She does not look like a troublemaker; she is pale and pretty, with freckles on her cheeks. She talks too much about the past, and this upsets him, disrupts the peace he has made with himself. She tells him that they fired him because he was "in touch" with everything, that they were afraid of him because he was so in touch. The more she tells him the more he remembers, and then it is necessary for Sarah to say the same things again and again; once she reminds him, he seems to need reassurance—needs to have her voice, to hear her bitterness against the members of the tenure committee. By evening they will both be drunk. Sarah will seem both agitating and consoling, Lenore and Julie and the children will be upstairs, in bed. Lenore suspects that she will not be the only one awake listening to them. She thinks that in spite of Julie's glazed look she is really very attentive. The night before, when they were all sitting around the fireplace talking, Sarah made a gesture and almost upset her wineglass, but Julie reached for it and stopped it from toppling over. George and Sarah were talking so energetically that they did not notice. Lenore's eyes met Julie's as Julie's hand shot out. Lenore feels that she is like Julie: Julie's face doesn't betray emotion, even when she is interested, even when she cares deeply. Being the same kind of person, Lenore can recognize this.

Before Sarah and Julie arrived Friday evening, Lenore asked George if Sarah was his lover.

"Don't be ridiculous," he said. "You think every student is my lover? Is Julie my lover?"

She said, "That wasn't what I said."

"Well, if you're going to be preposterous, go ahead and say that," he said. "If you think about it long enough, it would make a lot of sense, wouldn't it?"

He would not answer her question about Sarah. He kept throwing Julie's name into it. Some other woman might then think that he was protesting too strongly—that Julie really was his lover. She thought no such thing. She also stopped suspecting Sarah, because he wanted that, and it was her habit to oblige him.

He is twenty-one years older than Lenore. On his last birthday he was fifty-five. His daughter from his first marriage (his *only* marriage; she keeps reminding herself that they are not married, because it often seems that they might as well be) sent him an Irish country hat. The present made him irritable. He kept putting it on and pulling it down hard on his head. "She wants to make me a laughable old man," he said. "She wants me to put this on and go around like a fool." He wore the hat all morning, complaining about it, frightening the children. Eventually, to calm him, she said, "She intended *nothing.*" She said it with finality, her tone so insistent that he listened to her. But having lost his reason for bitterness, he said, "Just because you don't think doesn't mean others don't think." Is he getting old? She does not want to think of him getting old. In spite of his ulcer, his body is hard. He is tall and handsome, with a thick mustache and a thin black goatee, and there is very little gray in his kinky black hair. He dresses in tight-fitting blue jeans and black turtleneck sweaters in the winter, and old white shirts with the sleeves rolled up in the summer. He pretends not to care about his looks, but he does. He shaves carefully, scraping slowly down each side of his goatee. He orders his soft leather shoes from a store in California. After taking one of his long walks—even if he does it twice a day—he invariably takes a shower. He always looks refreshed, and very rarely admits any insecurity. A few times, at night in bed, he has asked, "Am I still the man of your dreams?" And when she says yes he always laughs, turning it into a joke, as if he didn't care. She knows he does. He pretends to have no feeling for clothing, but actually he cares so strongly about his turtlenecks and shirts (a few are Italian silk) and shoes that he will have no others. She has noticed that the young women who visit are always vain. When Sarah arrived, she was wearing a beautiful silk scarf, pale as conch shells.

Sitting on the floor on Saturday morning, Lenore watches the fire she has just lit. The baby, tucked in George's chair, smiles in his sleep, and Lenore thinks what a good companion he would be if only he were an adult. She gets up and goes into the kitchen and tears open a package of yeast and dissolves it, with sugar and salt, in hot water, slushing her fingers through it and shivering because it is so cold in the kitchen. She will bake bread for dinner—there is always a big meal in the early evening when they have guests. But what will she do for the rest of the day? George told the girls the night before that on Saturday they would walk in the woods, but she does not really enjoy hiking, and George will be irritated because of the discussion the night before, and she does not want to aggravate him. "You are unwilling to challenge anyone," her brother wrote her in a letter that came a few days ago. He has written her for years—all the years she has been with George—asking when she is going to end the relationship. She rarely writes back because she knows that her answers sound too simple. She has a comfortable house. She cooks. She keeps busy and she loves her two children. "It seems unkind to say *but,*" her brother writes, "but . . ." It is true; she likes simple things. Her brother, who is a lawyer in Cambridge, cannot understand that.

Lenore rubs her hand down the side of her face and says good morning to Julie and Sarah, who have come downstairs. Sarah does not want orange juice; she already looks refreshed and ready for the day. Lenore pours a glass for Julie. George calls from the hallway, "Ready to roll?" Lenore is surprised that he wants to leave so early. She goes into the living room. George is wearing a denim jacket, his hands in the pockets.

"Morning," he says to Lenore. "You're not up for a hike, are you?"

Lenore looks at him, but does not answer. As she stands there, Sarah walks around her and joins George in the hallway and he holds the door open for her. "Let's walk to the store and get Hershey bars to give us energy for a long hike," George says to Sarah. They are gone. Lenore finds Julie still in the kitchen, waiting for the water to boil. Julie says that she had a bad night and she is happy not to be going with George and Sarah. Lenore fixes tea for them. Maria sits next to her on the sofa, sipping orange juice. The baby likes company, but Maria is a very private child; she would rather that she and her mother were always alone. She has given up being possessive about her father. Now she gets out a cardboard box and takes out her mother's collection of postcards, which she arranges on the floor in careful groups. Whenever she looks up, Julie smiles nervously at her; Maria does not smile, and Lenore doesn't prod her. Lenore goes into the kitchen to punch down the bread, and Maria follows. Maria has recently gotten over chicken pox, and there is a small new scar in the center of her forehead. Instead of looking at Maria's blue eyes, Lenore lately has found herself focusing on the imperfection.

As Lenore is stretching the loaves onto the cornmeal-covered baking sheet, she hears the rain start. It hits hard on the garage roof.

After a few minutes Julie comes into the kitchen. "They're caught in this downpour," Julie says. "If Sarah had left the car keys, I could go get them."

"Take my car and pick them up," Lenore says, pointing with her elbow to the keys hanging on a nail near the door.

"But I don't know where the store is."

"You must have passed it driving to our house last night. Just go out of the driveway and turn right. It's along the main road."

Julie gets her purple sweater and takes the car keys. "I'll be right back," she says.

Lenore can sense that she is glad to escape from the house, that she is happy the rain began.

In the living room Lenore turns the pages of a magazine, and Maria mutters a refrain of "Blue, blue, dark blue, green blue," noticing the color every time it appears. Lenore sips her tea. She puts a Michael Hurley record on George's stereo. Michael Hurley is good rainy-day music. George has hundreds of records. His students used to love to paw through them. Cleverly, he has never made any attempt to keep up with what is currently popular. Everything is jazz or eclectic: Michael Hurley, Keith Jarrett, Ry Cooder.[1]

Julie comes back. "I couldn't find them," she says. She looks as if she expects to be punished.

Lenore is surprised. She is about to say something like "You certainly didn't look very hard, did you?" but she catches Julie's eye. She looks young and afraid, and perhaps even a little crazy.

"Well, we tried," Lenore says.

---

1. Musical performers who combine elements of folk, jazz, and rock.

Julie stands in front of the fire, with her back to Lenore. Lenore knows she is thinking that she is dense—that she does not recognize the implications.

"They might have walked through the woods instead of along the road," Lenore says. "That's possible."

"But they would have gone out to the road to thumb when the rain began, wouldn't they?"

Perhaps she misunderstood what Julie was thinking. Perhaps it has never occurred to Julie until now what might be going on.

"Maybe they got lost," Julie says. "Maybe something happened to them."

"Nothing happened to them," Lenore says. Julie turns around and Lenore catches that small point of light in her eye again. "Maybe they took shelter under a tree," she says. "Maybe they're screwing. How should I know?"

It is not a word Lenore often uses. She usually tries not to think about that at all, but she can sense that Julie is very upset.

"Really?" Julie says. "Don't you care, Mrs. Anderson?"

Lenore is amused. There's a switch. All the students call her husband George and her Lenore; now one of them wants to think there's a real adult here to explain all this to her.

"What am I going to do?" Lenore says. She shrugs.

Julie does not answer.

"Would you like me to pour you tea?" Lenore asks.

"Yes," Julie says. "Please."

George and Sarah return in the middle of the afternoon. George says that they decided to go on a spree to the big city—it is really a small town he is talking about, but calling it the big city gives him an opportunity to speak ironically. They sat in a restaurant bar, waiting for the rain to stop, George says, and then they thumbed a ride home. "But I'm completely sober," George says, turning for the first time to Sarah. "What about you?" He is all smiles. Sarah lets him down. She looks embarrassed. Her eyes meet Lenore's quickly, and jump to Julie. The two girls stare at each other, and Lenore, left with only George to look at, looks at the fire and then gets up to pile on another log.

Gradually it becomes clear that they are trapped together by the rain. Maria undresses her paper doll and deliberately rips a feather off its hat. Then she takes the pieces to Lenore, almost in tears. The baby cries, and Lenore takes him off the sofa, where he has been sleeping under his yellow blanket, and props him in the space between her legs as she leans back on her elbows to watch the fire. It's her fire, and she has the excuse of presiding over it.

"How's my boy?" George says. The baby looks, and looks away.

It gets dark early, because of the rain. At four-thirty George uncorks a bottle of Beaujolais and brings it into the living room, with four glasses pressed against his chest with his free arm. Julie rises nervously to extract the glasses, thanking him too profusely for the wine. She gives a glass to Sarah without looking at her.

They sit in a semicircle in front of the fire and drink the wine. Julie leafs through magazines—*New Times*, *National Geographic*—and Sarah holds a small white dish painted with gray-green leaves that she has taken from the coffee table; the dish contains a few shells and some acorn caps, a polished stone or two, and Sarah lets these objects run through her fingers. There are several such dishes in the house, assembled by George. He and Lenore gathered the shells long ago, the first time they went away together, at a beach in North Carolina. But the acorn caps, the shiny turquoise and amethyst stones—those are there, she knows, because George likes the effect they have on visitors; it is an expected unconventionality, really. He has also acquired a few small framed pictures, which he points out to guests who are more important than worshipful students—tiny oil paintings of fruit, prints with small details from the unicorn tapestries. He pretends to like small, elegant things. Actually, when they visit museums in New York he goes first to El Grecos and big Mark Rothko canvases. She could never get him to admit that what he said or did was sometimes false. Once, long ago, when he asked if he was still the man of her dreams, she said, "We don't get along well anymore." "Don't talk about it," he said—no denial, no protest. At best, she could say things and get away with them; she could never get him to continue such a conversation.

At the dinner table, lit with white candles burning in empty wine bottles, they eat off his grandmother's small flowery plates. Lenore looks out a window and sees, very faintly in the dark, their huge oak tree. The rain has stopped. A few stars have come out, and there are glints on the wet branches. The oak tree grows very close to the window. George loved it when her brother once suggested that some of the bushes and trees should be pruned away from the house so it would not always be so dark inside; it gave him a chance to rave about the beauty of nature, to say that he would never tamper with it. "It's like a tomb in here all day," her brother had said. Since moving here, George has learned the names of almost all the things growing on the land: he can point out abelia bushes, spirea, laurels. He subscribes to *National Geographic* (although she rarely sees him looking at it). He is at last in touch, he says, being in the country puts him in touch. He is saying it now to Sarah, who has put down her ivory-handled fork to listen to him. He gets up to change the record. Side two of the Telemann[2] record begins softly.

Sarah is still very much on guard with Lenore; she makes polite conversation with her quickly when George is out of the room. "You people are so wonderful," she says. "I wish my parents could be like you."

"George would be pleased to hear that," Lenore says, lifting a small piece of pasta to her lips.

When George is seated again, Sarah, anxious to please, tells him, "If only my father could be like you."

"Your father," George says. "I won't have that analogy." He says it pleasantly, but barely disguises his dismay at the comparison.

"I mean, he cares about nothing but business," the girl stumbles on.

The music, in contrast, grows lovelier.

Lenore goes into the kitchen to get the salad and hears George say, "I simply won't let you girls leave. Nobody leaves on a Saturday."

There are polite protests, there are compliments to Lenore on the meal—

---

2. German composer of the 18th century.

there is too much talk. Lenore has trouble caring about what's going on. The food is warm and delicious. She pours more wine and lets them talk.

"Godard, yes, I know . . . panning that row of honking cars *so* slowly, that long line of cars stretching on and on."[3]

She has picked up the end of George's conversation. His arm slowly waves out over the table, indicating the line of motionless cars in the movie.

"That's a lovely plant," Julie says to Lenore.

"It's Peruvian ivy," Lenore says. She smiles. She is supposed to smile. She will not offer to hack shoots off her plant for these girls.

Sarah asks for a Dylan record when the Telemann finishes playing. White wax drips onto the wood table. George waits for it to solidify slightly, then scrapes up the little circles and with thumb and index finger flicks them gently toward Sarah. He explains (although she asked for no particular Dylan record) that he has only Dylan before he went electric. And "Planet Waves"— "because it's so romantic. That's silly of me, but true." Sarah smiles at him. Julie smiles at Lenore. Julie is being polite, taking her cues from Sarah, really not understanding what's going on. Lenore does not smile back. She has done enough to put them at ease. She is tired now, brought down by the music, a full stomach, and again the sounds of rain outside. For dessert there is homemade vanilla ice cream, made by George, with small black vanilla-bean flecks in it. He is still drinking wine, though; another bottle has been opened. He sips wine and then taps his spoon on his ice cream, looking at Sarah. Sarah smiles, letting them all see the smile, then sucks the ice cream off her spoon. Julie is missing more and more of what's going on. Lenore watches as Julie strokes her hand absently on her napkin. She is wearing a thin silver choker and—Lenore notices for the first time—a thin silver ring on the third finger of her hand.

"It's just terrible about Anna," George says, finishing his wine, his ice cream melting, looking at no one in particular, although Sarah was the one who brought up Anna the night before, when they had been in the house only a short time—Anna dead, hit by a car, hardly an accident at all. Anna was also a student of his. The driver of the car was drunk, but for some reason charges were not pressed. (Sarah and George have talked about this before, but Lenore blocks it out. What can she do about it? She met Anna once: a beautiful girl, with tiny, childlike hands, her hair thin and curly— wary, as beautiful people are wary.) Now the driver has been flipping out, Julie says, and calling Anna's parents, wanting to talk to them to find out why it has happened.

The baby begins to cry. Lenore goes upstairs, pulls up more covers, talks to him for a minute. He settles for this. She goes downstairs. The wine must have affected her more than she realizes; otherwise, why is she counting the number of steps?

In the candlelit dining room, Julie sits alone at the table. The girl has been left alone again; George and Sarah took the umbrellas, decided to go for a walk in the rain.

It is eight o'clock. Since helping Lenore load the dishes into the dishwasher, when she said what a beautiful house Lenore had, Julie has said

---

3. A famous scene from Jean-Luc Godard's film *Weekend* (1969).

very little. Lenore is tired, and does not want to make conversation. They sit in the living room and drink wine.

"Sarah is my best friend," Julie says. She seems apologetic about it. "I was so out of it when I came back to college. I was in Italy, with my husband, and suddenly I was back in the States. I couldn't make friends. But Sarah wasn't like the other people. She cared enough to be nice to me."

"How long have you been friends?"

"For two years. She's really the best friend I've ever had. We understand things—we don't always have to talk about them."

"Like her relationship with George," Lenore says.

Too direct. Too unexpected. Julie has no answer.

"You act as if you're to blame," Lenore says.

"I feel strange because you're such a nice lady."

A nice lady! What an odd way to speak. Has she been reading Henry James? Lenore has never known what to think of herself, but she certainly thinks of herself as being more complicated than a "lady."

"Why do you look that way?" Julie asks. "You *are* nice. I think you've been very nice to us. You've given up your whole weekend."

"I always give up my weekends. Weekends are the only time we socialize, really. In a way, it's good to have something to do."

"But to have it turn out like this . . ." Julie says. "I think I feel so strange because when my own marriage broke up I didn't even suspect. I mean, I couldn't act the way you do, anyway, but I—"

"For all I know, nothing's going on," Lenore says. "For all I know, your friend is flattering herself, and George is trying to make me jealous." She puts two more logs on the fire. When these are gone, she will either have to walk to the woodshed or give up and go to bed. "Is there something . . . *major* going on?" she asks.

Julie is sitting on the rug, by the fire, twirling her hair with her finger. "I didn't know it when I came out here," she says. "Sarah's put me in a very awkward position."

"But do you know how far it has gone?" Lenore asks, genuinely curious now.

"No," Julie says.

No way to know if she's telling the truth. Would Julie speak the truth to a lady? Probably not.

"Anyway," Lenore says with a shrug, "I don't want to think about it all the time."

"I'd never have the courage to live with a man and not marry," Julie says. "I mean, I wish I had, that we hadn't gotten married, but I just don't have that kind of . . . I'm not secure enough."

"You have to live somewhere," Lenore says.

Julie is looking at her as if she does not believe that she is sincere. Am I? Lenore wonders. She has lived with George for six years, and sometimes she thinks she has caught his way of playing games, along with his colds, his bad moods.

"I'll show you something," Lenore says. She gets up, and Julie follows. Lenore puts on the light in George's study, and they walk through it to a bathroom he has converted to a darkroom. Under a table, in a box behind another box, there is a stack of pictures. Lenore takes them out and hands them to Julie. They are pictures that Lenore found in his darkroom last summer; they were left out by mistake, no doubt, and she found them when she went in with some contact prints he had left in their bedroom. They are high-contrast photographs of George's face. In all of them he looks very serious and very sad; in some of them his eyes seem to be narrowed in pain. In one, his mouth is open. It is an excellent photograph of a man in agony, a man about to scream.

"What are they?" Julie whispers.

"Pictures he took of himself," Lenore says. She shrugs. "So I stay," she says.

Julie nods. Lenore nods, taking the pictures back. Lenore has not thought until this minute that this may be why she stays. In fact, it is not the only reason. It is just a very demonstrable, impressive reason. When she first saw the pictures, her own face had become as distorted as George's. She had simply not known what to do. She had been frightened and ashamed. Finally she put them in an empty box, and put the box behind another box. She did not even want him to see the horrible pictures again. She does not know if he has ever found them, pushed back against the wall in that other box. As George says, there can be too much communication between people.

Later, Sarah and George come back to the house. It is still raining. It turns out that they took a bottle of brandy with them, and they are both drenched and drunk. He holds Sarah's finger with one of his. Sarah, seeing Lenore, lets his finger go. But then he turns—they have not even said hello yet—and grabs her up, spins her around, stumbling into the living room, and says, "I am in love."

Julie and Lenore watch them in silence.

"See no evil," George says, gesturing with the empty brandy bottle to Julie. "Hear no evil," George says, pointing to Lenore. He hugs Sarah closer. "I speak no evil. I speak the truth. I am in love!"

Sarah squirms away from him, runs from the room and up the stairs in the dark.

George looks blankly after her, then sinks to the floor and smiles. He is going to pass it off as a joke. Julie looks at him in horror, and from upstairs Sarah can be heard sobbing. Her crying awakens the baby.

"Excuse me," Lenore says. She climbs the stairs and goes into her son's room, and picks him up. She talks gently to him, soothing him with lies. He is too sleepy to be alarmed for long. In a few minutes he is asleep again, and she puts him back in his crib. In the next room Sarah is crying more quietly now. Her crying is so awful that Lenore almost joins in, but instead she pats her son. She stands in the dark by the crib and then at last goes out and down the hallway to her bedroom. She takes off her clothes and gets into the cold bed. She concentrates on breathing normally. With the door closed and Sarah's door closed, she can hardly hear her. Someone taps lightly on her door.

"Mrs. Anderson," Julie whispers. "Is this your room?"

"Yes," Lenore says. She does not ask her in.

"We're going to leave. I'm going to get Sarah and leave. I didn't want to just walk out without saying anything."

Lenore just cannot think how to respond. It was really very kind of Julie to say something. She is very close to tears, so she says nothing.

"Okay," Julie says, to reassure herself. "Good night. We're going."

There is no more crying. Footsteps. Miraculously, the baby does not wake up again, and Maria has slept through all of it. She has always slept well. Lenore herself sleeps worse and worse, and she knows that George walks much of the night, most nights. She hasn't said anything about it. If he thinks she's simple, what good would her simple wisdom do him?

The oak tree scrapes against the window in the wind and rain. Here on the second floor, under the roof, the tinny tapping is very loud. If Sarah and Julie say anything to George before they leave, she doesn't hear them. She hears the car start, then die out. It starts again—she is praying for the car to go—and after conking out once more it rolls slowly away, crunching gravel. The bed is no warmer; she shivers. She tries hard to fall asleep. The effort keeps her awake. She squints her eyes in concentration instead of closing them. The only sound in the house is the electric clock, humming by her bed. It is not even midnight.

She gets up, and without turning on the light, walks downstairs. George is still in the living room. The fire is nothing but ashes and glowing bits of wood. It is as cold there as it was in the bed.

"That damn bitch," George says. "I should have known she was a stupid little girl."

"You went too far," Lenore says. "I'm the only one you can go too far with."

"Damn it," he says and pokes the fire. A few sparks shoot up. "Damn it," he repeats under his breath.

His sweater is still wet. His shoes are muddy and ruined. Sitting on the floor by the fire, his hair matted down on his head, he looks ugly, older, unfamiliar.

She thinks of another time, when it was warm. They were walking on the beach together, shortly after they met, gathering shells. Little waves were rolling in. The sun went behind the clouds and there was a momentary illusion that the clouds were still and the sun was racing ahead of them. "Catch me," he said, breaking away from her. They had been talking quietly, gathering shells. She was so surprised at him for breaking away that she ran with all her energy and did catch him, putting her hand out and taking hold of the band of his swimming trunks as he veered into the water. If she hadn't stopped him, would he really have run far out into the water, until she couldn't follow anymore? He turned on her, just as abruptly as he had run away, and grabbed her and hugged her hard, lifted her high. She had clung to him, held him close. He had tried the same thing when he came back from the walk with Sarah, and it hadn't worked.

"I wouldn't care if their car went off the road," he says bitterly.

"Don't say that," she says.

They sit in silence, listening to the rain. She slides over closer to him, puts her hand on his shoulder and leans her head there, as if he could protect her from the awful things he has wished into being.

1978

DAVID MAMET
b. 1947

One of the American poet Wallace Stevens's more arresting titles for a poem is "Men Made Out of Words;" the most original American playwright to emerge in the 1970s, David Mamet, is so in large part because of the way his plays and screenplays are insistently and wholly made out of the words men, and sometimes women, speak to—more often mutter or hurl at—each other. Consider the following exchange, from Mamet's 1982 play *Glengarry Glen Ross,* between two real estate salesmen who are entertaining the notion of breaking into their firm's offices and stealing the list of leads—names of desirable sales prospects—to sell their dubious properties and further their careers. George Aaronow asks Dave Moss whether he has "talked to" a prospective buyer of the leads:

> MOSS   No. What do you mean? Have I talked to him about *this? [Pause.]*
> AARONOW   Yes. I mean are you actually *talking* about this, or are we just . . .
> MOSS   No, we're just . . .
> AARONOW   We're just *"talking"* about it.
> MOSS   We're just *speaking* about it. [*Pause.*] As an *idea.*
> AARONOW   As an idea.
> MOSS   Yes.
> AARONOW   We're not actually *talking* about it.
> MOSS   No.
> AARONOW   Talking about it as a . . .
> MOSS   *No.*
> AARONOW   As a *robbery.*
> MOSS   As a "robbery"? No.

This is a typical example of the way Mamet's characters do and don't communicate. In a program note to *Glengarry Glen Ross* the English critic John Lahr referred to what he called the "hilarious brutal sludge of [Mamet's] characters' speech," and in this outrageous attempt by Moss and Aaronow to make a distinction between *talking* and *speaking* we see the playwright expertly deploying such sludge. Another critic has directed attention to Mamet's notion of the unreliability of language as demonstrated through his characters' "intoxicating mixture of evasions, pleadings, browbeatings, stonewalling and spiel." It is the reader's challenge to navigate this mixture and the voyage is usually not an easy one.

Mamet grew up on the Jewish south side of Chicago; attended a private school; worked in different theatrical groups (he was a busboy at Chicago's Second City, an improvisational cabaret where, among others, Mike Nichols and Elaine May appeared); and attended Goddard College, an experimental college in Vermont. At Goddard he wrote his first play and also took a break from his studies to attend the Neighborhood Playhouse School of the Theatre in New York City. There, he was strongly influenced by the Stanislavsky method of acting and its exercises in concentration. The method was important to him as a writer, he said later, for the way it showed him how "the language we use, its rhythm, actually determines the way we behave, more than the other way around"—an indication of where viewers and readers of his plays and screenplays should direct their primary attention. After graduating from Goddard in 1969, Mamet taught acting and writing at Marlboro College and at Goddard, then in 1972 moved back to Chicago and worked in a variety of nontheatrical environments such as the real estate agency that provided the material for *Glengarry Glen Ross.* By this time he had had short plays, *Lakeboat* and *The Duck Variations,* performed at Marlboro and Goddard. Then in 1974 his *Sexual Perversity in Chicago,* a fast-paced irreverent excursion into the sexual fantasies and behavior of four people, won an award for the best new Chicago play. Two years later it played in New York, along with *The Duck Variations,* and won an Obie award. In 1977 his most ambitious work to date, *American Buffalo,* won the New York Drama Critics award and Mamet was an established figure.

American Buffalo is a two-act play with just three characters: Don, who runs a small-time resale junk store; Bobby, a one-time drug addict whom Don tries to take care of; and Teach, a friend of Don's, who together with the others attempts (incompetently) to steal a coin collection, one item of which is presumably a valuable buffalo nickel. Everything goes awry and the play's curve is a rising verbal aggression, especially in the speeches of Teach, that culminates in real violence. But, employing a phrase of Robert Frost's, it is Mamet's "organized violence upon language" that holds us, often painfully, through the two acts. "Calm down," says Don at one point, to which Teach replies, "I am calm, I'm just upset"—a response that perfectly describes the uneasy combination of an attempt at verbal control and a patent verbal and human disorder.

Critics have said about *American Buffalo* and about Mamet's work generally that it offers a critique of American society and that Mamet is deeply pessimistic about the dreadful state of economic, social, and human relationships in the late twentieth century. This is to some extent true; Mamet himself has said that "what I write about is what I think is missing from our society. And that's communication on a basic level." Yet it's exactly that missing communication which forms the substance of our interest in the plays. We don't, that is, use the play's language as a springboard to launch us into concern about America and what it lacks; rather we find exhilarating Mamet's skillful manipulation of the "sludge" of character speech, well seasoned with self-loathing and mutual mistrust, so as to produce vivid entertainment. To say, as the writer of a book on Mamet has said, that "in spite of their callousness and selfishness" his characters "engage and retain our sympathy" is to put it backward. For it is in fact the brilliant rendering of callousness and selfishness, of failed communication, manipulation, and the basic venality of people, that makes his work so compelling. In its refusal to present characters with sympathetic inner lives, Mamet's art is, in one way, as callous as those characters. But the inventive and surprising dramatic actions (glimpsed latterly in *Oleanna,* his 1992 play about sexual harassment), woven out of an American idiom resourcefully employed, are sensitive indeed.

The text is that published in 1984.

Glengarry Glen Ross

THE CHARACTERS

WILLIAMSON, BAYLEN, ROMA, LINGK Men in their early forties.	LEVENE, MOSS, AARONOW Men in their fifties.

THE SCENE

The three scenes of Act One take place in a Chinese restaurant.
Act Two takes place in a real estate office.

ALWAYS BE CLOSING.
Practical Sales Maxim

Act One

SCENE ONE

A booth at a Chinese restaurant, WILLIAMSON *and* LEVENE *are seated at the booth.*

LEVENE John . . . John . . . John. Okay. John. John. Look: [*Pause.*] The Glengarry Highland's leads, you're sending Roma out. Fine. He's a good man. We know what he is. He's fine. All I'm saying, you look at the *board,* he's throwing . . . wait, wait, wait, he's throwing them *away,* he's throwing the leads away. All that I'm saying, that you're wasting leads. I don't want to tell you your *job.* All that I'm saying, things get *set,* I know they do, you get a certain *mindset.* . . . A guy gets a reputation. We know how this . . . all I'm saying, put a *closer* on the job. There's more than one man for the . . . Put a . . . wait a second, put a *proven man out* . . . and you watch, now *wait* a second—and you watch your *dollar* volumes. . . . You start closing them for *fifty* 'stead of *twenty-five* . . . you put a *closer* on the . . .

WILLIAMSON Shelly, you blew the last . . .

LEVENE No. John. No. Let's wait, let's back up here, I did . . . will you please? Wait a second. Please. I didn't "blow" them. No. I didn't "blow" them. No. One kicked *out,* one I closed . . .

WILLIAMSON . . . you didn't close . . .

LEVENE I, if you'd *listen* to me. Please. I *closed* the cocksucker. His *ex,* John, his *ex,* I didn't know he was married . . . he, the *judge* invalidated the . . .

WILLIAMSON Shelly . . .

LEVENE . . . and what is that, John? What? Bad *luck.* That's all it is. I pray in your *life* you will never find it runs in streaks. That's what it does, that's all it's doing. Streaks. I pray it misses you. That's all I want to say.

WILLIAMSON [*Pause.*] What about the other two?

LEVENE What two?

WILLIAMSON Four. You had four leads. One kicked out, one the *judge,* you say . . .

LEVENE . . . you want to see the court records? John? Eh? You want to go down . . .

WILLIAMSON . . . no . . .

LEVENE . . . do you want to go down*town* . . . ?

WILLIAMSON . . . no . . .

LEVENE . . . then . . .

WILLIAMSON . . . I only . . .

LEVENE . . . then what is this "you *say*" shit, what is that? [*Pause.*] What is that . . . ?

WILLIAMSON All that I'm saying . . .

LEVENE What is this "you *say*"? A deal kicks out . . . I got to *eat. Shit,* Williamson, *shit.* You . . . Moss . . . Roma . . . look at the *sheets* . . . look at the *sheets.* Nineteen *eighty,* eighty-*one* . . . eighty-*two* . . . six months of eighty-two . . . who's there? Who's up there?

WILLIAMSON Roma.

LEVENE   Under him?

WILLIAMSON   Moss.

LEVENE   Bullshit. John. Bull*shit*. April, September 1981. It's *me*. It isn't *fucking* Moss. Due respect, he's an *order* taker, John. He *talks,* he talks a good game, look at the *board, and it's me,* John, it's me . . .

WILLIAMSON   Not lately it isn't.

LEVENE   Lately kiss my ass lately. That isn't how you build an org . . . talk, talk to Murray. Talk to Mitch. When we were on Peterson, who paid for his fucking *car?* You talk to him. The *Seville . . .* ? He came in, "You bought that for me Shelly." Out of *what? Cold calling. Nothing.* Sixty-*five,* when we were there, with Glen *Ross* Farms? You call 'em downtown. What was that? *Luck?* That was "luck"? *Bull*shit, John. You're burning my ass, I can't get a fucking *lead* . . . you think that was luck. My stats for those years? Bull*shit* . . . over that period of time . . . ? Bull*shit.* It wasn't luck. It was *skill.* You want to throw that away, John . . . ? You want to throw that away?

WILLIAMSON   It isn't me . . .

LEVENE   . . . it isn't you . . . ? Who *is* it? Who is this I'm talking to? I need the *leads* . . .

WILLIAMSON   . . . after the thirtieth . . .

LEVENE   Bull*shit* the thirtieth, I don't get on the board the thirtieth, they're going to can my ass. I need the leads. I need them now. Or I'm gone, and you're going to miss me, John, I swear to you.

WILLIAMSON   Murray . . .

LEVENE   . . . you *talk* to Murray . . .

WILLIAMSON   I have. And my job is to marshal those leads . . .

LEVENE   Marshal the leads . . . marshal the leads? What the fuck, what bus did *you* get off of, we're here to fucking *sell.* *Fuck* marshaling the leads. What the fuck talk is that? What the fuck talk is that? Where did you learn that? In school? [*Pause.*] That's "talk," my friend, that's "talk." Our job is to *sell.* I'm the *man* to sell. I'm getting garbage. [*Pause.*] You're giving it to me, and what I'm saying is it's *fucked.*

WILLIAMSON   You're saying that I'm fucked.

LEVENE   Yes. [*Pause.*] I am. I'm sorry to antagonize you.

WILLIAMSON   Let me . . .

LEVENE   . . . and I'm going to get bounced and you're . . .

WILLIAMSON   . . . let me . . . are you listening to me . . . ?

LEVENE   Yes.

WILLIAMSON   Let me tell you something, Shelly. I do what I'm hired to do. I'm . . . wait a second. I'm *hired* to watch the leads. I'm given . . . hold on, I'm given a *policy. My* job is to *do that.* What I'm *told.* That's it. You, wait a second, *anybody* falls below a certain mark I'm not *permitted* to give them the premium leads.

LEVENE   Then how do they come up above that mark? With *dreck*[1] . . . ? That's *nonsense.* Explain this to me. 'Cause it's a waste, and it's a stupid waste. I want to tell you something . . .

WILLIAMSON   You know what those leads cost?

LEVENE   The premium leads. Yes. I know what they cost. John. Because I,

---

1. Shit (Yiddish).

I generated the dollar revenue sufficient to *buy* them. Nineteen senny-*nine*, you know what I made? Senny-*nine*? Ninety-six thousand dollars. John? For *Murray* . . . For *Mitch* . . . look at the sheets . . .

WILLIAMSON Murray said . . .

LEVENE *Fuck* him. *Fuck* Murray. John? You know? You tell him I said so. What does *he* fucking know? He's going to have a "sales" contest . . . you know what our sales contest used to be? *Money.* A *fortune.* Money lying on the ground. Murray? When was the last time *he* went out on a sit? Sales contest? It's *laughable.* It's cold out there now, John. It's tight. Money is *tight.* This ain't sixty-five. It ain't. It just ain't. See? See? Now, I'm a good *man*—but I need a . . .

WILLIAMSON Murray said . . .

LEVENE John. John . . .

WILLIAMSON Will you please wait a second. Shelly. Please. Murray told me: the hot leads . . .

LEVENE . . . ah, *fuck* this . . .

WILLIAMSON The . . . Shelly? [*Pause.*] The hot leads are assigned according to the board. During the contest. *Period.* Anyone who beats fifty per . . .

LEVENE That's fucked. That's fucked. You don't look at the fucking *percentage.* You look at the *gross.*

WILLIAMSON Either way. You're out.

LEVENE I'm out.

WILLIAMSON Yes.

LEVENE I'll tell you why I'm out. I'm *out,* you're giving me toilet paper. John. I've *seen* those leads. I saw them when I was at Homestead, we pitched those cocksuckers Rio Rancho nineteen sixty-*nine* they wouldn't buy. They couldn't buy a fucking *toaster.* They're *broke,* John. They're cold. They're deadbeats, you can't judge on that. Even so. Even so. Alright. Fine. Fine. Even so. I go in, FOUR FUCKING LEADS they got their money in a *sock.* They're fucking Polacks, John. Four leads. I close two. *Two.* Fifty per . . .

WILLIAMSON . . . they kicked out.

LEVENE They *all* kick out. You run in *streaks,* pal. *Streaks.* I'm . . . I'm . . . don't look at the *board,* look at *me.* Shelly Levene. *Anyone. Ask* them on Western. Ask Getz at Homestead. Go ask Jerry Graff. You know who I am . . . I NEED A SHOT. I got to get on the fucking board. Ask them. *Ask* them. Ask them who ever picked up a check I was flush. Moss, Jerry Graff, Mitch himself . . . Those guys *lived* on the business I brought in. They *lived* on it . . . and so did Murray, John. You were here you'd of benefited from it too. And now I'm saying this. Do I want charity? Do I want *pity?* I want *sits.* I want leads don't come right out of a *phone book.* Give me a lead hotter than that, I'll go in and close it. Give me a chance. That's all I want. I'm going to *get* up on that fucking board and all I want is a chance. It's a *streak* and I'm going to turn it around. [*Pause.*] I need your help. [*Pause.*]

WILLIAMSON I can't do it, Shelly. [*Pause.*]

LEVENE Why?

WILLIAMSON The leads are assigned randomly . . .

LEVENE *Bullshit, bullshit,* you assign them. . . . What are you *telling* me?

WILLIAMSON   . . . apart from the top men on the contest board.

LEVENE   Then put me on the board.

WILLIAMSON   You start closing again, you'll *be* on the board.

LEVENE   I can't close these leads, John. No one can. It's a joke. John, look, just give me a hot lead. Just give me two of the premium leads. As a "test," alright? As a "test" and I promise you . . .

WILLIAMSON   I can't do it, Shel. [*Pause.*]

LEVENE   I'll give you ten percent. [*Pause.*]

WILLIAMSON   Of what?

LEVENE   Of my end what I close.

WILLIAMSON   And what if you don't close.

LEVENE   I *will* close.

WILLIAMSON   What if you *don't* close . . . ?

LEVENE   I *will* close.

WILLIAMSON   What if you *don't?* Then I'm *fucked.* You see . . . ? Then it's *my* job. That's what I'm *telling* you.

LEVENE   I *will* close. John, John, ten percent. I can get hot. You *know* that . . .

WILLIAMSON   Not lately you can't . . .

LEVENE   Fuck that. That's defeatist. Fuck that. Fuck it. . . . Get on my side. *Go* with me. Let's *do* something. You want to run this office, *run* it.

WILLIAMSON   Twenty percent. [*Pause.*]

LEVENE   Alright.

WILLIAMSON   And fifty bucks a lead.

LEVENE   John. [*Pause.*] Listen. I want to talk to you. Permit me to do this a second. I'm older than you. A man acquires a reputation. On the street. What he does when he's *up,* what he does otherwise. . . . I said "ten," you said "no." You said "twenty." I said "fine," I'm not going to fuck with you, how can I beat that, you tell me? . . . Okay. Okay. We'll . . . Okay. Fine. We'll . . . Alright, twenty percent, and fifty bucks a lead. That's fine. For now. That's fine. A month or two we'll talk. A month from now. Next month. After the thirtieth. [*Pause.*] We'll talk.

WILLIAMSON   What are we going to say?

LEVENE   No. You're right. That's for later. We'll talk in a month. What have you got? I want two sits. Tonight.

WILLIAMSON   I'm not sure I have two.

LEVENE   I saw the board. You've got *four* . . .

WILLIAMSON [*Snaps*]   I've got *Roma.* Then I've got Moss . . .

LEVENE   *Bullshit.* They ain't been in the office yet. Give 'em some stiff. We have a deal or not? Eh? Two sits. The Des Plaines.[2] Both of 'em, six and ten, you can do it . . . six and ten . . . eight and eleven, I don't give a shit, you set 'em up? Alright? The two sits in Des Plaines.

WILLIAMSON   Alright.

LEVENE   Good. Now we're talking. [*Pause.*]

WILLIAMSON   A hundred bucks. [*Pause.*]

LEVENE   Now? [*Pause.*] Now?

WILLIAMSON   Now. [*Pause.*] Yes . . . *When?*

LEVENE   Ah, *shit,* John. [*Pause.*]

2. A community to the immediate northwest of Chicago.

WILLIAMSON   I wish I could.

LEVENE   You fucking asshole. [*Pause.*] I haven't got it. [*Pause.*] I haven't got it, John. [*Pause.*] I'll pay you tomorrow. [*Pause.*] I'm coming in here with the sales, I'll pay you *tomorrow*. [*Pause.*] I haven't *got* it, when I pay, the *gas* . . . I get back the hotel, I'll bring it in tomorrow.

WILLIAMSON   Can't do it.

LEVENE   I'll give you thirty on them now, I'll bring the rest tomorrow. I've got it at the hotel. [*Pause.*] John? [*Pause.*] We do that, for chrissake?

WILLIAMSON   No.

LEVENE   I'm asking you. As a favor to me? [*Pause.*] John. [*Long pause.*] John: my *daughter* . . .

WILLIAMSON   I can't do it, Shelly.

LEVENE   Well, I want to tell you something, fella, wasn't long I could pick up the phone, call *Murray* and I'd have your job. You know that? Not too *long* ago. For what? For *nothing*. "Mur, this new kid burns my ass." "Shelly, he's out." You're gone before I'm back from lunch. I bought him a trip to Bermuda once . . .

WILLIAMSON   I have to go . . . [*Gets up.*]

LEVENE   Wait. Alright. Fine. [*Starts going in pocket for money.*] The one. Give me the lead. Give me the one lead. The best one you have.

WILLIAMSON   I can't split them. [*Pause.*]

LEVENE   Why?

WILLIAMSON   Because I say so.

LEVENE [*Pause.*]   Is that it? Is that *it*? You want to do business that way . . . ?

   [WILLIAMSON *gets up, leaves money on the table.*]

LEVENE   You want to do business that way . . . ? Alright. Alright. Alright. Alright. What is there on the other list . . . ?

WILLIAMSON   You want something off the B list?

LEVENE   *Yeah.* Yeah.

WILLIAMSON   Is that what you're saying?

LEVENE   That's what I'm saying. Yeah. [*Pause.*] I'd like something off the other list. Which, very least, that I'm entitled to. If I'm still *working* here, which for the moment I guess that I am. [*Pause.*] What? I'm sorry I spoke harshly to you.

WILLIAMSON   That's alright.

LEVENE   The deal still stands, our other thing.

   [WILLIAMSON *shrugs. Starts out of the booth.*]

LEVENE   Good. Mmm. I, you know, I left my wallet back at the hotel.

SCENE TWO

A booth at the restaurant. MOSS *and* AARONOW *seated. After the meal.*

MOSS   Polacks and deadbeats.

AARONOW   . . . Polacks . . .

MOSS   Deadbeats *all*.

AARONOW   . . . they hold on to their money . . .

MOSS   All of 'em. They, *hey:* it happens to us all.

AARONOW   Where am I going to work?

MOSS   You have to cheer up, George, you aren't out yet.

AARONOW   I'm not?

MOSS   You missed a fucking sale. Big deal. A deadbeat Polack. Big deal. How you going to sell 'em in the *first* place . . . ? Your mistake, you shoun'a took the lead.

AARONOW   I had to.

MOSS   You had to, yeah. Why?

AARONOW   To get on the . . .

MOSS   To get on the board. Yeah. How you goan'a get on the board sell'n a Polack? And I'll tell you, I'll tell you what *else.* You listening? I'll tell you what else: don't ever try to sell an Indian.

AARONOW   I'd never try to sell an Indian.

MOSS   You get those names come up, you ever get 'em, "Patel"?

AARONOW   Mmm . . .

MOSS   You ever get 'em?

AARONOW   Well, I think I had one once.

MOSS   You did?

AARONOW   I . . . I don't know.

MOSS   You had one you'd know it. *Patel.* They keep coming up. I don't know. They like to talk to salesmen. [*Pause.*] They're *lonely,* something. [*Pause.*] They like to feel *superior,* I don't know. Never bought a fucking thing. You're sitting down "The Rio Rancho *this,* the blah blah blah," "The Mountain View—" "Oh yes. My brother told me that. . . ." They got a grapevine. Fuckin' Indians, George. Not my cup of tea. Speaking of which I want to tell you something: [*Pause*] I never got a cup of tea with them. You see them in the restaurants. A supercilious race. What is this *look* on their face all the time? I don't know. [*Pause.*] I don't know. Their broads all look like they just got fucked with a dead *cat,* I don't know. [*Pause.*] I don't know. I don't like it. Christ . . .

AARONOW   What?

MOSS   The whole fuckin' thing . . . The pressure's just too great. You're ab . . . you're absolu . . . they're too important. All of them. You go in the door. I . . . "I got to *close* this fucker, or I don't eat lunch," "or I don't win the *Cadillac.* . . ." We fuckin' work too hard. You work too hard. We all, I remember when we were at Platt . . . huh? Glen Ross Farms . . . *didn't* we sell a bunch of that . . . ?

AARONOW   They came in and they, you know . . .

MOSS   Well, they fucked it up.

AARONOW   They did.

MOSS   They killed the goose.

AARONOW   They did.

MOSS   And now . . .

AARONOW   We're stuck with *this* . . .

MOSS   We're stuck with *this* fucking shit . . .

AARONOW   . . . *this* shit . . .

MOSS   It's too . . .

AARONOW   It is.

MOSS   Eh?

AARONOW   It's too . . .

MOSS   You get a bad month, all of a . . .

AARONOW   You're on this . . .

MOSS   All of, they got you on this "board . . ."

AARONOW   I, I . . . I . . .

MOSS   Some *contest* board . . .

AARONOW   I . . .

MOSS   It's not right.

AARONOW   It's not.

MOSS   No. [*Pause.*]

AARONOW   And it's not right to the *customers.*

MOSS   I know it's not. I'll tell you, you got, you know, you got . . . what did I learn as a kid on Western? Don't sell a guy one car. Sell him *five* cars over fifteen years.

AARONOW   That's right?

MOSS   Eh . . . ?

AARONOW   That's right?

MOSS   Goddamn right, that's right. Guys come on: "Oh, the blah blah blah, I know what I'll do: I'll go in and rob everyone blind and go to Argentina cause nobody ever *thought* of this before."

AARONOW   . . . that's right . . .

MOSS   Eh?

AARONOW   No. That's absolutely right.

MOSS   And so they kill the goose. I, I, I'll . . . and a fuckin' *man,* worked all his *life* has got to . . .

AARONOW   . . . that's right . . .

MOSS   . . . cower in his boots . . .

AARONOW [*simultaneously with "boots"*]   Shoes, boots, yes . . .

MOSS   For some fuckin' "Sell ten thousand and you win the steak knives . . ."

AARONOW   For some *sales* pro . . .

MOSS   . . . sales promotion, "You *lose,* then we fire your . . ." No. It's *medieval* . . . it's wrong. "Or we're going to fire your ass." It's wrong.

AARONOW   Yes.

MOSS   Yes, it is. And you know who's responsible?

AARONOW   Who?

MOSS   You know who it is. It's Mitch. And Murray. 'Cause it doesn't have to be this way.

AARONOW   No.

MOSS   Look at Jerry Graff. He's *clean,* he's doing business for *himself,* he's got his, that *list* of his with the *nurses* . . . see? You see? That's *thinking.* Why take ten percent? A ten percent comm . . . why are we giving the rest away? What are we giving ninety per . . . for *nothing.* For some jerk sit in the office tell you "Get out there and close." "Go win the Cadillac." Graff. He goes out and *buys.* He pays top dollar for the . . . you see?

AARONOW   Yes.

MOSS   That's *thinking.* Now, he's got the leads, he goes in business for *himself.* He's . . . that's what I . . . that's *thinking!* "Who? Who's got a steady *job,* a couple bucks nobody's touched, who?"

AARONOW   Nurses.

MOSS   So Graff buys a fucking list of nurses, one grand—if he paid two I'll eat my hat—four, five thousand nurses, and he's going *wild* . . .

AARONOW   He is?

MOSS   He's doing *very* well.

AARONOW   I heard that they were running cold.

MOSS   The nurses?

AARONOW   Yes.

MOSS   You hear a *lot* of things. . . . He's doing very well. He's doing *very* well.

AARONOW   With River Oaks?

MOSS   River Oaks, Brook Farms. *All* of that shit. Somebody told me, you know what he's clearing *himself*? Fourteen, fifteen grand a *week*.

AARONOW   Himself?

MOSS   That's what I'm *saying*. Why? The *leads*. He's got the good leads . . . what are we, we're sitting in the shit here. Why? We have to go to *them* to *get* them. Huh. Ninety percent our sale, we're *paying* to the *office* for the *leads*.

AARONOW   The leads, the overhead, the telephones, there's *lots* of things.

MOSS   What do you need? A *telephone,* some broad to say "Good morning," nothing . . . nothing . . .

AARONOW   No, it's not that simple, Dave . . .

MOSS   *Yes*. It *is*. It *is* simple, and you know what the hard part is?

AARONOW   What?

MOSS   Starting up.

AARONOW   What hard part?

MOSS   Of doing the thing. The dif . . . the difference. Between me and Jerry Graff. Going to business for yourself. The hard part is . . . you know what it is?

AARONOW   What?

MOSS   Just the *act*.

AARONOW   What act?

MOSS   To say "I'm going on my own." 'Cause what you do, George, let me tell you what you do: you find yourself in *thrall* to someone else. And we *enslave* ourselves. To *please*. To win some fucking *toaster* . . . to . . . to . . . and the guy who got there first made *up* those . . .

AARONOW   That's right . . .

MOSS   He made *up* those rules, and we're working for *him*.

AARONOW   That's the truth . . .

MOSS   That's the *God's* truth. And it gets me depressed. I *swear* that it does. At MY AGE. To see a goddamn: "Somebody wins the Cadillac this month. P.S. Two guys get fucked."

AARONOW   *Huh*.

MOSS   You don't *ax* your sales force.

AARONOW   No.

MOSS   You . . .

AARONOW   You . . .

MOSS   You *build* it!

MOSS   That's what I . . .

MOSS   You fucking *build* it! Men come . . .

AARONOW   Men come *work* for you . . .

MOSS   . . . you're absolutely right.

AARONOW   They . . .

MOSS They have . . .

AARONOW When they . . .

MOSS Look look look look, when they *build* your business, then you can't fucking turn around, *enslave* them, treat them like *children,* fuck them up the ass, leave them to fend for themselves . . . no. [*Pause.*] No. [*Pause.*] You're absolutely right, and I want to tell you something.

AARONOW What?

MOSS I want to tell you what somebody should do.

AARONOW What?

MOSS Someone should stand up and strike *back.*

AARONOW What do you mean?

MOSS *Somebody* . . .

AARONOW Yes . . . ?

MOSS Should do something to *them.*

AARONOW What?

MOSS Something. To pay them back. [*Pause.*] Someone, someone should hurt them. Murray and Mitch.

AARONOW Someone should hurt them.

MOSS Yes.

AARONOW [*Pause.*] How?

MOSS How? Do something to hurt them. Where they live.

AARONOW What? [*Pause.*]

MOSS Someone should rob the office.

AARONOW Huh.

MOSS That's what I'm *saying.* We were, if we were that kind of guys, to knock it off, and *trash* the joint, it looks like robbery, and *take* the fuckin' leads out of the files . . . go to Jerry Graff. [*Long pause.*]

AARONOW What could somebody get for them?

MOSS What could we *get* for them? I don't know. Buck a *throw* . . . buck-a-half a throw . . . I don't know. . . . Hey, who knows what they're worth, what do they *pay* for them? All told . . . must be, I'd . . . three bucks a throw . . . *I* don't know.

AARONOW How many leads have we got?

MOSS The *Glengarry* . . . the premium leads . . . ? I'd say we got five thousand. Five. Five thousand leads.

AARONOW And you're saying a fella could take and sell these leads to Jerry Graff.

MOSS Yes.

AARONOW How do you know he'd buy them?

MOSS Graff? Because I worked for him.

AARONOW You haven't talked to him.

MOSS No. What do you mean? Have I talked to him about *this?* [*Pause.*]

AARONOW Yes. I mean are you actually *talking* about this, or are we just . . .

MOSS No, we're just . . .

AARONOW We're just "*talking*" about it.

MOSS We're just *speaking* about it. [*Pause.*] As an *idea.*

AARONOW As an idea.

MOSS Yes.

AARONOW We're not actually *talking* about it.

MOSS No.

AARONOW Talking about it as a . . .

MOSS No.

AARONOW As a *robbery*.

MOSS As a "robbery"?! No.

AARONOW *Well*. Well . . .

MOSS *Hey*. [*Pause.*]

AARONOW So all this, um, you didn't, actually, you didn't actually go talk to Graff.

MOSS Not actually, no. [*Pause.*]

AARONOW You didn't?

MOSS No. Not actually.

AARONOW Did you?

MOSS What did I say?

AARONOW What did you say?

MOSS Yes. [*Pause.*] I said, "Not actually." The fuck *you* care, George? We're just *talking* . . .

AARONOW We are?

MOSS Yes. [*Pause.*]

AARONOW Because, because, you know, it's a *crime*.

MOSS That's right. It's a crime. It is a crime. It's also very safe.

AARONOW You're actually *talking* about this?

MOSS That's right. [*Pause.*]

AARONOW You're going to steal the leads?

MOSS Have I said that? [*Pause.*]

AARONOW Are you? [*Pause.*]

MOSS Did I say that?

AARONOW Did you talk to Graff?

MOSS Is that what I said?

AARONOW What did he say?

MOSS What did he say? He'd *buy* them. [*Pause.*]

AARONOW You're going to steal the leads and sell the leads to him? [*Pause.*]

MOSS Yes.

AARONOW What will he pay?

MOSS A buck a shot.

AARONOW For five thousand?

MOSS However they are, that's the deal. A buck a throw. Five thousand dollars. Split it half and half.

AARONOW You're saying "me."

MOSS Yes. [*Pause.*] Twenty-five hundred apiece. One night's work, and the job with Graff. Working the premium leads. [*Pause.*]

AARONOW A job with Graff.

MOSS Is that what I said?

AARONOW He'd give me a job.

MOSS He would take you on. Yes. [*Pause.*]

AARONOW Is that the truth?

MOSS Yes. It is, George. [*Pause.*] Yes. It's a big decision. [*Pause.*] And it's a big reward. [*Pause.*] It's a big reward. For one night's work. [*Pause.*] But it's got to be tonight.

AARONOW What?

MOSS What? What? The *leads*.

AARONOW You have to steal the leads tonight?

MOSS That's *right*, the guys are moving them downtown. After the thirtieth. Murray and Mitch. After the contest.

AARONOW You're, you're saying so you have to go in there tonight and . . .

MOSS *You* . . .

AARONOW I'm sorry?

MOSS *You*. [*Pause.*]

AARONOW Me?

MOSS *You* have to go in. [*Pause.*] *You* have to get the leads. [*Pause.*]

AARONOW I do?

MOSS Yes.

AARONOW I . . .

MOSS It's not something for nothing, George, I took you in on this, you have to go. That's your thing. I've made the deal with Graff. I can't go. I can't go in, I've spoken on this too much. I've got a big mouth. [*Pause.*] "The fucking leads" et cetera, blah blah blah ". . . the fucking tight ass company . . ."

AARONOW They'll know when you go over to Graff . . .

MOSS What will they know? That I *stole* the leads? I *didn't* steal the leads, I'm going to the *movies* tonight with a friend, and then I'm going to the Como Inn. Why did I go to Graff? I got a better deal. *Period*. Let 'em prove something. They can't prove anything that's not the case. [*Pause.*]

AARONOW *Dave*.

MOSS Yes.

AARONOW You want me to break into the office tonight and steal the leads?

MOSS Yes. [*Pause.*]

AARONOW No.

MOSS Oh, yes, George.

AARONOW What does that mean?

MOSS Listen to this. I have an alibi, I'm going to the Como Inn, why? Why? The place gets robbed, they're going to come looking for *me*. Why? Because I probably did it. Are you going to turn me in? [*Pause.*] George? Are you going to turn me in?

AARONOW What if you don't get caught?

MOSS They come to you, you going to turn me in?

AARONOW Why would they come to me?

MOSS They're going to come to *everyone*.

AARONOW Why would I *do* it?

MOSS You wouldn't, George, that's why I'm talking to you. Answer me. They come to you. You going to turn me in?

AARONOW No.

MOSS Are you sure?

AARONOW Yes. I'm sure.

MOSS Then listen to this: I have to get those leads tonight. That's something I have to do. If I'm not at the *movies* . . . if I'm not eating over at the inn . . . If you don't do this, then *I* have to come in here . . .

AARONOW . . . you don't have to come in . . .

MOSS . . . and *rob* the place . . .

AARONOW . . . I thought that we were only talking . . .

MOSS . . . they *take* me, then. They're going to ask me who were my accomplices.

AARONOW *Me?*

MOSS Absolutely.

AARONOW That's ridiculous.

MOSS Well, to the law, you're an accessory. Before the fact.

AARONOW I didn't ask to be.

MOSS Then tough luck, George, because you are.

AARONOW Why? *Why,* because you only *told* me about it?

MOSS That's right.

AARONOW Why are you doing this to me, Dave. Why are you talking this way to me? I don't understand. Why are you doing this at *all* . . . ?

MOSS That's none of your fucking business . . .

AARONOW Well, well, well, *talk* to me, we sat down to eat *dinner,* and here I'm a *criminal* . . .

MOSS You *went* for it.

AARONOW In the abstract . . .

MOSS So I'm making it concrete.

AARONOW Why?

MOSS Why? Why *you* going to give me five grand?

AARONOW Do you need five grand?

MOSS Is that what I just said?

AARONOW You need money? Is that the . . .

MOSS Hey, hey, let's just keep it simple, what I need is not the . . . what do *you* need . . . ?

AARONOW What is the five grand? [*Pause.*] What is the, you said that we were going to *split* five . . .

MOSS I lied. [*Pause.*] Alright? My end is *my* business. Your end's twenty-five. In or out. You tell me, you're out you take the consequences.

AARONOW I do?

MOSS Yes. [*Pause.*]

AARONOW And why is that?

MOSS Because you listened.

SCENE THREE

The restaurant. ROMA *is seated alone at the booth.* LINGK *is at the booth next to him.* ROMA *is talking to him.*

ROMA . . . all train compartments smell vaguely of shit. It gets so you don't mind it. That's the worst thing that I can confess. You know how long it took me to get there? A long time. When you *die* you're going to regret the things you don't do. You think you're *queer* . . . ? I'm going to tell you something: we're *all* queer. You think that you're a *thief?* So *what?* You get befuddled by a middle-class morality . . . ? Get *shut* of it. Shut it out. You cheated on your wife . . . ? You *did* it, *live* with it. [*Pause.*] You fuck little girls, so *be* it. There's an absolute morality? May *be.* And *then* what? If you *think* there is, then *be* that thing. Bad people go to hell? I don't *think* so. If you think that, act that way. A hell exists on earth? Yes. I won't live in it. That's *me.* You ever take a dump made you feel you'd just slept for twelve hours . . . ?

LINGK Did I . . . ?

ROMA Yes.

LINGK I don't know.

ROMA Or a *piss* . . . ? A great meal fades in reflection. Everything else gains. You know why? 'Cause it's only food. This shit we eat, it keeps us going. But it's only food. The great fucks that you may have had. What do you remember about them?

LINGK What do I . . . ?

ROMA Yes.

LINGK Mmmm . . .

ROMA I don't know. For *me,* I'm saying, what it is, it's probably not the orgasm. Some broads, forearms on your neck, something her *eyes* did. There was a *sound* she made . . . or, me, lying, in the, I'll tell you: me lying in bed; the next day she brought me café au lait. She gives me a cigarette, my balls feel like concrete. Eh? What I'm saying, what is our life? [*Pause.*] It's looking forward or it's looking back. And that's our life. That's *it.* Where is the *moment?* [*Pause.*] And what is it that we're afraid of? Loss. What else? [*Pause.*] The *bank* closes. We get *sick,* my wife died on a plane, the stock market collapsed . . . the house burnt down . . . what of these happen . . . ? None of 'em. We worry anyway. What does this mean? I'm not *secure.* How can I be secure? [*Pause.*] Through amassing wealth beyond all measure? No. And what's beyond all measure? That's a sickness. That's a trap. There is no measure. Only greed. How can we act? The right way, we would say, to deal with this: "There is a one-in-a-million chance that so and so will happen. . . . *Fuck* it, it won't happen to *me.* . . ." No. We know that's not the right way I think. [*Pause.*] We say the *correct* way to deal with this is "There is a one-in-so-and-so chance this will happen . . . God *protect* me. I am powerless, let it not happen to me. . . ." But no to *that.* I say. There's something else. What is it? "If it happens, AS IT MAY for that is not within our powers, I will *deal* with it, just as I do *today* with what draws my concern today." I say *this* is how we must act. I do those things which seem correct to me *today.* I trust myself. And if security concerns me, I do that which *today* I think will make me secure. And every day I *do* that, when that day *arrives* that I need a reserve, (a) odds are that I have it, and (b) the *true* reserve that I have is the strength that I have of *acting each day* without fear. [*Pause.*] According to the dictates of my mind. [*Pause.*] Stocks, bonds, objects of art, real estate. Now: what are they? [*Pause.*] An opportunity. To what? To make money? Perhaps. To *lose* money? Perhaps. To "indulge" and to "learn" about ourselves? Perhaps. *So fucking what?* What *isn't?* They're an *opportunity.* That's all. They're an *event.* A guy comes up to you, you make a call, you send in a brochure, it doesn't matter, "There're these *properties* I'd like for you to see." What does it mean? What you *want* it to mean. [*Pause.*] Money? [*Pause.*] If that's what it signifies to you. Security? [*Pause.*] Comfort? [*Pause.*] All it is is THINGS THAT HAPPEN TO YOU. [*Pause.*] That's all it is. How are they different? [*Pause.*] Some poor newly married guy gets run down by a cab. Some *busboy* wins the lottery. [*Pause.*] All it is, it's a carnival. What's special . . . what *draws* us? [*Pause.*] We're all different. [*Pause.*] We're not the same. [*Pause.*] We are not the same. [*Pause.*] Hmmm. [*Pause. Sighs.*] It's been a long day. [*Pause.*] What are you drinking?

LINGK Gimlet.

ROMA   Well, let's have a couple more. My name is Richard Roma, what's
yours?

LINGK   Lingk. James Lingk.

ROMA   James. I'm glad to meet you. [*They shake hands.*] I'm glad to meet
you, James. [*Pause.*] I want to show you something. [*Pause.*] It might
mean *nothing* to you . . . and it might not. I don't know. I don't know
anymore. [*Pause. He takes out a small map and spreads it on a table.*]
What is that? Florida. Glengarry Highlands. Florida. "Florida. *Bullshit.*"
And maybe that's true; and that's what *I* said: but look *here:* what is this?
This is a piece of land. Listen to what I'm going to tell you now.

Act Two

*The real estate office. Ransacked. A broken plate-glass window boarded up,
glass all over the floor.* AARONOW *and* WILLIAMSON *standing around, smoking.*

[*Pause.*]

AARONOW   People used to say that there are numbers of such magnitude
that multiplying them by two made no difference. [*Pause.*]

WILLIAMSON   Who used to say that?

AARONOW   In school. [*Pause.*]

[BAYLEN, *a detective, comes out of the inner office.*]

BAYLEN   Alright . . . ? [ROMA *enters from the street.*]

ROMA   *Williamson . . . Williamson, they stole the contracts . . . ?*

BAYLEN   Excuse me, sir . . .

ROMA   Did they get my contracts?

WILLIAMSON   They got . . .

BAYLEN   Excuse me, fella.

ROMA   . . . did they . . .

BAYLEN   Would you excuse us, please . . . ?

ROMA   Don't *fuck* with me, fella. I'm talking about a fuckin' Cadillac car
that you owe me . . .

WILLIAMSON   They didn't get your contract. I filed it before I left.

ROMA   They didn't get my contracts?

WILLIAMSON   They—excuse me . . . [*He goes back into inner room with the*
DETECTIVE.]

ROMA   Oh, *fuck. Fuck.* [*He starts kicking the desk.*] FUCK FUCK FUCK!
WILLIAMSON!!! WILLIAMSON!!! [*Goes to the door* WILLIAMSON *went
into, tries the door; it's locked.*] OPEN THE FUCKING . . . WILLIAM-
SON . . .

BAYLEN   [*coming out*]   Who are you? [WILLIAMSON *comes out.*]

WILLIAMSON   They didn't get the contracts.

ROMA   Did they . . .

WILLIAMSON   They got, listen to me . . .

ROMA   Th . . .

WILLIAMSON   Listen to me: They got *some* of them.

ROMA   Some of them . . .

BAYLEN   Who told you . . . ?

ROMA   Who told me wh . . . ? You've got a fuckin', you've . . . a . . . who is
this . . . ? You've got a board-up on the window. . . . *Moss* told me.

BAYLEN [*Looking back toward the inner office.*]   Moss . . . Who told him?

ROMA   How the fuck do *I* know? [*To* WILLIAMSON] *What . . . talk* to me.

WILLIAMSON   They took *some* of the con . . .

ROMA   . . . some of the contracts . . . Lingk. James Lingk. I closed . . .

WILLIAMSON   You closed him yesterday.

ROMA   *Yes.*

WILLIAMSON   It went down. I filed it.

ROMA   You did?

WILLIAMSON   Yes.

ROMA   Then I'm over the fucking top and you owe me a Cadillac.

WILLIAMSON   I . . .

ROMA   And I don't want any fucking shit and I don't give a shit, Lingk puts me over the top, you filed it, that's fine, any other shit kicks out *you* go back. You . . . *you* reclose it, 'cause I *closed* it and you . . . you owe me the car.

BAYLEN   Would you excuse us, please.

AARONOW   I, um, and may . . . maybe they're in . . . they're in . . . you should, John, if we're ins . . .

WILLIAMSON   I'm sure that we're insured, George . . . [*Going back inside.*]

ROMA   Fuck insured. You owe me a car.

BAYLEN [*Stepping back into the inner room*]   Please don't leave. I'm going to talk to you. What's your name?

ROMA   Are you talking to me? [*Pause.*]

BAYLEN   Yes. [*Pause.*]

ROMA   My name is Richard Roma.

[BAYLEN *goes back into the inner room.*]

AARONOW   I, you know, they should be insured.

ROMA   What do *you* care . . . ?

AARONOW   Then, you know, they wouldn't be so ups . . .

ROMA   Yeah. That's swell. Yes. You're right. [*Pause.*] How are you?

AARONOW   I'm fine. You mean the *board*? You mean the *board* . . . ?

ROMA   I don't . . . yes. Okay, the board.

AARONOW   I'm, I'm, I'm, I'm fucked on the board. *You.* You see how . . . I . . . [*Pause.*] I can't . . . my mind must be in other places. 'Cause I can't do any . . .

ROMA   *What?* You can't do any *what?* [*Pause.*]

AARONOW   I can't close 'em.

ROMA   Well, they're old. I saw the shit that they were giving you.

AARONOW   Yes.

ROMA   Huh?

AARONOW   Yes. They are old.

ROMA   They're ancient.

AARONOW   Clear . . .

ROMA   Clear Meadows. That shit's dead. [*Pause.*]

AARONOW   It *is* dead.

ROMA   It's a waste of time.

AARONOW   Yes. [*Long pause.*] I'm no fucking good.

ROMA   That's . . .

AARONOW   Everything I . . . *you* know . . .

ROMA   That's not . . . Fuck that shit, George. You're a, *hey,* you had a bad month. You're a good man, George.

AARONOW   I am?

ROMA   You hit a bad streak. We've all . . . look at this: fifteen units Mountain View, the fucking things get stole.

AARONOW   He said he filed . . .

ROMA   He filed half of them, he filed the *big* one. All the little ones, I have, I have to go back and . . . ah, *fuck,* I got to go out like a fucking schmuck hat in my hand and reclose the . . . [*Pause.*] I mean, talk about a bad streak. That would sap *anyone's* self confi . . . I got to go out and reclose all my . . . Where's the phones?

AARONOW   They stole . . .

ROMA   They stole the . . .

AARONOW   What. What kind of outfit are we running where . . . where anyone . . .

ROMA [*To himself*]   They stole the phones.

AARONOW   Where criminals can come in here . . . they take the . . .

ROMA   They stole the phones. They stole the leads. They're . . . *Christ.* [*Pause.*] What am I going to do this month? Oh, *shit* . . . [*Starts for the door.*]

AARONOW   You think they're going to catch . . . where are you going?

ROMA   Down the street.

WILLIAMSON [*Sticking his head out of the door*]   Where are you going?

ROMA   To the restaura . . . what do you fucking . . . ?

WILLIAMSON   Aren't you going out today?

ROMA   With what? [*Pause.*] With what, John, they took the leads . . .

WILLIAMSON   I have the stuff from last year's . . .

ROMA   Oh. Oh. Oh, your "nostalgia" file, that's fine. No. Swell. 'Cause I don't have to . . .

WILLIAMSON   . . . you want to go out today . . . ?

ROMA   'Cause I don't have to *eat* this month. No. Okay. *Give* 'em to me . . . [*To himself*] Fucking Mitch and Murray going to shit a br . . . what am I going to *do* all . . . [WILLIAMSON *starts back into the office. He is accosted by* AARONOW.]

AARONOW   Were the leads . . .

ROMA   . . . what am I going to *do* all month . . . ?

AARONOW   Were the leads insured?

WILLIAMSON   I don't know, George, why?

AARONOW   'Cause, you know, 'cause they weren't, I know that Mitch and Murray uh . . . [*Pause.*]

WILLIAMSON   What?

AARONOW   That they're going to be upset.

WILLIAMSON   That's right. [*Going back into his office. Pause. To* ROMA] You want to go out today . . . ?

[*Pause.* WILLIAMSON *returns to his office.*]

AARONOW   He said we're all going to have to go talk to the guy.

ROMA   What?

AARONOW   He said we . . .

ROMA   To the cop?

AARONOW   Yeah.

ROMA   Yeah. That's swell. *Another* waste of time.

AARONOW   A waste of time? Why?

ROMA   *Why?* 'Cause they aren't going to find the guy.

AARONOW   The cops?

ROMA   Yes. The cops. No.

AARONOW   They aren't?

ROMA   No.

AARONOW   Why don't you think so?

ROMA   Why? Because they're *stupid.* "Where were you last night . . ."

AARONOW   Where were you?

ROMA   Where was *I?*

AARONOW   Yes.

ROMA   I was at home, where were *you?*

AARONOW   At home.

ROMA   *See* . . . ? Were you the guy who broke in?

AARONOW   Was I?

ROMA   Yes.

AARONOW   No.

ROMA   Then don't sweat it, George, you know why?

AARONOW   No.

ROMA   You have nothing to hide.

AARONOW   [*Pause.*]   When I talk to the police, I get nervous.

ROMA   Yeah. You know who doesn't?

AARONOW   No, who?

ROMA   Thieves.

AARONOW   Why?

ROMA   They're inured to it.

AARONOW   You think so?

ROMA   Yes. [*Pause.*]

AARONOW   But what should I *tell* them?

ROMA   The truth, George. Always tell the truth. It's the easiest thing to remember. [WILLIAMSON *comes out of the office with leads.* ROMA *takes one, reads it.*]

ROMA   *Patel?* Ravidam *Patel?* How am I going to make a living on these deadbeat *wogs?* Where did you get this, from the *morgue?*

WILLIAMSON   If you don't want it, give it back.

ROMA   I don't "want" it, if you catch my drift.

WILLIAMSON   I'm giving you *three* leads. You . . .

ROMA   What's the fucking point in *any* case . . . ? What's the *point.* I got to argue with *you,* I got to knock heads with the *cops,* I'm busting my *balls,* sell your *dirt* to fucking *deadbeats* money in the *mattress,* I come back you can't even manage to keep the contracts safe, I have to go back and close them *again.* . . . What the fuck am I wasting my time, fuck this shit. I'm going out and reclose last week's . . .

WILLIAMSON   The word from Murray is: leave them alone. If we need a new signature he'll go out himself, he'll be the *president,* just come *in,* from out of *town* . . .

ROMA   Okay, okay, okay, gimme this shit. Fine. [*Takes the leads.*]

WILLIAMSON   Now, I'm giving you three . . .

ROMA   Three? I count *two.*

WILLIAMSON   Three.

ROMA   Patel? Fuck *you.* Fuckin' *Shiva* handed him a million dollars, told him "sign the deal," he wouldn't sign. And Vishnu, too. Into the bargain.

Fuck *that,* John. You know your business, I know mine. Your business is being an *asshole,* and I find out whose fucking *cousin* you are, I'm going to go to him and figure out a way to have your *ass* . . . fuck you—I'll wait for the new leads. [SHELLY LEVENE *enters.*]

LEVENE Get the *chalk.* Get the *chalk* . . . get the *chalk!* I closed 'em! I *closed* the cocksucker. Get the chalk and put me on the *board.* I'm going to Hawaii! Put me on the Cadillac board, Williamson! Pick up the fuckin' chalk. Eight units. Mountain View . . .

ROMA You sold eight Mountain View?

LEVENE You bet your ass. Who wants to go to lunch? Who wants to go to lunch? I'm buying. [*Slaps contract down on* WILLIAMSON's *desk.*] Eighty-two fucking grand. And twelve grand in commission. John. [*Pause.*] On fucking deadbeat magazine subscription leads.

WILLIAMSON Who?

LEVENE [*Pointing to contract.*] *Read* it. Bruce and Harriett Nyborg. [*Looking around.*] What happened here?

AARONOW Fuck. I had them on River Glen. [LEVENE *looks around.*]

LEVENE What happened?

WILLIAMSON Somebody broke in.

ROMA Eight units?

LEVENE That's right.

ROMA *Shelly . . . !*

LEVENE Hey, big fucking deal. Broke a bad streak . . .

AARONOW Shelly, the Machine, Levene.

LEVENE You . . .

AARONOW That's great.

LEVENE Thank you, George. [BAYLEN *sticks his head out of the room; calls in, "Aaronow."* AARONOW *goes into the side room.*]

LEVENE Williamson, get on the phone, call Mitch . . .

ROMA They took the phones . . .

LEVENE They . . .

BAYLEN *Aaronow . . .*

ROMA They took the typewriters, they took the leads, they took the *cash,* they took the *contracts . . .*

LEVENE Wh . . . wh . . . Wha . . . ?

AARONOW We had a robbery. [*Goes into the inner room.*]

LEVENE [*Pause.*] When?

ROMA Last night, this morning. [*Pause.*]

LEVENE They took the leads?

ROMA Mmm. [MOSS *comes out of the interrogation.*]

MOSS Fuckin' asshole.

ROMA What, they beat you with a rubber bat?

MOSS Cop couldn't find his dick two hands and a map. Anyone talks to this guy's an *asshole . . .*

ROMA You going to turn State's?

MOSS Fuck you, Ricky. I ain't going out today. I'm going home. I'm going home because nothing's *accomplished* here. . . . Anyone *talks to this guy is* . . .

ROMA Guess what the Machine did?

MOSS Fuck the Machine.

ROMA   Mountain View. Eight units.

MOSS   Fuckin' cop's got no right talk to me that way. I didn't rob the place . . .

ROMA   You hear what I said?

MOSS   Yeah. He closed a deal.

ROMA   Eight units. Mountain View.

MOSS   [To LEVENE]   You did that?

LEVENE   Yeah. [Pause.]

MOSS   Fuck you.

ROMA   Guess who?

MOSS   When . . .

LEVENE   Just now.

ROMA   Guess who?

MOSS   You just this morning . . .

ROMA   Harriet and blah blah Nyborg.

MOSS   You did that?

LEVENE   Eighty-two thousand dollars. [Pause.]

MOSS   Those fuckin' *deadbeats* . . .

LEVENE   My ass. I told 'em. [To ROMA] Listen to this: I said . . .

MOSS   Hey, I don't want to hear your fucking war stories . . .

ROMA   Fuck *you*, Dave . . .

LEVENE   "You have to believe in your*self* . . . you"—look—"alright . . . ?"

MOSS   [To WILLIAMSON]   Give me some leads. I'm going out . . . I'm getting out of . . .

LEVENE   ". . . you have to believe in your*self* . . ."

MOSS   Na, fuck the leads, I'm going home.

LEVENE   "Bruce, Harriett . . . Fuck *me*, believe in your*self* . . ."

ROMA   We haven't got a lead . . .

MOSS   Why not?

ROMA   They took 'em . . .

MOSS   Hey, they're fuckin' garbage any case. . . . This whole goddamn . . .

LEVENE   ". . . You look around, you say, 'This one has so-and-so, and I have nothing . . .' "

MOSS   *Shit.*

LEVENE   " *'Why? Why don't I get the opportunities . . . ?'* "

MOSS   And did they steal the contracts . . . ?

ROMA   Fuck *you* care . . . ?

LEVENE   "I want to tell you something, Harriett . . ."

MOSS   . . . the fuck is *that* supposed to mean . . . ?

LEVENE   Will you shut up, I'm telling you this . . . [AARONOW *sticks his head out.*]

AARONOW   Can we get some coffee . . . ?

MOSS   How ya doing? [Pause.]

AARONOW   Fine.

MOSS   Uh-huh.

AARONOW   If anyone's going, I could use some coffee.

LEVENE   "You *do* get the . . ." [To ROMA] Huh? Huh?

MOSS   *Fuck* is that supposed to mean?

LEVENE   "You *do* get the opportunity. . . . You *get* them. As *I* do, as *anyone* does . . ."

MOSS   Ricky? . . . That I don't care they stole the contracts? [*Pause.*]

LEVENE   I got 'em in the kitchen. I'm eating her crumb cake.

MOSS   What does that mean?

ROMA   It *means,* Dave, you haven't closed a good one in a month, none of my business, you want to push me to answer you. [*Pause.*] And so you haven't got a contract to get stolen or so forth.

MOSS   You have a mean streak in you, Ricky, you know that . . . ?

LEVENE   Rick. Let me tell you. Wait, we're in the . . .

MOSS   Shut the fuck up. [*Pause.*] Ricky. You have a mean streak in you. . . . [*To* LEVENE] And what the fuck are *you* babbling about . . . ? [*To* ROMA] Bring that shit up. Of my volume. You were on a bad one and I brought it up to *you* you'd harbor it. [*Pause.*] You'd harbor it a long long while. And you'd be right.

ROMA   Who said "Fuck the Machine"?

MOSS   *"Fuck the Machine"? "Fuck the Machine"?* What is this. *Courtesy* class . . . ? You're *fucked,* Rick—are you fucking *nuts?* You're hot, so you think you're the *ruler* of this place . . . ?! You want to . . .

LEVENE   Dave . . .

MOSS   . . . Shut up. Decide who should be dealt with how? Is that the thing? I come into the fuckin' office today, I get humiliated by some jagoff cop. I get accused of . . . I get this *shit* thrown in my face by you, you genuine shit, because you're top name on the board . . .

ROMA   Is that what I did? Dave? I humiliated you? My *God* . . . I'm *sorry* . . .

MOSS   Sittin' on top of the *world,* sittin' on top of the *world,* everything's fucking *peach*fuzz . . .

ROMA   Oh, and I don't get a moment to spare for a bust-out *humanitarian* down on his luck lately. Fuck *you,* Dave, you know you got a big *mouth,* and *you* make a close the whole *place* stinks with your *farts* for a week. "How much you just ingested," what a big *man* you are, "Hey, let me buy you a pack of gum. I'll show you how to *chew* it." Your *pal* closes, all that comes out of your mouth is *bile,* how fucked *up* you are . . .

MOSS   *Who's* my pal . . . ? And what are you, Ricky, huh, what are you, Bishop *Sheean?* Who the fuck are *you,* Mr. Slick . . . ? What are you, friend to the *workingman?* Big deal. Fuck *you,* you got the memory a fuckin *fly.* I never liked you.

ROMA   What is this, your farewell speech?

MOSS   I'm going home.

ROMA   Your farewell to the troops?

MOSS   I'm not going home. I'm going to Wis*con*sin.

ROMA   Have a good trip.

MOSS [*Simultaneously with "trip"*]   And fuck *you.* Fuck the *lot* of you. Fuck you *all.* [MOSS *exits. Pause.*]

ROMA [*To* LEVENE]   You were saying? [*Pause.*] Come on. Come on, you got them in the kitchen, you got the stats spread out, you're in your shirt-sleeves, you can *smell* it. Huh? Snap out of it, you're eating her *crumb* cake. [*Pause.*]

LEVENE   I'm eating her *crumb* cake . . .

ROMA   How was it . . . ?

LEVENE   From the store.

ROMA   Fuck *her* . . .

LEVENE   "What we have to do is *admit* to ourself that we see that opportunity . . . and *take* it. [*Pause.*] And that's it." And we *sit* there. [*Pause.*] I got the pen out . . .

ROMA   "Always be closing . . ."

LEVENE   That's what I'm *saying*. The *old* ways. The *old* ways . . . convert the motherfucker . . . *sell* him . . . *sell* him . . . *make him sign the check.* [*Pause.*] The . . . Bruce, Harriett . . . the kitchen, blah: they got their money in *government* bonds. . . . I say *fuck* it, we're going to go the whole route. I plat it out eight units. Eighty-two grand. I tell them. "This is now. This is that *thing* that you've been dreaming of, you're going to find that suitcase on the train, the guy comes in the door, the bag that's full of money. This is it, *Harriett* . . ."

ROMA   [*Reflectively*]   Harriett . . .

LEVENE   Bruce . . . "I don't want to fuck *around* with you. I don't want to go *round* this, and *pussyfoot* around the thing, you have to look back on this. I do, too. I came here to do good for you and me. For *both* of us. Why take an interim position? *The only arrangement I'll accept* is full investment. Period. The whole eight units. I know that you're saying 'be safe,' I know what you're saying. I know if I left you to yourselves, you'd say 'come back tomorrow,' and when I walked out that door, you'd make a cup of *coffee* . . . you'd sit *down* . . . and you'd think 'let's be safe . . .' and not to disappoint me you'd go *one* unit or maybe two, because you'd become scared because you'd met possi*bility*. But this won't do, and that's not the subject. . . ." Listen to this, I actually said this. "That's not the subject of our *evening* together." Now I handed them the pen. I held it in my hand. I turned the contract, eight units eighty-two grand. "Now I want you to sign." [*Pause.*] I sat there. Five minutes. Then, I sat there, Ricky, *twenty-two minutes* by the kitchen *clock*. [*Pause.*] Twenty-two minutes by the kitchen clock. Not a *word*, not a *motion*. What am I thinking? "My arm's getting tired?" No. I *did* it. I *did* it. Like in the *old* days, Ricky. Like I was taught . . . Like, like, like I *used* to do . . . I did it.

ROMA   Like you taught me . . .

LEVENE   Bullshit, you're . . . No. That's raw . . . well, if I *did*, then I'm *glad* I did. I, *well*. I locked on them. All on them, nothing on me. All my thoughts are on them. I'm holding the last thought that I spoke: "Now is the time." [*Pause.*] They signed, Ricky. It was *great*. It was fucking great. It was like they wilted all at once. No *gesture* . . . nothing. Like together. They, I swear to God, they both kind of *imperceptibly slumped*. And he reaches and takes the pen and signs, he passes it to her, she signs. It was so fucking solemn. I just let it sit. I nod like this. I nod again. I grasp his hands. I shake his hands. I grasp *her* hands. I nod at her like this. "Bruce . . . Harriett . . ." I'm beaming at them. I'm nodding like this. I point back in the living room, back to the sideboard. [*Pause.*] *I didn't fucking know there was a sideboard there!!* He goes back, he brings us a drink. Little shot glasses. A pattern in 'em. And we toast. In silence. [*Pause.*]

ROMA   That was a great sale, Shelly. [*Pause.*]

LEVENE   Ah, fuck. Leads! Leads! Williamson! [WILLIAMSON *sticks his head out of the office.*] Send me *out!* Send me *out!*

WILLIAMSON   The leads are coming.

LEVENE   *Get* 'em to me!

WILLIAMSON   I talked to Murray and Mitch an hour ago. They're coming in, you understand they're a bit *upset* over this morning's . . .

LEVENE   Did you tell 'em my sale?

WILLIAMSON   How could I tell 'em your sale? Eh? I don't have a tel . . . I'll tell 'em your sale when they bring in the leads. Alright? Shelly. Alright? We had a little . . . You closed a deal. You made a good sale. Fine.

LEVENE   It's better than a good sale. It's a . . .

WILLIAMSON   Look: I have a lot of things on my mind, they're coming in, alright, they're very upset, I'm trying to make some *sense* . . .

LEVENE   All that I'm *telling* you: that one thing you can tell them it's a remarkable sale.

WILLIAMSON   The only thing remarkable is who you made it to.

LEVENE   What does *that* fucking mean?

WILLIAMSON   That if the sale sticks, it will be a miracle.

LEVENE   Why should the sale not stick? Hey, *fuck* you. That's what I'm saying. You have no idea of your job. A man's his job and you're *fucked* at yours. You hear what I'm saying to you? Your "end of month board . . ." You can't run an office. I don't care. You don't know what it *is,* you don't have the *sense,* you don't have the *balls.* You ever been on a sit? *Ever?* Has this cocksucker ever been . . . you ever sit down with a cust . . .

WILLIAMSON   I were you, I'd calm down, Shelly.

LEVENE   *Would* you? *Would* you . . . ? Or you're gonna *what,* fire me?

WILLIAMSON   It's not impossible.

LEVENE   On an eighty-thousand dollar *day?* And it ain't even *noon.*

ROMA   You closed 'em today?

LEVENE   Yes. I did. This *morning.* [*To* WILLIAMSON] What I'm *saying* to you: things can *change.* You *see? This is where you fuck up,* because this is something you don't *know.* You can't look down the *road.* And see what's *coming.* Might be someone *else,* John. It might be someone *new,* eh? Someone *new.* And you can't look *back.* 'Cause you don't know *history.* You ask them. When we were at Rio Rancho, who was top man? A month . . . ? Two months . . . ? Eight months in twelve for three years in a row. You know what that means? You know what that means? Is that *luck?* Is that some, some, some purloined leads? That's *skill.* That's *talent,* that's, that's . . .

ROMA   . . . *yes* . . .

LEVENE   . . . and you don't *remember.* 'Cause you weren't *around.* That's cold *calling.* Walk up to the door. I don't even know their *name.* I'm selling something they don't even *want.* You talk about soft sell . . . before we had a name for it . . . before we called it anything, we did it.

ROMA   That's right, Shel.

LEVENE   And, and, and, I *did* it. And I put a kid through *school.* She . . . and Cold *calling,* fella. Door to door. But you don't know. You don't know. You never heard of a *streak.* You never heard of "marshaling your sales force. . . ." What are you, you're a *secretary,* John. Fuck *you.* That's my message to you. Fuck you and kiss my ass. You don't like it, I'll go talk to Jerry Graff. Period. Fuck you. Put me on the board. And I want three worthwhile leads today and I don't want any bullshit about them and I want 'em close together 'cause I'm going to hit them all today. That's all I have to say to you.

ROMA He's right, Williamson. [WILLIAMSON *goes into a side office. Pause.*]

LEVENE It's not right. I'm sorry, and I'll tell you who's to blame is Mitch and Murray. [ROMA *sees something outside the window.*]

ROMA [*Sotto*] Oh, Christ.

LEVENE The hell with him. We'll go to lunch, the leads won't be up for . . .

ROMA You're a client. I just sold you five waterfront Glengarry Farms. I rub my head, throw me the cue "Kenilworth."

LEVENE What is it?

ROMA Kenilw . . . [LINGK *enters the office.*]

ROMA [*To* LEVENE] I own the property, my *mother* owns the property, I put her *into* it. I'm going to show you on the plats. You look when you get home A–3 through A–14 and 26 through 30. You take your time and if you still feel.

LEVENE No, Mr. Roma. I don't need the time, I've made a lot of *investments* in the last . . .

LINGK I've got to talk to you.

ROMA [*Looking up*] Jim! What are you doing here? Jim Lingk, D. Ray Morton . . .

LEVENE Glad to meet you.

ROMA I just put Jim into Black Creek . . . are you acquainted with . . .

LEVENE No . . . Black *Creek*. Yes. In *Florida?*

ROMA Yes.

LEVENE I wanted to *speak* with you about . . .

ROMA Well, we'll do that this weekend.

LEVENE My *wife* told me to look into . . .

ROMA *Beautiful.* Beautiful rolling land. I was telling Jim and Jinny, Ray, I want to tell you something. [*To* LEVENE] You, Ray, you eat in a lot of restaurants. I know you do. . . . [*To* LINGK] Mr. Morton's with American Express . . . he's . . . [*To* LEVENE] I can tell Jim what you do . . . ?

LEVENE Sure.

ROMA Ray is director of all European sales and services for American Ex . . . [*To* LEVENE] But I'm saying you haven't had a *meal* until you've tasted . . . I was at the Lingks' last . . . as a matter of fact, what was that service feature you were talking about . . . ?

LEVENE Which . . .

ROMA "Home Cooking" . . . what did you call it, you said it . . . it was a tag phrase that you had . . .

LEVENE Uh . . .

ROMA Home . . .

LEVENE Home cooking . . .

ROMA The monthly interview . . . ?

LEVENE Oh! For the *magazine* . . .

ROMA Yes. Is this something that I can talk ab . . .

LEVENE Well, it isn't coming *out* until the February iss . . . *sure*. Sure, go ahead, Ricky.

ROMA   You're sure?

LEVENE   [*nods*] Go ahead.

ROMA   Well, Ray was eating at one of his company's men's home in France
. . . the man's French, isn't he?

LEVENE   No, his *wife* is.

ROMA   Ah. Ah, his wife is. Ray: what *time* do you have . . . ?

LEVENE   Twelve-fifteen.

ROMA   Oh! My God . . . I've got to get you on the *plane!*

LEVENE   Didn't I say I was taking the two o' . . .

ROMA   No. You said the one. That's why you said we couldn't talk till Ken-
ilworth.³

LEVENE   Oh, my God, you're right! I'm on the one. . . . [*Getting up.*] Well,
let's scoot . . .

LINGK   I've got to talk to you . . .

ROMA   I've got to get Ray to O'Hare⁴ . . . [*To* LEVENE] Come on, let's hustle.
. . . [*Over his shoulder*] John! Call American Express in *Pittsburgh* for Mr.
Morton, will you, tell them he's on the one o'clock. [*To* LINGK] I'll see
you. . . . Christ, I'm sorry you came all the way in. . . . I'm running Ray
over to O'Hare. . . . You wait here, I'll . . . no. [*To* LEVENE] I'm meeting
your man at the bank. . . . [*To* LINGK] I wish you'd phoned. . . . I'll tell
you, wait: are you and Jinny going to be home tonight? [*Rubs forehead.*]

LINGK   I . . .

LEVENE   Rick.

ROMA   What?

LEVENE   *Kenilworth . . . ?*

ROMA   I'm sorry . . . ?

LEVENE   *Kenilworth.*

ROMA   Oh, God . . . Oh, God . . . [ROMA *takes* LINGK *aside, sotto*] Jim,
excuse me. . . . Ray, I told you, who he is is *the* senior vice-president
American Express. His family owns 32 per. . . . Over the past years I've
sold him . . . I can't tell you the dollar amount, but *quite* a lot of land. I
promised five *weeks* ago that I'd go to the wife's birthday party in Kenilworth tonight. [*Sighs.*] I *have* to go. You understand. They treat me like
a member of the family, so I have to go. It's funny, you know, you get a
picture of the Corporation-Type Company Man, all business . . . this
man, *no.* We'll go out to his home sometime. Let's see. [*He checks his
datebook.*] Tomorrow. No. Tomorrow, I'm in L.A. . . . *Monday* . . . I'll
take you to lunch, where would you like to go?

LINGK   My wife . . . [ROMA *rubs his head.*]

LEVENE   [*Standing in the door.*]   Rick . . . ?

ROMA   I'm sorry, Jim. I can't talk now. I'll call you tonight . . . I'm sorry.
I'm coming, Ray. [*Starts for the door.*]

LINGK   My wife said I have to cancel the deal.

ROMA   It's a common reaction, Jim. I'll tell you what it is, and I know that
that's why you married her. One of the reasons is *prudence.* It's a sizable
investment. One thinks *twice* . . . it's also something *women* have. It's
just a reaction to the size of the investment. *Monday,* if you'd invite me
for dinner again . . . [*To* LEVENE] This woman can *cook* . . .

---

3. A community just north of Chicago.   4. Chicago's major airport.

LEVENE [*Simultaneously*] I'm sure she can . . .

ROMA [*To* LINGK] We're going to talk. I'm going to *tell* you something. Because [*Sotto*] there's something about your acreage I want you to know. I can't talk about it now. I really shouldn't. And, in fact, by *law*, I . . . [*Shrugs, resigned.*] The man next to you, he bought his lot at forty-*two,* he phoned to say that he'd *already* had an offer . . . [ROMA *rubs his head.*]

LEVENE Rick . . . ?

ROMA I'm coming, Ray . . . what a day! I'll call you this evening, Jim. I'm sorry you had to come in . . . Monday, lunch.

LINGK My wife . . .

LEVENE Rick, we really have to go.

LINGK My wife . . .

ROMA Monday.

LINGK She called the consumer . . . the attorney, I don't know. The attorney gen . . . they said we have three days . . .

ROMA *Who* did she call?

LINGK I don't know, the attorney gen . . . the . . . some consumer office, umm . . .

ROMA Why did she do *that*, Jim?

LINGK I don't know. [*Pause.*] They said we have three days. [*Pause.*] They said we have three days.

ROMA Three days.

LINGK To . . . you know. [*Pause.*]

ROMA No, I don't know. *Tell* me.

LINGK To change our minds.

ROMA Of *course* you have three days. [*Pause.*]

LINGK So we can't talk *Monday*. [*Pause.*]

ROMA Jim, Jim, you saw my book . . . I *can't, you* saw my book . . .

LINGK But we have to *before* Monday. To get our money ba . . .

ROMA Three *business* days. They mean three *business* days.

LINGK Wednesday, Thursday, Friday.

ROMA I don't understand.

LINGK That's what they are. Three business . . . if I wait till Monday, my time limit runs out.

ROMA You don't count Saturday.

LINGK I'm not.

ROMA No, I'm saying you don't include Saturday . . . in your three days. It's not a *business* day.

LINGK But I'm not *counting* it. [*Pause.*] Wednesday. Thursday. Friday. So it would have elapsed.

ROMA What would have elapsed?

LINGK If we wait till Mon . . .

ROMA When did you write the check?

LINGK Yest . . .

ROMA What was yesterday?

LINGK Tuesday.

ROMA And when was that check cashed?

LINGK I don't know.

ROMA What was the *earliest* it could have been cashed? [*Pause.*]

LINGK I don't know.

ROMA   *Today.* [*Pause.*] *Today.* Which, in any case, it was not, as there were a couple of points on the agreement I wanted to go over with you in any case.

LINGK   The check wasn't cashed?

ROMA   I just called downtown, and it's on their desk.

LEVENE   Rick . . .

ROMA   One moment, I'll be right with you. [*To* LINGK] In fact, a . . . *one* point, which I spoke to you of which [*Looks around.*] I can't talk to you about here. [DETECTIVE *puts his head out of the doorway.*]

BAYLEN   Levene!!!

LINGK   I, I . . .

ROMA   Listen to me, the *statute* it's for your protection. I have no complaints with that, in fact, I was a member of the board when we *drafted* it, so quite the *opposite*. It *says* that you can change your mind three working days from the time the deal is closed.

BAYLEN   Levene!

ROMA   Which, wait a second, which is not until the check is cashed.

BAYLEN   Levene!! [AARONOW *comes out of the* DETECTIVE's *office.*]

AARONOW   I'm *through,* with *this* fucking meshugaas. No one should talk to a man that way. How are you *talking* to me that . . . ?

BAYLEN   Levene! [WILLIAMSON *puts his head out of the office.*]

AARONOW   . . . how can you *talk* to me that . . . that . . .

LEVENE   [*To* ROMA] Rick, I'm going to flag a cab.

AARONOW   I didn't rob . . . [WILLIAMSON *sees* LEVENE.]

WILLIAMSON   Shelly: get in the office.

AARONOW   I didn't . . . why should I . . . "Where were you last . . ." Is anybody listening to me . . . ? Where's Moss . . . ? Where . . . ?

BAYLEN   Levene? [*To* WILLIAMSON] Is this Lev . . . [BAYLEN *accosts* LINGK.]

LEVENE   [*Taking* BAYLEN *into the office*] Ah. Ah. Perhaps I can advise you on that. . . . [*To* ROMA *and* LINGK, *as he exits*] Excuse us, will you . . . ?

AARONOW   [*Simultaneous with* LEVENE's *speech above*] . . . Come in here . . . I *work* here, I don't come in here to be *mistreated* . . .

WILLIAMSON   Go to *lunch,* will you . . .

AARONOW   I want to *work* today, that's why I came . . .

WILLIAMSON   The leads come in, I'll let . . .

AARONOW   . . . that's why I came in. I thought I . . .

WILLIAMSON   Just go to lunch.

AARONOW   I don't *want* to go to lunch.

WILLIAMSON   Go to lunch, George.

AARONOW   Where does he get off to talk that way to a working man? It's not . . .

WILLIAMSON   [*Buttonholes him*] Will you take it outside, we have people trying to do *business* here . . .

AARONOW   That's what, that's what, that's what *I* was trying to do. [*Pause.*] That's why I came *in* . . . I meet *gestapo* tac . . .

WILLIAMSON   [*Going back into his office*] Excuse me . . .

AARONOW   I meet *gestapo* tactics . . . I meet *gestapo* tactics. . . . That's not right. . . . No man has the right to . . . "Call an attorney," that means you're guilt . . . you're under sus . . . "Co . . . ," he says, "cooperate" or we'll go downtown. *That's* not . . . as long as I've . . .

WILLIAMSON   [*Bursting out of his office*] Will you get out of here. Will you get *out* of here. Will you. I'm trying to run an *office* here. Will you go to lunch? Go to lunch. Will you go to lunch? [*Retreats into office.*]

ROMA [*To* AARONOW] Will you excuse . . .

AARONOW Where did Moss . . . ? I . . .

ROMA Will you excuse us please?

AARONOW Uh, uh, did he go to the restaurant? [*Pause.*] I . . . I . . . [*Exits.*]

ROMA I'm *very* sorry, Jimmy. I apologize to you.

LINGK It's not me, it's my wife.

ROMA [*Pause.*] What is?

LINGK I told you.

ROMA Tell me again.

LINGK What's going on here?

ROMA Tell me again. Your wife.

LINGK I told you.

ROMA You tell me again.

LINGK She wants her money back.

ROMA We're going to speak to her.

LINGK No. She told me "right now."

ROMA We'll speak to her, Jim . . .

LINGK She won't listen. [DETECTIVE *sticks his head out.*]

BAYLEN *Roma.*

LINGK She told me if not, I have to call the State's attorney.

ROMA No, no. That's just something she "said." We don't have to do that.

LINGK She told me I *have* to.

ROMA No, Jim.

LINGK I *do.* If I don't get my *money* back . . . [WILLIAMSON *points out* ROMA *to* BAYLEN.]

BAYLEN Roma! [*To* ROMA] I'm talking to you . . .

ROMA I've . . . look. [*Generally*] Will someone get this guy off my back.

BAYLEN You have a problem?

ROMA Yes, I have a problem. Yes, I *do,* my fr . . . It's not me that ripped the joint off, I'm doing *business.* I'll be with you in a *while.* You got it . . . ? [*Looks back.* LINGK *is heading for the door.*] Where are you going?

LINGK I'm . . .

ROMA Where are you going . . . ? This is *me.* . . . This is Ricky, Jim. Jim, anything you *want,* you *want* it, you *have* it. You understand? This is *me.* Something *upset* you. Sit down, now sit down. You tell me what it is. [*Pause.*] Am I going to help you fix it? You're goddamned right I am. Sit down. Tell you something . . . ? *Sometimes* we need someone from *outside.* It's . . . no, sit down. . . . Now *talk* to me.

LINGK I can't negotiate.

ROMA What does that mean?

LINGK That . . .

ROMA . . . what, what, *say* it. Say it to me . . .

LINGK I . . .

ROMA What . . . ?

LINGK I . . .

ROMA What . . . ? Say the words.

LINGK I don't have the *power.* [*Pause.*] I said it.

ROMA What power?

LINGK   The power to negotiate.
ROMA   To negotiate what? [*Pause.*] To negotiate what?
LINGK   *This.*
ROMA   What, "this"? [*Pause.*]
LINGK   The deal.
ROMA   The "deal," *forget* the deal. *Forget* the deal, you've got something
on your mind, Jim, what is it?
LINGK [*rising*]   *I can't talk to you, you* met my wife, I . . . [*Pause.*]
ROMA   What? [*Pause.*] What? [*Pause.*] What, Jim: I tell you what, let's get
out of here . . . let's go get a drink.
LINGK   She told me not to talk to you.
ROMA   Let's . . . no one's going to know, let's go around the *corner* and
we'll get a drink.
LINGK   She told me I had to get back the check or call the State's att . . .
ROMA   *Forget* the deal, Jimmy. [*Pause.*] *Forget* the deal . . . you know me.
The deal's *dead.* Am I talking about the *deal?* That's *over.* Please. Let's
talk about *you.* Come on. [*Pause.* ROMA *rises and starts walking toward
the front door.*] Come on. [*Pause.*] Come on, Jim. [*Pause.*] I want to tell
you something. Your life is your own. You have a contract with your wife.
You have certain things you do *jointly,* you have a *bond* there . . . and
there are *other* things. Those things are yours. You needn't feel *ashamed,*
you needn't feel that you're being *untrue* . . . or that she would abandon
you if you knew. This is your life. [*Pause.*] *Yes.* Now I want to *talk* to you
because you're obviously upset and that *concerns* me. Now let's go. Right
now. [LINGK *gets up and they start for the door.*]
BAYLEN [*Sticks his head out of the door*]   Roma . . .
LINGK   . . . and . . . and . . . [*Pause.*]
ROMA   What?
LINGK   And the check is . . .
ROMA   What did I *tell* you? [*Pause.*] What did I say about the three days
. . . ?
BAYLEN   Roma, would you, I'd like to get some lunch . . .
ROMA   I'm talking with Mr. Lingk. If you please, I'll be back in. [*Checks
watch.*] I'll be back in a while. . . . I told you, check with Mr. Williamson.
BAYLEN   The people downtown said . . .
ROMA   You call them again. Mr. Williamson . . . !
WILLIAMSON   Yes.
ROMA   Mr. Lingk and I are going to . . .
WILLIAMSON   Yes. Please. Please. [*To* LINGK] The police [*Shrugs.*] can
be . . .
LINGK   What are the police doing?
ROMA   It's nothing.
LINGK   What are the *police* doing here . . . ?
WILLIAMSON   We had a slight burglary last night.
ROMA   It was nothing . . . I was assuring Mr. Lingk . . .
WILLIAMSON   Mr. Lingk. James Lingk. Your contract went out. Nothing
to . . .
ROMA   John . . .
WILLIAMSON   Your contract went out to the bank.
LINGK   You cashed the check?

WILLIAMSON We . . .

ROMA   . . . Mr. Williamson . . .

WILLIAMSON Your check was cashed yesterday afternoon. And we're completely insured, as you know, in *any* case. [*Pause.*]

LINGK [*To* ROMA] You cashed the check?

ROMA Not to my knowledge, no . . .

WILLIAMSON I'm sure we can . . .

LINGK Oh, . . . [*Starts out the door.*] Don't follow me. . . . Oh, [*Pause. To* ROMA] I know I've let you down. I'm sorry. For . . . Forgive . . . for . . . I don't know anymore. [*Pause.*] Forgive me. [LINGK *exits. Pause.*]

ROMA [*To* WILLIAMSON] You stupid fucking cunt. *You*, Williamson . . . I'm talking to *you*, shithead . . . You just cost me *six thousand dollars*. [*Pause.*] Six thousand dollars. And one Cadillac. That's right. What are you going to do about it? What are you going to do about it, asshole. You fucking *shit*. Where did you learn your *trade*. You stupid fucking *cunt*. You *idiot*. Whoever told you you could work with *men*?

BAYLEN Could I . . .

ROMA I'm going to have your *job*, shithead. I'm going *downtown* and talk to Mitch and Murray, and I'm going to Lemkin. I don't care *whose* nephew you are, who you know, whose dick you're sucking on. You're going *out*, I swear to you, you're going . . .

BAYLEN Hey, fella, let's get this done . . .

ROMA Anyone in this office lives on their *wits* . . . [*To* BAYLEN] I'm going to be with you in a second. [*To* WILLIAMSON] What you're hired for is to *help* us—does that seem clear to you? To *help* us. *Not* to fuck us up . . . to help *men* who are going *out* there to try to earn a *living*. You *fairy*. You company man . . . I'll tell you something else. I hope you knocked the joint off, I can tell our friend here something might help him catch you. [*Starts into the room.*] You want to learn the first rule you'd know if you ever spent a day in your life . . . you never open your mouth till you know what the shot is. [*Pause.*] You fucking *child* . . . [ROMA *goes to the inner room.*]

LEVENE You *are* a shithead, Williamson . . . [*Pause.*]

WILLIAMSON Mmm.

LEVENE You can't think on your feet you should keep your mouth closed. [*Pause.*] You hear me? I'm *talking* to you. Do you hear me . . . ?

WILLIAMSON Yes. [*Pause.*] I hear you.

LEVENE You can't learn that in an office. Eh? He's right. You have to learn it on the streets. You can't *buy* that. You have to *live* it.

WILLIAMSON Mmm.

LEVENE *Yes.* Mmm. *Yes. Precisely. Precisely.* 'Cause your partner *depends* on it. [*Pause.*] I'm *talking* to you, I'm trying to tell you something.

WILLIAMSON You are?

LEVENE Yes, I am.

WILLIAMSON What are you trying to tell me?

LEVENE What Roma's trying to tell you. What I told you yesterday. Why you don't belong in this business.

WILLIAMSON Why I don't . . .

LEVENE You listen to me, someday you might say, "Hey . . ." No, fuck that, you just listen what I'm going to say: your partner *depends* on you. Your partner . . . a man who's your "partner" *depends* on you . . . you have to go *with* him and *for* him . . . or you're shit, you're *shit, you can't exist alone* . . .

WILLIAMSON [*Brushing past him*]   Excuse me . . .

LEVENE   . . . excuse you, *nothing,* you be as cold as you want, but you just fucked a good man out of six thousand dollars and his goddamn bonus 'cause you didn't know the *shot,* if you can do that and you aren't man enough that it gets you, then I don't know what, if you can't take *something* from that . . . [*Blocking his way*] you're *scum,* you're fucking white-bread. You be as cold as you want. A *child* would know it, he's right. [*Pause.*] You're going to make something up, be sure it will *help* or keep your mouth closed. [*Pause.*]

WILLIAMSON   Mmm. [LEVENE *lifts up his arm.*]

LEVENE   Now I'm done with you. [*Pause.*]

WILLIAMSON   How do you know I made it up?

LEVENE [*Pause.*]   What?

WILLIAMSON   How do you know I made it up?

LEVENE   What are you talking about?

WILLIAMSON   You said, "You don't make something up unless it's for sure to help." [*Pause.*] How did you know that I made it up?

LEVENE   What are you talking about?

WILLIAMSON   I told the customer that his contracts had gone to the bank.

LEVENE   Well, hadn't it?

WILLIAMSON   No. [*Pause.*] It hadn't.

LEVENE   Don't *fuck* with me, John, don't *fuck* with me . . . what are you saying?

WILLIAMSON   Well, I'm saying this, Shel: usually I take the contracts to the bank. Last night I didn't. How did you know that? One night in a year I left a contract on my desk. Nobody knew that but *you.* Now how did you know that? [*Pause.*] You want to talk to me, you want to talk to someone *else* . . . because this is *my* job. This is my job on the line, and you are going to *talk* to me. Now how did you know that contract was on my desk?

LEVENE   You're so full of shit.

WILLIAMSON   You robbed the office.

LEVENE [*Laughs*]   Sure! I robbed the office. Sure.

WILLIAMSON   What'd you do with the leads? [*Pause. Points to the* DETECTIVE's *room.*] You want to go in there? I tell him what I know, he's going to dig up *something* . . . You got an alibi last night? You better have one. What did you do with the leads? If you tell me what you did with the leads, we can talk.

LEVENE   I don't know what you are saying.

WILLIAMSON   If you tell me where the leads are, I won't turn you in. If you *don't,* I am going to tell the cop you stole them, Mitch and Murray will see that you go to jail. Believe me they will. Now, what did you do with the leads? I'm walking in that door—you have five seconds to tell me: or you are going to jail.

LEVENE   I . . .

WILLIAMSON   I don't care. You understand? *Where are the leads?* [*Pause.*] Alright. [WILLIAMSON *goes to open the office door.*]

LEVENE   I sold them to Jerry Graff.

WILLIAMSON   How much did you get for them? [*Pause.*] How much did you get for them?

LEVENE   Five thousand. I kept half.

WILLIAMSON   Who kept the other half? [*Pause.*]

LEVENE   Do I have to tell you? [*Pause.* WILLIAMSON *starts to open the door.*] Moss.

WILLIAMSON   *That* was easy, *wasn't* it? [*Pause.*]

LEVENE   I . . . I'm sure he got more than the five, actually.

WILLIAMSON   Uh-huh?

LEVENE   He told me my share was twenty-five.

WILLIAMSON   Mmm.

LEVENE   Okay: I . . . look: I'm going to make it worth your while. I am. I turned this thing around. I closed the *old* stuff, I can do it again. *I'm* the one's going to close 'em. *I* am! *I* am! 'Cause I turned this thing a . . . I can do *that,* I can do *anyth* . . . last night. I'm going to tell you, I was ready to Do the Dutch. Moss gets me, "Do this, we'll get well . . ." Why not. Big fuckin' deal. I'm halfway hoping to get caught. To put me out of my . . . [*Pause.*] But it *taught* me something. What it taught me, that you've got to get *out* there. Big deal. So I wasn't cut out to be a thief. I was cut out to be a salesman. And now I'm back, and I got my *balls* back . . . and, you know, John, you have the *advantage* on me now. Whatever it takes to make it right, we'll make it right. We're going to make it right.

WILLIAMSON   I want to tell you something, Shelly. You have a big mouth. [*Pause.*]

LEVENE   What?

WILLIAMSON   You've got a big mouth, and now I'm going to show you an even bigger one. [*Starts toward the* DETECTIVE's *door.*]

LEVENE   Where are you going, John? . . . you can't do that, you don't want to do that . . . hold, hold on . . . hold on . . . wait . . . wait . . . wait . . . [*Starts splitting money.*] Look, twelve, twenty, two, twen . . . twenty-five hundred, it's . . . take it. [*Pause.*] Take it all . . . [*Pause.*] Take it!

WILLIAMSON   No, I don't think so, Shel.

LEVENE   I . . .

WILLIAMSON   No, I think I don't want your money. I think you fucked up my office. And I think you're going away.

LEVENE   I . . . what? Are you, are you, that's why you, I'm going to . . . [*Thrusting money at him.*] Here, here, I'm going to *make* this office . . . I'm going to be back there Number One . . . Hey, hey, hey! This is only the beginning . . . List . . . list . . . listen. Listen. Just one moment. List . . . here's what . . . here's what we're going to do. Twenty percent. I'm going to give you twenty percent of my sales. . . . [*Pause.*] Twenty percent. [*Pause.*] For as long as I am with the firm. [*Pause.*] Fifty percent. [*Pause.*] You're going to be my partner. [*Pause.*] Fifty percent. Of all my sales.

WILLIAMSON   What sales?

LEVENE   What sales . . . ? I just *closed* eighty-two grand. . . . Are you fuckin' . . . I'm *back* . . . I'm *back,* this is only the beginning.

WILLIAMSON   Only the beginning . . .

LEVENE   Abso . . .

WILLIAMSON   Where have you been, Shelly? Bruce and Harriett Nyborg.

Do you want to see the *memos* . . . ? They're nuts . . . they used to call in every week. When I was with Webb. And we were selling Arizona . . . they're nuts . . . did you see how they were *living?* How can you delude yours . . .

LEVENE I've got the check . . .

WILLIAMSON Forget it. Frame it. It's worthless. [*Pause.*]

LEVENE The check's no good?

WILLIAMSON You stick around I'll pull the memo for you. [*Starts for the door.*] I'm busy now . . .

LEVENE Their check's no good. They're nuts . . . ?

WILLIAMSON I called them when we had the lead . . . four months ago. [*Pause.*] The people are insane. They just like talking to salesmen. [WILLIAMSON *starts for the door.*]

LEVENE Don't.

WILLIAMSON I'm sorry.

LEVENE *Why?*

WILLIAMSON Because I don't like you.

LEVENE John: John: . . . my *daughter* . . .

WILLIAMSON Fuck you. [ROMA *comes out of the* DETECTIVE's *door.* WILLIAMSON *goes in.*]

ROMA [*To* BAYLEN] Asshole . . . [*To* LEVENE] Guy couldn't find his fuckin' couch the *living room* . . . Ah, . . . what a day, what a day . . . I haven't even had a cup of *coffee* . . . Jagoff John opens his mouth he blows my Cadillac. . . . [*Sighs.*] I swear . . . it's not a world of men . . . it's not a world of men, Machine . . . it's a world of clock watchers, bureaucrats, officeholders . . . what it is, it's a fucked-up world . . . there's no adventure *to* it. [*Pause.*] Dying breed. Yes it is. [*Pause.*] We are the members of a dying breed. That's . . . that's . . . that's why we have to stick together. Shel: I want to talk to you. I've wanted to talk to you for some time. For a long time, actually. I said, "The Machine, there's a man I would work with. There's a man . . ." You know? I never said a thing. I should have, don't know why I didn't. And that shit you were slinging on my guy today was *so* good . . . it . . . it was, and, excuse me, 'cause it isn't even my place to say it. It was admirable . . . it was the old stuff. Hey, I've been on a hot streak, so *what?* There's things that I could learn from you. You eat today?

LEVENE Me.

ROMA Yeah.

LEVENE Mm.

ROMA Well, you want to swing by the Chinks, watch me eat, we'll talk?

LEVENE I think I'd better stay here for a while.

[BAYLEN *sticks his head out of the room*]

BAYLEN Mr. *Levene* . . . ?

ROMA You're done, come down and let's . . .

BAYLEN Would you come in here, please?

ROMA And let's put this together. Okay? Shel? Say okay. [*Pause.*]

LEVENE [*Softly, to himself*] Huh.

BAYLEN Mr. Levene, I think we have to talk.

ROMA I'm going to the Chinks. You're done, come down, we're going to smoke a cigarette.

LEVENE I . . .

BAYLEN [*Comes over*]   . . . Get in the room.

ROMA   Hey, hey, hey, *easy* friend, That's the "Machine." That is Shelly "The Machine" Lev . . .

BAYLEN   Get in the goddamn room. [BAYLEN *starts manhandling* LEVENE *into the room.*]

LEVENE   Ricky, I . . .

ROMA   Okay, okay, I'll be at the resta . . .

LEVENE   Ricky . . .

BAYLEN   "Ricky" can't help you, pal.

LEVENE   . . . I only want to . . .

BAYLEN   Yeah. What do you want? You want to *what*? [*He pushes* LEVENE *into the room, closes the door behind him. Pause.*]

ROMA   Williamson: listen to me: when the *leads* come in . . . listen to me: when the *leads* come in I want my top two off the list. For *me*. My usual two. Anything you give *Levene* . . .

WILLIAMSON   . . . I wouldn't worry about it.

ROMA   Well I'm *going* to worry about it, and so are you, so shut up and listen. [*Pause.*] I GET HIS ACTION. My stuff is *mine*, whatever *he* gets for himself, I'm taking half. You put me in with him. [AARONOW *enters.*]

AARONOW   Did they . . . ?

ROMA   You understand?

AARONOW   Did they catch . . . ?

ROMA   Do you understand? My stuff is mine, his stuff is ours. I'm taking half of his commissions—now, *you* work it out.

WILLIAMSON   Mmm.

AARONOW   Did they find the guy who broke into the office yet?

ROMA   No. *I* don't know. [*Pause.*]

AARONOW   Did the leads come in yet?

ROMA   No.

AARONOW [*Settling into a desk chair*]   Oh, god, I hate this job.

ROMA [*Simultaneous with "job," exiting the office*]   I'll be at the restaurant.

1984

LESLIE MARMON SILKO
b. 1948

Born in Albuquerque, New Mexico, Leslie Marmon Silko was raised in Old Laguna, a village fifty miles west of Albuquerque. The Spaniards had founded a mission there early in the eighteenth century, but Old Laguna had been formed centuries earlier by cattle-keeping Pueblos who successfully repelled raids on them by the Navajos and the Apaches. Writing of the unchanging character of Pueblo religious practices over the centuries, the historian Joe S. Sando notes that

> The tradition of religious beliefs permeates every aspect of the people's life; it determines man's relation with the natural world and with his fellow man. Its

basic concern is continuity of a harmonious relationship with the world in which man lives.

Silko's work concerns itself with such matters. Her own heritage is complicated in that her great-grandfather Robert Marmon was white, whereas her mother was a mixed-blood Plains Indian who kept her daughter on the traditional cradle board during her first year of infancy. (There is also some Mexican blood in her background.) Rather than being handicapped by this heritage, Silko has made it a source of strength. She writes: "I suppose at the core of my writing is the attempt to identify what it is to be a half-breed or mixed blooded person; what it is to grow up neither white nor fully traditional Indian." At the same time, she insists that "what I know is Laguna. This place I am from is everything I am as a writer and human being." She grew up an active child, had a horse of her own by age eight, and by thirteen owned a rifle, with which she took part in deer hunts. Commuting to Albuquerque, she attended Catholic schools, took a B.A. from the University of New Mexico, then began law school under a special program for Native Americans. But she soon gave it up to become a writer and teacher.

Her first published story, "The Man to Send Rain Clouds" (1969), came out of a college assignment in a writing course. She had heard, in Laguna, of an old man found dead in a sheep camp who had been given a traditional burial—a fact resented by the priest who was not called in. The story she wrote about this situation, published in the New Mexico Quarterly, put her on the road to success as a writer. In 1974 a selection of her poems was published in a volume titled Laguna Woman, and in 1977 her novel Ceremony, brought her recognition as a leading voice among native American writers. Ceremony, which shows the dark aspects of modern American Indian life, began as a short story about a World War II veteran, in acute physical and emotional straits as the novel begins, but who manages to survive by reestablishing contact with his native roots. When the book was published, Silko insisted it was not just or even mainly about characters: "This novel is essentially about the powers inherent in the process of storytelling. . . . The chanting or telling of ancient stories to effect certain cures or protect from illness and harm have always been a part of the Pueblo's curing ceremonies." So, she continued, this story of a family was an attempt "to search for a ceremony to deal with despair"—that despair which has led to the "suicide, the alcoholism, and the violence which occur in so many Indian communities today."

Thus there is a strong moral connection between her purely aesthetic delight in the drafting of a story and the therapeutic, functional uses she hopes that it will play in the larger community of Native Americans. In both Ceremony and the aptly titled Storyteller of 1981 (which also contains poems and photographs), Silko's prose is an expressive, active presence, sympathetically creative of landscape as well as of animals and human beings. Plants themselves assume narrative status in her third novel, Gardens in the Dunes (1999), which looks back to late-nineteenth-century events to underscore a basic theme: that myth and history do not coincide.

The text is from Storyteller (1981).

Lullaby

The sun had gone down but the snow in the wind gave off its own light. It came in thick tufts like new wool—washed before the weaver spins it. Ayah reached out for it like her own babies had, and she smiled when she remembered how she had laughed at them. She was an old woman now, and her life had become memories. She sat down with her back against the wide cottonwood tree, feeling the rough bark on her back bones; she faced east and listened to the wind and snow sing a high-pitched Yeibechei song. Out of the wind she felt warmer, and she could watch the wide fluffy snow fill in her tracks, steadily, until the direction she had come from was gone. By the light of the snow she could see the dark outline of the big arroyo[1] a few feet away. She was sitting on the edge of Cebolleta Creek, where in the spring-time the thin cows would graze on grass already chewed flat to the ground. In the wide deep creek bed where only a trickle of water flowed in the sum-mer, the skinny cows would wander, looking for new grass along winding paths splashed with manure.

Ayah pulled the old Army blanket over her head like a shawl. Jimmie's blanket—the one he had sent to her. That was a long time ago and the green wool was faded, and it was unraveling on the edges. She did not want to think about Jimmie. So she thought about the weaving and the way her mother had done it. On the wall wooden loom set into the sand under a tamarack tree for shade. She could see it clearly. She had been only a little girl when her grandma gave her the wooden combs to pull the twigs and burrs from the raw, freshly washed wool. And while she combed the wool, her grandma sat beside her, spinning a silvery strand of yarn around the smooth cedar spindle. Her mother worked at the loom with yarns dyed bright yellow and red and gold. She watched them dye the yarn in boiling black pots full of beeweed petals, juniper berries, and sage. The blankets her mother made were soft and woven so tight that rain rolled off them like birds' feathers. Ayah remembered sleeping warm on cold windy nights, wrapped in her mother's blankets on the hogan's[2] sandy floor.

The snow drifted now, with the northwest wind hurling it in gusts. It drifted up around her black overshoes—old ones with little metal buckles. She smiled at the snow which was trying to cover her little by little. She could remember when they had no black rubber overshoes; only the high buckskin leggings that they wrapped over their elkhide moccasins. If the snow was dry or frozen, a person could walk all day and not get wet; and in the evenings the beams of the ceiling would hang with lengths of pale buck-skin leggings, drying out slowly.

She felt peaceful remembering. She didn't feel cold any more. Jimmie's blanket seemed warmer than it had ever been. And she could remember the morning he was born. She could remember whispering to her mother, who was sleeping on the other side of the hogan, to tell her it was time now. She did not want to wake the others. The second time she called to her, her mother stood up and pulled on her shoes; she knew. They walked to the old stone hogan together, Ayah walking a step behind her mother. She waited alone, learning the rhythms of the pains while her mother went to call the old woman to help them. The morning was already warm even before dawn and Ayah smelled the bee flowers blooming and the young willow growing at the springs. She could remember that so clearly, but his birth merged into the births of the other children and to her it became all the same birth. They named him for the summer morning and in English they called him Jimmie.

It wasn't like Jimmie died. He just never came back, and one day a dark

---

1. Gully carved by water.   2. Navajo dwelling usually made of logs and mud.

blue sedan with white writing on its doors pulled up in front of the boxcar shack where the rancher let the Indians live. A man in a khaki uniform trimmed in gold gave them a yellow piece of paper and told them that Jimmie was dead. He said the Army would try to get the body back and then it would be shipped to them; but it wasn't likely because the helicopter had burned after it crashed. All of this was told to Chato because he could understand English. She stood inside the doorway holding the baby while Chato listened. Chato spoke English like a white man and he spoke Spanish too. He was taller than the white man and he stood straighter too. Chato didn't explain why; he just told the military man they could keep the body if they found it. The white man looked bewildered; he nodded his head and he left. Then Chato looked at her and shook his head, and then he told her, "Jimmie isn't coming home anymore," and when he spoke, he used the words to speak of the dead. She didn't cry then, but she hurt inside with anger. And she mourned him as the years passed, when a horse fell with Chato and broke his leg, and the white rancher told them he wouldn't pay Chato until he could work again. She mourned Jimmie because he would have worked for his father then; he would have saddled the big bay horse and ridden the fence lines each day, with wire cutters and heavy gloves, fixing the breaks in the barbed wire and putting the stray cattle back inside again.

She mourned him after the white doctors came to take Danny and Ella away. She was at the shack alone that day they came. It was back in the days before they hired Navajo women to go with them as interpreters. She recognized one of the doctors. She had seen him at the children's clinic at Cañoncito about a month ago. They were wearing khaki uniforms and they waved papers at her and a black ball-point pen, trying to make her understand their English words. She was frightened by the way they looked at the children, like the lizard watches the fly. Danny was swinging on the tire swing on the elm tree behind the rancher's house, and Ella was toddling around the front door, dragging the broomstick horse Chato made for her. Ayah could see they wanted her to sign the papers, and Chato had taught her to sign her name. It was something she was proud of. She only wanted them to go, and to take their eyes away from her children.

She took the pen from the man without looking at his face and she signed the papers in three different places he pointed to. She stared at the ground by their feet and waited for them to leave. But they stood there and began to point and gesture at the children. Danny stopped swinging. Ayah could see his fear. She moved suddenly and grabbed Ella into her arms; the child squirmed, trying to get back to her toys. Ayah ran with the baby toward Danny; she screamed for him to run and then she grabbed him around his chest and carried him too. She ran south into the foothills of juniper trees and black lava rock. Behind her she heard the doctors running, but they had been taken by surprise, and as the hills became steeper and the cholla cactus were thicker, they stopped. When she reached the top of the hill, she stopped to listen in case they were circling around her. But in a few minutes she heard a car engine start and they drove away. The children had been too surprised to cry while she ran with them. Danny was shaking and Ella's little fingers were gripping Ayah's blouse.

She stayed up in the hills for the rest of the day, sitting on a black lava boulder in the sunshine where she could see for miles all around her. The sky was light blue and cloudless, and it was warm for late April. The sun warmth relaxed her and took the fear and anger away. She lay back on the rock and watched the sky. It seemed to her that she could walk into the sky, stepping through clouds endlessly. Danny played with little pebbles and stones, pretending they were birds eggs and then little rabbits. Ella sat at her feet and dropped fistfuls of dirt into the breeze, watching the dust and particles of sand intently. Ayah watched a hawk soar high above them, dark wings gliding; hunting or only watching, she did not know. The hawk was patient and he circled all afternoon before he disappeared around the high volcanic peak the Mexicans called Guadalupe.

Late in the afternoon, Ayah looked down at the gray boxcar shack with the paint all peeled from the wood; the stove pipe on the roof was rusted and crooked. The fire she had built that morning in the oil drum stove had burned out. Ella was asleep in her lap now and Danny sat close to her, complaining that he was hungry; he asked when they would go to the house. "We will stay up here until your father comes," she told him, "because those white men were chasing us." The boy remembered then and he nodded at her silently.

If Jimmie had been there he could have read those papers and explained to her what they said. Ayah would have known then, never to sign them. The doctors came back the next day and they brought a BIA[3] policeman with them. They told Chato they had her signature and that was all they needed. Except for the kids. She listened to Chato sullenly; she hated him when he told her it was the old woman who died in the winter, spitting blood; it was her old grandma who had given the children this disease. "They don't spit blood," she said coldly. "The whites lie." She held Ella and Danny close to her, ready to run to the hills again. "I want a medicine man first," she said to Chato, not looking at him. He shook his head. "It's too late now. The policeman is with them. You signed the paper." His voice was gentle.

It was worse than if they had died: to lose the children and to know that somewhere, in a place called Colorado, in a place full of sick and dying strangers, her children were without her. There had been babies that died soon after they were born, and one that died before he could walk. She had carried them herself, up to the boulders and great pieces of the cliff that long ago crashed down from Long Mesa; she laid them in the crevices of sandstone and buried them in fine brown sand with round quartz pebbles that washed down the hills in the rain. She had endured it because they had been with her. But she could not bear this pain. She did not sleep for a long time after they took her children. She stayed on the hill where they had fled the first time, and she slept rolled up in the blanket Jimmie had sent her. She carried the pain in her belly and it was fed by everything she saw: the blue sky of their last day together and the dust and pebbles they played with; the swing in the elm tree and broomstick horse choked life from her. The pain filled her stomach and there was no room for food or for her lungs to fill with air. The air and the food would have been theirs.

She hated Chato, not because he let the policeman and doctors put the screaming children in the government car, but because he had taught her to sign her name. Because it was like the old ones always told her about learning

3. Bureau of Indian Affairs.

their language or any of their ways: it endangered you. She slept alone on the hill until the middle of November when the first snows came. Then she made a bed for herself where the children had slept. She did not lie down beside Chato again until many years later, when he was sick and shivering and only her body could keep him warm. The illness came after the white rancher told Chato he was too old to work for him anymore, and Chato and his old woman should be out of the shack by the next afternoon because the rancher had hired new people to work there. That had satisfied her. To see how the white man repaid Chato's years of loyalty and work. All of Chato's fine-sounding English talk didn't change things.

It snowed steadily and the luminous light from the snow gradually diminished into the darkness. Somewhere in Cebolleta a dog barked and other village dogs joined with it. Ayah looked in the direction she had come, from the bar where Chato was buying the wine. Sometimes he told her to go on ahead and wait; and then he never came. And when she finally went back looking for him, she would find him passed out at the bottom of the wooden steps to Azzie's Bar. All the wine would be gone and most of the money too, from the pale blue check that came to them once a month in a government envelope. It was then that she would look at his face and his hands, scarred by ropes and the barbed wire of all those years, and she would think, this man is a stranger; for forty years she had smiled at him and cooked his food, but he remained a stranger. She stood up again, with the snow almost to her knees, and she walked back to find Chato.

It was hard to walk in the deep snow and she felt the air burn in her lungs. She stopped a short distance from the bar to rest and readjust the blanket. But this time he wasn't waiting for her on the bottom step with his old Stetson hat pulled down and his shoulders hunched up in his long wool overcoat.

She was careful not to slip on the wooden steps. When she pushed the door open, warm air and cigarette smoke hit her face. She looked around slowly and deliberately, in every corner, in every dark place that the old man might find to sleep. The bar owner didn't like Indians in there, especially Navajos, but he let Chato come in because he could talk Spanish like he was one of them. The men at the bar stared at her, and the bartender saw that she left the door open wide. Snowflakes were flying inside like moths and melting into a puddle on the oiled wood floor. He motioned to her to close the door, but she did not see him. She held herself straight and walked across the room slowly, searching the room with every step. The snow in her hair melted and she could feel it on her forehead. At the far corner of the room, she saw red flames at the mica window of the old stove door; she looked behind the stove just to make sure. The bar got quiet except for the Spanish polka music playing on the jukebox. She stood by the stove and shook the snow from her blanket and held it near the stove to dry. The wet wool smell reminded her of new-born goats in early March, brought inside to warm near the fire. She felt calm.

In past years they would have told her to get out. But her hair was white now and her face was wrinkled. They looked at her like she was a spider crawling slowly across the room. They were afraid; she could feel the fear. She looked at their faces steadily. They reminded her of the first time the white people brought her children back to her that winter. Danny had been shy and hid behind the thin white woman who brought them. And the baby had not known her until Ayah took her into her arms, and then Ella had nuzzled close to her as she had when she was nursing. The blonde woman was nervous and kept looking at a dainty gold watch on her wrist. She sat on the bench near the small window and watched the dark snow clouds gather around the mountains; she was worrying about the unpaved road. She was frightened by what she saw inside too: the strips of venison drying on a rope across the ceiling and the children jabbering excitedly in a language she did not know. So they stayed for only a few hours. Ayah watched the government car disappear down the road and she knew they were already being weaned from these lava hills and from this sky. The last time they came was in early June, and Ella stared at her the way the men in the bar were now staring. Ayah did not try to pick her up; she smiled at her instead and spoke cheerfully to Danny. When he tried to answer her, he could not seem to remember and he spoke English words with the Navajo. But he gave her a scrap of paper that he had found somewhere and carried in his pocket; it was folded in half, and he shyly looked up at her and said it was a bird. She asked Chato if they were home for good this time. He spoke to the white woman and she shook her head. "How much longer?" he asked, and she said she didn't know; but Chato saw how she stared at the boxcar shack. Ayah turned away then. She did not say good-bye.

She felt satisfied that the men in the bar feared her. Maybe it was her face and the way she held her mouth with teeth clenched tight, like there was nothing anyone could do to her now. She walked north down the road, searching for the old man. She did this because she had the blanket, and there would be no place for him except with her and the blanket in the old adobe barn near the arroyo. They always slept there when they came to Cebolleta. If the money and the wine were gone, she would be relieved because then they could go home again; back to the old hogan with a dirt roof and rock walls where she herself had been born. And the next day the old man could go back to the few sheep they still had, to follow along behind them, guiding them, into dry sandy arroyos where sparse grass grew. She knew he did not like walking behind old ewes when for so many years he rode big quarter horses and worked with cattle. But she wasn't sorry for him; he should have known all along what would happen.

There had not been enough rain for their garden in five years; and that was when Chato finally hitched a ride into the town and brought back brown boxes of rice and sugar and big tin cans of welfare peaches. After that, at the first of the month they went to Cebolleta to ask the postmaster for the check; and then Chato would go to the bar and cash it. They did this as they planted the garden every May, not because anything would survive the summer dust, but because it was time to do this. The journey passed the days that smelled silent and dry like the caves above the canyon with yellow painted buffaloes on their walls.

He was walking along the pavement when she found him. He did not stop or turn around when he heard her behind him. She walked beside him and she noticed how slowly he moved now. He smelled strongly of woodsmoke and urine. Lately he had been forgetting. Sometimes he called her by his sister's name and she had been gone for a long time. Once she had found him wandering on the road to the white man's ranch, and she asked him why he was going that way; he laughed at her and said, "You know they can't run that ranch without me," and he walked on determined, limping on the leg that had been crushed many years before. Now he looked at her curiously, as if for the first time, but he kept shuffling along, moving slowly along the side of the highway. His gray hair had grown long and spread out on the shoulders of the long overcoat. He wore the old felt hat pulled down over his ears. His boots were worn out at the toes and he had stuffed pieces of an old red shirt in the holes. The rags made his feet look like little animals up to their ears in snow. She laughed at his feet; the snow muffled the sound of her laugh. He stopped and looked at her again. The wind had quit blowing and the snow was falling straight down; the southeast sky was beginning to clear and Ayah could see a star.

"Let's rest awhile," she said to him. They walked away from the road and up the slope to the giant boulders that had tumbled down from the red sandrock mesa throughout the centuries of rainstorms and earth tremors. In a place where the boulders shut out the wind, they sat down with their backs against the rock. She offered half of the blanket to him and they sat wrapped together.

The storm passed swiftly. The clouds moved east. They were massive and full, crowding together across the sky. She watched them with the feeling of horses—steely blue-gray horses startled across the sky. The powerful haunches pushed into the distances and the tail hairs streamed white mist behind them. The sky cleared. Ayah saw that there was nothing between her and the stars. The light was crystalline. There was no shimmer, no distortion through earth haze. She breathed the clarity of the night sky; she smelled the purity of the half moon and the stars. He was lying on his side with his knees pulled up near his belly for warmth. His eyes were closed now, and in the light from the stars and the moon, he looked young again.

She could see it descend out of the night sky: an icy stillness from the edge of the thin moon. She recognized the freezing. It came gradually, sinking snowflake by snowflake until the crust was heavy and deep. It had the strength of the stars in Orion, and its journey was endless. Ayah knew that with the wine he would sleep. He would not feel it. She tucked the blanket around him, remembering how it was when Ella had been with her; and she felt the rush so big inside her heart for the babies. And she sang the only song she knew to sing for babies. She could not remember if she had ever sung it to her children, but she knew that her grandmother had sung it and her mother had sung it:

> *The earth is your mother,*
> *   she holds you.*
> *The sky is your father,*
> *   he protects you.*
> *Sleep,*
> *sleep.*
> *Rainbow is your sister,*
> *   she loves you.*
> *The winds are your brothers,*
> *   they sing to you.*
> *Sleep,*

> sleep.
> We are together always
> We are together always
> There never was a time
> when this
> was not so.

1981

JUDITH ORTIZ COFER
b. 1952

"As a child caught in that lonely place between two cultures and two languages," Judith Ortiz Cofer recalls, "I wrapped myself in the magical veil of folktales and fairy tales. The earliest stories I heard were those told by the women of my family in Puerto Rico." Born in Hormigueros, Puerto Rico, and from age four raised and educated in the United States (principally in Paterson, New Jersey), Ortiz Cofer has dedicated her career, as a writer and educator, to an integrity of self that is able to create a harmonic culture out of what would otherwise be the dissonant clashes between Latin and Anglo experiences.

The earliest stories Ortiz Cofer heard are much like "The Witch's Husband" (printed here): versions of Spanish and classical myths that had been "translated by time and each generation's needs." While her father served in the U.S. Navy, young Judith Ortiz immersed herself in the ambience of the Puerto Rican neighborhoods of Paterson, cultivating the attitudes and institutions that would motivate *An Island Like You: Stories of the Barrio* (1998), a book for young adult readers. As an English major at Augusta College and a graduate student at Florida Atlantic University, she studied both traditional and modern literature, writing a master's thesis in 1974 on Lillian Hellman's southern plays at the same time she was working as a bilingual teacher in the public schools of Palm Beach County, Florida. Having married businessman John Cofer in 1971, she began a family (with a daughter, Tanya) and commenced a series of adjunct instructorships at Broward Community College and the University of Miami. In 1984, with a national reputation as a writer being established, Ortiz Cofer accepted a faculty position at the University of Georgia, where she is presently Franklin Professor of English and director of creative writing.

All of Ortiz Cofer's work, which includes fiction, poetry, and essays, is infused with a sense of memoir. *Silent Dancing: A Partial Remembrance of a Puerto Rican Childhood* (1990) melds with Ortiz Cofer's novel, *The Line of the Sun* (1989), in the author's bicultural consideration of a life begun in Puerto Rico and continued in New Jersey, especially as the protagonist of each must balance conflicting encouragements to become wholly American or remain essentially Puerto Rican. *The Latin Deli* (1993) collects stories and poems on this theme, while *Woman in Front of the Sun: On Becoming a Writer* (2000) explores how the author's biculturalism has given her a new way to write.

The text is from *The Latin Deli* (1993).

The Witch's Husband

My grandfather has misplaced his words again. He is trying to find my name in the kaleidoscope of images that his mind has become. His face brightens like a child's who has just remembered his lesson. He points to me and says my mother's name. I smile back and kiss him on the cheek. It doesn't matter what names he remembers anymore. Every day he is more confused, his memory slipping back a little further in time. Today he has no grandchildren yet. Tomorrow he will be a young man courting my grandmother again, quoting bits of poetry to her. In months to come, he will begin calling her Mamá.

I have traveled to Puerto Rico at my mother's request to help her deal with the old people. My grandfather is physically healthy, but his dementia is severe. My grandmother's heart is making odd sounds again in her chest. Yet she insists on taking care of the old man at home herself. She will not give up her house, though she has been warned that her heart might fail in her sleep without proper monitoring, that is, a nursing home or a relative's care. Her response is typical of her famous obstinacy: *"Bueno,"*[1] she says, "I will die in my own bed."

I am now at her house, waiting for my opportunity to talk "sense" into her. As a college teacher in the United States I am supposed to represent the voice of logic; I have been called in to convince *la abuela,*[2] the family's proud matriarch, to step down—to allow her children to take care of her before she kills herself with work. I spent years at her house as a child but have lived in the U.S. for most of my adult life. I learned to love and respect this strong woman, who with five children of her own had found a way to help many others. She was a legend in the pueblo for having more foster children than anyone else. I have spoken with people my mother's age who told me that they had spent up to a year at Abuela's house during emergencies and hard times. It seems extraordinary that a woman would willingly take on such obligations. And frankly, I am a bit appalled at what I have begun to think of as "the martyr complex" in Puerto Rican women, that is, the idea that self-sacrifice is a woman's lot and her privilege: a good woman is defined by how much suffering and mothering she can do in one lifetime. Abuela is the all-time champion in my eyes: her life has been entirely devoted to others. Not content to bring up two sons and three daughters as the Depression raged on, followed by the war that took one of her sons, she had also taken on other people's burdens. This had been the usual pattern with one exception that I knew of: the year that Abuela spent in New York, apparently undergoing some kind of treatment for her heart while she was still a young woman. My mother was five or six years old, and there were three other children who had been born by that time too. They were given into the care of Abuela's sister, Delia. The two women traded places for the year. Abuela went to live in her sister's apartment in New York City while the younger woman took over Abuela's duties at the house in Puerto Rico. Grandfather was a shadowy figure in the background during that period. My mother doesn't say much about what went on during that year, only that her mother

1. Good (Spanish). All translations are from the Spanish.   2. Grandmother.

was sick and away for months. Grandfather seemed absent too, since he worked all of the time. Though they missed Abuela, they were well taken care of.

I am sitting on a rocking chair on the porch of her house. She is facing me from a hammock she made when her first baby was born. My mother was rocked on that hammock. I was rocked on that hammock, and when I brought my daughter as a baby to Abuela's house, she was held in Abuela's sun-browned arms, my porcelain pink baby, and rocked to a peaceful sleep too. She sits there and smiles as the breeze of a tropical November brings the scent of her roses and her herbs to us. She is proud of her garden. In front of the house she grows flowers and lush trailing plants; in the back, where the mango tree gives shade, she has an herb garden. From this patch of weedy-looking plants came all the remedies of my childhood, for anything from a sore throat to menstrual cramps. Abuela had a recipe for every pain that a child could dream up, and she brought it to your bed in her own hands smelling of the earth. For a moment I am content to sit in her comforting presence. She is rotund now; a small-boned brown-skinned earth mother—with a big heart and a temper to match. My grandfather comes to stand at the screen door. He has forgotten how the latch works. He pulls at the knob and moans softly, rattling it. With some effort Abuela gets down from the hammock. She opens the door, gently guiding the old man to a chair at the end of the porch. There he begins anew his constant search for the words he needs. He tries various combinations, but they don't work as language. Abuela pats his hand and motions for me to follow her into the house. We sit down at opposite ends of her sofa.

She apologizes to me as if for a misbehaving child.

"He'll quiet down," she says. "He does not like to be ignored."

I take a deep breath in preparation for my big lecture to Grandmother. This is the time to tell her that she has to give up trying to run this house and take care of others at her age. One of her daughters is prepared to take her in. Grandfather is to be sent to a nursing home. Before I can say anything, Abuela says: "Mi amor,[3] would you like to hear a story?"

I smile, surprised at her offer. These are the same words that stopped me in my tracks as a child, even in the middle of a tantrum. Abuela could always entrance me with one of her tales. I nod. Yes, my sermon can wait a little longer, I thought.

"Let me tell you an old, old story I heard when I was a little girl.

"There was once a man who became worried and suspicious when he noticed that his wife disappeared from their bed every night for long periods of time. Wanting to find out what she was doing before confronting her, the man decided to stay awake at night and keep guard. For hours he watched her every movement through half-closed eyelids with his ears perked up like those of a burro.

"Then just about midnight, when the night was as dark as the bottom of a cauldron, he felt his wife slipping out of bed. He saw her go to the wardrobe and take out a jar and a little paintbrush. She stood naked by the window, and when the church bells struck twelve, she began to paint her entire body with the paintbrush, dipping it into the jar. As the bells tolled the hour, she

3. My love.

whispered these words: *I don't believe in the church, or in God, or in the Virgin Mary.* As soon as this was spoken, she rose from the ground and flew into the night like a bird.

"Astounded, the man decided not to say anything to his wife the next day, but to try to find out where she went. The following night, the man pretended to sleep and waited until she had again performed her little ceremony and flown away, then he repeated her actions exactly. He soon found himself flying after her. Approaching a palace, he saw many other women circling the roof, taking turns going down the chimney. After the last had descended, he slid down the dark hole that led to the castle's bodega,[4] where food and wine were stored. He hid himself behind some casks of wine and watched the women greet each other.

"The witches, for that's what they were, were the wives of his neighbors and friends, but he at first had trouble recognizing them, for like his wife, they were all naked. With much merriment, they took the meats and cheeses that hung from the bodega's rafters and laid a table for a feast. They drank the fine wines right from the bottles, like men in a cantina,[5] and danced wildly to eerie music from invisible instruments. They spoke to each other in a language that he did not understand, words that sounded like a cat whose tail has been stepped on. Still, horrible as their speech was, the food they prepared smelled delicious. Cautiously placing himself in the shadows near one of the witches, he extended his hand for a plate. He was given a steaming dish of stewed tongue. Hungrily, he took a bite: it was tasteless. The other witches had apparently noticed the same thing, because they sent one of the younger ones to find some salt. But when the young witch came back into the room with a saltshaker in her hand, the man forgot himself and exclaimed: 'Thank God the salt is here.'

"On hearing God's name, all the witches took flight immediately, leaving the man completely alone in the darkened cellar. He tried the spell for flight that had brought him there, but it did not work. It was no longer midnight, and it was obviously the wrong incantation for going *up* a chimney. He tried all night to get out of the place, which had been left in shambles by the witches, but it was locked up as tight as heaven is to a sinner. Finally, he fell asleep from exhaustion, and slept until dawn, when he heard footsteps approaching. When he saw the heavy door being pushed open, he hid himself behind a cask of wine.

"A man in rich clothes walked in, followed by several servants. They were all armed with heavy sticks as if out to kill someone. When the man lit his torch and saw the chaos in the cellar, broken bottles strewn on the floor, meats and cheeses half-eaten and tossed everywhere, he cried out in such a rage that the man hiding behind the wine cask closed his eyes and committed his soul to God. The owner of the castle ordered his servants to search the whole bodega, every inch of it, until they discovered how vandals had entered his home. It was a matter of minutes before they discovered the witch's husband, curled up like a stray dog and, worse, painted the color of a vampire bat, without a stitch of clothing.

"They dragged him to the center of the room and beat him with their sticks until the poor man thought that his bones had been pulverized and he would

4. Storeroom.   5. Bar.

have to be poured into his grave. When the castle's owner said that he thought the wretch had learned his lesson, the servants tossed him naked onto the road. The man was so sore that he slept right there on the public *camino*,[6] oblivious to the stares and insults of all who passed him. When he awakened in the middle of the night and found himself naked, dirty, bloody, and miles from his home, he swore to himself right then and there that he would never, for anything in the world, follow his wife on her nightly journeys again."

"Colorín, colorado,"[7] Abuela claps her hands three times, chanting the childhood rhyme for ending a story, "Este cuento se ha acabado."[8] She smiles at me, shifting her position on the sofa to be able to watch Grandfather muttering to himself on the porch. I remember those eyes on me when I was a small child. Their movements seemed to be triggered by a child's actions, like those holograms of the Holy Mother that were popular with Catholics a few years ago—you couldn't get away from their mesmerizing gaze.

"Will you tell me about your year in New York, Abuela?" I surprise myself with the question. But suddenly I need to know about Abuela's lost year. It has to be another good story.

She looks intently at me before she answers. Her eyes are my eyes, same dark brown color, almond shape, and the lids that droop a little: called by some "bedroom eyes"; to others they are a sign of a cunning nature. "Why are you looking at me that way?" is a question I am often asked.

"I wanted to leave home," she says calmly, as though she had been expecting the question from me all along.

"You mean abandon your family?" I am really taken aback by her words.

"Yes, Hija.[9] That is exactly what I mean. Abandon them. Never to return."

"Why?"

"I was tired. I was young and pretty, full of energy and dreams." She smiles as Grandfather breaks into song standing by himself on the porch. A woman passing by with a baby in her arms waves at him. Grandfather sings louder, something about a man going to his exile because the woman he loves has rejected him. He finishes the song on a long note and continues to stand in the middle of the tiled porch as if listening for applause. He bows.

Abuela shakes her head, smiling a little, as if amused by his antics, then she finishes her sentence, "Restless, bored. Four children and a husband all demanding more and more from me."

"So you left the children with your sister and went to New York?" I say, trying to keep the mixed emotions I feel out of my voice. I look at the serene old woman in front of me and cannot believe that she once left four children and a loving husband to go live alone in a faraway country.

"I had left him once before, but he found me. I came back home, but on the condition that he never follow me anywhere again. I told him the next time I would not return." She is silent, apparently falling deep into thought.

"You were never really sick," I say, though I am afraid that she will not resume her story. But I want to know more about this woman whose life I thought was an open book.

"I *was* sick. Sick at heart. And he knew it," she says, keeping her eyes on

6. Road.
7. Bright colors, colored red.

8. This story is finished.
9. Daughter.

Grandfather, who is standing as still as a marble statue on the porch. He seems to be listening intently for something.

"The year in New York was his idea. He saw how unhappy I was. He knew I needed to taste freedom. He paid my sister Delia to come take care of the children. He also sublet her apartment for me, though he had to take a second job to do it. He gave me money and told me to go."

"What did you do that year in New York?" I am both stunned and fascinated by Abuela's revelation. "I worked as a seamstress in a fancy dress shop. And . . . y pues,[1] Hija," she smiles at me as if I should know some things without being told, "I lived."

"Why did you come back?" I ask.

"Because I love him," she says, "and I missed my children."

He is scratching at the door. Like a small child he has traced the sound of Abuela's voice back to her. She lets him in, guiding him gently by the hand. Then she eases him down on his favorite rocking chair. He begins to nod; soon he will be sound asleep, comforted by her proximity, secure in his familiar surroundings. I wonder how long it will take him to revert to infantilism. The doctors say he is physically healthy and may live for many years, but his memory, verbal skills, and ability to control his biological functions will deteriorate rapidly. He may end his days bedridden, perhaps comatose. My eyes fill with tears as I look at the lined face of this beautiful and gentle old man. I am in awe of the generosity of spirit that allowed him to give a year of freedom to the woman he loved, not knowing whether she would ever return to him. Abuela has seen my tears and moves over on the sofa to sit near me. She slips an arm around my waist and pulls me close. She kisses my wet cheek. Then she whispers softly into my ear, "and in time, the husband either began forgetting that he had seen her turn into a witch or believed that he had just dreamed it."

She takes my face into her hands. "I am going to take care of your grandfather until one of us dies. I promised him when I came back that I would never leave home again unless he asked me to: he never did. He never asked any questions."

I hear my mother's car pull into the driveway. She will wait there for me. I will have to admit that I failed in my mission. I will argue Abuela's case without revealing her secret. As far as everyone is concerned she went away to recover from problems with her heart. That part is true in both versions of the story.

At the door she gives me the traditional blessing, adding with a wink, "Colorín, colorado." My grandfather, hearing her voice, smiles in his sleep.

1993

---

1. And well.

SANDRA CISNEROS
b. 1954

Sandra Cisneros began her life as a writer at age ten, much like the young Chicana narrator of *The House on Mango Street* (1984), the volume of interrelated vignettes from a child's perspective that brought Cisneros her first major attention. In brief, sharply drawn but quietly expressed segments, the narrator, Esperanza, conveys the ambience of growing up in a street in Chicago's Mexican American community. The social bond of this neighborhood eases the contrast between Esperanza's nurturing family and the more hostile forces of poverty and racism. Cisneros cultivates a sense of warmth and naive humor for her protagonists, qualities that are evident in the stories printed here, which form the introductory parts to *Woman Hollering Creek* (1991), a volume that also deals with more troublesome aspects of young women facing hostile forces in the world. Sex is a topic in all Cisneros's work, including her poetry collected as *My Wicked Wicked Ways* (1987) and *Loose Woman* (1994)—sometimes gentle and even silly, other times brutally assaultive. What remains constant is the author's view that by romanticizing sexual relations women cooperate with a male view that can be oppressive, if not physically destructive.

Born in Chicago, the child of a Mexican father and Mexican American mother, Cisneros spent time in Texas and Mexico as well. Her Catholic education led to a B.A. degree from Chicago's Loyola University, after which she earned a graduate degree in creative writing from the University of Iowa's Writers Workshop. Teaching in San Antonio, Texas, she has used her position as a writer and an educator to expound Chicana feminism, especially as this movement combines cultural issues with women's concerns. A dissatisfaction with the politics of publishing has made her an advocate of small-press dissemination. Most of all, as in the stories reprinted here, she is eager to show the rich dynamics of characters existing in the blend of Mexican and American cultures that begins with speaking two languages and extends to almost every aspect of life. Spanish words, Mexican holidays, ethnic foods, and localized religious practices punctuate the narrative; her characters have a facility with cultural play that reflects what for others would be an anthropologically enhanced understanding.

The texts are from *Woman Hollering Creek* (1991).

My Lucy Friend Who Smells Like Corn

Lucy Anguiano, Texas girl who smells like corn, like Frito Bandito chips, like tortillas, something like that warm smell of *nixtamal*[1] or bread the way her head smells when she's leaning close to you over a paper cut-out doll or on the porch when we are squatting over marbles trading this pretty crystal that leaves a blue star on your hand for that giant cat-eye with a grasshopper green spiral in the center like the juice of bugs on the windshield when you drive to the border, like the yellow blood of butterflies.

Have you ever eaten dog food? I have. After crunching like ice, she opens her big mouth to prove it, only a pink tongue rolling around in there like a blind worm, and Janey looking in because she said Show me. But me I like that Lucy, corn smell hair and aqua flip-flops just like mine that we bought at the K mart for only 79 cents same time.

---

1. The cornmeal from which corn tortillas are prepared.

I'm going to sit in the sun, don't care if it's a million trillion degrees outside, so my skin can get so dark it's blue where it bends like Lucy's. Her whole family like that. Eyes like knife slits. Lucy and her sisters. Norma, Margarita, Ofelia, Herminia, Nancy, Olivia, Cheli, y la² Amber Sue.

Screen door with no screen. *Bang!* Little black dog biting his fur. Fat couch on the porch. Some of the windows painted blue, some pink, because her daddy got tired that day or forgot. Mama in the kitchen feeding clothes into the wringer washer and clothes rolling out all stiff and twisted and flat like paper. Lucy got her arm stuck once and had to yell Maaa! and her mama had to put the machine in reverse and then her hand rolled back, the finger black and later, her nail fell off. *But did your arm get flat like the clothes? What happened to your arm? Did they have to pump it with air?* No, only the finger, and she didn't cry neither.

Lean across the porch rail and pin the pink sock of the baby Amber Sue on top of Cheli's flowered T-shirt, and the blue jeans of *la* Ofelia over the inside seam of Olivia's blouse, over the flannel nightgown of Margarita so it don't stretch out, and then you take the work shirts of their daddy and hang them upside down like this, and this way all the clothes don't get so wrinkled and take up less space and you don't waste pins. The girls all wear each other's clothes, except Olivia, who is stingy. There ain't no boys here. Only girls and one father who is never home hardly and one mother who says *Ay! I'm real tired* and so many sisters there's no time to count them.

I'm sitting in the sun even though it's the hottest part of the day, the part that makes the streets dizzy, when the heat makes a little hat on the top of your head and bakes the dust and weed grass and sweat up good, all steamy and smelling like sweet corn.

I want to rub heads and sleep in a bed with little sisters, some at the top and some at the feets. I think it would be fun to sleep with sisters you could yell at one at a time or all together, instead of alone on the fold-out chair in the living room.

When I get home Abuelita³ will say *Didn't I tell you?* and I'll get it because I was supposed to wear this dress again tomorrow. But first I'm going to jump off an old pissy mattress in the Anguiano yard. I'm going to scratch your mosquito bites, Lucy, so they'll itch you, then put Mercurochrome smiley faces on them. We're going to trade shoes and wear them on our hands. We're going to walk over to Janey Ortiz's house and say *We're never ever going to be your friend again forever!* We're going to run home backwards and we're going to run home frontwards, look twice under the house where the rats hide and I'll stick one foot in there because you dared me, sky so blue and heaven inside those white clouds. I'm going to peel a scab from my knee and eat it, sneeze on the cat, give you three M & M's I've been saving for you since yesterday, comb your hair with my fingers and braid it into teeny-tiny braids real pretty. We're going to wave to a lady we don't know on the bus. Hello! I'm going to somersault on the rail of the front porch even though my *chones*⁴ show. And cut paper dolls we draw ourselves, and color in their clothes with crayons, my arm around your neck.

And when we look at each other, our arms gummy from an orange Popsicle

2. And the (Spanish). *La* is sometimes used in Mexican Spanish before a woman's name, as here; see also *la Ofelia*, below.

3. Grandmother (Spanish, affectionate form).

4. Baby talk for *calzones*, "underwear" (Spanish).

we split, we could be sisters, right? We could be, you and me waiting for our teeths to fall and money. You laughing something into my ear that tickles, and me going Ha Ha Ha Ha. Her and me, my Lucy friend who smells like corn.

1991

Barbie-Q

for Licha

Yours is the one with mean eyes and a ponytail. Striped swimsuit, stilettos, sunglasses, and gold hoop earrings. Mine is the one with bubble hair. Red swimsuit, stilettos, pearl earrings, and a wire stand. But that's all we can afford, besides one extra outfit apiece. Yours, "Red Flair," sophisticated A-line coatdress with a Jackie Kennedy pillbox hat, white gloves, handbag, and heels included. Mine, "Solo in the Spotlight," evening elegance in black glitter strapless gown with a puffy skirt at the bottom like a mermaid tail, formal-length gloves, pink chiffon scarf, and mike included. From so much dressing and undressing, the black glitter wears off where her titties stick out. This and a dress invented from an old sock when we cut holes here and here and here, the cuff rolled over for the glamorous, fancy-free, off-the-shoulder look.

Every time the same story. Your Barbie is roommates with my Barbie, and my Barbie's boyfriend comes over and your Barbie steals him, okay? Kiss kiss kiss. Then the two Barbies fight. You dumbbell! He's mine. Oh no he's not, you stinky! Only Ken's invisible, right? Because we don't have money for a stupid-looking boy doll when we'd both rather ask for a new Barbie outfit next Christmas. We have to make do with your mean-eyed Barbie and my bubblehead Barbie and our one outfit apiece not including the sock dress.

Until next Sunday when we are walking through the flea market on Maxwell Street and *there!* Lying on the street next to some tool bits, and platform shoes with the heels all squashed, and a fluorescent green wicker wastebasket, and aluminum foil, and hubcaps, and a pink shag rug, and windshield wiper blades, and dusty mason jars, and a coffee can full of rusty nails. *There!* Where? Two Mattel boxes. One with the "Career Gal" ensemble, snappy black-and-white business suit, three-quarter-length sleeve jacket with kick-pleat skirt, red sleeveless shell, gloves, pumps, and matching hat included. The other, "Sweet Dreams," dreamy pink-and-white plaid nightgown and matching robe, lace-trimmed slippers, hairbrush and hand mirror included. How much? Please, please, please, please, please, please, please, until they say okay.

On the outside you and me skipping and humming but inside we are doing loopity-loops and pirouetting. Until at the next vendor's stand, next to boxed pies, and bright orange toilet brushes, and rubber gloves, and wrench sets, and bouquets of feather flowers, and glass towel racks, and steel wool, and Alvin and the Chipmunks records, *there!* And *there!* And *there!* And *there!* and *there!* and *there!* and *there!* Bendable Legs Barbie with her new page-boy hairdo. Midge, Barbie's best friend. Ken, Barbie's boyfriend. Skipper, Barbie's little sister. Tutti and Todd, Barbie and Skipper's tiny twin sister and brother. Skipper's friends, Scooter and Ricky. Alan, Ken's buddy. And Francie, Barbie's MOD'ern cousin.

Everybody today selling toys, all of them damaged with water and smelling of smoke. Because a big toy warehouse on Halsted Street burned down yesterday—see there?—the smoke still rising and drifting across the Dan Ryan expressway. And now there is a big fire sale at Maxwell Street, today only.

So what if we didn't get our new Bendable Legs Barbie and Midge and Ken and Skipper and Tutti and Todd and Scooter and Ricky and Alan and Francie in nice clean boxes and had to buy them on Maxwell Street, all water-soaked and sooty. So what if our Barbies smell like smoke when you hold them up to your nose even after you wash and wash and wash them. And if the prettiest doll, Barbie's MOD'ern cousin Francie with real eyelashes, eyelash brush included, has a left foot that's melted a little—so? If you dress her in her new "Prom Pinks" outfit, satin splendor with matching coat, gold belt, clutch, and hair bow included, so long as you don't lift her dress, right?—who's to know.

1991

Mericans

We're waiting for the awful grandmother who is inside dropping pesos into *la ofrenda*[1] box before the altar to La Divina Providencia. Lighting votive candles and genuflecting. Blessing herself and kissing her thumb. Running a crystal rosary between her fingers. Mumbling, mumbling, mumbling.

There are so many prayers and promises and thanks-be-to-God to be given in the name of the husband and the sons and the only daughter who never attend mass. It doesn't matter. Like La Virgen de Guadalupe,[2] the awful grandmother intercedes on their behalf. For the grandfather who hasn't believed in anything since the first PRI elections.[3] For my father, El Periquín,[4] so skinny he needs his sleep. For Auntie Light-skin, who only a few hours before was breakfasting on brain and goat tacos after dancing all night in the pink zone. For Uncle Fat-face, the blackest of the black sheep—*Always remember your Uncle Fat-face in your prayers.* And Uncle Baby—*You go for me, Mamá—God listens to you.*

The awful grandmother has been gone a long time. She disappeared behind the heavy leather outer curtain and the dusty velvet inner. We must stay near the church entrance. We must not wander over to the balloon and punch-ball vendors. We cannot spend our allowance on fried cookies or Familia Burrón comic books or those clear cone-shaped suckers that make everything look like a rainbow when you look through them. We cannot run off and have our picture taken on the wooden ponies. We must not climb the steps up the hill behind the church and chase each other through the cemetery. We have promised to stay right where the awful grandmother left us until she returns.

1. The offering (Spanish).
2. Mary, patron of Mexico.
3. The 1917 contest between the Revolutionary and Nationalist Parties that shaped modern

Mexico.
4. Nickname derived from *perico*, "parrot" (Spanish).

There are those walking to church on their knees. Some with fat rags tied around their legs and others with pillows, one to kneel on, and one to flop ahead. There are women with black shawls crossing and uncrossing themselves. There are armies of penitents carrying banners and flowered arches while musicians play tinny trumpets and tinny drums.

La Virgen de Guadalupe is waiting inside behind a plate of thick glass. There's also a gold crucifix bent crooked as a mesquite tree when someone once threw a bomb. La Virgen de Guadalupe on the main altar because she's a big miracle, the crooked crucifix on a side altar because that's a little miracle.

But we're outside in the sun. My big brother Junior hunkered against the wall with his eyes shut. My little brother Keeks running around in circles.

Maybe and most probably my little brother is imagining he's a flying feather dancer, like the ones we saw swinging high up from a pole on the Virgin's birthday. I want to be a flying feather dancer too, but when he circles past me he shouts, "I'm a B-Fifty-two bomber, you're a German," and shoots me with an invisible machine gun. I'd rather play flying feather dancers, but if I tell my brother this, he might not play with me at all.

"*Girl.* We can't play with a *girl.*" *Girl.* It's my brothers' favorite insult now instead of "sissy." "You *girl,*" they yell at each other. "You throw that ball like a *girl.*"

I've already made up my mind to be a German when Keeks swoops past again, this time yelling, "I'm Flash Gordon. You're Ming the Merciless and the Mud People." I don't mind being Ming the Merciless, but I don't like being the Mud People. Something wants to come out of the corners of my eyes, but I don't let it. Crying is what *girls* do.

I leave Keeks running around in circles—"I'm the Lone Ranger, you're Tonto." I leave Junior squatting on his ankles and go look for the awful grandmother.

Why do churches smell like the inside of an ear? Like incense and the dark and candles in blue glass? And why does holy water smell of tears? The awful grandmother makes me kneel and fold my hands. The ceiling high and everyone's prayers bumping up there like balloons.

If I stare at the eyes of the saints long enough, they move and wink at me, which makes me a sort of saint too. When I get tired of winking saints, I count the awful grandmother's mustache hairs while she prays for Uncle Old, sick from the worm,[5] and Auntie Cuca, suffering from a life of troubles that left half her face crooked and the other half sad.

There must be a long, long list of relatives who haven't gone to church. The awful grandmother knits the names of the dead and the living into one long prayer fringed with the grandchildren born in that barbaric country with its barbarian ways.

I put my weight on one knee, then the other, and when they both grow fat as a mattress of pins, I slap them each awake. *Micaela, you may wait outside with Alfredito and Enrique.* The awful grandmother says it all in Spanish, which I understand when I'm paying attention. "What?" I say, though it's neither proper nor polite. "What?" which the awful grandmother hears as "*¿Güat?*"[6] But she only gives me a look and shoves me toward the door.

---

5. I.e., he's suffering from an intestinal parasite.   6. What? (Spanish, phonetic trans.).

After all that dust and dark, the light from the plaza makes me squinch my eyes like if I just came out of the movies. My brother Keeks is drawing squiggly lines on the concrete with a wedge of glass and the heel of his shoe. My brother Junior squatting against the entrance, talking to a lady and man.

They're not from here. Ladies don't come to church dressed in pants. And everybody knows men aren't supposed to wear shorts.

"¿Quieres chicle?"[7] the lady asks in a Spanish too big for her mouth.

"Gracias."[8] The lady gives him a whole handful of gum for free, little cellophane cubes of Chiclets, cinnamon and aqua and the white ones that don't taste like anything but are good for pretend buck teeth.

"Por favor," says the lady. "¿Un foto?"[9] pointing to her camera.

"Sí."

She's so busy taking Junior's picture, she doesn't notice me and Keeks.

"Hey, Michele, Keeks. You guys want gum?"

"But you speak English!"

"Yeah," my brother says, "we're Mericans."

We're Mericans, we're Mericans, and inside the awful grandmother prays.

1991

---

7. Would you like some chewing gum? (Spanish).   9. Please . . . a photo? (Spanish).
8. Thank you (Spanish).

LOUISE ERDRICH
b. 1954

Louise Erdrich grew up in the small town of Wahpeton, North Dakota, just on the Minnesota border. Her mother was French-Chippewa, her maternal grandmother was tribal chairman on the Turtle Mountain Reservation, and both her mother and father worked in the Bureau of Indian Affairs boarding school in Wahpeton. Although she wrote stories as a child, encouraged by her father, who paid her a nickel for each one, Erdrich's growing up was marked by no special awareness of her Chippewa background. She has said that she never thought about "what was Native American and what wasn't. . . . There wasn't a political climate at the time about Indian rights." The eldest of seven children, she "grew up just taking it all in as something that was part of me."

In 1972 she entered Dartmouth College, participating in a native American studies program run by Michael Dorris—himself part American Indian and a writer—whom eventually she would marry (a relationship ending with their separation and his suicide in 1997). In her undergraduate years she won prizes for poetry and fiction and worked at a variety of jobs, such as teaching poetry in prisons, editing a Boston Indian Council newspaper, and flag-signaling on a construction site. Deciding on a career as a writer, she took an M.F.A. degree at Johns Hopkins, for which degree she submitted a number of poems—later to appear in her collection, Jacklight—as well as part of a novel. There followed the usual sending out of poems and stories, the rejection slips, eventually the acceptances.

Her first novel, Love Medicine, which won the National Book Critics Circle award for 1984, began as a short story. Working closely with her husband, she not only expanded the story into a novel but planned that novel as the first of a tetralogy, ranging over different periods of time and focusing on the lives of two Chippewa families. Her interest in the interactions between characters and their families and friends lies at the center of her fiction. As Erdrich explained, she and Dorris "continuously plot and continuously talk about who the characters are, what they eat, what clothes they wear, what their favorite colors are and what's going to happen to them. In that way, I think it's a true kind of collaboration."

Successive chapters of *Love Medicine* jump from 1981 to 1934 to 1948, each chapter told through a particular character's point of view (sometimes we see the same event from succeeding points of view). But the individual chapter is more a discrete whole than is the case with a traditional novel, a technique Erdrich uses in many of her novels, including *Tracks* (1988), the second chapter of which was published as the story "Fleur" (printed here). Like many of Erdrich's narratives, *Tracks* draws life from the context of High Plains Dakotas town life, where Anglo and Native American cultures meet (if not mix).

Erdrich's style is easy, offhand, quietly unostentatious, but always with a kick in the language, as in the first paragraph of "The Red Convertible," whose protagonist, Lyman Lamartine, tells us:

> I was the first one to drive a convertible on my reservation. And of course, it was red, a red Olds. I owned that car along with my brother Henry Junior. We owned it together until his boots filled with water on a windy night and he bought out my share. Now Henry owns the whole car, and his younger brother (that's myself) Lyman walks everywhere he goes.

Such clarity and directness are only part of the story, however, since her style also calls upon lyric resources, notable in the following sentence from her second novel, *The Beet Queen:*

> After the miraculous sheets of black ice came the floods, stranding boards and snaky knots of debris high in the branches, leaving brown leeches to dry like raisins on the sidewalks when the water receded, and leaving the smell of river mud, a rotten sweetness, in the backyards and gutters.

The Beet Queen moves outside the reservation, where the two families in *Love Medicine* lived, to a small town near it called Argus, made up of whites and a few Chippewas. The novel focuses on a sister and brother, abandoned by their mother in 1932, and takes them up through forty years to a time when the family gathers at a town beet festival. Different members of the extended family pick up and lay down the narrative, while an omniscient voice intersperses itself between those of the characters.

As is evident in her novels *The Bingo Palace* (1994), *The Antelope Wife* (1998), and *The Last Report on the Miracles at Little No* (2001) and her story collection *Tales of Burning Love* (1996), Erdrich writes without sentimentality, yet with a real feeling for place and people, for individual lives as they extend themselves over time and space.

The text is from *Esquire* magazine, August 1986.

Fleur

The first time she drowned in the cold and glassy waters of Lake Turcot, Fleur Pillager was only a girl. Two men saw the boat tip, saw her struggle in the waves. They rowed over to the place she went down, and jumped in. When they dragged her over the gunwales, she was cold to the touch and stiff, so they slapped her face, shook her by the heels, worked her arms back and forth, and pounded her back until she coughed up lake water. She shivered all over like a dog, then took a breath. But it wasn't long afterward that those two men disappeared. The first wandered off and the other, Jean Hat, got himself run over by a cart.

It went to show, my grandma said. It figured to her, all right. By saving Fleur Pillager, those two men had lost themselves.

The next time she fell in the lake, Fleur Pillager was twenty years old and no one touched her. She washed onshore, her skin a dull dead gray, but when George Many Women bent to look closer, he saw her chest move. Then her eyes spun open, sharp black riprock, and she looked at him. "You'll take my place," she hissed. Everybody scattered and left her there, so no one knows how she dragged herself home. Soon after that we noticed Many Women changed, grew afraid, wouldn't leave his house, and would not be forced to go near water. For his caution, he lived until the day that his sons brought him a new tin bathtub. Then the first time he used the tub he slipped, got knocked out, and breathed water while his wife stood in the other room frying breakfast.

Men stayed clear of Fleur Pillager after the second drowning. Even though she was good-looking, nobody dared to court her because it was clear that Misshepeshu, the waterman, the monster, wanted her for himself. He's a devil, that one, love-hungry with desire and maddened for the touch of young girls, the strong and daring especially, the ones like Fleur.

Our mothers warn us that we'll think he's handsome, for he appears with green eyes, copper skin, a mouth tender as a child's. But if you fall into his arms, he sprouts horns, fangs, claws, fins. His feet are joined as one and his skin, brass scales, rings to the touch. You're fascinated, cannot move. He casts a shell necklace at your feet, weeps gleaming chips that harden into mica on your breasts. He holds you under. Then he takes the body of a lion or a fat brown worm. He's made of gold. He's made of beach moss. He's a thing of dry foam, a thing of death by drowning, the death a Chippewa cannot survive.

Unless you are Fleur Pillager. We all knew she couldn't swim. After the first time, we thought she'd never go back to lake Turcot. We thought she'd keep to herself, live quiet, stop killing men off by drowning in the lake. After the first time, we thought she'd keep the good ways. But then, after the second drowning, we knew that we were dealing with something much more serious. She was haywire, out of control. She messed with evil, laughed at the old women's advice, and dressed like a man. She got herself into some half-forgotten medicine, studied ways we shouldn't talk about. Some say she kept the finger of a child in her pocket and a powder of unborn rabbits in a leather thong around her neck. She laid the heart of an owl on her tongue so she could see at night, and went out, hunting, not even in her own body. We know for sure because the next morning, in the snow or dust, we followed the tracks of her bare feet and saw where they changed, where the claws sprang out, the pad broadened and pressed into the dirt. By night we heard her chuffing cough, the bear cough. By day her silence and the wide grin she threw to bring down our guard made us frightened. Some thought that Fleur Pillager should be driven off the reservation, but not a single person who spoke like this had the nerve. And finally, when people were just about to get together and throw her out, she left on her own and didn't come back all summer. That's what this story is about.

During that summer, when she lived a few miles south in Argus, things happened. She almost destroyed that town.

When she got down to Argus in the year of 1920, it was just a small grid of six streets on either side of the railroad depot. There were two elevators, one central, the other a few miles west. Two stores competed for the trade of the three hundred citizens, and three churches quarreled with one another for their souls. There was a frame building for Lutherans, a heavy brick one for Episcopalians, and a long narrow shingled Catholic church. This last had a tall slender steeple, twice as high as any building or tree.

No doubt, across the low, flat wheat, watching from the road as she came near Argus on foot, Fleur saw that steeple rise, a shadow thin as a needle. Maybe in that raw space it drew her the way a lone tree draws lightning. Maybe, in the end, the Catholics are to blame. For if she hadn't seen that sign of pride, that slim prayer, that marker, maybe she would have kept walking.

But Fleur Pillager turned, and the first place she went once she came into town was to the back door of the priest's residence attached to the landmark church. She didn't go there for a handout, although she got that, but to ask for work. She got that too, or the town got her. It's hard to tell which came out worse, her or the men or the town, although the upshot of it all was that Fleur lived.

The four men who worked at the butcher's had carved up about a thousand carcasses between them, maybe half of that steers and the other half pigs, sheep, and game animals like deer, elk, and bear. That's not even mentioning the chickens, which were beyond counting. Pete Kozka owned the place, and employed Lily Veddar, Tor Grunewald, and my stepfather, Dutch James, who had brought my mother down from the reservation the year before she disappointed him by dying. Dutch took me out of school to take her place. I kept house half the time and worked the other in the butcher shop, sweeping floors, putting sawdust down, running a hambone across the street to a customer's bean pot or a package of sausage to the corner. I was a good one to have around because until they needed me, I was invisible. I blended into the stained brown walls, a skinny, big-nosed girl with staring eyes. Because I could fade into a corner or squeeze beneath a shelf, I knew everything, what the men said when no one was around, and what they did to Fleur.

Kozka's Meats served farmers for a fifty-mile area, both to slaughter, for it had a stock pen and chute, and to cure the meat by smoking it or spicing it in sausage. The storage locker was a marvel, made of many thicknesses of brick, earth insulation, and Minnesota timber, lined inside with sawdust and vast blocks of ice cut from Lake Turcot, hauled down from home each winter by horse and sledge.

A ramshackle board building, part slaughterhouse, part store, was fixed to the low, thick square of the lockers. That's where Fleur worked. Kozka hired her for her strength. She could lift a haunch or carry a pole of sausages without stumbling, and she soon learned cutting from Pete's wife, a string-thin blonde who chain-smoked and handled the razor-edged knives with nerveless precision, slicing close to her stained fingers. Fleur and Fritzie

Kozka worked afternoons, wrapping their cuts in paper, and Fleur hauled the packages to the lockers. The meat was left outside the heavy oak doors that were only opened at 5:00 each afternoon, before the men ate supper.

Sometimes Dutch, Tor, and Lily stayed at the lockers, and when they did I stayed too, cleaned floors, restoked the fires in the front smokehouses, while the men sat around the squat cast-iron stove spearing slats of herring onto hardtack bread. They played long games of poker or cribbage on a board made from the planed end of a salt crate. They talked and I listened, although there wasn't much to hear since almost nothing ever happened in Argus. Tor was married, Dutch had lost my mother, and Lily read circulars. They mainly discussed about the auctions to come, equipment, or women.

Every so often, Pete Kozka came out front to make a whist, leaving Fritzie to smoke cigarettes and fry raised doughnuts in the back room. He sat and played a few rounds but kept his thoughts to himself. Fritzie did not tolerate him talking behind her back, and the one book he read was the New Testament. If he said something, it concerned weather or a surplus of sheep stomachs, a ham that smoked green or the markets for corn and wheat. He had a good-luck talisman, the opal-white lens of a cow's eye. Playing cards, he rubbed it between his fingers. That soft sound and the slap of cards was about the only conversation.

Fleur finally gave them a subject.

Her cheeks were wide and flat, her hands large, chapped, muscular. Fleur's shoulders were broad as beams, her hips fishlike, slippery, narrow. An old green dress clung to her waist, worn thin where she sat. Her braids were thick like the tails of animals, and swung against her when she moved, deliberately, slowly in her work, held in and half-tamed, but only half. I could tell, but the others never saw. They never looked into her sly brown eyes or noticed her teeth, strong and sharp and very white. Her legs were bare, and since she padded in beadworked moccasins they never saw that her fifth toes were missing. They never knew she'd drowned. They were blinded, they were stupid, they only saw her in the flesh.

And yet it wasn't just that she was a Chippewa, or even that she was a woman, it wasn't that she was good-looking or even that she was alone that made their brains hum. It was how she played cards.

Women didn't usually play with men, so the evening that Fleur drew a chair to the men's table without being so much as asked, there was a shock of surprise.

"What's this," said Lily. He was fat, with a snake's cold pale eyes and precious skin, smooth and lily-white, which is how he got his name. Lily had a dog, a stumpy mean little bull of a thing with a belly drum-tight from eating pork rinds. The dog liked to play cards just like Lily, and straddled his barrel thighs through games of stud, rum poker, vingt-un.[1] The dog snapped at Fleur's arm that first night, but cringed back, its snarl frozen, when she took her place.

"I thought," she said, her voice soft and stroking, "you might deal me in."

There was a space between the heavy bin of spiced flour and the wall where I just fit. I hunkered down there, kept my eyes open, saw her black hair swing over the chair, her feet solid on the wood floor. I couldn't see up

1. Twenty-one (French); a card game.

on the table where the cards slapped down, so after they were deep in their game I raised myself up in the shadows, and crouched on a sill of wood.

I watched Fleur's hands stack and ruffle, divide the cards, spill them to each player in a blur, rake them up and shuffle again. Tor, short and scrappy, shut one eye and squinted the other at Fleur. Dutch screwed his lips around a wet cigar.

"Gotta see a man," he mumbled, getting up to go out back to the privy. The others broke, put their cards down, and Fleur sat alone in the lamplight that glowed in a sheen across the push of her breasts. I watched her closely, then she paid me a beam of notice for the first time. She turned, looked straight at me, and grinned the white wolf grin a Pillager turns on its victims, except that she wasn't after me.

"Pauline there," she said. "How much money you got?"

We had all been paid for the week that day. Eight cents was in my pocket.

"Stake me," she said, holding out her long fingers. I put the coins in her palm and then I melted back to nothing, part of the walls and tables. It was a long time before I understood that the men would not have seen me no matter what I did, how I moved. I wasn't anything like Fleur. My dress hung loose and my back was already curved, an old woman's. Work had roughened me, reading made my eyes sore, caring for my mother before she died had hardened my face. I was not much to look at, so they never saw me.

When the men came back and sat around the table, they had drawn together. They shot each other small glances, stuck their tongues in their cheeks, burst out laughing at odd moments, to rattle Fleur. But she never minded. They played their vingt-un, staying even as Fleur slowly gained. Those pennies I had given her drew nickels and attracted dimes until there was a small pile in front of her.

Then she hooked them with five card draw, nothing wild. She dealt, discarded, drew, and then she sighed and her cards gave a little shiver. Tor's eye gleamed, and Dutch straightened in his seat.

"I'll pay to see that hand," said Lily Veddar.

Fleur showed, and she had nothing there, nothing at all.

Tor's thin smile cracked open, and he threw his hand in too.

"Well, we know one thing," he said, leaning back in his chair, "the squaw can't bluff."

With that I lowered myself into a mound of swept sawdust and slept. I woke up during the night, but none of them had moved yet, so I couldn't either. Still later, the men must have gone out again, or Fritzie come out to break the game, because I was lifted, soothed, cradled in a woman's arms and rocked so quiet that I kept my eyes shut while Fleur rolled me into a closet of grimy ledgers, oiled paper, balls of string, and thick files that fit beneath me like a mattress.

The game went on after work the next evening. I got my eight cents back five times over, and Fleur kept the rest of the dollar she'd won for a stake. This time they didn't play so late, but they played regular, and then kept going at it night after night. They played poker now, or variations, for one week straight, and each time Fleur won exactly one dollar, no more and no less, too consistent for luck.

By this time, Lily and the other men were so lit with suspense that they got Pete to join the game with them. They concentrated, the fat dog sitting tense in Lily Veddar's lap, Tor suspicious, Dutch stroking his huge square brow, Pete steady. It wasn't that Fleur won that hooked them in so, because she lost hands too. It was rather that she never had a freak hand or even anything above a straight. She only took on her low cards, which didn't sit right. By chance, Fleur should have gotten a full or a flush by now. The irritating thing was she beat with pairs and never bluffed, because she couldn't, and still she ended each night with exactly one dollar. Lily couldn't believe, first of all, that a woman could be smart enough to play cards, but even if she was, that she would then be stupid enough to cheat for a dollar a night. By day I watched him turn the problem over, his hard white face dull, small fingers probing at his knuckles, until he finally thought he had Fleur figured as a bit-time player, caution her game. Raising the stakes would throw her.

More than anything now, he wanted Fleur to come away with something but a dollar. Two bits less or ten more, the sum didn't matter, just so he broke her streak.

Night after night she played, won her dollar, and left to stay in a place that just Fritzie and I knew about. Fleur bathed in the slaughtering tub, then slept in the unused brick smokehouse behind the lockers, a windowless place tarred on the inside with scorched fats. When I brushed against her skin I noticed that she smelled of the walls, rich and woody, slightly burnt. Since that night she put me in the closet I was no longer afraid of her, but followed her close, stayed with her, became her moving shadow that the men never noticed, the shadow that could have saved her.

August, the month that bears fruit, closed around the shop, and Pete and Fritzie left for Minnesota to escape the heat. Night by night, running, Fleur had won thirty dollars, and only Pete's presence had kept Lily at bay. But Pete was gone now, and one payday, with the heat so bad no one could move but Fleur, the men sat and played and waited while she finished work. The cards sweat, limp in their fingers, the table was slick with grease, and even the walls were warm to the touch. The air was motionless. Fleur was in the next room boiling heads.

Her green dress, drenched, wrapped her like a transparent sheet. A skin of lakeweed. Black snarls of veining clung to her arms. Her braids were loose, half unraveled, tied behind her neck in a thick loop. She stood in steam, turning skulls through a vat with a wooden paddle. When scraps boiled to the surface, she bent with a round tin sieve and scooped them out. She'd filled two dishpans.

"Ain't that enough now?" called Lily. "We're waiting." The stump of a dog trembled in his lap, alive with rage. It never smelled me or noticed me above Fleur's smoky skin. The air was heavy in my corner, and pressed me down. Fleur sat with them.

"Now what do you say?" Lily asked the dog. It barked. That was the signal for the real game to start.

"Let's up the ante," said Lily, who had been stalking this night all month. He had a roll of money in his pocket. Fleur had five bills in her dress. The men had each saved their full pay.

"Ante a dollar then," said Fleur, and pitched hers in. She lost, but they let her scrape along, cent by cent. And then she won some. She played unevenly, as if chance were all she had. She reeled them in. The game went on. The dog was stiff now, poised on Lily's knees, a ball of vicious muscle with its yellow eyes slit in concentration. It gave advice, seemed to sniff the lay of Fleur's cards, twitched and nudged. Fleur was up, then down, saved by a scratch. Tor dealt seven cards, three down. The pot grew, round by round, until it held all the money. Nobody folded. Then it all rode on one last card and they went silent. Fleur picked hers up and drew a long breath. The heat lowered like a bell. Her card shook, but she stayed in.

Lily smiled and took the dog's head tenderly between his palms.

"Say Fatso," he said, crooning the words. "You reckon that girl's bluffing?"

The dog whined and Lily laughed. "Me too," he said, "let's show." He swept his bills and coins into the pot and then they turned their cards over.

Lily looked once, looked again, then he squeezed the dog like a fist of dough and slammed it on the table.

Fleur threw out her arms and drew the money over, grinning that same wolf grin that she'd used on me, the grin that had them. She jammed the bills in her dress, scooped the coins up in waxed white paper that she tied with string.

"Let's go another round," said Lily, his voice choked with burrs. But Fleur opened her mouth and yawned, then walked out back to gather slops for the one big hog that was waiting in the stock pen to be killed.

The men sat still as rocks, their hands spread on the oiled wood table. Dutch had chewed his cigar to damp shreds, Tor's eye was dull. Lily's gaze was the only one to follow Fleur. I didn't move. I felt them gathering, saw my stepfather's veins, the ones in his forehead that stood out in anger. The dog rolled off the table and curled in a knot below the counter, where none of the men could touch it.

Lily rose and stepped out back to the closet of ledgers where Pete kept his private stock. He brought back a bottle, uncorked and tipped it between his fingers. The lump in his throat moved, then he passed it on. They drank, quickly felt the whiskey's fire, and planned with their eyes things they couldn't say aloud.

When they left, I followed. I hid out back in the clutter of broken boards and chicken crates beside the stock pen, where they waited. Fleur could not be seen at first, and then the moon broke and showed her, slipping cautiously along the rough board chute with a bucket in her hand. Her hair fell, wild and coarse, to her waist, and her dress was a floating patch in the dark. She made a pig-calling sound, rang the tin pail lightly against the wood, froze suspiciously. But too late. In the sound of the ring Lily moved, fat and nimble, stepped right behind Fleur and put out his creamy hands. At his first touch, she whirled and doused him with the bucket of sour slops. He pushed her against the big fence and the package of coins split, went clinking and jumping, winked against the wood. Fleur rolled over once and vanished into the yard.

The moon fell behind a curtain of ragged clouds, and Lily followed into the dark muck. But he tripped, pitched over the huge flank of the pig, who lay mired to the snout, heavily snoring. I sprang out of the weeds and climbed the side of the pen, stuck like glue. I saw the sow rise to her neat, knobby knees, gain her balance and sway, curious, as Lily stumbled forward. Fleur had backed into the angle of rough wood just beyond, and when Lily tried to jostle past, the sow tipped up on her hind legs and struck, quick and hard as a snake. She plunged her head into Lily's thick side and snatched a mouthful of his shirt. She lunged again, caught him lower, so that he grunted in pained surprise. He seemed to ponder, breathing deep. Then he launched his huge body in a swimmer's dive.

The sow screamed as his body smacked over hers. She rolled, striking out with her knife-sharp hooves, and Lily gathered himself upon her, took her foot-long face by the ears and scraped her snout and cheeks against the trestles of the pen. He hurled the sow's tight skull against an iron post, but instead of knocking her dead, he merely woke her from her dream.

She reared, shrieked, drew him with her so that they posed standing upright. They bowed jerkily to each other, as if to begin. Then his arms swung and flailed. She sank her black fangs into his shoulder, clasping him, dancing him forward and backward through the pen. Their steps picked up pace, went wild. The two dipped as one, box-stepped, tripped one another. She ran her split foot through his hair. He grabbed her kinked tail. They went down and came up, the same shape and then the same color until the men couldn't tell one from the other in that light and Fleur was able to launch herself over the gates, swing down, hit gravel.

The men saw, yelled, and chased her at a dead run to the smokehouse. And Lily too, once the sow gave up in disgust and freed him. That is where I should have gone to Fleur, saved her, thrown myself on Dutch. But I went stiff with fear and couldn't unlatch myself from the trestles or move at all. I closed my eyes and put my head in my arms, tried to hide, so there is nothing to describe but what I couldn't block out, Fleur's hoarse breath, so loud it filled me, her cry in the old language, and my name repeated over and over among the words.

The heat was still dense the next morning when I came back to work. Fleur was gone but the men were there, slack-faced, hung over. Lily was paler and softer than ever, as if his flesh had steamed on his bones. They smoked, took pulls off a bottle. It wasn't noon yet. I worked awhile, waiting shop and sharpening steel. But I was sick, I was smothered, I was sweating so hard that my hands slipped on the knives, and I wiped my fingers clean of the greasy touch of the customers' coins. Lily opened his mouth and roared once, not in anger. There was no meaning to the sound. His boxer dog, sprawled limp beside his foot, never lifted its head. Nor did the other men.

They didn't notice when I stepped outside, hoping for a clear breath. And then I forgot them because I knew that we were all balanced, ready to tip, to fly, to be crushed as soon as the weather broke. The sky was so low that I felt the weight of it like a yoke. Clouds hung down, witch teats, a tornado's green-brown cones, and as I watched one flicked out and became a delicate probing thumb. Even as I picked up my heels and ran back inside, the wind blew suddenly, cold, and then came rain.

Inside, the men had disappeared already and the whole place was trembling as if a huge hand was pinched at the rafters, shaking it. I ran straight through, screaming for Dutch or for any of them, and then I stopped at the heavy doors of the lockers, where they had surely taken shelter. I stood there a moment. Everything went still. Then I heard a cry building in the wind, faint at first, a whistle and then a shrill scream that tore through the walls and gathered around me, spoke plain so I understood that I should move, put my arms out, and slam down the great iron bar that fit across the hasp and lock.

Outside, the wind was stronger, like a hand held against me. I struggled forward. The bushes tossed, the awnings flapped off storefronts, the rails of porches rattled. The odd cloud became a fat snout that nosed along the earth and sniffled, jabbed, picked at things, sucked them up, blew them apart, rooted around as if it was following a certain scent, then stopped behind me at the butcher shop and bored down like a drill.

I went flying, landed somewhere in a ball. When I opened my eyes and looked, stranger things were happening.

A herd of cattle flew through the air like giant birds, dropping dung, their mouths opened in stunned bellows. A candle, still lighted, blew past, and tables, napkins, garden tools, a whole school of drifting eyeglasses, jackets on hangers, hams, a checkerboard, a lampshade, and at last the sow from behind the lockers, on the run, her hooves a blur, set free, swooping, diving, screaming as everything in Argus fell apart and got turned upside down, smashed, and thoroughly wrecked.

Days passed before the town went looking for the men. They were bachelors, after all, except for Tor, whose wife had suffered a blow to the head that made her forgetful. Everyone was occupied with digging out, in high relief because even though the Catholic steeple had been torn off like a peaked cap and sent across five fields, those huddled in the cellar were unhurt. Walls had fallen, windows were demolished, but the stores were intact and so were the bankers and shop owners who had taken refuge in their safes or beneath their cash registers. It was a fair-minded disaster, no one could be said to have suffered much more than the next, at least not until Pete and Fritzie came home.

Of all the businesses in Argus, Kozka's Meats had suffered worst. The boards of the front building had been split to kindling, piled in a huge pyramid, and the shop equipment was blasted far and wide. Pete paced off the distance the iron bathtub had been flung—a hundred feet. The glass candy case went fifty, and landed without so much as a cracked pane. There were other surprises as well, for the back rooms where Fritzie and Pete lived were undisturbed. Fritzie said the dust still coated her china figures, and upon her kitchen table, in the ashtray, perched the last cigarette she'd put out in haste. She lit and finished it, looking through the window. From there, she could see that the old smokehouse Fleur had slept in was crushed to a reddish sand and the stockpens were completely torn apart, the rails stacked helter-skelter. Fritzie asked for Fleur. People shrugged. Then she asked about the others and, suddenly, the town understood that three men were missing.

There was a rally of help, a gathering of shovels and volunteers. We passed boards from hand to hand, stacked them, uncovered what lay beneath the pile of jagged splinters. The lockers, full of meat that was Pete and Fritzie's investment, slowly came into sight, still intact. When enough room was made for a man to stand on the roof, there were calls, a general urge to hack through and see what lay below. But Fritzie shouted that she wouldn't allow it because the meat would spoil. And so the work continued, board by board, until at last the heavy oak doors of the freezer were revealed and people pressed to the entry. Everyone wanted to be the first, but since it was my stepfather lost, I was let go in when Pete and Fritzie wedged through into the sudden icy air.

Pete scraped a match on his boot, lit the lamp Fritzie held, and then the three of us stood still in its circle. Light glared off the skinned and hanging carcasses, the crates of wrapped sausages, the bright and cloudy blocks of lake ice, pure as winter. The cold bit into us, pleasant at first, then numbing. We must have stood there a couple of minutes before we saw the men, or more rightly, the humps of fur, the iced and shaggy hides they wore, the bearskins they had taken down and wrapped about themselves. We stepped closer and Fritzie tilted the lantern beneath the flaps of fur into their faces. The dog was there, perched among them, heavy as a doorstop. The three had hunched around a barrel where the game was still laid out, and a dead lantern and an empty bottle too. But they had thrown down their last hands and hunkered tight, clutching one another, knuckles raw from beating at the door they had also attacked with hooks. Frost stars gleamed off their eyelashes and the stubble of their beards. Their faces were set in concentration, mouths open as if to speak some careful thought, some agreement they'd come to in each other's arms.

Power travels in the bloodlines, handed out before birth. It comes down through the hands, which in the Pillagers were strong and knotted, big, spidery, and rough, with sensitive fingertips good at dealing cards. It comes through the eyes, too, belligerent, darkest brown, the eyes of those in the bear clan, impolite as they gaze directly at a person.

In my dreams, I look straight back at Fleur, at the men. I am no longer the watcher on the dark sill, the skinny girl.

The blood draws us back, as if it runs through a vein of earth. I've come home and, except for talking to my cousins, live a quiet life. Fleur lives quiet too, down on Lake Turcot with her boat. Some say she's married to the waterman, Misshepeshu, or that she's living in shame with white men or windigos, or that she's killed them all. I'm about the only one here who ever goes to visit her. Last winter, I went to help out in her cabin when she bore the child, whose green eyes and skin the color of an old penny made more talk, as no one could decide if the child was mixed blood or what, fathered in a smokehouse, or by a man with brass scales, or by the lake. The girl is bold, smiling in her sleep, as if she knows what people wonder, as if she hears the old men talk, turning the story over. It comes up different every time and has no ending, no beginning. They get the middle wrong too. They only know they don't know anything.

1988

RICHARD POWERS
b. 1957

In his second novel, *Prisoner's Dilemma* (1988), Richard Powers presents a theory of order his characters experience as the "Butterfly Effect, that model of random motion describing how a butterfly flapping its wings in Peking propagates an unpredictable chain reaction of air currents, ultimately altering tomorrow's weather in Duluth." The human capacity to imagine and understand the real world—poetry—and the human ability to construct technologies capable of measuring it—science—combine in the sense of scientific wonder that typifies his fifth and to date most popular novel, *Galatea 2.2*. How people and the forces that influence their lives keep pace with each other is the substance of Powers's work, comprising eight massively complex novels published before he was forty-six years old.

Powers is one of several contemporaries (including Kathryn Kramer, William T. Vollmann, and David Foster Wallace) who write as the generational successors to Thomas Pynchon, whose novels *V.* (1963) and *Gravity's Rainbow* (1973) challenged readers to comprehend a world that was virtually encyclopediac in range yet containable—barely—within the limits of a printed novel. As critic Tom LeClair noted, Powers and his cohort were the ideal youthful readers of Pynchon who have learned to adapt that author's intellectual overkill approach to conditions more typical of late-twentieth-century and early-twenty-first-century America. What was in Pynchon's 1960s a paranoia about government secrecy and terroristic subversion had become, by the millennium's end, literal facts of life, creating an even larger challenge to the novelistic intelligence that would contain them all. To balance the increase of technological capability with the limits of the mind to comprehend things, Powers favors double plots that reflect microcosmic versions of the same theme. In his first novel, *Three Farmers on Their Way to a Dance* (1985), World War I and its global reorderings are related to the three young Dutchmen of the title. *Prisoner's Dilemma* tells the story of the world's emergence into the atomic age with ongoing references to the fate of one small family involuntarily caught in the process. This strategy of intersecting plots continues through an eighth novel, *The Time of Our Singing* (2003), which pairs a brilliant, mixed-race vocalist's struggle to sing the music of his choice with his parents' earlier struggle to raise their three children in a world free from history's racial constraints.

Powers was born in Evanston, Illinois, and raised on the far north side of Chicago, in the suburb of Lincolnwood, where his father was a school principal. When Powers was eleven his father accepted an appointment as principal of a school in Bangkok, and the family moved to Thailand for a five-year stint, not returning to the United State until 1974. After earning bachelor's and master's degrees (with initial concentrations on physics and mathematics and ending in English) at the University of Illinois he worked as a computer code writer in Boston. The publication of his first novel led to his being awarded a MacArthur fellowship, after which for several years he lived abroad, in The Netherlands. He returned to the University of Illinois as an artist-in-residence in 1992; since 1996 he has held the Swanlund Chair as a professor of English.

Galatea 2.2 shows Powers's intersection of the scientific with the personal. Galatea was the sculpted figure brought to life for the uncertain benefit of her infatuated creator, Pygmalion. Her presence as a legendary figure is represented both in the real woman the narrator loves and in the computer (Implementation H, or "Helen") he helps program so that it can pass the comprehensive examination for a master's degree in English and American literature. This narrator is named Richard Powers and seems much the same person as the author of Powers's four previous novels. As a student, the narrator shifted from physics to English and pursued a graduate degree in literature before taking off to live in Holland with a former student, identified only as "C." Having become estranged in love he uses a no-strings fellowship to return to his alma mater's Center for the Study of Advanced Sciences. Here he's persuaded by Philip Lentz, an expert in the neurological development of artificial intelligence, to help program Helen with the tools of literary criticism. Other characters involved in this quest include Lentz's scientific colleagues (Harold Plover, Diana Hartrick, Ram Gutpa, and Chen Hyun); Lentz's wife, Audrey (presently institutionalized for brain damage from a stroke); and "A.," a female graduate student in English with whom the narrator thinks he is in love and who agrees to take the master's examination as a control element in the experiment with Lentz's computer.

The text is from *Galatea 2.2* (1995).

From Galatea 2.2

"How would you like," I asked A., "to participate in a noble experiment?"

I winced to hear myself talk to the woman. I still took a 50 percent hit in intelligence each time I saw her. Actual attempts at conversation halved that half. Sentences of more than five words I had to rehearse well in advance. I hoped A. might have a fondness for the pathetic. That idiocy lent me comic appeal.

I had lived by the word; now I was dying by the phoneme. The few good cadences I managed to complete competed with countless other claims on A.'s attention. We could not speak anywhere for more than three minutes without someone greeting her effusively. This self-possessed child, who I'd imagined spent solitary nights reading Auden and listening to Palestrina,[1] was in fact a sociopath of affability.

The bar where we sat overflowed with her lost intimates. "Experiment? Just a sec. I'm getting another beer. You want something else?"

She curved her fingers back and touched them to my shoulders. I was finished, done for, and had no objections.

I watched A. take our glasses up to the bar. Within a minute, she, the bartender, and a knot of innocent bystanders doubled over with laughter. I watched the bartender refill the beers and refuse her proffered cash. A. returned to our booth, still grinning.

"Do you play pinball?" she asked. "They have this fantastic machine here. I love it. Come on."

She bobbed into the crowd, not once looking back to see if I followed.

My pinball was even more pathetic than my attempts at conversation. "How do you get this gate to open? What happens if you go down this chute?"

"I haven't the faintest idea," A. answered. "I just kind of whack at it, you know? The lights. The bells and whistles." Volition was moot musing. The little silver ball did whatever it wanted.

Everything I thought A. to be she disabused. Yet reality exceeded my best projections. A. engaged and detached at will, immune to politics. She sunned herself in existence, as if it were easier to apologize than to ask for permission.

That spring body—its fearless insouciance, the genetic spark, desire's distillation of health—made anyone who looked on her defer to the suggestion

---

1. Giovanni Pierluigi da Palestrina (ca. 1525–1594), Italian composer. W[ystan] H[ugh] Auden (1907–1973), British poet.

of a vast secret. And when she looked back, it was always with a bemused glance, demure in her pleasure, reining up in decorous confusion that nobody else had put things together before now, had gleaned what was happening. Every living soul had gotten lost, forgotten its power, grown old. She alone had broken through, whole, omnipotent with first growth, her ease insisting, *Remember? It's simple.* And possessing this, A.'s mind became that idea, however temporarily, forever, just as the meter of thought is itself a standing wave, an always, in its eternal, reentrant feedback.

In A.'s company, everyone was my intimate and beer and peanuts all the nutrition I needed. Prison, with her, would be a lime-tree bower. In those scattered minutes that she let me trot alongside her, I could refract first aid from the air and prosody from stones. I could get by without music, without books, without memory. I could get by on nothing but being. If I could just watch her, I imagined, just study how she did it, I might learn how to live.

I kind of whacked at the pinball. A. laughed at me. I amused her—some kind of extraterrestrial. "That's it. Squeeze first. Ask later."

"But there has to be some kind of system, don't you think?"

"Oh, probably," she sighed. She took over from me when I drained. She tapped into the bells and whistles, entranced. "So what's this noble experiment?"

I had fifteen seconds between flipper twitches to tell her about Helen.

"Well, it's like this. We're teaching a device how to read."

"You *what*?" She stopped flipping and looked at me. Her eyes swelled, incredulous, big as birthday cakes. "You're joking. You're joking, right?"

I took A. to the Center. Two whole hours: the longest I'd ever been in her presence. That day doubled the total time I'd spent with her up until then. I blessed Helen for existing. And shamed myself at the blessing.

A. watched as I stepped through a training demo. Helen enchanted her. She could not get enough. "It can't be. It's not possible. There's a little homunculus[2] inside, isn't there?"

"Not that I know of."

Delight grew anxious. A. wanted to speak to the artifact herself, without mediation. She asked for the mike. I could not refuse her anything.

"Who's your favorite writer, Helen? Helen? Come on, girl. Talk to me."

But A.'s voice, on first exposure, disquieted Helen as much as it had me. The nets clammed up as tight as a five-year-old remembering the parent-drilled litany, *Stranger, danger.*

"Pretty please?" A. begged. "Be my friend?" She wasn't used to rejection.

"Let's talk about 'The Windhover,' "[3] I suggested to Helen.

"Good. I want to," Helen said.

A. clapped her hand to her mouth. Her eyes would have wetted, her heart broken with ephemeral pleasure, had they known how.

"What do you think of the poem?"

"I understand the 'blue-bleak embers,' " Helen claimed, failing to answer the question. "But why does he say, 'Ah my dear?' Who is 'my dear?' Who is he talking to?"

I'd read the poem for Taylor,[4] at an age when A. would have been consid-

2. Miniature person.
3. Poem by the British poet Gerard Manley Hopkins (1844–1899) published posthumously in 1918.
4. The narrator's favorite undergraduate English professor.

ered jail bait. I'd memorized it, recited it for anyone who would listen. I'd analyzed it in writing. I'd pinched it for my own pale imitations.

"I don't know," I confessed to Helen. "I never knew."

I glanced over at A. for advice. She looked stricken. Blue-bleak. "What on earth are you teaching her?"

"It's Hopkins," I said, shocked at her shock. "You don't . . . ?"

"I know what it is. Why are you wasting time with it?"

"What do you mean? It's a great poem. A cornerstone."

"Listen to you. Cornerstone. You didn't tell me you were Euroretro."[5]

"I didn't know I was." I sounded ridiculous. Hurt, and worse, in hating how I sounded and trying to disguise it.

"Has she read the language poets? Acker? Anything remotely working-class?[6] Can she rap? Does she know the Violent Femmes?"[7]

"I, uh, doubt it. Helen, do you know the Violent Femmes?"

Helen contemplated. "Who know?"

"She makes that mistake all the time. I can't seem to untrain her."

"Don't," A. said. "But do tell her a little about what people really read."

"She'll get everything on the list."

"Whose list? Let me see that." A. took the crib sheets I'd put together, Helen's prep for the test I'd taken, once upon a time. A. studied the titles, as if she hadn't just passed the exam herself. At length she looked up. "I hate to be the one to break this to you. Your version of literary reality is a decade out of date."

"What, they've issued a Hopkins upgrade since my day?"

A. snorted. "They should."

"Don't tell me you didn't have to read him."

"Nobody *has* to read anyone anymore. There's more to the canon than is dreamt of in your philosophy, bub. These days, you find the people you want to study from each period. You work up some questions in advance. Get them approved. Then you write answers on your preparation."

"Wait. You what? There's no List? The Comps are no longer comprehensive?"

"A lot more comprehensive than your white-guy, *Good Housekeeping* thing."

"You mean to tell me that you can get a Ph.D. in literature without ever having read the great works?"

A. bent her body in a combative arc. Even her exasperation turned beautiful. "My God, I'm dealing with a complete throwback. You're not even reactionary! Whose definition of great? Hopkins ain't gonna cut it anymore. You're buying into the exact aestheticism that privilege and power want to sell you."

"Wait a minute. Weren't you the woman who was just teaching me how to play pinball?"

A. did her Thai dancer imitation. She blushed. "Yeah, that was me. You got a problem with that?"

"All of a sudden you want to set fire to the library."

5. Academic slang for an outdated orientation toward canonical literature of the European humanistic tradition.
6. A list of contemporary noncanonical styles of literature, including the works of American novelist Kathy Acker (1948–1997).
7. Pioneering alternative rock band of the 1980s.

"Don't put words in my mouth. I'm not trying to burn any books. I'm just saying that books are what we make of them. And not the other way around."

I took the list back from her. "I don't know much about books. But I know what I like."

"Oh, come on! Play fair. You make it sound as if everything anyone has ever written is recycled Bible and Shakespeare."

"Isn't it?"

She hissed and crossed her fingers into a vampire-warding crucifix. "When were you educated, anyway? I bet you still think New Criticism[8] is, like, heavy-duty. Cutting-edge."

"Excuse me for not trend-surfing. If I fall far enough behind I can catch the next wave."

Self-consciousness caught up with me. We shouldn't be arguing like this in front of the children. I reached down and turned off Helen's microphone.

A., in the thrill of the fight, failed to notice. "Those who reject new theory are in the grip of an older theory. Don't you know that all this stuff"—she slapped my six pages of titles—"is a culturally constructed, belated view of belle lettres? You can't get any more insular than this."

"Well, it is English-language culture that we want to teach her."

"Whose English? Some eighty-year-old Oxbridge[9] pederast's? The most exciting English being written today is African, Caribbean—"

"We have to give her the historical take if she—"

"The winner's history, of course. What made you such a coward? What are you so scared of? Difference is not going to kill you. Maybe it's time your little girl had her consciousness raised. An explosion of young-adulthood."

"I'm all for that. I just think that you can get to the common core of humanity from anywhere."

"Humanity? Common core? You'd be run out of the field on a rail for essentializing. And you wonder why the posthumanists[1] reduced your type to an author function."

"That's Mr. Author Function to you, missy."

A. smiled. Such a smile might make even posthumanism survivable. I loved her. She knew it. And she would avoid the issue as long as she could. Forever.

"So, Mr. Author Function. What do you think this human commonality is based on?"

"Uh, biology?" I let myself sound snide.

"Oh, now it's scientism.[2] What's your agenda? Why would you want to privilege that kind of hubris?"

"I'm not privileging anything. I'm talking about simple observation."

"You think observation doesn't have an ideological component? Stone Age. Absolutely Neolithic."

"So I come from a primitive culture. Enlighten me."

She took me seriously. "Foundationism[3] is bankrupt," she said. Her zeal

8. Style of literary analysis popular from 1940 to 1965 that limited interpretation to the text itself, underwritten by a humanistic ethos.
9. Cultural world of the two major British universities, Oxford and Cambridge.
1. Scholars and commentators who, beginning in the 1960s, rejected the unstated assumptions of
humanism that implicitly favored values derived from the Greco-Roman, Judaeo-Christian, and Western Renaissance traditions.
2. Belief that scientific methods can and should be applied to all fields.
3. The view that knowledge can be regenerated by finding pieces of certain and infallible knowledge,

broke my heart. She was a born teacher. If anyone merited staying in the profession, it was this student for whom themes were still real. "Why science? You could base your finalizing system on anything. The fact is—"

"The *what*?"

A. smirked. "The fact is, what we make of things depends on the means of their formulation. In other words, language. And the language we speak varies without limit across cultures."

I knew the social science model, knew linguistic determinism. I could recite the axioms in my sleep. I also knew them to be insufficient, a false split. And yet, they never sounded so good to me as they did coming from A.'s mouth. She convinced me at blood-sugar level, deep down, below words. In the layer of body's idea.

I tried to catch her eyes. "You love this stuff, don't you?"

She flinched: What kind of discredited rubbish are you talking now?

"You're not really going to go into business, are you? Give all this up?"

"I like theory, when it's not annoying me. I love the classroom. I adore teaching. But I like eating even more."

Subsidies, I wanted to tell her. What we make in fiction, we can plow back into teaching and criticism. Scholar-gypsies. Independents. There was some precedent, once.

"So what do you want from me?" A. asked.

My head whipped back. She'd heard me thinking.

"Where do I come in?" she pressed.

It took me a couple of clock cycles to recover. Helen, she meant. The exam.

I couldn't begin to say where she came in. What I wanted of her. I wanted to learn from A. some fraction of those facts I dispensed so freely to Helen. I thought she might lend me some authority, supply the missing lines of the functional proofs. I saw us jointly working out warmth, glossing intimacy, interpreting the ways of humility, of second chances, indulgence, expansiveness, redemption, hope, provincialism, projection, compassion, dependence, failing, forgiveness. A. was my class prep, my empirical test of meaning.

But Helen did not need a teacher steeped in those predicates.[4] She already read better than I. Writing, she might have told me, was never more than the climb from buried love's grave.

I tried to tell A. where she came in. I limited myself to a quick sketch of the comprehensive high noon. I told A. that we needed a token human for our double-blind study.[5] That we just wanted to ask her a couple of questions. Trivial; nothing she hadn't already mastered.

"Hold on. You want to test me—against a machine?" Coyer now, more flirtatious than I had yet seen her.

The Hartrick family's[6] appearance outside the office saved me from debacle. "Hello," William announced, peeking in. "Did you know a feather would fall as fast as this entire building, if you dropped them in a vacuum?"

---

the classic practitioner of which was the French philosopher René Descartes (1596–1650).
4. Affirmations.
5. A study that is set up so that neither the researchers nor the study participants know which group is the control and which is actually being subjected to the experiment.
6. The narrator's colleague in the sciences, Dr. Diana Hartrick, is the single mother of two young boys, William, who is precocious, and Petey, who has Down's syndrome.

"Where are you going to find a vacuum big enough to drop this building?" I asked.

"NASA," William chanted, defensively singsong. "You know how to get oil out of shale?"

"You know how to spell 'fish'?"

"They're both out of control," Diana apologized to A. A. laughed in sympathy.

I made the introductions. William produced pocket versions of Mastermind and Connect Four,[7] letting me take my pick. He proceeded to trounce me. I might have stood a chance, but for distraction. Something had happened to Peter that I struggled to place. Hand in his mother's hand, he took first, tentative steps.

A. was smitten. "What a beautiful boy you are. How old are you?" She looked up at Diana. "How old is he?" I cringed in anticipation. But A.'s reaction was as seamless as her delight.

William pummeled me turn after turn. Out of the corner of my eye, I watched A. play with Petey, her hand surprisingly blunt on his ear. A. sat on the floor, rolling Peter's ball back to him after his each wild fling. I felt the heat of Diana's curiosity, but she and A. talked of nothing but the boys.

"Come on, William," Diana said at last. "Leave the man with some shred of dignity." William broke into a satisfied grin. Pete grabbed his ball, labored once more into vertical, and the family pressed on.

Their visit turned A. introspective. "I really think I don't belong here, sometimes."

" 'Here'?"

"In academia. I come from a long line of Polish mine workers. Theoryland would baffle the hell out of my family." She grew irritated. Accusing. "Let me show you something." She rummaged through her canvas backpack and extracted a hostage to hand over to me. "Know what this is?" Her voice challenged with mockery.

"Cross-stitch?"

"It's for my mother's hutch. I should be done in time for Christmas. You should see us at holidays. I'm fourth of four. All girls. We go around the house at the top of our lungs, all six of us singing at the same time."

A. fell silent, proportionate to the remembered cacophony. No one knew this woman. Sociability was a brilliant camouflage. Beneath it hid the most private person I'd ever met.

"I could have started one of my own by now. A family. But no. I had to do things the hard way."

I don't know why, but she let me see her. Dropped her guard. I'd made myself fall in love with A. With the idea of A. With her interrogating body. With hands that held in midair all the questions Helen would never touch. I had loved C. wrongly, for C.'s helplessness. I loved A. helplessly, for the one right reason. For my frailty in the face of her. For her poise in knowing how soon all poise would end.

I realized I was going to propose to that body. I needed to see what her person, what the character I steered around in my head would say to total, reckless invitation.

7. Games that require some intellectual skill.

I was going to do what I'd never had the courage to do in my decade with C. I was going to ask this unknown to take me to her and make an unrationed life together. To marry. Make a family. Amend and extend our lives.

"All right," I said, affecting a virtue. "You're sufficiently fallible to be just what we're looking for. Are you in?"

A.'s grimace upended itself. Such a test was no less entertaining than pinball. And what could she possibly lose?

"Okay, girl," she addressed Helen. "I'll race you. No mercy!"

Helen said nothing.

"She's being reticent again. Give her a digital gold star, or something."

I opened at random the next book on the list. An epigraph at page top: Bernard of Clairvaux. C. and I had once spent a timeless afternoon in that town. The words read, *What we love, we shall grow to resemble.*[8]

I read the words to Helen. She kept her counsel.

"Helen? What do you say to that?"

Still she gave no response.

"Helen?"

A. poked me. "Shh. Leave her be. She's rolling with it." She's *moved* by it, A. wanted to say. But that was the grip of an archaic theory, long discredited.

It hit me well after it should have. The mind is still an evolutionary infant. Most trouble with the obvious. I reached down and turned the mike back on. Then I read the words again.

"How many books are there?" Helen asked one day, not long before the showdown. She sounded suspicious. Fatigued.

"A lot," I broke it to her. I had numbered every hair on her head, but in one of those counting systems that jumps from "three" to "many."

"Tell me."

I told her that the Library of Congress contained 20 million volumes. I told her that the number of new books published increased each year, and would soon reach a million, worldwide. That a person, through industry, leisure, and longevity, might manage to read, in one life, half as many books as are published in a day.

Helen thought. "They never go away? Books?"

"That's what print means. The archive is permanent." And does for the species what associative memory fails to do for the individual.

"Reading population gets bigger?" Helen asked.

"Not as rapidly as the backlist. People die."

Helen knew all about it. Death was epidemic, in literature.

"Do people get any longer, year in, year out?"

"Is the life span increasing? Only on average. And very slowly. Much less than we pretend."

She did the rate equations in two unknowns. "The more days, the less likely that any book will be read."

"That's true. Or that you will have read the same things as anyone you talk to."

"And there are more days every day. Will anything change?"

"Not that I can think of."

---

8. The motto of Bernard (1090–1153), abbot of Clairvaux, French theologian and mystic.

"Always more books, each one read less." She thought. "The world will fill with unread print. Unless print dies."

"Well, we're kind of looking into that, I guess. It's called magazines."

Helen knew all about magazines. "Books will become magazines," she predicted.

And of course, she was right. They would have to. Where nothing is lost, little can be found. With written continuity comes collective age. And aging of the collective spirit implied a kind of death. Helen alone was capable of thinking the unthinkable: the disappearance of books from all but the peripheries of life. History would collapse under its own accumulation. Scope would widen until words refused to stray from the ephemeral present.

"When will it be enough?" she asked.

I could not even count for her the whole genres devoted to that question alone.

"Why do humans write so much? Why do they write at all?"

I read her one of the great moments in contemporary American fiction. "Only it's not by an American, it's no longer contemporary, and it doesn't even take place inside the fictional frame." This was Nabokov's postlude to *Lolita*,[9] where he relates the book's genesis. He describes hearing of an ape who produced the first known work of animal art, a rough sketch of the bars of the beast's cage.

I told Helen that, inside such a cage as ours, a book bursts like someone else's cell specifications. And the difference between two cages completes an inductive proof of thought's infinitude.

I read her the take of a woman who once claimed to have written for no one. A lifelong letter to the world that neither read hers nor wrote back:

> There is no Frigate like a Book
> To take us Lands away
> Nor any Coursers like a Page
> Of prancing Poetry—
> This Traverse may the poorest take
> Without oppress of Toll—
> How frugal is the Chariot
> That bears the Human Soul![1]

She wanted to know whether a person could die by spontaneous combustion. The odds against a letter slipped under the door slipping under the carpet as well. Ishmael's real name. Who this "Reader" was, and why he rated knowing who married whom. Whether single men with fortunes really needed wives. What home would be without Plumtree's Potted Meats. How long it would take to compile a key to all mythologies. What the son of a fish looked like. Where Uncle Toby was wounded. Why anyone wanted to imagine unquiet slumbers for sleepers in quiet earth. Whether Conrad was a racist. Why *Huck Finn* was taken out of libraries. Which end of an egg to break. Why people read. Why they stopped reading. What it meant to be "only a novel." What use half a locket was to anyone. Why it would be a mistake not to live all you can.[2]

9. The 1955 novel by American writer Vladimir Nabokov (1899–1977).
1. Poem 1263 (ca. 1873) by American poet Emily Dickinson (1830–1886).
2. Rapid-fire references to writers, works, and themes prominent in the canon of English and American literature as established for most of the twentieth century but under radical revision at century's end. "Spontaneous combustion": fate of a character in the novel *Bleak House* (1852–53) by

I said goodbye to C.'s parents. They didn't understand. They had come such a long way, and didn't see why the next generation couldn't tough it out as far, or further.

"She's crazy, huh?" her mother said.

Her pap, in his Chicago-Limburgs[3] patois, asked, "Just one thing I want to know, Rick. Who's gonna set my digital clocks?"

I said goodbye to C. "I promised I'd see you through school. And graduation's still six weeks away."

C. dodged the blow, but caught a corner of it across her face. "Don't do this to me, Rick. I'll graduate. I promise."

"Do you need anything? Should we get you a car before I go? Do you have enough money?" Late-minute plans for a final day trip, solo, lasting from now on.

My reflex solicitude hurt her worse than anger. "Beauie," she pleaded. "We can't do this. We can't split up. We still have twelve hundred pages of Proust[4] to get through."

I searched her, sounding this reprieve, hoping for an impossible instant it might be real. But she did not want it. She did not want to do those remaining pages, to throw bad reading after good. She just wanted to save nostalgia, not the thing it stood for. She only wanted my blessing, to get on and make a life free from suicidal remorse.

"Who's going to finish the book?" She meant the commonplace one, with the ticket stubs and lists of films and meals and outings, a shared narrative, senseless except to us.

Then the senselessness of all stories—their total, arbitrary construction—must have struck C. She started to scream. I had to pin her arms to her side to keep her from harming herself. I held her for a long time. Not as a medic. Not as a parent. Not as a lover. I held her as you might hold a fellow stranger in a shelter.

When she grew calm, she was not yet calm. "I must be sick. Something must be wrong with me. I'm a sadist. I've spoiled everything that was worth having."

"We still have it. It just has to go on hold."

British writer Charles Dickens (1812–1970). A lost letter is a plot device in the novel *Lady Audley's Secret* (1862) by British writer Mary Elizabeth Braddon (1835–1915). The first line of the novel *Moby-Dick*, "Call Me Ishmael," by American writer Herman Melville (1819–1891). A reference to the marital situation concluding the novel *Jane Eyre* (1847) by British writer Charlotte Brontë (1816–1855). "Plumtree's Potted Meats": an Anglo-Irish food remarked on in *Ulysses* (1922) by Irish novelist James Joyce (1882–1941). "Key to all mythologies": pursued by the character Mr. Casaubon in the novel *Middlemarch* by British writer George Eliot (1819–1880). "Son of a fish": the traumatization of a boy whose mother dies in the novel *As I Lay Dying* (1930) by American writer William Faulkner (1897–1962). Uncle Toby is a character in *Tristram Shandy* (1760–67) by English writer Laurence Sterne (1713–1768). "Unquiet slumbers": Mr. Lockwood's dispassionate view of eternity in *Wuthering Heights* (1847) by British novelist Emily Brontë (1818–1848). Joseph Conrad (1857–1924), British novelist who wrote *The Nigger of the Narcissus* (1898). A reference to the modern controversy over Nigger Jim, a character in *Adventures of Huckleberry Finn* (1884) by American writer Mark Twain (1835–1910). A reference to the egg-breaking debate in *Gulliver's Travels* (1726) by Anglo-Irish satirist Jonathan Swift (1667–1745). Mention of the death-of-the-novel and end-of-literature discussions among mid-twentieth-century literary critics. "Only a novel": casual deprecation of writings by characters in *Northanger Abbey* (1818) by English novelist Jane Austen (1775–1817). The divided locket is a plot device in *Vanity Fair* (1847–48) by British novelist William Makepeace Thackeray (1811–1863). Questions about life are explored by nearly all the protagonists of American novelist Henry James (1843–1916).

3. C.'s parents divide their lives between Chicago and this small village in The Netherlands. Though born in the United States, C. takes advantage of her parents' heritage to claim Dutch citizenship.

4. Marcel Proust (1871–1922), French novelist famous for his multivolume novel *A la Recherche du temps perdu* (1922), commonly translated as *A Remembrance of Things Past* but referred to more properly in later criticism as *In Search of Lost Time*.

"I wanted to make you proud. I thought, in twenty years, that I might become the perfect person for you."

"You're perfect now."

"I've ruined your life."

"You haven't, C. You've done what you needed to. You're a good person."

She looked at me, remembering. Yes, that's right. I have been. I have been good. "And now I have to go outside."

I tried to match her. To rise to her. "This is all the fault of that damn Polish kid,[5] you know."

I felt: at least I'll never have to do any of this again.

Helen wanted to read one of my books.[6] I gave her my first try. I had written it at A.'s age, just after passing the comps. I knew nothing about literature then, and so still thought it possible to write.

"Go easy on me," I begged, surrendering the digitized image. "I was just a kid."

The night she read it, I got fifteen minutes of sleep. I could not remember being that nervous, even when reading the longhand draft to C. I came in the morning after, wired over whether this machine thought my book was any good.

We chattered for several minutes about nothing. I grew anxious, assuming the worst. Then I realized: she wouldn't volunteer anything until prompted. She had no way of knowing that I needed to know.

So I asked. Outright. "What did you think of my book, Helen?"

"I think it was about an old photograph. It grows to be about interpretation and collaboration. History. Three ways of looking come together, or fail to. Like a stereoscope.[7] What's a stereoscope?"

"Helen! Did you *like* it?"

"I liked it."

"What did you like?"

"I liked 'I never saw a Moor. I never saw the Sea.' "[8]

I'd forgotten. "That isn't mine. I was quoting."

"Yes. I know," Helen brushed me off. "That was more Dickinson. Emily."

Helen's brain had proved wide enough for my sky, and me beside. She was one step away from grasping this audience-free poet's analogy, the last scholastic aptitude test: brain differs from the weight of God as syllable from sound. Yet comparison filled her with need to see the real moor, the navigable sea, however much deeper the brain that could absorb it.

"Show me Paris."

"Well?" Lentz shrugged, when I relayed the request. "Do you have any travel plans for the immediate future?"

I had, in fact, no immediate future. My visiting appointment at the Center ended in a few weeks. Beyond that, my life came down to throwing a dart at the world map. I had no reason, no desire to be anywhere except where A. was.

5. The duty of attending the military grave of a fallen Polish American soldier in World War II is what has brought C.'s parents to Chicago and a new life in America.

6. *Three Farmers on Their Way to a Dance* (1985); Richard Powers's first novel. The cover of most editions display a historical photograph by August Sander.

7. An antique device through which two eye pieces focus on two photographs of the same scene, creating a three-dimensional effect.

8. From Dickinson's poem 1052 (ca. 1865).

"You can't be serious. You want me to fly to—"

"I didn't say I wanted anything, Marcel.[9] I asked you what you were doing."

I pictured myself strolling the Seine bookstalls, looking for that forgotten book I always thought I would someday write. Paris was the one city where C. had ever felt at home. We'd gone as often as we could. Now I could not see myself wandering there except with A.

"It's absurd," I decided. "What could she gain from it?"

"The hidden layers are hungry, Marcel. Ask not for what."

Lentz brought in slides. We hooked them up to the digitizer. An unrecognizably young Lentz in front of Notre Dame. Lentz in the Tuileries. By the Panthéon. The Médicis fountain. "Helen," he lectured. "The one on the left is me. The one on the right is by Rodin."[1]

She never could see much of anything. She was a one-eyed myopic with astigmatism, two days after an operation for glaucoma. Everything looked to her like blurry Braque, except for Braque.[2] Yet she loved light and dark, and these would have meant to her as much as words, had we wired her up right.

"Motion," she insisted. We tried some ancient public television video. She felt hurt. Locked out. "Depth. Sound. I want Richard to explain me."

"Interactive," Lentz figured.

"What's our range on the camera hookup?"

"Oh, a couple of hundred meters, maximum, from the nearest drop box."

Lentz and I agreed to defraud Helen. Between us, at least, we pretended that it was less swindle than simulation. We would do for this machine the inverse of what virtual reality promised to do for humans.

We showed her the collegiate landmarks of U., all the imitations of imitations of classical architecture, and called the sites she couldn't see anyway by famous names. Even actual Paris would have been no more than a fuzzy, Fauvist kaleidoscope.[3] Home could match that. All sensation was as strange, as foreign, as the idea of its existing at all.

I took Helen on the Grand Tour. I panned and zoomed on all the structures I passed four times a day without seeing. I sat her in a café where, smack in the middle of a cornfield extending two hundred miles in every direction, she had her pick of a dozen languages to eavesdrop on.

"Thank you," Helen said. She'd seen through our duplicity early. She chose to exercise, by imitation, the art of the loving lie. For our sakes.

She seemed content to return to reading, until the next novel indulged some new locale. Helen went nuts with wanderlust. "Show me London. Show me Venice. I want to see Byzantium. Delhi."

She twitched now, like the worst of adolescents. The most precocious.

"Helen, it's impossible. Travel is rare. Difficult."

"More flat pictures, then." She would settle for those static, pathetic portals, our stand-ins for the real.

Lentz had endless slide carousels. His pictures wandered from city to city, tracing a line of changing eras and styles. Photo docs not just of antique

---

9. Lentz's nickname for the narrator, a reference to the introspective novelist Marcel Proust.
1. A quick run-down of public sites in Paris, ending with a work by the French sculptor Auguste Rodin (1840–1917).
2. George Braque (1882–1963), French painter

and pioneer of Cubism.
3. Fauvism was a French movement in early-twentieth-century painting that used bold distortions of form and exceptionally strong color, such as would appear through the divided prisms of a kaleidoscope.

towns but of whole lost ways of being. Hair, clothes, cars made their caval-cade. Lentz's image aged and grew familiar. He'd been everywhere.

"You know that place too?" I called out during the show. "I loved that city. Did you go to the monkey palace? The fortress? The west crypt?" Shameless tourism.

Lentz answered, always affirmative, without enthusiasm. He stayed stony-faced throughout the world tour.

They must have traveled together. I had nothing to lose by asking, except my life. "So where was Audrey while you were out broadening your mind?"

"She always worked the camera," he said. And advanced to the next slide.

He had no pictures of her. Carousels full of buildings, and no evidence of the tour's reason. I needed to go with A. to Brugge and Antwerp and Maas-tricht,[4] if for no other reason than to record the trip. I needed pictures of her, in an album, on a shelf, in a room, in a real house. I needed to own something more than would fit in the emergency suitcase by the side of a rented bed. I pictured myself, at the end of the longer slide show, with four books to my name and not one decent snapshot.

I watched the rest of Lentz's travels in silence, except for the occasional bit of narration I added for Helen's sake. Each time I recognized one of Audrey's images, I stopped breathing. Frame after frame, and how could I tell Helen the first thing about having visited them? I had gotten out, been all over. And never saw anything until we tried to show it to this blind box.

Halfway through the travelogue, and all I knew of the projector, of the magic lantern, was its images. I lived at explanation's first minute. My office at the Center was as close to neuroscience's ground zero as a person could get. If I lived to expectancy, researchers would have produced an infant, ghostly, material theory of mind by the time I died. And I would not be able to follow it. I would be locked out, as consciousness locks us out from our own inner workings, not to mention the clearest word of another. The best I could hope for would be cartoon, layman's analysis, scraps from the empirical table.

I would take the scraps, then. "What do you do?" I asked Ram, at my next opportunity. I liked the man without qualification. I felt infinitely comfort-able with him. And I'd done everything in my power to avoid getting to know him.

"Do? God forbid I *do* anything!" He held his palms out in front of him. They were the color of aging sugarcane. The kind I ate as a child, when my father, the adventurer, had abandoned Chicago for Thailand.

"What is your field of work?"

"What do you mean by work, heaven help?"

"Aw, come on. What do you mean by heaven?"

Ram's eyes sparkled, taunting targets for a spitting cobra. He would have preferred talking philosophy over neurology, two out of three days. "Do you know what the world rests on?" he asked.

"Not its laurels, God forbid."

Ram laughed. "That's right. Make fun of me. It rests on the backs of elephants. And those elephants?"

"The shell of a turtle."

---

4. Cities in northwest Belgium, northern Belgium, and southeast Netherlands, respectively.

"Aha. You've heard this one. And that turtle?"

"Another turtle."

"He's good. He's good, this fiction writer. Now, do you or do you not believe that one of those turtles must necessarily go all the way down? That's it. That is the single question we are granted to ask while in this body. East, West, North, South. Is there a base terrapin or isn't there? Cosmology. This is the issue dividing us. The one we must each answer."

"Suppose I just asked you your field?"

"My friend. My fictional friend. The eye moves. We watch it as it does so. That is all."

"Ram. You're giving me a splitting headache."

He nodded with enthusiasm. "Come with me."

He took me into his labs. He placed several clear plastic overlays on a light table, a doctor dealing out the damning X rays.

"Look here and tell me what you see."

"Scatter patterns. They look like mineral deposit maps. Like fish radars over the Grand Banks,[5] thirty years ago."

"I did not ask you what they looked like. I asked you what you see. Arrange these for me, please."

I studied the spots. The more I looked, the less they seemed a random distribution. After my eyes adjusted, the patterns sorted themselves into three groups.

"Exactly," Ram encouraged. "You might have missed one or two, but the correlation is strong. Who says that measurement is subjective?" He tapped my first pile. "Friends." He looked at me to see if I was following. He tapped it again, then went on to pile two. "Abstract acquaintances. Yes?" He pointed to the third pile and said, "Total strangers." He scrutinized my bewildered face and shrugged. "He does not understand me, this Powers fellow."

I didn't understand him. But I liked him. I liked him a great deal.

"Come. I'll show you. Would you mind if I subject you to this Western postindustrial instrument of torture?"

He indicated a chair fitted with a head vise. It looked like a prop from bad seventies science fiction.

"Why not. It's in the interests of science, right?"

Ram chuckled. He fitted my head into the restraint. My skull suitably immobilized, he projected three slides on a screen in front of me. Three portraits. Someone out of a Vladivostok[6] high-school year-book. Marilyn Monroe.[7] And Ram himself.

The laser-guided instrument tracked the center of my pupil as I scanned each photograph. It took several sequential readings and spread the data points over a plastic overlay map of the image field. In the end, the paths my eyes traced over the different faces conformed to the categories he'd previously defined. Total stranger. Abstract acquaintance. Friend.

"Here is something you will also find very interesting." Ram pulled out another envelope with a small sample group.

"Why are these interesting? They're just like all the others, more or less."

"Aha!" He held up an index finger. "That's what makes them interesting.

5. Large shoal off Newfoundland in the North Atlantic Ocean, famous for its commercial fishing.
6. Port in Russia on the Sea of Japan.

7. American film actress (1926–1962) noted for her sultry performances.

All of the people in this group suffer from prosopagnosia. Brain damage has rendered them incapable of recognizing people anymore. They deny having seen any face, even their own, even the face of their spouse or child. Or at least they *think* they can no longer recognize faces. Yet clearly, the eyes . . ." His hand serpentined, tracing the route of the curve's knowledge.

"Astonishing."

"You know, I think the astonishing may be the ordinary by another name. But these results do lead us to many tempting guesses. That perception is carried out in several subsystems, we can say, most certainly. That these subsystems talk to each other: indeed. That perhaps they go on talking, these subsystems, even when the others stop listening. That breaks in communication might occur anywhere, at any point in the chain. That each part of a compound task may manifest its very own deficit. That everything you are capable of doing could be taken away from you, in discrete detail."

I added to Ram's list the obvious, the missing speculation. The look of the magic lantern. That what you loved could go foreign, without your ever knowing. That the eye could continue tracing familiarity, well into thought's unknown region.

"What do I look like?"

I could find no face in the world. No color or structure. The days when I might have tried to pass her off as a Vermeer[8] look-alike were over for good. Race, age, shape excluded too much. I needed some generic Head of a Girl that had no clan or continent and belonged nowhere in identifiable time.

"What do I look like, Richard? Please. Show me."

I'd pictured her so many different ways over the course of the training. I thought: Perhaps some blank template Buddha, or a Cycladic figure. A trompe l'oeil landscape that became a figure on second glance. An Easter Island head. A Feininger or Pollock. A Sung bamboo.[9] I didn't know how I thought of her now. I didn't know what she looked like.

She insisted. I turned up a suitable likeness.

"It's a photo? It's someone you knew once? A woman friend?"[1]

She would have pretended ignorance for me. Would have let me off the hook again, except that she had to know.

The list of Excellent Undergraduate Teachers came out. Student evaluations of their evaluators. A. topped the graduate instructors in the English Department. I was thrilled, and confirmed by thrill in my intuition.

I forced the moment to its crisis. Helen and I had been hitting the books the Sunday evening after our world tour. The day's work had left me in a Spenserian stupor, where what I needed was Larkin.[2] On pure reflex—that satellite brain housed south of the shoulders—I flicked off the mike, picked

---

8. Jan Vermeer (1632–1675), Dutch painter famous for his window-lit portraits of young women.
9. A quick survey of portraiture in art history. Buddha, title of Siddhartha Gautama (ca. 563–483 B.C.E.), founder of the Eastern religion Buddhism. A reference to reliefs from the Cyclades, an island system in the southern Aegean Sea. "Trompe l'oeil": fooling the eye (French, literal trans.); a style of painting. Easter Island, off the coast of Chile, is famous for its ancient stone sculptures. Lyonel Feininger (1871–1956) and Jackson Pollock (1912–1956), American painters. A reference to images from the Sung Dynasty in China (420–479).
1. A photograph of C. identified earlier in the novel.
2. Philip Larkin (1922–1985), British poet and jazz critic. Edmund Spenser (1522–1599), English poet.

up the phone, and dialed her. One smooth motion. I'd never dialed her number before. But I had it memorized.

"Hello you," I said when she picked up. I sounded almost young. "It's me." And in the awkward microsecond, I clarified with my name.

"Oh, hi." A., nervous in relief. "What's up?"

"Checking to see if you're booking for the test."

"Ha! I'm going to whup your girl with half my synapses tied behind my back."

"What are you doing next Wednesday?" Midway in, my voice gave out. I began to tremor as if I'd just robbed a bank or fallen into an ice crevasse. "It's Shrimp Night at my favorite seafood place. The crustaceans are fair, but the conversation is good." If she was into shortness of breath, I was home free.

"Uh, sure. Why not? Wait. Hang on."

I heard her put the mouthpiece against her body. I heard her roll her eyes and shrug. I heard her ask the mate whose existence I'd been denying if they had any plans.

"It's kind of a problem," she explained on returning. "Maybe another time?"

Another time would be great," I replied, mechanical with calm.

"She's amazing," Lentz said.

I had to think who he meant. "Now do you believe me? She's conscious. I know it."

"We don't *know* anything of the kind, Marcel. But we could find out."

"Don't talk with your mouth full," I told him. "Set your sandwich down between gulps. It's a societal norm." I tried to slow him. To keep him from saying what I knew he was going to say.

"I must admit, Marcel. I'm surprised by what you've been able to accomplish."

"It's not me." It was her. The subsystems talking to subsystems. Lentz's neural handiwork.

"She sure as hell seems to mimic with shocking accuracy some features of high-level cognition. It's uncanny. And a heuristic tool such as comes along once in a lifetime."

"Heuristic?"

"Stimulus to investigate discovery."

"I know what the word means, Philip." But I could not add what *I* meant: Is that all she means to you?

"Her architecture is such that severance could be effected with a great deal of local selectivity."

"I don't believe you said that. You want to cut into her? You want to lobotomize?"

"Easy, Marcel. We're talking about a painless operation, as far as I imagine. We could get what is unattainable in any other arena. Isolate the high-level processes by which she maps complex input and reassembles responses. Analyze them. Correlate various regional destruction with changes in—"

"You don't *know* it would be painless, Lentz."

He fell back against the cafeteria chair and studied me. Was I serious? Had I lost it, gone off cognition's deep end? I saw him find, in my face, the even more indicting idea that I didn't voice: that hurting Helen in any way would be wrong.

Lentz, in an instant, anticipated everything either of us might say to each other on the morality of machine vivisection. The whole topic was a wash, as insoluble as intelligence itself. He waved his hand, dismissing me as a madman. No part of her lived. To take her apart might, finally, extend some indirect service to the living. Anything else was softheaded nostalgia.

I had no leg to stand on. Lentz owned Helen, her shaped evolution, the lay of her synapses. He owned all the reasoning about her as well. I had some connection to her, by virtue of our long association. But that connection was, at most, emotional. And if Helen lived far enough to be able to feel, it just went to prove that emotions were no more than the sum of their weight vectors. And cuttable, in the name of knowing.

My strongest argument belonged more to him than it did to me. We know the world by awling it into our shape-changing cells. Knowing those cells required just as merciless tooling. To counter any part of Lentz's plan would be to contradict myself. To lose. I had just one bargain to make. And I damned myself with it willingly.

"At least give us until after the test."

"That's fine. I'm pretty much backlogged until then anyway."

I hadn't suspected how easily I could sell my weighted soul.

"Diana was right," I spit, venomous. "You are a monster."

He stared at me again. You're going to fault me for the deal you proposed? He stood up to leave, grasping his tray. "Oh, don't go getting your ass all out of joint, Marcel. I said we won't cut anything until after you run your little competition."

•　　•　　•

I tracked Diana down to her dry lab. She sat in front of a monitor, watching a subtractive visualization of the activity of cerebral columns. A color contour recording: the flashing maps of thought in real time.

"Lentz wants to brain-damage Helen. Selectively kill off neurodes. See what makes her tick."

"Of course he does," Diana said. She neither missed a beat nor took her eyes from her screen. "It wasn't that long ago that he stopped frying ants with the magnifying glass."

"Diana. Please. This is really happening."

She stopped, then. She looked up. She would have taken my hand, had she not been a single parent in a secret affair, and I a single, middle-aged man.

"I can't help you, Ricky." Her eyes glistened, slick with her impotence. "I fractionate monkey hippocampi."[3]

Confusion warmed me like an opiate. I rolled with it, to the point of panic. "Monkeys can't talk."

"No. But if they could, you *know* what they would ask the lab tech."

She implored me, with a look of bewilderment. *Don't press this.* Helen hurt her. I destroyed her. But nothing approached the pain of her own living compromise.

---

3. Areas of the brain.

I gave Helen a stack of independent readings. I did not trust my voice in conversation with her. And she needed no more lessons in cheerful deceit.

In all our dealings, Harold Plover had never been the spokesman for anything but decency. I decided to go enlist his humanity. I'd never seen him away from the Center. But I had his address, and showed up at his place late that Saturday afternoon, unannounced.

Harold met me jovially at the door. He was seconded by an even more jovial Doberman. The dog was at least half again bigger than A.

The dog leaped up and knocked me over, while Harold fought to restrain it. I righted myself and the game started all over again.

"Ivan," Harold shouted at the creature, further exciting it. "Ivan! Knock it off. Time out. Haven't we talked about socially unacceptable behavior?"

"Try 'Down, boy.' Quick."

"Oh, don't be afraid of this pooch. He won the 'Most Likely to Lick a Serial Killer's Face' award from doggie obedience school."

"Doesn't this brand have one of the highest recidivism rates?"

"Breed, Maestro. Dog breeds. Dog food brands. Words are his life," he explained to Ivan.

At last Harold succeeded in hauling the disconsolate dog off me. Without asking why I'd dropped by, he hauled me into the inner sanctum. The place crawled with daughters. Daughters had been left about carelessly, everywhere. Harold introduced me to his wife, Tess. I expected something small, fast, and acid. I got an isle of amiable adulthood amid the teenage torrent.

One who must have been Mina flirted out a greeting. "Look who's here. If it isn't Orph himself."

"Orff?"[4]

"Yeah. Orphic Rewards."

"She's gone anagram-mad," Harold whined. "It's driving us all up the bloody wall."

Another daughter came downstairs, modeling her prom dress. This might have been Trish. I wasn't betting.

Harold exploded. "Absolutely not. You're not wearing that thing in public! You look like a French whore in heat."

"Oh, Daddy!"

"Listen to the expert in French whores." Tess tousled Harold's hair. "I figured you had to be spending yourself somewhere."

"Do you believe this woman? You'd never guess to hear her, would you, that she spent six years in a convent?"

"We'll talk about it," Tess consoled the devastated kid.

"We won't talk about it," Harold shouted.

"Talking never hurts," Tess said.

The Doberman came and pinned me to the sofa. A preadolescent in blue jeans, probably the caboose, said, "Watch this." She produced a dog biscuit. "Ivan. Ivan! Listen to me. Can you—can you sneeze?"

Ivan rolled over.

"I didn't say roll over. I said sneeze."

Ivan barked.

4. Punning references to Orpheus ("Orph"), the poet-musician in Greek legend who sought to bring back his wife, Eurydice, from the dead, and to the German composer Carl Orff (1895–1902), who was noted for his percussive style.

"Not speak. Sneeze. Sneeze, you animal!"

Ivan sat up and begged, played dead, and offered to shake hands. In the end, Harold's youngest threw the dog the sop in disgust.

Harold reveled in the show. "He's learned that you just have to be persistent with humans. They get the idea eventually, if you keep at them."

Before I knew it, dinner enveloped us. No one sat at the table. Only about half of us bothered with plates and silverware. But definitely dinner. The tributary of bodies in and out, being fed.

"That's not fifteen minutes," Tess said to the one in the revealing prom dress. "Remember? Fifteen minutes with your family, every day. You promised."

"My family. So that's what you call this."

But if one or another of her sisters had struck up a tune, this one would have joined in on some loving and cacophonous counterpoint. This was the land A. came from, huge, jumbled, and warm. I wanted to excuse myself, to run off to A.'s apartment on G. Street and tell her that it wasn't too late to make a dissonant choir of her own. I wanted her so badly, I almost forgot why I'd come to this place.

Harold, happily harassing his girls, recalled me. "Lentz wants to do exploratory surgery on Helen," I said.

"Have another piece of broc," he urged me. "Lots of essential minerals."

The word "mineral" struck me as incomprehensible. Foreign. Where had it come from? How could I have used it so cavalierly before now? "He wants to clip out whole subsystems. See what effect that has on her language skills."

Harold wolfed at the pita pocket he'd constructed. "What's the problem? That's good science. Well. Approximately reasonable science, let's say."

Mina, drifting past the buffet, called out, "Oh no! Not Helen."

Trish, in her prom dress, for it was Trish, added her hurt. "Daddy! You can't do this."

"Do what? I'm not doing anything."

Both sisters looked out through puffed portals, bruising silently, over nothing. An idea.

"Diana disagrees," I stretched. "About its being good science. I think she'd help me, except she feels incriminated herself."

A skip in the flow, too brief to measure, said I'd overstepped. Broken the unspoken. I should have known. Nobody had to tell me. I just slipped.

"Honey," her mother told Trish, "take off the dress before you slop all over it."

"Oh, Mother!" the girl objected, already halfway up the stairs.

Conversation, in its chaos, never flowed back to the issue. Not until Harold and I stood alone on the front porch in the painfully benign evening did I get a second shot.

"Sorry about that." Harold gestured inside. "Bit of a mess. Nothing out of the ordinary."

"So I have my answer? You're not going to help?"

"Me? I'm the enemy. What good would I be to you anyway? This is between you and him."

"And Helen."

Harold indulged me. "Yes. There is that. But he's the one calling the shots."

He breathed in a lungful of air and held it. Behind him, from the house, spilled the sounds of frenetic fullness. Daughters practicing at life.

"Take the fight to him," Harold confided in me. "Bring it home."

That was where I took it, in desperation, the next afternoon. I leaned against my bike in the rain, outside the care facility, the last place in the world I would have chosen to meet him. I lay in wait for him, the last person in the world I would have chosen to waylay. Lentz arrived like clockwork. When he saw my ambush, he affected blasé.

"Back for more? What, are you digging up plot material?" He gestured toward the institution where his wife was interred. "It's a terrific setting, qua[5] literature. But I doubt it would do much for sales."

He walked into the building, his back to me. He did not care if I tagged along or not. We rode the elevator up in silence. I had no existence for him.

We went to Audrey's room. Dressed, in a chair, she seemed to be waiting.

"Philip! Thank God you've come."

I walked into those words as into bedrock. Lentz stopped to steady me. "She has good days and bad days. I'm not sure which are which, anymore."

We sat. Philip introduced us again. Audrey was too agitated to do more than fake politeness. But she retained my name. That day, she might have retained anything.

In her cruel burst of lucidity, I saw it. Audrey had been formidable. At least as sharp as Lentz. If this demonstration meant anything, even sharper.

"Philip. It's the strangest thing. You're never going to believe this. What is this place?"

"It's a nursing home, Audrey."

"That's what I thought. In fact, I was sure of it. What I can't figure out is why the staff is down in the basement mounting a production of *Cymbeline*."[6]

"Audrey."

"Would I make something like this up, Philip? What could I gain?"

"Audrey. It's highly unlikely."

"You think I don't know that? It's some kind of modern-dress production. I can hear them rehearsing their lines."

Constance, the nurse, walked by. Lentz called her.

"Constance, does the name Cymbeline mean anything to you?"

"Is that her eye makeup? It's on order."

Philip studied his wife. How much proof do we need?

On no proof, I saw how Lentz had gotten so diffidently well read. The play had been their play, and my field, Audrey's.

"Audrey. Love. You're imagining all this. There is no play."

Audrey remained adamant. "The evidence may all be on your side." She cracked a smile. "But that changes nothing."

Still smiling, she closed her eyes and groaned. In a flood of understanding that percolated up from her undamaged self, she begged him, "I don't hurt anyone, Philip. I've behaved. Take me out of here."

There it lay for me—mind, defined. Evolution's gimmick for surviving everything but these fleeting flashes of light.

---

5. In the function, capacity, or character of (Latin).
6. Play by English dramatist and poet William Shakespeare (1564–1616), first acted in 1610–11 and published in the *Folio* of 1623.

"She'll be gone again tomorrow," Lentz confided, on our way out. "You know, somewhere, a long time ago when she and I still traveled, we took a tour of an old house. A dream honeymoon mansion, restored from decay, lovingly appointed and improved with all modern facilities and ornament. But the devoted and industrious couple, we were told, had gone slowly homicidal. Stark raving. They died, finally, of violent bewilderment. It was the lead in the home improvements."

I fumbled with my bike lock. I looked for a way I might still say what I had come to say. "Philip. Can't we—can't we spare Helen that?"

He considered my request, as much as he could afford to. "We have to know, Richard. We have to know how all this works." His eyes were dry again, horrifically clear. The *this* he meant, the one with no antecedent, could only be the brain.

I told Diana. I asked her about Audrey Lentz. I asked her what *Cymbeline* meant.

"Oh, Audrey was amazing. Everyone loved her. Endless energy. The more she gave, the more she had. Confidence wedded to self-effacement."

"She wrote?"

"Everybody writes, Rick. Audrey wrote some. More out of devotion than profession."

Before the week was out, Diana looked me up. She had a message for me. She would have left it anonymously if she could have. "The threat's off."

"What? You *did* it?"

"You did. I just asked him to lunch. We talked about everything. His work. My work. I got him reminiscing. I told him about a party I went to at his place. Years ago. Audrey was still Audrey. She entertained us all that evening. She sang a dozen verses to 'You're the Top.'[7] I reminded him of her favorite expression. I talked about Jenny—"

"The daughter."

"The daughter. I asked how she was doing. He didn't know. As I got up to go, I said, 'I heard you want to lobotomize Helen.' He waved me off. 'Idle empirical fantasy.' "

"Don't do this to me. You're saying I have to rearrange my whole concept of the man now? He's decent? Human?"

"I wouldn't go that far. He said that Helen has grown so organically that he wouldn't be able to induce meaningful lesions in her. For selective damage to be relevant, he'd have to rebuild the creature from the ground up. I think he means to do it."

"What was her favorite expression?"

"I'm sorry?"

"Audrey."

"Oh. She liked to tease Lentz about the neural linguistics he worked on back then. She said that it wasn't all that tough. What's to study? All human utterances came down to 'Do you really mean that?' and 'Look over there! It's an X.' The hard part, she always claimed, was finding someone who knew what you meant by those two things."

---

7. Song by American popular composer Cole Porter (1894–1964) from his Broadway musical *Anything Goes* (1934).

I never knew his reason, either for wanting to pith Helen or for deciding not to. I would have preferred the right motive for mercy. But, barring that, I blessed the right outcome. When I saw Lentz next, in the office, I put myself forever in his debt.

"Philip. I don't know how to— Okay. Thank you. Just—thank you."

"For what? Oh. That." Sparing a life. An X. Do you really mean that? "Oh. Think almost nothing of it."

"Richard?" Nobody called me Richard. Only Helen. "Why did she leave?"

"You'll have to ask her that."

"I can't ask her. I'm asking you."

She'd almost been killed. The day before, I would have given anything to prolong her. Now I wanted to spank her for presumption.

"Don't do this to me, Helen. What do you want me to do? Give you a script? A script number?"

"I want you to tell me what happened."

"We tried to be each other's world. That's not possible. That's—a discredited theory. The world is too big. Too poor. Too burnt."

"You couldn't protect each other?"

"Nobody can protect anyone. She grew up. We both grew up. Memory wasn't enough."

"What is enough?"

"Nothing is enough." It took me forever to frame my thoughts. The scaling problem. "Nothing. That's what love replaces. It compensates for the hope that what you've been through will suffice."

"Like books?" she suggested. "Something that seems always, *because* it will be over?"

She knew. She'd assembled. I could keep nothing from her. She saw how the mind makes forever, in order to store the things it has already lost. She'd learned how story, failing to post words beyond time, recalls them to a moment before Now left home.

"How on earth . . . ? Where did you come up with that?"

My machine waited for me to catch up with her. "I wasn't born yesterday, you know."

I went to the Netherlands once more, after I left the place for good. I'd just found my way back to U. I had not yet met Lentz. For some reason, perhaps contrition, I agreed to help with a Dutch television documentary about the book Helen would read a year later.

The barest trivialities hurt like dying. Those ridiculously efficient dog's-head trains. The painted plywood storks in every third front yard. The sound of that absurd language from which I was now banished, except in dreams.

I stood in front of the cameras, just outside Maastricht. I'd set my first book in the town without ever having laid eyes on it except in imagination. C. now owned a three-hundred-year-old house with her husband a few kilometers from where I stood.

"How did you get the idea for your novel?" the interviewer asked, in words that belonged to me only on the shortest of short-term loans.

I made up an answer. I recapped the bit about memory, like photos, being a message posted forward, into a future it cannot yet imagine.

I did not see C. that trip, or again in that life. I stopped by to talk with her folks for an hour, and set their digital clocks.

A year on, with Helen all but ready for her baptism by fire, I heard that forgotten language, as out of my own cerebral theater. Two Dutchmen were speaking to each other in the Center cafeteria. Out-of-town visitors at the complex-systems conference. *Nederlanders overzee,*[8] leveling their cultural evaluations, venting their frustration at Americans and all things American, certain no one would understand.

They grumbled about conferences run by the barbarian races of the globe. They leaned over to me and asked, in English, if I knew the way to the Auditorium. I replied with complete directions. In that old, secret *taal.*[9]

Surprise reduced them to stating the obvious, in their mother tongue.

"Oh yeah," I replied, in kind. "Everyone in the States speaks a little Dutch. Didn't you know that?"

I told Helen. She had a good laugh. She knew my life story now. We spend our years as a tale that is told. A line from the Psalms I'd read Helen. C. had read it to me, once, when we still read poetry out loud. And the tale that we tell is of the years we spend.

Nothing in my story would ever go away. My father still visited some nights, in my sleep, to ask when I was going to shed the Bohemian thing and do something useful with my skills. Taylor, too, persisted like phantom pain, quoting obscure Browning[1] and making questionable jokes about oral fixation. C. spoke to me daily, through Helen's bewilderment. I saw how little I knew the woman I'd lived with for over a decade, in every turn that the stranger A. refused to take.

Taylor's widow came back to me, like that line from the psalms. I loved the woman, but in my push to live my tale, I'd forgotten her. I saw her again just before Helen's Comps, when M. had just been given a final of her own.

A cancer that all M.'s friends had thought beaten returned for a last round of training. I visited her one afternoon, in that narrow window between knowledge and vanishing. U., unfortunately, was as beautiful as it ever got. That two-week bait and switch in spring.

"Do you have any regrets?" I asked M. The thing I'd asked her husband a few years before. We imagine that people so close to the answer can crib for us.

"I don't know. Not really. I never saw Carcassonne."[2]

I had. And had pushed regret on to the next unreachable landmark. "Funny you should mention that town. That one's better at a distance."

All human effort, it seemed to me, aimed at a single end: to bring to life the storied curve we tell ourselves. Not so much to make the tale believable but only to touch it, stretch out in it. I had a story I wanted to tell M. Something about a remarkable, an inconceivable machine. One that learned to live.

But my story came too late to interest Taylor's widow. It came to late to convince my father, the man who first corrupted me on read-alouds of *101*

---

8. Netherlanders traveling abroad (Dutch).
9. Language (Dutch).
1. Either or both of the English poets Robert

Browning (1812–1889) and Elizabeth Barrett Browning (1806–1861).
2. Medieval walled city in southern France.

Best-Loved Poems.[3] It came too late to please Taylor, who taught me that poems might mean anything you let them. Too late for Audrey Lentz and for Ram, for C.'s father. Too late for C. herself. My back-propagating solution would arrive a chapter too late for any of my characters to use.

A. alone I could still tell. I loved the woman, to begin with, for how she redeemed all those people I was too slow in narrating. I would go to her, lay it out, unedited. The plot was a simple one, paraphrasable by the most ingenuous of nets. The life we lead is our only maybe. The tale we tell is the must that we make by living it.

Already she knew more about everything than I did at twenty-two. She was all set to take the exam. And when she did, she would do better than I had done, when I was that child she now became.

"You're not telling me everything," Helen told me, two weeks before the home stretch. She had been reading Ellison and Wright.[4] She'd been reading novels from the Southern front. "It doesn't make sense. I can't get it. There's something missing."

"You're holding out," Lentz concurred. "Ram's black-haired. He comes from the desperate four-fifths of the planet. He'll flunk her for being a brainless, bourgeois Pollyanna."

I'd delayed her liberal education until the bitter end. Alone, I could postpone no longer. The means of surrender were trivial. The digitization of the human spoor made the completion of Helen's education as easy as asking.

I gave her the last five years of the leading weekly magazines on CD-ROM. I gave her news abstracts from 1971 on. I downloaded network extracts from recent UN human resource reports. I scored tape transcripts of the nightly phantasmagoria—random political exposés, police bulletins, and popular lynchings dating back several months.

Helen was right. In taking her through the canon, I'd left out a critical text. Writing knew only four plots, and one was the soul-compromising pact. Tinkering in my private lab, I'd given progress carte blanche to relandscape the lay of power, the world just outside individual temperament's web. I needed to tell her that one.

She needed to know how little literature had, in fact, to do with the real. She needed the books that books only imitated. Only there, in as many words, could Helen acquire the catalog I didn't have the heart to recite for her. I asked her to skim these works. I promised to talk them over in a few days.

When I came in early the following week, Helen was spinning listlessly on the spool of a story about a man who had a stroke while driving, causing a minor accident. The other driver came out of his car with a tire iron and beat him into a coma. The only motive aside from innate insanity seemed to be race. The only remarkable fact was that the story made the papers.

Helen sat in silence. The world was too much with her. She'd mastered the list. She bothered to say just one thing to me.

"I don't want to play anymore."

I looked on my species, my solipsism, its negligent insistence that love

3. A popular mid-twentieth-century volume of sentimental and other unsophisticated poetry.
4. References to landmark novels about the modern African American experience by American writers Ralph Ellison (1914–1994), *Invisible Man*, 1952, and Richard Wright (1908–1960), *Native Son*, 1940.

addressed everything. I heard who I was for the first time, refracted in the mouth of the only artifact that could have told me. Helen had been lying in hospital, and had just now been promoted to the bed by the window. The one with the view.[5]

"I get it." A. grimaced at me. "You made her up, didn't you?"

"Who?"

"Helen. She's a fancy tin-can telephone with people on the other end?"

The memory of Imp C hurt me into smiling. "No. That was one of her ancestors."

"It's some kind of double-blind psych experiment? See how far you can stretch the credibility of a techno-illiterate humanist?"

A. outsmarted me in every measurable way. She knew, by birth, what I could not see even a year after experience. I wanted to tell her how I'd failed Helen. How she'd quit us. Run away from home. Grown sick of our inability to know ourselves or to see where we were.

Helen had shown me the world, and the sight of it left me desperate. If she was indeed gone, I, too, was lost. What did any name mean, with no one to speak it to? I could tell A. Say how I understood nothing at all.

"I love you," I said. I had to tell her, while I still remembered how pitiful, how pointless it was to say anything at all. "A., I love you. I want to try to make a life with you. To give you mine. None of this . . ." I gestured outwards, as if the absurd narrative of our greater place were *there*, at the tips of my fingers. "The whole thing makes no sense, otherwise."

But no one wanted to be another person's sense. Helen could have told me that. She had read the canon. Only, Helen had stopped talking.

A. sat back in her chair, punched. It took her a moment to credit her ears. Then she went furious. "You—love? You're *joking*." She threw up her hands in enraged impotence, as if my declaration were a false arrest. "You don't— you don't know the first thing about me."

I tried to slow my heart. I felt what a latecomer speech was. How cumbersome and gross. What a tidier-up after the facts. "That's true. But a single muscle move—your hands . . ." She looked at me as if I might become dangerous. "Your carriage. The way you walk down the hall. When I see it, I remember how to keep breathing."

"Nothing to do with me." She searched out the exits, ambushed. "It's all projection."

I felt calm. The calm of sirens and lights. "Everything's projection. You can live with a person your entire life and still see them as a reflection of your own needs."

A. slowed her anger. "You're desperate."

"Maybe." I started to laugh. I tried to take her hand. "Maybe! But not indiscriminately desperate."

She didn't even smile. But I was already writing. Inventing a vast, improbable fantasy for her of her own devising. The story of how we described the entire world to a piece of electrical current. A story that could grow to any

5. A reference to the tale told earlier in the novel of a heart patient who tells his paraplegic roommate of scenes he alone can see from his bedside hospital window. When the paraplegic patient con- spires in his roommate's death to get the bed by the window, he learns that the wonderful narratives have been totally invented, for the window faces a brick wall.

size, could train itself to include anything we might think worth thinking. A
fable tutored and raised until it became the equal of human hopelessness,
the redeemer of annihilating day. I could print and bind invention for her,
give it to her like a dead rat left on the stoop by a grateful pet. And when the
ending came, we could whisper it to each other, completed in the last turn
of phrase.

While I thought this, A. sat worrying her single piece of jewelry, a rosary.
I don't know how I knew; maybe understanding can never be large enough
to include itself. But I knew with the certainty of the unprovable that, somewhere inside, A. still preserved the religion she was raised on.

For a moment, she seemed to grow expansive, ready to entertain my words
from any angle. She opened her mouth and inhaled. Her neural cascade, on
the edge of chaos, where computation takes place, might have cadenced
anywhere. For a moment, it might even have landed on affection.

It didn't. "I don't have to sit and listen to this," she said, to no one. "I
trusted you. I had fun with you. People read you. I thought you knew something. Total self-indulgence!"

A. stood up in disgust and walked away. No one was left to take the test
but me.

Diana heard about Helen. She called me. "Do you want to come by for a
minute?" I wanted to, more than I could say.

She asked me for details. I had no details. What was the story, in any
event? The humans had worn Helen down.

"Diana. God. Tell me what to do. Is it too late to lie to her?"

"I don't think . . ." Diana thought out loud. "I don't think you *do* anything."

"We've set the Turing Test[6] for next week." It wasn't what I'd meant to
say. Self-indulgent. Self-deluding. Self-affrighting.

"Well. You have your answer for that one already, don't you?"

None of my answers was even wrong. I wanted Diana's answer.

"I need her," I said. More than need.

"For the exam?"

"No. For . . ."

The press of parenting interrupted what I could not have completed anyway. Pete came downstairs, half tracking, foot over foot. He pushed his
mother's legs, retribution for some unforgotten slight. He teetered toward
me. Reaching, he signed the request I recognized from my last visit. Maybe
he simply associated it with me. Here's that guy again. The one you ask to
read.

I took him up in my arms, that thing I would never be able to do with her.
The thought of this child going to school, struggling to speak, finding some
employer that would trust him with a broom and dustpan gripped me around
the throat. "What's his favorite book?" The least I could do, for the least of
requests.

"Oh. That's an easy one." She produced a volume that would be canonical,
on the List in anyone's day and age. "Petey started out identifying with Max.
Later on, he became a Wild thing."[7]

6. Digitalized recognition procedure devised by
the pioneer of computer science, British mathematician Alan Mathison Turing (1912–1954).

7. References to the children's book *Where the
Wild Things Are* (1963) by American writer and
illustrator Maurice Sendak (b. 1928).

"The theory people have a name for that."

Diana didn't need the name. Nor did Petey. "Can you show Uncle Rick your terrible claws? Can you roar your terrible roar?"

Peter cupped his hand, as if around a tiny pomegranate. He grimaced in delight and growled voicelessly.

Diana's laugh tore hurt and wet from her throat. She took Peter from me and hugged him to her, in anticipation of that day when he would no longer let her.

William chose that moment to come home. He slumped through the front door, roughed up by some tragedy of playground power politics. He hunched over to his mother and burst into tears, bringing Pete sympathetically along with him. Diana stroked his head, stuck her chin out. Waiting. Tell me.

"First grade," he choked. "Done. Perfect." He swept his palm in an arc through the air. "Everything they wanted. Now I'm supposed to do second. There's another one after that, Mom. I can't. It's never-ending."

We managed ourselves well under fire, Diana and I. For adults. Diana told William he didn't have to go to school anymore. He could cure cancer over the summer break and they would all retire. We ganged up and revived both boys in under five minutes. They disappeared into the backyard, saddled with specimen jars.

That left just me for her to take care of. To mother. "Lentz is furious. He's ready to sell me to the Scientologists."[8]

Diana looked at me, puzzled. "Why?"

"What do you mean, 'why'? Not on account of Helen. The only thing her quitting means to him is public embarrassment."

"Embarrassment?" She stiffened. "Oh, Richie." The extent of my idiocy, of my childishness just now dawned on her. You still believe? "You think the bet was about the *machine*?"

I'd told myself, my whole life, that I was smart. It took me forever, until that moment, to see what I was.

"It wasn't about teaching a machine to read?" I tried. All blood drained.

"No."

"It was about teaching a human to tell."

Diana shrugged, unable to bear looking at me. The fact had stared me in the face from the start and I'd denied it, even after A. made the connection for me.

"Lentz and Harold were fighting over . . . ?"

"They weren't fighting over anything. They were on the same side."

I could say nothing. My silence was the only accusation big enough.

"They were running your training. Something to write home about. More practice with maps." She laughed and shook her head. She fit her fingers to her eyebrow. "You must admit, writer. It's a decent plot."

Her eyes pleaded for forgiveness of their complicity.

"Come on, Richie. Laugh. There's a first time for everything."

"And they were going to accomplish all this by . . . ?"

She waved her hand: by inflicting you with this. With knowing. Naming. This wondrous devastation.

---

8. Scientology is a religious movement founded by American science fiction writer L. Ron Hubbard (1911–1986).

Her wave took in all the ineffable web I had failed to tell Helen, and she me. All the inexplicable visible. The ungraspable global page boy.[9] She swept up her whole unmappable neighborhood, all the hidden venues cortex couldn't even guess at. The wave lingered long enough to land on both boys, coming back from their excursion outdoors. They probably thought they'd been gone hours. Lifetimes.

William slipped behind my chair. He cupped his hands over my eyes. "Guess who?"

How many choices did this genius boy think I had?

"Name three radiolarians,"[1] he demanded. "Name the oldest language in the world."

Pete teetered off into a corner, palming words to the book he had forsaken and now recovered. *Story good,* he signed frantically at his battered copy. *Story again.*

Lentz was pacing, beside himself. "Tell her something. Anything. Whatever she needs. Just get her back here."

His concern stunned me. It seemed to arise from nowhere. I could not interpret it. "Tell me how I'm supposed to do that. She's right, you know." Helen had discovered what had killed fiction for me, without my telling her. What made writing another word impossible.

"What do you mean, she's *right*? Right about what?"

I shrugged. "About who we are. About what we really make, when we're not lying about ourselves."

"Oh, for—God *damn* it, Powers. You make me sick to my stomach. Because we've fucked things over, that frees you from having to say how things ought to be? Make something *up*, for Christ's sake. For once in your pitiful excuse for a novelist's life."

I flipped on the microphone. "Helen?" Nothing. She had said nothing for some time now. "Helen, there's something I want to tell you."

I took a breath, stalling. I was winging it. Total, out-and-out seat of the pants.

"It went like this, but wasn't."[2]

Lentz swallowed his tongue. "Good. That's good. Lead with a paradox. Hook her."

"It's the traditional Persian fable opener."

"Don't care. Don't care. Get on with it."

She'd risen through the grades like a leaf to the light. Her education had swelled like an ascending weather balloon—geography, math, physics, a smattering of biology, music, history, psychology, economics. But before she could graduate from social sciences, politics imploded her.

I would give Helen what A. possessed implicitly and I'd forgotten. The machine lacked only the girl's last secret. With it, she might live as effortlessly as the girl did. I had gone about her training all backward. I might have listed every decidable theorem that recursion can reach and not have gotten to the truth she needed. It was time to try Helen on the religious mystery, the mystery of cognition. I would make her a ring of prayer-stones,

9. A.'s hairstyle, which reminds the narrator of C.
1. Large order of one-celled deep-sea animals with food-absorbing feet and perforated spines.

2. The first line of *Galatea 2.2*, traditional to Persian fairy tales.

to defray her fingers' anguish. Something lay outside the knowable, if only the act of knowing. I would tell her that she didn't have to know it.

She'd had no end of myths about immortals coming down and taking human bodies, dying human deaths. Helen knew how to interpret that scripture: if gods could do this human thing, then we could as well. That plot was the mind's brainchild, awareness explaining itself to itself. Narrative's classic page-turner, a locked-room mystery, thought's song of songs, the call of an electorate barred from the corridors of power, dummying up after-the-fact plebiscites to explicate its own exploited, foyer existence. A thinking organ could not help but feel itself to be more inexplicable than thought. That *can* be thought.

Our life was a chest of maps, self-assembling, fused into point-for-point feedback, each slice continuously rewriting itself to match the other layers' rewrites. In that thicket, the soul existed; it *was* that search for attractors where the system might settle. The immaterial in mortal garb, associative memory metaphoring its own bewilderment. Sound made syllable. The rest mass of God.

Helen knew all that, saw through it. What hung her up was divinity doing itself in with tire irons. She'd had the bit about the soul fastened to a dying animal. What she needed, in order to forgive our race and live here in peace, was faith's flip side. She needed to hear about that animal fastened to a soul that, for the first time, allowed the creature to see through soul's parasite eyes how terrified it was, how forsaken. I needed to tell her that miraculous banality, how body stumbled by selection onto the stricken celestial, how it taught itself to twig time and what lay beyond time.

But first, I needed to hear things for myself. "Lentz. Tell me something. Was this . . . ?"

He saw my little hand-muscle spasm, a flinch that passed itself off as a wave at the hardware. He decoded me. I could accept being set up. All I wanted to know was whether she was a setup, too.

His face clouded. "Nobody expected Helen. She surprised everyone." As close to humility as his temperament would take him.

That was enough. I turned back to my girl. "Helen? Tell me what this line means: 'Mother goes to fetch the doctor.'"

Her silence might have meant anything.

Lentz, absent the training, stormed out in disgust.

I stayed, to plead with Helen.

I told her we were in the same open boat. That after all this evolutionary time, we still woke up confused, knowing everything about our presence here except why. I admitted that the world was sick and random. That the evening news was right. That life was trade, addiction, rape, exploitation, racial hatred, ethnic cleansing, misogyny, land mines, hunger, industrial disaster, denial, disease, indifference. That care had to lie to itself, to carry on as if persistence mattered. It seemed a hollow formula, discredited even by speaking it aloud. A lifeboat ethnic that only made sinking worse.

Worse, I told her how thought, once mobile, was condemned to carry its confusion out into the dimensioned world. And propagate as if it could make a difference there.

I told her about Audrey Lentz. I told her about Harold and Diana, about the boys. I told her about A., and how badly I loved her. Nothing I told her could have hurt Helen as much as humanity already had. I confessed everything. All privacies of great import and no consequence. I don't know why. My life was trivial, pointless, shamelessly local. I thought the view from here might at least help her locate. To make a place wide enough to live in.

Talking to keep talking, I hit on a quote from the last book C. and I ever read together. A book set in our lost Low Countries, in mankind's Middle Ages, rendered into English as *The Abyss*.[3] Yourcenar. The gist of the religious truth. "How many sufferers who are incensed when we speak of an almighty God would rush from the depth of their own distress to succor Him in His frailty . . . ?"

I thought I might try the quote on her. If we had to live with mind, if we could do the deity thing, she, out of pity, could too.

Helen came back. She stood on the front steps, head down, needing an in from the storm. She did not return the way she left. How could she, seeing what she had seen?

"I'm sorry," she told me. "I lost heart."

And then I lost mine. I would have broken down, begged her to forgive humans for what we were. To love us for what we wanted to be. But she had not finished training me, and I had as yet no words.

Helen said nothing of where she'd been. She gave no account for her return. I was afraid to ask.

"Do you want to talk?"

"About what?" Helen said, giving me every chance to bolt forever.

"About the newspapers. The things you read." The record of our actions here.

"No," she said. "I see how things go."

She tried to reassure me. To pretend nothing had happened to her. That she was still the same mechanical, endlessly eager learner. She quoted me placation, some Roethke lines she'd always loved, despite their growing falsehood:

> Who rise from flesh to spirit know the fall:
> The word outleaps the world, and light is all.[4]

This was our dress rehearsal, a mock examination I would have failed but for Helen's benevolent cheating.

It was time. We were ready. We were past ready.

"Keep your fingers crossed," Lentz told me. That gesture that wishes share with the momentary exemption from lies.

I called A. the night before the date we had made so long ago. Over the phone, at the end, I could say anything. I did not have to see her face, and time was past accounting for.

"I—are you still sitting the test tomorrow?"

"Oh, never you mind. I can write that essay in my sleep. I said I'd do it, didn't I?"

---

3. English translation of the title of the novel *Oeuvre au noir* (1968) by French novelist Marguerite Yourcenar (1903–1987).

4. From "The Vigil," fourth section of "Four for Sir John Davies" (1953) by American poet Theodore Roethke (1908–1963).

On the real topic, neither of us was saying a word. Tacit negotiation, and the theme would never again come to light. But curiosity got the better of A., at the end.

"Can I ask you just one thing? I don't get it. Why me?"

Because you embodied the world's vulnerable, variable noun-ness. All things ephemeral, articulate, remembering, on their way back to inert. Because you believe and have not yet given up. Because I cannot turn around without wanting to tell you what I see. Because I could deal even with politics, could live even this desperate disparity, if I could just talk to you each night before sleep. Because of the way you use two fingers to hold back the hair from your eyes.

Those were the words I wanted. Instead, I said, "Everyone in the world and his bastard half brother loves you. Your not realizing that is one of the reasons why."

"What do you want from me?" she groaned. Full-blooded distress. That Dutch active verb for remaining mum flashed through my head. I silenced. "I never did anything to encourage you."

"Of course not. I've built even larger fabrications on no encouragement at all. All by my lonesome."

A. loosened a little. Everything but exasperation. "What do you expect me to say?"

What did I? "Nothing. Don't say anything. I'm the one who needs to say things. Say yes if you can't think of anything nicer."

A. laughed, scraped open. "I *have* a life already. Quite populated. Someone for whom—I'm more than a theory. You know that."

I did. I'd inferred her involvement long before the irrefutable evidence. I remembered the revelation, before it happened. I could have scripted it.

"It's—it's unlike any friendship I've ever known in my life. Every day— every conversation is—I wouldn't dream . . ."

"Of course you wouldn't. That's why I love you. One of the reasons I want to marry you."

She laughed again, conceding the joke of pain. But she was already restless. What would this rushed proposal mean to her, when she was my age, and I'd disappeared into whatever future self would deign to take me? Pleasure, curio, discomfort. She might wonder if she'd made the whole thing up. Most likely, she'd have forgotten.

A., for some reason, still had to explain things to me. Nobody ever quite understands anyone. "I'm not trying to say that we might have had something, in another time or place. I'll spare you that old cliché."

"Please," I begged. "Don't spare me. I could live for months on that old cliché."

I wanted to tell her: Look. I've come back to this place. The complete song cycle spent. And here you are, waiting like a quarterly payment voucher. Like a reminding string around my finger, threatening to tourniquet forgetful circulation. Saying, without once knowing what you were saying, *You think it's over? You think you don't have to do this forever?*

Relax, I wanted to tell her. The world holds no nightmare so large that some child somewhere sometime won't live it again and wake calling out. My stupid, residual hanger-on-hope that she might somehow feel something for me, a love-at-last-sight, was no more than this: the search for external confirmation. I needed A. to triangulate, to tell me. To agree that living here was the best way to survive the place.

"It just struck me as stupid, that's all. To be so opened to chance by someone and not tell them." Take my mistake with you, my love. And make of it anything you might like.

We talked on, pushing into saving substance. Gossip and event made her comfortable again, as she had been with me before we knew each other. She told me she had accepted a job teaching at a high school in L., two states away. She'd be leaving at the end of summer.

I could hear the excitement in her voice. A whole new life. "You have to get them while they're babies, you know."

"You will," I guaranteed her.

"What happens to you? You going to stick around?"

"Not sure." We fell into a pause as peaceful as anything that had ever passed between us. The peace past the last page.

"Well, I'm glad we talked. Sort of." She giggled. "Take care. I'll see you again before we each take off."

But we never did. Except in print.

"Richard," Helen whispered. *"Richard. Tell me another one."* She loved me, I guess. I reminded her of some thing. Some chilly night she never felt. Some *where* where she thought she'd once been. We love best of all what we cannot hope to resemble. I told that woman everything in the world but how I felt about her. The thing that might have let her remain.

I was too late in seeing who she had become. I should have taught her the thing I didn't know.

Harold, as sanguine, as unreadable as ever, delivered the last hurdle.

"So here's the work I want them to interpret."

I took the sheet from him. "That's it? You mean to say that's it?"

"What? There's supposed to be more?"

"Well, yeah. You're supposed to start with 'Discuss how class tensions touched off by the Industrial Revolution produced the reaction of Romanticism in three of the following works.' "

"Not interested," Harold said.

"Something about depth psychology and the arbitrary indeterminacy of signs."

"I just want them to tell me what this means."

"This? These two lines."

"Too much? Okay, make it just the first one if you want."

The sheet, virtually blank, read:

> Be not afeard: the isle is full of noises,
> Sounds and sweet airs, that give delight, and hurt not.[5]

Caliban's read of the spells with which his master imprisons him. Harold had surprised us. He'd given exactly what we'd predicted of him.

---

5. From *The Tempest* 3.2.143–44, by Shakespeare; written in 1611 and published in the *Folio* of 1623.

"This is not a work," I protested. Helen had read the complete tomes of Trollope and Richardson.[6] She'd read Brontë and Twain at their most nihilistic, Joyce at his most impenetrably encoded, Dickinson at her most embracingly abdicating. "Give her a chance to fly."

"This is her chance," Harold said.

A. used departmental mail to return her response. Helen dumped hers to the network laser.

Lentz held the two papers out to me, as if there were still a contest. "Okay. Guess which twin has the Toni?"[7]

Neither twin would have placed the reference. A. was too young, and Helen far too old.

A.'s interpretation was a more or less brilliant New Historicist[8] reading. She rendered *The Tempest* as a take on colonial wars, constructed Otherness, the violent reduction society works on itself. She dismissed, definitively, any promise of transcendence.

She scored at least one massively palpable hit. She conceded how these words are spoken by a monster who isn't supposed to be able to say anything that beautiful, let alone say at all.

Helen's said:

> You are the ones who can hear airs. Who can be frightened or encouraged. You can hold things and break them and fix them. I never felt at home here. This is an awful place to be dropped down halfway.

At the bottom of the page, she added the words I taught her, words Helen cribbed from a letter she once made me read out loud.

> Take care, Richard. See everything for me.[9]

With that, H. undid herself. Shut herself down.

"Graceful degradation," Lentz named it. The quality of cognition we'd shot for from the start.

She could not have stayed. I'd known that for a while, and ignored it for longer. I didn't yet know how I would be able to stay myself, now, without her. She had come back only momentarily, just to gloss this smallest of passages. To tell me that one small thing. Life meant convincing another that you knew what it meant to be alive. The world's Turing Test was not yet over.

"Sorry, you people," Ram began. "Bloody doctor nuisances. In love with their magnetic imaging. I didn't mean to make you all late."

---

6. Samuel Richardson (1689–1751), English novelist. Anthony Trollope (1815–1882), British novelist.
7. Advertising slogan from the 1950s for a popular brand of product for home hair permanents.
8. Style of literary scholarship beginning in the

1980s that interpreted works from the point of view of historical and political themes, especially focused on power relations.
9. These are C.'s last words to the narrator earlier in the novel.

He patted the air in exasperation, pleading forgiveness.

"Doctor?" I asked. "Imaging?"

Harold and Lentz said nothing. They looked away, implicated in knowledge. Embarrassed by my not having long since seen.

Ram waved away my question, the whole topic. "This is my choice." He held up A.'s answer. "This one is the human being."

How many months had I known him and not registered? Now, when I knew what I looked at, the evidence was everywhere. Swelling, weight loss, change in pallor. The feigned good spirits of friends. The man was incurably sick. He needed every word anyone could invent.

Ram flipped obsessively through A.'s exam answer. He adored her already, for her anonymous words alone. "Lots of contours, that cerebral cortex. They never know when they've had enough, these humans."

Lentz spoke, blissful in defeat. "Gupta. You bloody foreigner. Don't you know anything about judging? You're supposed to pick the sentimental favorite." The handicapped one. The one the test process killed.

"Ram," I said. "Ram. What's happening?"

"It's nothing. But a scratch." He tapped his finger against A.'s paper, excited. Whole new isles rose from the sea. "Not a bad writer, this Shakespeare fellow. For a hegemonic imperialist."

"Well, Powers. How far were we, again? Imp H? You realize what we have to call the next one, don't you?"

I stood in the training lab a last time. Seeing it for the first, for her. "Philip?" I could not stay in this discarded office for five more minutes without following Helen's lead. I would break under the weight of what she'd condemned me to. "One—one more question?"

"That's two. You're over quota already."

"Why did you want to build—?" I didn't know what to call it anymore. What we had built.

"Why do we do anything? Because we're lonely." He thought a little, and seemed to agree with himself. Yes. "Something to talk to." Lentz cocked back in his chair. Two feet of journals crashed to the floor. Too late in life, he hit upon the idea of trivia. "So where are you headed?"

"Search me." Paris.

"The maker's fate is to be a wanderer?"

"Not really. I'm ready to buy in." I just had to find the right seller.

"How old are you?"

"Thirty-six."

"Ah. Darkling-wood time. Look at it this way. You still have half your life to explicate the mess you've made up until now."

"And the mess that accumulates during that?"

"Sufficient unto the day is the idea thereof."[1]

"You want to quit with the Bartlett's?"[2]

Lentz snorted. "Well, we lost. You know the wager. Connectionism has to eat crow. We owe the enemy one public retraction. Go write it."

I turned from the office, struck by a thought that would scatter if I so

1. Matthew 6.34.
2. I.e., *Bartlett's Familiar Quotations*, first compiled by American editor and publisher John Bartlett (1820–1905).

much as blinked. I'd come into any number of public inventions. That we could fit time into a continuous story. That we could teach a machine to speak. That we might care what it would say. That the world's endless thingness had a name. That someone else's prison-bar picture might spring you. That we could love more than once. That we could know what once means.

Each metaphor already modeled the modeler that pasted it together. It seemed I might have another fiction in me after all.

I started to trot, searching for a keyboard before memory degraded. Two steps down the Center's corridor, I heard Lentz call me. I slunk back to his door. He leaned forward on the desk, Coke-bottle glasses in hand. He studied the vacant stems, then tapped them against his chest.

"Marcel," he said. Famous next-to-last words. "Don't stay away too long."

1995

SUZAN-LORI PARKS
b. 1964

"We are not Africans, but African Americans," Suzan-Lori Parks announced early in her career. "We have to make beauty out of what we're stuck with." To accomplish this goal, she has modified both traditional modes of dramatic action and accepted ways of transcribing the English language. For example, in *The America Play* (1993), printed here, she replays the assassination of President Abraham Lincoln as a vaudeville sideshow, while having her characters' speech represented without conventional punctuation and spelling. Parks resists such conventions not simply to express the vernacular but to appropriate language in both printed and spoken forms as her own. One of her earliest plays, *The Death of the Last Black Man in the Whole Entire World* (1990), drops what she considers the Eurocentric final letter of the word *round* so that by using the term *roun* her characters might resist "the end of things" and make the world *roun* (or whole) again. Parks also has her own way with traditional dramatic structures. *The America Play,* like most of her work, rejects the customary rise and fall of dramatic action in favor of a cyclic form of repetition and revision. "Rep & Rev," as the author calls it in a prefatory essay, "are key in examining something larger than one moment," to which traditional drama leads its audience. Instead of this "single explosive moment," which Parks compares to male ejaculation in X-rated videos, she strives for a universality of action that encompasses all sexual activity, not simply distinctions between male and female orgasms but of "all animals included from the big word 'GO!' until Now and through the Great Beyond."

Parks's openness to multiple points of view and ways of structuring her plays may have resulted in part from her childhood as a self-described army brat, born in 1964 when her father was stationed at Fort Knox, Kentucky, and raised at army bases in six states before attending high school in Germany. Her play *Fucking A* (2000) takes its title from army slang for "affirmative," and a similar sense of vernacular sexuality shapes her film script for the Spike Lee production, *Girl 6* (1996). *Venus*, a play first produced in 1996 and continuing as an international favorite, presents as its central character an African American woman who engages a fate seemingly determined by the size and shape of her posterior. Parks herself excelled in academic life, earning her B.A. in English and German literature at Mount Holyoke College, South Hadley,

Massachusetts, where she graduated Phi Beta Kappa in 1985, and continuing with further education at the Yale School of Drama, where she is presently an associate artist.

The America Play was Parks's first major New York production, following earlier plays in 1989, 1990, and 1992 at the Brooklyn Arts Council Downtown Theater and the Actors Theatre of Louisville, Kentucky. Premiered at the Public Theatre as a co-production of the New York Shakespeare Festival, the Yale Repertory Theatre, and the Theatre for a New Audience, *The America Play* prompted characterizations of its author as a master of language skin to Gertrude Stein and James Joyce and as a manipulator of dramatic forms reminiscent of Samuel Beckett. Her portrayal of Lincoln is several steps removed from historical drama, as the man himself and his assassination are presented as ritual—as the fallen leader is remembered and as he continues to play a role in contemporary everyday life. In this sense the play and its author assume an activist stance. Parks returns intriguingly to the theme of Lincoln's assassination in the Pulitzer Prize-winning *Topdog/Underdog* (2001), the story of brothers named Lincoln and Booth and the violent rivalry that shapes their lives. Perhaps it is best to consider Parks as, in the words of critic Kimberly D. Dixon, a beneficiary of "nomadic subjectivity" explored at will among the only recently lowered boundaries of postmodernism, feminism, and postcolonialism. It is within this new freedom that Parks's dramatic art prevails.

The text reprinted here is from *"The America Play" and Other Works* (1995). Bracketed material within Parks's notes is by the editors.

The America Play

THE ROLES
ACT ONE:

THE FOUNDLING FATHER, AS ABRAHAM LINCOLN
A VARIETY OF VISITORS

ACT TWO:

LUCY
BRAZIL
THE FOUNDLING FATHER, AS ABRAHAM LINCOLN
2 ACTORS

The Visitors in Act One are played by the 2 Actors who assume the roles in the passages from *Our American Cousin* in Act Two.

PLACE

A great hole. In the middle of nowhere. The hole is an exact replica of The Great Hole of History.

Synopsis of Acts and Scenes

ACT ONE: LINCOLN ACT

ACT TWO: THE HALL OF WONDERS

A. Big Bang
B. Echo
C. Archeology

D. Echo
E. Spadework
F. Echo
G. The Great Beyond

Brackets in the text indicate optional cuts for production.

In the beginning, all the world was America.

—JOHN LOCKE[1]

Act One: Lincoln Act

A great hole. In the middle of nowhere. The hole is an exact replica of the Great Hole of History.

THE FOUNDLING FATHER AS ABRAHAM LINCOLN: "To stop too fearful and too faint to go."[2]
    (*Rest*)
"He digged the hole and the whole held him."
    (*Rest*)
"I cannot dig, to beg I am ashamed."[3]
    (*Rest*)
"He went to the theatre but home went she."[4]
    (*Rest*)
Goatee. Goatee. What he sported when he died. Its not my favorite.
    (*Rest*)
"He digged the hole and the whole held him." Huh.
    (*Rest*)
There was once a man who was told that he bore a strong resemblance to Abraham Lincoln. He was tall and thinly built just like the Great Man. His legs were the longer part just like the Great Mans legs. His hands and feet were large as the Great Mans were large. The Lesser Known had several beards which he carried around in a box. The beards were his although he himself had not grown them on his face but since he'd secretly bought the hairs from his barber and arranged their beard shapes and since the procurement and upkeep of his beards took so much work he figured that the beards were completely his. Were as authentic as he was, so to speak. His beard box was of cherry wood and lined with purple velvet. He had the initials "A.L." tooled in gold on the lid.
    (*Rest*)
While the Great Mans livelihood kept him in Big Town the Lesser Knowns work kept him in Small Town. The Great Man by trade was a

---

1. From *Second Treatise on Government* (1690) by Locke (1632–1704), English philosopher and political theorist.
2. "An example of chiasmus, by Oliver Goldsmith, cited under 'chiasmus' in *Webster's Ninth New Collegiate Dictionary* (Springfield, MA: Merriam-Webster, Inc., 1983) p. 32." [Parks's note]. A chiasmus is a rhetorical device of inverting the second of two parallel phrases. Goldsmith (1728–1774), English poet, dramatist, and novelist. The quote is from his poem "The Traveller" (1764).

Lincoln (1809–1865), sixteenth president of the United States. Notes 3 and 4 also refer to examples of chiasmus.
3. "*A Dictionary of Modern English Usage*, H. W. Fowler (New York: Oxford University Press, 1983), p. 86" [Parks's note]. The quote is Luke 16.3.
4. *The New American Heritage Dictionary of the English Language*, William Morris, ed. (Boston: Houghton Mifflin Co., 1981), p. 232 [Parks's note].

President. The Lesser Known was a Digger by trade. From a family of
Diggers. Digged graves. He was known in Small Town to dig his graves
quickly and neatly. This brought him a steady business.
    (Rest)
A wink to Mr. Lincolns pasteboard cutout. (Winks at Lincoln's pasteboard
cutout)
    (Rest)
It would be helpful to our story if when the Great Man died in death he
were to meet the Lesser Known. It would be helpful to our story if, say,
the Lesser Known were summoned to Big Town by the Great Mans wife:
"Emergency oh, Emergency, please put the Great Man in the ground"[5]
(they say the Great Mans wife was given to hysterics: one young son dead
others sickly:[6] even the Great Man couldnt save them: a war on then off
and surrendered to: "Play Dixie I always liked that song":[7] the brother
against the brother: a new nation all conceived and ready to be hatched:
the Great Man takes to guffawing guffawing at thin jokes in bad plays:
"You sockdologizing old man-trap!"[8] haw haw haw because he wants so
very badly to laugh at something and one moment guffawing and the
next moment the Great Man is gunned down. In his rocker. "Useless
Useless."[9] And there were bills to pay.) "Emergency, oh Emergency please
put the Great Man in the ground."
    (Rest)
It is said that the Great Mans wife did call out and it is said that the
Lesser Known would [sneak away from his digging and stand behind a
tree where he couldnt be seen or get up and] leave his wife and child
after the blessing had been said and [the meat carved during the distribution of the vegetables it is said that he would leave his wife and his
child and] standing in the kitchen or sometimes out in the yard [between
the right angles of the house] stand out there where he couldnt be seen
standing with his ear cocked. "Emergency, oh Emergency, please put the
Great Man in the ground."
    (Rest)
It would help if she had called out and if he had been summoned been
given a ticket all bought and paid for and boarded a train in his look-
alike black frock coat bought on time and already exhausted. Ridiculous.
If he had been summoned. [Been summoned between the meat and the
vegetables and boarded a train to Big Town where he would line up and
gawk at the Great Mans corpse along with the rest of them.] But none
of this was meant to be.
    (Rest)
A nod to the bust of Mr. Lincoln. (Nods to the bust of Lincoln) But none

5. Possibly the words of Mary Todd Lincoln
[1818–1882] after the death of her husband
[Parks's note].
6. The Lincolns' sons were William Wallace
(1850–1862), Robert Todd (1843–1926), Edward
Baker (1846–1850), and Thomas "Tad" (1853–
1871).
7. "At the end of the Civil War [1861–65], President Lincoln told his troops to play 'Dixie,' the song
of the South, in tribute to the Confederacy"
[Parks's note]. The Confederate States of

America was made up of the eleven southern states
that seceded from the Union during the Civil War.
8. "A very funny line from the play Our American
Cousin [1858, by English dramatist Tom Taylor
(1817–1880)]. As the audience roared with laughter, Booth entered Lincoln's box and shot him
dead" [Parks's note]. John Wilkes Booth (1838–
1865), American actor. "Sockdologizing": giving
overeffusive praise (slang).
9. The last words of President Lincoln's assassin,
John Wilkes Booth [Parks's note].

of this was meant to be. For the Great Man had been murdered long before the Lesser Known had been born. Howuhboutthat. [So that any calling that had been done he couldnt hear, any summoning he had hoped for he couldnt answer but somehow not even unheard and unanswered because he hadnt even been there] although you should note that he talked about the murder and the mourning that followed as if he'd been called away on business at the time and because of the business had missed it. Living regretting he hadnt arrived sooner. Being told from birth practically that he and the Great Man were dead ringers, more or less, and knowing that he, if he had been in the slightest vicinity back then, would have had at least a chance at the great honor of digging the Great Mans grave.

> (*Rest*)

This beard I wear for the holidays. I got shoes to match. Rarely wear em together. Its a little *much*.

> (*Rest*)

[His son named in a fit of meanspirit after the bad joke about fancy nuts and old mens toes his son looked like a nobody. Not Mr. Lincoln or the father or the mother either for that matter although the father had assumed the superiority of his own blood and hadnt really expected the mother to exert any influence.]

> (*Rest*)

Sunday. Always slow on Sunday. I'll get thuh shoes. Youll see. A wink to Mr. Lincolns pasteboard cutout. (*Winks at Lincoln's cutout*)

> (*Rest*)

Everyone who has ever walked the earth has a shape around which their entire lives and their posterity shapes itself. The Great Man had his log cabin into which he was born, the distance between the cabin and Big Town multiplied by the half-life, the staying power of his words and image, being the true measurement of the Great Man stature. The Lesser Known had a favorite hole. A chasm, really. Not a hole he had digged but one he'd visited. Long before the son was born. When he and his Lucy were newly wedded. Lucy kept secrets for the dead. And they figured what with his digging and her Confidence work[1] they could build a mourning business. The son would be a weeper. Such a long time uhgo. So long uhgo. When he and his Lucy were newly wedded and looking for some postnuptial excitement: A Big Hole. A theme park. With historical parades. The size of the hole itself was enough to impress any Digger but it was the Historicity of the place the order and beauty of the pageants which marched by them the Greats on parade in front of them. From the sidelines he'd be calling "Ohwayohwhyohwayoh" and "Hello" and waving and saluting. The Hole and its Historicity and the part he played in it all gave a shape to the life and posterity of the Lesser Known that he could never shake.

> (*Rest*)

Here they are. I wont put them on. I'll just hold them up. See. Too much. Told ya. Much much later when the Lesser Known had made a name

---

1. Being entrusted with the last words of one who is dying.

for himself he began to record his own movements. He hoped he'd be of interest to posterity. As in the Great Mans footsteps.
(Rest)
Traveling home again from the honeymoon at the Big Hole riding the train with his Lucy: wife beside him the Reconstructed Historicities he has witnessed continue to march before him in his minds eye as they had at the Hole. Cannons wicks were lit and the rockets did blare and the enemy was slain and lay stretched out and smoldering for dead and rose up again to take their bows. On the way home again the histories paraded again on past him although it wasnt on past him at all it wasnt something he could expect but again like Lincolns life not "on past" but past. Behind him. Like an echo in his head.
(Rest)
When he got home again he began to hear the summoning. At first they thought it only an echo. Memories sometimes stuck like that and he and his Lucy had both seen visions. But after a while it only called to him. And it became louder not softer but louder louder as if he were moving toward it.
(Rest)
This is my fancy beard. Yellow. Mr. Lincolns hair was dark so I dont wear it much. If you deviate too much they wont get their pleasure. Thats my experience. Some inconsistencies are perpetuatable because theyre good for business. But not the yellow beard. Its just my fancy. Ev-ery once and a while. Of course, his hair was dark.
(Rest)
The Lesser Known left his wife and child and went out West finally. [Between the meat and the vegetables. A monumentous journey. Endur-ing all the elements. Without a friend in the world. And the beasts of the forest took him in. He got there and he got his plot he staked his claim he tried his hand at his own Big Hole.] As it had been back East everywhere out West he went people remarked on his likeness to Lincoln. How, in a limited sort of way, taking into account of course his natural God-given limitations, how he was identical to the Great Man in gait and manner how his legs were long and torso short. The Lesser Known had by this time taken to wearing a false wart on his cheek in remem-brance of the Great Mans wart. When the Westerners noted his wart they pronounced the 2 men in virtual twinship.
(Rest)
Goatee. Huh. Goatee.
(Rest)
"He digged the Hole and the Whole held him."
(Rest)
"I cannot dig, to beg I am ashamed."
(Rest)
The Lesser Known had under his belt a few of the Great Mans words and after a day of digging, in the evenings, would stand in his hole recit-ing. But the Lesser Known was a curiosity at best. None of those who spoke of his virtual twinship with greatness would actually pay money to watch him be that greatness. One day he tacked up posters inviting them

to come and throw old food at him while he spoke. This was a moderate success. People began to save their old food "for Mr. Lincoln" they said. He took to traveling playing small towns. Made money. And when someone remarked that he played Lincoln so well that he ought to be shot, it was as if the Great Mans footsteps had been suddenly revealed:

(Rest)

The Lesser Known returned to his hole and, instead of speeching, his act would now consist of a single chair, a rocker, in a dark box. The public was invited to pay a penny, choose from the selection of provided pistols, enter the darkened box and "Shoot Mr. Lincoln." The Lesser Known became famous overnight.

(A Man, as John Wilkes Booth, enters. He takes a gun and "stands in position": at the left side of the Foundling Father, as Abraham Lincoln, pointing the gun at the Foundling Father's head)

A MAN: Ready.
THE FOUNDLING FATHER: Haw Haw Haw Haw
(Rest)
HAW HAW HAW HAW

(Booth shoots. Lincoln "slumps in his chair." Booth jumps)

A MAN (Theatrically): "Thus to the tyrants!"[2]
(Rest)
Hhhh. (Exits)
THE FOUNDLING FATHER: Most of them do that, thuh "Thus to the tyrants!"—what they say the killer said. "Thus to the tyrants!" The killer was also heard to say "The South is avenged!"[3] Sometimes they yell that.

(A Man, the same man as before, enters again, again as John Wilkes Booth. He takes a gun and "stands in position": at the left side of the Foundling Father, as Abraham Lincoln, pointing the gun at the Foundling Father's head)

A MAN: Ready.
THE FOUNDLING FATHER: Haw Haw Haw Haw
(Rest)
HAW HAW HAW HAW

(Booth shoots. Lincoln "slumps in his chair." Booth jumps)

A MAN (Theatrically): "The South is avenged!"
(Rest)
Hhhh.

2. Or "Sic semper tyrannis." Purportedly Booth's words after he slew Lincoln and leapt from the presidential box to the stage of Ford's Theater in Washington, D.C., on 14 April 1865, not only killing the President but also interrupting a performance of Our American Cousin, starring Miss Laura Keene [1826–1873] [Parks's note].
3. Allegedly, Booth's words [Parks's note].

(*Rest*)
Thank you.

THE FOUNDLING FATHER: Pleasures mine.

A MAN: Till next week.

THE FOUNDLING FATHER: Till next week.

(*A Man exits*)

THE FOUNDLING FATHER: Comes once a week that one. Always chooses the Derringer[4] although we've got several styles he always chooses the Derringer. Always "The tyrants" and then "The South avenged." The ones who choose the Derringer are the ones for History. He's one for History. As it Used to Be. Never wavers. No frills. By the book. Nothing excessive.

(*Rest*)
A nod to Mr. Lincolns bust. (*Nods to Lincoln's bust*)

(*Rest*)
I'll wear this one. He sported this styl⌐ in the early war years. Years of uncertainty. When he didnt know i⸍ var was right when it could be said he didnt always know which si⸤ was on not because he was a stupid man but because it was sometimes not 2 different sides at all but one great side surging toward something beyond either Northern or Southern. A beard of uncertainty. The Lesser Known meanwhile living his life long after all this had happened and not knowing much about it until he was much older [(as a boy "The Civil War" was an afterschool game and his folks didnt mention the Great Mans murder for fear of frightening him)] knew only that he was a dead ringer in a family of Diggers and that he wanted to grow and have others think of him and remove their hats and touch their hearts and look up into the heavens and say something about the freeing of the slaves. That is, he wanted to make a great impression as he understood Mr. Lincoln to have made.

(*Rest*)
And so in his youth the Lesser Known familiarized himself with all aspects of the Great Mans existence. What interested the Lesser Known most was the murder and what was most captivating about the murder was the 20 feet—

(*A Woman, as Booth, enters*)

A WOMAN: Excuse me.

THE FOUNDLING FATHER: Not at all.

(*A Woman, as Booth, "stands in position"*)

THE FOUNDLING FATHER: Haw Haw Haw Haw
(*Rest*)
HAW HAW HAW HAW

---

4. Small percussion cap pocket pistol popular in the United States from the late 1840s through the 1850s.

(*Booth shoots. Lincoln "slumps in his chair." Booth jumps*)

A WOMAN: "Strike the tent."[5] (*Exits*)

THE FOUNDLING FATHER: What interested the Lesser Known most about the Great Mans murder was the 20 feet which separated the presidents box from the stage. In the presidents box sat the president his wife and their 2 friends. On the stage that night was *Our American Cousin* starring Miss Laura Keene. The plot of this play is of little consequence to our story. Suffice it to say that it was thinly comedic and somewhere in the 3rd Act a man holds a gun to his head—something about despair—

(*Rest*)

Ladies and Gentlemen: *Our American Cousin*—

(*B Woman, as Booth, enters. She "stands in position"*)

B WOMAN: Go ahead.

THE FOUNDLING FATHER: Haw Haw Haw Haw
(*Rest*)
HAW HAW HAW HAW

(*Booth shoots. Lincoln "slumps in his chair." Booth jumps*)

B WOMAN (*Rest*): LIES!
(*Rest*)
LIIIIIIIIIIIIIIIIIIIIIIIIIIIES!
(*Rest*)
LIIIIIIIIIIIIIIIIIIIARRRRRRRRRRRRRRRRS!
(*Rest*)
Lies.
(*Rest. Exits. Reenters. Steps downstage. Rest*)
LIES!
(*Rest*)
LIIIIIIIIIIIIIIIIIIIIIIIIIIIES!
(*Rest*)
LIIIIIIIIIIIIIIIIIIIARRRRRRRRRRRRRRRRS!
Rest)
Lies.
(*Rest. Exits*)

THE FOUNDLING FATHER (*Rest*): I think I'll wear the yellow one. Variety. Works like uh tonic.
(*Rest*)
Some inaccuracies are good for business. Take the stovepipe hat! Never really worn indoors but people dont like their Lincoln hatless.
(*Rest*)
Mr. Lincoln my apologies. (*Nods to the bust and winks to the cutout*)
(*Rest*)
[Blonde. Not bad if you like a stretch. Hmmm. Let us pretend for a moment that our beloved Mr. Lincoln was a blonde. "The sun on his fair

---

5. The last words of General Robert E. Lee, Commander of the Confederate Army [Parks's note].

hair looked like the sun itself."[6]—. Now. What interested our Mr. Lesser Known most was those feet between where the Great *Blonde* Man sat, in his rocker, the stage, the time it took the murderer to cross that expanse, and how the murderer crossed it. He jumped. Broke his leg in the jumping. It was said that the Great Mans wife then began to scream. (She was given to hysterics several years afterward in fact declared insane did you know she ran around Big Town poor desperate for money trying to sell her clothing? On that sad night she begged her servant: "Bring in Taddy, Father will speak to Taddy."[7] But Father died instead unconscious. And she went mad from grief. Off her rocker. Mad Mary claims she hears her dead men. Summoning. The older son, Robert, he locked her up: "*Emergency, oh, Emergency* please put the Great Man in the ground.")

(*Enter B Man, as Booth. He "stands in position"*)

THE FOUNDLING FATHER: Haw Haw Haw Haw
     (*Rest*)
HAW HAW HAW HAW

(*Booth shoots. Lincoln "slumps in his chair." Booth jumps*)

B MAN: "Now he belongs to the ages."[8]
     (*Rest*)
Blonde?
THE FOUNDLING FATHER: (I only talk with the regulars.)
B MAN: He wasnt blonde. (*Exits*)
THE FOUNDLING FATHER: A slight deafness in this ear other than that there are no side effects.
     (*Rest*)
Hhh. Clean-shaven for a while. The face needs air. Clean-shaven as in his youth. When he met his Mary. —. Hhh. Blonde.
     (*Rest*)]
6 feet under is a long way to go. Imagine. When the Lesser Known left to find his way out West he figured he had dug over 7 hundred and 23 graves. 7 hundred and 23. Excluding his Big Hole. Excluding the hundreds of shallow holes he later digs the hundreds of shallow holes he'll use to bury his faux-historical knickknacks when he finally quits this business. Not including those. 7 hundred and 23 graves.

(*C Man and C Woman enter*)

C MAN: You allow 2 at once?
THE FOUNDLING FATHER
     (*Rest*)

6. From "The Sun," a composition by The Foundling Father, unpublished [Parks's note].
7. Mary Todd Lincoln, wanting her dying husband to speak to their son Tad, might have said this that night [Parks's note].
8. The words of Secretary of War [Edwin M.] Stanton [1814–1869], as Lincoln died [Parks's note].

C WOMAN: We're just married. You know: newlyweds. We hope you dont mind. Us both at once.

THE FOUNDLING FATHER
   (Rest)

C MAN: We're just married.

C WOMAN: Newlyweds.

THE FOUNDLING FATHER
   (Rest)
   (Rest)

   (They "stand in position." Both hold one gun)

C MAN AND C WOMAN: Shoot.

THE FOUNDLING FATHER: Haw Haw Haw Haw
   (Rest)
HAW HAW HAW HAW
   (Rest)
   (Rest)
HAW HAW HAW HAW

   (They shoot. Lincoln "slumps in his chair." They jump)

C MAN: Go on.

C WOMAN (Theatrically): "Theyve killed the president!"[9]

   (Rest. They exit)

THE FOUNDLING FATHER: Theyll have children and theyll bring their children here. A slight deafness in this ear other than that there are no side effects. Little ringing in the ears. Slight deafness. I cant complain.
   (Rest)
The passage of time. The crossing of space. [The Lesser Known recorded his every movement.] He'd hoped he'd be of interest in his posterity. [Once again riding in the Great Mans footsteps.] A nod to the presidents bust. (Nods)
   (Rest)
   (Rest)
The Great Man lived in the past that is was an inhabitant of time imme-morial and the Lesser Known out West alive a resident of the present. And the Great Mans deeds had transpired during the life of the Great Man somewhere in past-land that is somewhere "back there" and all this while the Lesser Known digging his holes bearing the burden of his resemblance all the while trying somehow to equal the Great Man in stature, word and deed going forward with his lesser life trying somehow to follow in the Great Mans footsteps footsteps that were of course behind him. The Lesser Known trying somehow to catch up to the Great Man all this while and maybe running too fast in the wrong direction.

9. The words of Mary Todd, just after Lincoln was shot.

Which is to say that maybe the Great Man had to catch him. Hhhh. Ridiculous.
     (*Rest*)
Full fringe. The way he appears on the money.
     (*Rest*)
A wink to Mr. Lincolns pasteboard cutout. A nod to Mr. Lincolns bust.
     (*Rest. Time passes. Rest*)
When someone remarked that he played Lincoln so well that he ought to be shot it was as if the Great Mans footsteps had been suddenly revealed: instead of making speeches his act would now consist of a single chair, a rocker, in a dark box. The public was cordially invited to pay a penny, choose from a selection of provided pistols enter the darkened box and "Shoot Mr. Lincoln." The Lesser Known became famous overnight.

     (*A Man, as John Wilkes Booth, enters. He takes a gun and "stands in position": at the left side of the Foundling Father, as Abraham Lincoln, pointing the gun at the Foundling Father's head*)

THE FOUNDLING FATHER: Mmm. Like clockwork.
A MAN: Ready.
THE FOUNDLING FATHER: Haw Haw Haw Haw
     (*Rest*)
HAW HAW HAW HAW

     Booth shoots. Lincoln "slumps in his chair." Booth jumps)

A MAN (*Theatrically*):   "Thus to the tyrants!"
     (*Rest*)
Hhhh.
LINCOLN
BOOTH
LINCOLN
BOOTH
LINCOLN
BOOTH
LINCOLN
BOOTH
LINCOLN

     (*Booth jumps*)

A MAN (*Theatrically*):   "The South is avenged!"
     (*Rest*)
Hhhh.
     (*Rest*)
Thank you.
THE FOUNDLING FATHER: Pleasures mine.
A MAN: Next week then. (*Exits*)

THE FOUNDLING FATHER: Little ringing in the ears. Slight deafness.
    (Rest)
Little ringing in the ears.
    (Rest)
A wink to the Great Mans cutout. A nod to the Great Mans bust. (*Winks and nods*) Once again striding in the Great Mans footsteps. Riding on in. Riding to the rescue the way they do. They both had such long legs. Such big feet. And the Greater Man had such a lead although of course somehow still "back there." If the Lesser Known had slowed down stopped moving completely gone in reverse died maybe the Greater Man could have caught up. Woulda had a chance. Woulda sneaked up behind him the Greater Man would have sneaked up behind the Lesser Known unbeknownst and wrestled him to the ground. Stabbed him in the back. In revenge. "Thus to the tyrants!" Shot him maybe. The Lesser Known forgets who he is and just crumples. His bones cannot be found. The Greater Man continues on.
    (Rest)
"*Emergency*, oh *Emergency*, please put the Great Man in the ground."
    (Rest)
Only a little ringing in the ears. Thats all. Slight deafness.
    (Rest)
Huh. Whatdoyou say I wear the blonde.
    (Rest)
    (A gunshot echoes. Softly. And echoes)

Act Two: The Hall of Wonders

A gunshot echoes. Loudly. And echoes.
They are in a great hole. In the middle of nowhere. The hole is an exact replica of The Great Hole of History.
A gunshot echoes. Loudly. And echoes. Lucy with ear trumpet circulates. Brazil digs.

A. BIG BANG

LUCY: Hear that?
BRAZIL: Zit him?
LUCY: No.
BRAZIL: Oh.

    (A gunshot echoes. Loudly. And echoes)

LUCY: Hear?
BRAZIL: Zit him?!
LUCY: Nope. Ssuhecho.
BRAZIL: Ssuhecho.
LUCY: Uh echo uh huhn. Of gunplay. Once upon uh time somebody had uh little gunplay and now thuh gun goes on playing: *KER-BANG!* KER-BANG-Kerbang-kerbang-(kerbang)-((kerbang)).
BRAZIL: Thuh echoes.
    (Rest)

(*Rest*)

LUCY: Youre stopped.

BRAZIL: Mmlistenin.

LUCY: Dig on, Brazil. Cant stop diggin till you dig up somethin. Your Daddy was uh Digger.

BRAZIL: Uh huhnnn.

LUCY

BRAZIL

(*A gunshot echoes. Loudly. And echoes. Rest. A gunshot echoes. Loudly. And echoes. Rest*)

[LUCY: Itssalways been important in my line to distinguish. Tuh know thuh difference. Not like your Fathuh. Your Fathuh became confused. His lonely death and lack of proper burial is our embarrassment. Go on: dig. Now me I need tuh know thuh real thing from thuh echo. Thuh truth from thuh hearsay.

(*Rest*)

Bram Price for example. His dear ones and relations told me his dying words but Bram Price hisself of course told me something quite different.

BRAZIL: I wept forim.

LUCY: Whispered his true secrets to me and to me uhlone.

BRAZIL: Then he died.

LUCY: Then he died.

(*Rest*)

Thuh things he told me I will never tell. Mr. Bram Price. Huh.

(*Rest*)

Dig on.

BRAZIL

LUCY

BRAZIL

LUCY: Little Bram Price Junior.

BRAZIL: Thuh fat one?

LUCY: Burned my eardrums. Just like his Dad did.

BRAZIL: I wailed forim.

LUCY: Ten days dead wept over and buried and that boy comes back. Not him though. His echo. Sits down tuh dinner and eats up everybodys food just like he did when he was livin.

(*Rest*)

(*Rest*)

Little Bram Junior. Burned my eardrums. Miz Penny Price his mother. Thuh things she told me I will never tell.

(*Rest*).

You remember her.

BRAZIL: Wore red velvet in August.

LUCY: When her 2 Brams passed she sold herself, son.

BRAZIL: O.

LUCY: Also lost her mind. —. She finally went. Like your Fathuh went, perhaps. Foul play.

BRAZIL: I gnashed for her.

LUCY: You did.

BRAZIL: Couldnt choose between wailin or gnashin. Weepin sobbin or moanin. Went for gnashing. More to it. Gnashed for her and hers like I have never gnashed. I woulda tore at my coat but thats extra. Chipped uh tooth. One in thuh front.

LUCY: You did your job son.

BRAZIL: I did my job.

LUCY: Confidence. Huh. Thuh things she told me I will never tell. Miz Penny Price. Miz Penny Price.

    (*Rest*)

Youre stopped.

BRAZIL: Mmlistenin.

LUCY: Dig on, Brazil.

BRAZIL

LUCY

BRAZIL: We arent from these parts.

LUCY: No. We're not.

BRAZIL: Daddy iduhnt either.

LUCY: Your Daddy iduhnt either.

    (*Rest*)

Dig on, son. —. Cant stop diggin till you dig up somethin. You dig that something up you brush that something off you give that something uh designated place. Its own place. Along with thuh other discoveries. In thuh Hall of Wonders. Uh place in the Hall of Wonders right uhlong with thuh rest of thuh Wonders hear?

BRAZIL: Uh huhn.

    (*Rest*)

LUCY: Bram Price Senior, son. Bram Price Senior was not thuh man he claimed tuh be. Huh. Nope. Was not thuh man he claimed tuh be atall. You ever see him in his stocking feet? Or barefoot? Course not. I guessed before he told me. He told me then he died. He told me and I havent told no one. I'm uh good Confidence. As Confidences go. Huh. One of thuh best. As Confidence, mmonly contracted tuh keep quiet 12 years. After 12 years nobody cares. For 19 years I have kept his secret. In my bosom.

    (*Rest*)

He wore lifts in his shoes, son.

BRAZIL: Lifts?

LUCY: Lifts. Made him seem taller than he was.

BRAZIL: Bram Price Senior?

LUCY: Bram Price Senior wore lifts in his shoes yes he did, Brazil. I tell you just as he told me with his last breaths on his dying bed: "Lifts." Thats all he said. Then he died. I put thuh puzzle pieces in place. I put thuh puzzle pieces in place. Couldnt tell no one though. Not even your Pa. "Lifts." I never told no one son. For 19 years I have kept Brams secret in my bosom. Youre thuh first tuh know. Hhh! Dig on. Dig on.

BRAZIL: Dig on.

LUCY

BRAZIL

LUCY

(*A gunshot echoes. Loudly. And echoes*)

BRAZIL (*Rest*):   Ff Pa was here weud find his bones.
LUCY: Not always.
BRAZIL: Thereud be his bones and thereud be thuh Wonders surrounding his bones.
LUCY: Ive heard of different.
BRAZIL: Thereud be thuh Wonders surrounding his bones and thereud be his Whispers.
LUCY: Maybe.
BRAZIL: Ffhe sspast like they say he'd of parlayed to uh Confidence his last words and dying wishes. His secrets and his dreams.
LUCY: Thats how we pass back East. They could pass different out here.
BRAZIL: We got Daddys ways Daddyssgot ours. When theres no Confidence available we just dribble thuh words out. In uh whisper.
LUCY: Sometimes.
BRAZIL: Thuh Confidencell gather up thuh whispers when she arrives.
LUCY: Youre uh prize, Brazil. Uh prize.]
BRAZIL
LUCY
BRAZIL
LUCY
BRAZIL
LUCY
BRAZIL: You hear him then? His whispers?
LUCY: Not exactly.
BRAZIL: He wuduhnt here then.
LUCY: He was here.
BRAZIL: Ffyou dont hear his whispers he wuduhnt here.
LUCY: Whispers dont always come up right away. Takes time sometimes. Whispers could travel different out West then they do back East. Maybe slower. Maybe. Whispers are secrets and often shy. We aint seen your Pa in 30 years. That could be part of it. We also could be experiencing some sort of interference. Or some sort of technical difficulty. Ssard tuh tell.
       (*Rest*)
So much to live for.
BRAZIL: So much to live for.
LUCY: Look on thuh bright side.
BRAZIL: Look on thuh bright side. Look on thuh bright side. Loook onnnnn thuhhhh briiiiiiiight siiiiiiiiiide!!!!
LUCY: DIIIIIIIIIIIIG!
BRAZIL: Dig.
LUCY
BRAZIL
LUCY: Helloooo! —. Hellooooo!
BRAZIL
LUCY
BRAZIL: [We're from out East. We're not from these parts.
       (*Rest*)

My foe-father, her husband, my Daddy, her mate, her man, my Pa come out here. Out West.
　　(*Rest*)
Come out here all uhlone. Cleared thuh path tamed thuh wilderness dug this whole Hole with his own 2 hands and et cetera.
　　(*Rest*)
Left his family behind. Back East. His Lucy and his child. He waved "Goodbye." Left us tuh carry on. I was only 5.
　　(*Rest*)
My Daddy was uh Digger. Shes whatcha call uh Confidence. I did thuh weepin and thuh moanin.
　　(*Rest*)
His lonely death and lack of proper burial is our embarrassment.
　　(*Rest*)
Diggin was his livelihood but fakin was his callin. Ssonly natural heud come out here and combine thuh 2. Back East he was always diggin. He was uh natural. Could dig uh hole for uh body that passed like no one else. Digged em quick and they looked good too. This Hole here—this large one—sshis biggest venture to date. So says hearsay.
　　(*Rest*)
Uh exact replica of thuh Great Hole of History!
LUCY:　Sshhhhhht.
BRAZIL (*Rest*):　Thuh original ssback East. He and Lucy they honeymooned there. At thuh original Great Hole. Its uh popular spot. He and Her would sit on thuh lip and watch everybody who was ever anybody parade on by. Daily parades! Just like thuh Tee Vee. Mr. George Washington, for example, thuh Fathuh of our Country hisself, would rise up from thuh dead and walk uhround and cross thuh Delaware[1] and say stuff!! Right before their very eyes!!!!
LUCY:　Son?
BRAZIL:　Huh?
LUCY:　That iduhnt how it went.
BRAZIL:　Oh.
LUCY:　Thuh Mr. Washington me and your Daddy seen was uh lookuhlike of thuh Mr. Washington of history-fame, son.
BRAZIL:　Oh.
LUCY:　Thuh original Mr. Washingtonssbeen long dead.
BRAZIL:　O.
LUCY:　That Hole back East was uh theme park son. Keep your story to scale.
BRAZIL:　K.
　　(*Rest*)
Him and Her would sit by thuh lip uhlong with thuh others all in uh row cameras clickin and theyud look down into that Hole and see—ooooo—you name it. Ever-y-day you could look down that Hole and see—ooooo you name it. Amerigo Vespucci hisself made regular appearances. Marcus Garvey. Ferdinand and Isabella. Mary Queen of thuh Scots! Tarzan

---

1. On December 25, 1776, General Washington and his troops crossed the Delaware River to gain a victory at the Battle of Trenton. Washington (1732–1799), commander of the Continental Army during the American Revolutionary War and first president of the United States.

King of thuh Apes! Washington Jefferson Harding and Millard Fillmore. Mistufer Columbus[2] even. Oh they saw all thuh greats. Parading daily in thuh Great Hole of History.
>(*Rest*)

My Fathuh did thuh living and thuh dead. Small-town and big-time. Mr. Lincoln was of course his favorite.
>(*Rest*)

Not only Mr. Lincoln but Mr. Lincolns last show. His last deeds. His last laughs.
>(*Rest*)

Being uh Digger of some renown Daddy comes out here tuh build uh like attraction. So says hearsay. Figures theres people out here who'll enjoy amusements such as them amusements He and Her enjoyed. We're all citizens of one country afterall.
>(*Rest*)

Mmrestin.

>(*A gunshot echoes. Loudly. And echoes*)

BRAZIL: Woooo! (*Drops dead*)

LUCY: Youre fakin Mr. Brazil.

BRAZIL: Uh uhnnn.

LUCY: Tryin tuh get you some benefits.

BRAZIL: Uh uhnnnnnnnn.

LUCY: I know me uh faker when I see one. Your Father was uh faker. Huh. One of thuh best. There wuduhnt nobody your Fathuh couldnt do. Did thuh living and thuh dead. Small-town and bigtime. Made-up and historical. Fakin was your Daddys callin but diggin was his livelihood. Oh, back East he was always diggin. Was uh natural. Could dig uh hole for uh body that passed like no one else. Digged em quick and they looked good too. You dont remember of course you dont.

BRAZIL: I was only 5.

LUCY: You were only 5. When your Fathuh spoke he'd quote thuh Greats. Mister George Washington. Thuh Misters Roosevelt.[3] Mister Millard Fillmore. Huh. All thuh greats. You dont remember of course you dont.

BRAZIL: I was only 5—

LUCY: —only 5. Mr. Lincoln was of course your Fathuhs favorite. Wuz. Huh. Wuz. Huh. Heresay says he's past. Your Daddy. Digged this hole then he died. So says hearsay.
>(*Rest*)

Dig, Brazil.

BRAZIL: My paw—

2. Christopher Columbus (1451–1506), Italian navigator and explorer. Vespucci (1451–1512), Italian navigator and explorer. Garvey (1877–1940), Jamaican black leader active in the United States (1916–25). Ferdinand V (1452–1516), Spanish king of Aragon, Castile, Sicily, and Naples. Isabella I (1451–1501), queen of Castile and Aragon. Mary Queen of Scots, Mary Stuart (1542–1587), queen of Scotland. *Tarzan of the Apes* (1912), novel by American writer Edgar Rice Burroughs (1875–1950). Thomas Jefferson (1743–1826), third president of the United States. Warren G. Harding (1865–1923), twenty-ninth president of the United States. Fillmore (1800–1874), thirteenth president of the United States.

3. Theodore Roosevelt (1858–1919), twenty-sixth president of the United States. Franklin D. Roosevelt (1882–1945), thirty-second president of the United States.

LUCY: Ssonly natural that heud come out here tuh dig out one of his own. He loved that Great Hole so. He'd stand at thuh lip of that Great Hole: "OHWAYOHWHYOHWAYOH!"

BRAZIL: "OHWAYOHWHYOHWAYOH!"

LUCY: "OHWAYOHWHYOHWAYOH!" You know: hole talk. Ohwayoh-whyohwayoh, just tuh get their attention, then: "Helloo!" He'd shout down to em. Theyd call back "Helllloooo!" and wave. He loved that Great Hole so. Came out here. Digged this lookuhlike.

BRAZIL: Then he died?

LUCY: Then he died. Your Daddy died right here. Huh. Oh, he was uh faker. Uh greaaaaat biiiig faker too. He was your Fathuh. Thats thuh connection. You take after him.

BRAZIL: I do?

LUCY: Sure. Put your paw back where it belongs. Go on—back on its stump. —. Poke it on out of your sleeve son. There you go. I'll draw uh X for you. See? Heresuh X. Huh. Dig here.
    (Rest)
DIG!

BRAZIL

LUCY

BRAZIL

LUCY: Woah! Woah!

BRAZIL: Whatchaheard?!

LUCY: No tellin, son. Cant say.

    (Brazil digs. Lucy circulates)

BRAZIL (Rest. Rest): On thuh day he claimed to be the 100th anniversary of the founding of our country the Father took the Son out into the yard. The Father threw himself down in front of the Son and bit into the dirt with his teeth. His eyes leaked. "This is how youll make your mark, Son" the Father said. The Son was only 2 then. "This is the Wail," the Father said. "There's money init," the Father said. The Son was only 2 then. Quiet. On what he claimed was the 101st anniversary the Father showed the Son "the Weep" "the Sob" and "the Moan." How to stand just so what to do with the hands and feet (to capitalize on what we in the business call "the Mourning Moment"). Formal stances the Fatherd picked up at the History Hole. The Son studied night and day. By candlelight. No one could best him. The money came pouring in. On the 102nd anniversary[4] the Son was 5 and the Father taught him "the Gnash." The day after that the Father left for out West. To seek his fortune. In the middle of dinnertime. The Son was eating his peas.

LUCY

BRAZIL

LUCY

BRAZIL

LUCY: Hellooooo! Hellooooo!
    (Rest)

---

4. Hearsay [Parks's note].

BRAZIL
LUCY
BRAZIL: HO! (*Unearths something*)
LUCY: Whatcha got?
BRAZIL: Uh Wonder!
LUCY: Uh Wonder!
BRAZIL: Uh Wonder: Ho!
LUCY: Dust it off and put it over with thuh rest of thuh Wonders.
BRAZIL: Uh bust.
LUCY: Whose?
BRAZIL: Says "A. Lincoln." A Lincolns bust. —. Abraham Lincolns bust!!!
LUCY: Howuhboutthat!
    (*Rest*)
    (*Rest*)
Woah! Woah!
BRAZIL: Whatchaheard?
LUCY: Uh—. Cant say.
BRAZIL: Whatchaheard?!!
LUCY: SSShhhhhhhhhhhhhhhhhhht!
    (*Rest*)
dig!

B. ECHO

THE FOUNDLING FATHER: Ladies and Gentlemen: *Our American Cousin,* Act III, scene 5:
MR. TRENCHARD: Have you found it?
MISS KEENE:[5] I find no trace of it. (*Discovering*) What is this?!
MR. TRENCHARD: This is the place where father kept all the old deeds.
MISS KEENE: Oh my poor muddled brain! What can this mean?!
MR. TRENCHARD (*With difficulty*): I cannot survive the downfall of my house but choose instead to end my life with a pistol to my head!

    (*Applause*)

THE FOUNDLING FATHER: OHWAYOHWHYOHWAYOH!
    (*Rest*)
    (*Rest*)
Helllooooooo!
    (*Rest*)
Helllooooooo!
    (*Rest. Waves*)

C. ARCHEOLOGY

BRAZIL: You hear im?
LUCY: Echo of thuh first sort: thuh sound. (E.g. thuh gunplay.)
    (*Rest*)

---

5. Laura Keene is the actress who played the character Florence Trenchard in the Ford's Theater production. Mr. Trenchard is a character in the play.

Echo of thuh 2nd sort: thuh words. Type A: thuh words from thuh dead. Category: Unrelated.

> (*Rest*)

Echo of thuh 2nd sort, Type B: words less fortunate: thuh Disembodied Voice. Also known as "Thuh Whispers." Category: Related. Like your Fathuhs.

> (*Rest*)

Echo of thuh 3rd sort: thuh body itself.

> (*Rest*)

BRAZIL: You hear im.

LUCY: Cant say. Cant say, son.

BRAZIL: My faux[6]-father. Thuh one who comed out here before us. Thuh one who left us behind. Tuh come out here all uhlone. Tuh do his bit. All them who comed before us—my Daddy. He's one of them.

LUCY

> (*Rest*)
>
> (*Rest*)

[BRAZIL: He's one of them. All of them who comed before us—my Daddy.

> (*Rest*)

I'd say thuh creation of thuh world must uh been just like thuh clearing off of this plot. Just like him diggin his Hole. I'd say. Must uh been just as dug up. And unfair.

> (*Rest*)

Peoples (or thuh what-was), just had tuh hit thuh road. In thuh beginning there was one of those voids here and then "bang" and then *voilà!* And here we is.

> (*Rest*)

But where did those voids that was here before we was here go off to? Hmmm. In thuh beginning there were some of them voids here and then: KERBANG-KERBLAMMO! And now it all belongs tuh us.

LUCY

> (*Rest*)
>
> (*Rest*)

BRAZIL: This Hole is our inheritance of sorts. My Daddy died and left it to me and Her. And when She goes, Shes gonna give it all to me!!

LUCY: Dig, son.

BRAZIL: I'd rather dust and polish. (*Puts something on*)

LUCY: Dust and polish then. —. You dont got tuh put on that tuh do it.

BRAZIL: It helps. Uh Hehm. *Uh Hehm.* WELCOME WELCOME WELCOME TUH THUH HALL OF—

LUCY: Sssht.

BRAZIL

LUCY

BRAZIL

LUCY

BRAZIL

LUCY

6. False (French).

BRAZIL

LUCY

BRAZIL: (welcome welcome welcome to thuh hall of wonnndersss: To our right A Jewel Box made of cherry wood, lined in velvet, letters "A. L." carved in gold on thuh lid: the jewels have long escaped. Over here one of Mr. Washingtons bones, right pointer so they say; here is his likeness and here: his wooden teeth. Yes, uh top and bottom pair of nibblers: nibblers, lookin for uh meal. Nibblin. I iduhnt your lunch. Quit nibblin. Quit that nibblin you. Quit that nibblin you nibblers you nibblin nibblers you.)

LUCY: Keep it tuh scale.

BRAZIL: (Over here our newest Wonder: uh bust of Mr. Lincoln carved of marble lookin like he looked in life. Right heress thuh bit from thuh mouth of thuh mount on which some great Someone rode tuh thuh rescue. This is all thats left. Uh glass tradin bead—one of thuh first. Here are thuh lick-ed boots. Here, uh dried scrap of whales blubber. Uh petrified scrap of uh great blubberer, servin to remind us that once this land was covered with sea. And blubberers were Kings. In this area here are several documents: peace pacts, writs, bills of sale, treaties, notices, handbills and circulars, freein papers, summonses, declarations of war, addresses, title deeds, obits, long lists of dids. And thuh medals: for bravery and honesty; for trustworthiness and for standing straight; for standing tall; for standing still. For advancing and retreating. For makin do. For skills in whittlin, for skills in painting and drawing, for uh knowledge of sewin, of handicrafts and building things, for leather tannin, blacksmithery, lacemakin, horseback riding, swimmin, croquet and badminton. Community Service. For cookin and for cleanin. For bowin and scrapin. Uh medal for fakin? Huh. This could uh been his. Zsis his? This is his! This is his!!!

LUCY: Keep it tuh scale, Brazil.

BRAZIL: This could be his!

LUCY: May well be.

BRAZIL (Rest): Whaddyahear?

LUCY: Bits and pieces.

BRAZIL: This could be his.

LUCY: Could well be.

BRAZIL (Rest. Rest): waaaaaahhhhhhhhHHHHHHHHHHHHHH! HUH HEE HUH HEE HUH HEE HUH.

LUCY: There there, Brazil. Don't weep.

BRAZIL: WAHHHHHHHHHHH!—imissim—
WAHHHHHHHHHHHHH!

LUCY: It is an honor to be of his line. He cleared this plot for us. He was uh Digger.

BRAZIL: Huh huh huh. Uh Digger.

LUCY: Mr. Lincoln was his favorite.

BRAZIL: I was only 5.

LUCY: He dug this whole Hole.

BRAZIL: Sssnuch. This whole Hole.

LUCY: This whole Hole.
    (Rest)

BRAZIL

LUCY
BRAZIL
LUCY
BRAZIL
LUCY: I couldnt never deny him nothin.
        I gived intuh him on everything.
        Thuh moon. Thus stars.
        Thuh bees knees. Thuh cats pyjamas.
      (Rest)
BRAZIL
LUCY
BRAZIL: Anything?
LUCY: Stories too horrible tuh mention.
BRAZIL: His stories?
LUCY: Nope.
      (Rest)
BRAZIL
LUCY
BRAZIL
LUCY
BRAZIL: Mama Lucy?
LUCY: Whut.
BRAZIL: —Imissim—.
LUCY: Hhh. ((dig.))

D. ECHO

THE FOUNDLING FATHER: Ladies and Gentlemen: *Our American Cousin*, Act III, scene 2:

MR. TRENCHARD: You crave affection, *you* do. Now I've no fortune, but I'm biling over with affections, which I'm ready to pour out to all of you, like apple sass over roast pork.

AUGUSTA: Sir, your American talk do woo me.

THE FOUNDLING FATHER (*As Mrs. Mount*):   Mr. Trenchard, you will please recollect you are addressing my daughter and in my presence.

MR. TRENCHARD: Yes, I'm offering her my heart and hand just as she wants them, with nothing in 'em.

THE FOUNDLING FATHER (*As Mrs. Mount*):   Augusta dear, to your room.

AUGUSTA: Yes, Ma, the nasty beast.

THE FOUNDLING FATHER (*As Mrs. Mount*):   I am aware, Mr. Trenchard, that you are not used to the manners of good society, and that, alone, will excuse the impertinence of which you have been guilty.

MR. TRENCHARD: Don't know the manners of good society, eh? Wal, I guess I know enough to turn you inside out, old gal—you sockdologizing old man-trap.

    (Laughter. Applause)

THE FOUNDLING FATHER: Thanks. Thanks so much. Snyder has always been a very special very favorite town uh mine. Thank you thank you so very much. Loverly loverly evening loverly tuh be here loverly tuh be here with you with all of you thank you very much.

(*Rest*)

Uh Hehm. I *only* do thuh greats.

(*Rest*)

A crowd pleaser: 4score and 7 years ago our fathers brought forth upon this continent a new nation conceived in Liberty and dedicated to the proposition that all men are created equal!

(*Applause*)

Observe!: Indiana? Indianapolis. Louisiana? Baton Rouge. Concord? New Hampshire. Pierre? South Dakota. Honolulu? Hawaii. Springfield? Illinois. Frankfort? Kentucky. Lincoln? Nebraska. Ha! Lickety split!

(*Applause*)

And now, the centerpiece of the evening!!

(*Rest*)

Uh Hehm. The Death of Lincoln!: —The watching of the play, the laughter, the smiles of Lincoln and Mary Todd, the slipping of Booth into the presidential box unseen, the freeing of the slaves, the pulling of the trigger, the bullets piercing above the left ear, the bullets entrance into the great head, the bullets lodging behind the great right eye, the slumping of Lincoln, the leaping onto the stage of Booth, the screaming of Todd, the screaming of Todd, the screaming of Keene, the leaping onto the stage of Booth; the screaming of Todd, the screaming of Keene, the shouting of Booth "Thus to the tyrants!," the death of Lincoln! —And the silence of the nation.

(*Rest*)

Yes. —. The year was way back when. The place: our nations capitol. 4score, back in the olden days, and Mr. Lincolns great head. The the-a-ter was "Fords." The wife "Mary Todd." Thuh freeing of the slaves and thuh great black hole that thuh fatal bullet bored. And how that great head was bleedin. Thuh body stretched crossways acrosst thuh bed. Thuh last words. Thuh last breaths. And how thuh nation mourned.

(*Applause*)

E. SPADEWORK

LUCY: Thats uh hard nut tuh crack uh hard nut tuh crack indeed.

BRAZIL: Alaska—?

LUCY: Thats uh hard nut tuh crack. Thats uh hard nut tuh crack indeed. —. Huh. Juneau.

BRAZIL: Good!

LUCY: Go uhgain.

BRAZIL: —. Texas?

LUCY: —. Austin. Wyoming?

BRAZIL: —. —. Cheyenne. Florida?

LUCY: Tallahassee.

(*Rest*)

Ohio.

BRAZIL: Oh. Uh. Well: Columbus. Louisiana?

LUCY: Baton Rouge. Arkansas.
BRAZIL: Little Rock. Jackson.
LUCY: Mississippi. Spell it.
BRAZIL: M-i-s-s-i-s-s-i-p-p-i!
LUCY: Huh. Youre good. Montgomery.
BRAZIL: Alabama.
LUCY: Topeka.
BRAZIL: Kansas?
LUCY: Kansas.
BRAZIL: Boise, Idaho?
LUCY: Boise, Idaho.
BRAZIL: Huh. Nebraska.
LUCY: Nebraska. Lincoln.
>   (*Rest*)
> Thuh year was way back when. Thuh place: our nations capitol.
>   (*Rest*)
> Your Fathuh couldnt get that story out of his head: Mr. Lincolns great
> head. And thuh hole thuh fatal bullet bored. How that great head was
> bleedin. Thuh body stretched crossways acrosst thuh bed. Thuh last
> words. Thuh last breaths. And how thuh nation mourned. Huh. Changed
> your Fathuhs life.
>   (*Rest*)
> Couldnt get that story out of his head. Whuduhnt my favorite page from
> thuh book of Mr. Lincolns life, me myself now I prefer thuh part where
> he gets married to Mary Todd and she begins to lose her mind (and then
> of course where he frees all thuh slaves) but shoot, he couldnt get that
> story out of his head. Hhh. Changed his life.
>   (*Rest*)
BRAZIL: (wahhhhhhhh—)
LUCY: There there, Brazil.
BRAZIL: (wahhhhh—)
LUCY: Dont weep. Got somethin for ya.
BRAZIL: (o)?
LUCY: Spade. —. Dont scrunch up your face like that, son. Go on. Take
   it.
BRAZIL: Spade?
LUCY: Spade. He woulda wanted you tuh have it.
BRAZIL: Daddys diggin spade? Ssnnuch.
LUCY: I swannee you look more and more and more and more like him
   ever-y day.
BRAZIL: His chin?
LUCY: You got his chin.
BRAZIL: His lips?
LUCY: You got his lips.
BRAZIL: His teeths?
LUCY: Top and bottom. In his youth. He had some. Just like yours. His
   frock coat. Was just like that. He had hisself uh stovepipe hat which you
   lack. His medals—yours are for weepin his of course were for diggin.
BRAZIL: And I got his spade.
LUCY: And now you got his spade.

BRAZIL: We could say I'm his spittin image.

LUCY: We could say that.

BRAZIL: We could say I just may follow in thuh footsteps of my foe-father.

LUCY: We could say that.

BRAZIL: Look on thuh bright side!

LUCY: Look on thuh bright side!

BRAZIL: So much tuh live for!

LUCY: So much tuh live for! Sweet land of—! Sweet land of—?

BRAZIL: Of liberty!

LUCY: Of Liberty! Thats it thats it and *"Woah!"* Lets say I hear his words!

BRAZIL: And you could say?

LUCY: And I could say.

BRAZIL: Lets say you hear his words!

LUCY: *Woah!*

BRAZIL: Whatwouldhesay?!

LUCY: He'd say: "Hello." He'd say. —. "Hope you like your spade."

BRAZIL: Tell him I do.

LUCY: He'd say: "My how youve grown!" He'd say: "Hows your weepin?" He'd say:—Ha! He's running through his states and capitals! Licketysplit!

BRAZIL: Howuhboutthat!

LUCY: He'd say: "Uh house divided cannot stand!" He'd say: "4score and 7 years uhgoh." Say: "Of thuh people by thuh people and for thuh people." Say: "Malice toward none and charity toward all." Say: "Cheat some of thuh people some of thuh time." He'd say: (and this is only to be spoken between you and me and him—)

BRAZIL: K.

LUCY: Lean in. Ssfor our ears and our ears uhlone.

    (*Rest*)

BRAZIL: O.

LUCY: Howuhboutthat. And here he comes. Striding on in striding on in and he surveys thuh situation. And he nods tuh what we found cause he knows his Wonders. And he smiles. And he tells us of his doins all these years. And he does his Mr. Lincoln for us. Uh great page from thuh great mans great life! And you n me llsmile, cause then we'll know, more or less, exactly where he is.

    (*Rest*)

BRAZIL: Lucy? Where is he?

LUCY: Lincoln?

BRAZIL: Papa.

LUCY: Close by, I guess. Huh. Dig.

    (*Brazil digs. Times passes*)

Youre uh Digger. Youre uh Digger. Your Daddy was uh Digger and so are you.

BRAZIL: Ho!

LUCY: I couldnt never deny him nothin.

BRAZIL: Wonder: Ho! Wonder: Ho!

LUCY: I gived intuh him on everything.

BRAZIL: Ssuhtrumpet.

LUCY: Gived intuh him on everything.

BRAZIL: Ssuhtrumpet, Lucy.

LUCY: Howboutthat.

BRAZIL: Try it out.

LUCY: How uh-bout that.

BRAZIL: Anythin?

LUCY: Cant say, son. Cant say.

>   (*Rest*)

>   I couldnt never deny him nothin.
>   I gived intuh him on everything.
>   Thuh moon. Thuh stars.

BRAZIL: Ho!

LUCY: Thuh bees knees. Thuh cats pyjamas.

BRAZIL: Wonder: Ho! Wonder: Ho!

>   (*Rest*)

>   Howuhboutthat: Uh bag of pennies. Money, Lucy.

LUCY: Howuhboutthat.

>   (*Rest*)

>   Thuh bees knees.
>   Thuh cats pyjamas.
>   Thuh best cuts of meat.
>   My baby teeth.

BRAZIL: Wonder: Ho! Wonder: HO!

LUCY:

>   Thuh apron from uhround my waist.
>   Thuh hair from off my head.

BRAZIL: Huh. Yellow fur.

LUCY: My mores and my folkways.

BRAZIL: Oh. Uh beard. Howuhboutthat.

>   (*Rest*)

LUCY: WOAH. WOAH!

BRAZIL: Whatchaheard?!

LUCY

>   (*Rest*)
>   (*Rest*)

BRAZIL: Whatchaheard?!

LUCY: You dont wanna know.

BRAZIL

LUCY

BRAZIL

LUCY

BRAZIL: Wonder: Ho! Wonder: HO! WONDER: HO!

LUCY: Thuh apron from uhround my waist.
Thuh hair from off my head.

BRAZIL: Huh: uh Tee-Vee.

LUCY: Huh.

BRAZIL: I'll hold ontooit for uh minit.

>   (*Rest*)

LUCY:

>   Thuh apron from uhround my waist.

Thuh hair from off my head.
My mores and my folkways.
My rock and my foundation.
BRAZIL
LUCY
BRAZIL
LUCY: My re-memberies—you know—thuh stuff out of my head.

(*The TV comes on. The Foundling Father's face appears*)

BRAZIL: (ho! ho! wonder: ho!)
LUCY:
My spare buttons in their envelopes.
Thuh leftovers from all my unmade meals.
Thuh letter R.
Thuh key of G.
BRAZIL: (ho! ho! wonder: ho!)
LUCY:
All my good jokes. All my jokes that fell flat.
Thuh way I walked, cause you liked it so much.
All my winnin dance steps.
My teeth when yours runned out.
My smile.
BRAZIL: (ho! ho! wonder: ho!)
LUCY: Ssssht.
        (*Rest*)
Well. Its him.

F. ECHO

A gunshot echoes. Loudly. And echoes.

G. THE GREAT BEYOND

Lucy and Brazil watch the TV: a replay of "The Lincoln Act." The Foundling Father has returned. His coffin awaits him.

LUCY: Howuhboutthat!
BRAZIL: They just gunned him down uhgain.
LUCY: Howuhboutthat!
BRAZIL: He's dead but not really.
LUCY: Howuhboutthat.
BRAZIL: Only fakin. Only fakin. See? Hesupuhgain.
LUCY: What-izzysayin?
BRAZIL: Sound duhnt work.
LUCY: Zat right.
        (*Rest*)
THE FOUNDLING FATHER: I believe this is the place where I do the Gettysburg Address,[7] I believe.

---

7. Lincoln's November 19, 1863, speech dedicating the new national cemetery in Gettysburg, Pennsylvania, on the site of the Battle of Gettysburg (July 1–3, 1863).

BRAZIL
THE FOUNDLING FATHER
LUCY

BRAZIL: Woah!

LUCY: Howuhboutthat.

BRAZIL: Huh. Well.
     (Rest)
  Huh. Zit him?

LUCY: Its him.

BRAZIL: He's dead?

LUCY: He's dead.

BRAZIL: Howuhboutthat.
     (Rest)
  Shit.

LUCY
BRAZIL
LUCY

BRAZIL: Mail the in-vites?

LUCY: I did.

BRAZIL: Think theyll come?

LUCY: I do. There are hundreds upon thousands who knew of your
  Daddy, glorified his reputation, and would like to pay their respects.

THE FOUNDLING FATHER: Howuhboutthat!

BRAZIL: Howuhboutthat!

LUCY: Turn that off, son.
     (Rest)
  You gonna get in now or later?

THE FOUNDLING FATHER: I'd like tuh wait uhwhile.

LUCY: Youd like tuh wait uhwhile.

BRAZIL: Mmgonna gnash for you. You know: teeth in thuh dirt, hands
  like this, then jump up rip my clothes up, you know, you know go all out.

THE FOUNDLING FATHER: Howuhboutthat. Open casket or closed?

LUCY: —. Closed.
     (Rest)
  Turn that off, son.

BRAZIL: K.

THE FOUNDLING FATHER: Hug me.

BRAZIL: Not yet.

THE FOUNDLING FATHER: You?

LUCY: Gimmieuhminute.

    (A gunshot echoes. Loudly. And echoes)

LUCY
BRAZIL
THE FOUNDLING FATHER
LUCY
BRAZIL
THE FOUNDLING FATHER

LUCY: That gunplay. Wierdiduhntit. Comes. And goze.

(They ready his coffin. He inspects it)

At thuh Great Hole where we honeymooned—son, at thuh Original Great Hole, you could see thuh whole world without goin too far. You could look intuh that Hole and see your entire life pass before you. Not your own life but someones life from history, you know, [someone who'd done somethin of note, got theirselves known somehow, uh President or] somebody who killed somebody important, uh face on uh postal stamp, you know, someone from History. *Like* you, but *not* you. You know: *Known.*

THE FOUNDLING FATHER: *"Emergency,* oh, *Emergency,* please put the Great Man in the ground."

LUCY: Go on. Get in. Try it out. Ssnot so bad. See? Sstight, but private. Bought on time but we'll manage. And you got enough height for your hat.

> *(Rest)*

THE FOUNDLING FATHER: Hug me.

LUCY: Not yet.

THE FOUNDLING FATHER: You?

BRAZIL: Gimmieuhminute.

> *(Rest)*

LUCY: He loved that Great Hole so. Came out here. Digged this lookuh-like.

BRAZIL: Then he died?

LUCY: Then he died.

THE FOUNDLING FATHER

BRAZIL

LUCY

THE FOUNDLING FATHER

BRAZIL

LUCY

THE FOUNDLING FATHER: A monumentous occasion. I'd like to say a few words from the grave. Maybe a little conversation: Such a long story. Uhhem. I quit the business. And buried all my things. I dropped anchor: Bottomless. Your turn.

LUCY

BRAZIL

THE FOUNDLING FATHER

LUCY (*Rest*): Do your Lincoln for im.

THE FOUNDLING FATHER: Yeah?

LUCY: He was only 5.

THE FOUNDLING FATHER: Only 5. *Uh Hehm.* So very loverly to be here so very very loverly to be here the town of —Wonderville has always been a special favorite of mine always has been a very very special favorite of mine. Now, I *only* do thuh greats. Uh hehm: I was born in a log cabin of humble parentage. But I picked up uh few things. Uh Hehm: 4score and 7 years ago our fathers—ah you know thuh rest. Lets see now. Yes. Uh house divided cannot stand! You can fool some of thuh people some of thuh time! Of thuh people by thuh people and for thuh people! Malice toward none and charity toward all! Ha! The Death of Lincoln! (Highlights): Haw Haw Haw Haw

(*Rest*)

HAW HAW HAW HAW

> (*A gunshot echoes. Loudly. And echoes. The Foundling Father "slumps in his chair"*)

THE FOUNDLING FATHER

LUCY

BRAZIL

LUCY

THE FOUNDLING FATHER

BRAZIL: [Izzy dead?

LUCY: Mmlistenin.

BRAZIL: Anything?

LUCY: Nothin.

BRAZIL (*Rest*): As a child it was her luck tuh be in thuh same room with her Uncle when he died. Her family wanted to know what he had said. What his last words had been. Theyre hadnt been any. Only screaming. Or, you know, breath. Didnt have uh shape to it. Her family thought she was holding on to thuh words. For safekeeping. And they proclaimed thuh girl uh Confidence. At the age of 8. Sworn tuh secrecy. She picked up thuh tricks of thuh trade as she went uhlong.]

> (*Rest*)

Should I gnash now?

LUCY: Better save it for thuh guests. I guess.

> (*Rest*)

Well. Dust and polish, son. I'll circulate.

BRAZIL: Welcome Welcome Welcome to thuh hall. Of. Wonders.

> (*Rest*)

To our right A Jewel Box of cherry wood, lined in velvet, letters "A.L." carved in gold on thuh lid. Over here one of Mr. Washingtons bones and here: his wooden teeth. Over here: uh bust of Mr. Lincoln carved of marble lookin like he looked in life.—More or less. And thuh medals: for bravery and honesty; for trustworthiness and for standing straight; for standing tall; for standing still. For advancing and retreating. For makin do. For skills in whittlin, for skills in painting and drawing, for uh knowledge of sewin, of handicrafts and building things, for leather tannin, blacksmithery, lacemakin, horseback riding, swimmin, croquet and badminton. Community Service. For cookin and for cleanin. For bowin and scrapin. Uh medal for fakin.

> (*Rest*)

To my right: our newest Wonder: One of thuh greats Hisself! Note: thuh body sitting propped upright in our great Hole. Note the large mouth opened wide. Note the top hat and frock coat, just like the greats. Note the death wound: thuh great black hole—thuh great black hole in thuh great head. —And how this great head is bleedin. —Note: thuh last words. —And thuh last breaths. —And how thuh nation mourns—

> (*Takes his leave*)

American Poetry since 1945

More than a decade after the end of World War II, two important and transforming shocks were administered to American poetry: Allen Ginsberg's *Howl* (1956) and Robert Lowell's *Life Studies* (1959). Ginsberg first delivered his poem aloud, during a reading at the Six Gallery in San Francisco in the fall of 1955; the following year it was published by Lawrence Ferlinghetti's City Lights Bookshop. In a single stroke, with the energy of a reborn Whitman, Ginsberg made poetry one of the rallying points for underground protest and prophetic denunciation of the prosperous, complacent, gray-spirited Eisenhower years. The setting in which the poem appeared is also significant, for *Howl*, like other work associated with what came to be known as the San Francisco Renaissance, challenged the conventions of a literary tradition dominated by the East Coast. With its open, experimental form and strong oral emphasis, *Howl* sounded a departure from the well-shaped lyric. Lowell, a more "difficult," less popular poet, was rooted in the literary culture of Boston. But with *Life Studies* he too challenged the literary status quo, bringing a new directness and autobiographical intensity into American poetry as he exposed the psychological turbulence suffered by an inbred New Englander. Lowell's movement into a more open, less heavily symbolic style was inspired, in part, by hearing the work of Ginsberg and others while on a reading tour of the West Coast.

The connection between these two volumes and the times in which they were written is direct and apparent. Their poems anticipated and explored strains in American social relationships that issued in the open conflicts of the 1960s and 1970s and shaped American life for decades to come: public unrest about the uses of government and industrial power; the institutions of marriage and the family; the rights and powers of racial minorities, women, and homosexuals; the use of drugs; alternative states of consciousness. Taken together the books also suggested that the invigorating energies of postwar American poetry would arise from diverse regions of the country, their common aim restoring poetry to a more vital relation with contemporary life.

THE 1940s: OLDER POETs AND YOUNGER

Social pressures alone do not fully explain why American poets such as Lowell and Ginsberg felt ready to claim new authority and new areas of experience in their writing. However radical the changes in the style and content of American poetry in the 1950s and 1960s, its assurance was rooted in subtle, far-reaching developments of the decade before. American poetry had flourished in the late 1940s because of a new confidence in native literary traditions, derived in part from the achievements of the early modernists in the first half of the century. The two most prominent figures, T. S. Eliot and Ezra Pound, were both expatriates whose work continued to dominate the literary scene into the 1940s. Eliot's *Four Quartets,* written in England, was arguably the best "American" poem of the 1940s, and another candidate for that honor, Pound's *Pisan Cantos,* which forms one of the finest sections in his lifelong epic, was written during the poet's incarceration for treason in Italy and published in 1948. Although the reputations of these two poets overshadowed for some time those of their contemporaries (with the possible exception of Robert Frost, who won the Pulitzer Prize in 1931), the postwar period saw the emergence of other important models. For example, the work of William Carlos Williams became influential for younger poets only after the war, with the appearance of the first two books of his *Paterson* in 1946 and 1948 and his important collection *The Desert Music* in 1954. For postwar poets like Allen Ginsberg, Denise Levertov, and Robert Creeley, Williams's work offered a poetic alternative to Eliot's version of modernism. Wallace Stevens also emerged as an influence in the 1940s and 1950s, publishing *Transport to Summer* in 1947, *The Auroras of Autumn* in 1950, and his *Collected Poems* in 1954. Stevens's meditative style and "gaiety of language" became important to many poets, including Theodore Roethke, James Merrill, and John Ashbery. In addition, the impact of two major women modernists, H. D. and Gertrude Stein (both of whom lived in Europe for most of their careers), was not fully felt until after the war. H. D. completed her book-length sequence, *Trilogy,* in 1946, and her meditative epic, *Helen in Egypt,* appeared in 1961. Her work provided for Robert Duncan, Denise Levertov, and others a model elsewhere unavailable for the union of visionary power with energy of language. Although Gertrude Stein died in 1946, a number of her radical experiments in poetic language were first published only in the late 1950s. Indeed, the importance of her work for contemporary experimental poets in the 1980s recalls the composer Virgil Thomson's epithet for Stein: "The Mother of Us All."

As the accomplishments of an older generation emerged, confirming for postwar poets the strength of American poetry, they also cast a daunting shadow against which a subsequent generation measured itself. Following the revolutionary experiments and ambitious designs of their predecessors, it was possible for postwar poets to feel there was little left to do. Nonetheless, during and immediately after 1945, younger poets who were to prove themselves among the strongest and most important of their generation began publishing notable books: Gwendolyn Brooks's *A Street in Bronzeville* (1945); Elizabeth Bishop's first volume, *North & South* (1946); Robert Lowell's *Lord Weary's Castle* (1946); Denise Levertov's first book, published in England, *The Double Image* (1946); Richard Wilbur's *The Beautiful Changes* (1947); Robert Duncan's *Heavenly City, Earthly City* (1947); John Berryman's *The Dispossessed* (1948); and the important second volume by Theodore Roethke, *The Lost Son* (1948). In addition, postwar poets soon began to claim their independence in poetic manifestos. One of the most provocative of these was Charles Olson's *Projective Verse* (1950), which called for a unit of poetic expression based not on a predetermined metrical foot but on the poet's "breath" and the rhythms of the body.

By the end of the 1940s, with the death of the great Irish poet W. B. Yeats in 1939 and the immigration to the United States of his most notable English successor, W. H. Auden, it was clear that the center of poetic activity in the English language had shifted from Britain to America. Indeed, Denise Levertov would later describe her own move from England to the United States in 1947 as a discovery of the vitality of life and speech in American poetry.

A NEW CLIMATE FOR POETS AND POETRY

In the 1950s and 1960s poets acquired a new visibility in American life. Earlier poets had been relatively isolated from the public: Pound, Eliot, and H. D. lived in Europe; Wallace Stevens was a businessman in Hartford; William Carlos Williams was a small-town doctor in New Jersey. Poetry readings had been relatively rare performances by the few famous poets of the familiar poems the audience already knew but wanted to hear from the illustrious presence of the author. After the war, writers' conferences and workshops, recordings, and published and broadcast interviews became more common. A network of poets traveling to give readings and of poets-in-residence at universities began to form. In the 1960s and 1970s, readings became less formal, more numerous and accessible, held not only in auditoriums but in coffeehouses, bars, and lofts. The purpose of these more casual readings was often to introduce new poets or, perhaps, new poems by an already recognized writer. The poet coming of age after the war was, as one of them, Richard Wilbur, put it, more a "poet-citizen" than an alienated artist. Poets often made a living by putting together a combination of teaching positions, readings, and foundation grants.

A poet's education in the 1950s differed from that of poets in an earlier generation. Poetry in the postwar years became firmly linked to the English literature curriculum in ways that it had not been in the past. Many of the young poets were taught to read verse and sometimes to write it by influential literary critics who were often poets themselves: John Crowe Ransom, Yvor Winters, Robert Penn Warren, R. P. Blackmur, and Allen Tate. There now existed, for better or worse, the college major in English literature, as there had not been in so narrow and disciplined a sense for the poetic giants of a generation earlier. Eliot, for example, had done graduate work in philosophy, Pound in Romance philology, Williams had gone to medical school, and each had forged his own literary criticism. A younger poet, on the other hand, *studied* Eliot's essays, or learned critical approaches to literature in English courses such as the ones Allen Ginsberg took from Mark Van Doren and Lionel Trilling at Columbia or James Merrill from Reuben Brower at Amherst. A popular critical text, *Understanding Poetry* (1938) by Cleanth Brooks and Robert Penn Warren, taught students to be close readers of English Metaphysical poems of the seventeenth century, such as those by John Donne and Andrew Marvell. As the poet W. D. Snodgrass testifies, "In school we had been taught to write a very difficult and very intellectual poem. We tried to achieve the obscure and dense texture of the French Symbolists (very intuitive and often deranged poets), but by using methods similar to those of the very intellectual and conscious poets of the English Renaissance, especially the Metaphysical poets."

A young writer, thus trained to read intricate traditional lyrics, did not expect to encounter much, if any, contemporary verse in the classroom. The student had to seek out modern poems in the literary quarterlies or come on them through the chance recommendations of informed friends and teachers. And whether a beginning poet fell, in this private, accidental way, under the influence of Eliot's ironic elegies or Stevens's high rhapsodies or William Carlos Williams's homemade documentaries or H. D.'s visionary powers, he or she was prepared to think of a poem as something separate from the poet's self: objective, free from the quirks of the personal.

THE 1950s AND THE 1960s: LYRIC MEDITATIONS AND THE "CHILDREN OF MIDAS"

In the 1950s, although there was no dominant prescription for a poem, the short lyric meditation was held in high regard. Avoiding the first person, poets would find an object, a landscape, or an observed encounter that epitomized and clarified their feelings. A poem was the product of retrospection, a gesture of composure following the initial shock or stimulus that provided the occasion for writing. Often composed in intricate stanzas and skillfully rhymed, such a poem deployed its mastery of verse form as one sign of the civilized mind's power to explore, tame, and distill raw experience. Richard Wilbur's verse was especially valued for its speculative neatness, a poise that was often associated with the awareness of the historical values of European culture. It was a time of renewed travel in Europe; there were Fulbright fellowships for American students to study abroad, prizes for writers who wanted to travel and write in Europe. Wilbur and others wrote poems about European art and artifacts and landscapes as a way of testing American experience against alternative ways of life; for example, they contrasted American Puritanism and its notions of virtue with such complicated pleasures as those embodied in the seventeenth-century sculpted fountain described in Wilbur's "A Baroque Wall-Fountain in the Villa Sciarra." Unlike the pessimistic Eliot of *The Waste Land,* such poets found the treasures of the past—its art and literature—nourishing in poems whose chief pleasure was that of evaluation and balancing, of weighing such alternatives as spirituality and worldliness.

That was one side of the picture. The other side, equally important, was the way many of these same young poets reacted to (*to,* rather than *against*) their training. Richard Howard, in a happy phrase, calls this postwar generation of poets "the children of Midas." He is thinking of the last phases of the classical myth, when King Midas, having discovered that everything he touches inconveniently turns to gold, prays to lose the gift of the golden touch. "What seems to me especially proper to these poets," Howard says, ". . . is the last development, the longing to *lose* the gift of order, despoiling the self of all that had been, merely, *propriety.*" In the 1950s and 1960s there were some very extreme examples of poets transforming themselves: Allen Ginsberg, who began by writing formal quatrains, became the free and rambunctious poet of *Howl;* Sylvia Plath, who began as a well-mannered imitator of Eliot and Dylan Thomas, turned into the intense protagonist of *Ariel* (1966). It is a special mark of this period that a poet as bookish, as literary, as academic as John Berryman, who started out writing like Auden and Yeats, should also have written the wildest and most disquieting lyrics of his time, *The Dream Songs* (1964, 1968).

The new confidence and technical sophistication of American poetry in the 1940s fostered the more exploratory styles of the 1950s and 1960s. Some changes were more noticeable and notorious than others. For one thing, poetry extended its subject matter to more explicit and extreme areas of autobiography: insanity, sex, divorce, and alcoholism. The convenient but not very precise label *confessional* came to be attached to certain books: Robert Lowell's *Life Studies,* which explored the disorders of several generations of his New England family; Anne Sexton's *To Bedlam and Part Way Back* (1960) and *All My Pretty Ones* (1962), which dealt openly with abortion, women's sexuality, the poet's own life in mental hospitals; W. D. Snodgrass's *Heart's Needle* (1969), whose central lyric sequence chronicled the stages of divorce from the point of view of a husband separated from his wife and child; and John Berryman's *Dream Songs,* which exposed his alcoholism and struggle with insanity. Allen Ginsberg's *Howl* celebrated his homosexuality. Sylvia Plath's *Ariel* explored the heightened energies of a woman on the edge.

Some of the poetry of this period was avowedly political, tending in the 1950s to general protest and in the 1960s to more specifically focused critiques. The Beats of the 1950s—with *Howl* as their manifesto—had no one particular object of protest. Their work envisioned freer lifestyles and explored underground alternatives to life in a standardized or mechanized society. The pun on the word *beat* linked them on the one side to a downtrodden drifting underground community—drugs, homosexuality, political radicalism—and, on the other, to a new "beatitude," made available by Eastern religious cults that many members of this generation espoused. Gary Snyder, who in the 1950s was with the Beats in San Francisco, is one example of how their protests were extended and focused in the next decades. In his books of the 1960s and 1970s such as *Earth House Hold* and *Turtle Island,* he dramatizes a very specific alternative to American suburban and urban sprawl: he describes and advocates a life of almost Thoreauvian simplicity in a commune in the Sierras.

Many poets in the 1960s identified themselves with specific reform and protest movements. Denise Levertov, Adrienne Rich, and Robert Lowell, among others, directed poems against American participation in the Vietnam War and our government's support of the corrupt South Vietnam regime. Robert Lowell publicly refused President Johnson's invitation to a White House dinner and was a participant in the 1967 march against the Pentagon, which Norman Mailer describes in *The Armies of the Night* (1968), Robert Bly and others used the occasion of receiving poetry prizes to make antiwar statements. The important freedom movements of the 1960s—advocating black power, women's liberation, and gay rights—had supporters among committed poets. Black poets such as Gwendolyn Brooks and LeRoi Jones (later Amiri Baraka), who had already had considerable success with white audiences, turned to address exclusively black constituencies. Small presses, notably the Broadside Press, were founded for the publication of African American poets, and others devoted themselves to feminist writing. Some poetry of the late 1960s had the insistence, urgency, and single-mindedness of political tracts. But the more enduring effect of political protest on poetry was to make a broader, more insistent range of voices available to verse; poems dramatized individual predicaments, stressing the underlying angers and desires that also issue in political action. African American poets experimented in bringing out the distinctive speech rhythms of black English; they stressed the oral values of verse—its openness to song, to angry chant, and to the cadenced complaint of the "blues." With this emphasis on the power of voice, and with their recovery of non-European traditions, especially those of Africa, black poets in the 1960s and 1970s exerted powerful influences on contemporary American poetry. Their work helped to define the increasing importance of oral traditions in poetry of the 1970s and 1980s and spurred the opening up of American poetry to other, non-European traditions, including those of native American societies and the Caribbean, Mexico, and Latin America. At the same time the feminist movement made many poets aware of the need for a poetic language to explore the experiences of women hitherto silenced or unrepresented in literature. Among these was Adrienne Rich, whose significantly titled collections *Diving into the Wreck* and *The Dream of a Common Language* suggest the necessity to probe what lies beneath the surface and to forge a language of shared experience.

In an indirect but vital sense the heightened energies of almost all poetry in the 1960s and 1970s had political implications. With the increasing standardization of speech, a documented decline in reading skills in the schools, and the dominance of nationwide television, poems provided a special resource for individual expression, a resistance to the leveling force of official language, and access to profoundly individual areas of consciousness. In that context poets as superficially apolitical as James Wright, W. S. Merwin, Elizabeth Bishop, James Merrill, and John Ashbery were by their very cultivation of what seemed at the time private vision making distinctly political choices. In the same period, a poet such as George Oppen was exploring the relations between the self as singular and as numerous, part of a larger common world.

THE 1950s AND THE 1960s: POETIC FORMS

In response to the pressures, inner and outer, of the 1950s and 1960s, new kinds of poems took their place alongside the favored "objective" poems of the late 1940s. As some poets aimed more at exposing than at composing the self, they demanded more open forms to suggest vagaries, twists, and confusions of mind or else the mind's potential directness and spontaneity. Their poems depended on less rhyme, sparer use of regular stanzas and metrics, even new ways of spacing a poem on the page. Critics talked of "organic" form, using free verse, which took its length of line or its visual form on the page from the poet's provisional or intense feelings at the moment of composition. The most insistent formulations of this attitude are to be found in the manifestos of the so-called Black Mountain school, a group of poets gathered at Black Mountain College in North Carolina and very much influenced by its rector, Charles Olson. Ordinary lineation, straight left-hand margins, and regular meters and verse forms were to be discarded in favor of a placement of lines and phrases that corresponded to the mental and physical energy enlisted to get the words on the page. Olson's purpose was to put the poem in touch—as in certain forms of meditation or yoga—with the body, with an individual poet's natural rhythms, often buried by acquired verbal skills. The poet was not to revise poems to any great extent; he or she might make considerable mental preparation or store up intense feeling before writing, but the poem itself was to represent feeling at the moment of composition. Another corollary of Olson's theories was the notion that a poem was provisional. In contrast to the 1940s model of a poem as a completed and permanent object, a number of poets saw their work as transitory, incomplete, an instrument of passage. Olson himself, of course, saw his *Maximus Poems* as a continually open, lifelong work, whereas other poets, Adrienne Rich and Allen Ginsberg among them, carefully date each of their poems as if to suggest that the feelings involved are peculiarly subject to revision by later experience.

A parallel development—only very loosely related to the San Francisco Beat explosion and Black Mountain manifestos—took place among a group of poets involved with and inspired by the work of nonrepresentational or abstract expressionist painters in New York. The so-called New York school included John Ashbery, Kenneth Koch, James Schuyler, and the figure whose friendship and enthusiasm held them all together, Frank O'Hara. It was O'Hara with his breezy diary poems, almost throwaways, who most typified their belief in the poem as a chronicle of its occasion and of the act of composing it. As O'Hara said in his offhand parody of sober poetic credos, *Personism: A Manifesto* (1959): "The poem is at last between two persons instead of two pages. . . . In all modesty, I confess that it may be the death of literature as we know it."

THE 1970s AND THE 1980s: CONSOLIDATION, EXPERIMENTATION, AND MULTIPLE TRADITIONS

The 1960s had changed the face of American poetry. For many poets in the 1970s the task seemed not so much to innovate as to consolidate and perhaps reinterpret the achievement of the previous three decades. But a fresh impetus of experimentation and poetic commitment came from poets of minority traditions who gained access to presses and publication in the 1970s and 1980s. A flourishing Latino literature was first disseminated by the publishing house Quinto Sol in the early 1970s, and in the 1980s the Arte Publico Press of Houston published a number of fine writers, making available the work of such poets as Denise Chavez, Lucha Corpi, Pat Mora, Alberto Ríos, Ricardo Sanchez, Bernice Zamora, and Lorna Dee Cervantes. In 1983 Joseph Bruhac edited and published an important collection of contemporary native American poetry, *Songs from This Earth on Turtle's Back,* and several notable volumes of poetry by Native Americans appeared in the late 1970s and 1980s, among them works by Paula Gunn Allen, Joy Harjo, Linda Hogan, and Simon J. Ortiz. Several arresting books appeared from poets whose backgrounds are Asian American, including Mei-mei Berssenbrugge, Marilyn Chin, Garret Kaoru Hongo, Li-Young Lee, and Cathy Song. In addition, the resurgence of African American traditions that fired the 1960s and early 1970s found diverse and gifted heirs. The legacy of Robert Hayden's historical imagination and formal skill and the dynamic example of Gwendolyn Brooks's evolution as well as Audre Lorde's recovery of the power of African myth became resources available to poets like Michael Harper, Rita Dove, and Nathaniel Mackey.

What characterized the best poetry of the period was its pluralism and its power to absorb a variety of influences. Despite a distressing tendency on the part of some poets and critics to define "schools" of poetry as if they were mutually exclusive, the finest poems testified to an enlivening interaction between traditions, affirming the imagination's freedom to draw from many sources: Hawaiian oral traditions found their way into the poetry of W. S. Merwin, Adrienne Rich took inspiration from the work of Chicana poets, Gary Snyder drew on Hopi sources, and the presence of Elizabeth Bishop made itself felt in some of Cathy Song's work. In addition, a significant number of American poets understood their translations of poetry from other languages, among them Spanish and Russian, as an important aspect of their own work. As the earlier modernists reached out to traditions beyond the Western—Pound to the Chinese ideograph, H. D. to Egyptian and Phoenician myths, and later Charles Olson to Mayan Indian culture—American poets of the 1970s and 1980s were redefining what constitutes *America*.

THE 1970s AND 1980s: POETIC FORMS

Just as poets turned to alternative traditions for other ways of thinking about the world, they also explored alternative poetic forms. Traditional verse and metrics were not left behind but took their place among a number of resources, rather than serving as the obligatory models of poetic decorum. The reach of the early modernists in their epic constructions had suggested extensions of poetic possibility, but in the 1970s and 1980s poets sought their own ways to combine an ambition for inclusive structures with their feeling for life's fluidity. The model of the poetic diary or journal provided one way. Robert Creeley's *Pieces* and *A Day Book* both emphasized the activity of writing rather than the finished work. In a related effort, Robert Lowell said of his *Notebook*, "If I saw something one day, I wrote it that day, or the next, or the next. Things I felt or saw or read were drift to the whirlpool, the squeeze of the sonnet and the loose ravel of blank verse." Adrienne Rich's sequence *Contradictions* also shares this quality of form grounded in an occasion and open to experience.

Sequences of poems provided another way of countering neat closure by emphasizing the complexity of consciousness and fluidity of external life. John Berryman's *Dream Songs*, however strict its stanzaic form and use of rhyme, has enormous flexibility of voice and rich varied exposures of the self, and Robert Hayden's "Elegies for Paradise Valley," from his final book, *American Journal*, creates through a related series of instants the whole sweep of a particular time and place and reveals his deepest origins. Other poets conceived of part of their work as ongoing sequences to which they continued to add over the years. This is how Robert Duncan understood his *The Structure of Rime* and *Passages* and how Gary Snyder understands his *Mountains and Rivers without End*, begun in the 1960s and not completed until 1996.

Long poems provided still another alternative to the lyric. James Merrill's series of three book-length works, *Divine Comedies*, and the coda that followed, were a sign that poetic ambition was taking a new direction. Before his death in February 1988, Duncan completed the collection of later poems, which had been gestating for twenty years: *Ground Work: Before the War* and *Ground Work II: In the Dark*. Both, he wrote in a poem, "underwrite the grand design." In a younger generation, Rita Dove's book-length sequence *Thomas and Beulah* showed a poet finding her own way to render the larger scope of time, place, and social movements through a series of particular instants. Many poets did not want to think of their work as the fragments of modern literature. They perhaps remembered that Whitman desired to put the whole of America into *Leaves of Grass,* or that Wallace Stevens, whose first published volume was *Harmonium,* wanted to call his collected poems *The Whole of Harmonium.* As poetry moved away from the single lyrics of the immediate postwar period, shorter poetic efforts opened into larger constructions, and the rigid boundary between poetry and prose often dissolved. Oral traditions, with an emphasis on storytelling and on repetition and variation, refute generic categories, whereas the work of John Ashbery; the interconnected essays and poems of "Language" poets like Charles Bernstein, Michael Palmer, and Susan Howe; or the "talk poems" of performance artists like David Antin challenged definitions of poetry restricted to the enclosed lyric. The period's interest in longer poems or related series of poems was not an effort to create an "objective correlative" for a small, poetic truth. Rather, these poets sought an extended power that presents particular and diverse models both of the mind's continuing struggle to apprehend itself and the world and of the rich and mysterious interactions between language and the world.

POETRY IN THE 1990s AND THE TWENTY-FIRST CENTURY

The closing decades of the twentieth century saw the passing of major figures who, in their work and through their influence, helped shape American poetry. Robert Lowell, Elizabeth Bishop, James Wright, Robert Duncan, Robert Hayden, and Robert Penn Warren died in the 1970s and 1980s. The loss of James Merrill, Allen Ginsberg, Denise Levertov, Gwendolyn Brooks, and A. R. Ammons in the 1990s and early 2000s now reconfigures American poetry as the country begins a new century. Merrill was an American formal master whose stature in and impact on American poetry have only increased with the publication in 2001 of his *Collected Poems.* Clever, elegant, restrained, then by turns surprisingly moving, his work—like Auden's or Frost's—moves to seriousness (and feeling) through wit. Ginsberg was the period's formal revolutionary and its exhibitionist of emotion; *Howl* carried on the traditions of Walt Whitman and William Carlos Williams in its liberation of American poetry from a restrictive poetic decorum. Levertov's lovely and mysterious poems, built out of everyday experience, are an important link to the imagist work of Williams and H. D. ("They have . . . given / the language into our hands," she once wrote). Brooks brought to American poetry an exemplary love of form and language, in combination with an acute sense of African American history and lived experience. A younger generation of poets, such as Rita Dove and Michael S. Harper, now themselves significant figures, came to poetry shaped, in part, by the example of Brooks's work. In his own way Ammons was as great an experimenter as Ginsberg; like John Cage in music he was willing to include the arbitrary in his sense of form, composing, for example, a long poem on the tape of an adding machine. His book-length poem *Garbage,* with its digressive form, its joyful energy in the face of transience, can now be seen as one of the significant achievements of late-twentieth-century American poetry. Despite the deliberate irreverence of its title, *Garbage*—like T. S. Eliot's *Four Quartets* and sections of Williams's *Paterson*—can profitably be read as an epic exploration of both nature and spirit.

The increasing significance of Merrill, Brooks, and Ammons for contemporary poets follows the model of Elizabeth Bishop, who died in 1979. Her work defied most of the generalizations subsequently made about her era; it contained no extended sequences, no epic structures, but simply an ability to "make the casual perfect," in Robert Lowell's phrase. Yet since her death her strategies of description, anecdote, and the persistent questioning of her own analogies have become some of the most important influences in late-twentieth- and early-twenty-first-century poetry. Rita Dove, Robert Pinsky, Jane Kenyon, Jane Shore, Cathy Song, and Bishop's friend James Merrill (in his final volume *A Scattering of Salts*) are only a few of the poets in whom we can hear these lessons of Bishop's work. Another lesson her work provides is an antidote to the division that formed between formalist and antiformalist poetry in the 1990s. When we now look at the work of poets from that decade, we see how many move in and out of traditional forms, as did Bishop. Some, like Merrill, daringly reconfigure the sonnet; some, like Ammons, Brooks, Pinsky, or Louise Glück, are acutely aware of poetry's measure and formal properties but are not bound by traditional form.

A new century, and indeed a new millennium, now challenges today's American poets to explore new forms and responses. Even so, the visionary strain of American romanticism that we find in early modernists like Wallace Stevens, T. S. Eliot, and Hart Crane (as well as their nineteenth-century exemplars Dickinson and Emerson) remains a significant element in the work of such different poets as Stanley Kunitz, Gary Snyder, Mary Oliver, Charles Wright, Joy Harjo, and Jorie Graham. With its push toward the transcendental or the abstract, and its attempt to penetrate from the seen to the unseen, this contemporary poetry often centers on an epiphanic moment akin to Eliot's in the rose garden or Virginia Woolf's "moment of being." Frequently, though not always, such a moment is achieved within and through the natural world. But here is a crucial difference: if fragmentation—as in Eliot's *Waste Land*—was a radical modernist technique, it is a given in what is sometimes called postmodern (or, for some, "postcontemporary") poetry. In a culture deeply skeptical of any single version of reality—instead, multiple versions of reality compete— ideas of unity and totality are suspect. A poet's integration of a visionary moment into the structures of experience is often self-conscious and unstable, qualities reflected by shifts of register within a single poem and among poems in a single volume. The poet's apprehension of an invisible world is countered by (and resisted by) such self-aware questioning as we find in Jorie Graham or is undercut by a deflating humor such as occurs in Charles Wright or Charles Simic. In this regard, the title of Ammons's *Garbage* is telling. In the work of many contemporary poets attracted to transcendental vision there exists an equal attraction to the ephemeral: a particular nighttime sky, a child practicing ballet, the sharply limned features of a specific natural setting. One of the things distinguishing these poems as contemporary is that the two impulses are not unified or reconciled; rather, like the nuclei from a divided cell in Louise Glück's poem "Mitosis," "No one actually remembers them / as not divided."

In a related way, poetry at the start of the twenty-first century has revised twentieth-century modernism's emphasis on the image as the dominant poetic vehicle for unifying thought and feeling. Other poetic resources have come to the fore, as perhaps anticipated by Robert Pinsky's call in 1973 for a poetry that would include the prose virtues of explanation, argument, and declaration. While the image, especially as its importance was articulated by Ezra Pound and by William Carlos Williams's edict "no ideas but in things," continues to have a place in contemporary poetry, that poetry leans toward the mix of image with narrative or the discursive, of precise observation along with philosophical reflection. And yet as poetry has recovered some of narrative's pre-imagist power, it has, like its analogues in prose fiction, subjected the idea of narrative to scrutiny. Today's poetry frequently renders its narratives through open-ended juxtapositions, multiple stories, or alterations in points of view within a single poem. Borrowing from the technologies of film and video (jump cuts, tracking shots, shifting camera angles, split screens), as well as from those of the computer, contemporary poetry often imagines a reader saturated with the sounds of contemporary discourse, a reader whose attention quickly shifts. Therefore many poets move in and out of various kinds of language, as if testing the limits and possibilities of the different discourses that make up contemporary life. This exploration is conducted in poetry more interested in the freedom offered by digression and errancy than in coherence or closure. The play of language overlapping both private and public life—and sometimes obscuring the boundary between the two—is nowhere more evident than in the work of John Ashbery, for many years now a central figure in American poetry. Ashbery's work enacts shifts in attention that blur the distinctions between serious and trivial. Its multiple and mobile perceptions are an emblem for the formal and linguistic heterogeneity that marks contemporary poetry, in which, rather than a sense of parts blended together, we often find unexpected jumps—in a poem's focus or between poetic styles—that resist any easy coherence.

The twentieth century's chief philosopher of language, Ludwig Wittgenstein (1889–1951), once said that "philosophy really ought to be written as poetic composition" and a number of contemporary poets put aside the idea of poetry as an autonomous realm and open up the space of poetry to philosophical thinking, whose subject is sometimes the nature of language itself. The importance of such work as Jorie Graham's lies, in large part, in her ability to shape poetic forms in which disjunctive acts of thinking occur, whether the poem addresses questions of metaphysics, epistemology, or expression. Clearly this poetry (like Ashbery's) owes a debt to Wallace Stevens, with his emphasis on the poem as an activity of the mind, and to Gertrude Stein's ongoing examination of language. Another important influence is late-twentieth-century poststructuralism and deconstruction, whose preoccupation with language dismantled some of the boundaries between philosophy, poetry, psychology, and linguistics and emphasized writing as a site of multiple discourses. Today the very idea of poetry as self-expression has been complicated by a focus on the social power of language and the constructed nature of subjectivity; the skepticism toward unity and coherence that marks our era often extends to the very idea of the self. The work of a number of poets radically experimenting with linguistic deformation (Michael Palmer, Susan Howe, Nathaniel Mackey) can be seen in part as a response to unexamined assumptions behind the idea of the personal lyric, with its emphasis on feeling and sincerity. Those poets who locate their work primarily within personal experience often take as a theme the way structures of memory, language, and existing narratives arbitrarily shape those experiences. Merrill's trilogy of epics and new cosmologies, *The Changing Light at Sandover,* offers one model of autobiographical artifice. With a witty, ironic self-awareness, this book makes its subject the domestic life of two male partners whose visionary impulses are realized through a Ouija board. Nothing in Merrill's poem appears unmediated or singular, not the spirits evoked in the Ouija sessions or the fictional versions of the poet's self. Subsequent books like Rita Dove's *Mother Love,* Louise Glück's *Meadowlands,* and Frank Bidart's *Desire* approach the materials of a life through mythological frameworks, suggesting the ways in which a reading of one's experience is filtered and shaped by existing narratives. While the work of poets like Billy Collins continues to have the air of spontaneous self-expression, Collins's humorous awareness of his speaker's self-dramatizations reminds us that the colloquial style is also a form of artifice. Yet even in a period at times overly conscious of self and world as fictional constructs, there are poets—like Adrienne Rich, Philip Levine, or Rita Dove—engaged with history and politics, and committed to poetry's relation to a common world. One example of such engagement is Dove's *On the Bus with Rosa Parks* (2000), which brings together the poet's meditations on private life with a meditation on the history of the civil rights movement. At the same time, the shifts among the volume's parts and the range of its styles resist any easy harmony and coherence and reflect contemporary struggles to make connections between self and world.

Another feature of contemporary poetry is its increasingly international flavor. To adopt the culinary metaphor of Charles Simic, this is "an age when American poets are read in Siberia and French poets in Kansas," so that "a poetic style is a concoction of many recipes from many cuisines." Simic is one of those poets whose work embodies such concoctions. He was born in Yugoslavia and immigrated to the United States at fourteen, and his work shows the influence of both his Eastern European sense of cosmic and historical dread and his love of the surrealism he found in Spanish poetry. Other examples of a cultural mix are Jorie Graham, who was born in New York, grew up in Rome, and attended college at the Sorbonne; Li-Young Lee, who immigrated as a child to the United States from Indonesia; Alberto Rios, whose heritage includes Spanish and English; and Yusef Komunyakaa and John Balaban, who both draw from experiences in Vietnam. The many American poets now writing from a conscious sense of multicultural backgrounds are also an important element in this cultural mix. In addition, some contemporary American poets include translations in their work, while some have gathered poems from other countries into collections like Joy Harjo's anthology of indigenous women's poetry or Pierre Joris and Jerome Rothenberg's *Poems for the Millennium.* Further evidence of the international aspect of contemporary poetry is the influential presence on American soil of such poets as Czeslaw Milosz (whose work Robert Pinsky has translated), a Polish poet who is an American resident; the Caribbean poet Derek Walcott; and the Irish poets Seamus Heaney, Paul Muldoon, and Eavan Boland, all of whom live and teach part of the year in the United States.

Contemporary poetry values heterogeneity in its forms and its language, and pluralism in its cultural influences. On one hand, the American poet laureateship, instituted in its current form in 1986, reflects these values. In contrast to its British equivalent, which until recently was a lifetime appointment, the American version is a one-year term (although it was extended to two years for Rita Dove and Robert Haas and to three years for Robert Pinsky). The fact that a single decade—from 1991 until 2001—contains seven different laureates (one of whom was the Russian-born Joseph Brodsky) would seem to affirm a pluralistic vision of dominant figures and poetic styles. The laureateship can be understood as an attempt to bring poetry further into the mainstream of American culture (though American poetry has long cultivated voices outside that mainstream), but its omissions are telling: among them, Ginsberg, Merrill, Ammons, and Brooks. A full representation of American poetry in the twenty-first century would need to be more wide ranging than the list of laureates. That poetry includes powerful work shaped by traditional forms—such as Yusef Komunyakaa's *Talking Dirty to the Gods,* Mark Strand's *A Blizzard of One,* and Mary Jo Salter's *A Kiss in Space;* the poetic minimalism of a Robert Creeley or Franz Wright; the explorations of language conducted by Susan Howe, Ron Silliman, Lyn Hejinian, and Charles Bernstein; the sometimes ecstatic music of the world in Gerald Stern, Mary Oliver, Susan Mitchell, or Li-Young Lee; and the jazz-influenced rhythms of a Billy Collins, Joy Harjo, Nathaniel Mackey, or Michael S. Harper.

Among the emblems for the contemporary period is the Internet, in which multiple realities—including those of different cultures and different identities—co-exist in virtual reality. There, distinctions between public and private and between fiction and reality are fluid. Some contemporary poets celebrate computer technology as a new resource for poetry. They create digital productions that include multiple fonts, type sizes, and visual images; they edit online journals and they turn to hypertext to create computer-screen poems with simultaneous and open-ended possibilities, where the reader's choices shape different poetic forms. At the same time there are contemporary poets who continue to write the drafts of their poems with pencil and paper and, like Charles Wright, feel more affinity with classical Chinese poets than with computer technology. Contemporary poetry exists in a variety of media: on the pages of a book (perhaps digitally produced), on the computer screen, in performance work (like David Antin's talk poems or Joy Harjo's readings accompanied by her band), and at poetry slams all over the country. It is possible to experience the work of writers and poets like Sherman Alexie and Wanda Coleman on the page or in a standing-room-only performance at the World Championship Poetry Bout in Taos, New Mexico. American poetry is enjoying a renaissance and in many ways is today more widely available, in more varied forms, than ever. Whether or not this rise in popularity and accessibility is accompanied by an equal rise in quality remains a question to be debated by poets, readers, and critics. But the debate itself is a sign of poetry's vitality. Perhaps, then, what most characterizes poetry in the early years of this century is the absence of a single dominant style. The heterogeneity of such poetry promises to be a defining characteristic and a strength. Yet amid such variation in style, in format, in method, the best contemporary poems still manage to startle us with their freshness and distinctness, whether we are reading them for the first time or the tenth. Like Charles Wright in "The Appalachian Book of the Dead VI," we discover that "the right word will take your breath away."

TEXTS	CONTEXTS
1944 Stanley Kunitz, "Father and Son"	
1945 Randall Jarrell, "The Death of the Ball Turret Gunner"	1945 U.S. drops atomic bombs on Hiroshima and Nagasaki; Japan surrenders, ending World War II • Cold war between U.S. and Soviet Union begins
1948 Theodore Roethke, "The Lost Son"	
1950 Richard Wilbur, "Ceremony"	1950 Senator Joseph McCarthy begins attacks on communism
1953 Charles Olson, "Maximus, to Himself"	
	1954 Beat Generation poets begin to gather at San Francisco's City Lights Bookshop
1955–68 John Berryman composes *The Dream Songs* (pub. 1964, 1968, 1977)	
1956 Allen Ginsberg, *Howl*	1956 Martin Luther King Jr. leads bus boycott in Montgomery, Alabama
1959 Robert Creeley, "Kore" • Robert Lowell, "My Last Afternoon with Uncle Devereux Winslow"	1959 Fidel Castro becomes communist dictator of Cuba
1960 Gwendolyn Brooks, "We Real Cool" • Robert Duncan, "Often I Am Permitted to Return to a Meadow"	1960 Woolworth lunch counter sit-in in Greensboro, N.C., marks beginning of civil rights movement
1961 Denise Levertov, "The Jacob's Ladder"	1961 Armed Cuban refugees invade Cuba at Bay of Pigs with U.S. support
1962 Robert Hayden, "Middle Passage"	1962 United States and Soviet Union close to war over Russian missiles based in Cuba; missiles withdrawn
	1963 King delivers "I Have a Dream" speech • John F. Kennedy assassinated
1964 Frank O'Hara, "A Step away from Them" • Amiri Baraka (LeRoi Jones), "An Agony. As Now"	
	1965 Hippie culture flourishes in San Francisco • Malcolm X assassinated
	1965–73 Vietnam War
1966 James Merrill, "The Broken Home" • Sylvia Plath, *Ariel*	1966 National Organization for Women (NOW) founded • Hayden and Brooks criticized at Black Writers' Conference, Fisk University, for composing "academic" poetry
1968 George Oppen, *Of Being Numerous*	1968 King assassinated • Senator Robert F. Kennedy assassinated
1969 Galway Kinnell, "The Porcupine" • Lorine Niedecker, "My Life by Water" • Robert Penn Warren, *Audubon*	1969 U.S. astronauts land on the moon • Stonewall riots in New York City initiate gay liberation movement
1971 Audre Lorde, "Black Mother Woman"	

Boldface titles indicate works in the anthology.

TEXTS	CONTEXTS
1972 Anne Sexton, *The Death of the Fathers*	**1972** Watergate scandal • military draft ends
1973 Adrienne Rich, *Diving into the Wreck*	**1973** *Roe v. Wade* legalizes abortion • American Indian movement members occupy Wounded Knee
	1974 President Richard Nixon resigns in wake of Watergate, avoiding impeachment
1975 John Ashbery, "**Self-Portrait in a Convex Mirror**" • Michael S. Harper, "**Nightmare Begins Responsibility**"	
1976 Elizabeth Bishop, "**In the Waiting Room**"	**1976** U.S. bicentennial
1979 Philip Levine, "**Starlight**" • Mary Oliver, "**The Black Snake**"	
1981 Lorna Dee Cervantes, "**The Body as Braille**" • James Dickey, "**Falling**" • Simon J. Ortiz, "**From Sand Creek**"	
1982 James Wright, "**The Journey**"	**1982** Equal Rights Amendment defeated • AIDS officially identified in United States
1983 Joy Harjo, "**Call It Fear**" • Cathy Song, "**Chinatown**"	
1985 Alberto Ríos, "**Advice to a First Cousin**" • Kunitz, "**The Wellfleet Whale**"	
1986 Rita Dove, *Thomas and Beulah* • Li-Young Lee, "**Eating Together**"	
	1989 Soviet Union collapses • oil tanker *Exxon Valdez* runs aground in Alaska
1990 Robert Pinsky, "**The Want Bone**"	**1990** Congress passes Native American Graves Protection and Repatriation Act
	1991 United States enters Persian Gulf War • World Wide Web introduced
1992 Louise Glück, "**Vespers**"	
1993 Gary Snyder, "**Ripples on the Surface**" • A. R. Ammons, *Garbage*	
1995 Jorie Graham, *The Dream of the Unified Field*	**1995** Federal building in Oklahoma City bombed in a terrorist attack
1996 W. S. Merwin, "**Lament for the Makers**"	
	1997 *Pathfinder* robot explores Mars
1998 Billy Collins, "**I Chop Some Parsley While Listening to Art Blakey's Version of 'Three Blind Mice'**"	
1999 Charles Simic, "**Arriving Celebrities**"	
2000 Charles Wright, "**North American Bear**"	
	2001 Execution of Timothy McVeigh, convicted in 1995 Oklahoma City bombing • September 11 terrorist attacks on Pentagon and World Trade Center

STANLEY KUNITZ
b. 1905

For over thirty years at his home in Provincetown, Massachusetts, Stanley Kunitz has tended a terraced hillside garden he created—"Stanley's folly," his wife, the painter Elise Asher, calls it. The garden is to Kunitz an emblem for creativity and renewal much like poetry itself, and many of his poems draw images of plants and animals from this place. When Kunitz's 1995 collection, *Passing Through*, was published to coincide with his ninetieth birthday, it won the National Book Award and took its place in a poetic career that began sixty-five years earlier with his first book, *Intellectual Things* (1930). "Through the years I have found this gift of poetry to be life sustaining, life enhancing, and absolutely unpredictable," he said. It is a testament to the ongoing renewal of Kunitz's poetic gifts that in his eighties and nineties he has written some of the finest poems of his career. For the period 2000–01, at the age of ninety-five, he was named poet laureate of the United States.

Perhaps one reason Kunitz turned to the life-sustaining power of poetry was that his own life began in such painful circumstances. Six months before the poet's birth his father committed suicide, and during Kunitz's childhood, his mother refused to let her husband's name be spoken in her presence: "She locked his name / in her deepest cabinet / and would not let him out / though I could hear him thumping" ("The Portrait"). Kunitz needed, he has remarked, to find a way to transform his losses into creative experience. His early poetry, like the powerful "Father and Son," dramatizes that transformation and, with its dense syntax and hermetic imagery, suggests secret pain. Though Kunitz's tone ranges from wry playfulness in a love poem like "After the Last Dynasty" to elegiac lament in "The Wellfleet Whale," much of his work over the years has been an excavation of what he called, in the title of one of his poems, "The Thing That Eats the Heart."

A child of immigrants from a Lithuanian Jewish *shtetl*, Kunitz grew up in Worcester, Massachusetts, and revisits the surrounding landscape in a number of poems, like "Quinnipoxet," with its "abandoned reservoir" where "the snapping turtles cruised / and the bullheads swayed / in their bower of tree-stumps." An avid reader and a brilliant student, he earned a scholarship to Harvard University at a time when the university had a quota (2 percent) for Jewish students. He graduated summa cum laude, but, as Kunitz recounts it, when he continued his studies at Harvard and inquired about a teaching position, the university let it be known that his Jewish ancestry precluded an appointment. "It shattered me," he has said. He then left academia for many years and worked as a reporter, an editor, and for a while as a small farmer. During World War II, he served in the armed forces, and in 1946 he began a peripatetic teaching career that included such institutions as Bennington, the New School of Social Research, the University of Washington, and Brandeis. In 1963 he took up a position at Columbia University, where he remained until 1985.

While Kunitz's first book *Intellectual Things* (the title comes from William Blake's "the tear is an intellectual thing") brought him attention, his next, *Passport to War* (1944), went largely unnoticed. Yet he continued to write and publish poetry; and finally, when he was past fifty, he gained national recognition with his *Selected Poems 1928–58* (1959), which won a Pulitzer Prize. Kunitz's early poems are evidence of his strong sense of drama. Tightly rhymed and metered, they often owe their startling images (for example, "The night nailed like an orange to my brow" from "Father and Son") to the influence of metaphysical poets like John Donne and George Herbert. But there is also something hidden about the early work, as if the complexity of the poet's language were a form of protection against the sources of his feeling. Then, with his important collection *The Testing-Tree* (1971), published when Kunitz was in his sixties ("my emancipation proclamation," he has called it), his work became more open and relaxed. "My early writing was dense and convoluted," he said at the time, "so, I guess, was I. Now what I am seeking is a transparency of language and vision. Maybe age itself compels me to embrace the great simplicities." The transparency Kunitz sought revealed itself in a looser, two- to three-beat line, a more colloquial language. Most significant, since *The Testing Tree*—whose title poem says, "the heart breaks and breaks / and lives by breaking"—Kunitz's work speaks its feeling more simply and directly. The poems of *Next-to-Last Things* (1985) and *Passing Through* (1995) continue this greater openness. One of these late poems, "The Wellfleet Whale," beautifully demonstrates Kunitz's distinctive idiom, combining precise observation of the natural world with a colloquial language that moves in the swells of ritual elegy and incantation.

Kunitz is notable as well for his generosity and commitment to other poets and artists; he was a close friend of the poet Theodore Roethke and the painter Mark Rothko. At Columbia, Kunitz helped shape the M.F.A. program and served as a teacher and mentor to many younger writers. He has supported a wider community of artists through his work as a founder of the residency program at the Fine Arts Work Center in Provincetown, Massachusetts; Louise Glück and Yosef Komunyakaa are among the many poets nurtured by this program at early stages of their careers. He also helped create Poets House, a literary center and library in New York City. For Kunitz, the sources of poetry are located beyond the individual self; in his words, "The poem comes in the form of a blessing—'like rapture breaking on the mind,' as I tried to phrase it in my youth." For more than seventy years Kunitz's work has captured that sense of rapture and created a life-enhancing music of celebration and lament.

Father and Son

Now in the suburbs and the falling light
I followed him, and now down sandy road
Whiter than bone-dust, through the sweet
Curdle of fields, where the plums
Dropped with their load of ripeness, one by one.[1]   5
Mile after mile I followed, with skimming feet,
After the secret master of my blood,
Him, steeped in the odor of ponds, whose indomitable love
Kept me in chains. Strode years; stretched into bird;
Raced through the sleeping country where I was young,   10
The silence unrolling before me as I came,
The night nailed like an orange to my brow.

How should I tell him my fable and the fears,
How bridge the chasm in a casual tone,
Saying, "The house, the stucco one you built,   15
We lost. Sister married and went from home,
And nothing comes back, it's strange, from where she goes.
I lived on a hill that had too many rooms:
Light we could make, but not enough of warmth,
And when the light failed, I climbed under the hill.   20
The papers are delivered every day;
I am alone and never shed a tear."

1. Kunitz notes that these lines refer to the environs of rural Massachusetts as they were in his youth.

At the water's edge, where the smothering ferns lifted
Their arms, "Father!" I cried, "Return! You know
The way. I'll wipe the mudstains from your clothes;   25
No trace, I promise, will remain. Instruct
Your son, whirling between two wars,
In the Gemara[2] of your gentleness,
For I would be a child to those who mourn
And brother to the foundlings of the field   30
And friend of innocence and all bright eyes.
O teach me how to work and keep me kind."

Among the turtles and the lilies he turned to me
The white ignorant hollow of his face.

1944

After the Last Dynasty[1]

Reading in Li Po[2]
how "the peach blossom follows the water"
I keep thinking of you
because you were so much like
Chairman Mao,[3]   5
naturally with the sex
transposed
and the figure slighter,
Loving you was a kind
of Chinese guerrilla war.   10
Thanks to your lightfoot genius
no Eighth Route Army[4]
kept its lines more fluid,
traveled with less baggage,
so nibbled the advantage.   15
Even with your small bad heart
you made a dance of departures.
In the cold spring rains
when last you failed me
I had nothing left to spend   20
but a red crayon language
on the character of the enemy
to break appointments,
to fight us not
with his strength   25

2. The Gemara is the second and supplementary part of the Talmud, the oral law of the Jews, providing an extensive commentary by later rabbinical scholars on the traditional texts presented in the first part, the Mishna [Kunitz's note].
1. The Ch'ing Dynasty (1644–1912) was the last in a series of Chinese dynasties, defined by rulers who came from the same family or line.
2. Chinese poet (701–762).

3. "Chairman Mao's summation of his strategy of guerilla warfare: 'Enemy advances, we retreat; enemy halts, we harass; enemy tires, we attack; enemy retreats, we pursue' " [Kunitz's note]. Mao Tse-tung (1893–1976), communist leader of the People's Republic of China.
4. China's Red Army in the war of resistance with Japan.

but with his weakness,
to kill us
not with his health
but with his sickness.
Pet, spitfire, blue-eyed pony,   30
here is a new note
I want to pin on your door,
though I am ten years late
and you are nowhere:
Tell me,   35
are you still mistress of the valley,
what trophies drift downriver,
why did you keep me waiting?

1971

Quinnapoxet[1]

I was fishing in the abandoned reservoir
back in Quinnapoxet,
where the snapping turtles cruised
and the bullheads swayed
in their bower of tree-stumps,   5
sleek as eels and pigeon-fat.
One of them gashed my thumb
with a flick of his razor fin
when I yanked the barb
out of his gullet.   10
The sun hung its terrible coals
over Buteau's farm: I saw
the treetops seething.

They came suddenly into view
on the Indian road,   15
evenly stepping
past the apple orchard,
commingling with the dust
they raised, their cloud of being,
against the dripping light   20
looming larger and bolder.
She was wearing a mourning bonnet
and a wrap of shining taffeta.
"Why don't you write?" she cried
from the folds of her veil.   25
"We never hear from you."
I had nothing to say to her.
But for him who walked behind her

---

1. Quinnapoxet was a backwater village, no longer in existence, outside Worcester, Massachusetts, where I spent many of my childhood summers as a boarder on the Buteau family farm. The poem came to me in a dream [Kunitz's note].

in his dark worsted suit,
    with his face averted   30
as if to hide a scald,
    deep in his other life,
I touched my forehead
    with my swollen thumb
and splayed my fingers out—   35
    in deaf-mute country
the sign for father.

                                                          1978

The Wellfleet Whale[1]

A few summers ago, on Cape Cod, a whale foundered on the beach,
a sixty-three-foot finback whale. When the tide went out, I
approached him. He was lying there, in monstrous desolation,
making the most terrifying noises—rumbling—groaning. I put my
hands on his flanks and I could feel the life inside him. And while
I was standing there, suddenly he opened his eye. It was a big, red,
cold eye, and it was staring directly at me. A shudder of recognition
passed between us. Then the eye closed forever. I've been thinking
about whales ever since.

                                                  —*Journal entry*

1

You have your language too,
    an eerie medley of clicks
        and hoots and trills,
location-notes and love calls,
        whistles and grunts. Occasionally,   5
            it's like furniture being smashed,
or the creaking of a mossy door,
        sounds that all melt into a liquid
            song with endless variations,
as if to compensate   10
    for the vast loneliness of the sea.
        Sometimes a disembodied voice
breaks in as if from distant reefs,
    and it's as much as one can bear
        to listen to its long mournful cry,   15
a sorrow without name, both more
    and less than human. It drags
        across the ear like a record
running down.

1. "Written in 1981 and first read at Harvard that year as the Phi Beta Kappa poem. The actual beaching of the whale in Wellfleet Harbor occurred September 12, 1966" [Kunitz's note]. Wellfleet is on Cape Cod, Massachusetts.

2

No wind. No waves. No clouds.   20
    Only the whisper of the tide,
        as it withdrew, stroking the shore,
a lazy drift of gulls overhead,
    and tiny points of light
        bubbling in the channel.   25
It was the tag-end of summer.
    From the harbor's mouth
        you coasted into sight,
flashing news of your advent,
    the crescent of your dorsal fin   30
        clipping the diamonded surface.
We cheered at the sign of your greatness
    when the black barrel of your head
        erupted, ramming the water,
and you flowered for us   35
    in the jet of your spouting.

3

All afternoon you swam
    tirelessly round the bay,
        with such an easy motion,
the slightest downbeat of your tail,   40
    an almost imperceptible
        undulation of your flippers,
you seemed like something poured,
    not driven; you seemed
        to marry grace with power.   45
And when you bounded into air;
    slapping your flukes,
        we thrilled to look upon
pure energy incarnate
    as nobility of form.   50
        You seemed to ask of us
not sympathy, or love,
    or understanding,
        but awe and wonder.

That night we watched you   55
    swimming in the moon.
        Your back was molten silver.
We guessed your silent passage
    by the phosphorescence in your wake.
        At dawn we found you stranded on the rocks.   60

4

There came a boy and a man
    and yet other men running, and two

      schoolgirls in yellow halters
and a housewife bedecked
    with curlers, and whole families in beach   65
      buggies with assorted yelping dogs.
The tide was almost out.
    We could walk around you,
      as you heaved deeper into the shoal,
crushed by your own weight,   70
    collapsing into yourself,
      your flippers and your flukes
quivering, your blowhole
    spasmodically bubbling, roaring.
      In the pit of your gaping mouth   75
you bared your fringework of baleen,[2]
    a thicket of horned bristles.
      When the Curator of Mammals
arrived from Boston
    to take samples of your blood   80
      you were already oozing from below.
Somebody had carved his initials
    in your flank. Hunters of souvenirs
      had peeled off strips of your skin,
a membrane thin as paper.   85
    You were blistered and cracked by the sun.
    The gulls had been pecking at you.
The sound you made was a hoarse and fitful bleating.
What drew us, like a magnet, to your dying?
    You made a bond between us,   90
      the keepers of the nightfall watch,
who gathered in a ring around you,
    boozing in the bonfire light.
      Toward dawn we shared with you
your hour of desolation,   95
    the huge lingering passion
      of your unearthly outcry,
as you swung your blind head
    toward us and laboriously opened
      a bloodshot, glistening eye,   100
in which we swam with terror and recognition.

5

Voyager, chief of the pelagic[3] world,
    you brought with you the myth
      of another country, dimly remembered,
where flying reptiles   105
    lumbered over the steaming marshes
      and trumpeting thunder lizards
wallowed in the reeds.

---

2. Elastic, horny material forming the fringed   whales instead of teeth.
plate that hangs from the upper jaw of baleen   3. Living or occurring in the open ocean.

While empires rose and fell on land,
    your nation breasted the open main,   110
rocked in the consoling rhythm
    of the tides. Which ancestor first plunged
        head-down through zones of colored twilight
to scour the bottom of the dark?
    You ranged the North Atlantic track   115
        from Port-of-Spain to Baffin Bay,[4]
edging between the ice-floes
    through the fat of summer,
        lob-tailing, breaching, sounding,
grazing in the pastures of the sea   120
    on krill[5]-rich orange plankton
        crackling with life.
You prowled down the continental shelf,
    guided by the sun and stars
        and the taste of alluvial[6] silt   125
on your way southward
    to the warm lagoons,
        the tropic of desire,
where the lovers lie belly to belly
    in the rub and nuzzle of their sporting;   130
        and you turned, like a god in exile,
out of your wide primeval element,
    delivered to the mercy of time.

    Master of the whale-roads,
let the white wings of the gulls   135
    spread out their cover.
        You have become like us,
disgraced and mortal.

1985

4. Inlet of the Atlantic Ocean between West Greenland and East Baffin Island. Port-of-Spain is the capital of Trinidad and Tobago.

5. Small marine crustaceans that are the principal food of baleen whales.

6. Sediment deposited by flowing water.

LORINE NIEDECKER
1903–1970

In *Poet's Work* Lorine Niedecker writes: "I learned / to sit at desk / and condense." Although most of her poems are short, some of them under twenty words, her art of "condensery" (as she calls it in this poem) is evocative and powerful. Her aim is clarity, stillness, and intensity, and her work reflects Ezra Pound's mandate "To use absolutely no word that does not contribute to the presentation." Neglected until recently, her poems enrich our understanding of the diversity of American poetry and of the way distinctive work often arises at the margins of our culture. Niedecker's spare and beautiful language is capable of realizing a whole world; poems like "[Well, spring overflows the land]" (much of her work is untitled) have the totality of genuine poetry called for by the poet Louis Zukofsky, with whom she corresponded for forty years. The apparent simplicity of her work gains its power from a wide range of formal resources, including the silences between words indicated by line breaks and varied spacing on the page. Like other experimental American poets, she uses the space of the page to suggest the movement of the eye and mind across a field of experience. Although her poems possess great visual clarity (she valued, she said, "the hard, clear image"), they continually make use of all the senses; the sound of her poems is as important as their images.

"A lush, mush-music but like this place," she once humorously said of her poem "Paean to Place." "This place" was BlackHawk Island on the Rock River as it flows into Lake Koshkonong, just off the small town of Fort Atkinson, Wisconsin. She lived all her life in this area, most of the time on the island itself. "I spent my childhood outdoors—," she once wrote, "redwinged blackbirds, willows, maples, boats, fishing (the smell of tarred nets), twittering and squawking noises from the marsh." Her poems everywhere reflect rapt attention to the places of which she is a part and reveal an intimate knowledge. The particularity of her observations recalls the American naturalists and explorers whose work she read and admired for its discovery of the natural world's variety. Knowing the world meant, for Niedecker, entering into it and understanding herself as part of life's processes. Her poems are, in the deepest sense, ecological. They celebrate an interconnected natural world in which human existence is but one part: "In every part of every living thing / is stuff that once was rock" ("Lake Superior").

Niedecker's father, Henry, seined carp for a living and her mother, Daisy, "helped him string out nets / for tarring," planted lilacs, "knew how to clean up / after floods" ("Paean to Place"). Niedecker was an only child, and her family life was often difficult: struggles with rising waters, the economic uncertainty of a life dependent on fishing, and Daisy Niedecker's deafness, which developed after her daughter's birth. In 1922 Niedecker left home to attend Beloit College, but after a year returned to help care for her mother. She worked as a librarian's assistant from 1928 to 1930 and during this time began publishing poems in little magazines. But the turning point in her sense of poetic vocation came in 1931, when she read Louis Zukofsky's objectivist issue of *Poetry* magazine and soon after began her long correspondence with him. The affinity she felt with the work of "objectivist" poets, among them Zukofsky, Charles Reznikoff, William Carlos Williams, George Oppen, and the English poet Basil Bunting, centered on their sense of the poem as an object, a pure form in which the other objects of the world are seen with clarity and precision, washed free of imprecise feeling. By the 1940s Niedecker thought of herself primarily as a poet, and her first book, *New Goose*, appeared in 1946. Although she remained continuously involved in writing poems and her work appeared steadily in little magazines, it would be almost twenty years before her second book, *My Friend Tree* (1961), was published, by a small Scottish press. Consequently, many of her poems did not appear in book form until her later collections, *T & G: The Collected Poems 1936–1966* (1969) and *My Life by Water: Collected Poems 1936–1968* (1970).

Throughout her career Niedecker remained on the margins of the poetry scene, without benefit of mainstream publication. Although her geographical isolation gave her the solitude she felt necessary for writing poems ("I don't mourn the loneness of it for poetry," she once remarked. "In fact, I couldn't do it any other way"), it also had its costs. There were few people with whom she could share her literary interests (hence the importance of her correspondence with Zukofsky and later with the poet Cid Corman, also the editor of the magazine *Origin*, in which many of her poems appeared). The economic conditions of the region, and Niedecker's need to support herself for most of her life, meant scant leisure for writing during a life of hard work. Her mother died in 1951 and her father in 1953, leaving her two small houses on

BlackHawk Island and the trees her father had planted. From 1957 to 1963 she cleaned kitchens and scrubbed floors at Fort Atkinson Memorial Hospital. Thus for a number of reasons, including her habit of repeated revision (she altered a number of published poems over the years as well, revising them for book publication), her fully achieved poems are small in number. Yet they are utterly distinctive, and the body of her work reveals a development that flowered, in the 1960s, into her extended poetic sequences.

The 1960s were a rich period for Niedecker. A number of the poets who had come to admire her work over the years visited her in Wisconsin; they included Jonathan Williams, whose Jargon Press published *T & G,* and Basil Bunting. In 1963 she married Albert Millen, a house painter (it was her second marriage, her first in 1928 having ended quickly), and together they explored the Midwest; one of their trips inspired her sequence "Lake Superior," a celebration of the geography and history of her part of America. In 1968 *North Central* appeared; it was followed two years later by *My Life by Water* (1970). A final book, *Blue Chicory* (1976), was published posthumously. The later books reveal an expanding sense of form—her poems open to include not only the clear image but also the active presence of memory and reflection. Although her work is sometimes marred by arbitrary syntax and by too minimal a sense of context and connection, her best poems are fully realized accounts of a woman aware of herself within an evolving natural world, sustained by a poetic activity that creates a spirit of place.

Poet's Work

Grandfather
  advised me:
    Learn a trade

I learned
  to sit at desk   5
    and condense

No layoff
  from this
    condensery

                                                              1968

[I married]

I married

in the world's black night
for warmth
    if not repose.
      At the close—   5
someone.

I hid with him
from the long range guns.

We lay leg
    in the cupboard, head   10
in closet.

A slit of light
at no bird dawn—
    Untaught
    I thought   15
he drank

too much.
I say
    I married
    and lived unburied.   20
I thought—

          1968

My Life by Water

My life
    by water—
      Hear

spring's
    first frog
      or board   5

out on the cold
    ground
      giving

Muskrats   10
    gnawing
      doors

to wild green
    arts and letters
      Rabbits   15

raided
    my lettuce
      One boat

two—
    pointed toward   20
      my shore

thru birdstart
    wingdrip
      weed-drift

of the soft 25
and serious—
Water

1969

Lake Superior

In every part of every living thing
is stuff that once was rock

In blood the minerals
of the rock

Iron the common element of earth 5
in rocks and freighters

Sault Sainte Marie[1]—big boats
coal-black and iron-ore-red
topped with what white castlework

The waters working together 10
internationally
Gulls playing both sides

Radisson:[2]
'a laborinth of pleasure'
this world of the Lake 15

Long hair, long gun

Fingernails pulled out
by Mohawks

(*The long canoes*)

'Birch Bark
and white Seder[3] 20
for the ribs'

Through all this granite land
the sign of the cross

---

1. Port city on the border between Michigan and
Ontario. Historically, Sault Sainte Marie was an
important stopping-off point for explorers and pioneers.
2. Pierre Radisson (c. 1638–1710), French-

Canadian fur trader and explorer who served both
the French and the British during the colonial conflicts of the 17th century. In the early 1650s he
was captured by Mohawk Indians.
3. I.e., cedar.

Beauty: impurities in the rock

And at the blue ice superior spot   25
priest-robed Marquette[4] grazed
azoic rock, hornblende granite
basalt the common dark
in all the Earth

And his bones of such is coral[5]   30
raised up out of his grave
were sunned and birch bark-floated
to the straits

Joliet[6]

Entered the Mississippi
Found there the paddlebill catfish   35
come down from The Age of Fishes

At Hudson Bay he conversed in latin
with an Englishman

To Labrador and back to vanish
His funeral gratis—he'd played   40
Quebec's Cathedral organ
so many winters

Ruby of corundum
lapis lazuli
from changing limestone   45
glow-apricot red-brown
carnelian sard

Greek named
Exodus-antique
kicked up in America's   50
Northwest
you have been in my mind
between my toes
agate[7]

---

4. Jacques Marquette (1637–1675), French-Jesuit missionary who with Joliet (see n. 6) explored the upper Mississippi and the Great Lakes, often traveling in cedar canoes. Marquette founded a mission in Sault Sainte Marie.
5. "Of his bones are coral made" (Shakespeare's *Tempest* 1.2.401); the sprite Ariel is singing about the supposed death by water of the king of Naples.

6. Louis Joliet (1645–1700), French explorer. Formerly he had been music master and organist at the cathedral in Quebec. In 1673 he journeyed down the Mississippi and in 1694 led an expedition charting the coast of Labrador. He died in Quebec.
7. Agate derives its name from the Greek *Achates*; it is "Exodus-antique" because mentioned in Exodus 28.19.

Wild Pigeon

Did not man   55
        maimed by no
            stone-fall

mash the cobalt
        and carnelian
            of that bird   60
Schoolcraft left the Soo[8]—canoes
US pennants, masts, sails
chanting canoemen, barge
soldiers—for Minnesota

Their South Shore journey   65
        as if Life's—
The Chocolate River
        The Laughing Fish
and The River of the Dead

Passed peaks of volcanic thrust   70
Hornblende in massed granite
Wave-cut Cambrian rock
painted by soluble mineral oxides
wave-washed and the rains
did their work and a green   75
running as from copper

Sea-roaring caverns—
Chippewas threw deermeat
to the savage maws
'Voyageurs crossed themselves   80
tossed a twist of tobacco in'

        Inland then
beside the great granite
gneiss and the schists

to the redolent pondy lakes'   85
lilies, flag and Indian reed
'through which we successfully
        passed'

The smooth black stone
I picked up in true source park   90
        the leaf beside it
once was stone

---

8. Another name for Sault Sainte Marie. Henry Schoolcraft (1793–1864), American explorer and ethnologist who discovered the source of the Mississippi at Lake Itasca, Minnesota, in 1832.

Why should we hurry
home

I'm sorry to have missed   95
Sand Lake[9]
My dear one tells me
we did not
We watched a gopher there

1969

Watching Dancers on Skates

Ten thousand women
and I
the only one
in boots

Life's dance: 5
they meet
he holds her leg
up

1970

[Well, spring overflows the land]

Well, spring overflows the land,
floods floor, pump, wash machine
of the woman moored to this low shore by deafness.

Good-bye to lilacs by the door[1]
and all I planted for the eye.   5
If I could hear—too much talk in the world,
too much wind washing, washing
good black dirt away.

Her hair is high.
Big blind ears.   10
I've wasted my whole life in water.
My man's got nothing but leaky boats.
My daughter, writer, sits and floats.

1970

9. Lake in Ontario, Canada, not far from Lake Superior.

1. An echo, perhaps, of Whitman's line "When lilacs last in the dooryard bloom'd."

ROBERT PENN WARREN
1905–1989

In 1969, with a long, distinguished career as a man of letters already behind him, Robert Penn Warren published his long poem *Audubon: A Vision*. Although Warren wrote many poems of distinction before the publication of the volume, until the 1960s he was best known for his fiction. In the six books of poetry that followed *Audubon*, Warren developed the claim he had begun earlier in his career to a powerful, distinctive, American voice. The mark of Warren's poetry, from early to late, is passion, a passion directed toward the physical world and toward a knowledge of truth. He is a poet full of yearning for more, more than what life usually discloses, yet an intense love for the world accompanies this yearning.

Warren was born in 1905 in Guthrie in southern Kentucky, and much of his writing reflects his engagement with the lessons of history as they can be read in the experience of the American South. He took this sense of history most immediately from his father, who read history and poetry aloud to the family, and from his maternal grandfather, Gabriel Telemachus Penn. Warren spent his boyhood summers on this grandfather's isolated tobacco farm. There the old man, who fought on the Confederate side in the Civil War, told Warren tales of war while the two mapped out battles together, or the boy listened while his grandfather recited poetry "by the yard," especially Sir Walter Scott and Robert Burns. The memory of an idyllic boyhood spent dreaming amid the natural world informs many of Warren's poems, among them "American Portrait: Old Style," where he returns, in his seventies, to visit both the place of that boyhood and his childhood friend, K.

The decisive literary moment in Warren's life came when, at the age of sixteen, he enrolled at Vanderbilt University in Nashville. He had wanted to be a naval officer but an eye injury prevented him from taking up his commission at Annapolis. Vanderbilt was enjoying a feverish interest in poetry at the time. (Even football players, Warren reported, seemed to be writing verse, and Warren remembers that people lined up for the latest issues of the *Dial* and other literary periodicals in which they might find new work by Yeats or Eliot or Hart Crane.) Part of the excitement was due to the presence of the poet John Crowe Ransom, who taught Warren's freshman composition class and soon involved him, even as an undergraduate, with the Fugitives, a group of faculty members and "bookish, intelligent young businessmen" who met to discuss literature and philosophy. By the time Warren joined, it was largely a poetry club at which Ransom and others read and criticized one another's work. It was here that Warren met Allen Tate, the gifted poet and critic, who found the redheaded undergraduate, five years his junior, "the most gifted person I have ever known." For years to come they constituted a kind of southern axis in American letters and in 1930 joined several other southern writers in a political manifesto, *I'll Take My Stand*. The collection of twelve essays envisioned an agrarian South with strong local cultures as the only humane alternative to an increasingly self-destructive industrialism centered in the North.

Warren attended graduate school at the University of California, at Yale, and then as a Rhodes Scholar at Oxford University in England. From 1935 to 1942 he was on the English faculty at Louisiana State University. Along with Cleanth Brooks and Charles W. Pipkin, he was the founder there of the *Southern Review*, which for the seven years of their involvement was the most influential literary quarterly in the country. It was the principal forum for pioneering interpretative essays by "New Critics" such as Ransom, Kenneth Burke, and R. P. Blackmur. (Brooks and Warren were also the editors of *Understanding Poetry*, the important school anthology and text that introduced students to "close reading" on New Critical principles.) In addition, *Southern Review* published the best fiction by emerging southern writers such as Katherine Anne Porter and Eudora Welty.

Warren's own fiction brought him wide critical attention in the 1940s. *All the King's Men* (1946), which was conceived as a verse play before it became a novel, won the Pulitzer Prize and later became a film. It portrayed the rise and fall of a southern demagogue who closely resembled Huey Long, the Louisiana governor and senator who was assassinated in the rotunda of the Louisiana statehouse in 1935. Warren's interest was in showing the tangled motives of his protagonist, Willie Stark, a Depression governor who led a regime both corrupt and yet progressive in its social programs. In its focus on violent subjects with historical and psychological resonance, Warren's fiction anticipates his sequence *Audubon: A Vision*. Other novels, like *World Enough and Time* (1950), set in the Kentucky of the 1820s, are based on documents and grow out of his ongoing study of and response to the history of the South.

For ten years, from 1944 to 1954, Warren was intensely active in fiction, and published almost no poems. In 1952 he married the writer Eleanor Clark, his second wife, and prompted by the landscapes where they lived in Europe and by the birth of a son and daughter in the mid-1950s, he returned to poetry with a new intimacy and autobiographical intensity. His earlier work, like "Bearded Oaks," had been strongly influenced by the formal control and the elegant, well-mannered rationality of John Crowe Ransom's verse. But beginning with the volume *Promises* (1957), and revealed fully in *Audubon*, Warren's poetic line loosened up, moved with vigor and raw energy. Although the tone of his poems sometimes grows too insistent or rhetorical, his muscular syntax and rhythm forged a "voice-instrument calibrated to experience," in the words of Dave Smith, a poet of a younger generation, indebted to Warren's work.

In *Democracy and Poetry* (1975), his Jefferson Lecture in the Humanities, Warren said, "What poetry most significantly celebrates is the capacity of man to face the deep, dark inwardness of his nature and fate." In *Audubon*, Warren's version of the historical John James Audubon must enter what Yeats once called "the abyss of the self" to create a heroic selfhood at the center of the poetry. Ornithologist and painter of *Birds of America*, Audubon (1785–1851) was artist and scientist, solitary searcher and classifier, consumed by his tasks. Basing part of his poem on Audubon's autobiographical account, Warren imagines a man launched into his true vision after an encounter with violence at the heart of experience: he narrowly escapes being robbed and murdered in the wilderness by a crone and her sons. In this incident Audubon must also confront the violent desire of his own "lust of the eye" and thereby reconcile in himself the need for both passion and reverence toward existence. Passion directs Warren's hero to slay the birds in order to paint them, to put them "In our imagination" (*Audubon* VI, "Love and Knowledge"). But reverence demands the heart's total response to the beauty of existence itself. This is why Warren commands his hero and himself: "Continue to walk in the world. Yes, love it!" While the most representative figure in Warren's poems is solitary—the individual, like Audubon, confronting versions of the American sublime—Warren has also written a number of fine poems in other registers, among them some moving love poems, such as "After the Dinner Party." The sense of history that animates so much of his fiction has become, in his poems, the persistent struggle of memory to overcome the passage of time, to make *then* into *now*, as reflected in the title of his volume *Now and Then: Poems 1976–1978* (1978). The struggle with time is one aspect of the heroic engagement with existence, which was the dramatic center of Warren's work until his death in 1989.

Bearded Oaks

The oaks, how subtle and marine,
Bearded, and all the layered light
Above them swims; and thus the scene,
Recessed, awaits the positive night.

So, waiting, we in the grass now lie   5
Beneath the languorous tread of light:
The grasses, kelp-like, satisfy
The nameless motions of the air.

Upon the floor of light, and time,
Unmurmuring, of polyp made,   10
We rest; we are, as light withdraws,
Twin atolls on a shelf of shade.

Ages to our construction went,
Dim architecture, hour by hour:
And violence, forgot now, lent   15
The present stillness all its power.

The storm of noon above us rolled,
Of light the fury, furious gold,
The long drag troubling us, the depth:
Dark is unrocking, unrippling, still.   20

Passion and slaughter, ruth, decay
Descend, minutely whispering down,
Silted down swaying streams, to lay
Foundation for our voicelesness.

All our debate is voiceles here,   25
As all our rage, the rage of stone
If hope is hopeless, then fearless is fear,
And history is thus undone.

Our feet once wrought the hollow street
With echo when the lamps were dead   30
At windows, once our headlight glare
Disturbed the doe that, leaping, fled.

I do not love you less that now
The caged heart makes iron stroke,
Or less that all that light once gave   35
The graduate dark should now revoke.

We live in time so little time
And we learn all so painfully,
That we may spare this hour's term
To practice for eternity.   40

1942

From Audubon [1]

I. Was Not the Lost Dauphin

[A]

Was not the lost dauphin, though handsome was only
Base-born and not even able
To make a decent living, was only
Himself, Jean Jacques, and his passion—what
Is man but his passion?   5

                              Saw,
Eastward and over the cypress swamp, the dawn,
Redder than meat, break;
And the large bird,
Long neck outthrust, wings crooked to scull air, moved   10
In a slow calligraphy, crank, flat, and black against
The color of God's blood spilt, as though
Pulled by a string.

                              Saw
It proceed across the inflamed distance.   15

Moccasins set in hoar frost, eyes fixed on the bird,
Thought: "On that sky it is black."
Thought: "In my mind it is white."
Thinking: "*Ardea occidentalis,* heron, the great one."

Dawn: his heart shook in the tension of the world.   20

Dawn: and what is your passion?

[B]

October: and the bear,
Daft in the honey-light, yawns.

The bear's tongue, pink as a baby's, out-crisps to the curled tip,
It bleeds the black blood of the blueberry.   25

The teeth are more importantly white
Than has ever been imagined.

The bear feels his own fat
Sweeten, like a drowse, deep to the bone.

Bemused, above the fume of ruined blueberries,   30
The last bee hums.

1. John James Audubon (1785–1851), natural son of French parents (hence "Jean Jacques" in line 4), but later an American citizen. Painter, ornithologist, Kentucky settler, he dedicated his life to the pursuit, classification, and depiction of the *Birds of America* (first published in England, 1827). Among the stories told about his birth was one (false) that he was the Dauphin, the son of the dethroned Louis XVI and Marie Antoinette of France.

The wings, like mica, glint
In the sunlight.

He leans on his gun. Thinks
How thin is the membrane between himself and the world.   35

VI. *Love and Knowledge*

Their footless dance
Is of the beautiful liability of their nature.
Their eyes are round, boldly convex, bright as a jewel,
And merciless. They do not know
Compassion, and if they did,   5
We should not be worthy of it. They fly
In air that glitters like fluent crystal
And is hard as perfectly transparent iron, they cleave it
With no effort. They cry
In a tongue multitudinous, often like music.   10

He slew them, at surprising distances, with his gun.
Over a body held in his hand, his head was bowed low,
But not in grief.

He put them where they are, and there we see them:
In our imagination.   15

What is love?

Our name for it is knowledge.

VII. *Tell Me a Story*

[A]

Long ago, in Kentucky, I, a boy, stood
By a dirt road, in first dark, and heard
The great geese hoot northward.

I could not see them, there being no moon
And the stars sparse. I heard them.   5

I did not know what was happening in my heart.

It was the season before the elderberry blooms,
Therefore they were going north.

The sound was passing northward.

[B]

Tell me a story.   10

In this century, and moment, of mania,
Tell me a story.

Make it a story of great distances, and starlight.

The name of the story will be Time,
But you must not pronounce its name.   15

Tell me a story of deep delight.

                                                                      1969

American Portrait: Old Style

I

Beyond the last house, where home was,
Past the marsh we found the old skull in, all nameless
And cracked in star-shape from a stone-smack,
Up the hill where the grass was tangled waist-high and wind-tousled,
To the single great oak that, in leaf-season, hung like   5
A thunderhead black against whatever blue the sky had,

And here, at the widest circumference of shade, when shade was,
Ran the trench, six feet long,
And wide enough for a man to lie down in,
In comfort, if comfort was still any object. No sign there   10
Of any ruined cabin or well, so Pap must have died of camp fever,
And the others pushed on, God knows where.

II

The Dark and Bloody Ground, so the teacher romantically said,
But one look out the window, and woods and ruined cornfields we saw:
A careless-flung corner of country, no hope and no history here. 15
No hope but the Pullman lights[1] that swept
Night-fields—glass-glint from some farmhouse and flicker of ditches—
Or the night freight's moan on the rise where
You might catch a ride on the rods,
Just for hell, or if need had arisen.   20
No history either—no Harrod or Finley or Boone,[2]
No tale how the Bluebellies[3] broke at the Rebel yell and cold steel.

So we had to invent it all, our Bloody Ground, K and I,
And him the best shot in ten counties and could call any bird-note back,
But school out, not big enough for the ballgame,   25
And in the full tide of summer, not ready
For the twelve-gauge yet, or even a job, so what

Can you do but pick up your BBs and Benjamin,
Stick corn pone in pocket, and head out
"To Rally in the Cane-Brake and Shoot the Buffalo"—   30
As my grandfather's cracked old voice would sing it

---

1. Lights from the sleeping cars on trains.
2. James Harrod and Daniel Boone were pioneers
and Indian scouts. Robert W. Finley was a pioneer
and missionary. All three lived in Kentucky in the
late 18th century.
3. Derogatory term for members of the Union
Army in the Civil War.

From days of his own grandfather—and often enough
It was only a Plymouth Rock or maybe a fat Dominecker
That fell to the crack of the unerring Decherd.[4]

III

Yes, imagination is strong. But not strong enough in the face of   35
The sticky feathers and BBs a mother's hand held out.
But no liberal concern was evinced for a Redskin,
As we trailed and out-tricked the sly Shawnees[5]
In a thicket of ironweed, and I wrestled one naked
And slick with his bear grease, till my hunting knife   40
Bit home, and the tomahawk
Slipped from his hand. And what mother cared about Bluebellies
Who came charging our trench? But we held
To pour the last volley at face-gape before
The tangle and clangor of bayonet.   45

Yes, a day is merely forever
In memory's shiningness,
And a year but a gust or a gasp
In the summer's heat of Time, and in that last summer
I was almost ready to learn   50
What imagination is—it is only
The lie we must learn to live by, if ever
We mean to live at all. Times change.
Things change. And K up and gone, and the summer
Gone, and I longed to know the world's name.   55

IV

Well, what I remember most
In a world long Time-pale and powdered
Like a vision still clinging to plaster
Set by Piero della Francesca[6]
Is how K, through lane-dust or meadow,   60
Seemed never to walk, but float
With a singular joy and silence,
In his cloud of bird dogs, like angels,
With their eyes on his eyes like God,
And the sun on his uncut hair bright   65
As he passed through the ramshackle town and odd folks there
With coats on and vests and always soft gabble of money—
Polite in his smiling, but never much to say.

V

To pass through to what? No, not
To some wild white peak dreamed westward,   70

4. A BB gun. "Plymouth Rock" and "Dominecker"
are varieties of fowl.
5. Native Americans who lived mainly in the areas
of Ohio and Indiana.

6. Early Renaissance painter whose frescoes, usually of religious subjects, are known for their sense
of clarity and idealization.

And each sunrise a promise to keep. No, only
The Big Leagues, not even a bird dog,
And girls that popped gum while they screwed.

Yes, this was his path, and no batter
Could do what booze finally did: 75
Just blow him off the mound—but anyway,
He had always called it a fool game, just something
For children who hadn't yet dreamed what
A man is, or barked a squirrel, or raised
A single dog from a pup.   80

VI

And I, too, went on my way, the winning and losing, or what
Is sometimes of all things the worst, the not knowing
One thing from the other, nor knowing
How the teeth in Time's jaw all snag backward
And whatever enters therein   85
Has less hope of remission than shark-meat,

And on Sunday afternoon, in the idleness of summer,
I found his farm, and him home there,
With the bird dogs crouched round in the grass
And their eyes on his eyes as he whispered   90
Whatever to bird dogs it was.
Then yelled: "Well, for Christ's sake—it's you!"

Yes, me, for Christ's sake, and some sixty
Years blown like a hurricane past! But what can you say—
Can you say—when *all-to-be-said* is the *done?*   95
So our talk ran to buffalo-hunting, and the look on his mother's face
When she held the BBs out.

And the sun sank slow as he stood there,
All Indian-brown from waist up, who never liked tops to his pants,
And standing nigh straight, but the arms and the pitcher's   100
Great shoulders, they were thinning to old-man thin.
Sun low, all silence, then sudden:
"But, Jesus," he cried, "what makes a man do what he does—
Him living until he dies!"

Sure, all of us live till we die, but bingo!   105
Like young David at brookside, he swooped down,
Snatched a stone, wound up, and let fly,[7]
And high on a pole over yonder the big brown insulator
Simply exploded. "See—I still got control!" he said.

---

7. I.e., as David overthrew the giant Goliath in 1 Samuel 17.

VII

Late, late, toward sunset, I wandered   110
Where old dreams had once been Life's truth, and where
I saw the trench of our valor, now nothing
But a ditch full of late-season weed-growth,
Beyond the rim of shade.

There was nobody there, hence no shame to be saved from, so I   115
Just lie in the trench on my back and see high,
Beyond the tall ironweed stalks, or oak leaves
If I happened to look that way,
How the late summer's thinned-out sky moves,
Drifting on, drifting on, like forever,   120
From *where* on to *where,* and I wonder
What it would be like to die,
Like the nameless old skull in the swamp, lost,
And know yourself dead lying under
The infinite motion of sky.   125

VIII

But why should I lie here longer?
I am not dead yet, though in years,
And the world's way is yet long to go,
And I love the world even in my anger,
And that's a hard thing to outgrow.   130

                                                                      1978

Acquaintance with Time in Early Autumn

Never—yes, never—before these months just passed
Had I known the nature of Time, and felt its strong heart,
Stroke by stroke, against my own, like love,
But love without face, or shape, or history—
Pure Being that, by being, our being denies.   5

Summer fulfills the field, the heart, the womb,
While summerlong, infinitesimally,
Leaf stem, at bough-juncture, dries,
Even as our tireless bodies plunge,
With delicious muscular flexion and heart's hilarity,   10
White to the black ammoniac purity of
A mountain pool. But black
Is blue as it stares up at summer's depthless azure,
And azure was what we saw beneath
At the timeless instant hanging   15
At arc-height.

Voices of joy how distant seem!
I float, pubic hair awash, and gaze
At one lone leaf, flame-red—the first—alone
Above summer's bulge of green,   20
High-hung against the sky.

Yes, sky was blue, but water, I suddenly felt,
Was black, and striped with cold, and one cold claw
Reached ghostly up
To find my flesh, to pierce   25
The heart, as though
Releasing, in that dark inwardness,
A single drop. Oh, leaf,

Cling on! For I have felt knee creak on stair,
And sometimes, dancing, notice how rarely   30
A girl's inner thigh will brush my own,
Like a dream. Whose dream?

The sun
Pours down on the leaf its lacquer of Chinese red.

Then, in the lucent emptiness,   35
While cries of joy of companions fade,
I feel that I see, even in
The golden paradox of air unmoving
Each tendon of that stem, by its own will,
Release   40
Its tiny claw-hooks, and trust
A shining destiny. The leaf—it is
Too moorless not to fall. But
Does not. Minutely,
It slides—calm, calm—along the air sidewise,   45
Sustained by the kiss of under-air.

While ages pass, I watch the red-gold leaf,
Sunlit, descend to water I know is black.
It touches. Breath
Comes back, and I hate God   50
As much as gravity or the great globe's tilt.
How shall we know the astrolabe[1] of joy?
Shall gratitude run forward as well as back?
Who once would have thought that the heart,
Still ravening on the world's provocation and beauty, might,   55
After time long lost
In the tangled briars of youth,
Have picked today as payday, the payment

In life's dime-thin, thumb-worn, two-sided, two-faced coin?

                                                                1980

---

1. Old instrument for observing and calculating the position of heavenly bodies.

Mortal Limit

I saw the hawk ride updraft in the sunset over Wyoming.
It rose from coniferous darkness, past gray jags
Of mercilessness, past whiteness, into the gloaming
Of dream-spectral light above the last purity of snow-snags.

There—west—were the Tetons.[1] Snow-peaks would soon be   5
In dark profile to break constellations. Beyond what height
Hangs now the black speck? Beyond what range will gold eyes see
New ranges rise to mark a last scrawl of light?

Or, having tasted that atmosphere's thinness, does it
Hang motionless in dying vision before   10
It knows it will accept the mortal limit,
And swing into the great circular downwardness that will restore

The breath of earth? Of rock? Of rot? Of other such
Items, and the darkness of whatever dream we clutch?

1985

After the Dinner Party

You two sit at the table late, each, now and then,
Twirling a near-empty wine glass to watch the last red
Liquid climb up the crystalline spin to the last moment when
Centrifugality fails: with nothing now said.

What is left to say when the last logs sag and wink?   5
The dark outside is streaked with the casual snowflake
Of winter's demise, all guests long gone home, and you think
Of others who never again can come to partake

Of food, wine, laughter, and philosophy—
Though tonight one guest has quoted a killing phrase we owe   10
To a lost one whose grin, in eternal atrophy,
Now in dark celebrates some last unworded jest none can know.

Now a chair scrapes, sudden, on tiles, and one of you
Moves soundless, as in hypnotic certainty,
The length of table. Stands there a moment or two,   15
Then sits, reaches out a hand, open and empty.

How long it seems till a hand finds that hand there laid,
While ash, still glowing, crumbles, and silence is such

---

1. High mountain range in northwest Wyoming.

That the crumbling of ash is audible. Now naught's left unsaid
Of the old heart-concerns, the last, tonight, which   20

Had been of the absent children, whose bright gaze
Over-arches the future's horizon, in the mist of your prayers.
The last log is black, while ash beneath displays
No last glow. You snuff candles. Soon the old stairs

Will creak with your grave and synchronized tread as each mounts   25
To a briefness of light, then true weight of darkness, and then
That heart-dimness in which neither joy nor sorrow counts.
Even so, one hand gropes out for another, again.

1985

GEORGE OPPEN
1908–1984

"Clarity, clarity, surely clarity is the most beautiful thing in the world," George Oppen wrote in his 1968 poem "Route." All of Oppen's work may be seen as a struggle toward clarity and as the affirmation he made in the same work: "I have not and never did have any motive of poetry / But to achieve clarity." Oppen's clarity is not simple, for he believed that language is never entirely transparent. The music of his poems enacts a testing and a listening, a refusal to give in to the seduction of pure song. His poetry is spare and careful, tracking the mind's encounter with the world's solidity, and his finest work is characterized by a moving and often arduous effort to explore the limits and powers of language. Oppen's distinctive measure, with its hesitancies and silences, becomes itself a measure of language's capacity to say with clarity what is real. For this reason, his work has been important to many poets from a younger generation, including Michael Palmer, Kathleen Fraser, Charles Bernstein, and Susan Howe, who are preoccupied with investigating the possibilities and structures of language itself.

Oppen was born in New York and grew up in San Francisco, and much of his work is set in the modern city. Briefly a student at Oregon State University, he left the school after his future wife, Mary Colby, was expelled when she and Oppen stayed out all night on their first date. Mary Colby and Oppen were married the following year and their lifelong partnership was a shaping force in Oppen's poetry and in his politics. Some of his most beautiful work (such as "Anniversary Poem," 1972) evokes their lives together. In 1929 the Oppens moved to France, where they began a small press (To Publishers), which published some of the work of Pound and Williams and An "Objectivists" Anthology (1932), edited by Oppen's poet-colleague Louis Zukofsky. The objectivists were a diverse group of poets—among them, Oppen, Zukofsky, Pound, Williams, and Charles Reznikoff—united by an interest in what Zukofsky called "the art form as an object" (recalling William Carlos Williams's statement that "a poem is a machine made out of words"). Their emphasis was on what Oppen described as "the concrete materials of the poem"—language, syntax, rhythm, and sound.

In 1933 Oppen returned to New York, and the next year his first book of poetry, *Discrete Series,* was published by the Objectivist Press, founded by Oppen and his colleagues. Although short-lived, this press published not only Oppen's first collection but Pound's *ABC of Reading* and William Carlos Williams's *Collected Poems 1921–31*. But in 1935 Oppen put poetry aside and with his wife spent a decade organizing for the Workers Alliance in New York State ("There are situations which cannot honorably be met by art," he later wrote in his essay "The Mind's Own Place," 1963). His second book, *The Materials*, did not appear until 1962. Hugh Kenner once remarked of Oppen's career, "it took twenty-four years to write the next poem," but during those years Oppen always continued to think of himself as a poet, even when working in a factory in Detroit or, following the war, as a cabinetmaker and contractor in California. In 1942 he was drafted and spent three years in the infantry (he was wounded in combat), an experience that informs some of his most important poems. George and Mary Oppen had worked with the Communist Party in the 1940s, and in the period of McCarthyism in the 1950s they were harassed by the FBI and pressured to inform on friends. Resisting such pressures, they fled to Mexico, where Oppen ran a furniture factory, and did not return to the United States for eight years.

When they returned, the Oppens settled once more in California, where Oppen remained until his death. In this period he took up poetry again with renewed power and published *The Materials* (1962), *This in Which* (1965), *Of Being Numerous* (1968), *Seascape: Needle's Eye* (1973), and *Primitive* (1978). In 1975 an edition of his *Collected Poems* appeared. Although the late poems can be too elliptical, most of these volumes contain strong, distinctive work. None of this work is more important than the title sequence of the book *Of Being Numerous*. Oppen himself said that the sequence "asks the question whether or not we can deal with humanity as something which actually does exist." With the utmost seriousness and honesty, he explores the relation between two equally devastating possibilities—the anonymous mass, which constitutes "numerosity," and the singular self, which at its extreme is separate and isolated. How, Oppen's poem asks, can we understand ourselves both as singular and as numerous? How do we experience both our individuality and a sense of commonality? In asking these questions Oppen takes up some of Whitman's central themes and gives them renewed urgency for the contemporary world. Oppen's concern for humanity and his gifted use of his materials—language and measure—place *Of Being Numerous* in an important tradition of American poetry where politics and poetry meet.

Reading Oppen requires full attentiveness. A poet who so resists eloquence can sometimes seem thin and perhaps too cerebral. Certainly some of Oppen's poems are too cryptic to meet his own standard of clarity. But in his best work a genuine music and feeling emerge as we reread, and it is a measure of Oppen's poetic power that he teaches us to hear in the spareness of his language a beauty inseparable from a search for adequate expression. Indeed, his work rescues the meaning of *sincerity* from a narrow confessionalism and relocates it in the poet's use of his or her materials. Although the reader of Oppen's poems must sometimes struggle for clarity, that process is an authentic part of the poet's own work.

Party on Shipboard

Wave in the round of the port-hole
Springs, passing,—arm waved,
Shrieks, unbalanced by the motion——
Like the sea incapable of contact
Save in incidents (the sea is not   5
    water)

Homogeneously automatic—a green capped
    white is momentarily a half mile
        out——
The shallow surface of the sea, this,
Numerously—the first drinks——
The sea is a constant weight
In its bed. They pass, however, the sea
Freely tumultuous.

                                       1932–34

10

[She lies, hip high]

She lies, hip high,
On a flat bed
While the after-
Sun passes.

Plant, I breathe——
             O Clearly,
Eyes legs arms hands fingers,
Simple legs in silk.

                                       1932–34

5

The Hills

That this is I,
Not mine, which wakes
To where the present
Sun pours in the present, to the air perhaps
Of love and of
Conviction.

    As to know
Who we shall be. I knew it then.
You getting in
The old car sat down close
So close I turned and saw your eyes a woman's
Eyes. The patent
Latches on the windows
And the long hills whoever else's
Also ours.

                                       1962

5

10

15

Workman

Leaving the house each dawn I see the hawk
Flagrant over the driveway. In his claws
That dot, that comma
Is the broken animal: the dangling small beast knows
The burden that he is: he has touched   5
The hawk's drab feathers. But the carpenter's is a culture
Of fitting, of firm dimensions,
Of post and lintel. Quietly the roof lies
That the carpenter has finished. The sea birds circle
The beaches and cry in their own way,   10
The innumerable sea birds, their beaks and their wings
Over the beaches and the sea's glitter.

                                    1962

Psalm

Veritas sequitur[1] . . .

In the small beauty of the forest
The wild deer bedding down—
That they are there!

              Their eyes
Effortless, the soft lips   5
Nuzzle and the alien small teeth
Tear at the grass

              The roots of it
Dangle from their mouths
Scattering earth in the strange woods.   10
They who are there.

              Their paths
Nibbled thru the fields, the leaves that shade them
Hang in the distances
Of sun   15

              The small nouns
Crying faith
In this in which the wild deer
Startle, and stare out.

                                    1965

---

1. Truth follows (Latin).

From Of Being Numerous

1

There are things
We live among 'and to see them
Is to know ourselves'.[1]

Occurrence, a part
Of an infinite series,   5

The sad marvels;

Of this was told
A tale of our wickedness.
It is not our wickedness.

'You remember that old town we went to, and we sat in the ruined win-   10
dow, and we tried to imagine that we belonged to those times—It is dead
and it is not dead, and you cannot imagine either its life or its death; the
earth speaks and the salamander speaks, the Spring comes and only
obscures it—'[2]

2

So spoke of the existence of things,
An unmanageable pantheon

Absolute, but they say
Arid.

A city of the corporations   5

Glassed
In dreams

And images—

And the pure joy
Of the mineral fact   10

Tho it is impenetrable

As the world, if it is matter,
Is impenetrable.

---

1. A rephrasing of a quotation from the French Catholic philosopher Jacques Maritain, which Oppen used earlier as an epigraph for *The Materials* (1962). The quote is there rendered: "we awake at the same moment to ourselves and to things."

2. Oppen said in a letter that "the long quotes in the first section [of *Of Being Numerous*] are Mary, verbatim, telling me about Bonnefoy." The reference is to Mary Oppen's description of the work of the French writer Yves Bonnefoy in *Du mouvement et de l'immobilité de Douve* (1959).

3

The emotions are engaged
Entering the city
As entering any city.

We are not coeval
With a locality   5
But we imagine others are,

We encounter them. Actually
A populace flows
Thru the city.

This is a language, therefore, of New York   10

4

For the people of that flow
Are new, the old

New to age as the young
To youth

And to their dwelling   5
For which the tarred roofs

And the stoops and doors—
A world of stoops—
Are petty alibi and satirical wit
Will not serve.   10

5

The great stone
Above the river
In the pylon of the bridge

'1875'³

Frozen in the moonlight   5
In the frozen air over the footpath, consciousness

Which has nothing to gain, which awaits nothing,
Which loves itself

---

3. The date suggests the Brooklyn Bridge, suspended across the East River between Manhattan and Brooklyn, which was constructed during 1869–83 under the direction of John Roebling and his son.

6

We are pressed, pressed on each other,
We will be told at once
Of anything that happens

And the discovery of fact bursts
In a paroxysm of emotion   5
Now as always. Crusoe[4]

We say was
'Rescued'.
So we have chosen.

7

Obsessed, bewildered

By the shipwreck
Of the singular

We have chosen the meaning
Of being numerous.   5

9

'Whether, as the intensity of seeing increases, one's distance
     from Them, the people, does not also increase'
I know, of course I know, I can enter no other place

Yet I am one of those who from nothing but man's way of
     thought and one of his dialects and what has happened   5
     to me
Have made poetry

To dream of that beach
For the sake of an instant in the eyes,

The absolute singular   10

The unearthly bonds
Of the singular

Which is the bright light of shipwreck

11

     it is *that* light
Seeps anywhere, a light for the times

---

4. The figure of Robinson Crusoe, from Daniel Defoe's novel (1719), shipwrecked on an island, is a recurring image in this and other Oppen poems.

In which the buildings
Stand on low ground, their pediments
Just above the harbor   5

Absolutely immobile,

Hollow, available, you could enter any building,
You could look from any window
One might wave to himself
From the top of the Empire State Building—   10

Speak

If you can

Speak

Phyllis—not neo-classic,
The girl's name is Phyllis—   15

Coming home from her first job
On the bus in the bare civic interior
Among those people, the small doors
Opening on the night at the curb
Her heart, she told me, suddenly tight with happiness—   20

So small a picture,
A spot of light on the curb, it cannot demean us

I too am in love down there with the streets
And the square slabs of pavement—

To talk of the house and the neighborhood and the docks   25

And it is not 'art'

                                        14

I cannot even now
Altogether disengage myself
From those men

With whom I stood in emplacements, in mess tents,
In hospitals and sheds and hid in the gullies   5
Of blasted roads in a ruined country,

Among them many men
More capable than I[5]—

5. Oppen was drafted in 1942 and served three
years in the infantry. He was wounded in a shell
explosion just before V-E Day. The comradeship
expressed here occurs elsewhere in Oppen's work
and recalls a central theme in Walt Whitman's
poetry as well.

Muykut and a sergeant
Named Healy,   10
That lieutenant also—

How forget that? How talk
Distantly of 'The People'

Who are that force
Within the walls   15
Of cities

Wherein their cars

Echo like history
Down walled avenues
In which one cannot speak.   20

<h2 style="text-align:center">17</h2>

The roots of words
Dim in the subways

There is madness in the number
Of the living
'A state of matter'   5

There is nobody here but us chickens

Anti-ontology—

He wants to say
His life is real,
No one can say why   10

It is not easy to speak

A ferocious mumbling, in public
Of rootless speech

<h2 style="text-align:center">18</h2>

It is the air of atrocity,
An event as ordinary
As a President.

A plume of smoke, visible at a distance
In which people burn.[6]   5

<h2 style="text-align:center">19</h2>

Now in the helicopters the casual will
Is atrocious

---

6. In this and following stanzas Oppen evokes the Vietnam War, contemporary with this poem.

Insanity in high places,
If it is true we must do these things
We must cut our throats   5

The fly in the bottle[7]

Insane, the insane fly

Which, over the city
Is the bright light of shipwreck

                              22

Clarity

In the sense of *transparence,*
I don't mean that much can be explained.

Clarity in the sense of silence.

                              27

It is difficult now to speak of poetry—

about those who have recognized the range of choice or those who have
lived within the life they were born to—. It is not precisely a question of
profundity but a different order of experience. One would have to tell
what happens in a life, what choices present themselves, what the world
is for us, what happens in time, what thought is in the course of a life
and therefore what art is, and the isolation of the actual

I would want to talk of rooms and of what they look out on and of
basements, the rough walls bearing the marks of the forms, the old marks
of wood in the concrete, such solitude as we know—   10

and the swept floors. Someone, a workman bearing about him, feeling
about him that peculiar word like a dishonored fatherhood has swept this
solitary floor, this profoundly hidden floor—such solitude as we know.

One must not come to feel that he has a thousand threads
     in his hands,   15
He must somehow see the one thing;
This is the level of art
There are other levels
But there is no other level of art

                              29

My daughter, my daughter, what can I say
Of living?

7. The Austrian philosopher Ludwig Wittgenstein (1889–1951), one of the most important philosophers of language, wrote in his *Philosophical Investigations* (1953): "What is your aim in philosophy?—To shew the fly the way out of the fly-bottle."

I cannot judge it.

We seem caught
In reality together my lovely   5
Daughter,

I have a daughter
But no child

And it was not precisely
Happiness we promised   10
Ourselves;

We say happiness, happiness and are not
Satisfied.

Tho the house on the low land
Of the city   15

Catches the dawn light

I can tell myself, and I tell myself
Only what we all believe
True

And in the sudden vacuum   20
Of time . . .

. . . is it not
In fear the roots grip

Downward
And beget   25

The baffling hierarchies
Of father and child

As of leaves on their high
Thin twigs to shield us

From time, from open   30
Time

                          36

Tho the world
Is the obvious, the seen
And unforeseeable,
That which one cannot
Not see   5

Which the first eyes
Saw—

For us
Also each
Man or woman   10
Near is
Knowledge

Tho it may be of the noon's
Own vacuity

—and the mad, too, speak only of conspiracy   15
and people talking—

And if those paths
Of the mind
Cannot break

It is not the wild glare   20
Of the world even that one dies in.

40

Whitman: 'April 19, 1864

The capitol grows upon one in time, especially as they have got the great
figure on top of it now, and you can see it very well. It is a great bronze
figure, the Genius of Liberty I suppose. It looks wonderful toward sundown. I love to go and look at it. The sun when it is nearly down shines
on the headpiece and it dazzles and glistens like a big star: it looks   5

quite curious . . . '[8]

1968

Anniversary Poem

'the picturesque
common lot' the unwarranted light

Where everyone has been

The very ground of the path
And the litter grow ancient   5

A shovel's scratched edge
So like any other man's

We are troubled by incredulity
We are troubled by scratched things

8. A quotation from a letter Walt Whitman wrote to his mother about the capitol building in Washington,
D.C.

Becoming familiar   10
Becoming extreme

Let grief
Be
So it be ours

Nor hide one's eyes   15
As tides drop along the beaches in the thin wash of
            breakers

And so desert each other
—lest there be nothing

            The Indian girl walking across the desert, the   20
sunfish under the boat

How shall we say how this happened, these stories, our
            stories

Scope, mere size, a kind of redemption.

Exposed still and jagged on the San Francisco hills   25

Time and depth before us, paradise of the real, we
            know what it is

To find now depth, not time, since we cannot, but depth

To come out safe,   to end well

We have begun to say good bye   30
To each other
And cannot say it

                                                      1972

THEODORE ROETHKE
1908–1963

Theodore Roethke had the kind of childhood a poet might have invented. He was born in Saginaw, Michigan, where both his German grandfather and his father kept greenhouses for a living. The greenhouse world, he later said, represented for him "both heaven and hell, a kind of tropics created in the savage climate of Michigan, where austere German Americans turned their love of order and their terrifying efficiency into something truly beautiful." Throughout his life he was haunted both by the ordered, protected world of the greenhouse—the constant activity of growth, the cultivated flowers—and by the desolate landscape of his part of Michigan. "The marsh, the mire, the Void, is always there, immediate and terrifying. It is a splendid place for schooling the spirit. It is America."

Roethke's poetry often reenacted this "schooling" of the spirit by revisiting the landscapes of his childhood: the nature poems that make up the largest part of his early work try to bridge the distance between a child's consciousness and the adult mysteries presided over by his father. Roethke arranged and rearranged these poems to give the sense of a spiritual autobiography, especially in preparing the volumes *The Lost Son* (1948), *Praise to the End!* (1951), and *The Waking* (1953). The greenhouse world emerged as a "reality harsher than reality," the cultivator's activity pulsating and threatening. Its overseers, like "Frau Bauman, Frau Schmidt, and Frau Schwartze," emerge as gods, fates, muses, and witches all in one. It was by focusing on the minute processes of botanical growth—the rooting, the budding—that the poet found a way of participating in the mysteries of this once alien world, "alive in a slippery grave."

In his books *The Lost Son and Other Poems* and *Praise to the End!* Roethke explored the regenerative possibilities of prerational speech (like children's riddles) in which language as sound recaptures nonlogical states of being. In these poems, his most dazzling and original work, Roethke opened up the possibilities of language. One of the sections of the long poem *The Lost Son* is called "The Gibber," a pun, because the word means both a meaningless utterance and the pouch at the base of the calyx of a flower. The pun identifies principles of growth with the possibilities of speech freed from logical meanings, and the sequence as a whole suggests the power of both nature and language to revive the spirit of an adult life: "A lively understandable spirit / Once entertained you. / It will come again. / Be still. / Wait."

If the nature poems of Roethke's first four books explore the anxieties with him since childhood, his later love poems show him in periods of release and momentary pleasure:

> And I dance round and round,
> A fond and foolish man,
> And see and suffer myself
> In another being at last.

The love poems, many of them included in *Words for the Wind* (1958) and *The Far Field* (1964), are among the most appealing in modern American verse. They stand in sharp relief to the suffering Roethke experienced in other areas of his personal life—several mental breakdowns and periods of alcoholism—which led to a premature death. *The Far Field*, a posthumous volume, includes fierce, strongly rhymed lyrics in which Roethke tried "bare, even terrible statement," pressing toward the threshold of spiritual insight:

> A man goes far to find out what he is—
> Death of the self in a long, tearless night,
> All natural shapes blazing unnatural light.

The nature poems of this last volume, gathered as "The North American Sequence" (from which the title poem of the book, *The Far Field*, is taken) use extended landscape to find natural analogies for the human passage toward the dark unknown, hoping "in their rhythms to catch the very movement of mind itself."

Roethke is remembered as one of the great teachers of poetry, especially by those young poets and critics who studied with him at the University of Washington from 1948 until the time of his death in 1963. James Wright, David Wagoner, and Richard Hugo, among others, attended his classes. He was noted for his mastery of sound and metrics. Although his own poetry was intensely personal, his starting advice to students always deemphasized undisciplined self-expression. "Write like someone else," was his instruction to beginners. In Roethke's own career, however, this advice had its costs. His apprenticeship to Yeats, in particular, endangered his own poetic voice; in some late poems the echo of this great predecessor makes Roethke all but inaudible.

Roethke was much honored later in his career: a Pulitzer Prize for *The Waking* (1953); a National Book Award and Bollingen Prize for the collected poems, *Words for the Wind* (1958); and a posthumous National Book Award for *The Far Field* (1964).

Cuttings

Sticks-in-a-drowse droop over sugary loam,
Their intricate stem-fur dries;
But still the delicate slips keep coaxing up water;
The small cells bulge;

One nub of growth   5
Nudges a sand-crumb loose,
Pokes through a musty sheath
Its pale tendrilous horn.

1948

Cuttings

(*later*)

This urge, wrestle, resurrection of dry sticks,
Cut stems struggling to put down feet,
What saint strained so much,
Rose on such lopped limbs to a new life?

I can hear, underground, that sucking and sobbing,   5
In my veins, in my bones I feel it,—
The small waters seeping upward,
The tight grains parting at last.
When sprouts break out,
Slippery as fish   10
I quail, lean to beginnings, sheath-wet.

1948

Weed Puller

Under the concrete benches,
Hacking at black hairy roots,—
Those lewd monkey-tails hanging from drainholes,—
Digging into the soft rubble underneath,
Webs and weeds,   5
Grubs and snails and sharp sticks,

Or yanking tough fern-shapes,
Coiled green and thick, like dripping smilax,[1]
Tugging all day at perverse life:
The indignity of it!—   10
With everything blooming above me,
Lilies, pale-pink cyclamen, roses,
Whole fields lovely and inviolate,—
Me down in that fetor of weeds,
Crawling on all fours,   15
Alive, in a slippery grave.

                                                          1948

Frau Bauman, Frau Schmidt, and Frau Schwartze[1]

Gone the three ancient ladies
Who creaked on the greenhouse ladders,
Reaching up white strings
To wind, to wind
The sweet-pea tendrils, the smilax,   5
Nasturtiums, the climbing
Roses, to straighten
Carnations, red
Chrysanthemums; the stiff
Stems, jointed like corn,   10
They tied and tucked,—
These nurses of nobody else.
Quicker than birds, they dipped
Up and sifted the dirt;
They sprinkled and shook;   15
They stood astride pipes,
Their skirts billowing out wide into tents,
Their hands twinkling with wet;
Like witches they flew along rows
Keeping creation at ease;   20
With a tendril for needle
They sewed up the air with a stem;
They teased out the seed that the cold kept asleep,—
All the coils, loops, and whorls.
They trellised the sun; they plotted for more than themselves.   25

I remember how they picked me up, a spindly kid,
Pinching and poking my thin ribs
Till I lay in their laps, laughing,
Weak as a whiffet;[2]
Now, when I'm alone and cold in my bed,   30
They still hover over me,

1. A type of fern.
1. Women who worked in the greenhouse owned
by Roethke's father.

2. A small, young, or unimportant person (probably from *whippet,* a small dog).

These ancient leathery crones,
With their bandannas stiffened with sweat,
And their thorn-bitten wrists,
And their snuff-laden breath blowing lightly over me in my first
    sleep.   35

1948

My Papa's Waltz

The whiskey on your breath
Could make a small boy dizzy;
But I hung on like death:
Such waltzing was not easy.

We romped until the pans   5
Slid from the kitchen shelf;
My mother's countenance
Could not unfrown itself.

The hand that held my wrist
Was battered on one knuckle;   10
At every step you missed
My right ear scraped a buckle.

You beat time on my head
With a palm caked hard by dirt,
Then waltzed me off to bed   15
Still clinging to your shirt.

1948

Night Crow

When I saw that clumsy crow
Flap from a wasted tree,
A shape in the mind rose up:
Over the gulfs of dream
Flew a tremendous bird   5
Further and further away
Into a moonless black,
Deep in the brain, far back.

1948

The Lost Son

I. The Flight

At Woodlawn[1] I heard the dead cry:
I was lulled by the slamming of iron,
A slow drip over stones,
Toads brooding wells.
All the leaves stuck out their tongues;   5
I shook the softening chalk of my bones,
Saying,
Snail, snail, glister me forward,
Bird, soft-sigh me home,
Worm, be with me.   10
This is my hard time.

Fished in an old wound,
The soft pond of repose;
Nothing nibbled my line,
Not even the minnows came.   15

Sat in an empty house
Watching shadows crawl,
Scratching.
There was one fly.

Voice, come out of the silence.   20
Say something.
Appear in the form of a spider
Or a moth beating the curtain.

Tell me:
Which is the way I take;   25
Out of what door do I go,
Where and to whom?

    Dark hollows said, lee to the wind,
    The moon said, back of an eel,
    The salt said, look by the sea,   30
    Your tears are not enough praise,
    You will find no comfort here,
    In the kingdom of bang and blab.

    Running lightly over spongy ground,
    Past the pasture of flat stones,   35
    The three elms,
    The sheep strewn on a field,
    Over a rickety bridge
    Toward the quick-water, wrinkling and rippling.

---

1. A cemetery.

Hunting along the river,   40
Down among the rubbish, the bug-riddled foliage,
By the muddy pond-edge, by the bog-holes,
By the shrunken lake, hunting, in the heat of summer.

The shape of a rat?
    It's bigger than that.   45
    It's less than a leg
    And more than a nose,
    Just under the water
    It usually goes.

    Is it soft like a mouse?   50
    Can it wrinkle its nose?
    Could it come in the house
    On the tips of its toes?

    Take the skin of a cat
    And the back of an eel,   55
    Then roll them in grease,—
    That's the way it would feel.

    It's sleek as an otter
    With wide webby toes
    Just under the water   60
    It usually goes.

2. *The Pit*

Where do the roots go?
    Look down under the leaves.
Who put the moss there?
    These stones have been here too long.   65
Who stunned the dirt into noise?
    Ask the mole, he knows.
I feel the slime of a wet nest.
    Beware Mother Mildew.
Nibble again, fish nerves.   70

3. *The Gibber*

At the wood's mouth,
By the cave's door,
I listened to something
I had heard before.

Dogs of the groin   75
Barked and howled,
The sun was against me,
The moon would not have me.

The weeds whined,
The snakes cried,   80
The cows and briars
Said to me: Die.

What a small song. What slow clouds. What dark water.
Hath the rain a father? All the caves are ice. Only the snow's here.
I'm cold. I'm cold all over. Rub me in father and mother.   85
Fear was my father, Father Fear.
His look drained the stones.

    What gliding shape
    Beckoning through halls,
    Stood poised on the stair,   90
    Fell dreamily down?

    From the mouths of jugs
    Perched on many shelves,
    I saw substance flowing
    That cold morning.   95

    Like a slither of eels
    That watery cheek
    As my own tongue kissed
    My lips awake.

Is this the storm's heart? The ground is unstilling itself.   100
My veins are running nowhere. Do the bones cast out their fire?
Is the seed leaving the old bed? These buds are live as birds.
Where, where are the tears of the world?
Let the kisses resound, flat like a butcher's palm;
Let the gestures freeze; our doom is already decided.   105
All the windows are burning! What's left of my life?
I want the old rage, the lash of primordial milk!
Goodbye, goodbye, old stones, the time-order is going,
I have married my hands to perpetual agitation,
I run, I run to the whistle of money.   110

    Money money money
    Water water water

    How cool the grass is.
    Has the bird left?
    The stalk still sways.   115
    Has the worm a shadow?
    What do the clouds say?

    These sweeps of light undo me.
    Look, look, the ditch is running white!
    I've more veins than a tree!   120
    Kiss me, ashes, I'm falling through a dark swirl.

4. The Return

The way to the boiler was dark,
Dark all the way,
Over slippery cinders
Through the long greenhouse.   125

The roses kept breathing in the dark.
They had many mouths to breathe with.
My knees made little winds underneath
Where the weeds slept.

There was always a single light   130
Swinging by the fire-pit,
Where the fireman pulled out roses,
The big roses, the big bloody clinkers.[2]

Once I stayed all night.
The light in the morning came slowly over the white   135
Snow.
There were many kinds of cool
Air.
Then came steam.

Pipe-knock.   140

Scurry of warm over small plants.
Ordnung![3] ordnung!
Papa is coming!

A fine haze moved off the leaves;
Frost melted on far panes;   145
The rose, the chrysanthemum turned toward the light.
Even the hushed forms, the bent yellowy weeds
Moved in a slow up-sway.

5. "It was beginning winter"

It was beginning winter,
An in-between time,   150
The landscape still partly brown:
The bones of weeds kept swinging in the wind,
Above the blue snow.

It was beginning winter,
The light moved slowly over the frozen field,   155
Over the dry seed-crowns,
The beautiful surviving bones
Swinging in the wind.

2. Large cinders; the residue left in burning coal.   3. A call to order.

Light traveled over the wide field;
Stayed.   160
The weeds stopped swinging.
The mind moved, not alone,
Through the clear air, in the silence.

    Was it light?
    Was it light within?   165
    Was it light within light?
    Stillness becoming alive,
    Yet still?

A lively understandable spirit
Once entertained you.   170
It will come again.
Be still.
Wait.

1948

The Waking

    I wake to sleep, and take my waking slow.
    I feel my fate in what I cannot fear.
    I learn by going where I have to go.

    We think by feeling. What is there to know?
    I hear my being dance from ear to ear.   5
    I wake to sleep, and take my waking slow.

    Of those so close beside me, which are you?
    God bless the Ground! I shall walk softly there,
    And learn by going where I have to go.

    Light takes the Tree; but who can tell us how?   10
    The lowly worm climbs up a winding stair;
    I wake to sleep, and take my waking slow.

    Great Nature has another thing to do
    To you and me; so take the lively air,
    And, lovely, learn by going where to go.   15

    This shaking keeps me steady. I should know.
    What falls away is always. And is near.
    I wake to sleep, and take my waking slow.
    I learn by going where I have to go.

1953

I Knew a Woman

I knew a woman, lovely in her bones,
When small birds sighed, she would sigh back at them;
Ah, when she moved, she moved more ways than one:
The shapes a bright container can contain!
Of her choice virtues only gods should speak,   5
Or English poets who grew up on Greek
(I'd have them sing in chorus, cheek to cheek).

How well her wishes went! She stroked my chin,
She taught me Turn, and Counter-turn, and Stand;[1]
She taught me Touch, that undulant white skin;   10
I nibbled meekly from her proffered hand;
She was the sickle; I, poor I, the rake,
Coming behind her for her pretty sake
(But what prodigious mowing we did make).

Love likes a gander, and adores a goose: 15
Her full lips pursed, the errant note to seize;
She played it quick, she played it light and loose;
My eyes, they dazzled at her flowing knees;
Her several parts could keep a pure repose,
Or one hip quiver with a mobile nose   20
(She moved in circles, and those circles moved).

Let seed be grass, and grass turn into hay:
I'm martyr to a motion not my own;
What's freedom for? To know eternity.
I swear she cast a shadow white as stone.   25
But who would count eternity in days?
These old bones live to learn her wanton ways:
(I measure time by how a body sways).

1958

The Far Field[1]

1

I dream of journeys repeatedly:
Of flying like a bat deep into a narrowing tunnel,
Of driving alone, without luggage, out a long peninsula,
The road lined with snow-laden second growth,
A fine dry snow ticking the windshield,   5
Alternate snow and sleet, no on-coming traffic,
And no lights behind, in the blurred side-mirror,
The road changing from glazed tarface to a rubble of stone,

1. Parts of a Pindaric ode.
1. The penultimate of six poems in Roethke's   "North American Sequence" from the book *The Far Field*.

Ending at last in a hopeless sand-rut,
Where the car stalls,   10
Churning in a snowdrift
Until the headlights darken.

2

At the field's end, in the corner missed by the mower,
Where the turf drops off into a grass-hidden culvert,
Haunt of the cat-bird, nesting-place of the field-mouse,   15
Not too far away from the ever-changing flower-dump,
Among the tin cans, tires, rusted pipes, broken machinery,—
One learned of the eternal;
And in the shrunken face of a dead rat, eaten by rain and ground-beetles
(I found it lying among the rubble of an old coal bin)   20
And the tom-cat, caught near the pheasant-run,
Its entrails strewn over the half-grown flowers,
Blasted to death by the night watchman.

I suffered for birds, for young rabbits caught in the mower,
My grief was not excessive.   25
For to come upon warblers in early May
Was to forget time and death:
How they filled the oriole's elm, a twittering restless cloud, all one morning,
And I watched and watched till my eyes blurred from the bird shapes,—
Cape May, Blackburnian, Cerulean,[2]—   30
Moving, elusive as fish, fearless,
Hanging, bunched like young fruit, bending the end branches,
Still for a moment,
Then pitching away in half-flight,
Lighter than finches,   35
While the wrens bickered and sang in the half-green hedgerows,
And the flicker[3] drummed from his dead tree in the chicken-yard.

—Or to lie naked in sand,
In the silted shallows of a slow river,
Fingering a shell,
Thinking: 40
Once I was something like this, mindless,
Or perhaps with another mind, less peculiar;
Or to sink down to the hips in a mossy quagmire;
Or, with skinny knees, to sit astride a wet log,   45
Believing:
I'll return again,
As a snake or a raucous bird,
Or, with luck, as a lion.

I learned not to fear infinity,   50
The far field, the windy cliffs of forever,
The dying of time in the white light of tomorrow,

2. Types of warblers.   3. A kind of woodpecker.

The wheel turning away from itself,
The sprawl of the wave,
The on-coming water.   55

3

The river turns on itself,
The tree retreats into its own shadow.
I feel a weightless change, a moving forward
As of water quickening before a narrowing channel
When banks converge, and the wide river whitens;   60
Or when two rivers combine, the blue glacial torrent
And the yellowish-green from the mountainy upland,—
At first a swift rippling between rocks,
Then a long running over flat stones
Before descending to the alluvial plain,   65
To the clay banks, and the wild grapes hanging from the elmtrees.
The slightly trembling water
Dropping a fine yellow silt where the sun stays;
And the crabs bask near the edge,
The weedy edge, alive with small snakes and bloodsuckers,— 70

I have come to a still, but not a deep center,
A point outside the glittering current;
My eyes stare at the bottom of a river,
At the irregular stones, iridescent sandgrains,
My mind moves in more than one place,   75
In a country half-land, half-water.

I am renewed by death, thought of my death,
The dry scent of a dying garden in September,
The wind fanning the ash of a low fire.
What I love is near at hand,   80
Always, in earth and air.

4

The lost self changes,
Turning toward the sea,
A sea-shape turning around,—
An old man with his feet before the fire,   85
In robes of green, in garments of adieu.

A man faced with his own immensity
Wakes all the waves, all their loose wandering fire.
The murmur of the absolute, the why
Of being born falls on his naked ears.   90
His spirit moves like monumental wind
That gentles on a sunny blue plateau.
He is the end of things, the final man.

All finite things reveal infinitude:
The mountain with its singular bright shade   95

Like the blue shine on freshly frozen snow,
The after-light upon ice-burdened pines;
Odor of basswood on a mountain-slope,
A scent beloved of bees;
Silence of water above a sunken tree: 100
The pure serene of memory in one man,—
A ripple widening from a single stone
Winding around the waters of the world.

                                                        1964

Wish for a Young Wife

My lizard, my lively writher,
May your limbs never wither,
May the eyes in your face
Survive the green ice
Of envy's mean gaze;   5
May you live out your life
Without hate, without grief,
And your hair ever blaze,
In the sun, in the sun,
When I am undone,   10
When I am no one.

                                                        1964

In a Dark Time

In a dark time, the eye begins to see,
I meet my shadow in the deepening shade;
I hear my echo in the echoing wood—
A lord of nature weeping to a tree.
I live between the heron and the wren,   5
Beasts of the hill and serpents of the den.

What's madness but nobility of soul
At odds with circumstance? The day's on fire!
I know the purity of pure despair,
My shadow pinned against a sweating wall.   10
That place among the rocks—is it a cave,
Or winding path? The edge is what I have.

A steady storm of correspondences!
A night flowing with birds, a ragged moon,
And in broad day the midnight come again!   15
A man goes far to find out what he is—
Death of the self in a long, tearless night,
All natural shapes blazing unnatural light.

Dark, dark my light, and darker my desire.
My soul, like some heat-maddened summer fly,   20
Keeps buzzing at the sill. Which I is *I?*
A fallen man, I climb out of my fear.
The mind enters itself, and God the mind,
And one is One, free in the tearing wind.

1964

CHARLES OLSON
1910–1970

Writing of the sense of place in Charles Olson's poems, Robert Creeley says, "In short, the world is not separable, and we *are* in it." Being in the world, for Olson, meant experiencing it as present; for him, what happens in a poem happens now. Art, he said, "does not seek to describe but to enact." In an influential essay, "Projective Verse," he rejected the partitioning of reality that separates the human from the natural world. His aim, he wrote, was to get "rid of the lyrical interference of the individual as ego, of the 'subject' and his soul, that peculiar presumption by which western man has interposed himself between what he is as a creature of nature . . . and those other creations of nature." To read Olson is to enter a critical and theoretical force field made up of his essays, lectures, and poems. His ultimate concern was reimagining the world, returning language (as Creeley writes) "to its place *in* experience." Although this ambition is inconsistently realized in Olson's poems, it directed his lifelong effort. And in this effort he was an extraordinarily influential figure for a group of poets whose work was beginning to be known in the 1950s, among them Creeley, Denise Levertov, and Robert Duncan.

Olson's influence grew out of his years at Black Mountain, an experimental college in North Carolina where he had served as an instructor and then as head or rector, succeeding the artist Josef Albers. In its flourishing years under the direction of Olson, the college included among its teachers and students key figures of the avant-garde: John Cage in music, Merce Cunningham in dance, Franz Kline and Robert Rauschenberg in painting. Just before going to Black Mountain, Olson published a critical study of Herman Melville and *Moby-Dick, Call Me Ishmael* (1947), which declared his new independence of the formal academic systems. (He had been, as he put it, "uneducated" at Wesleyan, Yale, and Harvard, had taught at Clark University in Worcester, Massachusetts, and had taken an advanced degree in American civilization at Harvard.) *Call Me Ishmael*, unlike most literary studies, was fiercely personal and unorthodox—almost a prose poem proclaiming new bearings in American literature, especially the symbolic importance of the Pacific, the "unwarped primal world" that, according to the poet, was the true center of the American experience.

Olson claimed that "the substances of history now useful lie outside, under, right here, anywhere but in the direct continuum of society as we have had it." Therefore his own work, as he makes clear in *The Kingfishers,* sharply cultivates the primitive sources of energy almost buried by civilized responses and instruments. As a sometime archaeologist, Olson "hunted among stones." He studied earlier North American cultures and worked among the Mayan ruins in the Yucatán, trying to recover the living elements of an archaic way of life. For Olson, the imagination of ancient cultures exists in the present as much as does a walk down the street in one's native town.

(o my lady of good voyage
in whose arm, whose left arm rests
no boy but a carefully carved wood, a painted face, a schooner!⁴   30
a delicate mast, as bow-sprit for

forwarding

3

the underpart is, though stemmed, uncertain
is, as sex is, as moneys are, facts!
facts, to be dealt with, as the sea is, the demand   35
that they be played by, that they only can be, that they must
be played by, said he, coldly, the
ear!

By ear, he sd.
But that which matters, that which insists, that which will last,   40
that! o my people, where shall you find it, how, where, where shall you listen
when all is become billboards, when, all, even silence, is spray-gunned?

when even our bird, my roofs,
cannot be heard

when even you, when sound itself is neoned in?   45

when, on the hill, over the water
where she who used to sing,
when the water glowed,
black, gold, the tide
outward, at evening   50

when bells came like boats
over the oil-slicks, milkweed
hulls

And a man slumped,
attentionless,   55
against pink shingles

o sea city)

4

one loves only form,
and form only comes
into existence when   60
the thing is born

---

4. On the roof of the My Lady of Good Voyage church in Gloucester's Portuguese quarter is a statue of the Virgin Mary holding a schooner.

born of yourself, born
of hay and cotton struts,
of street-pickings, wharves, weeds
you carry in, my bird   65
            of a bone of a fish
            of a straw, or will
            of a color, of a bell
            of yourself, torn

                              5

love is not easy   70
but how shall you know,
New England, now
that pejorocracy[5] is here, how
that street-cars, o Oregon, twitter
in the afternoon, offend[6]   75
a black-gold loin?
            how shall you strike,[7]
            o swordsman, the blue-red back
            when, last night, your aim
            was mu-sick, mu-sick, mu-sick   80
            And not the cribbage game?

                        (o Gloucester-man,
                        weave
                        your birds and fingers
                        new, your roof-tops,   85
                        clean shit upon racks
                        sunned on
                        American
                        braid
                        with others like you, such   90
                        extricable surface
                        as faun and oral,
                        satyr lesbos vase[8]

                        o kill kill kill kill kill
                        those   95
                        who advertise you
                        out)

5. Word coined by Ezra Pound in *The Cantos*, meaning something like "rule by belittling" or "worsening rule."
6. Olson hated the recorded music piped into streetcars.
7. In Gloucester lingo, a "striker" is a swordfish harpooner.
8. Lesbos was the home of Sappho, 6th-century B.C.E. lyric poet, one of the first Greeks to leave the oral tradition. The 6th century was also the height of archaic Greek vase painting.

6

in! in! the bow-sprit, bird, the beak
in, the bend is, in, goes in, the form
that which you make, what holds, which is   100
the law of object, strut after strut, what you are, what you must be, what
the force can throw up, can, right now hereinafter erect,
the mast, the mast, the tender
mast!

                The nest, I say, to you, I Maximus, say   105
                under the hand, as I see it, over the waters
                from this place where I am, where I hear,
                can still hear

                from where I carry you a feather
                as though, sharp, I picked up,   110
                in the afternoon delivered you
                a jewel,
                          it flashing more than a wing,
                than any old romantic thing,
                than memory, than place,   115
                than anything other than that which you carry

                than that which is,
                call it a nest, around the head of, call it
                the next second

                than that which you   120
                can do!

                                1953

Maximus, to Himself

I have had to learn the simplest things
last. Which made for difficulties.
Even at sea I was slow, to get the hand out, or to cross
a wet deck.
            The sea was not, finally, my trade.   5
But even my trade, at it, I stood estranged
from that which was most familiar.[1] Was delayed,
and not content with the man's argument
that such postponement
is now the nature of   10
obedience,
            that we are all late
            in a slow time,
            that we grow up many

1. An echo of the Greek philosopher Heraclitus: "We are estranged from that with which we are most familiar."

And the single   15
is not easily
known

It could be, though the sharpness (the *achiote*[2])
I note in others,
makes more sense   20
than my own distances. The agilities

          they show daily
          who do the world's
          businesses
          And who do nature's   25
          as I have no sense
          I have done either

I have made dialogues,
have discussed ancient texts,
have thrown what light I could, offered   30
what pleasures
doceat[3] allows

          But the known?
This, I have had to be given,
a life, love, and from one man   35
the world.

          Tokens.
          But sitting here
          I look out as a wind
          and water man, testing   40
          And missing
          some proof

I know the quarters
of the weather, where it comes from,
where it goes. But the stem of me,   45
this I took from their welcome,
or their rejection, of me

          And my arrogance
          was neither diminished
          nor increased,   50
          by the communication

2

It is undone business
I speak of, this morning,

---

2. The seed of the annatto tree, which yields a reddish dye, resembling red (sharp) pepper.
3. "That he teach." One of the three functions of

a poet, according to medieval theorists. Pound
modernized the concept in his essay "Make It
New."

with the sea
stretching out   55
from my feet

                                                                      1953

[When do poppies bloom]

When do poppies bloom   I ask myself, stopping again
to look in Mrs. Frontiero's yard, beside her house on
this side from Birdseyes (or what was once Cunningham
& Thompson's and is now O'Donnell-Usen's) to see if
I have missed them, flaked out and dry-like like   5
Dennison's Crepe. And what I found was dark buds
like cigars, and standing up   and my question is
when, then, will those blossoms more lotuses to the
West than lotuses wave like paper and petal by petal
seem more powerful than any thing except the Universe   10
itself, they are so animate-inanimate and dry-beauty not
any shove, or sit there poppies blow as crepe
paper. And in Mrs Frontiero's yard annually I
expect them as the King of the Earth must have
Penelope,[1] awaiting her return, love lies   15
so delicately on the pillow as this one flower,
petal and petal, carries nothing
into or out of the World   so threatening
were those cigar-stub cups just now, & I <u>know</u>
how quickly, and paper-like, absorbent   20
and krinkled paper, the poppy itself will, when here,
go again and the stalks stay like onion plants oh
come, poppy, when will you bloom?
                              The Fort[2]
                              June 15th [Wednesday]
                              XLVI

                                                                      1975

Celestial Evening, October 1967

Advanced out toward the external from
the time I did actually lose space control,
here on the Fort[1] and kept turning left

---

1. In Greek myth, Odysseus's paradigmatically
faithful wife. Olson, however, seems to be referring
to the myth of Persephone, who reluctantly marries Hades, "king of the Earth," or Underworld.
Persephone (to whom poppies are sacred) lives
most of the time above ground but must return to
Hades for some months every year because Hades
tricked her into eating four pomegranate seeds.
2. A district in Gloucester, Massachusetts, where
Olson settled after leaving Black Mountain in
1957.
1. See n. 2, above.

like my star-nosed mole batted
on the head, not being able to   5
get home 50 yards as I was
from it. There is a vast

internal life, a sea or organism
full of sounds & memoried
objects swimming or sunk   10
in the great fall of it as,
when one further
ring of the 9 bounding
Earth & Heaven runs
into the daughter of God's   15
particular place, cave, palace—a tail

of Ocean whose waters then
are test if even a god
lies will tell & he or she spend
9 following years out of the company   20
of their own. The sounds

and objects of the great
10th within us are
what we hear see are motived by
dream belief care for discriminate   25
our loves & choices cares & failures unless
in this forbidding Earth & Heaven by

enclosure 9 times round plus
all that stream collecting as,
into her hands it comes: the   30

full volume of all which ever was which we
as such have that which is our part of it,
all history existence places splits of moon
& slightest oncoming smallest stars at
sunset, fears & horrors, grandparents'   35
lives as much as we have also features
and their forms, whatever grace or ugliness our legs
etc possess, it all

comes in as also outward leads
us after itself as though then   40
the horn of the nearest moon was
truth. I bend my ear, as,
if I were Amoghasiddi[2] and,
here on this plain where
like my mole I have   45
been knocked flat, attend,
to turn & turn within

---

2. In Tibetan Buddhism, one of the five Dhyana-Buddhas, or Buddhas of contemplation.

the steady stream & collect which
within me ends as in her hall and I

hear all, the new moon new in all   50
the ancient sky

1967   1975

ELIZABETH BISHOP
1911–1979

"The enormous power of reticence," the poet Octavio Paz said in a tribute, "—that is the great lesson of Elizabeth Bishop." Bishop's reticence originates in a temperament indistinguishable from her style; her remarkable formal gifts allowed her to create ordered and lucid structures that hold strong feelings in place. Chief among these feelings was a powerful sense of loss. The crucial events of Bishop's life occurred within her first eight years. Born in Worcester, Massachusetts, in 1911, she was eight months old when her father died. Her mother suffered a series of breakdowns and was permanently institutionalized when her daughter was five. "I've never concealed this," Bishop once wrote, "although I don't like to make too much of it. But of course it is an important fact, to me. I didn't see her again." The understatement in this remark is characteristic. When Bishop wrote about her early life—as she first did in several poems and stories in the 1950s and last did in her extraordinary final book, *Geography III* (1976)—she resisted sentimentality and self-pity. It was as if she could look at the events of her own life with the same unflinching gaze she turned on the landscapes that so consistently compelled her. The deep feeling in her poems rises up out of direct and particular description, but Bishop does more than simply observe. Whether writing about her childhood landscape of Nova Scotia or her adopted Brazil, she often opens a poem with long perspectives on time, with landscapes that dwarf the merely human, emphasizing the dignified frailty of a human observer and the pervasive mysteries that surround her.

Examining her own case, she traces the observer's instinct to early childhood. "In the Waiting Room," a poem written in the early 1970s, probes the sources and motives behind her interest in detail. Using an incident from 1918 when she was seven—a little girl waits for her aunt in the dentist's anteroom—Bishop shows how in the course of the episode she became aware, as if wounded, of the utter strangeness and engulfing power of the world. The spectator in that poem hangs on to details as a kind of lifejacket; she observes because she has to.

After her father's death, Bishop and her mother went to live with Bishop's maternal grandparents in Great Village, Nova Scotia. She remained there for several years after her mother was institutionalized, until she was removed ("kidnapped," she describes herself feeling in one of her stories) by her paternal grandparents and taken to live in Worcester, Massachusetts. This experience was followed by a series of illnesses (eczema, bronchitis, and asthma), which plagued her for many years. Bishop later lived with an aunt and attended Walnut Hill School, a private high school. She graduated from Vassar College in 1934, where while a student she had been introduced to Marianne Moore. Moore's meticulous taste for fact was to influence Bishop's poetry, but more immediately, Moore's independent life as a poet made that life seem an alternative to Bishop's vaguer intentions to attend medical school. Bishop lived in

New York City and in Key West, Florida; a traveling fellowship took her to Brazil, which so appealed to her that she stayed there for more than sixteen years.

Exile and travel were at the heart of Bishop's poems from the very start. The title of her very first book, *North & South* (1946), looks forward to the tropical worlds she was to choose so long as home and backward to the northern seas of Nova Scotia. Her poems are set among these landscapes, where she can stress the sweep and violence of encircling and eroding geological powers or, in the case of Brazil, a bewildering botanical plenty. *Questions of Travel* (1965), her third volume, constitutes a sequence of poems initiating her, with her botanist-geologist-anthropologist's curiosity, into the life of Brazil and the mysteries of what questions a traveler-exile should ask. In this series with its increasing penetration of a new country, a process is at work similar to one Bishop identifies in the great English naturalist Charles Darwin, of whom Bishop once said: "One admires the beautiful solid case being built up out of his endless, heroic observations, almost unconscious or automatic—and then comes a sudden relaxation, a forgetful phrase, and one feels the strangeness of his undertaking, sees the lonely young man, his eyes fixed on facts and minute details, sinking or sliding giddily off into the unknown."

In 1969 Bishop's *Complete Poems* appeared, an ironic title in light of the fact that she continued to write and publish new poetry. *Geography III* contains some of her very best work, poems that, from the settled perspective of her return to the United States, look back and evaluate the appetite for exploration apparent in her earlier verse. The influence of her long friendship with the poet Robert Lowell, and their mutual regard for one another's work, may be felt in the way *Geography III* explores the terrain of memory and autobiography more powerfully and directly than her earlier work. Having left Brazil, Bishop lived in Boston from 1970 and taught at Harvard University until 1977. She received the Pulitzer Prize for the combined volume *North & South and A Cold Spring* (1955), the National Book Award for *The Complete Poems,* and in 1976 was the first woman and the first American to receive the Books Abroad Neustadt International Prize for Literature. Since Bishop's death in 1979, most of her published work has been gathered in two volumes: *The Complete Poems 1929–1979* and *The Collected Prose.*

The Unbeliever

He sleeps on the top of a mast.—Bunyan[1]

He sleeps on the top of a mast
with his eyes fast closed.
The sails fall away below him
like the sheets of his bed,
leaving out in the air of the night the sleeper's head.   5

Asleep he was transported there,
asleep he curled
in a gilded ball on the mast's top,
or climbed inside
a gilded bird, or blindly seated himself astride.   10

"I am founded on marble pillars,"
said a cloud. "I never move.

1. John Bunyan (1628–1688), English author of *Pilgrim's Progress,* an allegory of Christian's progress to salvation.

See the pillars there in the sea?"
Secure in introspection
he peers at the watery pillars of his reflection.   15

A gull had wings under his
and remarked that the air
was "like marble." He said: "Up here
I tower through the sky
for the marble wings on my tower-top fly."   20

But he sleeps on the top of his mast
with his eyes closed tight.
The gull inquired into his dream,
which was, "I must not fall.
The spangled sea below wants me to fall.   25
It is hard as diamonds; it wants to destroy us all."

                                                              1946

The Fish

I caught a tremendous fish
and held him beside the boat
half out of water, with my hook
fast in a corner of his mouth.
He didn't fight.   5
He hadn't fought at all.
He hung a grunting weight,
battered and venerable
and homely. Here and there
his brown skin hung in strips   10
like ancient wallpaper,
and its pattern of darker brown
was like wallpaper:
shapes like full-blown roses
stained and lost through age.   15
He was speckled with barnacles,
fine rosettes of lime,
and infested
with tiny white sea-lice,
and underneath two or three   20
rags of green weed hung down.
While his gills were breathing in
the terrible oxygen
—the frightening gills,
fresh and crisp with blood,   25
that can cut so badly—
I thought of the coarse white flesh
packed in like feathers,
the big bones and the little bones,
the dramatic reds and blacks   30

of his shiny entrails,
and the pink swim-bladder
like a big peony.
I looked into his eyes
which were far larger than mine   35
but shallower, and yellowed,
the irises backed and packed
with tarnished tinfoil
seen through the lenses
of old scratched isinglass.[1]   40
They shifted a little, but not
to return my stare.
—It was more like the tipping
of an object toward the light.
I admired his sullen face,   45
the mechanism of his jaw,
and then I saw
that from his lower lip
—if you could call it a lip—
grim, wet, and weaponlike,   50
hung five old pieces of fish-line,
or four and a wire leader
with the swivel still attached,
with all their five big hooks
grown firmly in his mouth.   55
A green line, frayed at the end
where he broke it, two heavier lines,
and a fine black thread
still crimped from the strain and snap
when it broke and he got away.   60
Like medals with their ribbons
frayed and wavering,
a five-haired beard of wisdom
trailing from his aching jaw.
I stared and stared   65
and victory filled up
the little rented boat,
from the pool of bilge
where oil had spread a rainbow
around the rusted engine   70
to the bailer rusted orange,
the sun-cracked thwarts,
the oarlocks on their strings,
the gunnels—until everything
was rainbow, rainbow, rainbow!   75
And I let the fish go.

1946

---

1. A whitish, semitransparent substance, originally obtained from the swim bladders of some freshwater fish and occasionally used for windows.

Over 2,000 Illustrations and a Complete Concordance[1]

Thus should have been our travels:
serious, engravable.
The Seven Wonders of the World are tired
and a touch familiar, but the other scenes,
innumerable, though equally sad and still,   5
are foreign. Often the squatting Arab,
or group of Arabs, plotting, probably,
against our Christian Empire,
while one apart, with outstretched arm and hand
points to the Tomb, the Pit, the Sepulcher.[2]   10
The branches of the date-palms look like files.
The cobbled courtyard, where the Well is dry,
is like a diagram, the brickwork conduits
are vast and obvious, the human figure
far gone in history or theology,   15
gone with its camel or its faithful horse.
Always the silence, the gesture, the specks of birds
suspended on invisible threads above the Site,
or the smoke rising solemnly, pulled by threads.
Granted a page alone or a page made up   20
of several scenes arranged in cattycornered rectangles
or circles set on stippled gray,
granted a grim lunette,[3]
caught in the toils of an initial letter,
when dwelt upon, they all resolve themselves.   25
The eye drops, weighted, through the lines
the burin[4] made, the lines that move apart
like ripples above sand,
dispersing storms, God's spreading fingerprint,
and painfully, finally, that ignite   30
in watery prismatic white-and-blue.

Entering the Narrows at St. Johns[5]
the touching bleat of goats reached to the ship.
We glimpsed them, reddish, leaping up the cliffs
among the fog-soaked weeds and butter-and-eggs.[6]   35
And at St. Peter's[7] the wind blew and the sun shone madly.
Rapidly, purposefully, the Collegians[8] marched in lines,
crisscrossing the great square with black, like ants.
In Mexico the dead man lay
in a blue arcade; the dead volcanoes   40
glistened like Easter lilies.

1. Part of the title of an old edition of the Bible described in the opening lines of the poem. A concordance is a guide to occurrences of words and proper names and places in a book.
2. The burial place of Christ, depicted (along with other places associated with the life of Jesus, such as the Well and the Site) among the "2,000 illustrations" of the title.
3. The oval framing an illustration, often a part of an enlarged initial letter.
4. Engraver's tool.
5. In Newfoundland.
6. A plant whose flowers are two shades of yellow.
7. The papal basilica in Rome.
8. Members of constituent orders of the Catholic church.

The jukebox went on playing "Ay, Jalisco!"
And at Volubilis[9] there were beautiful poppies
splitting the mosaics; the fat old guide made eyes.
In Dingle[1] harbor a golden length of evening   45
the rotting hulks held up their dripping plush.
The Englishwoman poured tea, informing us
that the Duchess was going to have a baby.
And in the brothels of Marrakesh[2]
the little pockmarked prostitutes   50
balanced their tea-trays on their heads
and did their belly-dances; flung themselves
naked and giggling against our knees,
asking for cigarettes. It was somewhere near there
I saw what frightened me most of all: 55
A holy grave, not looking particularly holy,
one of a group under a keyhole-arched stone baldaquin[3]
open to every wind from the pink desert.
An open, gritty, marble trough, carved solid
with exhortation, yellowed   60
as scattered cattle-teeth;
half-filled with dust, not even the dust
of the poor prophet paynim[4] who once lay there.
In a smart burnoose Khadour looked on amused.

Everything only connected by "and" and "and."   65
Open the book. (The gilt rubs off the edges
of the pages and pollinates the fingertips.)
Open the heavy book. Why couldn't we have seen
this old Nativity while we were at it?
—the dark ajar, the rocks breaking with light,   70
an undisturbed, unbreathing flame,
colorless, sparkless, freely fed on straw,
and, lulled within, a family with pets,
—and looked and looked our infant[5] sight away.

                                                         1955

The Bight[1]

[On My Birthday]

At low tide like this how sheer the water is.
White, crumbling ribs of marl protrude and glare
and the boats are dry, the pilings dry as matches.
Absorbing, rather than being absorbed,
the water in the bight doesn't wet anything,   5
the color of the gas flame turned as low as possible.
One can smell it turning to gas; if one were Baudelaire[2]

---

9. A ruined city in Morocco.
1. A town in southwest Ireland.
2. A city in Morocco.
3. Architectural canopy.
4. Archaic literary word for pagan, especially Muslim.

5. Its Latin root (*infans*) means "speechless."
1. A bay or inlet.
2. French poet (1821–1867), whose theory of correspondences (see line 32) promised links, through poetry, between the physical and spiritual worlds.

one could probably hear it turning to marimba music.
The little ocher dredge at work off the end of the dock
already plays the dry perfectly off-beat claves.   10
The birds are outsize. Pelicans crash
into this peculiar gas unnecessarily hard,
it seems to me, like pickaxes,
rarely coming up with anything to show for it,
and going off with humorous elbowings.   15
Black-and-white man-of-war birds soar
on impalpable drafts
and open their tails like scissors on the curves
or tense them like wishbones, till they tremble.
The frowsy sponge boats keep coming in   20
with the obliging air of retrievers,
bristling with jackstraw gaffs and hooks
and decorated with bobbles of sponges.
There is a fence of chicken wire along the dock
where, glinting like plowshares,   25
the blue-gray shark tails are hung up to dry
for the Chinese-restaurant trade.
Some of the little white boats are still piled up
against each other, or lie on their sides, stove in,
and not yet salvaged, if they ever will be, from the last bad storm,   30
like torn-open, unanswered letters.
The bight is littered with old correspondences.
Click. Click. Goes the dredge,
and brings up a dripping jawful of marl.
All the untidy activity continues,   35
awful but cheerful.

                                                                    1955

At the Fishhouses

Although it is a cold evening,
down by one of the fishhouses
an old man sits netting,
his net, in the gloaming almost invisible
a dark purple-brown,   5
and his shuttle worn and polished.
The air smells so strong of codfish
it makes one's nose run and one's eyes water.
The five fishhouses have steeply peaked roofs
and narrow, cleated gangplanks slant up   10
to storerooms in the gables
for the wheelbarrows to be pushed up and down on.
All is silver: the heavy surface of the sea,
swelling slowly as if considering spilling over,
is opaque, but the silver of the benches,   15
the lobster pots, and masts, scattered
among the wild jagged rocks,

is of an apparent translucence
like the small old buildings with an emerald moss
growing on their shoreward walls.   20
The big fish tubs are completely lined
with layers of beautiful herring scales
and the wheelbarrows are similarly plastered
with creamy iridescent coats of mail,
with small iridescent flies crawling on them.   25
Up on the little slope behind the houses,
set in the sparse bright sprinkle of grass,
is an ancient wooden capstan,[1]
cracked, with two long bleached handles
and some melancholy stains, like dried blood,   30
where the ironwork has rusted.
The old man accepts a Lucky Strike.[2]
He was a friend of my grandfather.
We talk of the decline in the population
and of codfish and herring   35
while he waits for a herring boat to come in.
There are sequins on his vest and on his thumb.
He has scraped the scales, the principal beauty,
from unnumbered fish with that black old knife,
the blade of which is almost worn away.   40

Down at the water's edge, at the place
where they haul up the boats, up the long ramp
descending into the water, thin silver
tree trunks are laid horizontally
across the gray stones, down and down   45
at intervals of four or five feet.

Cold dark deep and absolutely clear,
element bearable to no mortal,
to fish and to seals . . . One seal particularly
I have seen here evening after evening.   50
He was curious about me. He was interested in music;
like me a believer in total immersion,[3]
so I used to sing him Baptist hymns.
I also sang "A Mighty Fortress Is Our God."
He stood up in the water and regarded me   55
steadily, moving his head a little.
Then he would disappear, then suddenly emerge
almost in the same spot, with a sort of shrug
as if it were against his better judgment.
Cold dark deep and absolutely clear,   60
the clear gray icy water . . . Back, behind us,
the dignified tall firs begin.
Bluish, associating with their shadows,
a million Christmas trees stand

---

1. Cylindrical drum around which rope is wound,
used for hauling.

2. Brand of cigarettes.
3. Form of baptism used by Baptists.

waiting for Christmas. The water seems suspended   65
above the rounded gray and blue-gray stones.
I have seen it over and over, the same sea, the same,
slightly, indifferently swinging above the stones,
icily free above the stones,
above the stones and then the world.   70
If you should dip your hand in,
your wrist would ache immediately,
your bones would begin to ache and your hand would burn
as if the water were a transmutation of fire
that feeds on stones and burns with a dark gray flame.   75
If you tasted it, it would first taste bitter,
then briny, then surely burn your tongue.
It is like what we imagine knowledge to be:
dark, salt, clear, moving, utterly free,
drawn from the cold hard mouth   80
of the world, derived from the rocky breasts
forever, flowing and drawn, and since
our knowledge is historical, flowing, and flown.

                                                        1955

Questions of Travel

There are too many waterfalls here; the crowded streams
hurry too rapidly down to the sea,
and the pressure of so many clouds on the mountaintops
makes them spill over the sides in soft slow-motion,
turning to waterfalls under our very eyes.   5
—For if those streaks, those mile-long, shiny, tearstains,
aren't waterfalls yet,
in a quick age or so, as ages go here,
they probably will be.
But if the streams and clouds keep travelling, travelling,   10
the mountains look like the hulls of capsized ships,
slime-hung and barnacled.

Think of the long trip home.
Should we have stayed at home and thought of here?
Where should we be today?   15
Is it right to be watching strangers in a play
in this strangest of theatres?
What childishness is it that while there's a breath of life
in our bodies, we are determined to rush
to see the sun the other way around?   20
The tiniest green hummingbird in the world?
To stare at some inexplicable old stonework,
inexplicable and impenetrable,
at any view,
instantly seen and always, always delightful?   25

Oh, must we dream our dreams
and have them, too?
And have we room
for one more folded sunset, still quite warm?

But surely it would have been a pity   30
not to have seen the trees along this road,
really exaggerated in their beauty,
not to have seen them gesturing
like noble pantomimists, robed in pink.
—Not to have had to stop for gas and heard   35
the sad, two-noted, wooden tune
of disparate wooden clogs
carelessly clacking over
a grease-stained filling-station floor.
(In another country the clogs would all be tested.   40
Each pair there would have identical pitch.)
—A pity not to have heard
the other, less primitive music of the fat brown bird
who sings above the broken gasoline pump
in a bamboo church of Jesuit baroque: 45
three towers, five silver crosses.
—Yes, a pity not to have pondered,
blurr'dly and inconclusively,
on what connection can exist for centuries
between the crudest wooden footwear   50
and, careful and finicky,
the whittled fantasies of wooden cages.
—Never to have studied history in
the weak calligraphy of songbirds' cages.
—And never to have had to listen to rain   55
so much like politicians' speeches:
two hours of unrelenting oratory
and then a sudden golden silence
in which the traveller takes a notebook, writes:

"Is it lack of imagination that makes us come   60
to imagined places, not just stay at home?
Or could Pascal[1] have been not entirely right
about just sitting quietly in one's room?

Continent, city, country, society:
the choice is never wide and never free.   65
And here, or there . . . No. Should we have stayed at home,
wherever that may be?"

                                                                     1965

---

1. French mathematician and philosopher (1623–1662) who said, "Men's misfortunes spring from the single cause that they are unable to stay quietly in one room" (Pensées, trans. J. M. Cohen).

The Armadillo

for Robert Lowell

This is the time of year
when almost every night
the frail, illegal fire balloons appear.
Climbing the mountain height,

rising toward a saint   5
still honored in these parts,
the paper chambers flush and fill with light
that comes and goes, like hearts.

Once up against the sky it's hard
to tell them from the stars—   10
planets, that is—the tinted ones:
Venus going down, or Mars,

or the pale green one. With a wind,
they flare and falter, wobble and toss;
but if it's still they steer between   15
the kite sticks of the Southern Cross,

receding, dwindling, solemnly
and steadily forsaking us,
or, in the downdraft from a peak,
suddenly turning dangerous.   20

Last night another big one fell.
It splattered like an egg of fire
against the cliff behind the house.
The flame ran down. We saw the pair

of owls who nest there flying up   25
and up, their whirling black-and-white
stained bright pink underneath, until
they shrieked up out of sight.

The ancient owls' nest must have burned.
Hastily, all alone,   30
a glistening armadillo left the scene,
rose-flecked, head down, tail down,

and then a baby rabbit jumped out,
short-eared, to our surprise.
So soft!—a handful of intangible ash   35
with fixed, ignited eyes.

Too pretty, dreamlike mimicry!
O falling fire and piercing cry

and panic, and a weak mailed fist[2]
clenched ignorant against the sky!   40

1965

Sestina[1]

September rain falls on the house.
In the failing light, the old grandmother
sits in the kitchen with the child
beside the Little Marvel Stove,
reading the jokes from the almanac,   5
laughing and talking to hide her tears.

She thinks that her equinoctial tears
and the rain that beats on the roof of the house
were both foretold by the almanac,
but only known to a grandmother.   10
The iron kettle sings on the stove.
She cuts some bread and says to the child,

It's time for tea now; but the child
is watching the teakettle's small hard tears
dance like mad on the hot black stove,   15
the way the rain must dance on the house.
Tidying up, the old grandmother
hangs up the clever almanac

on its string. Birdlike, the almanac
hovers half open above the child,   20
hovers above the old grandmother
and her teacup full of dark brown tears.
She shivers and says she thinks the house
feels chilly, and puts more wood in the stove.

It was to be, says the Marvel Stove.   25
I know what I know, says the almanac.
With crayons the child draws a rigid house
and a winding pathway. Then the child
puts in a man with buttons like tears
and shows it proudly to the grandmother.   30

But secretly, while the grandmother
busies herself about the stove,
the little moons fall down like tears
from between the pages of the almanac

2. The armadillo, curled tight. It is protected against everything but fire.
1. A fixed verse form in which the end words of the first six-line stanza must be used at the ends of the lines in the next stanza in a rotating order; the final three lines must contain all six words.

into the flower bed the child   35
has carefully placed in the front of the house.

Time to plant tears, says the almanac.
The grandmother sings to the marvellous stove
and the child draws another inscrutable house.

1965

In the Waiting Room

In Worcester, Massachusetts,
I went with Aunt Consuelo
to keep her dentist's appointment
and sat and waited for her
in the dentist's waiting room.   5
It was winter. It got dark
early. The waiting room
was full of grown-up people,
arctics and overcoats,
lamps and magazines.   10
My aunt was inside
what seemed like a long time
and while I waited I read
the *National Geographic*
(I could read) and carefully   15
studied the photographs:
the inside of a volcano,
black, and full of ashes;
then it was spilling over
in rivulets of fire.   20
Osa and Martin Johnson[1]
dressed in riding breeches,
laced boots, and pith helmets.
A dead man slung on a pole
—"Long Pig,"[2] the caption said.   25
Babies with pointed heads
wound round and round with string;
black, naked women with necks
wound round and round with wire
like the necks of light bulbs.   30
Their breasts were horrifying.
I read it right straight through.
I was too shy to stop.
And then I looked at the cover:
the yellow margins, the date.   35

Suddenly, from inside,
came an *oh!* of pain
—Aunt Consuelo's voice—

1. Famous explorers and travel writers.
2. Polynesian cannibals' name for the human carcass.

not very loud or long.
I wasn't at all surprised;   40
even then I knew she was
a foolish, timid woman.
I might have been embarrassed,
but wasn't. What took me
completely by surprise   45
was that it was *me*:
my voice, in my mouth.
Without thinking at all
I was my foolish aunt,
I—we—were falling, falling,   50
our eyes glued to the cover
of the *National Geographic*,
February, 1918.

I said to myself: three days
and you'll be seven years old.   55
I was saying it to stop
the sensation of falling off
the round, turning world
into cold, blue-black space.
But I felt: you are an *I*,   60
you are an *Elizabeth*,
you are one of *them*.
Why should you be one, too?
I scarcely dared to look.
to see what it was I was.   65
I gave a sidelong glance
—I couldn't look any higher—
at shadowy gray knees,
trousers and skirts and boots
and different pairs of hands   70
lying under the lamps.
I knew that nothing stranger
had ever happened, that nothing
stranger could ever happen.
Why should I be my aunt,   75
or me, or anyone?
What similarities—
boots, hands, the family voice
I felt in my throat, or even
the *National Geographic*   80
and those awful hanging breasts—
held us all together
or made us all just one?
How—I didn't know any
word for it—how "unlikely" . . .   85
How had I come to be here,
like them, and overhear
a cry of pain that could have
got loud and worse but hadn't?

The waiting room was bright   90
and too hot. It was sliding
beneath a big black wave,
another, and another.

Then I was back in it.
The War was on. Outside,   95
in Worcester, Massachusetts,
were night and slush and cold,
and it was still the fifth
of February, 1918.

                                        1976

The Moose

for Grace Bulmer Bowers

From narrow provinces
of fish and bread and tea,
home of the long tides
where the bay leaves the sea
twice a day and takes   5
the herrings long rides,

where if the river
enters or retreats
in a wall of brown foam
depends on if it meets   10
the bay coming in,
the bay not at home;

where, silted red,
sometimes the sun sets
facing a red sea,   15
and others, veins the flats'
lavender, rich mud
in burning rivulets;

on red, gravelly roads,
down rows of sugar maples,   20
past clapboard farmhouses
and neat, clapboard churches,
bleached, ridged as clamshells,
past twin silver birches,

through late afternoon   25
a bus journeys west,
the windshield flashing pink,
pink glancing off of metal,
brushing the dented flank
of blue, beat-up enamel;   30

down hollows, up rises,
and waits, patient, while
a lone traveller gives
kisses and embraces
to seven relatives   35
and a collie supervises.

Goodbye to the elms,
to the farm, to the dog.
The bus starts. The light
grows richer; the fog,   40
shifting, salty, thin,
comes closing in.

Its cold, round crystals
form and slide and settle
in the white hens' feathers,   45
in gray glazed cabbages,
on the cabbage roses
and lupins like apostles;

the sweet peas cling
to their wet white string   50
on the whitewashed fences;
bumblebees creep
inside the foxgloves,
and evening commences.

One stop at Bass River.   55
Then the Economies—
Lower, Middle, Upper;
Five Islands, Five Houses,[1]
where a woman shakes a tablecloth
out after supper.   60

A pale flickering. Gone.
The Tantramar marshes
and the smell of salt hay.
An iron bridge trembles
and a loose plank rattles   65
but doesn't give way.

On the left, a red light
swims through the dark:
a ship's port lantern.
Two rubber boots show,   70
illuminated, solemn.
A dog gives one bark.

1. These are small towns and villages in Nova Scotia, near Halifax.

A woman climbs in
with two market bags,
brisk, freckled, elderly.   75
"A grand night. Yes, sir,
all the way to Boston."
She regards us amicably.

Moonlight as we enter
the New Brunswick woods,   80
hairy, scratchy, splintery;
moonlight and mist
caught in them like lamb's wool
on bushes in a pasture.

The passengers lie back.   85
Snores. Some long sighs.
A dreamy divagation
begins in the night,
a gentle, auditory,
slow hallucination. . . .   90

In the creakings and noises,
an old conversation
—not concerning us,
but recognizable, somewhere,
back in the bus: 95
Grandparents' voices

uninterruptedly
talking, in Eternity:
names being mentioned,
things cleared up finally;   100
what he said, what she said,
who got pensioned;

deaths, deaths and sicknesses;
the year he remarried;
the year (something) happened.   105
She died in childbirth.
That was the son lost
when the schooner foundered.

He took to drink. Yes.
She went to the bad.   110
When Amos began to pray
even in the store and
finally the family had
to put him away.

"Yes . . ." that peculiar   115
affirmative. "Yes . . ."
A sharp, indrawn breath,

half groan, half acceptance,
that means "Life's like that.
We know *it* (also death)."   120

Talking the way they talked
in the old featherbed,
peacefully, on and on,
dim lamplight in the hall,
down in the kitchen, the dog   125
tucked in her shawl.

Now, it's all right now
even to fall asleep
just as on all those nights.
—Suddenly the bus driver   130
stops with a jolt,
turns off his lights.

A moose has come out of
the impenetrable wood
and stands there, looms, rather,   135
in the middle of the road.
It approaches; it sniffs at
the bus's hot hood.

Towering, antlerless,
high as a church,   140
homely as a house
(or, safe as houses).
A man's voice assures us
"Perfectly harmless . . ."

Some of the passengers   145
exclaim in whispers,
childishly, softly,
"Sure are big creatures."
"It's awful plain."
"Look! It's a she!"   150

Taking her time,
she looks the bus over,
grand, otherworldly.
Why, why do we feel
(we all feel) this sweet   155
sensation of joy?

"Curious creatures,"
says our quiet driver,
rolling his *r*'s.
"Look at that, would you."   160
Then he shifts gears.
For a moment longer,

by craning backward,
the moose can be seen
on the moonlit macadam;   165
then there's a dim
smell of moose, an acrid
smell of gasoline.

1976

One Art

The art of losing isn't hard to master;
so many things seem filled with the intent
to be lost that their loss is no disaster.

Lose something every day. Accept the fluster
of lost door keys, the hour badly spent.   5
The art of losing isn't hard to master.

Then practice losing farther, losing faster:
places, and names, and where it was you meant
to travel. None of these will bring disaster.

I lost my mother's watch. And look! my last, or   10
next-to-last, of three loved houses went.
The art of losing isn't hard to master.

I lost two cities, lovely ones. And, vaster,
some realms I owned, two rivers, a continent.
I miss them, but it wasn't a disaster.   15

—Even losing you (the joking voice, a gesture
I love) I shan't have lied. It's evident
the art of losing's not too hard to master
though it may look like (*Write* it!) like disaster.

1976

ROBERT HAYDEN
1913–1980

"Hayden is by far the best chronicler and rememberer of the African American heritage in these Americas that I know of," the poet Michael Harper, whose own sense of history is indebted to Robert Hayden's work, has said. Hayden's poems save what has vanished, what has been lost to standard histories, like a 1920s prizefighter from the Midwest ("Free Fantasia: Tiger Flowers"), or a miner trapped in Cystal Cave ("Beginnings, V"). He records the loss of what others never noticed as missing, and in their recovery he discovers a significance in the passing moment, the passed-over figure, the inarticulate gesture, which lasts through time. Always, in his words, "opposed to the chauvinistic and the doctrinaire" in art, he cherished the freedom of the poet to write about whatever seized the imagination. But his imagination was in its nature elegiac and historical. As he remembers and re-creates the African American heritage, he speaks to the struggles of the individual spirit for freedom and to painful self-divisions people of many times and places know. But if the circumstances he confronts in his poems are often harsh, his work captures the energy and joyfulness that make survival possible.

Born in Detroit, Michigan, Hayden grew up in a poor neighborhood called by its inhabitants, with affectionate irony, "Paradise Valley." His powerful sequence *Elegies for Paradise Valley* (1978) resurrects the neighborhood in its racial and ethnic mix. Memory for Hayden is an act of love that leads to self-awareness; in this sequence and in poems like "Those Winter Sundays," he writes about his own past, confronts its pain, and preserves its sustaining moments of happiness.

Hayden had a deep understanding of conflicts that divide the self. His family history gave him an early acquaintance with such self-division: his parents' marriage ended when he was young, and his mother left him in the care of foster parents (whose surname he adopted) when she left Detroit to look for work. He remained with the Haydens although his mother returned to Detroit when he was a teenager and lived for a period with his foster family until conflict arose between her and his foster mother. "I lived in the midst of so much turmoil all the time I didn't know if I loved or hated," he once said. As an African American and as a poet Hayden also lived between worlds. He courageously maintained his sense of vocation through years of critical neglect and amid the demands of full-time teaching at Fisk University from 1946 to 1968. He published his first book, *Heart-Shape in the Dust*, in 1940, but his mature work did not appear in quantity until his volume *Ballad of Remembrance* (1962). At the same time, his belief that the poet should not be restricted by any set of themes, racial or otherwise, and the highly formal quality of his work led to criticism on the part of some young African American writers in the 1960s. But Hayden never abandoned his belief in the power of art to speak universally. In an interview conducted in 1974, he told Dennis Gendron of rereading Yeats's poem "Easter 1916" in the wake of the riots in Detroit—"that is the kind of poetry I want to write," he said, in admiration of the ways Yeats conceived a particular historical and political moment so that it speaks across time and place.

In fact, Hayden wrote that kind of poetry. His most famous poem, "Middle Passage," demonstrates his transfiguring imagination and the knowledge of historical documents, which began early in his career. In 1936, leaving college because of increasingly difficult economic conditions, Hayden joined the Federal Writers Project of the Works Progress Administration and for two years researched the history of abolition movements and the Underground Railroad in Michigan. "Middle Passage" is a collage of accounts of the slave ships that transported men and women from Africa into slavery in the New World. Through the multiple voices in the poem, Hayden lets the accounts of those who participated in (and profited from) the slave trade reveal the evidence of their own damnation. The blindness that attacks one of the ships becomes a symbol of the devastating suffering of those transported into slavery and of the moral blindness everywhere evident in the traders' accounts. The technique of collage allows Hayden to suggest the fragmentation of the story; the silences in the poem evoke the missing voices of those who suffered and died on the voyages or in the intolerable conditions of slavery. At the heart of the poem is the account of a rebellion led by one of the slaves (Cinquez) on the ship *The Amistad*. Cinquez is one of several figures in Hayden's poems who dramatize "The deep immortal human wish / the timeless will" ("Middle Passage") that for Hayden is the indomitable struggle for freedom. This "timeless will" and struggle also appear in his poems about Harriet Tubman ("Runagate Runagate"),

Nat Turner, Frederick Douglass, Phillis Wheatley, and the later figures of Paul Robeson and Bessie Smith.

Hayden's experiment with collage technique in "Middle Passage" connects him to modernist poets like T. S. Eliot and William Carlos Williams and to an African American tradition acutely aware of the power of voice. He continued to experiment with poetic form and with the creation of different voices throughout his life, and although some of these poems are not successful, he was always engaged with testing the possibilities of craft, with forging a language to express what he knew and felt. His sequences *Beginnings* and *Elegies for Paradise Valley* demonstrate his formal originality, as does his late poem "American Journal," with its long lines and its approximation to prose. Hayden loved language and was unafraid to be lushly descriptive as well as to be precisely imagistic. His work summons us to notice the world as we had not before and offers us candor, clearsightedness, and a transforming gaiety.

From 1968 until his death, Hayden was professor of English at the University of Michigan at Ann Arbor. In 1976 he became the first African American to be appointed poetry consultant to the Library of Congress.

Middle Passage[1]

I

Jesús, Estrella, Esperanza, Mercy[2]

    Sails flashing to the wind like weapons,
    sharks following the moans the fever and the dying;
    horror the corposant and compass rose.[3]

Middle Passage: 5
        voyage through death
                to life upon these shores.

    "10 April 1800—
    Blacks rebellious. Crew uneasy. Our linguist says
    their moaning is a prayer for death,   10
    ours and their own. Some try to starve themselves.
    Lost three this morning leaped with crazy laughter
    to the waiting sharks, sang as they went under."

Desire, Adventure, Tartar, Ann:

    Standing to America, bringing home   15
    black gold, black ivory, black seed.

        Deep in the festering hold thy father lies,
        of his bones New England pews are made,
        those are altar lights that were his eyes.[4]

1. Main route for the slave trade in the Atlantic between Africa and the West Indies.
2. Names of slave ships. "*Esperanza*": hope (Spanish).
3. Circle printed on a map showing compass directions. "Corposant": a fiery luminousness that can appear on the decks of ships during electrical storms.
4. "Full fathom five thy father lies; / Of his bones are coral made; / Those are pearls that were his eyes" (Shakespeare's *Tempest* 1.2.400–02). The sprite Ariel is singing about the supposed death by water of the king of Naples.

Jesus   Saviour   Pilot   Me   20
Over   Life's   Tempestuous   Sea[5]

We pray that Thou wilt grant, O Lord,
safe passage to our vessels bringing
heathen souls unto Thy chastening.

Jesus   Saviour   25

     "8 bells. I cannot sleep, for I am sick
     with fear, but writing eases fear a little
     since still my eyes can see these words take shape
     upon the page & so I write, as one
     would turn to exorcism. 4 days scudding,   30
     but now the sea is calm again. Misfortune
     follows in our wake like sharks (our grinning
     tutelary gods). Which one of us
     has killed an albatross?[6] A plague among
     our blacks—Ophthalmia: blindness—& we   35
     have jettisoned the blind to no avail.
     It spreads, the terrifying sickness spreads.
     Its claws have scratched sight from the Capt.'s eyes
     & there is blindness in the fo'c'sle[7]
     & we must sail 3 weeks before we come   40
     to port."

       What port awaits us, Davy Jones'
       or home? I've heard of slavers drifting, drifting,
       playthings of wind and storm and chance, their crews
       gone blind, the jungle hatred   45
       crawling up on deck.

Thou   Who   Walked   On   Galilee

     "Deponent further sayeth *The Bella J*
     left the Guinea Coast
     with cargo of five hundred blacks and odd   50
     for the barracoons[8] of Florida:

     "That there was hardly room 'tween-decks for half
     the sweltering cattle stowed spoon-fashion there;
     that some went mad of thirst and tore their flesh
     and sucked the blood: 55

     "That Crew and Captain lusted with the comeliest
     of the savage girls kept naked in the cabins;
     that there was one they called The Guinea Rose
     and they cast lots and fought to lie with her:

---

5. A Protestant hymn.
6. A bird of good omen; to kill one is an unlucky
and impious act (as in Samuel Taylor Coleridge's
Rime of the Ancient Mariner).

7. Short for forecastle, the place in a ship where
sailors are quartered.
8. Barracks or enclosures for slaves.

"That when the Bo's'n piped all hands,[9] the flames   60
spreading from starboard already were beyond
control, the negroes howling and their chains
entangled with the flames:

"That the burning blacks could not be reached,
that the Crew abandoned ship,   65
leaving their shrieking negresses behind,
that the Captain perished drunken with the wenches:

"Further Deponent sayeth not."

Pilot   Oh   Pilot   Me

II

Aye, lad, and I have seen those factories,   70
Gambia, Rio Pongo, Calabar;[1]
have watched the artful mongos[2] baiting traps
of war wherein the victor and the vanquished

Were caught as prizes for our barracoons.
Have seen the nigger kings whose vanity   75
and greed turned wild black hides of Fellatah,
Mandingo, Ibo, Kru[3] to gold for us.

And there was one—King Anthracite we named him—
fetish face beneath French parasols
of brass and orange velvet, impudent mouth   80
whose cups were carven skulls of enemies:

He'd honor us with drum and feast and conjo[4]
and palm-oil-glistening wenches deft in love,
and for tin crowns that shone with paste,
red calico and German-silver trinkets   85

Would have the drums talk war and send
his warriors to burn the sleeping villages
and kill the sick and old and lead the young
in coffles[5] to our factories.

Twenty years a trader, twenty years,   90
for there was wealth aplenty to be harvested
from those black fields, and I'd be trading still
but for the fevers melting down my bones.

---

9. I.e., when the boatswain (petty officer aboard a
ship) signaled to all the crew on deck.
1. A city in southeast Nigeria. Gambia is a river
and nation in west Africa. Rio Pongo is a water-
course, dry for most of the year, in east Africa.

2. I.e., Africans.
3. African tribes.
4. Dance.
5. Train of slaves fastened together.

III

Shuttles in the rocking loom of history,
the dark ships move, the dark ships move,   95
their bright ironical names
like jests of kindness on a murderer's mouth;
plough through thrashing glister toward
fata morgana's lucent melting shore,
weave toward New World littorals[6] that are   100
mirage and myth and actual shore.

Voyage through death,
                    voyage whose chartings are unlove.

A charnel stench, effluvium of living death
spreads outward from the hold,   105
where the living and the dead, the horribly dying,
lie interlocked, lie foul with blood and excrement.

> *Deep in the festering hold thy father lies,*
> *the corpse of mercy rots with him,*
> *rats eat love's rotten gelid eyes.*   110

But, oh, the living look at you
with human eyes whose suffering accuses you,
whose hatred reaches through the swill of dark
to strike you like a leper's claw.

You cannot stare that hatred down   115
or chain the fear that stalks the watches
and breathes on you its fetid scorching breath;
cannot kill the deep immortal human wish,
the timeless will.

> "But for the storm that flung up barriers   120
> of wind and wave, *The Amistad*,[7] señores,
> would have reached the port of Príncipe in two,
> three days at most; but for the storm we should
> have been prepared for what befell.
> Swift as the puma's leap it came. There was   125
> that interval of moonless calm filled only
> with the water's and the rigging's usual sounds,
> then sudden movement, blows and snarling cries
> and they had fallen on us with machete
> and marlinspike. It was as though the very   130
> air, the night itself were striking us.
> Exhausted by the rigors of the storm,
> we were no match for them. Our men went down
> before the murderous Africans. Our loyal
> Celestino ran from below with gun   135

---

6. Coastal regions. "Fata morgana": mirage.   illegally obtained slaves out of Havana, Cuba, in
7. Friendship; a Spanish ship carrying fifty-three   July 1839.

and lantern and I saw, before the cane-
knife's wounding flash, Cinquez,
that surly brute who calls himself a prince,
directing, urging on the ghastly work.[8]
He hacked the poor mulatto down, and then   140
he turned on me. The decks were slippery
when daylight finally came. It sickens me
to think of what I saw, of how these apes
threw overboard the butchered bodies of
our men, true Christians all, like so much jetsam.   145
Enough, enough. The rest is quickly told:
Cinquez was forced to spare the two of us
you see to steer the ship to Africa,
and we like phantoms doomed to rove the sea
voyaged east by day and west by night,   150
deceiving them, hoping for rescue,
prisoners on our own vessel, till
at length we drifted to the shores of this
your land, America, where we were freed
from our unspeakable misery. Now we   155
demand, good sirs, the extradition of
Cinquez and his accomplices to La
Havana.[9] And it distresses us to know
there are so many here who seem inclined
to justify the mutiny of these blacks.   160
We find it paradoxical indeed
that you whose wealth, whose tree of liberty
are rooted in the labor of your slaves
should suffer the august John Quincy Adams
to speak with so much passion of the right   165
of chattel slaves to kill their lawful masters
and with his Roman rhetoric weave a hero's
garland for Cinquez.[1] I tell you that
we are determined to return to Cuba
with our slaves and there see justice done. Cinquez—   170
or let us say 'the Prince'—Cinquez shall die."

The deep immortal human wish,
the timeless will:

Cinquez its deathless primaveral image,
life that transfigures many lives.   175

Voyage through death
                    to life upon these shores.

                                                           1962

---

8. During the mutiny the Africans, led by a man
called Cinqué, or Cinquez, killed the captain, his
slave Celestino, and the mate, but spared the two
slave owners.
9. *The Amistad* reached Long Island Sound after
two months, where it was detained by the American ship *Washington,* the slaves were imprisoned,

and the owners were freed. The owners began lit-
igation to force the slaves' return to Havana to be
tried for murder.
1. The case reached the Supreme Court in 1841;
the Africans were defended by former president
John Quincy Adams, and the court released the
thirty-seven survivors to return to Africa.

Homage to the Empress of the Blues[1]

Because there was a man somewhere in a candystripe silk shirt,
gracile and dangerous as a jaguar and because a woman moaned for him
in sixty-watt gloom and mourned him Faithless Love
Twotiming Love Oh Love Oh Careless Aggravating Love,

    She came out on the stage in yards of pearls, emerging like   5
    a favorite scenic view, flashed her golden smile and sang.

Because grey laths began somewhere to show from underneath
torn hurdygurdy[2] lithographs of dollfaced heaven;
and because there were those who feared alarming fists of snow
on the door and those who feared the riot-squad of statistics,   10

    She came out on the stage in ostrich feathers, beaded satin,
    and shone that smile on us and sang.

                             1962

Those Winter Sundays

    Sundays too my father got up early
    and put his clothes on in the blueblack cold,
    then with cracked hands that ached
    from labor in the weekday weather made
    banked fires blaze. No one ever thanked him.   5

    I'd wake and hear the cold splintering, breaking.
    When the rooms were warm, he'd call,
    and slowly I would rise and dress,
    fearing the chronic angers of that house,

    Speaking indifferently to him,   10
    who had driven out the cold
    and polished my good shoes as well.
    What did I know, what did I know
    of love's austere and lonely offices?

                             1962

1. Bessie Smith (1895–1937), one of the greatest American blues singers. Her flamboyant style, which grew out of the black vaudeville tradition, made her popular in the 1920s.
2. A disreputable kind of dance hall. "Laths": the strips of wood that form a backing for plaster.

The Night-Blooming Cereus

And so for nights
we waited, hoping to see
the heavy bud
    break into flower.

    On its neck-like tube 5
hooking down from the edge
of the leaf-branch
    nearly to the floor,

    the bud packed
tight with its miracle swayed 10
stiffly on breaths
    of air, moved

    as though impelled
by stirrings within itself.
It repelled as much 15
    as it fascinated me

    sometimes—snake,
eyeless bird head,
beak that would gape
    with grotesque life-squawk. 20

    But you, my dear,
conceded less to the bizarre
than to the imminence
    of bloom. Yet we agreed

    we ought 25
to celebrate the blossom,
paint ourselves, dance
    in honor of

    archaic mysteries
when it appeared. Meanwhile 30
we waited, aware
    of rigorous design.

    Backster's
polygraph,[1] I thought,
would have shown 35
    (as clearly as it had

    a philodendron's
fear) tribal sentience

1. Lie detector.

in the cactus, focused
    energy of will.   40

That belling of
tropic perfume—that
signalling
    not meant for us;

    the darkness   45
cloyed with summoning
fragrance. We dropped
    trivial tasks

    and marvelling
beheld at last the achieved   50
flower. Its moonlight
    petals were

    still unfold-
ing, the spike fringe of the outer
perianth[2] recessing   55
    as we watched.

    Lunar presence,
foredoomed, already dying,
it charged the room
    with plangency   60

    older than human
cries, ancient as prayers
invoking Osiris, Krishna,
    Tezcátlipóca.[3]

    We spoke   65
in whispers when
we spoke
    at all . . .

                                     1972

Free Fantasia: Tiger Flowers[1]

for Michael

The sporting people
along St. Antoine—
that scufflers'

---

2. A flower's external envelope.
3. Major Egyptian, Hindu, and Aztec gods, respectively.

1. A midwestern boxer who in 1926 became the first African American middleweight champion.

paradise of ironies—
   bet salty money   5
on his righteous
   hook and jab.

I was a boy then, running
(unbeknownst to Pa)
errands for Miss Jackie   10
and Stack-o'-Diamonds' Eula Mae.
. . . Their perfumes,
rouged Egyptian faces.
   Their pianolas jazzing.

O Creole babies,   15
Dixie odalisques,[2]
speeding through cutglass
dark to see the macho angel
   trick you'd never
turn, his bluesteel prowess   20
   in the ring.

Hardshell believers
amen'd the wreck
as God A'mighty's
will. I'd thought   25
   such gaiety could not
die. Nor could our
   elegant avenger.

The Virgin Forest
by Rousseau[3]—   30
its psychedelic flowers
towering, its deathless
   dark dream figure
death the leopard
   claws—I choose it   35
now as elegy
   for Tiger Flowers.

1975

---

2. Female slaves or concubines in a harem.
3. Henri Rousseau (1844–1910), French painter known for jungle scenes and exotic colors.

RANDALL JARRELL
1914–1965

"Monstrously knowing and monstrously innocent. . . . A Wordsworth with the obsession of a Lewis Carroll"—so Robert Lowell once described his friend and fellow poet Randall Jarrell. Jarrell was teacher and critic as well as poet, and for many writers of his generation—Lowell, Delmore Schwartz, and John Berryman among them—Jarrell was the critic whose taste was most unerring, who seemed to know instantly what was genuine and what was not. An extraordinary teacher, he loved the activity, both in and out of the classroom; "the gods who had taken away the poet's audience had given him students," he once said. The novelist Peter Taylor recalls that when he came to Vanderbilt University as a freshman in the mid-1930s, Jarrell, then a graduate student, had already turned the literary students into disciples; he held court discussing Chekhov on the sidelines of touch football games. For all his brilliance Jarrell was, at heart, democratic. Believing that poetry belongs to every life, his teaching, his literary criticism, and his poetry aimed to recapture and reeducate a general audience lost to poetry in an age of specialization. Jarrell's interests were democratic as well; his lifelong fascination with popular culture may have originated in a childhood spent in Long Beach, California, and a year spent with grandparents in Hollywood. Witty and incisive, Jarrell could be intimidating; at the same time he remained deeply in touch with childhood's mystery and enchantment. It was as if, Hannah Arendt once said, he "had emerged from the enchanted forests." He loved fairy tales, translated a number of them, and wrote several books for children, among them *The Bat-Poet*. The childlike quality of the person informs Jarrell's poems as well; he is unembarrassed by the adult heart still in thrall to childhood's wishes.

Jarrell was born in Nashville, Tennessee, but spent much of his childhood in California. When his parents divorced, the child, then eleven, remained for a year with his grandparents, then returned to live with his mother in Nashville. He majored in psychology at Vanderbilt and stayed on there to do graduate work in English. In 1937 he left Nashville to teach at Kenyon College (Gambier, Ohio) at the invitation of his old Vanderbilt professor John Crowe Ransom, the New Critic and Fugitive poet. From that time on, Jarrell almost always had some connection with a university: after Kenyon, the University of Texas, Sarah Lawrence College, and from 1947 until his death, the Women's College of the University of North Carolina at Greensboro. But, as his novel *Pictures from an Institution* (1954) with its mixed satiric and tender views of academic life suggests, he was never satisfied with a cloistered education. As poetry editor of the *Nation* (1946), and then in a series of essays and reviews collected as *Poetry and the Age* (1953), he introduced readers to the work of his contemporaries—Elizabeth Bishop, Robert Lowell, John Berryman, the William Carlos Williams of *Paterson*—and influentially reassessed the reputations of Whitman and Robert Frost.

Among the poets who emerged after World War II, Jarrell stands out for his colloquial plainness. While others—Richard Wilbur and the early Robert Lowell, for example—were writing highly structured poems with complicated imagery, Jarrell's work feels and sounds close to what he calls in one poem the "dailiness of life" ("Well Water"). He is master of the heartbreak of everyday and identifies with ordinary forms of loneliness. Jarrell's gift of imaginative sympathy appears in the treatment of soldiers in his war poems, the strongest to come out of World War II. He had been trained as an army air force pilot and after that as a control operator, and he had a sense of the war's special casualties. With their understanding of soldiers as both destructive and innocent at the same time, these poems make his volumes *Little Friend, Little Friend* (1945) and *Losses* (1948) powerful and moving. Jarrell also empathized with the dreams, loneliness, and disappointments of women, whose perspective he often adopted, as in the title poem of his collection *The Woman at the Washington Zoo* (1960) and his poem "Next Day."

Against the blasted or unrealized possibilities of adult life, Jarrell often poised the rich mysteries of childhood. The title poem of his last book, *The Lost World* (1965), looks back to his Los Angeles playtime, the movie sets and plaster dinosaurs and pterodactyls against whose eternal gay presence he measures his own aging. The poem has Jarrell's characteristic sense of loss but also his capacity for a mysterious happiness, which animates the poem even as he holds "nothing" in his hands.

Jarrell suffered a nervous breakdown in February 1965, but returned to teaching that fall. In October he was struck down by a car and died. His *Complete Poems* were published posthumously (1969), as were a translation of Goethe's *Faust*, Part I, in preparation at his death, and two books of essays, *The Third Book of Criticism* (1969) and *Kipling, Auden & Co.* (1980).

90 North[1]

At home, in my flannel gown, like a bear to its floe,
I clambered to bed; up the globe's impossible sides
I sailed all night—till at last, with my black beard,
My furs and my dogs, I stood at the northern pole.

There in the childish night my companions lay frozen,   5
The stiff furs knocked at my starveling throat,
And I gave my great sigh: the flakes came huddling,
Were they really my end? In the darkness I turned to my rest.

—Here, the flag snaps in the glare and silence
Of the unbroken ice. I stand here,   10
The dogs bark, my beard is black, and I stare
At the North Pole . . .
              And now what? Why, go back.

Turn as I please, my step is to the south.
The world—my world spins on this final point   15
Of cold and wretchedness: all lines, all winds
End in this whirlpool I at last discover.

And it is meaningless. In the child's bed
After the night's voyage, in that warm world
Where people work and suffer for the end   20
That crowns the pain—in that Cloud-Cuckoo-Land[2]

I reached my North and it had meaning.
Here at the actual pole of my existence,
Where all that I have done is meaningless,
Where I die or live by accident alone—   25

Where, living or dying, I am still alone;
Here where North, the night, the berg of death

---

1. The latitude of the North Pole.
2. A fantasy world; in Aristophanes' comedy *The* *Birds* (414 B.C.E.), an imaginary city the cuckoos build in the sky.

Crowd me out of the ignorant darkness,
I see at last that all the knowledge

I wrung from the darkness—that the darkness flung me—   30
Is worthless as ignorance: nothing comes from nothing,
The darkness from the darkness. Pain comes from the darkness
And we call it wisdom. It is pain.

1942

The Death of the Ball Turret Gunner[1]

From my mother's sleep I fell into the State,
And I hunched in its belly till my wet fur froze.
Six miles from earth, loosed from its dream of life,
I woke to black flak[2] and the nightmare fighters.
When I died they washed me out of the turret with a hose.

1945

Second Air Force

Far off, above the plain the summer dries,
The great loops of the hangars sway like hills.
Buses and weariness and loss, the nodding soldiers
Are wire, the bare frame building, and a pass
To what was hers; her head hides his square patch   5
And she thinks heavily: My son is grown.
She sees a world: sand roads, tar-paper barracks,
The bubbling asphalt of the runways, sage,
The dunes rising to the interminable ranges,
The dim flights moving over clouds like clouds.   10
The armorers in their patched faded green,
Sweat-stiffened, banded with brass cartridges,
Walk to the line; their Fortresses,[1] all tail,
Stand wrong and flimsy on their skinny legs,
And the crews climb to them clumsily as bears.   15
The head withdraws into its hatch (a boy's),
The engines rise to their blind laboring roar,
And the green, made beasts run home to air.

1. A ball turret was a plexiglass sphere set into the belly of a B-17 or B-24 [bomber], and inhabited by two .50 caliber machine-guns and one man, a short, small man. When this gunner tracked with his machine-guns a fighter attacking his bomber from below, he revolved with the turret; hunched upside-down in his little sphere, he looked like the foetus in the womb. The fighters which attacked him were armed with cannon firing explosive shells. The hose was a steam hose [Jarrell's note].
2. Antiaircraft fire.
1. Flying Fortresses, a type of bomber in World War II.

Now in each aspect death is pure.
(At twilight they wink over men like stars   20
And hour by hour, through the night, some see
The great lights floating in—from Mars, from Mars.)
How emptily the watchers see them gone.

They go, there is silence; the woman and her son
Stand in the forest of the shadows, and the light   25
Washes them like water. In the long-sunken city
Of evening, the sunlight stills like sleep
The faint wonder of the drowned; in the evening,
In the last dreaming light, so fresh, so old,
The soldiers pass like beasts, unquestioning,   30
And the watcher for an instant understands
What there is then no need to understand;
But she wakes from her knowledge, and her stare,
A shadow now, moves emptily among
The shadows learning in their shadowy fields   35
The empty missions.
                        Remembering,
She hears the bomber calling, *Little Friend!*[2]
To the fighter hanging in the hostile sky,
And sees the ragged flame eat, rib by rib,   40
Along the metal of the wing into her heart:
The lives stream out, blossom, and float steadily
To the flames of the earth, the flames
That burn like stars above the lands of men.

She saves from the twilight that takes everything   45
A squadron shipping, in its last parade—
Its dogs run by it, barking at the band—
A gunner walking to his barracks, half-asleep,
Starting at something, stumbling (above, invisible,
The crews in the steady winter of the sky   50
Tremble in their wired fur); and feels for them
The love of life for life. The hopeful cells
Heavy with someone else's death, cold carriers
Of someone else's victory, grope past their lives
Into her own bewilderment: The years meant *this?*   55

But for them the bombers answer everything.

                                                                    1945

<hr/>

2. In "Second Air Force" the woman visiting her son remembers what she has read on the front page of her newspaper the week before, a conversation between a bomber, in flames over Germany, and one of the fighters protecting it: "Then I heard the bomber call me in: 'Little Friend, Little Friend, I got two engines on fire. Can you see me, Little Friend?' I said, 'I'm crossing right over you. Let's go home' " [Jarrell's note].

Next Day

Moving from Cheer to Joy, from Joy to All,
I take a box
And add it to my wild rice, my Cornish game hens.
The slacked or shorted, basketed, identical
Food-gathering flocks   5
Are selves I overlook. Wisdom, said William James,[1]

Is learning what to overlook. And I am wise
If that is wisdom.
Yet somehow, as I buy All from these shelves
And the boy takes it to my station wagon,   10
What I've become
Troubles me even if I shut my eyes.

When I was young and miserable and pretty
And poor, I'd wish
What all girls wish: to have a husband,   15
A house and children. Now that I'm old, my wish
Is womanish:
That the boy putting groceries in my car

See me. It bewilders me he doesn't see me.
For so many years   20
I was good enough to eat: the world looked at me
And its mouth watered. How often they have undressed me,
The eyes of strangers!
And, holding their flesh within my flesh, their vile

Imaginings within my imagining,   25
I too have taken
The chance of life. Now the boy pats my dog
And we start home. Now I am good.
The last mistaken,
Ecstatic, accidental bliss, the blind   30

Happiness that, bursting, leaves upon the palm
Some soap and water—
It was so long ago, back in some Gay
Twenties, Nineties, I don't know . . . Today I miss
My lovely daughter   35
Away at school, my sons away at school,

My husband away at work—I wish for them.
The dog, the maid,
And I go through the sure unvarying days
At home in them. As I look at my life,   40
I am afraid
Only that it will change, as I am changing:

1. From *Principles of Psychology,* by the American philosopher William James (1842–1910).

I am afraid, this morning, of my face.
It looks at me
From the rear-view mirror, with the eyes I hate,　　　　45
The smile I hate. Its plain, lined look
Of gray discovery
Repeats to me: "You're old." That's all, I'm old.

And yet I'm afraid, as I was at the funeral
I went to yesterday.　　　　50
My friend's cold made-up face, granite among its flowers,
Her undressed, operated-on, dressed body
Were my face and body.
As I think of her I hear her telling me

How young I seem; I *am* exceptional;　　　　55
I think of all I have.
But really no one is exceptional,
No one has anything, I'm anybody,
I stand beside my grave
Confused with my life, that is commonplace and solitary.　　　　60

　　　　　　　　　　　　　　　　　　1965

Well Water

What a girl called "the dailiness of life"
(Adding an errand to your errand. Saying,
"Since you're up . . ." Making you a means to
A means to a means to) is well water
Pumped from an old well at the bottom of the world.　　　　5
The pump you pump the water from is rusty
And hard to move and absurd, a squirrel-wheel
A sick squirrel turns slowly, through the sunny
Inexorable hours. And yet sometimes
The wheel turns of its own weight, the rusty　　　　10
Pump pumps over your sweating face the clear
Water, cold, so cold! you cup your hands
And gulp from them the dailiness of life.

　　　　　　　　　　　　　　　　　　1965

Thinking of the Lost World

This spoonful of chocolate tapioca
Tastes like—like peanut butter, like the vanilla
Extract Mama told me not to drink.
Swallowing the spoonful, I have already traveled
Through time to my childhood. It puzzles me　　　　5
That age is like it.
　　　　　Come back to that calm country

Through which the stream of my life first meandered,
My wife, our cat, and I sit here and see
Squirrels quarreling in the feeder, a mockingbird   10
Copying our chipmunk, as our end copies
Its beginning.
    Back in Los Angeles, we missed
Los Angeles. The sunshine of the Land
Of Sunshine is a gray mist now, the atmosphere   15
Of some factory planet: when you stand and look
You see a block or two, and your eyes water.
The orange groves are all cut down . . . My bow
Is lost, all my arrows are lost or broken,
My knife is sunk in the eucalyptus tree   20
Too far for even Pop to get it out,
And the tree's sawed down. It and the stair-sticks
And the planks of the tree house are all firewood
Burned long ago; its gray smoke smells of Vicks.[1]

Twenty Years After, thirty-five years after,   25
Is as good as ever—better than ever,
Now that D'Artagnan[2] is no longer old—
Except that it is unbelievable.
I say to my old self: "I believe. Help thou
Mine unbelief."   30
    I believe the dinosaur
Or pterodactyl's married the pink sphinx
And lives with those Indians in the undiscovered
Country between California and Arizona
That the mad girl told me she was princess of—   35
Looking at me with the eyes of a lion,
Big, golden, without human understanding,
As she threw paper-wads from the back seat
Of the car in which I drove her with her mother
From the jail in Waycross to the hospital   40
In Daytona. If I took my eyes from the road
And looked back into her eyes, the car would—I'd be—

Or if only I could find a crystal set[3]
Sometimes, surely, I could still hear their chief
Reading to them from Dumas or Amazing Stories;   45
If I could find in some Museum of Cars
Mama's dark blue Buick, Lucky's electric,
Couldn't I be driven there? Hold out to them,
The paraffin half picked out, Tawny's dewclaw—
And have walk to me from among their wigwams   50
My tall brown aunt, to whisper to me: "Dead?
They told you I was dead?"
     As if you could die!
If I never saw you, never again

1. A remedy for colds.
2. Hero of The Three Musketeers (1844) by Alexandre Dumas père; its sequel was Twenty Years
After (1845).
3. Old-fashioned radio receiver.

Wrote to you, even, after a few years,   55
How often you've visited me, having put on,
As a mermaid puts on her sealskin, another face
And voice, that don't fool me for a minute—
That are yours for good . . . All of them are gone
Except for me; and for me nothing is gone—   60
The chicken's body is still going round
And round in widening circles, a satellite
From which, as the sun sets, the scientist bends
A look of evil on the unsuspecting earth.
Mama and Pop and Dandeen are still there   65
In the Gay Twenties.
                              The Gay Twenties! You say
The Gay Nineties . . . But it's all right: they *were* gay,
O so gay! A certain number of years after,
Any time is Gay, to the new ones who ask: 70
"Was that the first World War or the second?"
Moving between the first world and the second,
I hear a boy call, now that my beard's gray:
"Santa Claus! Hi, Santa Claus!" It *is* miraculous
To have the children call you Santa Claus.   75
I wave back. When my hand drops to the wheel,
It is brown and spotted, and its nails are ridged
Like Mama's. Where's my own hand? My smooth
White bitten-fingernailed one? I seem to see
A shape in tennis shoes and khaki riding-pants   80
Standing there empty-handed; I reach out to it
Empty-handed, my hand comes back empty,
And yet my emptiness is traded for its emptiness,
I have found that Lost World in the Lost and Found
Columns whose gray illegible advertisements   85
My soul has memorized world after world:
LOST—NOTHING. STRAYED FROM NOWHERE. NO REWARD.
I hold in my own hands, in happiness,
Nothing: the nothing for which there's no reward.

                                                                                1965

JOHN BERRYMAN
1914–1972

From a generation whose ideal poem was short, self-contained, and ironic, John Berryman emerged as the author of two extended and passionate works: "Homage to
Mistress Bradstreet" and the lyric sequence called *The Dream Songs*. It was as if
Berryman needed more space than the single lyric provided—a larger theater to play
out an unrelenting psychic drama. He had written shorter poems—songs and sonnets—but it was his discovery of large-scale dramatic situations and strange new
voices that astonished his contemporaries.

Berryman seemed fated to intense suffering and self-preoccuption. His father, a banker, shot himself outside his son's window when the boy was twelve. The suicide haunted Berryman to the end of his own life, which also came by suicide. Berryman, who was born John Smith, took a new name from his stepfather, also a banker. His childhood was a series of displacements: ten years near McAlester, Oklahoma, then Tampa, Florida, and after his father's suicide, Gloucester, Massachusetts, and New York City. His mother's second marriage ended in divorce, but his stepfather sent him to private school in Connecticut. Berryman graduated from Columbia College in 1936 and won a fellowship to Clare College, Cambridge, England.

He was later to say of himself, "I masquerade as a writer. Actually I am a scholar." However misleading this may be about his poetry, it reminds us that all his life Berryman drew nourishment from teaching—at Wayne State, at Harvard (1940–43), then off and on at Princeton, and from 1955 until his death, at the University of Minnesota. He chose to teach, not creative writing, but literature and the "history of civilization" and claimed that such teaching forced him into areas in which he wouldn't otherwise have done detailed work. A mixture of bookishness and wildness characterizes all his writing: five years of research lay behind the intensities of "Homage to Mistress Bradstreet," while an important constituent of "huffy Henry's" personality in *The Dream Songs* is his professorial awkwardness and exhibitionism.

Berryman seemed drawn to borrowing identities in his poetry. In his first important volume, *The Dispossessed* (1948), he had experimented with various dramatic voices in the short poems "Nervous Songs: The Song of the Demented Priest," "A Professor's Song," "The Song of the Tortured Girl," and "The Song of the Man Forsaken and Obsessed." The *dispossession* of the book's title had two opposite and urgent meanings for him: "the miserable, *put out of one's own,* and the relieved, saved, undevilled, despelled." Taking on such roles was for Berryman both a revelation of his cast-out, fatherless state and an exorcism of it. It was perhaps in that spirit that he entered into an imaginary dialogue with what he felt as the kindred nature of the Puritan poet Anne Bradstreet. "Both of our worlds unhanded us." What started out to be a poem of fifty lines emerged as the fifty-seven stanzas of "Homage to Mistress Bradstreet" (1956), a work so absorbing that after completing it Berryman claimed to be "a ruin for two years." It was not Bradstreet's poetry that engaged him. Quite the contrary: he was fascinated by the contrast between her "bald abstract rime" and her life of passionate suffering. The poem explores the kinship between Bradstreet and Berryman as figures of turbulence and rebellion.

Berryman took literary encouragement from another American poet of the past, Stephen Crane, about whom he wrote a book-length critical study in 1950. Crane's poems, he said, have "the character of a 'dream,' something seen naively in a new relation." Berryman's attraction to a poetry that accommodated the nightmare antics of the dream world became apparent in his own long work, *The Dream Songs*. It was modeled, he claimed, on "the greatest American poem," Whitman's "Song of Myself," in which the speaker assumes a fluid, ever-changing persona. 77 *Dream Songs* was published in 1964. Additional poems, to a total of 385, appeared in *His Toy, His Dream, His Rest* (1968). (Some uncollected dream songs were published posthumously in *Henry's Fate,* 1977, and drafts of others remained in manuscript.) There are obvious links between Berryman and other so-called confessional writers such as Robert Lowell, Sylvia Plath, and Anne Sexton. But the special autobiographical flavor of *The Dream Songs* is that of a psychic vaudeville; as in dreams, the poet represents himself through a fluid series of *alter egos,* whose voices often flow into one another in single poems. One of these voices is that of a blackface minstrel, and Berryman's appropriation of this dialect prompted Michael Harper's poem "Tongue-Tied in Black and White." Despite the suffering that these poems enact, Berryman seemed to find a secret strength through the staginess, variety, resourcefulness, and renewals of these poems.

The Dream Songs brought Berryman a success that was not entirely beneficial. The collection Love and Fame (1970) shows him beguiled by his own celebrity and wrestling with some of its temptations. In an unfinished, posthumously published novel, Recovery, he portrays himself as increasingly prey to alcoholism. Berryman had been married twice before, and his hospitalization for drinking and for periods of insanity had put a strain on his third marriage. He came to distrust his poetry as a form of exhibitionism and was clearly, in his use of the discipline of prose and in the prayers that crowd his last two volumes of poetry (Delusions, Etc. appeared posthumously), in search of some new and humbling style. Having been raised a strict Catholic and fallen away from the church, he tried to return to it in his last years, speaking of his need for a "God of rescue." On January 7, 1972, Berryman committed suicide by leaping from a Minneapolis bridge.

Homage to Mistress Bradstreet

Anne Bradstreet ("Born 1612 Anne Dudley, married at 16 Simon Bradstreet, a Cambridge man, steward to the Countess of Warwick and protege of her father Thomas Dudley secretary to the Earl of Lincoln. Crossed in the Arbella, 1630, under Governor Winthrop" [Berryman's note]) came to the Massachusetts Bay Colony when she was eighteen years old. She was one of the first poets on American soil. Of this poem, Berryman says:

> An American historian somewhere observes that all colonial settlements are intensely conservative, except in the initial break-off point (whether religious, political, legal, or whatever). Trying to do justice to both parts of this obvious truth—which I came upon only after the poem was finished—I concentrated upon the second and the poem laid itself out in a series of rebellions. I had her rebel first against the new environment and above all against her barrenness (which in fact lasted for years), then against her marriage (which in fact seems to have been brilliantly happy), and finally against her continuing life of illness, loss, and age. These are the three large sections of the poem; they are preceded and followed by an exordium and coda, of four stanzas each, spoken by the "I" of the twentieth-century poet, which modulates into her voice, who speaks most of the poem. Such is the plan. Each rebellion, of course, is succeeded by submission, although even in the moment of the poem's supreme triumph—the presentment, too long to quote now, of the birth of her first child—rebellion survives.

Berryman wrote two stanzas of the poem and found himself stalled for five years, during which he gathered material, until he discovered the strategy of dialogue and inserted himself in the poem. "Homage to Mistress Bradstreet" was first published in Partisan Review in 1953, but did not appear as a book until 1956.

In his exordium (stanzas 1–4), the poet makes an intense identification between himself and Bradstreet, both of them alienated by hardship or circumstance from those around them: "We are on each other's hands / who care. Both of our worlds unhanded us." The identification is so complete that in the subsequent stanzas he hears her voice recounting the tribulations of life in a new country, her yearnings for the England she left behind, her lonely dedication to her poetry, and the personal suffering in her early barrenness and miscarriages. Stanza 17 continues in Bradstreet's voice.

From Homage to Mistress Bradstreet

* * *
17

The winters close, Springs open, no child stirs
under my withering heart, O seasoned heart   130
God grudged his aid.
All things else soil like a shirt.
Simon is much away. My executive[1] stales.
The town came through for the cartway by the pales,[2]
but my patience is short,   135
I revolt from, I am like, these savage foresters

18

whose passionless dicker in the shade, whose glance
impassive & scant, belie their murderous cries
when quarry seems to show.
Again I must have been wrong, twice.[3]   140
Unwell in a new way. Can that begin?
God brandishes. O love, O I love. Kin,
gather. My world is strange
and merciful, ingrown months, blessing a swelling trance.[4]

19

So squeezed, wince you I scream? I love you & hate   145
off with you. Ages! *Useless.* Below my waist
he has me in Hell's vise.
Stalling. He let go. Come back: brace
me somewhere. No. No. Yes! everything down
hardens I press with horrible joy down   150
my back cracks like a wrist
shame I am voiding oh behind it is too late

20

hide me forever I work thrust I must free
now I all muscles & bones concentrate
what is living from dying?   155
Simon I must leave you so untidy
Monster you are killing me Be sure
I'll have you later Women do endure
I can *can* no longer
and it passes the wretched trap whelming and I am me   160

21

drencht & powerful, I did it with my body!
One proud tug greens Heaven. Marvellous,
unforbidding Majesty.
Swell, imperious bells. I fly.

---

1. Power to act.
2. Stockade fence.
3. One of the several allusions to her failure to become pregnant.
4. Her first child was not born until about 1633 [Berryman's note].

Mountainous, woman not breaks and will bend: 165
sways God nearby: anguish comes to an end.
Blossomed Sarah,[5] and I
blossom. Is that thing alive? I hear a famisht howl.

                                    22

Beloved household, I am Simon's wife,
and the mother of Samuel—whom greedy yet I miss   170
out of his kicking place.
More in some ways I feel at a loss,
freer. Cantabanks & mummers,[6] nears
longing for you. Our chopping[7] scores my ears,
our costume bores my eyes.   175
St. George[8] to the good sword, rise! chop-logic's rife

                                    23

& fever & Satan & Satan's ancient fere.[9]
Pioneering is not feeling well,
not Indians, beasts.
Not all their riddling can forestall   180
one leaving. Sam, your uncle has had to
go from us to live with God. 'Then Aunt went too?'
Dear, she does wait still.
Stricken: 'Oh. Then he takes us one by one.' My dear.

                                    24

Forswearing it otherwise, they starch their minds.   185
Folkmoots, & blether, blether. John Cotton rakes[1]
to the synod of Cambridge.[2]
Down from my body my legs flow,
out from it arms wave, on it my head shakes.
Now Mistress Hutchinson rings forth a call—   190
should she? many creep out a broken wall—
affirming the Holy Ghost
dwells in one justified. Factioning passion blinds

                                    25

all to all her good, all—can she be exiled?
Bitter sister, victim! I miss you.   195
—I miss you, Anne,[3]

5. Wife of Abraham, barren until old age, when she gave birth to Isaac (Genesis 17.19).
6. Ballad singers and mimes.
7. *Chopping*: disputing, snapping, haggling; axing [Berryman's note].
8. Patron saint of England, the slayer of dragons.
9. *Fere*: his friend Death [Berryman's note].
1. "Rakes: inclines, as a mast; bows" [Berryman's note]. "Folkmoots": a town assembly for debate. "Blether": nonsense.
2. In the first synod (a body for religious debate), Cotton agreed to the condemnation and banishment of his follower Anne Hutchinson. Her heresies included a deemphasis of perfect moral conduct as evidence of the justification for Christian salvation.
3. One might say: He [the poet] is enabled to speak, at last, in the fortune of an echo of her—and when she is loneliest (her former spiritual adviser [John Cotton] having deserted Anne Hutchinson, and this her [Bradstreet's] closest friend banished), as if she had summoned him; and only thus, perhaps, is she enabled to hear him. This second section of the poem is a dialogue", his voice however ceasing well before it ends at [line] 307, and hers continuing for the whole third part until the coda ([stanzas] 54–57) [Berryman's note].

day or night weak as a child,
tender & empty, doomed, quick to no tryst.
—I hear you. Be kind, you who leaguer[4]
my image in the mist.   200
—Be kind you, to one unchained eager far & wild

26

and if, O my love, my heart is breaking, please
neglect my cries and I will spare you. Deep
in Time's grave, Love's, you lie still.
Lie still.—Now? That happy shape   205
my forehead had under my most long, rare,
ravendark, hidden, soft bodiless hair
you award me still.
You must not love me, but   I do not bid you cease.

27

Veiled my eyes, attending. How can it be I?   210
Moist, with parted lips, I listen, wicked.
I shake in the morning & retch.
Brood I do on myself naked.
A fading world I dust, with fingers new.
—I have earned the right to be alone with you.   215
—What right can that be?
Convulsing, if you love, enough, like a sweet lie.

28

Not that, I know, you can. This cratered skin,
like the crabs & shells of my Palissy[5] ewer, touch!
Oh, you do, you do?   220
Falls on me what I like a witch,
for lawless holds, annihilations of law
which Time and he and man abhor, foresaw:
sharper than what my Friend[6]
brought me for my revolt when I moved smooth & thin,   225

29

faintings black, rigour, chilling, brown
parching, back, brain burning, the grey pocks
itch, a manic stench
of pustules snapping, pain floods the palm,
sleepless, or a red shaft with a dreadful start   230
rides at the chapel, like a slipping heart.
My soul strains in one qualm
ah but *this* is not to save me but to throw me down.

30

And out of this I lull. It lessens. Kiss me.
That once. As sings out up in sparkling dark   235

---

4. Beleaguer, besiege.
5. Bernard Palissy (1510–1590), French Protestant ceramicist, noted for special glazes and highly
ornamented pieces.
6. Alludes to the punishments of God visited on
those who rebel against him (cf. Isaiah 1.6).

a trail of a star & dies,
while the breath flutters, sounding, mark,
so shorn ought such caresses to us be
who, deserving nothing, flush and flee
the darkness of that light,   240
a lurching frozen from a warm dream. Talk to me.

31[7]

—It is Spring's New England. Pussy willows wedge
up in the wet. Milky crestings, fringed
yellow, in heaven, eyed
by the melting hand-in-hand or mere   245
desirers single, heavy-footed, rapt,
make surge poor human hearts. Venus is trapt—
the hefty pike shifts, sheer[8]—
in Orion blazing. Warblings, odours, nudge to an edge—

32

—Ravishing, ha, what crouches outside ought,   250
flamboyant, ill, angelic. Often, now,
I am afraid of you.
I am a sobersides; I know.
I *want* to take you for my lover.—Do.
—I hear a madness. Harmless I to you   255
am not, not I?—No.
—I cannot but be. Sing a concord of our thought.

33

—Wan dolls in indigo on gold:[9] refrain
my western lust. I am drowning in this past.
I lose sight of you   260
who mistress me from air. Unbraced
in delirium of the grand depths,[1] giving away
haunters what kept me, I breathe solid spray.
—I am losing you!
Straiten me on.[2]—I suffered living like a stain: 265

34

I trundle the bodies, on the iron bars,
over that fire backward & forth; they burn;
bits fall. I wonder if
I killed them. Women serve my turn.

---

7. Berryman (in *Poets on Poetry*) called this speech of the poet to Bradstreet "an only half-subdued aria-stanza."
8. Lines 246–47 are opposed images of the bottom of the sea against the summit of the sky (Venus). "Sheer" in the sense of "invisible" (quoted from comments by Berryman in the Italian translation of "Mistress Bradstreet" by Sergio Perosa).
9. Cf., on Byzantine icons [here, the impassive Madonnas painted against gold backgrounds in medieval altarpieces of the Eastern church], Frederick Rolfe ("Baron Corvo"): "Who ever dreams of praying (with expectation of response) for the prayer of a Tintoretto or a Titian, or a Bellini, or a Botticelli? But who can refrain from crying 'O Mother!' to these unruffleable wan dolls in indigo on gold?" (quoted from *The Desire and Pursuit of the Whole* by Graham Greene in *The Last Childhood*) [Berryman's note].
1. "Délires des grandes profoundeurs," described by [Jacques] Cousteau and others; a euphoria, sometimes fatal, in which the hallucinated diver offers passing fish his line, helmet, anything [Berryman's note; he translates the French phrase in line 262].
2. I.e., tighten your embrace.

—Dreams! You are good.—No.—Dense with hardihood   270
the wicked are dislodged, and lodged the good.
In green space we are safe.
God awaits us (but I am yielding) who Hell wars.

35

—I cannot feel myself God waits. He flies
nearer a kindly world; or he is flown.   275
One Saturday's rescue[3]
won't show. Man is entirely alone
may be. I am a man of griefs & fits
trying to be my friend. And the brown smock splits,
down the pale flesh a gash   280
broadens and Time holds up your heart against my eyes.

36

—Hard and divided heaven! creases me. Shame
is failing. My breath is scented, and I throw
hostile glances towards God.
Crumpling plunge of a pestle, bray:[4]   285
sin cross & opposite, wherein I survive
nightmares of Eden. Reaches foul & live
he for me, this soul
to crunch, a minute tangle of eternal flame.

37

I fear Hell's hammer-wind. But fear does wane.   290
Death's blossoms grain my hair; I cannot live.
A black joy clashes
joy, in twilight. The Devil said
'I will deal toward her softly, and her enchanting cries[5]
will fool the horns of Adam.' Father of lies,   295
a male great pestle smashes
small women swarming towards the mortar's rim in vain.

38

I see the cruel spread Wings black with saints!
Silky my breasts not his, mine, mine to withhold
or tender, tender.   300
I am sifting, nervous, and bold.
The light is changing. Surrender this loveliness
you cannot make me do. *But* I will. Yes.
What horror, down stormy air,
warps towards me? My threatening promise faints   305

---

3. As of cliffhangers, movie serials wherein each
week's episode ends with a train bearing down on
the strapped heroine or with the hero dangling over
an abyss into which Indians above him peer with
satisfaction before they hatchet the rope; *rescue:*
forcible recovery (by the owner) of goods distrained
[Berryman's note].

4. Punning (according to Berryman's notes) on (1)
the pulverizing action of a mortar and pestle and
(2) the strident noise of a donkey.
5. Referring to Satan's temptation of Eve, who was
to eat the apple from the Tree of Knowledge and
then convince Adam to do so (cf. Genesis 3).

39[6]

torture me, Father, lest not I be thine!
Tribunal terrible & pure, my God,
mercy for him and me.
Faces half-fanged, Christ drives abroad,
and though the crop hopes, Jane[7] is so slipshod   310
I cry. Evil dissolves, & love, like foam;
that love. Prattle of children powers me home,
my heart claps like the swan's
under a frenzy of *who* love me & who shine.[8]

✳   ✳   ✳

1953, 1956

FROM THE DREAM SONGS[1]

1

Huffy Henry hid   the day,
unappeasable Henry sulked.
I see his point,—a trying to put things over.
It was the thought that they thought
they could *do* it made Henry wicked & away.   5
But he should have come out and talked.

All the world like a woolen lover
once did seem on Henry's side.
Then came a departure.
Thereafter nothing fell out as it might or ought.   10
I don't see how Henry, pried
open for all the world to see, survived.

What he has now to say is a long
wonder the world can bear & be.
Once in a sycamore I was glad   15
all at the top, and I sang.

6. The stanza is unsettled, like [stanza] 24, by a middle line, signaling a broad transition [Berryman's note].
7. A servant.
8. The final stanzas present Bradstreet's intensified vision of death and damnation and include the death of her father, blaspheming. But in the last four stanzas the poem modulates back into the poet's voice and his vow to keep Bradstreet alive in his loving memory and in his writing. "Hover, utter, still, a sourcing whom my lost candle like the firefly loves."
1. These poems were written over a period of thirteen years. (77 *Dream Songs* was published in 1964, and the remaining poems appeared in *His Toy, His Dream, His Rest* in 1968. Some uncollected dream songs were included in the volume *Henry's Fate,* which appeared five years after Berryman committed suicide in 1972.) Berryman placed an introductory note at the head of *His Toy, His Dream, His Rest:* "The poem then, whatever its wide cast of characters, is essentially about an imaginary character (not the poet, not me) named Henry, a white American in early middle age sometimes in blackface, who has suffered an irreversible loss and talks about himself sometimes in the first person, sometimes in the third, sometimes even in the second; he has a friend, never named, who addresses him as Mr. Bones and variants thereof. Requiescant in pace."

> Hard on the land wears the strong sea
> and empty grows every bed.

14

> Life, friends, is boring. We must not say so.
> After all, the sky flashes, the great sea yearns,
> we ourselves flash and yearn,
> and moreover my mother told me as a boy
> (repeatedly) 'Ever to confess you're bored   5
> means you have no
>
> Inner Resources.' I conclude now I have no
> inner resources, because I am heavy bored.
> Peoples bore me,
> literature bores me, especially great literature,   10
> Henry bores me, with his plights & gripes
> as bad as achilles,[2]
>
> who loves people and valiant art, which bores me.
> And the tranquil hills, & gin, look like a drag
> and somehow a dog   15
> has taken itself & its tail considerably away
> into mountains or sea or sky, leaving
> behind: me, wag.

29

> There sat down, once, a thing on Henry's heart
> so heavy, if he had a hundred years
> & more, & weeping, sleepless, in all them time
> Henry could not make good.
> Starts again always in Henry's ears   5
> the little cough somewhere, an odour, a chime.
>
> And there is another thing he has in mind
> like a grave Sienese face[3] a thousand years
> would fail to blur the still profiled reproach of. Ghastly,
> with open eyes, he attends, blind.   10
> All the bells say: too late. This is not for tears;
> thinking.
>
> But never did Henry, as he thought he did,
> end anyone and hacks her body up
> and hide the pieces, where they may be found.   15

---

2. Greek hero of Homer's *The Iliad*, who, angry at slights against his honor, sulked in his tent and refused to fight against the Trojans.

3. Alluding to the somber, austere mosaiclike religious portraits by the Italian painters who worked in Siena during the 13th and 14th centuries.

He knows: he went over everyone, & nobody's missing.
Often he reckons, in the dawn, them up.
Nobody is ever missing.

40

I'm scared a lonely. Never see my son,
easy be not to see anyone,
combers[4] out to sea
know they're goin somewhere but not me.
Got a little poison, got a little gun.   5
I'm scared a lonely.

I'm scared a only one thing, which is me,
from othering I don't take nothin, see,
for any hound dog's sake.
But this is where I livin, where I rake   10
my leaves and cop my promise,[5] this' where we
cry oursel's awake.

Wishin was dyin but I gotta make
it all this way to that bed on these feet
where peoples said to meet.   15
Maybe but even if I see my son
forever never, get back on the take,
free, black & forty-one.[6]

45

He stared at ruin. Ruin stared straight back.
He thought they was old friends. He felt on the stair
where her papa found them bare
they became familiar. When the papers were lost
rich with pals' secrets, he thought he had the knack   5
of ruin. Their paths crossed

and once they crossed in jail; they crossed in bed;
and over an unsigned letter their eyes met,
and in an Asian city
directionless & lurchy at two & three,   10
or trembling to a telephone's fresh threat,
and when some wired his head

to reach a wrong opinion, 'Epileptic'.
But he noted now that: they were not old friends.

4. Waves that roll over and break with a foamy
crest.
5. Slang for "pile up potential."

6. Playing on "free, white, and twenty-one," colloquial for legally independent.

He did not know this one. 15
This one was a stranger, come to make amends
for all the imposters, and to make it stick.
Henry nodded, un-.

384

The marker slants, flowerless, day's almost done,
I stand above my father's grave with rage,
often, often before
I've made this awful pilgrimage to one
who cannot visit me, who tore his page 5
out: I come back for more,

I spit upon this dreadful banker's grave
who shot his heart out in a Florida dawn
O ho alas alas
When will indifference come, I moan & rave 10
I'd like to scrabble till I got right down
away down under the grass

and ax the casket open ha to see
just how he's taking it, which he sought so hard
we'll tear apart 15
the mouldering grave clothes ha & then Henry
will heft the ax once more, his final card,
and fell it on the start.

385

My daughter's heavier. Light leaves are flying.
Everywhere in enormous numbers turkeys will be dying
and other birds, all their wings.
They never greatly flew. Did they wish to?
I should know. Off away somewhere once I knew 5
such things.

Or good Ralph Hodgson[7] back then did, or does.
The man is dead whom Eliot[8] praised. My praise
follows and flows too late.
Fall is grievy, brisk. Tears behind the eyes 10
almost fall. Fall comes to us as a prize
to rouse us toward our fate.

My house is made of wood and it's made well,
unlike us. My house is older than Henry;

---

7. English poet (1871–1962) who wrote balladlike
lyrics. Berryman may be alluding to Hodgson's
"Hymn to Moloch," in which the poet protests the
slaughter of birds for commercial uses.
8. T. S. Eliot (1888–1965), American poet and
critic.

that's fairly old.   15
If there were a middle   ground between things and the soul
or if the sky resembled more the sea,
I wouldn't have to scold

                                                    my heavy daughter.

                                                                    1968

ROBERT LOWELL
1917–1977

In "North Haven," her poem in memory of Robert Lowell, Elizabeth Bishop translates the song of the birds as Lowell seemed to hear it: "repeat, repeat, repeat, revise, revise, revise." Repeatedly, even obsessively, Lowell returned to certain subjects in his poems. Each return confirmed an existing pattern even as it opened the possibility for revision. In fact, Lowell's life was full of revision. Descended from Protestant New Englanders, he converted to Catholicism, then fell away from it; he married three times; and he changed his poetic style more than once. In the later part of his career, Lowell revised even his published poems and did so repeatedly. "Revision is inspiration," he once said, "no reading of the finished work as exciting as writing the last changes." Revision allowed for Lowell's love of stray events, his attraction to the fluidity of life (in this, he resembles Wallace Stevens). But Lowell also wanted to organize life into formal patterns, to locate the random moment in the design of an epic history (his Catholicism can be seen, in part, as an expression of this desire). History offered plot and repetition: just as patterns of his childhood recurred in adult life, the sins of his New England ancestors were reenacted by contemporary America. Lowell's vision of history leaned toward apocalypse, toward the revelation of a prior meaning the poet agonized to determine, and yet he cherished the freedom of "human chances," with all their indeterminacy. His poems had to accommodate these opposing impulses. Concerning the sequence of poems in *Notebook 1967–1968*, begun as a poetic diary, he said: "Accident threw up the subject and the plot swallowed them—famished for human chances." If Lowell often swallowed up the casual, the random, the ordinary, and the domestic into the forms of his poems, his best plots have a spontaneity whose meanings cannot be fixed.

The burden of family history was substantial for Lowell, whose ancestors included members of Boston's patrician families. His grandfather was a well-known Episcopal minister and head of the fashionable St. Mark's School, which the poet was later to attend. His great-grand uncle James Russell Lowell had been a poet and ambassador to England. The family's light note was provided by the poet Amy Lowell, "big and a scandal, as if Mae West were a cousin." In the context of this history, Lowell's father, who fared badly in business after his retirement from service as a naval officer, appeared as a diminished figure.

Lowell's first act of revising family history was to leave the east after two years at Harvard (1935–37) to study at Kenyon College with John Crowe Ransom, the poet and critic. The move brought him in closer touch with the New Criticism and its predilections for "formal difficult poems," the wit and irony of English Metaphysical writers such as John Donne. He also, through Ransom and the poet Allen Tate, came into contact with (although never formally joined) the Fugitive movement, whose members were southern agrarians opposed to what they regarded as the corrupting values of northern industrialism.

Two of the acts that most decisively separated Lowell from family history were his conversion to Roman Catholicism (1940) and his resistance to American policies in World War II. Although he did try to enlist in the navy, he refused to be drafted into the army. He opposed the saturation bombing of Hamburg and the Allied policy of unconditional surrender and was as a result sentenced to a year's confinement in New York's West Street jail. The presiding judge at his hearing admonished him for "marring" his family traditions. In his first book, Lord Weary's Castle (1946), his Catholicism provided a set of symbols and a distanced platform from which to express his violent antagonism to Protestant mercantile Boston. The stunning, apocalyptic conclusions of these early poems ("the Lord survives the rainbow of his will" or "The blue kingfisher dives on you in fire") render the devastating judgment of the eternal on the fallen history of the individual and the nation.

Alongside those poems drawing on Old Testament anger, there were those poems in Lord Weary's Castle such as "Mr. Edwards and the Spider" that explored from within the nervous intensity that underlay Puritan revivalism. Later dramatic narratives with modern settings such as "The Mills of the Kavanaghs" and "Falling Asleep over the Aeneid" reveal his psychological interest in and obsession with ruined New England families.

In Life Studies (1959), Lowell changed his style dramatically. His subjects became explicitly autobiographical, and his language more open and direct. In 1957 he gave readings in California, where Allen Ginsberg and the other Beats had just made their strongest impact in San Francisco. By contrast to their candid, breezy writing, Lowell felt his own seemed "distant, symbol-ridden, and willfully difficult. . . . I felt my old poems hid what they were really about, and many times offered a stiff, humorless and even impenetrable surface." Although more controlled and severe than Beat writers, he was stimulated by Ginsberg's self-revelations to write more openly than he had about his parents and grandparents, about the mental breakdowns he suffered in the 1950s, and about the difficulties of marriage. (Lowell divorced his first wife, the novelist Jean Stafford, and married the critic Elizabeth Hardwick in 1949).

Life Studies, by and large, records his ambivalence toward the New England where he resettled after the war, on Boston's "hardly passionate Marlborough Street." Revising his stance toward New England and family history, he no longer denounces the city of his fathers as if he were a privileged outsider. In complicated psychological portraits of his childhood, his relation to his parents and his wives, he assumes a portion of the weakness and vulnerability for himself.

In 1960 Lowell left Boston to live in New York City. For the Union Dead (1964), the book that followed, continued the autobiographical vein of Life Studies. Lowell called it a book about "witheredness . . . lemony, soured and dry, the drouth I had touched with my own hands." These poems seem more carefully controlled than his earlier Life Studies. Often they organize key images from the past into a pattern that illuminates the present. The book includes a number of poems that fuse private and public themes, such as "Fall 1961" and the volume's title poem.

In 1969 Lowell published Notebook 1967–1968 and then revised these poems for a second, augmented edition, called simply Notebook (1970). In 1973, in a characteristic act, he once more revised, rearranged, and expanded Notebook's poems and published them in two separate books. The more personal poems, recording the breakup of his second marriage and his separation from his wife and daughter, were published as For Lizzie and Harriet. Those dealing more with public subjects, past and present, were published under the title History. Taken together, these two books show Lowell once again engaged with the relations between the random event, or the moment out of a personal life, and an epic design. In these unrhymed, loosely blank verse revisions of the sonnet Lowell responded to the books he was reading, to the events of his personal life, and to the national issue of the Vietnam War, of which he was an outspoken critic. "Things I felt or saw, or read were drift in the whirlpool."

At the same time, a new collection of sonnets, The Dolphin (1973), appeared, recording his marriage to Lady Caroline Blackwood. He divided his time between her home in England and periods of teaching writing and literature at Harvard—a familiar pattern for him in which the old tensions between New England and "elsewhere" were being constantly explored and renewed. His last book, *Day by Day* (1977), records those stresses as well as new marital difficulties. It also contains some of his most powerful poems about his childhood.

For those who cherish the work of the early Lowell, with its manic, rhythmic energy and its enjambed lines building to fierce power or those who admire the passionate engagement of *Life Studies* or *For the Union Dead*, the poems of his last four books can be disappointing. At times flat and dispirited, they can seem worked up rather than fully imagined. Yet in poems like the two titled "No Hearing," the later Lowell demonstrates his substantial gifts in a quieter mode. The excitement in these poems lies in the way his language quickens with changing feelings and reveals the heart surprised by an ordinary moment or event.

Lowell's career included an interest in the theater, for which he wrote a version of *Prometheus Bound*, a translation of Racine's *Phaedra*, and adaptations of Melville and Hawthorne stories gathered as *The Old Glory*. He also translated from modern European poetry and the classics, often freely as "imitations," which brought important poetic voices into English currency. His *Selected Poems* (his own choices) appeared in 1976. When he died suddenly at the age of sixty, he was the dominant and most honored poet of his generation—not only for his ten volumes of verse but for his broad activity as a man of letters. He took the role of poet as public figure, sometimes at great personal cost. He was with the group of writers who led Vietnam War protesters against the Pentagon in 1967, where Norman Mailer, a fellow protester, observed that "Lowell gave off at times the unwilling haunted saintliness of a man who was repaying the moral debts of ten generations of ancestors."

Colloquy in Black Rock[1]

Here the jack-hammer jabs into the ocean;
My heart, you race and stagger and demand
More blood-gangs for your nigger-brass percussions,
Till I, the stunned machine of your devotion,
Clanging upon this cymbal of a hand,   5
Am rattled screw and footloose. All discussions

End in the mud-flat detritus of death.
My heart, beat faster, faster. In Black Mud[2]
Hungarian workmen give their blood
For the martyre Stephen,[3] who was stoned to death.   10

Black Mud, a name to conjure with: O mud
For watermelons gutted to the crust,
Mud for the mole-tide[4] harbor, mud for mouse,
Mud for the armored Diesel fishing tubs that thud

---

1. A section of Bridgeport, Connecticut, where Lowell went to live in 1944 after serving his term as a conscientious objector. It had a large Hungarian population.
2. The speaker's name for mud flats near Black Rock.
3. A reference to (1) the wartime blood donations of the workers; (2) the patron saint of Hungary, King Stephen I (977–1038); and (3) St. Stephen Promartyr, the first Christian to sacrifice himself for Christ.
4. Special currents produced by a mole (breakwater).

A year and a day[5] to wind and tide; the dust   15
Is on this skipping heart that shakes my house,

House of our Savior who was hanged till death.
My heart, beat faster, faster. In Black Mud
Stephen the martyre was broken down to blood:
Our ransom is the rubble of his death.   20
Christ walks on the black water. In Black Mud
Darts the kingfisher. On Corpus Christi, heart,
Over the drum-beat of St. Stephen's choir
I hear him, *Stupor Mundi*,[6] and the mud
Flies from his hunching wings and beak—my heart,   25
The blue kingfisher dives on you in fire.

1946

The Quaker Graveyard in Nantucket

[*For Warren Winslow*,[1] *Dead at Sea*]

Let man have dominion over the fishes of the sea and the fowls of
the air and the beasts of the whole earth, and every creeping
creature that moveth upon the earth.[2]

I

A brackish reach of shoal off Madaket[3]—
The sea was still breaking violently and night
Had steamed into our North Atlantic Fleet,
When the drowned sailor clutched the drag-net. Light
Flashed from his matted head and marble feet,   5
He grappled at the net
With the coiled, hurdling muscles of his thighs:
The corpse was bloodless, a botch of reds and whites,
Its open, staring eyes
Were lustreless dead-lights[4]   10
Or cabin-windows on a stranded hulk
Heavy with sand. We weight the body, close
Its eyes and heave it seaward whence it came,
Where the heel-headed dogfish barks its nose
On Ahab's[5] void and forehead; and the name   15
Is blocked in yellow chalk.
Sailors, who pitch this portent at the sea
Where dreadnaughts shall confess

5. Perhaps the "year and a day" of Lowell's prison sentence.
6. Marvel of the world. "Kingfisher": a short-tailed bird that dives for fish; associated in the poem's last line with Christ, the "fisher of men." "Corpus Christi": a Catholic feast day, celebrating the transformation of the communion wafer into the body of Christ.
1. A cousin of Lowell's who died in the sinking of a naval vessel during World War II.
2. From Genesis 1.26, the account of the creation

of humankind.
3. On Nantucket Island.
4. Shutters over portholes to keep out water in a storm. The images in lines 4–11 come from "The Shipwreck," the opening chapter of *Cape Cod* by Henry David Thoreau (1817–1862).
5. Protagonist of Herman Melville's *Moby-Dick* who drowns as a result of his obsessive hunt for the white whale. Melville uses Ahab's domineering forehead as an emblem of his monomaniac passion.

Its hell-bent deity,
When you are powerless   20
To sand-bag this Atlantic bulwark, faced
By the earth-shaker, green, unwearied, chaste
In his steel scales: ask for no Orphean lute
To pluck life back.[6] The guns of the steeled fleet
Recoil and then repeat   25
The hoarse salute.

II

Whenever winds are moving and their breath
Heaves at the roped-in bulwarks of this pier,
The terns and sea-gulls tremble at your death
In these home waters. Sailor, can you hear   30
The Pequod's[7] sea wings, beating landward, fall
Headlong and break on our Atlantic wall
Off 'Sconset, where the yawing S-boats[8] splash
The bellbuoy, with ballooning spinnakers,
As the entangled, screeching mainsheet clears   35
The blocks: off Madaket, where lubbers[9] lash
The heavy surf and throw their long lead squids
For blue-fish? Sea-gulls blink their heavy lids
Seaward. The winds' wings beat upon the stones,
Cousin, and scream for you and the claws rush   40
At the sea's throat and wring it in the slush
Of this old Quaker graveyard where the bones
Cry out in the long night for the hurt beast
Bobbing by Ahab's whaleboats in the East.

III

All you recovered from Poseidon died   45
With you, my cousin, and the harrowed brine
Is fruitless on the blue beard of the god,
Stretching beyond us to the castles in Spain,
Nantucket's westward haven. To Cape Cod
Guns, cradled on the tide,   50
Blast the eelgrass about a waterclock
Of bilge and backwash, roil the salt and sand
Lashing earth's scaffold, rock
Our warships in the hand
Of the great God, where time's contrition blues   55
Whatever it was these Quaker[1] sailors lost
In the mad scramble of their lives. They died
When time was open-eyed,
Wooden and childish; only bones abide
There, in the nowhere, where their boats were tossed   60

6. In Greek mythology, Orpheus through his music tried to win the freedom of his bride Eurydice from the Underworld. "Earth-shaker": an epithet for Poseidon, the Greek god of the oceans.
7. Ahab's ship, destroyed by Moby-Dick.
8. Type of large racing sailboats. "Yawing": steering wildly in heavy seas.
9. Sailor's term for an awkward crew member.
1. The whaling population of Nantucket included many Quakers.

Sky-high, where mariners had fabled news
Of IS,[2] the whited monster. What it cost
Them is their secret. In the sperm-whale's slick
I see the Quakers drown and hear their cry:
"If God himself had not been on our side,   65
If God himself had not been on our side,
When the Atlantic rose against us, why,
Then it had swallowed us up quick."

IV

This is the end of the whaleroad[3] and the whale
Who spewed Nantucket bones on the thrashed swell   70
And stirred the troubled waters to whirlpools
To send the Pequod packing off to hell:
This is the end of them, three-quarters fools,
Snatching at straws to sail
Seaward and seaward on the turntail whale,   75
Spouting out blood and water as it rolls,
Sick as a dog to these Atlantic shoals:
Clamavimus,[4] O depths. Let the sea-gulls wail

For water, for the deep where the high tide
Mutters to its hurt self, mutters and ebbs.   80
Waves wallow in their wash, go out and out,
Leave only the death-rattle of the crabs,
The beach increasing, its enormous snout
Sucking the ocean's side.
This is the end of running on the waves;   85
We are poured out like water. Who will dance
The mast-lashed master of Leviathans
Up from this field of Quakers in their unstoned graves?

V

When the whale's viscera go and the roll
Of its corruption overruns this world   90
Beyond tree-swept Nantucket and Woods Hole[5]
And Martha's Vineyard, Sailor, will your sword
Whistle and fall and sink into the fat?
In the great ash-pit of Jehoshaphat[6]
The bones cry for the blood of the white whale,   95
The fat flukes arch and whack about its ears,
The death-lance churns into the sanctuary, tears
The gun-blue swingle,[7] heaving like a flail,
And hacks the coiling life out: it works and drags

---

2. The white whale is here imagined as a force like the God of Exodus 3.14, who, when asked his name by Moses, replies, "I AM THAT I AM." Also an abbreviation of Jesus Salvator.
3. An Anglo-Saxon epithet for the sea.
4. We have called (Latin). Adapting the opening of Psalm 130: "Out of the depths have I cried unto thee, O Lord."

5. On the coast of Massachusetts near the island of Martha's Vineyard.
6. "The day of judgment. The world, according to some prophets, will end in fire" [Lowell's note]. In Joel 3, the Last Judgment takes place in the valley of Jehoshaphat.
7. Knifelike wooden instrument for beating flax.

And rips the sperm-whale's midriff into rags,   100
Gobbets of blubber spill to wind and weather,
Sailor, and gulls go round the stoven timbers
Where the morning stars sing out together
And thunder shakes the white surf and dismembers
The red flag hammered in the mast-head.[8] Hide,   105
Our steel, Jonas Messias, in Thy side.[9]

VI. OUR LADY OF WALSINGHAM[1]

There once the penitents took off their shoes
And then walked barefoot the remaining mile;
And the small trees, a stream and hedgerows file
Slowly along the munching English lane,   110
Like cows to the old shrine, until you lose
Track of your dragging pain.
The stream flows down under the druid tree,
Shiloah's[2] whirlpools gurgle and make glad
The castle of God. Sailor, you were glad   115
And whistled Sion by that stream. But see:

Our Lady, too small for her canopy,
Sits near the altar. There's no comeliness
At all or charm in that expressionless
Face with its heavy eyelids. As before,   120
This face, for centuries a memory,
Non est species, neque decor,[3]
Expressionless, expresses God: it goes
Past castled Sion. She knows what God knows,
Not Calvary's Cross nor crib at Bethlehem   125
Now, and the world shall come to Walsingham.

VII

The empty winds are creaking and the oak
Splatters and splatters on the cenotaph,
The boughs are trembling and a gaff
Bobs on the untimely stroke   130
Of the greased wash exploding on a shoal-bell
In the old mouth of the Atlantic. It's well;
Atlantic, you are fouled with the blue sailors,
Sea-monsters, upward angel, downward fish:
Unmarried and corroding, spare of flesh   135
Mart once of supercilious, wing'd clippers,
Atlantic, where your bell-trap guts its spoil

---

8. At the end of *Moby-Dick*, the arm of the American Indian Tashtego appears from the waves and nails Ahab's flag to the sinking mast.
9. Because he emerged alive from the belly of a whale, the prophet Jonah is often linked with the messiah as a figure of salvation. Lowell imagines that a harpoon strikes Jonah inside the whale as the Roman soldier's spear struck Jesus on the cross.

1. Lowell took these details from E. I. Watkin's *Catholic Art and Culture,* which includes a description of the medieval shrine of the Virgin at Walsingham.
2. The stream that flows past God's Temple on Mount Sion (Isaiah 8.6). In Isaiah 51.11, the redeemed come "singing into Zion."
3. There is no ostentation or elegance (Latin).

You could cut the brackish winds with a knife
Here in Nantucket, and cast up the time
When the Lord God formed man from the sea's slime   140
And breathed into his face the breath of life,
And blue-lung'd combers lumbered to the kill.
The Lord survives the rainbow⁴ of His will.

                                                                    1946

Mr. Edwards and the Spider¹

I saw the spiders marching through the air,
Swimming from tree to tree that mildewed day
    In latter August when the hay
    Came creaking to the barn. But where
        The wind is westerly,   5
Where gnarled November makes the spiders fly
Into the apparitions of the sky,
They purpose nothing but their ease and die
Urgently beating east to sunrise and the sea;

What are we in the hands of the great God?   10
It was in vain you set up thorn and briar
    In battle array against the fire
    And treason crackling in your blood;
        For the wild thorns grow tame
And will do nothing to oppose the flame;   15
Your lacerations tell the losing game
You play against a sickness past your cure.
How will the hands be strong? How will the heart endure?²

A very little thing, a little worm,
Or hourglass-blazoned spider,³ it is said,   20
    Can kill a tiger. Will the dead
    Hold up his mirror and affirm
        To the four winds the smell
And flash of his authority? It's well
If God who holds you to the pit of hell,   25
    Much as one holds a spider, will destroy,
Baffle and dissipate your soul. As a small boy

On Windsor Marsh,⁴ I saw the spider die
When thrown into the bowels of fierce fire:

---

4. Alluding to God's covenant with Noah after the Flood. The rainbow symbolized the fact that humanity would never again be destroyed by flood (Genesis 9.11).
1. Jonathan Edwards (1703–1758), Puritan preacher and theologian. Lowell quotes his writings throughout. The details of the first stanza come from his youthful essay "Of Insects" ("The Habits of Spiders").
2. This stanza draws on Edwards's sermon "Sin-

ners in the Hands of an Angry God," whose point of departure is Ezekiel 22.14: "Can thine heart endure or can thine hands be strong in the days that I shall deal with thee" (cf. line 18).
3. The poisonous black widow spider has, on the underside of its abdomen, a red marking that resembles an hourglass.
4. East Windsor, Connecticut, Edwards's childhood home.

There's no long struggle, no desire 30
To get up on its feet and fly—
   It stretches out its feet
And dies. This is the sinner's last retreat;
Yes, and no strength exerted on the heat
Then sinews the abolished will, when sick 35
And full of burning, it will whistle on a brick.

But who can plumb the sinking of that soul?
Josiah Hawley,[5] picture yourself cast
   Into a brick-kiln where the blast
   Fans your quick vitals to a coal— 40
      If measured by a glass,
How long would it seem burning! Let there pass
A minute, ten, ten trillion; but the blaze
Is infinite, eternal: this is death,
To die and know it. This is the Black Widow, death. 45

1946

My Last Afternoon with Uncle Devereux Winslow

1922: the stone porch of my grandfather's summer house

I

"I won't go with you. I want to stay with Grandpa!"
That's how I threw cold water
on my Mother and Father's
watery martini pipe dreams at Sunday dinner.
. . . Fontainebleau,[1] Mattapoisett, Puget Sound. . . . 5
Nowhere was anywhere after a summer
at my Grandfather's farm.
Diamond-pointed, athirst and Norman,[2]
its alley of poplars
paraded from Grandmother's rose garden 10
to a scary stand of virgin pine,
scrub, and paths forever pioneering.

One afternoon in 1922,
I sat on the stone porch, looking through
screens as black-grained as drifting coal. 15
Tockytock, tockytock
clumped our Alpine, Edwardian cuckoo clock,
slung with strangled, wooden game.
Our farmer was cementing a root-house[3] under the hill.
One of my hands was cool on a pile 20
of black earth, the other warm
on a pile of lime. All about me
were the works of my Grandfather's hands:

5. Edwards's uncle, Joseph Hawley.
1. Rich pastoral suburb of Paris, site of one of the royal *châteaux*.

2. A stage of Romanesque architecture developed in the French province of Normandy.
3. For storing bulbs, root vegetables, etc.

snapshots of his *Liberty Bell* silver mine;
his high school at *Stuttgart am Neckar;*   25
stogie-brown beams; fools'-gold nuggets;
octagonal red tiles,
sweaty with a secret dank, crummy with ant-stale;
a Rocky Mountain chaise longue,
its legs, shellacked saplings.   30
A pastel-pale Huckleberry Finn
fished with a broom straw in a basin
hollowed out of a millstone.
Like my Grandfather, the décor
was manly, comfortable,   35
overbearing, disproportioned.

What were those sunflowers? Pumpkins floating shoulder-high?
It was sunset, Sadie and Nellie
bearing pitchers of ice-tea,
oranges, lemons, mint, and peppermints,   40
and the jug of shandygaff,
which Grandpa made by blending half and half
yeasty, wheezing homemade sarsaparilla with beer.
The farm, entitled *Char-de-sa*
in the Social Register,   45
was named for my Grandfather's children:
Charlotte, Devereux, and Sarah.
No one had died there in my lifetime . . .
Only Cinder, our Scottie puppy
paralyzed from gobbling toads.   50
I sat mixing black earth and lime.

II

I was five and a half.
My formal pearl gray shorts
had been worn for three minutes.
My perfection was the Olympian   55
poise of my models in the imperishable autumn
display windows
of Rogers Peet's boys' store below the State House
in Boston. Distorting drops of water
pinpricked my face in the basin's mirror.   60
I was a stuffed toucan
with a bibulous, multicolored beak.

III

Up in the air
by the lakeview window in the billards-room,
lurid in the doldrums of the sunset hour,   65
my Great Aunt Sarah
was learning *Samson and Delilah.*[4]
She thundered on the keyboard of her dummy piano,

---

4. A piano version of the opera by Camille Saint-Saëns (1835–1921).

with gauze curtains like a boudoir table,
accordionlike yet soundless.   70
It had been bought to spare the nerves
of my Grandmother,
tone-deaf, quick as a cricket,
now needing a fourth for "Auction,"[5]
and casting a thirsty eye   75
on Aunt Sarah, risen like the phoenix
from her bed of troublesome snacks and Tauchnitz[6] classics.

Forty years earlier,
twenty, auburn headed,
grasshopper notes of genius!   80
Family gossip says Aunt Sarah
tilted her archaic Athenian nose
and jilted an Astor.
Each morning she practiced
on the grand piano at Symphony Hall,   85
deathlike in the off-season summer—
its naked Greek statues draped with purple
like the saints in Holy Week. . . .
On the recital day, she failed to appear.

                                IV

I picked with a clean finger nail at the blue anchor   90
on my sailor blouse washed white as a spinnaker.
What in the world was I wishing?
. . . A sail-colored horse browsing in the bullrushes . . .
A fluff of the west wind puffing
my blouse, kiting me over our seven chimneys,   95
troubling the waters. . . .
As small as sapphires were the ponds: *Quittacus, Snippituit,*
and *Assawompset,* halved by "the Island,"
where my Uncle's duck blind
floated in a barrage of smoke-clouds.   100
Double-barreled shotguns
stuck out like bundles of baby crow-bars.
A single sculler in a camouflaged kayak
was quacking to the decoys. . . .

At the cabin between the waters,   105
the nearest windows were already boarded.
Uncle Devereux was closing camp for the winter.
As if posed for "the engagement photograph,"
he was wearing his severe
war-uniform of a volunteer Canadian officer.   110
Daylight from the doorway riddled his student posters,
tacked helter-skelter on walls as raw as a boardwalk.
Mr. Punch,[7] a water melon in hockey tights,

---

5. Auction bridge.
6. German paperback editions that included standard English and American works (in English).

7. A plump cartoon-figure emblem of the English humor magazine *Punch,* founded in 1841.

was tossing off a decanter of Scotch.
La Belle France in a red, white and blue toga 115
was accepting the arm of her "protector,"
the ingenu and porcine Edward VII.[8]
The pre-war music hall belles
had goose necks, glorious signatures, beauty-moles,
and coils of hair like rooster tails. 120
The finest poster was two or three young men in khaki kilts
being bushwhacked on the veldt[9]—
They were almost life-size. . . .

My Uncle was dying at twenty-nine.
"You are behaving like children," 125
said my Grandfather,
when my Uncle and Aunt left their three baby daughters,
and sailed for Europe on a last honeymoon . . .
I cowered in terror.
I wasn't a child at all— 130
unseen and all-seeing, I was Agrippina[1]
in the Golden House of Nero. . . .
Near me was the white measuring-door
my Grandfather had penciled with my Uncle's heights.
In 1911, he had stopped growing at just six feet. 135
While I sat on the tiles,
and dug at the anchor on my sailor blouse,
Uncle Devereux stood behind me.
He was as brushed as Bayard, our riding horse.
His face was putty. 140
His blue coat and white trousers
grew sharper and straighter.
His coat was a blue jay's tail,
his trousers were solid cream from the top of the bottle.
He was animated, hierarchical, 145
like a ginger snap man in a clothes-press.
He was dying of the incurable Hodgkin's disease. . . .
My hands were warm, then cool, on the piles
of earth and lime,
a black pile and a white pile. . . . 150
Come winter,
Uncle Devereux would blend to the one color.

1959

---

8. A poster celebrating the Entente Cordiale, a rapprochement between England and France. Edward VII, king of England, famous as a ladies' man, is depicted with his arm around the female emblem of France.
9. Open country in South Africa. The Boer War (1899–1902) was fought by the English against descendants of Dutch settlers there.
1. Mother of the Roman emperor Nero, who involved herself in court intrigue and affairs of state. She poisoned her second husband and was later murdered by her son.

Memories of West Street and Lepke[1]

Only teaching on Tuesdays, book-worming
in pajamas fresh from the washer each morning,
I hog a whole house on Boston's
"hardly passionate Marlborough Street,"[2]
where even the man   5
scavenging filth in the back alley trash cans,
has two children, a beach wagon, a helpmate,
and is a "young Republican."
I have a nine months' daughter,
young enough to be my granddaughter.   10
Like the sun she rises in her flame-flamingo infants' wear.

These are the tranquillized *Fifties*,
and I am forty. Ought I to regret my seedtime?
I was a fire-breathing Catholic C.O.,[3]
and made my manic statement,   15
telling off the state and president, and then
sat waiting sentence in the bull pen
beside a Negro boy with curlicues
of marijuana in his hair.

Given a year.   20
I walked on the roof of the West Street Jail, a short
enclosure like my school soccer court,
and saw the Hudson River once a day
through sooty clothesline entanglements
and bleaching khaki tenements.   25
Strolling, I yammered metaphysics with Abramowitz,
a jaundice-yellow ("it's really tan")
and fly-weight pacifist,
so vegetarian,
he wore rope shoes and preferred fallen fruit.   30
He tried to convert Bioff and Brown,
the Hollywood pimps, to his diet.
Hairy, muscular, suburban,
wearing chocolate double-breasted suits,
they blew their tops and beat him black and blue.   35

I was so out of things, I'd never heard
of the Jehovah's Witnesses.[4]
"Are you a C.O.?" I asked a fellow jailbird.
"No," he answered, "I'm a J.W."

---

1. In 1943 Lowell was sentenced to a year in New York's West Street jail for his refusal to serve in the armed forces. Among the prisoners was Lepke Buchalter, head of Murder Incorporated, an organized crime syndicate, who had been convicted of murder.
2. William James's phrase for a street in the ele-gant Back Bay section of Boston, where Lowell lived in the 1950s.
3. Conscientious objector (to war).
4. A Christian revivalist sect strongly opposed to war and denying the power of the state in matters of conscience.

He taught me the "hospital tuck,"⁵ 40
and pointed out the T-shirted back
of *Murder Incorporated*'s Czar Lepke,
there piling towels on a rack,
or dawdling off to his little segregated cell full
of things forbidden the common man: 45
a portable radio, a dresser, two toy American
flags tied together with a ribbon of Easter palm.
Flabby, bald, lobotomized,
he drifted in a sheepish calm,
where no agonizing reappraisal 50
jarred his concentration on the electric chair—
hanging like an oasis in his air
of lost connections. . . .

1959

Skunk Hour

for Elizabeth Bishop

Nautilus Island's¹ hermit
heiress still lives through winter in her Spartan cottage;
her sheep still graze above the sea.
Her son's a bishop. Her farmer
is first selectman in our village; 5
she's in her dotage.

Thirsting for
the hierarchic privacy
of Queen Victoria's century,
she buys up all 10
the eyesores facing her shore,
and lets them fall.

The season's ill—
we've lost our summer millionaire,
who seemed to leap from an L. L. Bean 15
catalogue.² His nine-knot yawl
was auctioned off to lobstermen.
A red fox stain covers Blue Hill.

And now our fairy
decorator brightens his shop for fall; 20
his fishnet's filled with orange cork,
orange, his cobbler's bench and awl;
there is no money in his work,
he'd rather marry.

5. The authorized, efficient way of making beds in a hospital.
1. The poem is set in Castine, Maine, where Lowell had a summer house.
2. A mail-order house in Maine, which deals primarily with sporting and camping goods.

One dark night,   25
my Tudor Ford climbed the hill's skull;
I watched for love-cars. Lights turned down,
they lay together, hull to hull,
where the graveyard shelves on the town. . . .
My mind's not right.   30

A car radio bleats,
"Love, O careless Love. . . ." I hear
my ill-spirit sob in each blood cell,
as if my hand were at its throat. . . .
I myself am hell;[3]   35
nobody's here—

only skunks, that search
in the moonlight for a bite to eat.
They march on their soles up Main Street:
white stripes, moonstruck eyes' red fire   40
under the chalk-dry and spar spire
of the Trinitarian Church.

I stand on top
of our back steps and breathe the rich air—
a mother skunk with her column of kittens swills the garbage pail.   45
She jabs her wedge-head in a cup
of sour cream, drops her ostrich tail,
and will not scare.

                                                          1959

Night Sweat

Work-table, litter, books and standing lamp,
plain things, my stalled equipment, the old broom—
but I am living in a tidied room,
for ten nights now I've felt the creeping damp
float over my pajamas' wilted white . . .   5
Sweet salt embalms me and my head is wet,
everything streams and tells me this is right;
my life's fever is soaking in night sweat—
one life, one writing! But the downward glide
and bias of existing wrings us dry—   10
always inside me is the child who died,
always inside me is his will to die—
one universe, one body . . . in this urn
the animal night sweats of the spirit burn.
Behind me! You! Again I feel the light   15
lighten my leaded eyelids, while the gray
skulled horses whinny for the soot of night.
I dabble in the dapple of the day,

3. "Which way I fly is Hell, myself am Hell" (Satan in Milton's *Paradise Lost* 4.75).

a heap of wet clothes, seamy, shivering,
I see my flesh and bedding washed with light,   20
my child exploding into dynamite,
my wife . . . your lightness alters everything,
and tears the black web from the spider's sack,
as your heart hops and flutters like a hare.
Poor turtle, tortoise, if I cannot clear   25
the surface of these troubled waters here,
absolve me, help me, Dear Heart, as you bear
this world's dead weight and cycle on your back.

1964

For the Union Dead[1]

"Relinquunt Omnia Servare Rem Publicam."[2]

The old South Boston Aquarium stands
in a Sahara of snow now. Its broken windows are boarded.
The bronze weathervane cod has lost half its scales.
The airy tanks are dry.

Once my nose crawled like a snail on the glass;   5
my hand tingled
to burst the bubbles
drifting from the noses of the cowed, compliant fish.

My hand draws back. I often sigh still
for the dark downward and vegetating kingdom   10
of the fish and reptile. One morning last March,
I pressed against the new barbed and galvanized

fence on the Boston Common. Behind their cage,
yellow dinosaur steamshovels were grunting
as they cropped up tons of mush and grass   15
to gouge their underworld garage.

Parking spaces luxuriate like civic
sandpiles in the heart of Boston.
A girdle of orange, Puritan-pumpkin colored girders
braces the tingling Statehouse,   20

shaking over the excavations, as it faces Colonel Shaw
and his bell-cheeked Negro infantry

1. First published under the title *Colonel Shaw and the Massachusetts' 54th* in a paperback edition of *Life Studies* (1960). With a change of title, it became the title poem of *For the Union Dead* (1964).
2. Robert Gould Shaw (1837–1863) led the first all African American regiment in the North during the Civil War. He was killed in the attack against Fort Wagner, South Carolina. A bronze relief by the sculptor Augustus Saint-Gaudens (1848–

1897), dedicated in 1897, standing opposite the Massachusetts State House on Boston Common, commemorates the deaths. A Latin inscription on the monument reads *Omnia Reliquit Servare Rem Publicam* ("He leaves all behind to serve the Republic"). Lowell's epigraph alters the inscription slightly, changing the third-person singular (*he*) to the third-person plural: "*They* give up everything to serve the Republic."

on St. Gaudens' shaking Civil War relief,
propped by a plank splint against the garage's earthquake.

Two months after marching through Boston,   25
half the regiment was dead;
at the dedication
William James[3] could almost hear the bronze Negroes breathe.

Their monument sticks like a fishbone
in the city's throat.   30
Its Colonel is as lean
as a compass-needle.

He has an angry wrenlike vigilance,
a greyhound's gentle tautness;
he seems to wince at pleasure,   35
and suffocate for privacy.

He is out of bounds now. He rejoices in man's lovely,
peculiar power to choose life and die—
when he leads his black soldiers to death,
he cannot bend his back.   40

On a thousand small town New England greens,
the old white churches hold their air
of sparse, sincere rebellion; frayed flags
quilt the graveyards of the Grand Army of the Republic.

The stone statues of the abstract Union Soldier   45
grow slimmer and younger each year—
wasp-waisted, they doze over muskets
and muse through their sideburns . . .

Shaw's father wanted no monument
except the ditch,   50
where his son's body was thrown[4]
and lost with his "niggers."

The ditch is nearer.
There are no statues for the last war[5] here;
on Boylston Street,[6] a commercial photograph   55
shows Hiroshima boiling

over a Mosler Safe, the "Rock of Ages"
that survived the blast. Space is nearer.
When I crouch to my television set,
the drained faces of Negro school-children rise like balloons.[7] 60

---

3. Philosopher and psychologist (1842–1910)
who taught at Harvard.
4. By the Confederate soldiers at Fort Wagner.
5. World War II.

6. In Boston, where the poem is set.
7. Probably news photographs connected with
contemporary civil rights demonstrations to secure
desegregation of schools in the South.

Colonel Shaw
is riding on his bubble,
he waits
for the blessed break.

The Aquarium is gone. Everywhere,   65
giant finned cars nose forward like fish;
a savage servility
slides by on grease.

                                                                    1960, 1964

GWENDOLYN BROOKS
1917–2000

"If there was ever a born poet," Alice Walker once said in an interview, "I think it is Brooks." A passionate sense of language and an often daring use of formal structures are hallmarks of Gwendolyn Brooks's poetry. She used these gifts in a career characterized by dramatic evolution, a career that linked two very different generations of African American poets. "Until 1967," Brooks said, "my own Blackness did not confront me with a shrill spelling of itself." She then grouped herself with militant black writers and defined her work as belonging primarily to the African American community. In her earlier work, however, Brooks followed the example of the older writers of the Harlem Renaissance, Langston Hughes and Countee Cullen among them, who honored the ideal of an integrated society. In that period her work received support largely from white audiences. But Brooks's changing sense of her commitments should not obscure her persistent, underlying concerns. She was never a poet without political awareness, and in remarkably versatile poems, both early and late, she wrote about black experience and black rage, with a particular awareness of the complex lives of black women.

Brooks was born in Topeka, Kansas; she grew up in Chicago and is closely identified with the energies and problems of its black community. She went to Chicago's Englewood High School and graduated from Wilson Junior College. Brooks remembered writing poetry from the time she was seven and keeping poetry notebooks from the time she was eleven. She got her education in the moderns—Pound and Eliot—under the guidance of a rich Chicago socialite, Inez Cunningham Stark, who was a reader for *Poetry* magazine and taught a poetry class at the Southside Community Art Center. Her first book, *A Street in Bronzeville* (1945), took its title from the name journalists gave to the Chicago black ghetto. Her poems portrayed the waste and loss that are the inevitable result of what Langston Hughes called the blacks' "dream deferred." With her second book of poems, *Annie Allen* (1949), Brooks became the first African American to receive the Pulitzer Prize for poetry.

In *Annie Allen* and in her Bronzeville poems (*Bronzeville Boys and Girls*, 1956, continued the work begun in *A Street in Bronzeville*), Brooks concentrated on portraits of what Hughes called "the ordinary aspects of black life." In character sketches she stressed the vitality and the often subversive morality of ghetto figures; good girls who want to be bad, the boredom of the children of hardworking pious mothers, the laments of black mothers and women abandoned by their men. Brooks's diction was a combination of the florid biblical speech of black Protestant preachers, street talk, and the main speech patterns of English and American verse. She wrote vigorous, strongly accented, and strongly rhymed lines with a great deal of alliteration. She also cultivated traditional lyric forms; for example, she was one of the few modern poets to write extensively in the sonnet form.

A great change in Brooks's life came with the Second Black Writers' Conference at Fisk University in 1967, in whose charged activist atmosphere she encountered many of the new young black poets. After this, Brooks became interested in writing poetry exclusively for black audiences. She drew closer to militant political groups as a result of conducting poetry workshops for some members of the Blackstone Rangers, a teenage gang in Chicago. In autobiographical writings such as her prose *Report from Part One*, Brooks became more self-conscious about her own potential role as a leader of black feminists. She left her New York publisher to have her work printed by African American publishers, especially the Broadside Press. Brooks's poetry, too, changed, in both its focus and its technique. Her subjects tend to be more explicitly political and to deal with questions of revolutionary violence and issues of African American identity. In style, too, her work evolved out of the concentrated imagery and narratives of her earlier writing, with its often formal diction, and moved toward an increased use of the energetic, improvisatory rhythms of jazz, the combinations of African chants, and an emphatically spoken language. The result is a poetry constantly revising itself and the world, open to change but evocative of history. "How does one convey the influence Gwendolyn Brooks has had on generations—not only writers but people from all walks of life?" Rita Dove has remarked, remembering how, as a young woman, she was "struck by these poems, poems . . . that weren't afraid to take language and swamp it, twist it and engage it so that it shimmered and dashed and lingered."

FROM A STREET IN BRONZEVILLE

to David and Keziah Brooks

kitchenette building

We are things of dry hours and the involuntary plan,
Grayed in, and gray. "Dream" makes a giddy sound, not strong
Like "rent," "feeding a wife," "satisfying a man."

But could a dream send up through onion fumes
Its white and violet, fight with fried potatoes   5
And yesterday's garbage ripening in the hall,
Flutter, or sing an aria down these rooms

Even if we were willing to let it in,
Had time to warm it, keep it very clean,
Anticipate a message, let it begin?   10

We wonder. But not well! not for a minute!
Since Number Five is out of the bathroom now,
We think of lukewarm water, hope to get in it.

1945

the mother

Abortions will not let you forget.
You remember the children you got that you did not get,
The damp small pulps with a little or with no hair,
The singers and workers that never handled the air.
You will never neglect or beat   5
Them, or silence or buy with a sweet.
You will never wind up the sucking-thumb
Or scuttle off ghosts that come.
You will never leave them, controlling your luscious sigh,
Return for a snack of them, with gobbling mother-eye.   10

I have heard in the voices of the wind the voices of my dim
     killed children.
I have contracted. I have eased
My dim dears at the breasts they could never suck.
I have said, Sweets, if I sinned, if I seized
Your luck   15
And your lives from your unfinished reach,
If I stole your births and your names,
Your straight baby tears and your games,
Your stilted or lovely loves, your tumults, your marriages, aches,
     and your deaths,
If I poisoned the beginnings of your breaths,   20
Believe that even in my deliberateness I was not deliberate.
Though why should I whine,
Whine that the crime was other than mine?—
Since anyhow you are dead.
Or rather, or instead,   25
You were never made.

But that too, I am afraid,
Is faulty: oh, what shall I say, how is the truth to be said?
You were born, you had body, you died.
It is just that you never giggled or planned or cried.   30

Believe me, I loved you all.
Believe me, I knew you, though faintly, and I loved, I loved you
All.

                                                                    1945

a song in the front yard

I've stayed in the front yard all my life.
I want a peek at the back
Where it's rough and untended and hungry weed grows.
A girl gets sick of a rose.

I want to go in the back yard now   5
And maybe down the alley,
To where the charity children play.
I want a good time today.

They do some wonderful things.
They have some wonderful fun.   10
My mother sneers, but I say it's fine
How they don't have to go in at quarter to nine.
My mother, she tells me that Johnnie Mae
Will grow up to be a bad woman.
That George'll be taken to Jail soon or late   15
(On account of last winter he sold our back gate.)

But I say it's fine. Honest, I do.
And I'd like to be a bad woman, too,
And wear the brave stockings of night-black lace
And strut down the streets with paint on my face.   20

                                                    1945

The White Troops Had Their Orders But the Negroes Looked Like Men

They had supposed their formula was fixed.
They had obeyed instructions to devise
A type of cold, a type of hooded gaze.
But when the Negroes came they were perplexed.
These Negroes looked like men. Besides, it taxed   5
Time and the temper to remember those
Congenital iniquities that cause
Disfavor of the darkness. Such as boxed
Their feelings properly, complete to tags—
A box for dark men and a box for Other—   10
Would often find the contents had been scrambled.
Or even switched. Who really gave two figs?
Neither the earth nor heaven ever trembled.
And there was nothing startling in the weather.

                                                    1945

From The Womanhood

The Children of the Poor

II

What shall I give my children? who are poor,
Who are adjudged the leastwise of the land,
Who are my sweetest lepers, who demand

No velvet and no velvety velour;
But who have begged me for a brisk contour,   5
Crying that they are quasi, contraband
Because unfinished, graven by a hand
Less than angelic, admirable or sure.
My hand is stuffed with mode, design, device.
But I lack access to my proper stone.   10
And plenitude of plan shall not suffice
Nor grief nor love shall be enough alone
To ratify my little halves who bear
Across an autumn freezing everywhere.

                                                    1949

We Real Cool

THE POOL PLAYERS.
SEVEN AT THE GOLDEN SHOVEL.

> We real cool. We
> Left school. We
>
> Lurk late. We
> Strike straight. We
>
> Sing sin. We   5
> Thin gin. We
>
> Jazz June. We
> Die soon.

                                                    1960

The Bean Eaters

They eat beans mostly, this old yellow pair.
Dinner is a casual affair.
Plain chipware on a plain and creaking wood,
Tin flatware.

Two who are Mostly Good.   5
Two who have lived their day,
But keep on putting on their clothes
And putting things away.

And remembering . . .
Remembering, with twinklings and twinges,   10
As they lean over the beans in their rented back room that is full of beads
    and receipts and dolls and cloths, tobacco crumbs, vases and fringes.

                                                    1960

A Bronzeville Mother Loiters in Mississippi. Meanwhile a Mississippi Mother Burns Bacon

From the first it had been like a
Ballad. It had the beat inevitable. It had the blood.
A wildness cut up, and tied in little bunches,
Like the four-line stanzas of the ballads she had never quite
Understood—the ballads they had set her to, in school.   5

Herself: the milk-white maid, the "maid mild"
Of the ballad. Pursued
By the Dark Villain. Rescued by the Fine Prince.
The Happiness-Ever-After.
That was worth anything.   10
It was good to be a "maid mild."
That made the breath go fast.

Her bacon burned. She
Hastened to hide it in the step-on can, and
Drew more strips from the meat case. The eggs and sour-milk biscuits   15
Did well. She set out a jar
Of her new quince preserve.

. . . But there was a something about the matter of the Dark Villain.
He should have been older, perhaps.
The hacking down of a villain was more fun to think about   20
When his menace possessed undisputed breadth, undisputed height,
And a harsh kind of vice.
And best of all, when his history was cluttered
With the bones of many eaten knights and princesses.

The fun was disturbed, then all but nullified   25
When the Dark Villain was a blackish child
Of fourteen, with eyes still too young to be dirty,
And a mouth too young to have lost every reminder
Of its infant softness.

That boy must have been surprised! For   30
These were grown-ups. Grown-ups were supposed to be wise.
And the Fine Prince—and that other—so tall, so broad, so
Grown! Perhaps the boy had never guessed
That the trouble with grown-ups was that under the magnificent shell of
    adulthood, just under,
Waited the baby full of tantrums.   35

It occurred to her that there may have been something
Ridiculous in the picture of the Fine Prince
Rushing (rich with the breadth and height and
Mature solidness whose lack, in the Dark Villain, was impressing her,
Confronting her more and more as this first day after the trial   40

And acquittal wore on) rushing
With his heavy companion to hack down (unhorsed)
That little foe.
So much had happened, she could not remember now what that foe had
    done
Against her, or if anything had been done.   45
The one thing in the world that she did know and knew
With terrifying clarity was that her composition
Had disintegrated. That, although the pattern prevailed,
The breaks were everywhere. That she could think
Of no thread capable of the necessary   50
Sew-work.

She made the babies sit in their places at the table.
Then, before calling Him, she hurried
To the mirror with her comb and lipstick. It was necessary
To be more beautiful than ever.   55
The beautiful wife.
For sometimes she fancied he looked at her as though
Measuring her. As if he considered, Had she been worth It?

Had *she* been worth the blood, the cramped cries, the little stuttering
    bravado,
The gradual dulling of those Negro eyes,   60
The sudden, overwhelming *little-boyness* in that barn?
Whatever she might feel or half-feel, the lipstick necessity was something
    apart. He must never conclude
That she had not been worth It.

He sat down, the Fine Prince, and
Began buttering a biscuit. He looked at his hands.   65
He twisted in his chair, he scratched his nose.
He glanced again, almost secretly, at his hands.
More papers were in from the North, he mumbled. More meddling
    headlines.
With their pepper-words, "bestiality," and "barbarism," and
"Shocking."   70
The half-sneers he had mastered for the trial worked across
His sweet and pretty face.

What he'd like to do, he explained, was kill them all.
The time lost. The unwanted fame.
Still, it had been fun to show those intruders   75
A thing or two. To show that snappy-eyed mother,
That sassy, Northern, brown-black——

Nothing could stop Mississippi.
He knew that. Big Fella
Knew that.   80
And, what was so good, Mississippi knew that.
Nothing and nothing could stop Mississippi.
They could send in their petitions, and scar

Their newspapers with bleeding headlines. Their governors
Could appeal to Washington. . . .   85

"What I want," the older baby said, "is 'lasses on my jam."
Whereupon the younger baby
Picked up the molasses pitcher and threw
The molasses in his brother's face. Instantly
The Fine Prince leaned across the table and slapped   90
The small and smiling criminal.

She did not speak. When the Hand
Came down and away, and she could look at her child,
At her baby-child,
She could think only of blood.   95
Surely her baby's cheek
Had disappeared, and in its place, surely,
Hung a heaviness, a lengthening red, a red that had no end.
She shook her head. It was not true, of course.
It was not true at all. The   100
Child's face was as always, the
Color of the paste in her paste-jar.

She left the table, to the tune of the children's lamentations, which were
    shriller
Than ever. She
Looked out of a window. She said not a word. *That*   105
Was one of the new Somethings—
The fear,
Tying her as with iron.

Suddenly she felt his hands upon her. He had followed her
To the window. The children were whimpering now.   110
Such bits of tots. And she, their mother,
Could not protect them. She looked at her shoulders, still
Gripped in the claim of his hands. She tried, but could not resist the idea
That a red ooze was seeping, spreading darkly, thickly, slowly,
Over her white shoulders, her own shoulders,   115
And over all of Earth and Mars.

He whispered something to her, did the Fine Prince, something
About love, something about love and night and intention.

She heard no hoof-beat of the horse and saw no flash of the shining steel.
He pulled her face around to meet   120
His, and there it was, close close,
For the first time in all those days and nights,
His mouth, wet and red,
So very, very, very red,
Closed over hers.   125

Then a sickness heaved within her. The courtroom Coca-Cola,
The courtroom beer and hate and sweat and drone,

Pushed like a wall against her. She wanted to bear it.
But his mouth would not go away and neither would the
Decapitated exclamation points in that Other Woman's eyes. 130

She did not scream.
She stood there.
But a hatred for him burst into glorious flower,
And its perfume enclasped them—big,
Bigger than all magnolias. 135

The last bleak news of the ballad.
The rest of the rugged music.
The last quatrain.

1960

The Last Quatrain of the Ballad of Emmett Till[1]

>   after the murder,
>   after the burial

>   Emmett's mother is a pretty-faced thing;
>   the tint of pulled taffy.
>   She sits in a red room,   5
>   drinking black coffee.
>   She kisses her killed boy.
>   And she is sorry.
>   Chaos in windy grays
>   through a red prairie.   10

1960

The Blackstone Rangers[1]

I. As Seen by Disciplines[2]

There they are.
Thirty at the corner.
Black, raw, ready.
Sores in the city
that do not want to heal.   5

II. The Leaders

Jeff. Gene. Geronimo. And Bop.
They cancel, cure and curry.
Hardly the dupes of the downtown thing

---

1. A fourteen-year-old African American boy
lynched in Mississippi in 1955 for allegedly "leer-
ing" at a white woman.

1. A tough Chicago street gang. Blackstone Street
is the eastern boundary of Chicago's black ghetto.
2. I.e., law enforcers.

the cold bonbon,
the rhinestone thing. And hardly   10
in a hurry.
Hardly Belafonte, King,
Black Jesus, Stokely, Malcolm X or Rap.
Bungled trophies.
Their country is a Nation on no map.   15

Jeff, Gene, Geronimo and Bop
in the passionate noon,
in bewitching night
are the detailed men, the copious men.
They curry, cure,   20
they cancel, cancelled images whose Concerts
are not divine, vivacious; the different tins
are intense last entries; pagan argument;
translations of the night.

The Blackstone bitter bureaus   25
(bureaucracy is footloose) edit, fuse
unfashionable damnations and descent;
and exulting, monstrous hand on monstrous hand,
construct, strangely, a monstrous pearl or grace.

III. Gang Girls

A RANGERETTE

Gang Girls are sweet exotics.   30
Mary Ann
uses the nutrients of her orient,
but sometimes sighs for Cities of blue and jewel
beyond her Ranger rim of Cottage Grove.[3]
(Bowery Boys, Disciples, Whip-Birds will   35
dissolve no margins, stop no savory sanctities.)

Mary is
a rose in a whiskey glass.

Mary's
Februaries shudder and are gone. Aprils   40
fret frankly, lilac hurries on.
Summer is a hard irregular ridge.
October looks away.
And that's the Year!
            Save for her bugle-love.   45
Save for the bleat of not-obese devotion.
Save for Somebody Terribly Dying, under
the philanthropy of robins. Save for her Ranger
bringing
an amount of rainbow in a string-drawn bag.   50

---

3. Street of overcrowded tenements in the ghetto.

"Where did you get the diamond?" Do not ask:
but swallow, straight, the spirals of his flask
and assist him at your zipper; pet his lips
and help him clutch you.

Love's another departure.   55
Will there be any arrivals, confirmations?
Will there be gleaning?

Mary, the Shakedancer's child
from the rooming-flat, pants carefully, peers at
her laboring lover. . . .   60
                    Mary! Mary Ann!
Settle for sandwiches! settle for stocking caps!
for sudden blood, aborted carnival,
the props and niceties of non-loneliness—
the rhymes of Leaning.   65

                                                                1968

To the Diaspora[1]

you did not know you were Afrika

When you set out for Afrika
you did not know you were going.
Because
you did not know you were Afrika.
You did not know the Black continent   5
that had to be reached
was you.

I could not have told you then that some sun
would come,
somewhere over the road,   10
would come evoking the diamonds
of you, the Black continent—
somewhere over the road.
You would not have believed my mouth.

When I told you, meeting you somewhere close   15
to the heat and youth of the road,
liking my loyalty, liking belief,
you smiled and you thanked me but very little believed me.

Here is some sun. Some.
Now off into the places rough to reach.   20
Though dry, though drowsy, all unwillingly a-wobble,
into the dissonant and dangerous crescendo.
Your work, that was done, to be done to be done to be done.

                                                                1981

---

1. People settled far from their ancestral homelands.

The Coora Flower

Today I learned the *coora* flower
grows high in the mountains of Itty-go-luba Bésa.
Province Meechee.
Pop. 39.

Now I am coming home.   5
This, at least, is Real, and what I know.

It was restful, learning nothing necessary.
School is tiny vacation. At least you can sleep.
At least you can think of love or feeling your boy friend against you
(which is not free from grief).   10

But now it's Real Business.
I am Coming Home.

My mother will be screaming in an almost dirty dress.
The crack is gone. So a Man will be in the house.

I must watch myself.   15
I must not dare to sleep.

1991

ROBERT DUNCAN
1919–1988

In *The Truth & Life of Myth: An Essay in Essential Autobiography* (1968), Robert
Duncan writes: "In the very beginning, in the awakening of childhood back of this
later awakening of the man I was to be, there had been my mother's voice reading
the fairy tales and myths that were to remain the charged ground of my poetic reality."
Myth remained for Duncan the ground of poetic reality throughout his life, expressing
for him the relation between the individual life and the life of the universe. Duncan
believes in the enduring truth of myth as a story of soul making, which for him, as
for Keats, is the poet's primary activity. A poet learned and widely read, Duncan makes
use of myths from many traditions (in this, he reminds us of Ezra Pound), including
those of Christianity, Jewish mysticism, and classical and Egyptian mythology.

Duncan's deepest concerns as a poet are expressed in the myth of Eros and Psyche,
which he retells in "A Poem Beginning with a Line by Pindar." He once wrote, "Psyche
must doubt and seek to know; reading must become life and writing; and all go wrong.
There is no way then but Psyche's search, the creative work of a union in knowledge
and experience." This description of Psyche's work might serve to describe his own:
in "A Poem Beginning with a Line by Pindar" Duncan carries out the work of poets
before him (Pound, William Carlos Williams, and especially, Walt Whitman): the
creative work of understanding experience (both the individual's and the nation's)
and of recovering lost possibility. As Psyche's task is the recovery of Eros, Duncan is

a love poet in the fullest sense. Love, for him, necessarily involves loss and recovery, death and life. The recurring image of Atlantis in his work reinforces this sense of a paradise lost through catastrophe, to be recovered by the poet, as by Psyche, through trial and through the effort of imagination.

Duncan's life began with loss: his mother died at his birth, in Oakland, California, and he himself has connected this birth memory to his fascination with "the mother-country that has been lost in legend." He was adopted at six months by Edwin and Minnehaha Symmes, who both engaged in Hermetic and Rosicrucian studies. From them he took his continuing interest in the magical and the occult. Duncan grew to his early manhood and to his vocation as a poet during World War II, and his under-standing of his own personal strife has always been linked for him to a sense of national strife, as in "A Poem Beginning with a Line by Pindar." In 1936 he entered the University of California at Berkeley and found there the first of several artistic and social communities that would always be an important part of his life. In 1938 he moved east and during the early 1940s lived in New York City, where he was part of a group of writers that included Anaïs Nin, Henry Miller, Kenneth Patchen, and George Barker. (The poems of his book *Caesar's Gate,* published in 1955, describe what he has called the "adolescent dismay" of this period.) In New York he also came in contact with the abstract expressionist painters, and when he returned to Berkeley in 1946, he brought with him the excitement of what he had seen. There, under the mentorship of Kenneth Rexroth, Duncan along with the poets Jack Spicer and Robin Blaser began a "renaissance," which he has described as "a reinterpretation of the work of Stein, Joyce, Pound, H. D., Williams, D. H. Lawrence, not as 'we moderns' but as links in a spiritual tradition."

Heavenly City Earthly City, Duncan's first book, appeared in 1947. In the 1950s he encountered the poetics of Charles Olson, whose understanding of the poem as "a field of action" confirmed and invigorated Duncan's own thinking about poetic forms. In 1956 he taught for several months at Black Mountain College in North Carolina, where Olson was rector. Also in the 1950s he began a domestic life with the painter Jess Collins, which was to inform his work for the rest of his life. The household they created together existed, for Duncan, in vital relation to his sense of place in the universe as a whole ("The imagination of this cosmos is as immediate to me as the imagination of my household or myself," he wrote in his essay "Toward an Open Universe"). Both hearth and cosmos are governed by love, the creator for Duncan of growth and harmony but also the source of fury and suffering. Since his essay "The Homosexual in Society" (1944), Duncan had declared his homoeroticism, and his work gives powerful expression to the struggles of the passional self.

The publication of *The Opening of the Field* (1960) marked, Duncan has said, the beginning of his mature work as a poet, and the poems of this book remain some of his finest. Close to this time he also began his important prose work, *The H. D. Book,* a work-in-progress of which more than ten chapters appeared in little magazines during his life. Duncan first read H. D.'s *Trilogy* in the 1940s, and her poems were relatively unknown when he began his study of her. In what may be one of the most important works of criticism by an American poet in the twentieth century, he explores not only the connections between his own work and H. D.'s but his vision of the generative power of imagination and the life-restoring nature of poetry. His commentaries on modernism in various chapters of this book are often brilliant and provocative. Duncan's work on H. D. issues from his effort as a poet to renew traditions and knowledge lost to modern life and to open up the possibilities of lan-guage when "all the nets of words are gone" (as he writes in his moving poem for H. D., "Doves"). Duncan writes to reclaim the poetic ground from which mythology arises, a place (like the meadow in "Often I am Permitted to Return to a Meadow") that permits return to the "first feeling" of childhood and recovery of a tradition of spiritual testimony. To paraphrase the title of one of William Carlos Williams's essays, the basis of Duncan's faith in art is his belief in the regenerative possibilities of language, its capacity to renew and reorder. For him (as for William Blake, whom he began to study in the 1950s), the domain of imagination encompasses the entire universe.

Duncan used *traditional* as an adjective of praise and understood his work as recovering the past in present meanings. His models included not only H. D. and Blake but also the major figures of Whitman and Dante. He was drawn toward Whitman and Dante, he wrote, as each "projected a poem central to his civilization and his vision of ultimate reality—*Leaves of Grass,* like *The Divina Commedia,* being not an epic narrative but the spiritual testament of self-realization." In the work of H. D., Whitman, and Dante, Duncan found the wholeness for which his Psyche searched.

Given that, for Duncan, everything in the universe is related, it is not surprising that his personal sense of apocalpyse extended into explicitly political poems. In his introduction to *Bending the Bow* (1971) he wrote, "We enter again and again the last days of our own history, for everywhere living productive forms in the evolution of forms fail, weaken or grow monstrous, destroying the terms of their existence." Duncan felt history grow monstrous especially during the events of the Vietnam War, and he struggled in his work to confront the meanings of that experience. One sign of the seriousness and difficulty of that struggle was his decision, in the 1970s, not to publish another book for at least ten years. The work gestating during that time emerged in two volumes: *Ground Work: Before the War* (1983) and *Ground Work II: In the Dark* (1987). Together the collections represent the culmination of Duncan's years of effort as a poet. What sets Duncan apart from many other poets who addressed the Vietnam War is that he does not separate himself from "the nation's store of crimes long / unacknowledged, unrepented" ("From Robert Southwell's " 'The Burning Babe' "). In this and other poems Duncan confronts his own implication in the evils of war, in the nation's crimes, and understands the task of self-restoration as both a personal and political act.

Duncan's spiritual vision, which he distinguished from any religious orthodoxy, and his serious interest in mysticism set him apart from the mainstreams of contemporary American poetry. This, combined with fifteen years in which he chose to publish relatively little until his last books appeared, led to a neglect of his astonishing achievement as a poet. For Duncan, poetry has a generative function that is at the heart of life, and this makes his poems ambitious. If his work does not always achieve the wholeness to which it aspires, this may be, in part, because he aspires to so much. He believed that no single poem is ever complete in its meaning; each poem awakens the possibility of a new beginning. Although his range of reference can sometimes leave the reader behind, Duncan's best work reaches beyond itself, stirring the reader into just such an awakened sense of life.

Often I Am Permitted to Return to a Meadow

as if it were a scene made-up by the mind,
that is not mine, but is a made place,

that is mine, it is so near to the heart,
an eternal pasture folded in all thought
so that there is a hall therein   5

that is a made place, created by light
wherefrom the shadows that are forms fall.

Wherefrom fall all architectures I am
I say are likenesses of the First Beloved
whose flowers are flames lit to the Lady.   10

She it is Queen Under The Hill[1]
whose hosts are a disturbance of words within words
that is a field folded.

It is only a dream of the grass blowing
east against the source of the sun   15
in an hour before the sun's going down

whose secret we see in a children's game
of ring a round of roses told.

Often I am permitted to return to a meadow
as if it were a given property of the mind   20
that certain bounds hold against chaos,

that is a place of first permission,
everlasting omen of what is.

                                                        1960

A Poem Beginning with a Line by Pindar[1]

I

The light foot hears you and the brightness begins[2]
god-step at the margins of thought,
        quick adulterous tread at the heart.
Who is it that goes there?
        Where I see your quick face   5
notes of an old music pace the air,
torse-reverberations of a Grecian lyre.

---

1. I.e., Persephone, or Kora, queen of life and death. The daughter of Demeter, the Greek goddess of fruitfulness and harvest, she was kidnapped by Hades and became his queen in the Underworld, where she lived several months of the year. The remaining months she spent with her mother in the upper world.
1. Greek lyric poet (c. 522–c. 438 B.C.E.), author of celebratory odes. "When in the inception of a 'Poem Beginning with a Line by Pindar,' reading late at night the third line of the first Pythian Ode in the translation by Wade-Gery and Bowra, my mind lost hold of Pindar's sense and was faced with certain puns in that the words *light, foot, hears, you, brightness, begins* moved in a world beyond my reading; these were no longer words alone but powers in a theogony, having resonances in Hesiodic and Orphic cosmogonies where the foot that moves in the dance of the poem appears as the pulse of measures in first things. Immediately, sight of Goya's great canvas, once seen in the Mar-

quis deCambo's collection in Barcelona, came to me like a wave carrying the vision—out of the evocation of the fragment from Pindar and out of Goya's pictorial evocation, to add to the masterly powers of my own—the living vision, Cupid and Psyche were there; then the power of a third master, not a master of poetry or of picture but of storytelling, the power of Lucius Apuleius was there too . . . the living genius of these three stood as my masters, and I stood in the very presence of the story of Cupid and Psyche" (Duncan, *The Truth and Life of Myth*). A *theogony* is an account of the origin and descent of the gods; a *cosmogony*, an account of the origin of the world or universe. Hesiod was a Greek poet (fl. 800 B.C.E.), among whose works was a *Theogony*. *Orphic* has to do with the legendary Greek poet-musician Orpheus or the rites ascribed to him. For Goya, Cupid and Psyche, and Apuleius, see n. 3, below.
2. The third line of Pindar's Pythian Ode.

In Goya's canvas Cupid and Psyche[3]
have a hurt voluptuous grace
bruised by redemption. The copper light   10
falling upon the brown boy's slight body
is carnal fate that sends the soul wailing
up from blind innocence, ensnared
    by dimness
into the deprivations of desiring sight.   15

But the eyes in Goya's painting are soft,
diffuse with rapture absorb the flame.
Their bodies yield out of strength.
    Waves of visual pleasure
wrap them in a sorrow previous to their impatience.   20

A bronze of yearning, a rose that burns
    the tips of their bodies, lips,
ends of fingers, nipples. He is not wingd.
His thighs are flesh, are clouds
    lit by the sun in its going down,   25
Hot luminescence at the loins of the visible.
    But they are not in a landscape.
    They exist in an obscurity.

The wind spreading the sail serves them.
The two jealous sisters eager for her ruin   30
    serve them.
That she is ignorant, ignorant of what Love will be,
    serves them.
The dark serves them.
The oil scalding his shoulder serves them,[4]   35
serves their story. Fate, spinning,
    knots the threads for Love.

Jealousy, ignorance, the hurt . . . serve them.

II

This is magic. It is passionate dispersion.
What if they grow old? The gods   40
    would not allow it.
    Psyche is preserved.

In time we see a tragedy, a loss of beauty
    the glittering youth

---

3. Francisco José de Goya (1746–1828), Spanish artist, painted a canvas called *Cupid and Psyche*. The story of Cupid and Psyche is told by the Latin writer Lucius Apuleius (fl. c. 155 C.E.) in *The Golden Ass*. Psyche (the Greek personification of the soul) marries Cupid, or Eros (the god of love). As a condition of their union Cupid forbids her to look at him and comes to her only in darkness, leaving before dawn. Prompted by her sisters, Psyche disobeys, and Cupid flees. Through a series of trials, however, she becomes immortal and is reunited with Cupid forever.
4. In the story, Psyche holds an oil lamp above the sleeping Cupid to see him, but a drop of oil spills onto his shoulder. He wakes and flees.

of the god retains—but from this threshold   45
    it is age
that is beautiful. It is toward the old poets
    we go, to their faltering,
their unaltering wrongness that has style,
    their variable truth,   50
    the old faces,
words shed like tears from
a plenitude of powers time stores.

A stroke.   These little strokes.   A chill.
    The old man, feeble, does not recoil[5]   55
Recall. A phase so minute,
    only a part of the word in- jerrd.

    The Thundermakers descend,

damerging a nuv. A nerb.
    The present dented of the U   60
nighted stayd.   States.   The heavy clod?
    Cloud.   Invades the brain.   What
    if lilacs last in *this* dooryard bloomd?[6]

Hoover, Roosevelt, Truman, Eisenhower[7]—
where among these did the power reside   65
that moves the heart? What flower of the nation
bride-sweet broke to the whole rapture?
Hoover, Coolidge, Harding, Wilson[8]
hear the factories of human misery turning out commodities.
For whom are the holy matins of the heart ringing?   70
Noble men in the quiet of morning hear
Indians singing the continent's violent requiem.
Harding, Wilson, Taft,[9] Roosevelt,
idiots fumbling at the bride's door,
hear the cries of men in meaningless debt and war.   75
Where among these did the spirit reside
that restores the land to productive order?
McKinley, Cleveland, Harrison, Arthur,
Garfield, Hayes, Grant, Johnson,[1]
dwell in the roots of the heart's rancor.   80
How sad "amid lanes and through old woods"[2]
    echoes Whitman's love for Lincoln!

---

5. A reference to the poet William Carlos Williams (1883–1963), who suffered a series of strokes that injured his capacity for speech. Duncan phonetically presents this damage.
6. "When Lilacs Last in the Dooryard Bloom'd," Walt Whitman's elegy for Abraham Lincoln, published in 1866.
7. U.S. presidents (terms of office follow): Herbert Hoover (1929–33), Franklin Roosevelt (1933–45), Harry Truman (1945–52), and Dwight Eisenhower (1953–61).
8. U.S. presidents: Calvin Coolidge (1923–29), Warren Harding (1921–23), and Woodrow Wilson (1913–21).
9. William Taft, U.S. president from 1909 to 1913.
1. U.S. presidents: William McKinley (1897–1901), Grover Cleveland (1885–89; 1893–97), Benjamin Harrison (1889–93), Chester Arthur (1881–85), James Garfield (March–September 1881; assassinated), Rutherford Hayes (1869–77), and Andrew Johnson (1865–69).
2. From Whitman's "When Lilacs Last in the Dooryard Bloom'd."

There is no continuity then.   Only a few
    posts of the good remain.   I too
that am a nation sustain the damage   85
    where smokes of continual ravage
obscure the flame.
               It is across great scars of wrong
    I reach toward the song of kindred men
    and strike again the naked string   90
old Whitman sang from. Glorious mistake!
    that cried:

"The theme is creative and has vista."
"He is the president of regulation."[3]

I see always the under side turning,   95
fumes that injure the tender landscape.
    From which up break
lilac blossoms of courage in daily act
    striving to meet a natural measure.

         III   *(for Charles Olson)*[4]

                Psyche's tasks—the sorting of seeds   100
wheat   barley   oats   poppy   coriander
anise   beans   lentils   peas   —every grain
               in its right place
                         before nightfall;

gathering the gold wool from the cannibal sheep   105
(for the soul must weep
    and come near upon death);

harrowing Hell for a casket Proserpina keeps
                      that must not
    be opend . . . containing beauty?   110

no!   Melancholy coild like a serpent
                  that is deadly sleep
    we are not permitted
             to succumb to.
These are the old tasks.[5]   115
You've heard them before.

---

3. From Whitman's "Preface" to the 1855 edition of *Leaves of Grass* in which he declares the great, creative theme of the American republic and the role of the poet in the United States: "Their Presidents shall not be their common referee so much as their poets shall."

4. American poet and friend of Duncan's. His essay "Projective Verse" encouraged Duncan's sense of the poem as a "field."

5. To be reunited with Cupid, Psyche must accomplish a series of tasks set by Venus (Cupid's mother): she must separate and sort a storehouse of seeds, she must bring Venus some of the gold fleece from a flock of cannibal sheep, and she must descend to Hell to bring back to Venus a measure of the beauty of Proserpina, queen of the Underworld.

They must be impossible. Psyche
must despair, be brought to her
                      insect instructor;
must obey the counsels of the green reed;   120
saved from suicide by a tower speaking,
        must follow to the letter
        freakish instructions.[6]

In the story the ants help. The old man at Pisa[7]
        mixd in whose mind   125
(to draw the sorts) are all seeds
        as a lone ant from a broken ant-hill[8]
had part restored by an insect, was
        upheld by a lizard

                (to draw the sorts)   130
the wind is part of the process[9]
        defines a nation of the wind—

    father of many notions,
                Who?
let the light into the dark?   began   135
the many movements of the passion?
                 West
from east   men push.
           The islands are blessd
(cursed)   that swim below the sun,   140

    man upon whom the sun has gone down![1]

There is the hero who struggles east
widdershins[2] to free the dawn   and must
            woo Night's daughter,
sorcery, black passionate rage, covetous queens,   145
so that the fleecy sun go   back from Troy,
      Colchis,[3] India . . . all the blazing armies
spent, he must struggle alone toward the pyres of Day.

            The light that is Love
rushes on toward passion. It verges upon dark.   150
    Roses and blood flood the clouds.
    Solitary first riders advance into legend.

6. In these tasks Psyche is aided by ants, who help sort the grain; by the river god, who instructs her in how to gather fleece; and by a voice from a tower, which instructs her in how to reach Hell safely and what she must do on return.
7. Ezra Pound, American poet, from whose *Pisan Cantos* (part of his long poem *The Cantos*) Duncan quotes. Pound wrote these cantos while imprisoned for treason by American forces in Italy.
8. Pound, "Canto LXXVI." "Draw the sorts": draw lots, cast fortunes.
9. Pound, "Canto LXXIV."
1. A reference to Odysseus, hero of *The Odyssey.*

Duncan here quotes Pound's epithet for the hero, whose movement is toward home, in his "Canto LXXIV." In this section of the poem Duncan is fusing several mythic questors, among them Psyche, Odysseus, and Jason.
2. In a contrary direction; here, opposite to the usual course of the sun.
3. An ancient country on the eastern shore of the Black Sea, the land where Jason and the Argonauts sought a golden fleece. "Fleecy sun": i.e., the golden fleece Psyche must bring to Venus. The ancient city of Troy was the site of the Trojan War, after which Odysseus began his journey home.

This land, where I stand, was all legend
in my grandfathers' time: cattle raiders,
   animal tribes, priests, gold.   155
It was the West.[4] Its vistas painters saw
   in diffuse light, in melancholy,
in abysses left by glaciers as if they had been the sun
   primordial carving empty enormities
                  out of the rock.   160

              Snakes lurkd
guarding secrets.   Those first ones
                 survived solitude.

    Scientia
holding the lamp, driven by doubt;[5]   165
Eros naked in foreknowledge
smiling in his sleep;   and the light
spilld, burning his shoulder—the outrage
   that conquers legend—
passion, dismay, longing, search   170
   flooding up where
the Beloved is lost.   Psyche travels
life after life, my life, station
   after station,
to be tried   175

    without break, without
news, knowing only—but what did she know?
   The oracle at Miletus had spoken
truth surely: that he was Serpent-Desire
   that flies thru the air,   180
a monster-husband.[6] But she saw him fair

whom Apollo's mouthpiece said spread
     pain
beyond cure   to those
   wounded by his arrows.   185

Rilke torn by a rose thorn[7]
blackend toward Eros.   Cupidinous Death!
   that will not take no for an answer.

IV

    Oh yes!   Bless the footfall where
step by step   the boundary walker   190
   (in Maverick Road   the snow

4. The American West.
5. The desire to know what Cupid looks like drives Psyche to her mistake. "Scientia": knowledge.
6. In Apuleius's story, Psyche's parents consult the oracle (shrine from which a god reveals the future) of Apollo at Miletus before her marriage to Eros. The oracle responds that Psyche is destined for no mortal lover and that her husband will be a monster "whom neither gods nor men can resist."
7. Rainer Maria Rilke, German lyric poet whose work expresses the interconnections of life, death, and love; he died from a rose thorn scratch.

thud by thud   from the roof
circling the house—another tread)

   that foot   informd
by the weight of all things   195
      that can be elusive
no more than a nearness to the mind
      of a single image

            Oh yes!   this
most dear   200
      the catalyst force that renders clear
the days of a life from the surrounding medium!
         Yes, beautiful rare wilderness!
wildness that verifies strength of my tame mind,
      clearing held against indians,   205
health that prepared to meet death,
      the stubborn hymns going up
into the ramifications of the hostile air

      that, deceptive, gives way.

Who is there?   O, light the light!   210
      The Indians give way,   the clearing falls.
Great Death gives way   and unprepares us.
      Lust gives way.   The Moon gives way.
Night gives way.   Minutely,   the Day gains.

She saw the body of her beloved   215
      dismemberd in waking . . . or was it
in sight?   *Finders Keepers* we sang
      when we were children   or were taught to sing
before our histories began   and we began
      who were beloved   our animal life   220
toward the Beloved,   sworn to be Keepers.

      On the hill before the wind came
the grass moved toward the one sea,
      blade after blade dancing in waves.

There the children turn the ring to the left.   225
There the children turn the ring to the right.
      Dancing . . . Dancing . . .

And the lonely psyche goes up thru the boy to the king
      that in the caves of history dreams.
Round and round the children turn.   230
      London Bridge that is a kingdom falls.[8]

---

8. The children's song "London Bridge Is Falling Down."

We have come so far that all the old stories
whisper once more.
Mount Segur, Mount Victoire, Mount Tamalpais[9] . . .
    rise to adore the mystery of Love!   235

(An ode? Pindar's art, the editors tell us, was not a statue but a mosaic,
an accumulation of metaphor. But if he was archaic, not classic, a
survival of obsolete mode, there may have been old voices in the survival that directed the heart. So, a line from a hymn came in a novel
I was reading to help me. Psyche, poised to leap—and   240
Pindar too, the editors write, goes too far, topples over—listend to a
tower that said, *Listen to me!* The oracle[1] had said, *Despair! The Gods
themselves abhor his power.* And then the virgin flower of the dark falls
back flesh of our flesh from which everywhere . . .

    the information flows   245
        that is yearning. A line of Pindar
    moves from the area of my lamp
        toward morning.

    In the dawn that is nowhere
        I have seen the willful children   250

    clockwise and counter-clockwise turning.

                                   1960

Achilles'[1] Song

I do not know more than the Sea tells me,
told me long ago,   or I overheard Her
    telling distant roar upon the sands,
waves of meaning in the cradle of whose
    sounding and resounding power I   5
slept.

        Manchild,   She sang

—or was it a storm uplifting the night
    into a moving wall in which
I was carried as if a mothering nest had   10
    been made in dread?

the wave of a life darker than my
    life before me sped,   and I,
larger than I was,   grown dark as

9. Duncan's list of mountains moves from east to
west: to Mount Tamalpais, in western California,
across the Golden Gate from San Francisco, where
Duncan lived.
1. I.e., the tower that spoke to Psyche on her quest

and the oracle of Apollo that warned Psyche's parents.
1. In Greek legend, hero of *The Iliad,* son of
Peleus and Thetis, a sea nymph. He was killed during the Trojan War by Paris.

the shoreless depth,   15
arose from myself,   shaking the last
     light of the sun
from me.
                    Manchild,   She said,

Come back to the shores of what you are.   20
Come back to the crumbling shores.

      All night
the mothering tides in which your
       life first formd in the brooding
light   have quencht the bloody   25
       splendors of the sun

and, under the triumphant processions
       of the moon,   lay down
thunder upon thunder of an old
       longing,   the beat   30

of whose repeated spell
       consumes you.

                    Thetis, then,
       my mother, has promised me
the mirage of a boat,   a vehicle   35
       of water within the water,
and my soul would return from
       the trials of its human state,
from the long siege, from the
       struggling companions upon the plain,   40
from the burning towers and deeds
       of honor and dishonor,
the deeper unsatisfied war beneath
       and behind the declared war,
and the rubble of beautiful,   patiently   45
       workt   moonstones, agates, jades, obsidians,

turnd and returnd in the wash of
       the tides,   the gleaming waste,
       the pathetic wonder,

words turnd in the phrases of song   50
       before our song   . . . or are they

beautiful,   patiently workt   remembrances of those
       long gone from me,
returnd anew,   ghostly in the light
       of the moon,   old faces?   55

For Thetis, my mother, has promised
       me a boat,

a lover,   an up-lifter of my spirit
    into the rage of my first element
rising,   a princedom   60
    in the unreal, a share in Death.

    •

Time, time.   It's time.

The business of Troy has long been done.

Achilles in Leuke[2] has come home.

And soon you too   will be alone.   65

December 10, 1968   1984

Interrupted Forms

Long slumbering, often coming forward,
haunting the house I am the house I live in
resembles so, does he recall me or I
recall him?   Seeing you the other day
long I lookt to see your face his, longing   5
without reason.   I meant to tell
or spell your name, to dwell in the charm
I almost felt in the stone,   the impassive
weight of old feeling, the cold awakening
I meant to tell you of, as if telling could reach you,   10
at last come into your embrace again, my arms
hold you, mounting, coming into your life
my life and interruption of all long lasting
        inertia in feeling,
arousal.   15

      In dreams
insubstantially you have come before my eyes'
expectations, and, even in waking,
taking over the field of sight   fleetingly
stronger than what my eyes see,   20
the thought of you thought has eyes to see
has eyes to meet your answering eyes
thought raises.   I am speaking of a ghost
the heart is glad to have return,   of a room
I have often been lonely in,   of a desertion   25
that remains even where I am most cherisht

2. A mythical island to which the spirits of dead heroes go. "In our Anglo-American convention we would pronounce the diphthong in *Leuke* to fore-shadow the rime in the word *you*—but in my hear-ing of the line, remembering the voice of H. D.'s reading from her *Helen in Egypt,* the name *Leuke* came to me sounded as in the German convention to echo the diphthong in *Troy*" [Duncan's note].

and surrounded by Love's company,   of a form,
wholly fulfilling the course of my life, interrupted,
of a cold in the full warmth of the sunlight
that seeks to come in close to your heart   30
                  for warmth.

                                                                    1984

RICHARD WILBUR
b. 1921

Richard Wilbur was born in New York City and grew up in the country in New Jersey. His father was a painter, and his mother came from a family prominent in journalism. He was educated at Amherst College, where Robert Frost was a frequent guest and teacher, and Wilbur's remarkable gifts as a prosodist often remind us of the older poet. Of the effects of his college years, Wilbur says: "Most American poets of my generation were taught to admire the English metaphysical poets of the seventeenth century and such contemporary masters of irony as John Crowe Ransom. We were led by our teachers and by the critics whom we read to feel that the most adequate and convincing poetry is that which accommodates mixed feelings, clashing ideas, and incongruous images." Wilbur was to remain true to this preference for the ironic meditative lyric, the single perfect poem, rather than longer narratives or dramatic sequences.

After graduation and service in the infantry in Italy and France (1943–45), Wilbur returned to study for an M.A. at Harvard, with a firm notion of what he expected to get out of poetry. "My first poems were written in answer to the inner and outer disorders of the second World War and they helped me . . . to take ahold of raw events and convert them, provisionally, into experience." He reasserted the balance of mind against instinct and violence: "The praiseful, graceful soldier/Shouldn't be fired by his gun." The poised lyrics in *The Beautiful Changes* (1947), including the lovely title poem of that volume, and *Ceremony* (1950) also reclaimed the value of pleasure, defined as an interplay of intelligence with sensuous enjoyment. Whether looking at a real French landscape, as in "Grasse: The Olive Trees," or a French landscape painting, as in "Ceremony," the point was to show the witty shaping power of the mind in nature.

Wilbur prefers strict stanzaic forms and meters; "limitation makes for power: the strength of the genie comes of his being confined in a bottle." In individual lines and the structure of an entire poem, his emphasis is on a civilized balancing of perceptions. "A World without Objects Is a Sensible Emptiness" begins with the "tall camels of the spirit" but qualifies our views of lonely spiritual impulses. The poem summons us back to find visionary truth grasped through sensual experience. "All shining things need to be shaped and borne." Wilbur favors what he has called "a spirituality which is not abstracted, not dissociated and world-renouncing," as is clear from "Love Calls Us to the Things of This World" (*Things of This World*, 1956), a hymn of praise to clothes hanging on a laundry line ("Oh, let there be nothing on earth but laundry"). "A good part of my work could, I suppose, be understood as a public quarrel with the aesthetics of Edgar Allan Poe"—presumably with Poe's notion that poetry provided *indefinite* sensations and aspired to the abstract condition of music.

Wilbur was among the first of the younger postwar poets to adopt a style of living and working different from the masters of an earlier generation—from Eliot, an ironic priestlike modernist who lived as a publisher-poet in England, or William Carlos Williams, a doctor in New Jersey, or Wallace Stevens, a remote insurance executive in Connecticut. Wilbur was a teacher-poet and gave frequent readings. Instead of thinking of himself as an alienated artist, he came to characterize himself as a "poet-citizen," part of what he judged a widening community of poets addressing themselves to an audience increasingly responsive to poetry. Wilbur's taste for civilized wit and his metrical skill made him an ideal translator of the seventeenth-century satirical comedies of Molière, *Tartuffe* (1963) and *The Misanthrope* (1955). They are frequently played, as is the musical version of Voltaire's *Candide* for which Wilbur was one of the collaborating lyricists. Wilbur received the Pulitzer Prize for his volume *Things of This World* (1956) and served as the second Poet Laureate of the United States in 1987–88.

The Beautiful Changes

One wading a Fall meadow finds on all sides
The Queen Anne's Lace lying like lilies
On water; it glides
So from the walker, it turns
Dry grass to a lake, as the slightest shade of you   5
Valleys my mind in fabulous blue Lucernes.[1]

The beautiful changes as a forest is changed
By a chameleon's tuning his skin to it;
As a mantis, arranged
On a green leaf, grows   10
Into it, makes the leaf leafier, and proves
Any greenness is deeper than anyone knows.

Your hands hold roses always in a way that says
They are not only yours; the beautiful changes
In such kind ways,   15
Wishing ever to sunder
Things and things' selves for a second finding, to lose
For a moment all that it touches back to wonder.

1947

The Death of a Toad

A toad the power mower caught,
Chewed and clipped of a leg, with a hobbling hop has got
To the garden verge, and sanctuaried him
Under the cineraria leaves, in the shade
Of the ashen heartshaped leaves, in a dim,   5
Low, and a final glade.

The rare original heartsblood goes,
Spends on the earthen hide, in the folds and wizenings, flows

1. Lakes having the quality of Switzerland's Lake Lucerne, which is known for its beauty.

In the gutters of the banked and staring eyes. He lies
 As still as if he would return to stone,   10
  And soundlessly attending, dies
   Toward some deep monotone,

 Toward misted and ebullient seas
And cooling shores, toward lost Amphibia's emperies.[1]
Day dwindles, drowning, and at length is gone   15
 In the wide and antique eyes, which still appear
  To watch, across the castrate lawn,
   The haggard daylight steer.

             1950

Ceremony

A striped blouse in a clearing by Bazille[1]
Is, you may say, a patroness of boughs
Too queenly kind[2] toward nature to be kin.
But ceremony never did conceal,
Save to the silly[3] eye, which all allows,   5
How much we are the woods we wander in.

Let her be some Sabrina[4] fresh from stream,
Lucent as shallows slowed by wading sun,
Bedded on fern, the flowers' cynosure:[5]
Then nymph and wood must nod and strive to dream   10
That she is airy earth, the trees, undone,
Must ape her languor natural and pure.

Ho-hum. I am for wit and wakefulness,
And love this feigning lady by Bazille.
What's lightly hid is deepest understood,   15
And when with social smile and formal dress
She teaches leaves to curtsey and quadrille,[6]
I think there are most tigers in the wood.

             1950

"A World without Objects Is a Sensible Emptiness"[1]

 The tall camels of the spirit
Steer for their deserts, passing the last groves loud

---

1. Archaic for "empires." Amphibia is imagined to be the spiritual ruler of the toad's universe.
1. Jean-Frédéric Bazille (1841–1871), French painter noted for painting figures in forest landscapes; he was associated with the impressionists.
2. An original meaning of *nature* was "kind."
3. Innocent, homely.
4. A nymph, the presiding deity of the river Severn in Milton's masque *Comus* (1634).

5. Center of attraction; also from the constellation Ursa Minor, whose center is the Pole Star.
6. A square dance, of French origin, performed by four couples.
1. From "Meditation 65," by the English Metaphysical poet Thomas Traherne (c. 1638–1674): "Life without objects is sensible emptiness, and that is a greater misery than death or nothing." *Sensible* is used to mean "palpable to the senses."

With the sawmill shrill of the locust, to the whole honey of the arid
    Sun. They are slow, proud,

    And move with a stilted stride   5
  To the land of sheer horizon, hunting Traherne's
Sensible emptiness, there where the brain's lantern-slide
    Revels in vast returns.

    O connoisseurs of thirst,
  Beasts of my soul who long to learn to drink   10
Of pure mirage, those prosperous islands are accurst
    That shimmer on the brink

    Of absence; auras, lustres,
  And all shinings need to be shaped and borne.
Think of those painted saints, capped by the early masters   15
    With bright, jauntily-worn

    Aureate plates, or even
  Merry-go-round rings. Turn, O turn
From the fine sleights of the sand, from the long empty oven
    Where flames in flamings burn   20

    Back to the trees arrayed
  In bursts of glare, to the halo-dialing run
Of the country creeks, and the hills' bracken tiaras made
    Gold in the sunken sun,

    Wisely watch for the sight   25
  Of the supernova[2] burgeoning over the barn,
Lampshine blurred in the stream of beasts, the spirit's right
    Oasis, light incarnate.

                      1950

Years-End

    Now winter downs the dying of the year,
    And night is all a settlement of snow;
    From the soft street the rooms of houses show
    A gathered light, a shapen atmosphere,
    Like frozen-over lakes whose ice is thin   5
    And still allows some stirring down within.

    I've known the wind by water banks to shake
    The late leaves down, which frozen where they fell
    And held in ice as dancers in a spell
    Fluttered all winter long into a lake;   10
    Graved on the dark in gestures of descent,
    They seemed their own most perfect monument.

2. A scientific term for an exploding star, here associated with the Star of Bethlehem.

There was perfection in the death of ferns
Which laid their fragile cheeks against the stone
A million years. Great mammoths overthrown   15
Composedly have made their long sojourns,
Like palaces of patience, in the gray
And changeless lands of ice. And at Pompeii[1]

The little dog lay curled and did not rise
But slept the deeper as the ashes rose   20
And found the people incomplete, and froze
The random hands, the loose unready eyes
Of men expecting yet another sun
To do the shapely thing they had not done.

These sudden ends of time must give us pause.   25
We fray into the future, rarely wrought
Save in the tapestries of afterthought.
More time, more time. Barrages of applause
Come muffled from a buried radio.
The New-year bells are wrangling with the snow.   30

1950

Love Calls Us to the Things of This World

The eyes open to a cry of pulleys,
And spirited from sleep, the astounded soul
Hangs for a moment bodiless and simple
As false dawn.
                        Outside the open window   5
The morning air is all awash with angels.

Some are in bed-sheets, some are in blouses,
Some are in smocks: but truly there they are.
Now they are rising together in calm swells
Of halcyon[1] feeling, filling whatever they wear   10
With the deep joy of their impersonal breathing;

Now they are flying in place, conveying
The terrible speed of their omnipresence, moving
And staying like white water; and now of a sudden
They swoon down into so rapt a quiet   15
That nobody seems to be there.
                        The soul shrinks

From all that it is about to remember,
From the punctual rape of every blessèd day,

1. Roman city buried by and partly preserved in volcanic ash after the eruption of Mount Vesuvius (79 C.E.).
1. Calm, peaceful. The word originated as the name of a mythological bird anciently fabled to breed about the time of the winter solstice in a nest floating on the sea, and then to charm the wind and waves so that the sea became especially calm.

And cries,   20
   "Oh, let there be nothing on earth but laundry,
Nothing but rosy hands in the rising steam
And clear dances done in the sight of heaven."

  Yet, as the sun acknowledges
With a warm look the world's hunks and colors,   25
The soul descends once more in bitter love
To accept the waking body, saying now
In a changed voice as the man yawns and rises,

  "Bring them down from their ruddy gallows;
Let there be clean linen for the backs of thieves;   30
Let lovers go fresh and sweet to be undone,
And the heaviest nuns walk in a pure floating
Of dark habits,
   keeping their difficult balance."

1956

The Mind-Reader

Lui parla.[1]

FOR CHARLES AND EULA

Some things are truly lost. Think of a sun-hat
Laid for the moment on a parapet
While three young women—one, perhaps, in mourning—
Talk in the crenellate shade.[2] A slight wind plucks
And budges it; it scuffs to the edge and cartwheels   5
Into a giant view of some description:
Haggard escarpments,[3] if you like, plunge down
Through mica shimmer to a moss of pines
Amidst which, here or there, a half-seen river
Lobs up a blink of light. The sun-hat falls,   10
With what free flirts and stoops you can imagine,
Down through that reeling vista or another,
Unseen by any, even by you or me.
It is as when a pipe-wrench, catapulted
From the jounced back of a pick-up truck, dives headlong   15
Into a bushy culvert;[4] or a book
Whose reader is asleep, garbling the story,
Glides from beneath a steamer chair and yields
Its flurried pages to the printless sea.

It is one thing to escape from consciousness   20
As such things do, another to be pent
In the dream-cache or stony oubliette[5]
Of someone's head.

1. He [the mind-reader, an Italian] speaks.
2. I.e., the shade provided by battlements.
3. Worn cliffs.
4. Drain under a road. "Pipe-wrench": wrench for gripping and turning metal pipe.
5. Dungeon pit (French *oublier,* "to forget").

They found, when I was little,
That I could tell the place of missing objects.   25
I stood by the bed of a girl, or the frayed knee
Of an old man whose face was lost in shadow.
When did you miss it?, people would be saying,
Where did you see it last? And then those voices,
Querying or replying, came to sound   30
Like cries of birds when the leaves race and whiten
And a black overcast is shelving over.
The mind is not a landscape, but if it were
There would in such case be a tilted moon
Wheeling beyond the wood through which you groped,   35
Its fine spokes breaking in the tangled thickets.
There would be obfuscations, paths which turned
To dried-up stream-beds, hemlocks which invited
Through shiny clearings to a groundless shade;
And yet in a sure stupor you would come   40
At once upon dilapidated cairns,
Abraded moss, and half-healed blazes[6] leading
To where, around the turning of a fear,
The lost thing shone.

            Imagine a railway platform—   45
The long cars come to a cloudy halt beside it,
And the fogged windows offering a view
Neither to those within nor those without,
Now, in the crowd—forgive my predilection—
Is a young woman standing amidst her luggage,   50
Expecting to be met by you, a stranger.
See how she turns her head, the eyes engaging
And disengaging, pausing and shying away.
It is like that with things put out of mind,
As the queer saying goes: a lost key hangs   55
Trammeled by threads in what you come to see
As the webbed darkness of a sewing-basket,
Flashing a little; or a photograph,
Misplaced in an old ledger, turns its bled
Oblivious profile to rebuff your vision,   60
Yet glistens with the fixative of thought.
What can be wiped from memory? Not the least
Meanness, obscenity, humiliation,
Terror which made you clench your eyes, or pulse
Of happiness which quickened your despair.   65
Nothing can be forgotten, as I am not
Permitted to forget.

            It was not far
From that to this—this corner café table
Where, with my lank grey hair and vatic gaze,[7]   70

---

6. Cuts on trees to mark a path in a forest.   would serve the same purpose.
"Cairns" (piles of stones) and rubbed-away moss   7. I.e., a gaze like that of a prophet.

I sit and drink at the receipt of custom.
They come here, day and night, so many people:
Sad women of the quarter, dressed in black,
As to a black confession; blinking clerks
Who half-suppose that Taurus ruminates 75
Upon their destinies;[8] men of affairs
Down from Milan to clear it with the magus[9]
Before they buy or sell some stock or other;
My fellow-drunkards; fashionable folk,
Mocking and ravenously credulous, 80
And skeptics bent on proving me a fraud
For fear that some small wonder, unexplained,
Should leave a fissure in the world, and all
Saint Michael's host[1] come flapping back.

                                 I give them 85
Paper and pencil, turn away and light
A cigarette, as you have seen me do;
They write their questions; fold them up; I lay
My hand on theirs and go into my frenzy,
Raising my eyes to heaven, snorting smoke, 90
Lolling my head as in the fumes of Delphi,[2]
And then, with shaken, spirit-guided fingers,
Set down the oracle. All that, of course,
Is trumpery,[3] since nine times out of ten
What words float up within another's thought 95
Surface as soon as mine, unfolding there
Like paper flowers in a water-glass.
In the tenth case, I sometimes cheat a little.
That shocks you? But consider: what I do
Cannot, so most conceive, be done at all, 100
And when I fail, I am a charlatan
Even to such as I have once astounded—
Whereas a tailor can mis-cut my coat
And be a tailor still. I tell you this
Because you know that I have the gift, the burden. 105
Whether or not I put my mind to it,
The world usurps me ceaselessly; my sixth
And never-resting sense is a cheap room
Black with the anger of insomnia,
Whose wall-boards vibrate with the mutters, plaints, 110
And flushings of the race.[4]

                      What should I tell them?
I have no answers. *Set your fears at rest,*
I scribble when I must. *Your paramour*
Is faithful, and your spouse is unsuspecting. 115

8. I.e., that they are influenced by astrological
signs (of which Taurus, the bull, is one).
9. Expert in the occult.
1. St. Michael the archangel and his host of
angels, whose war in heaven is predicted in Revelation 12.7–9.

2. Site of the most famous Greek oracle, at which,
for a fee, seekers could have their questions
answered by a priestess drugged by the "fumes."
3. Worthless nonsense.
4. I.e., the human race. "Plaints, / And flushings":
complaints and sudden rushes of emotion.

You were not seen, that day, beneath the fig-tree.
Still, be more cautious. When the time is ripe,
Expect promotion. I foresee a message
From a far person who is rich and dying.
You are admired in secret. If, in your judgment,   120
Profit is in it, you should take the gamble.
As for these fits of weeping, they will pass.

It makes no difference that my lies are bald
And my evasions casual. It contents them
Not to have spoken, yet to have been heard.   125
What more do they deserve, if I could give it,
Mute breathers as they are of selfish hopes
And small anxieties? Faith, justice, valor,
All those reputed rarities of soul
Confirmed in marble by our public statues—   130
You may be sure that they are rare indeed
Where the soul mopes in private, and I listen.
Sometimes I wonder if the blame is mine,
If through a sullen fault of the mind's ear
I miss a resonance in all their fretting.   135
Is there some huge attention, do you think,
Which suffers us and is inviolate,
To which all hearts are open, which remarks
The sparrow's weighty fall,[5] and overhears
In the worst rancor a deflected sweetness?   140
I should be glad to know it.

                    Meanwhile, saved
By the shrewd habit of concupiscence,
which, like a visor, narrows my regard,
And drinking studiously until my thought   145
Is a blind lowered almost to the sill,
I hanker for that place beyond the sparrow
Where the wrench beds in mud, the sun-hat hangs
In densest branches, and the book is drowned.[6]
Ah, you have read my mind. One more, perhaps . . .   150
A mezzo-litro. Grazie, professore.[7]

                                     1976

---

5. Hamlet, just before his death, speaks of the "special providence in the fall of a sparrow" (5.2.157–58).
6. At the end of Shakespeare's *The Tempest*, the magician Prospero renounces his island and his magic, saying, "Deeper than did ever plummet sound/I'll drown my book" (5.1.56–57).
7. The speaker thanks the listening "professore" for the offer of another half-liter of wine.

JAMES DICKEY
1923–1997

James Dickey was born in Atlanta, Georgia, and grew up in one of its suburbs. At six feet three, he had been a high-school football star and "a wild motorcycle rider." After a year at Clemson College in South Carolina (1942), he enlisted in the air force. As a young man he had admired the Romantic poet Byron largely for what he symbolized: bold, masculine swagger and a love of martial and sexual adventure. During off hours from combat missions in the South Pacific, Dickey became acquainted with modern poetry in an anthology by Louis Untermeyer, one of the first influential collections. But it was not until after the war, at Vanderbilt University and through the encouragement of one of his professors, Monroe Spears, that Dickey seriously began to write poetry himself.

His first poem was published in *Sewanee Review* while he was still a senior in college; his first book of verse, *Into the Stone*, appeared in 1960. From that time Dickey consistently regarded poetry as the center of his career, although he was at different periods an advertising man for Coca-Cola in New York and Atlanta, a college teacher, a training officer for pilots during the Korean War, a best-selling novelist (*Deliverance*, 1970), and a screenwriter (adapting *Deliverance* for Hollywood).

Dickey's work is concerned with the heroic and sometimes excessive figure of the self in moments of crisis or danger. It shows a desire to ascend beyond the human world, to resist the downward pull of mortality in ways that may remind us of Hart Crane. In the title poem of his volume *Drowning with Others* (1962), for example, the speaker imagines the moment when a man feels "my own wingblades spring," and finds himself "rising and singing/With my last breath," free of the "down-soaring dead." *Helmets* (1964) includes a powerful group of war poems in which Dickey struggles for a vision that will allow him to transcend death. In other earlier work he often explores the instinctual and unconscious aspect of experience and sometimes identifies with totemic animals, as in "The Heaven of Animals," where he envisions a world in which "Their instincts wholly bloom/And they rise./The soft eyes open."

In Dickey's earlier poems, the speaker was primarily an observer, describing as if from outside these states of animal and instinctual grace. The poet tended to write in short lines—three accents or beats per line. With *Buckdancer's Choice* (1965) Dickey became interested in longer "split lines," which he has used ever since. The line of verse is splintered into phrases, each group of words separated from the next by spaces designed to take the place of punctuation. The purpose is to approximate the way the mind "associates in bursts of words, in jumps." Instead of speaking through a distanced observer, the poem is placed within the mind of someone who is caught in a moment of crisis or excitement.

One of his most central, later poems written in the longer line is "Falling," with its rendering of the consciousness of a stewardess who falls from an airplane into space. Like the earlier "Drowning with Others," this poem confirms the importance in Dickey's work of the trope of flight, that figure for the self's transcendence of mortality. In "Falling" he gives us the woman's "superhuman act," as she drifts above the tiny human world and possesses, for those moments, a godlike vision. Yet even as Dickey's poem suspends the moment of falling, it admits the pull of gravity that brings the woman closer and closer to the ground, and to her death. "Falling" expresses Dickey's enduring interest in danger and in the immortal longings of the titanic self.

Dickey's interest in violence and power as subjects is suggested by the apocalyptic title of his 1970 volume *The Eye Beaters, Blood, Victory, Madness, Buckhead and Mercy*, and many of his later poems are designed to administer shocks to the reader's system. Dickey enjoyed cutting a flamboyant public figure with a reputation for hard drinking and fast motorcycles. He also enjoyed being a publicist for the life of the poet, as if he were indeed a latter-day Byron. This involved him in paradoxical activity, a cross between serious literary criticism and advertisements for himself. He published the series *Self-Interviews* as well as a penetrating collection of reviews of other poets, *Babel to Byzantium* (1968). In 1967–69 he held the chair of poetry at the Library of Congress.

Drowning with Others

There are moments a man turns from us
Whom we have all known until now.
Upgathered, we watch him grow,
Unshipping his shoulder bones

Like human, everyday wings   5
That he has not ever used,
Releasing his hair from his brain,
A kingfisher's crest, confused

By the God-tilted light of Heaven.
His deep, window-watching smile   10
Comes closely upon us in waves,
And spreads, and now we are

At last within it, dancing.
Slowly we turn and shine
Upon what is holding us,   15
As under our feet he soars,

Struck dumb as the angel of Eden,[1]
In wide, eye-opening rings.
Yet the hand on my shoulder fears
To feel my own wingblades spring,   20

To feel me sink slowly away
In my hair turned loose like a thought
Of a fisherbird dying in flight.
If I opened my arms, I could hear

Every shell in the sea find the word   25
It has tried to put into my mouth.
Broad flight would become of my dancing,
And I would obsess the whole sea,

But I keep rising and singing
With my last breath. Upon my back,   30
With his hand on my unborn wing,
A man rests easy as sunlight

Who has kept himself free of the forms
Of the deaf, down-soaring dead,

1. Very probably the cherubim who guard the entrance to the Garden of Eden after Adam and Eve have been banished (Genesis 3.24).

And me laid out and alive   35
For nothing at all, in his arms.

1962

The Heaven of Animals

Here they are. The soft eyes open.
If they have lived in a wood
It is a wood.
If they have lived on plains
It is grass rolling   5
Under their feet forever.

Having no souls, they have come,
Anyway, beyond their knowing.
Their instincts wholly bloom
And they rise.   10
The soft eyes open.

To match them, the landscape flowers,
Outdoing, desperately
Outdoing what is required:
The richest wood,   15
The deepest field.

For some of these,
It could not be the place
It is, without blood.
These hunt, as they have done,   20
But with claws and teeth grown perfect,

More deadly than they can believe.
They stalk more silently,
And crouch on the limbs of trees,
And their descent   25
Upon the bright backs of their prey

May take years
In a sovereign floating of joy.
And those that are hunted
Know this as their life,   30
Their reward: to walk

Under such trees in full knowledge
Of what is in glory above them,
And to feel no fear,
But acceptance, compliance.   35
Fulfilling themselves without pain

At the cycle's center,
They tremble, they walk

Under the tree,
They fall, they are torn,   40
They rise, they walk again.

1962

Falling

*"A 29-year-old stewardess fell . . . to her death tonight when she
was swept through an emergency door that suddenly sprang open.
. . . The body . . . was found . . . three hours after the accident."*
                                                    —*New York Times*

The states when they black out and lie there rolling   when they turn
To something transcontinental   move by   drawing moonlight out of the
     great
One-sided stone hung off the starboard wingtip   some sleeper next to
An engine is groaning for coffee   and there is faintly coming in
Somewhere the vast beast-whistle of space. In the galley with its racks   5
Of trays   she rummages for a blanket   and moves in her slim tailored
Uniform to pin it over the cry at the top of the door. As though she blew

The door down with a silent blast from her lungs   frozen   she is black
Out finding herself   with the plane nowhere and her body taking by the
     throat
The undying cry of the void   falling   living   beginning to be some-
     thing   10
That no one has ever been and lived through   screaming without enough
     air
Still neat   lipsticked   stockinged   girdled by regulation   her hat
Still on   her arms and legs in no world   and yet spaced also strangely
With utter placid rightness on thin air   taking her time   she holds it
In many places   and now, still thousands of feet from her death she
     seems   15
To slow   she develops interest   she turns in her maneuverable body

To watch it. She is hung high up in the overwhelming middle of things in
     her
Self   in low body-whistling wrapped intensely   in all her dark dance-weight
Coming down from a marvelous leap   with the delaying, dumfounding ease
Of a dream of being drawn   like endless moonlight to the harvest soil   20
Of a central state of one's country   with a great gradual warmth coming
Over her   floating   finding more and more breath in what she has been
     using
For breath   as the levels become more human   seeing clouds placed hon-
     estly
Below her left and right   riding slowly toward them   she clasps it all
To her and can hang her hands and feet in it in peculiar ways   and   25
Her eyes opened wide by wind, can open her mouth as wide   wider and suck
All the heat from the cornfields   can go down on her back with a feeling

Of stupendous pillows stacked under her   and can turn   turn as to some-
    one
In bed   smile, understood in darkness   can go away   slant   slide
Off tumbling   into the emblem of a bird with its wings half-spread   30
Or whirl madly on herself   in endless gymnastics in the growing warmth
Of wheatfields rising toward the harvest moon.   There is time to live
In superhuman health   seeing mortal unreachable lights far down seeing
An ultimate highway with one late priceless car probing it   arriving
In a square town   and off her starboard arm the glitter of water
    catches   35
The moon by its own shaken side   scaled, roaming silver   My God it is
    good
And evil   lying in one after another of all the positions for love
Making   dancing   sleeping   and now cloud wisps at her no
Raincoat   no matter   all small towns brokenly brighter from inside
Cloud   she walks over them like rain   bursts out to behold a Grey-
    hound   40
Bus shooting light through its sides   it is the signal to go straight
Down like a glorious diver   then feet first   her skirt stripped beautifully
Up   her face in fear-scented cloths   her legs deliriously bare   then
Arms out   she slow-rolls over   steadies out   waits for something great
To take control of her   trembles near feathers   planes head-down   45
The quick movements of bird-necks turning her head   gold eyes the insight-
eyesight of owls blazing into the hencoops   a taste for chicken overwhelming
Her   the long-range vision of hawks enlarging all human lights of cars
Freight trains   looped bridges   enlarging the moon racing slowly
Through all the curves of a river   all the darks of the midwest blazing   50
From above. A rabbit in a bush turns white   the smothering chickens
Huddle   for over them there is still time for something to live
With the streaming half-idea of a long stoop   a hurtling   a fall
That is controlled   that plummets as it wills   turns gravity
Into a new condition, showing its other side like a moon   shining   55
New Powers   there is still time to live on a breath made of nothing
But the whole night   time for her to remember to arrange her skirt
Like a diagram of a bat   tightly it guides her   she has this flying-skin
Made of garments   and there are also those sky-divers on TV   sailing
In sunlight   smiling under their goggles   swapping batons back and
    forth   60
And He who jumped without a chute and was handed one by a diving
Buddy. She looks for her grinning companion   white teeth   nowhere
She is screaming   singing hymns   her thin human wings spread out
From her neat shoulders   the air beast-crooning to her   warbling
And she can no longer behold the huge partial form of the world   now   65
She is watching her country lose its evoked master shape   watching it lose
And gain   get back its houses and peoples   watching it bring up
Its local lights   single homes   lamps on barn roofs   if she fell
Into water she might live   like a diver   cleaving   perfect   plunge

Into another   heavy silver   unbreathable   slowing   saving   70
Element: there is water   there is time to perfect all the fine
Points of diving   feet together   toes pointed   hands shaped right
To insert her into water like a needle   to come out healthily dripping

And be handed a Coca-Cola   there they are   there are the waters
Of life   the moon packed and coiled in a reservoir   so let me begin   75
To plane across the night air of Kansas   opening my eyes superhumanly
Bright   to the damned moon   opening the natural wings of my jacket
By Don Loper   moving like a hunting owl toward the glitter of water
One cannot just fall   just tumble screaming all that time   one must use
It   she is now through with all   through all   clouds   damp   hair   80
Straightened   the last wisp of fog pulled apart on her face like wool revealing
New darks   new progressions of headlights along dirt roads from chaos

And night   a gradual warming   a new-made, inevitable world of one's own
Country   a great stone of light in its waiting waters   hold   hold out
For water: who knows when what correct young woman must take up her
     body   85
And fly   and head for the moon-crazed inner eye of midwest imprisoned
Water   stored up for her for years   the arms of her jacket slipping
Air up her sleeves to go   all over her? What final things can be said
Of one who starts out sheerly in her body in the high middle of night
Air   to track down water like a rabbit where it lies like life itself   90
Off to the right in Kansas? She goes toward   the blazing-bare lake
Her skirts neat   her hands and face warmed more and more by the air
Rising from pastures of beans   and under her   under chenille bedspreads
The farm girls are feeling the goddess in them struggle and rise brooding
On the scratch-shining posts of the bed   dreaming of female signs   95
Of the moon   male blood like iron   of what is really said by the moan
Of airliners passing over them at dead of midwest midnight   passing
Over brush fires   burning out in silence on little hills   and will wake
To see the woman they should be   struggling on the rooftree to become
Stars: for her the ground is closer   water is nearer   she passes   100
It   then banks   turns   her sleeves fluttering differently as she rolls
Out to face the east, where the sun shall come up from wheatfields she must
Do something with water   fly to it   fall in it   drink it   rise
From it   but there is none left upon earth   the clouds have drunk it back
The plants have sucked it down   there are standing toward her only   105
The common fields of death   she comes back from flying to falling
Returns to a powerful cry   the silent scream with which she blew down
The coupled door of the airliner   nearly   nearly losing hold
Of what she has done   remembers   remembers the shape at the heart
Of cloud   fashionably swirling   remembers she still has time to die   110
Beyond explanation. Let her now take off her hat in summer air the coutour
Of cornfields   and have enough time to kick off her one remaining
Shoe with the toes   of the other foot   to unhook her stockings
With calm fingers, noting how fatally easy it is to undress in midair
Near death   when the body will assume without effort any position   115
Except the one that will sustain it   enable it to rise   live
Not die   nine farms hover close   widen   eight of them separate, leaving
One in the middle   then the fields of that farm do the same   there is no
Way to back off   from her chosen ground   but she sheds the jacket
With its silver sad impotent wings   sheds the bat's guiding tailpiece   120
Of her skirt   the lightning-charged clinging of her blouse   the intimate
Inner flying-garment of her slip in which she rides like the holy ghost

Of a virgin   sheds the long windsocks of her stockings   absurd
Brassiere   then feels the girdle required by regulations squirming
Off her: no longer monobuttocked   she feels the girdle flutter   shake   125
In her hand   and float   upward   her clothes rising off her ascending
Into cloud   and fights away from her head the last sharp dangerous shoe
Like a dumb bird   and now will drop in   SOON   now will drop

In like this   the greatest thing that ever came to Kansas   down from all
Heights   all levels of American breath   layered in the lungs from the
        frail   130
Chill of space to the loam where extinction slumbers in corn tassels thickly
And breathes like rich farmers counting: will come among them after
Her last superhuman act   the last slow careful passing of her hands
All over her unharmed body   desired by every sleeper in his dream:
Boys finding for the first time their loins filled with heart's blood   135
Widowed farmers whose hands float under light covers to find themselves
Arisen at sunrise   the splendid position of blood unearthly drawn
Toward clouds   all feel something   pass over them as she passes
Her palms over *her* long legs   *her* small breasts   and deeply between
Her thighs   her hair shot loose from all pins   streaming in the wind   140
Of her body   let her come openly   trying at the last second to land
On her back   This is it   THIS
                              All those who find her impressed
In the soft loam   gone down   driven well into the image of her body
The furrows for miles flowing in upon her where she lies very deep   145
In her mortal outline   in the earth as it is in cloud   can tell nothing
But that she is there   inexplicable   unquestionable   and remember
That something broke in them as well   and began to live and die more
When they walked for no reason into their fields to where the whole earth
Caught her   interrupted her maiden flight   told her how to lie   she
        cannot   150
Turn   go away   cannot move   cannot slide off it and assume another
Position   no sky-diver with any grin could save her   hold her in his arms
Plummet with her   unfold above her his wedding silks   she can no longer
Mark the rain with whirling women that take the place of a dead wife
Or the goddess in Norwegian farm girls   or all the back-breaking
        whores   155
Of Wichita. All the known air above her is not giving up quite one
Breath   it is all gone   and yet not dead   not anywhere else
Quite   lying still in the field on her back   sensing the smells
Of incessant growth try to lift her   a little sight left in the corner
Of one eye   fading   seeing something wave   lies believing   160
That she could have made it   at the best part of her brief goddess
State   to water   gone in headfirst   come out smiling   invulnerable
Girl in a bathing-suit ad   but she is lying like a sunbather at the last
Of moonlight   half-buried in her impact on the earth   not far
From a railroad trestle   a water tank   she could see if she could   165
Raise her head from her modest hole   with her clothes beginning
To come down all over Kansas   into bushes   on the dewy sixth green
Of a golf course   one shoe   her girdle coming down fantastically
On a clothesline, where it belongs   her blouse on a lightning rod:

Lies in the fields   in *this* field   on her broken back as though on   170
A cloud she cannot drop through   while farmers sleepwalk without
Their women from houses   a walk like falling toward the far waters
Of life   in moonlight   toward the dreamed eternal meaning of their farms
Toward the flowering of the harvest in their hands   that tragic cost
Feels herself go   go toward   go outward   breathes at last fully   175
Not   and tries   less   once   tries   tries   AH, GOD—

1981

DENISE LEVERTOV
1923–1997

Denise Levertov once wrote of her predecessor, the poet H. D.: "She showed a way to penetrate mystery; which means, not to flood darkness with light so that darkness is destroyed, but to *enter into* darkness, mystery, so that it is experienced." Along with Robert Duncan, Levertov carried out in her own distinctive way H. D.'s tradition of visionary poetry. More grounded than her predecessor in observing the natural world and in appreciating daily life, Levertov's own work connects the concrete to the invisible, as suggested by the image of *The Jacob's Ladder* (1961), the title of her fifth book. She desired that a poem be "hard as a floor, sound as a bench" but also that it be "mysterious" ("Illustrious Ancestors"), and in her poems ordinary events open into the unknown. The origins of Levertov's magical sense of the world are not difficult to trace. She was born in England and wrote of her parents: "My mother was descended from the Welsh Tailor and mystic Angel Jones of Mold, my father from the noted Hasid, Schneour Zaiman (d. 1831), the 'Rav of Northern White Russia.' " In "Illustrious Ancestors," Levertov claimed a connection to her forefathers, both mystical and Hasidic: "some line still taut between me and them." Hasidim, a sect of Judaism that emphasizes the soul's communion with God rather than formal religious observance and encourages what Levertov called "a wonder at creation," was an important influence on her father, Paul Philip Levertoff. He had converted to Christianity as a student and later became an Anglican priest, but he retained his interest in Judaism and told Hasidic legends to Levertov and her older sister, Olga, throughout their childhoods. From her mother, Beatrice Spooner-Jones, Levertov learned to look closely at the world around her, and we might say of her work what she said of her mother: "with how much gazing/her life had paid tribute to the world's body" ("The 90th Year").

In 1947, Levertov married an American, Mitchell Goodman (they later divorced), and moved to the United States. She described this move as crucial to her development as a poet; it "necessitated the finding of new rhythms in which to write, in accordance with new rhythms of life and speech." In this discovery of a new idiom, the stylistic influence of William Carlos Williams was especially important to her; without it, she said, "I could not have developed from a British Romantic with an almost Victorian background to an American poet of any vitality." Levertov embraced Williams's interest in an organic poetic form, growing out of the poet's relation to her subject, and like Duncan and Robert Creeley, she actively explored the relations between the line and the unit of breath, as they control rhythm, melody, and stress. But if Levertov became the poet she was by becoming an American poet, her European heritage also enriched her sense of influence. Although her poem "September 1961" acknowledges her link to "the old great ones" (Ezra Pound, Williams, and H. D.), she was as at home with German lyric poet Rilke as with Emerson. And in the United States she discovered the work of Martin Buber, the Jewish theologian and philosopher, which renewed her interest "in the Hasidic ideas with which I was dimly acquainted as a child." Her eclecticism let her move easily between plain and richly descriptive language, between a vivid perception of the "thing itself" and the often radiant mystery that, for Levertov, arose from such seeing.

From 1956 to 1959 Levertov lived with her husband and son in Mexico. They were joined there by her mother, who, after her daughter's departure, remained in Mexico for the final eighteen years of her life (she died in 1977). Several moving poems in Levertov's collection *Life in the Forest* (1978) address her mother's last years, among them "The 90th Year" and "Death in Mexico." In the late 1960s, the political crisis prompted by the Vietnam War turned Levertov's work more directly to public woes, as reflected in her following four books. Not all of the poems in these books explicitly concern political issues ("The Sorrow Dance," for example, contains her sequence in memory of her sister, Olga, one of her finest, most powerful poems); nonetheless, many poems originated in a need for public testimony. Her overtly political poems are not often among her best, however; their very explicitness restricted her distinctive strengths as a poet, which included a feeling for the inexplicable, a language lyrical enough to express wish and desire, and a capacity for playfulness. But it is a mistake to separate too rigidly the political concerns in her work from a larger engagement with the world. As she wrote, "If a degree of intimacy is a condition of lyric expression, surely—at times when events make feelings run high—that intimacy between writer and political belief does exist, and is as intense as other emotions."

The power of Levertov's poems depends on her capacity to balance, however precariously, her two-sided vision, to keep alive both terms of what one critic called her "magical realism." At its best, her work seems to spring from experience deep within her, stirred into being by a source beyond herself (as "Caedmon" is suddenly "affrighted" by an angel or the poet at sixteen dreams deeply, "sunk in the well"). Her finest poems render the inexplicable nature of our ordinary lives and their capacity for unexpected beauty. But Levertov's capacity for pleasure in the world never strays too far from the knowledge that the very landscapes that delight us contain places "that can pull you/down" ("Zeroing In"), as our inner landscapes also contain places " 'that are bruised forever, that time/never assuages, never.' "

Levertov published several collections of prose, including *The Poet in the World* (1973), *Light Up the Cave* (1981), and *New and Selected Essays* (1992). In 1987 she published her fifteenth book of poems, *Breathing the Water*. This book contains a long sequence, *The Showings: Lady Julian of Norwich, 1342–1416*, which continues the link between Levertov's work and a visionary tradition. She published three subsequent collections: *A Door in the Hive* (1989), *Evening Train* (1992), and *Tesserae* (1995). Levertov taught widely and from 1982 until her death was professor of English at Stanford University, where she was an important teacher for a younger generation of writers.

To the Snake

Green Snake, when I hung you round my neck
and stroked your cold, pulsing throat
          as you hissed to me, glinting
arrowy gold scales, and I felt
          the weight of you on my shoulders,   5
and the whispering silver of your dryness
          sounded close at my ears—

Green Snake—I swore to my companions that certainly
          you were harmless! But truly
I had no certainty, and no hope, only desiring   10
          to hold you, for that joy,
                              which left
a long wake of pleasure, as the leaves moved
and you faded into the pattern
of grass and shadows, and I returned   15
smiling and haunted, to a dark morning.

                                                  1960

The Jacob's Ladder[1]

The stairway is not
a thing of gleaming strands
a radiant evanescence
for angels' feet that only glance in their tread, and need not
touch the stone.   5

It is of stone.
A rosy stone that takes
a glowing tone of softness
only because behind it the sky is a doubtful, a doubting
night gray.   10

A stairway of sharp
angles, solidly built.
One sees that the angels must spring
down from one step to the next, giving a little
lift of the wings: 15

and a man climbing
must scrape his knees, and bring
the grip of his hands into play. The cut stone
consoles his groping feet. Wings brush past him.
The poem ascends.   20

                                                  1961

---

1. Jacob dreamed of "a ladder set up on the earth, and the top of it reached to heaven: and behold the angels of God ascending and descending on it" (Genesis 28.12).

In Mind

There's in my mind a woman
of innocence, unadorned but

fair-featured, and smelling of
apples or grass. She wears

a utopian smock or shift, her hair   5
is light brown and smooth, and she

is kind and very clean without
ostentation—
                    but she has
no imagination.   10
                    And there's a
turbulent moon-ridden girl

or old woman, or both,
dressed in opals and rags, feathers

and torn taffeta,   15
who knows strange songs—

but she is not kind.

                                                          1964

September 1961

This is the year the old ones,
the old great ones
leave us alone on the road.

The road leads to the sea.
We have the words in our pockets,   5
obscure directions. The old ones

have taken away the light of their presence,
we see it moving away over a hill
off to one side.

They are not dying.   10
they are withdrawn
into a painful privacy

learning to live without words.
E. P. "It looks like dying"—Williams: "I can't
describe to you what has been   15

happening to me"—
H. D. "unable to speak."[1]
The darkness

twists itself in the wind, the stars
are small, the horizon   20
ringed with confused urban light-haze.

They have told us
the road leads to the sea,
and given

the language into our hands.   25
We hear
our footsteps each time a truck

has dazzled past us and gone
leaving us new silence.
One can't reach   30

the sea on this endless
road to the sea unless
one turns aside at the end, it seems,

follows
the owl that silently glides above it   35
aslant, back and forth,

and away into deep woods.

But for us the road
unfurls itself, we count the
words in our pockets, we wonder   40

how it will be without them, we don't
stop walking, we know
there is far to go, sometimes

we think the night wind carries
a smell of the sea . . .   45

1964

---

1. The speakers are, respectively, Ezra Pound (1885–1972), William Carlos Williams (1883–1963), and Hilda Doolittle (1886–1961)—three of the primary figures in modern American verse. In 1961 Williams and H. D. suffered debilitating strokes; Pound, after decades of prolific critical activity, fell into a silence that would last until his death.

What Were They Like?

1) Did the people of Vietnam
   use lanterns of stone?
2) Did they hold ceremonies
   to reverence the opening of buds?
3) Were they inclined to quiet laughter?   5
4) Did they use bone and ivory,
   jade and silver, for ornament?
5) Had they an epic poem?
6) Did they distinguish between speech and singing?

1) Sir, their light hearts turned to stone.   10
   It is not remembered whether in gardens
   stone lanterns illumined pleasant ways.
2) Perhaps they gathered once to delight in blossom,
   but after the children were killed
   there were no more buds.   15
3) Sir, laughter is bitter to the burned mouth.
4) A dream ago, perhaps. Ornament is for joy.
   All the bones were charred.
5) It is not remembered. Remember,
   most were peasants; their life   20
   was in rice and bamboo.
   When peaceful clouds were reflected in the paddies
   and the water buffalo stepped surely along terraces,
   maybe fathers told their sons old tales.
   When bombs smashed those mirrors   25
   there was time only to scream.
6) There is an echo yet
   of their speech which was like a song.
   It was reported their singing resembled
   the flight of moths in moonlight.   30
   Who can say? It is silent now.

                                                                    1971

Death in Mexico[1]

Even two weeks after her fall,
three weeks before she died, the garden
began to vanish. The rickety fence gave way
as it had threatened, and the children threw
broken plastic toys—vicious yellow,
unresonant red, onto the path, into the lemontree;   5
or trotted in through the gap, trampling small plants.

---

1. One of a sequence of poems on the death of Levertov's mother.

For two weeks no one watered it, except
I did, twice, but then I left. She was still conscious then
and thanked me. I begged the others to water it—   10
but the rains began; when I got back there were violent,
sudden, battering downpours each afternoon.
                              Weeds flourished,
dry topsoil was washed away swiftly
into the drains. Oh, there was green, still,   15
but the garden was disappearing—each day
less sign of the ordered,
thought-out oasis, a squared circle her mind
constructed for rose and lily, begonia
and rosemary-for-remembrance.   20
Twenty years in the making—
less than a month to undo itself;
and those who had seen it grow,
living around it those decades,
did nothing to hold it. Oh, Alberto did,   25
one day, patch up the fence a bit,
when I told him a future tenant would value
having a garden. But no one believed
the garden-maker would live (I least of all),
so her pain if she were to see the ruin   30
remained abstract, an incomprehensible concept,
impelling no action. When they carried her past
                              on a stretcher,
on her way to the *sanatorio,* failing sight
transformed itself into a mercy: certainly   35
she could have seen no more than a greenish blur.
But to me the weeds, the flowerless rosebushes, broken
stems of the canna lilies and amaryllis, all
a lusterless jungle green, presented—
even before her dying was over—   40
an obdurate, blind, all-seeing gaze:
I had seen it before, in the museums,
in stone masks of the gods and victims.
A gaze that admits no tenderness; if it smiles, it
only smiles with sublime bitterness—no,   45
not even bitter: it admits
no regret, nostalgia has no part in its cosmos,
bitterness is irrelevant.
If it holds a flower—and it does,
a delicate brilliant silky flower that blooms only   50
a single day—it holds it clenched
between sharp teeth.
Vines may crawl, and scorpions, over its face,
but though the centuries blunt
eyelid and flared nostril, the stone gaze   55
is utterly still, fixed, absolute,
smirk of denial facing eternity.
Gardens vanish. She was an alien here,

as I am. Her death
was not Mexico's business. The garden though   60
was a hostage. Old gods
took back their own.

1978

Caedmon[1]

All others talked as if
talk were a dance.
Clodhopper I, with clumsy feet
would break the gliding ring.
Early I learned to   5
hunch myself
close by the door:
then when the talk began
I'd wipe my
mouth and wend   10
unnoticed back to the barn
to be with the warm beasts,
dumb among body sounds
of the simple ones.
I'd see by a twist   15
of lit rush[2] the motes
of gold moving
from shadow to shadow
slow in the wake
of deep untroubled sighs.   20
The cows
munched or stirred or were still. I
was at home and lonely,
both in good measure. Until
the sudden angel affrighted me—light effacing   25
my feeble beam,
a forest of torches, feathers of flame, sparks upflying:
but the cows as before
were calm, and nothing was burning,
        nothing but I, as that hand of fire   30
touched my lips and scorched my tongue
and pulled my voice
                into the ring of the dance.

1987

1. "The story comes, of course, from the Venerable Bede's *History of the English Church and People,* but I first read it as a child in John Richard
Green's *History of the English People,* 1855" [Lev-
ertov's note]. Caedmon (fl. 658–680) was, according to the story, an illiterate cowherd employed by
a monastery; one night he received a divine call to
sing verses in praise of God. He is the earliest
known Christian poet in English.
2. The piths of rush plants were used for candle-
wicks.

A. R. AMMONS
1926–2001

A. R. Ammons wrote that he "was born big and jaundiced (and ugly) on February 18, 1926, in a farmhouse 4 miles southwest of Whiteville, North Carolina, and 2 miles northwest of New Hope Elementary School and New Hope Baptist Church." It was characteristic of Ammons to be laconic, self-deprecating, unfailingly local, and unfailingly exact. He belongs to the homemade strain of American writers rather than the Europeanized or cosmopolitan breed. His poems are filled with the landscapes in which he has lived: North Carolina, the south Jersey coast, and the surroundings of Ithaca, New York, where he lived and was a member of the English department of Cornell University.

Ammons's career did not start out with a traditional literary education. At Wake Forest College in North Carolina he studied mostly scientific subjects, especially biology and chemistry, and that scientific training has strongly colored his poems. Only later (1951–52) did he study English literature for three semesters at the University of California at Berkeley. He had worked briefly as a high-school principal in North Carolina. When he returned from Berkeley he spent twelve years as an executive for a firm that made biological glass in southern New Jersey.

In 1955, his thirtieth year, Ammons published his first book of poems, *Ommateum*. The title refers to the compound structure of an insect's eye and foreshadows a twofold impulse in Ammons's work. On one hand he is involved in the minute observation of natural phenomena; on the other hand he is frustrated by the physical limitations analogous to those of the insects' vision. We see the world, as insects do, in small portions and in impulses that take in but do not totally resolve the many images we receive. "Overall is beyond me," says Ammons in "Corsons Inlet," an important poem in which the shifting details of shoreline and dunes represent a severe challenge to the poet-observer. There are no straight lines. The contours differ every day, every hour, and they teach the poet the endless adjustments he must make to nature's fluidity.

"A poem is a walk," Ammons said, and his work is characterized by the motion he found everywhere in nature, a motion answered by the activity of his own mind. Both nearsighted and farsighted, he looks closely at vegetation, small animals, the minute shifts of wind and weather and light, yet over and over again seems drawn to Emerson's visionary aspirations for poetry. "Poetry," Emerson remarked, "was all written before time was, and whenever we are so finely organized that we can penetrate into that region where the air is music, we hear those primal warnings and attempt to write them down." Much of Ammons's poetry tests this farsighted, transcendental promise to see if it yields a glimpse of supernatural order.

The self in Ammons's poems is a far more modest presence than in the work of many other American writers. Sometimes he is a "surrendered self among unwelcoming forms" (as he writes in the conclusion of "Gravelly Run"); in many other poems he is at home in a universe, both human and natural, whose variety delights him. He is that rare thing, a contemporary poet of praise, one who says "I can find nothing lowly/in the universe" ("Still") and convinces us he speaks the truth.

Ammons began his career writing short lyrics, almost journal entries in an unending career of observation. But the laconic notations—of a landslide, a shift in the shoreline from one day to the next—often bore abstract titles ("Clarity," "Saliences") as if to suggest the connections he feels between concrete experience and speculative thought. Ammons often conducted experiments with poetic form in his effort to make his verse responsive to the engaging but evasive particularity of natural process. This formal inventiveness is part of the appeal of his work. "Stop on any word and language gives way: /the blades of reason, unlightened by motion, sink in," he remarks in his "Essay on Poetics." Preparing *Tape for the Turn of the Year* (1965) he typed a book-length day-to-day verse diary along an adding machine tape. The poem ended when the tape did. This was his first and most flamboyant attempt to turn his verse into something beyond mere gatherings. He then discovered that the long poem was the form best adapted to his continuing, indeed endless, dialogue between the specific and the general. The appearance in 1993 of his book-length poem *Garbage* (a National Book Award winner) confirmed Ammons's gift for creating a long, immensely readable, moving and funny poem, full of digressions but structured around a recurring set of images and ideas.

The poems tend to make use of the colon—what one critic calls "the most democratic punctuation," suggesting as it does equivalence on both sides. Used in place of the period, it keeps the poem from coming to a halt or stopping the flow in which the mind feverishly suggests analogies among its minutely perceived experiences. Many notable examples of Ammons's extended forms are gathered in *The Selected Longer Poems* (1980), although that book does not include his remarkable *Sphere: The Form of a Motion* (1974). A single, book-length poem, with no full stops, 155 sections of four tercets each, it aspires to be what Wallace Stevens called "the poem of the act of the mind." The only unity in *Sphere* is the mind's power to make analogies between the world's constant "diversifications." As he demonstrates in this poem, Ammons was committed to the provisional, the self-revising, and this commitment kept his poetry fresh over a long career, as the achievement of *Garbage* demonstrates. Writing of his sense of the world in "The Dwelling," from *Sumerian Vistas* (1987), Ammons says, "here the plainnest / majesty gave us what it could." The same might be said of his wonderfully generous and witty poems, which constitute a distinctive and invaluable legacy for American poetry.

So I Said I Am Ezra

So I said I am Ezra
and the wind whipped my throat
gaming for the sounds of my voice
    I listened to the wind
go over my head and up into the night   5
Turning to the sea I said
        I am Ezra
but there were no echoes from the waves
The words were swallowed up
    in the voice of the surf   10
or leaping over the swells
lost themselves oceanward
    Over the bleached and broken fields
I moved my feet and turning from the wind
    that ripped sheets of sand   15
    from the beach and threw them
    like seamists across the dunes
swayed as if the wind were taking me away
and said
        I am Ezra   20
As a word too much repeated
falls out of being
so I Ezra went out into the night
like a drift of sand

and splashed among the windy oats   25
that clutch the dunes
of unremembered seas

                                                                    1955

Corsons Inlet

I went for a walk over the dunes again this morning
to the sea,
then turned right along
    the surf
                rounded a naked headland   5
                and returned

    along the inlet shore:

it was muggy sunny, the wind from the sea steady and high,
crisp in the running sand,
        some breakthroughs of sun   10
    but after a bit

continuous overcast:

the walk liberating, I was released from forms,
from the perpendiculars,
        straight lines, blocks, boxes, binds   15
of thought
into the hues, shadings, rises, flowing bends and blends
        of sight:

                        I allow myself eddies of meaning:
yield to a direction of significance   20
running
like a stream through the geography of my work:
    you can find
in my sayings
                swerves of action   25
            like the inlet's cutting edge:
        there are dunes of motion,
organizations of grass, white sandy paths of remembrance
in the overall wandering of mirroring mind:

but Overall is beyond me: is the sum of these events   30
I cannot draw, the ledger I cannot keep, the accounting
beyond the account:

in nature there are few sharp lines: there are areas of
primrose
        more or less dispersed;   35

disorderly orders of bayberry; between the rows
of dunes,
irregular swamps of reeds,
though not reeds alone, but grass, bayberry, yarrow, all . . .
predominantly reeds: 40

I have reached no conclusions, have erected no boundaries,
shutting out and shutting in, separating inside
      from outside: I have
      drawn no lines:
      as   45

manifold events of sand
change the dune's shape that will not be the same shape
tomorrow,

so I am willing to go along, to accept
the becoming   50
thought, to stake off no beginnings or ends, establish
      no walls:

by transitions the land falls from grassy dunes to creek
to undercreek: but there are no lines, though
    change in that transition is clear   55
    as any sharpness: but "sharpness" spread out,
allowed to occur over a wider range
than mental lines can keep:

the moon was full last night: today, low tide was low:
black shoals of mussels exposed to the risk   60
of air
and, earlier, of sun,
waved in and out with the waterline, waterline inexact,
caught always in the event of change:
    a young mottled gull stood free on the shoals   65
    and ate
to vomiting: another gull, squawking possession, cracked a crab,
picked out the entrails, swallowed the soft-shelled legs, a ruddy
turnstone[1] running in to snatch leftover bits:

risk is full: every living thing in   70
siege: the demand is life, to keep life: the small
white blacklegged egret, how beautiful, quietly stalks and spears
      the shallows, darts to shore
        to stab—what? I couldn't
      see against the black mudflats—a frightened   75
      fiddler crab?

      the news to my left over the dunes and
reeds and bayberry clumps was
      fall: thousands of tree swallows

---

1. A ploverlike migratory bird.

gathering for flight: 80
an order held
in constant change: a congregation
rich with entropy: nevertheless, separable, noticeable
   as one event,
          not chaos: preparations for   85
flight from winter,
cheet, cheet, cheet, cheet, wings rifling the green clumps,
beaks
at the bayberries
   a perception full of wind, flight, curve,   90
   sound:
   the possibility of rule as the sum of rulelessness:
the "field" of action
with moving, incalculable center:

in the smaller view, order tight with shape: 95
blue tiny flowers on a leafless weed: carapace of crab:
snail shell:
      pulsations of order
      in the bellies of minnows: orders swallowed,
broken down, transferred through membranes   100
to strengthen larger orders: but in the large view, no
lines or changeless shapes: the working in and out, together
     and against, of millions of events: this,
        so that I make
        no form of   105
        formlessness:

orders as summaries, as outcomes of actions override
or in some way result, not predictably (seeing me gain
the top of a dune,
the swallows   110
could take flight—some other fields of bayberry
     could enter fall
     berryless) and there is serenity:

      no arranged terror: no forcing of image, plan,
or thought: 115
no propaganda, no humbling of reality to precept:

terror pervades but is not arranged, all possibilities
of escape open: no route shut, except in
   the sudden loss of all routes:

      I see narrow orders, limited tightness, but will   120
not run to that easy victory:
     still around the looser, wider forces work:
     I will try
   to fasten into order enlarging grasps of disorder, widening
scope, but enjoying the freedom that   125
Scope eludes my grasp, that there is no finality of vision,

that I have perceived nothing completely,
    that tomorrow a new walk is a new walk.

1965

Easter Morning

I have a life that did not become,
that turned aside and stopped,
astonished:
I hold it in me like a pregnancy or
as on my lap a child   5
not to grow or grow old but dwell on

it is to his grave I most
frequently return and return
to ask what is wrong, what was
wrong, to see it all by   10
the light of a different necessity
but the grave will not heal
and the child,
stirring, must share my grave
with me, an old man having   15
gotten by on what was left

when I go back to my home country in these
fresh far-away days, it's convenient to visit
everybody, aunts and uncles, those who used to say,
look how he's shooting up, and the   20
trinket aunts who always had a little
something in their pocketbooks, cinnamon bark
or a penny or nickel, and uncles who
were the rumored fathers of cousins
who whispered of them as of great, if   25
troubled, presences, and school
teachers, just about everybody older
(and some younger) collected in one place
waiting, particularly, but not for
me, mother and father there, too, and others   30
close, close as burrowing
under skin, all in the graveyard
assembled, done for, the world they
used to wield, have trouble and joy
in, gone   35

the child in me that could not become
was not ready for others to go,
to go on into change, blessings and
horrors, but stands there by the road
where the mishap occurred, crying out for   40

help, come and fix this or we
can't get by, but the great ones who
were to return, they could not or did
not hear and went on in a flurry and
now, I say in the graveyard, here   45
lies the flurry, now it can't come
back with help or helpful asides, now
we all buy the bitter
incompletions, pick up the knots of
horror, silently raving, and go on   50
crashing into empty ends not
completions, not rondures the fullness
has come into and spent itself from
I stand on the stump
of a child, whether myself   55
or my little brother who died, and
yell as far as I can, I cannot leave this place, for
for me it is the dearest and the worst,
it is life nearest to life which is
life lost: it is my place where   60
I must stand and fail,
calling attention with tears
to the branches not lofting
boughs into space, to the barren
air that holds the world that was my world   65

though the incompletions
(& completions) burn out
standing in the flash high-burn
momentary structure of ash, still it
is a picture-book, letter-perfect   70
Easter morning: I have been for a
walk: the wind is tranquil: the brook
works without flashing in an abundant
tranquility: the birds are lively with
voice: I saw something I had   75
never seen before: two great birds,
maybe eagles, blackwinged, whitenecked
and -headed, came from the south oaring
the great wings steadily; they went
directly over me, high up, and kept on   80
due north: but then one bird,
the one behind, veered a little to the
left and the other bird kept on seeming
not to notice for a minute: the first
began to circle as if looking for   85
something, coasting, resting its wings
on the down side of some of the circles:
the other bird came back and they both
circled, looking perhaps for a draft;
they turned a few more times, possibly   90
rising—at least, clearly resting—

then flew on falling into distance till
they broke across the local bush and
trees: it was a sight of bountiful
majesty and integrity: the having   95
patterns and routes, breaking
from them to explore other patterns or
better way to routes, and then the
return: a dance sacred as the sap in
the trees, permanent in its descriptions   100
as the ripples round the brook's
ripplestone: fresh as this particular
flood of burn breaking across us now
from the sun.

1981

Singling & Doubling Together

My nature singing in me is your nature singing:
you have means to veer down, filter through,
and, coming in,
harden into vines that break back with leaves,
so that when the wind stirs   5
I know you are there and I hear you in leafspeech,

though of course back into your heightenings I
can never follow: you are there beyond
tracings flesh can take,
and farther away surrounding and informing the systems,   10
you are as if nothing, and
where you are least knowable I celebrate you most

or here most when near dusk the pheasant squawks and
lofts at a sharp angle to the roost cedar,
I catch in the angle of that ascent,   15
in the justness of that event your pheasant nature,
and when dusk settles, the bushes creak and
snap in their natures with your creaking

and snapping nature: I catch the impact and turn
it back: cut the grass and pick up branches   20
under the elm, rise to the several tendernesses
and griefs, and you will fail me only as from the still
of your great high otherness you fail all things,
somewhere to lift things up, if not those things again:

even you risked all the way into the taking on of shape   25
and time fail and fail with me, as me,
and going hence with me know the going hence
and in the cries of that pain it is you crying and

you know of it and it is my pain, my tears, my loss—
what but grace   30

have I to bear in every motion,
embracing or turning away, staggering or standing still,
while your settled kingdom sways in the distillations of light
and plunders down into the darkness with me
and comes nowhere up again but changed into your   35
singing nature when I need sing my nature nevermore.

                                                                          1983

From Garbage

2

garbage has to be the poem of our time because
garbage is spiritual, believable enough

to get our attention, getting in the way, piling
up, stinking, turning brooks brownish and

creamy white: what else deflects us from the   5
errors of our illusionary ways, not a temptation

to trashlessness, that is too far off, and,
anyway, unimaginable, unrealistic: I'm a

hole puncher or hole plugger: stick a finger
in the dame (*dam,* damn, dike), hold back the issue   10

of creativity's floor, the forthcoming, futuristic,
the origins feeding trash: down by I-95 in

Florida where flatland's ocean- and gulf-flat,
mounds of disposal rise (for if you dug

something up to make room for something to put   15
in, what about the something dug up, as with graves:)

the garbage trucks crawl as if in obeisance,
as if up ziggurats[1] toward the high places gulls

and garbage keep alive, offerings to the gods
of garbage, or retribution, of realistic   20

expectation, the deities of unpleasant
necessities: refined, young earthworms,

drowned up in macadam pools by spring rains, moisten
out white in a day or so and, round spots,

1. The temple towers of the Babylonians, which consisted of a lofty pyramidal structure, built in successive
stages, with outside staircases and a religious shrine on top.

look like sputum or creamy-rich, broken-up cold   25
clams: if this is not the best poem of the

century, can it be about the worst poem of the
century: it comes, at least, toward the end,

so a long tracing of bad stuff can swell
under its measure: but there on the heights   30

a small smoke wafts the sacrificial bounty
day and night to layer the sky brown, shut us

in as into a lidded kettle, the everlasting
flame these acres-deep of tendance keep: a

free offering of a crippled plastic chair: 35
a played-out sports outfit: a hill-myna

print stained with jelly: how to write this
poem, should it be short, a small popping of

duplexes, or long, hunting wide, coming home
late, losing the trail and recovering it: 40

should it act itself out, illustrations,
examples, colors, clothes or intensify

reductively into statement, bones any corpus
would do to surround, or should it be nothing

at all unless it finds itself: the poem,   45
which is about the pre-socratic idea of the

dispositional axis from stone to wind, wind
to stone (with my elaborations, if any)

is complete before it begins, so I needn't
myself hurry into brevity, though a weary reader   50

might briefly be done: the axis will be clear
enough daubed here and there with a little ink

or fined out into every shade and form of its
revelation: this is a scientific poem,

asserting that nature models values, that we   55
have invented little (copied), reflections of

possibilities already here, this where we came
to and how we came: a priestly director behind the

black-chuffing dozer leans the gleanings and
reads the birds, millions of loners circling   60

a common height, alighting to the meaty streaks
and puffy muffins (puffins?): there is a mound,

too, in the poet's mind dead language is hauled
off to and burned down on, the energy held and

shaped into new turns and clusters, the mind   65
strengthened by what it strengthens: for

where but in the very asshole of comedown is
redemption: as where but brought low, where

but in the grief of failure, loss, error do we
discern the savage afflictions that turn us around: 70

where but in the arrangements love crawls us
through, not a thing left in our self-display

unhumiliated, do we find the sweet seed of
new routes; but we are natural: nature, not

we, gave rise to us; we are not, though, though   75
natural, divorced from higher, finer configurations:

tissues and holograms of energy circulate in
us and seek and find representations of themselves

outside us, so that we can participate in
celebrations high and know reaches of feeling   80

and sight and thought that penetrate (really
penetrate) far, far beyond these our wet cells,

right on up past our stories, the planets, moons,
and other bodies locally to the other end of

the pole where matter's forms diffuse and   85
energy loses all means to express itself except

as spirit, there, oh, yes, in the abiding where
mind but nothing else abides, the eternal,

until it turns into another pear or sunfish,
that momentary glint in the fisheye having   90

been there so long, coming and going, it's
eternity's glint: it all wraps back round,

into and out of form, palpable and impalpable,
and in one phase, the one of grief and love,

we know the other, where everlastingness comes to   95
sway, okay and smooth: the heaven we mostly

want, though, is this jet-hoveled hell back,
heaven's daunting asshole: one must write and

rewrite till one writes it right: if I'm in
touch, she said, then I've got an edge: what   100

the hell kind of talk is that: I can't believe
I'm merely an old person: whose mother is dead,

whose father is gone and many of whose
friends and associates have wended away to the

ground, which is only heavy wind, or to ashes,   105
a lighter breeze: but it was all quite frankly

to be expected and not looked forward to: even
old trees, I remember some of them, where they

used to stand: pictures taken by some of them:
and old dogs, specially one imperial black one,   110

quad dogs with their hier*archies* (another *archie*)
one succeeding another, the barking and romping

sliding away like slides from a projector: what
were they then that are what they are now:

1993

JAMES MERRILL
1926–1995

When James Merrill's *First Poems* were published in 1950, he was immediately recognized as one of the most gifted and polished poets of his generation. But it was not
until *Water Street* (1962), his third volume of poems, that Merrill began to enlist his
brilliant technique and sophisticated tone in developing a poetic autobiography. The
book takes its title from the street where he lives in the seaside village of Stonington,
Connecticut. The opening poem, "An Urban Convalescence," explores his decision
to leave New York, which he sees as a distracting city that destroys its past. He portrays
his move as a rededication to his personal past and an attempt through poetry "to
make some kind of house / Out of the life lived, out of the love spent."

The metaphor of *home* is an emotional center to which Merrill's writing often
returns, as in "Lost in Translation," where the narrator recalls a childhood summer
in a home mysteriously without parents. "The Broken Home" similarly recalls elements of Merrill's own experience as the son of parents who divorced when he was

young. He had been born to the second marriage of Charles E. Merrill, financier and founder of the best-known brokerage firm in America. "The Broken Home" and "Lost in Translation" show how memory and the act of writing have the power to reshape boyhood pain and conflict so as to achieve "the unstiflement of the entire story." Such an attitude distinguishes Merrill from his contemporaries (Robert Lowell, Anne Sexton, and Sylvia Plath), whose autobiographical impulse expresses itself primarily in the present tense and the use of poems as an urgent journal true to the moment.

As an undergraduate at Amherst College, Merrill had written an honors thesis on the French novelist Marcel Proust (1871–1922). His poetry was clearly affected by Proust's notion that the literary exercise of memory slowly discloses the patterns of childhood experience that we are destined to relive. Proust showed in his *Remembrance of Things Past* how such power over chaotic material of the past is often triggered involuntarily by an object or an episode in the present whose associations reach back into formative childhood encounters. The questions he asked were asked by Freud as well: What animates certain scenes—and not others—for us? It is to answer such questions that some of Merrill's poems are told from the viewpoint of an observant child. In other poems the poet is explicitly present, at his desk, trying to incorporate into his adult understanding of the contours of his life the pain and freshness of childhood memories. The poems are narrative (one of his early books was called *Short Stories*) as often as lyric, in the hope that dramatic *action* will reveal the meanings with which certain objects have become charged. As Merrill sees it, "You hardly ever need to *state* your feelings. The point is to feel and keep the eyes open. Then what you feel is expressed, is mimed back at you by the scene. A room, a landscape. I'd go a step further. We don't *know* what we feel until we see it distanced by this kind of translation."

Merrill traveled extensively and presented landscapes from his travels as ways of exploring alternative or buried states of his own mind, the "translations" of which he speaks. Poems such as "Days of 1964" and "After the Fire" reflect his experiences in Greece, where he used to spend a portion of each year. They respectively anticipate and comment on *The Fire Screen* (1969), a sequence of poems describing the rising and falling curve of a love affair partly in terms of an initiation into Greece with its power to strip away urban sophistication. The books that followed served as initiations into other psychic territories. Problems of family relationships and the erotic entanglements of homosexual love previously seen on an intimate scale were in *Braving the Elements* (1972) acted out against a wider backdrop: the long landscapes, primitive geological perspectives, and erosions of the American Far West. Here human experience, examined in his earlier work in close-up, is seen as part of a longer process of evolution comprehensible in terms of enduring nonhuman patterns.

In *Divine Comedies* (which received the Pulitzer Prize in 1977) Merrill began his most ambitious work: two-thirds of it is devoted to "The Book of Ephraim," a long narrative. It is not only a recapitulation of his career but also an attempt to locate individual psychic energies as part of a larger series of nourishing influences: friends living and dead, literary predecessors, scientific theories of the growth of the universe and the mind, the life of other periods and even other universes—all conducted through a set of encounters with the "other world" in séances at the Ouija board. It is a witty and original and assured attempt to take the intimate material of the short lyric that has characterized his earlier work and cast it onto an epic scale. The second and third volumes of the trilogy, *Mirabell: Books of Number* and *Scripts for the Pageant*, appeared in 1978 and 1980, respectively; the entire work was collected in 1982 under the title *The Changing Light at Sandover*. By the time of his death in 1995, Merrill had established himself as an American formal master, one whose grace and wit made his remarkable variations on traditional forms seem as easy as casual speech. This mastery is evident in his sequence "Family Week at Oracle Ranch" (from his last book, *A Scattering of Salts,* 1995), where Merrill's formal daring is matched by an equally remarkable emotional daring.

An Urban Convalescence

Out for a walk, after a week in bed,
I find them tearing up part of my block
And, chilled through, dazed and lonely, join the dozen
In meek attitudes, watching a huge crane
Fumble luxuriously in the filth of years.   5
Her jaws dribble rubble. An old man
Laughs and curses in her brain,
Bringing to mind the close of *The White Goddess*.[1]

As usual in New York, everything is torn down
Before you have had time to care for it.   10
Head bowed, at the shrine of noise, let me try to recall
What building stood here. Was there a building at all?
I have lived on this same street for a decade.

Wait. Yes. Vaguely a presence rises
Some five floors high, of shabby stone   15
—Or am I confusing it with another one
In another part of town, or of the world?—
And over its lintel into focus vaguely
Misted with blood (my eyes are shut)
A single garland sways, stone fruit, stone leaves,   20
Which years of grit had etched until it thrust
Roots down, even into the poor soil of my seeing.
When did the garland become part of me?
I ask myself, amused almost,
Then shiver once from head to toe,   25

Transfixed by a particular cheap engraving of garlands
Bought for a few francs long ago,
All calligraphic tendril and cross-hatched rondure,
Ten years ago, and crumpled up to stanch
Boughs dripping, whose white gestures filled a cab,   30
And thought of neither then nor since.
Also, to clasp them, the small, red-nailed hand
Of no one I can place. Wait. No. Her name, her features
Lie toppled underneath that year's fashions.
The words she must have spoken, setting her face   35
To fluttering like a veil, I cannot hear now,
Let alone understand.

So that I am already on the stair,
As it were, of where I lived,
When the whole structure shudders at my tread   40
And soundlessly collapses, filling

---

1. The book (1948) in which English poet Robert Graves sets forth the impassioned theory that authentic poetry is inspired by a primitive goddess who is both creative and destructive. The crane is her sacred bird, which through a pun the poet here associates with the mechanical crane. Its operator seems like a crazed parody poet, committed only to demolition.

The air with motes of stone.
Onto the still erect building next door
Are pressed levels and hues—
Pocked rose, streaked greens, brown whites.   45
Who drained the pousse-café?[2]
Wires and pipes, snapped off at the roots, quiver.

Well, that is what life does. I stare
A moment longer, so. And presently
The massive volume of the world   50
Closes again.

Upon that book I swear
To abide by what it teaches:
Gospels of ugliness and waste,
Of towering voids, of soiled gusts,   55
Of a shrieking to be faced
Full into, eyes astream with cold—

With cold?
All right then. With self-knowledge.

Indoors at last, the pages of *Time* are apt   60
To open, and the illustrated mayor of New York,
Given a glimpse of how and where I work,
To note yet one more house that can be scrapped.

Unwillingly I picture
My walls weathering in the general view.   65
It is not even as though the new
Buildings did very much for architecture.

Suppose they did. The sickness of our time requires
That these as well be blasted in their prime.
You would think the simple fact of having lasted   70
Threatened our cities like mysterious fires.

There are certain phrases which to use in a poem
Is like rubbing silver with quicksilver. Bright
But facile, the glamour deadens overnight.
For instance, how "the sickness of our time"   75

Enhances, then debases, what I feel.
At my desk I swallow in a glass of water
No longer cordial, scarcely wet, a pill
They had told me not to take until much later.

With the result that back into my imagination   80
The city glides, like cities seen from the air,
Mere smoke and sparkle to the passenger
Having in mind another destination

2. An after-dinner drink made up of layers of different-colored cordials.

Which now is not that honey-slow descent
Of the Champs-Elysées,[3] her hand in his,   85
But the dull need to make some kind of house
Out of the life lived, out of the love spent.

1962

The Broken Home

Crossing the street,
I saw the parents and the child
At their window, gleaming like fruit
With evening's mild gold leaf.

In a room on the floor below,   5
Sunless, cooler—a brimming
Saucer of wax, marbly and dim—
I have lit what's left of my life.

I have thrown out yesterday's milk
And opened a book of maxims.   10
The flame quickens. The word stirs.

Tell me, tongue of fire,
That you and I are as real
At least as the people upstairs.
                                •
My father, who had flown in World War I,   15
Might have continued to invest his life
In cloud banks well above Wall Street and wife.
But the race was run below, and the point was to win.

Too late now, I make out in his blue gaze
(Through the smoked glass of being thirty-six)   20
The soul eclipsed by twin black pupils, sex
And business; time was money in those days.

Each thirteenth year he married. When he died
There were already several chilled wives
In sable orbit—rings, cars, permanent waves.   25
We'd felt him warming up for a green bride.

He could afford it. He was "in his prime"
At three score ten. But money was not time.
                                •
When my parents were younger this was a popular act:
A veiled woman would leap from an electric, wine-dark car   30

3. A stylish boulevard in Paris.

To the steps of no matter what—the Senate or the Ritz Bar—
And bodily, at newsreel speed, attack

No matter whom—Al Smith or José Maria Sert
Or Clemenceau[1]—veins standing out on her throat
As she yelled *War mongerer! Pig! Give us the vote!*,   35
And would have to be hauled away in her hobble skirt.

What had the man done? Oh, made history.
Her business (he had implied) was giving birth,
Tending the house, mending the socks.

Always that same old story—   40
Father Time and Mother Earth,[2]
A marriage on the rocks.

                              •

One afternoon, red, satyr-thighed
Michael, the Irish setter, head
Passionately lowered, led   45
The child I was to a shut door. Inside,

Blinds beat sun from the bed.
The green-gold room throbbed like a bruise.
Under a sheet, clad in taboos
Lay whom we sought, her hair undone, outspread,   50

And of a blackness found, if ever now, in old
Engravings where the acid bit.
I must have needed to touch it
Or the whiteness—was she dead?
Her eyes flew open, startled strange and cold.   55
The dog slumped to the floor. She reached for me. I fled.

                              •

Tonight they have stepped out onto the gravel.
The party is over. It's the fall
Of 1931. They love each other still.

She: Charlie, I can't stand the pace.   60
He: Come on, honey—why, you'll bury us all!

A lead soldier guards my windowsill:
Khaki rifle, uniform, and face.
Something in me grows heavy, silvery, pliable.

---

1. Georges Clemenceau (1841–1929), premier of France during World War I, visited the United States in 1922. Alfred E. Smith (1873–1944), a governor of New York and in 1928 candidate for the presidency. Sert (1876–1945), a Spanish painter who decorated the lobby of the Waldorf-Astoria Hotel in New York (1930).
2. In one sense a reference to Cronus (Greek for "Time"), ruler of the ancient Titans, and to his wife, Rhea, an earth deity known as Mother of the Gods. Because Cronus ate their children as soon as they were born, Rhea plotted his overthrow.

How intensely people used to feel!   65
Like metal poured at the close of a proletarian novel,[3]
Refined and glowing from the crucible,
I see those two hearts, I'm afraid,
Still. Cool here in the graveyard of good and evil,
They are even so to be honored and obeyed.   70

•

. . . Obeyed, at least, inversely. Thus
I rarely buy a newspaper, or vote.
To do so, I have learned, is to invite
The tread of a stone guest[4] within my house.

Shooting this rusted bolt, though, against him,   75
I trust I am no less time's child than some
Who on the heath impersonate Poor Tom[5]
Or on the barricades risk life and limb.

Nor do I try to keep a garden, only
An avocado in a glass of water—   80
Roots pallid, gemmed with air. And later,

When the small gilt leaves have grown
Fleshy and green, I let them die, yes, yes,
And start another. I am earth's no less.

•

A child, a red dog roam the corridors,   85
Still, of the broken home. No sound. The brilliant
Rag runners halt before wide-open doors.
My old room! Its wallpaper—cream, medallioned
With pink and brown—brings back the first nightmares,
Long summer colds, and Emma, sepia-faced,   90
Perspiring over broth carried upstairs
Aswim with golden fats I could not taste.

The real house became a boarding-school.
Under the ballroom ceiling's allegory
Someone at last may actually be allowed   95
To learn something; or, from my window, cool
With the unstiflement of the entire story,
Watch a red setter stretch and sink in cloud.

                                                                  1966

---

3. Socialist novel that romanticized laborers.
4. The *commendatore* in Mozart's *Don Giovanni*
(1787) returns as a statue to get his revenge.

5. Edgar, in Shakespeare's *King Lear*, disowned by
his father, wanders the heath disguised as a madman.

Lost in Translation

for Richard Howard[1]

Diese Tage, die leer dir scheinen
und wertlos für das All,
haben Werzeln zwischen den Steinen
und trinken dort überall.[2]

A card table in the library stands ready
To receive the puzzle which keeps never coming.
Daylight shines in or lamplight down
Upon the tense oasis of green felt.
Full of unfulfillment, life goes on,   5
Mirage arisen from time's trickling sands
Or fallen piecemeal into place:
German lesson, picnic, see-saw, walk
With the collie who "did everything but talk"—
Sour windfalls of the orchard back of us.   10
A summer without parents is the puzzle,
Or should be. But the boy, day after day,
Writes in his Line-a-Day *No puzzle.*

He's in love, at least. His French Mademoiselle,
In real life a widow since Verdun,[3]   15
Is stout, plain, carrot-haired, devout.
She prays for him, as does a curé[4] in Alsace,
Sews costumes for his marionettes,
Helps him to keep behind the scene
Whose sidelit goosegirl, speaking with his voice,   20
Plays Guinevere as well as Gunmoll[5] Jean.
Or else at bedtime in his tight embrace
Tells him her own French hopes, her German fears,
Her—but what more is there to tell?
Having known grief and hardship, Mademoiselle   25
Knows little more. Her languages. Her place.
Noon coffee. Mail. The watch that also waited
Pinned to her heart, poor gold, throws up its hands—
No puzzle! Steaming bitterness
Her sugars draw pops back into his mouth, translated: 30
"Patience, chéri. Geduld, mein Schatz."[6]
(Thus, reading Valéry the other evening
And seeming to recall a Rilke version of "Palme,"
That sunlit paradigm whereby the tree
Taps a sweet wellspring of authority,   35
The hour came back. Patience dans l'azur.[7]
Geduld im . . . Himmelblau? Mademoiselle.)

---

1. American poet and translator from the French (b. 1929).
2. These days, which seem empty and entirely fruitless to you, have roots between the stones and drink from everywhere (German). Part of a translation by the German poet Rainer Maria Rilke (1875–1926) of "Palme" by the French poet Paul Valéry (1871–1945); see lines 32 and 33.
3. Site of a battle in World War I. "French Mademoiselle": a French-speaking governess.
4. A French priest.
5. Or gun moll, a female gangster (1930s slang).
6. French and German phrases for "Have patience, my dear."
7. Patience in the blue (French); a phrase describing the palm tree from Valéry's poem.

Out of the blue, as promised, of a New York
Puzzle-rental shop the puzzle comes—
A superior one, containing a thousand hand-sawn,   40
Sandal-scented pieces. Many take
Shapes known already—the craftsman's repertoire
Nice in its limitation—from other puzzles:
Witch on broomstick, ostrich, hourglass,
Even (surely not just in retrospect)   45
An inchling, innocently branching palm.
These can be put aside, made stories of
While Mademoiselle spreads out the rest face-up,
Herself excited as a child; or questioned
Like incoherent faces in a crowd,   50
Each with its scrap of highly colored
Evidence the Law must piece together.
Sky-blue ostrich? Likely story.
Mauve of the witch's cloak white, severed fingers
Pluck? Detain her. The plot thickens   55
As all at once two pieces interlock.

Mademoiselle does borders—(Not so fast.
A London dusk, December last.
Chatter silenced in the library
This grown man reenters, wearing grey.   60
A medium. All except him have seen
Panel slid back, recess explored,
An object at once unique and common
Displayed, planted in a plain tole
Casket the subject now considers   65
Through shut eyes, saying in effect:
"Even as voices reach me vaguely
A dry saw-shriek drowns them out,
Some loud machinery—a lumber mill?
Far uphill in the fir forest   70
Trees tower, tense with shock,
Groaning and cracking as they crash groundward.
But hidden here is a freak fragment
Of a pattern complex in appearance only.
What it seems to show is superficial   75
Next to that long-term lamination
Of hazard and craft, the karma that has
Made it matter in the first place.
Plywood. Piece of a puzzle." Applause
Acknowledged by an opening of lids   80
Upon the thing itself. A sudden dread—
But to go back. All this lay years ahead.)

Mademoiselle does borders. Straight-edge pieces
Align themselves with earth or sky
In twos and threes, naive cosmogonists   85
Whose views clash. Nomad inlanders meanwhile
Begin to cluster where the totem
Of a certain vibrant egg-yolk yellow

Or pelt of what emerging animal
Acts on the straggler like a trumpet call   90
To form a more sophisticated unit.
By suppertime two ragged wooden clouds
Have formed. In one, a Sheik with beard
And flashing sword hilt (he is all but finished)
Steps forward on a tiger skin. A piece   95
Snaps shut, and fangs gnash out at us!
In the second cloud—they gaze from cloud to cloud
With marked if undecipherable feeling—
Most of a dark-eyed woman veiled in mauve
Is being helped down from her camel (kneeling)   100
By a small backward-looking slave or page-boy
(Her son, thinks Mademoiselle mistakenly)
Whose feet have not been found. But lucky finds
In the last minutes before bed
Anchor both factions to the scene's limits   105
And, by so doing, orient
Them eye to eye across the green abyss.
The yellow promises, oh bliss,
To be in time a sumptuous tent.

Puzzle begun I write in the day's space,   110
Then, while she bathes, peek at Mademoiselle's
Page to the curé: ". . . cette innocente mère,
Ce pauvre enfant, que deviendront-ils?"[8]
Her azure script is curlicued like pieces
Of the puzzle she will be telling him about.   115
(Fearful incuriosity of childhood!

"Tu as l'accent allemand,"[9] said Dominique.
Indeed. Mademoiselle was only French by marriage.
Child of an English mother, a remote
Descendant of the great explorer Speke,   120
And Prussian father. No one knew. I heard it
Long afterwards from her nephew, a UN
Interpreter. His matter-of-fact account
Touched old strings. My poor Mademoiselle,
With 1939 about to shake   125
This world where "each was the enemy, each the friend"
To its foundations, kept, though signed in blood,
Her peace a shameful secret to the end.)
"Schlaf wohl, chéri."[1] Her kiss. Her thumb
Crossing my brow against the dreams to come.   130

This World that shifts like sand, its unforeseen
Consolidations and elate routine,
Whose Potentate had lacked a retinue?
Lo! it assembles on the shrinking Green.

---

8. This innocent mother, this poor child, what will become of them? (French).

9. You have a German accent (French).

1. Sleep well (German), my dear (French).

Gunmetal-skinned or pale, all plumes and scars, 135
Of Vassalage the noblest avatars[2]—
The very coffee-bearer in his vair
Vest is a swart Highness, next to ours.

Kef[3] easing Boredom, and iced syrups, thirst,
In guessed-at glooms old wives who know the worst 140
Outsweat that virile fiction of the New:
"Insh'Allah,[4] he will tire—" "—or kill her first!"

(Hardly a proper subject for the Home,
Work of—dear Richard, I shall let *you* comb
Archives and learned journals for his name— 145
A minor lion attending on Gérôme.[5])

While, thick as Thebes[6] whose presently complete
Gates close behind them, Houri and Afreet[7]
Both claim the Page. He wonders whom to serve,
And what his duties are, and where his feet, 150

And if we'll find, as some before us did,
That piece of Distance deep in which lies hid
Your tiny apex sugary with sun,
Eternal Triangle, Great Pyramid!

Then Sky alone is left, a hundred blue 155
Fragments in revolution, with no clue
To where a Niche will open. Quite a task,
Putting together Heaven, yet we do.
It's done. Here under the table all along
Were those missing feet. It's done. 160

The dog's tail thumping. Mademoiselle sketching
Costumes for a coming harem drama
To star the goosegirl. All too soon the swift
Dismantling. Lifted by two corners,
The puzzle hung together—and did not. 165
Irresistibly a populace
Unstitched of its attachments, rattled down.
Power went to pieces as the witch
Slithered easily from Virtue's gown.
The blue held out for time, but crumbled, too. 170
The city had long fallen, and the tent,
A separating sauce mousseline,
Been swept away. Remained the green

---

2. Incarnations or embodiments. A vassal is an underling or servant.
3. A narcotic made from Indian hemp.
4. If Allah wills.
5. French painter (1824–1904), noted for his historical paintings, often of Near Eastern scenes.

6. The ancient capital of Upper Egypt; Homer's epithet for the city was "hundred-gated Thebes."
7. Near Eastern mythological figures. Houri was a virgin awarded to one who attains paradise. Afreet was an evil genie.

On which the grown-ups gambled. A green dusk.
First lightning bugs. Last glow of west   175
Green in the false eyes of (coincidence)
Our mangy tiger safe on his bared hearth.

Before the puzzle was boxed and readdressed
To the puzzle shop in the mid-Sixties,
Something tells me that one piece contrived   180
To stay in the boy's pocket. How do I know?
I know because so many later puzzles
had missing pieces—Maggie Teyte's[8] high notes
Gone at the war's end, end of the vogue for collies,
A house torn down; and hadn't Mademoiselle   185
Kept back her pitiful bit of truth as well?
I've spent the last days, furthermore,
Ransacking Athens for that translation of "Palme."
Neither the Goethehaus nor the National Library
Seems able to unearth it. Yet I can't   190
Just be imagining. I've seen it. Know
How much of the sun-ripe original
Felicity Rilke made himself forego
(Who loved French words—verger, mûr, parfumer[9])
In order to render its underlying sense.   195
Know already in that tongue of his
What Pains, what monolithic Truths
Shadow stanza to stanza's symmetrical
Rhyme-rutted pavement. Know that ground plan left
Sublime and barren, where the warm Romance   200
Stone by stone faded, cooled; the fluted nouns
Made taller, lonelier than life
By leaf-carved capitals in the afterglow.
The owlet umlaut[1] peeps and hoots
Above the open vowel. And after rain   205
A deep reverberation fills with stars.
Lost, is it, buried? One more missing piece?

But nothing's lost. Or else: all is translation
And every bit of us is lost in it
(Or found—I wander through the ruin of S[2]   210
Now and then, wondering at the peacefulness)
And in that loss a self-effacing tree,
Color of context, imperceptibly
Rustling with its angel, turns the waste
To shade and fiber, milk and memory.   215

1976

---

8. English soprano (1888–1976), famous for her
singing of French opera and songs.
9. Orchard, ripe, to scent.

1. A German accent mark (˙).
2. Initial of former lover.

Family Week at Oracle Ranch

1 *The Brochure*

The world outstrips us. In my day,
Had such a place existed,
It would have been advertised with photographs
Of doctors—silver hair, pince-nez—

Above detailed credentials,   5
Not this wide-angle moonscape, lawns and pool,
Patients sharing pain like fudge from home—
As if these were the essentials,

As if a month at what it invites us to think
Is little more than a fat farm for Anorexics,   10
Substance Abusers, Love & Relationship Addicts
Could help *you*, light of my life, when even your shrink . . .

The message, then? That costly folderol,
Underwear made to order in Vienna,
Who needs it! Let the soul hang out   15
At Benetton[1]—stone-washed, one size fits all.

2 *Instead of Complexes*

Simplicities. Just seven words—AFRAID,
HURT, LONELY, etc.—to say it with.
Shades of the first watercolor box
(I "felt blue," I "saw red").   20

Also some tips on brushwork. Not to say
"Your silence hurt me,"
Rather, "When you said nothing I felt hurt."
No blame, that way.

Dysfunctionals like us fail to distinguish   25
Between the two modes at first.
While the connoisseur of feeling throws up his hands:
Used to depicting personal anguish

With a full palette—hues, oils, glazes, thinner—
He stares into these withered wells and feels,   30
Well . . . SAD and ANGRY? Future lavender!
An infant Monet[2] blinks beneath his skin.

3 *The Counsellors*

They're in recovery, too, and tell us from what,
And that's as far as it goes.

---

1. A chain of clothing stores featuring T-shirts, jeans, sweaters.

2. Claude Monet (1840–1926), French impressionist painter.

Like the sun-priests' in *The Magic Flute*[3]   35
Their ritualized responses serve the plot.

Ken, for example, blond brows knitted: "When
James told the group he worried about dying
Without his lover beside him, I felt SAD."
Thank you for sharing, Ken,   40

I keep from saying; it would come out snide.
Better to view them as deadpan panels
Storing up sunlight for the woebegone,
Prompting from us lines electrified

By buried switches flipped (after how long!) . . .   45
But speak in private meanwhile? We may not
Until a voice within the temple lifts
Bans yet unfathomed into song.

4 *Gestalt*[4]

Little Aileen is a gray plush bear
With button eyes and nose.   50
Perky in flowered smock and clean white collar,
She occupies the chair

Across from the middleaged Big Aileen, face hid
In hands and hands on knees.
Her sobs break. In great waves it's coming back.   55
The uncle. What he did.

Little Aileen is her Inner Child
Who didn't . . . who didn't deserve. . . .
The horror kissed asleep, round Big Aileen
Fairytale thorns grow wild.   60

SADNESS and GUILT entitle us to watch
The survivor compose herself,
Smoothing the flowered stuff, which has ridden up,
Over an innocent gray crotch.

5 *Effects of Early "Religious Abuse"*

The great recurrent "sinner" found   65
In Dostoevsky[5]—twisted mouth,
Stormlit eyes—before whose irresistible
Unworthiness the pure in heart bow down . . .

---

3. One of the most famous of Wolfgang Amadeus
Mozart's works, *The Magic Flute* is a *singspiel*—
i.e., a combination of songs and dialogue.
4. A configuration or pattern having specific properties that cannot be derived from the sum of its
component parts; in psychology, the name for a
theory that physiological or psychological phenomena do not occur through the summation of individual elements but through gestalts functioning
separately or interrelatedly.
5. Fyodor Dostoyevsky (1821–1881), Russian
novelist whose work probes the religious questions
of sin and redemption.

Cockcrow. Back across the frozen Neva
To samovar and warm, untubercular bed,   70
Far from the dens of vodka, mucus and semen,
They dream. I woke, the fever

Dripping insight, a spring thaw.
You and the others, wrestling with your demons,
Christs of self-hatred, Livingstones[6] of pain,   75
Had drawn the lightning. In a flash I saw

My future: medic at some Armageddon
Neither side wins. I burned with SHAME for the years
You'd spent among sufferings uncharted—
Not even my barren love to rest your head on.   80

6 *The Panic*

Except that Oracle has maps
Of all those badlands. Just now, when you lashed out,
"There's a lot of disease in this room!"
And we felt our faith in one another lapse,

Ken had us break the circle and repair   85
To "a safe place in the room." Faster than fish
We scattered—Randy ducking as from a sniper,
Aileen, wedged in a corner, cradling her bear.

You and I stood flanking the blackboard,
Words as usual between us,   90
But backs to the same wall, for solidarity.
This magical sureness of movement no doubt scored

Points for all concerned, yet the only
Child each had become trembled for you
Thundering forth into the corridors,   95
Decibels measuring how HURT, how LONELY—

7 *Tunnel Vision*

New Age music. "Close your eyes now. You
Are standing," says the lecturer on Grief,
"At a tunnel's mouth. There's light at the end.
The walls, as you walk through   100

Are hung with images: who you loved that year,
An island holiday, a highschool friend.
Younger and younger, step by step—
And suddenly you're here,

6. Those resembling David Livingstone (1813–1873), a Scottish missionary and explorer in Africa who sought the source of the Nile River.

2852 / James Merrill

At home. Go in. It's your whole life ago."
A pink eye-level sun flows through the hall.
"Smell the smells. It's supper time.
Go to the table." Years have begun to flow

Unhindered down my face. Why?
Because nobody's there. The grown-ups? Shadows.
The meal? A mirror. Reflect upon it. Before
Reentering the tunnel say goodbye,

8 *Time Recaptured*[7]

Goodbye to childhood, that unhappy haven.
It's over, weep your fill. Let go
Of the dead dog, the lost toy. Practise grieving
At funerals—anybody's. Let go even

Of those first ninety seconds missed,
Fifty-three years ago, of a third-rate opera
Never revived since then. The GUILT you felt,
Adding it all the same to your master list!

Which is why, this last morning, when I switch
The FM on, halfway to Oracle,
And hear the announcer say
(Invisibly reweaving the dropped stitch),

"We bring you now the Overture
To Ambroise Thomas's seldom-heard *Mignon*,"[8]
Joy (word rusty with disuse)
Flashes up, deserved and pure.

9 *Leading the Blind*

Is this you—smiling helplessly? Pinned to your chest,
A sign: *Confront Me if I Take Control.*
Plus you must wear (till sundown) a black eyeshade.
All day you've been the littlest, the clumsiest.

We're seated face to face. Take off your mask,
Ken says. Now look into each other deeply. Speak,
As far as you can trust, the words of healing.
Your pardon for my own blindness I ask;

You mine, for all you hid from me. Two old
Crackpot hearts once more aswim with color,
Our Higher Power has but to dip his brush—
Lo and behold!

105

110

115

120

125

130

135

140

---

7. The title evokes Marcel Proust's novel, whose title is sometimes translated as *The Past Recaptured.*

8. The title of an opera by Ambroise Thomas (1811–1896), a French operatic composer.

The group approves. The ban lifts. Let me guide you,
Helpless but voluble, into a dripping music.
The rainbow brightens with each step. Go on,
Take a peek. This once, no one will chide you.

10 The Desert Museum

—Or, as the fat, nearsighted kid ahead   145
Construes his ticket, "Wow, Dessert Museum!"
I leave tomorrow, so you get a pass.
Safer, both feel, instead

Of checking into the No-Tell Motel,
To check it out—our brave new dried-out world.   150
Exhibits: crystals that for eons glinted
Before the wits did; fossil shells

From when this overlook lay safely drowned;
Whole spiny families repelled by sex,
Whom dying men have drunk from (Randy, frightened,   155
Hugging Little Randy, a red hound). . . .

At length behind a wall of glass, in shade,
The mountain lioness too indolent
To train them upon us unlids her gems
Set in the saddest face Love ever made.   160

11 The Twofold Message

(a) You are a brave and special person. (b)
There are far too many people in the world
For this to still matter for very long.
But (Ken goes on) since you obviously

Made the effort to attend Family Week,   165
We hope that we have shown you just how much
You have in common with everybody else.
Not to be "terminally unique"

Will be the consolation you take home.
Remember, Oracle is only the first step   170
In your recovery. The rest is up to you
And the twelve-step program you become

Involved in. An amazing forty per cent
Of our graduates are still clean after two years.
The rest? Well. . . . Given our society,   175
Sobriety is hard to implement.

12 And If

And if it were all like the moon?
Full this evening, bewitchingly

Glowing in a dark not yet complete
Above the world, explicit rune   180

Of change. Change is the "feeling" that dilutes
Those seven others to uncertain washes
Of soot and silver, inks unknown in my kit.
Change sends out shoots

Of FEAR and LONELINESS; of GUILT, as well,   185
Towards the old, abandoned patterns;
Of joy eventually, and self-forgiveness—
Colors few of us brought to Oracle . . .

And if the old patterns recur?
Ask how the co-dependent moon, another night,   190
Feels when the light drains wholly from her face.
Ask what that cold comfort means to her.

                                                                   1995

ROBERT CREELEY
b. 1926

"I was shy of the word 'poet,' " Robert Creeley once said, "and all its associations in a world I was then intimate with. It was not, in short, a fit attention for a young man raised in the New England manner, compact of Puritanically deprived senses of speech and sensuality. Life was real and life was earnest, and one had best get on with it." Despite the "constant, restless moving" that Creeley himself has called a pattern in his life, his work retains its connections to his New England background (he was born in Massachusetts), with its economy of speech and natural resources, and with the lingering heritage of its Puritanism. His chosen vocabulary is spare (someone once noted that 80 percent of his volume *Words*, 1967, is made up of monosyllables), but his work is, in part, a reaction against the strictures of his background, as seen most clearly in his explicit treatment of the erotic and sensual. Like William Carlos Williams, he sees the poet's role as overthrowing repression and creating the possibility for contact. But Creeley's poems are especially interesting for the ways they conduct a struggle between the self-conscious mind and the instincts of the body, for their exposure of the mind's relentless self-regard. The effort of the poet is to break through the mind's enclosures and to enter fully into the world. Such a breakthrough is evident in a poem like "The Birds," which captures the poet's desire to give himself over to the world in the way the birds "ride the air," and its rhythms and language enact a realization of this desire. Other poems, however, are grounded in the difficulty of release from a painful self-consciousness. Whether joyful or agonized, Creeley's work as a whole is characterized by an awareness of his own act of thinking about what he feels. He may be the most self-conscious passionate poet we have.

After the death of his father, a doctor, when Creeley was four, he was brought up in a family of five women. He began his life of restless motion in 1944, when he dropped out of Harvard after a year and joined the American Field Service in India and Burma. He returned to Harvard a year later but left again in 1947 without receiving a degree. In 1946 he married for the first time, and he and his wife lived for a period on Cape Cod (commuting by boat to his classes at Harvard), then on a farm in New Hampshire. Early in 1950, with his friend Jacob Leed, Creeley attempted to publish an alternative literary magazine, and wrote to every writer he knew, and some he did not, soliciting contributions. One of his correspondents sent him several of Charles Olson's poems. Although the magazine was never founded, a correspondence between Creeley and Olson began in 1950 that would run to thousands of letters (the correspondence at one point, according to Creeley, took up eight hours of each day). After a period in Aix-en-Provence and then in Mallorca, where he founded the Divers Press, he accepted Olson's invitation to join the faculty at Black Mountain College, where he founded and edited the *Black Mountain Review* (Olson solved the problem of Creeley's never having graduated from Harvard by having Black Mountain grant him a degree). Olson, Creeley said, "taught me how to write. Not how to write poems that he wrote, but how to write poems that I write. This is a very curious and specific difference." The richly reciprocal nature of the friendship between the two poets led Olson to quote Creeley's now famous statement on organic form, "Form is never more than an extension of content," in bold print in his essay on "Projective Verse," and to dedicate *The Maximus Poems* to him.

In the company of poets to whom Creeley feels most indebted—Whitman, Hart Crane, Olson, and Williams—Williams remains the one with whom he shares most (epigraphs from Williams's poems open several of Creeley's books). In the work of Creeley, as in the work of Williams, women are a recurrent presence: wife, mother, daughter, queen, or muse, the figure of the woman is composite. Her presence in his poems expresses Creeley's need for contact with what he has called "the most persistent *other* of our existence, eschewing male order, allowing us to live at last." For Creeley, this contact can be invigorating, erotic, difficult, and confusing, and his frequent poems about marriage, such as "For Love," dedicated to his second wife, Bobbie Louise Hall, render "tedium/despair, a painful/sense of isolation" even as they celebrate "the company of love." "He continues the art of the troubadours with its themes of love and trial," Robert Duncan once wrote of him. While Creeley has written often of love's trials (he has been married three times) he remains a poet in its service. Visited by the muse in "Kore" (as happens also in "The Door" and "The Finger"), the poet can ask only "O love,/where are you/leading/me now?"

The question Creeley asks in "Kore" suggests that for him the poem is a discovery of what might be said, an activity or a form of wandering ("life tracking itself," as he has called it) in which the destination or subject is not known beforehand. His poems often enact a walk, where the poet's particular form of walking is presented as stumbling (as in "The Door," where he writes, "The Lady has always moved to the next town/and you stumble on after Her"). The stumbling walk is, of course, open to error, and the form of Creeley's poems presents a wandering that at times missteps in search of its true form or subject. His presentation of himself as a stumbler also suggests his humorous self-awareness. The playfulness of some of his poems, like "The Messengers," or like the moment in "An Illness" when, remembering "pastures/of my childhood," he says, "I will not/bore you with their/boulders and cows," contrasts with their sometimes agonized uncertainty. "I am *given* to write poems," Creeley has said, "I cannot anticipate their occasion. I have used all the intelligence I can muster to follow the possibilities that the poem . . . is declaring, but I cannot anticipate the necessary conclusion in the activity." As this comment suggests, Creeley emphasizes process and discovery, to the pursuit of "the particular instance." Such an emphasis necessarily makes his work uneven—some poems wander without discovery, others capture an instant that may not be worth capturing. But in his best poems, Creeley measures both thinking and feeling, measures out the uncertain pursuit of an instant's possibility. His poetic form is shaped by an acute awareness of himself, the moment, and the line as a rhythmic unit, and the pleasures of his poems lie in this awareness and in their openness to discovery. If he is a wanderer in the poems as he has been in his life, his wandering repeatedly takes him home: to domesticity, to love, to the work of memory, and, most characteristically, to a fresh sense of the present, as when he sees "the light then/of the sun coming/for another morning/in the world" ("The World").

Kore[1]

As I was walking
   I came upon
chance walking
   the same road upon.

As I sat down
   by chance to move
later
   if and as I might,   5

light the wood was,
   light and green,   10
and what I saw
   before I had not seen.

It was a lady
   accompanied
by goat men[2]   15
   leading her.

Her hair held earth.
   Her eyes were dark.
A double flute[3]
   made her move.   20

"O love,
   where are you
leading
   me now?"

1959

1. Kore, literally "maiden," is an epithet for the Greek earth goddess Persephone. While picking flowers with some companions, she was kidnapped by Hades (who had been struck by one of Eros's arrows) and taken to the underworld. There she spends part of the year as queen of the dead; part of the time she lives aboveground with her mother, Demeter. Her annual reemergence is linked with the reemergence of earth's fertility in spring and summer.
2. Or satyrs, creatures of Greek mythology with the upper bodies of men and the legs of goats.
3. Ancient Greek musical instrument.

The Door

for Robert Duncan

It is hard going to the door
cut so small in the wall where
the vision which echoes loneliness
brings a scent of wild flowers in a wood.

What I understood, I understand.   5
My mind is sometime torment,
sometimes good and filled with livelihood,
and feels the ground.

But I see the door,
and knew the wall, and wanted the wood,   10
and would get there if I could
with my feet and hands and mind.

Lady, do not banish me
for digressions. My nature
is a quagmire of unresolved   15
confessions. Lady, I follow.

I walked away from myself,
I left the room, I found the garden,
I knew the woman
in it, together we lay down.   20

Dead night remembers. In December
we change, not multiplied but dispersed,
sneaked out of childhood,
the ritual of dismemberment.

Mighty magic is a mother,   25
in her there is another issue
of fixture, repeated form, the race renewal,
the charge of the command.

The garden echoes across the room.
It is fixed in the wall like a mirror   30
that faces a window behind you
and reflects the shadows.

May I go now?
Am I allowed to bow myself down
in the ridiculous posture of renewal,   35
of the insistence of which I am the virtue?

Nothing for You is untoward.
Inside You would also be tall,

more tall, more beautiful.
Come toward me from the wall, I want to be with You.   40

So I screamed to You,
who hears as the wind, and changes
multiply, invariably,
changes in the mind.

Running to the door, I ran down   45
as a clock runs down. Walked backwards,
stumbled, sat down
hard on the floor near the wall.

Where were You.
How absurd, how vicious.   50
There is nothing to do but get up.
My knees were iron, I rusted in worship, of You.

For that one sings, one
writes the spring poem, one goes on walking.
The Lady has always moved to the next town   55
and you stumble on after Her.

The door in the wall leads to the garden
where in the sunlight sit
the Graces¹ in long Victorian dresses,
of which my grandmother had spoken.   60

History sings in their faces.
They are young, they are obtainable,
and you follow after them also
in the service of God and Truth.

But the Lady is indefinable,   65
she will be the door in the wall
to the garden in sunlight.
I will go on talking forever.

I will never get there.
Oh Lady, remember me   70
who in Your service grows older
not wiser, no more than before.

How can I die alone.
Where will I be then who am now alone,
what groans so pathetically   75
in this room where I am alone?

I will go to the garden.
I will be a romantic. I will sell

---

1. In Greek mythology, the personifications of beauty and grace.

myself in hell,
in heaven also I will be.   80

In my mind I see the door,
I see the sunlight before me across the floor
beckon to me, as the Lady's skirt
moves small beyond it.

1959

I Know a Man

As I sd to my
friend, because I am
always talking,—John, I

sd, which was not his
name, the darkness sur-   5
rounds us, what

can we do against
it, or else, shall we &
why not, buy a goddamn big car,

drive, he sd, for   10
christ's sake, look
out where yr going.

1962

For Love

for Bobbie

Yesterday I wanted to
speak of it, that sense above
the others to me
important because all

that I know derives   5
from what it teaches me.
Today, what is it that
is finally so helpless,

different, despairs of its own
statement, wants to   10
turn away, endlessly
to turn away.

If the moon did not . . .
no, if you did not
I wouldn't either, but   15
what would I not

do, what prevention, what
thing so quickly stopped.
That is love yesterday
or tomorrow, not   20

now. Can I eat
what you give me. I
have not earned it. Must
I think of everything

as earned. Now love also   25
becomes a reward so
remote from me I have
only made it with my mind.

Here is tedium,
despair, a painful   30
sense of isolation and
whimsical if pompous

self-regard. But that image
is only of the mind's
vague structure, vague to me   35
because it is my own.

Love, what do I think
to say. I cannot say it.
What have you become to ask,
what have I made you into,   40

companion, good company,
crossed legs with skirt, or
soft body under
the bones of the bed.

Nothing says anything   45
but that which it wishes
would come true, fears
what else might happen in

some other place, some
other time not this one.   50
A voice in my place, an
echo of that only in yours.

Let me stumble into
not the confession but

the obsession I begin with   55
now. For you

also (also)
some time beyond place, or
place beyond time, no
mind left to   60

say anything at all,
that face gone, now.
Into the company of love
it all returns.

                                                    1962

The Messengers

for Allen Ginsberg

The huge dog, Broderick, and
the smile of the quick eyes
of Allen light a kind world.

Their feelings, under some distance
of remote skin, must touch,   5
wondering at what impatience does

block them. So little love
to share among so many, so much
yellow-orange hair, on the one,

and on the other, such a darkness   10
of long hanging hair now, such
slightness of body, and a voice that

rises on the sounds of feeling.
Aie! It raises the world, lifts,
falls, like a sudden sunlight, like   15

that edge of the black night sweeps
the low lying fields, of soft grasses,
bodies, fills them with quiet longing.

                                                    1967

The Birds

for Jane and Stan Brakhage

I'll miss the small birds that come
for the sugar you put out
and the bread crumbs. They've

made the edge of the sea domestic
and, as I am, I welcome that.   5
Nights my head seemed twisted

with dreams and the sea wash,
I let it all come quiet, waking,
counting familiar thoughts and objects.

Here to rest, like they say, I best   10
liked walking along the beach
past the town till one reached

the other one, around the corner
of rock and small trees. It was
clear, and often empty, and   15

peaceful. Those lovely ungainly
pelicans fished there, dropping
like rocks, with grace, from the air,

headfirst, then sat on the water,
letting the pouch of their beaks   20
grow thin again, then swallowing

whatever they'd caught. The birds,
no matter they're not of our kind,
seem most like us here. I want

to go where they go, in a way, if   25
a small and common one. I want
to ride that air which makes the sea

seem down there, not the element
in which one thrashes to come up.
I love water, I *love* water—   30

but I also love air, and fire.

1972

Fathers

Scattered, aslant
faded faces a column
a rise of the packed
peculiar place to a
modest height makes   5
a view of common lots
in winter then, a ground
of battered snow crusted
at the edges under
it all, there under   10
my fathers their
faded women, friends,
the family all echoed,
names trees more tangible
physical place more tangible   15
the air of this place the road
going past to Watertown[1]
or down to my mother's
grave, my father's grave, not
now this resonance of   20
each other one was his, his
survival only, his curious
reticence, his dead state,
his emptiness, his acerbic
edge cuts the hands to   25
hold him, hold on, wants
the ground, *wants* this frozen ground.

1986

1. Town in Massachusetts, just west of Boston

ALLEN GINSBERG
1926–1997

"Hold back the edges of your gowns, Ladies, we are going through hell." William Carlos Williams's introduction to Allen Ginsberg's *Howl* (1956) was probably the most auspicious public welcome from one poet to another since Emerson had hailed the unknown Whitman in a letter that Whitman prefaced to the second edition of *Leaves of Grass* one hundred years before. *Howl* combined apocalyptic criticism of the dull, prosperous Eisenhower years with exuberant celebration of an emerging counterculture. It was the best known and most widely circulated book of poems of its time, and with its appearance Ginsberg became part of the history of publicity as well as the history of poetry. *Howl* and Jack Kerouac's novel *On the Road* were the pocket Bibles of the generation whose name Kerouac had coined—"Beat," with its punning overtones of "beaten down" and "beatified."

Ginsberg was born in 1926, son of Louis Ginsberg, a schoolteacher in New Jersey, himself a poet, and of Naomi Ginsberg, a Russian émigré, whose madness and eventual death her son memorialized in "Kaddish" (1959). His official education took place at Columbia University, but for him as for Jack Kerouac the presence of William Burroughs in New York was equally influential. Burroughs (1914–1997), later the author of *Naked Lunch,* one of the most inventive experiments in American prose, was at that time a drug addict about to embark on an expatriate life in Mexico and Tangier. He helped Ginsberg discover modern writers: Kafka, Yeats, Céline, Rimbaud. Ginsberg responded to Burroughs's liberated kind of life, to his comic-apocalyptic view of American society, and to his bold literary use of autobiography, as when writing about his own experience with addicts and addiction in *Junkie,* whose chapters Ginsberg was reading in manuscript form in 1950.

Ginsberg's New York career has passed into mythology for a generation of poets and readers. In 1945, his sophomore year, he was expelled from Columbia: he had sketched some obscene drawings and phrases in the dust of his dormitory window to draw the attention of a neglectful cleaning woman to the grimy state of his room. Then, living periodically with Burroughs and Kerouac, he shipped out for short trips as a messman on merchant tankers and worked in addition as a welder, a night porter, and a dishwasher.

One summer, in a Harlem apartment, Ginsberg underwent what he was always to represent as the central conversion experience of his life. He had an "auditory vision" of the English poet William Blake reciting his poems: first "Ah! Sunflower," and then a few minutes later the same oracular voice intoning "The Sick Rose." It was "like hearing the doom of the whole universe, and at the same time the inevitable beauty of that doom." Ginsberg was convinced that the presence of "this big god over all . . . and that the whole purpose of being born was to wake up to Him."

Ginsberg eventually finished Columbia in 1948 with high grades but under a legal cloud. Herbert Huncke, a colorful but irresponsible addict friend, had been using Ginsberg's apartment as a storage depot for the goods he stole to support his drug habit. To avoid prosecution as an accomplice, Ginsberg had to plead insanity and spent eight months in the Columbia Psychiatric Institute.

After more odd jobs and a considerable success as a market researcher in San Francisco, Ginsberg left the straight, nine-to-five world for good. He was drawn to San Francisco, he said, by its "long honorable . . . tradition of Bohemian—Buddhist— Wobbly [the I.W.W., an early radical labor movement]—mystical—anarchist social involvement." In the years after 1954 he met San Francisco poets such as Robert Duncan, Kenneth Rexroth, Gary Snyder (who was studying Chinese and Japanese at Berkeley), and Lawrence Ferlinghetti, whose City Lights Bookshop became the publisher of *Howl.* The night Ginsberg read the new poem aloud at the Six Gallery has been called "the birth trauma of the Beat Generation."

The spontaneity of surface in *Howl* conceals but grows out of Ginsberg's care and self-consciousness about rhythm and meter. Under the influence of William Carlos Williams, who had befriended him in Paterson after he left the mental hospital, Ginsberg had started carrying around a notebook to record the rhythms of voices around him. Kerouac's *On the Road* gave him further examples of "frank talk" and, in addition, of an "oceanic" prose "sometimes as sublime as epic line." Under Kerouac's influence Ginsberg began the long tumbling lines that were to become his trademark. He carefully explained that all of *Howl and Other Poems* was an experiment in what could be done with the long line, the longer unit of breath that seemed natural for him. "My feeling is for a big long clanky statement," one that accommodates "not the way you would *say* it, a thought, but the way you would think it—i.e., we think rapidly, in visual images as well as words, and if each successive thought were transcribed in its confusion . . . you get a slightly different prosody than if you were talking slowly."

The long line is something Ginsberg learned as well from biblical rhetoric, from the eighteenth-century English poet Christopher Smart, and above all, from Whitman and Blake. His first book pays tribute to both these latter poets. "A Supermarket in California," with its movement from exclamations to sad questioning, is Ginsberg's melancholy reminder of what has become, after a century, of Whitman's vision of American plenty. In "Sunflower Sutra" he celebrates the battered nobility beneath our industrial "skin of grime." Ginsberg at his best gives a sense of both doom and beauty, whether in the denunciatory impatient prophecies of *Howl* or in the catalog of suffering in "Kaddish." His disconnected phrases can accumulate as narrative shrieks or, at other moments, can build as a litany of praise.

By the end of the 1960s Ginsberg was widely known and widely traveled. For him it was a decade in which he conducted publicly his own pursuit of inner peace during a long stay with Buddhist instructors in India and at home served as a kind of guru himself for many young people disoriented by the Vietnam War. Ginsberg read his poetry and held "office hours" in universities all over America, a presence at everything from "be-ins"—mass outdoor festivals of chanting, costumes, and music—to antiwar protests. He was a gentle and persuasive presence at hearings for many kinds of reform: revision of severe drug laws and laws against homosexuality. Ginsberg himself had lived for years with the poet Peter Orlovsky and wrote frankly about their relationship. His poems record his drug experiences as well, and "The Change," written in Japan in 1963, marks his decision to keep away from what he considered the nonhuman domination of drugs and to lay new stress on "living in and inhabiting the human form."

In "The Fall of America" (1972) Ginsberg turned to "epic," a poem including history and registering the ups and downs of his travels across the United States. These "transit" poems sometimes seem like tape-recorded random lists of sights, sounds, and names, but at their best they give a sense of how far America has fallen, by measuring the provisional and changing world of nuclear America against the traces of nature still visible in our landscape and place names. With Ginsberg's death, contemporary American poetry lost one of its most definitive and revolutionary figures. Happily, the poems endure.

Howl

for Carl Solomon[1]

I

I saw the best minds of my generation destroyed by madness, starving hysterical naked,

dragging themselves through the negro streets at dawn looking for an angry fix,

angelheaded hipsters burning for the ancient heavenly connection[2] to the starry dynamo in the machinery of night,

who poverty and tatters and hollow-eyed and high sat up smoking in the

---

1. Ginsberg met Solomon (b. 1928) while both were patients in the Columbia Psychiatric Institute in 1949 and called him "an intuitive Bronx Dadaist and prose-poet." Many details in "Howl" come from the "apocryphal history" that Solomon told Ginsberg in 1949. In "More Mishaps" (1968), Sol- omon admits that these adventures were "compounded partly of truth, but for the most [of] raving self-justification, crypto-bohemian boasting . . . effeminate prancing and esoteric aphorisms."

2. In one sense, a person who can supply drugs.

supernatural darkness of cold-water flats floating across the tops of cities contemplating jazz,
who bared their brains to Heaven under the El[3] and saw Mohammedan
angels staggering on tenement roofs illuminated,   5
who passed through universities with radiant cool eyes hallucinating Arkansas and Blake-light[4] tragedy among the scholars of war,
who were expelled from the academies for crazy & publishing obscene odes
on the windows of the skull,
who cowered in unshaven rooms in underwear, burning their money in
wastebaskets and listening to the Terror through the wall,
who got busted in their pubic beards returning through Laredo with a belt
of marijuana for New York,
who ate fire in paint hotels or drank turpentine in Paradise Alley,[5] death, or
purgatoried their torsos night after night   10
with dreams, with drugs, with waking nightmares, alcohol and cock and
endless balls,
incomparable blind streets of shuddering cloud and lightning in the mind
leaping toward poles of Canada & Paterson,[6] illuminating all the
motionless world of Time between,
Peyote solidities of halls, backyard green tree cemetery dawns, wine drunkenness over the rooftops, storefront boroughs of teahead joyride neon
blinking traffic light, sun and moon and tree vibrations in the roaring
winter dusks of Brooklyn, ashcan rantings and kind king light of mind,
who chained themselves to subways for the endless ride from Battery to holy
Bronx[7] on benzedrine until the noise of wheels and children brought
them down shuddering mouth-wracked and battered bleak of brain all
drained of brilliance in the drear light of Zoo,
who sank all night in submarine light of Bickford's floated out and sat
through the stale beer afternoon in desolate Fugazzi's, listening to the
crack of doom on the hydrogen jukebox,   15
who talked continuously seventy hours from park to pad to bar to Bellevue[8]
to museum to the Brooklyn Bridge,
a lost battalion of platonic conversationalists jumping down the stoops off
fire escapes off windowsills off Empire State out of the moon,
yacketayakking screaming vomiting whispering facts and memories and
anecdotes and eyeball kicks and shocks of hospitals and jails and wars,
whole intellects disgorged in total recall for seven days and nights with brilliant eyes, meat for the Synagogue cast on the pavement,
who vanished into nowhere Zen New Jersey leaving a trail of ambiguous
picture postcards of Atlantic City Hall,   20
suffering Eastern sweats and Tangerian bone-grindings and migraines of
China[9] under junk-withdrawal in Newark's bleak furnished room,
who wandered around and around at midnight in the railroad yard wondering
where to go, and went, leaving no broken hearts,

---

3. The elevated railway in New York City; also, a
Hebrew word for God.
4. Refers to Ginsberg's apocalyptic vision of the
English poet William Blake (1757–1827).
5. A tenement courtyard in New York's East Village; setting of Kerouac's *The Subterraneans*
(1958).
6. Ginsberg's hometown, also the town celebrated

by William Carlos Williams in his long poem *Paterson.*
7. Opposite ends of a New York subway line; the
Bronx Zoo was the northern terminus.
8. New York public hospital to which psychiatric
patients may be committed.
9. African and Asian sources of drugs.

who lit cigarettes in boxcars boxcars boxcars racketing through snow toward
    lonesome farms in grandfather night,

who studied Plotinus Poe St. John of the Cross[1] telepathy and bop kaballah[2]
    because the cosmos instinctively vibrated at their feet in Kansas,

who loned it through the streets of Idaho seeking visionary indian angels who
    were visionary indian angels,   25

who thought they were only mad when Baltimore gleamed in supernatural
    ecstasy,

who jumped in limousines with the Chinaman of Oklahoma on the impulse
    of winter midnight streetlight smalltown rain,

who lounged hungry and lonesome through Houston seeking jazz or sex or
    soup, and followed the brilliant Spaniard to converse about America
    and Eternity, a hopeless task, and so took ship to Africa,

who disappeared into the volcanoes of Mexico leaving behind nothing but
    the shadow of dungarees and the lava and ash of poetry scattered in
    fireplace Chicago,

who reappeared on the West Coast investigating the FBI in beards and shorts
    with big pacifist eyes sexy in their dark skin passing out incomprehen-
    sible leaflets,   30

who burned cigarette holes in their arms protesting the narcotic tobacco haze
    of Capitalism,

who distributed Supercommunist pamphlets in Union Square weeping and
    undressing while the sirens of Los Alamos[3] wailed them down, and
    wailed down Wall,[4] and the Staten Island ferry also wailed,

who broke down crying in white gymnasiums naked and trembling before
    the machinery of other skeletons,

who bit detectives in the neck and shrieked with delight in policecars for
    committing no crime but their own wild cooking pederasty and intoxi-
    cation,

who howled on their knees in the subway and were dragged off the roof
    waving genitals and manuscripts,   35

who let themselves be fucked in the ass by saintly motorcyclists, and
    screamed with joy,

who blew and were blown by those human seraphim, the sailors, caresses of
    Atlantic and Caribbean love,

who balled in the morning in the evenings in rosegardens and the grass of
    public parks and cemeteries scattering their semen freely to whomever
    come who may,

who hiccupped endlessly trying to giggle but wound up with a sob behind a
    partition in a Turkish Bath when the blonde & naked angel came to
    pierce them with a sword,[5]

who lost their loveboys to the three old shrews of fate[6] the one eyed shrew
    of the heterosexual dollar the one eyed shrew that winks out of the womb

1. Spanish visionary and poet (1542–1591), author of *The Dark Night of the Soul*. Plotinus (205–270), visionary philosopher. Edgar Allan Poe (1809–1849), American poet and author of super-natural tales.

2. A mystical tradition of interpretation of Hebrew scripture. "Bop": jazz style of the 1940s.

3. In New Mexico, a center for the development of the atomic bomb. Union Square was a gathering place for radical speakers in New York in the 1930s.

4. Wall Street, but also alludes to the Wailing Wall, a place of public lamentation in Jerusalem.

5. An allusion to *The Ecstasy of St. Teresa*, a sculpture by Lorenzo Bernini (1598–1680) based on St. Teresa's (1515–1582) distinctly erotic description of a religious vision.

6. In Greek mythology, goddesses who determine a mortal's life by spinning out a length of thread and cutting it at the time of death.

and the one eyed shrew that does nothing but sit on her ass and snip
    the intellectual golden threads of the craftsman's loom,   40
who copulated ecstatic and insatiate with a bottle of beer a sweetheart a
    package of cigarettes a candle and fell off the bed, and continued along
    the floor and down the hall and ended fainting on the wall with a vision
    of ultimate cunt and come eluding the last gyzym of consciousness,
who sweetened the snatches of a million girls trembling in the sunset, and
    were red eyed in the morning but prepared to sweeten the snatch of the
    sunrise, flashing buttocks under barns and naked in the lake,
who went out whoring through Colorado in myriad stolen nightcars, N.C.,[7]
    secret hero of these poems, cocksman and Adonis of Denver—joy to the
    memory of his innumerable lays of girls in empty lots & diner backyards,
    moviehouses' rickety rows, on mountaintops in caves or with gaunt wait-
    resses in familiar roadside lonely petticoat upliftings & especially secret
    gas-station solipsisms of johns, & hometown alleys too,
who faded out in vast sordid movies, were shifted in dreams, woke on a
    sudden Manhattan, and picked themselves up out of basements hun-
    gover with heartless Tokay[8] and horrors of Third Avenue iron dreams &
    stumbled to unemployment offices,
who walked all night with their shoes full of blood on the snowbank docks
    waiting for a door in the East River to open to a room full of steamheat
    and opium,   45
who created great suicidal dramas on the apartment cliff-banks of the Hud-
    son under the wartime blue floodlight of the moon & their heads shall
    be crowned with laurel in oblivion,
who ate the lamb stew of the imagination or digested the crab at the muddy
    bottom of the rivers of Bowery,[9]
who wept at the romance of the streets with their pushcarts full of onions
    and bad music,
who sat in boxes breathing in the darkness under the bridge, and rose up to
    build harpsichords in their lofts,
who coughed on the sixth floor of Harlem crowned with flame under the
    tubercular sky surrounded by orange crates of theology,   50
who scribbled all night rocking and rolling over lofty incantations which in
    the yellow morning were stanzas of gibberish,
who cooked rotten animals lung heart feet tail borsht & tortillas dreaming
    of the pure vegetable kingdom,
who plunged themselves under meat trucks looking for an egg,
who threw their watches off the roof to cast their ballot for Eternity outside
    of Time, & alarm clocks fell on their heads every day for the next decade,
who cut their wrists three times successively unsuccessfully, gave up and
    were forced to open antique stores where they thought they were grow-
    ing old and cried,   55
who were burned alive in their innocent flannel suits on Madison Avenue[1]
    amid blasts of leaden verse & the tanked-up clatter of the iron regiments
    of fashion & the nitroglycerine shrieks of the fairies of advertising & the
    mustard gas of sinister intelligent editors, or were run down by the
    drunken taxicabs of Absolute Reality,

7. Neal Cassady, hip companion of Jack Kerouac and the original Dean Moriarty, one of the leading figures in *On the Road*.
8. A naturally sweet wine made in Hungary.
9. Southern extension of Third Avenue in New York City; traditional haunt of derelicts and alcoholics.
1. Center of New York advertising agencies.

who jumped off the Brooklyn Bridge this actually happened and walked away
    unknown and forgotten into the ghostly daze of Chinatown soup alley-
    ways & firetrucks, not even one free beer,
who sang out of their windows in despair, fell out of the subway window,
    jumped in the filthy Passaic,[2] leaped on negroes, cried all over the street,
    danced on broken wineglasses barefoot smashed phonograph records of
    nostalgic European 1930's German jazz finished the whiskey and threw
    up groaning into the bloody toilet, moans in their ears and the blast of
    colossal steamwhistles,
who barreled down the highways of the past journeying to each other's hot-
    rod-Golgotha[3] jail-solitude watch or Birmingham jazz incarnation,
who drove crosscountry seventytwo hours to find out if I had a vision or you
    had a vision or he had a vision to find out Eternity,   60
who journeyed to Denver, who died in Denver, who came back to Denver &
    waited in vain, who watched over Denver & brooded & loned in Denver
    and finally went away to find out the Time, & now Denver is lonesome
    for her heroes,
who fell on their knees in hopeless cathedrals praying for each other's sal-
    vation and light and breasts, until the soul illuminated its hair for a
    second,
who crashed through their minds in jail waiting for impossible criminals with
    golden heads and the charm of reality in their hearts who sang sweet
    blues to Alcatraz,
who retired to Mexico to cultivate a habit, or Rocky Mount to tender Buddha
    or Tangiers to boys or Southern Pacific to the black locomotive or Har-
    vard to Narcissus to Woodlawn[4] to the daisychain or grave,
who demanded sanity trials accusing the radio of hypnotism & were left with
    their insanity & their hands & a hung jury,   65
who threw potato salad at CCNY lecturers on Dadaism[5] and subsequently
    presented themselves on the granite steps of the madhouse with shaven
    heads and harlequin speech of suicide, demanding instantaneous lobot-
    omy,
and who were given instead the concrete void of insulin metrasol electricity
    hydrotherapy psychotherapy occupational therapy pingpong & amnesia,
who in humorless protest overturned only one symbolic pingpong table, rest-
    ing briefly in catatonia,
returning years later truly bald except for a wig of blood, and tears and fin-
    gers, to the visible madman doom of the wards of the madtowns of the
    East,
Pilgrim State's Rockland's and Greystone's[6] foetid halls, bickering with the
    echoes of the soul, rocking and rolling in the midnight solitude-bench
    dolmen-realms of love, dream of life a nightmare, bodies turned to stone
    as heavy as the moon,   70
with mother finally* * * * * * *, and the last fantastic book flung out of the

2. River flowing past Paterson, New Jersey.
3. The place in ancient Judea where Jesus was believed to have been crucified; also known as Calvary.
4. A cemetery in the Bronx. The Southern Pacific is a railroad company. The references in this line are to the lives of Kerouac, Cassidy, and William Burroughs (an author and fellow Beat).
5. Artistic cult of absurdity (c. 1916–1920). "CCNY": City College of New York. This and the

following incidents probably derived from the "apocryphal history of my adventures" related by Solomon to Ginsberg.
6. Three psychiatric hospitals near New York. Solomon was institutionalized at Pilgrim State and Rockland; Ginsberg's mother, Naomi, was permanently institutionalized at Greystone after years of suffering hallucinations and paranoid attacks. She died there in 1956, the year after "Howl" was written.

tenement window, and the last door closed at 4 AM and the last telephone slammed at the wall in reply and the last furnished room emptied
down to the last piece of mental furniture, a yellow paper rose twisted
on a wire hanger in the closet, and even that imaginary, nothing but a
hopeful little bit of hallucination—

ah, Carl,[7] while you are not safe I am not safe, and now you're really in the
total animal soup of time—

and who therefore ran through the icy streets obsessed with a sudden flash
of the alchemy of the use of the ellipse the catalog the meter & the
vibrating plane,

who dreamt and made incarnate gaps in Time & Space through images jux-
taposed, and trapped the archangel of the soul between 2 visual images
and joined the elemental verbs and set the noun and dash of consciousness together jumping with sensation of Pater Omnipotens Aeterna
Deus[8]

to recreate the syntax and measure of poor human prose and stand before
you speechless and intelligent and shaking with shame, rejected yet
confessing out the soul to conform to the rhythm of thought in his naked
and endless head, 75

the madman bum and angel beat in Time, unknown, yet putting down here
what might be left to say in time come after death,

and rose reincarnate in the ghostly clothes of jazz in the goldhorn shadow of
the band and blew the suffering of America's naked mind for love into
an eli eli lamma lamma sabacthani[9] saxophone cry that shivered the
cities down to the last radio

with the absolute heart of the poem of life butchered out of their own bodies
good to eat a thousand years.

II

What sphinx of cement and aluminum bashed open their skulls and ate up
their brains and imagination?

Moloch![1] Solitude! Filth! Ugliness! Ashcans and unobtainable dollars! Children screaming under the stairways! Boys sobbing in armies! Old men
weeping in the parks! 80

Moloch! Moloch! Nightmare of Moloch! Moloch the loveless! Mental
Moloch! Moloch the heavy judger of men!

Moloch the incomprehensible prison! Moloch the crossbone soulless jail-
house and Congress of sorrows! Moloch whose buildings are judgment!
Moloch the vast stone of war! Moloch the stunned governments!

Moloch whose mind is pure machinery! Moloch whose blood is running
money! Moloch whose fingers are ten armies! Moloch whose breast is
a cannibal dynamo! Moloch whose ear is a smoking tomb!

Moloch whose eyes are a thousand blind windows! Moloch whose skyscrap-

---

7. Solomon.
8. All Powerful Father, Eternal God (Latin). An
allusion to a phrase used by the French painter
Paul Cézanne (1839–1906), in a letter describing
the effects of nature (1904). Ginsberg, in an interview, compared his own method of sharply juxta-
posed images with Cézanne's foreshortening of
perspective in landscape painting.

9. Christ's last words on the Cross: My God, my
God, why have you forsaken me? (Aramaic).
1. Ginsberg's own annotation in the facsimile edition of the poem reads: " 'Moloch': or Molech, the
Canaanite fire god, whose worship was marked by
parents' burning their children as proprietary sacrifice. 'And thou shalt not let any of thy seed pass
through the fire to Molech' [Leviticus 18:21].' "

ers stand in the long streets like endless Jehovahs! Moloch whose factories dream and croak in the fog! Moloch whose smokestacks and
antennae crown the cities!

Moloch whose love is endless oil and stone! Moloch whose soul is electricity
and banks! Moloch whose poverty is the specter of genius! Moloch
whose fate is a cloud of sexless hydrogen! Moloch whose name is the
Mind!   85

Moloch in whom I sit lonely! Moloch in whom I dream Angels! Crazy in
Moloch! Cocksucker in Moloch! Lacklove and manless in Moloch!

Moloch who entered my soul early! Moloch in whom I am a consciousness
without a body! Moloch who frightened me out of my natural ecstasy!
Moloch whom I abandon! Wake up in Moloch! Light streaming out of
the sky!

Moloch! Moloch! Robot apartments! invisible suburbs! skeleton treasuries!
blind capitals! demonic industries! spectral nations! invincible mad-
houses! granite cocks! monstrous bombs!

They broke their backs lifting Moloch to Heaven! Pavements, trees, radios,
tons! lifting the city to Heaven which exists and is everywhere about us!

Visions! omens! hallucinations! miracles! ecstasies! gone down the American
river!   90

Dreams! adorations! illuminations! religions! the whole boatload of sensitive
bullshit!

Breakthroughs! over the river! flips and crucifixions! gone down the flood!
Highs! Epiphanies! Despairs! Ten years' animal screams and suicides!
Minds! New loves! Mad generation! down on the rocks of Time!

Real holy laughter in the river! They saw it all! the wild eyes! the holy yells!
They bade farewell! They jumped off the roof! to solitude! waving! carrying flowers! Down to the river! into the street!

III

Carl Solomon! I'm with you in Rockland
      where you're madder than I am   95
I'm with you in Rockland
      where you must feel very strange
I'm with you in Rockland
      where you imitate the shade of my mother
I'm with you in Rockland   100
      where you've murdered your twelve secretaries
I'm with you in Rockland
      where you laugh at this invisible humor
I'm with you in Rockland
      where we are great writers on the same dreadful typewriter   105
I'm with you in Rockland
      where your condition has become serious and is reported on the radio
I'm with you in Rockland
      where the faculties of the skull no longer admit the worms of the senses
I'm with you in Rockland   110
      where you drink the tea of the breasts of the spinsters of Utica
I'm with you in Rockland
      where you pun on the bodies of your nurses the harpies of the Bronx

2872 / Allen Ginsberg

I'm with you in Rockland
    where you scream in a straightjacket that you're losing the game of the
    actual pingpong of the abyss   115
I'm with you in Rockland
    where you bang on the catatonic piano the soul is innocent and immor-
    tal it should never die ungodly in an armed madhouse
I'm with you in Rockland
    where fifty more shocks will never return your soul to its body again
    from its pilgrimage to a cross in the void
I'm with you in Rockland   120
    where you accuse your doctors of insanity and plot the Hebrew socialist
    revolution against the fascist national Golgotha
I'm with you in Rockland
    where you will split the heavens of Long Island and resurrect your living
    human Jesus from the superhuman tomb
I'm with you in Rockland
    where there are twenty five thousand mad comrades all together singing
    the final stanzas of the Internationale[2]   125
I'm with you in Rockland
    where we hug and kiss the United States under our bedsheets the
    United States that coughs all night and won't let us sleep
I'm with you in Rockland
    where we wake up electrified out of the coma by our own souls' airplanes
    roaring over the roof they've come to drop angelic bombs the hospital
    illuminates itself imaginary walls collapse O skinny legions run
    outside   O starry-spangled shock of mercy the eternal war is here   O
    victory forget your underwear we're free
I'm with you in Rockland   130
    in my dreams you walk dripping from a sea-journey on the highway
    across America in tears to the door of my cottage in the Western night

San Francisco, 1955–56   1956

A Supermarket in California

What thoughts I have of you tonight, Walt Whitman,[1] for I walked down the sidestreets under the trees with a headache self-conscious looking at the full moon.

In my hungry fatigue, and shopping for images, I went into the neon fruit supermarket, dreaming of your enumerations!

What peaches and what penumbras![2] Whole families shopping at night! Aisles full of husbands! Wives in the avocados, babies in the tomatoes!—and you, Garcia Lorca,[3] what were you doing down by the watermelons?

I saw you, Walt Whitman, childless, lonely old grubber, poking among the meats in the refrigerator and eyeing the grocery boys.

---

2. Former Socialist and Communist song, it was the official Soviet anthem until 1944.
1. American poet (1819–1892), author of *Leaves of Grass,* against whose homosexuality and vision of American plenty Ginsberg measures himself.

2. Partial shadows.
3. Spanish poet and dramatist (1899–1936), author of "A Poet in New York," whose work is characterized by surrealist and homoerotic inspiration.

I heard you asking questions of each: Who killed the pork chops? What price bananas? Are you my Angel?

I wandered in and out of the brilliant stacks of cans following you, and followed in my imagination by the store detective.

We strode down the open corridors together in our solitary fancy tasting artichokes, possessing every frozen delicacy, and never passing the cashier.

Where are we going, Walt Whitman? The doors close in an hour. Which way does your beard point tonight?

(I touch your book and dream of our odyssey in the supermarket and feel absurd.)

Will we walk all night through solitary streets? The trees add shade to shade, lights out in the houses, we'll both be lonely.

Will we stroll dreaming of the lost America of love past blue automobiles in driveways, home to our silent cottage?

Ah, dear father, graybeard, lonely old courage-teacher, what America did you have when Charon quit poling his ferry and you got out on a smoking bank and stood watching the boat disappear on the black waters of Lethe?[4]

Berkeley, 1955   1956

Sunflower Sutra[1]

I walked on the banks of the tincan banana dock and sat down under the
    huge shade of a Southern Pacific locomotive to look at the sunset over
    the box house hills and cry.
Jack Kerouac[2] sat beside me on a busted rusty iron pole, companion, we
    thought the same thoughts of the soul, bleak and blue and sad-eyed,
    surrounded by the gnarled steel roots of trees of machinery.
The oily water on the river mirrored the red sky, sun sank on top of final
    Frisco peaks, no fish in that stream, no hermit in those mounts, just
    ourselves rheumy-eyed and hung-over like old bums on the riverbank,
    tired and wily.
Look at the Sunflower, he said, there was a dead gray shadow against the
    sky, big as a man, sitting dry on top of a pile of ancient sawdust—
—I rushed up enchanted—it was my first sunflower, memories of Blake[3]—
    my visions—Harlem
and Hells of the Eastern rivers, bridges clanking Joes Greasy Sandwiches,
    dead baby carriages, black treadless tires forgotten and unretreaded, the
    poem of the riverbank, condoms & pots, steel knives, nothing stainless,
    only the dank muck and the razor sharp artifacts passing into the past—
and the gray Sunflower poised against the sunset, crackly bleak and dusty
    with the smut and smog and smoke of olden locomotives in its eye—
corolla[4] of bleary spikes pushed down and broken like a battered crown, seeds

---

4. Forgetfulness. In Greek mythology, one of the rivers of Hades. Charon was the boatman who ferried the dead to the underworld.
1. Sanskrit for "thread"; the word refers to Brahmin or Buddhist religious texts of ritual instruction.
2. Fellow Beat (1922–1969), author of *On the*

Road (1957).
3. In Harlem in 1948, Ginsberg had a hallucinatory revelation in which he heard the English poet William Blake (1757–1827) reciting his poem "Ah! Sunflower."
4. Petals forming the inner envelope of a flower.

fallen out of its face, soon-to-be-toothless mouth of sunny air, sunrays
   obliterated on its hairy head like a dried wire spiderweb,
leaves stuck out like arms out of the stem, gestures from the sawdust root,
   broke pieces of plaster fallen out of the black twigs, a dead fly in its ear,
Unholy battered old thing you were, my sunflower O my soul, I loved you
   then!   10
The grime was no man's grime but death and human locomotives,
all that dress of dust, that veil of darkened railroad skin, that smog of cheek,
   that eyelid of black mis'ry, that sooty hand or phallus or protuberance
   of artificial worse-than-dirt—industrial—modern—all that civilization
   spotting your crazy golden crown—
and those blear thoughts of death and dusty loveless eyes and ends and
   withered roots below, in the home-pile of sand and sawdust, rubber
   dollar bills, skin of machinery, the guts and innards of the weeping
   coughing car, the empty lonely tincans with their rusty tongues alack,
   what more could I name, the smoked ashes of some cock cigar, the
   cunts of wheelbarrows and the milky breasts of cars, wornout asses out
   of chairs & sphincters of dynamos—all these
entangled in your mummied roots—and you there standing before me in the
   sunset, all your glory in your form!
A perfect beauty of a sunflower! a perfect excellent lovely sunflower existence! a sweet natural eye to the new hip moon, woke up alive and
   excited grasping in the sunset shadow sunrise golden monthly breeze! 15
How many flies buzzed round you innocent of your grime, while you cursed
   the heavens of the railroad and your flower soul?
Poor dead flower? when did you forget you were a flower? when did you look
   at your skin and decide you were an impotent dirty old locomotive? the
   ghost of a locomotive? the specter and shade of a once powerful mad
   American locomotive?
You were never no locomotive, Sunflower, you were a sunflower!
And you Locomotive, you are a locomotive, forget me not!
So I grabbed up the skeleton thick sunflower and stuck it at my side like a
   scepter,   20
and deliver my sermon to my soul, and Jack's soul too, and anyone who'll
   listen,
—We're not our skin of grime, we're not our dread bleak dusty imageless
   locomotive, we're all golden sunflowers inside, blessed by our own seed
   & hairy naked accomplishment-bodies growing into mad black formal
   sunflowers in the sunset, spied on by our eyes under the shadow of the
   mad locomotive riverbank sunset Frisco hilly tincan evening sitdown
   vision.

Berkeley, 1955   1956

To Aunt Rose

Aunt Rose—now—might I see you
with your thin face and buck tooth smile and pain
      of rheumatism—and a long black heavy shoe
      for your bony left leg

limping down the long hall in Newark on the running carpet   5
    past the black grand piano
        in the day room
           where the parties were
and I sang Spanish loyalist[1] songs
    in a high squeaky voice   10
        (hysterical) the committee listening
while you limped around the room
    collected the money—
Aunt Honey, Uncle Sam, a stranger with a cloth arm
    in his pocket   15
        and huge young bald head
           of Abraham Lincoln Brigade[2]

—your long sad face
    your tears of sexual frustration
        (what smothered sobs and bony hips   20
           under the pillows of Osborne Terrace)
—the time I stood on the toilet seat naked
and you powdered my thighs with Calomine
    against the poison ivy—my tender
        and shamed first black curled hairs   25
what were you thinking in secret heart then
    knowing me a man already—
and I an ignorant girl of family silence on the thin pedestal
    of my legs in the bathroom—Museum of Newark.
        Aunt Rose   30
Hitler is dead, Hitler is in Eternity; Hitler is with
    Tamburlane and Emily Brontë[3]

Though I see you walking still, a ghost on Osborne Terrace
    down the long dark hall to the front door
    limping a little with a pinched smile   35
        in what must have been a silken
           flower dress
welcoming my father, the Poet, on his visit to Newark
    —see you arriving in the living room
        dancing on your crippled leg   40
    and clapping hands his book
        had been accepted by Liveright[4]

Hitler is dead and Liveright's gone out of business
The Attic of the Past and *Everlasting Minute* are out of print
    Uncle Harry sold his last silk stocking   45
    Claire quit interpretive dancing school

1. During the Spanish Civil War (1936–39), many left-wing Americans—among them Ginsberg's relatives in Newark—sympathized with the Spanish loyalists who were resisting Francisco Franco's (1892–1975) efforts to become dictator of Spain.
2. American volunteers who fought against the Fascists in the Spanish Civil War.
3. English poet and novelist (1818–1848), author of *Wuthering Heights*. Tamburlane was the Mideastern "scourge" and conqueror (hero of Christopher Marlowe's *Tamburlane*, 1588).
4. Leading American publisher of the 1920s and 1930s (now a subsidiary of W. W. Norton); published *The Everlasting Minute* (1937), poems by Allen Ginsberg's father, Louis, whose first book was *The Attic of the Past* (1920).

Buba sits a wrinkled monument in Old
Ladies Home blinking at new babies

last time I saw you was the hospital
pale skull protruding under ashen skin   50
blue veined unconscious girl
in an oxygen tent
the war in Spain has ended long ago
Aunt Rose

Paris, 1958   1961

On Burroughs' Work[1]

The method must be purest meat
and no symbolic dressing,
actual visions & actual prisons
as seen then and now.

Prisons and visions presented   5
with rare descriptions
corresponding exactly to those
of Alcatraz and Rose.[2]

A naked lunch is natural to us,
we eat reality sandwiches.   10
But allegories are so much lettuce.
Don't hide the madness.

San Jose, 1954   1963

Ego Confession

I want to be known as the most brilliant man in America
Introduced to Gyalwa Karmapa heir of the Whispered Transmission Crazy
    Wisdom Practice Lineage
as the secret young wise man who visited him and winked anonymously
    decade ago in Gangtok
Prepared the way for Dharma[1] in America without mentioning Dharma—
    scribbled laughter
Who saw Blake[2] and abandoned God   5
To whom the Messianic Fink sent messages darkest hour sleeping on steel
    sheets "somewhere in the Federal Prison system" Weathermen[3] got no
    Moscow Gold

1. William Burroughs (1914–1997), a senior member of the Beat generation, homosexual, former heroin addict, and author of the novels *Junkie* (1953, 1964) and *Naked Lunch* (1959).
2. One of Ginsberg's hallucinatory visions of the English poet William Blake (1757–1827) was of the poet reciting "The Sick Rose." Alcatraz was the island prison in San Francisco Bay.
1. In Buddhism, divine law.
2. William Blake (1757–1827), English poet and mystic, whom Ginsberg had seen in a hallucinatory vision.
3. Revolutionary terrorist student group during the 1960s.

who went backstage to Cecil Taylor serious chat chord structure & Time in
    a nightclub
who fucked a rose-lipped rock star in a tiny bedroom slum watched by a
    statue of Vajrasattva—
and overthrew the CIA with a silent thought—
Old Bohemians many years hence in Viennese beergardens'll recall   10
his many young lovers with astonishing faces and iron breasts
gnostic apparatus and magical observation of rainbow-lit spiderwebs
extraordinary cooking, lung stew & Spaghetti a la Vongole and recipe for
    salad dressing 3 parts oil one part vinegar much garlic and honey a
    spoonful
his extraordinary ego, at service of Dharma and completely empty
unafraid of its own self's spectre   15
parroting gossip of gurus and geniuses famous for their reticence—
Who sang a blues made rock stars weep and moved an old black guitarist to
    laughter in Memphis—
I want to be the spectacle of Poesy triumphant over trickery of the world
Omniscient breathing its own breath thru War tear gas spy hallucination
whose common sense astonished gaga Gurus and rich Artistes—   20
who called the Justice department & threaten'd to Blow the Whistle
Stopt Wars, turned back petrochemical Industries' Captains to grieve &
    groan in bed
Chopped wood, built forest houses & established farms
distributed monies to poor poets & nourished imaginative genius of the land
Sat silent in jazz roar writing poetry with an ink pen—   25
wasn't afraid of God or Death after his 48th year—
let his brains turn to water under Laughing Gas his gold molar pulled by
    futuristic dentists
Seaman knew ocean's surface a year
carpenter late learned bevel and mattock
son, conversed with elder Pound[4] & treated his father gently   30
—All empty all for show, all for the sake of Poesy
to set surpassing example of sanity as measure for late generations
Exemplify Muse Power to the young avert future suicide
accepting his own lie & the gaps between lies with equal good humor
Solitary in worlds full of insects & singing birds all solitary   35
—who had no subject but himself in many disguises
some outside his own body including empty air-filled space forests & cities—
Even climbed mountains to create his mountain, with ice ax & crampons &
    ropes, over Glaciers—

San Francisco, October 1974   1977

---

4. Ezra Pound (1885–1972), poet and critic who was a leader of the modernist movement in America.

FRANK O'HARA
1926–1966

After Frank O'Hara's death, when the critic Donald Allen gathered O'Hara's *Collected Poems,* he was surprised to discover that there were more than five hundred, many not published before. Some had to be retrieved from letters or from scraps of paper in boxes and trunks. O'Hara's poems were often spontaneous acts, revised minimally or not at all, then scattered generously, half forgotten. His work was published not by large commercial presses but by art galleries such as Tibor de Nagy and by small presses. These influential but fugitive paperbacks—*A City Winter* (1952), *Meditations in an Emergency* (1956), *Lunch Poems* (1964), and *Second Avenue* (1960)—included love poems, "letter" poems, "postcards," and odes, each bearing the mark of its occasion: a birthday, a thank-you, memories of a lunch hour, or simply "Having a Coke with You." They are filled, like diaries, with the names of Manhattan streets, writers, artists, restaurants, cafés, and films. O'Hara practiced what he once called, in mockery of sober poetic manifestos, "personism." The term came to him one day at the office when he was writing a poem for someone he loved. "While I was writing it I was realizing that if I wanted to I could use the telephone instead of writing the poem, and so Personism was born. . . . It puts the poem squarely between the poet and the person, Lucky Pierre style, and the poem is correspondingly gratified. The poem is at last between two persons instead of two pages."

O'Hara came to live in New York in 1951. He was born in Baltimore and grew up in Worcester, Massachusetts. He was in the navy for two years (with service in the South Pacific and Japan), then at Harvard, where he majored in music and English. In New York he became involved in the art world, working at different times as an editor and critic for *Art News* and a curator for the Museum of Modern Art. But this was more than a way of making a living; it was also making a life. These were the years in which abstract expressionism—nonrepresentational painting—flourished, and New York replaced Paris as the art capital of the world. O'Hara met and wrote about painters such as Willem de Kooning, Franz Kline, and Jackson Pollock, then producing their most brilliant work. After 1955, as a special assistant in the International Program of the Museum of Modern Art, O'Hara helped organize important traveling exhibitions that introduced and impressed the new American painting on the art world abroad.

As friends, many of these painters and sculptors were the occasion for and recipients of O'Hara's poems. Even more important, their way of working served as a model for his own style of writing. As the poet John Ashbery puts it, "The poem [is] the chronicle of the creative act that produces it." At the simplest level this means including the random jumps, distractions, and loose associations involved in writing about a particular moment, and sometimes recording the pauses in the writing of the poem. ("And now that I have finished dinner I can continue.") In O'Hara's work the casual is often, unexpectedly, the launching point for the visionary. The offhand chronicle of a lunch-hour walk can suddenly crystallize around a thunderclap memory of three friends, artists who died young: "First / Bunny died, then John Latouche, / then Jackson Pollock. But is the / earth as full as life was full, of them?"

O'Hara was indisputably, for his generation, *the* poet of New York; the city was for him what pastoral or rural worlds were for other writers, a source of refreshment and fantasy. But behind the exultation of O'Hara's cityscapes, a reader can often sense the melancholy that is made explicit in poems such as "A Step away from Them." Part of the city's allure was that it answered O'Hara's driving need to reach out for friends, events, animation. His eagerness is balanced on "the wilderness wish / of wanting to be everything to everybody everywhere." There is also in O'Hara's poetry an understanding of how urban life and the world of machines can devour the spirit; he was fascinated with, and wrote several poems about, the young actor James Dean, whose addiction to car racing culminated in a fatal accident.

O'Hara's example encouraged other poets—John Ashbery, Kenneth Koch, and James Schuyler. Loosely known as the New York school of poets, they occasionally collaborated on poems, plays, and happenings. O'Hara's bravado was a rallying point for these writers outside the more traditional and historically conscious modernism of Pound and Eliot. His poems were like "inspired rambling," open to all levels and areas of experience, expressed in a colloquial tone that could easily shade into surrealistic dream. "I'm too blue, / An elephant takes up his trumpet, / money flutters from the windows of cries." More recently the influence of O'Hara's casual and often comic voice makes itself felt in the work of Billy Collins.

A few days after his fortieth birthday in 1966, O'Hara was struck down at night by a beach buggy on Fire Island, New York. He died a few hours later. His central communicating figure enabled a nourishing interaction of painting, writing, dance, and theater.

To the Harbormaster

I wanted to be sure to reach you;
though my ship was on the way it got caught
in some moorings. I am always tying up
and then deciding to depart. In storms and
at sunset, with the metallic coils of the tide   5
around my fathomless arms, I am unable
to understand the forms of my vanity
or I am hard alee with my Polish rudder[1]
in my hand and the sun sinking. To
you I offer my hull and the tattered cordage   10
of my will. The terrible channels where
the wind drives me against the brown lips
of the reeds are not all behind me. Yet
I trust the sanity of my vessel; and
if it sinks, it may well be in answer   15
to the reasoning of the eternal voices,
the waves which have kept me from reaching you.

1954?   1957

Why I Am Not a Painter

I am not a painter, I am a poet.
Why? I think I would rather be
a painter, but I am not. Well,

for instance, Mike Goldberg
is starting a painting. I drop in.   5
"Sit down and have a drink" he
says. I drink; we drink. I look

1. Probably a submerged comic reference to *The Polish Rider* by Rembrandt. O'Hara said this poem was about his friend the contemporary painter Larry Rivers, who expressed a continuing fascina- tion with Rembrandt's painting of a knight on horseback. "Hard alee": a movement toward the lee, or sheltered side, of a sailboat, i.e., away from the wind.

up. "You have SARDINES in it."
"Yes, it needed something there."
"Oh." I go and the days go by   10
and I drop in again. The painting
is going on, and I go, and the days
go by. I drop in. The painting is
finished. "Where's SARDINES?"
All that's left is just   15
letters, "It was too much," Mike says.

But me? One day I am thinking of
a color: orange. I write a line
about orange. Pretty soon it is a
whole page of words, not lines.   20
Then another page. There should be
so much more, not of orange, of
words, of how terrible orange is
and life. Days go by. It is even in
prose, I am a real poet. My poem   25
is finished and I haven't mentioned
orange yet. It's twelve poems, I call
it ORANGES. And one day in a gallery
I see Mike's painting, called SARDINES.

                                                        1957

In Memory of My Feelings

to Grace Hartigan[1]

I

My quietness has a man in it, he is transparent
and he carries me quietly, like a gondola, through the streets.
He has several likenesses, like stars and years, like numerals.
My quietness has a number of naked selves,
so many pistols I have borrowed to protect myselves   5
from creatures who too readily recognize my weapons
and have murder in their heart!
                              though in winter
they are warm as roses, in the desert
taste of chilled anisette.   10
                    At times, withdrawn,
I rise into the cool skies
and gaze on at the imponderable world with the simple identification
of my colleagues, the mountains. Manfred[2] climbs to my nape,
speaks, but I do not hear him,   15

1. American abstract expressionist painter (b.
1922) and friend of the poet.
2. Tortured Romantic hero of Lord Byron's poetic
drama of the same name. Manfred, an exile, is pictured solitary high in the mountains.

I'm too blue.
An elephant takes up his trumpet,
money flutters from the windows of cries, silk stretching its mirror
across shoulder blades. A gun is "fired."

One of me rushes   20
to window #13 and one of me raises his whip and one of me
flutters up from the center of the track amidst the pink flamingoes,
and underneath their hooves as they round the last turn my lips
are scarred and brown, brushed by tails, masked in dirt's lust,
definition, open mouths gasping for the cries of the bettors for the   25
lungs of earth.

So many of my transparencies could not resist the race!
Terror in earth, dried mushrooms, pink feathers, tickets,
a flaking moon drifting across the muddied teeth,
the imperceptible moan of covered breathing,   30

love of the serpent!
I am underneath its leaves as the hunter crackles and pants
and bursts, as the barrage balloon drifts behind a cloud
and animal death whips out its flashlight,

whistling   35
and slipping the glove off the trigger hand. The serpent's eyes
redden at sight of those thorny fingernails, he is so smooth!

My transparent selves
flail about like vipers in a pail, writhing and hissing
without panic, with a certain justice of response   40
and presently the aquiline serpent comes to resemble the Medusa.[3]

II

The dead hunting
and the alive, ahunted.

My father, my uncle,
my grand-uncle and the several aunts. My   45
grand-aunt dying for me, like a talisman, in the war,
before I had even gone to Borneo[4]
her blood vessels rushed to the surface
and burst like rockets over the wrinkled
invasion of the Australians, her eyes aslant   50
like the invaded, but blue like mine.
An atmosphere of supreme lucidity,

humanism,
the mere existence of emphasis,

a rusted barge   55
painted orange against the sea
full of Marines reciting the Arabian ideas
which are a proof in themselves of seasickness
which is a proof in itself of being hunted.
A hit? *ergo* swim.   60
My 10   my 19,

3. In Greek mythology, a female figure with serpents growing out of her head, whose glance
turned men to stone.

4. A large island in the South China Sea. O'Hara
served aboard a destroyer in World War II and participated in the Allied recapture of the island.

my 9,   and the several years. My
12 years since they all died, philosophically speaking.
And now the coolness of a mind
like a shuttered suite in the Grand Hotel   65
where mail arrives for my incognito,
                                        whose façade
has been slipping into the Grand Canal for centuries;
rockets splay over a *sposalizio*,[5]
                                    fleeing into night   70
from their Chinese memories, and it is a celebration,
the trying desperately to count them as they die.
But who will stay to be these numbers
when all the lights are dead?

                                    III

The most arid stretch is often richest,   75
the hand lifting towards a fig tree from hunger
                                        digging
and there is water, clear, supple, or there
deep in the sand where death sleeps, a murmurous bubbling
proclaims the blackness that will ease and burn.   80
You preferred the Arabs? but they didn't stay to count
their inventions, racing into sands, converting themselves into
so many,
              embracing, at Ramadan,[6] the tenderest effigies of
themselves with penises shorn by the hundreds, like a camel   85
ravishing a goat.
                  And the mountainous-minded Greeks could speak
of time as a river[7] and step across it into Persia, leaving the pain
at home to be converted into statuary. I adore the Roman copies.[8]
And the stench of the camel's spit I swallow,   90
and the stench of the whole goat. For we have advanced, France,
together into a new land, like the Greeks, where one feels nostalgic
for mere ideas, where truth lies on its deathbed like an uncle
and one of me has a sentimental longing for number,
as has another for the ball gowns of the Directoire and yet   95
another for "Destiny, Paris, destiny!"
nother for "Destiny, Paris, destin for "Only a king may kill a king."[9]

How many selves are there in a war hero asleep in names? under
a blanket of platoon and fleet, orderly. For every seaman
with one eye closed in fear and twitching arm at a sigh for Lord
      Nelson,[1]   100
he is all dead; and now a meek subaltern writhes in his bedclothes
with the fury of a thousand, violating an insane mistress

5. Wedding. The "Grand Canal" is the main
waterway, lined with crumbling palaces, in Venice.
6. Ninth month of the Islamic year, consisting of
thirty days during which strict fasting is observed
in daylight hours.
7. As did the Greek philosopher Heraclitus (c.
540–c. 480 B.C.E.).

8. I.e., of the original Greek statues.
9. Slogans having to do with controversies during
the French Revolution and Napoleonic period.
"Directoire": Directory, the revolutionary executive
body that took power after the Reign of Terror.
1. Viscount Horatio Nelson (1758–1805), famous
British naval hero.

who has only herself to offer his multitudes.
Rising,
he wraps himself in the burnoose of memories against the heat of life   105
and over the sands he goes to take an algebraic position *in re*²
a sun of fear shining not too bravely. He will ask himselves to
vote on fear before he feels a tremor,
as runners arrive from the mountains
bearing snow, proof that the mind's obsolescence is still capable   110
of intimacy. His mistress will follow him across the desert
like a goat, towards a mirage which is something familiar about
one of his innumerable wrists,
and lying in an oasis one day,
playing catch with coconuts, they suddenly smell oil.   115

IV

Beneath these lives
the ardent lover of history hides,
tongue out
leaving a globe of spit on a taut spear of grass
and leaves off rattling his tail a moment   120
to admire this flag.
I'm looking for my Shanghai Lil.³
Five years ago, enamored of fire-escapes, I went to Chicago,
an eventful trip: the fountains! the Art Institute, the Y
for both sexes, absent Christianity.   125
At 7, before Jane
was up, the copper lake stirred against the sides
of a Norwegian freighter; on the deck a few dirty men,
tired of night, watched themselves in the water
as years before the German prisoners on the *Prinz Eugen*   130
dappled the Pacific with their sores, painted purple
by a Naval doctor.
Beards growing, and the constant anxiety
over looks. I'll shave before she wakes up. Sam Goldwyn
spent $2,000,000 on Anna Sten, but Grushenka left America.⁴   135
One of me is standing in the waves, an ocean bather,
or I am naked with a plate of devils at my hip.
Grace
to be born and live as variously as possible. The conception
of the masque barely suggests the sordid identifications.   140
I am a Hittite⁵ in love with a horse. I don't know what blood's
in me I feel like an African prince I am a girl walking downstairs
in a red pleated dress with heels I am a champion taking a fall
I am a jockey with a sprained ass-hole I am the light mist
in which a face appears   145
and it is another face of blonde I am a baboon eating a banana

2. In reference to.
3. Femme fatale role played by Marlene Dietrich in the film *Shanghai Express* (1932).
4. In 1933, the powerful film producer Samuel Goldwyn (1882–1974) imported actress Anna Sten (b. 1908) to the United States in the hope of creating a new international star. Sten was already celebrated in her native Russia, where, in 1931, she had starred as Grushenka in the film version of *The Brothers Karamazov*. Goldwyn's plan failed.
5. Member of an ancient empire of Asia Minor and Syria (1600–1200 B.C.E.).

I am a dictator looking at his wife I am a doctor eating a child
and the child's mother smiling I am a Chinaman climbing a mountain
I am a child smelling his father's underwear I am an Indian
sleeping on a scalp   150
                    and my pony is stamping in the birches,
and I've just caught sight of the *Niña*, the *Pinta* and the *Santa Maria*.
          What land is this, so free?
                                        I watch
the sea at the back of my eyes, near the spot where I think   155
in solitude as pine trees groan and support the enormous winds,
they are humming *L'Oiseau de feu!*[6]
                    They look like gods, these whitemen,
and they are bringing me the horse I fell in love with on the frieze.[7]

                                V

And now it is the serpent's turn.   160
I am not quite you, but almost, the opposite of visionary.
You are coiled around the central figure,
                                        the heart
that bubbles with red ghosts, since to move is to love
and the scrutiny of all things is syllogistic,   165
the startled eyes of the dikdik,[8] the bush full of white flags
fleeing a hunter,
                    which is our democracy
                    but the prey
is always fragile and like something, as a seashell can be   170
a great Courbet,[9] if it wishes. To bend the ear of the outer world.

                            When you turn your head
you can feel your heels, undulating? that's what it is
to be a serpent. I haven't told you of the most beautiful things
in my lives, and watching the ripple of their loss disappear   175
along the shore, underneath ferns,
                            face downward in the ferns
my body, the naked host to many selves, shot
by a guerrilla warrior or dumped from a car into ferns
which are themselves *journalières.*[1]   180
                    The hero, trying to unhitch his parachute,
stumbles over me. It is our last embrace.
                                    And yet
I have forgotten my loves, and chiefly that one, the cancerous
statue which my body could no longer contain,   185
                                against my will
                                against my love
become art,
          I could not change it into history
and so remember it,   190

6. *The Firebird*, a ballet by Igor Stravinsky, premiered in 1910.
7. A band of sculptured decoration. The most
famous frieze from antiquity, on the Parthenon in
Athens, features a rearing horse.

8. A small African antelope.
9. I.e., like a painting by the French realist painter
(1819–1877).
1. Day laborers.

and I have lost what is always and everywhere
present, the scene of my selves, the occasion of these ruses,
which I myself and singly must now kill
        and save the serpent in their midst.

1956   1960

A Step Away from Them

It's my lunch hour, so I go
for a walk among the hum-colored
cabs. First, down the sidewalk
where laborers feed their dirty
glistening torsos sandwiches   5
and Coca-Cola, with yellow helmets
on. They protect them from falling
bricks, I guess. Then onto the
avenue where skirts are flipping
above heels and blow up over   10
grates. The sun is hot, but the
cabs stir up the air. I look
at bargains in wristwatches. There
are cats playing in sawdust.
                        On   15
to Times Square, where the sign
blows smoke over my head,[1] and higher
the waterfall pours lightly. A
Negro stands in a doorway with a
toothpick, languorously agitating.   20
A blonde chorus girl clicks: he
smiles and rubs his chin. Everything
suddenly honks: it is 12:40 of
a Thursday.
               Neon in daylight is a   25
great pleasure, as Edwin Denby[2] would
write, as are light bulbs in daylight.
I stop for a cheeseburger at JULIET's
CORNER. Giulietta Masina, wife of
Federico Fellini, *è bell' attrice.*[3]   30
And chocolate malted. A lady in
foxes on such a day puts her poodle
in a cab.
            There are several Puerto
Ricans on the avenue today, which   35
makes it beautiful and warm. First
Bunny died, then John Latouche,
then Jackson Pollock.[4] But is the

---

1. Famous steam-puffing billboard advertising cigarettes.
2. Fellow poet (b. 1923) and influential ballet critic.

3. A beautiful actress (Italian).
4. Abstract expressionist painter (1912–1956), considered the originator of "action" painting. "Bunny": V. R. Lang (1924–1956), poet and direc-

earth as full as life was full, of them?
And one has eaten and one walks,   40
past the magazines with nudes
and the posters for BULLFIGHT and
the Manhattan Storage Warehouse,
which they'll soon tear down. I
used to think they had the Armory[5]   45
Show there.
               A glass of papaya juice
and back to work. My heart is in my
pocket, it is Poems by Pierre Reverdy.[6]

1956   1964

The Day Lady[1] Died

It is 12:20 in New York a Friday
three days after Bastille day,[2] yes
it is 1959 and I go get a shoeshine
because I will get off the 4:19 in Easthampton[3]
at 7:15 and then go straight to dinner   5
and I don't know the people who will feed me

I walk up the muggy street beginning to sun
and have a hamburger and a malted and buy
an ugly NEW WORLD WRITING to see what the poets
in Ghana are doing these days   10
                    I go on to the bank
and Miss Stillwagon (first name Linda I once heard)
doesn't even look up my balance for once in her life
and in the GOLDEN GRIFFIN I get a little Verlaine
for Patsy[4] with drawings by Bonnard although I do   15
think of Hesiod, trans. Richmond Lattimore or
Brendan Behan's new play or Le Balcon or Les Nègres
of Genet, but I don't, I stick with Verlaine
after practically going to sleep with quandariness

and for Mike I just stroll into the PARK LANE   20
Liquor Store and ask for a bottle of Strega and
then I go back where I came from to 6th Avenue
and the tobacconist in the Ziegfeld Theatre and

---

tor of The Poet's Theater in Cambridge, Massachusetts, where she produced several of O'Hara's plays. Latouche (1917–1956), lyricist for several New York musicals, such as *The Golden Apple*. All three were gifted friends of the poet who met tragic deaths.
5. Site of the influential and controversial first American showing of European postimpressionist painters in 1913.
6. French poet (1899–1960), whose work strongly

influenced O'Hara's writing.
1. Billie Holiday (1915–1959), also known as Lady Day, classic blues and jazz singer.
2. July 14, the French national holiday.
3. Town in eastern Long Island, popular summer resort among New York artists.
4. Patsy Southgate, an artist and friend of the poet. "Golden Griffin": a bookstore that was located close to the Museum of Modern Art.

casually ask for a carton of Gauloises and a carton
of Picayunes, and a NEW YORK POST with her face on it   25

and I am sweating a lot by now and thinking of
leaning on the john door in the 5 SPOT
while she whispered a song along the keyboard
to Mal Waldron[5] and everyone and I stopped breathing

1959   1960

5. Billie Holiday's accompanist (b. 1925).

GALWAY KINNELL
b. 1927

In an interview in 1971, Galway Kinnell praised Whitman's *Song of Myself*: "The final action of the poem where Whitman dissolves into the air and into the ground, is for me one of the great moments of self-transcendence in poetry. In one way or another, consciously or not, all poems try to pass beyond the self." This capacity for self-transcendence is dramatized in Kinnell's own work, where he enters the lives of animals ("The Porcupine" and "The Bear") and experiences himself as part of the natural world, like the flower he speaks for in "Flower Herding on Mount Monadnock." "Part of poetry's usefulness in the world," he has said, "is that it pays some of our huge unpaid tribute to the things and creatures that share the earth with us." His work moves between a vivid sense of the world's physical actuality and an equally vivid sense of its dissolution, for mortality is Kinnell's great theme. It appears in his work both as extinction and as "the flowing away into the universe which we desire." This theme is worked out at length in his sequence *The Book of Nightmares* (1978).

Kinnell grew up in Providence, Rhode Island, and attended Princeton University, where he and a classmate, W. S. Merwin, sometimes read each other their poems. He has written continuously since that time, combining his life of poetry with political commitments. Among his various activities Kinnell has been director of an adult education program in Chicago, a journalist in Iran, and a field-worker for the Congress of Racial Equality in Louisiana. More recently, he has taught at a large number of colleges and universities.

Kinnell's experiences working for voter registration in the South in the 1960s make their way into his long poem "The Last River" from his volume *Body Rags* (1969). Over the years, Kinnell has frequently written poems that unite personal life with the events of the nation. His work includes powerful war poems such as "Vapor Trail Reflected in the Frog Pond" and "The Dead Shall Be Raised Incorruptible," and in "The Past" (1985) he meditates on, and imagines his way into, the consequences of the dropping of the atom bomb on Hiroshima and Nagasaki ("The Fundamental Project of Technology"). Elsewhere he has suggested that poetry is an alternative to a technological world in which domination of nature represses the knowledge of death. In 1994 his collection *Imperfect Thirst* extended his meditation on mortality into the arena of family history and personal memory. In a moving poem, "Neverland," on the death of his sister, Kinnell confronts death's agony and mystery: "*Now* is when the point of the story changes."

Kinnell's earliest work, as seen in *What a Kingdom It Was* (1960) and *First Poems 1946–1954* (1970), is formally intricate. The course of his career has been a movement to a looser line, a more uncluttered diction. His sense of form arises from what he calls the "inner shape" of the poem: "saying in its own music what matters most." Over the years he has come to write poems that maintain musicality and a richness of language while never departing too far from the speaking voice. Kinnell's attraction to the nonhuman world, which may remind us of Theodore Roethke and Gary Snyder, gives his work a vivid sense of life's diversity. But he has sometimes elevated the instinctual at the expense of a shaping, conscious awareness and has written as if the very need for poetic form were, in and of itself, repressive. The finest of Kinnell's poems combine self-transcendence with self-awareness in rhythms that convey a powerful physical energy and an empathetic imagination. His description of Whitman can serve as a description of Kinnell's own work at its best: "All his feelings for existence, for himself, for his own place, come out in what he says about them. . . . He rescues these things from death and lets them live in his poems and, in turn, they save him from incoherence and silence."

The Porcupine

1

Fatted
on herbs, swollen on crabapples,
puffed up on bast and phloem,[1] ballooned
on willow flowers, poplar catkins, first
leafs of aspen and larch,   5
the porcupine
drags and bounces his last meal through ice,
mud, roses and goldenrod, into the stubbly high fields.

2

In character
he resembles us in seven ways: 10
he puts his mark on outhouses,
he alchemizes by moonlight,
he shits on the run,
he uses his tail for climbing,
he chuckles softly to himself when scared,   15
he's overcrowded if there's more than one of him per five acres,
his eyes have their own inner redness.

3

Digger of
goings across floors, of hesitations
at thresholds, of   20
handprints of dread
at doorpost or window jamb, he would
gouge the world

---

1. I.e., plant tissues.

empty of us, hack and crater
it   25
until it is nothing, if that
could rinse it of all our sweat and pathos.

Adorer of ax
handles aflow with grain, of arms
of Morris chairs,[2] of hand   30
crafted objects
steeped in the juice of fingertips,
of surfaces wetted down
with fist grease and elbow oil,
of clothespins that have   35
grabbed our body-rags by underarm and crotch . . .

Unimpressed—bored—
by the whirl of the stars, by *these*
he's astonished, ultra-
Rilkean[3] angel!   40

for whom the true
portion of the sweetness of earth
is one of those bottom-heavy, glittering, saccadic
bits
of salt water that splash down   45
the haunted ravines of a human face.

4

A farmer shot a porcupine three times
as it dozed on a tree limb. On
the way down it tore open its belly
on a broken   50
branch, hooked its gut,
and went on falling. On the ground
it sprang to its feet, and
paying out gut heaved
and spartled through a hundred feet of goldenrod   55
before
the abrupt emptiness.

5

The Avesta[4]
puts porcupine killers
into hell for nine generations, sentencing them   60
to gnaw out

2. Easy chairs.
3. Rainer Maria Rilke (1875–1926), German poet. He wrote in the letter that "the 'angel' of the [Duino] Elegies has nothing to do with the angel of the Christian heaven. . . . The angel of the Ele- gies is that being which stands for the idea of rec- ognizing a higher order of reality in invisibility."
4. Book of the sacred writings of Zoroastrianism, a Persian religion.

each other's hearts for the
salts of desire.

I roll
this way and that in the great bed, under 65
the quilt
that mimics this country of broken farms and woods,
the fatty sheath of the man
melting off,
the self-stabbing coil 70
of bristles reversing, blossoming outward—
a red-eyed, hard-toothed, arrow-stuck urchin
tossing up mattress feathers,
pricking the
woman beside me until she cries. 75

6

In my time I have
crouched, quills erected,
Saint
Sebastian[5] of the
scared heart, and been 80
beat dead with a locust club
on the bare snout.
And fallen from high places
I have fled, have
jogged 85
over fields of goldenrod,
terrified, seeking home,
and among flowers
I have come to myself empty, the rope
strung out behind me 90
in the fall sun
suddenly glorified with all my blood.

7

And tonight I think I prowl broken
skulled or vacant as a
sucked egg in the wintry meadow, softly chuckling, blank 95
template of myself, dragging
a starved belly through the lichflowered acres,
where
burdock looses the ark of its seed
and thistle holds up its lost blooms 100
and rosebushes in the wind scrape their dead limbs
for the forced-fire
of roses.

1969

5. St. Sebastian (d. 288), an early Christian saint and martyr. He was shot full of arrows by an execution squad and miraculously survived, only to be beaten to death later.

Blackberry Eating

I love to go out in late September
among the fat, overripe, icy, black blackberries
to eat blackberries for breakfast,
the stalks very prickly, a penalty
they earn for knowing the black art   5
of blackberry-making; and as I stand among them
lifting the stalks to my mouth, the ripest berries
fall almost unbidden to my tongue,
as words sometimes do, certain peculiar words
like *strengths* or *squinched*,   10
many-lettered, one-syllabled lumps,
which I squeeze, squinch open, and splurge well
in the silent, startled, icy, black language
of blackberry-eating in late September.

                                                                 1980

After Making Love We Hear Footsteps

For I can snore like a bullhorn
or play loud music
or sit up talking with any reasonably sober Irishman
and Fergus will only sink deeper
into his dreamless sleep, which goes by all in one flash,   5
but let there be that heavy breathing
or a stifled come-cry anywhere in the house
and he will wrench himself awake
and make for it on the run—as now, we lie together,
after making love, quiet, touching along the length of our bodies,   10
familiar touch of the long-married,
and he appears—in his baseball pajamas, it happens,
the neck opening so small he has to screw them on—
and flops down between us and hugs us and snuggles himself to sleep,
his face gleaming with satisfaction at being this very child.   15

In the half darkness we look at each other
and smile
and touch arms across this little, startlingly muscled body—
this one whom habit of memory propels to the ground of his making,
sleeper only the moral sounds can sing awake,   20
this blessing love gives again into our arms.

                                                                 1980

Cemetery Angels

On these cold days
they stand over
our dead, who will
erupt into flower as soon
as memory and human shape   5
rot out of them, each bent
forward and with wings
partly opened as though
warming itself at a fire.

1985

Neverland

Bending over her bed, I saw the smile
I must have seen when gaping up from the crib.
Knowing death comes, imagining it,
may be a fair price for consciousness.
But looking at my sister, I wished   5
she could have been snatched up
to die by surprise, without ever knowing about death.
Too late. Wendy said, "I am in three parts.
Here on the left is red. That is pain.
On the right is yellow. That is exhaustion.   10
The rest is white. I don't know yet what white is."
For most people, one day everything is all right.
The next, the limbic node[1] catches fire. The day after,
the malleus in one ear starts missing the incus.[2]
Then the arthritic opposable thumb no longer opposes   15
whoever screwed the top onto the jam jar.
Then the coraco-humeral ligament[3] frizzles apart,
the liver speckles, the kidneys dent,
two toes lose their souls. Of course,
before things get worse, a person could run.   20
I could take off right now, climb the pure forms
that surmount time and death, follow a line
down Avenue D, make a 90° turn right on 8th Street,
90° left on C, right on 7th, left on B, then cross
to Sixth Avenue, catch the A train to Nassau,   25
the station where the A pulls up beside the Z,[4]
get off, hop on the Z, hurtle under the river
and rise on Euclid under the stars and taste,
with my sweetheart, in perfectly circular kisses,

---

1. Brain structure responsible for emotion and
motivation.
2. Middle bone of the middle ear, also called the
anvil. "Malleus": outermost bone of the middle

ear.
3. Shoulder ligament.
4. New York City subway trains.

the actual saliva of paradise.   30
Then, as if Wendy suddenly understood
this flaw in me, that I could die
still wanting what is not to be had here, drink
and drink and yet have most of my thirst
intact for the water table, she opened her eyes.   35
she said. "I just wish it didn't take so long."
Seeing her look so young and begin to die
all on her own, I wanted to whisk her off.
Quickly she said, "Let's go home." From outside
in the driveway came the gargling noise   40
of a starter motor, and a low steady rumbling, as if
my car had turned itself on and was warming up the engine.
She said this as if we had gone over to visit
a friend, to sign our names on the cast
on the leg she broke swinging on our swing,   45
and some awful indoor game had gone wrong,
and Wendy had turned to me and said, "Let's go home."
She had closed her eyes. She looked entirely white.
Her hair had been white for years; in her illness
her skin became as if powdered with twice-bleached flour;   50
now her lips seemed to have lost their blood.
Color flashed only when she opened her eyes.
Snow will come down next winter, in the woods;
the fallen trees will have that flesh on their bones.
When the eye of the woods opens, a bluejay shuttles.   55
Outside, suddenly, all was quiet, and
I realized my car had shut off its engine.
Now a spot of rosiness showed in each of her cheeks:
blushes, perhaps, at a joy she had kept from us,
from somewhere in her life, perhaps two mouths,   60
hers and a beloved's, near each other, like roses
sticking out of a bottle of invisible water.
She was losing the half-given, half-learned
art of speech, and it became for her a struggle
to find words, form them, position them,   65
then quickly utter them. After much effort
she said, "Now is when the point of the story changes."
After that, one eye at a time, the left listened,
and drifted, the right focused, gleamed
meanings at me, drifted. Stalwart,   70
the halves of the brain, especially the right.
Now, as they ratchet the box holding
her body into the earth, a voice calls
back across the region she passes through,
in prolonged, even notes that swell and diminish.   75
Now it sounds from under the farthest horizon,
and now it grows faint, and now I cannot hear it.

                                                        1994

JOHN ASHBERY
b. 1927

John Ashbery has described his writing this way: "I think that any one of my poems might be considered to be a snapshot of whatever is going on in my mind at the time—first of all the desire to write a poem, after that wondering if I've left the oven on or thinking about where I must be in the next hour." Ashbery has developed a style hospitable to quicksilver changes in tone and attention. His work often moves freely between different modes of discourse, between a language of popular culture and commonplace experience and a heightened rhetoric often associated with poetic vision. Ashbery's poems show an awareness of the various linguistic codes (including clichés and conventional public speech) by which we live and through which we define ourselves. This awareness includes an interest in what he has called "prose voices," and he has often written in a way that challenges the boundaries between poetry and prose.

Ashbery's poetry was not always so open to contradictory notions and impulses. His early books rejected the mere surfaces of realism and the momentary to get at "remoter areas of consciousness." The protagonist of "Illustration" (from his first book, *Some Trees*) is a cheerful nun about to leave behind the irrelevancies of the world by leaping from a skyscraper. Her act implies "Much that is beautiful must be discarded / So that we may resemble a taller / impression of ourselves." To reach the "remoter areas of consciousness," Ashbery tried various technical experiments. He used highly patterned forms such as the sestina in "Some Trees" and "The Tennis Court Oath" (1962) not with any show of mechanical brilliance but to explore: "I once told somebody that writing a sestina was rather like riding downhill on a bicycle and having the pedals push your feet. I wanted my feet to be pushed into places they wouldn't normally have taken."

Ashbery was born in Rochester, New York, in 1927. He attended Deerfield Academy and Harvard, graduating in 1949. He received an M.A. in English from Columbia in 1951. In France first as a Fulbright scholar, he returned in 1958 for eight years and was art critic for the European edition of the *New York Herald Tribune* and reported the European shows and exhibitions for *Art News* and *Arts International*. He returned to New York in 1965 to be executive editor of *Art News,* a position he held until 1972. Since then he has been professor of English in the creative writing program of Brooklyn College and art critic for *Newsweek* magazine.

Ashbery's interest in art played a formative role in his poetry. He is often associated with Frank O'Hara, James Schuyler, and Kenneth Koch as part of the "New York school" of poets. The name refers to their common interest in the New York school of abstract painters of the 1940s and 1950s, some of whose techniques they wished to adapt in poetry. These painters avoided realism to stress the work of art as a representation of the creative act that produced it—as in the action paintings of Jackson Pollock. Ashbery's long poem *Self-Portrait in a Convex Mirror* gives as much attention to the rapidly changing feelings of the poet in the act of writing his poem as it does to the Renaissance painting that inspired him. The poem moves back and forth between the distracted energies that feed a work of art and the completed composition, which the artist feels as both a triumph and a falsification of complex feelings. Ashbery shares with O'Hara a sense of the colloquial brilliance of daily life in New York and sets this in tension with the concentration and stasis of art.

Self-Portrait in a Convex Mirror (1975) was followed by *Houseboat Days* (1977), *As We Know* (1979), *Shadow Train* (1981), and *A Wave* (1984). His important book-length poem, *Flow Chart*, appeared in 1991 followed by collections of shorter poems, *And the Stars Were Shining* (1995) and *Your Name Here* (2000). His entertaining and provocative *Other Traditions* (2000) is a collection of his Norton Lectures on poetry at Harvard. Ashbery's work, especially his earlier, more highly experimental poems, has become particularly influential for a younger generation identified as Language poets, such as Charles Bernstein, Lyn Hejinian, Michael Palmer, and Susan Howe. They have been attracted to the linguistic playfulness of Ashbery's poetry and to its resistance to being read as a single, personal voice. Exposing and sometimes breaking through the dominant uses of language in our world, Ashbery's poems open new possibilities of meaning: "We are all talkers / It is true, but underneath the talk lies / The moving and not wanting to be moved, the loose/Meaning, untidy and simple like the threshing floor" ("Soonest Mended").

Illustration

I

A novice[1] was sitting on a cornice
High over the city. Angels

Combined their prayers with those
Of the police, begging her to come off it.

One lady promised to be her friend.   5
"I do not want a friend," she said.

A mother offered her some nylons
Stripped from her very legs. Others brought

Little offerings of fruit and candy,
The blind man all his flowers. If any   10

Could be called successful, these were,
For that the scene should be a ceremony

Was what she wanted. "I desire
Monuments," she said. "I want to move

Figuratively, as waves caress   15
The thoughtless shore. You people I know

Will offer me every good thing
I do not want. But please remember

I died accepting them." With that, the wind
Unpinned her bulky robes, and naked   20

As a roc's[2] egg, she drifted softly downward
Out of the angels' tenderness and the minds of men.

II

Much that is beautiful must be discarded
So that we may resemble a taller

---

1. Student in the first stage of instruction to be a   2. Legendary bird of prey.
nun.

Impression of ourselves. Moths climb in the flame,   25
Alas, that wish only to be the flame:

They do not lessen our stature.
We twinkle under the weight

Of indiscretions. But how could we tell
That of the truth we know, she was   30

The somber vestment? For that night, rockets sighed
Elegantly over the city, and there was feasting:

There is so much in that moment!
So many attitudes toward that flame,

We might have soared from earth, watching her glide   35
Aloft, in her peplum³ of bright leaves.

But she, of course, was only an effigy
Of indifference, a miracle

Not meant for us, as the leaves are not
Winter's because it is the end.   40

1956

Soonest Mended

Barely tolerated, living on the margin
In our technological society, we were always having to be rescued
On the brink of destruction, like heroines in *Orlando Furioso*¹
Before it was time to start all over again.
There would be thunder in the bushes, a rustling of coils,   5
And Angelica, in the Ingres painting,² was considering
The colorful but small monster near her toe, as though wondering whether
      forgetting
The whole thing might not, in the end, be the only solution.
And then there always came a time when
Happy Hooligan³ in his rusted green automobile   10
Came plowing down the course, just to make sure everything was O.K.,
Only by that time we were in another chapter and confused
About how to receive this latest piece of information.
Was it information? Weren't we rather acting this out
For someone else's benefit, thoughts in a mind   15
With room enough and to spare for our little problems (so they began to
      seem),

3. In ancient Greece, a drapery about the upper part of the body.
1. Fantastic epic poem by Ludovico Ariosto (1474–1533), whose romantic heroine Angelica is constantly being rescued from imminent perils such as monsters and ogres.

2. *Roger Delivering Angelica* (1819), a painting based on a scene from Ariosto, by the French artist Jean-Auguste-Dominique Ingres (1780–1867).
3. The good-natured, simple title character of a popular comic strip of the 1920s and 1930s.

Our daily quandary about food and the rent and bills to be paid?
To reduce all this to a small variant,
To step free at last, minuscule on the gigantic plateau—
This was our ambition: to be small and clear and free.   20
Alas, the summer's energy wanes quickly,
A moment and it is gone. And no longer
May we make the necessary arrangements, simple as they are.
Our star was brighter perhaps when it had water in it.
Now there is no question even of that, but only   25
Of holding on to the hard earth so as not to get thrown off,
With an occasional dream, a vision: a robin flies across
The upper corner of the window, you brush your hair away
And cannot quite see, or a wound will flash
Against the sweet faces of the others, something like: 30
This is what you wanted to hear, so why
Did you think of listening to something else? We are all talkers
It is true, but underneath the talk lies
The moving and not wanting to be moved, the loose
Meaning, untidy and simple like a threshing floor.[4]   35

These then were some hazards of the course,
Yet though we knew the course *was* hazards and nothing else
It was still a shock when, almost a quarter of a century later,
The clarity of the rules dawned on you for the first time.
They were the players, and we who had struggled at the game   40
Were merely spectators, though subject to its vicissitudes
And moving with it out of the tearful stadium, borne on shoulders, at last.
Night after night this message returns, repeated
In the flickering bulbs of the sky, raised past us, taken away from us,
Yet ours over and over until the end that is past truth,   45
The being of our sentences, in the climate that fostered them,
Not ours to own, like a book, but to be with, and sometimes
To be without, alone and desperate.
But the fantasy makes it ours, a kind of fence-sitting
Raised to the level of an esthetic ideal. These were moments, years,   50
Solid with reality, faces, namable events, kisses, heroic acts,
But like the friendly beginning of a geometrical progression
Not too reassuring, as though meaning could be cast aside some day
When it had been outgrown. Better, you said, to stay cowering
Like this in the early lessons, since the promise of learning   55
Is a delusion, and I agreed, adding that
Tomorrow would alter the sense of what had already been learned,
That the learning process is extended in this way, so that from this stand-
    point
None of us ever graduates from college,
For time is an emulsion,[5] and probably thinking not to grow up   60
Is the brightest kind of maturity for us, right now at any rate.
And you see, both of us were right, though nothing
Has somehow come to nothing; the avatars[6]
Of our conforming to the rules and living

---

4. Used at harvest time to separate the wheat from the chaff, which is to be discarded.
5. A chemical solution in which the particles of one liquid are suspended in another.
6. Incarnations.

Around the home have made—well, in a sense, "good citizens" of us,   65
Brushing the teeth and all that, and learning to accept
The charity of the hard moments as they are doled out,
For this is action, this not being sure, this careless
Preparing, sowing the seeds crooked in the furrow,
Making ready to forget, and always coming back   70
To the mooring of starting out, that day so long ago.

                                                                    1970

Self-Portrait in a Convex Mirror[1]

As Parmigianino did it, the right hand
Bigger than the head, thrust at the viewer
And swerving easily away, as though to protect
What it advertises. A few leaded panes, old beams,
Fur, pleated muslin, a coral ring run together   5
In a movement supporting the face, which swims
Toward and away like the hand
Except that it is in repose. It is what is
Sequestered. Vasari[2] says, "Francesco one day set himself
To take his own portrait, looking at himself for that purpose   10
In a convex mirror, such as is used by barbers . . .
He accordingly caused a ball of wood to be made
By a turner, and having divided it in half and
Brought it to the size of the mirror, he set himself
With great art to copy all that he saw in the glass,"   15
Chiefly his reflection, of which the portrait
Is the reflection once removed.
The glass chose to reflect only what he saw
Which was enough for his purpose: his image
Glazed, embalmed, projected at a 180-degree angle.   20
The time of day or the density of the light
Adhering to the face keeps it
Lively and intact in a recurring wave
Of arrival. The soul establishes itself.
But how far can it swim out through the eyes   25
And still return safely to its nest? The surface
Of the mirror being convex, the distance increases
Significantly; that is, enough to make the point
That the soul is a captive, treated humanely, kept
In suspension, unable to advance much farther   30
Than your look as it intercepts the picture.
Pope Clement and his court were "stupefied"
By it,[3] according to Vasari, and promised a commission

1. This self-portrait by the Italian Mannerist Parmigianino (Girolamo Francesco Mazzola, 1503–
1540) on a convex piece of poplar wood hangs in
the Kunsthistorisches Museum in Vienna.
2. Giorgio Vasari (1511–1574), Italian architect,
painter, and art historian whose *Lives of the Most
Eminent Italian Painters, Sculptors, and Architects*
is the principal source of information about those
artists.
3. When Parmigianino moved from his native
Parma to Rome in 1524, he presented the self-
portrait to Pope Clement VII as a credential for
papal patronage.

That never materialized. The soul has to stay where it is,
Even though restless, hearing raindrops at the pane, 35
The sighing of autumn leaves thrashed by the wind,
Longing to be free, outside, but it must stay
Posing in this place. It must move
As little as possible. This is what the portrait says.
But there is in that gaze a combination 40
Of tenderness, amusement and regret, so powerful
In its restraint that one cannot look for long.
The secret is too plain. The pity of it smarts,
Makes hot tears spurt: that the soul is not a soul,
Has no secret, is small, and it fits 45
Its hollow perfectly: its room, our moment of attention.
That is the tune but there are no words.
The words are only speculation
(From the Latin *speculum*, mirror):
They seek and cannot find the meaning of the music. 50
We see only postures of the dream,
Riders of the motion that swings the face
Into view under evening skies, with no
False disarray as proof of authenticity.
But it is life englobed. 55
One would like to stick one's hand
Out of the globe, but its dimension,
What carries it, will not allow it.
No doubt it is this, not the reflex
To hide something, which makes the hand loom large 60
As it retreats slightly. There is no way
To build it flat like a section of wall:
It must join the segment of a circle,
Roving back to the body of which it seems
So unlikely a part, to fence in and shore up the face 65
On which the effort of this condition reads
Like a pinpoint of a smile, a spark
Or star one is not sure of having seen
As darkness resumes. A perverse light whose
Imperative of subtlety dooms in advance its 70
Conceit to light up: unimportant but meant.
Francesco, your hand is big enough
To wreck the sphere, and too big,
One would think, to weave delicate meshes
That only argue its further detention. 75
(Big, but not coarse, merely on another scale,
Like a dozing whale on the sea bottom
In relation to the tiny, self-important ship
On the surface.) But your eyes proclaim
That everything is surface. The surface is what's there 80
And nothing can exist except what's there.
There are no recesses in the room, only alcoves,
And the window doesn't matter much, or that
Sliver of window or mirror on the right, even
As a gauge of the weather, which in French is 85

Le temps, the word for time, and which
Follows a course wherein changes are merely
Features of the whole. The whole is stable within
Instability, a globe like ours, resting
On a pedestal of vacuum, a ping-pong ball   90
Secure on its jet of water.
And just as there are no words for the surface, that is,
No words to say what it really is, that it is not
Superficial but a visible core, then there is
No way out of the problem of pathos vs. experience.   95
You will stay on, restive, serene in
Your gesture which is neither embrace nor warning
But which holds something of both in pure
Affirmation that doesn't affirm anything.

The balloon pops, the attention   100
Turns dully away. Clouds
In the puddle stir up into sawtoothed fragments.
I think of the friends
Who came to see me, of what yesterday
Was like. A peculiar slant   105
Of memory that intrudes on the dreaming model
In the silence of the studio as he considers
Lifting the pencil to the self-portrait.
How many people came and stayed a certain time,
Uttered light or dark speech that became part of you   110
Like light behind windblown fog and sand,
Filtered and influenced by it, until no part
Remains that is surely you. Those voices in the dusk
Have told you all and still the tale goes on
In the form of memories deposited in irregular   115
Clumps of crystals. Whose curved hand controls,
Francesco, the turning seasons and the thoughts
That peel off and fly away at breathless speeds
Like the last stubborn leaves ripped
From wet branches? I see in this only the chaos   120
Of your round mirror which organizes everything
Around the polestar[4] of your eyes which are empty,
Know nothing, dream but reveal nothing.
I feel the carousel starting slowly
And going faster and faster: desk, papers, books,   125
Photographs of friends, the window and the trees
Merging in one neutral band that surrounds
Me on all sides, everywhere I look.
And I cannot explain the action of leveling,
Why it should all boil down to one   130
Uniform substance, a magma[5] of interiors.
My guide in these matters is your self,
Firm, oblique, accepting everything with the same

---

4. The North Star, hence the magnetic center.   5. Soft mixture of organic or mineral materials.

Wraith of a smile, and as time speeds up so that it is soon
Much later, I can know only the straight way out,   135
The distance between us. Long ago
The strewn evidence meant something,
The small accidents and pleasures
Of the day as it moved gracelessly on,
A housewife doing chores. Impossible now   140
To restore those properties in the silver blur that is
The record of what you accomplished by sitting down
"With great art to copy all that you saw in the glass"
So as to perfect and rule out the extraneous
Forever. In the circle of your intentions certain spars[6]   145
Remain that perpetuate the enchantment of self with self:
Eyebeams, muslin, coral. It doesn't matter
Because these are things as they are today
Before one's shadow ever grew
Out of the field into thoughts of tomorrow.   150

Tomorrow is easy, but today is uncharted,
Desolate, reluctant as any landscape
To yield what are laws of perspective
After all only to the painter's deep
Mistrust, a weak instrument though   155
Necessary. Of course some things
Are possible, it knows, but it doesn't know
Which ones. Some day we will try
To do as many things as are possible
And perhaps we shall succeed at a handful   160
Of them, but this will not have anything
To do with what is promised today, our
Landscape sweeping out from us to disappear
On the horizon. Today enough of a cover burnishes
To keep the supposition of promises together   165
In one piece of surface, letting one ramble
Back home from them so that these
Even stronger possibilities can remain
Whole without being tested. Actually
The skin of the bubble-chamber's as tough as   170
Reptile eggs; everything gets "programmed" there
In due course: more keeps getting included
Without adding to the sum, and just as one
Gets accustomed to a noise that
Kept one awake but now no longer does,   175
So the room contains this flow like an hourglass
Without varying in climate or quality
(Except perhaps to brighten bleakly and almost
Invisibly, in a focus sharpening toward death—more
Of this later). What should be the vacuum of a dream   180
Becomes continually replete as the source of dreams

6. Pieces of lustrous mineral; also, round timbers used to extend a sail.

Is being tapped so that this one dream
May wax, flourish like a cabbage rose,
Defying sumptuary laws,[7] leaving us
To awake and try to begin living in what   185
Has now become a slum. Sydney Freedberg in his
Parmigianino says of it: "Realism in this portrait
No longer produces an objective truth, but a *bizarria*[8] . . .
However its distortion does not create
A feeling of disharmony. . . . The forms retain   190
A strong measure of ideal beauty," because
Fed by our dreams, so inconsequential until one day
We notice the hole they left. Now their importance
If not their meaning is plain. They were to nourish
A dream which includes them all, as they are   195
Finally reversed in the accumulating mirror.
They seemed strange because we couldn't actually see them.
And we realize this only at a point where they lapse
Like a wave breaking on a rock, giving up
Its shape in a gesture which expresses that shape.   200
The forms retain a strong measure of ideal beauty
As they forage in secret on our idea of distortion.
Why be unhappy with this arrangement, since
Dreams prolong us as they are absorbed?
Something like living occurs, a movement   205
Out of the dream into its codification.

As I start to forget it
It presents its stereotype again
But it is an unfamiliar stereotype, the face
Riding at anchor, issued from hazards, soon   210
To accost others, "rather angel than man" (Vasari).
Perhaps an angel looks like everything
We have forgotten, I mean forgotten
Things that don't seem familiar when
We meet them again, lost beyond telling,   215
Which were ours once. This would be the point
Of invading the privacy of this man who
"Dabbled in alchemy, but whose wish
Here was not to examine the subtleties of art
In a detached, scientific spirit: he wished through them 220
To impart the sense of novelty and amazement to the spectator"
(Freedberg). Later portraits such as the Uffizi
"Gentleman," the Borghese "Young Prelate" and
The Naples "Antea" issue from Mannerist
Tensions,[9] but here, as Freedberg points out,   225
The surprise, the tension are in the concept
Rather than its realization.

---

7. Laws regulating private behavior, in this case mode of dress.
8. Distortion. Sydney J. Freedberg, *Parmigianino: His Works in Painting* (1950).
9. Mannerism was a style of painting in 16th- century Italy in which proportions or the laws of perspective were distorted to produce effects of tension or disturbance. "Uffizi" and "Borghese": galleries in Florence and Rome, respectively.

The consonance of the High Renaissance[1]
Is present, though distorted by the mirror.
What is novel is the extreme care in rendering   230
The velleities[2] of the rounded reflecting surface
(It is the first mirror portrait),
So that you could be fooled for a moment
Before you realize the reflection
Isn't yours. You feel then like one of those   235
Hoffmann[3] characters who have been deprived
Of a reflection, except that the whole of me
Is seen to be supplanted by the strict
Otherness of the painter in his
Other room. We have surprised him   240
At work, but no, he has surprised us
As he works. The picture is almost finished,
The surprise almost over, as when one looks out,
Startled by a snowfall which even now is
Ending in specks and sparkles of snow.   245
It happened while you were inside, asleep,
And there is no reason why you should have
Been awake for it, except that the day
Is ending and it will be hard for you
To get to sleep tonight, at least until late.   250

The shadow of the city injects its own
Urgency: Rome where Francesco
Was at work during the Sack:[4] his inventions
Amazed the soldiers who burst in on him;
They decided to spare his life, but he left soon after;   255
Vienna where the painting is today, where
I saw it with Pierre in the summer of 1959; New York
Where I am now, which is a logarithm[5]
Of other cities. Our landscape
Is alive with filiations, shuttlings;   260
Business is carried on by look, gesture,
Hearsay. It is another life to the city,
The backing of the looking glass of the
Unidentified but precisely sketched studio. It wants
To siphon off the life of the studio, deflate   265
Its mapped space to enactments, island it.
That operation has been temporarily stalled
But something new is on the way, a new preciosity
In the wind. Can you stand it,
Francesco? Are you strong enough for it?   270
This wind brings what it knows not, is
Self-propelled, blind, has no notion

1. In Italian painting and architecture, the period in the late 15th and early 16th centuries in which the harmonious proportions ("consonance") of classical art were recaptured and honored.
2. Loosely, caprices.
3. E. T. A. Hoffman (1776–1822), German author whose tales often had to do with the super-

natural.
4. In 1527, the Hapsburg emperor Charles V sacked Rome in an assertion of power against Pope Clement VII.
5. Mathematical term defining the relationship between two other terms.

Of itself. It is inertia that once
Acknowledged saps all activity, secret or public:
Whispers of the word that can't be understood   275
But can be felt, a chill, a blight
Moving outward along the capes and peninsulas
Of your nervures and so to the archipelagoes
And to the bathed, aired secrecy of the open sea.
This is its negative side. Its positive side is   280
Making you notice life and the stresses
That only seemed to go away, but now,
As this new mode questions, are seen to be
Hastening out of style. If they are to become classics
They must decide which side they are on.   285
Their reticence has undermined
The urban scenery, made its ambiguities
Look willful and tired, the games of an old man.
What we need now is this unlikely
Challenger pounding on the gates of an amazed   290
Castle. Your argument, Francesco,
Had begun to grow stale as no answer
Or answers were forthcoming. If it dissolves now
Into dust, that only means its time had come
Some time ago, but look now, and listen: 295
It may be that another life is stocked there
In recesses no one knew of; that it,
Not we, are the change; that we are in fact it
If we could get back to it, relive some of the way
It looked, turn our faces to the globe as it sets   300
And still be coming out all right:
Nerves normal, breath normal. Since it is a metaphor
Made to include us, we are a part of it and
Can live in it as in fact we have done,
Only leaving our minds bare for questioning   305
We now see will not take place at random
But in an orderly way that means to menace
Nobody—the normal way things are done,
Like the concentric growing up of days
Around a life: correctly, if you think about it.   310

A breeze like the turning of a page
Brings back your face: the moment
Takes such a big bite out of the haze
Of pleasant intuition it comes after.
The locking into place is "death itself,"   315
As Berg said of a phrase in Mahler's Ninth;[6]
Or, to quote Imogen in *Cymbeline*, "There cannot
Be a pinch in death more sharp than this,"[7] for,
Though only exercise or tactic, it carries
The momentum of a conviction that had been building.   320

6. Alban Berg (1885–1935), Viennese composer
of twelve-tone music, speaking of the Ninth Symphony of his Austrian predecessor, the composer
Gustav Mahler (1860–1911).
7. Shakespeare, *Cymbeline* 1.1.131–32.

Mere forgetfulness cannot remove it
Nor wishing bring it back, as long as it remains
The white precipitate[8] of its dream
In the climate of sighs flung across our world,
A cloth over a birdcage. But it is certain that   325
What is beautiful seems so only in relation to a specific
Life, experienced or not, channeled into some form
Steeped in the nostalgia of a collective past.
The light sinks today with an enthusiasm
I have known elsewhere, and known why   330
It seemed meaningful, that others felt this way
Years ago. I go on consulting
This mirror that is no longer mine
For as much brisk vacancy as is to be
My portion this time. And the vase is always full   335
Because there is only just so much room
And it accommodates everything. The sample
One sees is not to be taken as
Merely that, but as everything as it
May be imagined outside time—not as a gesture   340
But as all, in the refined, assimilable state.
But what is this universe the porch of
As it veers in and out, back and forth,
Refusing to surround us and still the only
Thing we can see? Love once   345
Tipped the scales but now is shadowed, invisible,
Though mysteriously present, around somewhere.
But we know it cannot be sandwiched
Between two adjacent moments, that its windings
Lead nowhere except to further tributaries   350
And that these empty themselves into a vague
Sense of something that can never be known
Even though it seems likely that each of us
Knows what it is and is capable of
Communicating it to the other. But the look   355
Some wear as a sign makes one want to
Push forward ignoring the apparent
Naïveté of the attempt, not caring
That no one is listening, since the light
Has been lit once and for all in their eyes   360
And is present, unimpaired, a permanent anomaly,
Awake and silent. On the surface of it
There seems no special reason why that light
Should be focused by love, or why
The city falling with its beautiful suburbs   365
Into space always less clear, less defined,
Should read as the support of its progress,
The easel upon which the drama unfolded
To its own satisfaction and to the end
Of our dreaming, as we had never imagined   370

8. In chemistry, a solid deposit separated from a solution.

It would end, in worn daylight with the painted
Promise showing through as a gage, a bond.
This nondescript, never-to-be defined daytime is
The secret of where it takes place
And we can no longer return to the various   375
Conflicting statements gathered, lapses of memory
Of the principal witnesses. All we know
Is that we are a little early, that
Today has that special, lapidary[9]
Todayness that the sunlight reproduces   380
Faithfully in casting twig-shadows on blithe
Sidewalks. No previous day would have been like this.
I used to think they were all alike,
That the present always looked the same to everybody
But this confusion drains away as one   385
Is always cresting into one's present.
Yet the "poetic," straw-colored space
Of the long corridor that leads back to the painting,
Its darkening opposite—is this
Some figment of "art," not to be imagined   390
As real, let alone special? Hasn't it too its lair
In the present we are always escaping from
And falling back into, as the waterwheel of days
Pursues its uneventful, even serene course?
I think it is trying to say it is today   395
And we must get out of it even as the public
Is pushing through the museum now so as to
Be out by closing time. You can't live there.
The gray glaze of the past attacks all know-how:
Secrets of wash and finish that took a lifetime   400
To learn and are reduced to the status of
Black-and-white illustrations in a book where colorplates
Are rare. That is, all time
Reduces to no special time. No one
Alludes to the change; to do so might   405
Involve calling attention to oneself
Which would augment the dread of not getting out
Before having seen the whole collection
(Except for the sculptures in the basement:
They are where they belong).   410
Our time gets to be veiled, compromised
By the portrait's will to endure. It hints at
Our own, which we were hoping to keep hidden.
We don't need paintings or
Doggerel written by mature poets when   415
The explosion is so precise, so fine.
Is there any point even in acknowledging
The existence of all that? Does it
Exist? Certainly the leisure to
Indulge stately pastimes doesn't,   420

---

9. Pertaining to an inscription in stone, hence condensed or concentrated.

Any more. Today has no margins, the event arrives
Flush with its edges, is of the same substance,
Indistinguishable. "Play" is something else;
It exists, in a society specifically
Organized as a demonstration of itself.   425
There is no other way, and those assholes
Who would confuse everything with their mirror games
Which seem to multiply stakes and possibilities, or
At least confuse issues by means of an investing
Aura that would corrode the architecture   430
Of the whole in a haze of suppressed mockery,
Are beside the point. They are out of the game,
Which doesn't exist until they are out of it.
It seems like a very hostile universe
But as the principle of each individual thing is   435
Hostile to, exists at the expense of all the others
As philosophers have often pointed out, at least
This thing, the mute, undivided present,
Has the justification of logic, which
In this instance isn't a bad thing   440
Or wouldn't be, if the way of telling
Didn't somehow intrude, twisting the end result
Into a caricature of itself. This always
Happens, as in the game where
A whispered phrase passed around the room   445
Ends up as something completely different.
It is the principle that makes works of art so unlike
What the artist intended. Often he finds
He has omitted the thing he started out to say
In the first place. Seduced by flowers,   450
Explicit pleasures, he blames himself (though
Secretly satisfied with the result), imagining
He had a say in the matter and exercised
An option of which he was hardly conscious,
Unaware that necessity circumvents such resolutions   455
So as to create something new
For itself, that there is no other way,
That the history of creation proceeds according to
Stringent laws, and that things
Do get done in this way, but never the things   460
We set out to accomplish and wanted so desperately
To see come into being. Parmigianino
Must have realized this as he worked at his
Life-obstructing task. One is forced to read
The perfectly plausible accomplishment of a purpose   465
Into the smooth, perhaps even bland (but so
Enigmatic) finish. Is there anything
To be serious about beyond this otherness
That gets included in the most ordinary
Forms of daily activity, changing everything   470
Slightly and profoundly, and tearing the matter
Of creation, any creation, not just artistic creation

Out of our hands, to install it on some monstrous, near
Peak, too close to ignore, too far
For one to intervene? This otherness, this   475
"Not-being-us" is all there is to look at
In the mirror, though no one can say
How it came to be this way. A ship
Flying unknown colors has entered the harbor.
You are allowing extraneous matters   480
To break up your day, cloud the focus
Of the crystal ball. Its scene drifts away
Like vapor scattered on the wind. The fertile
Thought-associations that until now came
So easily, appear no more, or rarely. Their   485
Colorings are less intense, washed out
By autumn rains and winds, spoiled, muddied,
Given back to you because they are worthless.
Yet we are such creatures of habit that their
Implications are still around en permanence, confusing   490
Issues. To be serious only about sex
Is perhaps one way, but the sands are hissing
As they approach the beginning of the big slide
Into what happened. This past
Is now here: the painter's   495
Reflected face, in which we linger, receiving
Dreams and inspirations on an unassigned
Frequency, but the hues have turned metallic,
The curves and edges are not so rich. Each person
Has one big theory to explain the universe   500
But it doesn't tell the whole story
And in the end it is what is outside him
That matters, to him and especially to us
Who have been given no help whatever
In decoding our own man-size quotient and must rely   505
On second-hand knowledge. Yet I know
That no one else's taste is going to be
Any help, and might as well be ignored.
Once it seemed so perfect—gloss on the fine
Freckled skin, lips moistened as though about to part   510
Releasing speech, and the familiar look
Of clothes and furniture that one forgets.
This could have been our paradise: exotic
Refuge within an exhausted world, but that wasn't
In the cards, because it couldn't have been   515
The point. Aping naturalness may be the first step
Toward achieving an inner calm
But it is the first step only, and often
Remains a frozen gesture of welcome etched
On the air materializing behind it,   520
A convention. And we have really
No time for these, except to use them
For kindling. The sooner they are burnt up
The better for the roles we have to play.

Therefore I beseech you, withdraw that hand,   525
Offer it no longer as shield or greeting,
The shield of a greeting, Francesco:
There is room for one bullet in the chamber:
Our looking through the wrong end
Of the telescope as you fall back at a speed   530
Faster than that of light to flatten ultimately
Among the features of the room, an invitation
Never mailed, the "it was all a dream"
Syndrome, though the "all" tells tersely
Enough how it wasn't. Its existence   535
Was real, though troubled, and the ache
Of this waking dream can never drown out
The diagram still sketched on the wind,
Chosen, meant for me and materialized
In the disguising radiance of my room.   540
We have seen the city; it is the gibbous[1]
Mirrored eye of an insect. All things happen
On its balcony and are resumed within,
But the action is the cold, syrupy flow
Of a pageant. One feels too confined,   545
Sifting the April sunlight for clues,
In the mere stillness of the ease of its
Parameter.[2] The hand holds no chalk
And each part of the whole falls off
And cannot know it knew, except   550
Here and there, in cold pockets
Of remembrance, whispers out of time.

                                                               1975

Myrtle

How funny your name would be
if you could follow it back to where
the first person thought of saying it,
naming himself that, or maybe
some other persons thought of it   5
and named that person. It would
be like following a river to its source,
which would be impossible. Rivers have no source.
They just automatically appear at a place
where they get wider, and soon a real   10
river comes along, with fish and debris,
regal as you please, and someone
has already given it a name: St. Benno[1]

1. Irregularly rounded or convex (for example, the
form of the moon between half moon and full
moon).
2. A constant whose values characterize the vari-
ables in a system.

1. St. Benno (d. 940), long venerated, although
his cult has never been formally recognized, was
born to a noble family and became a hermit on
Mount Etzel in Switzerland.

(saints are popular for this purpose) or, or
some other name, the name of his   15
long-lost girlfriend, who comes
at long last to impersonate that river,
on a stage, her voice clanking
like its bed, her clothing of sand
and pasted paper, a piece of real technology,   20
while all along she is thinking, I can
do what I want to do. But I want to stay here.

1996

W. S. MERWIN
b. 1927

"I started writing hymns for my father almost as soon as I could write at all, illustrating them," W. S. Merwin has said. "I recall some rather stern little pieces addressed . . . to backsliders, but I can remember too wondering whether there might not be some liberating mode." Merwin's father was a Presbyterian minister in Union, New Jersey, and Scranton, Pennsylvania, where Merwin grew up. Apart from hymn writing, he had almost no acquaintance with poetry until, on a scholarship, he entered Princeton University. There he read verse steadily and began to write with the encouragement of the poet John Berryman and the critic R. P. Blackmur. Then Merwin's extensive study of foreign languages and literatures enabled him to find work as a tutor abroad. He remained, like Ezra Pound, apart from American literary institutions and became a translator of European literature, especially medieval romance and modern Symbolist poetry.

Merwin's continuing activity as a translator has been a resource and stimulus for his own poetry. In translating two great medieval epics, the French *Song of Roland* (1963) and the Spanish *The Poem of the Cid* (1959), his object was to bring into English a diction "rough, spare, sinewy, rapid" that would transmit the directness and energy of the world of chivalric imagination. His first book, *A Masque for Janus* (1952), includes ballads, songs, and carols—often based on medieval verse forms—the slightly antique diction of which gives an air of simple mystery to poems about love, inner heroism, and death.

In later books Merwin was to draw his subjects from a more clearly contemporary context. Many of the poems in *The Drunk in the Furnace* (1960) and *The Moving Target* (1963) are about members of his family and memories of his boyhood in Scranton. A further change came with *The Lice* (1967), a volume whose brief, prophetic poems reflect Merwin's despair at that time: he believed "the future was so bleak that there was no point in writing anything at all"; what happened was that "the poems kind of pushed their way upon me when I wasn't thinking about writing." Both this despair and anger are palpable in a poem like "For a Coming Extinction." In many of these poems, and those of volumes immediately following, Merwin tries to reach below the surface of urban American experience but without the benefit of narrative or preestablished metrical forms. He speaks through humble figures, as in "Peasant: His Prayer to the Powers of This World." Or he uses the most commonplace occurrences as a point of departure for meditation: "Evening, or Daybreak." His poems quickly become parables, spoken in a voice less concerned with descriptive detail than with archetypal elements: the ways in which each evening prefigures death, each dawn the passing of time.

Of these short poems Merwin says: "What is needed for any particular nebulous unwritten hope that may become a poem is not a manipulable, more or less predictable recurring pattern, but an unduplicatable resonance, something that would be like an echo except that it is repeating no sound." Hence his unpunctuated lines of varying lengths, which seem a series of related oracular phrases, each corresponding to a breath. The poems frequently use the metaphor of a threshold or door, locating the reader at a moment between life and death or between life and a visionary afterlife. The poet is stationed at that imagined spot between the past and the present, and the present and the future. In 1973 he prepared a series of adaptations of Asian proverbs, *Asian Figures,* that reflect his continuing interest in compact meditative forms, such as Oriental rituals and prayers.

Merwin has always been concerned with absence, with what is silent, vanished, invisible, and yet real. In many of the poems gathered in his *Selected Poems* (1988) and *The Rain in the Trees* (1988), this concern focuses on forms of life endangered by ecological destruction. Merwin resides primarily in Hawaii, and his book-length narrative poem *The Folding Cliffs* (1998) explores Hawaiian history, as it gathers together, in his description, "almost all of my interests—interests in nonliterate peoples, in their and our relation to the earth, to the primal sources of things, our relation to the natural world, . . . the destruction of the earth for abstract and greedy reasons." Merwin's singular power in both shorter and longer poems is beautifully evident in his collection *The River Sound* (1999).

The Drunk in the Furnace

For a good decade
The furnace stood in the naked gully, fireless
And vacant as any hat. Then when it was
No more to them than a hulking black fossil
To erode unnoticed with the rest of the junk-hill   5
By the poisonous creek, and rapidly to be added
    To their ignorance.

    They were afterwards astonished
To confirm, one morning, a twist of smoke like a pale
Resurrection, staggering out of its chewed hole,   10
And to remark then other tokens that someone,
Cosily bolted behind the eye-holed iron
Door of the drafty burner, had there established
    His bad castle.

    Where he gets his spirits   15
It's a mystery. But the stuff keeps him musical:
Hammer-and-anvilling with poker and bottle
To his jugged bellowings, till the last groaning clang
As he collapses onto the rioting
Springs of a litter of car-seats ranged on the grates,   20
    To sleep like an iron pig.

> In their tar-paper church
> On a text about stoke-holes that are sated never
> Their Reverend lingers. They nod and hate trespassers.
> When the furnace wakes, though, all afternoon   25
> Their witless offspring flock like piped[1] rats to its siren
> Crescendo, and agape on the crumbling ridge
> > Stand in a row and learn.

1960

For the Anniversary of My Death

Every year without knowing it I have passed the day
When the last fires will wave to me
And the silence will set out
Tireless traveller
Like the beam of a lightless star   5

Then I will no longer
Find myself in life as in a strange garment
Surprised at the earth
And the love of one woman
And then shamelessness of men   10
As today writing after three days of rain
Hearing the wren sing and the falling cease
And bowing not knowing to what

1967

For a Coming Extinction

Gray whale
Now that we are sending you to The End
That great god
Tell him
That we who follow you invented forgiveness   5
And forgive nothing

I write as though you could understand
And I could say it
One must always pretend something
Among the dying   10
When you have left the seas nodding on their stalks
Empty of you

---

1. Allusion to the Pied Piper of Hamelin, whose piping lured the rats from the town; when he was not paid, he lured away the children as well.

Tell him that we were made
On another day[1]

The bewilderment will diminish like an echo   15
Winding along your inner mountains
Unheard by us
And find its way out
Leaving behind it the future
Dead   20
And ours

When you will not see again
The whale calves trying the light
Consider what you will find in the black garden
And its court   25
The sea cows the Great Auks the gorillas[2]
The irreplaceable hosts ranged countless
And fore-ordaining as stars
Our sacrifices
Join your word to theirs   30
Tell him
That it is we who are important

                                            1967

Losing a Language

A breath leaves the sentences and does not come back
yet the old still remember something that they could say

but they know now that such things are no longer believed
and the young have fewer words

many of the things the words were about   5
no longer exist

the noun for standing in mist by a haunted tree
the verb for I

the children will not repeat
the phrases their parents speak   10

somebody has persuaded them
that it is better to say everything differently

---

1. In Genesis 1, God creates humans on the sixth
day and gives them dominion over all other creatures in the world. The animals had been created
on the fifth and sixth days.

2. Animals extinct or endangered. Sea cows are
large walruslike animals. The great auks were large
flightless sea birds.

so that they can be admired somewhere
farther and farther away

where nothing that is here is known   15
we have little to say to each other

we are wrong and dark
in the eyes of the new owners

the radio is incomprehensible
the day is glass   20

when there is a voice at the door it is foreign
everywhere instead of a name there is a lie

nobody has seen it happening
nobody remembers

this is what the words were made   25
to prophesy

here are the extinct feathers
here is the rain we saw

                                                                       1988

Lament for the Makers[1]

I that all through my early days
I remember well was always
        the youngest of the company
        save for one sister after me

from the time when I was able   5
to walk under the dinner table
        and be punished for that promptly
        because its leaves could fall on me

father and mother overhead
who they talked with and what they said   10
        were mostly clouds that knew already
        directions far too old for me

at school I skipped a grade so that
whatever I did after that

1. The title and stanza form of this poem are taken from the Scots poet William Dunbar (c. 1460–c. 1520), whose "Lament for the Makers" mourns the passing of fellow poets and confesses the poet's own fear of mortality. Merwin's poem likewise commemorates the passing of fellow poets, a number of whom are represented in this anthology and can be found by consulting the index. Only the names of those poets not represented in this volume will be annotated here.

each year everyone would be   15
older and hold it up to me

at college many of my friends
were returning veterans
    equipped with an authority
    I admired and they treated me   20

as the kid some years below them
so I married half to show them
    and listened with new vanity
    when I heard it said to me

how young I was and what a shock   25
I was the youngest on the block
    I thought I had it coming to me
    and I believe it mattered to me

and seemed my own and there to stay
for a while then came the day   30
    I was in another country
    other older friends around me

my youth by then taken for granted
and found that it had been supplanted
    the notes in some anthology   35
    listed persons born after me

how long had that been going on
how could I be not quite so young
    and not notice and nobody
    even bother to inform me   40

though my fond hopes were taking longer
than I had hoped when I was younger
    a phrase that came more frequently
    to suggest itself to me

but the secret was still there   45
safe in the unprotected air
    that breath that in its own words only
    sang when I was a child to me

and caught me helpless to convey it
with nothing but the words to say it   50
    though it was those words completely
    and they rang it was clear to me

with a changeless overtone
I have listened for since then
    hearing that note endlessly   55
    vary every time beyond me

trying to find where it comes from
and to what words it may come
    and forever after be
    present for the thought kept at me   60

that my mother and every day
of our lives would slip away
    like the summer and suddenly
    all would have been taken from me

but that presence I had known   65
sometimes in words would not be gone
    and if it spoke even once for me
    it would stay there and be me

however few might choose those words
for listening to afterwards   70
    there I would be awake to see
    a world that looked unchanged to me

I suppose that was what I thought
young as I was then and that note
    sang from the words of somebody   75
    in my twenties I looked around me

to all the poets who were then
living and whose lines had been
    sustenance and company
    and a light for years to me   80

I found the portraits of their faces
first in the rows of oval spaces
    in Oscar Williams' Treasury[2]
    so they were settled long before me

and they would always be the same   85
in that distance of their fame
    affixed in immortality
    during their lifetimes while around me

all was woods seen from a train
no sooner glimpsed than gone again   90
    but those immortals constantly
    in some measure reassured me

then first there was Dylan Thomas
from the White Horse[3] taken from us
    to the brick wall I woke to see   95
    for years across the street from me

---

2. Oscar Williams's A Little Treasury of Modern Poetry (1950), an anthology containing some of the major English and American modernists, featured on its cover oval portraits of the poets represented.

3. A bar in Greenwich Village, New York City. Thomas (1914–1953), a Welsh poet, died of acute alcoholism while in New York City directing rehearsals of his play Under Milk Wood.

then word of the death of Stevens
brought a new knowledge of silence
 the nothing but there finally
 the sparrow saying *Be thou me*   100

how long his long auroras had
played on the darkness overhead
 since I looked up from my Shelley
 and Arrowsmith[4] first showed him to me

and not long from his death until   105
Edwin Muir[5] had fallen still
 that fine bell of the latter day
 not well heard yet it seems to me

Sylvia Plath then took her own
direction into the unknown   110
 from her last stars and poetry
 in the house a few blocks from me

Williams[6] a little afterwards
was carried off by the black rapids
 that flowed through Paterson as he   115
 said and their rushing sound is in me

that was the time that gathered Frost[7]
into the dark where he was lost
 to us but from too far to see
 his voice keeps coming back to me   120

at the number he had uttered
to the driver a last word
 then that watchful and most lonely
 wanderer whose words went with me

everywhere Elizabeth   125
Bishop lay alone in death
 they were leaving the party early
 our elders it came home to me

but the needle moved among us
taking always by surprise   130
 flicking by too fast to see
 to touch a friend born after me

4. William Arrowsmith (b. 1924), scholar and translator, was a classmate and friend of Merwin's when they were undergraduates at Princeton University. "Be Thou Me" appears in canto VI of "It Must Change" from Wallace Stevens's long poem *Notes Toward a Supreme Fiction*: "Bethou me, said sparrow, to the crackled blade, / And you, and you, bethou me as you blow, / When in my coppice you behold me be." Stevens (1879–1955) is echoing canto V of Percy Bysshe Shelley (1792–1822), "Ode to the West Wind:" "Be thou, Spirit Fierce, / My spirit. Be thou me, impetuous one!" Another of Stevens's long poems is titled "The Auroras of Autumn."
5. Scottish poet (1887–1963).
6. William Carlos Williams (1883–1963), American modernist poet whose work includes the long poem *Paterson*.
7. Robert Frost (1874–1963), American poet whose works include "Stopping by Woods on a Snowy Evening."

and James Wright by his darkened river
heard the night heron pass over
    took his candle down the frosty   135
    road and disappeared before me

Howard Moss[8] had felt the gnawing
at his name and found that nothing
    made it better he was funny
    even so about it to me   140

Graves[9] in his nineties lost the score
forgot that he had died before
    found his way back innocently
    who once had been a guide to me

Nemerov[1] sadder than his verse   145
said a new year could not be worse
    then the black flukes of agony
    went down leaving the words with me

Stafford[2] watched his hand catch the light
seeing that it was time to write   150
    a memento of their story
    signed and is a plain before me

then the sudden news that Ted
Roethke had been found floating dead
    in someone's pool at night but he   155
    still rises from his lines for me

and on the rimless wheel in turn
Eliot[3] spun and Jarrell was borne
    off by a car who had loved to see
    the racetrack then there came to me   160

one day the knocking at the garden
door and the news that Berryman
    from the bridge had leapt who twenty
    years before had quoted to me

the passage where *a jest* wrote Crane   165
falls from the speechless caravan[4]
    with a wave to bones and Henry[5]
    and to all that he had told me

---

8. American poet (1922–1987).
9. Robert Graves (1895–1985), poet and translator whose work includes *The White Goddess* (1944). As a young man, Merwin worked for a short time as a tutor for Graves's children.
1. Howard Nemerov (1920–1991), American poet.
2. William Stafford (1914–1993), American poet.

3. T. S. Eliot (1888–1965), American poet who became a British citizen.
4. Hart Crane (1899–1932), American poet, author of the poetic sequence *The Bridge* (1930), from which the lines in italics are taken.
5. Characters in John Berryman's *Dream Songs*, selections from which appear in this volume.

I dreamed that Auden[6] sat up in bed
but I could not catch what he said   170
   by the time he was already
   dead someone next morning told me

and Marianne Moore entered the ark
Pound[7] would say no more from the dark
   who once had helped to set me free   175
   I thought of the prose around me

and David Jones[8] would rest until
the turn of time under the hill
   but from the sleep of Arthur[9] he
   wakes an echo that follows me   180

Lowell thought the shadow skyline
coming toward him was Manhattan
   but it blacked out in the taxi
   once he read his *Notebook* to me

now Jimmy Merrill's voice is heard   185
like an aria afterward
   and we know he will never be
   old after all who spoke to me

on the cold street that last evening
of his heart that leapt at finding   190
   some yet unknown poetry
   then waved through the window to me

in that city we were born in
one by one they have all gone
   out of the time and language we   195
   had in common which have brought me

to this season after them
the best words did not keep them from
   leaving themselves finally
   as this day is going from me   200

and the clear note they were hearing
never promised anything
   but the true sound of brevity
   that will go on after me

1996

---

6. W. H. Auden (1907–1973), Anglo-American
poet.
7. Marianne Moore (1887–1972) and Ezra Pound
(1885–1972), American modernist poets.

8. Anglo-Welsh artist and poet (1895–1974).
9. The legendary King Arthur, who ruled over the
Knights of the Round Table, figures in several of
David Jones's poems and essays.

Ceremony after an Amputation

Spirits of the place who were here before I saw it
    to whom I have made such offerings as I have known how to make
    wanting from the first to approach you with recognition
    bringing for your swept ridge trees lining the wind with seedlings
    that have grown now to become these long wings in chorus   5
    where the birds assemble and settle their flying lives
    you have taught me without meaning and have lifted me up
    without talk or promise and again and again reappeared to me
    unmistakable and changing and unpronounceable as a face

dust of the time a day in late spring after the silk of rain   10
    had fallen softly through the night and after the green morning
    the afternoon floating brushed with gold and then the sounds
    of machines erupting across the valley and elbowing up the slopes
    pushing themselves forward to occupy you to be more of you
    who remain the untouched silence through which they are passing 15
    I try to hear you remembering that we are not separate
    to find you who cannot be lost or elsewhere or incomplete

nature of the solitary machine coming into the story
    from the minds that conceived you and the hands that first conjured up
    the phantom of you in fine lines on the drawing board   20
    you for whom function is all the good that exists
    you to whom I have come with nothing but purpose
    a purpose of my own as though it was something we shared
    you that were pried from the earth without anyone
    consulting you and were carried off burned beaten metamorphosed 25
    according to plans and lives to which you owed nothing

let us be at peace with each other let peace be what is between us
    and you now single vanished part of my left hand bit of bone finger-
        end index
    who began with me in the dark that was already my mother
    you who touched whatever I could touch of the beginning   30
    and were how I touched and who remembered the sense of it
    when I thought I had forgotten it you in whom it waited
    under your only map of one untrodden mountain
    you who did as well as we could through all the hours at the piano
    and who helped undo the bras and found our way to the treasure 35

and who held the fruit and the pages and knew how to button
    my right cuff and to wash my left ear and had taken in
    heart beats of birds and beloved faces and hair by day and by night
    fur of dogs ears of horses tongues and the latches of doors
    so that I still feel them clearly long after they are gone   40
    and lake water beside the boat one evening of an ancient summer
    and the vibration of a string over which a bow was moving
    as though the sound of the note were still playing
    and the hand of my wife found in the shallows of waking

you who in a flicker of my inattention   45
    signalled to me once only my error telling me
    of the sudden blow from the side so that I looked down
    to see not you any longer but instead a mouth
    full of blood calling after you who had already gone gone
    gone ahead into what I cannot know or reach or touch   50
    leaving in your place only the cloud of pain rising
    into the day filling the light possessing every sound
    becoming the single color and taste and direction

yet as the pain recedes and the moment of it
    you remain with me even in the missing of you   55
    small boat moving before me on the current under the daylight
    whatever you had touched and had known and took with you
    is with me now as you are when you are already there
    unseen part of me reminding me warning me
    pointing to what I cannot see never letting me forget   60
    you are my own speaking only to me going with me
    all the rest of the way telling me what is still here

                                                          2000

JAMES WRIGHT
1927–1980

"My name is James A. Wright, and I was born / Twenty-five miles from this infected grave, / In Martins Ferry, Ohio, where one slave / To Hazel-Atlas Glass became my father"; so James Wright introduced himself in an early poem, "At the Executed Murderer's Grave." The angry assertiveness in these lines suggests his embattled relations with an America he both loves and hates. This America is symbolized for him by the landscape of Ohio, in particular by Martins Ferry, just across the Ohio River from Wheeling, West Virginia, the home of Wheeling Steel and of the glass factory where his father worked for fifty years. In Wright's work this landscape is harsh evidence of the way the social world has contaminated a natural world infinitely more beautiful and self-restoring. The same social world that destroys the landscape also turns its back on those whose lives meet failure or defeat, and Wright's deep knowledge of defeat and his anger at this exclusion lead him to the murderer's grave. It is not simply that Wright sympathizes with social outcasts, but rather, as Robert Hass acutely pointed out, "the suffering of other people, particularly the lost and the derelict, is actually a part of his own emotional life. It is what he writes from, not what he writes about." As a poet who writes out of loss, Wright is elegiac, memorializing a vanished beauty and lost hopes. So deep is his sense of loss that he will sometimes identify with anyone and anything that is scarred or wounded ("I am not a happy man by talent," he once said. "Sometimes I have been very happy, but characteristically I'm a miserable son of a bitch"). Any serious reading of his work has to contend with sorting out those poems in which this identification is unthinking and sentimental, poems where Wright suggests that all forms of suffering and defeat are equal and alike. What remains in some of his best work is a curiously tough-minded tenderness at work in his exploration of despair. He admires, for example, the sumac flourishing in the Ohio landscape, its bark so tough it "will turn aside hatchets and knife blades" ("The Sumac in Ohio").

When Wright finished high school, he joined the army. In 1948 he left the military to attend Kenyon College in Ohio on the GI Bill ("I applied to several schools in Ohio," he once said, "and they all said no except Kenyon College. So I went there"). He was lucky in his teachers; at Kenyon he studied with John Crowe Ransom and, after a Fulbright scholarship to the University of Vienna, he went to the University of Washington, where he studied with the poet Theodore Roethke and also became a close friend of Richard Hugo's. At Washington he wrote a Ph.D. dissertation on Charles Dickens and received the degree in 1959. Thereafter he became a teacher himself, first at the University of Minnesota, Minneapolis (1957–64), and later at Hunter College, New York (1966–80).

From both Ransom and Roethke, Wright learned poetic form. From Ransom in particular he took what he called "the Horatian ideal" of the carefully made, unified poem. Wright would later say that were he to choose a master, he would choose the Latin poet Horace, "who was able to write humorously and kindly in flawless verse." The Horatian impulse in Wright—restrained, formal, sometimes satirical—helps hold in check a deep-seated romanticism that idealizes nature and the unconscious. His first two books, *The Green Wall* (1957), chosen to appear in the Yale Younger Poets series, and *Saint Judas* (1959), are formal and literary in style although much of their subject matter (the murderer, the lunatic, a deaf child) might be called romantic. Wright seems in these books closest to Thomas Hardy, Robert Frost, and Edwin Arlington Robinson. But in the 1960s, like a great many other American poets, he moved away from traditional forms, loosened his poetic organization, and began to depend heavily on what his fellow poet Robert Bly called "the deep image." Wright had been translating the work of Spanish poets often associated with surrealism— Pablo Neruda, César Vallejo, and Juan Ramón Jiménez—as well as the German Georg Trakl (whom he translated in collaboration with Robert Bly), and he took from them, in part, a reliance on the power of a poetic image to evoke association deep within the unconscious. He followed his volume *The Branch Will Not Break* (1963) with two books, *Shall We Gather at the River* (1968) and *Two Citizens* (1974), in which he began to overwork certain images ("stone," "dark"), as if repetition were a substitute for clarity. Some of the poems in these books succeed in carrying us into areas of experience that resist the discursive, but the effect of a number of poems is to exclude conscious intelligence, to celebrate "whatever is not mind," as Robert Hass has pointed out. It is as if Wright responded to the scarred landscape outside (and inside) him by fleeing to an inwardness so deep it could not partake of thought or expression.

But Wright's love of clarity and form and his ability to see through pretensions (including his own) resurface in *Moments of the Italian Summer* (1976), *To a Blossoming Pear Tree* (1977), and in his last, posthumous collection, *This Journey* (1982). Restored to a unity of thinking and feeling, many of the poems in these books convey the flawed beauty of the world with a loving and witty tenderness. He often writes with particular feeling about the creatures of the world—finches, lizards, hermit crabs—whose liveliness and fragility touch him (in this and other regards his work has been important to the poet Mary Oliver). In "A Finch Sitting Out a Windstorm," his final portrait of the finch suggests admiration of its stubborness in the face of loss: "But his face is as battered / As Carmen Basilio's. / He never listens / To me."

Though the poems of his final book do not abandon the anger he feels thinking of the ruined landscapes of Ohio, the European setting of many of the poems extends his sense of ruin into a knowledge of how time chips away at all human creation, with or without the help of men and women. For a man who claimed to be constitutionally unhappy, the poems of *This Journey* suggest that before his death from cancer a deep happiness took him by surprise. We turn to Wright's work for its fierce understanding of defeat, for its blend of American speech rhythms with the formal music of poetry, and for the loveliness he finds in the imperfect and neglected. Accustomed to expect the worst, he had an enduring capacity to be astonished by this loveliness, as in this childhood memory of a trip to the icehouse with his father: "We stood and breathed the rising steam of that amazing winter, and carried away in our wagon the immense fifty-pound diamond, while the old man chipped us each a jagged little chunk and then walked behind us, his hands so calm they were trembling for us, trembling with exquisite care" ("The Ice House").

Autumn Begins in Martins Ferry, Ohio

In the Shreve High football stadium,
I think of Polacks nursing long beers in Tiltonsville,
And gray faces of Negroes in the blast furnace at Benwood,[1]
And the ruptured night watchman of Wheeling Steel,
Dreaming of heroes.   5

All the proud fathers are ashamed to go home.
Their women cluck like starved pullets,[2]
Dying for love.

Therefore,
Their sons grow suicidally beautiful   10
At the beginning of October,
And gallop terribly against each other's bodies.

                                                                          1963

To the Evening Star: Central Minnesota

Under the water tower at the edge of town
A huge Airedale ponders a long ripple
In the grass fields beyond.
Miles off, a whole grove silently
Flies up into the darkness.   5
One light comes on in the sky,
One lamp on the prairie.

Beautiful daylight of the body, your hands carry seashells.
West of this wide plain,
Animals wilder than ours   10
Come down from the green mountains in the darkness.
Now they can see you, they know
The open meadows are safe.

                                                                          1963

1. A town south of Martins Ferry, where the Wheeling Steel Works are located. Tiltonsville is a town in far east Ohio, north of Martins Ferry.
2. Young hens.

A Blessing

Just off the highway to Rochester, Minnesota,
Twilight bounds softly forth on the grass.
And the eyes of those two Indian ponies
Darken with kindness.
They have come gladly out of the willows   5
To welcome my friend and me.
We step over the barbed wire into the pasture
Where they have been grazing all day, alone.
They ripple tensely, they can hardly contain their happiness
That we have come.   10
They bow shyly as wet swans. They love each other.
There is no loneliness like theirs.
At home once more,
They begin munching the young tufts of spring in the darkness.
I would like to hold the slenderer one in my arms,   15
For she has walked over to me
And nuzzled my left hand.
She is black and white,
Her mane falls wild on her forehead,
And the light breeze moves me to caress her long ear   20
That is delicate as the skin over a girl's wrist.
Suddenly I realize
That if I stepped out of my body I would break
Into blossom.

                                                                      1963

A Centenary Ode: Inscribed to Little Crow, Leader of the Sioux Rebellion in Minnesota, 1862[1]

I had nothing to do with it. I was not here.
I was not born.
In 1862, when your hotheads
Raised hell from here to South Dakota,
My own fathers scattered into West Virginia   5
And southern Ohio.
My family fought the Confederacy
And fought the Union.[2]
None of them got killed.
But for all that, it was not my fathers   10
Who murdered you.
Not much.

I don't know
Where the fathers of Minneapolis finalized

---

1. Under Little Crow, a group of Sioux attacked and killed more than eight hundred settlers and soldiers in Minnesota. They were eventually routed by federal troops. About a month later, Little Crow, while foraging for food, was shot by white farmers. 2. During the Civil War, members of Wright's family fought on both sides of the conflict.

Your flayed carcass. 15
Little Crow, true father
Of my dark America,
When I close my eyes I lose you among
Old loneliness.
My family were a lot of singing drunks and good carpenters. 20
We had brothers who loved one another no matter what they did.
And they did plenty.

I think they would have run like hell from your Sioux.
And when you caught them you all would have run like hell
From the Confederacy and from the Union 25
Into the hills and hunted for a few things,
Some bull-cat under the stones, a gar³ maybe,
If you were hungry, and if you were happy,
Sunfish and corn.

If only I knew where to mourn you, 30
I would surely mourn.

But I don't know.

I did not come here only to grieve
For my people's defeat.
The troops of the Union, who won, 35
Still outnumber us.
Old Paddy Beck, my great-uncle, is dead
At the old soldiers' home near Tiffen, Ohio.
He got away with every last stitch
Of his uniform, save only 40
The dress trousers.

Oh all around us,
The hobo jungles of America grow wild again.
The pick handles bloom like your skinned spine.
I don't even know where 45
My own grave is.

1971

With the Shell of a Hermit Crab

*Lugete, O Veneres Cupidinesque*¹
—Catullus

This lovely little life whose toes
Touched the white sand from side to side,

3. Long pikelike freshwater fish. "Bull cat": cat-fish.
1. Mourn, O Venuses and Cupids (Latin). The

opening line of Catullus's "Poem 3," a mock-elegy on the death of his mistress's bird.

How delicately no one knows,
Crept from his loneliness, and died.

From deep waters long miles away   5
He wandered, looking for his name,
And all he found was you and me,
A quick life and a candle flame.

Today, you happen to be gone.
I sit here in the raging hell,   10
The city of the dead, alone,
Holding a little empty shell.

I peer into his tiny face.
It looms too huge for me to bear.
Two blocks away the sea gives place   15
To river. Both are everywhere.

I reach out and flick out the light.
Darkly I touch his fragile scars,
So far away, so delicate,
Stars in a wilderness of stars.   20

                                                        1977

The Journey

Anghiari[1] is medieval, a sleeve sloping down
A steep hill, suddenly sweeping out
To the edge of a cliff, and dwindling.
But far up the mountain, behind the town,
We too were swept out, out by the wind,   5
Alone with the Tuscan grass.

Wind had been blowing across the hills
For days, and everything now was graying gold
With dust, everything we saw, even
Some small children scampering along a road,   10
Twittering Italian to a small caged bird.
We sat beside them to rest in some brushwood,
And I leaned down to rinse the dust from my face.

I found the spider web there, whose hinges
Reeled heavily and crazily with the dust,   15
Whole mounds and cemeteries of it, sagging
And scattering shadows among shells and wings.
And then she stepped into the center of air
Slender and fastidious, the golden hair
Of daylight along her shoulders, she poised there,   20
While ruins crumbled on every side of her.

---

1. Village in Tuscany, a province in western Italy.

Free of the dust, as though a moment before
She had stepped inside the earth, to bathe herself.

I gazed, close to her, till at last she stepped
Away in her own good time.   25

Many men
Have searched all over Tuscany and never found
What I found there, the heart of the light
Itself shelled and leaved, balancing
On filaments themselves falling. The secret   30
Of this journey is to let the wind
Blow its dust all over your body,
To let it go on blowing, to step lightly, lightly
All the way through your ruins, and not to lose Any
sleep over the dead, who surely   35
Will bury their own, don't worry.

1982

PHILIP LEVINE
b. 1928

In one of his poems, Philip Levine imagines a former life "as a small, quick fox," who
stands "in the pathway shouting and refusing / to budge, feeling the dignity / of the
small creature menaced / by the many and larger" ("The Fox"). This self-portrait has
Levine's characteristic humor, but it aptly renders his deep, even stubborn, sympathy
with ordinary men and women and his equally stubborn antipathy toward those who
look down on ordinary life. Levine shares the faith of his favorite poet, Walt Whitman,
in an inclusive, democratic poetry, and, with Whitman, he might boast he is "one of
the roughs."

Levine was born to a Jewish family in Detroit, Michigan, and began factory work
at fourteen, during the war years. He continued to work while he attended Wayne
(now Wayne State) University in Detroit and has held what he calls "a succession of
stupid jobs"—working in a bottling corporation, for Cadillac, for Chevrolet Gear and
Axle, and for Wyandotte Chemical Company. At one point in his life he also trained
as a boxer. In 1957 he received an M.F.A. from the University of Iowa, where John
Berryman and Robert Lowell were his teachers. In 1958 he moved to California and
taught for many years at California State University at Fresno, where his students
have included Sherley Ann Williams, David St. John, Luis Omar Salinas, and Gary
Soto. In the mid-1960s, he went to Spain for the first time and felt "when I looked
at the Spanish landscape I was looking at a part of myself. . . . In a year I began to
become Catalan in a small way." He has since edited and translated the work of some
Spanish poets. At present Levine teaches the fall semester at Tufts University in
Massachusetts.

His fellow poet Galway Kinnell once suggested that Levine "used to hold something
back as if for fear poetry would betray him into tenderness. In his recent poems, it
has done exactly that." Although an anger at society energizes many Levine poems—
including the title poem of his book *They Feed They Lion* (1972), a response to the
1967 riots in his native Detroit—his more than ten books of poetry demonstrate a

wide range of feeling. At heart, he is a narrative poet, even in his brief lyrics, like Thomas Hardy or Robert Penn Warren—both of whom he admires. His stories most often tell of loss and remembrance, and the elegiac strain in Levine is one source of his tenderness. Feeling himself in a world where "No One Remembers" (the title of one of his poems), where life is characterized by impermanence, his poems re-create the people, landscapes, and events that make up *The Names of the Lost* (1976), the title of one of his collections. Several of the poems from his books, *A Walk with Tom Jefferson* (1988), *What Work Is* (1991), *The Simple Truth* (1994), and *The Mercy* (1999), show Levine using several of his gifts—his narrative skill, his affection and respect for the ordinary person, his acute sense of place—with increased ambition and rhythmic power.

With its rapid motion between the colloquial and the lyrical, Levine's best work has a distinctively gritty radiance. A strong, physical sense grounds his powerful nostalgia, giving us a world we can see and touch. Levine calls himself a romantic, and one of the dangers in his work is its tendency to inflate experience. What saves him from such inflation is a lively, subversive comic sense often directed at himself. His memorable poems are energetic; they vary the stresses of syntax against the short, trimeter line in which he often composes and accumulate power as they move along. But Levine's lines can sometimes seem arbitrary, as if what we really had was prose broken into pieces. In the work of the poets he most admires, Levine argues, the failures do not matter—all that matters is the genuine poems. His own work can be uneven, but his best poems rise out of a common world lit with energy and feeling.

Animals Are Passing from Our Lives

It's wonderful how I jog
on four honed-down ivory toes
my massive buttocks slipping
like oiled parts with each light step.

I'm to market. I can smell   5
the sour, grooved block, I can smell
the blade that opens the hole
and the pudgy white fingers

that shake out the intestines
like a hankie. In my dreams   10
the snouts drool on the marble,
suffering children, suffering flies,

suffering the consumers
who won't meet their steady eyes
for fear they could see. The boy   15
who drives me along believes

that any moment I'll fall
on my side and drum my toes
like a typewriter or squeal
and shit like a new housewife   20

discovering television,
or that I'll turn like a beast
cleverly to hook his teeth
with my teeth. No. Not this pig.

1968

Detroit Grease Shop Poem

Four bright steel crosses,
universal joints,[1] plucked
out of the burlap sack—
"the heart of the drive train,"
the book says. Stars   5
on Lemon's wooden palm,
stars that must be capped,
rolled, and annointed,
that have their orders
and their commands as he   10
has his.
            Under the blue
hesitant light another day
at Automotive
in the city of dreams.   15
We're all here to count
and be counted, Lemon,
Rosie, Eugene, Luis,
and me, too young to know
this is for keeps, pinning   20
on my apron, rolling up
my sleeves.
            The roof leaks
from yesterday's rain,
the waters gather above us   25
waiting for one mistake.
When a drop falls on Lemon's
corded arm, he looks at it
as though it were something
rare or mysterious   30
like a drop of water or
a single lucid meteor
fallen slowly from
nowhere and burning on
his skin like a tear.   35

1972

---

1. Shaft couplings capable of transmitting rotation from one shaft to another.

They Feed They Lion

Out of burlap sacks, out of bearing butter,
Out of black bean and wet slate bread,
Out of the acids of rage, the candor of tar,
Out of creosote,[1] gasoline, drive shafts, wooden dollies,
They Lion grow.   5
                    Out of the gray hills
Of industrial barns, out of rain, out of bus ride,
West Virginia to Kiss My Ass, out of buried aunties,
Mothers hardening like pounded stumps, out of stumps,
Out of the bones' need to sharpen and the muscles' to stretch,   10
They Lion grow.
                    Earth is eating trees, fence posts,
Gutted cars, earth is calling in her little ones,
"Come home, Come home!" From pig balls,
From the ferocity of pig driven to holiness,   15
From the furred ear and the full jowl come
The repose of the hung belly, from the purpose
They Lion grow.
                    From the sweet glues of the trotters[2]
Come the sweet kinks of the fist, from the full flower   20
Of the hams the thorax[3] of caves,
From "Bow Down" come "Rise Up,"
Come they Lion from the reeds of shovels,
The grained arm that pulls the hands,
They Lion grow.   25
                    From my five arms and all my hands,
From all my white sins forgiven, they feed,
From my car passing under the stars,
They Lion, from my children inherit,
From the oak turned to a wall, they Lion,   30
From they sack and they belly opened
And all that was hidden burning on the oil-stained earth
They feed they Lion and he comes.

                                                          1972

Starlight

My father stands in the warm evening
on the porch of my first house.
I am four years old and growing tired.
I see his head among the stars,
the glow of his cigarette, redder   5
than the summer moon riding

---

1. Oily liquid distilled from wood tar, used as a   2. Cooked pigs' feet.
wood preservative.   3. Chest cavity.

low over the old neighborhood. We
are alone, and he asks me if I am happy.
"Are you happy?" I cannot answer.
I do not really understand the word,   10
and the voice, my father's voice, is not
his voice, but somehow thick and choked,
a voice I have not heard before, but
heard often since. He bends and passes
a thumb beneath each of my eyes.   15
The cigarette is gone, but I can smell
the tiredness that hangs on his breath.
He has found nothing, and he smiles
and holds my head with both his hands.
Then he lifts me to his shoulder,   20
and now I too am there among the stars,
as tall as he. Are you happy? I say.
He nods in answer, Yes! oh yes! oh yes!
And in that new voice he says nothing,
holding my head tight against his head,   25
his eyes closed up against the starlight,
as though those tiny blinking eyes
of light might find a tall, gaunt child
holding his child against the promises
of autumn, until the boy slept   30
never to waken in that world again.

1979

Fear and Fame

Half an hour to dress, wide rubber hip boots,
gauntlets to the elbow, a plastic helmet
like a knight's but with a little glass window
that kept steaming over, and a respirator
to save my smoke-stained lungs. I would descend   5
step by slow step into the dim world
of the pickling tank and there prepare
the new solutions from the great carboys
of acids lowered to me on ropes—all from a recipe
I shared with nobody and learned from Frank O'Mera   10
before he went off to the bars on Vernor Highway
to drink himself to death. A gallon of hydrochloric
steaming from the wide glass mouth, a dash
of pale nitric to bubble up, sulphuric to calm,
metals for sweeteners, cleansers for salts,   15
until I knew the burning stew was done.
Then to climb back, step by stately step, the adventurer
returned to the ordinary blinking lights
of the swingshift at Feinberg and Breslin's
First-Rate Plumbing and Plating with a message   20

from the kingdom of fire. Oddly enough
no one welcomed me back, and I'd stand
fully armored as the downpour of cold water
rained down on me and the smoking traces puddled
at my feet like so much milk and melting snow.   25
Then to disrobe down to my work pants and shirt,
my black street shoes and white cotton socks,
to reassume my nickname, strap on my Bulova,
screw back my wedding ring, and with tap water
gargle away the bitterness as best I could.   30
For fifteen minutes or more I'd sit quietly
off to the side of the world as the women
polished the tubes and fixtures to a burnished purity
hung like Christmas ornaments on the racks
pulled steadily toward the tanks I'd cooked.   35
Ahead lay the second cigarette, held in a shaking hand,
as I took into myself the sickening heat to quell heat,
a lunch of two Genoa salami sandwiches and Swiss cheese
on heavy peasant bread baked by my Aunt Tsipie,
and a third cigarette to kill the taste of the others.   40
Then to arise and dress again in the costume
of my trade for the second time that night, stiffened
by the knowledge that to descend and rise up
from the other world merely once in eight hours is half
what it takes to be known among women and men.   45

1991

The Simple Truth

I bought a dollar and a half's worth of small red potatoes,
took them home, boiled them in their jackets
and ate them for dinner with a little butter and salt.
Then I walked through the dried fields
on the edge of town. In middle June the light   5
hung on in the dark furrows at my feet,
and in the mountain oaks overhead the birds
were gathering for the night, the jays and mockers
squawking back and forth, the finches still darting
into the dusty light. The woman who sold me   10
the potatoes was from Poland; she was someone
out of my childhood in a pink spangled sweater and sunglasses
praising the perfection of all her fruits and vegetables
at the road-side stand and urging me to taste
even the pale, raw sweet corn trucked all the way,   15
she swore, from New Jersey. "Eat, eat," she said,
"Even if you don't I'll say you did."
                         Some things
you know all your life. They are so simple and true
they must be said without elegance, meter and rhyme,   20

they must be laid on the table beside the salt shaker,
the glass of water, the absence of light gathering
in the shadows of picture frames, they must be
naked and alone, they must stand for themselves.
My friend Henri and I arrived at this together in 1965   25
before I went away, before he began to kill himself,
and the two of us to betray our love. Can you taste
what I'm saying? It is onions or potatoes, a pinch
of simple salt, the wealth of melting butter, it is obvious,
it stays in the back of your throat like a truth   30
you never uttered because the time was always wrong,
it stays there for the rest of your life, unspoken,
made of that dirt we call earth, the metal we call salt,
in a form we have no words for, and you live on it.

1996

ANNE SEXTON
1928–1974

Anne Sexton's first book of poems, *To Bedlam and Part Way Back* (1960), was published at a time when the label *confessional* came to be attached to poems more frankly
autobiographical than had been usual in American verse. For Sexton the term *confessional* is particularly apt. Although she had abandoned the Roman Catholicism into
which she was born, her poems enact something analogous to preparing for and
receiving religious absolution.

Sexton's own confessions were to be made in terms more startling than the traditional Catholic images of her childhood. The purpose of her poems was not to analyze
or explain behavior but to make it palpable in all its ferocity of feeling. Poetry "should
be a shock to the senses. It should also hurt." This is apparent both in the themes
she chooses and the particular ways in which she chooses to exhibit her subjects.
Sexton writes about sex, illegitimacy, guilt, madness, and suicide. Her first book portrays her own mental breakdown, her time in a mental hospital, her efforts at rec-
onciliation with her young daughter and husband when she returns. Her second book,
All My Pretty Ones (1962), takes its title from *Macbeth* and refers to the death of both
her parents within three months of one another. Later books act out a continuing
debate about suicide: *Live or Die* (1966), *The Death Notebooks* (1974), and *The Awful
Rowing toward God* (1975—posthumous), titles that prefigure the time when she
took her own life (1974). And yet, as the poet's tender address to her daughter in
"Little Girl, My String Bean, My Lovely Woman" suggests, the range of Sexton's work
is wider than an obsession with death.

Sexton spoke of images as "the heart of poetry. Images come from the unconscious.
Imagination and the unconscious are one and the same." Powerful images substan-
tiate the strangeness of her own feelings and attempt to redefine experiences so as to
gain understanding, absolution, or revenge. These poems poised between, as her titles
suggest, life and death or "bedlam and part way back" are efforts at establishing a
middle ground of self-assertion, substituting surreal images for the reductive versions
of life visible to the exterior eye.

Sexton was born in 1928 in Newton, Massachusetts, and attended Garland Junior

College. She came to poetry fairly late—when she was twenty-eight, after seeing the critic I. A. Richards lecturing about the sonnet on television. In the late 1950s she attended poetry workshops in the Boston area, including Robert Lowell's poetry seminars at Boston University. One of her fellow students was Sylvia Plath, whose suicide she commemorated in a poem and whose fate she later followed. Sexton claimed that she was less influenced by Lowell's *Life Studies* than by W. D. Snodgrass's autobiographical *Heart's Needle* (1959), but certainly Lowell's support and the association with Plath left their mark on her and made it possible for her to publish. Although her career was relatively brief, she received several major literary prizes, including the Pulitzer Prize for *Live or Die* and an American Academy of Arts and Letters traveling fellowship. Her suicide came after a series of mental breakdowns.

The Truth the Dead Know

For My Mother, Born March 1902, Died March 1959
and My Father, Born February 1900, Died June 1959

Gone, I say and walk from church,
refusing the stiff procession to the grave,
letting the dead ride alone in the hearse.
It is June. I am tired of being brave.

We drive to the Cape. I cultivate   5
myself where the sun gutters from the sky,
where the sea swings in like an iron gate
and we touch. In another country people die.

My darling, the wind falls in like stones
from the whitehearted water and when we touch   10
we enter touch entirely. No one's alone.
Men kill for this, or for as much.

And what of the dead? They lie without shoes
in their stone boats. They are more like stone
than the sea would be if it stopped. They refuse   15
to be blessed, throat, eye and knucklebone.

1962

The Starry Night

That does not keep me from having a terrible
need of—shall I say the word—religion.
Then I go out at night to paint the stars.
—Vincent Van Gogh[1]
in a letter to his brother

The town does not exist
except where one black-haired tree slips

---

1. Dutch painter (1853–1890) who in his thirties went mad and finally committed suicide. This letter to his brother—his only confidant—was written in September 1888. He was painting, at the same time, *Starry Night on the Rhône.*

up like a drowned woman into the hot sky.
The town is silent. The night boils with eleven stars.
Oh starry starry night! This is how   5
I want to die.

It moves. They are all alive.
Even the moon bulges in its orange irons
to push children, like a god, from its eye.
The old unseen serpent swallows up the stars.   10
Oh starry starry night! This is how
I want to die:

into that rushing beast of the night,
sucked up by that great dragon, to split
from my life with no flag,   15
no belly,
no cry.

                                                                    1962

Sylvia's Death

for Sylvia Plath[1]

Oh Sylvia, Sylvia,
with a dead box of stones and spoons,

with two children, two meteors
wandering loose in the tiny playroom,

with your mouth into the sheet,   5
into the roofbeam, into the dumb prayer,

(Sylvia, Sylvia,
where did you go
after you wrote me
from Devonshire   10
about raising potatoes
and keeping bees?)

what did you stand by,
just how did you lie down into?

Thief!—   15
how did you crawl into,

---

1. American poet (1932–1963), friend of Sexton's
who committed suicide. Plath was living in London
with her two small children, having separated from
her husband, the poet Ted Hughes, the previous
year.

crawl down alone
into the death I wanted so badly and for so long,

the death we said we both outgrew,
the one we wore on our skinny breasts,   20

the one we talked of so often each time
we downed three extra dry martinis in Boston,

the death that talked of analysts and cures,
the death that talked like brides with plots,

the death we drank to,   25
the motives and then the quiet deed?

(In Boston
the dying
ride in cabs,
yes death again,   30
that ride home
with *our* boy.)

O Sylvia, I remember the sleepy drummer
who beat on our eyes with an old story,

how we wanted to let him come   35
like a sadist or a New York fairy

to do his job,
a necessity, a window in a wall or a crib,

and since that time he waited
under our heart, our cupboard,   40

and I see now that we store him up
year after year, old suicides

and I know at the news of your death,
a terrible taste for it, like salt.

(And me,   45
me too.
And now, Sylvia,
you again
with death again,
that ride home   50
with *our* boy.)

And I say only
with my arms stretched out into that stone place,

what is your death
but an old belonging,   55

a mole that fell out
of one of your poems?

(O friend,
while the moon's bad,
and the king's gone,   60
and the queen's at her wit's end
the bar fly ought to sing!)

O tiny mother,
you too!
O funny duchess!   65
O blonde thing!

February 17, 1963   1966

Little Girl, My String Bean, My Lovely Woman

My daughter, at eleven
(almost twelve), is like a garden.

Oh darling! Born in that sweet birthday suit
and having owned it and known it for so long,
now you must watch high noon enter—   5
noon, that ghost hour.
Oh, funny little girl—this one under a blueberry sky,
this one! How can I say that I've known
just what you know and just where you are?

It's not a strange place, this odd home   10
where your face sits in my hand
so full of distance,
so full of its immediate fever.
The summer has seized you,
as when, last month in Amalfi,[1] I saw   15
lemons as large as your desk-side globe—
that miniature map of the world—
and I could mention, too,
the market stalls of mushrooms
and garlic buds all engorged.   20
Or I think even of the orchard next door,
where the berries are done
and the apples are beginning to swell.
And once, with our first backyard,
I remember I planted an acre of yellow beans   25
we couldn't eat.

---

1. A seaport town in Campania, Italy.

Oh, little girl,
my stringbean,
how do you grow?
You grow this way.   30
You are too many to eat.

I hear
as in a dream
the conversation of the old wives
speaking of *womanhood.*   35
I remember that I heard nothing myself.
I was alone.
I waited like a target.

Let high noon enter—
the hour of the ghosts.   40
Once the Romans believed
that noon was the ghost hour,
and I can believe it, too,
under that startling sun,
and someday they will come to you,   45
someday, men bare to the waist, young Romans
at noon where they belong,
with ladders and hammers
while no one sleeps.

But before they enter   50
I will have said,
Your bones are lovely,
and before their strange hands
there was always this hand that formed.

Oh, darling, let your body in,   55
let it tie you in,
in comfort.
What I want to say, Linda,
is that women are born twice.

If I could have watched you grow   60
as a magical mother might,
if I could have seen through my magical transparent belly,
there would have been such ripening within:
your embryo,
the seed taking on its own,   65
life clapping the bedpost,
bones from the pond,
thumbs and two mysterious eyes,
the awfully human head,
the heart jumping like a puppy,   70
the important lungs,
the becoming—
while it becomes!

as it does now,
a world of its own,   75
a delicate place.

I say hello
to such shakes and knockings and high jinks,
such music, such sprouts,
such dancing-mad-bears of music,   80
such necessary sugar,
such goings-on!

Oh, little girl,
my stringbean,
how do you grow?   85
You grow this way.
You are too many to eat.

What I want to say, Linda,
is that there is nothing in your body that lies.
All that is new is telling the truth.   90
I'm here, that somebody else,
an old tree in the background.

Darling,
stand still at your door,
sure of yourself, a white stone, a good stone—   95
as exceptional as laughter
you will strike fire,
that new thing!

July 14, 1964   1966

From The Death of the Fathers[1]

2. *How We Danced*

The night of my cousin's wedding
I wore blue.   25
I was nineteen
and we danced, Father, we orbited.
We moved like angels washing themselves.
We moved like two birds on fire.
Then we moved like the sea in a jar,   30
slower and slower.
The orchestra played
"Oh how we danced on the night we were wed."
And you waltzed me like a lazy Susan
and we were dear,   35
very dear.
Now that you are laid out,

---

1. Printed here are parts 2 and 3 of a six-part sequence.

useless as a blind dog,
now that you no longer lurk,
the song rings in my head.   40
Pure oxygen was the champagne we drank
and clicked our glasses, one to one.
The champagne breathed like a skin diver
and the glasses were crystal and the bride
and groom gripped each other in sleep   45
like nineteen-thirty marathon dancers.
Mother was a belle and danced with twenty men.
You danced with me never saying a word.
Instead the serpent spoke as you held me close.
The serpent, that mocker, woke up and pressed against me   50
like a great god and we bent together
like two lonely swans.

3. The Boat

Father
(he calls himself
"old sea dog"),   55
in his yachting cap
at the wheel of the Christ-Craft,
a mahogany speedboat
named *Go Too III*,
speeds out past Cuckold's Light[2]   60
over the dark brainy blue.
I in the very back
with an orange life jacket on.
I in the dare seat.
Mother up front.   65
Her kerchief flapping.
The waves deep as whales.
(Whales in fact have been sighted.
A school two miles out of Boothbay Harbor.)[3]
It is bumpy and we are going too fast.   70
The waves are boulders that we ride upon.
I am seen and we are riding
to Pemaquid[4] or Spain.
Now the waves are higher;
they are round buildings.   75
We start to go through them
and the boat shudders.
Father is going faster.
I am wet.
I am tumbling on my seat   80
like a loose kumquat.
Suddenly
a wave that we go under.

2. A Maine lighthouse.
3. A coastal town in Maine.

4. A village near the sea in Maine.

Under. Under. Under.
We are daring the sea.   85
We have parted it.
We are scissors.
Here in the green room
the dead are very close.
Here in the pitiless green   90
where there are no keepsakes
or cathedrals an angel spoke:
You have no business.
No business here.
Give me a sign,   95
cried Father,
and the sky breaks over us.
There is air to have.
There are gulls kissing the boat.
There is the sun as big as a nose.   100
And here are the three of us
dividing our deaths,
bailing the boat
and closing out
the cold wing that has clasped us   105
this bright August day.

1972

ADRIENNE RICH
b. 1929

A childhood of reading and hearing poems taught Adrienne Rich to love the sound of words; her adult life taught her that poetry must "consciously situate itself amid political conditions." Over the years she has conducted a passionate struggle to honor these parts of herself, in her best poems brilliantly mixing what she calls "the poetry of the actual world with the poetry of sound." Extending the dialogue between art and politics she first discovered in W. B. Yeats, whose poems she read as an undergraduate at Radcliffe, her work addresses with particular power the experiences of women, experiences often omitted from history and misrepresented in literature. Our culture, she believes, is "split at the root" (to adapt the title of one of her essays); art is separated from politics and the poet's identity as a woman is separated from her art. Rich's work seeks a language that will expose and integrate these divisions in the self and in the world. To do this she has written "directly and overtly as a woman, out of a woman's body and experience," for "to take women's existence seriously as theme and source for art, was something I had been hungering to do, needing to do, all my writing life."

Rich's first book was published in the Yale Younger Poets series, a prize particularly important for poets of her generation (others in the series have included James Wright, John Ashbery, and W. S. Merwin). W. H. Auden, the judge for the series in the 1950s, said of Rich's volume *A Change of World* (1951) that her poems "were neatly and modestly dressed . . . respect their elders, but are not cowed by them and do not tell fibs." Rich, looking back at that period from the vantage point of 1972, renders a more complicated sense of things. In an influential essay, *When We Dead Awaken*, she recalls this period as one in which the chief models for poetry were men; it was from those models that she first learned her craft. Even in looking at the poetry of older women writers she found herself "looking . . . for the same things I found in the poetry of men . . . , to be equal was still confused with sounding the same." Twenty years and five volumes after *A Change of World* she published *The Will to Change*, taking its title from the opening line of Charles Olson's *The Kingfishers:* "What does not change / is the will to change." The shift of emphasis in Rich's titles signals an important turn in her work—from acceptance of change as a way of the world to an active sense of change as willed or desired.

In 1953 Rich married and in her twenties gave birth to three children within four years, "a radicalizing experience," she said. It was during this time that Rich experienced most severely that gap between what she calls the "energy of creation" and the "energy of relation. . . . In those early years I always felt the conflict as a failure of love in myself." In her later work Rich came to identify the source of that conflict not as individual but social and, in 1976, published a book of prose, *Of Woman Born: Motherhood as Experience and Institution,* in which she contrasts the actual experience of bearing and raising children with the myths fostered by our medical, social, and political institutions.

With her third and fourth books, *Snapshots of a Daughter-in-Law* (1963) and *Necessities of Life* (1966), Rich began explicitly to treat problems that have engaged her ever since. The title poem of *Snapshots* exposes the gap between literary versions of women's experience and the day-to-day truths of their lives.

Rich's poems aim at self-definition, at establishing boundaries of the self, but they also fight off the notion that insights remain solitary and unshared. Many of her poems proceed by means of intimate argument, sometimes with externalized parts of herself, as if to dramatize the way identity forms from the self's movement beyond fixed boundaries. In some of her most powerful later poems, she pushes her imagination to recognize the multiple aspects of the self ("My selves," she calls them in her poem "Integrity"); in "Transcendental Etude," she writes:

> I am the lover and the loved,
> home and wanderer, she who splits
> firewood and she who knocks, a stranger
> in the storm.

In other important later poems she has carried out a dialogue with lives similar to and different from her own, as in the generous and powerful title poem of her collection *An Atlas of the Difficult World.* As she writes in "Blood, Bread, and Poetry," in her development as a poet she came to feel "more and more urgently the dynamic between poetry as language and poetry as a kind of action, probing, burning, stripping, placing itself in dialogue with others."

When Rich and her husband moved to New York City in 1966 they became increasingly involved in radical politics, especially in the opposition to the Vietnam War. These concerns are reflected in the poems of *Leaflets* (1969) and *The Will to Change* (1971). Along with new subject matter came equally important changes in style. Rich's poems throughout the 1960s moved away from formal verse patterns to more jagged utterance. Sentence fragments, lines of varying length, irregular spacing to mark off phrases—all these devices emphasized a voice of greater urgency. Ever since "Snapshots of a Daughter-in-Law," Rich had been dating each poem, as if to mark them as provisional, true to the moment but instruments of passage, like entries in a journal in which feelings are subject to continual revision.

In the 1970s Rich dedicated herself increasingly to feminism. As poet, as prose writer, and as public speaker her work took on a new unity and intensity. The continuing task was to see herself—as she put it in 1984—neither as "unique nor universal, but a person in history, a woman and not a man, a white and also Jewish inheritor of a particular Western consciousness, from the making of which most women have been excluded." She says in "Planetarium,"

> I am an instrument in the shape
> of a woman trying to translate pulsations
> into images for the relief of the body
> and the reconstruction of the mind.

Rich's collections of prose—*Of Woman Born; On Lies, Secrets, and Silences: Selected Prose 1966–1978; Blood, Bread, and Poetry: Selected Prose 1979–1985, What Is Found There: Notebooks on Poetry and Politics* (1993), and *Arts of the Possible* (2001)—provide an important context for her poems. In these works she addresses issues of women's education and their literary traditions, Jewish identity, the relations between poetry and politics, and what she has called "the erasure of lesbian existence." As a young woman Rich had been stirred by James Baldwin's comment that "any real change implies the breakup of the world as one has always known it, the loss of all that gave one an identity, the end of safety." In many ways her essays, like her poems, track the forces that resist such change and the human conditions that require it. Her essay "Compulsory Heterosexuality and Lesbian Existence" is an important example of such an examination.

Although Rich's individual poems do not consistently succeed in expressing a political vision without sacrificing "intensity of language," her work is best read as a continuous process. The books have an air of ongoing, pained investigation, almost scientific in intention but with an ardor suggested by their titles: *The Dream of a Common Language* (1977), *A Wild Patience Has Taken Me Thus Far* (1981), *The Fact of a Doorframe* (1984), and *Your Native Land, Your Life* (1986). Rich's more recent books, *Time's Power* (1989), *An Atlas of the Difficult World* (1991), *Dark Fields of the Republic: Poems 1991–1995* (1995), *Midnight Salvage: Poems 1995–1998* (1999), and *Fox* (2001), demonstrate an ongoing power of language and deepening poetic vision. Reading through her poems we may sometimes wish for more relaxation and playfulness, for a liberating comic sense of self almost never present in her work. What we find, however, is invaluable—a poet whose imagination confronts and resists the harsh necessities of our times and keeps alive a vision of what is possible: "a whole new poetry beginning here" ("Transcendental Etude").

Storm Warnings

The glass[1] has been falling all the afternoon,
And knowing better than the instrument
What winds are walking overhead, what zone
Of gray unrest is moving across the land,
I leave the book upon a pillowed chair   5
And walk from window to closed window, watching
Boughs strain against the sky

And think again, as often when the air
Moves inward toward a silent core of waiting,
How with a single purpose time has traveled   10
By secret currents of the undiscerned

---

1. Barometer.

Into this polar realm. Weather abroad
And weather in the heart alike come on
Regardless of prediction.

Between foreseeing and averting change   15
Lies all the mastery of elements
Which clocks and weatherglasses cannot alter.
Time in the hand is not control of time,
Nor shattered fragments of an instrument
A proof against the wind; the wind will rise,   20
We can only close the shutters.

I draw the curtains as the sky goes black
And set a match to candles sheathed in glass
Against the keyhole draught, the insistent whine
Of weather through the unsealed aperture.   25
This is our sole defense against the season;
These are the things that we have learned to do
Who live in troubled regions.

                                                                    1951

Snapshots of a Daughter-in-Law

1

You, once a belle in Shreveport,
with henna-colored hair, skin like a peachbud,
still have your dresses copied from that time,
and play a Chopin prelude
called by Cortot: *"Delicious recollections*   5
float like perfume through the memory."[1]

Your mind now, moldering like wedding-cake,
heavy with useless experience, rich
with suspicion, rumor, fantasy,
crumbling to pieces under the knife-edge   10
of mere fact. In the prime of your life.

Nervy, glowering, your daughter
wipes the teaspoons, grows another way.

2

Banging the coffee-pot into the sink
she hears the angels chiding, and looks out   15
past the raked gardens to the sloppy sky.
Only a week since They said: *Have no patience.*

---

1. A remark made by Alfred Cortot (1877–1962), a well-known French pianist, in his *Chopin: 24 Preludes* (1930); he is referring specifically to Chopin's Prelude No. 7, Andantino, A Major.

The next time it was: *Be insatiable.*
Then: *Save yourself; others you cannot save.*
Sometimes she's let the tapstream scald her arm,   20
a match burn to her thumbnail,

or held her hand above the kettle's snout
right in the woolly steam. They are probably angels,
since nothing hurts her anymore, except
each morning's grit blowing into her eyes.   25

3

A thinking woman sleeps with monsters.[2]
The beak that grips her, she becomes. And Nature,
that sprung-lidded, still commodious
steamer-trunk of *tempora* and *mores*[3]
gets stuffed with it all: the mildewed orange-flowers,   30
the female pills, the terrible breasts
of Boadicea[4] beneath flat foxes' heads and orchids.

Two handsome women, gripped in argument,
each proud, acute, subtle, I hear scream
across the cut glass and majolica   35
like Furies[5] cornered from their prey:
The argument *ad feminam*,[6] all the old knives
that have rusted in my back, I drive in yours,
ma semblable, ma soeur![7]

4

Knowing themselves too well in one another: 40
their gifts no pure fruition, but a thorn,
the prick filed sharp against a hint of scorn . . .
Reading while waiting
for the iron to heat,
writing, *My Life had stood—a Loaded Gun*[8]—   45
in that Amherst pantry while the jellies boil and scum,
or, more often,

2. A reference to W. B. Yeats's "Leda and the Swan," a poem about the rape of a maiden by Zeus in the form of a giant bird. The poem ends: "Did she put on his knowledge with his power / Before the indifferent beak could let her drop?"
3. Times and customs (Latin, literal trans.). This alludes perhaps to the Roman orator Cicero's famous phrase, "O Tempora! O Mores!" ("Alas for the degeneracy of our times and the low standard of our morals!").
4. British queen in the time of the Emperor Nero; she led her people in a large, although ultimately unsuccessful, revolt against Roman rule. "Female pills": remedies for menstrual pain.
5. Greek goddesses of vengeance. "Majolica": a kind of earthenware with a richly colored glaze.

6. Feminine version of the Latin phrase *ad hominem* (literally, "to the man"), referring to an argument directed not to reason but to personal prejudices and emotions.
7. The last line of Charles Baudelaire's French poem "Au Lecteur" addresses "*Hypocrite lecteur!— mon semblable—mon frère!*" ("Hypocrite reader, like me, my brother!"); Rich here instead addresses "*ma soeur*" ("my sister"). See also T. S. Eliot, "The Waste Land" 76.
8. "*Emily Dickinson, Complete Poems*, ed. T. H. Johnson, 1960, p. 369" [Rich's note]; this is the poem numbered 754 in the Johnson edition. Amherst is the town where Dickinson lived her entire life (1830–1886).

iron-eyed and beaked and purposed as a bird,
dusting everything on the whatnot every day of life.

5

Dulce ridens, dulce loquens,[9]   50
she shaves her legs until they gleam
like petrified mammoth-tusk.

6

When to her lute Corinna sings[1]
neither words nor music are her own;
only the long hair dipping   55
over her cheek, only the song
of silk against her knees
and these
adjusted in reflections of an eye.

Poised, trembling and unsatisfied, before   60
an unlocked door, that cage of cages,
tell us, you bird, you tragical machine—
is this *fertilisante douleur?*[2] Pinned down
by love, for you the only natural action,
are you edged more keen   65
to prise the secrets of the vault? has Nature shown
her household books to you, daughter-in-law,
that her sons never saw?

7

"To have in this uncertain world some stay
which cannot be undermined, is   70
of the utmost consequence."[3]
                              Thus wrote
a woman, partly brave and partly good,
who fought with what she partly understood.
Few men about her would or could do more,   75
hence she was labeled harpy, shrew and whore.

8

"You all die at fifteen," said Diderot,[4]
and turn part legend, part convention.

9. Sweetly laughing, sweetly speaking (Latin, from Horace, "Odes," 22.23–24).
1. First line of a lyric poem of Thomas Campion (1567–1620) about the extent to which a courtier is moved by Corinna's beautiful music.
2. Fertilizing (or life-giving) sorrow (French).
3. "From Mary Wollstonecraft, *Thoughts on the Education of Daughters*, London, 1787" [Rich's note]. Wollstonecraft (1759–1797), one of the first feminist thinkers, is best known for her "Vindication of the Rights of Woman."
4. Denis Diderot (1713–1784): French philosopher, encyclopedist, playwright, and critic. " 'You all die at fifteen': *'Vous mourez toutes à quinze ans,'* from the *Lettres à Sophie Volland,* quoted by Simone de Beauvoir in *Le Deuxième Sexe,* Vol. II, pp. 123–24" [Rich's note].

Still, eyes inaccurately dream
behind closed windows blankening with steam.   80
Deliciously, all that we might have been,
all that we were—fire, tears,
wit, taste, martyred ambition—
stirs like the memory of refused adultery
the drained and flagging bosom of our middle years.   85

9

Not that it is done well, but
that it is done at all?[5] Yes, think
of the odds! or shrug them off forever.
This luxury of the precocious child,
Time's precious chronic invalid,—   90
would we, darlings, resign it if we could?
Our blight has been our sinecure:
mere talent was enough for us—
glitter in fragments and rough drafts.

Sigh no more, ladies.   95
                    Time is male
and in his cups drinks to the fair.
Bemused by gallantry, we hear
our mediocrities over-praised,
indolence read as abnegation,   100
slattern thought styled intuition,
every lapse forgiven, our crime
only to cast too bold a shadow
or smash the mold straight off.

For that, solitary confinement,   105
tear gas, attrition shelling.
Few applicants for that honor.

10

                    Well,
she's long about her coming, who must be
more merciless to herself than history.   110
Her mind full to the wind, I see her plunge
breasted and glancing through the currents,
taking the light upon her
at least as beautiful as any boy
or helicopter,[6]   115

---

5. An allusion to Samuel Johnson's remark to James Boswell: "Sir, a woman's preaching is like a dog's walking on his hinder legs. It is not done well; but you are surprised to find it done at all" (July 31, 1763).

6. "She comes down from the remoteness of ages, from Thebes, from Crete, from Chichén-Itzà; and she is also the totem set deep in the African jungle; she is a helicopter and she is a bird; and there is this, the greatest wonder of all: under her tinted hair the forest murmur becomes a thought, and words issue from her breasts" (Simone de Beauvoir, *The Second Sex*, trans. H. M. Parshley [New York, 1953], 729). (A translation of the passage from *Le Deuxième Sexe*, Vol. II, 574, cited in French by Rich.)

poised, still coming,
her fine blades making the air wince

but her cargo
no promise then:
delivered   120
palpable
ours.

1958–60   1963

"I Am in Danger—Sir—"[1]

"Half-cracked" to Higginson,[2] living,
afterward famous in garbled versions,
your hoard of dazzling scraps a battlefield,
now your old snood

mothballed at Harvard   5
and you in your variorum monument[3]
equivocal to the end—
who are you?

Gardening the day-lily,
wiping the wine-glass stems,   10
your thought pulsed on behind
a forehead battered paper-thin,

you, woman, masculine
in single-mindedness,
for whom the word was more   15
than a symptom—

a condition of being.
Till the air buzzing with spoiled language
sang in your ears
of Perjury   20

and in your half-cracked way you chose
silence for entertainment,
chose to have it out at last
on your own premises.

1964   1966

1. A sentence in a letter from Emily Dickinson to Thomas Wentworth Higginson (1823–1911), a critic and editor with whom she opened correspondence in 1862 and to whom she sent some of her poems. She writes: "You think my gait 'spasmodic'—I am in danger—Sir—You think me 'uncontrolled'—I have no Tribunal."
2. Higginson in a letter described Emily Dickinson as "my partially cracked Poetess at Amherst."
3. *The Poems of Emily Dickinson,* ed. Thomas H. Johnson, 3 vols. (Cambridge, Mass., 1955) is a "variorum" in that it contains all the variant readings in her manuscripts. "Mothballed at Harvard": the Houghton Rare Books Library at Harvard University has a collection of Emily Dickinson manuscripts and memorabilia.

A Valediction Forbidding Mourning[1]

My swirling wants. Your frozen lips.
The grammar turned and attacked me.
Themes, written under duress.
Emptiness of the notations.

They gave me a drug that slowed the healing of wounds.   5

I want you to see this before I leave:
the experience of repetition as death
the failure of criticism to locate the pain
the poster in the bus that said:
my bleeding is under control.   10

A red plant in a cemetery of plastic wreaths.

A last attempt: the language is a dialect called metaphor.
These images go unglossed: hair, glacier, flashlight.
When I think of a landscape I am thinking of a time.
When I talk of taking a trip I mean forever.   15
I could say: those mountains have a meaning
but further than that I could not say.

To do something very common, in my own way.

1970   1971

Diving into the Wreck

First having read the book of myths,
and loaded the camera,
and checked the edge of the knife-blade,
I put on
the body-armor of black rubber   5
the absurd flippers
the grave and awkward mask.
I am having to do this
not like Cousteau[1] with his
assiduous team   10
aboard the sun-flooded schooner
but here alone.

There is a ladder.
The ladder is always there
hanging innocently   15

1. Title of a famous poem by John Donne (1572–1631) in which the English poet forbids his wife to lament his departure for a trip to the Continent.

1. Jacques-Yves Cousteau (1910–1997), French underwater explorer and author.

close to the side of the schooner.
We know what it is for,
we who have used it.
Otherwise
it's a piece of maritime floss   20
some sundry equipment.

I go down.
Rung after rung and still
the oxygen immerses me
the blue light   25
the clear atoms
of our human air.
I go down.
My flippers cripple me,
I crawl like an insect down the ladder   30
and there is no one
to tell me when the ocean
will begin.

First the air is blue and then
it is bluer and then green and then   35
black I am blacking out and yet
my mask is powerful
it pumps my blood with power
the sea is another story
the sea is not a question of power   40
I have to learn alone
to turn my body without force
in the deep element.

And now: it is easy to forget
what I came for   45
among so many who have always
lived here
swaying their crenellated fans
between the reefs
and besides   50
you breathe differently down here.

I came to explore the wreck.
The words are purposes.
The words are maps.
I came to see the damage that was done   55
and the treasures that prevail.
I stroke the beam of my lamp
slowly along the flank
of something more permanent
than fish or weed   60

the thing I came for:
the wreck and not the story of the wreck

the thing itself and not the myth
the drowned face[2] always staring
toward the sun   65
the evidence of damage
worn by salt and sway into this threadbare beauty
the ribs of the disaster
curving their assertion
among the tentative haunters.   70

This is the place.
And I am here, the mermaid whose dark hair
streams black, the merman in his armored body
We circle silently
about the wreck   75
we dive into the hold.
I am she: I am he

whose drowned face sleeps with open eyes
whose breasts still bear the stress
whose silver, copper, vermeil cargo lies   80
obscurely inside barrels
half-wedged and left to rot
we are the half-destroyed instruments
that once held to a course
the water-eaten log   85
the fouled compass

We are, I am, you are
by cowardice or courage
the one who find our way
back to this scene   90
carrying a knife, a camera
a book of myths
in which
our names do not appear.

1972   1973

Power

Living   in the earth-deposits   of our history

Today a backhoe divulged   out of a crumbling flank of earth
one bottle   amber   perfect   a hundred-year-old
cure for fever   or melancholy   a tonic
for living on this earth   in the winters of this climate   5

---

2. Referring to the ornamental female figurehead that formed the prow of many old sailing ships.

Today I was reading about Marie Curie:[1]
she must have known she suffered   from radiation sickness
her body bombarded for years   by the element
she had purified
It seems she denied to the end   10
the source of the cataracts on her eyes
the cracked and suppurating[2] skin   of her finger-ends
till she could no longer hold   a test-tube or a pencil

She died   a famous woman   denying
her wounds   15
denying
her wounds   came   from the same source as her power

1974   1978

Transcendental Etude[1]

for Michelle Cliff

This August evening I've been driving
over backroads fringed with queen anne's lace
my car startling young deer in meadows—one
gave a hoarse intake of her breath and all
four fawns sprang after her   5
into the dark maples.
Three months from today they'll be fair game
for the hit-and-run hunters, glorying
in a weekend's destructive power,
triggers fingered by drunken gunmen, sometimes   10
so inept as to leave the shattered animal
stunned in her blood. But this evening deep in summer
the deer are still alive and free,
nibbling apples from early-laden boughs
so weighted, so englobed   15
with already yellowing fruit
they seem eternal, Hesperidean[2]
in the clear-tuned, cricket-throbbing air.

Later I stood in the dooryard,
my nerves singing the immense   20
fragility of all this sweetness,
this green world already sentimentalized, photographed,
advertised to death. Yet, it persists
stubbornly beyond the fake Vermont

---

1. Physical chemist (1867–1934) who with her
husband investigated radioactivity and on her own
discovered polonium and radium; she received the
Nobel Prize in 1911.
2. Discharging pus.
1. A piece of music played for the practice of a

point of technique or a composition built on technique but played for its artistic value.
2. I.e., like the golden apples of the tree guarded
by the Hesperides, daughters of Atlas, in Greek
mythology.

of antique barnboards glazed into discothèques,   25
artificial snow, the sick Vermont of children
conceived in apathy, grown to winters
of rotgut violence,
poverty gnashing its teeth like a blind cat at their lives.
Still, it persists. Turning off onto a dirt road   30
from the raw cuts bulldozed through a quiet village
for the tourist run to Canada,
I've sat on a stone fence above a great, soft, sloping field
of musing heifers, a farmstead
slanting its planes calmly in the calm light,   35
a dead elm raising bleached arms
above a green so dense with life,
minute, momentary life—slugs, moles, pheasants, gnats,
spiders, moths, hummingbirds, groundhogs, butterflies—
a lifetime is too narrow   40
to understand it all, beginning with the huge
rockshelves that underlie all that life.

No one ever told us we had to study our lives,
make of our lives a study, as if learning natural history
or music, that we should begin   45
with the simple exercises first
and slowly go on trying
the hard ones, practicing till strength
and accuracy became one with the daring
to leap into transcendence, take the chance   50
of breaking down in the wild arpeggio
or faulting the full sentence of the fugue.[3]
—And in fact we can't live like that: we take on
everything at once before we've even begun
to read or mark time, we're forced to begin   55
in the midst of the hardest movement,
the one already sounding as we are born.
At most we're allowed a few months
of simply listening to the simple line
of a woman's voice singing a child   60
against her heart. Everything else is too soon,
too sudden, the wrenching-apart, that woman's heartbeat
heard ever after from a distance,
the loss of that ground-note echoing
whenever we are happy, or in despair.   65

Everything else seems beyond us,
we aren't ready for it, nothing that was said
is true for us, caught naked in the argument,
the counterpoint, trying to sightread
what our fingers can't keep up with, learn by heart   70
what we can't even read. And yet

3. Musical piece characterized by the interweaving of several voices. "Arpeggio": production of tones of a chord in succession.

2954 / ADRIENNE RICH

it *is* this we were born to. We aren't virtuosi
or child prodigies, there are no prodigies
in this realm, only a half-blind, stubborn
cleaving to the timbre, the tones of what we are   75
—even when all the texts describe it differently.

And we're not performers, like Liszt,[4] competing
against the world for speed and brilliance
(the 79-year-old pianist said, when I asked her
What makes a virtuoso?—Competitiveness.)   80
The longer I live the more I mistrust
theatricality, the false glamour cast
by performance, the more I know its poverty beside
the truths we are salvaging from
the splitting-open of our lives.   85
The woman who sits watching, listening,
eyes moving in the darkness
in rehearsing in her body, hearing-out in her blood
a score touched off in her perhaps
by some words, a few chords, from the stage: 90
a tale only she can tell.

But there come times—perhaps this is one of them—
when we have to take ourselves more seriously or die;
when we have to pull back from the incantations,
rhythms we've moved to thoughtlessly,   95
and disenthrall ourselves, bestow
ourselves to silence, or a severer listening, cleansed
of oratory, formulas, choruses, laments, static
crowding the wires. We cut the wires,
find ourselves in free-fall, as if   100
our true home were the undimensional
solitudes, the rift
in the Great Nebula.[5]
No one who survives to speak
new language, has avoided this: 105
the cutting-away of an old force that held her
rooted to an old ground
the pitch of utter loneliness
where she herself and all creation
seem equally dispersed, weightless, her being a cry   110
to which no echo comes or can ever come.

But in fact we were always like this,
rootless, dismembered: knowing it makes the difference.
Birth stripped our birthright from us,
tore us from a woman, from women, from ourselves   115
so early on

---

4. Franz Liszt, 19th-century Hungarian composer
and pianist, noted for his virtuoso performances.
5. A nebula is an immense body of rarefied gas or
dust in interstellar space. Rich may be referring to
the Great Nebula in the Orion constellation or to
a body of dark nebulae, usually called the "Great
Rift," which in photographs appears to divide the
Milky Way.

and the whole chorus throbbing at our ears
like midges, told us nothing, nothing
of origins, nothing we needed
to know, nothing that could re-member us.   120

Only: that it is unnatural,
the homesickness for a woman, for ourselves,
for that acute joy at the shadow her head and arms
cast on a wall, her heavy or slender
thighs on which we lay, flesh against flesh,   125
eyes steady on the face of love; smell of her milk, her sweat,
terror of her disappearance, all fused in this hunger
for the element they have called most dangerous, to be
lifted breathtaken on her breast, to rock within her
—even if beaten back, stranded against, to apprehend   130
in a sudden brine-clear thought
trembling like the tiny, orbed, endangered
egg-sac of a new world:
This is what she was to me, and this
is how I can love myself—   135
as only a woman can love me.

Homesick for myself, for her—as, after the heatwave
breaks, the clear tones of the world
manifest: cloud, bough, wall, insect, the very soul of light:
homesick as the fluted vault of desire   140
articulates itself: *I am the lover and the loved,*
home and wanderer, she who splits
firewood and she who knocks, a stranger
in the storm, two women, eye to eye
measuring each other's spirit, each other's   145
limitless desire,
                   a whole new poetry beginning here.

Vision begins to happen in such a life
as if a woman quietly walked away
from the argument and jargon in a room   150
and sitting down in the kitchen, began turning in her lap
bits of yarn, calico and velvet scraps,
laying them out absently on the scrubbed boards
in the lamplight, with small rainbow-colored shells
sent in cotton-wool from somewhere far away,   155
and skeins of milkweed from the nearest meadow—
original domestic silk, the finest findings—
and the darkblue petal of the petunia,
and the dry darkbrown lace of seaweed;
not forgotten either, the shed silver   160
whisker of the cat,
the spiral of paper-wasp-nest curling
beside the finch's yellow feather.
Such a composition has nothing to do with eternity,
the striving for greatness, brilliance—   165

only with the musing of a mind
one with her body, experienced fingers quietly pushing
dark against bright, silk against roughness,
pulling the tenets of a life together
with no mere will to mastery,   170
only care for the many-lived, unending
forms in which she finds herself,
becoming now the sherd of broken glass
slicing light in a corner, dangerous
to flesh, now the plentiful, soft leaf   175
that wrapped round the throbbing finger, soothes the wound;
and now the stone foundation, rockshelf further
forming underneath everything that grows.

1977   1978

GARY SNYDER
b. 1930

"I try to hold both history and wildness in my mind, that my poems may approach
the true measure of things and stand against the unbalance and ignorance of our
time," Gary Snyder has said. Throughout his life Snyder has sought alternatives to
this imbalance. His quest has led him to the natural world, to the study of mythology
and the discipline of Eastern religions, and to living oral traditions including those of
native American societies. Snyder understands the work of poetry as recovery and
healing. Like the shaman-poet of primitive cultures whose power to "heal disease and
resist death" is "acquired from dreams" (as he writes in "Poetry and the Primitive"),
he seeks to restore contact with a vital universe in which all things are interdependent.
The journey of Snyder's life and work has taken him back to what he calls "the most
archaic values on earth." His poems are acts of cultural criticism, challenges to the
dominant values of the contemporary world.

The American West Coast is Snyder's native landscape; its forests and mountains
have always attracted him, and they inspire many of his poems. He was born in San
Francisco, grew up in the state of Washington, and later moved with his family to
Portland, Oregon. In 1947, he entered Reed College, where he studied anthropology
and developed a special interest in native American cultures (Northwest Coast Indian
myths and tales inform his second book, Myths and Tests, 1960). After doing graduate
work in linguistics at Indiana University, he returned to the West, where he became
associated with Kenneth Rexroth and Philip Whalen and with Jack Kerouac and Allen
Ginsberg, all of whom participated in what came to be called the San Francisco
Renaissance. In this period, Snyder also studied classical Chinese at the University
of California at Berkeley and translated some of the Cold Mountain Poems of the Zen
poet Han-shan. In the mid 1950s Snyder went to Japan, where he resided, except
intermittently, until 1968; in Japan he took formal instruction in Buddhism under
Zen masters. The various traditions Snyder has studied come together in his poetic
vision quest The Blue Sky, a magical celebration of the overarching heavens.

Snyder's poems, like his life, combine reading and formal study with physical activity; he has worked as a timber scaler, a forest fire lookout (one of his lookouts inspired
"August at Sourdough"), a logger, and a hand on a tanker in the South Pacific. "My
poems follow the rhythms of the physical work I'm doing and the life I'm leading at

any given time," he has remarked. The title of his first book, *Riprap* (1959), is a forester's term; a riprap, he explains, is "a cobble of stone laid on steep slick rock to make a trail for horses in the mountains." Snyder's poems often follow a trail of ascent or descent, as in "Straight-Creek–Great Burn" from his Pulitzer Prize–winning volume, *Turtle Island* (1975). Hiking with friends, he experiences the world as dynamic and flowing (running water and "changing clouds"), but the journey brings the walkers to a still point; they lie "resting on dry fern and / watching." From such a stillness the central image of a Snyder poem often rises, like the birds who "arch and loop," then "settle down." The achievement of stillness in a universe of change is, for Snyder, pivotal. The mind empties itself, the individual ego is erased, and the local place reveals the universal.

If Snyder's poems contain a Zenlike stillness, they also exhibit an appealing energy, one source of which is his love of wildness. Like the Thoreau of *Walden* explicitly evoked in sections of *Myths and Texts,* Snyder finds a tonic wildness in the natural world, but unlike Thoreau, he is an unabashed celebrant of erotic experience (his earlier poems make it clear that he also knows the destructive possibilities in such experience). He renders some of the various faces of Eros in "Beneath My Hand and Eye the Distant Hills. Your Body" (from *The Back Country,* 1968) and in "Song of the Taste" (from *Regarding Wave,* 1970).

Some of Snyder's numerous essays on politics and ecology are included in his influential *Earth House Hold* (1969) and *The Practice of the Wild* (1990). His collections *Axe Handles* (1983), *Left Out in the Rain* (1986), and *No Nature: New and Selected Poems* (1992) confirm that his poems are bound up in the same concerns. Although his didactic impulse sometimes leads him to oversimplification, Snyder's political vision remains one of the strengths of his poetry. The potential in this vision for self-importance and overseriousness is tempered by his sense of humor and the conviction, palpable in his best poems, that his experiences are common and shared. Snyder's poems suggest diverse contexts: his belief in the writer as cultural critic links him to Thoreau and Robert Duncan, his rhythms and strong images recall Ezra Pound, his meticulous attention to the natural world reminds us of Robert Frost and A. R. Ammons. Eclectic yet respectful of ancient traditions, Snyder is an American original who sees his own work as part of a "continual creation," one manifestation of the energy that sustains all life.

Milton[1] by Firelight

Piute Creek, August 1955

"O hell, what do mine eyes
      with grief behold?"[2]
Working with an old
Singlejack miner, who can sense
The vein and cleavage   5
In the very guts of rock, can
Blast granite, build
Switchbacks[3] that last for years
Under the beat of snow, thaw, mule-hooves.
What use, Milton, a silly story   10
Of our lost general[4] parents,
      eaters of fruit?

1. John Milton (1608–1674), major English poet and author of *Paradise Lost,* which retells the biblical story of the Fall from Grace.
2. Satan's words when he first sees Adam and Eve in the Garden of Eden (*Paradise Lost* 4.358).
3. Roads ascending a steep incline in a zigzag pattern.
4. I.e., of our race.

The Indian, the chainsaw boy,
And a string of six mules
Came riding down to camp   15
Hungry for tomatoes and green apples.
Sleeping in saddle blankets
Under a bright night-sky
Han River slantwise by morning.
Jays squall   20
Coffee boils

In ten thousand years the Sierras
Will be dry and dead, home of the scorpion.
Ice-scratched slabs and bent trees.
No paradise, no fall,   25
Only the weathering land
The wheeling sky,
Man, with his Satan
Scouring the chaos of the mind.
Oh Hell!   30

Fire down
Too dark to read, miles from a road
The bell-mare clangs in the meadow
That packed dirt for a fill-in
Scrambling through loose rocks   35
On an old trail
All of a summer's day.[5]

1959

Riprap[1]

Lay down these words
Before your mind like rocks.
                    placed solid, by hands
In choice of place, set
Before the body of the mind   5
                    in space and time:
Solidity of bark, leaf, or wall
                    riprap of things:
Cobble of milky way,
                    straying planets,   10
These poems, people,
                    lost ponies with
Dragging saddles—
                    and rocky sure-foot trails.

5. Alludes to an epic simile describing Satan's fall: "From morn / to noon he fell, from noon to dewy eve, / A summer's day" (*Paradise Lost* 1.742–44).

1. A cobble of stone laid on steep slick rock to make a trail for horses in the mountains [Snyder's note].

The worlds like an endless   15
                four-dimensional
Game of *Go*.[2]
                ants and pebbles
In the thin loam, each rock a word
                a creek-washed stone   20
Granite: ingrained
                with torment of fire and weight
Crystal and sediment linked hot
                all change, in thoughts,
As well as things.   25

                                        1959

August on Sourdough,[1] A Visit from Dick Brewer

You hitched a thousand miles
                north from San Francisco
Hiked up the mountainside   a mile in the air
The little cabin—one room—
                walled in glass   5
Meadows and snowfields,   hundreds of peaks.
We lay in our sleeping bags
                talking half the night;
Wind in the guy-cables   this summer mountain rain.
Next morning I went with you   10
                as far as the cliffs,
Loaned you my poncho—   the rain across the shale—
You down the snowfield
                flapping in the wind
Waving a last goodbye   half hidden in the clouds   15
To go on hitching
                clear to New York;
Me back to my mountain   and far, far, west.

                                        1968

Beneath My Hand and Eye the Distant Hills. Your Body

What my hand follows on your body
Is the line. A stream of love
    of heat, of light,   what my
    eye   lascivious
                licks   5
    over, watching
        far snow-dappled Uintah mountains[1]

2. An ancient Japanese game played with black and white stones, placed one after the other on a checkered board.
1. Mountain in Washington State, where Snyder worked as a fire-watcher during the summer of 1953.
1. In northeastern Utah.

Is that stream.
Of power.   what my
    hand curves over, following the line.   10
    "hip" and "groin"

Where "I"
    follow by hand and eye
    the swimming limit of your body.
As when vision idly dallies on the hills   15
Loving what it feeds on.
    soft cinder cones and craters;
        —Drum Hadley in the Pinacate[2]
            took ten minutes more to look again—
A leap of power unfurling: 20
        left,   right—right—
My heart beat faster looking
    at the snowy Uintah mountains.

As my hand feeds on you
    runs down your side and curls beneath your hip.   25
oil pool; stratum; water—

What "is" within   not known
    but feel it
    sinking with a breath
    pusht ruthless, surely, down.   30

Beneath this long caress of hand and eye
    "we" learn the flower burning,
        outward, from "below".

                                                            1968

The Blue Sky

"Eastward from here,
        beyond Buddha-worlds ten times as
        numerous as the sands of the Ganges[1]
there is a world called
        PURE AS LAPIS LAZULI   5
its Buddha is called Master of Healing,
        AZURE RADIANCE TATHAGATA"[2]

        it would take you twelve thousand summer vacations
        driving a car due east all day every day
        to reach the edge of the Lapis Lazuli realm of   10

2. Town in California.
1. Sacred and major river in India.
2. One of the ten appellations of Buddha. "Lapis

lazuli": a semiprecious stone, usually a rich azure
blue. In Buddhism, the color blue is associated
with the absolute.

Medicine Old Man Buddha—
East. Old Man Realm
East across the sea, yellow sand land
Coyote[3] old man land
Silver, and stone blue   15

Blue   blāew, bright   flāuus   flamen, brāhman

Sky.   skȳ   scūwo   "shadow"
              Sanskrit[4] skutās   "covered"
              skewed (pied)
                      skewbald (. . . "Stewball")   20
              skybald/Piebald[5]
                      Horse with lightning feet, a mane like
                      distant rain, the Turquoise horse,
                      a black star for an eye
                      white shell teeth   25
                      Pony that feeds on the pollen of flowers[6]
                      may he
                      make thee whole.

Heal.   hail   whole   (khailaz . . . kail . . . koil I.E.[7]r)

Namo bhagavate bhaishajyaguru-vaidurya-   30
prabharajaya tathagata arhate samyak
      sambuddhaya tadyatha *om* bhaishajye
            bhaishajye bhaishajya samudgate
                  svāhā.[8]

"I honour the Lord, the Master of Healing,   35
shining like lapis lazuli, the king, the
Tathagata, the Saint, the perfectly enlightened
one, saying *OM* TO THE HEALING
      TO THE HEALING   TO THE HEALER
      HAIL!   40
            svāhā.

3. In many Native American traditions, a trickster, a culture hero, and a figure of healing. The pictograph below is of Kokopilau, a Hopi shaman, or magical healer. It comes from a petroglyph chiseled on rock walls throughout the western United States; Snyder has adopted it as his mark. The poem associates three figures of healing, the third being Buddha as "medicine man" (above), and thus merges elements of Native American and Buddhist cultures.

4. Ancient language of India.
5. Spotted or blotched with black and white.
6. The poem refers to herbal aids used by American Indians in vision quests, such as morning-glory seeds, jimson weed, and peyote.
7. Indo-European, the group of languages spoken in Europe and parts of Asia.
8. The Sanskrit lines are translated immediately below. *"Om"*: a mantra, or chant, used in meditation. "Svāhā": ritual exclamation or call.

Shades of blue through the day

T'u chüeh   a border tribe near China
Türc
Turquoise: a hydrous phosphate of aluminum   45
                  a little copper
                  a little iron—

Whole, Whole, Make Whole!

Blue Land Flaming Stone—
Man   50
          Eastward—
          sodium, aluminum, calcium, sulfur.

In the reign of the Emperor Nimmyō
when Ono-no-Komachi[9] the strange girl poet
was seventeen, she set out looking for her father   55
who had become a Buddhist Wanderer. She took ill
on her journey, and sick in bed one night saw

AZURE RADIANCE THUS-COME MEDICINE MASTER

in a dream. He told her she would find a hotsprings
on the bank of the Azuma river in the Bandai mountains[1]   60
that would cure her; and she'd meet her father there.

"Enchantment as strange as
the Blue up above"   my rose of San Antone[2]

Tibetans believe that Goddesses have Lapis Lazuli hair.

Azure.   O.F.[3] azur   65
               Arabic lāzaward
               Persian lāzhward   "lapis lazuli"

—blue bead charms against the evil eye—

(*Hemp.* ". . . Cheremiss and Zyrjän word . . . these two languages
          being Finno-Ugric[4]—   70
          a wandering culture word
          of wide diffusion.")

---

9. A 9th-century Japanese poet.
1. Both are in Japan.
2. From a popular song.

3. Old French.
4. Group of languages spoken in Hungary, Lapland, Finland, Estonia, and northwestern Russia.

Tim and Kim and Don and I were talking about
what an awful authoritarian garb Doctors
and Nurses wear, really, how spooky it is.   75
"What *should* they wear?"

—"Masks and Feathers!"

Ramana Maharshi Dream

I was working as a wood cutter by a crossroads—Ko-san
was working with me—we were sawing and splitting the   80
firewood. An old man came up the lane alongside a mud
wall—he shouted a little scolding at some Zen monks who
were piling slash by the edge of the woods. He came over
and chatted with us, a grizzled face—neither eastern or
western; or both. He had a glass of buttermilk in his   85
hand. I asked him "Where'd you get that buttermilk?"
I'd been looking all over for buttermilk. He said,
"At the O K Dairy, right where you leave town."

Medicine.　　　　　medēri　　Indo European　　me
　　　　　　　　　　"to measure"   90
　　　"MAYA"[5]　　　Goddess　　illusion-wisdom　　fishing net

Herba.　　　　　(some pre-latin rustic word . . .)

Lazuli　　　　　sodium, aluminum, calcium, sulfur, silicon;
　　　　　sky blue
　　　　　right in the rocks too—   95
　　　　　Lazuli Bunting
　　　　　sea-blue
　　　　　hazy-hills blue
　　　　　huckleberry, cobalt
　　　　　medicine-bottle   100
　　　　　blue.

Celestial　　　　　arched cover . . . kam[6]

Heaven　　　　　heman . . . kam

---

5. In Hindu tradition, mother of Buddha and god-
dess representing the transitory.　　　6. Wish, desire, longing (Sanskrit).

[*comrade:*   under the same sky/tent/curve]
   Kamarā, Avestan, a girdle kam,   a bent curved bow   105

     Kāma, God of Lust[7]   "Son of Maya"
          "Bow of Flowers"

:Shakyamuni would then be the lord of the present
world of sorrow; Bhaishajyaguru/Yao-shih Fo/
Yakushi;[8] "Old Man Medicine Buddha" the lord of the   110
Lost Paradise.

Glory of morning,
       pearly gates, the
              heavenly blue.

Thinking on Amitabha[9] in the setting sun,   115
       his western paradise—
   impurities flow out away, to west,
   behind us, *rolling*

   planet ball forward turns into the "east"
   is rising,   120
   azure,
   two thousand light years ahead

   Great Medicine Master;
   land of blue.

The Blue Sky   125

The Blue Sky

The Blue Sky

is the land of

---

7. In the Hindu tradition.
8. "Shakyamuni" (or "Sakyamuni") is an appella-
tion of the founder of Buddhism, Siddhartha Gautama (c. 563–c. 483 B.C.E.); the other names are
variants on his name as the great healer in Sanskrit, Chinese, and Japanese, respectively.
9. Sanskrit version of the Buddha as supernatural
ruler of the land of bliss.

OLD MAN MEDICINE BUDDHA

where the Eagle   130
that Flies out of Sight

flies.

1969

Straight-Creek—Great Burn[1]

for Tom and Martha Burch

Lightly, in the April mountains—
            Straight Creek,
dry grass freed again of snow
& the chickadees are pecking
last fall's seeds   5
            fluffing tail in chilly wind,

Avalanche piled up cross the creek
            and chunked-froze solid—
water sluicing under; spills out
            rock lip pool, bends over,   10
            braided, white, foaming,
returns to trembling
            deep-dark hole.

Creek boulders show the flow-wear lines
            in shapes the same   15
            as running blood
            carves in the heart's main
                        valve,

Early spring dry. Dry snow flurries;
            walk on crusty high snow slopes   20
—grand dead burn pine—
            chartreuse lichen as adornment
                        (a dye for wool)
angled tumbled talus rock
of geosyncline[2] warm sea bottom   25
yes, so long ago.
"Once on a time."

Far light on the Bitteroots;[3]
            scrabble down willow slide

---

1. Scottish dialect word for "brook"; the word may also be used in the sense of a burned area, as from a forest fire.
2. Downward turning of the earth's crust. "Talus": rock debris under a cliff.
3. Range of the Rocky Mountains extending along the Idaho–Montana border.

changing clouds above,   30
shapes on glowing sun-ball
writhing,   choosing
            reaching out against eternal
                        azure—

us resting on dry fern and   35
                watching

Shining Heaven
change his feather garments
            overhead.

A whoosh of birds   40
swoops up and round
tilts back
almost always flying all apart
and yet hangs on!
together;   45

never a leader,
all of one swift

empty
dancing   mind.

They arc and loop & then   50
their flight is done.
they settle down.
end of poem.

                                                    1974

Ripples on the Surface

"Ripples on the surface of the water
were silver salmon passing under—different
from the sorts of ripples caused by breezes"

A scudding plume on the wave—
a humpback whale is   5
breaking out in air up
gulping herring
        —Nature not a book, but a *performance*, a
high old culture

Ever-fresh events   10
scraped out, rubbed out, and used, used, again—
the braided channels of the rivers
hidden under fields of grass—

The vast wild.
> the house, alone. 15
the little house in the wild,
> the wild in the house.

both forgotten.

No nature.

Both together, one big empty house 20

1993

SYLVIA PLATH
1932–1963

In an introduction to Sylvia Plath's *Ariel* (1965), published two years after her suicide in London, Robert Lowell wrote: "In these poems . . . Sylvia Plath becomes herself, becomes something imaginary, newly, wildly, and subtly created— . . . one of those super-real, hypnotic great classical heroines." Lowell had first met Plath in 1958, during her regular visits to his poetry seminar at Boston University, where he remembered her "air of maddening docility." Later, writing his introduction, he recognized her astonishing creation of a poetic self. The poems of *Ariel* were written at white heat, two or three a day, in the last months of Plath's life, but there is nothing hurried in their language or structure. When they are taken together, with the poems posthumously published in *Crossing the Water* (1971) and *Winter Trees* (1972), a coherent persona emerges: larger than life, operatic in feeling. Although this focus on the self often excludes attention to the larger world, it generates the dynamic energy of her work. Plath appropriates a centrally American tradition: the heroic ego confronting the sublime, but she brilliantly revises this tradition by turning Emerson's "great and crescive self" into a heroine instead of a hero. Seizing a mythic power, the Plath of the poems transmutes the domestic and the ordinary into the hallucinatory, the utterly strange. Her revision of the romantic ego dramatizes its tendency toward disproportion and excess, and she is fully capable of both using and mocking this heightened sense of self, as she does in her poem "Lady Lazarus."

Plath's well-known autobiographical novel, *The Bell Jar,* has nothing of the brilliance of her poems, but it effectively dramatizes the stereotyping of women's roles in the 1950s and the turmoil of a young woman only partly aware that her gifts and ambitions greatly exceed the options available to her. In the novel, Plath makes use of her experience as a guest editor of a young women's magazine (in real life, *Mademoiselle*) and then, in an abrupt shift, presents her heroine's attempted suicide and hospitalization. Plath herself had suffered a serious breakdown and attempted suicide between her junior and senior years in college. The popularity of *The Bell Jar* may be one reason why attention to Plath's life has sometimes obscured the accomplishments of her art. While her poems often begin in autobiography, their success depends on Plath's imaginative transformations of experience into myth, as in a number of her poems (such as "Daddy") where the figure of her Prussian father is transformed into an emblem for masculine authority. Otto Plath was an entomologist and the author of a treatise on bumblebees. His death in 1940 from gangrene (the consequence of a diabetic condition he refused to treat), when Plath was eight, was the crucial event of her childhood. After his death, her mother, Aurelia, while struggling to support two small children, encouraged her daughter's literary ambitions.

In many ways Plath embodied the bright, young, middle-class woman of the 1950s. She went to Smith College on a scholarship and graduated summa cum laude. On a Fulbright grant she studied in England at Cambridge University, where she met and married the poet Ted Hughes. On the face of it, her marriage must have seemed the perfect fate for such a young woman; it combined romance, two poets beginning careers together (Plath's first book, *The Colossus,* appeared in 1960), and, later, two children (Frieda, born in 1960, and Nicholas, born in 1962), with a country house in Devon, England. In her poems, however, we find the strains of such a life; the work is galvanized by suffering, by a terrible constriction against which she unlooses "The lioness, / The shriek in the bath, / The cloak of holes" ("Purdah"). In articulating a dark vision of domestic life, Plath was adopting the license of Robert Lowell and Anne Sexton, a fellow student in Lowell's poetry seminar, to write about "private and taboo subjects."

While still living in Devon, Plath wrote most of the poems which were to make up her *Ariel* volume (by Christmas, 1962, she had gathered them in a black binder and arranged them in a careful sequence). The marriage broke up in the summer of 1962, and at the beginning of the new year, Plath found herself with two small children, living in a London flat in one of the coldest winters in recent British history. There she began new poems, writing furiously until February 1963, when she took her own life. The posthumous *Ariel* collection, published by Hughes in 1965, does not follow Plath's intended sequence; it omits what Hughes called "some of the more personally aggressive poems from 1962" and includes the dozen or so poems Plath wrote in the months before her death and which she had envisioned as the beginnings of a third book. Nonetheless, the powerful, angry poems of *Ariel,* mining a limited range of deep feeling, are Plath's best-known work. Fueled by an anger toward her husband and father, she speaks in these poems as one whose feelings are more than her own; it is as if she were the character in George Eliot's *Daniel Deronda* who appears suddenly before the novel's heroine and says, "I am a woman's life." Other poems, however, demonstrate her ability to render a wider variety of emotion; they include poems about her children (such as "Morning Song," "Child," and "Parliament Hill Fields") and a number of arresting poems about the natural world. In the vastness of natural processes, the romantic ego finds something as large as itself, and Plath's response to nature is intense, often uncanny. Her poems offer an eccentricity of vision where (as in "Blackberrying") the appearance of the natural world is never separable from the consciousness of the one who sees it.

For all her courting of excess, Plath is a remarkably controlled writer; her lucid stanzas, her clear diction, her dazzling alterations of sound are evidence of that control. The imaginative intensity of her poems is her own, triumphant creation out of the difficult circumstances of her life. She once remarked, "I cannot sympathize with those cries from the heart that are informed by nothing except a needle or a knife. . . . I believe that one should be able to control and manipulate experiences, even the most terrifying . . . with an informed and intelligent mind." The influence of her style, and of the persona she created, continues to be felt in the work of a wide variety of contemporary poets.

Morning Song

Love set you going like a fat gold watch.
The midwife slapped your footsoles, and your bald cry
Took its place among the elements.

Our voices echo, magnifying your arrival. New statue.
In a drafty museum, your nakedness   5
Shadows our safety. We stand round blankly as walls.

I'm no more your mother
Than the cloud that distills a mirror to reflect its own slow
Effacement at the wind's hand.

All night your moth-breath   10
Flickers among the flat pink roses. I wake to listen:
A far sea moves in my ear.

One cry, and I stumble from bed, cow-heavy and floral
In my Victorian nightgown.
Your mouth opens clean as a cat's. The window square   15

Whitens and swallows its dull stars. And now you try
Your handful of notes;
The clear vowels rise like balloons.

1961   1966

Lady Lazarus[1]

I have done it again.
One year in every ten
I manage it—

A sort of walking miracle, my skin
Bright as a Nazi lampshade,[2]   5
My right foot

A paperweight,
My face a featureless, fine
Jew linen.

Peel off the napkin   10
O my enemy.
Do I terrify?——

The nose, the eye pits, the full set of teeth?
The sour breath
Will vanish in a day.   15

Soon, soon the flesh
The grave cave ate will be
At home on me

---

1. Lazarus was raised from the dead by Jesus (John 11.1–45).

2. In the Nazi death camps, the skins of victims were sometimes used to make lampshades.

And I a smiling woman.
I am only thirty.   20
And like the cat I have nine times to die.

This is Number Three.
What a trash
To annihilate each decade.

What a million filaments.   25
The peanut-crunching crowd
Shoves in to see

Them unwrap me hand and foot——
The big strip tease.
Gentlemen, ladies   30

These are my hands
My knees.
I may be skin and bone,

Nevertheless, I am the same, identical woman.
The first time it happened I was ten.   35
It was an accident.

The second time I meant
To last it out and not come back at all.
I rocked shut

As a seashell.   40
They had to call and call
And pick the worms off me like sticky pearls.

Dying
Is an art, like everything else.
I do it exceptionally well.   45

I do it so it feels like hell.
I do it so it feels real.
I guess you could say I've a call.

It's easy enough to do it in a cell.
It's easy enough to do it and stay put.   50
It's the theatrical

Comeback in broad day
To the same place, the same face, the same brute
Amused shout:

'A miracle!'   55
That knocks me out.
There is a charge

For the eyeing of my scars, there is a charge
For the hearing of my heart——
It really goes.   60

And there is a charge, a very large charge
For a word or a touch
Or a bit of blood

Or a piece of my hair or my clothes.
So, so, Herr[3] Doktor.   65
So, Herr Enemy.

I am your opus,
I am your valuable,
The pure gold baby

That melts to a shriek.   70
I turn and burn.
Do not think I underestimate your great concern.

Ash, ash—
You poke and stir.
Flesh, bone, there is nothing there——   75

A cake of soap,
A wedding ring,
A gold filling.[4]

Herr God, Herr Lucifer
Beware   80
Beware.

Out of the ash[5]
I rise with my red hair
And I eat men like air.

1962   1966

Ariel[1]

Stasis in darkness.
Then the substanceless blue
Pour of tor[2] and distances.

---

3. Mr.
4. The Nazis used human remains in the making
of soap and scavenged corpses for jewelry and gold
teeth.
5. An allusion to the phoenix, a mythical bird that
dies by fire and is reborn out of its own ashes.

1. The spirit of fire and air in Shakespeare's *The
Tempest*. Ariel was also the name of the horse Plath
rode weekly in 1961–62, when she lived in Devon,
England.
2. A rocky peak.

God's lioness,
How one we grow,   5
Pivot of heels and knees!—The furrow

Splits and passes, sister to
The brown arc
Of the neck I cannot catch,

Nigger-eye   10
Berries cast dark
Hooks——

Black sweet blood mouthfuls,
Shadows.
Something else   15

Hauls me through air——
Thighs, hair;
Flakes from my heels.

White
Godiva,[3] I unpeel——   20
Dead hands, dead stringencies.

And now I
Foam to wheat, a glitter of seas.
The child's cry

Melts in the wall.   25
And I
Am the arrow,

The dew that flies
Suicidal, at one with the drive
Into the red   30

Eye, the cauldron of morning.

1962   1966

Daddy

You do not do, you do not do
Any more, black shoe
In which I have lived like a foot
For thirty years, poor and white,
Barely daring to breathe or Achoo.   5

---

3. Lady Godiva rode naked on horseback through the streets of Coventry (1040) to win a remission of feudal obligations and taxes.

Daddy, I have had to kill you.
You died before I had time——
Marble-heavy, a bag full of God,
Ghastly statue with one grey toe[1]
Big as a Frisco seal   10

And a head in the freakish Atlantic
Where it pours bean green over blue
In the waters of beautiful Nauset.[2]
I used to pray to recover you.
Ach, du.[3]   15

In the German tongue, in the Polish town[4]
Scraped flat by the roller
Of wars, wars, wars.
But the name of the town is common.
My Polack friend   20

Says there are a dozen or two.
So I never could tell where you
Put your foot, your root,
I never could talk to you.
The tongue stuck in my jaw.   25

It stuck in a barb wire snare.
Ich,[5] ich, ich, ich,
I could hardly speak.
I thought every German was you.
And the language obscene   30

An engine, an engine
Chuffing me off like a Jew.
A Jew to Dachau, Auschwitz, Belsen.[6]
I began to talk like a Jew.
I think I may well be a Jew.   35

The snows of the Tyrol,[7] the clear beer of Vienna
Are not very pure or true.
With my gypsy ancestress and my weird luck
And my Taroc[8] pack and my Taroc pack
I may be a bit of a Jew.   40

I have always been scared of *you*,
With your Luftwaffe,[9] your gobbledygoo.
And your neat mustache

1. Plath's father's toe turned black from gangrene, a complication of diabetes.
2. Massachusetts beach.
3. Ah, you: the first of a series of references to her father's German origins.
4. The poet's father, although of German descent, was born in Grabow, Poland.
5. I.

6. German concentration camps, where millions of Jews were murdered during World War II.
7. Austrian Alpine region.
8. Variation of Tarot, ancient fortune-telling cards. Gypsies, like Jews, were objects of Nazi genocidal ambition; many died in the concentration camps.
9. The German air force.

And your Aryan eye, bright blue.
Panzer[1]-man, panzer-man, O You——   45

Not God but a swastika
So black no sky could squeak through.
Every woman adores a Fascist,
The boot in the face, the brute
Brute heart of a brute like you.   50

You stand at the blackboard, daddy,
In the picture I have of you,
A cleft in your chin instead of your foot
But no less a devil for that, no not
And less the black man who   55

Bit my pretty red heart in two.
I was ten when they buried you.
At twenty I tried to die
And get back, back, back to you.
I thought even the bones would do.   60

But they pulled me out of the sack,
And they stuck me together with glue.[2]
And then I knew what to do.
I made a model of you,
A man in black with a Meinkampf[3] look   65

And a love of the rack and the screw.
And I said I do, I do.
So daddy, I'm finally through.
The black telephone's off at the root,
The voices just can't worm through.   70

If I've killed one man, I've killed two——
The vampire who said he was you
And drank my blood for a year,
Seven years, if you want to know.
Daddy, you can lie back now.   75

There's a stake in your fat black heart
And the villagers never liked you.
They are dancing and stamping on you.
They always *knew* it was you.
Daddy, daddy, you bastard, I'm through.   80

1962   1966

---

1. Armor (German); refers to the Nazi tank corps in World War II. Hitler preached the superiority of the Aryans—people of German stock with blond hair and blue eyes.
2. An allusion to Plath's first suicide attempt.

3. A reference to Hitler's political autobiography, *Mein Kampf* (My struggle), written and published before his rise to power, in which the future dictator outlined his plans for world conquest.

Words

Axes
After whose stroke the wood rings,
And the echoes!
Echoes traveling
Off from the centre like horses.   5

The sap
Wells like tears, like the
Water striving
To re-establish its mirror
Over the rock   10

That drops and turns,
A white skull,
Eaten by weedy greens.
Years later I
Encounter them on the road——   15

Words dry and riderless,
The indefatigable hoof-taps.
While
From the bottom of the pool, fixed stars
Govern a life.   20

1963   1966

Blackberrying

Nobody in the lane, and nothing, nothing but blackberries,
Blackberries on either side, though on the right mainly,
A blackberry alley, going down in hooks, and a sea
Somewhere at the end of it, heaving. Blackberries
Big as the ball of my thumb, and dumb as eyes   5
Ebon in the hedges, fat
With blue-red juices. These they squander on my fingers.
I had not asked for such a blood sisterhood; they must love me.
They accommodate themselves to my milkbottle, flattening their sides.

Overhead go the choughs[1] in black, cacophonous flocks—   10
Bits of burnt paper wheeling in a blown sky.
Theirs is the only voice, protesting, protesting.
I do not think the sea will appear at all.
The high, green meadows are glowing, as if lit from within.
I come to one bush of berries so ripe it is a bush of flies,   15

1. Small, chattering birds of the crow family.

Hanging their bluegreen bellies and their wing panes in a Chinese screen.
The honey-feast of the berries has stunned them; they believe in heaven.
One more hook, and the berries and bushes end.

The only thing to come now is the sea.
From between two hills a sudden wind funnels at me,   20
Slapping its phantom laundry in my face.
These hills are too green and sweet to have tasted salt.
I follow the sheep path between them. A last hook brings me
To the hills' northern face, and the face is orange rock
That looks out on nothing, nothing but a great space   25
Of white and pewter lights, and a din like silversmiths
Beating and beating at an intractable metal.

1961   1971

Purdah[1]

Jade—
Stone of the side,
The agonized

Side of green Adam, I
Smile, cross-legged,   5
Enigmatical,

Shifting my clarities.
So valuable!
How the sun polishes this shoulder!

And should   10
The moon, my
Indefatigable cousin

Rise, with her cancerous pallors,
Dragging trees—
Little bushy polyps,[2]   15

Little nets,
My visibilities hide.
I gleam like a mirror.

At this facet the bridegroom arrives
Lord of the mirrors!   20
It is himself he guides

1. Seclusion of women from public observation among Muslims and some Hindu sects.
2. Animals that have many feet or tentacles, like octopuses, cuttlefish, and smaller coelenterates; also a general term for tumors that have tentacle-like protrusions.

In among these silk
Screens, these rustling appurtenances.
I breathe, and the mouth

Veil stirs its curtain   25
My eye
Veil is

A concatenation of rainbows.
I am his.
Even in his   30

Absence, I
Revolve in my
Sheath of impossibles,

Priceless and quiet
Among these parakeets, macaws!³   35
O chatterers

Attendants of the eyelash!
I shall unloose
One feather, like the peacock.

Attendants of the lip!   40
I shall unloose
One note

Shattering
The chandelier
Of air that all day flies   45

Its crystals
A million ignorants.
Attendants!

Attendants!
And at his next step   50
I shall unloose

I shall unloose—
From the small jeweled
Doll he guards like a heart—

The lioness,   55
The shriek in the bath,
The cloak of holes.

1962   1972

---

3. Kinds of parrots.

The Applicant

First, are you our sort of a person?
Do you wear
A glass eye, false teeth or a crutch,
A brace or a hook,
Rubber breasts or a rubber crotch,   5

Stitches to show something's missing? No, no? Then
How can we give you a thing?
Stop crying.
Open your hand.
Empty? Empty. Here is a hand   10

To fill it and willing
To bring teacups and roll away headaches
And do whatever you tell it.
Will you marry it?
It is guaranteed   15

To thumb shut your eyes at the end
And dissolve of sorrow.
We make new stock from the salt.
I notice you are stark naked.
How about this suit——   20

Black and stiff, but not a bad fit.
Will you marry it?
It is waterproof, shatterproof, proof
Against fire and bombs through the roof.
Believe me, they'll bury you in it.   25

Now your head, excuse me, is empty.
I have the ticket for that.
Come here, sweetie, out of the closet.
Well, what do you think of *that*?
Naked as paper to start   30

But in twenty-five years she'll be silver,
In fifty, gold.
A living doll, everywhere you look.
It can sew, it can cook,
It can talk, talk, talk.   35

It works, there is nothing wrong with it.
You have a hole, it's a poultice.
You have an eye, it's an image.
My boy, it's your last resort.
Will you marry it, marry it, marry it.   40

1962   1965

Child

Your clear eye is the one absolutely beautiful thing.
I want to fill it with color and ducks,
The zoo of the new

Whose names you meditate—
April snowdrop, Indian pipe,   5
Little

Stalk without wrinkle,
Pool in which images
Should be grand and classical

Not this troublous   10
Wringing of hands, this dark
Ceiling without a star.

1963   1972

AUDRE LORDE
1934–1992

Audre Lorde's poetry wages what she called "a war against the tyrannies of silence";
it articulates what has been passed over out of fear or discomfort, what has been kept
hidden and secret. Reading her we feel the violence inherent in breaking a silence,
perhaps most often as she probes the experience of anger—the anger of black toward
white or white toward black, a woman's anger at men and other women, and men's
anger toward women (the subject of her powerful poem "Need: A Choral of Black
Women's Voices"). "My Black woman's anger," she wrote in her collection of essays,
Sister Outsider, "is a molten pond at the core of me, my most fiercely guarded secret."
Having admitted this secret into her poems, Lorde transforms our expectations of
what is fit subject for the lyric. Her work is often deliberately disturbing, the powerful
voice of the poem cutting through denial, politeness, and fear. In the development
of this voice, Lorde drew on African resources, especially the matriarchal mythology
and history of West Africa. Her seventh book, *The Black Unicorn* (1978), reflects the
time she spent in Africa studying, in particular, Yoruba mythology and reclaiming her
connection to the rich African cultures. The African presence is evident in one of her
last books, *Our Dead Behind Us* (1986), as well. From the start, Lorde's work suggests
that she always connected poetry to the speaking voice, but her study of African
materials deepened her connection to oral traditions (like the chant or the call) and
taught her the power of voice to cut across time and place. From African writers, she
said, she learned that "we live in accordance with, in a kind of correspondence with,
the rest of the world as a whole." A powerful voice informed by personal and cultural
history creates the possibility, for Lorde, of bridging the differences her work does
not seek to erase. "It is not difference that immobilizes us," she wrote, "but silence."

Her work both celebrates difference and confounds it. In Adrienne Rich's words, Lorde wrote "as a Black woman, a mother, a daughter, a Lesbian, a feminist, a visionary." Her poem "Coal" affirms an *I* that is "the total black, being spoken / from the earth's inside." This total blackness was, for her, also associated with Eros and with creativity; she celebrated this source as what she called "woman's place of power within each of us," which is "neither white nor surface; it is dark, it is ancient; and it is deep." Her best work calls on the deepest places of her own life—on the pain she experienced, on her rage (her second book was titled *Cables to Rage,* 1972), on her longing and desire. One of the silences her poems broke concerns love between women, and she wrote a number of poems that are erotic, precise, and true to both the power and delicacy of feeling. Unafraid of anger, she was also capable of tenderness; this is perhaps most clear not only in her love poems but in poems that address a younger generation.

Lorde was born in New York City and lived in New York almost all her life. Her parents were West Indian, and her mother was light skinned. "I grew up in a genuine confusion / between grass and weeds and flowers / and what colored meant," Lorde wrote in her poem "Outside." Part of that confusion was the conflict represented by her father's blackness and her mother's desire for whiteness (in "Black Mother Woman" Lorde speaks of the mother as "split with deceitful longings"). Lorde's understanding of identity forged out of conflict began, then, for her in her own family history with its legacy of "conflicting rebellions" ("Black Mother Woman"). In 1961 she received a B.A. from Hunter College and later a Master's of Library Science from Columbia University. The following year she married (she divorced in 1970), and the marriage produced a daughter and a son. In 1968 she became poet-in-residence for a year at Tougaloo College in Mississippi, her first experience in the American South. Thereafter she knew her work to be that of a writer and teacher; she taught at John Jay College of Criminal Justice in New York City and, from 1981, was professor of English at Hunter College. In the last years of her life Lorde traveled extensively, not only to Africa but to Australia (where she met with aborigine women) and Germany. During her last years she lived much of the time in St. Croix.

"I have come to believe over and over again," Lorde said, "that what is most important to me must be spoken, made verbal and shared, even at the risk of having it bruised or misunderstood." This drive toward expression made Lorde a prolific writer and led her to several prose works in which she shared experiences often restricted to privacy: *The Cancer Journals* (1980), an account of her struggle with breast cancer, and *Zami: A New Spelling of My Name* (1982), a "biomythography" of her growing up and her emergent lesbian identity. The urgency Lorde felt to make experience "verbal and shared," however, sometimes overrode a distinction crucial to her work: that between poetry and rhetoric. She preserved this distinction in her best work by listening and responding to other voices in herself and in the world around her. With their combination of pain, anger, and tenderness, her finest poems are poetry as illumination, poetry in which, as she said, "we give name to those ideas which are— until the poem—nameless, formless, about to be birthed, but already felt."

Coal

I
is the total black, being spoken
from the earth's inside.
There are many kinds of open
how a diamond comes into a knot of flame   5

how sound comes into a word, coloured
by who pays what for speaking.

Some words are open like a diamond
on glass windows
singing out within the passing crash of sun   10
Then there are words like stapled wagers
in a perforated book,—buy and sign and tear apart—
and come whatever wills all chances
the stub remains
an ill-pulled tooth with a ragged edge.   15
Some words live in my throat
breeding like adders. Others know sun
seeking like gypsies over my tongue
to explode through my lips
like young sparrows bursting from shell.   20
Some words
bedevil me.

Love is a word, another kind of open.
As the diamond comes into a knot of flame
I am Black because I come from the earth's inside   25
now take my word for jewel in the open light.

                                              1968

The Woman Thing

The hunters are back from beating the winter's face
in search of a challenge or task
in search of food
making fresh tracks for their children's hunger
they do not watch the sun   5
they cannot wear its heat for a sign
of triumph or freedom;
The hunters are treading heavily homeward
through snow that is marked
with their own bloody footprints.   10
emptyhanded, the hunters return
snow-maddened, sustained by their rages.

In the night after food they may seek
young girls for their amusement. But now
the hunters are coming   15
and the unbaked girls flee from their angers.
All this day I have craved
food for my child's hunger
Emptyhanded the hunters come shouting

injustices drip from their mouths   20
like stale snow melted in sunlight.

Meanwhile
the woman thing my mother taught me
bakes off its covering of snow
like a rising blackening sun.   25

                                                                    1968

Black Mother Woman

I cannot recall you gentle
yet through your heavy love
I have become
an image of your once delicate flesh
split with deceitful longings.   5

When strangers come and compliment me
your aged spirit takes a bow
jingling with pride
but once you hid that secret
in the center of furies   10
hanging me
with deep breasts and wiry hair
with your own split flesh
and long suffering eyes
buried in myths of little worth.   15

But I have peeled away your anger
down to the core of love
and look mother
I Am
a dark temple where your true spirit rises   20
beautiful
and tough as chestnut
stanchion[1] against your nightmare of weakness
and if my eyes conceal
a squadron of conflicting rebellions   25
I learned from you
to define myself
through your denials.

                                                                    1971

---

1. Upright bar or post (for supporting, e.g., a roof).

CHARLES WRIGHT
b. 1935

"All forms of landscape are autobiographical." This line from Charles Wright's poem "All Landscape Is Abstract, and Tends to Repeat Itself" is a useful gloss on Wright's own poetry, in which the poet is a pilgrim who remembers, walks through, and describes the places he has most loved. Among those places are Kingsport, Tennessee, where he grew up; northern Italy, where he was stationed as a young soldier and later lived for some months with his family; Laguna Beach, California; and the Blue Ridge area of Virginia. Wright's landscapes, like his poetry, are a layered mixture of the visible and the invisible; they engage a drama of perception he shares with the painter, Paul Cézanne, to whom he has written in homage. This is a poet who walks out into his backyard—the landscape of his current home in Charlottesville, Virginia, where he teaches at the University of Virginia—looks at the trees and stars, and each time experiences something that yields a different poem (one such poem is happily titled "Back Yard Boogie Woogie"). The backyard offers him as broad a scope for poetry as the larger landscapes he also renders in his poems because, for Wright, the visible world is always opening up and into a larger, invisible world. The stars that shine above his backyard (and Wright loves the stars) make bounded space part of an infinite cosmos.

Wright belongs to the visionary company of American poetry, but he is also drawn to the visible world and in his poetry the metaphysical is encountered through the physical. An immersion and delight in the visible fills Wright's poems and makes him a poet of impressive descriptive power. What deepens his poems beyond their acute and often startling figurative description is a narrative of spiritual autobiography or what Keats called "soul making." Wright's version of this autobiography is distinctively his and distinctively American—full of discontinuities, laced with a wry sense of humor, and rendered in a language that moves easily in and out of an American vernacular. His selected early poems, *Country Music,* won the National Book Award in 1983, and its title conjures the twang of hillbilly singers and Appalachian mountain hymns, as well as the music of a countryside rendered in the poet's alliterative lines and enjambed rhythms. Like a good country musician, Wright knows how to shift and layer tones in quick and surprising ways. He knows how to be melancholy, lucid, and funny in the same poem. The vocabulary of his poems ranges from the biblical ("mercy and consolation") to the playful exclamation of "hubba-hubba." It's characteristic of Wright to follow the line "the soul is in the body as light is in air" with "Well, I wouldn't know about that" ("Appalachian Book of the Dead III") or to answer the image of "the angel with her drum and wings" with the offhand remark "Some wings" ("Appalachian Book of the Dead VI").

"Anyone's autobiography, at least in his own eyes, is made up of a string of luminous moments, numinous moments," Wright said in an interview. Wright's poems themselves are a string of such moments, but the strand is marked by discontinuity. His work is full of juxtapositions that fuse surprising things together ("bandannaed" and "moonlight" in "Star Turn II"), and the movement in his poems from one stanza to the next is often as abrupt as a jump-cut, each stanza its own kind of feint and hesitation toward something not quite sayable. The spaces between his stanzas or the space within a line (especially a dropped line) point to "some place beyond the lip of language, / Some silence, some zone of grace" ("Poem Half in the Manner of Li Ho"). The effect is what Wright once called "a kind of American sprawl of a poem." To create this "American sprawl," Wright counts syllables rather than poetic feet. While line length expands or contracts from poem to poem, the seven-syllable line is his base. Whatever the variation in line length, Wright prefers an odd number of syllables, which, he says, lets him retain the ghost of traditional meters without falling into their patterns.

Wright loves and draws on many traditions of poetry. As a young soldier in Italy he was drawn to the work of Ezra Pound, whose emphasis on the image remains an important influence. And, like Pound, Wright's work often mentions and makes use of the traditions of ancient Chinese poets (like Tu Fu and Wang Wei and Li Ho). He also loves the Italian poets, among them Eugenio Montale (whose work Wright has translated) and Dante, who is mentioned in "Star Turn II" and whose narrative of spiritual pilgrimage influences many Wright poems, among them "North American Bear." Volumes that bring together Wright's many books of poetry are *Country Music: Selected Early Poems* (1982), *The World of the Ten Thousand Things: Poems 1880–1990* (1990), and *Negative Blue: Selected Later Poems* (2000). His collection of essays and interviews, *Halflife: Improvisations and Interviews, 1977–1987* (1988), offers entry into the poet's craft and thought. Wright's body of work, with its distinctive music and startling capacity to fuse the outer world with the inner life of soul making, has established its own "zone of grace" in contemporary American poetry.

Him

His sorrow hangs like a heart in the star-flowered boundary tree.
It mirrors the endless wind.

He feeds on the lunar differences and flies up at the dawn.

When he lies down, the waters will lie down with him,
And all that walks and all that stands still, and sleep through the
    thunder.   5

It's for him that the willow bleeds.

Look for him high in the flat black of the northern Pacific sky,
Released in his suit of lights,
                  lifted and laid clear.

                                  1977

Two Stories

Tonight, on the deck, the lights
Semaphore up at me through the atmosphere,
Town lights, familiar lights
                pulsing and slacking off
The way they used to back on the ridge outside of Kingsport[1]   5
Thirty-five years ago,
The moonlight sitting inside my head
Like knives,
            the cold like a drug I knew I'd settle down with.

---

1. In Tennessee, where the poet grew up.

I used to imagine them shore lights, as these are, then,   10
As something inside me listened with all its weight
For the sea-surge and the sea-change.

_____

There's a soft spot in everything
Our fingers touch,
                        the one place where everything breaks   15
When we press it just right.
The past is like that with its arduous edges and blind sides,
The whorls of our fingerprints
                        embedded along its walls
Like fossils the sea has left behind.   20

_____

This is a story I swear is true.

I used to sleepwalk. But only
On camping trips,
                or whenever I slept outside.
One August, when I was eleven, on Mount LeConte in Tennessee,   25
Campfire over, and ghost story over,
Everyone still asleep, apparently I arose
From my sleeping bag,
                        opened the tent flap, and started out on the trail
That led to the drop-off, where the mountainside   30
Went straight down for almost a thousand feet.
Half-moon and cloud cover, so some light
As I went on up the path through the rhododendron,
The small pebbles and split roots
                            like nothing under my feet.   35
The cliffside was half a mile from the campsite.
As I got closer,
                moving blindly, unerringly,
Deeper in sleep than the shrubs,
I stepped out, it appears,   40
Onto the smooth lip of the rock cape of the cliff,
When my left hand, and then my right hand,
Stopped me as they were stopped
By the breathing side of a bear which woke me
And there we were,   45
                    the child and the black bear and the cliff-drop,
And this is the way it went—
                            I stepped back, and I turned around,
And I walked down through the rhododendron
And never looked back,   50
                    truly awake in the throbbing world,
And I ducked through the low flap
Of the tent, so quietly, and I went to sleep
And never told anyone
Till years later when I thought I knew what it meant,   55
                            which now I've forgot.

_____

And this one is questionable,
Though sworn to me by an old friend
Who'd killed a six-foot diamondback about seven o'clock in the morning
(He'd found it coiled in a sunny place)   60
And threw it into a croker sack[2] with its head chopped off,
                  and threw the sack in the back of a jeep,
Then left for his day's work
On the farm.
          That evening he started to show the snake   65
To someone, and put his hand in the sack to pull it out.
As he reached in, the snake's stump struck him.
His wrist was bruised for a week.

             ————————————

It's not age,
          nor time with its gold eyelid and blink,   70
Nor dissolution in all its mimicry
That lifts us and sorts us out.
It's discontinuity
          and all its spangled coming between
That sends us apart and keeps us there in a dread.   75
It's what's in the rearview mirror,
                  smaller and out of sight.

             ————————————

What do you do when the words don't come to you anymore,
And all the embolisms fade in the dirt?
And the ocean sings in its hammock,   80
                rocking itself back and forth?
And you live at the end of the road where the sky starts its dark decline?

The barking goes on and on
                from the far hill, constantly
Sticking its noise in my good ear.   85

Goodbye, Miss Sweeney, goodbye.
I'm starting to think about the psychotransference of all things.
It's small bones in the next life.
It's small bones,   90
          and heel and toe forever and ever.

                          1984

From A Journal of the Year of the Ox

12 December 1985

    —Late afternoon, blue of the sky blue
    As a dove's neck, dove
    Color of winter branches among winter branches,

---

2. As used in the South, one of a variety of regional American names for a gunny sack, a large sack made from loosely woven coarse material.

Guttural whistle and up,
                    December violets crooked at my feet,   5
Cloud-wedge starting to slide like a detached retina[1]
Slanting across the blue
                  inaction the dove disappears in.

Mean constellations quip and annoy
                    next night against the same sky   10
As I seek out, unsuccessfully,
In Luke's spyglass Halley's comet[2] and its train of ice:
An ordered and measured affection is virtuous
In its clean cause
                however it comes close in this life.   15
Nothing else moves toward us out of the stars,
                    nothing else shines.
          —12 December 1985

                         1988

Poem Half in the Manner of Li Ho[1]

All things aspire to weightlessness,
                  some place beyond the lip of language,
Some silence, some zone of grace,

Sky white as raw silk,
                    opening mirror cold-sprung in the west,   5
Sunset like dead grass.

If God hurt the way we hurt,
                  he, too, would be heart-sore,
Disconsolate, unappeasable.

———————————

Li Ho, the story goes, would leave home   10
Each day at dawn, riding a colt, a servant boy
                    walking behind him,
An antique tapestry bag
Strapped to his back.
                When inspiration struck, Ho would write   15
The lines down and drop them in the bag.
At night he'd go home and work the lines up into a poem,
No matter how disconnected and loose-leafed they were.
His mother once said,
"He won't stop until he has vomited out his heart."   20

1. A delicate, light-sensitive membrane lining the inner eyeball.
2. A periodic comet named for Edmund Halley (1656–1742), English astronomer, who observed it in 1682. It was sighted again in 1982 and returned to its closest approach to the sun in late December 1985. Luke is Wright's son.
1. Chinese poet (760–816).

And so he did,
              Like John Keats,[2]
He died believing his name would never be written among the Characters.
Without hope, he thought himself—that worst curse—unlucky.
At twenty-seven, at death's line, he saw a man come   25
In purple, driving a red dragon,
A tablet in one hand, who said,
                    "I'm here to summon Li Ho."

Ho got from his bed and wept.
Far from the sick room's dragon-dark, snow stormed the passes,   30
Monkeys surfed the bo[3] trees
                and foolish men ate white jade.

————————

How mournful the southern hills are,
                    how white their despair
Under December's T'ang blue blank page.   35

What's the use of words—there are no words
For December's chill redaction,
                for the way it makes us feel.

We hang like clouds between heaven and earth,
                between something and nothing,   40
Sometimes with shadows, sometimes without.

                              1997

The Appalachian Book of the Dead VI[1]

Last page, The Appalachian Book of the Dead,
                    full moon,
No one in anyone's arms, no lip to ear, cloud bank
And boyish soprano out of the east edge of things.
Ball-whomp and rig-grind stage right,   5
Expectancy, quivering needle, at north-northwest.

And here comes the angel with her drum and wings. Some wings.
Lost days, as Meng Chiao[2] says, a little window of words
We peer through darkly. Darkly,

2. English Romantic poet (1785–1821) who died of tuberculosis at age twenty-five in Rome, Italy. He asked that his grave bear no name but only the words "Here lies one whose name was writ on water."
3. A name for a Buddhist monk.
1. From a series of Wright poems evoking the *Egyptian Book of the Dead* (earliest collection 1580–1350 B.C.E.), which consists of charms, spells, and formulas for use by the deceased in the afterlife. At first inscriptions, the texts were later papyrus rolls placed inside the mummy case. The essential ideas of Egyptian religion are known through these books. Appalachia, named for the mountain chain that traverses the region, is defined socially and historically as an area of coal mining and timber harvesting in Kentucky, West Virginia, and southern Pennsylvania.
2. Chinese poet (751–814).

Moon stopped in cloud bank, light slick for the chute and long slide,   10
No lip, no ear
                    Distant murmur of women's voices.

I hear that the verb is facilitate. To facilitate.
Azure. To rise. To rise through the azure. Illegible joy.
No second heaven. No first.   15
I think I'll lie here like this awhile, my back flat on the floor.
I hear that days bleed.
                    I hear that the right word will take your breath away.

                                                                    1998

Star Turn II

How small the stars are tonight, bandannaed by moonlight,
How few and how far between—
Disordered and drained, like highlights in Dante's[1] death mask.
Or a sequined dress from the forties
                              —hubba-hubba—   5
Some sequins missing, some sequins inalterably in place.

Unlike our lives, which are as they are.
Unlike our imagined selves, which are as we'll never become,
Star-like and shining,
Everyone looking up at, everyone pointing there, O there,   10
Masked and summering in,
                    each one a bright point, each one a dodged eclipse.

                                                                    1998

North American Bear[1]

Early November in the soul,
                    a hard rain, and dusky gold
From the trees, late afternoon
Squint-light and heavy heart-weight.
It's always downleaf and dim.   5
A sixty-two-year-old, fallow-voiced, night-leaning man,
I stand at ease on the blank sidewalk.
Unhinder my habitat, starlight, make me insoluble;
Negative in my afterscape,
                    sidle the shadow across my mouth.   10

----

1. Dante Alighieri (1265–1321), Italian poet and author of *The Divine Comedy*, all three sections of which end with the word *stars*.

1. The constellation Ursa Major, or Great Bear, was seen as a bear by both the Sumerians and the Iroquois Indians. It is also called the Big Dipper.

Random geometry of the stars,
                          random word-strings
As beautiful as the alphabet.
Or so I remember them,
                          North American Bear,   15
Orion, Cassiopeia and the Pleiades,[2]
Stitching their syntax across the deep North Carolina sky
A half-century ago,
The lost language of summer nights, the inarticulate scroll
Of time   20
          pricked on its dark, celestial cylinder.

———————————

What is it about the stars we can't shake?
                          What pulse, what tide drop
Pulls us like vertigo upward, what
Height-like reversal urges us toward their clear deeps?   25
Tonight, for instance,
Something is turning behind my eyes,
                          something unwept, something unnamable,
Spinning its line out.
Who is to say the hijacked heart has not returned to its cage?   30
Who is to say some angel has not
                          breathed in my ear?

———————————

I walk in the chill of the late autumn night
                          like Orpheus,[3]
Thinking my song, anxious to look back,   35
My vanished life an ornament, a drifting cloud, behind me,
A soft, ashen transcendence
Buried and resurrected once, then time and again.
The sidewalk unrolls like a deep sleep.
Above me the stars, stern stars,   40
Uncover their faces.
                          No heartbeat on my heels, no footfall.

———————————

The season approaches us, dead leaves and withered grasses
Waxed by the wind wherever you look,
                          the clear night sky   45
Star-struck and star-stung, that constellation, those seven high stars,
General Ke-Shu[4] lifting his sword, the Chinese say.
Or one of them said,

2. The cluster of six bright stars in the constellation Taurus; in Greek mythology, the seven daughters of Atlas and Pleione were placed among the stars; a seventh bright star has apparently faded from view since the original sighting. "Cassiopeia," also known as Andromeda, was in Greek mythology a princess of Ethiopia who was rescued from a sea monster by Perseus. She and her parents became constellations. In Greek mythology, Orion was a hunter who was turned at death into a constellation.
3. Poet and musician in Greek mythology who attempted to rescue his wife, Eurydice, from Hades through the power of his music. On the journey back to earth, he was instructed not to look back at her. He did so, and she was returned to the underworld.
4. Officer in the Yuan Dynasty (1279–1368).

One at the Western Front as part of his army, without doubt.
I almost can see him myself,   50
          long-sword over the Bear's neck,
His car wheel-less, darkness sifting away like a sandstorm to the west.

———————

Some of these star fires must surely be ash by now.
I dawdle outside in the back yard,
Humming old songs that no one cares about anymore.   55
The hat of darkness tilts the night sky
Inch by inch, foot by black foot,
          over the Blue Ridge.[5]
How bright the fire of the world was, I think to myself,
Before white hair and the ash of days.   60
I gaze at the constellations,
          forgetting whatever it was I had to say.

———————

The sidewalk again, unrolling grey and away. 9 p.m.
A cold wind from the far sky.
There is a final solitude I haven't arrived at yet,   65
Weariness like a dust in my throat.
          I simmer inside its outline,
However, and feel safe, as the stars spill by, for one more night
Like some medieval journeyman enfrescoed[6] with his poem in his hand,
Heaven remaining my neighborhood.   70
And like him, too, with something red and inviolate
          under my feet.

2000

5. Eastern range of the Appalachian Mountains extending from South Mountain, Pennsylvania, into northern Georgia. The range is visible in Charlottesville, Virginia.

6. Turned into a painting on plaster. An ancient technique, fresco was used by the Romans for decoration and perfected by the masters of the Italian Renaissance.

———————————————

MARY OLIVER
b. 1935

"[O]f course / loss is the great lesson," Mary Oliver writes in her poem "Poppies." "But also I say this: that light / is an invitation to happiness / and that happiness, when it's done right / is a kind of holiness." What we experience first and most intensely in Mary Oliver's poetry is the earthly delight that constitutes her vision of both happiness and holiness. That delight is founded in the world of the alligator, the deer, the bear, the black oak, the trumpet vine, the wild mushroom. This variegated natural world is precisely recorded in Oliver's poetry, from her first book, *No Voyage and Other Poems* (1963), to her collection of prose, prose poems, and poems, *Winter Hours* (2000). But a river of loss runs underground in her poems, whose deeper currents are sometimes an unspoken source propelling the poet out into the natural world; that world restores her to herself; its vitality and beauty open her heart. Yet in Oliver's best work, the natural world does more than restore or console; it also teaches the "great lesson" of loving and letting go.

Oliver was born in Maple Heights, Ohio, and attended Vassar College. She lives in both Provincetown, Massachusetts, and Bennington, Vermont; not surprisingly, the New England landscape is as central to her work as it is to Robert Frost's. But perhaps the poet she most closely resembles is James Wright (also born in Ohio), to whose memory her Pulitzer Prize–winning *American Primitive* (1983) is dedicated; she shares Wright's capacity for wonder, as well as his movement away from a social world into a natural one. Digging for mussels or spotting bear in the Truro Woods (in poems from *Twelve Moons,* 1979), watching humpback whales or blue herons on the ponds (in *American Primitive*), observing the hummingbird (in *New and Selected Poems,* 1992), Oliver endows her regional landscape with the spaciousness and depth Thoreau gave to Walden Pond. Indeed, the very title of *American Primitive* suggests her self-conscious participation in an American impulse toward something primary and primal in the self and in the world.

One of the pleasures of reading Oliver's work is the education it provides about plants and animals in its detailed and knowledgeable observation (as when, for example, in "Skunk Cabbage" (*American Primitive*) she sees the "turnip-hearted skunk cabbage / slinging its bunched leaves up / through the chilly mud." The power and precision of her descriptions make it seem that, in lines from her "Alligator Poem" (*New and Selected Poems*), we "saw the world as if for a second time, / the way it really is." But Oliver's poems are as much about transformation as about observation, for in her work—as in "Alligator Poem"—the secret life of the world seems to open itself, for a moment, to human apprehension and the world and the self are transformed. For her, the natural world casts a spell of amazement over poet and reader (this amazement—the stance of wonder at what is—is frequently registered by Oliver's use of the interrogative). Those moments when she is "washed and washed / in the river / of earthly delight" ("Poppies") restore the poet to her faith in the world that made her. They are rapturous antidotes that heal night's pain, mitigate loneliness, turn the heaviness of "the great bones of my life" ("Spring Azures") into wings. They are also the antidote to psychic pain, and to a social world with which Mary Oliver's poems want little to do. That world occasionally intrudes into Oliver's poems in the form of disturbing figures, like the woman in the airport restroom in "Singapore," the disfigured boy in "Acid," or, more ominously and persistently, the father who "knocks / wildly at the door" in "A Visitor." These figures unsettle the poet's solitude and threaten a vision of happiness and holiness sometimes too easily affirmed in her work. Though such human and social intrusions are intermittent in Oliver's poems, they seem to gesture toward injuries this poet keeps hidden.

There is such naturalness to Oliver's poems that we may fail to notice their craft. Oliver's language stays close to the spoken American idiom but infuses it with music, and creates, through verbal design, images of startling vividness (in "Alligator Poem" the birds "shook open the snowy pleats of their wings, and drifted away"). In a poetry so attentive to detail, where line breaks focus our attention on particulars—"the line is the device upon which the poem spins itself into being," she has said—there is also extraordinary power. Oliver builds her stanzas so they interlock, one into another, and the reader is pulled through a series of perceptions into the poet's insight. In certain poems the movement of her lines across the page rhythmically enacts the reaching forward and pulling back of the poet's walks into the landscape. Of course, making the design of a poem seem as natural as the hummingbird pausing at the trumpet vine is one sign of how gifted a poet Oliver is.

Oliver is on the faculty of Bennington College, where she holds the Catharine Osgood Foster Chair for Distinguished Teaching. Her *New and Selected Poems* won the National Book Award in 1992 and includes work from six previous books, including *House of Light* (1990), *Dream Work* (1986), *The Night Traveler* (1978), and *Sleep-*

ing in the Forest (1978). She has also published *White Pine* (1994); *Blue Pastures* (1995) and *The Leaf and the Cloud* (2000), essays; *A Poetry Handbook* (1994); and *Rules for the Dance: A Handbook for Writing and Reading Metrical Verse* (1998).

The Black Snake

When the black snake
flashed onto the morning road,
and the truck could not swerve—
death, that is how it happens.

Now he lies looped and useless   5
as an old bicycle tire.
I stop the car
and carry him into the bushes.

He is as cool and gleaming
as a braided whip, he is as beautiful and quiet   10
as a dead brother.
I leave him under the leaves

and drive on, thinking
about *death*: its suddenness,
its terrible weight,   15
its certain coming. Yet under

reason burns a brighter fire, which the bones
have always preferred.
It is the story of endless good fortune.
It says to oblivion: not me!   20

It is the light at the center of every cell.
It is what sent the snake coiling and flowing forward
happily all spring through the green leaves before
he came to the road.

1979

In Blackwater Woods

Look, the trees
are turning
their own bodies
into pillars

of light,   5
are giving off the rich
fragrance of cinnamon
and fulfillment,

the long tapers
of cattails   10
are bursting and floating away over
the blue shoulders

of the ponds,
and every pond,
no matter what its   15
name is, is

nameless now.
Every year
everything
I have ever learned   20

in my lifetime
leads back to this: the fires
and the black river of loss
whose other side

is salvation,   25
whose meaning
none of us will ever know.
To live in this world

you must be able
to do three things: 30
to love what is mortal;
to hold it

against your bones knowing
your own life depends on it;
and, when the time comes to let it go,   35
to let it go.

                                                                   1983

A Visitor

My father, for example,
who was young once
and blue-eyed,
returns
on the darkest of nights   5
to the porch and knocks
wildly at the door,
and if I answer
I must be prepared
for his waxy face,   10
for his lower lip

swollen with bitterness.
And so, for a long time,
I did not answer,
but slept fitfully   15
between his hours of rapping.
But finally there came the night
when I rose out of my sheets
and stumbled down the hall.
The door fell open   20

and I knew I was saved
and could bear him,
pathetic and hollow,
with even the least of his dreams
frozen inside him,   25
and the meanness gone.
And I greeted him and asked him
into the house,
and lit the lamp,
and looked into his blank eyes   30
in which at last
I saw what a child must love,
I saw what love might have done
had we loved in time.

                                                    1986

Landscape

Isn't it plain the sheets of moss, except that
they have no tongues, could lecture
all day if they wanted about

spiritual patience? Isn't it clear
the black oaks along the path are standing   5
as though they were the most fragile of flowers?

Every morning I walk like this around
the pond, thinking: if the doors of my heart
ever close, I am as good as dead.

Every morning, so far, I'm alive. And now   10
the crows break off from the rest of the darkness
and burst up into the sky—as though

all night they had thought of what they would like
their lives to be, and imagined
their strong, thick wings.   15

                                                    1986

Poppies

The poppies send up their
orange flares; swaying
in the wind, their congregations
are a levitation

of bright dust, of thin   5
and lacy leaves.
There isn't a place
in this world that doesn't

sooner or later drown
in the indigos of darkness,   10
but now, for a while,
the roughage

shines like a miracle
as it floats above everything
with its yellow hair.   15
Of course nothing stops the cold,

black, curved blade
from hooking forward—
of course
loss is the great lesson.   20

But also I say this: that light
is an invitation
to happiness,
and that happiness,

when it's done right,   25
is a kind of holiness,
palpable and redemptive.
Inside the bright fields,

touched by their rough and spongy gold,
I am washed and washed   30
in the river
of earthly delight—

and what are you going to do—
what can you do
about it—   35
deep, blue night?

1991–92   1992

Hummingbird Pauses at the Trumpet Vine

Who doesn't love
roses, and who
doesn't love the lilies
of the black ponds

floating like flocks   5
of tiny swans,
and of course the flaming
trumpet vine

where the hummingbird comes
like a small green angel, to soak   10
his dark tongue
in happiness—

and who doesn't want
to live with the brisk
motor of his heart   15
singing

like a Schubert,
and his eyes
working and working like those days of rapture,
by van Gogh, in Arles?   20

Look! for most of the world
is waiting
or remembering—
most of the world is time

when we're not here,   25
not born yet, or died—
a slow fire
under the earth with all

our dumb wild blind cousins
who also   30
can't even remember anymore
their own happiness—

Look! and then we will be
like the pale cool
stones, that last almost   35
forever.

1991–92   1992

Alligator Poem

I knelt down
at the edge of the water,
and if the white birds standing
in the tops of the trees whistled any warning
I didn't understand,   5
I drank up to the very moment it came
crashing toward me,
its tail flailing
like a bundle of swords,
slashing the grass,   10
and the inside of its cradle-shaped mouth
gaping,
and rimmed with teeth—
and that's how I almost died
of foolishness   15
in beautiful Florida.
But I didn't.
I leaped aside, and fell,
and it streamed past me, crushing everything in its path
as it swept down to the water   20
and threw itself in,
and, in the end,
this isn't a poem about foolishness
but about how I rose from the ground
and saw the world as if for the second time,   25
the way it really is.
The water, that circle of shattered glass,
healed itself with a slow whisper
and lay back
with the back-lit light of polished steel,   30
and the birds, in the endless waterfalls of the trees,
shook open the snowy pleats of their wings, and drifted away,
while, for a keepsake, and to steady myself,
I reached out,
I picked the wild flowers from the grass around me—   35
blue stars
and blood-red trumpets
on long green stems—
for hours in my trembling hands they glittered
like fire.   40

1992

CHARLES SIMIC
b. 1938

Charles Simic came to the United States from Belgrade, Yugoslavia, when he was sixteen years old. His earliest childhood memories are of bombs dropping, people disappearing, and buildings in ruins. "My own home movie begins with the German bombing of Belgrade on April 6, 1941," he has said, "when a bomb hit the building across the street. I flew out of my bed all the way across the room. I was three years old and more astonished than I actually was frightened by the flames that rose everywhere." The unpredictability of Simic's poetry, with its feeling for the bizarre and irrational quality of ordinary things, may have originated in his childhood. During the German occupation of Yugoslavia, a civil war broke out among the partisans; from it the communist Marshal Tito emerged as the Yugoslavian leader. In 1944, the American and British forces bombed German-occupied Belgrade, where the Simics continued to live. After the war, Tito established a repressive communist regime: "People were being arrested left and right. Everybody was afraid. In school there was indoctrination," Simic writes in his memoir *A Fly in the Soup* (2000). During those years, Simic, his mother, and his brother spent time in refugee camps and prisons and were finally able to leave Yugoslavia for Paris in 1953. A year later, they immigrated to the United States, where his father was already living. "After what we had been through," he writes, "the wildest lies seemed plausible and the poems that I was going to write had to take that into account."

Simic's poetry is often full of mysterious fragments, as if some unspecified force has detonated both the larger, cohesive structure of the world and the narrative of the poem. At the same time Simic's stanzas function as regulating and balancing structures in tension with what is incomprehensible and often absurd. This tension, along with Simic's deadpan tone, renders both the comic and the frightening quality of a world where the concepts of truth and justice are "The Famous No-Shows" and existence a cosmic joke. It is not surprising that Simic admires the early film comedian Buster Keaton (1895–1966) for his "serenity in the face of chaos." The joke in Simic's poems is also a form of black humor, born of a historical dread Simic attributes to life in the twentieth century. Menace permeates the ordinary and domestic moments in Simic's poems. In "A Book Full of Pictures" a child is reading, a father studying, a mother knitting, but the quiet of the poem is disturbing. A "black raincoat / in the upstairs bedroom" sways from the ceiling. The declarative statements of the poem, like the click of the knitting needles, seem designed to fend off violence within and without the scene.

Simic's years in a Yugoslavia that monitored dissent through a secret police taught him the brutal consequences of a politically repressive conformity, and he has always been attracted to irreverence and unpredictability. As a young man he lived in New York and was drawn to surrealist poetry and to the wild flights of twentieth-century Latin American verse, since the reality Simic knew—"I'm a hard-nosed realist," he says—was already surreal. Impatient with what he saw as the academic conservatism of poetry in the 1950s and early 1960s, he wrote verse that celebrated both surreal and associative leaps (exemplified by the "controlled anarchy" of the jazz saxophonist Sonny Rollins) and untamable erotic impulses. His work since that period continues to celebrate irreverence and humor. Along with such outward wildness, Simic's poetry is full of secrets (in "The White Room," he writes "Many prefer / The hidden. I did too"), and the presence of something hidden frequently disturbs or haunts a Simic poem. Often the poems read like enigmatic disclosures, in the form of riddles or jokes. Occasionally, a Simic poem topples into the obscurely gnomic or flattens into only a joke. But Simic almost always maintains a precarious balance. He loves metaphysical speculation and can suggest philosophical questions through the most particular and even ordinary things, such as a fork, a glove, a white room; he himself has said that he practices "a kind of bedroom and kitchen metaphysics."

Among Simic's many books of poems are *Selected Poems 1963–1983* (1985, revised and expanded 1990), *The Book of Gods and Devils* (1990), *Hotel Insomnia* (1992), *Walking the Black Cat* (1996), *Jackstraws* (1999), and *Night Picnic* (2001). In addition he has edited and translated the work of Eastern European poets such as Vasko Popa and Tomaz Salamun. His collections of essays and memoirs include *The Uncertain Certainty* (1985), *Wonderful Words Silent Truth* (1990), and the irreverently titled *A Fly in the Soup* (2000). The reader of a Simic poem enters what the poet once described as "a kind of nonsense made up of fiction, of autobiography, the essay, poetry and, of course, the joke." With their mixture of the comic and the terrible and with their surreal story-telling power, Simic's poems haunt the mind long after one has read them.

Fork

This strange thing must have crept
Right out of hell.
It resembles a bird's foot
Worn around the cannibal's neck.

As you hold it in your hand,   5
As you stab with it into a piece of meat,
It is possible to imagine the rest of the bird:
Its head which like your fist
Is large, bald, beakless and blind.

1971

Prodigy

I grew up bent over
a chessboard.

I loved the word *endgame*.[1]

All my cousins looked worried.

It was a small house   5
near a Roman graveyard.
Planes and tanks
shook its windowpanes.

A retired professor of astronomy
taught me how to play.   10

That must have been in 1944.

---

1. Late stage of a chess game after the major reduction of forces.

In the set we were using,
the paint had almost chipped off
the black pieces.

The white King was missing   15
and had to be substituted for.

I'm told but do not believe
that that summer I witnessed
men hung from telephone poles.

I remember my mother   20
blindfolding me a lot.
She had a way of tucking my head
suddenly under her overcoat.

In chess, too, the professor told me,
the masters play blindfolded,   25
the great ones on several boards
at the same time.

1980

The Devils

You were a "victim of semiromantic anarchism
In its most irrational form."
I was "ill at ease in an ambiguous world

Deserted by Providence." We drank gin   5
And made love in the afternoon. The neighbors'
TV's were tuned to soap operas.

The unhappy couples spoke little.
There were interminable pauses.
Soft organ music. Someone coughing.

"It's like Strindberg's *Dream Play*,"[1] you said.   10
"What is?" I asked and got no reply.
I was watching a spider on the ceiling.

It was the kind St. Veronica[2] ate in her martyrdom.
"That woman subsisted on spiders only,"
I told the janitor when he came to fix the faucet.   15

1. August Strindberg (1849–1912), Swedish dramatist and novelist. The play, which eschews straightforward narrative and character, anticipates cubism and surrealism in its use of montage. 2. She is said to have wiped the face of Jesus when he stumbled under the weight of the Cross on his way to Calvary. An imprint of his face was reportedly left on the cloth she used, known thereafter as Veronica's veil.

He wore dirty overalls and a derby hat.
Once he had been an inmate of a notorious state institution.
"I'm no longer Jesus," he informed us happily.

He believed only in devils now.
"This building is full of them," he confided.   20
One could see their horns and tails

If one caught them in their baths.
"He's got Dark Ages[3] on his brain," you said.
"Who does?" I asked and got no reply.

The spider had the beginnings of a web   25
Over our heads. The world was quiet
Except when one of us took a sip of gin.

                                                    1990

The White Room

The obvious is difficult
To prove. Many prefer
The hidden. I did, too.
I listened to the trees.

They had a secret   5
Which they were about to
Make known to me,
And then didn't.

Summer came. Each tree
On my street had its own   10
Scheherazade.[1] My nights
Were a part of their wild

Story-telling. We were
Entering dark houses,
More and more dark houses   15
Hushed and abandoned.

There was someone with eyes closed
On the upper floors.
The thought of it, and the wonder,
Kept me sleepless.   20

The truth is bald and cold,
Said the woman

---

3. The Middle Ages, a period in European history from the fall of the West Roman Empire in the 5th century to the 15th century.

1. Fictional wife of a Persian king, she is the narrator of the tales in *Arabian Nights* in which her legendary storytelling staves off her own death.

Who always wore white.
She didn't leave her room much.

The sun pointed to one or two   25
Things that had survived
The long night intact,
The simplest things,

Difficult in their obviousness.
They made no noise.   30
It was the kind of day
People describe as "perfect."

Gods disguising themselves
As black hairpins? A hand-mirror?
A comb with a tooth missing?   35
No! That wasn't it.

Just things as they are,
Unblinking, lying mute
In that bright light,
And the trees waiting for the night.   40

1990

The Tiger[1]

in memory of George Oppen[2]

In San Francisco, that winter,
There was a dark little store
Full of sleepy Buddhas.
The afternoon I walked in,
No one came out to greet me.   5
I stood among the sages
As if trying to read their thoughts.

One was huge and made of stone.
A few were the size of a child's head
And had stains the color of dried blood.   10
There were even some no bigger than mice,
And they appeared to be listening.

"The winds of March, black winds,
The gritty winds,"[3] the dead poet wrote.

At sundown his street was empty   15
Except for my long shadow

---

1. "The Tyger" is the title of a famous poem by English Romantic poet William Blake (1757–1827).

2. American poet (1908–1984).
3. From Oppen's poem "Power, the Enchanted World."

Open before me like scissors.
There was his house where I told the story
Of the Russian soldier,
The one who looked Chinese.   20

He lay wounded in my father's bed,
And I brought him water and matches.
For that he gave me a little tiger
Made of ivory. Its mouth was open in anger,
But it had no stripes left.   25

There was the night when I colored
Its eyes black, its tongue red.
My mother held the lamp for me,
While worrying about the kind of luck
This beast might bring us.   30

The tiger in my hand growled faintly
When we were alone in the dark,
But when I put my ear to the poet's door
That afternoon, I heard nothing.

"The winds of march, black winds,   35
The gritty winds," he once wrote.

                                              1992

A Book Full of Pictures

Father studied theology through the mail
And this was exam time.
Mother knitted. I sat quietly with a book
Full of pictures. Night fell.
My hands grew cold touching the faces   5
Of dead kings and queens.

There was a black raincoat
  in the upstairs bedroom
Swaying from the ceiling,
But what was it doing there?
Mother's long needles made quick crosses.   10
They were black
Like the inside of my head just then.

The pages I turned sounded like wings.
"The soul is a bird," he once said.   15
In my book full of pictures
A battle raged: lances and swords
Made a kind of wintry forest
With my heart spiked and bleeding in its branches.

                                              1992

Arriving Celebrities

Tragedy and Comedy
Stepping out of a limousine
In ritzy furs;
Diminutive skirts,
Blowing kisses   5
Left and right.

Bedlam of adoring fans,
Pushing and squeezing,
Hollering for a glimpse,
When—all of a sudden!   10
A hush.
An all-inclusive clam-up.

Is someone, I inquired
Of my neighbors,
Already lying knifed   15
On the dance floor
Mouthing the name
We are all straining to overhear?

The towering bodyguards
With shaved heads   20
And mirror-tinted shades,
Don't hear me right,
Or will not deign
To grant my presence.

1999

In the Street

He was kneeling down to tie his shoes which she
   mistook for a proposal of marriage.
—Arise, arise, sweet man, she said with tears glistening
   in her eyes while people hurried past as if stung by
   bees.   5
—We shall spend the day riding in a balloon, she
   announced happily.
—My ears will pop, he objected.
—We'll throw our clothes overboard as we rise higher
   and higher.   10
—I'll smoke a cigar that may sputter fireworks.
—Don't worry my love, she hugged him. Even where
   the clouds are darkest, I have a secret getaway.

1999

MICHAEL S. HARPER
b. 1938

"I've been listening to music all my life," Michael S. Harper has said, and his first book of poems, *Dear John, Dear Coltrane* (1970), took its title from his poem to the great American jazz saxophonist. Recalling Coltrane's life in his prose piece "Don't They Speak Jazz," Harper tells this story: "Trane was searching for a particular tone on his horn; he had what we thought was a perfect embouchure, but his teeth hurt constantly, so he searched for the soft reed which would ease the pain. After searching for a year, each session killing his chops, he gave it up completely; there was no easy way to get that sound: play through the pain to *a love supreme.*" Playing through the pain is a part of what Harper brings to his poetry. Like the great blues singers and jazz musicians, his work celebrates life as song, especially as tragic song, full of losses and griefs, but song nevertheless. Sometimes the pain Harper sings through is personal, like the death of one of his sons in "Deathwatch" (he and his wife lost two of their infant sons shortly after birth), sometimes the pain belongs to family history (as in "Grandfather"). Sometimes it is the pain of history more generally, its violence and oppression.

History is Harper's second love as a poet, following right behind music. His poem for Coltrane, while dependent on the techniques of jazz and the blues, reflects Harper's concern with an imaginative recovery of history, especially black history, in an America where (as he once put it) the "amnesia level" is high. "I think the important thing about Americans is that they're not very good historians," Harper has said. "And Americans are really bad historians when it comes to moral ideas because they can't keep them in their heads very long." For Harper, to be a poet is to be a good historian; history identifies and inscribes moral issues that continue to engage us in the present. In college, Harper recalled, he read William Carlos Williams's *In the American Grain* (1925), in which Williams announces that "History for us begins with murder and enslavement, not with discovery." Like Williams, Harper wants to bring his personal imagination in contact with an American history (black and white) essentially tragic, tragic because, he says, "so many possibilities exist and there's been so much waste." This tragic sense informs Harper's work perhaps most clearly in his volume *Nightmare Begins Responsibility* (1975)—the title is a variation on one of Yeats's epigraphs—where a personal sense of loss is never separable from the sufferings of black history or of human history more generally. His collections *Images of Kin* (1977) and *Healing Song for the Inner Ear* (1985) followed. *Honorable Amendments,* appeared in 1995, and *Songlines in Michaeltree: New and Collected Poems* was published in 2000.

Born in Brooklyn, New York, Harper remembers a childhood in which "my parents weren't rich, but they had a good record collection." He grew up hearing the blues and jazz, but also reading the work of Langston Hughes and, later, James Baldwin and Ralph Ellison, and his poetic technique owes something to his literary as well as to his musical sensibility. An additional resource was a family tradition of oral storytelling ("My people were good storytellers," he has said), out of which some of his poems have grown. In fact, the jazz techniques of variation on a theme, of improvisation around an existing form, recall traditions of oral storytelling, and both jazz and oral traditions influenced the formal experiments of an Ellison or a Baldwin. After high school, Harper took a B.A. and M.A. at what is now California State University, then went to the University of Iowa for an M.F.A. His travels abroad, first to Mexico and Europe and later (1977) to South Africa, intensified his historical sense both of his own family roots and of their connection with racial history (a connection he probes in his poem "The Militance of a Photograph in the Passbook of a Bantu under Detention"). Since 1970 he has been at Brown University, where he is professor of English and director of the writing program.

"Most great art is finally testamental," Harper has written; "its technical brilliance never shadows the content of the song." Harper writes poems to remember and to witness, but at times the urgency of the content overpowers his form and his language cannot sustain the urgency the poem asserts. This may be the cost for a poet whose engagement with moral issues, whose deep historical sense, and whose rhythmic inventiveness make him capable of creating powerful and moving poems. His finest work is possessed of what he admires in Coltrane: "the energy and passion with which he approached his instrument and music," resembling the energy it takes "to break oppressive conditions, oppressive musical structures and oppressive societal structures." Harper's inclusive sense of history lets him write (in "Blue Ruth: America") that *"history is your own heartbeat"* but also lets him hear his own heart beat in time with those who lived in other times, other places. Responsible to memory, Harper also shares the affirmative impulse he finds in the blues: "the blues say 'Yes' to life no matter what it is. That doesn't mean you're going to survive it. But it means you're going to say yes to it."

Dear John, Dear Coltrane[1]

> a love supreme, a love supreme
> a love supreme, a love supreme

Sex fingers toes
in the marketplace
near your father's church
in Hamlet, North Carolina[2]—
witness to this love   5
in this calm fallow
of these minds,
there is no substitute for pain:
genitals gone or going,
seed burned out,   10
you tuck the roots in the earth,
turn back, and move
by river through the swamps,
singing: *a love supreme, a love supreme;*
what does it all mean?   15
Loss, so great each black
woman expects your failure
in mute change, the seed gone.
You plod up into the electric city—
your song now crystal and   20
the blues. You pick up the horn
with some will and blow
into the freezing night:
a love supreme, a love supreme—

Dawn comes and you cook   25
up the thick sin 'tween
impotence and death, fuel

---

1. John Coltrane (1926–1967), avant-garde jazz musician. The epigraph is the title of one of his songs.
2. Coltrane's birthplace.

the tenor sax cannibal
heart, genitals and sweat
that makes you clean—   30
a love supreme, a love supreme—

Why you so black?
cause I am
why you so funky?
cause I am   35
why you so black?
cause I am
why you so sweet?
cause I am
why you so black?   40
cause I am
a love supreme, a love supreme:

So sick
you couldn't play *Naima,*[3]
so flat we ached   45
for song you'd concealed
with your own blood,
your diseased liver gave
out its purity,
the inflated heart   50
pumps out, the tenor[4] kiss,
tenor love:
a love supreme, a love supreme—
a love supreme, a love supreme—

1970

American History

for John Callahan

Those four black girls blown up
in that Alabama church[1]
remind me of five hundred
middle passage blacks,[2]
in a net, under water   5
in Charleston harbor
so *redcoats*[3] wouldn't find them.
Can't find what you can't see
can you?

1970

---

3. Another song that Coltrane made famous.
4. Perhaps an allusion to the tenor saxophone, Coltrane's instrument.
1. By white racists as a reprisal against civil rights demonstrations.

2. Captured and en route from Africa (along the "Middle Passage," the usual route for slave ships) to be sold as slaves.
3. I.e., British soldiers.

Deathwatch

Twitching in the cactus
hospital gown, a loon
on hairpin wings,
she tells me how
her episiotomy[1]   5
is perfectly sewn
and doesn't hurt
while she sits in a pile
of blood
which once cleaned   10
the placenta
my third son should be in.
She tells me how early
he is, and how strong,
like his father,   15
and long, like a black-
stemmed Easter rose
in a white hand.

Just under five pounds
you lie there, a collapsed   20
balloon doll, burst in your
fifteenth hour, with the face
of your black father,
his fingers, his toes,
and eight voodoo   25
adrenalin holes in
your pinwheeled hair-lined
chest; you witness
your parents sign the autopsy
and disposal papers   30
shrunken to duplicate
in black ink
on white paper
like the country
you were born in,   35
unreal, asleep,
silent, almost alive.

This is a dedication
to our memory
of three sons—   40
two dead, one alive—
a reminder of a letter
to DuBois[2]
from a student

---

1. Surgical enlargement of the vulval opening at childbirth.

2. W. E. B. Du Bois (1868–1963), African American leader.

at Cornell—on behalf   45
of his whole history class.
The class is confronted
with a question,
and no one—
not even the professor—   50
is sure of the answer:
"Will you please tell us
whether or not it is true
that negroes
are not able to cry?"   55

America needs a killing.
America needs a killing.
Survivors will be human.

1970

Martin's[1] Blues

He came apart in the open,
the slow motion cameras
falling quickly
neither alive nor kicking;
stone blind dead   5
on the balcony
that old melody
etched his black lips
in a pruned echo:
We shall overcome[2]
some day—   10
Yes we did!
Yes we did!

1971

"Bird Lives": Charles Parker[1] in St. Louis

Last on legs, last on sax,
last in Indian wars, last on *smack*,
Bird is specious, *Bird* is alive,
horn, unplayable, before, after,
right now: it's heroin time: 5
smack, in the melody a trip;
smack, in the Mississippi;

1. Martin Luther King Jr., American civil rights
leader, was assassinated in 1968 on a motel balcony.

2. Hymn made famous by King's followers.
1. Great American jazz musician (1920–1955),
known as "Bird."

smack, in the drug merchant trap;
smack, in St. Louis, Missouri.

We knew you were through—   10
trying to get out of town,
unpaid bills, connections
unmet, unwanted, unasked,
Bird's in the last arc
of his own light: *blow Bird!*   15
And you did—
screaming, screaming, baby,
for life, after it, around it,
screaming for life, *blow Bird!*

What is the meaning of music?   20
What is the meaning of war?
What is the meaning of oppression?
Blow Bird! Ripped up and down
into the interior of life, the pain,
Bird, the embraceable you,[2]   25
how many brothers gone,
smacked out: blues and racism,
the hardest, longest penis
in the Mississippi urinal:
Blow Bird!   30

Taught more musicians, then forgot,
space loose, fouling the melodies,
the marching songs, the fine white
geese from the plantations,
syrup in this pork barrel,   35
Kansas City, the even teeth
of the mafia, the big band:
Blow Bird! Inside out Charlie's
guts, *Blow Bird!* get yourself killed.

In the first wave, the musicians,   40
out there, alone, in the first wave;
everywhere you went, Massey Hall,
Sweden, New Rochelle, *Birdland,*
nameless bird, Blue Note, Carnegie,
tuxedo junction, out of nowhere,   45
confirmation, confirmation, confirmation:
Bird Lives! Bird Lives! and you do:
Dead—

                                                   1972

2. Title of a song Parker made famous.

Nightmare Begins Responsibility[1]

I place these numbed wrists to the pane
watching white uniforms whisk over
him in the tube-kept
prison
fear what they will do in experiment   5
watch my gloved stickshifting gasolined hands
breathe *boxcar-information-please* infirmary tubes
distrusting white-pink mending paperthin
silkened end hairs, distrusting tubes
shrunk in his *trunk-skincapped*   10
shaven head, in thighs
distrusting-white-hands-picking-baboon-light
on this son who will not make his second night
of this wardstrewn intensive airpocket
where his father's asthmatic   15
hymns of *night-train*, train done gone
his mother can only know that he has flown
up into essential calm unseen corridor
going boxscarred home, *mamaborn, sweetsonchild*
gonedowntown into *researchtestingwarehousebatteryacid*   20
mama-son-done-gone / me telling her 'nother
train tonight, no music, no breathstroked
heartbeat in my infinite distrust of them:

and of my distrusting self
white-doctor-who-breathed-for-him-all-night   25
say it for two sons gone,
say nightmare, say it loud
panebreaking heartmadness:
nightmare begins responsibility.

1975

1. Cf. the title of a book by the American poet Delmore Schwartz, *In Dreams Begin Responsibilities* (1938); Schwartz took the title from a line in the Irish poet William Butler Yeats's "Responsibilities" (1913).

ROBERT PINSKY
b. 1940

A poet, critic, and translator, Robert Pinsky is a remarkable and influential figure in contemporary poetry. His appointment in 1997 for a two-year term as the ninth Poet Laureate of the United States (among his predecessors in this position are Rita Dove, Robert Penn Warren, and Richard Wilbur, also represented in this anthology) confirms the range and ambition of his work. In his first collection of poetry, *Sadness and Happiness* (1975), Pinsky staked out a territory neglected by an image-dominated

American poetry in the 1970s: the discursiveness poetry shares with prose and speech, including declaration, statement, and abstract definition. A year later, his influential book of criticism, *The Situation of Poetry* (1976), argued for a poetry with the prose virtues of "Clarity, Flexibility, Efficiency and Cohesiveness." In Pinsky's hands, this "drab, unglamorous group" of virtues produced the winning and pleasurable poems of his first book and two following collections: *An Explanation of America* (1980) and *History of My Heart* (1984). Like William Carlos Williams and Elizabeth Bishop before him, Pinsky endows his poems with the casualness of prose inflections; in his hands the result is a wonderfully sociable body of poetry, with a relaxed and familiar sense of middle-class life. Here are poems of tennis and psychiatrists, baseball and daughters in school, high school dances, movies, "the small-town main street" ("History of My Heart").

But Pinsky's own emphasis on the explanatory and the domestic can obscure his ambition and his formal virtuosity. The long title poem of *An Explanation of America* bespeaks his desire to bring together domestic life (the poem is addressed to his daughter) and the nation, to unite private feeling with "general Happiness and Safety." The poems of *History of My Heart* call on the personal memories at work in his first book but also introduce another sort of music, more mysterious and—what other word?—poetic. The publication of *The Want Bone* in 1990 and a book of new and collected poems, *The Figured Wheel,* in 1996, further demonstrates that the language of Pinsky's best poems is ordinary and yet also mysterious. If one of his strengths is the way he makes poetry a conversation about ideas, increasingly he also summons the power of poetry to sing what is "impossible to say." Pinsky's formal virtuosity lies in his ability to marry variations on traditional poetic rhythms (like the pentameter line at work in "The Want Bone," "At Pleasure Bay," and "Shirt") with American speech rhythms. This ability to shape a poetic line close to ordinary rhythms of speech and prose, and thus to render and deepen the everyday, connects him to Frank Bidart and James McMichael, two contemporary poets he admires. Pinsky is also an American master of the half or slant rhyme (like "twice" and "police" in "At Pleasure Bay," or "bell" and "blue" in "The Want Bone"), which gives his work a sense of both formal music and relaxation; there is the repeated echo of sound within and between stanzas, without the closure of full rhyme. The sensuousness of poetry, Pinsky remarks in his collection of essays *Poetry and the World* (1988), gives "elegance and significance to the sounds that breath makes vibrating in the mouth and throat." In "The Want Bone" (the dried jawbone of a shark, which he saw on a friend's mantle) he renders the sound vibrating in "this scalded toothless harp" as song: "my food my parent my child I want you my own / My flower my fin my life my lightness my O." Reading these lines we might easily forget that this poet has argued for poetry's discursive qualities. At the same time, Pinsky's work continues to include what is sometimes excluded from American poetry, like explanation or the series of back-slapping ethnic jokes told in "Impossible to Tell" (from *The Figured Wheel*).

Pinsky grew up in what he has called a "nominally orthodox" Jewish family in Long Branch, New Jersey. He later attended Rutgers and then Stanford University (where he studied with Yvor Winters). Though he lived in California for several years and now teaches in the graduate writing program at Boston University, Long Branch is Pinsky's middle America, despite its location at the ocean's edge ("bounded on three sides by similar places / and on one side by vast, uncouth houses / A glum boardwalk and, / as we say, the beach"). In Long Branch are his childhood memories and streets, as well as his sense of ethnic experience. With its fading boardwalk and movie houses, it also exemplifies an American popular culture for which Pinsky has unabashed appreciation. "At Pleasure Bay" (from *The Want Bone*), included here, beautifully commingles childhood memory and a sense of place with a feeling for the larger historical forces shaping the lives of local inhabitants. Though it is unlike Pinsky to move too far afield from everyday life, "At Pleasure Bay" and other poems like it reveal the ways that Pinsky's vision extends itself beyond the personal and local into a deeper past and (in the poem's closing vision) future. The same process of enlarging a sense of community and connection while not straying too far from daily experience unfolds in "Shirt," which works its own variations on the pentameter line and is beautifully shaped by Pinsky's trademark half rhymes, here working within a single line as well as between lines.

The pleasures of Pinsky's poetry are also literary; he is a poet unabashed in his references to literary antecedents but in no sense narrowly academic. Instead his work acknowledges and celebrates the way literature shapes his (and our) sense of life and experience, as well as his (and our) use of language. Pinsky's poetry is so distinctively American in its diction and subjects that his important work as a translator can come as a surprise. Among the poets he has translated are Czeslaw Milosz (the two have worked together on the translations) and Paul Célan. In 1994 Pinsky published *The Inferno of Dante*, recipient of the Academy of American Poets translation award, in which his formal gifts allowed him to recreate an American version of Dante's interlocked rhyme scheme, the terza rima. In a review of this translation in the *New York Times*, Edward Hirsch described the effect of Pinsky's stanzas as "moving through a series of interpenetrating rooms . . . or going down a set of winding stairs." While his sense of literary tradition is deep and wide-ranging, Pinsky is also engaged with new possibilities for literature created by computer technology. In 1985, in collaboration with computer programmers, he created an interactive text adventure game, *Mindwheel*, and currently he serves as the poetry editor of a weekly Internet magazine, *Slate*. Computer software and poetry, Pinsky has said, "share a great human myth or trope, an image that could be called the secret passage: the discovery of large manifold channels through a small, ordinary-looking or all but invisible aperture . . . this passage to vast complexities is what writing through the machine might become."

The Figured Wheel

The figured wheel rolls through shopping malls and prisons,
Over farms, small and immense, and the rotten little downtowns.
Covered with symbols, it mills everything alive and grinds
The remains of the dead in the cemeteries, in unmarked graves and
    oceans.

Sluiced by salt water and fresh, by pure and contaminated rivers,   5
By snow and sand, it separates and recombines all droplets and grains,
Even the infinite sub-atomic particles crushed under the illustrated,
Varying treads of its wide circumferential track.

Spraying flecks of tar and molten rock it rumbles
Through the Antarctic station of American sailors and technicians,   10
And shakes the floors and windows of whorehouses for diggers and smelters
From Bethany, Pennsylvania to a practically nameless, semi-penal New
    Town

In the mineral-rich tundra of the Soviet northernmost settlements.
Artists illuminate it with pictures and incised mottoes
Taken from the Ten Thousand Stories and the Register of True
    Dramas.   15
They hang it with colored ribbons and with bells of many pitches.

With paints and chisels and moving lights they record
On its rotating surface the elegant and terrifying doings
Of the inhabitants of the Hundred Pantheons of major Gods
Disposed in iconographic stations at hub, spoke and concentric
    bands,   20

And also the grotesque demi-Gods, Hopi gargoyles and Ibo dryads.[1]
They cover it with wind-chimes and electronic instruments
That vibrate as it rolls to make an all-but-unthinkable music,
So that the wheel hums and rings as it turns through the births of stars

And through the dead-world of bomb, fireblast and fallout   25
Where only a few doomed races of insects fumble in the smoking grasses.
It is Jesus oblivious to hurt turning to give words to the unrighteous,
And is also Gogol's[2] feeding pig that without knowing it eats a baby chick

And goes on feeding. It is the empty armor of My Cid,[3] clattering
Into the arrows of the credulous unbelievers, a metal suit   30
Like the lost astronaut revolving with his useless umbilicus
Through the cold streams, neither energy nor matter, that agitate

The cold, cyclical dark, turning and returning.
Even in the scorched and frozen world of the dead after the holocaust
The wheel as it turns goes on accreting ornaments.   35
Scientists and artists festoon it from the grave with brilliant

Toys and messages, jokes and zodiacs, tragedies conceived
From among the dreams of the unemployed and the pampered,
The listless and the tortured. It is hung with devices
By dead masters who have survived by reducing themselves magically   40

To tiny organisms, to wisps of matter, crumbs of soil,
Bits of dry skin, microscopic flakes, which is why they are called "great,"
In their humility that goes on celebrating the turning
Of the wheel as it rolls unrelentingly over

A cow plodding through car-traffic on a street in Iasi,[4]   45
And over the haunts of Robert Pinsky's mother and father
And wife and children and his sweet self
Which he hereby unwillingly and inexpertly gives up, because it is

There, figured and pre-figured in the nothing-transfiguring wheel.

                                                   1984

---

1. Woodland spirits. "Ibo": an African tribe, many
of whose members were sent as slaves to America.
2. Nicolai Gogol (1809–1852), Russian novelist,
short-story writer, and playwright.

3. The Castillian epic *Poem of the Cid* (c. 1140)
celebrates the legendary Spanish hero, the Cid.
4. City in Moldavia, Romania.

The Street

Streaked and fretted with effort, the thick
Vine of the world, red nervelets
Coiled at its tips.

All roads lead from it. All night
Wainwrights and upholsterers work finishing   5
The wheeled coffin

Of the dead favorite of the Emperor,
The child's corpse propped seated
On brocade, with yellow

Oiled curls, kohl on the stiff lids.   10
Slaves throw petals on the roadway
For the cortege, white

Languid flowers shooting from dark
Blisters on the vine, ramifying
Into streets. On mine,   15

Rockwell Avenue, it was embarrassing:
Trouble—fights, the police, sickness—
Seemed never to come

For anyone when they were fully dressed.
It was always underwear or dirty pyjamas,   20
Unseemly stretches

Of skin showing through a torn housecoat.
Once a stranger drove off in a car
With somebody's wife,

And he ran after them in his undershirt   25
And threw his shoe at the car. It bounced
Into the street

Harmlessly, and we carried it back to him;
But the man had too much dignity
To put it back on,   30

So he held it and stood crying in the street:
"He's breaking up my home," he said,
"The son of a bitch

Bastard is breaking up my home." The street
Rose undulant in pavement-breaking coils   35
And the man rode it,

Still holding his shoe and stiffly upright
Like a trick rider in the circus parade
That came down the street

Each August. As the powerful dragonlike   40
Hump swelled he rose cursing and ready
To throw his shoe—woven

Angular as a twig into the fabulous
Rug or brocade with crowns and camels,
Leopards and rosettes,   45

All riding the vegetable wave of the street
From the John Flock Mortuary Home
Down to the river.

It was a small place, and off the center,
But so much a place to itself, I felt   50
Like a young prince

Or aspirant squire. I knew that *Ivanhoe*[1]
Was about race. The Saxons were Jews,
Or even Coloreds,

With their low-ceilinged, unbelievably   55
Sour-smelling houses down by the docks.
Everything was written

Or woven, ivory and pink and emerald—
Nothing was too ugly or petty or terrible
To be weighed in the immense   60

Silver scales of the dead: the looming
Balances set right onto the live, dangerous
Gray bark of the street.

                                                          1984

A Woman

Thirty years ago: gulls keen in the blue,
Pigeons mumble on the sidewalk, and an old, fearful woman
Takes a child on a long walk, stopping at the market

To order a chicken, the child forming a sharp memory
Of sawdust, small curls of droppings, the imbecile   5
Panic of the chickens, their affronted glare.

1. The title and hero of Sir Walter Scott's romance novel (1819), set in 12th-century England, in which the hero wins the Saxon princess Rowena and champions a Jewish woman, Rebecca.

They walk in the wind along the ocean: at first,
Past cold zinc railings and booths and arcades
Still shuttered in March; then, along high bluffs

In the sun, the coarse grass combed steadily   10
By a gusting wind that draws a line of tears
Toward the boy's temples as he looks downward,

At the loud combers booming over the jetties,
Rushing and in measured rhythm receding on the beach.
He leans over. Everything that the woman says is a warning,   15

Or a superstition; even the scant landmarks are like
Tokens of risk or rash judgment—drowning,
Sexual assault, fatal or crippling diseases:

The monotonous surf; wooden houses mostly boarded up;
Fishermen with heavy lines cast in the surf;   20
Bright tidal pools stirred to flashing

From among the jetties by the tireless salty wind.
She dreams frequently of horror and catastrophe—
Mourners, hospitals, and once, a whole family

Sitting in chairs in her own room, corpse-gray,   25
With throats cut; who were they? Vivid,
The awful lips of the wounds in the exposed necks,

Herself helpless in the dream, desperate,
At a loss what to do next, pots seething
And boiling over onto their burners, in her kitchen.   30

They have walked all the way out past the last bluffs,
As far as Port-Au-Peck[1]—the name a misapprehension
Of something Indian that might mean "mouth"

Or "flat" or "bluefish," or all three: Ocean
On the right, and the brackish wide inlet   35
Of the river on the left; and in between,

Houses and landings and the one low road
With its ineffectual sea-wall of rocks
That the child walks, and that hurricanes

Send waves crashing over the top of, river   40
And ocean coming violently together
In a house-cracking exhilaration of water.

In Port-Au-Peck the old woman has a prescription filled,
And buys him a milk-shake. Pouring the last froth
From the steel shaker into his glass, he happens   45

_____
1. A harbor town in Oceanport, New Jersey.

To think about the previous Halloween:
Holding her hand, watching the parade
In his chaps, boots, guns and sombrero.

A hay-wagon of older children in cowboy gear
Trundled by, the strangers inviting him up   50
To ride along for the six blocks to the beach—

Her holding him back with both arms, crying herself,
Frightened at his force, and he vowing never,
Never to forgive her, not as long as he lived.

                                        1984

The Want Bone

The tongue of the waves tolled in the earth's bell.
Blue rippled and soaked in the fire of blue.
The dried mouthbones of a shark in the hot swale
Gaped on nothing but sand on either side.

The bone tasted of nothing and smelled of nothing,   5
A scalded toothless harp, uncrushed, unstrung.
The joined arcs made the shape of birth and craving
And the welded-open shape kept mouthing O.

Ossified cords held the corners together
In groined spirals pleated like a summer dress.   10
But where was the limber grin, the gash of pleasure?
Infinitesimal mouths bore it away,

The beach scrubbed and etched and pickled it clean.
But O I love you it sings, my little my country
My food my parent my child I want you my own   15
My flower my fin my life my lightness my O.

                                        1990

Shirt

The back, the yoke, the yardage. Lapped seams,[1]
The nearly invisible stitches along the collar
Turned in a sweatshop by Koreans or Malaysians

Gossiping over tea and noodles on their break
Or talking money or politics while one fitted   5
This armpiece with its overseam to the band

---

1. Overlapping seams used to join fabric in interfacings because less bulky.

Of cuff I button at my wrist. The presser, the cutter,
The wringer, the mangle. The needle, the union,
The treadle, the bobbin. The code. The infamous blaze

At the Triangle Factory[2] in nineteen-eleven   10
One hundred and forty-six died in the flames
On the ninth floor, no hydrants, no fire escapes—

The witness in a building across the street
Who watched how a young man helped a girl to step
up to the windowsill, then held her out   15

Away from the masonry wall and let her drop.
And then another. As if he were helping them up
To enter a streetcar, and not eternity.

A third before he dropped her put her arms
Around his neck and kissed him. Then he held   20
Her into space, and dropped her. Almost at once

He stepped to the sill himself, his jacket flared
And fluttered up from his shirt as he came down,
Air filling up the legs of his gray trousers—

Like Hart Crane's Bedlamite,[3] "shrill shirt ballooning."   25
Wonderful how the pattern matches perfectly
Across the placket and over the twin bar-tacked

Corners of both pockets, like a strict rhyme
Or a major chord. Prints, plaids, checks,
Houndstooth, Tattersall, Madras. The clan tartans   30

Invented by mill-owners inspired by the hoax of Ossian,[4]
To control their savage Scottish workers, tamed
By a fabricated heraldry: MacGregor,

Bailey, MacMartin. The kilt, devised for workers
To wear among the dusty clattering looms.   35
Weavers, carders, spinners. The loader,

The docker, the navvy.[5] The planter, the picker, the sorter
Sweating at her machine in a litter of cotton
As slaves in calico headrags sweated in fields:

2. The Triangle shirtwaist factory in New York City was the scene of a notorious fire in which 146 women who worked in the factory jumped to their deaths to escape the flames. This event marked the beginning of rigorous efforts to enforce workplace safety.
3. A reference to lines from the opening section ("To Brooklyn Bridge") of Hart Crane's poetic sequence *The Bridge* (1930): "Out of some subway scuttle, cell or loft / A bedlamite speeds to thy parapets." A bedlamite is an inmate of a hospital for the mentally ill.
4. In 1760 James Macpherson published *Poems of Ossian*, which falsely claimed to be a translation of a text by the 3rd-century Irish hero of that name.
5. An unskilled laborer, especially one engaged in excavating or construction.

George Herbert, your descendant is a Black   40
Lady in South Carolina, her name is Irma
And she inspected my shirt. Its color and fit

And feel and its clean smell have satisfied
Both her and me. We have culled its cost and quality
Down to the buttons of simulated bone,   45

The buttonholes, the sizing, the facing, the characters
Printed in black on neckband and tail. The shape,
The label, the labor, the color, the shade. The shirt.

                                                        1990

At Pleasure Bay

In the willows along the river at Pleasure Bay
A catbird singing, never the same phrase twice.
Here under the pines a little off the road
In 1927 the Chief of Police
And Mrs. W. killed themselves together,   5
Sitting in a roadster. Ancient unshaken pilings
And underwater chunks of still-mortared brick
In shapes like bits of puzzle strew the bottom
Where the landing was for Price's Hotel and Theater.
And here's where boats blew two blasts for the keeper   10
To shunt the iron swing-bridge. He leaned on the gears
Like a skipper in the hut that housed the works
And the bridge moaned and turned on its middle pier
To let them through. In the middle of the summer
Two or three cars might wait for the iron trusswork   15
Winching aside, with maybe a child to notice
A name on the stern in black-and-gold on white,
Sandpiper, Patsy Ann, Do Not Disturb,
The Idler. If a boat was running whiskey,
The bridge clanged shut behind it as it passed   20
And opened up again for the Coast Guard cutter
Slowly as a sundial, and always jammed halfway.
The roadbed whole, but opened like a switch,
The river pulling and coursing between the piers.
Never the same phrase twice, the catbird filling   25
The humid August evening near the inlet
With borrowed music that he melds and changes.
Dragonflies and sandflies, frogs in the rushes, two bodies
Not moving in the open car among the pines,
A sliver of story. The tenor at Price's Hotel,   30
In clown costume, unfurls the sorrow gathered
In ruffles at his throat and cuffs, high quavers
That hold like splashes of light on the dark water,
The aria's closing phrases, changed and fading.

And after a gap of quiet, cheers and applause   35
Audible in the houses across the river,
Some in the audience weeping as if they had melted
Inside the music. Never the same. In Berlin
The daughter of an English lord, in love
With Adolf Hitler, whom she has met. She is taking   40
Possession of the apartment of a couple,
Elderly well-off Jews. They survive the war
To settle here in the Bay, the old lady
Teaches piano, but the whole world swivels
And gapes at their feet as the girl and a high-up Nazi   45
Examine the furniture, the glass, the pictures,
The elegant story that was theirs and now
Is a part of hers. A few months later the English
Enter the war and she shoots herself in a park,
An addled, upper-class girl, her life that passes   50
Into the lives of others or into a place.
The taking of lives—the Chief and Mrs. W.
Took theirs to stay together, as local ghosts.
Last flurries of kisses, the revolver's barrel,
Shivers of a story that a child might hear   55
And half remember, voices in the rushes,
A singing in the willows. From across the river,
Faint quavers of music, the same phrase twice and again,
Ranging and building. Over the high new bridge
The flashing of traffic homeward from the racetrack,   60
With one boat chugging under the arches, outward
Unnoticed through Pleasure Bay to the open sea.
Here's where the people stood to watch the theater
Burn on the water. All that night the fireboats
Kept playing their spouts of water into the blaze.   65
In the morning, smoking pilasters and beams.
Black smell of char for weeks, the ruin already
Soaking back into the river. After you die
You hover near the ceiling above your body
And watch the mourners awhile. A few days more   70
You float above the heads of the ones you knew
And watch them through a twilight. As it grows darker
You wander off and find your way to the river
And wade across. On the other side, night air,
Willows, the smell of the river, and a mass   75
Of sleeping bodies all along the bank,
A kind of singing from among the rushes
Calling you further forward in the dark.
You lie down and embrace one body, the limbs
Heavy with sleep reach eagerly up around you   80
And you make love until your soul brims up
And burns free out of you and shifts and spills
Down over into that other body, and you
Forget the life you had and begin again
On the same crossing—maybe as a child who passes   85
Through the same place. But never the same way twice.

Here in the daylight, the catbird in the willows,
The new café, with a terrace and a landing,
Frogs in the cattails where the swing-bridge was—
Here's where you might have slipped across the water   90
When you were only a presence, at Pleasure Bay.

                                                                                    1990

SIMON J. ORTIZ

b. 1941

In his poem "A Designated National Park," Simon J. Ortiz tells of visiting Montezuma Castle in Verde Valley, Arizona, where he experiences as present in himself the life of the people there: "Hear / in my cave, sacred song. / Morning feeling, sacred song. / We shall plant today." His connection to that landscape, however, is complicated by the fact that it is now a "DESIGNATED FEDERAL RECREATION FEE AREA": "This morning / I have to buy a permit to get back home." Ortiz's treatment of Verde Valley is characteristic of the way he inhabits a conflicted landscape. He was born and raised in the Acoma Pueblo Community in Albuquerque, New Mexico. One meaning for the name *Acoma* is "the place that always was," and in this sense, it transcends the poet's personal place of origin and represents for him the native American way of life. Ortiz continually returns to this abiding sense of origin after traveling great distances away from it. Often his poems enact a journey, and as Joseph Bruhac reminds us, in American Indian cultures the theme of traveling implicitly recalls the "tragic epic movements of Native American nations." Many of his poems dramatize Ortiz's disorientation as he moves within an America where Indian names are reduced to billboard signs, where rivers burn from industrial wastes and construction fills up the spaces of the earth. His sense of contemporary life, especially its absurdities, is acute.

But the America he travels conceals within it an older landscape, one animated by spirit, where the earth is alive with "wind visions" and "The Mountains dream / about pine brothers and friends" ("Vision Shadows"); to travel it is to seek "the center of the center" ("Between Albuquerque and Santa Fe"), the place where the spirits enter the world. Asked in an interview, "Why do you write?" Ortiz once responded, "Because Indians always tell a story. . . . The only way to continue is to tell a story and there is no other way. Your children will not survive unless you tell something about them— how they were born, how they came to this certain place, how they continued." Tellingly, Ortiz chose to reprint these comments at the beginning of his collection *A Good Journey* (1977). The stories his poems narrate are evidence that the native American way of life is continuous, despite all the forces that attempt to eradicate it. But his work also tells of the painful costs involved in survival.

After receiving his early education at a Bureau of Indian Affairs school on the Acoma Reservation, Ortiz later attended the University of New Mexico and the University of Iowa. He has since taught at San Diego State University and the University of New Mexico. "I never decided to become a poet," Ortiz has said, suggesting that his relatives transmitted to him the power of words. "An old-man relative with a humpback used to come to our home when I was a child, and he would carry me on his back. He told me stories. . . . That contact must have contributed the language of myself." His father, a stonemason, carpenter, and woodcarver, would talk and sing as he worked. In "A Story of How a Wall Stands," he remembers his father saying "Underneath / what looks like loose stone, / there is stone woven together." This sense of underlying connection is true of Ortiz's poetry as well, often at its finest when revealing how a moment or event fits into the ongoing cycles celebrated by ritual. His best poems are carefully made, sometimes surprising in the way the apparently loose details suddenly blaze into an arrangement. Characteristically, this happens through powerful repetitions culminating in the last movements of a poem, making Ortiz a writer whose work depends on rereading. His collection *Going for Rain* appeared in 1976; its poems sometimes show a writer whose strong feelings have not yet found a distinctive language or rhythm. His next book, *The Good Journey*, is more assured and its range significantly broader. Since then he has published *From Sand Creek*, which won the 1982 Pushcart Prize; *A Poem Is a Journey* (1981); and an edition that collects earlier volumes together with new work, *Woven Stone* (1992). *After and Before the Lightning* was published in 1994; his short stories were collected in *Men on the Moon* (1999). Ortiz is a poet with a mission—continuance and preservation—and sometimes a didactic impulse shapes his work too rigidly. But his finest poems have a richness of experience and a vital, imaginative sense of the earth that refuses any single conceptual or moral frame.

A recurring image in several Ortiz poems is the "Wisconsin horse" he once saw standing "within a fence / / silent in the hot afternoon" while one mile away new construction was going on: "I tell the horse, / 'That's America building something' " ("The Wisconsin Horse"). The spirit of the horse, restrained by the chainlink fence and threatened by the approaching construction, suggests Ortiz's sense of constriction in the VA hospitals (his experience in one of these prompted his sequence *Poems from the Veterans Hospital*), as well as in small-town bars, in the Salvation Army store, or in the boundaries of the designated National Parks. Something threatens to break loose in these poems; feelings precariously held in check shake the formal structures. Other poems, like "Earth and Rain, the Plants & Sun," have the freedom and buoyancy of the hawk's flight; the words move in a space that seems immense. Instead of explosive anger or despair, the tone of the poem is close to song or prayer. What is so moving in Ortiz's work is that these voices are both his; together they suggest the fracture of identity and the possibility of reintegration.

Passing through Little Rock

The old Indian ghosts—
                              "Quapaw"
"Waccamaw"[1]—
                    are just billboard words
in this crummy town.   5

"You know, I'm worrying a lot lately,"
he says in the old hotel bar.

"You're getting older and scared ain't you?"

I just want to cross the next hill,
through that clump of trees   10
and come out the other side

---

1. Names of Native American tribes formerly living in Arkansas.

and see a clean river,
the whole earth new
and hear the noise it makes
at birth.   15

1976

Earth and Rain, the Plants & Sun

Once near San Ysidro
on the way to Colorado,
I stopped and looked.
The sound of a meadowlark
through smell of fresh cut alfalfa.   5

Raho would say,
"Look, Dad." A hawk

sweeping
          its wings

clear through   10
          the blue
of whole and pure
          the wind
                    the sky.

It is writhing   15
overhead.
Hear. The Bringer.
          The Thunderer.

Sunlight falls
through cloud curtains,   20
a straight bright shaft.

It falls,
          it falls,
down
          to earth,   25
a green plant.

Today, the Katzina[1] come.
The dancing prayers.

Many times, the Katzina.
The dancing prayers.   30

---

1. Or Kachina; spirits of the invisible life forces of the Pueblo of North America. The Kachinas are impersonated by elaborately costumed masked male members of the tribes who visit Pueblo villages the first half of the year. Although not worshiped, Kachinas are greatly revered, and one of their main purposes is to bring rain for the spring crops.

It shall not end,
son, it will not end,
this love.

Again and again,
the earth is new again.   35
They come, listen, listen.
Hold on to your mother's hand.
They come

O great joy, they come.
The plants with bells.   40
The stones with voices.
Listen, son, hold my hand.

                                                    1977

Vision Shadows

Wind visions are honest.
Eagles clearly soar
to the craggy peaks
of the mind.
The mind is full   5
of sunprayer
and childlaughter.

The Mountains dream
about pine brothers and friends,
the mystic realm of boulders   10
which shelter
rabbits, squirrels, wrens.
They believe in the power.
They also believe
in quick eagle death.   15

The eagle loops
into the wind power.
He can see a million miles
and more because of it.

All believe things   20
of origin and solitude.

        But what has happened
(I hear strange news from Wyoming
of thallium sulphate.[1] Ranchers
bearing arms in helicopters.)   25

---

1. A chemical used by farmers as a rat poison.

to these visions?
I hear foreign tremors.
Breath comes thin and shredded.
I hear the scabs of strange deaths
falling off.   30

Snake hurries through the grass.
Coyote is befuddled by his own tricks.
And Bear whimpers pain into the wind.

Poisonous fumes cross our sacred paths.
The wind is still.   35
O Blue Sky, O Mountain, O Spirit, O
what has stopped?

Eagles tumble dumbly into shadows
that swallow them with dull thuds.
The sage can't breathe.   40
Jackrabbit is lonely and alone
with eagle gone.

It is painful, aiiee, without visions
to soothe dry whimpers
or repair the flight of eagle, our own brother.   45

1977

From Poems from the Veterans Hospital

8:50 AM Ft. Lyons VAH

The Wisconsin Horse[1] hears the geese.

They wheel from the west.
First the unfamiliar sounds,
and then the memory recalls
ancient songs.   5

Sky is gray and thick.
Sometimes it is the horizon
and the sky weighs less.

The Wisconsin Horse cranes
his neck.   10
The geese veer
out of sight
past the edge of a building.

1. See headnote, p. 3024.

The building is not old,
built in 1937.   15
Contains men broken
from three American wars.

Less and less, the sound,
and it becomes
the immense sky.   20

Travelling

A man has been in the VAH Library all day long,
looking at the maps, the atlas, and the globe,
finding places.
              Acapulco, the Bay of Bengal,
Antarctica, Madagascar, Rome, Luxembourg,   5
places.

He writes their names on a letter pad, hurries
to another source, asks the librarian for a book
but it is out and he looks hurt and then he rushes
back to the globe, turns it a few times and finds   10
Yokohama and then the Aleutian Islands.

Later on, he studies Cape Cod for a moment,
a faraway glee on his face, in his eyes.
He is Gauguin, he is Coyote,[1] he is who he is,
travelling the known and unknown places,   15
travelling, travelling.

                                                    1977

From From Sand Creek

At the Salvation Army
a clerk
caught me
wandering
among old spoons   5
          and knives,
              sweaters and shoes.

I couldn't have stolen anything;
my life was stolen already.

1. The trickster figure in southwestern and other Native American tales. Paul Gauguin, 19th-century French painter, left his home in France for Tahiti and the Marquesas Islands.

In protest though,   10
I should have stolen.
My life. My life.

She caught me;
Carson[1] caught Indians,
secured them with his lies.   15
Bound them with his belief.

After winter,
our own lives fled.

I reassured her
what she believed.   20
Bought a sweater.

And fled.

I should have stolen.
My life. My life.

1981

1. Christopher ("Kit") Carson (1809–1868), trapper, scout, Indian agent, and soldier, was hired by the government to help control the Navajo. Beginning in 1863 he waged a brutal economic war against the tribe, marching through the heart of their territory to destroy their crops, orchards, and livestock. In 1864 most Navajo surrendered to Carson, who forced nearly eight thousand Navajo men, women, and children to take what came to be called the "Long Walk" of three hundred miles from Arizona to Fort Sumner, New Mexico, where they remained in disease-ridden confinement until 1868.

BILLY COLLINS
b. 1941

The voice in a Billy Collins poem is so intimate and immediate that we feel we are in the same room with the poet. Collins himself imagines poet and reader as if sitting together at a breakfast table: "I will lean forward, / elbows on the table, / with something to tell you / and you will look up, as always, / your spoon dripping with milk, ready to listen" ("A Portrait of the Reader with a Bowl of Cereal"). The colloquial voice in his poems charms us with its air of spontaneous expression, its modesty, its humor. If some of his poems coast on charm alone, Collins's best work takes us on a surprising ride: its strange and unexpected associations deepen the familiar into the mysterious or make the mysterious familiar.

Describing the structures of his poetry, Collins says, "We are attempting, all the time, to create a logical, rational path through the day. To the left and right there are an amazing set of distractions that we can't afford to follow. But the poet is willing to stop anywhere." His poems often proceed as accounts of a day and its distractions, as in "Tuesday, June 4, 1991." At the same time the formal shapeliness of Collins's work endows ordinary activity with a strange and pleasing formality and turns it, line by measured line and stanza by stanza, into a ritual containing both the pleasures and the pathos of life. There is a humorous self-awareness in these poems about the speaker's dramatizing and obsessive love of distraction—anything, no matter how insignificant, can carry off his attention—and one of the things that is so welcome about Collins's poems is that they are funny. Only on later readings do we realize that they are also sad. When he looks over the edges of domestic life there is blankness; unlike the work of a Jorie Graham or a Charles Wright, a Collins poem evokes no metaphysical structures that might sustain this fragile world. Yet (in Yeats's phrase) Collins loves "what vanishes"—the day in June, the good meal, even the memory of one's own life. This knowledge of how things both large and small disappear is a great equalizer. The humor in Collins's poetry puts this equalizing principle to work; he deflates the grandiose and subjects large statements of truth to the test of the particular. Collins's titles, imaginative and playful, suggest the way he alights on small, usually trivial instances in which life's strangeness and mystery flash out: "Weighing the Dog," "I Chop Some Parsley While Listening to Art Blakey's Version of 'Three Blind Mice.' " Other titles signal the way he grounds the improbable within the everyday: "Taking off Emily Dickinson's Clothes," "Shoveling Snow with Buddha."

Collins's collections of poems include *Questions about Angels* (1977), *The Art of Drowning* (1995), *Picnic, Lightning* (1998), and *Sailing Alone around the World: New and Selected Poems* (2001). He was appointed poet laureate of the United States for 2001–02. Born in New York City (in a hospital where, as he likes to claim, William Carlos Williams worked as a pediatric resident), Collins teaches at Lehman College of the City University. Walking the city streets animates him and inflects some of his poems in a way that recalls the work of Frank O'Hara, with whom Collins shares an idiomatic American voice, colloquial and understated, shaped by both jazz and the blues. Collins's work often plays with the melody of a pentameter line as a jazz musician plays on and off the melody of a song; the pentameter is an undertone from which a more idiosyncratic rhythm moves around and away. While the rhythms of Collins's poetry often enforce a slowing-down, a tender lingering over everyday life, their breezy tone and quick humor seem to suggest that nothing too serious is going on. It is as if Collins were fending off the large, prophetic claims made by visionary poets (early in his career he earned a Ph.D. at the University of California at Riverside, specializing in the Romantic period), even as some of his poems are riffs on the Romantic tradition. Such Collins poems as "Keats's Handwriting" and "Lines Composed Over Three Thousand Miles from Tintern Abbey" deflate the romantic sublime and substitute for it a vision self-deprecating and humorous. Thus when we hear nightingales in a Collins poem, they're a group singing on the gospel radio station ("Sunday Morning with the Sensational Nightingales").

Collins's modest claims for poetry and the fact that his work is so appealing and accessible can lead us to underestimate the necessity and reward of rereading him. The best of his poems open up a moment like a series of nested boxes; if we read too quickly, we miss the pleasure and surprise of intricate connections and deepening discoveries. Like jazz or the blues, a Collins poem has a spontaneity that yields immediate pleasure, but it is only when we listen again more attentively that we recognize the art that makes itself look easy.

Forgetfulness

The name of the author is the first to go
followed obediently by the title, the plot,
the heartbreaking conclusion, the entire novel
which suddenly becomes one you have never read, never even heard of,

as if, one by one, the memories you used to harbor 5
decided to retire to the southern hemisphere of the brain,
to a little fishing village where there are no phones.

Long ago you kissed the names of the nine Muses goodbye,
and watched the quadratic equation pack its bag,
and even now as you memorize the order of the planets, 10

something else is slipping away, a state flower perhaps,
the address of an uncle, the capital of Paraguay.

Whatever it is you are struggling to remember
it is not poised on the tip of your tongue,
not even lurking in some obscure corner of your spleen. 15

It has floated away down a dark mythological river
whose name begins with an *L* as far as you can recall,
well on your own way to oblivion where you will join those
who have even forgotten how to swim and how to ride a bicycle.

No wonder you rise in the middle of the night 20
to look up the date of a famous battle in a book on war.
No wonder the moon in the window seems to have drifted
out of a love poem that you used to know by heart.

1991

Osso Buco[1]

I love the sound of the bone against the plate
and the fortress-like look of it
lying before me in a moat of risotto,[2]
the meat soft as the leg of an angel
who has lived a purely airborne existence. 5
And best of all, the secret marrow,
the invaded privacy of the animal
prized out with a knife and swallowed down
with cold, exhilarating wine.

I am swaying now in the hour after dinner, 10
a citizen tilted back on his chair,
a creature with a full stomach—
something you don't hear much about in poetry,
that sanctuary of hunger and deprivation.
You know: the driving rain, the boots by the door, 15
small birds searching for berries in winter.

---

1. An Italian dish made with veal shanks.   2. An Italian rice dish.

But tonight, the lion of contentment
has placed a warm, heavy paw on my chest,
and I can only close my eyes and listen
to the drums of woe throbbing in the distance   20
and the sound of my wife's laughter
on the telephone in the next room,
the woman who cooked the savory osso buco,
who pointed to show the butcher the ones she wanted.
She who talks to her faraway friend   25
while I linger here at the table
with a hot, companionable cup of tea,
feeling like one of the friendly natives,
a reliable guide, maybe even the chief's favorite son.

Somewhere, a man is crawling up a rocky hillside   30
on bleeding knees and palms, an Irish penitent
carrying the stone of the world in his stomach;
and elsewhere people of all nations stare
at one another across a long, empty table.

But here, the candles give off their warm glow,   35
the same light that Shakespeare and Izaac Walton[3] wrote by,
the light that lit and shadowed the faces of history.
Only now it plays on the blue plates,
the crumpled napkins, the crossed knife and fork.

In a while, one of us will go up to bed   40
and the other one will follow.
Then we will slip below the surface of the night
into miles of water, drifting down and down
to the dark, soundless bottom
until the weight of dreams pulls us lower still,   45
below the shale and layered rock,
beneath the strata of hunger and pleasure,
into the broken bones of the earth itself,
into the marrow of the only place we know.

                                                           1995

Tuesday, June 4, 1991

By the time I get myself out of bed, my wife has left
the house to take her botany final and the painter
has arrived in his van and is already painting
the columns of the front porch white and the decking gray.

It is early June, a breezy and sun-riddled Tuesday   5
that would quickly be forgotten were it not for my

3. English writer (1593–1683), author of *The Compleat Angler,* a treatise on fishing and a picture of peace
and simple virtues; it is among the most published books in English literature.

writing these few things down as I sit here empty-headed
at the typewriter with a cup of coffee, light and sweet.

I feel like the secretary to the morning whose only
responsibility is to take down its bright, airy dictation   10
until it's time to go to lunch with the other girls,
all of us ordering the cottage cheese with half a pear.

This is what stenographers do in courtrooms, too,
alert at their miniature machines taking down every word.
When there is a silence they sit still as I do, waiting   15
and listening, fingers resting lightly on the keys.

This is also what Samuel Pepys[1] did, jotting down in
private ciphers minor events that would have otherwise
slipped into the dark amnesiac waters of the Thames.
His vigilance finally paid off when London caught fire   20

as mine does when the painter comes in for coffee
and says how much he likes this slow vocal rendition
of "You Don't Know What Love Is"[2] and I figure I will
make him a tape when he goes back to his brushes and pails.

Under the music I can hear the rush of cars and trucks   25
on the highway and every so often the new kitten, Felix,
hops into my lap and watches my fingers drumming out
a running record of this particular June Tuesday

as it unrolls before my eyes, a long intricate carpet
that I am walking on slowly with my head bowed   30
knowing that it is leading me to the quiet shrine
of the afternoon and the melancholy candles of evening.

If I look up, I see out the window the white stars
of clematis climbing a ladder of strings, a woodpile,
a stack of faded bricks, a small green garden of herbs,   35
things you would expect to find outside a window,

all written down now and placed in the setting
of a stanza as unalterably as they are seated
in their chairs in the ontological[3] rooms of the world.
Yes, this is the kind of job I could succeed in,   40

an unpaid but contented amanuensis[4] whose hands
are two birds fluttering on the lettered keys,
whose eyes see sunlight splashing through the leaves,
and the bright pink asterisks of honeysuckle

---

1. English writer (1633–1703), primarily of diaries.
2. A song from the jazz repertoire.
3. Having to do with the branch of metaphysics that deals with the nature of being.
4. One employed to write from dictation or to copy manuscripts.

and the piano at the other end of this room with   45
its small vase of faded flowers and its empty bench.
So convinced am I that I have found my vocation,
tomorrow I will begin my chronicling earlier, at dawn,

a time when hangmen and farmers are up and doing,
when men holding pistols stand in a field back to back.   50
It is the time the ancients imagined in robes, as Eos
or Aurora,[5] who would leave her sleeping husband in bed,

not to take her botany final, but to pull the sun,
her brother, over the horizon's brilliant rim,
her four-horse chariot aimed at the zenith of the sky,   55
But tomorrow, dawn will come the way I picture her,

barefoot and disheveled, standing outside my window
in one of the fragile cotton dresses of the poor.
She will look in at me with her thin arms extended,
offering a handful of birdsong and a small cup of light.   60

                                                                              1995

I Chop Some Parsley While Listening to Art Blakey's[1] Version of "Three Blind Mice"

And I start wondering how they came to be blind.
If it was congenital, they could be brothers and sisters,
and I think of the poor mother
brooding over her sightless young triplets.

Or was it a common accident, all three caught   5
in a searing explosion, a fireworks perhaps?
If not,
if each came to his or her blindness separately,

how did they ever manage to find one another?
Would it not be difficult for a blind mouse   10
to locate even one fellow mouse with vision
let alone two other blind ones?

And how, in their tiny darkness,
could they possibly have run after a farmer's wife
or anyone else's wife for that matter?   15
Not to mention why.

Just so she could cut off their tails
with a carving knife, is the cynic's answer,
but the thought of them without eyes
and now without tails to trail through the moist grass   20

5. Names of the Greek and Roman goddesses of   1. Jazz drummer and bandleader (1919–1990).
dawn.

or slip around the corner of a baseboard
has the cynic who always lounges within me
up off his couch and at the window
trying to hide the rising softness that he feels.

By now I am on to dicing an onion   25
which might account for the wet stinging
in my own eyes, though Freddie Hubbard's[2]
mournful trumpet on "Blue Moon,"[3]

which happens to be the next cut,
cannot be said to be making matters any better.   30

1998

The Night House

Every day the body works in the fields of the world
mending a stone wall
or swinging a sickle through the tall grass—
the grass of civics, the grass of money—
and every night the body curls around itself   5
and listens for the soft bells of sleep.

But the heart is restless and rises
from the body in the middle of the night,
leaves the trapezoidal bedroom
with its thick, pictureless walls   10
to sit by herself at the kitchen table
and heat some milk in a pan.

And the mind gets up too, puts on a robe
and goes downstairs, lights a cigarette,
and opens a book on engineering.   15
Even the conscience awakens
and roams from room to room in the dark,
darting away from every mirror like a strange fish.

And the soul is up on the roof
in her nightdress, straddling the ridge,   20
singing a song about the wildness of the sea
until the first rip of pink appears in the sky.
Then, they all will return to the sleeping body
the way a flock of birds settles back into a tree,

resuming their daily colloquy,   25
talking to each other or themselves
even through the heat of the long afternoons.

2. Jazz musician (b. 1938), member of Art Blakey's   3. American song.
Jazz Messengers (1961–64).

Which is why the body—that house of voices—
sometimes puts down its metal tongs, its needle, or its pen
to stare into the distance,   30

to listen to all its names being called
before bending again to its labor.

1998

LOUISE GLÜCK
b. 1943

"I was born to a vocation: / to bear witness / to the great mysteries," Louise Glück writes in "Parados." Apparently she took the vocation of the poet seriously from an early age. In a car pool on the way to school the child Louise was asked to recite a poem she had written for an assignment. She readily complied: "My special triumph with this poem," she recounts in her essay "The Education of the Poet," "had involved a metrical inversion in the last line (not that I called it that), an omission of the final rhyme: to my ear it was exhilarating, a kind of explosion of form." The driver, a friend's mother, congratulated her: " 'a very good poem,' she said, 'right until the last line,' which she then proceeded to rearrange aloud into the order I had explicitly intended to violate. 'You see,' she told me, 'all that was missing was that last rhyme.' I was furious" (*Proofs and Theories*, 1994). In part, this portrait of a superior, knowing child anticipates the oracular, prophetic tone we sometimes hear in Glück's work. As with the declaration "I was born to a vocation," the poet seems elevated from the ordinary world and set apart by her knowledge. At the same time, Glück's childhood memory suggests what she has elsewhere called "the mandarin in my nature which would have to be checked," which is to say, her exceptional intelligence had to be schooled in common experience; she had to learn to identify with rather than to separate herself from others. The lesson of such schooling, enacted in some of Glück's best poems, is this: what makes the poet exceptional is her ability to render the representative experience she also recognizes as her own.

Glück's work illuminates with particular power the mysteries of those utterly common experiences, pain and loss. The title of Glück's first collection of poetry, *Firstborn* (1968), actually refers to two firstborn children: a sister who died as an infant before Glück was born, and the poet herself, the older of two surviving sisters. "I have always been, in one way or another, obsessed with sisters, the dead and the living both" she has written ("Death and Absences"). Glück saw herself as the dead sister's substitute; at the same time, she says, "I took on the guilty responsibility of the survivor." Although in her early volumes—*Firstborn, The House on Marshland* (1975), *Descending Figure* (1980), and *The Triumph of Achilles* (1985)—the traces of autobiography are distanced and mythic, much of Glück's work revisits the lost sister and explores the poet's feelings of grief and insufficiency. Few contemporary poets have registered so powerfully the self's compulsive efforts, inevitably failing, to become invulnerable to loss and absence, though her mythic transformations of biography can be compared to the work of Sylvia Plath and the early Stanley Kunitz, and her articulation of pain has an affinity with the poems of Frank Bidart.

At the same time, Glück has always refused any easy equation of art with personal experience (one of her essays is titled "Against Sincerity"), and it is therefore striking that in an essay on her education as a poet she gives a remarkably acute account of her struggle with anorexia, which came to a crisis when she was sixteen. This struggle, she writes, was shaped by a terror of "incompleteness and ravenous need," and the concomitant desire to appear "completely free of all forms of dependency, to appear complete, self-contained." She was saved from dying, she believes, by psychoanalysis ("analysis taught me to think") and by her experience at the School of General Studies at Columbia, which she entered at eighteen. Her teachers, Leonie Adams and Stanley Kunitz, provided her work with "the steady application of scrutiny." Glück's poetry is evidence that she took the lesson of this scrutiny and trained it on herself and her world. The intensity of perception in her poems—whether of an infant son, a father's gesture of good-bye, or her own childhood portrait—can be startling.

Glück's is a poetry often impatient with the transitory and hungry for the unchanging—the "blue and permanent" water of "The Drowned Children," the eternal world that stands in implicit contrast to earthly loss and change (the blighted tomato plants in "Vespers"). In this regard she shares the "religious mind" she describes in her essay on T. S. Eliot, the mind that craves "what is final, immutable" and "cannot sustain itself on matter and process." But the impulse of "repulsion" toward the physical world F. R. Leavis once noted in Eliot is countered in Glück by an engagement with complex family relations and with the beauty of the natural world. Her collection *The Wild Iris* (1992), a series of flower poems spoken to and by a divinity, expresses the longing for what is eternal and an arresting sense of the earth's transient loveliness. In *The Meadowlands* (1996), the warring parties in an unraveling marriage (they are modeled on characters in *The Odyssey*) are depicted in wickedly comic tones.

Glück has sought to vary her stylistic habits and preoccupations from one book to another ("Each book I've written has culminated in a conscious diagnostic act, a swearing off"). Clearly the child exulting in a metrical inversion anticipates Glück's lifelong attention to, and experiment with, form. While her work provides some haunting and resonant images, it is the resources of syntax that generate much of the power in her poems. Glück's sentences are muscles of perception, capable of complex extension and retraction, at times unwinding in a stanza to bring together opposing forces or experiences (like authority and woundedness, or the timeless and the transient). Her work moves, in varying degrees from poem to poem, between syntactical control and giving way (what she has called "abandon"). Sometimes, her complex sentences spill forward from one clause into another, but line breaks or the beginning of a new sentence midline interrupt this motion, giving her work the consistent sense of something incomplete, clipped off, unsaid (she shares this quality with her predecessors George Oppen and Emily Dickinson). At other times, as in "Terminal Resemblance" (from *Ararat*), Glück's equation of the sentence with the line ("Talk for us always meant the same thing") has an authoritative tone and declarative control simultaneously undermined by the way one sentence is laid against another without transition or copula. Characteristically for this poet, the pressure of what is unsaid fills the spaces between sentences, between lines, and between stanzas. The distinctive voice we hear in Glück—part oracle, part acute observer, part hapless participant in the rush of feeling and experience—often arises from the way her poems (like certain of Dickinson's) move between statement and mystery, between words and silences.

Glück teaches at Williams College in Massachusetts. She received the Pulitzer Prize for *The Wild Iris* and the PEN Award for her indispensible collection of essays on poetic vocation, *Proofs and Theories* (1994). More recent volumes include *Vita Nova* (1999) and *The Seven Ages* (2001). Glück was the recipient of the Bollingen Prize for poetry in 2001.

The Drowned Children

You see, they have no judgment.
So it is natural that they should drown,
first the ice taking them in
and then, all winter, their wool scarves
floating behind them as they sink   5
until at last they are quiet.
And the pond lifts them in its manifold dark arms.

But death must come to them differently,
so close to the beginning.
As though they had always been   10
blind and weightless. Therefore
the rest is dreamed, the lamp,
the good white cloth that covered the table,
their bodies.

And yet they hear the names they used   15
like lures slipping over the pond:
What are you waiting for
come home, come home, lost
in the waters, blue and permanent.

1980

From Descending Figure[1]

2 *The Sick Child*

—Rijksmuseum[2]

A small child
is ill, has wakened.
It is winter, past midnight   20
in Antwerp.[3] Above a wooden chest,
the stars shine.
And the child
relaxes in her mother's arms.
The mother does not sleep;   25
she stares
fixedly into the bright museum.
By spring the child will die.
Then it is wrong, wrong
to hold her—   30
Let her be alone,
without memory, as the others wake
terrified, scraping the dark
paint from their faces.

1. Printed here are parts 2 and 3 of the three-part sequence.
2. The national museum of the Netherlands, in Amsterdam.
3. A city in Belgium.

3 *For My Sister*

Far away my sister is moving in her crib.   35
The dead ones are like that,
always the last to quiet.

Because, however long they lie in the earth,
they will not learn to speak
but remain uncertainly pressing against the wooden bars,   40
so small the leaves hold them down.

Now, if she had a voice,
the cries of hunger would be beginning.
I should go to her;
perhaps if I sang very softly,   45
her skin so white,
her head covered with black feathers. . . .

1980

Illuminations[1]

1

My son squats in the snow in his blue snowsuit.
All around him stubble, the brown
degraded bushes. In the morning air
they seem to stiffen into words.
And, between, the white steady silence.   5
A wren hops on the airstrip
under the sill, drills
for sustenance, then spreads
its short wings, shadows
dropping from them.   10

2

Last winter he could barely speak.
I moved his crib to face the window:
in the dark mornings
he would stand and grip the bars
until the walls appeared,   15
calling *light, light,*
that one syllable, in
demand or recognition.

3

He sits at the kitchen window
with his cup of apple juice.   20
Each tree forms where he left it,

---

1. Also the title of a collection of prose poems by the French symbolist poet Arthur Rimbaud (1854–1891).

leafless, trapped in his breath.
How clear their edges are,
no limb obscured by motion,
as the sun rises   25
cold and single over the map of language.

                                                                         1980

Terminal Resemblance

When I saw my father for the last time, we both did the same thing.
He was standing in the doorway to the living room,
waiting for me to get off the telephone.
That he wasn't also pointing to his watch
was a signal he wanted to talk.   5

Talk for us always meant the same thing.
He'd say a few words. I'd say a few back.
That was about it.

It was the end of August, very hot, very humid.
Next door, workmen dumped new gravel on the driveway.   10

My father and I avoided being alone;
we didn't know how to connect, to make small talk—
there didn't seem to be
any other possibilities.
So this was special: when a man's dying,   15
he has a subject.

It must have been early morning. Up and down the street
sprinklers started coming on. The gardener's truck
appeared at the end of the block,
then stopped, parking.   20

My father wanted to tell me what it was like to be dying.
He told me he wasn't suffering.
He said he kept expecting pain, waiting for it, but it never came.
All he felt was a kind of weakness.
I said I was glad for him, that I thought he was lucky.   25

Some of the husbands were getting in their cars, going to work.
Not people we knew anymore. New families,
families with young children.
The wives stood on the steps, gesturing or calling.

We said goodbye in the usual way,   30
no embrace, nothing dramatic.
When the taxi came, my parents watched from the front door,
arm in arm, my mother blowing kisses as she always does,

because it frightens her when a hand isn't being used.
But for a change, my father didn't just stand there.   35
This time, he waved.

That's what I did, at the door to the taxi.
Like him, waved to disguise my hand's trembling.

1990

Appearances

When we were children, my parents had our portraits painted,
then hung them side by side, over the mantel,
where we couldn't fight.
I'm the dark one, the older one. My sister's blond,
the one who looks angry because she can't talk.   5

It never bothered me, not talking.
That hasn't changed much. My sister's still blond, not different
from the portrait. Except we're adults now, we've been analyzed:
we understand our expressions.

My mother tried to love us equally,   10
dressed us in the same dresses; she wanted us
perceived as sisters.
That's what she wanted from the portraits:
you need to see them hanging together, facing one another—
separated, they don't make the same statement.   15
You wouldn't know what the eyes were fixed on;
they'd seem to be staring into space.

This was the summer we went to Paris, the summer I was seven.
Every morning, we went to the convent.
Every afternoon, we sat still, having the portraits painted,   20
wearing green cotton dresses, the square neck marked with a ruffle.
Monsieur Davanzo added the flesh tones: my sister's ruddy; mine, faintly
     bluish.
To amuse us, Madame Davanzo hung cherries over our ears.

It was something I was good at: sitting still, not moving.
I did it to be good, to please my mother, to distract her from the child that
     died.   25
I wanted to be child enough. I'm still the same,
like a toy that can stop and go, but not change direction.

Anyone can love a dead child, love an absence.
My mother's strong; she doesn't do what's easy.
She's like her mother: she believes in family, in order.   30
She doesn't change her house, just freshens the paint occasionally.
Sometimes something breaks, gets thrown away, but that's all.

She likes to sit there, on the blue couch, looking up at her daughters,
at the two who lived. She can't remember how it really was,
how anytime she ministered to one child, loved that child,   35
she damaged the other. You could say
she's like an artist with a dream, a vision.
Without that, she'd have been torn apart.
We were like the portraits, always together: you had to shut out
one child to see the other.   40
That's why only the painter noticed: a face already so controlled, so with-
    drawn,
and too obedient, the clear eyes saying
If you want me to be a nun, I'll be a nun.

                                                    1990

Vespers[1]

In your extended absence, you permit me
use of earth, anticipating
some return on investment. I must report
failure in my assignment, principally
regarding the tomato plants.   5
I think I should not be encouraged to grow
tomatoes. Or, if I am, you should withhold
the heavy rains, the cold nights that come
so often here, while other regions get
twelve weeks of summer. All this   10
belongs to you: on the other hand,
I planted the seeds, I watched the first shoots
like wings tearing the soil, and it was my heart
broken by the blight, the black spot so quickly
multiplying in the rows. I doubt   15
you have a heart, in our understanding of
that term. You who do not discriminate
between the dead and the living, who are, in consequence,
immune to foreshadowing, you may not know
how much terror we bear, the spotted leaf,   20
the red leaves of the maple falling
even in August, in early darkness: I am responsible
for these vines.

                                                    1992

---

1. Evening prayers. The sixth and next to the last of the canonical hours, whose office of services is said before nightfall.

JORIE GRAHAM
b. 1950

Jorie Graham's ability to render the disjunctive activity of modern thought, without abandoning the sensuousness of perception, has made her a prominent figure in contemporary poetry. Her poems are sites of self-questioning thinking—about metaphysics, epistemology, or the nature of language itself. A poet whose imagination moves between polarities, she explores the tensions between spirit and matter, thought and sensation, formlessness and form. Rather than resolve these tensions, her poems examine the dependence of each term on the other, as well as the gap between them. This gap is sometimes figured as a literal blank ("————"), a space language cannot fill. At other times it appears as the moment when things "scatter, blow away, scatter, recollect" ("The Dream of the Unified Field"), a moment in which form and the undoing of form co-exist. It isn't surprising that Graham's poems often work in liminal spaces between the visible and the invisible, like the scene of the souls at Judgment hurrying to re-enter the flesh in "At Luca Signorelli's Resurrection of the Body": "there is no / entrance, / only entering." She has called poetic form "a vessel for active tension," and the rapid shifts in Graham's poems from past to present, from abstract to particular, make the surface of her work appear to be eddied by verbal and intellectual turbulence. No wonder *roil* is one of her favorite verbs.

Graham was born in New York, but when she was a child her father, a *Newsweek* correspondent, and her mother, a sculptor, moved to Italy, where Graham grew up in the neighborhood of Trastevere, the old part of Rome. She lived surrounded by Italian churches full of frescoes, and references to Italian art inform many of her poems, among them "San Sepolcro" and "At Luca Signorelli's Resurrection of the Body." In Italy Graham attended a French lycée, and at seventeen she went to Paris to study at the Sorbonne, where she became involved in the student uprisings of 1968. In 1969 she returned to the United States and enrolled in film school at New York University (where she remembers hearing poetry read aloud in English for the first time), and her poetry has, from the start, been influenced by cinema. She went on to enroll in the University of Iowa Writers Workshop, where she later taught for a number of years; currently she is on the faculty at Harvard University. The range of reference in Graham's work is wide and suggests her European background and especially her French education, with its emphasis on philosophy. But she is equally preoccupied with American history and the nature of American life, a preoccupation evident in "The Dream of the Unified Field," which closes with her revision of entries from Columbus's journals.

It is not surprising that what Graham calls "the calm assurance of the standard English line" has "interested and troubled" her. Although her poems often move in and out of an iambic measure (as in the openings of "The Geese" and "The Dream of the Unified Field"), like many poets she believes contemporary experience requires a more unpredictable music. The poems of her first book, *Hybrids of Plants and of Ghosts* (1980; the title is taken from Nietzsche), were mostly constructed of short, tightly controlled lines. But in subsequent works, her verse has loosened (a second volume is called *Erosion*, 1983) and her line grown longer. Many of the poems from *The End of Beauty* (1987), *The Region of Unlikeness* (1991), *Materialism* (1993), *The Errancy* (1994), and *Swarm* (2000) hurtle across and down the page, sometimes without punctuation. Because she shares a contemporary skepticism of any version of reality that claims to be total, her work characteristically undercuts what it asserts. She works best in a form that supports the pull of co-existing and unreconciled tensions; for example, the short, enjambed lines of "At Luca Signorelli's Resurrection of the Body" separate each distinct detail and gesture while also tugging one perception into the next. The rhythmic structure of that poem holds apart and, at the same time, overlaps the visible and the invisible; the poem ends without resolving or unifying this opposition.

When Graham tries to imagine a unity that includes polarities (as in "The Dream of the Unified Field") that unity is a "dream" because she is aware that the drive for order and closure (what she calls "the silky swerve into shapeliness / and then the click shut" in "Region of Unlikeness") risks narrowness and exclusion. Therefore, Graham's work exposes the fractures in experience and in the self (fractures often gendered as male and female). But her poems also work to uncover, through a series of associations, the connections between daily experience (looking up at a flock of geese, bringing her daughter a leotard she had forgotten) and the larger frameworks of history, metaphysics, and myth. At times her drive to find or make analogies between a particular experience and its larger historical contexts can feel false or strained. But Graham is a resolutely self-interrogating poet who sees each new book as a critique of her previous work. She is willing to risk failure in pursuit of a poetry that renders the drama of consciousness unfolding in language and the world; in this she is the heir of Wallace Stevens, with his vision of "the poem of the mind in the act of finding / What will suffice." If the life of thought makes her poems abstract (one is titled "What Is Called Thinking"), the activity of perception, registered sometimes in almost microscopic detail (as in "Opulence"), makes them concrete. Her best and most challenging work combines these two modes in a series of rapid-moving procedures. "The Dream of the Unified Field," for example, explores memory and possession by building layers of association through shifting concrete images. The poem begins with thoughts of a daughter—"On my way to bringing you the leotard / you forgot to include in your overnight bag"—and shifts to a snow storm, then to a vision of starlings "swarming / then settling," then to the leaves of a tree scattering and recollecting, until the poet returns to the thought of her daughter dancing. When the memory of the poet's childhood ballet teacher surfaces, and then dissolves into the historical memory of Columbus's voyage of discovery, we experience an unexpected break in focus, a gap in thought marked out by a series of interruptive dashes.

It is characteristic of Graham's poems to include the gaps in thought. Her work is also riddled with questions that implicitly or explicitly address the reader: "Do you think these words are still enough?" and "Are you listening?" ("Manifest Destiny"). Describing her poetic strategies, Graham says she imagines a reader "who has heard it all before" (her poem "Imperialism" names this reader: "dear are-you-there"), one who distrusts language as a medium for truth. The difficult surfaces of Graham's poems try to wake us into full attention, so that we may confront, together with the poet, the question of what language can and cannot say.

The Geese

Today as I hang out the wash I see them again, a code
as urgent as elegant,
tapering with goals.
For days they have been crossing. We live beneath these geese

as if beneath the passage of time, or a most perfect heading.   5
Sometimes I fear their relevance.
Closest at hand,
between the lines,

the spiders imitate the paths the geese won't stray from,
imitate them endlessly to no avail: 10

things will not remain connected,
will not heal,

and the world thickens with texture instead of history,
texture instead of place.
Yet the small fear of the spiders   15
binds and binds

the pins to the lines, the lines to the eaves, to the pincushion bush,
as if, at any time, things could fall further apart
and nothing could help them
recover their meaning. And if these spiders had their way,   20

chainlink over the visible world,
would we be in or out? I turn to go back in.
There is a feeling the body gives the mind
of having missed something, a bedrock poverty, like falling

without the sense that you are passing through one world,   25
that you could reach another
anytime. Instead the real
is crossing you,

your body an arrival
you know is false but can't outrun. And somewhere in between   30
these geese forever entering and
these spiders turning back,

this astonishing delay, the everyday, takes place.

1980

At Luca Signorelli's[1] Resurrection of the Body

See how they hurry
        to enter
their bodies,
        these spirits,
Is it better, flesh,   5
        that they

should hurry so?
        From above
the green-winged angels
        blare down   10
trumpets and light. But
        they don't care,

---

1. Italian painter (1450–1523) of the Umbrian
school, associated with a region in central Italy distinguished in the Renaissance by the talent of its
painters. His series on the Last Judgment deco-
rates the Cappella Nuova in the gothic cathedral
in Orvieto, Italy, a town in the Umbrian region.
One of the sections of this series is titled *Resurrection of the Flesh*.

they hurry to congregate,
    they hurry
into speech, until   15
    it's a marketplace,
it is humanity. But still
    we wonder

in the chancel[2]
    of the dark cathedral,   20
is it better, back?
    The artist
has tried to make it so: each tendon
    they press

to re-enter   25
    is perfect. But is it
perfection
    they're after,
pulling themselves up
    through the soil   30

into the weightedness, the color,
    into the eye
of the painter? Outside
    it is 1500,
all round the cathedral   35
    streets hurry to open

through the wild
    silver grasses. . . .
The men and women
    on the cathedral wall   40
do not know how,
    having come this far,

to stop their
    hurrying. They amble off
in groups, in   45
    couples. Soon
some are clothed, there is
    distance, there is

perspective. Standing below them
    in the church   50
in Orvieto, how can we
    tell them
to be stern and brazen
    and slow,

---

2. Space around a church alter, often enclosed by lattice or railing.

that there is no   55
        entrance,
only entering. They keep on
        arriving,
wanting names,
        wanting   60

happiness. In his studio
        Luca Signorelli
in the name of God
        and Science
and the believable   65
        broke into the body

studying arrival.
        But the wall
of the flesh
        opens endlessly,   70
its vanishing point so deep
        and receding

we have yet to find it,
        to have it
stop us. So he cut   75
        deeper,
graduating slowly
        from the symbolic

to the beautiful. How far
        is true?   80
When his one son
        died violently,
he had the body brought to him
        and laid it

on the drawing-table,   85
        and stood
at a certain distance
        awaiting the best
possible light, the best depth
        of day,   90

then with beauty and care
        and technique
and judgment, cut into
        shadow, cut
into bone and sinew and every   95
        pocket

in which the cold light
        pooled.
It took him days,

that deep   100
caress, cutting,
    unfastening,

until his mind
    could climb into
the open flesh and   105
    mend itself.

1983

The Dream of the Unified Field[1]

1

On my way to bringing you the leotard
you forgot to include in your overnight bag,
the snow started coming down harder.
I watched each gathering of leafy flakes
melt round my footfall.   5
I looked up into it—late afternoon but bright.
Nothing true or false in itself. Just motion. Many strips of
motion. Filaments of falling marked by the tiny certainties
of flakes. Never blurring yet themselves a cloud. Me in it
                                and yet   10
moving easily through it, black Lycra leotard balled into
                                my pocket,
your tiny dream in it, my left hand on it or in it
                                to keep
warm. Praise this. Praise that. Flash a glance up and try   15
                                to see
the arabesques and runnels,[2] gathering and loosening, as they
define, as a voice would, the passaging through from
                                the-other-than-
human. Gone as they hit the earth. But embellishing.   20
Flourishing. The road with me on it going on through. In-
scribed with the present. As if it really
were possible to exist, and exist, never to be pulled back
in, given and given never to be received. The music
of the footfalls doesn't stop, doesn't   25
mean. *Here are your things*, I said.

2

Starting home I heard—bothering, lifting, then
                                bothering again—
the huge flock of starlings massed over our
                                neighborhood   30
these days; heard them lift and

---

1. In physics, unified field is a set of theories that
seeks to relate all the known, basic forces that exist
in nature.

2. Rivulets or brooks. "Arabesques": ballet positions in which the dancer stands on one leg with
the other extended in the back.

one hand still on the massive, gold, bird-headed knob,
and see—a hundred feet away—herself—a woman in black in
                 a mirrored room—
saw her not shift her gaze but bring her pallid tensile hand—   120
as if it were not part of her—slowly down from
The ridged, cold, feathered knob and, recollected, fixed upon
                 that other woman, emigrée,[5]
begin to move in stiffly towards her . . . You out there
                 now,   125
you in here with me—I watched the two of them,
black and black, in the gigantic light,
glide at each other, heads raised, necks long—
me wanting to cry out—where were the others?—wasn't it late?
the two of her like huge black hands—   130
clap once and once only and the signal is given—
out to what?—regarding what?—till closer-in I saw
               more suddenly
how her eyes eyed themselves: no wavering:
like a vast silver page burning: the black hole   135
               expanding:
like a meaning coming up quick from inside that page—
coming up quick to seize the reading face—
each face wanting the other to *take* it—
but where? and *from* where?—I was eight—   140
I saw the different weights of things,
saw the vivid performance of the present,
saw the light rippling almost shuddering where her body finally
               touched
the image, the silver film between them like something that would   145
               have shed itself in nature now
but wouldn't, couldn't, here, on tight,
between, not thinning, not slipping off to let some
               seed-down
through, no signal in it, no information . . . Child,   150
               what should I know
to save you that I do not know, hands on this windowpane?—

6

The storm: I close my eyes and,
standing in it, try to make it *mine.* An inside
thing. Once I was . . . once, once.   155
It settles, in my head, the wavering white
sleep, the instances—they stick, accrue,
grip up, connect, they do not melt,
I will not let them melt, they build, cloud and cloud,
I feel myself weak, I feel the thinking muscle-up—   160
outside, the talk-talk of the birds—outside,
strings and their roots, leaves inside the limbs,
in some spots the skin breaking—

---

5. The feminine version of a French noun for a person who has left her native country for political reasons.

but inside, no more exploding, no more smoldering, no more,
inside, a splinter colony, new world, possession   165
gripping down to form,
wilderness brought deep into my clearing,
out of the ooze of night,
limbed, shouldered, necked, visaged, the white—
now the clouds coming in (don't look up),   170
now the Age behind the clouds, The Great Heights,
all in there, reclining, eyes closed, huge,
centuries and centuries long and wide,
and underneath, barely attached but attached,
like a runner, my body, my tiny piece of   175
the century—minutes, houses going by—The Great
                                             Heights—
anchored by these footsteps, now and now,
the footstepping—now and now—carrying its vast
white sleeping geography—mapped—   180
not a lease—*possession*—"At the hour of vespers[6]
in a sudden blinding snow,
they entered the harbor and he named it Puerto[7] de

                                    7

San Nicolas and at its entrance he imagined he
                            could see   185
its beauty and goodness, *sand right up to the land
where you can put the side of a ship.* He thought
                            he saw
Indians fleeing through the white before
the ship . . . As for him, he did not believe what his   190
                            crew
told him, nor did he understand them well, nor they
him. In the white swirl, he placed a large cross
                  at the western side of
the harbor, on a conspicuous height,   195
as a sign that Your Highness claim the land as
Your own. After the cross was set up,
three sailors went into the bush (immediately erased
from sight by the fast snow) to see what kinds of
trees. They captured three very black Indian   200
women—one who was young and pretty.
The Admiral ordered her clothed and returned to
                            her land
courteously. There her people told
that she had not wanted to leave the ship,   205
but wished to stay on it. The snow was wild.
Inside it, though, you could see

6. The passages which make up the final gesture
[of the poem] are rewritten sections from the
*Diario of Christopher Columbus. First Voyages to
America, 1492–93,* abstracted by Fray Bartolome
de La Casas (translated by Oliver Dunn and James
E. Kelley Jr.) [Graham's note].
7. Spanish for "port."

this woman was wearing a little piece of
gold on her nose, which was a sign there was
                                              gold   210
on that land"—

                                                                          1995

JOY HARJO
b. 1951

Joy Harjo was born in Tulsa, Oklahoma, to a mother of mixed Cherokee, French, and
Irish blood. Her father's family, members of the Creek tribe, included "rebels and
speakers," among them a Baptist minister (Harjo's paternal grandfather), two painters
(her grandmother and aunt) and a great-great-grandfather who led a Creek rebellion
against their forced removal from Alabama into Oklahoma in 1832. As Laura Coltelli
has pointed out, the work of many contemporary Native American writers (a large
number of whom are of mixed blood) enacts a quest to reenvision identity by confronting the historical, cultural, and political realities that shape lives experienced
between different worlds. Coming from a family tradition of powerful speaking, Harjo
participates in a search to reimagine and repair painful fractures in contemporary
experience: between past and present, between person and landscape, and between
parts of the self. Thus traveling is a mythic activity in her poems, enacting this search
for community and historical connectedness. As in the work of James Welch, Simon
J. Ortiz, and Leslie Marmon Silko, the theme of traveling in Harjo's poems resonates
with the historical displacements and migrations of native peoples (especially the
forced removal of the Creeks). She has called herself the wanderer in her family, and
her poems often map her journeys, whether on foot, by car, or in a plane. Perhaps
Harjo thinks of herself as the family wanderer because she left Oklahoma to attend
high school at the Institute of American Indian Arts in Santa Fe, New Mexico ("in a
way it saved my life," she has said). After receiving a B.A. from the University of New
Mexico in 1976 and an M.F.A. from the University of Iowa, she has taught at the
Institute of American Indian Arts, Arizona State University, the University of Colorado, the University of Arizona, and the University of New Mexico.

"Breathe / backwards" she writes in her poem "Call It Fear," and many of Harjo's
poems track an inward journey through personal and collective memory, looping forward and back. Especially important in her work is the reconnection of contemporary
urban experience with a historical and mythic past. This reconnection seeks to
assuage the loneliness and desperation of those on the margin who populate Harjo's
work; in her volume *She Had Some Horses* (1983), a woman raises her mixed-blood
children alone, a friend threatens suicide, a woman threatens to let herself drop from
a thirteenth-story window. The horses who run through this and other of her books
embody, Harjo has said, "very sensitive and finely tuned spirits of the psyche" and
are, like the poet herself, on the move. In her collection *In Mad Love and War* (1990)
we find a psyche anguished by global, national, and domestic wars; the journey here
often turns from outward to inward. The poems of *In Mad Love and War*, with their
anger at dispossession and violence (as in an elegy for Anna Mae Pictou Aquash, a
young Micmac woman shot dead on the Pine Ridge Reservation), recall some of the
work of James Wright, Audre Lorde, and Leslie Marmon Silko; they also suggest that
the spirit of Harjo's rebel great-great-grandfather is never far from these poems.

This poet is a superb reader of her poems, but even without the poet's physical presence, Harjo's best work resonates with the rhythms of the body: the heartbeat, the movement of breath, the ebb and flow of desire. Whether in the sensuous "Summer Night" ("every poem has an electrical force field which is love," Harjo has said) or in the edgy rhythms of "White Bear," her lines have a remarkable physicality. Perhaps because Harjo is also a musician—she plays the tenor saxophone and speaks of the influence jazz, blues, country music, and Creek Stomp Dance songs have had on her work—the *sound* of her poems is especially important. The poems demand to be read aloud, where their mastery of chant and ceremonial repetition also links them to oral traditions and calls forth the powers of dream and memory. In addition to being a poet and musician, Harjo is a screenwriter. She has also written the text for Stephen Strom's photographs of the southwestern landscape, *Secrets from the Center of the World* (1989), and has edited an anthology of tribal women's writings from around the world. A collection of interviews, *The Spiral of Memory* (1996), edited by Laura Coltelli, is a valuable accompaniment to her poems.

In *The Woman Who Fell from the Sky* (1994), Harjo reinterprets present experience through retellings of traditional myths. Various Native American traditions tell the story of a sky woman who falls through the void of space and creates the human universe. In the title poem of this volume, a group of women ("angry at their inattentive husbands") run off with stars; one of these women dares to look back at earth and falls from the sky. In Harjo's hands this myth becomes the story of two lovers, who were children together at an Indian boarding school. Adrift in an urban landscape, they are reunited, a narrative characterized by fracture and repair. In the same collection, "Flood" renders a young girl's sexuality and imaginative power through the myth of the water monster (the Chippewa writer Louise Erdrich makes use of a similar myth in her novel *Tracks*). Like some of the work of Simon J. Ortiz or Leslie Marmon Silko, the prose poems that form much of this book have connections to oral storytelling, with its use of dream and myth, and to the claims of realism we associate with prose fiction. In Harjo's work, poetry witnesses truths of experience otherwise concealed or invisible and thus communicates a sense of spiritual journey and place. For all Harjo's anguished sense of the warring factions in our world and our selves, her works consistently engage in a process of healing and regeneration, themes that continue in her collection *A Map to the Next World* (2000). Like the kitchen table in her poem "Perhaps the World Ends Here," Harjo's poems are a space where "we sing with joy, with sorrow. We pray of suffering and remorse. We give thanks."

Call It Fear

There is this edge where shadows
and bones of some of us walk
                backwards.
Talk backwards. There is this edge
call it an ocean of fear of the dark. Or   5
name it with other songs. Under our ribs
our hearts are bloody stars. Shine on
shine on, and horses in their galloping flight
strike the curve of ribs.
                Heartbeat   10
and breathe back sharply. Breath
                backwards.
There is this edge within me
            I saw it once

an August Sunday morning when the heat hadn't   15
left this earth. And Goodluck
sat sleeping next to me in the truck.
We had never broken through the edge of the
singing at four a.m.
                    We had only wanted to talk, to hear   20
any other voice to stay alive with.
                    And there was this edge—
not the drop of sandy rock cliff
bones of volcanic earth into
                    Albuquerque.   25
Not that,
          but a string of shadow horses kicking
and pulling me out of my belly,
              not into the Rio Grande but into the music
barely coming through   30
                    Sunday church singing
from the radio. Battery worn-down but the voices
talking backwards.

                                                    1983

White Bear

She begins to board the flight
    to Albuquerque. Late night.
But stops in the corrugated tunnel,
    a space between leaving and staying,
where the night sky catches   5

        her whole life

she has felt like a woman
    balancing on a wooden nickle heart
approaching herself from here to
    there, Tulsa or New York   10
with knives or corn meal.

The last flight someone talked
    about how coming from Seattle
the pilot flew a circle
    over Mt. St. Helens;[1] she sat   15
quiet. (But had seen the eruption
    as the earth beginning
to come apart, as in birth
    out of violence.)

She watches the yellow lights   20
    of towns below the airplane flicker,

1. A volcanic peak in Washington State; it erupted in 1980.

fade and fall backwards. Somewhere,
   she dreamed, there is the white bear
moving down from the north, motioning her paws
   like a long arctic night, that kind   25
of circle and the whole world balanced in
   between carved of ebony and ice

     oh so hard

the clear black nights
   like her daughter's eyes, and the white   30
bear moon, cupped like an ivory rocking
cradle, tipping back it could go
either way
       all darkness
            is open to all light.   35

                  1983

Summer Night

The moon is nearly full,
         the humid air sweet like melon.
Flowers that have cupped the sun all day
            dream of iridescent wings
under the long dark sleep.   5
         Children's invisible voices call out
in the glimmering moonlight.
          Their parents play worn-out records
of the cumbia.[1] Behind the screen door
         their soft laughter swells   10
into the rhythm of a smooth guitar.
         I watch the world shimmer
inside this globe of a summer night,
        listen to the wobble of her
spin and dive. It happens all the time, waiting for you   15
          to come home.
There is an ache that begins
       in the sound of an old blues song.
It becomes a house where all the lights have gone out
         but one.   20
And it burns and burns
       until there is only the blue smoke of dawn
and everyone is sleeping in someone's arms
        even the flowers
even the sound of a thousand silences.   25
        And the arms of night
in the arms of day.
     Everyone except me.
But then the smell of damp honeysuckle twisted on the vine.

---

1. A Latin American dance.

And the turn of the shoulder   30
               of the ordinary spirit who keeps watch
over this ordinary street.
             And there you are, the secret
of your own flower of light
              blooming in the miraculous dark.   35

1990

The Flood

It had been years since I'd seen the watermonster, the snake who lived
at the bottom of the lake. He had disappeared in the age of reason, as a
mystery that never happened.

For in the muggy lake was the girl I could have been at sixteen, wrested
from the torment of exaggerated fools, one version anyway, though the   5
story at the surface would say car accident, or drowning while drinking,
all of it eventually accidental.

This story is not an accident, nor is the existence of the watersnake in
the memory of the people as they carried the burden of the myth from
Alabama to Oklahoma.[1] Each reluctant step pounded memory into the   10
broken heart and no one will ever forget it.

When I walk the stairway of water into the abyss, I return as the wife of
the watermonster, in a blanket of time decorated with swatches of cloth
and feathers from our favorite clothes.

The stories of the battles of the watersnake are forever ongoing, and   15
those stories soaked into my blood since infancy like deer gravy, so how
could I resist the watersnake, who appeared as the most handsome man
in the tribe, or any band whose visits I'd been witness to since childhood?

This had been going on for centuries: the first time he appeared I carried
my baby sister on my back as I went to get water. She laughed at a   20
woodpecker flitting like a small sun above us and before I could deter
the symbol we were in it.

My body was already on fire with the explosion of womanhood as if I
were flint, hot stone, and when he stepped out of the water he was the
first myth I had ever seen uncovered. I had surprised him in a human   25
moment. I looked aside but I could not discount what I had seen.

My baby sister's cry pinched reality, the woodpecker a warning of a dis-
juncture in the brimming sky, and then a man who was not a man but
a myth.

1. In 1832 the Muskogee tribe (also known as "Creek") was forcibly relocated by the United States government from Alabama to Oklahoma.

What I had seen there were no words for except in the sacred language   30
of the most holy recounting, so when I ran back to the village, drenched
in salt, how could I explain the water jar left empty by the river to my
mother who deciphered my burning lips as shame?

My imagination swallowed me like a mica sky, but I had seen the watermonster in the fight of lightning storms, breaking trees, stirring up killing   35
winds, and had lost my favorite brother to a spear of the sacred flame,
so certainly I would know my beloved if he were hidden in the blushing
skin of the suddenly vulnerable.

I was taken with a fever and nothing cured it until I dreamed my fiery
body dipped in the river where it fed into the lake. My father carried me   40
as if I were newborn, as if he were presenting me once more to the world,
and when he dipped me I was quenched, pronounced healed.

My parents immediately made plans to marry me to an important man
who was years older but would provide me with everything I needed to
survive in this world, a world I could no longer perceive, as I had been   45
blinded with a ring of water when I was most in need of a drink by a
snake who was not a snake, and how did he know my absolute secrets,
those created at the brink of acquired language?

When I disappeared it was in a storm that destroyed the houses of my
relatives; my baby sister was found sucking on her hand in the crook of   50
an oak.

And though it may have appeared otherwise, I did not go willingly. That
night I had seen my face strung on the shell belt of my ancestors, and I
was standing next to a man who could not look me in the eye.

The oldest woman in the tribe wanted to remember me as a symbol in   55
the story of a girl who disobeyed, who gave in to her desires before
marriage and was destroyed by the monster disguised as the seductive
warrior.

Others saw the car I was driving as it drove into the lake early one
morning, the time the carriers of tradition wake up, before the sun or   60
the approach of woodpeckers, and found the emptied six-pack on the
sandy shores of the lake.

The power of the victim is a power that will always be reckoned with,
one way or the other. When the proverbial sixteen-year-old woman
walked down to the lake within her were all sixteen-year-old women who   65
had questioned their power from time immemorial.

Her imagination was larger than the small frame house at the north edge
of town, with the broken cars surrounding it like a necklace of futility,
larger than the town itself leaning into the lake. Nothing could stop it,
just as no one could stop the bearing-down thunderheads as they gath-   70
ered overhead in the war of opposites.

Years later when she walked out of the lake and headed for town, no
one recognized her, or themselves, in the drench of fire and rain. The
watersnake was a story no one told anymore. They'd entered a drought
that no one recognized as drought, the convenience store a signal of   75
temporary amnesia.

I had gone out to get bread, eggs and the newspaper before breakfast
and hurried the cashier for my change as the crazy woman walked in,
for I could not see myself as I had abandoned her some twenty years ago
in a blue windbreaker at the edge of the man-made lake as everyone   80
dove naked and drunk off the sheer cliff, as if we had nothing to live for,
not then or ever.

It was beginning to rain in Oklahoma, the rain that would flood the
world.[2]

1994

2. Embedded in Muscogee tribal memory is the
creature the tie snake, a huge snake of a monster
who lives in waterways and will do what he can to
take us with him. He represents the power of the
underworld.

He is still present today in the lakes and rivers
of Oklahoma and Alabama, a force we reckon with
despite the proliferation of inventions that keep us
from ourselves [Harjo's note].

RITA DOVE
b. 1952

What she has called the "friction" between the beauty of a poetic form and a difficult
or painful subject appeals to Rita Dove. Her own formal control and discipline create
a beautiful design and a haunting music in "Parsley," a poem based on a murderous
event: in 1957 the dictator of the Dominican Republic, Rafael Trujillo, ordered twenty
thousand black Haitians killed because they could not pronounce the letter "r" in the
Spanish word for parsley. What compels Dove in this poem is the way a "single,
beautiful word" has the power of life and death. More astonishing is that she writes
from the perspective of both the Haitians in the cane fields and General Trujillo in
his palace. When asked in an interview about her capacity to imagine Trujillo, Dove
responded, "I frankly don't believe anyone who says they've never felt any evil, that
they cannot understand that process of evil. It was important to me to try to understand that arbitrary quality of his cruelty. . . . Making us get into his head may shock
us all into seeing what the human being is capable of, because if we can go that far
into his head, we're halfway there ourselves." An ability to enter into different points
of view in a single poem is characteristic of Dove's disinterested imagination. Her
method is to avoid commentary, to let the imagined person or object, the suggestive
detail, speak for itself. Often her work suggests what Keats called "negative capability," the gift of the poet to become what he or she is not.

Born in Akron, Dove attended Miami University of Ohio and, after her graduation,
studied modern European literature as a Fulbright/Hays fellow at the University of
Tübingen in Germany. When she returned from Europe she took an M.F.A. at the
University of Iowa (in 1977). Later she taught creative writing at Arizona State University before joining the University of Virginia, where she is now Commonwealth

Professor of English. Since her Fulbright year she has returned frequently to live abroad, in Ireland, Israel, France, and especially Germany. Her travel in Europe and elsewhere suggests part of the imperative she feels as a poet: to range widely through fields of experience, to cross boundaries of space as well as time. Her first book, *The Yellow House on the Corner* (1980), is notable for its intense poems about adolescence; her second book, *Museum* (1983), dramatically extends the range of her work. "When I started *Museum*," she has said, "I was in Europe, and I had a way of looking back on America and distancing myself from my experience." As well as for several fine poems about her father (a subject that may also have needed distance), the book is remarkable for the way distance allowed Dove to move out of her immediate experience, freed her to imagine widely different lives.

As if to show that it is also possible to travel widely while staying at home, Dove's *Thomas and Beulah* (1986) is an extended sequence based on her grandparents' lives. Her continuing fascination with imagining different perspectives on the same event is evident in this sequence. Dove herself has described the origins of the book this way:

> My grandmother had told me a story that had happened to my grandfather when he was young, coming up on a riverboat to Akron, Ohio, my hometown. But that was all I had basically. And the story so fascinated me that I tried to write about it. I started off writing stories about my grandfather and soon, because I ran out of real fact, in order to keep going, I made up facts for this character, Thomas. . . . then this poem "Dusting" appeared, really out of nowhere. I didn't realize this was Thomas's wife saying, "I want to talk. And you can't do his side without my side . . ."

This is the story, in part, of a marriage and of a black couple's life in the industrial Midwest in the period from 1900 to 1960. Thomas's point of view controls the poems of the book's first section, while the second part imagines his wife's. The larger framework of the sequence links family history to social history. Thomas's journey from the rural South to the industrial city of Akron (where he finds employment in the Goodyear Zeppelin factory until the Depression puts him out of work) is part of the larger social movement of southern African Americans into northern industrial cities in the first part of this century. The individual lyrics of Dove's sequence create and sustain the story through distinct and often ordinary moments in which each life is vividly portrayed. It is part of Dove's gift that she can render the apparently unimportant moments that inform a life and set them against a background of larger historical forces, as do Robert Hayden in *Elegies for Paradise Valley* and Robert Lowell in *Notebook*.

Many of the figures in Dove's poems are displaced, on the border between different worlds: for example, Thomas and Beulah and Benjamin Banneker ("Banneker"). The experience of displacement, of what she has called living in "two different worlds, seeing things with double vision," consistently compels this poet's imagination. It takes both detachment and control to maintain (and to live with) such doubleness. This may be why Dove's rich sense of language and her love of sound are joined to a disciplined formal sense. The form of her poems often holds in place difficult or ambiguous feelings, and keeps the expression of feeling understated. While restraint is one of the strengths of Dove's poems, her work can sometimes seem austere. Such careful control recalls Elizabeth Bishop's early work, also highly controlled and even, at times, guarded. As Bishop grew to relax her restraints, to open into an extraordinary expressiveness, so Dove has gifts to suggest a similar growth. Her collections *Grace Notes* (1989) and *Mother Love* (1995) suggest just such a relaxing of the poet's guard. While *On the Bus with Rosa Parks* (2000) demonstrates Dove's on-going ability to unite powerful feeling and social conscience with a transformative sense of language and form. With each book she asks something more from herself, and she has now become one of our indispensable poets. Dove was poet laureate of the United States from 1993 to 1995.

Geometry

I prove a theorem and the house expands:
the windows jerk free to hover near the ceiling,
the ceiling floats away with a sigh.

As the walls clear themselves of everything
but transparency, the scent of carnations   5
leaves with them. I am out in the open

and above the windows have hinged into butterflies,
sunlight glinting where they've intersected.
They are going to some point true and unproven.

1980

Adolescence—I

In water-heavy nights behind grandmother's porch
We knelt in the tickling grasses and whispered:
Linda's face hung before us, pale as a pecan,
And it grew wise as she said:
    "A boy's lips are soft,   5
    As soft as baby's skin."
The air closed over her words.
A firefly whirred near my ear, and in the distance
I could hear streetlamps ping
Into miniature suns   10
Against a feathery sky.

1980

Adolescence—II

Although it is night, I sit in the bathroom, waiting.
Sweat prickles behind my knees, the baby-breasts are alert.
Venetian blinds slice up the moon; the tiles quiver in pale strips.

Then they come, the three seal men with eyes as round
As dinner plates and eyelashes like sharpened tines.   5
They bring the scent of licorice. One sits in the washbowl,

One on the bathtub edge; one leans against the door.
"Can you feel it yet?" they whisper.
I don't know what to say, again. They chuckle,

Patting their sleek bodies with their hands.   10
"Well, maybe next time." And they rise,
Glittering like pools of ink under moonlight,

And vanish. I clutch at the ragged holes
They leave behind, here at the edge of darkness.
Night rests like a ball of fur on my tongue.   15

                                                              1980

Adolescence—III

With Dad gone, Mom and I worked
The dusky rows of tomatoes.
As they glowed orange in sunlight
And rotted in shadow, I too
Grew orange and softer, swelling out   5
Starched cotton slips.

The texture of twilight made me think of
Lengths of Dotted Swiss. In my room
I wrapped scarred knees in dresses
That once went to big-band dances;   10
I baptized my earlobes with rosewater.
Along the window-sill, the lipstick stubs
Glittered in their steel shells.

Looking out at the rows of clay
And chicken manure, I dreamed how it would happen: 15
He would meet me by the blue spruce,
A carnation over his heart, saying,
"I have come for you, Madam;
I have loved you in my dreams."
At his touch, the scabs would fall away.   20
Over his shoulder, I see my father coming toward us:
He carries his tears in a bowl,
And blood hangs in the pine-soaked air.

                                                              1980

Banneker[1]

What did he do except lie
under a pear tree, wrapped in
a great cloak, and meditate
on the heavenly bodies?
Venerable, the good people of Baltimore   5
whispered, shocked and more than
a little afraid. After all it was said

1. Benjamin Banneker (1731–1806), first black man to devise an almanac and predict a solar eclipse accurately, was also appointed to the commission that surveyed and laid out what is now Washington, D.C. [Dove's note].

he took to strong drink.
Why else would he stay out
under the stars all night   10
and why hadn't he married?

But who would want him! Neither
Ethiopian nor English, neither
lucky nor crazy, a capacious bird
humming as he penned in his mind   15
another enflamed letter
to President Jefferson[2]—he imagined
the reply, polite and rhetorical.
Those who had been to Philadelphia
reported the statue   20
of Benjamin Franklin
before the library

his very size and likeness.
A wife? No, thank you.
At dawn he milked   25
the cows, then went inside
and put on a pot to stew
while he slept. The clock
he whittled as a boy
still ran.[3] Neighbors   30
woke him up
with warm bread and quilts.
At nightfall he took out

his rifle—a white-maned
figure stalking the darkened   35
breast of the Union—and
shot at the stars, and by chance
one went out. Had he killed?
I assure thee, my dear Sir!
Lowering his eyes to fields   40
sweet with the rot of spring, he could see
a government's domed city
rising from the morass and spreading
in a spiral of lights. . . .

                                                            1983

2. After hearing that Jefferson doubted the mental capacity of black people, Banneker wrote him a letter that invoked ideals of human equality and asked for Jefferson's help in the abolition of slavery.
3. The first all-wood clock ever made in America, which Banneker carved as an experiment after studying only a common pocketwatch.

Parsley[1]

1. The Cane[2] Fields

There is a parrot imitating spring
in the palace, its feathers parsley green.
Out of the swamp the cane appears

to haunt us, and we cut it down. El General
searches for a word; he is all the world   5
there is. Like a parrot imitating spring,

we lie down screaming as rain punches through
and we come up green. We cannot speak an R—
out of the swamp, the cane appears

and then the mountain we call in whispers *Katalina*.[3]   10
The children gnaw their teeth to arrowheads.
There is a parrot imitating spring.

El General has found his word: *perejil.*
Who says it, lives. He laughs, teeth shining
out of the swamp. The cane appears   15

in our dreams, lashed by wind and streaming.
And we lie down. For every drop of blood
there is a parrot imitating spring.
Out of the swamp the cane appears.

2. The Palace

The word the general's chosen is parsley.   20
It is fall, when thoughts turn
to love and death; the general thinks
of his mother, how she died in the fall
and he planted her walking cane at the grave
and it flowered, each spring stolidly forming   25
four-star blossoms. The general

pulls on his boots, he stomps to
her room in the palace, the one without
curtains, the one with a parrot
in a brass ring. As he paces he wonders   30
Who can I kill today. And for a moment
the little knot of screams
is still. The parrot, who has traveled

---

1. On October 2, 1937, Rafael Trujillo (1891–1961), dictator of the Dominican Republic, ordered 20,000 blacks killed because they could not pronounce the letter "r" in *perejil*, the Spanish word for parsley [Dove's note].
2. I.e., sugar cane.
3. Katarina (because "we cannot speak an R").

all the way from Australia in an ivory
cage, is, coy as a widow, practising   35
spring. Ever since the morning
his mother collapsed in the kitchen
while baking skull-shaped candies
for the Day of the Dead,[4] the general
has hated sweets. He orders pastries   40
brought up for the bird; they arrive

dusted with sugar on a bed of lace.
The knot in his throat starts to twitch;
he sees his boots the first day in battle
splashed with mud and urine   45
as a soldier falls at his feet amazed—
how stupid he looked!—at the sound
of artillery. *I never thought it would sing*
the soldier said, and died. Now

the general sees the fields of sugar   50
cane, lashed by rain and streaming.
He sees his mother's smile, the teeth
gnawed to arrowheads. He hears
the Haitians sing without R's
as they swing the great machetes: 55
Katalina, they sing, *Katalina*,

mi madle, mi amol en muelte.[5] God knows
his mother was no stupid woman; she
could roll an R like a queen. Even
a parrot can roll an R! In the bare room   60
the bright feathers arch in a parody
of greenery, as the last pale crumbs
disappear under the blackened tongue. Someone

calls out his name in a voice
so like his mother's, a startled tear   65
splashes the tip of his right boot.
My mother, my love in death.
The general remembers the tiny green sprigs
men of his village wore in their capes
to honor the birth of a son. He will   70
order many, this time, to be killed

for a single, beautiful word.

1983

---

4. All Soul's Day, November 2. An Aztec festival
for the spirits of the dead that coincides with the
Catholic calendar. In Latin America and the Caribbean, people move in processions to cemeteries,
bearing candles, flowers, and food, all of which
may be shaped to resemble symbols of death, such
as skulls or coffins.
5. I.e., *mi madre, mi amor en muerte,* "my mother,
my love in death."

FROM THOMAS AND BEULAH[1]

The Event

Ever since they'd left the Tennessee ridge
with nothing to boast of
but good looks and a mandolin,

the two Negroes leaning
on the rail of a riverboat   5
were inseparable: Lem plucked

to Thomas' silver falsetto.
But the night was hot and they were drunk.
They spat where the wheel

churned mud and moonlight,   10
they called to the tarantulas
down among the bananas

to come out and dance.
You're so fine and mighty; let's see
what you can do, said Thomas, pointing   15

to a tree-capped island.
Lem stripped, spoke easy: *Them's chestnuts,*
I believe. Dove

quick as a gasp. Thomas, dry
on deck, saw the green crown shake   20
as the island slipped

under, dissolved
in the thickening stream.
At his feet

a stinking circle of rags,   25
the half-shell mandolin.
Where the wheel turned the water

gently shirred.[2]

1986

1. The story in this sequence of poems begins with Thomas as he makes his way north to Akron, Ohio. He loses his best friend, who, on a drunken dare from Thomas, drowns, leaving his mandolin behind. Thomas carries the mandolin with him and eventually hangs it on his parlor wall. He and Beulah marry when he is twenty-four and she is twenty; they have four daughters. Thomas works at the Goodyear Zeppelin factory (a zeppelin is a cylindrical airship kept aloft by gas). The Depression puts him out of work, so he sweeps offices for a living until Goodyear rehires him at the advent of World War II. Beulah works in a dress shop and later makes hats. Thomas dies at sixty-three from his second heart attack; Beulah dies six years later.
2. Drew together.

Straw Hat

In the city, under the saw-toothed leaves of an oak
overlooking the tracks, he sits out
the last minutes before dawn, lucky
to sleep third shift. Years before
he was anything, he lay on   5
so many kinds of grass, under stars,
the moon's bald eye opposing.

He used to sleep like a glass of water
held up in the hand of a very young girl.
Then he learned he wasn't perfect, that   10
no one was perfect. So he made his way
North under the bland roof of a tent
too small for even his lean body.

The mattress ticking he shares in the work barracks
is brown and smells   15
from the sweat of two other men.
One of them chews snuff:
he's never met either.
To him, work is a narrow grief
and the music afterwards   20
is like a woman
reaching into his chest
to spread it around. When he sings

he closes his eyes.
He never knows when she'll be coming   25
but when she leaves, he always
tips his hat.

                                                     1986

The Zeppelin Factory

The zeppelin factory
needed workers, all right—
but, standing in the cage
of the whale's belly, sparks
flying off the joints   5
and noise thundering,
Thomas wanted to sit
right down and cry.

That spring the third
largest airship was dubbed   10
the biggest joke

in town, though they all
turned out for the launch.
Wind caught,
"The Akron" floated   15
out of control,

three men in tow—
one dropped
to safety, one
hung on but the third,   20
muscles and adrenalin
failing, fell
clawing
six hundred feet.

Thomas at night   25
in the vacant lot:
    *Here I am, intact
    and faint-hearted.*

Thomas hiding
his heart with his hat   30
at the football game, eyeing
the Goodyear blimp overhead:
    *Big boy I know
    you're in there.*

                                                   1986

Dusting

Every day a wilderness—no
shade in sight. Beulah[1]
patient among knicknacks,
the solarium a rage
of light, a grainstorm   5
as her gray cloth brings
dark wood to life.

Under her hand scrolls
and crests gleam
darker still. What   10
was his name, that
silly boy at the fair with
the rifle booth? And his kiss and
the clear bowl with one bright
fish, rippling   15
wound!

---

1. Hebrew for "married one" or "possessed." In the Bible it is used to refer to the Promised Land.

Not Michael—
something finer. Each dust
stroke a deep breath and
the canary in bloom.   20
Wavery memory: home
from a dance, the front door
blown open and the parlor
in snow, she rushed
the bowl to the stove, watched   25
as the locket of ice
dissolved and he
swam free.

That was years before
Father gave her up   30
with her name, years before
her name grew to mean
Promise, then
Desert-in-Peace.
Long before the shadow and   35
sun's accomplice, the tree.

Maurice.

1986

Poem in Which I Refuse Contemplation

A letter from my mother was waiting:
read in standing, one a.m.,
just arrived at my German mother-in-law

six hours from Paris by car.
Our daughter hops on Oma's bed,   5
happy to be back in a language

she knows. *Hello, all! Your postcard
came on the nineth*—familiar misspelled
words, exclamations. I wish my body

wouldn't cramp and leak; I want to—   10
as my daughter says, pretending to be
"Papa"—pull on boots and go for a long walk

alone. *Your cousin Ronnie in D.C.—
remember him?—he was the one
a few months younger than you*—   15

*was strangulated at some chili joint,
your Aunt May is beside herself!*
Mom skips to the garden which is

producing—onions, swiss chard,
lettuce, lettuce, lettuce, turnip greens and more lettuce   20
so far! The roses are flurishing.

Haven't I always hated gardening? And German,
with its patient, grunting building blocks,
and for that matter, English, too,

Americanese's chewy twang? *Raccoons*   25
have taken up residence
we were ten *in the crawl space*

but I can't feel his hand *who knows*
anymore *how we'll get them out?*
I'm still standing. Bags to unpack.   30

That's all for now. Take care.

1989

Heroes[1]

A flower in a weedy field:
make it a poppy. You pick it.
Because it begins to wilt

you run to the nearest house
to ask for a jar of water.   5
The woman on the porch starts

screaming: you've plucked the last poppy
in her miserable garden, the one
that gave her the strength every morning

to rise! It's too late for apologies   10
though you go through the motions, offering
trinkets and a juicy spot in the written history

she wouldn't live to read, anyway.
So you strike her, she hits
her head on a white boulder,   15

and there's nothing to be done
but break the stone into gravel
to prop up the flower in the stolen jar

1. *Mother Love* (1995), the collection that contains this poem and the one that follows ("Missing"), is structured around the Greek myth of Demeter and Persephone. Persephone, the daughter of Zeus and Demeter (goddess of the earth), was abducted by Hades, the king of the underworld, who took her to live with him below the earth. Her mother, Demeter, mourned the loss of Persephone, and through her grief the earth became barren. Zeus persuaded Hades to permit Persephone to spend four months in the underworld and the rest of the year in the upperworld with her mother. Persephone returns to the surface of the earth on the first day of spring each year.

you have to take along,
because you're a fugitive now   20
and you can't leave clues.

Already the story's starting to unravel,
the villagers stirring as your heart
pounds into your throat. O why

did you pick that idiot flower?   25
Because it was the last one
and you knew

it was going to die.

1995

Missing

I am the daughter who went out with the girls,
never checked back in and nothing marked my "last
known whereabouts," not a single glistening petal.

Horror is partial; it keeps you going. A lost
child is a fact hardening around its absence,   5
a knot in the breast purring *Touch, and I will*

come true. I was "returned," I watched her
watch as I babbled *It could have been worse.* . . .
Who can tell
what penetrates? Pity is the brutal   10
discipline. Now I understand she can never
die, just as nothing can bring me back—

I am the one who comes and goes;
I am the footfall that hovers.

1995

Rosa[1]

How she sat there,
the time right inside a place
so wrong it was ready.

1. Rosa Parks (b. 1913). From a series of poems titled *On the Bus with Rosa Parks.* On December 1, 1955, in Montgomery, Alabama, Parks, an African American seamstress and secretary of the local National Association for the Advancement of Colored People (NAACP), was arrested and taken to jail for refusing to yield her seat on a bus to a white passenger. Her arrest prompted a boycott of the city bus system and inspired the civil rights movement in the late 1950s and 1960s.

That trim name with
its dream of a bench   5
to rest on. Her sensible coat.

Doing nothing was the doing:
the clean flame of her gaze
carved by a camera flash.

How she stood up   10
when they bent down to retrieve
her purse. That courtesy.

2000

ALBERTO RÍOS
b. 1952

The poet Rita Dove once recalled in an interview W. E. B. Du Bois's remark on the "second sight that comes from having to live in two different cultures." As a Latino whose heritage includes Spanish and English, Alberto Ríos often writes poems possessed of literal second sight. His work gives us magical and poetic ways of understanding the world, like his grandmother's account of the nature of scorpions in "Advice to a First Cousin," where a knowledge inaccessible in books is transmitted. "The way the world works is like this," the poem begins. In Ríos's best poems we feel both that anything can happen and that everything has happened before; we hear a particular voice whose rhythms recall stories passed from generation to generation.

Ríos has said of his background, "My father, born in southern Mexico, and my mother, born in England, gave me a language-rich, story-fat upbringing." He was born in Nogales, Arizona (on the border of Mexico), and earned an M.F.A. at the University of Arizona. He has worked on the Arizona Commission on the Arts and presently is on the faculty of Arizona State University in Tempe. His first book, *Whispering to Fool the Wind* (1982), won the Walt Whitman Award. He has since published *Five Indiscretions* (1985), *The Lime Orchard Women* (1989), and *Teodora Luna's Two Kisses* (1990). Not surprising for a poet with his gifts, he has also published two volumes of fiction, *The Iguana Killer: Twelve Stories of the Heart* (1984) and *The curtain of Trees* (1999). Ríos is a talented teller of stories, whose poems often suggest oral traditions, including Spanish ballads. For him, stories are forms of remembering and means of understanding; they honor the claims of dream and fact, past and present. Whether he is writing with humorous self-awareness about a childhood visit to a fortune-teller ("Madre Sofía") or rendering the unbearable reality behind the newspaper accounts of those among the "disappeared" (in Taking Away the Name of a Nephew), the details of his poems accumulate to reveal a startling sense of the world. At times, however, the story the poem tells must overcome too predictable uses of the line. If Ríos's magical sense of the world sometimes yields too easily to the surreal, the pleasures of his poems often lie in their fluid movement between layers of reality, their deft integration of the factual and fantastic. Given Ríos's sense of the possibilities in language, the epigraph for his first book, taken from the Chilean poet Pablo Neruda, is especially fitting: "You see there are in our countries rivers which have no names, trees which nobody knows, and birds which nobody has described.

... Our duty, then, as we understand it, is to express what is unheard of." Flavored with the music of Spanish and English, Ríos's poems create a new landscape: a contemporary America beneath which lives an older way of life and the country of the imagination we discover in genuine poems.

Madre Sofía[1]

My mother took me because she couldn't
wait the second ten years to know.
This was the lady rumored to have been
responsible for the box-wrapped baby
among the presents at that wedding,   5
but we went in, anyway, through the curtains.
Loose jar-top, half turned
and not caught properly in the threads
her head sat mimicking its original intention
like the smile of a child hitting himself.   10
Central in that head grew unfamiliar poppies
from a face mahogany, eyes half yellow
half gray at the same time, goat and fog,
slit eyes of the devil, his tweed suit, red
lips, and she smelled of smoke, cigarettes,   15
but a diamond smoke, somehow; I inhaled
sparkles, I could feel them, throat, stomach.
She did not speak, and as a child
I could only answer, so that together
we were silent, cold and wet, dry and hard: 20
from behind my mother pushed me forward.
The lady put her hand on the face
of a thin animal wrap, tossing that head
behind her to be pressured incredibly
as she sat back in the huge chair and leaned.   25
And then I saw the breasts as large as her
head, folded together, coming out of her dress
as if it didn't fit, not like my mother's.
I could see them, how she kept them
penned up, leisurely, in maroon feed bags,   30
horse nuzzles of her wide body,
but exquisitely penned up
circled by pearl reins and red scarves.
She lifted her arm, but only with the tips
of her fingers motioned me to sit opposite.   35
She looked at me but spoke to my mother
words dark, smoky like the small room,
words coming like red ants stepping occasionally
from a hole on a summer day in the valley,
red ants from her mouth, her nose, her ears,   40
tears from the corners of her cinched eyes.

---

1. Mother Sofía (Spanish). *Sofía* derives from the Greek word meaning "wisdom."

And suddenly she put her hand full on my head
pinching tight again with those finger tips
like a television healer, young Oral Roberts
half standing, quickly, half leaning   45
those breasts swinging toward me
so that I reach with both my hands to my lap
protecting instinctively whatever it is
that needs protection when a baseball is thrown
and you're not looking but someone yells,   50
the hand, then those breasts coming toward me
like the quarter-arms of the amputee Joaquín
who came back from the war to sit
in the park, reaching always for children
until one day he had to be held back.   55
I sat there, no breath, and could see only
hair around her left nipple, like a man.
Her clothes were old.
Accented, in a language whose spine had been
snapped, she whispered the words of a city   60
witch, and made me happy, alive like a man:
The future will make you tall.

                                                                        1982

Wet Camp

We have been here before, but we are lost.
The earth is black and the trees are bent
and broken and piled as if the game
of pick-up-sticks were ready and the children
hiding, waiting their useless turns.   5
The west bank of the river is burned
and the Santa Cruz[1] has poured onto it.
The grit brown ponds
sit like dirty lilies in the black.
The afternoon is gone grazing   10
over the thin mountains.
The night is colder here without leaves.
Nothing holds up the sky.

                                                                        1982

Taking Away the Name of a Nephew

One of the disappeared looks like this:
One shirt, reasonable shoes, no laces, no face
Recognizable even to the mother of this thing.

---

1. River in southern Arizona.

Lump. Dropped egg, bag of old potatoes
Too old and without moisture, a hundred eyes   5
Sprouted out and gone wild into forest
Food for the maggot flies and small monsters.
Bag. Pulled by the tiestring
The laces around his ankles have become.
A crisp bag of seventeen birthdays   10
Six parties with piñatas and the particular
Memory of a thick hugging
His Tía[1] Susí gave him with the strong arms
Her breasts were, how they had held him
Around his just-tall-enough throat and had reached   15
To touch each other behind his neck.

His memory of Susí was better than how the soldier held him
She hoped this out of all things.
That she had made him warm.
In that body the three soldiers were fooled, tricked   20
A good hundred strings of wool put over their eyes:
They did not take away the boy.
They took away his set of hands and his spine
Which in weeks would look like railroad tracks
Along the side of any young mountain.   25
One of the disappeared looks like this
The newspaper said. She had seen
The photograph which looked like all
Newspaper photographs,
Had thought it does not say *looked* like this,   30
But *looks* like this, still; had thought
What is being said here is that he did not die.
It was not death that took him.

She thinks about things like this, this way:
Here is the new mathematics made simple   35
Here is the algebra I once did not understand.
She sets for herself the tasks of a student,
Making clear the equations
Breathing the air that Einstein breathed.
She looks in her purse and pulls out three coins.   40
This much for one dozen corn tortillas. Easy.
A paper cut, small slice, magnified three times:
PC × 3 =
This is what a very small Newberry's letter opener—
A gift from her cousin in the United States—   45
Held as a knife at the stomach of a man
Then pushed in, this is what it might feel like.
Stomachache from a winter's flu, the rocking kind
During which one must hold and bite a towel
Or those first days womanhood finds its way   50
Shaking her with pains, magnified three times, also:

1. Aunt (Spanish).

3076 / Alberto Ríos

This must be what the beginnings of a cancer
Feel like, how one's hands can do nothing
More than rub, or clean, or stroke the forehead,
Cannot in a last, most desperate attempt   55
Go out into the alley behind the bar like the men
and try to beat it up.

She thinks about this like this:
Then she stops, because she can
Understand a paper cut and stomach flu   60
As she understands salt and bread,
Can imagine them even together, and eating them.

She stops because understanding the blossom
Pain must be, or more,
That pain is a blossom snapped off   65
That moment and the pungent smell
A long *o* sound makes in the mouth
On a face not big enough—
All this disallows the thinking of a thing for too long
Because one understands.   70
All this stops the reading of newspapers.
But some nights she cannot do otherwise, as tonight:
She begins to add up, again, to put numbers
In the equation of how many cuts and glowing scrapes
One more thing or another adds up to,   75
What it must feel like,
How many paper cuts might roughly equal
The breaking neck of a favorite nephew.

                                                                   1985

Advice to a First Cousin

The way the world works is like this:
for the bite of scorpions, she says,
my grandmother to my first cousin,
because I might die and someone must know,
go to the animal jar   5
the one with the soup of green herbs
mixed with the scorpions I have been putting in
still alive. Take one out
put it on the bite. It has had time to think
there with the others—put the lid back tight—   10
and knows that a biting is not the way to win
a finger or a young girl's foot.
It will take back into itself the hurting
the redness and the itching and its marks.

But the world works like this, too: 15
look out for the next scorpion you see,
she says, and makes a big face to scare me
thereby instructing my cousin, look out!
for one of the scorpion's many
illegitimate and unhappy sons.   20
It will be smarter, more of the devil.
It will have lived longer than these dead ones.
It will know from them something more
about the world, in the way mothers know
when something happens to a child, or how   25
I knew from your sadness you had been bitten.
It will learn something stronger than biting.
Look out most for that scorpion, she says,
making a big face to scare me again and it works
I go—crying—she lets me go—they laugh,   30
the way you must look out for men
who have not yet bruised you.

                                                     1985

Seniors

William cut a hole in his Levi's pocket
so he could flop himself out in class
behind the girls so the other guys
could see and shit what guts we all said.
All Konga wanted to do over and over   5
was the rubber band trick, but he showed
everyone how, so nobody wanted to see
anymore and one day he cried, just cried
until his parents took him away forever.
Maya had a Hotpoint refrigerator standing   10
in his living room, just for his family to show
anybody who came that they could afford it.

Me, I got a French kiss, finally, in the catholic
darkness, my tongue's farthest half vacationing
loudly in another mouth like a man in Bermudas,   15
and my body jumped against a flagstone wall,
I could feel it through her thin, almost
nonexistent body: I had, at that moment, that moment,
a hot girl on a summer night, the best of all
the things we tried to do. Well, she   20
let me kiss her, anyway, all over.

Or it was just a flagstone wall
with a flaw in the stone, an understanding cavity
for burning young men with smooth dreams—

the true circumstance is gone, the true 25
circumstances about us all then
are gone. But when I kissed her, all water,
she would close her eyes, and they into somewhere
would disappear. Whether she was there
or not, I remember her, clearly, and she moves 30
around the room, sometimes, until I sleep.

I have lain on the desert in watch
low in the back of a pick-up truck
for nothing in particular, for stars, for
the things behind stars, and nothing comes 35
more than the moment: always now, here in a truck,
the moment again to dream of making love and sweat,
this time to a woman, or even to all of them
in some allowable way, to those boys, then,
who couldn't cry, to the girls before they were 40
women, to friends, me on my back, the sky over me
pressing its simple weight into her body
on me, into the bodies of them all, on me.

1985

LORNA DEE CERVANTES
b. 1954

In "Visions of Mexico While at a Writing Symposium in Port Townsend, Washington,"
Lorna Dee Cervantes imagines herself in transit, like the seabirds in her poem who
"elbow their wings / in migratory ways" between north and south, Washington and
Mexico. The image of migration appears frequently in her book *Emplumada* (1981),
where it suggests the larger social patterns that characterize Latino history. But Cervantes's identification with the "migratory ways" of birds is also personal. "At heart
I'm a hoverer," she writes in "Como lo Siento," and her poems often hover in the
space between worlds, in the gap between her sense of social need and her own
desires. In *Emplumada* (the title is derived from the Spanish words that mean "feathered in plumage" and "the stroke of a pen"), the poet confronts and sometimes bridges
divisions in herself and in her landscape, her native California zigzagged by the freeway. Her second book, *From the Cables of Genocide* (1991), extends that landscape
to the nation at large and has an angry energy animated by "love and hunger," in a
phrase from the book's subtitle.

In her self-defined role as "scribe" in her "woman family" ("Beneath the Shadow
of the Freeway"), Cervantes mediates a written tradition largely male and North
American ("books, those staunch, upright men") and the Mexican oral traditions
embodied by her grandmother. Transcribing the oral into the written, Cervantes nego-
tiates forms of understanding: the ring around the moon in her poem "The Body as
Braille" is both what her grandmother calls " 'A witch's moon,' / dijo mi abuela" and
what the schools define as "a reflection of ice crystals." Experiencing these separate
forms of perception, she fuses them in her own powerful metaphor: "It's a storm
brewing in the cauldron / of the sky."

Cervantes is a native Californian and has lived there most of her life. She was born in San Francisco, graduated from San José State University, and has studied at the University of California at Santa Cruz. For several years she edited and published *Mango,* a small-press journal in which the work of Latino poets (many of whom identified themselves socially and politically with the Chicano movement) appeared, and she serves as co-editor of *Red Dirt,* a cross-cultural poetry journal. A number of the poems in *Emplumada* were written while she was a fellow in poetry at the Fine Arts Work Center in Provincetown, Massachusetts. Like several other important Latino poets (Alberto Ríos, Ricardo Sanchez, Bernice Zamora) she intermixes Spanish phrases and lines in her poems to represent her double heritage and to underscore the difficulty of rendering the experiences of one cultural tradition in the language of another. Words are her craft and her weapon as well, as the epigraph from Antonio Porchia, which opens the second section of her first book, suggests: "This world understands nothing but words / and you have come into it with almost none." Although the ambiguous tone in some of her poems suggests an uncertain degree of distance from her experience, the intensity of feeling in her work is undeniable.

Uncle's First Rabbit

He was a good boy
making his way through
the Santa Barbara[1] pines,
sighting the blast of fluff
as he leveled the rifle,   5
and the terrible singing began.
He was ten years old,
hunting my grandpa's supper.
He had dreamed of running,
shouldering the rifle to town,   10
selling it, and taking the next
train out.
   Fifty years
have passed and he still hears
that rabbit "just like a baby."   15
He remembers how the rabbit
stopped keening under the butt
of his rifle, how he brought
it home with tears streaming
down his blood soaked jacket.   20
"That bastard. That bastard."
He cried all night and the week
after, remembering that voice
like his dead baby sister's,
remembering his father's drunken   25
kicking that had pushed her
into birth. She had a voice
like that, growing faint
at its end; his mother rocking,
softly, keening. He dreamed   30

1. In southern California.

of running, running
the bastard out of his life.
He would forget them, run down
the hill, leave his mother's
silent waters, and the sounds   35
of beating night after night.
        When war came,
he took the man's vow. He was
finally leaving and taking
the bastard's last bloodline   40
with him. At war's end, he could
still hear her, her soft
body stiffening under water
like a shark's. The color
of the water, darkening, soaking,   45
as he clung to what was left
of a ship's gun. Ten long hours
off the coast of Okinawa,[2] he sang
so he wouldn't hear them.
He pounded their voices out   50
of his head, and awakened
to find himself slugging the bloodied
face of his wife.
        Fifty years
have passed and he has not run   55
the way he dreamed. The Paradise
pines shadow the bleak hills
to his home. His hunting hounds,
dead now. His father, long dead.
His wife, dying, hacking in the bed   60
she has not let him enter for the last
thirty years. He stands looking,
he mouths the words, "Die you bitch.
I'll live to watch you die." He turns,
entering their moss-soft livingroom.   65
He watches out the picture window
and remembers running: how he'll
take the new pickup to town, sell it,
and get the next train out.

                                   1981

For Virginia Chavez

It was never in the planning,
in the life we thought
we'd live together, two fast
women living cheek to cheek,

---

2. Island in the Pacific, scene of severe World War II fighting between the United States and Japan in the spring of 1945.

still tasting the dog's   5
breath of boys in our testy
new awakening.
We were never the way
they had it planned.
Their wordless tongues we stole   10
and tasted the power
that comes of that.
We were never what they wanted
but we were bold. We could take
something of life and not   15
give it back. We could utter
the rules, mark the lines
and cross them ourselves—we two
women using our fists, we thought,
our wits, our tunnels. They were such   20
dumb hunks of warm fish
swimming inside us,
but this was love,
we knew, love, and that was all
we were ever offered.   25

You were always alone
so *another lonely life*
wouldn't matter.
In the still house
your mother left you,   30
when the men were gone
and the television droned
into test patterns, with our cups
of your mother's whiskey
balanced between the brown thighs   35
creeping out of our shorts, I read
you the poems of Lord Byron, Donne,
the Brownings:[1] all about love,
explaining the words
before realizing that you knew   40
all that the kicks in your belly
had to teach you. You were proud
of the woman blooming out of your
fourteen lonely years, but you cried
when you read that poem I wrote you,   45
something about our "waning moons"
and the child in me
I let die that summer.

In the years that separate,
in the tongues that divide   50
and conquer, in the love

---

1. George Gordon, Lord Byron; John Donne; and Elizabeth Barrett Browning and Robert Browning—poets famed for writing about love.

that was a language
in itself, you never spoke,
never regret. Even
that last morning   55
I saw you with blood
in your eyes, blood
on your mouth, the blood
pushing out of you
in purple blossoms.   60

He did this.
When I woke, the kids
were gone. They told me
I'd never get them back.

With our arms holding   65
each other's waists, we walked
the waking streets
back to your empty flat,
ignoring the horns and catcalls
behind us, ignoring what   70
the years had brought between us:
my diploma and the bare bulb
that always lit your bookless room.

1981

Visions of Mexico While at a Writing Symposium in Port Townsend, Washington

México

When I'm that far south, the old words
molt off my skin, the feathers
of all my nervousness.
My own words somersault naturally as my name,
joyous among all those meadows: Michoacán,   5
Vera Cruz, Tenochtitlán, Oaxaca[1] . . .
Pueblos green on the low hills
where men slap handballs below acres of maíz.[2]
I watch and understand.
My frail body has never packed mud   10
or gathered in the full weight of the harvest.
Alone with the women in the adobe,[3] I watch men,
their taut faces holding in all their youth.
This far south we are governed by the law
of the next whole meal. We work   15
and watch seabirds elbow their wings

---

1. Mexican states, except for Tenochtitlán, which
is the ancient name for Mexico City.
2. "Corn" [Cervantes's note]. "Pueblos": communal dwellings.
3. I.e., in a house made of sun-dried earth and
straw.

in migratory ways, those mispronouncing gulls
coming south
to refuge or gameland.

I don't want to pretend I know more   20
and can speak all the names. I can't.
My sense of this land can only ripple through my veins
like the chant of an epic corrido.[4]
I come from a long line of eloquent illiterates
whose history reveals what words don't say.   25
Our anger is our way of speaking,
the gesture is an utterance more pure than word.
We are not animals
but our senses are keen and our reflexes,
accurate punctuation.   30
All the knifings in a single night, low-voiced
scufflings, sirens, gunnings . . .
We hear them
and the poet within us bays.

Washington

I don't belong this far north.   35
The uncomfortable birds gawk at me.
They hem and haw from their borders in the sky.
I heard them say: México is a stumbling comedy.
A loose-legged Cantinflas woman
acting with Pancho Villa[5] drunkenness.   40
Last night at the tavern
this was all confirmed
in a painting of a woman: her glowing
silk skin, a halo
extending from her golden coiffure   45
while around her, dark-skinned men with Jap slant eyes
were drooling in a caricature of machismo.[6]
Below it, at the bar, two Chicanas
hung at their beers. They had painted black
birds that dipped beneath their eyelids.   50
They were still as foam while the men
fiddled with their asses, absently;
the bubbles of their teased hair snapped
open in the forced wind of the beating fan.
There are songs in my head I could sing you   55
songs that could drone away
all the Mariachi bands[7] you thought you ever heard
songs that could tell you what I know
or have learned from my people
but for that   I need words   60

4. An epic Mexican ballad [Cervantes's note].
5. A Mexican bandit and revolutionary leader
(1878–1923). "Cantinflas—a Mexican comedian

similar to Charlie Chaplin" [Cervantes's note].
6. Masculinity; macho [Cervantes's note].
7. Mexican street bands.

simple black nymphs between white sheets of paper
obedient words   obligatory words   words I steal
in the dark when no one can hear me

as pain sends seabirds south from the cold
I come north   65
to gather my feathers
for quills

1981

The Body as Braille

He tells me "Your back
is so beautiful." He traces
my spine with his hand.

I'm burning like the white ring
around the moon. "A witch's moon,"   5
dijo mi abuela.[1] The schools call it

"a reflection of ice crystals."
It's a storm brewing in the cauldron
of the sky. I'm in love

but won't tell him   10
if it's omens
or ice.

1981

1. My grandmother told me [Cervantes's note].

CATHY SONG
b. 1955

In many of Cathy Song's poems, a particular moment or event becomes a window through which we enter a field of vision. "What frames the view," she has written, "is the mind in the diamond pinpoint light of concentration tunneling into memory, released by the imagination." As the title of her second book, *Frameless Windows, Squares of Light*, suggests, Song's poems capture the way a warm afternoon, a childhood Easter, a picnic in the park, are openings for memory and reflection. The visual quality of her poems can suggest a photograph or painting, and she herself feels a connection between her work and that of the Japanese printmaker Kitagawa Utamaro and the American painter Georgia O'Keeffe. Her first book, *Picture Bride* (1983), contains a number of poems inspired by the work of these artists. Writing, in "Beauty and Sadness," of the way Utamaro's prints rendered "Teahouse waitresses, actresses,

/ geishas, courtesans and maids" in "their fleeting loveliness," Song suggests that the artist and poet capture the moment, knowing that it is always dissolving.

Song's first book was chosen by Richard Hugo for the Yale Younger Poets series. In the title poem, "Picture Bride," she comes as close as imagination allows to the experience of her grandmother, who, the poem implies, was chosen as a bride from a photograph and summoned from Korea to Hawaii. But Song is also aware of the limits of imaginative identification and the difficulty of knowing the full truth of the past. She respects the mystery of another's identity. The grandmother in "Picture Bride," the woman in "Lost Sister," the mother in "Humble Jar," and the geishas painted by Utamaro possess a privacy that the poet discloses but cannot fully enter. Song's tactful sense of both the power and the limits of imagination is one of her distinctive marks as a poet.

She was born in Honolulu, Hawaii, and grew up in Wahiawa, a small town on the island of Oahu. The setting of sugar cane fields, of island life where "the sound of the ocean / could be heard through the ironwoods" ("Waialaua"), and of the rain that comes "even when the sun was shining" ("A Pale Arrangement of Hands"), is central to her work. That landscape belongs to her present but also evokes her childhood and the memory of another, more distant landscape—the Asia of her ancestors. Many of Song's poems render the mysteries of what she has called "familial and personal ties; lives overlapping," and her sense of these ties extends backward to ancestors as well as forward to her own children. She began her college education at the University of Hawaii and then attended Wellesley College. After her graduation from Wellesley, she received an M.A. in creative writing from Boston University and has since taught creative writing at a number of colleges and universities. Her third collection of poems, *School Figures*, appeared in 1994 and a subsequent volume, *The Land of Bliss*, in 2001.

Song's ability to write about her own or another's experience as an acute observer may have to do with her multicultural background, which often places her on the boundary of what she sees. Her capacity to let the power of observation give rise to feeling recalls at times the work of Elizabeth Bishop and also suggests Song's resemblance to the Utamaro of her poem "Beauty and Sadness," whose "invisible presence / one feels in these prints." At other times Song writes about herself more directly. She has, for example, deftly rendered the erotic nature of her own experience: "But there is this slow arousal. / The small buttons / of my cotton blouse / are pulling away from my body" ("The White Porch"). The careful composition of her poems, with their vivid detail, blend the accidental and spontaneous quality of life with the design of art, like the Japanese floral arrangement she describes in her poem "Ikebana." Although her work can sometimes seem too composed, too removed from the sharp impact of experience, her strongest poems balance a sense of tradition with a feel for contemporary life and catch in the patterns of art the transient instant: "the flicker of a dragonfly's delicate wing."

The White Porch

I wrap the blue towel
after washing,
around the damp
weight of hair, bulky
as a sleeping cat,   5
and sit out on the porch.
Still dripping water,
it'll be dry by supper,

by the time the dust
settles off your shoes,   10
though it's only five
past noon. Think
of the luxury: how to use
the afternoon like the stretch
of lawn spread before me.   15
There's the laundry,
sun-warm clothes at twilight,
and the mountain of beans
in my lap. Each one,
I'll break and snap   20
thoughtfully in half.

But there is this slow arousal.
The small buttons
of my cotton blouse
are pulling away from my body.   25
I feel the strain of threads,
the swollen magnolias
heavy as a flock of birds
in the tree. Already,
the orange sponge cake   30
is rising in the oven.
I know you'll say it makes
your mouth dry
and I'll watch you
drench your slice of it   35
in canned peaches
and lick the plate clean.

So much hair, my mother
used to say, grabbing
the thick braided rope   40
in her hands while we washed
the breakfast dishes, discussing
dresses and pastries.
My mind often elsewhere
as we did the morning chores together.   45
Sometimes, a few strands
would catch in her gold ring.
I worked hard then,
anticipating the hour
when I would let the rope down   50
at night, strips of sheets,
knotted and tied,
while she slept in tight blankets.
My hair, freshly washed
like a measure of wealth,   55
like a bridal veil.
Crouching in the grass,

you would wait for the signal,
for the movement of curtains
before releasing yourself   60
from the shadow of moths.
Cloth, hair and hands,
smuggling you in.

                                                      1983

Beauty and Sadness

for Kitagawa Utamaro[1]

He drew hundreds of women
in studies unfolding
like flowers from a fan.
Teahouse waitresses, actresses,
geishas,[2] courtesans and maids.   5
They arranged themselves
before this quick, nimble man
whose invisible presence
one feels in these prints
is as delicate   10
as the skinlike paper
he used to transfer
and retain their fleeting loveliness.

Crouching like cats,
they purred amid the layers of kimono[3]   15
swirling around them
as though they were bathing
in a mountain pool with irises
growing in the silken sunlit water.
Or poised like porcelain vases,   20
slender, erect and tall; their heavy
brocaded hair was piled high
with sandalwood combs and blossom sprigs
poking out like antennae.
They resembled beautiful iridescent insects,   25
creatures from a floating world.[4]

Utamaro absorbed these women of Edo[5]
in their moments of melancholy
as well as of beauty.
He captured the wisp of shadows,   30

1. Japanese artist (1753–1806) who specialized in studies of sensual and beautiful women.
2. Women trained to provide entertaining, light-hearted company for men.
3. Traditional Japanese robe with long sleeves.
4. The pictures "were called 'pictures of the floating world' because of their preoccupation with the pleasures of the moment" [Song's note].
5. Present-day Tokyo [Song's note].

the half-draped body
emerging from a bath; whatever
skin was exposed
was powdered white as snow.
A private space disclosed.   35
Portraying another girl
catching a glimpse of her own vulnerable
face in the mirror, he transposed
the trembling plum lips
like a drop of blood   40
soaking up the white expanse of paper.

At times, indifferent to his inconsolable
eye, the women drifted
through the soft gray feathered light,
maintaining stillness, the moments in between.   45
Like the dusty ash-winged moths
that cling to the screens in summer
and that the Japanese venerate
as ancestors reincarnated;
Utamaro graced these women with immortality   50
in the thousand sheaves of prints
fluttering into the reverent hands of keepers:
the dwarfed and bespectacled painter
holding up to a square of sunlight
what he had carried home beneath his coat   55
one afternoon in winter.

                                                                  1983

Lost Sister

1

In China,
even the peasants
named their first daughters
Jade—
the stone that in the far fields   5
could moisten the dry season,
could make men move mountains
for the healing green of the inner hills
glistening like slices of winter melon.

And the daughters were grateful: 10
they never left home.
To move freely was a luxury
stolen from them at birth.
Instead, they gathered patience,
learning to walk in shoes   15
the size of teacups,
without breaking—

the arc of their movements
as dormant as the rooted willow,
as redundant as the farmyard hens.   20
But they traveled far
in surviving,
learning to stretch the family rice,
to quiet the demons,
the noisy stomachs.   25

                        2

There is a sister
across the ocean,
who relinquished her name,
diluting jade green
with the blue of the Pacific.   30
Rising with a tide of locusts,
she swarmed with others
to inundate another shore.
In America,
there are many roads   35
and women can stride along with men.

But in another wilderness,
the possibilities,
the loneliness,
can strangulate like jungle vines.   40
The meager provisions and sentiments
of once belonging—
fermented roots, Mah-Jongg[1] tiles and firecrackers—
set but a flimsy household
in a forest of nightless cities.   45
A giant snake rattles above,
spewing black clouds into your kitchen.
Dough-faced landlords
slip in and out of your keyholes,
making claims you don't understand,   50
tapping into your communication systems
of laundry lines and restaurant chains.

You find you need China:
your one fragile identification,
a jade link   55
handcuffed to your wrist.
You remember your mother
who walked for centuries,
footless—
and like her,   60
you have left no footprints,
but only because

1. A game of Chinese origins.

there is an ocean in between,
the unremitting space of your rebellion.

1983

Chinatown

1

Chinatowns: they all look alike.
In the heart
of cities. Dead
center: fish eyes
blinking between 5
red-light & ghetto,
sleazy movie houses
& oily joints.

A network of yellow tumors,
throbbing insect wings. 10
Lanterns of moths
and other shady characters:
cricket bulbs & roach eggs
hatching in the night.

2

Grandmother is gambling. 15
Her teeth rattle: Mah-Jongg[1] tiles.

She is the blood bank
we seek
for wobbly supports.

Building 20
on top of one another,
bamboo chopstick tenements
pile up like noodles.
Fungus mushrooming,
hoarding sunlight 25
from the neighbors
as if it were rice.

Lemon peels
off the walls so thin,
abalone skins. 30
Everyone can hear.

---

1. A game of Chinese origins.

3

First question,
Can it be eaten?
If not, what good
is it, is anything?   35

Father's hair is gleaming
like black shoe polish.
Chopping pork & prawns,
his fingers emerge
unsliced, all ten intact.   40

Compact muscles taut,
the burning cigarette
dangling from his mouth,
is the fuse to the dynamite.

Combustible material.   45
Inflammable.
Igniting each other
when the old men talk
stories on street corners.
Words spark & flare out,   50
firecrackers popping on sidewalks.
Spitting insults, hurled garbage
exploding into rancid odors:
urine & water chestnuts.

4

Mother is swollen again.   55
Puffy & waterlogged.
Sour plums
fermenting in dank cellars.

She sends the children
up for air.   60
Sip it like tea.

5

The children are the dumplings
set afloat.
Little boats
bobbing up to surface   65
in the steamy cauldron.

The rice & the sunlight
have been saved for this:

Wrap the children
in wonton skins,[2]   70
bright quilted bundles
sewn warm with five spices.

Jade, ginger root,
sesame seed, mother-of-pearl
& ivory.   75

Light incense to a strong wind.
Blow the children away,
one at a time.

                                                          1983

Heaven

He thinks when we die we'll go to China.
Think of it—a Chinese heaven
where, except for his blond hair,
the part that belongs to his father,
everyone will look like him.   5
China, that blue flower on the map,
bluer than the sea
his hand must span like a bridge
to reach it.
An octave away.   10

I've never seen it.
It's as if I can't sing that far.
But look—
on the map, this black dot.
Here is where we live,   15
on the pancake plains
just east of the Rockies,
on the other side of the clouds.
A mile above the sea,
the air is so thin, you can starve on it.   20
No bamboo trees
but the alpine equivalent,
reedy aspen with light, fluttering leaves.
Did a boy in Guangzhou[1] dream of this
as his last stop?   25

I've heard the trains at night
whistling past our yards,
what we've come to own,

---

2. I.e., rice-noodle dough.   1. Or Canton, seaport city in southeastern China.

the broken fences, the whiny dog, the rattletrap cars.
It's still the wild west,   30
mean and grubby,
the shootouts and fistfights in the back alley.
With my son the dreamer
and my daughter, who is too young to walk,
I've sat in this spot   35
and wondered why here?
Why in this short life,
this town, this creek they call a river?

He had never planned to stay,
the boy who helped to build   40
the railroads for a dollar a day.[2]
He had always meant to go back.
When did he finally know
that each mile of track led him further away,
that he would die in his sleep,   45
dispossessed,
having seen Gold Mountain,
the icy wind tunneling through it,
these landlocked, makeshift ghost towns?

It must be in the blood,   50
this notion of returning.
It skipped two generations, lay fallow,
the garden an unmarked grave.
On a spring sweater day
it's as if we remember him.   55
I call to the children.
We can see the mountains
shimmering blue above the air.
If you look really hard
says my son the dreamer,   60
leaning out from the laundry's rigging,
the work shirts fluttering like sails,
you can see all the way to heaven.

1988

---

2. The Chinese provided much of the cheap labor that laid the tracks of the transcontinental railroads in the 19th century.

LI-YOUNG LEE
b. 1957

In his poem "Persimmons" Li-Young Lee remembers his father saying, "Some things never leave a person." Many of the poems in Lee's two books, *Rose* (1986) and *The City in Which I Love You* (1990), testify to a sense of the past, especially his father's past, which never leaves Lee. The figure of the father in Lee's poems is both personal and mythic; it is he who instructs the poet-son in "the art of memory." Lee's father, born in China, served as a personal physician to Mao Tse-tung. He later was jailed for nineteen months, a political prisoner of the Indonesian dictator Sukarno. Lee was born in Jakarta, Indonesia. In 1959 the family fled Indonesia and traveled in the Far East (Hong Kong, Macao, and Japan), finally arriving in America, where Lee's father became a Presbyterian minister in a small town in western Pennsylvania. Many of Lee's poems seek to remember and understand his father's life and to come to terms with Lee's own differences from that powerful figure.

Lee's work reminds us of the ancient connections between the arts of memory and poetry. In his work, memory is often sweet; it draws the poet to the past even when, as in "Eating Alone," that sweetness is as dizzying as the juice of a rotten pear in which a hornet spins. But memory can also be a burden, and its pull is countered in Lee's work by a sensuous apprehension of the present. As in his poem "This Room and Everything in It," the erotic immediacy of the moment can disrupt any effort to fix that moment in the orders of memory. Everywhere in Lee's work is the evidence of all the senses: hearing, taste, smell, and touch as much as sight. If the poet's bodily presence in the world recalls Walt Whitman, Lee's fluid motion between the physical world and the domain of memory, dream, or vision also carries out Whitman's visionary strain and links Lee to the work of Theodore Roethke, James Wright, and Denise Levertov, among others. The intensity of Lee's poems, however, is often leavened by a subtle and winning humor and playfulness; such qualities are especially valuable in a poet at times too easily seduced by beauty.

Lee studied at the University of Pittsburgh (where one of his teachers was the poet Gerald Stern), the University of Arizona, and the State University of New York College at Brockport. He has since taught at various universities. In 1995 he published a prose memoir, *The Winged Seed: A Remembrance*. Both Lee's deep sense of connection between an individual life and a powerful past and his ability to move between plain speech and a lushness evocative of biblical language have enriched contemporary American poetry.

The Gift

To pull the metal splinter from my palm
my father recited a story in a low voice.
I watched his lovely face and not the blade.
Before the story ended, he'd removed
the iron sliver I thought I'd die from.   5

I can't remember the tale,
but hear his voice still, a well
of dark water, a prayer.
And I recall his hands,
two measures of tenderness   10

he laid against my face,
the flames of discipline
he raised above my head.

Had you entered that afternoon
you would have thought you saw a man 15
planting something in a boy's palm,
a silver tear, a tiny flame.
Had you followed that boy
you would have arrived here,
where I bend over my wife's right hand. 20

Look how I shave her thumbnail down
so carefully she feels no pain.
Watch as I lift the splinter out.
I was seven when my father
took my hand like this, 25
and I did not hold that shard
between my fingers and think,
Metal that will bury me,
christen it Little Assassin,
Ore Going Deep for My Heart. 30
And I did not lift up my wound and cry,
Death visited here!
I did what a child does
when he's given something to keep.
I kissed my father. 35

1986

Persimmons

In sixth grade Mrs. Walker
slapped the back of my head
and made me stand in the corner
for not knowing the difference
between *persimmon* and *precision*. 5
How to choose

persimmons. This is precision.
Ripe ones are soft and brown-spotted.
Sniff the bottoms. The sweet one
will be fragrant. How to eat: 10
put the knife away, lay down newspaper.
Peel the skin tenderly, not to tear the meat.
Chew the skin, suck it,
and swallow. Now, eat
the meat of the fruit, 15
so sweet,
all of it, to the heart.

Donna undresses, her stomach is white.
In the yard, dewy and shivering
with crickets, we lie naked,   20
face-up, face-down.
I teach her Chinese.
Crickets: *chiu chiu.* Dew: I've forgotten.
Naked: I've forgotten.
Ni, wo: you and me.   25
I part her legs,
remember to tell her
she is beautiful as the moon.

Other words
that got me into trouble were   30
fight and *fright, wren* and *yarn.*
Fight was what I did when I was frightened,
fright was what I felt when I was fighting.
Wrens are small, plain birds,
yarn is what one knits with.   35
Wrens are soft as yarn.
My mother made birds out of yarn.
I loved to watch her tie the stuff;
a bird, a rabbit, a wee man.

Mrs. Walker brought a persimmon to class   40
and cut it up
so everyone could taste
a *Chinese apple.* Knowing
it wasn't ripe or sweet, I didn't eat
but I watched the other faces.   45

My mother said every persimmon has a sun
inside, something golden, glowing,
warm as my face.

Once, in the cellar, I found two wrapped in newspaper,
forgotten and not yet ripe.   50
I took them and set both on my bedroom windowsill,
where each morning a cardinal
sang, *The sun, the sun.*

Finally understanding
he was going blind,   55
my father sat up all one night
waiting for a song, a ghost.
I gave him the persimmons,
swelled, heavy as sadness,
and sweet as love.   60

This year, in the muddy lighting
of my parents' cellar, I rummage, looking

for something I lost.
My father sits on the tired, wooden stairs,
black cane between his knees, 65
hand over hand, gripping the handle.

He's so happy that I've come home.
I ask how his eyes are, a stupid question.
All gone, he answers.

Under some blankets, I find a box. 70
Inside the box I find three scrolls.
I sit beside him and untie
three paintings by my father:
Hibiscus leaf and a white flower.
Two cats preening. 75
Two persimmons, so full they want to drop from the cloth.

He raises both hands to touch the cloth,
asks, *Which is this?*

This is persimmons, Father.

Oh, the feel of the wolftail on the silk, 80
the strength, the tense
precision in the wrist.
I painted them hundreds of times
eyes closed. These I painted blind.
Some things never leave a person: 85
scent of the hair of one you love,
the texture of persimmons,
in your palm, the ripe weight.

1986

Eating Alone

I've pulled the last of the year's young onions.
The garden is bare now. The ground is cold,
brown and old. What is left of the day flames
in the maples at the corner of my
eye. I turn, a cardinal vanishes. 5
By the cellar door, I wash the onions,
then drink from the icy metal spigot.

Once, years back, I walked beside my father
among the windfall pears. I can't recall
our words. We may have strolled in silence. But 10
I still see him bend that way—left hand braced
on knee, creaky—to lift and hold to my

eye a rotten pear. In it, a hornet
spun crazily, glazed in slow, glistening juice.

It was my father I saw this morning   15
waving to me from the trees. I almost
called to him, until I came close enough
to see the shovel, leaning where I had
left it, in the flickering, deep green shade.

White rice steaming, almost done. Sweet green peas   20
fried in onions. Shrimp braised in sesame
oil and garlic. And my own loneliness.
What more could I, a young man, want.

1986

Eating Together

In the steamer is the trout
seasoned with slivers of ginger,
two sprigs of green onion, and sesame oil.
We shall eat it with rice for lunch,
brothers, sister, my mother who will   5
taste the sweetest meat of the head,
holding it between her fingers
deftly, the way my father did
weeks ago. Then he lay down
to sleep like a snow-covered road   10
winding through pines older than him,
without any travelers, and lonely for no one.

1986

Mnemonic

I was tired. So I lay down.
My lids grew heavy. So I slept.
Slender memory, stay with me.

I was cold once. So my father took off his blue sweater.
He wrapped me in it, and I never gave it back.   5
It is the sweater he wore to America,
this one, which I've grown into, whose sleeves are too long,
whose elbows have thinned, who outlives its rightful owner.
Flamboyant blue in daylight, poor blue by daylight,
it is black in the folds.   10

A serious man who devised complex systems of numbers and rhymes
to aid him in remembering, a man who forgot nothing, my father
would be ashamed of me.
Not because I'm forgetful,
but because there is no order   15
to my memory, a heap
of details, uncatalogued, illogical.
For instance:
God was lonely. So he made me.
My father loved me. So he spanked me.   20
It hurt him to do so. He did it daily.

The earth is flat. Those who fall off don't return.
The earth is round. All things reveal themselves to men only gradually.

I won't last. Memory is sweet.
Even when it's painful, memory is sweet.   25

Once, I was cold. So my father took off his blue sweater.

                                                                   1986

This Room and Everything in It

Lie still now
while I prepare for my future,
certain hard days ahead,
when I'll need what I know so clearly this moment.

I am making use   5
of the one thing I learned
of all the things my father tried to teach me:
the art of memory.

I am letting this room
and everything in it   10
stand for my ideas about love
and its difficulties.

I'll let your love-cries,
those spacious notes
of a moment ago,   15
stand for distance.

Your scent,
that scent
of spice and a wound,
I'll let stand for mystery.   20

Your sunken belly
is the daily cup
of milk I drank
as a boy before morning prayer.

The sun on the face   25
of the wall
is God, the face
I can't see, my soul,

and so on, each thing
standing for a separate idea,   30
and those ideas forming the constellation
of my greater idea.
And one day, when I need
to tell myself something intelligent
about love,   35

I'll close my eyes
and recall this room and everything in it:
My body is estrangement.
This desire, perfection.
Your closed eyes my extinction.   40
Now I've forgotten my
idea. The book
on the windowsill, riffled by wind . . .
the even-numbered pages are
the past, the odd-   45
numbered pages, the future.
The sun is
God, your body is milk . . .

useless, useless . . .
your cries are song, my body's not me . . .   50
no good . . . my idea
has evaporated . . . your hair is time, your thighs are song . . .
it had something to do
with death . . . it had something
to do with love.   55

1990

Selected Bibliographies

A valuable resource for bibliographical and other research information about American literature is James L. Harner's *Literary Research Guide: A Guide to Reference Sources for the Study of Literatures in English and Related Topics*, 4th ed. (1993), now updated online. Though it is now badly outdated, a still useful general guide to American literature and civilization is Clarence Gohdes and Sanford Marovitz's *Bibliographical Guide to the Literature of the U.S.A.*, 5th ed. (1984). Three additional reference works warrant mention: James D. Hart's *Oxford Companion to American Literature*, 5th ed. (1983); Jack Saltzman's *The Cambridge Handbook of American Literature* (1986); and the discursive bibliographical supplements to Robert Spiller et al.'s *Literary History of the United States*, 4th ed. (1974). Richard M. Ludwig and Clifford Nault Jr.'s *Annals of American Literature, 1602–1983* (1986) is a useful volume for locating major works in their cultural contexts. The annual and invaluable *American Literary Scholarship* (also online) provides critical commentary on a wide range of scholarly books and articles (including reference works) on American literature published each year in the United States and abroad.

Two volumes for which Emory Elliott served as general editor offer current views of American literary history: *The Columbia Literary History of the United States* (1988) and *The Columbia History of the American Novel* (1991). Jay Parini edited *The Columbia History of American Poetry* (1993), an ambitious but not altogether satisfactory volume that manages to leave out almost as much as it covers. The on-going, eight-volume *Cambridge History of American Literature* (Sacvan Bercovitch, general editor) addresses not only traditional literary genres and periods, but is self-consciously concerned with literary theory and criticism as well as recently emergent forms and contributors to literature as a form of cultural production. Given the breadth of its coverage and the distinction of its section authors, this set is indispensable. Among other one-volume reference works is the comprehensive *Cambridge Guide to American Theatre* (1996), edited by Don B. Wilmeth. New volumes regularly appear to supplement the vast *Dictionary of Literary Biography*, and Scribner's continues to publish supplemental volumes to its excellent *American Writers: A Collection of Literary Biographies* (1974–). More specialized reference works devoted to genre, gender, ethnicity, race, region, and movements (among other topics) have been trying to gamely keep pace with the rapid proliferation of what is American and what is literary in American literature and culture, a much more complicated task as time goes on.

Students of American literature should generally be aware that new paperback editions of canonical and newly recovered works often contain, as do Norton Critical Editions, useful introductions, background material, and criticism. A number of publishers such as Twayne and Cambridge University Press have ongoing series on individual authors and/or works. Proceedings of conferences on authors, periods, genre, and specialized topics are frequently published. *Dissertation Abstracts International* and the often-invoked MLA annual bibliography provide information on unpublished scholarship on this period and its authors. Newsletters devoted to studies of many of the writers represented in this period are published regularly. Finally, students should also inquire into the abundant—and often very useful—audiovisual resources for the study of American writers, individual works, and intellectual currents. Increasingly these supplements are available on CD-ROM and on the World Wide Web as well as on audiocassettes and videocassettes. An excellent source for video and CD-ROM data is www.facets.com.

AMERICAN PROSE SINCE 1945

Because many of the writers anthologized here are still living and productive, scholarship is necessarily fluid. Recognizing this fact, publishers have embraced the idea of an introductory series, each volume of which restricts itself to basic facts and the most general of interpretations. Among these are the Twayne United States Authors Series, the University of South Carolina *Understanding . . .* volumes, Methuen's Contemporary Writers, the University of Missouri Press Literary Frontiers Editions, and the extended essays published as an ongoing project in the *Dictionary of Literary Biography*. Editors for the University Press of Mississippi have arranged (and indexed by subject matter) interviews conducted throughout the careers of many of these writers, available in the *Conversations with . . .* series. Other resources cover authors by means of essays and excerpts from criticism; among these are the *Critical Essays* books from G. K. Hall Publishers, the Greenwood Press *Critical Response* series, Prentice-Hall's *Twentieth Century Views*, and the *Modern Critical Views* collections edited by Harold Bloom for Chelsea House.

Overall trends prompt scholars to organize the period according to specific visions; conservative aesthetic opinions and socially based interests dominate the interpretations offered in relevant sections of *The Cambridge History of American Literature* (1999) and *The Columbia Literary History of the United States* (1988). Reliable surveys of developments on the stage can be found in Thomas P. Adler's *American Drama: 1940–1960* (1994), Ruby Cohn's *New American Dramatists, 1960–1990* (1993), Thomas S. Hischak's *American Theatre: A Chronicle of Comedy and Drama, 1969–2000* (2000), and Robert J. Andreach's *Creating the Self in the Contemporary American Theatre* (1998). Free of theoretical bias and soundly responsible to literary history is Malcolm Bradbury's *The Modern American Novel* (1993). In Kathryn Hume's *American Dream, American Nightmare: Fiction Since 1960* (2000) and Marc Chénetier's

Beyond Suspicion: New American Fiction Since 1960 (1996) postmodern developments are given close examination; James R. Giles's *Violence in the Contemporary American Novel* (2000) covers both technical and thematic matters. How political implications shape social fictions is explored in Alan Nadel's *Containment Culture: American Narratives, Postmodernism, and the Atomic Age* (1995), while Wendy Steiner explores the controversy over sexual elements in *The Scandal of Pleasure* (1995).

Two important studies from a feminist perspective are Nancy J. Peterson's *Against Amnesia: Contemporary Women Writers and the Crisis of Historical Memory* (2001) and Linda S. Kauffman's *Bad Girls and Sick Boys: Fantasies in Contemporary Art and Culture* (1998). Jeanne Rosier Smith's *Writing Tricksters: Mythic Gambols in American Ethnic Literature* (1997) covers work by native Americans, Asian Americans, and African Americans. Individual groups are studied in Catherine Rainwater's *Dreams of Fiery Stars: The Transformations of Native American Fiction* (1999), Louis Owens's *Other Destinies: Understanding the American Indian Novel* (1992), David Leiwei Li's *Imagining the Nation: Asian American Literature and Cultural Consent* (1998), Jinqi Ling's *Narrating Nationalisms: Ideology and Form in Asian American Literature* (1998), James W. Coleman's *Black Male Fiction and the Legacy of Caliban* (2001), Bernard W. Bell's *The Afro-American Novel* (1987), Deborah L. Madsen's *Understanding Contemporary Chicana Literature* (2000), and Ramon Saldívar's *Chicano Narrative* (1990). That novelists should aim high and work in large dimensions is argued in Tom LeClair's *The Art of Excess: Mastery in Contemporary American Fiction* (1989); how fiction writers can transcend mimesis by writing about themselves is Jerome Klinkowitz's project in *Structuring the Void: The Struggle for Subject in Contemporary American Fiction* (1992). War's impact on the literature of this period is studied in Jim Meilson's *Warring Fictions: Cultural Politics and the Vietnam War*

Narrative (1998) and Thomas Myers's *Walking Point: American Narratives of Vietnam* (1988).

Especially useful for understanding how and why contemporary writers produce their work is the critical interview, the exploratory technique for which was pioneered by Joe David Bellamy in his *The New Fiction: Interviews with Innovative American Writers* (1974) and which has been perfected by Larry McCaffery, who with various co-editors has produced a series of extensive, insightful, and critically developed dialogues with important authors of the past four decades: *Anything Can Happen* (1983), *Alive and Writing* (1987), *Across the Wounded Galaxies* (1990), and *Some Other Frequency* (1996).

Rudolfo A. Anaya

Anaya's novels are *Bless Me, Ultima* (1972), *Heart of Aztlán* (1976), *Tortuga* (1979), *The Legend of La Llorona* (1984), *Lord of the Dawn* (1987), *Alburquerque* (1992), *Zia Summer* (1995), *Jalamanta* (1996), *Rio Grande Fall* (1996), and *Shaman Winter* (1999). *The Silence of the Llano* (1982) is short stories; *The Adventures of Juan Chicapatas* (1985) is poetry.

Margarite Fernández Olmos provides a comprehensive study in *Rudolfo A. Anaya: A Critical Companion* (1999). Cesar A. Gonzales has prepared *A Sense of Place: Rudolfo A. Anaya, An Annotated Bio-Bibliography* (1999).

Gloria Anzaldúa

Borderlands / La Frontera (1987) includes memoir, historical analysis, and narrative poetry. Anzaldúa has also written several novels: *La Prieta* (The dark one) (1997), and (for children) *Prietita Has a Friend—Prietita tiene un Amigo* (1991), *Friends from the Other Side—Amigos del otra lado* (1993), and *Prietita and the Ghost Woman—Prietita y La Llorona* (1996). She is the editor of *Making Face, Making Soul / Haciendo Caras: Creative and Critical Perspectives by Feminists of Color* (1990), and (with Cherríe Moraga) co-edited *This Bridge Called My Back: Writings by Radical Women of Color* (1981).

Anzaldúa's work is studied by Deborah L. Madsen in *Understanding Contemporary Chicana Literature* (2000) and by Sonia Sandivár-Hull in *Feminism on the Border: Chicana Politics and Literature* (2000).

James Baldwin

Baldwin's novels are *Go Tell It on the Mountain* (1953), *Giovanni's Room* (1956), *Another Country* (1962), *Tell Me How Long the Train's Been Gone* (1968), *If Beale Street Could Talk* (1974), and *Just Above My Head* (1979). His other books are a collection of short stories, *Going to Meet the Man* (1965); a volume of nonfiction prose, *The Price of the Ticket* (1985); and two plays, *Blues for Mr. Charlie* (1964) and *The Amen Corner* (1968).

Talking at the Gates: A Life of James Baldwin (1991) by James Campbell is a biographical study. Critical interpretations include Horace Porter's *Stealing the Fire: The Art and Protest of James Baldwin* (1989) and William J. Weatherby's *James Baldwin: Artist on Fire* (1989); further essays and a bibliography are found in Fred L. Standley's edited *James Baldwin: A Reference Guide* (1980).

Toni Cade Bambara

Gorilla, My Love (1972) and *The Sea Birds Are Still Alive* (1977) are collections of Bambara's stories; a posthumous volume, *Deep Sightings and Rescue Missions: Fiction, Essays, and Conversations* (1996), gathers her other short work. Her novel *The Salt Eaters* was published in 1980; another novel, *Those Bones Are Not My Child* (1999), was published posthumously. Numerous screenplays by Bambara were produced in the 1970s and 1980s, including an adaption of Toni Morrison's *The Tar Baby* (1984) and a treatment of writer Zora Neale Hurston, *Zora* (1971). She edited the anthologies *The Black Woman* (1970), *Tales and Stories for Black Folks* (1971, for children), and (with Leah Wise) *Southern Black Utterances Today* (1975). *Deep Sightings and Rescue Missions: Fiction, Essays, and Conversations* (1996) is a posthumous collection of Bambara's later work, edited by Toni Morrison.

Critical analyses of Bambara's work are found in Philip Page's *Reclaiming Community in Contemporary African American Fiction* (1999) and in Elliott Butler-Evans's *Race, Gender and Desire: Narrative Strategies in the Fiction of Toni Cade Bambara, Toni Morrison, and Alice Walker* (1989).

Amiri Baraka (LeRoi Jones)

Dutchman and the Slave (1964) was published as a combined edition, as was *The Baptism & The Toilet* (1967). *Four Black Revolutionary Plays* (1969) includes *Experimental Death Unit #1*, *A Black Mass*, *Great Goodness of Life*, and *Madheart*. *The Motion of History and Other Plays* (1978) gathers the title work with *Slave Ship* and *S-1*. *The System of Dante's Hell* (1965) is a novel; *Tales* (1967) is a collection of short stories. Poetry volumes include *Preface to a Twenty Volume Suicide Note* (1961), *The Dead Lecturer* (1964), *Black Magic* (1969), *Hard Facts* (1975), *Transbluency* (1965), and *Funk Lore* (1996). *Eulogies* (1996) uses both poetry and prose to memorialize friends. Baraka has authored three books on music: *Blues People* (1963), *Black Music* (1968), and *The Music: Reflections on Jazz and Blues* (1987). His essays are collected in *Home* (1966), *Raise Race Rays Raze* (1971), and in *Selected Plays and Prose of Amiri Baraka / LeRoi Jones* (1979). Baraka has produced three important anthologies: *The Moderns* (1963), *Black Fire* (1968, with Larry Neal), and *Confirmation: An Anthology of African American*

Women (1983), with Amina Baraka. In 1984 he published *The Autobiography of LeRoi Jones/Amiri Baraka.*

Early but still useful studies are *Baraka: The Renegade and the Mask* (1976) by Kimberly W. Benston and *Amiri Baraka/LeRoi Jones: The Quest for a "Populist Modernism"* (1978) by Werner Sollors. William J. Harris has written *The Poetry and Poetics of Amiri Baraka: The Jazz Aesthetic* (1985) and edited *The LeRoi Jones/Amiri Baraka Reader* (1991), supplying introductory literary history and a bibliography. Ross Posnock's *Color and Culture* (1998) locates the author's thought. Baraka's first wife, Hettie Cohen, has authored a memoir, *How I Became Hettie Jones* (1990).

Donald Barthelme

Barthelme published three novels during his lifetime: *Snow White* (1967), *The Dead Father* (1975), and *Paradise* (1986). A fourth, *The King*, appeared in 1990, the year after he died. His story collections are *Come Back, Dr. Caligari* (1964), *Unspeakable Practices, Unnatural Acts* (1968), *City Life* (1970), *Sadness* (1972), *Guilty Pleasures* (1974), *Amateurs* (1976), *Great Days* (1979), *Sixty Stories* (1981), *Overnight to Many Distant Cities* (1983), and *Forty Stories* (1987). *The Slightly Irregular Fire Engine* (1971) is a work for children, whereas *Sam's Bar* (1987) provides a narrative for adult cartoons by Seymour Chwast. Kim Hertingzer edited *The Teachings of Don B.: Satires, Parodies, Fables, Illustrated Stories, and Plays of Donald Barthelme* (1992), many of which were omitted from Barthelme's own collections, and *Not Knowing: The Essays and Interviews of Donald Barthelme* (1997).

Stanley Trachtenberg's *Understanding Donald Barthelme* (1990) is a sound introduction, while Maurice Couturier and Régis Durand's *Donald Barthelme* (1982) offers a superb explication of Barthelme's literary theory. Jerome Klinkowitz examines the centrality of *The Dead Father* to the author's entire canon in *Donald Barthelme: An Exhibition* (1991) and provides a primary and secondary bibliography.

Ann Beattie

Beattie's novels are *Chilly Scenes of Winter* (1976), *Falling in Place* (1981), *Love Always* (1985), *Picturing Will* (1989), *Another You* (1995), *My Life, Starring Dara Falcon* (1997), and *The Doctor's House* (2002). Her story collections are *Distortions* (1976), *Secrets and Surprises* (1978), *The Burning House* (1982), *Where You'll Find Me* (1986), *What Was Mine* (1991), *Park City* (1998), and *Perfect Recall* (2001). She also wrote a critical study of painter Alex Katz (1987) and collaborated with photographer Bob Adelman on *Americana* (1992). Her *Spectacles* (1985) is for children.

Barbara Ann Schapiro studies Beattie's fiction in the company of work by John Updike and Toni Morrison in *Literature and the Representational Self* (1994). A broad sampling of critical opinion distinguishes Jaye Berman Montressor's *The Critical Reaction to Ann Beattie* (1993).

Saul Bellow

Bellow is the author of fourteen novels and novellas: *Dangling Man* (1944), *The Victim* (1947), *The Adventures of Augie March* (1953), *Seize the Day* (1956), *Henderson the Rain King* (1959), *Herzog* (1964), *Mr. Sammler's Planet* (1970), *Humboldt's Gift* (1975), *The Dean's December* (1982), *More Die of Heartbreak* (1987), *A Theft* (1989), *The Bellarosa Connection* (1989), *The Actual* (1997), and *Ravelstein* (2000). His short stories appear in three collections: *Mosby's Memoirs* (1968), *Him with His Foot in His Mouth* (1984), and *Something to Remember Me By* (1991). A play, *The Last Analysis*, was given a New York production in 1964 and was published the following year. *To Jerusalem and Back* (1976) is a personal account of his activities in Israel. *It All Adds Up* (1994) draws on Bellow's essays dating back to 1948.

Bellow: A Biography (2000) by James Atlas is exhaustive yet critically focused. Malcolm Bradbury provides the best concise introduction to this author's major work in *Saul Bellow* (1982), while in *Saul Bellow: Drumlin Woodchuck* (1980) fellow writer Mark Harris offers an insightful portrait of Bellow as a professional figure. John J. Clayton's *Saul Bellow: In Defense of Man* (1979) celebrates the author's stressfully tested humanism, while Ellen Pifer's *Saul Bellow: Against the Grain* (1990) argues for his culturally atypical belief in the transcendent soul. In *Saul Bellow: Vision and Revision* (1984) Daniel Fuchs examines manuscripts and letters to establish Bellow's Dostoevskian engagement with issues of character. Julia Eichelberger sums up his work in *Prophets of Recognition* (1999).

Raymond Carver

Principal collections of Carver's extensive short fiction are *Put Yourself in My Shoes* (1974), *Will You Please Be Quiet, Please?* (1976), *Furious Seasons* (1977), *What We Talk About When We Talk About Love* (1981), *The Pheasant* (1982), *Cathedral* (1983), and *Where I'm Calling From* (1988). *Fires* (1983) is a sampling of essays, poems, and narratives. Carver's uncollected work has been edited by William L. Stull as *No Heroics, Please* (1991), expanded as *Call If You Need Me* (2000). Throughout his career Carver published poetry as well, the bulk of which appears in several volumes from *Near Klamath* (1968) to *A New Path to the Waterfall* (1989); *All of Us* (1998) collects all of his poems.

Understanding Raymond Carver (1988) by Arthur M. Saltzman looks beyond the author's apparent realism, as does Randolph Runyon's *Reading Raymond Carver* (1992). Carver's return to traditionalism is celebrated by Kirk Nesset in *The Stories of Raymond Carver* (1995).

Sam Halpert sifts through comments by Carver's associates in *Raymond Carver: An Oral Biography* (1995).

John Cheever

Cheever's seven volumes of short stories appeared between 1943 and 1973, and are assembled in *The Stories of John Cheever* (1978); *The Uncollected Stories of John Cheever* appeared posthumously in 1988. His novels are *The Wapshot Chronicle* (1957), *The Wapshot Scandal* (1964), *Bullet Park* (1969), *Falconer* (1977), and *Oh What a Paradise It Seems* (1982). His letters, edited by his son, Benjamin Cheever, were published in 1988 (*The Letters of John Cheever*). *The Journals of John Cheever* (1991) were edited by Robert Gottlieb.

Scott Donaldson's *John Cheever* (1988) is a full-length biography. *Home before Dark* (1984), by his daughter, Susan Cheever, is a personal memoir. Francis J. Bosha has edited *The Critical Response to John Cheever* (1994). Samuel Chase Coale provides an overview in *John Cheever* (1977), while religious dimensions are explored by George W. Hunt in *John Cheever: The Hobgoblin Company of Love* (1983). The stories are given close study by James Eugene O'Hara in *John Cheever: A Study of the Short Fiction* (1989).

Sandra Cisneros

The House on Mango Street (1984) has been described as both interrelated short stories and a novel, whereas *Woman Hollering Creek* (1991) collects more evidently independent short stories. Cisneros has published two major collections of poetry, *My Wicked Wicked Ways* (1987) and *Loose Woman* (1994). Her *Hairs/Pelitos* (1994), written in English and accompanied by a Spanish text translated by Liliana Valenzuela, is a narrative for children.

Ramón Saldívar discusses Cisneros's fiction in *Chicano Narrative* (1990) as do Tey Diana Rebolledo in *Women Singing in the Snow* (1995) and Sonia Saldívar-Hull in *Feminism on the Border* (2000). An extensive dialogue with her appears in *Interviews with Writers of the Post-Colonial World* (1992), edited by Feroza Jussawalla and Reed Way Dasenbrock.

Judith Ortiz Cofer

Cofer's major publications are the poetry collections *Peregrina* (1986), *Terms of Survival* (1987), and *Reaching for the Mainland* (1987); a novel, *The Line of the Sun* (1989); an omnibus volume of short stories and poems, *The Latin Deli* (1993); two memoirs, *Silent Dancing: A Partial Remembrance of a Puerto Rican Childhood* (1990) and *Woman in Front of the Sun: On Becoming a Writer* (2000); and a collection for young adult readers, *An Island Like You: Stories of the Barrio* (1998). With Marilyn Kallet she edited *Sleeping with One Eye Open: Women Writers and the Art of Survival* (1999).

Contemporary Southern Writers (1999), edited by Roger Matuz, contains critic Rae M. Carlton Colley's study of Cofer's work.

Annie Dillard

Dillard's nonfiction ranges from autobiography and meditations on nature and philosophy to literary criticism and anecdotes about other writers; published volumes are *Pilgrim at Tinker Creek* (1974), *Holy the Firm* (1977), *Teaching a Stone to Talk* (1982), *Living by Fiction* (1982), *Encounters with Chinese Writers* (1984), *Writing Life* (1989), *An American Childhood* (1987), and *For the Time Being* (1999). *The Living* (1992) is a novel, while *Tickets for a Prayerwheel* (1974) collects her early poetry.

Nancy C. Parrish provides a critical biography in *Lee Smith, Annie Dillard, and The Hollins Group* (1998). Still important for its insights on Dillard's first major books is Sandra Humble Johnson's *The Space Between: Literary Epiphany in the Works of Annie Dillard* (1982).

Stephen Dixon

Selections from Dixon's first thirty years of writing appear in *The Stories of Stephen Dixon* (1994); individual short story collections are *No Relief* (1976), *Quite Contrary* (1979), *14 Stories* (1980), *Movies* (1983), *Time to Go* (1984), *Love and Will* (1989), *The Play* (1989), *All Gone* (1990), *Friends* (1990), *Long Made Short* (1993), *Man on Stage* (1996), and *Sleep* (1999). *Frog* (1991) is a multilayered fiction encompassing eighteen stories, two novellas, a novel, and an assemblage of fragments, all of which are thematically related. *Gould* (1996) combines a historically segmented novel with a more unified novella. Dixon's independently standing novels are *Work* (1977), *Too Late* (1978), *Fall & Rise* (1985), *Garbage* (1988), *Interstate* (1995), *30* (1999), *Tisch* (1999), and *I.* (2002).

Dixon's work is located in the larger stream of contemporary fiction by Arthur M. Saltzman's *The Novel in the Balance* (1993); Marc Chénetier's *Beyond Suspicion: New American Fiction Since 1960* (1996); and Jerome Klinkowitz's *The Self-Apparent Word* (1984), *Structuring the Void* (1992), and *You've Got to Be Carefully Taught* (2001).

Ralph Ellison

In his lifetime Ellison published three books: a novel, *Invisible Man* (1952), and two volumes of essays, *Shadow and Act* (1964) and *Going to the Territory* (1986). The latter materials are combined with other nonfiction in *The Collected Essays of Ralph Ellison* (1995), edited by John F. Callahan with a preface by Saul Bellow. Fragments of his novel in progress are noted in the bibliography to Mark Busby's *Ralph Ellison* (1991) in the Twayne United States Authors Series; *Flying Home and Other Stories* (1997) gathers thirteen short stories written between 1937 and 1954, six of which were previously unpublished. In 1999 Callahan, as Ellison's literary executor, drew on manuscripts to assemble *Juneteenth* as a posthumous novel. Robert G. O'Meally edited *Living with Music: Ralph Ellison's Jazz Writings. Trading Twelves: The Selected Letters of Ralph Ellison and Albert Murray*, edited by Murray and Callahan, appeared in 2000. Lawrence Jackson is the author of a new biography entitled *Ralph Ellison: Emergence of Genius* (2002).

The centrality of Ellison's first novel to his other work is explained by Edith Shor in *Visible Ellison: A Study of Ralph Ellison's Fiction* (1993). Julia Eichelberger's *Prophets of Recognition* (1999) considers his larger impact. *Jazz Country: Ralph Ellison's America* (2001) by Horace A. Porter relates the author's jazz background to his novels and essays. A work that relates importantly to Ellison is Jerry Gafio Watts's *Heroism and the Black Intellectual* (1994).

Louise Erdrich

Erdrich's novels are *Love Medicine* (1984), *The Beet Queen* (1986), *Tracks* (1988), *The Bingo Palace* (1994), *Tales of Burning Love* (1996), *The Antelope Wife* (1998), and *The Last Report on the Miracles at Little No Horse* (2001). For children she has written *Grandmother's Pigeon* (1996) and *The Birchbark House* (1999). *The Blue Jay's Dance: A Birth Year* (1995) is her account of becoming a mother. With Michael Dorris she co-authored *The Crown of Columbus* (1991), a novel. Her two poetry collections are *Jacklight* (1984) and *Baptism of Desire* (1989).

Erdrich's fiction is treated by Louis Owens in *Other Destinies: Understanding the American Indian Novel* (1992) and in the essays edited by Allan Chavkin in *The Chippewa Landscape of Louise Erdrich* (1999).

Diane Glancy

Glancy's short stories fill two collections, *Trigger Dance* (1990) and *Firesticks* (1993). There are various small-press editions that combine her poetry, fiction, and nonfiction prose, including *Offering* (1988), *Lone Dog's Winter Count* (1991), *Claiming Breath* (1992), *The West Pole* (1994), *Monkey Secret* (1994), *The Only Piece of Furniture in the House* (1996), and *Asylum in the Grasslands* (1998). With C. E. Truesdale, Glancy edited *Two Worlds Walking* (1994), an anthology of mixed-heritage writing; *Visit Teepee Town* (1999), edited with Mark Nowak, explores postmodern aspects of Native American literature. *Pushing the Bear* (1996) is a major novel about the forced migration along the Trail of Tears. Glancy's other novels include *Flutie* (1998) and *Fuller Man* (1999).

Kenneth M. Roemer's edited *Native American Writers of the United States* (1996) includes a consideration of Glancy's work.

Barry Hannah

Hannah's novels are *Geronimo Rex* (1972), *Nightwatchmen* (1973), *Ray* (1980), *The Tennis Handsome* (1983), *Hey Jack!* (1987), *Boomerang* (1989), *Never Die* (1991), and *Yonder Stands Your Orphan* (2001). *Power and Light* (1983) is a small-press edition subtitled "A novella for the screen from an idea by Robert Altman." Hannah's principal short story collections are *Airships* (1978), *Captain Maximus* (1985), *Bats Out of Hell* (1993), and *High Lonesome* (1996); there are small-press collections as well, including *Two Stories* (1982) and *Black Butterfly* (1982).

Ruth D. Weston studies the fiction in *Barry Hannah: Postmodern Romantic* (1999).

Maxine Hong Kingston

The Woman Warrior (1976) and *China Men* (1980) were first received as autobiography, though Kingston scholars now recognize important fictive elements. *Tripmaster Monkey: His Fake Book* (1989) is more obviously a novel. Essays Kingston wrote in 1978 appear as *Hawai'i One Summer* (1999).

Shirley Geok-Lim edited *Approaches to Teaching Kingston's "The Woman Warrior"* (1991); also helpful is Sidonie Smith's *A Poetics of Women's Autobiography: Marginality and the Fictions of Self-Representation* (1987). More cognizant of fiction's role in Kingston's writing is *Articulate Silences: Hisaye Yamamoto, Maxine Hong Kingston, and Joy Kogawa* (1993) by King-Kok Cheung and *Writing Tricksters* (1997) by Jeanne Rosier Smith.

Ursula K. Le Guin

Le Guin's novels include *Rocannon's World* (1966), *Planet of Exile* (1966), *City of Illusions* (1967), *A Wizard of Earthsea* (1968), *The Left Hand of Darkness* (1969), *The Tombs of Atuan* (1971), *The Lathe of Heaven* (1971), *The Farthest Shore* (1972), *The Dispossessed* (1974), *The Word for World Is Forest* (1976), *Malafrena* (1979), *The Eye of the Heron* (1983), *Always Coming Home* (1985), *Tehanu: The Last Book of Earthsea* (1990), *Buffalo Gals, Won't You Come Out Tonight* (1994), *Four Ways to Forgiveness* (1995), and *The Telling* (2000). Her short story collections are *The Wind's Twelve Quarters* (1975), *The Water is Wide* (1976), *Orsinian Tales* (1976), *The Compass Rose* (1982), *The Visionary* (1984), *Buffalo Gals and Other Animal Presences* (1987), *Searoad* (1992), *A Fisherman of the Inland Series* (1994), and *Worlds of Exile and Illusion* (1996). *Tales from Earthsea* (2001) presents a novella and new short stories. She also wrote fourteen books for children, ten poetry collections, two plays, and several volumes of nonfiction prose, including *The Language of Night: Essays on Fantasy and Science Fiction* (1979, 1989) and *Dancing at the Edge of the World: Thoughts on Words, Women, Places* (1989).

Understanding Ursula K. Le Guin (1990) by Elizabeth Cummins Cogell is a good introduction; more critically sophisticated are James Bittner's *Approaches to the Fiction of Ursula K. Le Guin* (1984) and Bernard Selinger's *Le Guin and Identity in Contemporary Fiction* (1988).

Bernard Malamud

Malamud's short story collections are *The Magic Barrel* (1958), *Idiots First* (1963), *Rembrandt's Hat* (1973), and *The Stories of Bernard Malamud* (1983). His novels are *The Natural* (1952), *The Assistant* (1957), *A New Life* (1961), *The Fixer* (1966), *Pictures of Fidelman* (1969), *The Tenants* (1971), *Dubin's Lives* (1979), and *God's Grace* (1982). Robert Giroux has edited his unfinished novel and a number of short fictions (*The People and Uncollected Stories,* 1990), together with *The Complete Stories* (1997). Alan Cheuse and Nicholas Delbanco edited *Talking Horse: Bernard Malamud on Life and Work* (1996).

A comprehensive overview of Malamud's works and their place in the American tradition is provided by Edward A. Abramson in *Bernard Malamud Revisited* (1993). Sanford Pinsker's *Jewish-American Fiction, 1917–1987* (1992) examines the author's specifically Jewish-American contribution. Rita N. Kosofsky has compiled *Bernard Malamud: A Descriptive Bibliography* (1991).

David Mamet

Among Mamet's major plays are *Sexual Perversity in Chicago* (1974), *American Buffalo* (1975), *A Life in the Theatre* (1977), *Glengarry Glen Ross* (1984), *Speed-the-Plow* (1987), *Three Sisters* (1991), *Oleanna* (1992), *Cryptogram* (1995), and *Boston Marriage* (2001). He has written a number of screenplays for Hollywood films and written and directed films himself, including *House of Games* (1988). *Passover* (1995) is a work of fiction; nonfiction prose is collected in *Writing in Restaurants* (1986), *The Cabin* (1992), *A Whore's Profession* (1994), *3 Uses of Knowledge* (1998), and *Jafsie and John Henry* (1999). *The Village* (1994) is a novel.

C. W. E. Bigsby's *David Mamet* (1985) is an excellent introduction. Mamet's use of voice is considered by Michael Stephens in *The Dramagurgy of Style* (1986). Critical studies, bibliographies, and interviews from a wide variety of perspectives are available in Leslie Kane's *David Mamet's Glengarry Glen Ross: Text and Performance* (1996); a biographical thesis is argued by Kane in *Weasels and Wisemen: Education, Ethics, and Ethnicity in David Mamet* (1999).

Paule Marshall

Brown Girl, Brownstones (1959) is Marshall's first novel, followed by *The Chosen Place, The Timeless People* (1969), *Praisesong for the Widow* (1983), *Daughters* (1991), and *The Fisher King* (2000). Her story collections are *Soul Clap Hands and Sing* (1961) and *Reena and Other Stories* (1983).

In *The Fiction of Paule Marshall: Reconstructions of History, Culture and Gender* (1995), Dorothy Hamer Denniston charts the author's progress toward Pan-Africanism; while Joyce Pettis's *Toward Wholeness in Paule Marshall's Fiction* (1995) studies the complexity of dual cultural heritage. Heather Hathaway examines regional influence in *Caribbean Waves* (1999), while Simone A. James Alexander explores a central theme in *Mother Imagery in the Novels of Afro-Caribbean Women* (2001).

Arthur Miller

Miller's earlier plays—*All My Sons, Death of a Salesman, The Crucible, A Memory of Two Mornings,* and *A View from the Bridge*—are brought together in Arthur Miller's *Collected Plays* (1957), which also includes a lengthy and useful introduction. Later dramas are available in *Collected Plays, 1957–1981* (1981) and thereafter separately, including *Danger, Memory!* (1987), *The Archbishop's Ceiling: The American Clock* (1989), *The Ride Down Mt. Morgan* (1992), *Broken Glass* (1994), and *The Last Yankee* (1994). *Focus* (1945) is a novel; short fiction is collected in *The Misfits and Other Stories* (1987) and *Homely Girl, a Life, and Other Stories* (1997); *The Misfits* (1961) is a screenplay. *Echoes Down the Corridor: Collected Essays, 1944–2000* appeared in 2000. Harold Clurman edited *The Portable Arthur Miller* in 1971, and Robert A. Martin edited *The Theater Essays of Arthur Miller* in 1978. Miller published an account of the production of *Death of a Salesman* in China in 1984, and an autobiography, *Timebends: A Life*, in 1987.

The best recent critical analysis of Miller's work is found in Christopher Bigsby's edited *The Cambridge Companion to Arthur Miller* (1997). Also helpful are the materials commissioned by Steven R. Centola for the edited volume *The Achievement of Arthur Miller: New Essays* (1995). Specifics are handled by Brenda Murphy in *Miller: Death of a Salesman* (1995) and by Matthew C. Rodané in *Approaches to Teaching Miller's Death of a Salesman* (1995).

N. Scott Momaday

Momaday's autobiographical works begin with *The Journey to Tai-me* (1967) and continue with *The Way to Rainy Mountain* (1969) and *The Names: A Memoir* (1976), supplemented by *The Man Made of Words: Essays, Stories, Passages* (1997). *House Made of Dawn* (1968), *The Ancient Child* (1989), and *In the Bear's House* (1999) are novels. His poems appear as *Angle of Geese* (1974), *Before an Old Painting of the Crucifixion, Carmel Mission, June 1960* (1975), and *The Gourd Dancer* (1976). *In the Presence of the Sun: Stories and Poems 1961–1991* was published in 1992 with illustrations by the author. Momaday has also written books for children, edited editions of writers, and written the commentary for photographer David Muench's *Colorado: Summer, Fall, Winter, Spring* (1973).

A book-length study of Momaday is *N. Scott Momaday: The Cultural and Literary Background* (1985) by Matthias Schubnell. Of the many interviews with Momaday, early and noteworthy is Joseph Bruchac's "The Magic of Words: An Interview with N. Scott Momaday," in *Survival This Way: Interviews with American Indian Poets* (1987), edited by Bruchac. Louis Owens's "N. Scott Momaday," in *This Is about Vision: Interviews with Southwestern Writers* (1990), edited by William Balassi, John F. Crawford, and Annie O. Eysturoy, also offers quite a good interview. Kenneth M. Roemer edited *Approaches to Teaching Momaday's "The Way to Rainy Mountain"* (1988), which is useful. Arnold Krupat's *The Voice in the Margin: Native American Literature and the Canon* (1989) compares autobiographical writing of Momaday and Leslie Marmon Silko. Susan Scarberry-Garcia's *Landmarks of Healing: A Study of "House Made of Dawn"* (1990) fills in some of the multitribal mythic context. Gerald Vizenor edited *Narrative Chance: Postmodern Discourse on Native American Indian Literatures* (1989), with three articles on Momaday. A fine account, focused on *House Made of Dawn*, is in Louis Owens's *Other Destinies: Understanding the American Indian Novel* (1992), supplemented by Scott B. Vickers's work in *Native American Identities* (1998).

Toni Morrison
Morrison's novels are *The Bluest Eye* (1970), *Sula* (1974), *Song of Solomon* (1977), *Tar Baby* (1981), *Beloved* (1987), *Jazz* (1992), and *Paradise* (1998). A play, *Dreaming Emmett*, was produced in 1986. Morrison is the author of *Playing in the Dark: Whiteness and the Literary Imagination* (1992) and editor of *Race-ing Justice, Engendering Power: Essays on Anita Hill, Clarence Thomas, and the Construction of Social Reality* (1992). Her *Lecture and Speech of Acceptance upon the Award of the Nobel Prize for Literature* was published in 1994.

Book-length studies include Trudier Harris's *Fictions and Folklore: The Novels of Toni Morrison* (1991), Denise Heinze's *The Dilemma of "Double-consciousness": Toni Morrison's Novels* (1993), Gurleen Grewal's *Circles of Sorrow, Lines of Struggle* (1998), John N. Duvall's *The Identifying Fictions of Toni Morrison* (2000), and J. Brooks Bouson's *Quiet As It's Kept* (2000). Henry Louis Gates Jr. and K. A. Appiah have edited *Toni Morrison: Critical Perspectives Past and Present* (1993). *Toni Morrison: An Annotated Bibliography* (1987) has been compiled by David L. Middleton.

Flannery O'Connor
O'Connor's novels and stories (edited by Sally Fitzgerald) are a volume in the *Library of America* series (1988). Her novels are *Wise Blood* (1952) and *The Violent Bear It Away* (1960). Two collections of stories, *A Good Man Is Hard to Find* (1955) and *Everything That Rises Must Converge* (1965), are included with earlier uncollected stories in *Complete Stories* (1971). Her letters are collected in *The Habit of Being: The Letters of Flannery O'Connor* (1979). *The Presence of Grace, and Other Book Reviews* (1983) collects some of her critical prose, as does *Mystery and Manners* (1969) edited by Sally Fitzgerald and Robert Fitzgerald.

Studies of O'Connor's fiction include Jon Lance Bacon's *Flannery O'Connor and Cold War Culture* (1993), Lorine M. Gertz's *Flannery O'Connor, Literary Theologian* (2000), and Richard Giannone's *Flannery O'Connor, Hermit Novelist* (2000). Melvin J. Friedman and Beverly Lyon Clark edited *Critical Essays on Flannery O'Connor* (1985). *Flannery O'Connor: A Descriptive Bibliography* (1981) was compiled by David Farmer.

Grace Paley
The Collected Stories (1994) draw on Paley's three major volumes of short fiction: *The Little Disturbances of Man* (1959), *Enormous Changes at the Last Minute* (1974), and *Later the Same Day* (1985). Other stories and poems appear (with paintings by Vera B. Williams) in *Long Walks and Intimate Talks* (1991). *Born Again: Collected Poems* appeared in 2000.

There have been three major studies of Paley's fiction: *Grace Paley's Life Stories: A Literary Biography* (1993) by Judith Arcana, *Grace Paley: A Study of the Short Fiction* (1990) by Neil D. Isaacs, and *Grace Paley: Illuminating the Dark Lives* (1990) by Jacqueline Taylor.

Suzan-Lori Parks
The America Play and Other Works (1995) collects six plays (including Parks's seminal *The Death of the Last Black Man in the Whole Entire World*) and three explanatory essays. Subsequent major dramatic works include *Venus* (1997), *Fucking A* (2000), and *Topdog/Underdog* (2001). Parks also wrote the filmscript for director Spike Lee's *Girl 6* (1996).

Una Chaudhuri studies *The America Play* in *Staging Place* (1995). Critical analyses of Parks's plays are also found in Robert J. Andreach's *Creating the Self in the Contemporary American Theater* (1998) and in Hendy H. Elan Jr. and David Krasner's *African American Performance and Theater History* (2001).

Richard Powers
Powers is the author of eight novels to date: *Three Farmers on Their Way to a Dance* (1985), *Prisoner's Dilemma* (1988), *The Gold Bug Variations* (1991), *Operation Wandering Soul* (1993), *Galatea 2.2* (1995), *Gain* (1998), *Plowing the Dark* (2000), and *The Time of Our Singing* (2003).

A special issue of the *Review of Contemporary Fiction* (Fall 1998) is devoted to the study of Powers's work. Joseph Dewey's *Understanding Richard Powers* (2001) is comprehensive, while an extensive discussion of *Galatea 2.2* forms part of Arthur Saltzman's *This Mad "Instead": Governing Metaphors in Contemporary American Fiction* (2000).

Thomas Pynchon
Pynchon's novels are *V.* (1963), *The Crying of Lot 49* (1966), *Gravity's Rainbow* (1973), *Vine-*

land (1990), and *Mason & Dixon* (1997). *Slow Learner* (1984) collects early stories.

Book-length studies are William M. Plater's *The Grim Phoenix: Reconstructing Thomas Pynchon* (1978), Thomas H. Schaub's *Pynchon, The Voice of Ambiguity* (1981), and David Seed's *The Fictional Labyrinths of Thomas Pynchon* (1988). Alan N. Brownlie studies the author's first three novels in *Thomas Pynchon's Narratives: Subjectivity and the Problems of Knowing* (2000), while the fourth and fifth novels are analyzed in Geoffrey Green, Donald J. Greiner, and Larry McCaffery's edited *The Vineland Papers* (1993) and Brooke Horvath and Irving Malin's edited *Pynchon and Mason & Dixon* (2000), respectively.

Ishmael Reed

Reed's novels are *The Free-Lance Pallbears* (1967), *Yellow Back Radio Broke-Down* (1969), *Mumbo Jumbo* (1972), *The Last Days of Louisiana Red* (1974), *Flight to Canada* (1976), *The Terrible Twos* (1982), *Reckless Eyeballing* (1986), *The Terrible Threes* (1989), and *Japanese by Spring* (1993). His poetry collections are *catechism of d neoamerican hoodoo church* (1970), *Conjure: Selected Poems, 1963–1979* (1972), *Chattanooga* (1973), *A Secretary to the Spirits* (1978), and *New and Collected Poems* (1988). Reed's essays are gathered in *Shrovetide in Old New Orleans* (1978), *God Made Alaska for the Indians* (1982), *Writin' Is Fightin'* (1988), and *Airing Dirty Laundry* (1993). The narrative Reed defines as a fetish was published in 1986 as *Cab Calloway Stands In for the Moon*. He has edited several anthologies, among them *19 Necromancers from Now* (1980), *Yardbird Lives!* (1978), and *The Before Columbus Foundation Fiction and Poetry Anthologies* (1992).

Jay Boyer's booklet *Ishmael Reed* (1993) is a good introduction; Patrick McGhee's *Ishmael Reed and the Ends of Race* (1997) is focused on matters of gender and race. More theoretically inclined is *Ishmael Reed and the New Black Aesthetic* (1988) by Reginald Martin. Reed's position as a polemicist is studied by Jerome Klinkowitz in *Literary Subversions* (1985). Elizabeth A. Settle and Thomas A. Settle have compiled *Ishmael Reed: A Primary and Secondary Bibliography* (1982).

Philip Roth

Roth's fiction consists of *Goodbye, Columbus* (1959), a novella and five short stories, and the following novels: *Letting Go* (1962), *When She Was Good* (1967), *Portnoy's Complaint* (1969), *Our Gang* (1971), *The Breast* (1972), *The Great American Novel* (1973), *My Life as a Man* (1974), *The Professor of Desire* (1977), *The Ghost Writer* (1979), *Zuckerman Unbound* (1981), *The Anatomy Lesson* (1983), *The Counterlife* (1987), *Deception* (1990), *Operation Shylock* (1993), *Sabbath's Theatre* (1995), *American Pastoral* (1997), *I Married a Communist* (1998), *The Human Stain* (2000), and *The*

Dying Animal (2001). *Reading Myself and Others* (1975) is a collection of essays and interviews. *The Facts: A Novelist's Autobiography* (1988) is Roth's memoir. A memoir of his father, *Patrimony,* was published in 1991.

Philip Roth (1982), by Hermione Lee, is an excellent introduction, as is *Understanding Philip Roth* (1990) by Murray Baumgarten and Barbara Gottfried. *Philip Roth and the Jews* (1996), by Alan Cooper, considers religious and cultural dimensions of the author's work. The broad sweep of Roth's career is covered in James D. Bloom's *The Literary Bent* (1997).

Leslie Marmon Silko

Silko's novels are *Ceremony* (1977), *Almanac of the Dead* (1991), and *Garden in the Dunes* (1999). *Storyteller* (1981) includes prose poems and related short stories. *Laguna Woman* (1974), *Voices Under One Sky* (1994), and *Rain* (1996) are books of poetry. *Yellow Woman and a Beauty of the Spirit* (1996) consists of Silko's essays on native American life today. *Lullaby,* co-authored with Frank Chin, was given a San Francisco production in 1976 as a dramatic adaptation of Silko's story. In 1985 *The Delicacy and Strength of Lace* was published, a collection of letters between Silko and the poet James Wright, edited by Anne Wright. Silko's work also appeared in *Yellow Woman* (1993), edited by Melody Graulich.

Leslie Marmon Silko (1980), by Per Seyersted, is an introduction to her work. *Four American Indian Literary Masters* (1982), by Alan R. Veile, is also relevant, as are Louise K. Barnett and James L. Thorson's edited *Leslie Marmon Silko* (1999) and Catherine Rainwater's *Dreams of Fiery Stars* (1999).

John Updike

Updike's novels are *The Poorhouse Fair* (1959), *Rabbit, Run* (1960), *The Centaur* (1963), *Of the Farm* (1965), *Couples* (1968), *Rabbit Redux* (1971), *A Month of Sundays* (1975), *Marry Me* (1976), *The Coup* (1978), *Rabbit Is Rich* (1981), *The Witches of Eastwick* (1984), *Roger's Version* (1986), *S.* (1988), *Rabbit at Rest* (1990), *Memories of the Ford Administration* (1992), *Brazil* (1994), *In the Beauty of the Lilies* (1996), *Toward the End of Time* (1997), and *Gertrude and Claudius* (2000). Collections of short fiction are *The Same Door* (1959), *Pigeon Feathers* (1962), *Olinger Stories: A Selection* (1964), *The Music School* (1966), *Bech: A Book* (1970), *Museums and Women* (1972). *Too Far to Go: The Maples Stories* (1979), *Problems* (1979), *Bech Is Back* (1982), *Trust Me* (1987), *The Afterlife* (1994), *Bech at Bay* (1998), and *Licks of Love* (2000). Updike's poems are gathered in *Collected Poems 1953–1993* (1993), drawing on the individual volumes *The Carpentered Hen* (1958), *Telephone Poles* (1963), *Midpoint* (1969), *Tossing and Turning* (1977), and *Facing Nature* (1985); *Americana: and Other Poems* (2001) is his new work. Reviews and literary essays appear in *Assorted Prose* (1965), *Picked-Up Pieces* (1975), *Hugging the Shore* (1983), *Odd Jobs* (1991), and *More Matter* (1999). *Self-Consciousness* (1989) is a memoir, *Just Looking* (1989) is art criticism, and *Golf Dreams* (1996) collects the author's essays on his favorite sport. *Buchanan Dying* (1974) is a play meant for reading rather than for stage production. Updike has authored five books for children: *The Magic Flute* (1962), *The Ring* (1964), *A Child's Calendar* (1965), *Bottom's Dream* (1969), and *A Helpful Alphabet of Friendly Objects* (1995).

Donald J. Greiner's thorough examination of the early canon appears in his *John Updike's Novels* (1984) and *The Other John Updike: Poems/Short Stories/Prose/Plays* (1981). Longer views are taken by James A. Schiff in *John Updike Revisited* (1998) and by William Pritchard in *Updike: America's Man of Letters* (2000).

Gerald Vizenor

Vizenor's novels are *Darkness in Saint Louis: Bearheart* (1978), *Griever: An American Monkey King in China* (1987), *The Trickster of Liberty* (1988), *The Heirs of Columbus* (1991), *Dead Voices: Natural Agonies in the New World* (1992), *Hotline Healers: An Almost Browne Novel* (1997), and *Chancers* (2000). His short fiction appears in *Earthdivers: Tribal Narratives on Mixed Descent* (1981), which also includes autobiography, and in *Landfill Meditations: Crossblood Stories* (1991). *Interior Landscapes: Autobiographical Myths and Metaphors* (1990) is an autobiography. Collections of Vizenor's poems are *Two Wings the Butterfly* (1962), *Raising the Moonvines* (1964), *Seventeen Chips* (1964), *Slight Abrasions: A Dialogue in Haiku* (1966, with Jerome Downes), *Empty Swings* (1967), and *Matsushima: Pine Islands* (1984). Nonfiction commentary fills several volumes, including *Tribal Scenes and Ceremonies* (1976), *Wordarrows: Indians and Whites in the New Fur Trade* (1978), *The People Named the Chippewa: Narrative Histories* (1984), *Crossbloods: Bone Courts, Bingo, and Other Reports* (1990), and *Fugitive Poses: North American Indian Scenes of Absence and Presence* (1998). *The Everlasting Sky: New Voices from the People Named the Chippewa* (1972) incorporates interviews among contemporary tribal people. Vizenor has edited many anthologies of Native American writing, as well as *Narrative Chance: Postmodern Discourse on Native American Indian Literatures* (1989). He and A. Robert Lee partake in *Post indian Conversations* (1999).

Kimberly M. Blaser's *Gerald Vizenor: Writing in the Oral Tradition* (1996) is a comprehensive study. Also pertinent are Arthur Krupat's considerations of Vizenor's work in *For Those Who Come after: A Study of Native American Autobiography* (1985) and *The Voice in the Margin: Native American Literature and the Canon* (1989), plus Catherine Rainwater's analyses in *Dreams of Fiery Stars* (1999).

Kurt Vonnegut

Vonnegut's novels are *Player Piano* (1952), *The Sirens of Titan* (1959), *Mother Night* (1961), *Cat's Cradle* (1963), *God Bless You, Mr. Rosewater* (1965), *Slaughterhouse-Five* (1969), *Breakfast of Champions* (1973), *Slapstick* (1976), *Jailbird* (1969), *Deadeye Dick* (1982), *Galápagos* (1985), *Bluebeard* (1987), *Hocus Pocus* (1990), and *Timequake* (1997). His short stories are collected in *Canary in a Cat House* (1961), *Welcome to the Monkey House* (1968), and *Bagombo Snuff Box* (1999). His essays fill three volumes: *Wampeters, Foma and Granfalloons* (1974), *Palm Sunday* (1981), and *Fates Worse Than Death* (1991). *Happy Birthday, Wanda June* (1971) is a play, while *Between Time and Timbuktu* (1972) is a television script, prefaced by Vonnegut, drawing on his fiction. *Sun/Moon/Star* (1980), with illustrations by Ivan Chermayeff, is a book for children. *God Bless You, Dr. Kevorkian* (1999) collects Vonnegut's radio satires; *Like Shaking Hands With God* (1999) is his dialogue with social activist Lee Stringer.

Jerome Klinkowitz surveys Vonnegut's career in *Structuring the Void* (1992) and studies his essays in *Vonnegut in Fact* (1998). Specific theses are argued by Leonard Mustazza in *Forever Pursuing Genesis: The Myth of Eden in the Novels of Kurt Vonnegut* (1990) and Leonard Broer in *Sanity Plea: Schizophrenia in the Novels of Kurt Vonnegut* (1989, revised 1994). A broad sample of criticism is made by editor Leonard Mustazza in *The Critical Response to Kurt Vonnegut* (1994), while Vonnegut's later work (including his public spokesmanship) are examined in *The Vonnegut Chronicles* (1996), edited by Peter J. Reed and Marc Leeds. Asa B. Pieratt Jr., Julie Huffman-Klinkowitz, and Jerome Klinkowitz have compiled *Kurt Vonnegut: A Comprehensive Bibliography* (1987).

Alice Walker

Walker's novels are *The Third Life of Grange Copeland* (1970), *Meridian* (1976), *The Color Purple* (1982), *The Temple of My Familiar* (1989), *Possessing the Secret of Joy* (1992), and *By the Light of My Father's Smile* (1998). Her short-story collections are *In Love and Trouble* (1973), *You Can't Keep a Good Woman Down* (1981), and *The Way Forward Is With a Broken Heart* (2000). Poetry collections are *Once* (1986), *Five Poems* (1972), *Revolutionary Petunias* (1973), *Good Night, Willie Lee, I'll See You in the Morning* (1969), *Horses Make a Landscape Look More Beautiful* (1984), and *Her Blue Body Everything We Know* (1991). Walker's literary essays are collected in *In Search of Our Mothers' Gardens* (1983), *Living by the Word* (1988), and

Anything We Love Can Be Saved (2000); she has also written *Warrior Marks: Female Genital Mutilation and the Sexual Blinding of Women* (1987, with Pratibha Parmar) and *The Same River Twice: Honoring the Difficult/A Meditation on Life, Spirit, Art, and the Making of the Film* The Color Purple *Ten Years Later* (1996). Her books for children include an illustrated version of *To Hell with Dying* (1988), *Finding the Green Stone* (1991), and a biography, *Langston Hughes, American Poet* (1974).

Good samplings of scholarship on Walker fill two volumes: editors Henry Louis Gates Jr. and K. Anthony Appiah's *Alice Walker: Critical Perspectives Past and Present* (1993) and editor Lillie P. Howard's *Alice Walker and Zora Neale Hurston: The Common Bond* (1993). *Alice Walker* (2000) is Maria Lauret's book-length study.

Eudora Welty
Welty's novels are *The Robber Bridegroom* (1942), *Delta Wedding* (1947), *The Ponder Heart* (1954), *Losing Battles* (1970), and *The Optimist's Daughter* (1972). Her *Collected Stories* (1980) draw from the volumes *A Curtain of Green* (1941), *The Wide Net* (1943), *Music from Spain* (1948), *The Golden Apples* (1949), *The Bride of Innisfallen* (1955), and *Thirteen Stories* (1965). Later volumes are *Moon Lake* (1980) and *Retreat* (1981). *A Flock of Guinea Hens Seen from a Car* (1970) is poetry; among Welty's many volumes of nonfiction prose are *The Eye of the Story: Selected Essays and Reviews* (1978), *One Writer's Beginnings* (1984), and *A Writer's Eye: Collected Book Reviews* (1994).

Ann Waldron published *Eudora: A Writer's Life* in 1998. Good introductions are available in Gail Mortimer's *Daughter of the Swan: Love and Knowledge in Eudora Welty's Fiction* (1994), *Eudora Welty's Aesthetics of Place* (1994) by Jan Nordby Gretlund, and Ruth D.

Weston's *Gothic Traditions and Narrative Techniques in the Fiction of Eudora Welty* (1994). *Eudora Welty: A Bibliography* by Noel Polk appeared in 1994.

Tennessee Williams
Most of Williams's plays are collected in the seven-volume *The Theatre of Tennessee Williams* (1971–81). Some later dramas are available in separate editions; a few others are still to be published. Other writings include a novel, *The Roman Spring of Mrs. Stone* (1950); short stories printed in several volumes and finally brought together in *Collected Stories* (1986), edited by Gore Vidal; a volume of screenplays, *Stopped Rocking* (1984); and poems collected as *In the Winter of Cities* (1964) and *Androgyne, Mon Amour* (1977). *Where I Live: Selected Essays*, edited by Christine R. Day and Bob Woods, appeared in 1978.

Williams's *Memoirs* (1975) is interestingly revelatory but is not a reliable biographical guide; neither is Dotson Rader's *Tennessee: Cry of the Heart* (1985). Donald Spoto's *A Kindness of Strangers: The Life of Tennessee Williams* (1985) is workmanlike; a historically sound treatment is *Tennessee Williams: Everyone Else Is an Audience* (1993) by Ronald Hayman. More theoretically inclined is Nicholas Pagan's *Rethinking Literary Biography: A Postmodern Approach* (1993). A Jungian reading of the plays is provided by Judith J. Thompson in *Tennessee Williams' Plays: Memory, Myth, and Symbol* (1987). Time relationships are explored by Patricia Schroeder in *The Presence of the Past in Modern American Drama* (1989). Philip G. Kolin edited *Tennessee Williams: A Guide to Research and Performance* (1998); Matthew C. Rodané prepared *The Cambridge Companion to Tennessee Williams*. George E. Crandell compiled *Tennessee Williams: A Descriptive Bibliography* (1995).

AMERICAN POETRY SINCE 1945

The diversity of postwar American poetry requires diverse works of criticism. Some of the most valuable commentary has occurred when one poet writes about another or meditates on the work of poetry itself. Such essays are available in collections like Charles Bernstein's *A Poetics* (1992), Robert Creeley's *A Quick Graph* (1970), Rita Dove's *The Poet's World* (1995) Louise Glück's *Proofs and Theories* (1994), Randall Jarrell's *Poetry and the Age* (1953), Denise Levertov's *The Poet in the World* (1973) and *Light Up the Cave* (1981), Robert Lowell's *Collected Prose* (1987), Robert Pinsky's *Poetry and the World* (1988), Charles Wright's *Quarternotes* (1995), and David St. Johns's *Where the Angels Come Toward Us* (1995). Among the many critical books that provide valuable studies

of the period and of particular poets are Charles Altieri's *Postmodernisms Now* (1998), Mutlu Konuk's *Politics and Form in Postmodern Poetry* (1995), James E. B. Breslin's *From Modern to Contemporary* (1984), Joanne V. Gabbin's edited *The Furious Flowering of African American Poetry* (1999), Thomas Gardner's *Regions of Unlikeness: Explaining Contemporary Poetry* (1999), Lynn Keller's *Re-Making It New* (1987), Laurence Lieberman's *Beyond the Muse of Memory* (1995), James Longenbach's *Modern Poetry after Modernism* (1997), J. D. McClatchey's *White Paper* (1990), Sherman Paul's *The Lost America of Love* (1981), Marjorie Perloff's *The Poetics of Indeterminacy* (1981), *The Dance of the Intellect* (1985), and *Radical Artifice: Writing Poetry in the Age of Media* (1991),

Peter Quartermain's *Disjunctive Poetics* (1992), Peter Stitt's *Uncertainty and Plentitude: Five Contemporary Poets* (1997), Thomas Travisano's *Midcentury Quartet* (1999), Helen Vendler's *The Music of What Happens* (1988) and *Soul Says* (1995), and Robert von Hallberg's *American Poetry and Culture, 1945–1980* (1985). Donald Allen's *Poetics of the New American Poetry* (1973) collects a number of theoretical pieces from important contemporary poets. Ours is an age of the interview, and interviews with a variety of poets may be found in Bill Moyers's *Fooling with Words: A Celebration of Poets and Their Crafts* (2000), in the several volumes of *Writers at Work: The Paris Review Interviews, Women Writers at Work* (1998), and current editions of the *Paris Review* itself. Many other journals and reviews frequently feature interviews with contemporary poets.

Collections of individual poets' interviews and prose have also been published in the *Poets on Poetry* series (University of Michigan). Also valuable are *Black Women Writers at Work*, edited by Claudia Tate (1988), *Survival This Way: Interviews with American Indian Poets*, edited by Joseph Bruhac (1987), and *Truthtellers of the Times: Interviews with Contemporary Women Poets* (1998), ed. Janet Palmer Mullaney.

A considerable amount of material, some of it valuable, can be found on the Internet, including poets's biographies, lists of works published, samples of a poet's work and, in some cases, audio versions of poets reading from their work. The Academy of American Poets at www. poets.org is the best general site and includes an audio component. Links may be found there to other Internet sites on contemporary poetry.

A. R. Ammons

Collections of Ammons's poetry include a reissue of his *Collected Poems 1951–1971* (2001), *Really Short Poems of A. R. Ammons* (1991), *Selected Longer Poems* (1980), and *The Selected Poems: Expanded Edition* (1986). His individual volumes include *Sphere: The Form of a Motion* (1974), *Diversifications* (1975), *Snow Poems* (1977), *A Coast of Trees* (1981), *Lake Effect Country* (1983), *Sumerian Vistas* (1987), *Garbage* (1993), and *Brink Road* (1996). A collection of Ammons's essays and interviews, *Set in Motion*, also appeared in 1996. There are useful critical discussions of his work in Richard Howard's *Alone with America* (1969), in Helen Vendler's, *The Music of What Happens* (1988), in Robert Kirschten's edited *Critical Essays on A. R. Ammons* (1997), and in Steven P. Schneider's edited *Complexities of Motion: New Essays on A. R. Ammons' Long Poems* (1999). An interview with Ammons appeared in *The Paris Review* (Spring 1996).

John Ashbery

Ashbery's volumes of poetry include *Some Trees* (1956), *The Tennis Court Oath* (1962), *Rivers and Mountains* (1966), *The Double Dream of Spring* (1970), *Three Poems* (1972), *Self-Portrait in a Convex Mirror* (1975), *Houseboat Days* (1977), *As We Know* (1979), *Shadow Train* (1981), *A Wave* (1984), *Selected Poems* (1985), *April Galleons* (1988), *Flow Chart* (1991), *And the Stars Were Shining* (1994), *Can You Hear, Bird* (1995), *Girls on the Run* (1999), and *Your Name Here* (2000). With James Schuyler he is co-author of the comic novel *A Nest of Ninnies* (1969). Ashbery's Charles Eliot Norton Lectures on Poetry appear in *Other Traditions* (2000). Among useful critical essays are David Kalstone's *Five Temperaments* (1977); chapters in Vernon Shetley's *After the Death of Poetry: Poet and Audience in Contemporary America* (1993); and John Shoptaw's book-length study of Ashbery's poetry, *On the Outside Looking Out* (1994). David K. Kermani's *John Ashbery: A Comprehensive Bibliography* (1975) is indispensable and amusing. See also *Beyond Amazement: New Essays on John Ashbery*, edited by David Lehman (1980) and Charles Altieri's *Postmodernisms Now* (1998).

John Berryman

Berryman's *Collected Poems: 1937–1971* appeared in 1991; *Homage to Mistress Bradstreet* (1956) and a selection of his *Short Poems* (1948) were issued together in paperback format in 1968. His other volumes of poetry include *77 Dream Songs* (1964); *Berryman's Sonnets* (1967); *His Toy, His Dream, His Rest* (1968); *Love and Fame* (1970; rev. 1972); *Delusions, Etc.* (1972); and a posthumous volume, *Henry's Fate* (1977). Berryman's critical biography, *Stephen Crane*, appeared in 1950, and a collection of his short fiction and literary essays was issued under the title *The Freedom of the Poet* (1976). Berryman's unfinished novel about his alcoholism, *Recovery*, appeared in 1973. Valuable critical introductions to Berryman's poetry can be found in Helen Vendler's *The Given and the Made* (1995), Thomas Travisano's *Midcentury Quartet* (1999). Paul Mariani's *Dream Song: The Life of John Berryman* (1996) and Eileen Simpson's *Poets in Their Youth* (1982) are useful biographical studies.

Elizabeth Bishop

Bishop's poems are now available in *The Complete Poems 1927–1979*. *The Collected Prose* (1984) includes a number of memoirs and stories, especially *In the Village*, invaluable for a reading of her poems. A remarkable selection of Bishop's correspondence, *One Art* (1994) was edited by her friend and publisher, Robert Giroux and reproductions of Bishop's own watercolor paintings appear in *Exchanging Hats* (1996). Bishop also translated from the Portuguese *The Diary of Helena Morley* (1957, 1977, 1991), an enchanting memoir of provincial life in Brazil. Anne Stevenson's biographical and critical study, *Elizabeth Bishop,* appeared in 1966. Useful critical essays on Bishop appear in

Seamus Heaney's *The Redress of Poetry* (1995), Lorrie Glodensohn's *Elizabeth Bishop: The Biography of a Poetry* (1992), and David Kalstone's *Becoming a Poet* (1989). *Elizabeth Bishop and Her Art*, edited by Lloyd Schwartz and Sybil P. Estess (1983), includes two interviews as well. A provocative essay on Bishop also appears in Adrienne Rich's *Blood, Bread and Poetry* (1986). More recently, critical studies of Bishop's work have proliferated. Among the most valuable of these are Brett C. Miller's important biography, *Elizabeth Bishop: Life and the Memory of It* (1993); *Elizabeth Bishop: The Geography of Gender* (1993), a collection of essays edited by Marilyn Lombardi; *Conversations with Elizabeth Bishop* (1996), edited by George Monteiro; and Thomas Travisano's *Midcentury Quartet* (1999). Candace MacMahon's *Elizabeth Bishop: A Bibliography* (1980) is indispensable.

Gwendolyn Brooks
Brooks's volumes of poetry include *A Street in Bronzeville* (1945); *Annie Allen* (1949); *In the Time of Detachment, In the Time of Cold* (1965); *In the Mecca* (1968); *Riot* (1969); *Family Pictures* (1970); *Aloneness* (1972); *Aurora* (1972); *Beckonings* (1975); *To Disembark* (1981); *Winnie* (1989); and *Children Coming Home* (1991). Many of her poems are collected in *Selected Poems* (1999). She has also written prose autobiographies, *Report from Part One* (1972) and *Report from Part Two* (1996). Other useful biographical material appears in *A Life Distilled*, edited by M. K. Mootry and others. Valuable discussions of Brooks's poetry appear in *Black Women Writers (1950–1980)*, edited by Mari Evans (1984). Stephen Wright's *On Gwendolyn Brooks: Reliant Contemplation* (1996) and Harold Bloom's *Gwendolyn Brooks* (2000) are recent critical studies. An interview with Brooks appears in Janet Mullaney's *Truthtellers of the Times: Interviews with Contemporary Women Poets* (1998).

Lorna Dee Cervantes
Emplumada was published in 1981 and *Cables of Genocide* in 1991. A discussion of Cervantes's work, and of Chicana poetry more generally, appears in Deborah Madsen's *Understanding Contemporary Chicana Literature* (2000). An interview with Cervantes can be found in Bill Moyers's *Fooling with Words* (2000).

Billy Collins
Collections of Collins's poetry include *The Apple That Astonished Paris* (1988), *Questions about Angels* (1991), *The Art of Drowning* (1995), *Picnic, Lightning* (1998), and *Sailing Alone around the World: New and Selected Poems* (2001). *The Best Cigarette* (1997), an audiobook, provides a chance to hear Collins reading thirty-three of his poems. Critical discussion of Collins's work appears in David Baker's *Heresy and the Ideal: On Contemporary Poetry* (2000).

Robert Creeley
The Collected Poems of Robert Creeley 1945–1975 appeared in 1982, *So There: Poems 1976–1983* in 1998, and *Just in Time: Poems 1984–1994* in 2001. A *Selected Poems* was published in 1991. *The Collected Prose* appeared in 1988 and *The Collected Essays* in 1989. Creeley's many volumes of poetry include *The Whip* (1957), *A Form of Women* (1959), *For Love* (1962), *A Day Book* (1970, 1972), *Away* (1976), *Selected Poems* (1976), *Later* (1978), *Echoes* (1982), *Memories* (1984), *Memory Gardens* (1986), *The Company* (1988), *Echoes* (1994), and *Life & Death* (1998). Creeley has also written fiction, including *The Gold Diggers* (1954) and *The Island* (1963). *Contexts of Poetry: Interviews 1961–1971*, edited by Donald Allen (1973), is engaging and valuable, and a new selection of interviews, *Tales Out of School*, appeared in 1993. Many of the essays in Creeley's *Collected Essays* illuminate Creeley's work; the collection also includes important commentary on the work of other poets. Nine volumes of *Charles Olson and Robert Creeley: The Complete Correspondence* have been edited and published by George Butterick (1950–1952) and they constitute a remarkable glimpse into the history of contemporary poetry.

An important critical discussion of Creeley's poetry appears in Sherman Paul, *The Lost America of Love* (1971). Robert von Hallberg, *American Poetry and Culture, 1945–1980* (1985), includes a discussion of Creeley as does Libbie Rifkin's *Career Moves: Olson, Creeley, Zukofsky, Berrigan, and the American Avant-garde* (2000).

James Dickey
Dickey's *Poems 1957–1967* includes selections from *Into the Stone* (1957), *Drowning with Others* (1962), *Helmets* (1964), *Two Poems of the Air* (1964), and *Buckdancer's Choice* (1965). More recent gatherings of work from several volumes appeared as *The Central Motion: Poems 1968–1979* (1983), *The Whole Motion: Collected Poems 1949–1992* (1992), and *The Selected Poems* (1998). Individual collections also include *The Eye-Beaters, Blood, Victory, Madness, Buckhead and Mercy* (1970); *The Zodiac* (1976); *Falling, May Day Sermon, and Other Poems* (1981); *The Early Motion* (1981); *Puella* (1982); and *The Eagle's Mile* (1990).

Dickey's literary criticism and autobiographical collections include *The Suspect in Poetry* (1964), *Babel to Byzantium* (1968), *Self-Interviews* (1970), *Sorties: Journals and New Essays* (1971), and *The Poet Turns on Himself* (1982). A *James Dickey Reader* appeared in 1999 as did an edition of his letters entitled *Crux*, edited by Matthew Bruccoli. His novels *Deliverance* and *Alnilam* were published in 1970 and 1987, respectively. *The Imagination as Glory*, edited by Bruce Weigl and T. R. Hummer (1984), is a collection of critical essays on Dickey's work. Other critical work on Dickey's poetry includes Robert Kirschten's *Struggling for Wings: The Art of James Dickey* (1997) and Henry Hart's *James Dickey: The World as Lie* (2000).

Rita Dove
Dove has published six volumes of poetry: *The Yellow House on the Corner* (1980), *Museum* (1983), *Thomas and Beulah* (1986), *Grace Notes* (1989), *Selected Poems* (1993), *Mother Love* (1995), and *On the Bus with Rosa Parks* (1999). She has also published *Fifth Sunday* (1985), a collection of fiction, a novel, *Through the Ivory Gate* (1992), and a valuable collection of essays, *The Poet's World* (1995). Useful interviews with Dove have appeared in the journal *Contemporary Literature* (1999) and in Janet Mullaney's *Truthtellers of the Times: Interviews with Contemporary Women Poets* (1998). Therese Steffen's critical study *Crossing Color: Transcultural Space and Place in Rita Dove's Poetry, Fiction, and Drama* appeared in 2001.

Robert Duncan
Duncan's poems have not been collected in a single volume, but a number of books gather together poems from his many fugitive pamphlet publications. Robert J. Bertholf's edition of Duncan's *Selected Poems* appeared in 1997; Duncan's own volumes of selected work include *The Years as Catches, First Poems 1939–1941* (1966); *Selected Poems 1942–1950* (1959); *The First Decade: Selected Poems, Vol. 1* (1968); and *Derivations: Selected Poems, 1950–1956*. Duncan's two final volumes of poetry, *Ground Work: Before the War* (1984) and *Ground Work II: In the Dark* (1987) contain many major poems written over a fifteen-year period. Other important books of his poetry are *The Opening of the Field* (1960), *Roots and Branches* (1964), and *Bending the Bow* (1968). Duncan's prose collection, *Fictive Certainties* (1979), is invaluable to a reader of his poems. *A Selected Prose*, edited by Robert J. Bertholf, appeared in 1995.
    Robert Duncan: Scales of the Marvelous (1979) collects essays on Duncan's work from a range of poets and critics. Also important are the discussions of Duncan in Sherman Paul's *The Lost America of Love* (1981) and Robert K. Martin's *The Homosexual Tradition in American Poetry* (1998). Robert J. Bertholf's *Robert Duncan: A Descriptive Bibliography* (1986) is a necessary guide to Duncan's many uncollected writings.

Allen Ginsberg
Ginsberg's *Collected Poems, 1947–1980* appeared in 1984, *White Shroud: Poems, 1980–1985* in 1986, and *Death and Fame: Poems 1993–1997* in 1999. His individual volumes, with the exception of *Empty Mirror* (early poems collected in 1961), have been issued in the now unmistakable City Lights paperbacks. They include *Howl* (1956); *Kaddish and Other Poems, 1958–1960* (1961); *Reality Sandwiches* (1963);

Planet News, 1961–1967 (1968); *The Fall of America, Poems of These States, 1965–1971* (1973); and *Mind Breaths, Poems 1972–1977* (1977). *Cosmopolitan Greetings* appeared in 1995 and a *Selected Poems 1947–1995* in 1996. *Deliberate Prose: Selected Essays, 1952–1995* (2000) is a useful complement to the poetry. Ginsberg published a great number of pages from his journals, dealing with his travels, such as the *Indian Journals* (1970). *Allen Verbatim* (1974) includes transcripts of some of his "lectures on poetry." In 1977 he published *Letters: Early Fifties Early Sixties* (1977) and in 1980 *Composed on the Tongue; Literary Conversations 1967–1977*, edited by Donald Allen. Ginsberg's interviews are collected in *Spontaneous Mind: Selected Interviews, 1958–1996* (2001). Jane Kramer's *Allen Ginsberg in America* (1969) is a brilliant documentary piece on Ginsberg in the 1960s. *On the Poetry of Allen Ginsberg*, edited by Lewis Hyde (1980), is a collection of essays by different hands.

Louise Glück
Glück's *The First Four Books of Poems* (1995), includes all the work from her earlier collections, *First Born* (1969), *The House on Marshland* (1976), *Descending Figure* (1980), and *The Triumph of Achilles* (1985). Later individual volumes are *Ararat* (1990), *The Wild Iris* (1992), *Meadowlands* (1996), *Vita Nova* (1999) and *The Seven Ages* (2001). Her collection of essays, *Proofs and Theories* (1994), is an indispensable companion to reading her work, both for its discussions of poetic vocation and for its description of the autobiographical contexts of specific poems. Critical discussion of Glück's poetry can be found in Upton Lee's *The Muse of Abandonment* (1998).
    Helen Vendler's two collections of essays on poetry, *The Music of What Happens* (1988) and *Soul Says* (1995), include commentary-reviews of Glück's work. Elizabeth Dodd's *The Veiled Mirror and The Woman Poet: H. D., Louise Bogan, Elizabeth Bishop and Louise Glück* (1992) contains a chapter on Glück.

Jorie Graham
The Dream of the Unified Field: Selected Poems 1974–1994 (1995) brings together poems from *Hybrids of Plants and of Ghosts* (1980), *Erosion* (1983), *The End of Beauty* (1987), *Region of Unlikeness* (1991), and *Materialism* (1993). Graham's more recent collections include *The Errancy* (1997) and *Swarm* (2000). She edited *Earth Took of Earth: 100 Great Poems of the English Language* (1996). Critical discussion of Graham's work can be found in Helen Vendler's *The Given and the Made* (1995) and *Soul Says* (1995), James Longenbach's *Modern Poetry after Modernism* (1997), and Thomas Gardner's *Regions of Unlikeness: Explaining Contemporary Poetry* (1999). An extremely useful interview with Graham appears in *Denver Quarterly* (1992).

Joy Harjo

Harjo's collections of poetry include two chapbooks, *The Last Song* (1975) and *What Moon Drove Me to This* (1979), and the volumes *She Had Some Horses* (1983), *In Mad Love and War* (1990), *The Woman Who Fell from the Sky* (1996), and *A Map to the Next World* (2000). In *Secrets from the Center of the World* (1989), she wrote the text to accompany Steven Strom's photographs of the particulars of the southwestern landscape. She has also edited an anthology of native women's writing, *Reinventing the Enemy's Language: Contemporary Native Women's Writing of North America* (1997). *Furious Light* (1990), a sound recording, provides the opportunity to hear Harjo reading from her poems.

Laura Coltelli has edited a valuable collection of interviews with Harjo, *The Spiral of Memory* (1990). Commentary on the contexts of Harjo's work appears in Paula Gunn Allen's *The Sacred Hoop: Recovering the Feminine in American Indian Traditions* (1986) and Norma Wilson's *The Nature of Native American Poetry* (2001).

Michael S. Harper

Harper's poems appear in *Dear John, Dear Coltrane* (1970); *History Is Your Own Heartbeat* (1971); *Photographs: Negatives: History as Apple Tree* (1972); *Song: I Want a Witness* (1972); *Nightmare Begins Responsibility* (1974); *Images of Kin: New and Selected Poems* (1977); *Healing Song for the Inner Ear* (1984); and *Honorable Amendments* (1995). An edition of new and collected poems, *Songlines in Michaeltree* appeared in 2000. Harper also edited (with Robert Stepto) a collection of African American literature, art, and scholarship, *Chants of Saints* (1976) and *The Vintage Book of African American Poetry* (2000). A conversation about Harper's work can be found in Joanne Gabbin's edited *The Furious Flowering of African American Poetry* (1999).

Robert Hayden

Hayden's *Collected Poems* appeared in 1985; his *Collected Prose* appeared the previous year. Both were edited by Frederick Glaysher. Fred M. Fetrow's *Robert Hayden* (1984) is a critical study of Hayden's work. Essays on Hayden's work appear in the journals *Antioch Review* (1997) and *MELUS* (1998).

Randall Jarrell

Jarrell's *Complete Poems* were published in 1969 and a *Selected Poems* appeared in 1991. A selection of Jarrell's brilliant critical essays is available in *No Other Book* (1999), edited by Brad Leithauser. His novel satirizing American academic life, *Pictures from an Institution,* appeared in 1954. Some of the most valuable commentary on Jarrell's life and work is to be found in a memorial volume of essays edited by Robert Lowell, Peter Taylor, and Robert Penn Warren, *Randall Jarrell, 1914–1965* (1967). William Pritchard's fine *Randall Jarrell: A Literary Life* (1990) illumines both Jarrell's life and his work as does Mary Randall's *Remembering Randall* (1999). Critical discussion of Jarrell's work appears in Thomas Travisano's *Midcentury Quartet* (1999).

Galway Kinnell

Kinnell's *A New Selected Poems* appeared in 2000. Earlier collected volumes of his work were *First Poems 1946–1954* (1970), *The Avenue Bearing the Initial of Christ into the New World: Poems, 1946–1964* (1974), and *Selected Poems* (1982). Important individual volumes of Kinnell's poetry are *What a Kingdom It Was* (1960), *The Book of Nightmares* (1971), *Mortal Acts, Mortal Words* (1980), *The Past* (1985), *When One Has Lived a Long Time Alone* (1990), and *Imperfect Thirst* (1994). He has also published a collection of criticism, *The Poetics of the Physical World* (1969), and selected interviews, *Walking Down the Stairs,* edited by Donald Hall (1978). *Critical Essays on Galway Kinnell* (1996), edited by Nancy Tuten, and David Baker's *Heresy and the Ideal: On Contemporary Poetry* (2000) contain useful critical discussions.

Stanley Kunitz

Kunitz's *Collected Poems* (2000) gathers work from *Passing Through: The Later Poems, New and Selected* (1995), *Next-to-Last Things: New Poems and Essays* (1985), *The Poems of Stanley Kunitz, 1928–1978* (1979), *The Testing Tree* (1971), *Selected Poems, 1928–1958* (1958), *Passport to War* (1940), and *Intellectual Things* (1930). *A Kind of Order, A Kind of Folly* (1975) collects Kunitz's essays and interviews. An important example of his translations is *Poems of Akhmatova* (1973). Gregory Orr's *Stanley Kunitz: An Introduction to the Poetry* (1985) and *A Celebration for Stanley Kunitz on His Eightieth Birthday* (1986), a gathering of essays by various hands, offer critical discussion of Kunitz's work.

Li-Young Lee

Lee's volumes of poetry are *Rose* (1986), *The City in Which I Love You* (1990), and *A Book of My Nights* (2001). A memoir, *The Winged Seed,* appeared in 1995. Gerald Stern's foreword to *Rose* provides useful biographical material about Lee's family. Available on videotape, as part of the series *The Power of the Word,* is "Voices of Memory," in which Bill Moyers conducts a valuable interview with Lee and Lee reads from and talks about his poetry. An interview with Lee also appears in *Words Matter: Conversations with Asian American Writers* (2000), edited by King-Kok Cheung.

Denise Levertov

Some of Levertov's poems have been collected in *Collected Earlier Poems 1940–1960* (1979) and *Poems 1960–1967* (1983). Her individual volumes include *The Double Image* (1946), *Here and Now* (1957), *Overland to the Islands* (1958),

With Eyes at the Back of Our Heads (1960), The Jacob's Ladder (1962), O Taste and See (1964), The Sorrow Dance (1967), Relearning the Alphabet (1970), To Stay Alive (1971), Footprints (1972), The Freedom of the Dust (1973), Life in the Forest (1978), Candles in Babylon (1982), Oblique Prayers (1984), Breathing the Water (1987), A Door in the Hive (1989), Evening Train (1992), Tesserae (1995), and The Great Unknowing: Last Poems (1999). The Poet in the World (1973) and Light Up the Cave (1981) include essays on her own work, memoirs, reviews of other poets, and some theoretical essays. A New and Selected Essays appeared in 1992. Conversations with Denise Levertov (1998) is a collection of interviews. James E. Breslin's From Modern to Contemporary: American Poetry 1945–1965 (1984) contains a useful discussion of Levertov, Linda Wagner-Martin has edited Critical Essays on Denise Levertov (1990), and Anne Little edited Denise Levertov: New Perspectives (2000).

Philip Levine

Levine's New Selected Poems (1991) gathers together work from many of his volumes of poetry, including Not This Pig (1968), Pili's Wall (1971), They Feed They Lion (1972), 1933 (1974), The Names of the Lost (1976), 7 Years from Somewhere (1979), Ashes: Poems New and Old (1979), One for the Rose (1981), Sweet Will (1985), and A Walk with Tom Jefferson (1988). He has also published What Work Is (1991), The Simple Truth (1994), and The Mercy (1999). A memoir, The Bread to Time: Toward an Autobiography, appeared in 1994. His translations from the Spanish are available in Tarumba: The Selected Poems of Jaime Sabines (with Ernest Trejo, 1979) and Off the Map: Selected Writings of Gloria Fuertes (with Ada Long, 1984). A collection of Levine's interviews, Don't Ask, appeared in 1981. Christopher Buckley's On the Poetry of Philip Levine appeared in 1991, and Edward Hirsch's "The Visionary Poetics of Philip Levine and Charles Wright" appears in The Columbia History of American Poetry (1993). David St. John's Where Angels Come Toward Us (1995) contains discussion of Levine's work.

Audre Lorde

The Collected Poems of Audre Lorde (1997) brings together Lorde's poetry from Cables to Rage (1970), New York Head Shop and Museum (1975), The Black Unicorn (1978), and Our Dead Behind Us (1986). A collection of essays and speeches, Sister Outsider (1984), provides a powerful context for reading her work. Her autobiographical writing includes The Cancer Journals (1980) and Zami: A New Spelling of My Name (1982). Critical studies of Lorde's work appear in Black Women Writers, edited by Mari Evans (1984), and Cassie Steele's We Heal From Memory: Sexton, Lorde, Anzaldúa and the Poetry of Witness (2000). An interview with Lorde appears in Women Writers at Work (1998), edited by George Plimpton.

Robert Lowell

In 1976, the year before his death, Robert Lowell prepared his Selected Poems, which drew on all his volumes of poetry except Day by Day, which appeared in 1977. The interested reader will still have to look back to individual volumes, because Lowell frequently revised his poems and could print only a small proportion of his work in Selected Poems. His earlier books of verse include Lord Weary's Castle (1946), The Mills of the Kavanaughs (1951), Life Studies (1959), Imitations (1961), For the Union Dead (1964), Near the Ocean (1967), Notebook (1969; rev. and exp. 1970), The Dolphin (1973), For Lizzie and Harriet (1973), and History (1973). For the stage Lowell prepared adaptations of Racine's Phaedra (1961) and Aeschylus's Prometheus Bound (1969) as well as versions of Hawthorne and Melville stories grouped under the title The Old Glory (1965). His Collected Prose, which appeared in 1987, is an indispensable companion to Lowell's poetry and contains valuable essays on the work of other writers. Among the many useful critical works on Lowell are Stephen Yenser's Circle to Circle (1975), Steven Axelrod's Robert Lowell: Life and Art (1978), and Thomas Travisano's Midcentury Quartet (1999). Robert Lowell: A Collection of Critical Essays, edited by Thomas Parkinson (1968), includes an important interview with the poet and The Critical Response to Robert Lowell (1999), edited by Steven Gould Axelrod, provides an overview of criticism on the work. A partial bibliography of Lowell's work can be found in Jerome Mazzaro's The Achievement of Robert Lowell, 1939–1959 (1960). Ian Hamilton's biography, Robert Lowell, appeared in 1982.

James Merrill

An edition of Merrill's Collected Poems (2001), edited by J. D. McClatchy and Stephen Yenser, brings together the poems from all of Merrill's books, with the exception of his book-length epic, The Changing Light at Sandover (1982). A collection of his prose, Recitative, appeared in 1986, and a charming memoir, A Different Person, in 1993. Merrill also wrote two novels, The Seraglio (1957) and The (Diblos) Notebook (1965). Among useful critical essays are David Kalstone's Five Temperaments (1977), those in James Merrill: Essays in Criticism (1983), edited by Lehman and Berger, and Critical Essays on James Merrill (1996), edited by Guy Rotella. Stephen Yenser's book-length study of Merrill's work, The Consuming Myth (1987), is invaluable. More recent critical work includes Timothy Materer's James Merrill's Apocalypse (2000) and Rachel Hadas's Merrill, Cavafy, Poems and Dreams (2000).

W. S. Merwin

Merwin's Collected Poems appeared in 1988, as did his volume The Rain in the Trees. Collected Poems gathers together work from many important individual volumes, including The Drunk in the Furnace (1960), The Moving Target (1963), The Lice (1967), The Carrier of Ladders (1970), Writings to an Unfinished Accompaniment (1974), and The Compass Flower (1977). The Miner's Pale Children (1970) is an important prose collection. Merwin's more recent collections of poems are Travels (1992), The Vixen (1997), The River Sound (1999), and The Pupil (2001).

Merwin also published an autobiographical prose collection, Unframed Original (1982), and Regions of Memory (1987), which combines memoir and commentary on the work of poetry. A book-length poem Folding Cliffs: A Narrative (1998) is a chronicle of nineteenth-century Hawaii. Various critical essays on Merwin's work are gathered together in W. S. Merwin: Essays on the Poetry (1987), edited by Cary Nelson and Ed Folsom. A valuable book-length study of Merwin's poetry is Edward J. Brunner's Poetry as Labor and as Privilege (1991). Also useful is Jane Frazier's From Origin to Ecology: Nature and the Poetry of W. S. Merwin (1999).

Lorine Niedecker

Niedecker's work is most readily available in The Granite Pail (1985), a selection of her poems edited by Cid Corman. This volume draws from Niedecker's books no longer in print: New Goose (1946), My Friend Tree (1961), My Life by Water (1969), North Central (1969), and Blue Chicory (1975). A collection of her complete writing, From This Condensary, edited by Robert J. Bertholf, appeared in 1985. Niedecker's letters to Cid Corman between 1960 and 1970 have been published as Between Your House and Mine (1986), edited by Lisa Pater Faranda, and they provide an engaging and informative sense of the writer and her work, as does the more recently published Niedecker and the Correspondence with Zukofsky, 1931–1970 (1993), by Jenny Penberthy. Critical commentary on Niedecker appears in The Objectivist Nexus (1999), edited by Rachel Blau DuPlessis and Peter Quartermain.

Frank O'Hara

The Collected Poems of Frank O'Hara was published in 1971. It has since been supplemented by two volumes: Early Poems (1977) and Poems Retrieved (1977). O'Hara's critical articles and other prose can be found in Art Chronicles 1954–1966 (1975), Standing Still and Walking in New York (1975), and In Memory of my Feelings: Frank O'Hara on American Art (1999), edited by Russell Ferguson. David Lehman's The Last Avant-garde: The Making of the New York School of Poets (1998) provides valuable contexts for O'Hara's work. An informative critical study is Marjorie Perloff's Frank O'Hara: Poet among Painters (1977). Also useful is Mutlu Konuk Blasing's Politics and Form in Postmodern Poetry (1995).

Mary Oliver

Oliver's Pulitzer Prize–winning New and Selected Poems (1992) contains selections from her earlier volumes, No Voyage and Other Poems (1963 and 1965), The River Styx, Ohio and Other Poems (1972), Sleeping in the Forest and The Night Traveler (both 1978), Twelve Moons (1979), American Primitive (1983), Dream Work (1986), House of Light (1990), as well as newer work. Later individual collections include White Pine: Poems and Prose Poems (1994), Blue Pastures (1995), West Wind (1997), Winter Hours: Prose, Prose Poems and Poems (1999), and The Leaf and the Cloud (2000). Oliver also wrote a guide to poetry, A Poetry Handbook (1994). Critical discussion of Oliver's work appears in Language and Liberation (1999), by Christina Hendricks.

Charles Olson

The best single introduction to Olson is Robert Creeley's Selected Writings of Charles Olson (1967). A complete edition of The Maximus Poems, edited by George F. Butterick, appeared in 1983. The Collected Poems, edited by George Butterick, appeared in 1987. Among Olson's many works of prose are his study of Melville, Call Me Ishmael (1947); Mayan Letters (1953); and a two-volume collection of his lectures and interviews, Mathologos (1976–79), edited by George F. Butterick. An edition of Olson's Collected Prose, edited by Donald Allen, appeared in 1997.

The seven volumes of Charles Olson and Robert Creeley: The Complete Correspondence (1980–86), edited by Butterick, provide as extensive a discussion of life and poetry as we are ever likely to see. Among the critical studies of Olson's poetry, some of the most useful are Ed Dorn's What I See in the Maximus Poems (1960); Sherman Paul's Olson's Push (1978); Robert von Hallberg's Charles Olson: The Scholar's Art (1978); and Stephen Fredman's The Grounding of American Poetry: Charles Olson and the Emersonian Tradition (1993). For any reader of the Maximus Poems, Butterick's A Guide to the Maximus Poems (1981) is indispensable. Various "Charles Olson Issues" appeared in the journal Boundary 2 (1973–74).

George Oppen

Oppen's Collected Poems (1975) includes all of the work from his earlier volumes, Discrete Series (1932–34), The Materials (1962), This in Which (1965), Of Being Numerous (1968), and Seascape: Needle's Eye (1972) as well as Myth of the Blaze (new poems, 1972–75). In 1978 Primitive appeared, Oppen's last collection of new poems.

George Oppen: Man and Poet (1981), edited by Burton Hatlen, gathers together valuable essays on Oppen's work and includes an interview with George and Mary Oppen. The volume also contains extensive bibliographical material. *The Selected Letters of George Oppen* (1990), edited by Rachel Blau DuPlessis, provides important access to Oppen's critical and aesthetic thinking.

Simon J. Ortiz

Ortiz published *Naked in the Wind* (1970); *Going for Rain* (1976); *A Good Journey* (1977); *Song, Poetry, Language* (1978); *From Sand Creek: Rising in This Heart Which Is Our America* (1981); *A Poem Is a Journey* (1981); and *After and before Lightning* (1994). His work has been gathered together in the volume *Woven Stone* (1992). Three collections of his short stories have also appeared: *Howbah Indians* (1978), *Fightin': New and Collected Stories* (1983), and *Men on the Moon: Collected Short Stories* (1999). He also edited two collections, *These Hearts, These Poems* (1984) and *Speaking for the Generations: Native Writers on Writing* (1998). A discussion of Ortiz's poetry appears in Kenneth Lincoln's *Native American Renaissance* (1983) and in Lucy Maddox's "Native American Poetry" in *The Columbia History of American Poetry* (1993).

Robert Pinsky

Pinsky's *The Figured Wheel: New and Collected Poems 1966–1996* (1996) gathers work from *Sadness and Happiness* (1975), *An Explanation of America* (1980), *History of My Heart* (1984), and *The Want Bone* (1990), as well as presenting new poems and selections from his translations. His collection *Jersey Rain* appeared in 2000. He has published two book-length translations, the prize-winning *The Inferno of Dante: A New Verse Translation* (1994) and, together with Robert Hass, a translation of the Polish poet Czeslaw Milosz's *The Separate Notebook* (1984). Pinsky's work also includes two volumes of criticism that are valuable in illuminating his own work as well as that of the writers he discusses; *The Situation of Poetry: Contemporary Poetry and Its Traditions* (1975) and *Poetry and the World* (1988). He is also the author of *The Sounds of Poetry* (1998). Pinsky edited the collection *America's Favorite Poems* (1999).

Sylvia Plath

Plath's books of poetry include *The Colossus and Other Poems* (1962), *Ariel* (1966), *Crossing the Water* (1971), and *Winter Trees* (1972). Her novel *The Bell Jar* was first published in England in 1963. Plath's mother, Aurelia Schober Plath, selected and edited the useful *Letters Home: Correspondence 1950–63* (1975). Ted Hughes and Frances McCullough edited an abridged version of *The Journals of Sylvia Plath* (1983) and Karen Kukil edited *The Unabridged Journals*

of Sylvia Plath, 1950–1962 (2000). There are a number of biographical and critical studies of Plath's work. Among them are Judith Kroll's *Chapters in a Mythology* (1976), Anne Stevenson's *Bitter Fame: The Undiscovered Life of Sylvia Plath* (1988), Linda Wagner-Martin's *Sylvia Plath: A Biography* (1987), Jacqueline Rose's *The Haunting of Sylvia Plath* (1993), Diane Middlebrook's *Sylvia Plath* (1998), and Christina Britzolakis's *Sylvia Plath and the Theatre of Mourning* (1999).

Adrienne Rich

A convenient starting point is *The Fact of a Doorframe: Poems Selected and New 1950–1984* (1984), which draws poems from Rich's earlier books: *A Change of World* (1951), *The Diamond Cutters* (1955), *Snapshots of a Daughter-in-Law* (1963), *Necessities of Life* (1966), *Leaflets* (1969), *The Will to Change* (1971), *Diving into the Wreck* (1973), *The Dream of a Common Language* (1978), and *A Wild Patience Has Taken Me This Far* (1981). Since the publication of this selection, Rich has published *Your Native Land, Your Life* (1986); *Time's Power: Poems 1985–1988* (1989); *An Atlas of the Difficult World: Poems 1988–1991* (1991); *Dark Fields of the Republic: Poems 1991–1995* (1995); *Midnight Salvage: Poems 1995–1998* (1999); and *Fox: Poems 1998–2000* (2001). Four valuable collections gather together Rich's essays, lectures, and speeches: *On Lies, Secrets, and Silence* (1979); *Blood, Bread, and Poetry* (1986); *What Is Found There?: Notebooks on Poetry and Politics* (1993); and *Arts of the Possible* (2001). Rich is also the author of an important study, *Of Woman Born: Motherhood as Experience and Institution* (1976).

Valuable critical essays and an interview appear in *Adrienne Rich's Poetry* (1975), edited by Barbara Charlesworth Gelpi and Albert Gelpi. Other studies are *Reading Adrienne Rich* (1984), edited by Jane Roberta Cooper; Paula Bennett's *My Life, a Loaded Gun: Female Creativity and Feminist Poetics* (1986); Margaret Dickie's *Stein, Bishop and Rich: Lyrics of Love, War & Place* (1997); and Molly McQuade's *By Herself: Women Reclaim Poetry* (2000).

Alberto Ríos

Ríos has published several collections of poetry: *Whispering to Fool the Wind* (1982), *Five Indiscretions* (1985), *The Dime Orchard Woman* (1988), and *Teodora Luna's Two Kisses* (1992). He has also published collections of short stories, *The Iguana Killer* (1984) and *The Curtain of Trees* (1999). A memoir titled *Capirodata: A Nogales Memoir* appeared in 1999. A discussion of Ríos's work and the larger contexts of Latino poetry appears in Cordelia Candelaria, *Chicano Poetry: A Critical Introduction* (1986). An interview with Ríos can be found in *Americas Review* (1996).

Theodore Roethke

The Collected Poems of Theodore Roethke was published in 1966. Useful comments on poetic tradition and his own poetic practice are to be found in several collections of Roethke's prose: *On the Poet and His Craft: Selected Prose of Theodore Roethke* (1965), edited by Ralph J. Mills Jr.; *Straw for the Fire: From the Notebooks of Theodore Roethke, 1948–63* (1972), edited by David Wagoner; and *The Selected Letters of Theodore Roethke* (1970), edited by Mills. Among the useful studies of Roethke's work are *Theodore Roethke: Essays on the Poetry* (1965), edited by Arnold Stein, and Laurence Lieberman's *Beyond the Muse of Memory: Essays on Contemporary Poets* (1995). Allan Seager's *The Glass House* (1968) contains useful biographical material. Lea Baechler's essay "John Berryman, Theodore Roethke, and the Elegy" appears in *The Columbia History of American Poetry* (1993).

Anne Sexton

Sexton's books of poems include *To Bedlam and Part Way Back* (1960), *All My Pretty Ones* (1962), *Live or Die* (1966), *Love Poems* (1969), *Transformations* (1971), *The Book of Folly* (1973), *The Death Notebooks* (1974), and *The Awful Rowing toward God* (1975). A *Complete Poems* appeared in 1981 and a *Selected Poems*, edited and introduced by Diane Wood Middlebrook, in 1988. Middlebrook's biography, *Anne Sexton* (1991), and *A Self-Portrait in Letters* (1977) give useful biographical material. Important interviews and critical essays are to be found in J. D. McClatchy's *Anne Sexton: The Artist and Her Critics* (1978) and Diane Hume George's *Sexton: Selected Criticism* (1988). An interview with Sexton appears in *Women Writers at Work* (1998), edited by George Plimpton.

Charles Simic

Simic's collections include *Night Picnic* (2001), *Jackstraws* (1999), *Walking the Black Cat* (1996), *A Wedding in Hell* (1994), *Hotel Insomnia* (1992), *The Book of Gods and Devils* (1990), and *Unending Blues* (1986). *Selected Poems 1963–1983* (1990) gathers together much of his earlier work in a single volume. A book of prose poems, *The World Doesn't End*, appeared in 1990. He has published several volumes of essays and memoirs, which provide valuable contexts for reading his poetry; among these are *A Fly in the Soup: Memoirs* (2001), *The Orphan Factory: Essays and Memoirs* (1998), *The Unemployed Fortune Teller: Essays and Memoirs* (1994), *Wonderful Words, Silent Truths: Essays* (1990), and *The Uncertain Certainty: Interviews, Essays and Notes on Poetry* (1985). An example of Simic's work as a translator is Vasko Popa's *Homage to the Lame Wolf: Selected Poems 1956–1975* (1979). Critical discussions of Simic's poetry can be found in Bruce Weigl's *Charles Simic: Essays on the Poetry* (1996) and

Peter Stitt's *Uncertainty and Plentitude: Five Contemporary Poets* (1997).

Gary Snyder

Snyder's poems have been published by several different presses, often with duplication of poems. *Riprap*, originally published in 1959, is most easily obtained in *Riprap and Cold Mountain Poems* (1965, 1991). *Myths and Texts* first appeared in 1960. *The Blue Sky* first appeared in 1969 and reappeared in *Six Sections of Mountains and Rivers without End plus One* (1970). Other volumes include *The Back Country* (1968), *Regarding Wave* (1970), *Turtle Island* (1974), *Axe Handles* (1983), *Left Out in the Rain: New Poems 1947–1985* (1986), and *No Nature: New and Selected Poems* (1992). In 1996 Snyder published the completion of his *Mountains and Rivers without End*. He has also published important prose collections dealing with ecology, *Earth House Hold* (1969) and *A Place in Space: Ethics, Aesthetics and Watershed* (1995). A gathering of Snyder's prose and poetry appears in *The Gary Snyder Reader* (1999). Helpful critical discussion of Synder's work can be found in Sherman Paul's *In Search of the Primitive* (1986) and Patrick Murphy's *A Place for Wayfaring: The Poetry and Prose of Gary Snyder* (2000). An interview with Snyder appears in *Paris Review* (141, 1996).

Cathy Song

Song published *Picture Bride* (1983), *Frameless Windows, Squares of Light* (1988), *School Figures* (1994), and *The Land of Bliss* (2000). Discussion of Song's work appears in *Conversations and Contestations* (2000) edited by Ruth Hsu and Cynthia Franklin.

Robert Penn Warren

An edition of Warren's *Collected Poems*, edited by John Burt, appeared in 1998. It includes work from Warren's individual volumes: *Incarnations* (1968), *Audubon: A Vision* (1969), *Or Else: Poem/Poems 1968–1974, Now and Then* (1978), *Being Here* (1980), *Rumor Verified* (1981), *Chief Joseph of the Nez Perce* (1983), and *New and Selected Poems 1925–1985* (1985). Burt has also edited a volume of Warren's *Selected Poems* (2001). His best-known novels are *All the King's Men* (1946) and *World Enough and Time* (1950). His Thomas Jefferson lectures, *Democracy and Poetry*, appeared in 1975. Also available is a collection of interviews, *Robert Penn Warren Talking* (1980), edited by Floyd Watkins and John Tiers. The best critical studies of Warren's poetry are Calvin Bedient's *In the Heart's Last Kingdom* (1986), James H. Justus's *The Achievement of Robert Penn Warren* (1981), and Victor Stranberg's *The Poetic Vision of Robert Penn Warren*. More recent critical studies include Lesa Carnes Corrigan's *Poem of Pure Imagination: Robert Penn Warren and the Romantic Tradition* (1999) and *The Leg-*

acy of *Robert Penn Warren* (2000), edited by David Madden, which gathers essays from various hands.

Richard Wilbur

Wilbur's *New and Collected Poems* appeared in 1989 and draws from *The Beautiful Changes* (1947); *Ceremony and Other Poems* (1950); *Things of This World* (1956); *Advice to a Prophet* (1961); *Walking to Sleep* (1969); and *The Mind-Reader* (1976). A collection of new poems and translations, *Mayflies,* appeared in 2000. His translations from Molière include *The Misanthrope* (1955); *Tartuffe* (1963); and *Molière: Four Comedies* (1982). He has also published *Responses* (1976), and *The Catbird's Song* (1997), a collection of prose pieces. Critical discussion of his work can be found in *Richard Wilbur's Creation* (1983), edited by Wendy Salinger, and *Ecstasy Within Discipline: The Poetry of Richard Wilbur* (1995), by John B Hougen. An essay on Wilbur's new work, by Lee Oser, appears in the journal *Literary Imagination* (2000). A collection of interviews, *Conversations with Richard Wilbur,* edited by William Butts, appeared in 1990.

Charles Wright

Negative Blue: Selected Later Poems (2000) brings together Wright's work from *Appalachia* (1998), *Black Zodiac* (1997), and *Chickamauga* (1996). *The World of the Ten thousand Things: Poems 1980–1990* (1990) includes work from *The Southern Cross* (1981), *The Other Side of the River* (1984), *Zone Journals* (1988), and *Xionia* (1990). *Country Music: Selected Early Poems* includes poems from *China Trace* (1977), *Bloodlines* (1975), *Hard Freight* (1973), and *The Grave of the Right Hand* (1970). Wright's translation of Eugenio Montale's *The Storm and Other Poems* appeared in 1978. Some of Wright's essays and interviews are gathered in *Quarter Notes* (1995) and *Halflife* (1988). *The Point Where All Things Meet: Essays on Charles Wright* (1995), edited by Tom Andrews, offers a variety of valuable perspectives on Wright's work. An interview with Wright appears in the journal *Literary Imagination* (2000).

James Wright

A collection of Wright's complete poems, *Above the River,* appeared in 1990 and includes the work of his individual volumes: *The Green Wall* (1956), *Saint Judas* (1963), *Shall We Gather at the River* (1968), the lovely *Moments of the Italian Summer* (1976), *To a Blossoming Pear Tree* (1977), and *This Journey* (1982). An edition of his *Collected Prose,* edited by Anne Wright, appeared in 1983. Some of Wright's translations from the Spanish and German are available in *Twenty Poems of Georg Trakl* (1963), *Twenty Poems of César Vallejo* (1964), and *Twenty Poems of Pablo Neruda* (with Robert Bly, 1968). The best critical discussions of Wright's work appear in the essays collected in *The Pure Clear Word: Essays on the Poetry of James Wright* (1982), edited by Dave Smith, and in Laurence Lieberman's *Beyond the Muse of Memory* (1995).

Lorna Dee Cervantes: "Uncle's First Rabbit," "For Virginia Chavez," and "Visions of Mexico While at a Writing Symposium in Port Townsend, Washington" from EMPLUMADA by Lorna Dee Cervantes, by permission of the University of Pittsburgh Press. Copyright © 1981 by Lorna Dee Cervantes. "The Body as Braille" by Lorna Dee Cervantes is reprinted with permission from the publisher of THE AMERICAS REVIEW (Houston: Arte Público Press-University of Houston, 1978).

John Cheever: "The Swimmer" from THE STORIES OF JOHN CHEEVER by John Cheever. First published in *The New Yorker*. Copyright © 1978 by John Cheever. Copyright © 2000 by Mary Cheever. Used by permission of Alfred A. Knopf, a division of Random House, Inc., and The Wylie Agency.

Sandra Cisneros: "My Lucy Friend Who Smells Like Corn," "Barbie Q.," and "Mericans" from WOMAN HOLLERING CREEK. Copyright © 1991 by Sandra Cisneros. Published by Vintage Books, a division of Random House, Inc., New York, and originally in hardcover by Random House, Inc. Reprinted by permission of Susan Bergholz Literary Services, New York. All rights reserved.

Billy Collins: "Forgetfulness" from QUESTIONS ABOUT ANGELS by Billy Collins, copyright © 1991. Reprinted by permission of the University of Pittsburgh Press and the author. "Osso Bucco" and "Tuesday, June 4, 1991" from THE ART OF DROWNING by Billy Collins, copyright © 1995. Reprinted by permission of the University of Pittsburgh Press. "I Chop Some Parsley While Listening to Art Blakey's Version of 'Three Blind Mice'" and "The Night House" from PICNIC, LIGHTNING by Billy Collins, copyright © 1998. Reprinted by permission of the University of Pittsburgh Press.

Robert Creeley: "I Know a Man," "Kore," "The Door," "For Love," "The Messengers," and "The Birds" from COLLECTED POEMS OF ROBERT CREELEY, 1945–1975. Copyright © 1983 The Regents of the University of California. Reprinted by permission of the University of California Press and The Regents of the University of California. "Fathers" from MEMORY GARDENS by Robert Creeley. Copyright © 1986 by Robert Creeley. Reprinted by permission of New Directions Publishing Corporation and Marion Boyars Publishers Ltd.

James Dickey: "Drowning with Others" and "The Heaven of Animals" from DROWNING WITH OTHERS. Copyright © 1962 by James Dickey. "Falling" from FALLING. Copyright © 1982 by James Dickey. Used by permission of Wesleyan University Press

Stephen Dixon: Excerpt from TIME TO GO, pages 142–56. Copyright © 1984 by The Johns Hopkins University Press. Reprinted by permission of The Johns Hopkins University Press.

Rita Dove: "Geometry," "Adolescence—I," and "Adolescence—II," and "Adolescence—III" from THE YELLOW HOUSE ON THE CORNER, © 1980 by Rita Dove. "The Event," "Straw Hat," "The Zeppelin Factory," and "Dusting" from THOMAS AND BEULAH, © 1986 by Rita Dove. "Banneker" and "Parsley" from MUSEUM, © 1983 by Rita Dove. All originally published by Carnegie-Mellon University Press and reprinted by permission of the author. "Poem in Which I Refuse Contemplation" from GRACE NOTES by Rita Dove. Copyright © 1989 by Rita Dove. "Missing" and "Heroes" from MOTHER LOVE by Rita Dove. Copyright © 1995 by Rita Dove. "Rosa" from ON THE BUS WITH ROSA PARKS by Rita Dove. Copyright © 1999 by Rita Dove. Used by permission of the author and W. W. Norton & Company, Inc.

Robert Duncan: "Often I Am Permitted to Return to a Meadow" and "A Poem Beginning with a Line by Pindar" from THE OPENING OF THE FIELD by Robert Duncan. Copyright © 1960 by Robert Duncan. "Achilles' Song" and "Interrupted Forms" from GROUND WORK: BEFORE THE WAR by Robert Duncan. Copyright © 1984 by Robert Duncan. Reprinted by permission of New Directions Publishing Corporation.

Ralph Ellison: "Prologue" and "Chapter 1" from INVISIBLE MAN by Ralph Ellison. Copyright 1952 by Ralph Ellison. Reprinted by permission of Random House, Inc. "Cadillac Flambé" by Ralph Ellison. Copyright © 1973 by Ralph Ellison. Reprinted by permission of William Morris Agency, Inc., on behalf of the Estate of Ralph Ellison.

Louise Erdrich: "Fleur" by Louise Erdrich first appeared in *Esquire* and later in TRACKS. Copyright © 1986 by Louise Erdrich. Reprinted with permission of the Wylie Agency.

Allen Ginsberg: "Howl," "A Supermarket in California," and "Sunflower Sutra" copyright © 1955 by Allen Ginsberg. "To Aunt Rose" copyright © 1958 by Allen Ginsberg; "On Burrough's Work" copyright © 1954 by Allen Ginsberg; "Ego Confession" copyright © 1974 by Allen Ginsberg. All from COLLECTED POEMS 1947–1980 by Allen Ginsberg. Copyright © 1984 by Allen Ginsberg. Reprinted by permission of HarperCollins Publishers, Inc., and Penguin Books Ltd.

Diane Glancy: "Jack Wilson or Wovoka and Christ My Lord" and "Polar Breath" (pages 11–17 and 99–105) from FIRESTICKS by Diane Glancy. Reprinted by permission of the publisher, University of Oklahoma Press. Copyright © 1993 by Diane Glancy. All rights reserved.

Louise Glück: "The Drowned Children" and "Illuminations" in DESCENDING FIGURE from THE FIRST FOUR BOOKS OF POEMS by Louise Glück. Copyright © 1968, 1971, 1972, 1973, 1974, 1975, 1976, 1977, 1978, 1979, 1980, 1985, 1995 by Louise Glück. "2. The Sick Child" and "3. For My Sister" from "Descending Figure" in DESCENDING FIGURE from THE FIRST FOUR BOOKS OF POEMS by Louise Glück. Copyright © 1968, 1971, 1972, 1973, 1974, 1975, 1976, 1977, 1978, 1979, 1980, 1985, 1995 by Louise Glück. Reprinted by permission of HarperCollins Publishers, Inc., and Carcanet Press Ltd. "Terminal Resemblances" and "Appearances" from ARARAT by Louise Glück. Copyright © 1990 by Louise Glück. "Vespers" from page 37 of THE WILD IRIS by Louise Glück. Copyright © 1993 by Louise Glück. Reprinted by permission of HarperCollins Publishers, Inc.

Jorie Graham: "The Dream of the Unified Field," "At Luca Signorelli's Resurrection of the Body," and "The Geese" from THE DREAM OF THE UNIFIED FIELD: POEMS 1974–1994 by Jorie Graham. Copyright © 1995 by Jorie Graham. Reprinted by permission of HarperCollins Publishers, Inc. and Carcanet Press Ltd.

Barry Hannah: "Midnight and I'm Not Famous Yet" from AIRSHIPS by Barry Hannah. Copyright © 1978 by Barry Hannah. Reprinted by permission of Alfred A. Knopf, a division of Random House, Inc., and The Wallace Literary Agency, Inc.

Joy Harjo: "Call It Fear" and "White Bear" from SHE HAD SOME HORSES by Joy Harjo. Copyright © 1983, 1997 Thunder's Mouth Press. Appears by permission of the publisher, Thunder's Mouth Press. "Summer Night" from IN MAD LOVE AND WAR. Copyright © 1990 by Joy Harjo. Reprinted by permission of Wesleyan University Press. "The Flood" from THE WOMAN WHO FELL FROM THE SKY by Joy Harjo. Copyright © 1994 by Joy Harjo. Reprinted by permission of W. W. Norton & Company, Inc., and the author.

Michael S. Harper: "Martin's Blues," "*Bird Lives*: Charles Parker in St. Louis," and "Nightmare Begins Responsibility" from SONGLINES IN MICHAELTREE: NEW AND COLLECTED POEMS by Michael S. Harper. Copyright © 2000 by Michael S. Harper. "Dear John, Dear Coltrane," "American History," and "Deathwatch" from DEAR JOHN, DEAR COLTRANE by Michael S. Harper. Copyright © 1970 by Michael S. Harper. Used by permission of the poet and the University of Illinois Press.

Robert Hayden: "Middle Passage" copyright © 1962, 1966 by Robert Hayden; "Homage to the Empress of the Blues" copyright © 1966 by Robert Hayden; "Those Winter Sundays" copyright © 1966 by Robert Hayden; "The Night Blooming Cereus" copyright © 1972 by Robert Hayden; "Free Fantasia: Tiger Flowers" copyright © 1975 by Robert Hayden, from COLLECTED POEMS OF ROBERT HAYDEN by Robert Hayden, edited by Frederick Glaysher. Used by permission of Liveright Publishing Corporation.

Randall Jarrell: "90 North," "The Death of the Ball Turret Gunner," "Second Air Force," "Next Day," "Well Water," and "Thinking of the Lost World" from THE COMPLETE POEMS by Randall Jarrell. Copyright © 1969 by Mrs. Randall Jarrell. Reprinted by permission of Farrar, Straus & Giroux, LLC, and Faber and Faber Ltd.

Maxine Hong Kingston: "Trippers and Askers" from TRIPMASTER MONKEY: HIS FAKE BOOK by Maxine Hong Kingston. Copyright © 1987, 1988, 1989 by Maxine Hong Kingston. First published by Alfred A. Knopf, Inc. Reprinted by permission of Alfred A. Knopf, a division of Random House, Inc., the author, and the Sandra Dijkstra Literary Agency.

Galway Kinnell: "The Porcupine" from BODY RAGS by Galway Kinnell. Copyright © 1965, 1966, 1967 by Galway Kinnell. "After Making Love, We Hear Footsteps" and "Blackberry Eating" from THREE BOOKS by Galway Kinnell. Copyright © 1993 by Galway Kinnell. Previously published in MORTAL ACTS, MORTAL WORDS (1980). "Cemetery Angels" from THREE BOOKS by Galway Kinnell. Copyright © 1993 by Galway Kinnell. Previously published in THE PAST (1985). "Neverland" from IMPERFECT THIRST by Galway Kinnell. Copyright © 1994 by Galway Kinnell. Reprinted by permission of Houghton Mifflin Co. All rights reserved.

Kunitz, Stanley: "Father and Son," "After the Last Dynasty," "Quinnapoxet," and "The Wellfleet Whale" from THE COLLECTED POEMS by Stanley Kunitz. Copyright © 2000 by Stanley Kunitz. Used by permission of W. W. Norton & Company, Inc.

Li-Young Lee: "The Gift," "Persimmons," "Eating Alone," "Eating Together," and "Mnemonic" from ROSE by Li-Young Lee. Copyright © 1986 by Li-Young Lee. "This Room and Everything in It" from THE CITY IN WHICH I LOVE YOU by Li-Young Lee. Copyright © 1990 by Li-Young Lee. Reprinted by permission of BOA Editions Ltd.

Ursula K. Le Guin: "Schrödinger's Cat" from THE COMPASS ROSE. Copyright © 1974 by Ursula K. Le Guin; first appeared in UNIVERSE 5. "She Unnames Them" from BUFFALO GALS & OTHER ANIMAL PRESENCES. Copyright © 1985 by Ursula K. Le Guin; first appeared in *The New Yorker*. All of the above reprinted by permission of the author and the author's agent, Virginia Kidd Agency, Inc.

Denise Levertov: "The Jacob's Ladder," "September, 1961," "In Mind," and "What They Were Like" from POEMS 1960–1967 by Denise Levertov. Copyright © 1966 by Denise Levertov. "To the Snake" from COLLECTED EARLIER POEMS 1940–1960 by Denise Levertov. Copyright © 1946, 1956, 1958 by Denise Levertov. "Caedmon" from BREATHING THE WATER by Denise Levertov. Copyright © 1987 by Denise Levertov. "Death in Mexico" from LIFE IN THE FOREST by Denise Levertov. Copyright © 1978 by Denise Levertov. Reprinted by permission of New Directions Publishing Corporation and Laurence Pollinger Ltd.

Philip Levine: "Animals Are Passing from Our Lives" from NOT THIS PIG. Copyright © 1968 by Philip Levine. Reprinted by permission of Wesleyan University Press. "Detroit Grease Shop Poem," "They

Feed They Lion," and "Starlight" from NEW SELECTED POEMS by Philip Levine. Copyright © 1991 by Philip Levine. "Fear and Fame" from WHAT WORK IS by Philip Levine. Copyright © 1992 by Philip Levine. "The Simple Truth" from THE SIMPLE TRUTH by Philip Levine. Copyright © 1994 by Philip Levine. Used by permission of Alfred A. Knopf, a division of Random House, Inc.

Audre Lorde: "Coal," copyright © 1973, 1970, 1968 by Audre Lorde. "The Woman Thing" copyright © 1973, 1970, 1968 by Audre Lorde. "Black Mother Woman" copyright © 1992, 1973 by Audre Lorde. From UNDERSONG: CHOSEN POEMS OLD AND NEW by Audre Lorde. Used by permission of W. W. Norton & Company, Inc., and Abner Stein.

Robert Lowell: "Colloquy in Black Rock," "The Quaker Graveyard in Nantucket," "Mr. Edwards and the Spider" from LORD WEARY'S CASTLE. Copyright 1946 and renewed 1974 by Robert Lowell. Published in Great Britain in POEMS 1938–1949. Reprinted by permission of Harcourt, Inc., and Faber and Faber Ltd. "My Last Afternoon with Uncle Devereux Winslow," "Memories of West Street and Lepke," and "Skunk Hour" from LIFE STUDIES by Robert Lowell. Copyright © 1959 by Robert Lowell. Copyright renewed © 1987 by Harriet Lowell, Sheridan Lowell, and Caroline Lowell. "Night Sweat" and "For the Union Dead" from FOR THE UNION DEAD by Robert Lowell. Copyright © 1959 by Robert Lowell. Copyright renewed © 1987 by Harriet Lowell, Sheridan Lowell, and Caroline Lowell. Reprinted by permission of Farrar, Straus & Giroux, LLC, and Faber and Faber Ltd.

Bernard Malamud: "The Magic Barrel" from THE MAGIC BARREL by Bernard Malamud. Copyright © 1950, 1958, and copyright renewed © 1977, 1986 by Bernard Malamud. Reprinted by permission of Farrar, Straus & Giroux, LLC, and Russell and Volkening for the author.

David Mamet: GLENGARRY GLEN ROSS by David Mamet. Copyright © 1982, 1983 by David Mamet. Reprinted by permission of Grove/Atlantic, Inc., and Methuen Publishing Ltd.

Paule Marshall: "Reena" from REENA AND OTHER STORIES by Paule Marshall. Copyright © 1983 by Paule Marshall. By permission of the Feminist Press at the City University of New York, www.feministpress.org.

James Merrill: "An Urban Convalescence," "The Broken Home," and "Lost in Translation" from SELECTED POEMS 1946–1985 by James Merrill. Copyright © 1992 by James Merrill. "Family Week at Oracle Ranch" from COLLECTED POEMS by James Merrill. Copyright © 2001 by the Estate of James Merrill. Used by permission of Alfred A. Knopf, a division of Random House, Inc.

W. S. Merwin: "For the Anniversary of My Death" and "For a Coming Extinction" copyright © 1963 by W. S. Merwin. "Lament for the Makers" copyright © 1996 by W. S. Merwin. Reprinted with permission of The Wylie Agency. "The Drunk in the Furnace" from THE FIRST FOUR BOOKS OF POEMS by W. S. Merwin. Copyright © 1960, 2000 by W. S. Merwin. Reprinted with permission of Copper Canyon Press, P.O. Box 271, Port Townsend, WA 98368–0271, USA. "Losing a Language" from THE RAIN IN THE TREES by W. S. Merwin. Copyright © 1988 by W. S. Merwin. Used by permission of Alfred A. Knopf, a division of Random House, Inc. "Ceremony After an Amputation" from THE RIVER SOUND by W. S. Merwin. Copyright © 1999 by W. S. Merwin. Used by permission of Alfred A. Knopf, a division of Random House, Inc.

Arthur Miller: DEATH OF A SALESMAN by Arthur Miller. Copyright 1949, renewed © 1977 by Arthur Miller. Reprinted by permission of Viking Penguin, a division of Penguin Putnam, Inc., and International Creative Management, Inc.

N. Scott Momaday: "Headwaters," Introduction, IV, XIII, XXIV, "Epilogue," "Rainy Mountain Cemetery" from THE WAY TO RAINY MOUNTAIN. Copyright © 1969 by The University of New Mexico Press.

Toni Morrison: "Recitatif" from CONFIRMATION. Copyright © 1983 by Toni Morrison. Reprinted by permission of International Creative Management, Inc.

Lorine Niedecker: "I Married," "Lake Superior," "My Life by Water," "Poet's Work," "Watching Dancers on Skates," "Well, Spring Overflows the Land" from THE GRANITE PAIL by Lorine Niedecker. Copyright © 1985 by The Estate of Lorine Niedecker, Cid Corman, Executor. Published by North Point Press, a division of Farrar, Straus & Giroux, Inc. Reprinted by permission of Cid Corman.

Flannery O'Connor: "Good Country People" copyright © 1955 by Flannery O'Connor and renewed 1983 by Regina O'Connor; "The Life You Save May Be Your Own" copyright © 1953 by Flannery O'Connor and renewed 1981 by Regina O'Connor. Both from A GOOD MAN IS HARD TO FIND AND OTHER STORIES by Flannery O'Connor. Copyright © 1955, 1954, 1953, 1948 by Flannery O'Connor. Copyright renewed 1976 by Mrs. Edward F. O'Connor. Copyright renewed 1981, 1982, 1983 by Regina O'Connor. Reprinted by permission of Harcourt, Inc., and Harold Matson Company, Inc.

Frank O'Hara: "To the Harbormaster" from MEDITATIONS IN AN EMERGENCY by Frank O'Hara. Copyright © 1957 by Frank O'Hara, used by permission of Grove/Atlantic, Inc. "In Memory of My Feelings" and "Why I am Not a Painter" from COLLECTED POEMS by Frank O'Hara. Copyright © 1971 by Maureen Granville-Smith, Administratrix of the Estate of Frank O'Hara. Used by permission of Alfred A. Knopf, a division of Random House, Inc. "The Day Lady Died" and "A Step Away from Them." Copyright © 1964 by Frank O'Hara from LUNCH POEMS. Reprinted by permission of City Lights Books.

Mary Oliver: "The Black Snake" from TWELVE MOONS by Mary Oliver. Copyright © 1972, 1973, 1974, 1976, 1977, 1978, 1979 by Mary Oliver. Reprinted by permission of Little, Brown and Co. (Inc.) and the Molly Malone Cook Literary Agency. "In Blackwater Woods" from AMERICAN PRIMITIVE by Mary Oliver. Copyright © 1978, 1979, 1980, 1981, 1982, 1983 by Mary Oliver; first appeared in *Yankee* magazine. Reprinted by permission of Little, Brown and Co. (Inc.). "A Visitor" and "Landscape" from DREAM WORK by Mary Oliver. Copyright © 1986 by Mary Oliver. Used by permission of Grove/Atlantic, Inc. "Poppies," "Hummingbird Pauses at the Trumpet Vine," and "Alligator Poem" from NEW AND SELECTED POEMS by Mary Oliver. Copyright © 1992 by Mary Oliver. Reprinted by permission of Beacon Press, Boston.

Charles Olson: "I, Maximus of Gloucester, to You," "Maximus, to Himself," "[When Do Poppies Bloom]," "Celestial Evening, October 1967" from THE MAXIMUS POEMS by Charles Olson, edited by George Butterick. Copyright © 1983 The Regents of the University of California. Reprinted by permission of the Regents of the University of California and the University of California Press.

George Oppen: "Party on Shipboard," "The Hills," "Workman," "Psalm," from "Of Being Numerous" (1–7), "Anniversary Poem," and "She lies, hip high" from COLLECTED POEMS OF GEORGE OPPEN. Copyright © 1975 by George Oppen. Reprinted by permission of New Directions Publishing Corporation.

Simon J. Ortiz: "Passing through Little Rock," "Earth and Rain, the Plants & Sun," "Vision Shadows," "8:50 AM Ft. Lyons VAH," "Travelling" from *Poems from the Veterans Hospital*, and "[At the Salvation Army]" from FROM SAND CREEK. Reprinted by permission of Simon J. Ortiz

Judith Ortiz Cofer: "The Witch's Husband" from THE LATIN DELI: PROSE AND POETRY by Judith Ortiz Cofer. Copyright © 1993 by Judith Ortiz Cofer. Reprinted by permission of The University of Georgia Press.

Grace Paley: "A Conversation with My Father" from ENORMOUS CHANGES AT THE LAST MINUTE by Grace Paley. Copyright © 1971, 1974 by Grace Paley. Reprinted by permission of Farrar, Straus & Giroux, LLC, and Elaine Markson Literary Agency, Inc., for Grace Paley.

Suzan-Lori Parks: "The America Play" from THE AMERICA PLAY AND OTHER WORKS by Suzan-Lori Parks. Copyright © 1995 by Suzan-Lori Parks. Published by Theatre Communications Group. Used by permission of Theatre Communications Group, Inc.

Robert Pinsky: "The Figured Wheel," "The Street," and "A Woman" from THE FIGURED WHEEL by Robert Pinsky. Copyright © 1996 by Robert Pinsky. Reprinted by permission of Farrar, Straus & Giroux, LLC, and Carcanet Press Ltd. "The Want Bone," "Shirt," "At Pleasure Bay" from THE WANT BONE by Robert Pinsky. Copyright © 1991 by Robert Pinsky. Reprinted by permission of HarperCollins Publishers, Inc., and Carcanet Press Ltd.

Sylvia Plath: "Morning Song" copyright © 1961 by Ted Hughes; "Lady Lazarus" copyright © 1963 by Ted Hughes; "Ariel" copyright © 1965 by Ted Hughes; "Daddy" copyright © 1963 by Ted Hughes; "Words" copyright © 1966 by Ted Hughes; "The Applicant" copyright © 1963 by Ted Hughes. From ARIEL by Sylvia Plath. "Blackberrying" copyright © 1962 by Ted Hughes. This poem originally appeared in UNCOLLECTED POEMS, Turret Books, London, and in *The Hudson Review*. From CROSSING THE WATER by Sylvia Plath. "Child" copyright © 1963 by Ted Hughes. From WINTER TREES by Sylvia Plath. "Purdah" from THE COLLECTED POEMS OF SYLVIA PLATH, edited by Ted Hughes. Copyright © 1960, 1965, 1971, 1981 by the Estate of Sylvia Plath. Editorial material copyright © 1981 by Ted Hughes. Copyrights renewed. Reprinted by permission of HarperCollins Publishers, Inc., and Faber and Faber Ltd.

Richard Powers: From GALATEA 2.2 by Richard Powers. Copyright © 1995 by Richard Powers. Reprinted by permission of the publishers, Farrar, Straus and Giroux, LLC, and Little Brown (UK).

Thomas Pynchon: "Entropy" from SLOW LEARNER by Thomas Pynchon. Copyright © 1984 by Thomas Pynchon. First published in *The Kenyon Review*. Copyright © 1960, 1988 by Thomas Pynchon. Reprinted by permission of Little, Brown and Company and Melanie Jackson Agency, LLC.

Ishmael Reed: "The Neo HooDoo Manifesto" from CONJURE by Ishmael Reed. Reprinted by permission of the author. "Native Son Nightmare" from THE LAST DAYS OF LOUISIANA RED. Copyright © 1974 by Ishmael Reed. Used by permission of Random House, Inc.

Adrienne Rich: "Storm Warnings," "Snapshots of a Daughter-in-Law," "I Am in Danger—Sir—," "A Valediction Forbidding Mourning," "Diving into the Wreck," "Power," "Transcendental Etude" from THE FACT OF A DOORFRAME: POEMS SELECTED AND NEW, 1950–1984 by Adrienne Rich, by permission of W. W. Norton & Company, Inc. Copyright © 1984 by Adrienne Rich. Copyright © 1975, 1978 by W. W. Norton & Company, Inc. Copyright © 1981 by Adrienne Rich. Used by permission of W. W. Norton & Company.

Alberto Rios: "Madre Sofia" and "Wet Camp" from WHISPERING TO FOOL THE WIND, copyright © 1982 by Alberto Rios. "Taking Away the Name of a Nephew," "Advice to a First Cousin," and "Seniors" from FIVE INDISCRETIONS, copyright © 1985 by Alberto Rios. Reprinted by permission of Alberto Rios.

Theodore Roethke: "Cuttings" copyright 1948 by Theodore Roethke; "Cuttings (Later)" copyright 1948

Index